www.wadsworth.com

www.wadsworth.com is the World Wide Web site for
Thomson Wadsworth and is your direct source to dozens
of online resources.

At *www.wadsworth.com* you can find out about
supplements, demonstration software, and
student resources. You can also send email to many of our
authors and preview new publications and exciting new
technologies.

www.wadsworth.com
Changing the way the world learns®

Metaphysics

Classic and Contemporary Readings
Second Edition

Ronald C. Hoy
California University of Pennsylvania

L. Nathan Oaklander
University of Michigan–Flint

THOMSON

WADSWORTH

Australia • Canada • Mexico • Singapore • Spain • United Kingdom • United States

THOMSON
WADSWORTH

Publisher: *Holly J. Allen*
Philosophy Editor: *Steve Wainwright*
Assistant Editors: *Lee McCracken, Anna Lustig*
Editorial Assistant: *Barbara Hillaker*
Technology Project Manager: *Julie Aguilar*
Marketing Manager: *Worth Hawes*
Marketing Assistant: *Andrew Keay*
Advertising Project Manager: *Laurel Anderson*

Print/Media Buyer: *Karen Hunt*
Permissions Editor: *Stephanie Lee*
Production Service: *Buuji, Inc.*
Copy Editor: *Alan DeNiro, Buuji, Inc.*
Cover Designer: *Yvo Riezebos*
Cover Image: *Curling Wall/Getty Image*
Compositor: *Buuji, Inc.*
Printer: *Webcom, Ltd.*

Printed in Canada
1 2 3 4 5 6 7 08 07 06 05 04

For more information about our products,
contact us at:
Thomson Learning Academic Resource Center
1-800-423-0563

For permission to use material from this text
or product, submit a request online at
http://www.thomsonrights.com.

Any additional questions about permissions
can be submitted by email to
thomsonrights@thomson.com.

Library of Congress Control Number:
2004111046

ISBN 0-534-64134-2

Thomson Wadsworth
10 Davis Drive
Belmont, CA 94002-3098
USA

Asia
Thomson Learning
5 Shenton Way #01-01
UIC Building
Singapore 068808

Australia/New Zealand
Thomson Learning
102 Dodds Street
Southbank, Victoria 3006
Australia

Canada
Nelson
1120 Birchmount Road
Toronto, Ontario M1K 5G4
Canada

Europe/Middle East/Africa
Thomson Learning
High Holborn House
50/51 Bedford Row
London WC1R 4LR
United Kingdom

Latin America
Thomson Learning
Seneca, 53
Colonia Polanco
11560 Mexico D.F.
Mexico

Spain/Portugal
Paraninfo
Calle Magallanes, 25
28015 Madrid, Spain

Dedicated to our parents

E. A. and E. H. Hoy

the late Fay and Isadore Oaklander

Contents

Part III: Mind   213

Part IV: Freedom   345

Preface

Metaphysics is an ancient and honorable discipline that sometimes suffers from too much enthusiasm and sometimes from too much self-doubt. In the twentieth century, doubt tended to dominate, and this trend has continued into the twenty-first century. Metaphysics has been declared meaningless or fruitless, and it has been analyzed, psychoanalyzed, deconstructed, and sometimes left for dead in the dust of "semantic ascent." Nevertheless, philosophers have continued to propose and debate arguments about what really exists—to wonder about how to achieve the best possible view of the world. And students and the general public show irrepressible interest in metaphysics, though this is sometimes evidenced only by the popularity of books on the occult, which offer entertaining views of reality beyond the ordinary. The common confusion of metaphysics with the study of the supernatural should be remedied by accessible books that show how fascinating and challenging the attempt to understand "ordinary" reality can be.

The working assumption of the editors of this anthology has been that professors who teach metaphysics have been poorly served by the scarcity of available texts. Professors have tended to resort to a historical approach, having their students read the work of classical authors, or they have tended to focus on specific contemporary problems as they are dealt with in journal articles that are collected in specialized anthologies that soon go out of print. The result is that it has been difficult to do two desirable things: ground the study of metaphysics in its history *and* motivate and master contemporary theories, which are often quite technical. Accordingly, we have compiled an anthology that includes both classic and contemporary selections, and we have organized them around six topics of general and perennial interest. The readings represent alternative points of view and, hopefully, give some indication of the development of philosophical understanding.

Students taking metaphysics courses frequently have diverse backgrounds and preparation, so the anthology includes readings of varying degrees of difficulty. Enough material is included to allow professors flexibility in designing a variety of courses. For example, courses might be designed that follow the organization of the book and concentrate on selected problems, but it is also feasible to design a course by picking readings chronologically and using the problems covered as examples of how historically important philosophers dealt with metaphysical topics. Or a course might begin with a contemporary reading dealing with a popular topic like free will and then work backward, showing how the topic requires exploring theories of mind and time. Also, the variety of selections, and the relatedness of articles in different sections, should make the book useful in courses having a special focus, for example, philosophy of mind courses or seminars on free will or the nature of persons.

All the readings are from the Western philosophical tradition; many represent an analytic perspective, and many take seriously the metaphysical implications of advancing science. This second edition includes a new part dealing with arguments for the existence of God. We added this section for two reasons. First, many users of the first edition noted they wanted to cover this topic in their courses. Second, the last couple of decades has seen a renewed interest in cosmological arguments for the existence of God as science has made spectacular progress picturing the early and large-scale features of the universe. The addition of the new Part V led to the shortening of Part VI, Knowing Reality. In the first edition, this part included Kant, Hegel, and Heidegger. For the second edition, Part VI focuses on empiricist critiques of metaphysics (Berkeley and Hume), and then it leapfrogs over Kant to American pragmatism. While we feel that Kant and his German successors are very important,

the metaphysical issues raised by empiricism and pragmatism manageably cohere with an important theme of the rest of the anthology: coming to terms with evolving science.

We begin the book with time because we have had success beginning our metaphysics courses by introducing puzzles about the nature of time. Not only do students have a great interest in this topic, but it leads naturally (as it has in the history of metaphysics) to further questions; for example, to questions about identity and freedom.

We would like to acknowledge the comments of the following reviewers: David Berlinski, San Jose State University and Santa Clara University; Lewis Ford, Old Dominion University; Gary Gurtler, Loyola University of Chicago; Arthur Herman, University of Wisconsin, Stevens Point; Daniel Kolak, William Paterson College; Bradford Petrie, Union College; and Steven L. Reynolds, Arizona State University.

For any improvements in this second edition, we would like to acknowledge the heartening comments of many students and professors who used the first edition. In particular, we would like to thank Joe Camp of the University of Pittsburgh and Quentin Smith of Western Michigan State University.

R.C.H.
L.N.O.

Metaphysics

Classic and Contemporary Readings
Second Edition

Introduction

Metaphysics is the study of the general character of reality. What are the fundamental kinds of things that exist? Is reality logical? What is the true nature of familiar things? For example, are persons really material bodies or souls or minds or some combination of these things? Such questions are fascinating, but their boldness can be intimidating. And the diversity of exotic answers that philosophers have proposed can make one dizzy. This anthology focuses on six metaphysical topics that have natural interest to students: (1) What is time? (2) How can things change yet be the same—in particular, what constitutes the identity of a person? (3) What is the nature of mind? (4) If the structure of the world is fixed or determined, can people be free? (5) Can the existence of God be proven? (6) Can one know reality? These questions have been debated since the beginning of philosophy. Studying the diversity of answers that philosophers have proposed can enrich one's life by putting ordinary things in new perspectives. Hopefully, it will also show that philosophers have made some progress understanding reality.

Though everyone has probably wondered about metaphysical issues at some point, the study of metaphysics is bound to seem somewhat alien when compared with other subjects. Compare metaphysics with a familiar study, say, the study of rocks. Geologists ask, among other questions, What kinds of rocks exist? As they go about the business of classifying rocks, they can usually take it for granted they have working agreement about what counts as a rock. Philosophers would like to know, in most general terms, what kinds of things are real, but they do not always share working agreement about what counts as real. Instead of first agreeing about the criteria for reality and then looking to see what satisfies the criteria, philosophers spend much of their time proposing and debating different criteria. Thus, metaphysical theories can seem bewilderingly different from each other and difficult to evaluate.

To see how quickly metaphysical disagreements can escalate, consider the implications of endorsing the following two innocent-looking criteria for reality. Suppose one decides that for something to count as real it must be observable and have some definite location in space and time. Such things as individual rocks, trees, and birds meet these criteria, but what about abstract or ideal entities like numbers or justice? On reflection, most people will agree the square root of two, for example, cannot be seen and has no definite spatiotemporal location (though instances of its name can be seen and located). Should one conclude the square root of two does not exist? Similarly, though one might claim to be able to see people who are just, can one see justice itself, and, does it have a definite location? Some philosophers (for example, Plato) have denied justice can be seen or located in space and time, yet they have claimed since justice (like numbers) can be thought about and known, it must exist. Another example of something threatened by these innocent-looking criteria is God. God is often thought to be unobservable and to exist, somehow, beyond space and time. So would one's agreement with these criteria for reality (observability and spatiotemporal location) force one to deny the reality of God along with numbers and justice? If, however, one has good reasons for believing such things are real, then one should attack these criteria and propose some alternatives.

Suppose, on the other hand, you consider yourself to have a tough scientific temperament, and you are willing to hold onto the criteria and to deny the reality of numbers, justice, and God. Then you may still have cause to worry. You probably believe everyday objects are real and consist of matter. But physicists now explain matter in terms of strange subatomic things like quarks, virtual particles, or "superstrings." Many physicists claim these things are not observable and have no definite location. Are you then forced to deny the reality of these entities? Again, many scientists would answer affirmatively, saying the objects of quantum physics are merely parts of models, not much better than fictions that are useful only for making predictions. But if everyday material objects are not really, at their core, swarming clouds of subatomic particles, what are they?

After being introduced to puzzles about numbers, God, and theoretical scientific entities, it is tempting to try to take refuge in the reality of familiar, ordinary objects just as they appear. Surely, tables and trees are real; surely persons exist. It is an important historical fact, however, that metaphysics began in ancient Greece when people started asking simple but probing questions about ordinary things. For example, familiar things can change and yet still seem to be the same thing. But how can the *very same* thing have different, incompatible properties? Doesn't this involve a contradiction, and isn't being noncontradictory a minimum criterion for reality? Or can reality be contradictory? To avoid this problem, should one abandon the idea that self-identical things can endure change? (After all, are you *really* the same thing that had your name and social security number five years ago?) Or should one try to find some new view of things, change, and identity?

The early Greek philosophers were aware that ordinary objects present different appearances to different people. How are the different appearances of a table related to the table itself—to the *real* table? Once the distinction is made between appearance and reality, it is tempting to try to solve metaphysical puzzles by claiming they have their source in mistaking appearance for reality. In their different ways, thinkers like Parmenides, Zeno, and Plato used puzzles about change and identity to argue that the ordinary world of changing things is *mere* appearance. This is a disturbing conclusion, however, if you want to take refuge from questions about numbers, quarks, and God by holding fast to the reality of the ordinary world of perceived objects. So, one should not be too confident that even *that* world is real until one answers the challenges of those philosophers who maintain it is mere appearance.

Much of the history of metaphysics is the history of philosophers' claiming to find defects in some view of reality or claiming to find a new view that diagnoses and fixes the defects of earlier views. Often, the new theories are radical and fantastic. Imagine reality being entirely spiritual, consisting of an infinity of souls reflecting each other (a simplification of Leibniz's view). Or, imagine reality consisting only of dumb material atoms careening in the void (the view of some ancient and modem materialists). To read the history of metaphysics is to take a challenging journey, a journey where one is tempted to follow different ideas in different directions, and where each one offers some logic, some reason, to go in that direction.

The diversity of metaphysical theories may be entertaining, but it also can be confusing and disconcerting. How can intelligent people come to such different conclusions? How can each one be so sure his or her theory is correct? Why, after over 2,000 years of argumentation, does there appear to be so little agreement about which metaphysics is true?

Skepticism about metaphysics is itself a recurrent metaphysical theme, and it is usually accompanied by some analysis of the nature and limits of human knowledge. In the eighteenth century, for example, David Hume argued that all legitimate ideas must be analyzed in terms of sensations. He claimed that such metaphysical notions as ideas of causality and enduring substance could not be adequately grounded in experience. Skeptical critiques of metaphysics, however, eventually express or presuppose metaphysical theses of their own. Hume, for example, believed in the reality of sensations as inner, immediate objects of experience. Some later philosophers will try to understand perceptual experience without reifying sensations as inner objects, thereby denying the picture of consciousness on which Hume based his skepticism.

Closer to the present, some philosophers became skeptical about metaphysics either because they advocated science as the best way to know reality or, ironically, because they wondered about the metaphysics of science. Even if science is the best way to know the character of reality, is not science constantly evolving? If so, why think that any given theory of science at some stage of its development is literally true? Perhaps what matters is its utility or success in certain human projects?

This book will not treat very general questions about whether it is possible to know what is real until the final section. And it will not survey chronologically the grand metaphysical systems that individual philosophers have constructed to try to solve all metaphysical problems. Instead, its strategy is to have the reader work through five specific topics—time, identity, mind, God, and freedom—seeing how earlier and contemporary philosophers have attempted to deal with them. Not only will this approach help one decide whether progress has been made in understanding these important topics, but also it will give the reader the opportunity to evaluate different philosophical perspectives by seeing them in action. Several themes will recur, for example, the influence of changing scientific beliefs on metaphysics and the tension between one's ordinary experience and theoretical views of reality. It will also become clear why a position on one subject, say the nature of mind, may lead naturally to a position on another subject, for example, freedom. After wrestling with these particular topics, the reader will be able to appreciate better the general reflections on metaphysics contained in Part VI.

Part I

Time

Probably every reflective person has been struck by the importance of time and by its elusive, puzzling character. People see time as important because their hopes and fears concern the coming and going of events they enjoy or dread. Birthdays celebrate years of growth and success, but they also mark one's approach to death. Since so much that is vital is ruled by time, one is bound to wonder what kind of sovereign it is. Myth and poetry occasionally personify time. The Hindu god Vishnu declared, "Know that I am time, that makes the worlds to perish, when ripe, and come to bring destruction." And in the West, the familiar figure of Father Time is thought to be a renaissance combination of Cronus (the reaper god who, in

Greek myth, castrates his father), and Death. In some religions, people hope to escape time by trying to deny the importance of the transient events of life. Others use science and technology to wrestle with time, trying to win more free time and longer lives. But whether one battles, embraces, or flees time, one thereby acknowledges its significance.

When one wonders about time, each question asked seems to lead to others. How should one interpret the question What is time? Should time be treated as an entity whose parts are the past, present, and future? But what are these parts? The past and future do not exist now, so what kind of entity is it that appears to consist largely of what does not exist now? Is time not a thing at all, but rather some kind of "movement," "flow," or "passage"? But movement seems to occur *in time*, so what is clarified by saying time itself is movement?

When early philosophers asked such questions about time, they not only found them very difficult to answer, but they also discovered their confusion spread to different topics. Time has something to do with change, but how can anything change? How can something be one way at one time and some other way at another time, yet still be the *same* thing? Thus, questions about the nature of time can lead to questions about the nature of change and identity. Here is another example. People frequently talk about future events, and presumably some of what is said about future events is true. Does this mean future events must have some kind of reality? And if future events are real, does this mean the future is fixed or "fated"? Therefore, questions about the nature of time can lead to questions about truth and about the freedom of actions.

Puzzles about time are central to metaphysics not only because they generate and are involved in additional philosophical problems, but also because their difficulty has called into question the whole philosophical project of trying to understand reality. Is the nature of time so problematic that any attempt to understand it leads to paradoxes—to contradictions? Some philosophers have come to this conclusion, and they have been then faced with a difficult choice: either time is real and our reason is incapable of comprehending an irrational world, or, if reality must conform to reason and logic, then time cannot be real. Important philosophers such as Parmenides, Plato, Kant, McTaggart, and Bergson wrestled with this dilemma, and all were driven to the conclusion that reality must be quite different from how we ordinarily think of it. Thus, the puzzling nature of time has repeatedly forced philosophers to deal with such bold and disturbing claims as "time is not real," and "there must be something drastically wrong

with our ways of thinking." These general, skeptical challenges provide further motivation for philosophers to formulate a coherent metaphysics of time.

The study of time can take one in several different directions. The readings in Part I have been selected because they deal with central, perennial issues in the philosophy of time, and because they will be useful in motivating and understanding some of the other problems covered in this anthology. The articles in Part I concern two themes: (1) Is time real? (2) Should time be understood in terms of the passage of the present, or should time be viewed as a series of events standing in earlier-than and later-than relations? The first issue challenges one to formulate nonparadoxical accounts of change and identity. The second theme forces one to clarify the metaphysical status (the kind of reality) of the past and the future. It also has implications for analyses of change and identity, and it leads to further questions about truth and freedom.

Part I begins with the startling arguments of Parmenides and Zeno, according to whom time and motion are not real. Aristotle responded to this challenge, and his selection is a painstaking analysis of time that defends its reality. In the following article, Augustine is led to wonder about time by theological difficulties. But he, too, worries about the paradoxical character of time, and he is not content with Aristotle's analysis. Augustine hints that time has an important subjective aspect when he suggests it is some kind of "protraction" of mind. For Isaac Newton, on the other hand, time is the absolute flux of the present as it is represented by the true equations of mathematical physics. It is independent of both changing things and mind.

The remainder of the readings in Part I were originally published more recently. Bergson complains that logic and mathematics distort the true character of time, which he believes can be revealed in intuitive experience to be a *sui generis* flux of becoming (or the moving Now). McTaggart also worries that becoming does not obey logic, but he concludes that time, therefore, is not real. Donald C. Williams argues that becoming is merely subjective—it is just the perspective from which consciousness views the four-dimensional world pictured by modern physics. In their different ways, D. H. Mellor and John Perry continue to attack the apparent special metaphysical status of the moving present by showing that only facts involving relations are needed to explain what is true in statements about change and time.

After studying Part I, the reader will appreciate how theories of time become intertwined with other philosophical topics and why there are many questions left to explore. For example, What gives time its apparent direction? What is the relation between temporal and timeless things (if any)? How are people able to apprehend durations?

1. *Being Is Not Temporal*

PARMENIDES

Parmenides of Elea lived during the dawn of Greek philosophy. Born about 515 BC, he flourished in the generation before Socrates. He is given credit for focusing attention on the general question What is the nature of real being? Previous Presocratic thinkers had begun to break with the anthropomorphic explanation characteristic of early religions. Instead of being content to view the world in terms of the activities of human-like spiritual agencies, the Greek cosmologists had begun to speculate that the world might be intelligible in terms of generalizations like "everything is water" or "everything is fire." Parmenides did more than just debate or add to these theories. He purported to use only logic to argue for the startling view that reality is unchanging, undivided being—reality is One. Parmenides claimed to find something contradictory (and therefore impossible) in saying what exists is a created, changing, or diverse plurality of things.

Though Parmenides is not primarily concerned with the nature of time, it is appropriate to begin this section and this anthology with his writing. For in claiming reality has no beginning or end and does not change, he is denying that familiar temporal distinctions apply to it—in other words, time is not real. This implies that our familiar temporal world is an appearance or illusion. But do not appearances and illusions have some kind of reality? Is Parmenides' logic mistaken? Are there alternative strategies for analyzing time and change? Or should one conclude time is real, but not rational (or logical)? In this way, Parmenides' bold logic and implausible conclusion generated many of the metaphysical questions that concerned later philosophers.

In this work, a goddess distinguishes the way of appearances from the way of truth, and she shows how the way of truth leads to the One. Readers should be aware that there are rival interpretations of the poem that are still debated by scholars.

The mares that draw me wherever my heart would go escorted me, when the goddesses who were driving set me on the renowned road that leads through all cities the man who knows. Along this I was borne; for along it the wise horses drew at full stretch the chariot, and maidens led the way. The axle, urged round by the whirling wheels at either end, shrilled in its sockets and glowed, as the daughters of the sun, leaving the house of night and pushing the veils from their heads with their hands, hastened to escort me towards the light.

From *An Introduction to Early Greek Philosophy* by John Mansley Robinson. Copyright © 1968 by John M. Robinson. Reprinted by permission of the author.

There are the gates of the ways of night and day, enclosed by a lintel and a threshold of stone; and these, high in the ether, are fitted with great doors, and avenging Justice holds the keys which control these ways. The maidens entreated her with gentle words, and wisely persuaded her to thrust back quickly the bolts of the gate. The leaves of the door, swinging back, made a yawning gap as the brazen pins on either side turned in their sockets. Straight through them, along the broad way, the maidens guided mares and chariot; and the goddess received me kindly, and taking my right hand in hers spoke these words to me:

"Welcome, youth, who come attended by immortal charioteers and mares which bear you on your journey to our dwelling. For it is no evil fate that has set you to travel on this road, far from the beaten paths of men, but right and justice. It is meet that you learn all things—both the unshakable heart of well-rounded truth and the opinions of mortals in which there is no true belief. But these, too, you must learn completely, seeing that appearances have to be acceptable, since they pervade everything."

Come now, and I will tell you (and you, when you have heard my speech shall bear it away with you) the ways of inquiry which alone exist for thought. The one is the way of how it is, and how it is not possible for it not to be; this is the way of persuasion, for it attends Truth. The other is the way of how it is not, and how it is necessary for it not to be; this, I tell you, is a way wholly unknowable. For you could not know what is not—that is impossible—nor could you express it.

For thought and being are the same.

Thinking and the thought that it is are the same; for you will not find thought apart from what is, in relation to which it is uttered.

It is necessary to speak and to think what is; for being is, but nothing is not. These things I bid you consider. For I hold you back from this first way of inquiry; but also from that way on which mortals knowing nothing wander, of two minds. For helplessness guides the wandering thought in their breasts; they are carried along deaf and blind alike, dazed, beasts without judgment, convinced that to be and not to be are the same and not the same, and that the road of all things is a backward-turning one.

For never shall this prevail: that things that are not, are. But hold back your thought from this way of inquiry, nor let habit born of long experience force you to ply an aimless eye and droning ear along this road; but judge by reasoning the much-contested argument that I have spoken.

One way remains to be spoken of: the way how it is. Along this road there are very many indications that what is is unbegotten and imperishable; for it is whole and immovable and complete. Nor was it at any time, nor will it be, since it is now, all at once, one and continuous.

For what begetting of it would you search for? How and whence did it grow? I shall not let you say or think "from what is not"; for it is not possible either to say or to think how it is not. Again,

what need would have driven it, if it began from nothing, to grow later rather than sooner? Thus it must exist fully or not at all. Nor will the force of conviction ever allow anything over and above itself to arise out of what is not; wherefore Justice does not loosen her fetters so as to allow it to come into being or pass away, but holds it fast.

Concerning these things the decision lies here: either it is, or it is not. But it has been decided, as was necessary, that the one way is unknowable and unnamable (for it is no true road) and that the other is real and true. How could what is perish? How could it have come to be? For if it came into being, it is not; nor is it if ever it is going to be. Thus coming into being is extinguished, and destruction unknown.

Nor is it divisible, since it is all alike; nor is there any more or less of it in one place which might prevent it from holding together, but all is full of what is.

Look steadfastly at those things which, though absent, are firmly present to the mind. For it cannot cut off what is from clinging to what is, either scattering it in every direction in order or bringing it together.

But motionless in the limits of mighty bonds, it is without beginning or end, since coming into being and passing away have been driven far off, cast out by true belief. Remaining the same, and in the same place, it lies in itself, and so abides firmly where it is. For strong Necessity holds it in the bonds of the limit which shuts it in on every side, because it is not right for what is to be incomplete. For it is not in need of anything, but not-being would stand in need of everything.

But since there is a furthest limit, it is complete on every side, like the body of a well-rounded sphere, evenly balanced in every direction from the middle; for it cannot be any greater or any less in one place than in another. For neither is there what is not, which would stop it from reaching its like, nor could what is possibly be more in one place and less than another, since it is all inviolable. For being equal to itself in every direction it nevertheless meets with its limits.

For there is not, nor will there be, anything other than what is, since indeed Destiny has fettered it to remain whole and immovable. Therefore those things which mortals have established, believing them to be true, will be mere names: "coming into being and passing away," "being and not-being," "change of place and alteration of bright color."

It is all one to me where I begin, for I shall come back there again.

Here I end my trustworthy account and thought concerning truth. Learn henceforth the beliefs of mortals, harkening to the deceitful ordering of my words. For they have made up their minds to name two forms, one of which it is not right to name—here is where they have gone astray—and have distinguished them as opposite in bodily form and have assigned to them marks distinguishing them from one another: to one ethereal flame of fire, which is gentle, very light, the same with itself in every direction but not the same with the other. That other too, in itself, is opposite: dark night, dense in bodily form and heavy. The whole arrangement of these I tell to you as it seems likely, so that no thought of mortals shall ever outstrip you.

You shall know the nature of the ether and all the signs in the ether, and the unseen works of the pure torch of the bright sun and whence they came into being. And you shall know the wander-ing works of the round-faced moon and its nature, and you shall know, too, the heaven which sur-rounds all, whence it grew, and how Necessity, guiding it, fettered it to keep the limits of the stars.

[And you shall learn] how sun and moon, the ether which is common to all, the Milky Way and outermost Olympos, and the burning might of the stars, began to arise.

But now that all things have been named light and night, and their powers have been assigned to each, everything is full at once of light and obscure night, both equally, since neither has a share in nothingness.

The narrower rings are filled with unmixed fire, those next to them with night; and into the midst of these a portion of fire is discharged. In the middle of these is the goddess who steers all things; for she is the beginner of all hateful birth and all begetting, sending the female to mix with the male and the male in turn to the female.

First of all the gods she devised Eros.

For as at any time the mixture of their much-wandering limbs is, so thought comes to men. For to all men and to each the nature of the bodily frame is the same as that which it thinks. For what predominates in it is the thought.

2. A Contemporary Exposition of Zeno's Paradoxes

WESLEY C. SALMON

Zeno of Elea was one of Parmenides' students. He defended the view that reality is a changeless One by devising additional arguments trying to show that to believe otherwise is to have beliefs infected with paradox. So, if it is hard to believe reality is changeless, it also should be difficult to believe it changes (at least, after reading Zeno's arguments). Although directly concerned with attacking motion, the arguments can be viewed as attacking change in general by attacking a simple case of change; namely, change of location in time. The paradoxes are pertinent to the study of time not merely because they were used to defend the thesis that reality is not temporal, but also because in attempting to resolve them philosophers have been forced to carefully analyze and develop their views of time. For example, the Dichotomy Paradox forces one to wonder whether a duration can consist of an infinite sequence of events, and the Arrow Paradox forces one to wonder about the character of the present. Is the Now momentary? If so, how does change occur? If, on the other hand, it is not momentary, how can the present consist of events some of which are *not* simultaneous?

Knowledge of Zeno's paradoxes derives from the comments of later philosophers, chiefly Aristotle. Reprinted here is a lucid contemporary exposition by Wesley Salmon, excerpted from his book *Space, Time, and Motion*. (Readers should consult Salmon's book for a discussion of mathematical resolutions of the paradoxes.) Salmon (1925–2001) last taught at the University of Pittsburgh.

The intellectual heritage bequeathed to us by the ancient Greeks was rich indeed. The science of geometry and the entire course of Western philosophy, as we have noted, both had their beginnings with Thales. Both enjoyed fantastic development at the hands of his early successors, achieving a surprising degree of perfection during antiquity. During the same period, Aristotle provided the first systematic development of formal logic. But the fertile soil from which all of this grew also gave rise to a series of puzzles which have challenged successive generations of philosophers and scientists right down to the present. These are the famous paradoxes of Zeno of Elea who flourished about 500 BC.

Zeno was a devoted disciple of the philosopher Parmenides, who had held that reality consisted of one undifferentiated, unchanging motionless whole which was devoid of any parts. Motion, change, and plurality were, according to him, mere illusions. Not too many philosophers could accept this view, and Parmenides was apparently the object of some ridicule from those who disagreed. Zeno's main purpose, it is reported, was to refute those who made fun of his master. His aim was to show that those who believed in motion, change, and plurality were involved in even greater absurdities. Out of perhaps forty such puzzles that he propounded, fewer than ten have come down to us, but they involve some very subtle difficulties. Since motion involves the occupation of different *places* at different *times,* these paradoxes strike at the heart of our concepts of space and time.

Bertrand Russell once remarked that "Zeno's arguments, in some form, have afforded grounds for almost all theories of space and time and infinity which have been constructed from his time to our own." This statement was made in 1914, in an essay which contains a penetrating analysis of the paradoxes, but as we shall see, there were problems inherent in these puzzles that escaped even Russell.

The following paradoxes fall into two main categories, paradoxes of *motion* and paradoxes of *plurality*. The paradoxes of motion are the more famous ones, and I shall begin with them.

The Paradoxes of Motion

Our knowledge of the paradoxes of motion comes from Aristotle who, in the course of his discussions, offers a paraphrase of each. Zeno's original formulations have not survived.

1. *Achilles and the Tortoise.* Imagine that Achilles, the fleetest of Greek warriors, is to run a footrace against a tortoise. It is only fair to give the tortoise a head start. Under these circumstances, Zeno argues, Achilles can never catch up with the tortoise, no matter how fast he runs. In order to overtake the tortoise, Achilles must run from his starting point A to the tortoise's original starting point T_0 (see Figure 1). While he is doing that, the tortoise will have moved ahead to T_1. Now Achilles must reach the point T_1. While Achilles is covering this new distance, the tortoise moves still farther to T_2.

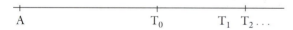

A T_0 T_1 T_2 . . .

Figure 1

Again, Achilles must reach this new position of the tortoise. And so it continues: whenever Achilles arrives at a point where the tortoise *was*, the tortoise has already moved a bit ahead. Achilles can narrow the gap, but he can never actually catch up with him. This is the most famous of all of Zeno's paradoxes. It is sometimes known simply as "The Achilles."

2. *The Dichotomy.* This paradox comes in two forms, progressive and regressive. According to the first, Achilles cannot get to the end of any racecourse, tortoise or no tortoise; indeed, he cannot even reach the original starting point T_0 of the tortoise in the previous paradox. Zeno argues as follows. Before the runner can cover the whole distance he must cover the first half of it (see Figure 2).

Figure 2

Then he must cover the first half of the remaining distance, and so on. In other words, he must first run one-half, then an additional one-fourth, then an additional one-eighth, etc., always remaining somewhere short of his goal. Hence, Zeno concludes, he can never reach it. This is the progressive form of the paradox, and it has very nearly the same force as Achilles and the Tortoise, the only difference being that in the Dichotomy the goal is stationary, while in Achilles and the Tortoise it moves, but at a speed much less than that of Achilles.

The regressive form of the Dichotomy attempts to show, worse yet, that the runner cannot even get started. Before he can complete the full distance, he must run half of it (see Figure 3). But before he can complete the first half, he must run half of that, namely, the first quarter.

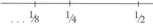

. . . ⅛   ¼   ½

Figure 3

Before he can complete the first quarter, he must run the first eighth. And so on. In order to cover any distance no matter how short, Zeno concludes, the runner must already have completed an infinite number of runs. Since the sequence of runs he must already have completed has the form of a regression,

$$\ldots \tfrac{1}{16}, \tfrac{1}{8}, \tfrac{1}{4}, \tfrac{1}{2}$$

it has no first member, and hence, the runner cannot even get started.

3. *The Arrow.* In this paradox, Zeno argues that an arrow in flight is always at rest. At any given instant, he claims, the arrow is where it is, occupying a portion of space equal to itself. During the instant it cannot move, for that would require the instant to have parts, and an instant is by definition a minimal and indivisible element of time. If the arrow did move during the instant it would have to be in one place at one part of the instant, and in a different place at another part of the instant. Moreover, for the arrow to move during the instant would require that during the instant it must occupy a space larger than itself, for otherwise it has no room to move. As Russell says, "It is never moving, but in some miraculous way the change of position has to occur *between* the instants, that is to say, not at any time whatever." This paradox is more difficult to understand than Achilles and the Tortoise or either form of the Dichotomy, but another remark by Russell is apt: "The more the difficulty is meditated, the more real it becomes."

4. *The Stadium.* Consider three rows of objects A, B, and C, arranged as in the first position of Figure 4. Then, while row A remains at rest, imagine rows B and C moving in opposite directions until all three rows are lined up as shown in the second position. In the process, C_1 passes twice as many B's as A's; it lines up with the first A to its left, but with the second B to its left. According to

First Position

	A_1	A_2	A_3
B_1	B_2	B_3	
	C_1	C_2	C_3

Second Position

A_1	A_2	A_3
B_1	B_2	B_3
C_1	C_2	C_3

Figure 4

Aristotle, Zeno concluded that "double the time is equal to half."

Some such conclusion would be warranted if we assume that the time it takes for a C to pass to the next B is the same as the time it takes to pass to the next A, but this assumption seems patently false. It appears that Zeno had no appreciation of relative speed, assuming that the speed of C relative to B is the same as the speed of C relative to A. If that were the only foundation for the paradox we would have no reason to be interested in it, except perhaps as a historical curiosity. It turns out, however, that there is an interpretation of this paradox which gives it serious import.

Suppose, as people occasionally do, that space and time are atomistic in character, being composed of space-atoms and time-atoms of non-zero size, rather than being composed of points and instants whose size is zero. Under these circumstances, motion would consist in taking up different discrete locations at different discrete instants. Now, if we suppose that the A's are not moving, but the B's move to the right at the rate of one place per instant while the C's move to the left at the same speed, some of the C's get past some of the B's without ever passing them. C_1 begins at the right of B_2 and it ends up at the left of B_2, but there is no instance at which it lines up with B_2; consequently, there is no time at which they pass each other—it never happens.

It has been suggested that Zeno's arguments fit into an overall pattern. Achilles and the Tortoise and the Dichotomy are designed to refute the doctrine that space and time are continuous, while the Arrow and the Stadium are intended to refute the view that space and time have an atomic structure. The paradox of plurality, which will be discussed later, also fits into the total schema. Thus, it has been argued, Zeno tries to cut off all possible avenues to escape from the conclusion that space, time, and motion are not real but illusory.

3. *Time Is a Measure of Change*

ARISTOTLE

Parmenides' view that the temporal world is not real had an influence on the two grandest metaphysical systems of ancient Greek philosophy, Plato's and Aristotle's. Plato basically agreed with Parmenides that real entities should be immune to puzzles surrounding time and change, and he claimed that only changeless, atemporal Forms (that is, ideal universals like circularity and justice) qualify as fully real objects. The ordinary particular things we perceive are only fleeting and imperfect instances of Forms. In this concession to Parmenides, Plato did not try to make time itself intelligible by developing a theory of time, though he did develop a picture of change according to which particulars "participate" in different Forms. Plato was content to poetically describe time as a (mere) moving image of eternity. (See his dialogue, *Timaeus* for remarks about time. Plato's *Phaedo* is reprinted in Part II; there Plato deals with the nature of change and the soul and claims that Forms cannot change).

In opposition to Plato (his teacher), Aristotle (384–322 BC) did not believe Forms existed separately from changing particulars. For him, ordinary objects (what he called "substances") were basic realities, and he tried to formulate a coherent account of change that did not cast doubt on their reality. As part of this effort, Aristotle wrestled with a variety of puzzles concerning time. What emerged was what might be viewed as the first relational theory of time. According to Aristotle, time is a measure (a way of numbering) change; so understanding time is a matter of understanding, in a particular way, how different states of substances are related. The selection reprinted here is from his *Physics*. Though Aristotle may have been trying to safeguard the world of common sense from views like Parmenides' and Plato's, his analyses are often technical and his writing style is compressed. It is believed that most of his surviving writings are not polished expositions, but rather notes for lectures. Readers should not be discouraged if they find this selection difficult.

Chapter 10

After what has been said, the next thing is to inquire into time. First, it is well to go through the problems about it, using the untechnical arguments as well [as technical ones]: whether it is among things that are or things that are not, and then what its nature is.

From *The Oxford Translation of Aristotle: Physics* (1942), edited by W. D. Ross, pp. 125–137. Reprinted by permission of Oxford University Press.

That it either is not at all or [only] scarcely and dimly is, might be suspected from the following considerations. (1) Some of it has been and is not, some of it is to be and is not yet. From these both infinite time and any arbitrary time are composed. But it would seem to be impossible that what is composed of things that are not should participate in being. (2) Further, it is necessary that, of everything that is resoluble into parts, if it is, either all the parts or some of them should be when it is. But of time, while it is resoluble into parts, some [parts] have been, some are to be, and none is. The now is not a part, for a part measures [the whole], and the whole must be composed of the parts, but time is not thought to be composed of nows. (3) Again, it is not easy to see whether the now, which appears to be the boundary between past and future, remains always one and the same or is different from time to time. (*a*) If it is always different, and if no two distinct parts of things that are in time are simultaneous—except those of which one includes the other, as the greater time includes the smaller—and if the now which is not but which previously was must have ceased to be at some time, then the nows too will not be simultaneous, and it must always be the case that the previous now has ceased-to-be. Now, that it has ceased-to-be in itself is not possible, because then it is; but it cannot be that the former now has ceased to be in another now, either. For we take it that it is impossible for the nows to be adjoining one another, as it is for a point to be adjoining a point; so, since the now has not ceased to be in the next now but in some other one, it will be simultaneously in the nows in between, which are infinitely many; but this is impossible. (*b*) Yet it is not possible either that the same now should always persist. For (*i*) nothing that is divisible and finite has [only] one limit, whether it is continuous in one direction or in more than one. But the now is a limit, and it is possible to take a finite time. Again (*ii*) if to be together in time and neither before or after, is to be in the one and the same now, and if both previous and subsequent [nows] are in this present now, then events of a thousand years ago will be simultaneous with those of today and none will be either previous or subsequent to any other.

Let this much, then, be our examination of difficulties about the properties of time. As to what time is and what its nature is, this is left equally unclear by the recorded opinions [of earlier thinkers] and by our own previous discussions. Some say it is the change of the universe, some the [celestial] sphere itself. Yet of the [celestial] revolution even a part is a time, though it is not a revolution. (The part considered is a part of a revolution, but not a revolution.) Again, if there were more than one world, time would equally be the change of any one whatever of them, so that there would be many times simultaneously. The sphere of the universe was thought to be time, by those who said it was, because everything is both in time and in the sphere of the universe; but this assertion is too simple-minded for us to consider the impossibilities it contains.

Since time is above all thought to be change, and a kind of alteration, this is what must be examined. Now the alteration and change of anything is only in the thing that is altering, or wherever the thing that is being changed and altering may chance to be; but time is equally everywhere and with everything. Again, alteration may be faster or slower, but not time; what is slow and what is fast is defined by time, fast being that which changes much in a short [time], slow that which changes little in a long [time]. But time is not defined by time, whether by its being so much or by its being of such a kind. It is manifest, then, that time is not change (let it make no difference to us, at present, whether we say 'change' or 'alteration').

Chapter 11

And yet [time is] not apart from alteration, either. When we ourselves do not alter in our mind or do not notice that we alter, then it does not seem to us that any time has passed, just as it does not seem so to the fabled sleepers in [the sanctuary of] the heroes in Sardinia, when they wake up; they join up the latter now to the former, and make it one, omitting what is in between because of failure to perceive it. So, just as, if the now were not different but one and the same, there would be no time, in the same way, even when the now *is* different but is not noticed to be different, what is in between does not seem to be any time. If, then, when we do not mark off any alteration, but the soul seems to remain in one indivisible, it happens as a consequence that we do not think there was any time, and if when we do perceive and mark off [an alteration], then we do say that some time has passed, then it is manifest that there is no time apart from change and alteration. It is manifest, then, that time neither is change nor is apart from change, and since we are looking for what time is we must start from this fact, and find what aspect of change it is. We perceive change and time together: even if it is dark and we are not acted upon through the body, but there is some change in the soul, it immediately seems to us that some time has passed together with the change. Moreover, whenever some time seems to have passed, some change seems to have occurred together with it. So that time is either change or some aspect of change; and since it is not change, it must be some aspect of change.

Now since what changes changes from something to something, and every magnitude is continuous, the change follows the magnitude: it is because the magnitude is continuous that the change is too. And it is because the change is that the time is. (For the time always seems to have been of the same amount as the change.)

Now the before and after is in place primarily; there, it is by convention. But since the before and after is in magnitude, it must also be in change, by analogy with what there is there. But in time, too, the before and after is present, because the one always follows the other of them. The before and after in change is, in respect of what makes it what it is, change; but its being is different and is not change.

But time, too, we become acquainted with when we mark off change, marking it off by the before and after, and we say that time has passed when we get a perception of the before and after in change. We mark off change by taking them to be different things, and some other thing between them; for whenever we conceive of the limits as other than the middle, and the soul says that the nows are two, one before and one after, then it is and this it is that we say time is. (What is marked off by the now is thought to be time: let this be taken as true.) So whenever we perceive the now as one, and not either as before and after in the change, or as the same but pertaining to something which is before and after, no time seems to have passed, because no change [seems to have occurred] either. But whenever [we do perceive] the before and after, then we speak of time.

For that is what time is: a number of change in respect of the before and after. So time is not change but in the way in which change has a number. An indication: we discern the greater and the less by number, and greater and less change by time; hence time is a kind of number. But number is [so called] in two ways: we call number both (*a*) that which is counted and countable, and (*b*) that by which we count. Time is that which is counted

and not that by which we count. (That by which we count is different from that which is counted.)

Just as the change is always other and other, so the time is too, though the whole time in sum is the same. For the now is the same X, whatever X it may be which makes it what it is; but its being is not the same. It is the now that measures time, considered as before and after. The now is in a way the same, and in a way not the same: considered as being at different stages, it is different—that is what it is for it to be a now—but whatever it is that makes it a now is the same. For change follows magnitude, as was said, and time, we assert, follows change. As it is with the point, then, so it is with the moving thing, by which we become acquainted with change and the before and after in it. The moving thing is, in respect of what makes it what it is, the same (as the point is, so is a stone or something else of that sort); but in definition it is different, in the way in which the sophists assume that being Coriscus-in-the-Lyceum is different from being Coriscus-in-the-marketplace. That, then, is different by being in different places, and the now follows the moving thing as time does change. For it is by the moving thing that we become acquainted with the before and after in change, and the before and after, considered as countable, is the now. Here too, then, whatever it is that makes it the now is the same—it is the before and after in change. But its being is different: the now is the before and after, considered as countable. Moreover, it is this that is most familiar; for the change too is known by that which changes, and the motion by the moving thing, because the moving thing is a 'this,' but the change is not. So the now is in a way the same always, and in a way not the same, since the moving thing too [is so].

It is manifest too that, if time were not, the now would not be either, and if the now were not, time would not be. For just as the moving thing and the motion go together, so too do the number of the moving thing and the number of the motion. Time is the number of the motion, and the now is, as the moving thing is, like a unit of number.

Moreover, time is both continuous, by virtue of the now, and divided at the now—this too follows the motion and the moving thing. For the change and the motion too are one by virtue of the moving thing, because that is one (not [one] X, whatever X it may be that makes it what it is—for then it might leave a gap—but [one] in definition). And this bounds the change before and after. This too in a sense follows the point: the point, too, both makes the length continuous and bounds it, being the beginning of one and the end of another. But when one takes it in this way, treating the one [point] as two, one must come to a halt, if the same point is to be both beginning and end. But the now is always different, because the moving thing changes. Hence time is a number, not as [a number] of the same point, in that it is beginning and end, but rather in the way in which the extremes [are the number] of the line—and not as the parts [of the line] are, both because of what has been said (one will treat the middle point as two, so that there will be rest as a result), and further [because] it is manifest that the now is no portion of time, nor [is] the division [a portion] of the change, any more than the point is of the line (it is the two lines that are portions of the one). So, considered as a limit, the now is not time but is accidentally so, while, considered as counting, it is a number. (For limits are of that alone of which they are limits, but the number of these horses, the ten, is elsewhere too.)

It is manifest then that time is a number of change in respect of the before and after, and is continuous, for it is [a number] of what is continuous.

Chapter 12

The least number, without qualification, is the two; but [a least] particular number there in a way is and in a way is not, e.g., of a line, the number least in multiplicity is two lines or one line, but in magnitude there is no least number, for every line always gets divided. So it is, then, with time too: the least time in respect of number is one time or two times, but in respect of magnitude there is none.

It is manifest too that it is not said to be fast or slow, but is said to be much and little, and long and short. It is as being continuous that it is long and short, and as a number that it is much and little. But it is not fast or slow—nor indeed is any number by which we count fast or slow.

It is the same time, too, everywhere together, but before and after it is not the same [time], since the present alteration is one, but the past alteration and the future one are different, and time is not the number by which we count but the number which is counted, and this number turns out to be always different before and after, because the nows are different. (The number of a hundred horses and that of a hundred men is one and the same, but the things of which it is the number are different—the horses are different from the men.) Again, in the sense in which it is possible for one and the same change to occur again and again, so too with time: e.g. a year, or spring or autumn.

Not only do we measure change by time, but time by change also, because they are defined by one another. The time defines the change, being its number, and the change the time. We speak of 'much time' and 'little time,' measuring it by change, just as we measure the number by what is countable: e.g. by the one horse we measure the number of the horses, for it is by number that we become acquainted with the multiplicity of the horses and, conversely, by the one horse that we become acquainted with the number of horses itself. Similarly, in the case of time and change, we measure the change by the time and the time by the change. It is reasonable that this should turn out so, because change follows magnitude, and time follows change, in being a quantity and continuous and divisible: for it is because the magnitude is of this kind that the change has these properties and because change is that time does. And we measure both magnitude by change and change by magnitude: we say the road is long, if the journey is long, and we say the journey is long, if the road is; and the time, if the change is, and the change, if the time is.

Since time is a measure of change and of being-in-change, and since it measures change by defining some change which will measure out the whole change (just as the cubit measures length by defining some magnitude which will measure off the whole magnitude), and since for a change the being in time is the being measured by time both of the change itself and of its being (time measures at once the change and the being of the change, and this is what it is, for the change, to be in time, viz. its being's being measured), it is clear, then, that for other things too this is what it is to be in time: their being's being measured by time. For to be in time is one or other of two things: *either,* to be when time is, *or,* [to be in it] in the way in which we say that some things are 'in number,' which means that [something is in number] *either* as a part or property of number, and, in general, that it is some aspect of number, *or* that there is a number of it. And since time is a number, the now and the before and everything of that kind are in time in the way in which the limit and the odd and the even are in number (they are aspects of number as the others are of time). But objects are [in time] as they are in number. If so, they are surrounded by time just as the things in number are by number and the things in place by place. It is manifest, too, that to be in time is not to be when time is, any more than to be in change or in place is to be when change is or place is. If this is what 'in something' is to mean, then all objects will be in anything whatever, and the world will be in the grain of millet, since when the grain is, the whole is too. This is accidentally so, but the other is a necessary consequence: for what is in time there must be some time when that too is, and for what is in change there must then be change.

Since what is in time is so as in a number, there will be found a time greater than anything that is in time, so that of necessity all things that are in time are surrounded by time, just like all other things that are in something: e.g. the things that are in place [are surrounded] by place. Moreover, they are acted upon in some respect by time, just as we are in the habit of saying 'time wears things away' and 'everything grows old through time' and 'forgets because of time'—but not 'learns because of time' or 'becomes young' or 'becomes beautiful.' For time, in itself, is responsible for ceasing-to-be rather [than for coming-to-be]; for it is the number of change, and change removes what is present. So it is manifest that the things that always are, considered as such, are not in time, for they are not surrounded by time, nor is their being measured by time, and an indication of this is that they are not acted on at all by time either, which shows that they are not in time.

And since time is the measure of change, it will be the measure of rest also. For all rest is in time; it is not the case that, as what is in change must change, so what is in time must, since time is not change but the number of change, and in the number of change there can also be that which is at rest. For it is not everything that is unchanging that is at rest, but that which, while deprived of change, has it in its nature to change, as was said earlier. For a thing to be in number is for there to be some number of the object, and for its being to be measured by the number in which it is, and so, if it is in time, by time. Time will measure what is changing and what is at rest, the one *qua* changing and the other *qua* at rest; for it will measure their change and their rest, [measuring] how great each is. Hence, what is changing is not measurable by time simply inasmuch as it is of some quantity, but inasmuch as its change is of some quantity. And so all that neither changes nor is at rest is not in time; for to be in time is to be measured by time, and time is a measure of change and rest.

It is manifest, therefore, that not everything that is not will be in time either; for example, all the things that cannot be otherwise [than not being], like the diagonal's being commensurate with the side. For in general, if time is a measure in itself of change and of other things accidentally, it is clear that all things of which it measures the being must have their being in being at rest or changing. Now all things that admit of ceasing-to-be and coming-to-be and, generally, that at some time are and at some time are not, must be in time—there will be some greater time which will exceed both their being and that [time] which measures their being. But, of things that are not, all that time surrounds either were (e.g. Homer once was) or will be (e.g. something future), on whichever side [of the present] it may surround them; and if on both sides, both. But all the things that it nowhere surrounds neither were nor are nor will be; and, among things that are not, such are all those that are such that their contraries always are: e.g. the diagonal's being incommensurable always is, and this will not be in time. So its being commensurable will not be [in time] either; so *that* always is not being opposite to what always is. But everything of which the opposite not always is, is capable of being and of not being, and there is coming-to-be of it and ceasing-to-be.

Chapter 13

The now is a link of time, as has been said, for it links together past and future time, and is a limit of time, since it is a beginning of one and an end of another. But this is not manifest, as it is in the case of the point at rest. It divides potentially, and *qua* such, the now is always different, but *qua* binding together it is always the same, just as in the case of mathematical lines: [a point is] not always the same point in thought, for if one divides the line it is different in different cases, but inasmuch as [the line] is one, [the point] is the same everywhere. So too the now is on the one hand a division of time, in potentiality, on the other hand the limit and union of both [times]; the division and the unification are the same thing and in respect of the same thing, but their being is not the same. This then is one sense of 'now'; another is when the time of a thing is close at hand: 'he will come now' because he will come today, 'he has now come,' because he came today. But it is not the case that the Trojan war has *now* occurred, or the deluge: the time *is* continuous [from now] to then, but they are not close at hand.

The 'at some time' is a time defined in relation to the now (in the former sense): e.g. 'Troy fell at some time,' 'the deluge will occur at some time'—the time must be finite in relation to the now. Therefore there will be a certain quantity of time from this to that, and there was [from this] to the past one. If there is no time which is not 'at some time,' every time will be finite. Will time then give out? Or not, if there always is change? Will it then be different, or the same many times over? It is clear that, as change is, so will time too be; if one and the same change comes to be at some time, the time too will be one and the same, and if not, not. Since the now is an end and a beginning of time, but not of the same time, being the end of past time and the beginning of future time, time will be like the circle—the convex and the concave are in what is in a sense the same—so too time is always at a beginning and at an end. And for this reason it is thought always different, for the now is not the beginning and the end of the same thing; otherwise opposites would hold simultaneously and in respect of the same thing.

And so time will not give out, for it is always at a beginning.

The *just* is that which is close to the present indivisible now, whether it is a part of future time ('when are you taking a walk?' 'I'm just taking it'—because the time in which he is going to go is near) or of past time, when it is not far from the now ('when are you taking a walk?' 'I've just taken it'). But to say that Troy has just fallen—we do not say it, because that is too far from the now. The *recently* is the portion of the past which is close to the present now. ('When did you come?' 'Recently,' if the time is close to the actual now.) What is far away [from the now] is *long ago*. The *suddenly* is that which removes out of its previous state in a time which is so small as to be imperceptible.

It is in time that everything comes to be and ceases to be. For this reason some called it the wisest of things, but the Pythagorean Paron the most foolish, because people forget in time too; and he was more correct. It is clear, then, that it is, in itself, responsible for ceasing-to-be rather than for coming-to-be, as was stated earlier, because alteration, in itself, is productive of removal from a previous state—but it is, accidentally, responsible for coming-to-be and for being. A sufficient indication is that nothing comes to be without its being changed in some way and being acted upon, but a thing may cease to be even though it is not changed, and this is above all what we usually call ceasing-to-be by the agency of time. Yet even this is not produced by time, but it happens that this alteration too occurs in time.

It has now been stated that time is, and what it is, and in how many ways 'now' is said, and what 'at some time' and 'recently' and 'just' and 'long ago' and 'suddenly' are.

Chapter 14

Now that we have determined these matters in this way, it is manifest that every alteration and all that changes is in time. 'Faster' and 'slower' apply to every alteration, since in every case this is obviously true. (I say that changes faster which is earlier to alter into a given [state], changing over the same extension and with a uniform change (e.g. in the case of locomotion, if both things are changing along the curve or along the straight line, and in other cases similarly).) But the before is in time, for we use 'before' and 'after' according to the distance from the now, and the now is the boundary of the past and the future. So, since the nows are in time, the before and after will also be in time; for the distance from the now will be in that in which the now is. ('Before' is applied in opposite ways in relation to past time and to future time: in the past, we call 'before' what is further from the now, and 'after' what is nearer to it, but in the future we call 'before' what is nearer and 'after' what is further.) So, since the before is in time, and the before accompanies every change, it is manifest that every alteration and every change is in time.

It is also worth investigating how time is related to the soul, and for what reason it is that time is thought to be in everything—on earth and in the sea and in the heavens. Is it that it is a property or a state of change, being the number [of it], and all these things are changeable, since they are all in place, and time and change are together both in potentiality and in actual operation? One might find it a difficult question, whether if there were no soul there would be time or not. For if it is impossible that there should be something to do the counting, it is also impossible that anything should be countable, so that it is clear that there would be no number either, for number is either that which has been counted or that which can be. But if there is nothing that has it in its nature to count except soul, and of soul [the part which is] intellect, then it is impossible that there should be time if there is no soul, except that there could be that X which time is, whatever X makes it what it is; as for example if it is possible for there to be change without soul. The before and after are in change, and time is these *qua* countable.

One might also find it a difficult question: of what kind of change is time a number? Perhaps of any kind whatever? After all, [things] come to be and cease to be and increase in size and change qualitatively and move in time. So it is a number of each change, in as much as there is change. Hence it is, without qualification, a number of continuous change, not of a particular [kind of] change. But it is possible that now something else as well has been made to change: so it would be

the number of either change. Is there then another time, and will there be two equal times together? Perhaps not, for the time which is equal and together is one and the same (and even those which are not together are the same in kind). Suppose there are some dogs and some horses, seven of each; the number is the same. In the same way, the time is the same of changes that reach a limit together, though one perhaps is fast and one not, one is locomotion and one a qualitative change. Still, the time is the same, if it is equal and together, of both the qualitative change and the locomotion. And this is why, while changes are various and in different places, time is everywhere the same, because the number, too, of things equal and together is one and the same everywhere.

Since there is locomotion, and, as a kind of locomotion, circular motion, and since each thing is counted by some one thing of the same kind (units by a unit, horses by a horse), and therefore time too by some definite time, and since, as we said, time is measured by change and change by time (that is, the quantity of the change and of the time is measured by the change defined by time)—if, then, that which is first is the measure of all things of the same sort, then uniform circular motion is most of all a measure, because the number of this is most easily known. (There is no uniform qualitative change or uniform increase in size or uniform coming-to-be, but there *is* uniform locomotion.) This is why time is thought to be the motion of the [celestial] sphere, because the other changes are measured by this one, and time by this change. And for this reason too, what is commonly said turns out true: people say that human affairs are a cycle, and so is what happens to the other things that have a natural motion and come to be and cease to be. This is so because all these things are discerned by means of time, and make an end and a beginning as if according to some circular course. Indeed, time itself is thought to be a kind of cycle, and this, in turn, is thought because it is the measure of what kind of motion and is itself measured by that kind. So that to say that those things that come to be are a cycle is to say that there is a kind of cycle of time; and this is so, because it is measured by circular motion. For, over and above the measure, nothing else is apparent which is obviously measured, but the whole is either one measure or more than one.

It is correct, too, to say that the number of the sheep and of the dogs is the same, if each number is equal, but that the ten is not the same [ten] nor [are there] ten of the same; just as the equilateral and the scalene are not the same triangles, though they are the same figure, in that both are triangles. For a thing is said to be the same X if it does not differ by the difference of an X, but not [the same X] if it does: e.g. a triangle differs from a triangle by the difference of a triangle, and therefore they are different triangles; but it does not [differ by the

difference] of a figure, but the two are in one and the same division. For one kind of figure is a circle, another a triangle, and one kind of triangle is equilateral, another is scalene. So they are the same figure, namely a triangle, but not the same triangle. And so too it is the same number, since the number of them does not differ by the difference of a number, but not the same ten, since the things it is said of are different: dogs in one case, horses in another.

An account, then, has been given both of time itself and of the connected matters proper to our inquiry.

4. *What Is Time?*

ST. AUGUSTINE

Augustine (354–430) lived in North Africa, where he experienced the social transformations associated with the decline of the Roman Empire. He converted to Christianity in 386, became bishop of Hippo in 395, and died when the Vandals were attacking his city. Augustine worried about the nature of time in response to theological challenges. Christian doctrine had maintained that God created the world from nothing, but Manichaean objectors wondered what God was doing *before* creation and why the world was created at one time rather than another. For Augustine, the challenge was to answer these questions without making God subject to change (that is, without making God something less than eternally perfect). In dealing with these issues, he was led to consider additional problems. What kind of reality do the past and the future have? How can the future be known by God and the prophets unless it already exists? And, much as Zeno and Aristotle wondered, how can there be change in the present if the present is a moment that does not have earlier and later parts? Like Aristotle, Augustine maintained that time is not something prior to, or independent of, change; so he concluded there is no time "before" creation. Not being willing to identify time with the numbering of change, however, Augustine drew attention to the possibility that temporal distinctions are subjective when he suggested that time may be a "protraction" of mind.

From *Confessions*, St. Augustine, Book XI, sections X–XXXI, trans. E. B. Pusey. Copyright © 1948 by Regnery Gateway. Reprinted by permission.

Lo are they not full of their old leaven, who say to us, "What was God doing before *He made heaven and earth?*" "For if (say they) He were unemployed and wrought not, why does He not also henceforth, and for ever, as He did heretofore? For did any new motion arise in God, and a new will to make a creature, which He had never before made, how then would that be a true eternity, where there ariseth a will, which was not? For the will of God is not a creature, but before the creature; seeing nothing could be created, unless the will of the Creator had preceded. The will of God then belongeth to His very Substance. And if aught have arisen in God's Substance, which before was not, that Substance cannot be truly called eternal. But if the will of God has been from eternity that the creature should be, why was not the creature also from eternity?"

Who speaks thus, do not yet understand Thee, O Wisdom of God, Light of souls, understand not yet how the things be made, which by Thee, and in Thee are made: yet they strive to comprehend things eternal, whilst their heart fluttereth between the motions of things past and to come, and is still unstable. Who shall hold it, and fix it, that it be settled awhile, and awhile catch the glory of that ever-fixed Eternity, and compare it with the times which are never fixed, and see that it cannot be compared; and that a long time cannot become long, but out of many motions passing by, which cannot be prolonged altogether; but that in the Eternal nothing passeth, but the whole is present; whereas no time is all at once present: and that all time past, is driven on by time to come, and all to come followeth upon the past; and all past and to come, is created, and flows out of that which is ever present? Who shall hold the heart of man, that it may stand still, and see how eternity ever still-standing, neither past nor to come, uttereth the times past and to come? Can my hand do this, or the hand of my mouth by speech bring about a thing so great?

See, I answer him that asketh, "What did God do before He *made heaven and earth?*" I answer not as one is said to have done merrily (eluding the pressure of the question) "He was preparing hell (saith he) for pryers into mysteries." It is one thing to answer enquiries, another to make sport of enquirers. So I answer not; for rather had I answer, "I know not," what I know not, than so as to raise a laugh at him who asketh deep things and gain praise for one who answereth false things. But I say that Thou, our God, art the Creator of every crea-

ture: and if by the name "heaven and earth," every creature be understood; I boldly say, "that before God made heaven and earth, He did not make any thing." For if He made, what did He make but a creature? And would I knew whatsoever I desire to know to my profit, as I know, that no creature was made, before there was made any creature.

But if any excursive brain rove over the images of forepassed times, and wonder that Thou the God Almighty and All-creating and All-supporting, Maker of heaven and earth, didst for innumerable ages forbear from so great a work, before Thou wouldest make it; let him awake and consider, that he wonders at false conceits. For whence could innumerable ages pass by, which Thou madest not, Thou the Author and Creator of all ages? or what times should there be, which were not made by Thee? or how should they pass by, if they never were? Seeing then Thou art the Creator of all times, if any time was before Thou *madest heaven and earth,* why say they that Thou didst forego working? For that very time didst Thou make, nor could times pass by, before Thou madest those times. But if before *heaven and earth* there was no time, why is it demanded, what Thou then didst? For there was no "then," when there was no time.

Nor dost Thou by time, precede time: else shouldest Thou not precede all times. But Thou precedest all things past, by the sublimity of an ever-present eternity; and surpassest all future because they are future, and when they come, they shall be past; *but Thou art the Same, and Thy years fail not.* Thy years neither come nor go; whereas ours both come and go, that they all may come. Thy years stand together, because they do stand; nor are departing thrust out by coming years, for they pass not away; but ours shall all be, when they shall no more be. Thy years are one day; and Thy day is not daily, but To-day, seeing Thy To-day gives not place unto to-morrow, for neither doth it replace yesterday. Thy To-day, is Eternity; therefore didst Thou beget The Coeternal, to whom Thou saidst, *This day have I begotten Thee.* Thou hast made all things; and before all times Thou art: neither in any time was time not.

At no time then hadst Thou not made any thing, because time itself Thou madest. And no times are coeternal with Thee, because Thou abidest; but if they abode, they should not be times. For what is time? Who can readily and briefly explain this? Who can even in thought comprehend it, so as to utter a word about it? But what in discourse do we mention more familiarly and knowingly, than time? And, we understand, when we speak of it; we understand also, when we hear it spoken of by another. What, then, is time? If no one asks me, I know: if I wish to explain it to one that asketh, I know not: yet I say boldly that I know, that if nothing passed away, time past were not; and if nothing were coming, a time to come were not; and if nothing were, time present were not. Those two times then, past and to come, how are they, seeing the past now is not, and that to come is not yet? But the present, should it always be present, and never pass into time past, verily it should not be time, but eternity. If time present (if it is to be time) only cometh into existence, because it passeth into time past, how can we say that either this is, whose cause of being is, that it shall not be; so, namely, that we cannot truly say that time is, but because it is tending not to be?

And yet we say, "a long time" and "a short time;" still, only of time past or to come. A long time past (for example) we call an hundred years since; and a long time to come, an hundred years hence. But a short time past, we call (suppose) ten days since; and a short time to come, ten days hence. But in what sense is that long or short, which is not? For the past, is not now; and the future, is not yet. Let us not then say, "it is long;" but of the past, "it hath been long;" and of the future, "it will be long." O my Lord, my Light, shall not here also Thy Truth mock at man? For that past time which was long, was it long when it was now past, or when it was yet present? For then might it be long, when there was, what could be long; but when past, it was no longer; wherefore neither could that be long, which was not at all. Let us not then say, "time past hath been long:" for we shall not find, what hath been long, seeing that since it was past, it is no more; but let us say, "that present time was long;" because, when it was present, it was long. For it had not yet passed away, so as not to be; and therefore there was, what could be long; but after it was past, that ceased also to be long, which ceased to be.

Let us see then, thou soul of man, whether present time can be long: for to thee it is given to feel and to measure length of time. What wilt thou answer me? Are an hundred years, when present, a long time? See first, whether an hundred years can be present. For if the first of these years be now current, it is present, but the other ninety and nine are to come, and therefore are not yet, but if the second year be current, one is now past, another present, the rest to come. And so if we assume any middle year of this hundred to be present, all before it, are past; all after it, to come; wherefore an hundred years cannot be present. But see at least whether that one which is now current, itself is present; for if the current month be its first, the rest are to come; if the second, the first is already past, and the rest are not yet. Therefore, neither is the year now current present; and if not present as a whole, then is not the year present. For twelve months are a year; of which whatever be the current month is present; the rest past, or to come. Although neither is that current month present; but one day only; the rest being to come, if it be the first; past, if the last; if any of the middle, then amid past and to come.

See how the present time, which alone we found could be called long, is abridged to the length scarce of one day. But let us examine that also; because neither is one day present as a whole. For it is made up of four and twenty hours of night and day: of which, the first hath the rest to come; the last hath them past; and any of the middle hath those before it past, those behind it to come. Yea, that one hour passeth away in flying particles. Whatsoever of it hath flown away, is past; whatsoever remaineth, is to come. If an instant of time be conceived, which cannot be divided into the smallest particles of moments, that alone is it, which may be called present. Which yet flies with such speed from future to past, as not to be lengthened out with the least stay. For if it be, it is divided into past and future. The present hath no space. Where then is the time, which we may call long? Is it to come? Of it we do not say, "it is long;" because it is not yet, so as to be long; but we say, "it will be long." When therefore will it be? For if even then, when it is yet to come, it shall not be long, (because what can be long, as yet is not,) and so it shall then be long, when from future which as yet is not, it shall begin now to be, and have become present, that so there should exist what may be long; then does time present cry out in the words above, that it cannot be long.

And yet, Lord, we perceive intervals of times, and compare them, and say, some are shorter, and others longer. We measure also, how much longer or shorter this time is than that; and we answer, "This is double, or treble; and that, but once, or only just so much as that." But we measure times as they are passing, by perceiving them; but past, which now are not, or the future, which are not yet, who can measure? unless a man shall presume to say, that can be measured, which is not. When time is passing, it may be perceived and measured; but when it is past, it cannot, because it is not.

I ask, Father, I affirm not: O my God, rule and guide me. "Who will tell me that there are not three times, (as we learned when boys, and taught boys,) past, present, and future; but present only, because those two are not? Or are they also; and when from future it becometh present, doth it come out of some secret place; and so, when retiring, from present it becometh past? For where did they, who foretold things to come, see them, if as yet they be not? For that which is not, cannot be seen. And they who relate things past, could not relate them, if in mind they did not discern them, and if they were not, they could no way be discerned. Things then past and to come are."

Permit me, Lord, to seek further. O my hope, let not my purpose be confounded. For if times past and to come be, I would know where they be. Which yet if I cannot, yet I know, wherever they be, they are not there as future, or past, but present. For if there also they be future, they are not yet there; if there also they be past, they are no longer there. Wheresoever then is whatsoever is, it is only as present. Although when past facts are related, there are drawn out of the memory, not the things themselves which are past, but words which, conceived by the images of the things, they, in passing, have through the senses left as traces in the mind. Thus my childhood, which now is not, is in time past, which now is not: but now when I recall its image, and tell of it, I behold it in the present, because it is still in my memory. Whether there be a like cause of foretelling things to come also; that of things which as yet are not, the images may be perceived before, already existing, I confess, O my God, I know not. This indeed I know, that we generally think before on our future actions, and that that forethinking is present, but the action whereof we forethink is not

yet, because it is to come. Which, when we have set upon, and have begun to do what we were forethinking, then shall that action be; because then it is no longer future, but present.

Which way soever then this secret fore-perceiving of things to come be; that only can be seen, which is. But what now is, is not future, but present. When then things to come are said to be seen, it is not themselves which as yet are not, (that is, which are to be,) but their causes perchance or signs are seen, which already are. Therefore they are not future but present to those who now see that, from which the future, being fore-conceived in the mind, is foretold. Which fore-conceptions again now are; and those who foretell those things, do behold the conceptions present before them. Let now the numerous variety of things furnish me some example. I behold the day-break, I foreshew, that the sun is about to rise. What I behold, is present; what I foresignify, to come; not the sun, which already is; but the sun-rising, which is not yet. And yet did I not in my mind imagine the sun-rising itself, (as now while I speak of it,) I could not foretell it. But neither is that daybreak which I discern in the sky, the sun-rising, although it goes before it; nor that imagination of my mind; which two are seen now present, that the other which is to be may be foretold. Future things then are not yet: and if they be not yet, they are not: and if they are not, they cannot be seen; yet foretold they may be from things present, which are already, and are seen.

Thou then, Ruler of Thy creation, by what way dost Thou teach souls things to come? For Thou didst teach Thy Prophets. By what way dost Thou, to whom nothing is to come, teach things to come, or rather of the future, dost teach things present? For, what is not, neither can it be taught. Too far is this way out of my ken: *it is too mighty for me, I cannot attain unto it;* but from Thee I can, when Thou shalt vouchsafe it, O sweet light of my hidden eyes.

What now is clear and plain is, that neither things to come nor past are. Nor is it properly said, "there be three times, past, present, and to come:" yet perchance it might be properly said, "there be three times; a present of things past, a present of things present, and a present of things future." For these three do exist in some sort, in the soul, but otherwhere do I not see them; present of things past, memory; present of things present, sight; present of things future, expectation. If thus we be permitted to speak, I see three times, and I confess there are three. Let it be said too, "there be three times, past, present, and to come:" in our incorrect way. See, I object not, nor gainsay, nor find fault, if what is so said be but understood, that neither what is to be, now is, nor what is past. For but few things are there, which we speak properly, most things improperly; still the things intended are understood.

I said then even now, we measure times as they pass, in order to be able to say, this time is twice so much as that one; or, this is just so much as that; and so of any other parts of time, which be measurable. Wherefore, as I said, we measure times as they pass. And if any should ask me, "How knowest thou?" I might answer, "I know, that we do measure, nor can we measure things that are not; and things past and to come, are not." But time present how do we measure, seeing it hath no space? It is measured while passing, but when it shall have passed, it is not measured; for there will be nothing to be measured. But whence, by what way, and whither passes it while it is a measuring? whence, but from the future? Which way, but through the present? whither, but into the past? From that therefore, which is not yet, through that, which hath no space, into that, which now is not. Yet what do we measure, if not time in some space? For we do not say, single, and double, and triple, and equal, or any other like way that we speak of time, except of spaces of times. In what space then do we measure time passing? In the future, whence it passeth through? But what is not yet, we measure not. Or in the present, by which it passes? but no space, we do not measure: or in the past, to which it passes? But neither do we measure that, which now is not.

My soul is on fire to know this most intricate enigma. Shut it not up, O Lord my God, good Father; through Christ I beseech Thee, do not shut up these usual, yet hidden things, from my desire, that it be hindered from piercing into them; but let them dawn through Thy enlightening mercy, O Lord. Whom shall I enquire of concerning these things? and to whom shall I more fruitfully confess my ignorance, than to Thee, to Whom these my studies, so vehemently kindled toward Thy Scriptures, are not troublesome? Give what I love; for I do love, and this hast Thou given me. Give, Father, Who *truly knowest to give good gifts unto Thy children*. Give, because I have taken upon me to know, and trouble is before me until Thou openest it. By Christ I beseech Thee, in His Name, Holy of holies, let no man disturb me. For *I believed, and therefore do I speak*. This is my hope, for this do I live, that *I may contemplate the delights of the Lord*. Behold, *Thou hast made my days* old, and they pass away, and how, I know not. And we talk of time, and time, and times, and times, "How long time is it since he said this;" "how long time since he did this;" and "how long time since I saw that;" and "this syllable hath double time to that single short syllable." These words we speak, and these we hear, and are understood, and understand. Most manifest and ordinary they are, and the self-same things again are but too deeply hidden, and the discovery of them were new.

I heard once from a learned man, that the motions of the sun, moon, and stars, constituted time, and I assented not. For why should not the motions of all bodies rather be times? Or, if the lights of heaven should cease, and a potter's wheel run round, should there be no time by which we might measure those whirlings, and say, that either it moved with equal pauses, or if it turned sometimes slower, otherwhiles quicker, that some rounds were longer, other shorter? Or, while we were saying this, should we not also be speaking in time? Or, should there in our words be some syllables short, others long, but because those sounded in a shorter time, these in a longer? God, grant to men to see in a small thing notices common to things great and small. The stars and lights of heaven, are also *for signs, and for seasons, and for years, and for days;* they are; yet neither should I say, that the going round of that wooden wheel was a day, nor yet he, that it was therefore no time.

I desire to know the force and nature of time, by which we measure the motions of bodies, and say (for example) this motion is twice as long as that. For I ask, seeing "day" denotes not the stay only of the sun upon the earth, (according to which day is one thing, night another;) but also its whole circuit from east to east again; according to which we say, "there passed so many days," the night being included when we say "so many days," and the nights not reckoned apart;—seeing then a day is completed by the motion of the sun and by his circuit from east to east again, I ask, does the motion alone make the day, or the stay in which that motion is completed, or both? For if the first be the day; then should we have a day, although the sun should finish that course in so small a space of time, as one hour comes to. If the second, then should not that make a day, if between one sunrise and another there were but so short a stay, as one hour comes to; but the sun must go four and twenty times about, to complete one day. If both, then neither could that be called a day, if the sun should run his whole round in the space of one hour; nor that, if, while the sun stood still, so much time should overpass, as the sun usually makes his whole course in, from morning to morning. I will not therefore now ask, what that is which is called day; but, what time is, whereby we, measuring the circuit of the sun, should say that it was finished in half the time it was wont, if so be it was finished in so small a space as twelve hours, and comparing both times, should call this a single time, that a double time; even supposing the sun to run his round from east to east, sometimes in that single, sometimes in that double time. Let no man then tell me, that the motions of the heavenly bodies constitute times, because, when at the prayer of one, the sun had stood still, till he could achieve his victorious battle, the sun stood still, but time went on. For in its own allotted space of time was that battle waged and ended. I perceive time then to be a certain extension. But do I perceive it, or seem to perceive it? Thou, Light and Truth, wilt shew me.

Dost Thou bid me assent, if any define time to be "motion of a body?" Thou dost not bid me. For that no body is moved, but in time, I hear; this Thou sayest; but that the motion of a body is time, I hear not; Thou sayest it not. For when a body is moved, I by time measure, how long it moveth, from the time it began to move, until it left off? And if I did not see whence it began; and it continue to move so that I see not when it ends, I cannot measure, save perchance from the time I began, until I cease to see. And if I took long, I can only pronounce it to be a long time, but not how long; because when we say "how long," we do it by comparison; as, "this is as long as that," or "twice so long as that," or the like. But when we can mark the distance of the places, whence and whither goeth the body moved, or his parts, if it moved as in a

lathe, then can we say precisely, in how much time the motion of that body or his part, from this place unto that, was finished. Seeing therefore the motion of a body is one thing, that by which we measure how long it is, another; who sees not, which of the two is rather to be called time? For and if a body be sometimes moved, sometimes stands still, then we measure, not his motion only, but his standing still too by time; and we say, "it stood still, as much as it moved;" or "it stood still twice or thrice so long as it moved;" or any other space which our measuring hath either ascertained, or guessed; more or less, as we use to say. Time then is not the motion of a body.

And I confess to Thee, O Lord, that I yet know not what time is, and again I confess unto Thee, O Lord, that I know that I speak this in time, and that having long spoken of time, that very "long" is not long, but by the pause of time. How then know I this, seeing I know not what time is? or is it perchance that I know not how to express what I know? Woe is me, that do not even know, what I know not. Behold, O my God, before Thee I lie not; but as I speak so is my heart. *Thou shalt light my candle; Thou O Lord my God, wilt enlighten my darkness.*

Does not my soul most truly confess unto Thee, that I do measure times? Do I then measure, O my God, and know not what I measure? I measure the motion of a body in time; and the time itself do I not measure? Or could I indeed measure the motion of a body how long it were, and in how long space it could come from this place to that, without measuring the time in which it is moved? This same time then, how do I measure? do we by a shorter time measure a longer, as by the space of a cubit, the space of a rood? for so indeed we seem by the space of a short syllable, to measure the space of a long syllable, and to say that this is double the other. Thus measure we the spaces of stanzas, by the spaces of the verses, and the spaces of the verses, by the spaces of the feet, and the spaces of the feet, by the spaces of the syllables, and the spaces of long, by the spaces of short syllables; not measuring by pages, (for then we measure spaces, not times;) but when we utter the words and they pass by, and we say "it is a long stanza, because composed of so many verses; long verses, because consisting of so many feet; long feet, because prolonged by so many syllables; a long syllable because double to a short one." But neither do we this way obtain any certain measure of time; because it may be, that a shorter verse, pronounced more fully, may take up more time than a longer, pronounced hurriedly. And so for a verse, a foot, a syllable. Whence it seemed to me, that time is nothing else than protraction; but of what, I know not; and I marvel, if it be not of the mind itself? For what I beseech Thee, O my God, do I measure, when I say, either indefinitely "this is a longer time than that," or definitely "this is double that?" That I measure time, I know; and yet I measure not time to come, for it is not yet; nor present, because it is not protracted by any space; nor past, because it now is not. What then do I measure? Times passing, not past? for so I said.

Courage, my mind, and press on mightily. God is our helper, He *made us, and not we ourselves*. Press on where truth begins to dawn. Suppose, now, the voice of a body begins to sound, and does sound, and sounds on, and list, it ceases; it is silence now, and that voice is past, and is no more a voice. Before it sounded, it was to come, and could not be measured, because as yet it was not, and now it cannot, because it is no longer. Then therefore while it sounded, it might; because there then was what might be measured. But yet even then it was not at a stay; for it was passing on, and passing away. Could it be measured the rather, for that? For while passing, it was being extended into some space of time, so that it might be measured, since the present hath no space. If therefore then it might, then, lo, suppose another voice hath begun to sound, and still soundeth in one continued tenor without any interruption; let us measure it while it sounds; seeing when it hath left sounding, it will then be past, and nothing left to be measured; let us measure it verily, and tell how much it is. But it sounds still, nor can it be measured but from the instant it began in, unto the end it left in. For the very space between is the thing we measure, namely, from some beginning unto some end. Wherefore, a voice that is not yet ended, cannot be measured, so that it may be said how long, or short it is; nor can it be called equal to another, or double to a single, or the like. But when ended, it no longer is. How may it then be measured? And yet we measure times; but yet neither those which are not yet, nor those which no longer are, nor those which are not lengthened out by some pause, nor those

which have no bounds. We measure neither times to come, nor past, nor present, nor passing; and yet we do measure times.

"Deus Creator omnium," this verse of eight syllables alternates between short and long syllables. The four short then, the first, third, fifth, and seventh, are but single, in respect of the four long, the second, fourth, sixth, and eighth. Every one of these, to every one of those, hath a double time: I pronounce them, report on them, and find it so, as one's plain sense perceives. By plain sense then, I measure a long syllable by a short, and I sensibly find it to have twice so much; but when one sounds after the other, if the former be short, the latter long, how shall I detain the short one, and how, measuring, shall I apply it to the long, that I may find this to have twice so much; seeing the long does not begin to sound, unless the short leaves sounding? And that very long one do I measure as present, seeing I measure it not till it be ended? Now his ending is his passing away. What then is it I measure? where is the short syllable by which I measure? where the long which I measure? Both have sounded, have flown, passed away, are no more; and yet I measure, and confidently answer (so far as is presumed on a practised sense) that as to space of time this syllable is but single, that double. And yet I could not do this, unless they were already past and ended. It is not then themselves, which now are not, that I measure, but something in my memory, which there remains fixed.

It is in thee, my mind, that I measure times. Interrupt me not, that is, interrupt not thyself with the tumults of thy impressions. In thee I measure times; the impression, which things as they pass by cause in thee, remains even when they are gone; this it is which, still present, I measure, not the things which pass by to make this impression. This I measure, when I measure times. Either then this is time, or I do not measure times. What when we measure silence, and say that this silence hath held as long time as did that voice? do we not stretch out our thought to the measure of a voice, as if it sounded that so we may be able to report of the intervals of silence in a given space of time? For though both voice and tongue be still, yet in thought we go over poems, and verses, and any other discourse, or dimensions of motions, and report as to the spaces of times, how much this is in respect of that, no otherwise than if vocally we did pronounce them. If a man would utter a lengthened sound, and had settled in thought how long it should be, he hath in silence already gone through a space of time, and committing it to memory, begins to utter that speech, which sounds on, until it be brought unto the end proposed. Yea it hath sounded, and will sound; for so much of it as is finished, hath sounded already, and the rest will sound. And thus passeth it on, until the present intent conveys over the future into the past; the past increasing by the diminution of the future, until by the consumption of the future, all is past.

But how is that future diminished or consumed, which as yet is not? or how that past increased, which is now no longer, save that in the mind which enacteth this, there be three things done? For it expects, it considers, it remembers; that so that which it expecteth, through that which it considereth, passeth into that which it remembereth. Who therefore denieth, that things to come are not as yet? and yet, there is in the mind an expectation of things to come. And who denies past things to be now no longer? and yet is there still in the mind a memory of things past. And who denieth that the present time hath no space, because it passeth away in a moment? and yet our consideration continueth, through which that which shall be present proceedeth to become absent. It is not then future time, that is long, for as yet it is not: but a "long future," is "a long expectation of the future," nor is it time past, which now is not, that is long; but a long past, is "a long memory of the past."

I am about to repeat a Psalm that I know. Before I begin, my expectation is extended over the whole; but when I have begun, how much soever of it I shall separate off into the past, is extended along my memory; thus the life of this action of mine is divided between my memory as to what I have repeated, and expectation as to what I am about to repeat; but "consideration" is present with me, that through it what was future, may be conveyed over, so as to become past. Which the more it is done again and again, so much the more the expectation being shortened, is the memory enlarged; till the whole expectation be at length exhausted, when that whole action being ended, shall have passed into memory. And

this which takes place in the whole Psalm, the same takes place in each several portion of it, and each several syllable; the same holds in that longer action, whereof this Psalm may be a part; the same holds in the whole life of man, whereof all the actions of man are parts; the same holds through the whole age of the sons of men, whereof all the lives of men are parts.

But because *Thy loving kindness is better than all lives,* behold, my life is but a distraction, and *Thy right hand upheld me,* in my Lord the *Son of man,* the *Mediator betwixt Thee,* The One, and us many, many also through our manifold distractions amid many things, that by Him *I may apprehend in Whom I have been apprehended,* and may be recollected from my old conversation, to follow The One, *forgetting what is behind, and* not distended, but *extended,* not to things which shall be and shall pass away, but *to those things which are before,* not distractedly but intently, *I follow on for the prize of my heavenly calling,* where I may *hear the voice* of Thy *praise,* and *contemplate* Thy *delights,* neither to come, nor to pass away. But now *are my years spent in mourning.* And Thou, O Lord, art my comfort, my Father everlasting, but I have been severed amid times, whose order I know not; and my thoughts, even the inmost bowels of my soul, are rent and mangled with tumultuous varieties, until I flow together into Thee, purified and molten by the fire of Thy love.

And now will I stand, and become firm in Thee, in my mould, Thy truth; nor will I endure the questions of men, who by a penal disease thirst for more than they can contain, and say, "what did God do before He *made heaven and earth?*" "Or, how came it into His mind to make anything, having never before made any thing?" Give them, O Lord, well to bethink themselves what they say, and to find, that "never" cannot be predicated, when "time" is not. This then that He is said "never to have made;" what else is it to say, than "in 'no time' to have made?" Let them see therefore, that time cannot be without created being, and cease to *speak* that *vanity.* May they also be *extended towards those things which are before;* and understand Thee before all times, the eternal Creator of all times, and that no times be coeternal with Thee, nor any creature, even if there be any creature before all times.

O Lord my God, what a depth is that recess of Thy mysteries, and how far from it have the consequences of my transgressions cast me! Heal mine eyes, that I may share the joy of Thy light. Certainly, if there be a mind gifted with such vast knowledge and foreknowledge, as to know all things past and to come, as I know one well-known Psalm, truly that mind is passing wonderful, and fearfully amazing; in that nothing past, nothing to come in after-ages, is any more hidden from him, than when I sung that Psalm, was hidden from me what, and how much of it had passed away from the beginning, what, and how much there remined unto the end. But far be it that Thou the Creator of the Universe, the Creator of souls and bodies, far be it, that Thou shouldest in such wise know all things past and to come. Far, far more wonderfully, and far more mysteriously, dost thou know them. For not, as the feelings of one who singeth what he knoweth, or heareth some well-known song, are through expectation of the words to come, and the remembering of those that are past, varied, and his senses divided,—not so doth any thing happen unto Thee, unchangeably eternal, that is, the eternal Creator of minds. Like then as Thou *in the Beginning* knewest *the heaven and the earth,* without any variety of Thy knowledge, so *madest* Thou *in the Beginning heaven and earth,* without any distraction of Thy action. Whoso understandeth, let him confess unto Thee; and whoso understandeth not, let him confess unto Thee. Oh how high art Thou, and yet the humble in heart are Thy dwelling-place; for Thou *raisest up those that are bowed down,* and they fall not, whose elevation Thou art.

---

5. *Time Is Absolute*

ISAAC NEWTON

Isaac Newton (1642–1727) was the English mathematician and physicist whose work ensured the success of the Scientific Revolution. In previous generations, people like Copernicus, Galileo, and Descartes had advanced the use of mathematics as a tool for describing the natural world. Newton's invention of the mathematics of "fluxions" (that is, calculus), his formulation of the laws of motion, and his mathematical treatment of gravity successfully showed how both earthly and celestial phenomena could be viewed as the predictable behavior of matter in motion. The new theories made frequent reference to time because they dealt with the velocity and acceleration of objects and with the duration that objects were acted upon by forces. Newton was aware that not every "sensible" measurement of time led to the right results, so he made a distinction between absolute and relative time. He made a similar distinction between absolute and relative space, believing real forces were the ones that produced accelerations with respect to absolute space and time. These distinctions were rejected by Leibniz (Newton's contemporary) and abandoned in 1905 by Einstein in his special theory of relativity. (Philosophers, however, still debate whether the "spacetime" of later physics is in some way absolute.) Nonetheless, Newton's characterization of absolute time is important not only because it was a significant part of science for 200 years, but also because it gave voice to the common idea that time flows independently whether or not things change. In this view, time is something that changes occur "in," and the distinction between the past, present, and future is *sui generis.*

Hitherto I have laid down the definitions of such words as are less known, and explained the sense in which I would have them to be understood in the following discourse. I do not define time, space, place, and motion, as being well known to all. Only I must observe, that the common people conceive those quantities under no other notions but from the relation they bear to sensible objects. And thence arise certain prejudices, for the removing of which it will be convenient to distinguish them into absolute and relative, true and apparent, mathematical and common.

I. Absolute, true, and mathematical time, of itself, and from its own nature, flows equably without relation to anything external, and by another name is called duration: relative, apparent, and common time, is some sensible and external (whether accurate or unequable) measure of duration by the means of motion, which is commonly used instead of true time; such as an hour, a day, a month, a year.

II. Absolute space, in its own nature, without relation to anything external, remains always similar and immovable. Relative space is some movable dimension or measure of the absolute spaces; which our senses determine by its position to bodies; and which is commonly taken for immovable space; such is the dimension of a subterraneous, an aerial, or celestial space, determined by its position in respect of the earth. Absolute and relative space are the same in figure and magnitude; but they do not remain always numerically the same. For if the earth, for instance, moves, a space of our air, which relatively and in respect of the earth remains always the same, will at one time be one part of the absolute space into which the air passes; at another time it will be another part of the same, and so,

absolutely understood, it will be continually changed.

III. Place is a part of space which a body takes up, and is according to the space, either absolute or relative. I say, a part of space; not the situation, nor the external surface of the body. For the places of equal solids are always equal; but their surfaces, by reason of their dissimilar figures, are often unequal. Positions properly have no quantity, nor are they so much the places themselves, as the properties of places. The motion of the whole is the same with the sum of the motions of the parts; that is, the translation of the whole, out of its place, is the same thing with the sum of the translations of the parts out of their places; and therefore the place of the whole is the same as the sum of the places of the parts, and for that reason, it is internal, and in the whole body.

IV. Absolute motion is the translation of a body from one absolute place into another; and relative motion, the translation from one relative place into another. Thus in a ship under sail, the relative place of a body is that part of the ship which the body possesses; or that part of the cavity which the body fills, and which therefore moves together with the ship: and relative rest is the continuance of the body in the same part of the ship, or of its cavity. But real, absolute rest, is the continuance of the body in the same part of that immovable space, in which the ship itself, its cavity, and all that it contains, is moved. Wherefore, if the earth is really at rest, the body, which relatively rests in the ship, will really and absolutely move with the same velocity which the ship has on the earth. But if the earth also moves, the true and absolute motion of the body will arise, partly from the true motion of the earth, in immovable space, partly from the relative motion of the ship on the earth; and if the body moves also relatively in the ship, its true motion will arise, partly from the true motion of the earth, in immovable space, and partly from the relative motions as well of the ship on the earth, as of the body in the ship; and from these relative motions will arise the relative motion of the body on the earth. As if that part of the earth, where the ship is, was truly moved towards the east, with a velocity of 10010 parts; while the ship itself, with a fresh gale, and full sails, is carried towards the west, with a velocity expressed by 10 of those parts; but a sailor walks in the ship towards the east, with 1 part of the said velocity; then the sailor will be moved truly in immovable space towards the east, with a velocity of 10001 parts, and relatively on the earth towards the west, with a velocity of 9 of those parts.

Absolute time, in astronomy, is distinguished from relative, by the equation or correction of the apparent time. For the natural days are truly unequal, though they are commonly considered as equal, and used for a measure of time; astronomers correct this inequality that they may measure the celestial motions by a more accurate time. It may be, that there is no such thing as an equable motion, whereby time may be accurately measured. All motions may be accelerated and retarded, but the flowing of absolute time is not liable to any change. The duration or perseverance of the existence of things remains the same, whether the motions are swift or slow, or none at all: and therefore this duration ought to be distinguished from what are only sensible measures thereof; and from which we deduce it, by means of the astronomical equation. The necessity of this equation, for determining the times of a phenomenon, is evinced as well from the experiments of the pendulum clock, as by eclipses of the satellites of Jupiter.

As the order of the parts of time is immutable, so also is the order of the parts of space. Suppose those parts to be moved out of their places, and they will be moved (if the expression may be allowed) out of themselves. For times and spaces are, as it were, the places as well of themselves as of all other things. All things are placed in time as to order of succession; and in space as to order of situation. It is from their essence or nature that they are places; and that the primary places of things should be movable, is absurd. These are therefore the absolute places; and translations out of those places, are the only absolute motions.

But because the parts of space cannot be seen, or distinguished from one another by our senses, therefore in their stead we use sensible measures of them. For from the positions and distances of things from any body considered as immovable, we define all places; and then with respect to such places, we estimate all motions, considering bodies as transferred from some of those places into others. And so, instead of absolute places and motions, we use relative ones; and that without any inconvenience in common affairs; but in philosophical disquisitions, we ought to abstract from our senses, and consider things themselves, distinct from what are only sensible measures of them. For it may be that there is no body really at rest, to which the places and motions of others may be referred.

But we may distinguish rest and motion, absolute and relative, one from the other by their properties, causes, and effects. It is a property of rest, that bodies really at rest do rest in respect to one another. And therefore as it is possible, that in the remote regions of the fixed stars, or perhaps far beyond them, there may be some body absolutely at rest; but impossible to know, from the position of bodies to one another in our regions, whether any of these do keep the same position to that remote body, it follows that absolute rest cannot be determined from the position of bodies in our regions.

It is a property of motion, that the parts, which retain given positions to their wholes, do partake of the motions of those wholes. For all the parts of revolving bodies endeavor to recede from the axis of motion; and the impetus of bodies moving forwards arises from the joint impetus of all the parts. Therefore, if surrounding bodies are moved, those that are relatively at rest within them will partake of their motion. Upon which account, the true and absolute motion of a body cannot be determined by the translation of it from those which only seem to rest; for the external bodies ought not only to appear at rest, but to be really at rest. For otherwise, all included bodies, besides their translation from near the surrounding ones, partake likewise of their true motions; and though that translation were not made, they would not be really at rest, but only seem to be so. For the surrounding bodies stand in the like relation to the surrounded as the exterior part of a whole does to the interior, or as the shell does to the kernel; but if the shell moves, the kernel will also move, as being part of the whole, without any removal from near the shell.

A property, near akin to the preceding, is this, that if a place is moved, whatever is placed therein moves along with it; and therefore a body, which is moved from a place in motion, partakes also of the motion of its place. Upon which account, all motions, from places in motion, are no other than parts of entire and absolute motions; and every entire motion is composed of the motion of the body out of its first place, and the motion of this place out of its place; and so on, until we come to some immovable place, as in the before-mentioned example of the sailor. Wherefore, entire and absolute motions can be no otherwise determined than by immovable places; and for that reason I did before refer those absolute motions to immovable places, but relative ones to movable places. Now no other places are immovable but those that, from infinity to infinity, do all retain the same given position one to another; and upon this account must ever remain unmoved; and do thereby constitute immovable space.

The causes by which true and relative motions are distinguished, one from the other, are the forces impressed upon bodies to generate motion. True motion is neither generated nor altered, but by some force impressed upon the body moved; but relative motion may be generated or altered without any force impressed upon the body. For it is sufficient only to impress some force on other bodies with which the former is compared, that by their giving way, that relation may be changed, in which the relative rest or motion of this other body did consist. Again, true motion suffers always some change from any force impressed upon the moving body; but relative motion does not necessarily undergo any change by such forces. For if the same forces are likewise impressed on those other bodies, with which the comparison is made, that the relative position may be preserved, then that condition will be preserved in which the relative motion consists. And therefore any relative motion may be changed when the true motion remains unaltered, and the relative may be preserved when the true suffers some change. Thus, true motion by no means consists in such relations.

The effects which distinguish absolute from relative motion are, the forces of receding from the axis of circular motion. For there are no such forces in a circular motion purely relative, but in a true and absolute circular motion, they are greater or less, according to the quantity of the motion. If a vessel, hung by a long cord, is so often turned about that the cord is strongly twisted, then filled with water, and held at rest together with the water; thereupon, by the sudden action of another force, it is whirled about the contrary way, and while the cord is untwisting itself, the vessel continues for some time in this motion; the surface of the water will at first be plain, as before the vessel began to move; but after that, the vessel, by gradually communicating its motion to the water, will make it begin sensibly to revolve, and recede by little and little from the middle, and ascend to the sides of the vessel, forming itself into a concave figure (as I have experienced), and the swifter the motion becomes, the higher will the water rise, till at last, performing its revolutions in the same times with the vessel, it becomes relatively at rest in it. This ascent of the water shows its endeavor to recede from the axis of its motion; and the true and absolute circular motion of the water, which is here directly contrary to the relative, becomes known, and may be measured by this endeavor. At first, when the relative motion of the water in the vessel was greatest, it produced no endeavor to recede from the axis; the water showed no tendency to the circumference, nor any ascent towards the sides of the vessel, but remained of a plain surface, and therefore its true circular motion had not yet begun. But afterwards, when the relative motion of the water had decreased, the ascent thereof towards the sides of the vessel proved its endeavor to recede from the axis; and this endeavor showed the real circular motion of the water continually increasing, till it had acquired its greatest quantity, when the water rested relatively in the vessel. And therefore this endeavor does not depend upon any translation of the water in respect of the ambient bodies, nor can true circular motion be defined by such translation. There is only one real circular motion of any one revolving body, corresponding to only one power of endeavoring to recede from its axis of motion, as its proper and adequate effect; but relative motions, in one and the same body, are innumerable, according to the various relations it bears to external bodies, and, like other relations, are altogether destitute of any real effect, any otherwise than they may perhaps partake of that one only true motion. And therefore in their system who suppose that our heavens, revolving below the sphere of the fixed stars, carry the planets along with them; the several parts of those heavens, and the planets, which are indeed relatively at rest in their heavens, do yet really move. For they change their position one to another (which never happens to bodies truly at rest), and being carried together with their heavens, partake of their motions, and as parts of revolving wholes, endeavor to recede from the axis of their motions.

Wherefore relative quantities are not the quantities themselves, whose names they bear, but those sensible measures of them (either accurate or inaccurate), which are commonly used instead of the measured quantities themselves. And if the meaning of words is to be determined by their use, then by the names time, space, place, and motion, their [sensible] measures are properly to be understood; and the expression will be unusual, and purely mathematical, if the measured quantities themselves are meant. On this account, those violate the accuracy of language, which ought to be kept precise, who interpret these words for the measured quantities. Nor do those less defile the purity of mathematical and philosophical truths, who confound real quantities with their relations and sensible measures.

It is indeed a matter of great difficulty to discover, and effectually to distinguish, the true motions of particular bodies from the apparent; because the parts of that immovable space, in which those motions are performed, do by no means come under the observation of our senses. Yet the thing is not altogether desperate; for we have some arguments to guide us, partly from the apparent motions, which are the differences of the true motions; partly from the forces, which are the causes and effects of the true motions. For instance, if two globes, kept at a given distance one from the other by means of a cord that connects them, were revolved about their common centre of gravity, we might, from the tension of the cord, discover the endeavor of the globes to recede from the axis of their motion, and from thence we might compute the quantity of their circular motions. And then if any equal forces should be impressed at once on the alternate faces of the globes to augment or diminish their circular motions, from the increase or decrease of the tension of the cord, we might infer the increment or decrement of their motions; and thence would be found on what faces those forces ought to be impressed, that the motions of the globes might be most augmented; that is, we might discover their hindmost faces, or those which, in the circular motion, do follow. But the faces which follow being known, and consequently the opposite ones that precede, we should likewise know the determination of their motions. And thus we might find both the quantity and the determination of this circular motion, even in an immense vacuum, where there was nothing external or sensible with which the globes could be compared. But now, if in that space some remote bodies were placed that kept always a given position one to another, as the fixed stars do in our regions, we could not indeed determine from the relative translation of the globes among those bodies, whether the motion did belong to the globes or to the bodies. But if we observed the cord, and found that its tension was that very tension which the motions of the globes required, we might conclude the motion to be in the globes, and the bodies to be at rest; and then, lastly, from the translation of the globes among the bodies, we should find the determination of their motions. But how we are to obtain the true motions from their causes, effects, and apparent differences, and the converse, shall be explained more [later]. For to this end it was that I composed it.

6. *Time Is the Flux of Duration*

HENRI BERGSON

Henri Bergson (1859–1941) was a French philosopher who believed the mathematical picture of the world developed by science was incomplete and distorting. He wanted to base metaphysical knowledge on experience, but he felt language and concepts (especially scientific ones) were clumsy tools that evolved for practical purposes—not for expressing metaphysical knowledge. Bergson advocated an intuitive form of knowing that focused on immediate experience. With this intuition, Bergson claimed to find "pure duration," a kind of present or period of becoming that is not just the juxtapositioning of successive, momentary events. He claimed time is the flux of pure duration, and *concepts* of momentary states of things are like snapshots that freeze and misrepresent this flux. Influenced by theories of organic evolution, Bergson believed making time fundamental in this way would leave room for creative novelty and freedom (purportedly, in contrast to the mechanical world of physics). Though Bergson objected to the mathematical "spatialization" of time, it should be observed that he agreed with Newton that time is not just a relation among events. The article reprinted here is an early (1903) essay in which Bergson argues the way to know time is via intuition.

If we compare the various ways of defining metaphysics and of conceiving the absolute, we shall find, despite apparent discrepancies, that philosophers agree in making a deep distinction between two ways of knowing a thing. The first implies going all around it, the second entering into it. The first depends on the viewpoint chosen and the symbols employed, while the second is taken from no viewpoint and rests on no symbol. Of the first kind of knowledge we shall say that it stops at the *relative;* of the second that, wherever possible, it attains the *absolute.*

Take, for example, the movement of an object in space. I perceive it differently according to the point of view from which I look at it, whether from that of mobility or of immobility. I express it differently, furthermore as I relate it to the system of axes or reference points, that is to say, according to the symbols by which I translate it. And I call it *relative* for this double reason: in either case,

I place myself outside the object itself. When I speak of an absolute movement, it means that I attribute to the mobile an inner being and, as it were, states of soul; it also means that I am in harmony with these states and enter into them by an effort of imagination. Therefore, according to whether the object is mobile or immobile, whether it adopts one movement or another, I shall not have the same feeling about it. And what I feel will depend neither on the point of view I adopt toward the object, since I am in the object itself, nor on the symbols by which I translate it, since I have renounced all translation in order to possess the original. In short, the movement will not be grasped from without and, as it were, from where I am, but from within, inside it, in what it is in itself. I shall have hold of an absolute.

Or again, take a character whose adventures make up the subject of a novel. The novelist may multiply traits of character, make his hero speak and act as much as he likes: all this has not the same value as the simple and indivisible feeling I should experience if I were to coincide for a single moment with the personage himself. The actions, gestures and words would then appear to flow naturally, as though from their source. They would no longer be accidents making up the idea I had of the character, constantly enriching this idea without ever succeeding in completing it. The character would be given to me all at once in its entirety, and the thousand and one incidents which make it manifest, instead of adding to the idea and enriching it, would, on the contrary, seem to me to fall away from it without in any way exhausting or impoverishing its essence. I get a different point of view regarding the person with every added detail I am given. All the traits which describe it to me, yet which can only enable me to know it by comparisons with persons or things I already know, are signs by which it is more or less symbolically expressed. Symbols and points of view then place me outside it; they give me only what it has in common with others and what does not belong properly to it. But what is properly itself, what constitutes its essence, cannot be perceived from without, being internal by definition, nor be expressed by symbols, being incommensurable with everything else. Description, history and analysis in this case leave me in the relative. Only by coinciding with the person itself would I possess the absolute.

It is in this sense, and in this sense alone, that *absolute* is synonymous with *perfection*. Though all the photographs of a city taken from all possible points of view indefinitely complete one another, they will never equal in value that dimensional object, the city along whose streets one walks. All the translations of a poem in all possible languages may add nuance to nuance and, by a kind of mutual retouching, by correcting one another, may give an increasingly faithful picture of the poem they translate, yet they will never give the inner meaning of the original. A representation taken from a certain point of view, a translation made with certain symbols still remain imperfect in comparison with the object whose picture has been taken or which the symbols seek to express. But the absolute is perfect in that it is perfectly what it is.

It is probably for the same reason that the *absolute* and the *infinite* are often taken as identical. If I wish to explain to someone who does not know Greek the simple impression that a line of Homer leaves upon me, I shall give the translation of the line, then comment on my translation, then

I shall develop my commentary, and from explanation to explanation I shall get closer to what I wish to express; but I shall never quite reach it. When you lift your arm you accomplish a movement the simple perception of which you have inwardly; but outwardly, for me, the person who sees it, your arm passes through one point, then through another, and between these two points there will be still other points, so that if I begin to count them, the operation will continue indefinitely. Seen from within, an absolute is then a simple thing; but considered from without, that is to say relative to something else, it becomes, with relation to those signs which express it, the piece of gold for which one can never make up the change. Now what lends itself at the same time to an indivisible apprehension and to an inexhaustible enumeration is, by definition, an infinite.

It follows that an absolute can only be given in an *intuition*, while all the rest has to do with *analysis*. We call intuition here the *sympathy* by which one is transported into the interior of an object in order to coincide with what there is unique and consequently inexpressible in it. Analysis, on the contrary, is the operation which reduces the object to elements already known, that is, common to that object and to others. Analyzing then consists in expressing a thing in terms of what is not it. All analysis is thus a translation, a development into symbols, a representation taken from successive points of view from which are noted a corresponding number of contacts between the new object under consideration and others believed to be already known. In its eternally unsatisfied desire to embrace the object around which it is condemned to turn, analysis multiplies endlessly the points of view in order to complete the ever incomplete representation, varies interminably the symbols with the hope of perfecting the always imperfect translation. It is analysis ad infinitum. But intuition, if it is possible, is a simple act.

This being granted, it would be easy to see that for positive science analysis is its habitual function. It works above all with symbols. Even the most concrete of the sciences of nature, the sciences of life, confine themselves to the visible form of living beings, their organs, their anatomical elements. They compare these forms with one another, reduce the more complex to the more simple, in fact they study the functioning of life in what is, so to speak, its visual symbol. If there exists a means of possessing a reality absolutely, instead of knowing it relatively, of placing oneself within it instead of adopting points of view toward it, of having the intuition of it instead of making the analysis of it, in short, of grasping it over and above all expression, translation or symbolical representation, metaphysics is that very means. *Metaphysics is therefore the science which claims to dispense with symbols.*

There is at least one reality which we all seize from within, by intuition and not by simple analysis. It is our own person in its flowing through time, the self which endures. With no other thing can we sympathize intellectually, or if you like, spiritually. But one thing is sure: we sympathize with ourselves.

When, with the inner regard of my consciousness, I examine my person in its passivity, like some superficial encrustment, first I perceive all the perceptions which come to it from the material world. These perceptions are clear-cut, distinct, juxtaposed or mutually juxtaposable; they seek to group themselves into objects. Next I perceive memories more or less adherent to these perceptions and which serve to interpret them; these memories are, so to speak, as if detached from the depth of my person and drawn to the periphery by perceptions resembling them; they are fastened on me without being absolutely myself. And finally, I become aware of tendencies, motor habits, a crowd of virtual actions more or less solidly bound to those perceptions and these memories. All these elements with their well-defined forms appear to me to be all the more distinct from myself the more they are distinct from one another. Turned outwards from within, together they constitute the surface of a sphere which tends to expand and loose itself in the external world. But if I pull myself in from the periphery toward the center, if I seek deep down within me what is the most uniformly, the most constantly and durably myself, I find something altogether different.

What I find beneath these clear-cut crystals and this superficial congelation is a continuity of flow comparable to no other flowing I have ever seen. It is a succession of states each one of which announces what follows and contains what precedes. Strictly speaking they do not constitute multiple states until I have already got beyond them, and turn around to observe their trail. While I was experiencing them they were so solidly organized, so profoundly animated with a common life, that I could never have said where any one of them finished or the next one began. In reality, none of them do begin or end; they all dove-tail into one another.

It is, if you like, the unrolling of a spool, for there is no living being who does not feel himself coming little by little to the end of his span; and living consists in growing old. But it is just as much a continual winding, like that of thread into a ball, for our past follows us, becoming larger and larger with the present it picks up on its way; and consciousness means memory.

To tell the truth, it is neither a winding nor an unwinding, for these two images evoke the representation of lines or surfaces whose parts are homogeneous to and superposable on one another. Now, no two moments are identical in a conscious being. Take for example the simplest feeling, suppose it to be constant, absorb the whole personality in it: the consciousness which will accompany this feeling will not be able to remain identical with itself for two consecutive moments, since the following moment always contains, over and above the preceding one, the memory the latter has left it. A consciousness which had two identical moments would be a consciousness without memory. It would therefore die and be reborn continually. How otherwise can unconsciousness be described?

We must therefore evoke a spectrum of a thousand shades, with imperceptible gradations leading from one shade to another. A current of feeling running through the spectrum, becoming tinted with each of these shades in turn, would suffer gradual changes, each of which would announce the following and sum up within itself the preceding ones. Even then the successive shades of the spectrum will always remain external to each other. They are juxtaposed. They occupy space. On the contrary, what is pure duration excludes all idea of juxtaposition, reciprocal exteriority and extension.

Instead, let us imagine an infinitely small piece of elastic, contracted, if that were possible, to a mathematical point. Let us draw it out gradually in such a way as to bring out of the point a line which will grow progressively longer. Let us fix our attention not on the line as line, but on the action which traces it. Let us consider that this action, in spite of its duration, is indivisible if one supposes that it goes on without stopping; that, if we intercalate a stop in it, we make two actions of it instead of one and that each of these actions will then be the indivisible of which we speak; that it is not the moving act itself which is never indivisible, but the motionless line it lays down beneath it like a track in space. Let us take our mind off the space subtending the movement and concentrate solely on the movement itself, on the act of tension or extension, in short, on pure mobility. This time we shall have a more exact image of our development in duration.

And yet that image will still be incomplete, and all comparison furthermore will be inadequate, because the unrolling of our duration in certain aspects resembles the unity of a movement which progresses, in others, a multiplicity of states spreading out, and because no metaphor can express one of the two aspects without sacrificing the other. If I evoke a spectrum of a thousand shades, I have before me a complete thing, whereas duration is the state of completing itself. If I think of an elastic being stretched, of a spring being wound or unwound, I forget the wealth of coloring characteristic of duration as something lived and see only the simple movement by which consciousness goes from one shade to the other. The inner life is all that at once, variety of qualities, continuity of progress, unity of direction. It cannot be represented by images.

But still less could it be represented by *concepts,* that is, by abstract ideas, whether general or simple. Doubtless no image will quite answer to the original feeling I have of the flowing of myself. But neither is it necessary for me to try to express it. To him who is not capable of giving himself the intuition of the duration constitutive of his being, nothing will ever give it, neither concepts nor images. In this regard, the philosopher's sole aim should be to start up a certain effort which the utilitarian habits of mind of everyday life tend, in most men, to discourage. Now the image has at least the advantage of keeping us in the concrete. No image will replace the intuition of duration, but many different images, taken from quite dif-

ferent orders of things, will be able, through the convergence of their action, to direct the consciousness to the precise point where there is a certain intuition to seize on. By choosing images as dissimilar as possible, any one of them will be prevented from usurping the place of the intuition it is instructed to call forth, since it would then be driven out immediately by its rivals. By seeing that in spite of their differences in aspect they all demand of our mind the same kind of attention and, as it were, the same degree of tension, one will gradually accustom the consciousness to a particular and definitely determined disposition, precisely the one it will have to adopt in order to appear unveiled to itself. But even then the consciousness must acquiesce in this effort; for we shall have shown it nothing. We shall simply have placed it in the attitude it must take to produce the desired effort and, by itself, to arrive at the intuition. On the other hand the disadvantage of too simple concepts is that they are really symbols which take the place of the object they symbolize and which do not demand any effort on our part. Upon close examination one would see that each of them retains of the object only what is common to that object and to others. Each of them is seen to express, even more than does the image, a *comparison* between the object and those objects resembling it. But as the comparison has brought out a resemblance, and as the resemblance is a property of the object, and as a property seems very much as though it were a *part* of the object possessing it, we are easily persuaded that by juxtaposing concepts to concepts we shall recompose the whole of the object with its parts and obtain from it, so to speak, an intellectual equivalent. We shall in this way think we are forming a faithful representation of duration by lining up the concepts of unity, multiplicity, continuity, finite or infinite divisibility, etc. That is precisely the illusion. And that, also, is the danger. In so far as abstract ideas can render service to analysis, that is, to a scientific study of the object in its relations with all others, to that very extent are they incapable of replacing intuition, that is to say, the metaphysical investigation of the object in what essentially belongs to it. On the one hand, indeed, these concepts placed end to end will never give us anything more than an artificial recomposition of the object of which they can symbolize only certain general and, as it were, impersonal aspects: therefore it is vain to believe that through them one can grasp a reality when all they present is its shadow. But on the other hand, alongside the illusion, there is also a very grave danger. For the concept generalizes at the same time that it abstracts. The concept can symbolize a particular property only by making it common to an infinity of things. Therefore it always more or less distorts this property by the extension it gives to it. A property put back into the metaphysical object to which it belongs coincides with the object, at least molds itself on it, adopting the same contours. Extracted from the metaphysical object and represented in a concept, it extends itself indefinitely, surpassing the object since it must henceforth contain it along with others. The various concepts we form of the properties of a thing are so many much larger circles drawn round it, not one of which fits it exactly. And yet, in the thing itself, the properties coincided with it and therefore with each other. We have no alternative then but to resort to some artifice in order to re-establish the coincidence. We shall take any one of these concepts and with it try to rejoin the others. But the junction will be brought about in a different way, depending upon the concept we start from. According to whether we start, for example, from unity or from multiplicity, we shall form a different conception of the multiple unity of duration. Everything will depend on the weight we assign to this or that concept, and this weight will always be arbitrary, since the concept, extracted from the object, has no weight, being nothing more than the shadow of a body. Thus a multiplicity of different *systems* will arise, as many systems as there are external viewpoints on the reality one is examining or as there are larger circles in which to enclose it. The simple concepts, therefore, not only have the disadvantage of dividing the concrete unity of the object into so many symbolical expressions; they also divide philosophy into distinct schools, each of which reserves its place, chooses its chips, and begins with the others a game that will never end. Either metaphysics is only this game of ideas, or else, if it is a serious occupation of the mind, it must transcend concepts to arrive at intuition. To be sure, concepts are indispensable to it, for all the other sciences ordinarily work with concepts, and metaphysics cannot get along without the other sciences. But it is strictly itself only when it goes

beyond the concept, or at least when it frees itself of the inflexible and ready-made concepts and creates others very different from those we usually handle, I mean flexible, mobile, almost fluid representations, always ready to mold themselves on the fleeting forms of intuition. I shall come back to this important point a little later. It is enough for us to have shown that our duration can be presented to us directly in an intuition, that it can be suggested indirectly to us by images, but that it cannot—if we give to the word *concept* its proper meaning—be enclosed in a conceptual representation.

Let us for an instant try to break it up into parts. We must add that the terms of these parts, instead of being distinguished like those of any multiplicity, encroach upon one another; that we can, no doubt, by an effort of imagination, solidify this duration once it has passed by, divide it into pieces set side by side and count all the pieces; but that this operation is achieved on the fixed memory of the duration, on the immobile track the mobility of the duration leaves behind it, not on the duration itself. Let us therefore admit that, if there is a multiplicity here, this multiplicity resembles no other. Shall we say then that this duration has unity? Undoubtedly a continuity of elements prolonged into one another partakes of unity as much as it does of multiplicity, but this moving, changing, colored and living unity scarcely resembles the abstract unity, empty and motionless, which the concept of pure unity circumscribes. Are we to conclude from this that duration must be defined by both unity and multiplicity at the same time? But curiously enough, no matter how I manipulate the two concepts, apportion them, combine them in various ways, practice on them the most delicate operations of mental chemistry, I shall never obtain anything which resembles the simple intuition I have of duration; instead of which, if I place myself back in duration by an effort of intuition, I perceive immediately how it is unity, multiplicity and many other things besides. These various concepts were therefore just so many external points of view on duration. Neither separated nor reunited have they made us penetrate duration itself.

We penetrate it, nevertheless, and the only way possible is by an intuition. In this sense, an absolute internal knowledge of the duration of the self by the self is possible. But if metaphysics demands and can obtain here an intuition, science has no less need of an analysis. And it is because of a confusion between the roles of analysis and intuition that the dissensions between schools of thought and the conflicts between systems will arise.

Psychology, in fact, like the other sciences, proceeds by analysis. It resolves the self, first given to it in the form of a simple intuition, into sensations, feelings, images, etc. which it studies separately. It therefore substitutes for the self a series of elements which are the psychological facts. But these *elements,* are they *parts?* That is the whole question, and it is because we have evaded it that we have often stated in insoluble terms the problem of the human personality. . . .

It is true that in order to do that one must institute a reversal of the habitual work of the intelligence. To think consists ordinarily in going from concepts to things, and not from things to concepts. To know a reality in the ordinary meaning of the word "to know," is to take ready-made concepts, apportion them, and combine them until one obtains a practical equivalent of the real. But it must not be forgotten that the normal work of the intelligence is far from being a disinterested work. We do not, in general, aim at knowing for the sake of knowing, but at knowing in order to take a stand, gain a profit, in fact to satisfy an interest. We try to find out up to what point the object to be known is *this* or *that,* into what known genus it fits, what kind of action, step or attitude it should suggest to us. These various possible actions and attitudes are so many *conceptual directions* of our thought, determined once and for all; nothing remains but for us to follow them; precisely in that consists the application of concepts to things. To try a concept on an object is to ask of the object what we have to do with it, what it can do for us. To label an object with a concept is to tell in precise terms the kind of action or attitude the object is to suggest to us. All knowledge properly so-called is, therefore, turned in a certain direction or taken from a certain point of view. It is true that our interest is often complex. And that is why we sometimes manage to turn our knowledge of the same object in several successive directions and to cause view-points concerning it to vary. This is what, in the ordinary meaning of these terms, a "wide" and "comprehensive" knowledge of the object consists in: the object,

then, is led back, not to a unique concept, but to several concepts in which it is deemed to "participate." How it is to participate in all these concepts at once is a question of no practical importance and one that need not be asked. It is, therefore, natural and legitimate that we proceed by juxtaposition and apportioning of concepts in every-day life: no philosophical difficulties will be born of this since, by tacit consent, we shall abstain from philosophizing. But to transfer this *modus operandi* to philosophy, to go—here again—from concepts to the thing, to employ for the disinterested knowledge of an object one now aims at attaining in itself, a manner of knowing inspired by a definite interest and consisting by definition in a view taken of the object externally, is to turn one's back on the goal at which one was aiming; it is to condemn philosophy to an eternal friction between the schools and set up a contradiction in the very heart of the object and the method. Either there is no philosophy possible and all knowledge of things is a practical knowledge turned to the profit to be gained from them, or philosophizing consists in placing oneself within the object itself by an effort of intuition.

But in order to comprehend the nature of this intuition, to determine precisely where intuition ends and analysis begins, we must return to what was said above concerning the flow of duration.

It is to be observed that the concepts or schemas, to which analysis leads, have the essential characteristic of being immobile while under consideration. I have isolated from the whole of the inner life that psychological entity which I call a simple sensation. So long as I study it I suppose it to remain what it is. If I were to find some change in it, I should say that it was not a single sensation, but several successive sensations; and it is to each one of the succeeding sensations that I should then transfer the immutability at first attributed to the whole sensation. In any case I shall, by carrying analysis far enough, be able to arrive at elements I shall hold to be immovable. It is there, and there only, that I shall find the solid base of operations which science needs for its proper development.

There is no mood, however, no matter how simple, which does not change at every instant, since there is no consciousness without memory, no continuation of a state without the addition, to the present feeling, of the memory of past moments. That is what duration consists of. Inner duration is the continuous life of a memory which prolongs the past into the present, whether the present distinctly contains the ever-growing image of the past, or whether, by its continual changing of quality, it attests rather the increasingly heavy burden dragged along behind one the older one grows. Without that survival of the past in the present there would be no duration but only instantaneity.

It is true that if I am criticized for abstracting the psychological state from duration by the mere fact of analyzing it, I shall defend myself against the charge by saying that each of these elementary psychological states to which my analysis leads is a state which still occupies time. "My analysis," I shall say, "easily resolves the inner life into states each of which is homogeneous to itself; only, since the homogeneity spreads out over a definite number of minutes or seconds, the elementary psychological state does not cease to have duration, though it does not change."

But who does not see that the definite number of minutes and seconds I attribute to the elementary psychological state, has no more than the value of an indication meant to remind me that the psychological state, supposedly homogeneous, is in reality a state which changes and endures? The state, taken in itself, is a perpetual becoming. I have extracted from this becoming a certain mean of quality which I have supposed invariable: I have thus constituted a state which is stable, and by that very fact, schematic. Again, I have extracted becoming in general, the becoming that would no more be the becoming of this than of that, and this is what I have called the *time* this state occupies. Were I to examine it closely, I should see that this abstract time is as immobile for me as the state I localize in it, that it could flow only by a continual changing of quality and that, if it is without quality, a simple theater of change, it thus becomes an immobile milieu. I should see that the hypothesis of this homogeneous time is simply meant to facilitate the comparison between the various concrete durations, to permit us to count simultaneities and to measure one flowing of duration in relation to another. And finally, I should understand that in fastening to the representation of an elementary psychological state the indication of a definite number of minutes and seconds, I am

merely recalling that the state has been detached from an ego which endures, and demarcating the place where it would have to be set in motion again in order to bring it, from the simple schema it has become, back to the concrete form it had at first. But I forget all that, having no use for it in analysis.

That is to say, analysis operates on immobility, while intuition is located in mobility or, what amounts to the same thing, in duration. That is the very clear line of demarcation between intuition and analysis. One recognizes the real, the actual, the concrete, by the fact that it is variability itself. One recognizes the element by the fact that it is invariable. And it is invariable by definition, being a schema, a simplified reconstruction, often a mere symbol, in any case, a view taken of the reality that flows.

But the mistake is to believe that with these schemas one could recompose the real. It cannot be too often repeated: from intuition one can pass on to analysis, but not from analysis to intuition.

With variability I shall make as many variations, as many qualities or modifications as I like because they are so many immobile views taken by analysis of the mobility given to intuition. But these modifications placed end to end will not produce anything resembling variability, because they were not parts of it but elements which is quite another thing.

Let us consider, for example, the variability nearest to homogeneity, movement in space. For the whole length of this movement I can imagine possible halts: they are what I call the positions of the mobile or the points through which the mobile passes. But with the positions, were they infinite in number, I shall not make movement. They are not parts of the movement; they are so many views taken of it; they are, we say, only halt suppositions. Never is the mobile really in any of these points; the most one can say is that it passes through them. But the passing, which is a movement, has nothing in common with a halt, which is immobility. A movement could not alight on an immobility for it would then coincide with it, which would be contradictory. The points are not *in* the movement as parts, nor even *under* the movement as places of the mobile. They are simply projected by us beneath the movement like so many places where, if it should stop, would be a mobile which by hypothesis does not stop. They are not, therefore, properly speaking, positions, but suppositions, views or mental viewpoints. How, with these points of view, could one construct a thing?

That, nevertheless, is what we try to do every time we reason about movement and also about time for which movement serves as representation. By an illusion deeply rooted in our mind, and because we cannot keep from considering analysis as equivalent to intuition, we begin by distinguishing, for the whole length of the movement, a certain number of possible halts or points which, willy-nilly, we make parts of the movement. Faced with our inability to recompose movement with these points we intercalate other points, in the belief that we are thus keeping closer to what mobility there is in movement. Then, as the mobility still escapes us, we substitute for a finite and definite number of points a number "infinitely increasing,"—trying thus, but vainly, through the movement of our thought, which indefinitely pursues the addition of points to points, to counterfeit the real and undivided movement of the mobile. Finally, we say that movement is made up of points, but that it comprises in addition the obscure, mysterious passing from one position to the next. As though the obscurity did not come wholly from the fact that we have assumed immobility to be clearer from mobility, the halt to precede movement! As though the mystery was not due to the fact that we claim to go from halts to movement by way of composition which is impossible, whereas we pass easily from movement to slowing down and to immobility! You have sought the meaning of a poem in the form of the letters which make it up, you have thought that in considering an increasing number of letters you would finally embrace the constantly fleeting meaning, and as a last resource, seeing that it was no use to seek a part of the meaning in each letter, you have assumed that between each letter and the one following was lodged the missing fragment of the mysterious meaning! But the letters, once more, are not parts of the thing, they are the elements of the symbol. The positions of the mobile are not parts of the movement: they are points of the space which is thought to subtend the movement. This empty and immobile space, simply *con*ceived, never *per*ceived, has exactly the value of a symbol.

By manipulating symbols, how are you going to manufacture reality?

But in this case the symbol meets the demands of our most inveterate habits of thought. We install ourselves ordinarily in immobility, where we find a basis for practice, and with it we claim to recompose mobility. We obtain thus only a clumsy imitation, a counterfeit of real movement, but this imitation is of much greater use to us in life than the intuition of the thing itself would be. Now our mind has an irresistible tendency to consider the idea it most frequently uses to be the clearest. That is why immobility seems clearer to it than mobility, the halt preceding movement.

This explains the difficulties raised by the problem of movement from earliest antiquity. They are due to the fact that we claim to go from space to movement, from the trajectory to the flight, from immobile positions to mobility, and pass from one to the other by way of composition. But it is movement which precedes immobility, and between positions and a displacement there is not the relation of parts to the whole, but that of the diversity of possible viewpoints to the real indivisibility of the object.

Many other problems are born of the same illusion. What the immobile points are to the movement of a mobile, so are the concepts of various qualities to the qualitative change of an object. The different concepts into which a variation is resolved are therefore so many stable visions of the instability of the real. And to think an object, in the usual sense of the word "think," is to take one or several of these immobile views of its mobility. It is, in short, to ask oneself from time to time just where it is, in order to know what to do with it. Nothing is more legitimate than this method of procedure, as long as it is only a question of practical knowledge of reality. Knowledge, in so far as it is directed toward the practical, has only to enumerate the possible principal attitudes of the thing in relation to us, as also our best possible attitudes in respect to it. That is the ordinary role of ready-made concepts, those stations with which we mark out the passage of the becoming. But to desire, with them, to penetrate to the innermost nature of things, is to apply to the mobility of the real a method designed to give of it immobile points of view. It is to forget that if metaphysics is possible, it can only be an effort to re-ascend the slope natural to the work of thought, to place oneself immediately, through a dilation of the mind, in the thing one is studying, in short, to go from reality to concepts and not from concepts to reality. Is it surprising that philosophers so often see the object they claim to embrace recede from them, like children trying to catch smoke by closing their fists? A good many quarrels are thus perpetuated between the schools, in which each one accuses the others of having let the real escape them.

But if metaphysics is to proceed by intuition, if intuition has as its object the mobility of duration, and if duration is psychological in essence, are we not going to shut the philosopher up in exclusive self-contemplation? Will not philosophy consist simply in watching oneself live, "as a dozing shepherd watches the running water"? To speak in this fashion would be to return to the error I have not ceased to emphasize from the very beginning of this study. It would be to fail to recognize the particular nature of duration and at the same time the essentially active character of metaphysical intuition. It would be to fail to see that only the method of which we are speaking allows one to pass beyond idealism as well as realism, to affirm the existence of objects both inferior and superior to us, though nevertheless in a certain sense inferior to us, to make them coexistent without difficulty, and progressively to dispel the obscurities that analysis accumulates around great problems. Without taking up the study of these different points here, let us confine ourselves to showing how the intuition we are discussing is not a single act but an indefinite series of acts, all doubtless of the same genus but each one of a very particular species, and how this variety of acts corresponds to the degrees of being.

If I try to *analyze* duration, that is, to resolve it into ready-made concepts, I am certainly obliged by the very nature of the concept and the analysis, to take two opposing views of *duration in general,* views with which I shall then claim to recompose it. This combination can present neither a diversity of degrees nor a variety of forms: it is or it is not. I shall say, for example, that there is, on the one hand, a *multiplicity* of successive states of consciousness and, on the other hand, a *unity* which binds them together. Duration will be the "syn-

thesis" of this unity and multiplicity, but how this mysterious operation can admit of shades or degrees—I repeat—is not quite clear. In this hypothesis there is, there can only be, a single duration, that in which our consciousness habitually operates. To make certain of what we mean, if we take duration under the simple aspect of a movement being accomplished in space and if we try to reduce to concepts movement considered as representative of time, we shall have on the one hand any desired number of points of the trajectory, and on the other hand an abstract unity joining them, like a thread holding together the beads of a necklace. Between this abstract multiplicity and this abstract unity their combination, once assumed to be possible, is some strange thing in which we shall find no more shadings than the addition of given numbers in arithmetic would allow. But if, instead of claiming to analyze duration (that is, in reality, to make a synthesis of it with concepts), one first installs oneself in it by an effort of intuition, one has the feeling of a certain well-defined *tension,* whose very definiteness seems like a choice between an infinity of possible durations. This being so one perceives any number of durations, all very different from one another, even though each one of them, reduced to concepts, that is to say, considered externally from two opposite points of view, is always brought back to the indefinable combination of the multiple and the one.

Let us express the same idea more precisely. If I consider duration as a multiplicity of moments bound to one another by a unity which runs through them like a thread, these moments, no matter how short the chosen duration, are unlimited in number. I can imagine them as close together as I like; there will always be, between these mathematical points, other mathematical points, and so on, ad infinitum. Considered from the standpoint of multiplicity, duration will therefore disappear in a dust of moments not one of which has duration, each one being instantaneous. If on the other hand I consider the unity binding the moments together, it is evident that it cannot have duration either since, by hypothesis, everything that is changing and really durable in duration has been put to the account of the multiplicity of the moments. This unity, as I examine its essence, will then appear to me as an immobile substratum of the moving reality, like some intemporal essence of time: that is what I shall call eternity—the eternity of death, since it is nothing else than movement emptied of the mobility which made up its life. Examining closely the opinions of the schools antagonistic to the subject of duration, one would see that they differ simply in attributing to one or the other of these two concepts a capital importance. Certain of them are drawn to the point of view of the multiple; they set up as concrete reality the distance moments of a time which they have, so to speak, pulverized; they consider as being far more artificial the unity which makes a powder of these grains. The others, on the contrary, set up the unity of duration as concrete reality. They place themselves in the eternal. But as their eternity nevertheless remains abstract, being empty, as it is the eternity of a concept which by hypothesis excludes the opposite concept, one cannot see how this eternity could allow an indefinite multiplicity of moments to coexist with it. In the first hypothesis one has a world suspended in mid-air which would have to end and begin again by itself each instant. In the second, one has an infinitely abstract eternity of which one can say that it is especially difficult to understand why it does not remain enveloped in itself and how it allows things to co-exist with it. But in either case, and no matter which one of the two metaphysics is chosen, time appears from the psychological point of view as a mixture of two abstractions neither one of which admits of either degrees or shadings. In either system, there is only a single duration which carries everything along with it, a river without bottom and without banks and flowing without assignable forces in a direction one cannot define. Even then it is a river and the river flows only because reality obtains this sacrifice from the two doctrines, taking advantage of an inadvertence in their logic. As soon as they regain possession of themselves, they congeal this flowing either into an immense solid sheet, or into an infinity of crystallized needles, but always in a *thing* which necessarily participates in the immobility of a *point of view*.

It is altogether different if one places oneself directly, by an effort of intuition, in the concrete flowing of duration. To be sure, we shall find no logical reason for positing multiple and diverse durations. Strictly speaking, there might exist no other duration than our own, as there might be no other color in the world than orange, for example. But just as a consciousness of color, which would harmonize inwardly with orange instead of perceiving it outwardly, would feel itself caught between red and yellow, would perhaps even have, beneath the latter color, a presentiment of a whole spectrum in which is naturally prolonged the continuity which goes from red to yellow, so the intuition of our duration, far from leaving us suspended in the void as pure analysis would do, puts us in contact with a whole continuity of durations which we should try to follow either downwardly or upwardly: in both cases we can dilate ourselves indefinitely by a more and more vigorous effort, in both cases transcend ourselves. In the first case, we advance toward a duration more and more scattered, whose palpitations, more rapid than ours, dividing our simple sensation, dilute its quality into quantity: at the limit would be the pure homogeneous, the pure *repetition* by which we shall define materiality. In advancing in the other direction, we go toward a duration which stretches, tightens, and becomes more and more intensified: at the limit would be eternity. This time not only conceptual eternity, which is an eternity of death, but an eternity of life. It would be a living and consequently still moving eternity where our own duration would find itself like the vibrations in light, and which would be the concretion of all duration as materiality is its dispersion. Between these two extreme limits moves intuition, and this movement is metaphysics itself.

7. Time Is Not Real

JOHN M. E. McTAGGART

John McTaggart (1866–1925) was a British philosopher who defended a variety of metaphysical idealism (that is, he believed reality consisted of minds and their contents). Like many turn-of-the-century philosophers, he was influenced by Hegel's idealism. McTaggart argued that space, time, and material objects, as we ordinarily conceive them, are not real. He believed they are misperceptions of spiritual entities. Though McTaggart's idealism has had few followers, his argument against the reality of time has been widely studied. He distinguishes two ways to think about time: we can view time either as a series of pasts, presents, and futures (what he calls the "*A* series") or as a series of events standing in earlier-than or later-than relations (the "*B* series"). McTaggart claimed that the *B* series does not capture the essence of time, namely, change. So for time to be real (for there to be real change), the *A* series must be real. Then McTaggart argues that time cannot be real because the *A* series leads to logical difficulties. McTaggart's position is doubly challenging. If one believes time is real and the distinction between the past, present, and future is the essence of time, then one should try to rescue the *A* series from the logical problems McTaggart claims to find. If, on the other hand, one believes time is real and adequately represented by earlier-later relations, then one must defend the *B* series from McTaggart's charge that it pictures a universe devoid of real change.

It will be convenient to begin our enquiry by asking whether anything existent can possess the characteristic of being in time. I shall endeavour to prove that it cannot.

It seems highly paradoxical to assert that time is unreal, and that all statements which involve its reality are erroneous. Such an assertion involves a departure from the natural position of mankind which is far greater than that involved in the assertion of the unreality of space or the unreality of matter. For in each man's experience there is a part—his own states as known to him by introspection—which does not even appear to be spatial or material. But we have no experience which does not appear to be temporal. Even our judgments that time is unreal appear to be themselves in time.

Yet in all ages and in all parts of the world the belief in the unreality of time has shown itself to be singularly persistent. In the philosophy and religion of the West—and still more, I suppose, in the philosophy and religion of the East—we find that the doctrine of the unreality of time continually recurs. Neither philosophy nor religion ever hold themselves apart from mysticism for any long period, and almost all mysticism denies the reality of time. In philosophy, time is treated as unreal by Spinoza, by Kant, and by Hegel. Among more modern thinkers, the same view is taken by Mr. Bradley. Such a concurrence of opinion is highly significant, and is not the less significant because the doctrine takes such different forms, and is supported by such different arguments.

I believe that nothing that exists can be temporal, and that therefore time is unreal. But I believe it for reasons which are not put forward by any of the philosophers I have just mentioned.

Positions in time, as time appears to us *prima facie*, are distinguished in two ways. Each position

From *The Nature of Existence*, Vol. II, John M. E. McTaggart and C. D. Broad, eds. Copyright © 1921–1927 by Cambridge University Press.

is Earlier than some and Later than some of the other positions. To constitute such a series there is required a transitive asymmetrical relation, and a collection of terms such that, of any two of them, either the first is in this relation to the second, or the second is in this relation to the first. We may take here either the relation of "earlier than" or the relation of "later than," both of which, of course, are transitive and asymmetrical. If we take the first, then the terms have to be such that, of any two of them, either the first is earlier than the second, or the second is earlier than the first.

In the second place, each position is either Past, Present, or Future. The distinctions of the former class are permanent, while those of the latter are not. If *M* is ever earlier than *N,* it is always earlier. But an event, which is now present, was future, and will be past.

Since distinctions of the first class are permanent, it might be thought that they were more objective, and more essential to the nature of time, than those of the second class. I believe, however, that this would be a mistake, and that the distinction of past, present, and future is as *essential* to time as the distinction of earlier and later, while in a certain sense it may, as we shall see, be regarded as more *fundamental* than the distinction of earlier and later. And it is because the distinctions of past, present, and future seem to me to be essential for time, that I regard time as unreal.

For the sake of brevity I shall give the name of the *A* series to that series of positions which runs from the far past through the near past to the present, and then from the present through the near future to the far future, or conversely. The series of positions which runs from earlier to later, or conversely, I shall call the *B* series. The contents of any position in time form an event. The varied simultaneous contents of a single position are, of course, a plurality of events. But, like any other substance, they form a group, and this group is a compound substance. And a compound substance consisting of simultaneous events may properly be spoken of as itself an event.[1]

The first question which we must consider is whether it is essential to the reality of time that its events should form an *A* series as well as a *B* series. It is clear, to begin with, that, in present experience, we never *observe* events in time except as forming both these series. We perceive events in

time as being present, and those are the only events which we actually perceive. And all other events which, by memory or by inference, we believe to be real, we regard as present, past, or future. Thus the events of time as observed by us form an *A* series.

It might be said, however, that this is merely subjective. It might be the case that the distinction of positions in time into past, present, and future, is only a constant illusion of our minds, and that the real nature of time contains only the distinctions of the *B* series—the distinctions of earlier and later. In that case we should not perceive time as it really is, though we might be able to *think* of it as it really is.

This is not a very common view, but it requires careful consideration. I believe it to be untenable, because, as I said above, it seems to me that the *A* series is essential to the nature of time, and that any difficulty in the way of regarding the *A* series as real is equally a difficulty in the way of regarding time as real.

It would, I suppose, be universally admitted that time involves change. In ordinary language, indeed, we say that something can remain unchanged through time. But there could be no time if nothing changed. And if anything changes, then all other things change with it. For its change must change some of their relations to it, and so their relational qualities. The fall of a sand-castle on the English coast changes the nature of the Great Pyramid.

If, then, a *B* series without an *A* series can constitute time, change must be possible without an *A* series. Let us suppose that the distinctions of past, present, and future do not apply to reality. In that case, can change apply to reality?

What, on this supposition, could it be that changes? Can we say that, in a time which formed a *B* series but not an *A* series, the change consisted in the fact that the event ceased to be an event, while another event began to be an event? If this were the case, we should certainly have got a change.

But this is impossible. If *N* is ever earlier than *O* and later than *M,* it will always be, and has always been, earlier than *O* and later than *M,* since the relations of earlier and later are permanent. *N* will thus always be in a *B* series. And as, by our present hypothesis, a *B* series by itself constitutes time, *N* will always have a position in a time-series, and always has had one. That is, it always has been an event, and always will be one, and cannot begin or cease to be an event.

Or shall we say that one event *M* merges itself into another event *N*, while still preserving a certain identity by means of an unchanged element, so that it can be said, not merely that *M* has ceased and *N* begun, but that it is *M* which has become *N*? Still the same difficulty recurs. *M* and *N* may have a common element, but they are not the same event, or there would be no change. If, therefore, *M* changed into *N* at a certain moment, then at that moment, *M* would have ceased to be *M*, and *N* would have begun to be *N*. This involves that, at that moment, *M* would have ceased to be an event, and *N* would have begun to be an event. And we saw, in the last paragraph, that, on our present hypothesis, this is impossible.

Nor can such change be looked for in the different moments of absolute time, even if such moments should exist. For the same argument will apply here. Each such moment will have its own place in the *B* series, since each would be earlier or later than each of the others. And, as the *B* series depends on permanent relations, no moment could ever cease to be, nor could it become another moment.

Change, then, cannot arise from an event ceasing to be an event, nor from one event changing into another. In what other way can it arise? If the characteristics of an event change, then there is certainly change. But what characteristics of an event can change? It seems to me that there is only one class of such characteristics. And that class consists of the determinations of the event in question by the terms of the *A* series.

Take any event—the death of Queen Anne, for example—and consider what changes can take place in its characteristics. That it is a death, that it is the death of Anne Stuart, that it has such causes, that it has such effects—every characteristic of this sort never changes. "Before the stars saw one another plain," the event in question was the death of a Queen. At the last moment of time—if time has a last moment—it will still be the death of a Queen. And in every respect but one, it is equally devoid of change. But in one respect it does change. It was once an event in the far future. It became every moment an event in the nearer future. At last it was present. Then it became past, and will always remain past, though every moment it becomes further and further past.[2]

Such characteristics as these are the only characteristics which can change. And, therefore, if there is any change, it must be looked for in the *A* series, and in the *A* series alone. If there is no real *A* series, there is no real change. The *B* series, therefore, is not by itself sufficient to constitute time, since time involves change.

The *B* series, however, cannot exist except as temporal, since earlier and later, which are the relations which connect its terms, are clearly time-relations. So it follows that there can be no *B* series when there is no *A* series, since without an *A* series there is no time.

We must now consider three objections which have been made to this position. The first is involved in the view of time which has been taken by Mr. Russell, according to which past, present, and future do not belong to time *per se,* but only in relation to a knowing subject. An assertion that *N* is present means that it is simultaneous with that assertion, an assertion that it is past or future means that it is earlier or later than that assertion. Thus it is only past, present, or future, in relation to some assertion. If there were no consciousness, there would be events which were earlier and later than others, but nothing would be in any sense past, present, or future. And if there were events earlier than any consciousness, those events would never be future or present, though they could be past.

If *N* were ever present, past, or future in relation to some assertion *V*, it would always be so, since whatever is ever simultaneous to, earlier than, or later than, *V*, will always be so. What, then, is change? We find Mr. Russell's views on this subject in his *Principles of Mathematics.* "Change is the difference, in respect of truth or falsehood, between a proposition concerning an entity and the time *T,* and a proposition concerning the same entity and the time *T′*, provided that these propositions differ only by the fact that *T* occurs in the one where *T′* occurs in the other." That is to say, there is change, on Mr. Russell's view, if the proposition "at the time *T* my poker is hot" is true, and the proposition "at the time *T′* my poker is hot" is false.

I am unable to agree with Mr. Russell. I should, indeed, admit that, when two such propositions were respectively true and false, there would be change. But then I maintain that there can be no time without an *A* series. If, with Mr. Russell, we reject the *A* series, it seems to me that change goes with it, and that therefore time, for which change is essential, goes too. In other words, if the *A* series is rejected, no proposition of the type "at the time *T* my poker is hot" can ever be true, because there would be no time.

It will be noticed that Mr. Russell looks for change, not in the events in the time-series, but in the entity to which those events happen, or of which they are states. If my poker, for example, is hot on a particular Monday, and never before or since, the event of the poker being hot does not change. But the poker changes, because there is a time when this event is happening to it, and a time when it is not happening to it.

But this makes no change in the qualities of the poker. It is always a quality of that poker that it is one which is hot on that particular Monday. And it is always a quality of that poker that it is one which is not hot at any other time. Both these qualities are true of it at any time—the time when it is hot and the time when it is cold. And therefore it seems to be erroneous to say that there is any change in the poker. The fact that it is hot at one point in a series and cold at other points cannot give change, if neither of these facts change—and neither of them does. Nor does any other fact about the poker change, unless its presentness, pastness, or futurity change.

Let us consider the case of another sort of series. The meridian of Greenwich passes through a series of degrees of latitude. And we can find two points in this series, *S* and *S'*, such that the proposition "at *S* the meridian of Greenwich is within the United Kingdom" is true, while the proposition "at *S'* the meridian of Greenwich is within the United Kingdom" is false. But no one would say that this gave us change. Why should we say so in the case of the other series?

Of course there is a satisfactory answer to this question if we are correct in speaking of the other series as a time-series. For where there is time, there is change. But then the whole question is whether it is a time-series. My contention is that if we remove the *A* series from the *prima facie* nature of time, we are left with a series which is not temporal, and which allows change no more than the series of latitudes does.

If, as I have maintained, there can be no change unless facts change, then there can be no change without an *A* series. For, as we saw with the death of Queen Anne, and also in the case of the poker, no fact about anything can change, unless it is a fact about its place in the *A* series. Whatever other qualities it has, it has always. But that which is future will not always be future, and that which was past was not always past.

It follows from what we have said that there can be no change unless some propositions are sometimes true and sometimes false. This is the case of propositions which deal with the place of anything in the *A* series—"the battle of Waterloo is in the past," "it is now raining." But it is not the case with any other propositions.

Mr. Russell holds that such propositions are ambiguous, and that to make them definite we must substitute propositions which are always true or always false—"the battle of Waterloo is earlier than this judgment," "the fall of rain is simultaneous with this judgment." If he is right, all judgments are either always true, or always false. Then, I maintain, no facts change. And then, I maintain, there is no change at all.

I hold, as Mr. Russell does, that there is no *A* series. (My reasons for this will be given below.) And, as I shall explain, I regard the reality lying behind the appearance of the *A* series in a manner not completely unlike that which Mr. Russell has adopted. The difference between us is that he thinks that, when the *A* series is rejected, change, time, and the *B* series can still be kept, while I maintain that its rejection involves the rejection of change, and, consequently, of time, and of the *B* series.

The second objection rests on the possibility of nonexistent time-series—such, for example, as the adventures of Don Quixote. This series, it is said, does not form part of the *A* series. I cannot at this moment judge it to be either past, present, or future. Indeed, I know that it is none of the three. Yet, it is said, it is certainly a *B* series. The adventure of the galley-slaves, for example, is later than the adventure of the windmills. And a *B* series involves time. The conclusion drawn is that an *A* series is not essential to time.

I should reply to this objection as follows. Time only belongs to the existent. If any reality is in time, that involves that the reality in question exists. This, I think, would be universally admitted. It may be questioned whether all of what exists is in time, or even whether anything really existent is in time, but it would not be denied that, if anything is in time, it must exist.

Now what is existent in the adventures of Don Quixote? Nothing. For the story is imaginary. The states of Cervantes' mind when he invented the story, the states of my mind when I think of the story—these exist. But then these form part of an *A* series. Cervantes' invention of the story is in the past. My thought of the story is in the past, the present, and—I trust—the future.

But the adventures of Don Quixote may be believed by a child to be historical. And in reading them I may, by an effort of my imagination, contemplate them as if they really happened. In this case, the adventures are believed to be existent, or are contemplated as existent. But then they are believed to be in the *A* series, or are contemplated as being in the *A* series. The child who believes them to be historical will believe that they happened in the past. If I contemplate them as existent, I shall contemplate them as happening in the past. In the same way, if I believed the events described in Jefferies' *After London* to exist, or contemplated them as existent, I should believe them to exist in the future, or contemplate them as existing in the future. Whether we place the object of our belief or of our contemplation in the present, the past, or the future, will depend upon the characteristics of that object. But somewhere in the *A* series it will be placed.

Thus the answer to the objection is that, just as far as a thing is in time, it is in the *A* series. If it is really in time, it is really in the *A* series. If it is believed to be in time, it is believed to be in the *A* series. If it is contemplated as being in time, it is contemplated as being in the *A* series.

The third objection is based on the possibility that, if time were real at all, there might be in reality several real and independent time-series. The objection, if I understand it rightly, is that every time-series would be real, while the distinctions of past, present, and future would only have a meaning within each series, and would not, therefore, be taken as absolutely real. There would be, for example, many presents. Now, of course, many points of time can be present. In each time-series

many points are present, but they must be present successively. And the presents of the different time-series would not be successive, since they are not in the same time.[3] And different presents, it would be said, cannot be real unless they are successive. So the different time-series, which are real, must be able to exist independently of the distinction between past, present, and future.

I cannot, however, regard this objection as valid. No doubt in such a case, no present would be *the* present—it would only be the present of a certain aspect of the universe. But then no time would be *the* time—it would only be the time of a certain aspect of the universe. It would be a real time-series, but I do not see that the present would be less real than the time.

I am not, of course, maintaining that there is no difficulty in the existence of several distinct *A* series. [Later] I shall endeavour to show that the existence of *any A* series is impossible. What I assert here is that, if there could be an *A* series at all, and if there were any reason to suppose that there were several distinct *B* series, there would be no additional difficulty in supposing that there should be a distinct *A* series for each *B* series.

We conclude, then, that the distinctions of past, present, and future are essential to time, and that, if the distinctions are never true of reality, then no reality is in time. This view, whether true or false, has nothing surprising in it. It was pointed out above that we always perceive time as having these distinctions. And it has generally been held that their connection with time is a real characteristic of time, and not an illusion due to the way in which we perceive it. Most philosophers, whether they did or did not believe time to be true of reality, have regarded the distinctions of the *A* series as essential to time.

When the opposite view has been maintained it has generally been, I believe, because it was held (rightly, as I shall try to show) that the distinctions of past, present, and future cannot be true of reality, and that consequently, if the reality of time is to be saved, the distinction in question must be shown to be unessential to time. The presumption, it was held, was for the reality of time, and this would give us a reason for rejecting the *A* series as unessential to time. But, of course, this could only give a presumption. If the analysis of the nature of time has shown that, by removing the *A* series, time is destroyed, this line of argument is no longer open.

I now pass to the second part of my task. Having, as it seems to me, succeeded in proving that there can be no time without an *A* series, it remains to prove that an *A* series cannot exist, and that therefore time cannot exist. This would involve that time is not real at all, since it is admitted that the only way in which time can be real is by existing.

Past, present, and future are characteristics which we ascribe to events, and also to moments of time, if these are taken as separate realities. What do we mean by past, present, and future? In the first place, are they relations or qualities? It seems quite clear to me that they are not qualities but relations, though, of course, like other relations, they will generate relational qualities in each of their terms.[4] But even if this view should be wrong, and they should in reality be qualities and not relations, it will not affect the result which we shall reach. For the reasons for rejecting the reality of past, present, and future, which we are about to consider, would apply to qualities as much as to relations.

If, then, anything is to be rightly called past, present, or future, it must be because it is in relation to something else. And this something else to which it is in relation must be something outside the time-series. For the relations of the *A* series are changing relations, and no relations which are exclusively between members of the time-series can ever change. Two events are exactly in the same places in the time-series, relatively to one another, a million years before they take place, while each of them is taking place, and when they are a million years in the past. The same is true of the relation of moments to one another, if moments are taken as separate realities. And the same would be true of the relations of events to moments. The changing relation must be to something which is not in the time-series.

Past, present, and future, then, are relations in which events stand to something outside the time-series. Are these relations simple, or can they be defined? I think that they are clearly simple and indefinable. But, on the other hand, I do not think that they are isolated and independent. It does not seem that we can know, for example, the meaning of pastness, if we do not know the meaning of presentness or of futurity.

We must begin with the *A* series, rather than with past, present, and future, as separate terms. And we must say that a series is an *A* series when each of its terms has, to an entity *X* outside the series, one, and only one, of three indefinable relations, pastness, presentness, and futurity, which are such that all the terms which have the relation of presentness to *X* fall between all the terms which have the relation of pastness to *X*, on the one hand, and all the terms which have the relation of futurity to *X*, on the other hand.

We have come to the conclusion that an *A* series depends on relations to a term outside the *A* series. This term, then, could not itself be in time, and yet must be such that different relations to it determine the other terms of those relations, as being past, present, or future. To find such a term would not be easy, and yet such a term must be found, if the *A* series is to be real. But there is a more positive difficulty in the way of the reality of the *A* series.

Past, present, and future are incompatible determinations. Every event must be one or the other, but no event can be more than one. If I say that any event is past, that implies that it is neither present nor future, and so with the others. And this exclusiveness is essential to change, and therefore to time. For the only change we can get is from future to present, and from present to past.

The characteristics, therefore, are incompatible. But every event has them all.[5] If M is past, it has been present and future. If it is future, it will be present and past. If it is present, it has been future and will be past. Thus all the three characteristics belong to each event. How is this consistent with their being incompatible?

It may seem that this can easily be explained. Indeed, it has been impossible to state the difficulty without almost giving the explanation, since our language has verb-forms for the past, present, and future, but no form that is common to all three. It is never true, the answer will run, that *M is* present, past, and future. It *is* present, *will be* past, and *has been* future. Or it *is* past, and *has been* future and present, or again *is* future, and *will be* present and past. The characteristics are only incompatible when they are simultaneous, and there is no contradiction to this in the fact that each term has all of them successively.

But what is meant by "has been" and "will be"? And what is meant by "is," when, as here, it is used with a temporal meaning, and not simply for prediction? When we say that X has been Y, we are asserting X to be Y at a moment of past time. When we say that X will be Y, we are asserting X to be Y at a moment of future time. When we say that X is Y (in the temporal sense of "is"), we are asserting X to be Y at a moment of present time.

Thus our first statement about M—that it is present, will be past, and has been future—means that M is present at a moment of present time, past at some moment of future time, and future at some moment of past time. But every moment, like every event, is both past, present, and future. And so a similar difficulty arises. If M is present, there is no moment of past time at which it is past. But the moments of future time, in which it is past, are equally moments of past time, in which it cannot be past. Again, that M is future and will be present and past means that M is future at a moment of present time, and present and past at different moments of future time. In that case it cannot be present or past at any moments of past time. But all the moments of future time, in which M will be present or past, are equally moments of past time.

And thus again we get a contradiction, since the moments at which M has any one of the three determinations of the A series are also moments at which it cannot have that determination. If we try to avoid this by saying of these moments what had been previously said of M itself—that some moment, for example, is future, and will be present and past—then "is" and "will be" have the same meaning as before. Our statement, then, means that the moment in question is future at a present moment, and will be present and past at different moments of future time. This, of course, is the same difficulty over again. And so on infinitely.

Such an infinity is vicious. The attribution of the characteristics past, present, and future to the terms of any series leads to a contradiction, unless it is specified that they have them successively. This means, as we have seen, that they have them in relation to terms specified as past, present, and future. These again, to avoid a like contradiction, must in turn be specified as past, present, and future. And, since this continues infinitely, the first set of terms never escapes from contradiction at all.[6]

The contradiction, it will be seen, would arise in the same way supposing that pastness, presentness, and futurity were original qualities, and not, as we have decided that they are, relations. For it would still be the case that they were characteristics which were incompatible with one another, and that whichever had one of them would also have the other. And it is from this that the contradiction arises.

The reality of the A series, then, leads to a contradiction, and must be rejected. And, since we have seen that change and time require the A series, the reality of change and time must be rejected. And so must the reality of the B series, since that requires time. Nothing is really present, past, or future. Nothing is really earlier or later than anything else or temporally simultaneous with it. Nothing really changes. And nothing is really in time. Whenever we perceive anything in time—which is the only way in which, in our present experience, we do perceive things—we are perceiving it more or less as it really is not.[7]

Dr. Broad, in his admirable book *Scientific Thought,* has put forward a theory of time which he maintains would remove the difficulties which have led me to treat time as unreal.[8] It is difficult to do justice to so elaborate and careful a theory by means of extracts. I think, however, that the following passages will give a fair idea of Dr. Broad's position. His theory, he tells us, "accepts the reality of the present and the past, but holds that the future is simply nothing at all. Nothing has happened to the present by becoming past except that fresh slices of existence have been added to the total history of the world. The past is thus as real as the present. On the other hand, the essence of a present event is, not that it precedes future events, but that there is quite literally *nothing* to which it has the relation of precedence. The sum total of existence is always increasing, and it is this which gives the time-series a sense as well as an order. A moment t is later than a moment t' if the sum total of existence at t includes the sum total of existence at t' together with something more."

Again, he says that "judgments which profess to be about the future do not refer to any fact, whether positive or negative, at the time when they are made. They are therefore at that time neither true nor false. They will become true or false when there is a fact for them to refer to; and after this they will remain true or false, as the case may be, for ever and ever. If you choose to define the word *judgment* in such a way that nothing is to be called a judgment unless it be either true or false, you must not, of course, count judgments that profess to be about the future as judgments. If you accept the latter, you must say that the Law of Excluded Middle does not apply to all judgments. If you reject them, you may say that the Law of Excluded Middle applies to all genuine judgments; but you must add that judgments which profess to be about the future are not genuine judgments when they are made, but merely enjoy a courtesy title by anticipation, like the elder sons of the higher nobility during the lifetime of their fathers." "I do not think that the laws of logic have anything to say against this kind of change; and, if they have, so much the worse for the laws of logic, for it is certainly a fact."

My first objection to Dr. Broad's theory is that, as he says, it would involve that "it will rain tomorrow" is neither true nor false, and that "England will be a republic in 1920," was not false in 1919. It seems to me quite certain that "it will rain tomorrow" is either true or false, and that "England will be a republic in 1920," was false in 1919. Even if Dr. Broad's theory did enable him to meet my objections to the reality of time (which I shall try to show later on is not the case) I should still think that my theory should be accepted in preference to his. The view that time is unreal is, no doubt, very different from the *prima facie* view of reality. And it involves that perception can be erroneous. But the *prima facie* view of reality need not be true, and erroneous perception is not impossible. And, I submit, it is quite impossible that "it will rain tomorrow" is neither true nor false.

In the second place it is to be noted that Dr. Broad's theory must be false if the past ever intrinsically determines the future. If X intrinsically determines a subsequent Υ, then (at any rate as soon as X is present or past, and therefore, on Dr. Broad's theory, real) it will be true that, since there is an X, there must be a subsequent Υ. Then it is true that there is a subsequent Υ. And if that Υ is not itself present or past, then it is true that there will be a future Υ, and so something is true about the future.

Now is it possible to hold that the past never does intrinsically determine the future? It seems to me that there is just as much reason to believe that the past determines the future as there is to believe that the earlier past determines the later past or the present.

We cannot, indeed, usually get a positive statement as simple as "the occurrence of X intrinsically determines the occurrence of a subsequent Υ." But the intrinsic determination of the events can often be summed up in a statement of only moderate complexity. If the moon was visible in a certain direction last midnight, this intrinsically determines that, either it will be visible in a rather different direction next midnight, or the night will be cloudy, or the universe will have come to an end, or the relative motions of the earth and moon will have changed. Thus it is true that in the future one of four things will happen. And thus a proposition about the future is true.

And there are other intrinsic determinations which can be summed up in very simple negative statements. If Smith has already died childless, this intrinsically determines that no future event will be a marriage of one of Smith's grandchildren.

It seems, then, impossible to deny that the truth of some propositions about the future is implied in the truth of some propositions about the past, and that, therefore, some propositions about the future are true. And we may go further. If no propositions abut the past implied propositions about the future, then no propositions about the past could imply propositions about the later past or the present.

If the proposition "the occurrence of X implies the occurrence of Υ" is ever true, it is always true, while X is real, and, therefore, even according to Dr. Broad's view of reality, it is always true while X is present and past. For it is dependent on the nature of X and the laws of implication. The latter are not changeable, and when an event has once happened, its nature remains unchangeable. Thus, if it were not true, in 1921, that the occurrence of any event in 1920 involved the occurrence of any event in 1922, then it could not be true in 1923, when both 1920 and 1922 are in the past. And this would apply to any two periods in time, as much as to 1920 and 1922.

There are, then, only two alternatives. Either propositions about the future are true, and Dr. Broad's theory is wrong. Or else no proposition about any one period of time implies the truth of a proposition about any other period of time. From this it follows that no event at any point of time intrinsically determines any event at any other point of time, and that there is no causal determination except what is strictly simultaneous.

It is clear, from the rest of his book, that Dr. Broad does not accept this last alternative, and it is difficult to conceive that anyone would do so, unless he were so complete a sceptic that he could have no theory as to the nature of time, or of anything else. For a person who accepted this alternative would not merely deny that complete causal determination could be proved, he would not merely deny that any causal determination could be proved, but he would assert that all causal determination, between nonsimultaneous events, was proved to be impossible. But if this is not accepted, then some propositions about the future must be true.[9]

In the third place, even if the two objections already considered should be disregarded, time would still, on Dr. Broad's theory, involve the contradiction described above. For although, if Dr. Broad were right, no moment would have the three incompatible characteristics of past, present, and future, yet each of them (except the last moment of time, if there should be a last moment) would have the two incompatible characteristics of past and present. And this would be sufficient to produce the contradiction.

The words past and present clearly indicate different characteristics. And no one, I think, would suggest that they are simply compatible, in the way that the characteristics red and sweet are. If one man should say "strawberries are red," and another should reply "that is false, for they are sweet," the second man would be talking absolute nonsense. But if the first should say "you are eating my strawberries," and the second should reply "that is false, for I have already eaten them," the remark is admittedly not absolute nonsense, though its precise relation to the truth would depend on the truth about the reality of matter and time.

The terms can only be made compatible by a qualification. The proper statement of that qualification seems to me to be, as I have said, that, when we say that M is present, we mean that it is present at a moment of present time, and will be past at some moment of future time, and that,

when we say that M is past we mean that it has been present at some moment of past time, and is past at a moment of present time. Dr. Broad will, no doubt, claim to cut out "will be past at some moment of future time." But even then it would be true that, when we say M is past, we mean that it has been present at some moment of past time, and is past at a moment of present time, and that, when we say M is present, we mean that it is present at a moment of present time. As much as this Dr. Broad can say, and as much as this he must say, if he admits that each event (except a possible last event) is both present and past.

Thus we distinguish the presentness and pastness of events by reference to past and present moments. But every moment which is past is also present. And if we attempt to remove this difficulty by saying that it *is* past and *has been* present, then we get an infinite vicious series.

For these three reasons it seems to me that Dr. Broad's theory of time is untenable, and that the reality of time must still be rejected.

It is sometimes maintained that we are so immediately certain of the reality of time, that the certainty exceeds any certainty which can possibly be produced by arguments to the contrary, and that such arguments, therefore, should be rejected as false, even if we can find no flaw in them.

It does not seem to me that there is any immediate certainty of the reality of time. It is true, no doubt, that we perceive things as in time, and that therefore the unreality of time involves the occurrence of erroneous perception. But, as I have said, I hope to prove later that there is no impossibility in erroneous perception. It may be worth while, however, to point out that any theory which treated time as objectively real could only do so by treating time, *as we observe it,* as being either unreal or merely subjective. It would thus have no more claim to support from our perceptions than the theories which deny the reality of time.[10]

I perceive as present at one time whatever falls within the limits of one specious present. Whatever falls earlier or later than this, I do not perceive at all, though I judge it to be past or future. The time-series then, of which any part is perceived by me, is a time-series in which the future and the past are separated by a present which is a specious present.

Whatever is simultaneous with anything present, is itself present. If, therefore, the objective time-series, in which events really are, is the series which I immediately perceive, whatever is simultaneous with my specious present is present. But the specious present varies in length according to circumstances. And it is not impossible that there should be another conscious being existing besides myself, and that his specious present and mine may at the same time be of different lengths. Now the event *M* may be simultaneous both with *X*'s perception *Q*, and with *Y*'s perception *R*. At a certain moment *Q* may have ceased to be a part of *X*'s specious present. *M*, therefore, will at that moment be past. But at the same moment *R* may still be a part of *Y*'s specious present. And, therefore, *M* will be present at some moment at which it is past.

This is impossible. If, indeed, the *A* series was something purely subjective, there would be no difficulty. We could say that *M* was past for *X* and present for *Y*, just as we could say that it was pleasant for *X* and painful for *Y*. But we are now considering the hypothesis that time is objective. And, since the *A* series is essential to time, this involves that the *A* series is objective. And, if so, then at any moment *M* must be present, past, or future. It cannot be both present and past.

The present, therefore, through which events are really to pass, cannot be determined as being simultaneous with a specious present. If it has a duration, it must be a duration which is independently fixed. And it cannot be independently fixed so as to be identical with the duration of all specious presents, since all specious presents have not the same duration. And thus an event may be past or future when I am perceiving it as present, and may be present when I am remembering it as past or anticipating it as future. The duration of the objective present may be the thousandth part of a second. Or it may be a century, and the coronations of George IV and of Edward VII may form part of the same present. What reasons can we find in the immediate certainties of our experience to believe in the existence of such a present, which we certainly do not observe to be a present, and which has no relation to what we do observe as a present?

If we take refuge from these difficulties in the view, which has sometimes been held, that the present in the *A* series is not a finite duration, but a single point, separating future from past, we shall find other difficulties as serious. For then the objective time, in which events are, would be something entirely different from the time in which we experience them as being. The time in which we experience them has a present of varying finite duration, and is therefore divided into three durations—the past, the present, and the future. The objective time has only two durations, separated by a present which has nothing but the name in common with the present of experience, since it is not a duration but a point. What is there in our perception which gives us the least reason to believe in such a time as this?

And thus the denial of the reality of time turns out not to be so very paradoxical. It was called paradoxical because it required us to treat our experience of time as illusory. But now we see that our experience of time—centring as it does about the specious present—would be no less illusory if there were a real time in which the realities we experience existed. The specious present of our observations cannot correspond to the present of the events observed. And consequently the past and future of our observations could not correspond to the past and future of the events observed. On either hypothesis—whether we take time as real or as unreal—everything is observed as in a specious present, but nothing, not even the observations themselves, can ever really *be* in a specious present. For if time is unreal, nothing can be in any present at all, and, if time is real, the present in which things are will not be a specious present. I do not see, therefore, that we treat experience as much more illusory when we say that nothing is ever present at all, than when we say that everything passes through some present which is entirely different from the only present we experience.

It must further be noted that the results at which we have arrived do not give us any reason to suppose that *all* the elements in our experience of time are illusory. We have come to the conclusion that there is no real *A* series, and that therefore there is no real *B* series, and no real time-series. But it does not follow that when we have experience of a time-series we are not observing a real series. It is possible that, whenever we have an illusory experience of a time-series, we are observing a real series, and that all that is illusory is the appearance that it is a time-series. Such a series as this—a series which is not a time-series, but under certain conditions appears to us to be one—may be called a C series.

There are good reasons for supposing that such a C series does actually exist, in every case in which there is the appearance of a time-series. For when we consider how an illusion of time can come about, it is very difficult to suppose, either that all the elements in the experience are illusory, or that the element of the serial nature is so. And it is by no means so difficult to account for the facts if we suppose that there is an existent C series. In this case the illusion consists only in our applying the A series to it, and in the consequent appearance of the C series as a B series, the relation, whatever it may be, which holds between the terms of the C series, appearing as a relation of earlier and later.

The C series, then, can be real, while the A and B series are merely apparent. But when we consider how our experience is built up, we must class C and A together as primary, while B is only secondary. The real C series and the appearance of the A series must be given, separately and independently, in order to have the experience of time. For, as we have seen, they are both essential to it, and neither can be derived from the other. The B series, on the other hand, can be derived from the other two. For if there is a C series, where the terms are connected by permanent relations, and if the terms of this series appear also to form an A series, it will follow that the terms of the C series will also appear as a B series, those which are placed first, in the direction from past to future, appearing as earlier than those whose places are further in the direction of the future.

And thus, if there is a C series, it will follow that our experience of the time-series will not be entirely erroneous. Through the deceptive form of time, we shall grasp some of the true relations of what really exists. If we say that the events M and N are simultaneous, we say that they occupy the same position in the time-series. And there will be some truth in this, for the realities, which we perceive as the events M and N, do really occupy the same position in a series, though it is not a temporal series.

Again, if we assert that the events M, N, O are all at different times, and are in that order, we assert that they occupy different positions in the

time-series, and that the position of N is between the positions of M and O. And it will be true that the realities which we see as these events will be in a series, though not in a temporal series, and that they will be in different positions in it, and that the position of the reality which we perceive as the event N will be between the positions of the realities which we perceive as the events M and O.

If this view is adopted, the result will so far resemble the views of Hegel rather than those of Kant. For Hegel regarded the order of the time-series as a reflection, though a distorted reflection, of something in the real nature of the timeless reality, while Kant does not seem to have contemplated the possibility that anything in the nature of the noumenon should correspond to the time-order which appears in the phenomenon.

Thus the C series will not be altogether unlike the time-series as conceived by Mr. Russell. The C series will include as terms everything which appears to us as an event in time, and the C series will contain the realities in the same order as the events are ranged in by the relations of earlier and later. And the time-series, according to Mr. Russell, does not involve the objective reality of the A series.

But there remain important differences. Mr. Russell's series is a time-series, and the C series is not temporal. And although Mr. Russell's time-series (which is identical with our B series) has a one-to-one correspondence with the C series, still the two series are very different. The terms of the B series are events, and the terms of the C series are not. And the relation which unites the terms of the B series is the relation of earlier and later, which is not the case with the C series.

Endnotes

[1]It is very usual to contemplate time by the help of a metaphor of spatial movement. But spatial movement in which direction? The movement of time consists in the fact that later and later terms pass into the present, or—which is the same fact expressed in another way—that presentness passes to later and later terms. If we take it the first way, we are taking the B series as sliding along a fixed A series. If we take it the second way, we are taking the A series as sliding along a fixed B series. In the first case time presents itself as a movement from future to past. In the second case it presents itself as a movement from earlier to later. And this explains why we say that events come out of

the future, while we say that we ourselves move towards the future. For each man identifies himself especially with his present state, as against his future or his past, since it is the only one which he is directly perceiving. And this leads him to say that he is moving with the present towards later events. And as those events are now future, he says that he is moving towards the future.

Thus the question as to the movement of time is ambiguous. But if we ask what is the movement of either series, the question is not ambiguous. The movement of the *A* series along the *B* series is from earlier to later. The movement of the *B* series along the *A* series is from future to past.

²The past, therefore, is always changing, if the *A* series is real at all, since at each moment a past event is further in the past than it was before. This result follows from the reality of the *A* series, and is independent of the truth of our view that all change depends exclusively on the *A* series. It is worth while to notice this, since most people combine the view that the *A* series is real with the view that the past cannot change—a combination which is inconsistent.

³Neither would they be simultaneous, since that equally involves being in the same time. They would stand in no time-relation to one another.

⁴It is true, no doubt, that my anticipation of an experience *M,* the experience itself, and the memory of the experience, are three states which have different original qualities. But it is not the future *M,* the present *M,* and the past *M,* which have these three different qualities. The qualities are possessed by three different events—the anticipation of *M, M* itself, and the memory of *M*—each of which in its turn is future, present, and past. Thus this gives no support to the view that the changes of the *A* series are changes of original qualities.

⁵If the time-series has a first term, that term will never be future, and if it has a last term, that term will never be past. But the first term, in that case, will be present and past, and the last term will be future and present. And the possession of two incompatible characteristics raises the same difficulty as the possession of three.

⁶It may be worth while to point out that the vicious infinite has not arisen from the impossibility of *defining* past, present, and future, without using the terms in their own definitions. On the contrary, we have admitted these terms to be indefinable. It arises from the fact that the nature of the terms involves a contradiction, and that the attempt to remove the contradiction involves the employment of the terms, and the generation of a similar contradiction.

⁷Even on the hypothesis that judgments are real it would be necessary to regard ourselves as perceiving things in time, and so perceiving them erroneously. And we shall see later that all cognition is perception, and that, therefore, all error is erroneous perception.

⁸I have published my views on time, pretty nearly in their present shape, in *Mind* for 1908.

⁹It might seem that the truth of propositions about the future would be as fatal to my theory as to Dr. Broad's, since I am denying the reality of time. But, as will be explained later, although there is no time-series, there is a nontemporal series which is misperceived as a time-series. An assertion at one point of this series may be true of a fact at some other point in this series, which appears as a future point. And thus statements about the future might have phenomenal validity—they might have a one-to-one correspondence with true statements, and they might themselves be as true as any statements about the past could be. But Dr. Broad's theory requires that they should have no truth whatever, while some statements about the past and present should be absolutely true.

¹⁰By objectively real time, I mean a common time in which all existent things exist, so that they stand in temporal relations to each other. By subjectively real time, I mean one in which only the different states of a single self exist, so that it does not connect any self with anything outside it.

8. *The Myth of Passage*

DONALD C. WILLIAMS

Donald C. Williams was an American philosopher who taught at Harvard University. His article, "The Myth of Passage," first appeared in the *Journal of Philosophy* in 1951. This article shows how empirically minded philosophers were assimilating new ideas in physics and defending a relational view of time. Newton, Bergson, and McTaggart had maintained that there is something *sui generis* about the present, the Now. Whether called the "flux of absolute time" or "pure duration" or "Becoming," such thinkers believed time has a dynamic aspect that cannot be accounted for solely in terms of relations like earlier-than or later-than. But early in the twentieth century, Einstein's successful special theory of relativity rejected Newton's absolute time. Not only did Relativity take a relational approach to time, it said there is no unique cosmic Now: different observers in different "reference frames" could all be right when they disagreed about which events were past, present, or future. This led some people to believe reality is a four-dimensional "manifold" of "tenselessly existing" events. But how can such a view explain the deep-seated belief (and one's experience) that the present is unique and passing? Williams addresses this issue.

At every moment each of us finds himself the apparent center of the world, enjoying a little lit foreground of the here and now, while around him there looms, thing beyond thing, event beyond event, the plethora of a universe. Linking the furniture of the foreground are sets of relations which he supposes also to bind the things beyond and to bind the foreground with the rest. Noteworthy among them are those queerly obvious relations, peculiarly external to their terms, which compose the systems of space and time, modes of connection exhaustively specifiable in a scheme of four dimensions at right angles to one another. Within this manifold, for all that it is so firmly integrated, we are immediately struck by a disparity between the three-dimensional spread of space and the one dimension of time. The spatial dimensions are in a literal and precise sense perpendicular to one another, and the submanifold which they compose is isotropic, the same in all directions. The one dimension of time, on the other hand, although it has the same formal properties as each of the other three, is at least sensuously different from them as they are not from one another, and the total manifold is apparently not isotropic. Whereas an object can preserve the same shape while it is so shifted that its height becomes its breadth, we cannot easily conceive how it could do so while being shifted so that its breadth becomes its duration.

The theory of the manifold, I think, is the one model on which we can describe and explain the foreground of experience, or can intelligibly and

credibly construct our account of the rest of the world, and this is so because in fact the universe is spread out in those dimensions. There may be Platonic entities which are foreign to both space and time; there may be Cartesian spirits which are foreign to space; but the homely realm of natural existence, the total of world history, is a spatiotemporal volume of somewhat uncertain magnitude, chockablock with things and events. Logic, with its law of excluded middle and its tenseless operators, and natural science, with its secular world charts, concur inexorably with the vision of metaphysics and high religion that truth and fact are thus eternal.

I believe that the universe consists, without residue, of the spread of events in space-time, and that if we thus accept realistically the four-dimensional fabric of juxtaposed actualities we can dispense with all those dim nonfactual categories which have so bedeviled our race: the potential, the subsistential, and the influential, the noumenal, the numinous, and the nonnatural. But I am arguing here, not that there is nothing outside the natural world of events, but that the theory of the manifold is anyhow literally true and adequate to that world: true, in that the world contains no less than the manifold; adequate, in that it contains no more.

Since I think that this philosophy offers correct and coherent answers to real questions, I must think that metaphysical difficulties raised against it are genuine too. There are facts, logical and empirical, which can be described and explained only by the concept of the manifold; there are facts which some honest men deem irreconcilable with it. Few issues can better deserve adjudication. The difficulties which we need not take seriously are those made by primitive minds, and by new delib-

From Donald C. Williams, "The Myth of Passage," *The Journal of Philosophy*, Vol. 48, 1951, pp. 457–472. Reprinted by permission of *The Journal of Philosophy* and the estate of Donald C. Williams.

erate primitivists, who recommend that we follow out the Augustinian clue, as Augustine did not, that the man who best feels he understands time is he who refuses to think about it.

Among philosophical complainants against the manifold, some few raise difficulties about space—there are subjectivistic epistemologists, for example, who grant more reality to their own past and future than to things spatially beyond themselves. The temporal dimension of the manifold, however, bears the principal brunt. Sir James Jeans regretted that time is mathematically attached to space by so "weird" a function as the square root of minus one,[1] and the very word "weird," being cognate with *"werden,"* to become, is a monument to the uncanniness of our fourth dimension. Maintaining that time is in its essence something wholly unique, a flow or passage, the "time snobs" (as Wyndham Lewis called them) either deny that the temporal spread is a reality at all, or think it only a very abstract phase of real time. Far from disparaging time itself, they conceive themselves thus to be "taking time seriously" in a profounder sense than our party who are content with the vasty reaches of what is, was, and will be.

The more radical opposition to the manifold takes time with such Spartan seriousness that almost none of it is left—only the pulse of the present, born virginally from nothing and devouring itself as soon as born, so that whatever past and future there be are strictly only the memory and anticipation of them in this Now.[2] One set of motives for this view is in the general romantic polemic against logic and the competence of concepts. The theory of the manifold is the logical account of events par excellence, the teeth by which the jaws of the intellect grip the flesh of occurrence. The Bergsonian, who thinks that concepts cannot convey the reality of time because they are "static," the Marxist who thinks that process defies the cadres of two-valued logic, and the Heideggerian who thinks that temporality, history, and existence are leagued outside the categories of the intellect, thus have incentives for denying, in effect, all the temporal universe beyond what is immanent in the present flare and urge.

To counter their attack, it is a nice and tempting question whether and how concepts are "static," whether and how, in any case, a true concept must be similar to its object, and whether and how

history and existence are any more temporal than spatial. But we cannot here undertake the whole defense of the intellect against its most violent critics. We shall rather notice such doubters as trust and use conceptual analysis and still think there are cogent arguments against the manifold. One argument to that effect is an extreme sharpening of the positivistic argument from the egocentric predicament. For if it is impossible for my concepts to transcend experience in general, it may well be impossible for them to transcend the momentary experience in which they are entertained. Conversely, however, anybody who rejects the arguments for instantaneous solipsism, as most people do, must reject this argument for diminishing the manifold. The chief mode of argument is rather the finding of an intolerable anomaly in the statement that what was but has ceased, or what will be but has not begun, nevertheless is. This reflection has been used against the reality of the future, in particular, by philosophers as miscellaneous as Aristotle and neoscholastics, C. D. Broad, Paul Weiss, and Charles Hartshorne. In so far as it is an argument from logic, charging the manifold with self-contradiction, it would be as valid against the past as against the future; but, I have argued, it is by no means valid.[3]

The statement that a sea fight not present in time nevertheless exists is no more contradictory than that one not present in space nevertheless exists. If it seems so, this is only because there happens to be a temporal reference (tense) built into our verbs rather than a spatial reference (as in some languages) or than no locative reference (as in canonical symbolic transcriptions into logic).

I am not to contend now for the reality of the manifold, however, but against the extra *weirdness* alleged for time both by some champions who reject the manifold out of hand and by some who contend anyhow that it is not the whole story, both parties agreeing that the temporal dimension is not "real time," not "the genuine creative flux." If our temporalist means by this that the theory of temporal extension, along with the spatial models provided by calendars, kymographs, and statistical time charts, is in the last analysis fictitious, corresponding to nothing in the facts, he is reverting, under a thin cloak of dissimulation, to the mere rejection which we have agreed to leave aside. If he means, at the other extreme, no more than that the theory and the models themselves are not identical, either numerically or qualitatively, with the actual temporal succession which they represent, he is uttering a triviality which is true of every theory or representation. If he means that the temporal spread, though real and formally similar to a spatial spread, is qualitatively or intuitively very different from it, or lies in a palpably and absolutely unique direction, he says something plausible and important but not at all incompatible with the philosophy of the manifold.

He is most likely to mean, however, another proposition which is never more than vaguely expressed: that over and above the sheer spread of events, with their several qualities, along the time axis, which is analogous enough to the spread of space, there is something extra, something active and dynamic, which is often and perhaps best described as "passage." This something extra, I am going to plead, is a myth: not one of those myths which foreshadow a difficult truth in a metaphorical way, but altogether a false start, deceiving us about the facts, and blocking our understanding of them.

The literature of "passage" is immense, but it is naturally not very exact and lucid, and we cannot be sure of distinguishing in it between mere harmless allegorical phenomenology and the special metaphysical declaration which I criticize. But "passage," it would seem, is a character supposed to inhabit and glorify the present, "the passing present,"[4] "the moving present,"[5] the "travelling now."[6] It is "the passage of time as actual . . . given now with the jerky or whooshy quality of transience."[7] It is James' "passing moment."[8] It is what Broad calls "the transitory aspect" of time, in contrast with the "extensive."[9] It is Bergson's living felt duration. It is Heidegger's *Zeitlichkeit*. It is Tillich's "moment that is creation and fate."[10] It is "the act of becoming," the mode of potency and generation, which Hugh King finds properly appreciated only by Aristotle and Whitehead.[11] It is Eddington's "ongoing" and "the formality of taking place,"[12] and Dennes' "surge of process."[13] It is the dynamic essence which Ushenko believes that Einstein omits from the world.[14] It is the mainspring of McTaggart's "A-series" which puts movement in time,[15] and it is Broad's pure becoming.[16] Withal it is the flow and go of very existence, nearer to us than breathing, closer than hands and feet.

So far as one can interpret these expressions into a theory, they have the same purport as all the immemorial turns of speech by which we describe time as *moving*, with respect to the present or with respect to our minds. Time flows or flies or marches, years roll, hours pass. More explicitly we may speak as if the perceiving mind were stationary while time flows by like a river, with the flotsam of events upon it; or as if presentness were a fixed pointer under which the tape of happenings slides; or as if the time sequence were a moving-picture film, unwinding from the dark reel of the future, projected briefly on the screen of the present, and rewound into the dark can of the past. Sometimes, again, we speak as if the time sequence were a stationary plain or ocean on which we voyage, or a variegated river gorge down which we drift; or, in Broad's analogy, as if it were a row of house fronts along which the spotlight of the present plays. "The essence of nowness," Santayana says, "runs like fire along the fuse of time."[17]

Augustine pictures the present passing into the past, where the modern pictures the present as invading the future,[18] but these do not conflict, for Augustine means that the *events* which were present become past, while the modern means that *presentness* encroaches on what was previously the future. Sometimes the surge of presentness is conceived as a mere moving illumination by consciousness, sometimes as a sort of vivification and heightening, like an ocean wave heaving along beneath a stagnant expanse of floating seaweed, sometimes as no less than the boon of existence itself, reifying minute by minute a limbo of unthings.

Now, the most remarkable feature of all this is that while the modes of speech and thought which enshrine the idea of passage are universal and perhaps ineradicable, the instant one thinks about them one feels uneasy, and the most laborious effort cannot construct an intelligible theory which admits the literal truth of any of them. The obvious and notorious fault of the idea, as we have now localized it, is this. Motion is already defined and explained in the dimensional manifold as consisting of the presence of the same individual in different places at different times. It consists of bends or quirks in the world line, or the space-time worm, which is the four-dimensional totality of the individual's existence. This is motion in space, if you like; but we can readily define a corresponding "motion in time." It comes out as nothing more dramatic than an exact equivalent: "motion in time" consists of being at different times in different places.

True motion then is motion at once in time and space. Nothing can "move" in time alone any more than in space alone, and time itself cannot "move" any more than space itself. "Does this road go anywhere?" asks the city tourist. "No, it stays right along here," replies the countryman. Time "flows" only in the sense in which a line flows or a landscape "recedes into the west." That is, it is an ordered extension. And each of us proceeds through time only as a fence proceeds across a farm: that is, parts of our being, and the fence's, occupy successive instants and points, respectively. There is passage, but it is nothing extra. It is the mere happening of things, their existence strung along in the manifold. The term "the present" is the conventional way of designating the cross section of events which are simultaneous with the uttering of the phrase, and "the present moves" only in that when similar words occur at successively different moments, they denote, by a twist of language essentially the same as that of all "egocentric particulars," like "here" and "this," different cross sections of the manifold.

Time travel, prima facie, then, is analyzable either as the banality that at each different moment we occupy a different moment from the one we occupied before, or the contradiction that at each different moment we occupy a different moment from the one which we are then occupying—that five minutes from now, for example, I may be a hundred years from now.[19]

The tragedy then of the extra idea of passage or absolute becoming, as a philosophical principle, is that it incomprehensibly doubles its world by reintroducing terms like "moving" and "becoming" in a sense which both requires and forbids interpretation in the preceding ways. For as soon as we say that time or the present or we move in the odd extra way which the doctrine of passage requires, we have no recourse but to suppose that this movement in turn takes time of a special sort: $time_1$ moves at a certain rate in $time_2$, perhaps one $second_1$ per one $second_2$, perhaps slower, perhaps faster. Or, conversely, the moving present slides over so many seconds of $time_1$ in so many seconds of $time_2$. The history of the new moving present,

in $time_2$, then composes a new and higher time dimension again, which cries to be vitalized by a new level of passage, and so on forever.

We hardly needed to point out the unhappy regress to which the idea of time's motion commits us, for any candid philosopher, as soon as he looks hard at the idea, must *see* that it is preposterous. "Taking place" is not a formality to which an event incidentally submits—it is the event's very being. World history consists of actual concrete happenings in a temporal sequence; it is not necessary or possible that happening should happen to them all over again. The system of the manifold is thus "complete" in something like the technical logical sense, and any attempted addition to it is bound to be either contradictory or supererogatory.

Bergson, Broad, and some of the followers of Whitehead[20] have tried to soften the paradoxes of passage by supposing that the present does not move across the total time level, but that it is the very fountain where the river of time gushes out of nothingness (or out of the power of God). The past, then, having swum into being and floated away, is eternally real, but the future has no existence at all. This may be a more appealing figure, but logically it involves the same anomalies of metahappening and metatime which we observed in the other version.

What, then, we must ask, were the motives which drove men to the staggering philosophy of passage? One of them, I believe, we can dispose of at once. It is the innocent vertigo which inevitably besets a creature whose thinking is strung out in time, as soon as he tries to think of the time dimension itself. He finds it easiest to conceive and understand purely geometrical structures. Motion is more difficult, and generally remains vague, while time per se is very difficult indeed, but being now identified as the principle which imports motion into space, it is put down as a kind of quintessential motion itself. The process is helped by the fact that the mere further-along-ness of successive segments, either of a spatial or of a temporal stretch, can quite logically be conceived as a degenerate sort of change, as when we speak of the flow of a line or say that the scenery changes along the Union Pacific.

A rather more serious excuse for the idea of passage is that it is supposed necessary and sufficient for adding to the temporal dimension that intrinsic *sense* from earlier to later in which time is supposed to differ radically from any dimension of space.[21] A meridian of longitude has only a direction, but a river has a "sense," and time is in this like the river. It is, as the saying goes, irreversible and irrevocable. It has a "directed tension."[22] The mere dimension of time, on the other hand, would seem to be symmetrical. The principle of absolute passage is bidden to rectify this symmetry with what Eddington called "time's arrow."

It might be replied that science does not supply an arrow for time because it has no need of it. But I think it plain that time does have a sense, from early to late. I only think that it can be taken care of on much less draconian principles than absolute passage. There is nothing in the dimensional view of time to preclude its being generated by a uniquely asymmetrical relation, and experience suggests powerfully that it is so generated. But the fact is that every real series has a "sense" anyhow. This is provided, if by nothing else, then by the sheer numerical identity and diversity of terms.

In the line of individual things or events, *a, b, c, . . . z,* whether in space or in time, the "sense" from *a* to *z* is *ipso facto* other than the "sense" from *z* to *a.* Only because there is a difference between the ordered couple *a;z* and the couple *z;a* can we define the difference between a symmetrical and an asymmetrical relation. Only because there are already two distinguishable "ways" on a street, determined by its individual ends, can we decide to permit traffic to move one way and prohibit it the other. But a sufficient difference of sense, finally, would appear to be constituted, if nothing else offered, by the inevitably asymmetrical distribution of properties along the temporal line (or any other). Eddington has been only one of many scientists who think the arrow is provided for the cosmos by the principle of entropy, and entropy has been only one principle thus advocated.[23]

In so far as what men mean by "the irrevocability of the past" is the causal circumstance that we can affect the future in a way we cannot affect the past, it is just a trait of the physicist's arrow. They often mean by it, however, only the inexorability of fact, that what is the case is the case, past, present, or future; or the triviality that the particular events of 1902, let us say, cannot also be the events of 1952. Very similar events might be so, however, and if very few of them are, this is the fault of the concrete nature of things and not of any grudge on the part of time.[24]

The final motive for the attempt to consummate or supplant the fourth dimension of the manifold with the special perfection, the grace and whiz, of passage is the vaguest but the most substantial and incorrigible. It is simply that we *find* passage, that we are immediately and poignantly involved in the whoosh of process, the felt flow of one moment into the next. Here is the focus of being. Here is the shore whence the youngster watches the golden mornings swing toward him like serried bright breakers from the ocean of the future. Here is the flood on which the oldster wakes in the night to shudder at its swollen black torrent cascading him into the abyss.

It would be futile to try to deny these experiences, but their correct description is another matter. If they are in fact consistent with our theory, they are no evidence against it; and if they are entailed by it, they are evidence in its favor. Since the theory was originally constructed to take account of them, it would be odd if they were inconsistent with it or even irrelevant to it. I believe that in fact they are neither, and that the theory of the manifold provides the true and literal description of what the enthusiastic metaphors of passage have deceptively garbled.

The principal reason why we are troubled to accommodate our experience of time to the intellectual theory of time goes very deep in the philosophy of philosophy. It is that we must here scrutinize the undoctored fact of perception, on the one hand, and must imagine our way into a conceptual scheme, and envisage the true intrinsic being of its objects, on the other hand, and then pronounce on the numerical identity of the first with the second. This is a very rare requirement. Even such apt ideas as those of space and of physical objects, as soon as we contemplate them realistically, begin to embarrass us, so that we slip into the assumption that the real objects of the conceptions, if they exist at all, exist on a different plane or in a different realm from the sensuous spread and lumpiness of experience. The ideas of time and of the mind, however, do not permit of such evasion. Those beings are given in their own right and person, filling the foreground. Here for once we must fit the fact directly into the intellectual form, without benefit of precedent or accustomed criteria.

First off, then, comparing the calm conceptual scheme with the turbid event itself, we may be repelled by the former, not because it is not true to the latter, but because it *is* not the latter. When we see that this kind of diversity is inevitable to every concept and its object, and hence is irrelevant to the validity of any, we demur because the conceptual scheme is indifferently flat and third-personal, like a map, while the experienced reality is centripetal and perspectival, piled up and palpitating where we are, gray and retiring elsewhere.

But this is only because every occasion on which we compare the world map with experience has itself a single specific location, confronting part of the world, remote from the rest. The perspectivity of the view is exactly predictable from the map. The deception with respect to time is worse than with respect to space because our memories and desires run timewise and not spacewise. The jerk and whoosh of this moment, which are simply the real occurrence of one particular batch of events, are no different from the whoosh and being of any other patch of events up and down the eternal timestretch. Remembering some of the latter, however, and anticipating more, and bearing in mind that while they happen they are all called "the present," we mistakenly hypostatize *the* Present as a single surge of bigness which rolls along the time axis. There is in fact no more a single rolling Now than there is a single rolling Here along a spatial line—a standing line of soldiers, for example, though each of them has the vivid presentment of his own here.

Let us hug to us as closely as we like that there is real succession, that rivers flow and winds blow, that things burn and burst, that men strive and guess and die. All this is the concrete stuff of the manifold, the reality of serial happening, one event after another, in exactly the time spread which we have been at pains to diagram. What does the theory allege except what we find, and what do we find that is not accepted and asserted by the theory? Suppose a pure intelligence, bred outside of time, instructed in the nature of the manifold and the design of the human spacetime worm, with its mnemic organization, its particular delimited but overlapping conscious fields, and the strands of world history which flank them, and suppose him incarnated among us: what could he have expected the temporal experience to be like except just

about what he actually discovers it to be? How, in brief, could processes and experiences which endure and succeed each other along the time line appear as anything other than enduring and successive processes and a stream of consciousness?

The theory of the manifold leaves abundant room for the sensitive observer to record any describable difference he may find, in intrinsic quality, relational texture, or absolute direction, between the temporal dimension and the spatial ones. He is welcome to mark it so on the map. The very singleness of the time dimension, over against the amalgamated three dimensions of space, may be an idiosyncrasy with momentous effects; its *fourthness*, so to speak, so oddly and immensely multiplying the degrees of freedom embodied in the familiar spatial complex, was bound to seem momentous too.

The theory has generally conceded or emphasized that time is unique in these and other respects, and I have been assuming that it was right to do so. In the working out of this thesis, however, and in considering the very lame demurrals which oppose it, I have come a little uneasily to the surmise that the idea of an absolute or intrinsic difference of texture or orientation is superfluous, and that the four dimensions of the manifold compose a perfectly homogeneous scheme of location relations, the same in all directions, and that the oddity of temporal distances is altogether a function of features which occupy them—a function of *de facto* pattern like the shape of an arrow, like the difference between the way in and the way out of a flytrap, and like the terrestrial difference between up and down.

Even a person who believes that temporal distances are a categorically peculiar mode of relation, intrinsically different from spatial distance, regardless of how they are filled, must grant that they nevertheless *are* filled differently: things, persons, and events, as a matter of natural fact, are strung along with respect to the time axis in rhythms and designs notably different from those in which they are deployed spacewise. Entropy and the other scientific criteria for the "sense" from past to future distinguish no less the whole temporal direction from the spatial ones. The very concept of "things" or "individual substances" derives from a peculiar kind of coherence and elongation of clumps of events in the time direction. Living bodies in particular have a special organized trend timewise, a *conatus sese conservandi,* which nothing has in spatial section. Characteristic themes of causation run in the same direction, and paralleling all these, and accounting for their importance and obviousness to us, is the pattern of mental events, the stream of consciousness, with its mnemic cumulation and that sad anxiety to *keep going* futureward which contrasts strangely with our comparative indifference to our spatial girth.

The same fact of the grain and configuration of events which, if it does not constitute, certainly accompanies and underlines the "senses" of space and time, has other virtues which help to naturalize experience in the manifold. It accounts for the apparent *rate* of happening, for example; for the span of the specious present; and for the way in which the future is comparatively malleable to our present efforts and correspondingly dark to our present knowledge. An easy interpretation would be that the world content is uniquely organized in the time direction because the time direction itself is aboriginally unique. Modern philosophical wisdom, however, consists mostly of trying the cart before the horse, and I find myself more than half convinced by the oddly repellent hypothesis that the peculiarity of the time dimension is not thus primitive but is wholly a resultant of those differences in the mere *de facto* run and order of the world's filling.

It is conceivable, then, though perhaps physically impossible, that one four-dimensional part of the manifold of events be slued around at right angles to the rest, so that the time order of that area, as composed by its interior lines of strain and structure, runs parallel with a spatial order in its environment. It is conceivable, indeed, that a single whole human life should lie thwartwise of the manifold, with its belly plump in time, its birth at the east and its death in the west, and its conscious stream perhaps running alongside somebody's garden path.[25]

It is conceivable too then that a human life be twisted, not 90° but 180°, from the normal temporal grain of the world. F. Scott Fitzgerald tells the story of Benjamin Button who was born in the last stages of senility and got younger all his life till he died a dwindling embryo.[26] Fitzgerald imagined the reversal to be so imperfect that Benjamin's stream of consciousness ran, not back-

ward with his body's gross development, but in the common clockwise manner. We might better conceive a reversal of every cell twitch and electron whirl, and hence suppose that he experienced his own life stages in the same order as we do ours, but that he observed everyone around him moving backward from the grave to the cradle. True time travel, then, is conceivable after all, though we cannot imagine how it could be caused by beings whose lives are extended in the normal way: it would consist of a man's life-pattern, and the pattern of any appliances he employed, running at an abnormal rate or on an abnormal heading across the manifold.

As the dimensional theory accommodates what is true in the notion of passage, that is, the occurrence of events, in contrast with a mythical rearing and charging of time itself, so it accounts for what is true in the notions of "flux," "emergence," "creative advance," and the rest. Having learned the trick of mutual translation between theory and experience, we see where the utter misrepresentation lies in the accusation that the dimensional theory denies that time is "real," or that it substitutes a safe and static world, a block universe, a petrified *fait accompli,* a *totum simul,* for the actuality of risk and change.

Taking time with the truest seriousness, on the contrary, it calmly diagnoses "novelty" or "becoming," for example, as the existence of an entity, or kind of entity, at one time in the world continuum which does not exist at any previous time. No other sort of novelty than this, I earnestly submit, is discoverable or conceivable—or desirable. In practice, the modern sciences of the manifold have depicted it as a veritable caldron of force and action. Although the theory entails that it is true at every time that events occur at other times, it emphatically does not entail that all events happen at the same time or at every time, or at no time. It does not assert, therefore, that future things "already" exist or exist "forever." Emphatically also it does not, as is frequently charged, "make time a dimension of space,"[27] any more than it makes space a dimension of time.

The theory of the manifold, which is thus neutral with respect to the amount of change and permanence in the world, is surprisingly neutral also toward many other topics often broached as though they could be crucial between it and the extra idea of passage. It is neutral, so far, toward whether space and time are absolute and substantival in the Democritean and Newtonian way, or relative and adjectival in Spencer's and Whitehead's way, or further relativistic in Einstein's way. The theory of space does not, as Bergson pretended, have any preference for discontinuity over continuity, and while a time order in which nothing exists but the present would be fatal to any real continuity, the philosophy of the manifold is quite prepared to accept any verdict on whether space or time or both are continuous or discrete, as it is also on whether they are finite or infinite. Instead of "denying history," it preserves it, and is equally hospitable to all philosophies of history except such as themselves deny history by disputing the objectivity and irrevocability of historical truth. It does not care whether events eternally recur, or run along forever on the dead level as Aristotle thought, or enact the ringing brief drama of the Christian episode, or strive into the Faustian boundless. It is similarly neutral toward theories of causation and of knowledge.

The world manifold of occurrences, each eternally deter*minate* at its own place and date, may and may not be so deter*mined* in its texture that what occurs at one juncture has its sufficient reason at others. If it does evince such causal connections, these may be either efficient (as apparently they are) or final (as apparently they are not). The core of the causal nexus itself may be, so far as the manifold is concerned, either a real connection of Spinoza's sort, or Whitehead's, or the scholastics', or the mere regular succession admitted by Hume and Russell. It was a mistake for Spinoza to infer, if he did, that the eternal manifold and strict causation entail one another, as it is a worse mistake for the scholastics, Whitehead, Ushenko, and Weiss to infer the opposite (as they seem to), that "real time" and "real causation" entail one another.[28] The theory is similarly noncommittal toward metaphysical accounts of individual substances, which it can allow to be compounds of form and matter or mere sheaves of properties.

The theory of the manifold makes a man at home in the world to the extent that it guarantees that intelligence is not affronted at its first step into reality. Beyond that, the cosmos is as it is. If there is moral responsibility, if the will is free, if there is reasonableness in regret and hope in deci-

sion, these must be ascertained by more particular observations and hypotheses than the doctrine of the manifold. It makes no difference to our theory whether we are locked in an ice pack of fate, or whirled in a tornado of chance, or are firmfooted makers of destiny. It will accept benignly either the Christian Creator, or the organic and perfect Absolute, or Hume's sand pile of sensation, or the fluid melee of contextualism, or the structured world process of materialism.

The service which the theory performs with respect to all these problems is other than dictating solutions of them. It is the provision of a lucent frame or arena where they and their solutions can be laid out and clearheadedly appraised in view of their special classes of evidence. Once under this kind of observation, for example, the theories of change which describe becoming as a marriage of being and not-being, or an interpenetration of the present with the future and the past, become repulsive, not because they conflict especially with the philosophy of the manifold, but because if they are not mere incantations they contradict themselves. When we see that the problem how Achilles can overtake the tortoise is essentially the same as the problem how two lines can intersect one another obliquely, we are likely to be content with the simple mathematical intelligibility of both. When we see that the "change" of a leaf's color from day to day is of the same denomination as its "change" from inch to inch of its surface, we are less likely to hope that mysterious formulas about the actualization of the potential and the perdurance of a substratum are of any use in accounting for either of them.

If then there is some appearance of didactic self-righteousness in my effort here to save the pure theory of the manifold from being either displaced or amended by what I think is the disastrous myth of passage, this is because I believe that the theory of the manifold is the very paradigm of philosophic understanding. It grasps with a firm logic, so far as I can see, the most intimate and pervasive of facts; it clarifies the obscure and assimilates the apparently diverse.

Most of the effect of the prophets of passage, on the other hand, is to melt back into the primitive magma of confusion and plurality the best and sharpest instruments which the mind has forged. Some of those who do this have a deliberate preference for the melting pot of mystery as an end in itself. Others, I suppose, hope eventually to cast from it a finer metal and to forge a sharper point. No hope of that sort is altogether chimerical. But I suggest that if a tithe of the animus and industry invested in that ill-omened enterprise were spent on the refinement and imaginative use of the instrument we have, whatever difficulties still attend it would soon be dissipated.

Endnotes

[1] *The Mysterious Universe*. New York, 1930, p. 118.

[2] This I think is a fair description of G. H. Mead's doctrine in *The Philosophy of the Present*. See also, e.g., Schopenhauer: *The World as Will and Idea*, Bk. 4, Sec. 54.

[3] "The Sea Fight Tomorrow," Williams, *Principles of Empirical Realism*.

[4] W. R. Dennes, in California, University, Philosophical Union, *The Problem of Time*. Berkeley, Calif., 1935, p. 103.

[5] I. Stearns, in *Review of Metaphysics*, 4 (1950), 198.

[6] Santayana: *Realms of Being*, in *Works*, Vol. 14, p. 254.

[7] Lewis: *An Analysis of Knowledge and Valuation*, p. 19. This is pretty surely phenomenology, not metaphysics, but it is too good to omit.

[8] James: *A Pluralistic Universe*, p. 254.

[9] Broad: *An Examination of McTaggart's Philosophy*, Vol. 2, Pt. 1, p. 271.

[10] Paul Tillich: *The Interpretation of History*. New York, 1936, p. 129.

[11] H. R. King, in *Journal of Philosophy*, 46 (1949), 657–70. This is an exceptionally ingenious, serious, and explicit statement of the philosophy which I am opposing.

[12] Arthur S. Eddington: *Space, Time, and Gravitation*, New York, 1920, p. 51; *The Nature of the Physical World*, New York, 1928, p. 68.

[13] Dennes: op. cit., pp. 91, 93.

[14] Andrew P. Ushenko: *Power and Events*. Princeton, 1946, p. 146.

[15] John M. E. McTaggart: *The Nature of Existence*. Cambridge, 1927, Vol. 2, Bk. 5, Chap. 33.

[16] Broad: *Scientific Thought*, p. 67; *An Examination of McTaggart's Philosophy*, Vol. 2, Pt. 1, p. 277.

[17] *Realms of Being*, in *Works*, Vol. 15, p. 90.

[18] *Confessions*, Bk. 11, Chap. 14; cf. E. B. McGilvary, in *Philosophical Review*, 23 (1914), 121–45.

[19] "He may even now—if I may use the phrase—be wandering on some plesiosaurus-haunted oolitic coral reef, or beside the lonely saline seas of the Triassic Age"—H. G. Wells, *The Time Machine*, epilogue. This book, perhaps the best yarn ever written, contains such early and excellent accounts of the theory of the manifold that it has been quoted and requoted by scientific writers. Though it makes slips, its logic is better than that of later such stories.

[20] Bergson's theory of the snowball of time may be thus understood: the past abides in the center while ever new presents accrete around it. For Broad, see *Scientific Thought*, p. 66, and on Whitehead, see King, op. cit., esp. p. 663.

[21] See, for example, Broad: *Scientific Thought*, p. 57.

[22] Tillich, op. cit., p. 245.

[23] *The Nature of the Physical World*, Chap. 3. For the present scientific state of the question, see Adolf Grünbaum: *Philosophical Problems of Space and Time*, New York, 1963.

[24] Dennes argues thus, loc. cit.

[25] I should expect the impact of the environment on such a being to be so wildly queer and out of step with the way he is put together, that his mental life must be a dragged-out monstrous delirium. Professor George Burch has suggested to me that it might be the mystic's timeless illumination. Whether these diagnoses are different I shall not attempt to say.

[26] "The Curious Case of Benjamin Button," in *Tales of the Jazz Age*. New York, 1922.

[27] See Charles Hartshorne: *Man's Vision of God, and the Logic of Theism*, Chicago, 1941, p. 140, and Tillich, op. cit., pp. 132, 248; and remember Bergson's allegation that the principle of the manifold "spatializes" time.

[28] See, for example, Whitehead: *Process and Reality*, p. 363; Paul Weiss: *Nature and Man*, New York, 1947.

9. McTaggart, Fixity and Coming True*

D. H. MELLOR

Many twentieth-century philosophers have debated the metaphysical significance of language. This is in keeping with an ancient tradition that recognizes meaning is itself a puzzling phenomenon and philosophical
disagreements and errors might result from faulty analyses of what people
say. Modern logical and semantic theories have become quite technical in an
effort to settle the question What exactly must exist if our statements are
true? An important issue regarding time has been the significance of tense.
Some philosophers have claimed tensed statements are indispensible and
have no tenseless equivalents. They argue that this fact, if it is a fact, proves
the Now is *sui generis* and, hence, tenseless views of time that reduce the
present to earlier-later relations are false. The relevance of tense to the metaphysics of time is the central topic of D. H. Mellor's 1981 paper,
"McTaggart, Fixity and Coming True."

In this selection, which is developed more fully in his book *Real Time*,
Mellor offers a "token-reflexive analysis" of tense, according to which, a present tense sentence token is true if and only if it occurs (exists tenselessly) at
(roughly) the same time as the event it is about; a past tense token is true if
and only if it occurs at a time later than the event it refers to, and so on. In
Real Time II (1998), Mellor abandoned the token-reflexive analysis and
replaced it by the "date-analysis." According to the date-analysis, the truth
conditions of a tensed sentence are determined by the time at which it is
uttered. For example, "It is now raining," uttered at t1 is true if it is raining
at t1. The meaning of a tensed sentence is thus a function from the time of
its occurrence to that sentence's truth conditions at that time.

D. H. Mellor is an Emeritus Professor of Philosophy in the Faculty of
Philosophy at the University of Cambridge and Fellow of Darwin College.

1. Introduction

Some events are past, some present and some, I
expect, are still to come. These are at once the
most obvious, the most basic and the most disputed facts about time. I am one of those who dispute them. I maintain with McTaggart (1908;
1927: ch. 33) that in reality nothing is either past,
present or future. Since, however, I part from him
by thinking that reality need not be tensed to be
temporal, I am not led, as he is, to deny the reality of time itself. Indeed I believe that, paradoxically, time needs to be both real and tenseless to

From *Reduction, Time, and Reality*, R. Healey, ed.
Copyright © 1981 by Cambridge University Press.
Reprinted by permission of Cambridge University Press.

* This paper developed out of classes given at
Stanford University in the Fall of 1978, during a visit
made possible by the grant of a Radcliffe Fellowship and
a British Academy Overseas Visiting Fellowship, for
which I owe thanks to the Radcliffe Trust and the British
Academy. I am indebted for helpful comment and criticism to several Stanford students, to Professors John
Perry, Nancy Cartwright and David Lewis, and to those
taking part in the March 1979 meeting of the Thyssen
U.K. Philosophy Group, at which the original version of
it was discussed. In rewriting I have been further assisted
by the replies of Professor Jeffrey and Mr. Mackie to my
critique, and also by detailed comments from Jeremy
Butterfield.

explain how and why people come to think of events as being past, present and future.

These propositions are, I fear, still contentious, so they will have to be defended in what follows. But my main object is not merely to promote and sugar McTaggart's pill. I want also to prescribe it: specifically, for R. C. Jeffrey's 'conceit that the world grows by accretion of facts'; or, in other words, that only when an event happens does the proposition saying so 'come true' (1980: 253). It will also serve to purge J. L. Mackie's closely related conceit that events become 'fixed and settled and unalterable' (1974: 178) as soon as their 'preceding sufficient causes . . . have occurred' (181). These are serious conceits, though not new ones: McTaggart himself (1927: §337) appeals to the second while disposing of Broad's (1923: ch. II) version of the first. But as they have been newly reconceived, so they need renewed purgation. They are, I shall argue, only trivially true if time is tenseless. And rather than tax my distinguished colleagues with triviality, I prefer to conclude that they are wrong.

2. *Time without* T*ense*

First, however, we must get rid of tense, and I will not pretend that this is easy. Consider for example the fundamental relation '. . . is earlier than . . .' (or its converse, 'later than'). What makes this relation temporal? One persuasive answer is: one event, e, being earlier than another, e', implies such tensed facts as that sometime e' is present and e past but never *vice versa*. What makes the 'earlier' relation temporal, in other words, is that it determines the order in which the events it relates become successively present and then past. But if there are in reality no such tensed facts as events being present or past, something else must make 'earlier' temporal—and it is no easy task to find something else that will do the job. As McTaggart saw, it is not enough for a tenseless relation between events merely to reproduce the order in which they appear to become present. If, for example, everything in the universe was always at the same temperature at the same time, but always cooling, the 'cooler' relation would do that: but that would not make 'cooler' a temporal relation.

Advocates of tenseless time have, I admit, mostly shirked the task, e.g. of saying what is temporal about the nonspatial dimension of their four-dimensional Minkowski manifolds. Their 'block' universes have no more real time in them than McTaggart's does—the difference being that McTaggart sees this and they, by and large, do not. I too will shirk the task here, but I do acknowledge it, since I am not willing to give up real time, and I undertake to tackle it elsewhere. All I can say here is that the materials I will use are the direct perception of one event being later than another, which occurs whenever we see something move or change in some other definite way, and the role causation plays in that perception.

There is another task, however, which I must attempt here: namely, to give a tenseless account of change. Time is essentially the dimension of change, and any theory of time has to account for that fact. Now McTaggart thought that change needed tense, since he thought change to be impossible without events moving from the future *via* the present to the past, a movement I shall call 'McTaggart change'. Without real tense, of course, McTaggart change does not exist, so a tenseless account of change must find a way of doing without it. My account derives from Russell (1903: §442): 'Change is the difference, in respect of truth or falsehood, between a proposition concerning an entity and the time T, and a proposition concerning the same entity and the time T', provided that these propositions differ only by the fact that T occurs in the one where T' occurs in the other.' This is what Geach has called 'Cambridge change' and, as he says, actual change is only one species of it (1979: 90–2). To adapt an example of McTaggart's (1927: §309), 'the fall of a sandcastle on the English coast' effects a Cambridge change in the Great Pyramid, by changing a relation in which it stands to the sand; but clearly the Pyramid itself does not actually change as the sand does. The difference between actual and what Geach calls 'merely' Cambridge change is causal: actual changes are events, with spatiotemporally contiguous effects, and merely Cambridge changes are not.

I follow Davidson (1969) in taking events, including changes, to be individuated by their causes and effects. But not all events are changes; nor do events themselves change. Change occurs in things, i.e. individual substances, in one standard sense of that term. (The difference between things and events I take to be that whereas events, if extended in time, have temporal parts, things do not. People are things in this sense, and so are common objects such as tables, chairs—and McTaggart's (1927: §313) poker. For a longer list, and some reasons why the thing/event distinction matters, see my 1982: §6.) A thing may have a nontemporal property at one date incompatible with those it has at earlier or later dates; and when such a fact constitutes an event, with effects spatiotemporally contiguous to the thing, the thing has undergone an actual change between these dates. We may indeed use this as a criterion for distinguishing real from merely apparent properties of things, thus ruling out such spurious properties as being forty, famous, the tallest man in the room and 'grue' (Goodman 1965: ch. III). Real properties of things and people, loss or gain of which is actual change in them, rather than the merely Cambridge variety, include temperatures, masses, colours, shapes—and both physical dispositions such as solubility (Mellor 1974: §I-II), and mental states such as particular beliefs and desires (Mellor 1978: §II).

Now suppose some thing, *a*, has a pair, *G* and *G**, of such incompatible real properties (e.g. temperatures) during two separate stretches of time *t* and *t**: i.e.

$$a \text{ is } G \text{ during } t \qquad (1)$$

and

$$a \text{ is } G^* \text{ during } t^* \qquad (2)$$

If *a* were an event, it would have different temporal parts containing *a*-during-*t* and *a*-during-*t**, and the supposed change would reduce to these different parts having different properties:

$$G(a\text{-during-}t) \qquad (3)$$

and

$$G^*(a\text{-during-}t^*) \qquad (4)$$

But that different entities differ in their properties does not amount to change, even if one is earlier than the other and both are parts of something

else. (3) and (4) would no more constitute a case of change than would *a*'s spatial parts differing in their properties—e.g. McTaggart's poker being hot at one end and cool at the other.

I take change to require a difference between the state of a *whole* thing at two different times. That is, real changeable non-temporal properties of a thing are in fact relations it has to the various times and stretches of times at which it exists. I.e. (1) and (2) should be read as

$$G(a, t) \qquad (5)$$

and

$$G^*(a, t^*) \qquad (6)$$

Treating temperatures, colours, shapes etc. as relations between things and times may seem odd, but it is only a way of making two indubitable points about facts like (1):

(a) Both the contexts

$$\ldots \text{ is } G \text{ during } t'$$

and

$$'a \text{ is } G \text{ during } \ldots$$

are transparent, i.e. (1) remains true however *a* and *t* are referred to.

(b) For (1) to be true, both *a* and *t* must exist. (This need not of course imply a Newtonian conception of absolute time: it does not follow that time could exist without events—times may still need specifying by events, such as Christ's birth, and their temporal relations, such as the earth's period of rotation on its axis and about the sun.)

I should emphasise at once that (5) and (6) in no way beg the question against tenses. Nothing prevents *t* and *t** taking tensed values like 'yesterday' and 'tomorrow' as well as tenseless ones like '9 January' and '10 January'. Nor do (5) and (6) conflict with the use of sentential operators which Prior's work has made usual in tense-logic; i.e., in this case,

$$\text{During } t, Ga \qquad (7)$$

and

$$\text{During } t^*, G^*a \qquad (8)$$

On the contrary, a relational reading of tensed facts is standardly used to supply 'semantics' for these operators (McArthur 1976: ch. 1.3). In other words, even tense-logicians take (7) and (8), with appropriately tensed t and t^*, to be made true by the corresponding relational facts as stated in (5) and (6).

However, as an advocate of tenseless time, I will restrict t and t^* to tenseless values. Change, I maintain, consists in a thing's having a real non-temporal property at one date which it lacks at others, i.e. respectively having and lacking, to those dates, the corresponding real non-temporal relation.

McTaggart would not agree; but not because he disputes—he does not draw—my distinctions between things and events and between actual and merely Cambridge change. For McTaggart, (1) and (2), however construed, would not constitute change because they are themselves unchanging facts about a. His poker being 'hot on a particular Monday' and cool thereafter (1927: §315) is no change in it, he says, since it always was and always will be a fact that it is hot that Monday and cool thereafter. And as McTaggart says, neither this 'nor any other fact about the poker change[s], unless its presentness, pastness, or futurity change'. McTaggart change, in other words, is the only kind of change tenseless facts are capable of. But why, in order for a change to be a fact, must that fact also change? I see no reason to believe it must, nor hence any good argument from real change to McTaggart change and hence real tense. We can quite well deny both, and still insist that McTaggart's poker changes as it cools.

3. Tenses and Dates

We can, I believe, account for time and change without real tense: but why should we try to? Because real tense implies McTaggart change, and that, as he showed, is a myth—the 'myth of passage' as it has been called (Williams 1951). But it is a very powerful myth, and undoubtedly expresses something real and important about time. As the persistent rejection of McTaggart's own sound and simple disproof of it shows, its grip

will not be broken until something better is put in its place. In what follows, therefore, I shall put up a tenseless surrogate for it; to which end, I must first lay down more precisely the specification the surrogate has to satisfy.

The myth of time passing, i.e. of McTaggart change, combines two ways of locating events in time: by their dates, and by their temporal distance, past or future, from the present. These two ways locate events in two series of temporal positions which McTaggart called the '*B* series' and the '*A* series' respectively. McTaggart change consists in the relative motion of these two series. Events of given date become less future or more past, as the present time moves from earlier to later dates.

(There may in fact be several *A* and *B* series. In both, events get the same location just in case they are simultaneous; and relativity theory may make the simultaneity of distant events depend, within causal limits, on an arbitrary choice of a so-called 'reference frame', to settle what is to count as being at rest. Physical fact may fail to settle that question: so different but equally good reference frames may make quite different celestial events simultaneous with the terrestrial events of 1 January 1984, for example, thus filling that *B* series position quite differently. But the same goes for the *A* series: whatever celestial events get that terrestrial date will *ipso facto* then count as temporally present. So there is, as McTaggart conjectured (1927: §323), a distinct A series corresponding to each distinct *B* series. For present purposes, however, I can afford to ignore these relativistic complications, since I am concerned only with the apparent relative movement of corresponding *A* and *B* series. In referring to 'the' *A* and *B* series, then, I shall henceforth mean any relativistically acceptable *B* series, and the *A* series corresponding to it.)

Positions in the *B* series I shall call 'dates', stretching that term to cover locations of all sizes from nanoseconds to millennia. Thus BC is a date, and so is the first p.m. second of 1 January 1984. (Events have any date that includes all their temporal parts, just as things have any spatial location that includes all their spatial parts. Thus the end of World War II has, *inter alia*, the dates AD, the twentieth century and 1945, just as London has the locations Earth, Europe and England. When I refer to 'the' date of an event, I mean the shortest date that includes all its temporal parts.) Dates may be regarded as intervals of *B* series instants, such as noon precisely on 1 January 1984, ordered by the 'earlier' relation. I do not of course mean by this that instants exist: if there are any such things, they will be spatiotemporal entities—space-time points—not purely temporal ones. Instants are no more than convenient theoretical devices for generating indefinitely divisible systems for dating events.

Positions in the *A* series I shall reluctantly follow custom and call 'tenses', though they are mostly marked, not by verbal inflection but by adverbs and phrases such as 'today', 'ten days hence' and 'last year'; and given these, verbal tenses are redundant—'last year' already implies the past tense, as 'today' implies the present. Tense in the sense of *A* series position must therefore be sharply distinguished from verbal tense, which is merely one very crude way of marking it; and the former, not the latter, is what I shall mean by 'tense' hereafter unless I explicitly say otherwise.

Tenses, like dates in the *B* series, may be regarded as intervals of instants, and these are likewise ordered by the 'earlier' relation. McTaggart (1927: §305) characterises the *B* series as ordered by 'earlier', as opposed to the *A* series, which is ordered by degrees of pastness or futurity; but this is a false contrast. 'Earlier' orders both series. Ten days ago, an *A* series position, is earlier than today in just the same sense in which 1 January is ten days earlier than 11 January. In fact, the *A* and *B* series have exactly the same temporal structure. They use the very same 'earlier' relation to order the very same collections of simultaneous events. Fix which *B* series instant is the *A* series' present instant, and either series is immediately definable in terms of the other. To every *B* series instant there then corresponds the *A* series instant which is that much earlier or later than the present instant; and hence to every date, i.e. interval of *B* series instants, there corresponds a tense, and *vice versa*. Thus, when it is now noon on 1 January 1984, 10 a.m. is two hours past, 11 January is ten days hence, and the next century is the twenty-first.

Seeing that the *A* and *B* series are so similar, and so simply interdefinable, what is the difference between them? The difference is that whereas an event's dates are fixed, its tenses are not. By this I mean that its tenses vary with time (this of course being just what McTaggart change is), and its dates do not. Suppose for example that it is now May 1984 and the Queen is 58. That is, she was born 58 years ago; in other words, that event has the tense: 58 years past. The tense of this event obviously varies with time: in 1974, the Queen was only 48 years old; in 1994, she will be 68. Note that the event's tense varies just the same if the time itself is reckoned by tense rather than by date: thus, ten years ago, the Queen's birth was 48 years past; ten years hence, it will be 68 years past. These facts, of course, follow from each other, the general study of such temporal entailments being the business of so-called 'tense-logic'. The reason there is no comparable 'date-logic' is simply that an event's dates, unlike its tenses, do not vary with time, whether the time be reckoned in tenses or dates. The fact now, in May 1984, is that the Queen was born on 21 April 1926; and that always was and always will be the date of her birth. (Some indeed think that before 1926, when the Queen's birth was future, it did not yet exist, and so had no date at all. But no one thinks it ever had, or ever will have, any date other than 21 April 1926.) Date-logic, then, is not studied, because it is too simple. Temporal operators, be they dated or tensed, and however they are iterated, have no effect at all on the classical truth value (if any) of '*e* occurs at *T*'.

Dates, unlike tenses, are outright, temporally unqualified properties of events. That is the essential characteristic of the *B*, as opposed to the *A*, series—and why, provided tenseless sense can be made of 'earlier', it is the fundamental series. The *B* series is definable as the definite temporal structure of all the world's events (on a relational view of time), or of all instants (on an absolute view). The *A* series is neither: it has to be defined in terms of the *B* series plus a present instant. And the present instant has to move: there has to be McTaggart change, or the *A* series would be identical with the *B* series. Past, present and future, therefore, as aspects of reality, stand or fall with McTaggart change. They fall—as we shall see in the course of constructing something tenseless to put in their place. But first let us look at the reasons that support them.

4. *Tensed Truth, Tenseless Fact*

There are two chief reasons for believing in real tense, and in particular in a real present. One is experiential, the other linguistic. The former is what many take to be an irreducible experience of events being present as they happen to us (or, in the case of actions, as we perform them); in other words, its sheer presentness seems to be an undeniable part of our every experience. A credible surrogate is needed for this. To produce it, however, I must first dispose of the latter, linguistic reason for believing in real tense: namely, that our judgments about the tenses of events are generally either objectively true or objectively false, and real tenses are needed to make them so. In May 1984, for example, it is objectively true to think or say that the Queen is 58. What makes that true seems to be that she *is* then 58, i.e. that at that date her birth really does have the tense: 58 years past. But if reality has no tense, there is no such fact, and we must give this indisputably objective judgment alternative tenseless truth conditions. And once that has been done, explaining away the apparent presentness of our experience will turn out to pose no great problem.

The truth conditions I need are really quite obvious, and also quite indisputable. Even if events have tenses, it turns out that these have nothing to do with making what I shall call 'tensed judgments' about them true or false. The truth value of a tensed judgment is determined entirely by how much earlier (or later) it is than the event it is about. A judgment that the Queen is *N* years old, for example, is objectively true just in case its date is between *N* and *N* + 1 years later than that of her birth. It is quite immaterial whether the Queen's birth, or the tensed judgment about it, is past, present or future.

The truth conditions of all tensed judgments are fixed in reality by dates. A present tense judgment is true if, and only if, it differs no more in date from the event it is about than the span of tense it ascribes to that event. E.g. '*e* occurs today' is true just in case it is said or thought on the same day as *e*; '*e* occurs this week' just in case it is said or thought the same week. Past and future tense judgments are true if and only if they have dates as much later or earlier respectively than the events they are about as the tenses they ascribe to them are than the

present. Tensed judgments can of course be more complex than the simple ascription of an *A* series position to an event. There are, for example, the judgments commonly expressed in English by verbal tenses such as the future perfect. But the truth conditions of these too are fixed by how much earlier or later their dates are than those of events they are about and other dates definable from these. 'Next year the Queen will have reigned 33 years', for instance, is true just in case the Queen is still Queen the year after that judgment is made, and that year is 33 years later than her accession. And similarly for tensed judgments of any complexity. The real usefulness, indeed, of the standard 'semantics' of tense-logic referred to in Section 2, is that it shows how to derive any tensed judgment's truth conditions from its date in this sort of way.

Dates are not only sufficient to fix the truth conditions of tensed judgments, they are also necessary. Suppose a tensed judgment, e.g. that the Queen is 58, had no date—being, perhaps, one of God's judgments if, as some have said, He is 'outside time'. What could make it true? Not that the Queen really is 58 when the judgment is made; for, given that the Queen was born in 1926, that gives the judgment a date, namely 1984. Without a date, in short, a tensed judgment has no definite truth conditions; and with one, its truth conditions contain no tenses. These facts seem to me to make the idea of real tense not merely redundant, but incredible. Try to suppose that there really is in 1984 such a tensed fact as that the Queen is 58. This supposed fact turns out to be no part of what makes the corresponding judgment true: what does that job is simply the date of the Queen's birth being 58 years earlier. Now a fact which has nothing to do with making any tensed judgment true is surely no tensed fact. But these supposed facts are by definition tensed. Yet in reality no such supposedly tensed facts make any tensed judgment true. So I conclude that in reality there are no such facts: there is no real *A* series, and therefore no McTaggart change.

5. *Experience and Indexicals*

But what then of our experience of tense and of McTaggart change? Tenseless truth conditions seem not to dispose of that. Consider Prior's famous example: 'Thank goodness that's over!', said after a painful experience (Prior 1959). 'That's over' is indeed true if and only if said or thought later than whatever experience the 'that' refers to. But why thank goodness for such a tenseless fact, which could be recognised as such at any time, before or during, as well as after, the pain in question: surely the thanks are given in sheer relief for the pain's becoming past and thereby ceasing to be present?

Not necessarily. 'Thank goodness' certainly expresses relief, and is thus appropriately said or thought just when relief is appropriately felt. But when is that? Prior says it is when a pain is past, as opposed to present or future; whereas I say it is just after the pain, as opposed to during or before it. I cannot see that Prior's tensed account of when relief is appropriate is any better than my tenseless one. And mine does make sense of the whole remark: since 'thank goodness', said of a pain, is appropriate just when 'that's over', said of it, is true, it is always right to say both (or neither) at the same time.

This account of Prior's case gives the clue to a tenseless analysis of the apparent presentness of experience. Like his case, it involves self-consciousness; only here one is making tensed judgments of experience as it occurs, rather than afterwards. Now simultaneity with its subject matter is the defining truth condition of a present tense judgment, as opposed to a past or future tense one; so if I am thinking of my actions or experiences as happening *while* I am thinking of them, I am *ipso facto* thinking of them as being present. And that, I suggest, is all there is to the much vaunted presentness of our experience. Experiences in themselves, like events of every other kind, are neither past, present nor future. It is only our simultaneous consciousness of them, as being simultaneous, which necessarily both has, and satisfies, the tenseless truth conditions of present tense judgments.

Our being trapped forever in the present is not a profound metaphysical constraint on our temporal location: it is a trivial consequence of the essential indexicality of tensed judgment. It is like everyone being condemned to be himself and, wherever he is, to being—as he sees it—here. The judgments 'I am X' and 'Here is Y', made respec-

tively by person X and at place Y, are as objectively and inevitably true for all X and Y as 'It is now T', made at time T, is for all T: but not because X and Y have respectively such real properties as 'being me' and 'being here'. Obviously there are no such personal and spatial equivalents of our supposed tensed facts; and if there were, they would, like tensed facts, be no part of what makes the corresponding judgments true. 'I am X' is true if and only if X judges it; 'Here is Y' is true if and only if it is judged at Y. So anyone who judges, of the place that he is at, that it is here, is bound to be right, wherever he is; and similarly, *mutatis mutandis*, for judgments of one's own first person identity. That is all the inescapability of being oneself and being here amounts to: and so it is with the inescapability of the present.

I conclude that neither our experience of time nor the objective truth of tensed judgments requires, or indeed admits of, real tense. Tensed judgments are simply a kind of indexical judgment, with tenseless truth conditions. But this does not mean either that tensed judgments themselves are really tenseless, or that we could do without them. Tense may not be an aspect of the world; but, as Perry (1979) has shown, it is, like personal and spatial indexicality, an irreducible and indispensable aspect of our thought.

That a tensed judgment is not equivalent to any tenseless one is easily seen. If it were, it would be equivalent to the tenseless judgment that its own truth conditions obtain. For example, a particular judgment J, a 'token' of the 'type' 'It is now T', is true if and only if it is made at T. Let J' be the tenseless judgment that this is so, i.e. 'J is made at T'. J is true if and only if J' is. But they are not the same judgment. In particular, if J' is true at all, it is true whenever it is made, whereas J is only true at T.

In other words, as upholders of tense have rightly insisted, tensed truths cannot be translated into tenseless ones. Neither the sentence type 'It is now T', nor Prior's 'Thank goodness that's over', nor any other tensed sentence type, means the same as any tenseless sentence. That is because tensed sentence types are indexical: it is part of their meaning that the truth conditions of their tokens vary with time, which is not true of tokens of tenseless types. But there is no tense in the truth conditions themselves; just as the truth conditions of tokens of 'Here is Υ' are (literally!) neither here nor there, despite its being different from any non-indexical spatial judgment.

Not only is indexical judgment untranslatable, it is also indispensable. To suppose that we could make do with a tenseless language is as much a mirage as is real tense itself. Suppose I want to do something at T. Some change in my state of mind is needed to prompt me to act at T rather than some other time. The change of course is my coming to judge 'It is now T', where before I judged, 'It is not yet T.' And for this kind of change of tensed belief there is no tenseless substitute. Because the truth value of tenseless beliefs does not change with time, mere lapse of time gives no cause to change them. But it does give us cause to change our tensed beliefs if we are to keep them true, which it is the object of all our belief to be. And these changes, especially changes of belief from the future to the present tense, are the immediate and indispensable causes of our actions. Whether they cause us to act in time is of course another matter: our mental clocks are as fallible as any others. But without them, i.e. without making tensed judgments, we should have no cause to act at all.

This is my surrogate for the myth of passage: the tensed judgments we need to have, and therefore continually to change, in order to be capable of timely action. This is the truth behind the myth. The error is to misread the tense of these judgments as part of their non-indexical content, and hence to see it as an extra, ever-changing aspect of the objective world. Having exposed the error, we may hope at last to break the myth, and begin to repair the havoc it has wreaked in the philosophy of time.

6. Fixity and Coming True

Tense has not wreaked all its havoc under its own name. Jeffrey's conceit of propositions about events 'coming true' as the events happen, is stated explicitly in tenseless terms; and Mackie's, of events acquiring 'fixity', easily can be. Nonetheless, these specious happenings are nothing if not kinds of McTaggart change. Without real tense they are trivial; and with it, impossible, as I will now attempt to show.

Jeffrey gives events no tenses, only dates; but says that before the date of an event its happening is no fact. In other words, the corresponding tenseless proposition is not then true; though it may be 'ineluctable', if its 'final truth' is determined by the facts to date. As time goes on, therefore, propositions come true, and the number of facts increases: 'the world grows by accretion of facts'. What is wrong with this picture?

For a start, Jeffrey's use of 'true' and 'finally true'. In calling a tenseless proposition 'finally true', he means what most of us would mean by calling it plain 'true'. At any rate, what he calls 'final truth' is what our tenseless judgments aim at, and that is what matters. Given his 'final truth', what he calls 'truth' is entirely immaterial. Suppose I do not know whether the third Test in a (current) 1984 Australian series has finished yet, and so am unsure what tense to give my judgment that England win it. My judgment still has a perfectly definite tenseless content, and attains its object provided England do win, whether they have done so yet or not. That question, whose answer decides whether my judgment is 'true' in Jeffrey's sense, is of no interest to me whatever: 'final truth' is all I am after.

More seriously, suppose that at the end of 1984 I make some tenseless judgment about an event (picked out by a non-temporal description) that happens in a distant galaxy after the light I see left it and before its reflection would return there. If that event is as I judge it to be, my judgment attains its object: it is 'finally true'. Whether, for Jeffrey, it is also 'true' depends on the event's date not being later than 1984, which, according to relativity, may be a matter of an arbitrary choice of reference frame (see Section 3 above): a matter which concerns me not at all, and is certainly not one I can credit with marking the boundaries of objective fact (see Mellor, 1974a; this objection is not met by the modification Jeffrey proposes in his n. 1, p. 259).

I propose to restore 'true' to its customary and proper use, for the intended attribute of all our judgments, tensed and tenseless alike. That is, I shall call 'true' what Jeffrey calls 'finally true'. So I need another term for what he calls 'true'. Since he applies the term to tenseless propositions just when it should be applied to the corresponding past and present tense ones, I shall take the liberty of saying instead that they have 'come to pass'.

I have no objection to Jeffrey's use of 'ineluctable'. By it he means 'necessary', in the sense in which 'it is necessary that p is true if the present state of affairs makes it certain that the p-event will occur, or again if the p-event has already occurred' (Ackrill 1963: 139). The peculiarity of this sense of 'necessary' (in which, for example, p entails its own necessity) is quite enough to justify Jeffrey's preference for 'ineluctable'. It is also what Mackie (1974: ch. 7) means in ascribing 'fixity' to past and present events and the future events they determine. Ackrill and Mackie put the matter in tensed terms, but that, as Jeffrey shows, is by no means essential: an event is 'fixed', we may say, only on and after the date it, or an earlier sufficient cause of it, happens. The tenseless proposition that it happens is likewise 'ineluctable' only on and after the date it, or some other true proposition that determines its truth, 'comes to pass'.

Events therefore, and true tenseless propositions about them, are credited with the ability to undergo at least two sorts of change: (i) the events happen, and the propositions come to pass; and (ii), then or earlier the events become fixed and the propositions ineluctable. What sort of sense can be made of these supposed changes? Tenseless propositions, after all, are normally thought to be unchanging; and while in Section 2 I have admitted that some events *are* changes, I have denied that events themselves change. Nevertheless, sense can be made of (i) and (ii)—only not, as we shall see in Section 7, a sense sufficient for their authors' needs.

Suppose an event e happens at date T. Let H be the property of having happened, and let t and t^* be any dates entirely earlier or later respectively than (every temporal part of) e. Then the change (i) consists in the facts that

$$e \text{ is } \sim H \text{ during } t \qquad (9)$$

and

$$e \text{ is } H \text{ during } t^* \qquad (10)$$

for all t and t^*.

Do (9) and (10) constitute a change in the sense of Section 2? Certainly, even though e itself is an event and not a thing, (9) and (10) do not reduce to any difference between temporal parts. The parts that would be required, e-during-t and

e-during-t^*, are not parts of e, since t is by definition earlier than every temporal part of e, and t^* is later. They would have to be parts of some *ersatz* e-thing, say E, which changes from being $\sim H$ to being H. But since t is *any* date before e, and t^* any date after it, E would have to span the whole history of the world (except perhaps when e itself is). And in reality there are obviously no such things. An everlasting whole of which World War II-during-5000 BC, and World War II-during-20,000 AD are temporal parts, for example, is not a credible substitute for World War II itself.

So (9) and (10) must be read along the lines of (5) and (6), not (3) and (4): i.e. as

$$\sim H(e, t) \qquad (11)$$

and

$$H(e, t^*) \qquad (12)$$

H is thus some relation that any event e has to every date later than itself, but lacks to any earlier date. The relation is, of course, a familiar one: 'earlier' is its common name! For an event to 'happen' at a date is simply for it to be earlier than all later dates, and later than all earlier ones.

Now this is not of course a change in e, as it would be were H a real non-temporal relation. Instances of (5) and (6) are indeed taken to imply that a's temporal location includes both t and t^*: it exists at both dates, and at some time between them changes from being G to being G^*. But (11) and (12) imply no such thing about e: on the contrary, they imply that e is *not* located at t and t^*, or it would not be later and earlier respectively than those dates. So e is not an everlasting thing, existing during all the dates t and t^* and changing at T in respect of having happened. Put like that, I dare say no one thinks it is. But there is evidently a recurrent temptation to harbour an equivalent thought: namely, that e's happening is another event, apart from e, and constituting some sort of change in it. Not so: e is all there is, and talk of it happening at T is just a way of saying that T is its date, its temporal location—i.e. that e is later than all times earlier than T and earlier than all later times.

T being e's date is also all there is to the proposition that says this 'coming to pass' (and hence all other true propositions about e doing so). Let p be this true tenseless proposition, and

C be the supposed property of having come to pass (i.e. of being 'true' in Jeffrey's eccentric sense). As before, t and t^* are any dates earlier and later respectively than e. Then the facts are that

$$p \text{ is } {\sim}C \text{ during } t \qquad (13)$$

and

$$p \text{ is } C \text{ during } t^* \qquad (14)$$

Now Jeffrey in effect construes (13) along the lines of (3) and (4), not (5) and (6); i.e. he credits propositions with temporal parts:

$${\sim}C(p\text{-during-}t) \qquad (15)$$

and

$$C(p\text{-during-}t^*) \qquad (16)$$

Once these temporal parts have come to pass, Jeffrey accumulates them into what he calls 'stages': 'Stages do duty (in the formal mode of speech) for all the facts so far' (253). We may reconstruct his stages from (15) and (16) as follows. For any t (before or after e), let p-through-t be the whole whose temporal parts are p-during-t' for all dates t' containing no instants later than t. Let C^* be the property such that p-through-t is C^* if and only if some temporal part of it is C. Then for any given t, the conjunction of all C^* p-through-t is the stage of the world at t's last instant. In other words, as true tenseless propositions come to pass, they become parts of all later stages of the world.

The mundane facts behind this formal farrago are actually more visible in the relational reading of (13) and (14):

$${\sim}C(p, t) \qquad (17)$$

and

$$C(p, t^*) \qquad (18)$$

Tenseless propositions, unlike events, admittedly have no dates; so C cannot just be the 'earlier' relation, i.e. H. But H suffices to define it:

$$C(p,t^*) =_{df} H(e,t^*) \qquad (19)$$

In other words, e's being earlier than t^* is the fact that makes p have come to pass at that date. p's coming to pass at T, like e's happening then, is in reality nothing more than T being e's date.

So much for (i); what of (ii)? (ii) in fact depends on (i), since fixity depends on events happening, ineluctability on propositions coming to pass. The mere happening of an event fixes it, if the earlier happening of a sufficient cause has not already done so. And no event is fixed until it, or some preceding sufficient cause of it, has happened. Now we have seen that for an event to have happened by a certain date is simply for it to be earlier than that date. The supposed property, H, of having happened is in reality just the 'earlier' relation between events and dates. The supposed property, F, of being fixed is likewise in reality a relation events have to dates: a relation entailed by H but not entailing it, since the earlier happening of a sufficient cause may fix an event before it happens. F is thus definable by H, and by the relation S (= 'is a sufficient cause of'):

$$F(e, t) =_{df} H(e,t) \vee (\exists\, e^*) [H(e^*, t) \,\&\, S(e^*, e)] \qquad (20)$$

As for events, so for propositions. A proposition's coming to pass suffices to make it ineluctable, if it has not already been made so by the earlier coming to pass of a proposition that determines its truth. And no proposition is ineluctable until it, or some such determining proposition, has come to pass. The parallel between propositions and events here is obvious and exact. By definition, p becomes ineluctable just when e becomes fixed: i.e.

$$I(p,t) =_{df} F(e,t) \qquad (21)$$

so the reality of ineluctability is just that of fixity, *viz* the conditions given in (20). All that fixity and ineluctability need are events, their dates, and the tenseless relations 'earlier' and 'sufficient cause'. (And if, as Hume thought, there is in reality no such relation as S, the second disjunct of (20) is always false, and both fixity and ineluctability reduce to events happening, i.e. to their having dates.)

7. *Fixity, Coming True and Tense*

I have given the simple relational conditions of happening, coming to pass, being fixed and being ineluctable. These conditions are undeniable, but they will hardly satisfy the authors of these conceits. Jeffrey, for example, is trying to conceive the world as 'growing by accretion of facts'. But the reality of his accretion turns out to be nothing more than the truism that the later a date is, the more events are earlier than it. There is no growth in that fact, any more than there is shrinkage in the fact that the earlier a date is, the more events are later than it. Jeffrey must be after something more.

So must Mackie. He hopes to find 'in this notion of fixity a basis for the concept of causal priority' (183). Specifically, causes are distinguished by being fixed at times when their effects are not, but not conversely (180). Since events are fixed at the latest when they happen, this is supposed to explain why causes mostly precede their effects (the exception being later causes fixed before their effects by the still earlier happening of sufficient causes of them). But for this to be an explanation, fixity must not itself be defined by the very fact Mackie wants to derive from it. But in (20) it is. When two causally related events e and e' have no preceding sufficient causes, e is fixed when e' is not just in case e is earlier than e'. So Mackie's definition of causal priority reduces in this case to the cause being the earlier of two causally related events, which is just what he is trying to explain. And when e does have sufficient causes, the arbitrary restriction in (20)'s second disjunct, to $e^\star$s earlier than e, likewise begs the question it is supposed to answer. Later events, after all, exist no less than earlier ones, and are as capable of being sufficient causes of e. If any are, the restriction in (20) discriminates without reason against them; and if none are, it is superfluous.

The fact is that Mackie's theory, like Jeffrey's, is useless and trivial unless having happened and being fixed are something more than the relations I have reduced them to. H and F must be real nonrelational properties of events, acquired at times that are their, or their sufficient causes', dates, for the facts of causal priority to be explained by them. And similarly for C and I, the coming to pass and becoming ineluctable of Jeffrey's true tenseless propositions. Real accretion must be more than a relational fact: more, at any rate, than the different relations events have to different dates. Can we meet these seemingly modest demands?

Whatever these nonrelational properties H, F, C and I are, their ascription will still have to satisfy the relational conditions I have stated. Maybe 'earlier', as a relation between events and dates, should be defined by 'has happened' rather than *vice versa:* but either way, their equivalence must follow. And even if (19), (20) and (21) will not do as definitions, they must still come out as necessary truths.

What this comes to is that, for example, any judgment to the effect that an event e has the property H must come out true just in case e is not later than the date of the judgment itself. But this is to say that the judgment is indexical: specifically, that its truth conditions are those of the simultaneous judgment that e is past or present. In other words, the nonrelational property H simply *is* that rather imprecise tense: to have happened is to be either past or present.

Ascriptions of fixity are indexical in a slightly more complex way. A judgment that an event e has the property F is true if and only if its date is not earlier than e or some sufficient cause of e. For e to be fixed, therefore, is just for it, or a sufficient cause of it, to be past or present.

Jeffrey's properties C and I likewise turn out to depend on tense, despite his tenseless pretensions. If p says that e's date is T, I judge truly that p is C if and only if I do so no earlier than e itself. So for p to have come to pass is for e to be past or present. Similarly, for p to be ineluctable, either e or a sufficient cause of e must be past or present.

Mackie and Jeffrey thus both require events to have positions in McTaggart's A series, and the changes they postulate are a species of McTaggart change. Events happen and become fixed, propositions come to pass and become ineluctable, as the tense of events changes from future to present. Jeffrey's world growing by accretion of facts is Broad's (1923: ch. 11) world growing by accretion of present facts.

We can now, therefore, use the results of Sections 2–5 to extract the truth in Mackie's and Jeffrey's conceits from their error. The truth is that nonrelational ascriptions of H, F, C and I, because they are indexical, do not mean the same as nonindexical statements of the relational facts to which I have reduced them. A judgment *J*, that *e* is *H*, is never the same as the simultaneous judgment *J'*, that *e* is earlier than *J*. Yet they both have the same truth conditions, namely those stated by *J'*. And such truth conditions consist entirely of events, including judgments, having dates and being more or less earlier than, or simultaneous with, each other. In the real world that makes these judgments objectively true or false, the nonrelational *H, F, C* and *I* do not figure at all. Because there is in reality no tense, so there is no real happening of events (apart from the events themselves) and no acquisition of fixity by them; no coming to pass, or becoming ineluctable, of true tenseless propositions.

Fixity, then, since it does not exist, cannot be the real basis of causal priority, nor can the world really grow by accretion of facts. In their intended substance, these conceits will have to go. Still, they will go in good company. Three quarters of a century after McTaggart demolished them, much writing, in many areas of philosophy, still appeals to real, nonrelational nonindexical differences between past, present and future. All of that will have to go too. But not from here; despatching so great a multitude of errors must be matter for another place.

References

Ackrill, J. L., transl. 1963., *Aristotle: De Interpretatione*. London: Oxford University Press.

Broad, C. D. 1923. *Scientific Thought*. London: Kegan Paul, Trench and Trubner.

Davidson, Donald. 1969. 'The individuation of events.' *Essays in Honor of Carl G. Hempel*, ed. N. Rescher, pp. 216–34. Dordrecht: Reidel.

Geach, P. T. 1979. *Truth, Love and Immortality*. London: Hutchinson.

Goodman, Nelson. 1965. *Fact, Fiction and Forecast*, 2nd ed. New York: Bobbs-Merrill.

Jeffrey, R. C. 1980. 'Coming true.' *Intention and Intentionality*, ed. C. Diamond and J. Teichman, pp. 251–60. London: Harvester.

Mackie, J. L. 1974. *The Cement of the Universe*. Oxford: Clarendon Press.

McArthur, R. P. 1976. *Tense Logic*. Dordrecht: Reidel.

McTaggart, J. McT. E. 1908. 'The unreality of time.' *Mind* 18, 457–84.

McTaggart, J. McT. E. 1927. *The Nature of Existence*, vol. II. Cambridge: Cambridge University Press.

Mellor, D. H. 1974. 'In defense of dispositions.' *Philosophical Review* 83, 157–81.

Mellor, D. H. 1974a. 'Special relativity and present truth.' *Analysis* 34, 74–8.

Mellor, D. H. 1978. 'Conscious belief.' *Proceedings of the Aristotelian Society* 78, 87–101.

Mellor, D. H. 1982. 'The reduction of society.' *Philosophy* 57.

Perry, John. 1979. 'The problem of the essential indexical.' *Nous* 13, 3–21.

Prior, A. N. 1959. 'Thank goodness that's over.' *Philosophy* 34, 12–17.

Russell, B. 1903. *The Principles of Mathematics*. Cambridge: Cambridge University Press.

Williams, Donald C. 1951. 'The myth of passage.' *Journal of Philosophy* 48, 457–72.

10. *Time, Consciousness and the Knowledge Argument*

JOHN PERRY

Various B-theory analyses of tense, like the one offered by Mellor in the previous selection, have been refined and debated by several authors. Mellor himself offers a somewhat different theory in his 1998 book, *Real Time II*. Some critics of B-theories continue to maintain that something is missing from B-theories; for example, they can seem to fail to capture what we know to be true when we say that some event is happening *now*. In this selection,

John Perry sees a connection between these complaints and similar arguments in debates about the nature of mind (see Part III of this anthology). His attempt to diagnose why these arguments fail should also be relevant to some of the issues in Part III.

John Perry is Henry Waldgrave Stuart Professor of Philosophy at Stanford University.

Introduction

Hugh Mellor's *Real Time II* is an excellent book, for the following reasons. First it deals with an important and difficult philosophical problem, the passage, or apparent passage, of time. Second, Mellor is basically right. Mellor is a B-theorist, in the sense that he thinks that the B-facts, the facts that are not relative to a time, provide all the truthmakers we need. I was convinced that this must be right by reading D. C. William's "The Myth of Passage" a long time ago, when I was in graduate school. But although I knew which side I was on, this conviction was based more on seeing problems for the A-theory, and thinking that the A-arguments weren't very convincing, than on understanding how the B-theory could account for everything. And this is the third thing I like about Mellor's book. As I read it, I really felt, for the first time, that I understood, or at least began to understand, how the B-theory not only must be right, but could be right.

In this paper, I will argue that at the heart of the A-position is an argument analogous to Frank Jackson's knowledge argument and that Mellor's approach in *Real Time II* can be extended to deal with Jackson's argument.[1]

Time and the Knowledge Argument

Jackson's famous argument goes as follows. There is a young woman raised in a Black and White Room, and never allowed to have any color experiences. She knows all the physical facts, for she is

From John Perry, "Time, Consciousness and the Knowledge Argument," in *The Importance of Time*, L. N. Oaklander, ed., pp. 81–94. Copyright © 2001 Kluwer Academic Publishers. Reprinted with kind permission of Kluwer Academic Publishers.

quite bright and reads all the books there are to read, and from them learns all the physical facts. But when she is let out of the room, she learns what it is like to see red. So she learns something, a fact, that she did not know. So there is a fact she did not know. It isn't a physical fact, for she knew all of them, so it is a non-physical fact, and so there are non-physical facts.

Suppose now that there is a young man named Larry, who is raised in a room in the Claremont Hotel with no up-to-date calendars. That is, he is never allowed to know what day it is, or even what year it is. This young man has a passionate interest in the Pacific Division of the APA, and is allowed to read all of the APA publications there ever have been, including programs of all of the past APA's and also future APA's for the next twenty years. (Let's pretend that Anita Silvers is part of this experiment, and that, motivated by a terrific deal on printing programs, she has decided on the schedule of talks for the next twenty years. She will rely on her vast knowledge of the membership of the Pacific APA to make sure things turn out right, making deft suggestions to the key committee members at the right times.) So Larry knows all the B-facts there are to know about events at the APA meetings: which talks come before which talks, which sessions are concurrent, and so forth. He knows, for example that in 1999 on April 1 there was or will be a meeting about the views of Hugh Mellor. He knows also

(1)   The 1999 Presidential Address is on April 2, 1999.

Every year or so he can tell, from the small window in his room at the Claremont Hotel, that the Pacific APA meetings are starting, because he can see the sign out in front that says, "Welcome Pacific Division, APA." But he doesn't know what year it is. Larry waits patiently for his release, but he is proud to be part of a philosophical experi-

ment. As a matter of fact, Larry has just been
released, stepped out of the room in which he was
kept, and joined us here at the symposium. Larry
peeked at the Palm Pilot of the person sitting next
to him—the first up to date calendar he has seen—
and realized:

(2)   Today is April 1, 1999.

and from that and what he already knew already,
he inferred

(3)   The 1999 Pacific Division APA
         Presidential Address is tomorrow.

(3) is new knowledge for Larry. (3) expresses
something that Larry did not know before his
release, while (1) expresses something he did
know before his release. So (1) and (3) seem to be
different bits of knowledge. And they both seem
to be APA facts in the sense above, facts about
when the APA sessions are held. But (3) cannot be
identified with (1), since Larry knew (1) without
knowing (3). The same goes for any other of the
APA B-facts Larry knew. So there are not just APA
B-facts. There are non-B APA facts as well, and
these are what we all call A-facts.

Space and Knowledge Argument

In *Real Time II* Mellor often defuses arguments
about time by looking at the analogues for space.
Space seems to be inherently less mysterious than
time, and so we are less willing to accept arguments that lead to mysterious conclusions. This is
a well-known strategy in teaching philosophy.
Students will accept forms of argument if they are
presented as having some fairly profound conclusion, say that people don't really survive from
moment to moment. But they will see through the
forms of argument very quickly if they are used to
show something relatively trivial, say that the ham
sandwich they are about to eat really doesn't
belong to them, since it really isn't the one they
paid for at the counter (it was at the counter, and
this one is on their plate, and so they have different properties, so they are not the same).

Can we construct a knowledge argument for
space? Certainly. Put Larry in a windowless hut
across from Little America, just off Interstate 80 in
western Wyoming (Little America is a gas station
with a restaurant and souvenir shop. It has more
gas pumps than anyplace in the world.) Give him
an Interstate Road Map to memorize. Larry may
know all the B-type Interstate 80-facts—the order
of states, cities, towns and villages as one progresses east to west or west to east along Interstate
80, from Berkeley through Reno, Salt Lake City,
Little America, Cheyenne, Lincoln, and so on. But
he isn't allowed to look out of his hut so he
doesn't know where he is. Eventually let him out.
He sees all the gas pumps, realizes he is in Little
America, and immediately knows a number of
facts that seem to be Interstate 80 facts, although
they are not B-facts. He already knew the B-fact

(4)   Salt Lake City is west of Little
         America.

Now he learns,

(5)   Little America is here,

and infers

(6)   Salt Lake city is west of here.

And so on for many other things. Since he knew
all of the 80 B-facts before he was let out, but
didn't know these facts, these are clearly not
B-facts, so there are Interstate 80 A-facts as well as
Interstate 80 B-facts.

Beliefs and Facts

I think the key move in the knowledge argument
is the move from

(7)   Larry (or Mary) has a new bit of
         knowledge

which seems to me to be true, to

(8)   There is an X-fact that Larry (or Mary)
         did not know

where X is the type of fact at issue, viz., about the mind in Mary's case, about the APA in our first Larry case, and about Interstate 80 in our second. I think this step is a fallacy, which rests on a mistake about the structure of knowledge.

Mellor's conceptual framework in *Real Time II* provides an analysis of what is wrong with this argument. Mellor is not an across the board enemy of A things. He allows A-representations, but not A-facts. He allows A-perceptions, A-thoughts, A-utterances, A-propositions and A-beliefs. But he does not have A-facts or *truthmakers*. Once you have all of the B-facts, you have all of the facts. You have all of the truthmakers for the A things as well as the B things. An inventory of the B-facts of a world is a complete inventory, nothing is left out.

Mellor thinks of A-beliefs as beliefs in A-propositions. We can say that Larry did acquire new beliefs, beliefs in A-propositions, that he did not have before. And these beliefs were true. So he acquired bits of knowledge he did not have before. But it does not follow from this that there are facts he didn't know before, only that there are true A-propositions that he didn't believe before. So (8) simply does not follow from (7).[2]

Think of a possible world as telling us, for each time, what happens. Call these the B-facts of the world. Think of a proposition as a set of such possible worlds. Think of a B-belief as a relation that an agent has to such a proposition at a time. If the proposition is true, call this B-knowledge. Then the inference from 7B to 8B seems valid:

(7B) Larry has a new bit of B-knowledge
(8B) There is a B-fact that Larry (or Mary) did not know

Let an agent and a time and a place, where the agent is at the place at the time, be an *occasion* of belief. Let an A-proposition be a function from occasions to B-propositions. A belief in an A-proposition is a true belief, if the B-proposition that is the value of the A-proposition at the occasion of belief is true.

For example, Larry's A-belief, that he expresses with

(6)   Salt Lake city is west of here,

is a belief in an A-proposition. This proposition is a function that will yield the B-proposition that Salt Lake City is west of p at an occurrence a, t, p. The truthmakers for Larry's belief consist of

(i)   The facts of the occurrence of the belief, that it is a belief of Larry's at t at Little America (where t is the time his utterance);

(ii)   The facts about the subject matter of the belief, that at t Salt Lake City is west of Little America.

Both of these truthmakers are perfectly good B-facts. There is no need for A-facts. So Larry has a new bit of knowledge, but this knowledge doesn't consist of knowing a new fact. The knowledge argument gives us no reason to suppose that there are A-facts in addition to B-facts.

Now let's turn to Larry, who until a few minutes ago was locked in the Claremont without an up-to-date calendar. Larry's beliefs change as he emerges and sees the date on the Palm Pilot next to him. He comes to believe something he expresses with

(2)   Today is April 1, 1999,

and this leads to many more new beliefs.

Larry's new belief is a belief in an A-proposition, a function from occurrences of belief a,t,p to the B-proposition that at p, t occurs during April 1, 1999. This would exclude worlds in which Larry emerges from the room just as he does, but the room is in Tokyo, where the present moment is a part of April 2, 1999, not April 1st. It excludes worlds in which Larry comes out on April 4, 2003, and sits next to someone with a defective Palm Pilot, which leads him to say (2). But in fact Larry is here in the Claremont, and emerged today, so his belief is true. The truthmakers are:

(i)   the fact about when and where his belief occurs, namely, right at this moment in the Claremont,

and

(ii)   the fact that in California, where the Claremont is, this moment is a part of April 1, 1999,

which are both perfectly good B-facts.

In both cases, then, when Larry acquires a new bit of knowledge, he does so by acquiring a new A-belief which is true. But the truth of the A-belief does not require any A truthmakers or facts.

The Classic Knowledge Argument

If we follow Mellor, and break the move from (7) to (8), we can diagnose what is wrong with the knowledge argument. Mary emerges from the Black and White room and sees a fireplug. She knows, as a matter of general knowledge picked up in the Black and White Room, that fireplugs are red. She attends to the experience she has when she looks at the fireplug, the experience of seeing red, and forms a belief she might express with

(9)   This is what it is like to see red,

or perhaps,

(10)   This quale is the what-it-is-like aspect of the experience of seeing red,

or perhaps

(11)   This quale is the seeing-red quale.

Mary has a belief she didn't have before, that she expresses in one of these ways.

Antecedent Physicalism

Now let me digress for a moment, and quickly explain a perspective that I call "antecedent physicalism." The word "antecedent" is a nod to Hume, in the *Dialogues on Natural Religion,* where he observes that although all the pain and suffering we find in the world are not what we would expect from an all-perfect God, they do not logically contradict the existence of such a being.

Hence, if we are *antecedently convinced* of such a God, these phenomena will not disprove it.

Similarly, qualia, the what-it-is-like aspects of experiences, are not something that strike us as all that physical. But it seems to be that if we are antecedently convinced of physicalism, they do not give us a good reason to abandon it.

The antecedent physicalist (me), is not skeptical about qualia, but quite enamored of them. Consider the taste of a warm Mrs. Fields chocolate chip cookies as you chew it, trying hard not to swallow so the qualia will last as long as possible. Or the taste of a handful of zinc-covered nails, that you accidentally put in your mouth while working on the roof, forgetting that the mouth is not a good storage spot for zinc covered nails, although it works well for most other kinds.

Since I am an antecedent physicalist, I must regard these experiences as physical states and processes, brain-events, as it were. And I also think they have only physical properties. So the aspect of my experience, of my brain state, that I am aware of and enjoy as I eat the cookie, is a physical aspect of my brain state.

This view has often been thought to be absurd. Leibniz asks us to imagine a brain as big as a factory. Walk into it. Could you see the experience of tasting a chocolate chip cookie? A. C. Ewing asks the physicalist to pick up a hot coal from the barbecue. Carefully attend to the searing, unendurable pain that rises in your consciousness. Does that seem like a brain state?

The fallacy of these arguments is that there is no reason to suppose that what-it-is-like to see a brain state, is anything like what-it-is-like to be in that brain state. The knowledge argument, I think (and Chalmer's Zombie argument too, by the way), is simply a fancy version of the Leibniz-Ewing argument, a fancy version that allows us to see the structural relation between this argument and Passage of Time arguments.

So, metaphysically, the antecedent physicalist thinks that experiences are brain events, and qualia are real physical properties of those brain events. There are lots of sentient beings, in the sense of having brain states such that it is like something to have them. The antecedent physicalist believes sentience is a central and important part of the architecture of the beings that have it. The basic idea is very old-fashioned. A basic part of being an animal is to avoid pain and seek pleasure.

We humans, and no doubt many other kinds of animals as well, are not only sentient, we are aware of our sentient states. That is, we not only have brain states it is like something to be in, we note such states, think about them, classify them, notice the kinds of situations in which they occur, and adopt elaborate plans to avoid being in them or promote being in them. I might base my whole day, for example, on walking past a Mrs. Fields shop so I can get a cookie. I may brush and floss every day for years to avoid having a cavity that needs to be drilled and filled. I make these plans because I know what it is like to have one's tooth drilled, and I think I know what sorts of situations lead to, and prevent, experiences of these sorts.

This inner awareness we have our own what-it-is-like states has some analogies with perception, and some disanalogies. There is not as far as we know some kind of organ, like the eye or the ear, involved in awareness of our experiences. Nor is there, as far as we know, a transmission through medium of some sort of disturbance, as with hearing and seeing. But there are clear analogies with perception of things that are close by. We can only be aware of experiences when we have them. Later on we can remember them; beforehand we can anticipate them, but we can only be aware of them when they occur. And, like the things we are looking at or listening to or smelling, we can direct our attention and focus to some of the things we are aware of. I can focus on my experience of red, or my headache, or the minor pain in my finger.

And, as with things we perceive, the natural way to talk about what I am aware of, when I attend to it and focus on various aspects of it, are demonstratives: "this feeling," "this emotion," "this ache," and the like.

Back to Mary

Armed now with Mellor's break between objects of knowledge and facts, and the perspective of antecedent physicalism, let's return to Mary in the Black and White Room. The natural way for Mary to express her new bit of knowledge, when she leaves the Black and White Room is,

(9)   This qualia is what its like to see red.

How should we think of this use of "this qualia?" "This qualia," in the use Mary is making of it, will refer, on a given occasion of awareness, to the qualia to which the agent is attending. So, in Mary's case, it will refer to the what-it-is-like aspect of her experience of seeing red. But, in other cases, it will refer to other qualia. Suppose Mary is confused, and a bit later, while looking at something that is lavender, and attending to the lavender quale, utters (9) again. In this case, "this qualia" will refer to the quale she is attending to, the quale that occurs when people look at something lavender, and so she will have said and thought something that is false.

From our physicalist point of view, we want to think that all the facts there are, are the physical facts. They play the role of the B-facts in this dialectic. And we think that the physical facts *are* B-facts; that is, physical events happening at times. So we want the truthmakers for Mary's beliefs to be physical facts. The knowledge argument challenges this, but using lessons from Mellor we can see what to say.

Let us say that physical B-worlds are B-worlds in which only physical things happen. Physical B-propositions are sets of such worlds. And physical A-propositions are functions from episodes of directed inner awareness to physical B-propositions. An episode of directed inner awareness will involve an agent, a time, and a quale, such that the agent is having and attending to the quale at the time.

Let us label the quale which a person with normal vision has when he sees something red in normal circumstances Q_r. Mary is attending to Q_r in the original case. So, what we want to say about Mary is:

(A)   The object of her belief is the physical A-proposition expressed with "This qualia is what it is like to see red."

(B)   This physical A-proposition is a function f from occasions of directed inner awareness c to physical B-propositions P:

$f(c)=P$, where for each world w in P, in w the quale that the agent of c is attending to at the time of c is what it is like in w to see red.

(C)   The truthmakers for Mary's belief are the B-facts:

(i)   Mary inner attends to Q_r
(ii) Q_r is what it is like to see red

both of which are physical B-facts.

On this account, there is nothing about Mary's case that counts against physicalism.

The Myth of Objective Knowledge

The knowledge arguments, in all their applications, move from a new bit of knowledge, to a newly known fact. This is the step from (7) to (8):

(7)   Larry (or Mary) has a new bit of knowledge
(8)   There is an X-fact that Larry (or Mary) did not know

The strategy we have been looking at for blocking this step is to allow two kinds of belief, and hence two kinds of knowledge. For B-belief or knowledge, belief is a relation to a B-proposition. A B-proposition is true or false independently of who believes and when or where; it is objective. In contrast, we have A-beliefs, which are beliefs in A-propositions, which are not true independently of who believes them and when and where.

Now I'd like to explore a somewhat different option, a somewhat different way of looking at this. This option says that there are not really two kinds of belief. There is really just one kind, with all sorts of variations. Each episode of belief involves a believer in a belief state at a time, a way of believing, and a B-proposition believed. What differs is the extent to which the same ways of believing yield the same proposition believed, given changes in the facts about the episode. Being in the sort of belief state one expresses with "It is raining here now" constitutes belief in quite different propositions, depending on when and where the belief takes place. Being in the sort of belief state one expresses with "It is raining in Berkeley, California, now"

constitutes belief in different propositions depending on the time of the episode, but the place does not matter. Being in the sort of belief state one expresses with "2 + 2 = 4" constitutes belief in the same proposition, no matter who is in the state, when, and where. So on this view, we characterize the belief-state with something like what Mellor calls A-propositions, but we don't think of the entities as *propositions,* but as abstract objects that characterize an important property of belief states, by characterizing them as relations between the relevant facts about the belief episode, the context, and the proposition believed.

Let's start with Larry's "A-belief" of twenty minutes ago, that he expressed with "Today is April 1, 1999." On our treatment of this belief there are three basic elements:

(i)   The circumstance of the belief: the agent, time and place where the belief occurs (Larry, a time **t** about twenty minutes ago; this room in the Claremont);
(ii)   The nature of the belief (It is the kind of belief expressible by "Today is now April 1, 1999");
(iii) The proposition Larry believes in virtue of having that sort of belief in those circumstances, the B-proposition that in Berkeley **t** occurs on April 1, 1999.

If we fix the nature of a belief, we establish a *relation* between the other two factors, the circumstance of the belief, and the proposition believed. That is, given we are dealing with a type (ii) belief, what we fill in for (i) constrains what we can fill in for (ii) (and vice versa).

Determining the circumstances of the belief, who has it, where, and when, determines what the subject matter has to be like for the belief to be true, that is, which proposition is believed. For example, once we have fixed the nature of the belief as being of the same type that Larry had, the type one expresses with (3),

(3)   The 1999 Pacific Division APA Presidential Address is tomorrow

the following pairs of "belief context" and "belief content" will be appropriately related:

First pair:

(i)   Yoshi, Tokyo, and the time **t′** 24 hours before **t**;

(iii) That the 1999 Pacific Division APA Presidential Address is/was/will be April 2, 1999.

That is, twenty four hours ago, by being in the same state Larry is in now, Yoshi would have believed the same B-proposition as Larry now does. Of course, if he were in that state at the same time as Larry is—that is, right now—he would not believe the same thing as Larry, since it is already April 2 in Japan. And if Larry had been in that state at **t′**, he would have believed something false, that the Presidential Address was April 1, since, in Berkeley, **t′** occurred during March 31.

Second pair:

(i)   Malcolm, London, and the time **t′** 4 hours before **t**

(iii) That the 1999 Pacific Division APA is/was/will be April 2, 1999.

And so forth...

What I want to suggest, then, is that we can characterize the contribution of the subject's brain, to the truth or falsity of the belief, with a relation between (i) B-facts and (iii) B-propositions, what we might call generally, *facts about context of representation facts* and *the proposition believed*. What Mellor calls A-propositions are better thought of, I think, as abstract objects characterizing these belief types.

Compare now

(4)   Salt Lake City is west of Little America.

(6)   Salt Lake City is west of here.

Whether you think of (4) and (6) as English sentences, or as the belief states that might be expressed with such English sentences, they differ dramatically in the relationships they impose. An occurrence, belief or utterance, of (4) will be true no matter where it is spoken or thought, any time after the construction of Little America and before some cataclysm destroys one or the other or moves the surface of the U.S. around quite a bit. An occurrence of (6) will be true if it is spoken or

thought at some place p and time t, such that it is a fact that p is east of Salt Lake City at t. The difference isn't that what is believed in the case of (6) is much more dynamic and fragile than what is believed in (4). It is rather that the sentence (or type of belief) in (6) has a much more fragile relationship with the non-fragile truth that Salt Lake City is west of Little America. It only expresses that truth from some places. So, in a way, one needs to know more to assert (4) than (6), one needs to know the facts of one's context of utterance or belief, which is what Larry learned when he stepped out of the hut.

This relational perspective is more or less that recommended in my 1983 book with Jon Barwise, *Situations and Attitudes*. Since that time I have developed an account I call the reflexive/referential account, and applied it to a number of philosophical issues, including the knowledge argument. The underlying picture of belief states as classifiable by relations between facts about the episode and states of affairs involving the subject matter remains intact, however.

Endnotes

[1] See Robert Coburn (1990) for Jackson's argument. See A. C. Ewing (1962) for a discussion of A and B dichotomies with respect to time, space, and possible worlds.

[2] The way Mellor thinks of this isn't quite the same as I do; I say a little bit about this below, and quite a bit in John Perry (1997) and (1993). The differences between us have to do with the philosophies of language and propositional attitudes, however, rather than with the issues about time and consciousness that concern us here. The key point is that Mellor's set-up allows us to block the step from (7) to (8).

References

Barwise, J. and Perry, J. (1983), *Situations and Attitudes* (Cambridge, MA: Bradford-MIT Press).

Chalmers, D. (1996), *The Conscious Mind* (New York: Oxford University Press).

Ewing, A. C. (1962), *The Fundamental Questions of Philosophy* (New York: Collier Books).

Coburn, R. C. (1990), *The Strangeness of the Ordinary: Problems and Issues in Contemporary Metaphysics* (Savage, MD: Rowman and Littlefield).

Jackson, F. (1986), "What Mary Didn't Know," *Journal of Philosophy*, LXXXIII: 291–295.

Mellor, H. (1998), *Real Time II* (London: Routledge).

Perry, J. (1993), *The Problem of the Essential Indexical and Other Essays* (New York: Oxford University Press).

Perry, J. (1997), "Indexicals and Demonstratives," in Robert Hale and Crispin Wright (eds.), *Companion to the Philosophy of Language* (Oxford: Blackwell Publishers Ltd.): 586–612.

Further Reading

Albert, D. Z., *Time and Chance* (Cambridge: Harvard University Press, 2000).

Barbour, J., *The End of Time* (Oxford: Oxford University Press, 1999).

Butterfield, J., *The Arguments of Time* (Oxford: Oxford University Press, 1999).*

Callender, C., ed., *Time, Reality and Experience* (Cambridge: Cambridge University Press, 2002).

Capek, M., ed., *The Concepts of Space and Time* (Dordrecht: D. Reidel, 1976).

Dainton, B., *Time and Space* (Chesham, UK: Acumen Publishing Ltd., 2001).

Davies, P., *The Physics of Time Asymmetry* (Berkeley: University of California Press, 1977).*

Davies, P., *Space and Time in the Modern Universe* (Cambridge: Cambridge University Press, 1977).

Durato, M., *Time and Reality* (Bologna: CLUEB, 1995).

Earman, J., *World Enough and Space-Time* (Cambridge: MIT Press, 1989).*

Earman, J., et al., eds., *Foundations of Space-Time Theories, Minnesota Studies in the Philosophy of Science, VIII* (Minneapolis: University of Minnesota Press, 1977).*

Flood, R., and Lockwood, M., eds., *The Nature of Time* (Oxford: Blackwell, 1986).

Fraser, J., et al., eds., *The Study of Time*, Vol. 3 (New York: Springer-Verlag, 1978).

Friedman, M., *Foundations of Space-Time Theories* (Princeton: Princeton University Press, 1983).

Gale, R., *The Language of Time* (New York: Humanities, 1968).

Gale, R., ed., *The Philosophy of Time* (Garden City, N.Y.: Anchor, 1967).

Greene, B., *The Fabric of the Cosmos—Space, Time and the Texture of Reality* (New York: Knopf, 2004).

Grünbaum, A., *Modern Science and Zeno's Paradoxes* (Middletown, Conn.: Wesleyan University Press, 1967).

Grünbaum, A., *Philosophical Problems of Space and Time*, 2d ed. (Dordrecht: Reidel, 1973).*

Hawking, S., *A Brief History of Time* (New York: Bantam, 1988).

Horwich, P., *Asymmetries in Time* (Cambridge: MIT Press, 1987).

Jokic, A., and Smith, Q., eds., *Time, Tense and Reference* (Cambridge: MIT Press, 2003).

Le Poidevin, R., *Travels in Four Dimensions: The Enigmas of Space and Time* (Oxford: Oxford University Press, 2003).

Le Poidevin, R., ed., *Questions of Time and Tense* (Oxford: Clarendon Press, 1998).

Le Poidevin, R., *Change, Cause and Contradiction* (New York: St. Martin's Press, 1991).

Machamer, P., and Turnbull, R., eds., *Motion and Time, Space and Matter* (Columbus: Ohio University Press, 1976).

*May require familiarity with some advanced mathematics.

Mellor, D. H., *Real Time* (Cambridge: Cambridge University Press, 1981).

Mellor, D. H., *Real Time II* (London: Routledge, 1998).

Newton-Smith, W., *The Structure of Time* (London: Routledge & Kegan Paul, 1980).

Oaklander, L. N., *Temporal Relations and Temporal Becoming* (Lanham, Md.: University Press of America, 1984).

Oaklander, L. N., ed., *The Importance of Time* (Dordrecht: Kluwer, 2001).

Oaklander, L. N., *The Ontology of Time* (Amherst, N.Y.: Prometheus Books, 2004).

Oaklander, L. N., and Smith, Q., eds., *The New Theory of Time* (New Haven: Yale University Press, 1994).

Park, D., *The Image of Eternity* (Amherst: University of Massachusetts Press, 1980).

Price, H., *Time's Arrow and Archimedes' Point* (New York: Oxford University Press, 1996).

Prigogine, I., and Stenger, I., *Order out of Chaos* (New York: Bantam, 1984).

Prior, A., and Fine, K., *Worlds, Times, and Selves* (Amherst: University of Massachusetts Press, 1977).

Salmon, W., *Space, Time, and Motion*, 2d ed. (Minneapolis: University of Minnesota Press, 1980).

Schlesinger, G., *Aspects of Time* (Indianapolis: Hackett, 1980).

Sherover, C., ed., *The Human Experience of Time* (New York: New York University Press, 1975).

Sklar, L., *Space, Time and Space-Time* (Berkeley: University of California Press, 1974).*

Smart, J., ed., *Problems of Space and Time* (New York: Macmillan, 1964).

Smith, Q., *Language and Time* (New York: Oxford University Press, 1993).

Sorabi, R., *Time, Creation, and the Continuum* (Ithaca, N.Y.: Cornell University Press, 1983).

Swinburne, R., ed., *Space, Time and Causality* (Dordrecht: Reidel, 1981).

Tooley, M., *Time, Tense and Causation* (Oxford: Oxford University Press, 1997).

van Fraassen, B., *An Introduction to the Philosophy of Time and Space* (New York: Random House, 1970).

van Inwagen, P., ed., *Time and Cause* (Dordrecht: Reidel, 1980).

Whitrow, G., *The Natural Philosophy of Time,* 2d ed. (Oxford: Oxford University Press, 1980).

Yourgrau, P., *The Disappearance of Time* (Cambridge: Cambridge University Press, 1991).

Part II

Identity

In the fifth century BC, the Greek philosopher Heraclitus said that you cannot step into the same river twice because rivers are constantly changing. He is also famous for such epigrams as "winter is summer" and "war is peace." Although little of Heraclitus' writings has been preserved, his brief remarks have ensured him a prominent place in the history of philosophy because he raised general problems about change and identity that stimulated later philosophers to try to find metaphysical solutions. Though he suggested there is some law governing change, Heraclitus used contradictory sentences to point to patterns of change. This might give the impression that change is contradictory; it is thought that Parmenides' belief that change is contradictory and therefore not real was, in part, a reaction to Heraclitus (see Chapter 1). The challenge to later philosophers was to explain how things could change yet, in some important sense, be the same; that is, retain their identity. Many of the problems of change and identity are still puzzling, and they are especially provocative when one considers *personal* identity. Part II begins with readings representing classic treatments of the general problem of change and identity, and proceeds to articles focusing on the nature of personal identity.

It will help explain some of the issues if you first reflect on the everyday experience of change. The experience of change is pervasive. Consider any object: an apple, a tree, a chair, this book, or yourself. There is one undeniable fact about them all—they change. Apples change color, trees grow taller, chairs become dirty, books become worn, and people change in more ways than can be described. If everything is constantly changing, then is there no permanence at all (is this Heraclitus' point)? Yet this cannot be entirely correct, because change also seems to require some permanence. Common sense says it is one and the same rose that was once in bloom and fragrant, but is now dry and odorless. Indeed, how could it be *the rose* that changes unless it is the same rose? Common sense seems to assume change involves identity, but how? How can the changing thing not be what it formerly was *and* be what it was?

Plato took very seriously the view that there is something contradictory about change, and this is the basis of his belief that a world of things that did not change would be perfectly real. Moreover, Plato claimed to discover such a world: the world of Forms (the world of general properties existing by themselves, "above" all change). Plato thought everyday objects (the objects of perceptual experience) were inferior entities infected by change. The best we can do, according to Plato, is to describe ordinary objects as at one time "participating" in (or exemplifying) one Form and later participating in another Form. For example, an apple changing from being green to red involves first participating in the Form, Greenness, and then participating in Redness. Though Plato may have invented some of the logical distinctions useful for describing change, he left changing things themselves in metaphysical limbo. What, exactly, is it that participates in Forms?

Aristotle's answer was that changing things (or substances) are combinations of matter and form, and they—not the Forms themselves—are fundamental realities. As seen in Part I, Aristotle believed time is a property of change, and change is a property of substances. Without substances there would be no properties (or

Forms), and without change there would be no time. But it is one thing to affirm the reality of change and time and another to give a coherent account of what constitutes the identity of something undergoing change. Here, though Aristotle starts with common sense, his analyses become complex and subtle. He claims individual things consist of some material having some essential form (some essential properties) and some accidental properties. When one asks whether an object is the same, the question can be ambiguous—it can be relative to whether one is asking about an object's essential properties, its accidental properties, or its matter.

Consider again the apple that changes from green to red. According to Aristotle, it is a substance having the essential property, being an apple. Its color is an accidental property. If, when one asks whether the apple is the same, one means *same apple*, then the answer is yes; because apples can change their color. Suppose, however, one means instead Is it the same *as it was* two weeks ago? Then, though it is the same apple, the answer is no, because it has changed its color. Suppose the apple is squashed so it becomes a puddle of apple juice. Now, even though the matter is the same matter, it is not the same apple because the matter no longer has the essential properties of an apple—the apple has ceased to exist altogether. Usually, for Aristotle, questions about the identity of an object involved determining whether some matter continued to have the same essential properties.

During the rise of modern science, Aristotle's notion of essential forms and their explanatory power came under attack. Materialists wanted to explain things in terms of their material constituents. From this perspective, the seventeenth-century philosopher Thomas Hobbes tried to solve an ancient puzzle: Suppose a ship's parts are gradually replaced over time so eventually the original ship no longer has any of the parts with which it began. And suppose the original parts are saved and gradually put together to make a second ship. Is the original ship identical with the one with new parts, or identical with the ship consisting of the old parts? Is the answer in some way arbitrary, to be decided by social conventions or laws?

Supposing that one could analyze the identity of such changing things as dogs or ships in the ways recommended by either Aristotle or Hobbes, many philosophers have nevertheless believed that the topic of personal identity raises new issues. Clearly, one's body changes dramatically during one's life: not only does its shape, size, and weight change, but also there are numerous complete replacements of its molecular constituents. Also, one's personality and memory can undergo significant changes. Yet, through all such changes it is common to believe that some identical person persists. It is not very helpful in understanding personal identity to be told that it is a matter of an individual maintaining the same essence. One would like to know what the exact *criteria* are for being the same person. Moreover, the issue of one's identity has ethical and value implications that make it seem vital in the way the identity of a ship is not. Whereas one might allow social or linguistic conventions to decide the identity of a ship, many believe that there must be more to personal identity. In this volume, Plato, Reid, and Chisholm represent the position that this something more is a unity (a soul, for example) that persists through all change. Other philosophers, however, are skeptical about this solution and try to formulate bodily or psychological criteria (see the articles by Perry, Parfit, Whiting, and Nagel). Challenging all theories is the debate, inspired by Parfit and discussed by Perry and Whiting, concerning the reasons we have to care about our own future selves, and how they differ from the reasons we have for the concern we have for others. Continuing to motivate and challenge much of this work is David Hume's skeptical worry that personal identity is a metaphysical illusion.

11. *Phaedo*

PLATO

Plato (470–347 BC) of Athens was closely associated with Socrates during the last years before his death. In his writings, which were primarily dialogues, Socrates is usually Plato's spokesperson. In the *Phaedo,* Plato is concerned with the question of immortality. The issue has dramatic significance, for the discussion takes place in the prison where Socrates is sentenced to die. Socrates expresses the view that the presence of the soul in the body is what gives it life, and that the soul is also crucial to personal identity. He argues that true philosophers should look forward to death because then, and only then, will they be able to attain their lifelong goal, namely, better knowledge of Reality. In order to render this view plausible Socrates considers several arguments for the immortality of the soul, all of which are included in this selection. Though the focus of the discussion is on the immortality of the soul, the *Phaedo* is also important because it shows how Plato analyzed change.

Socrates, sitting up on the couch, began to bend and rub his leg, saying, as he rubbed: How singular is the thing called pleasure, and how curiously related to pain, which might be thought to be the opposite of it; for they never come to a man together, and yet he who pursues either of them is generally compelled to take the other. They are two, and yet they grow together out of one head or stem; and I cannot help thinking that if Aesop had noticed them, he would have made a fable about God trying to reconcile their strife, and when he could not, he fastened their heads together; and this is the reason why when one comes the other follows, as I find in my own case pleasure comes following after the pain in my leg, which was caused by the chain.

Upon this Cebes said: I am very glad indeed, Socrates, that you mentioned the name of Aesop. For that reminds me of a question which has been asked by others, and was asked of me only the day before yesterday by Evenus the poet, and as he will be sure to ask again, you may as well tell me what I should say to him, if you would like him to have an answer. He wanted to know why you who never before wrote a line of poetry, now that you

are in prison are putting Aesop into verse, and also composing that hymn in honor of Apollo.

Tell him, Cebes, he replied, that I had no idea of rivalling him or his poems; which is the truth, for I knew that I could not do that. But I wanted to see whether I could purge away a scruple which I felt about certain dreams. In the course of my life I have often had intimations in dreams "that I should make music." The same dream came to me sometimes in one form, and sometimes in another, but always saying the same or nearly the same words: Make and cultivate music, said the dream. And hitherto I had imagined that this was only intended to exhort and encourage me in the study of philosophy, which has always been the pursuit of my life, and is the noblest and best of music. The dream was bidding me to do what I was already doing, in the same way that the competitor in a race is bidden by the spectators to run when he is already running. But I was not certain of this, as the dream might have meant music in the popular sense of the word, and being under sentence of death, and the festival giving me a respite, I thought that I should be safer if I satisfied the scruple, and, in obedience to the dream, composed a few verses before I departed. And first I made a hymn in honor of the god of the festival, and then considering that a poet, if he is really to

From Plato's *Phaedo,* translated by Benjamin Jowett, first published in 1909.

be a poet or maker, should not only put words together but make stories, and as I have no invention, I took some fables of Aesop, which I had ready at hand and knew, and turned them into verse. Tell Evenus this, and bid him be of good cheer; that I would have him come after me if he be a wise man, and not tarry; and that today I am likely to be going, for the Athenians say that I must.

Simmias said: What a message for such a man! Having been a frequent companion of his, I should say that, as far as I know him, he will never take your advice unless he is obliged.

Why, said Socrates, is not Evenus a philosopher?

I think that he is, said Simmias.

Then he, or any man who has the spirit of philosophy, will be willing to die, though he will not take his own life, for that is held not to be right.

Here he changed his position, and put his legs off the couch on to the ground, and during the rest of the conversation he remained sitting.

Why do you say, inquired Cebes, that a man ought not to take his own life, but that the philosopher will be ready to follow the dying?

Socrates replied: And have you, Cebes and Simmias, who are acquainted with Philolaus, never heard him speak of this?

I never understood him, Socrates.

My words, too, are only an echo; but I am very willing to say what I have heard: and indeed, as I am going to another place, I ought to be thinking and talking of the nature of the pilgrimage which I am about to make. What can I do better in the interval between this and the setting of the sun?

Then tell me, Socrates, why is suicide held not to be right? as I have certainly heard Philolaus affirm when he was staying with us at Thebes: and there are others who say the same, although none of them has ever made me understand him.

But do your best, replied Socrates, and the day may come when you will understand. I suppose that you wonder why, as most things which are evil may be accidentally good, this is to be the only exception (for may not death, too, be better than life in some cases?), and why, when a man is better dead, he is not permitted to be his own benefactor, but must wait for the hand of another.

By Jupiter! yes, indeed, said Cebes, laughing, and speaking in his native Doric.

I admit the appearance of inconsistency, replied Socrates, but there may not be any real inconsistency after all in this. There is a doctrine uttered in secret that man is a prisoner who has no right to open the door of his prison and run away; this is a great mystery which I do not quite understand. Yet I, too, believe that the gods are our guardians, and that we are a possession of theirs. Do you not agree?

Yes, I agree to that, said Cebes.

And if one of your own possessions, an ox or an ass, for example took the liberty of putting himself out of the way when you had given no intimation of your wish that he should die, would you not be angry with him, and would you not punish him if you could?

Certainly, replied Cebes.

Then there may be reason in saying that a man should wait, and not take his own life until God summons him, as he is now summoning me.

Yes, Socrates, said Cebes, there is surely reason in that. And yet how can you reconcile this seemingly true belief that God is our guardian and we his possessions, with that willingness to die which we were attributing to the philosopher? That the wisest of men should be willing to leave this service in which they are ruled by the gods who are the best of rulers is not reasonable, for surely no wise man thinks that when set at liberty he can take better care of himself than the gods take of him. A fool may perhaps think this—he may argue that he had better run away from his master, not considering that his duty is to remain to the end, and not to run away from the good, and that there is no sense in his running away. But the wise man will want to be ever with him who is better than himself. Now this, Socrates, is the reverse of what was just now said; for upon this view the wise man should sorrow and the fool rejoice at passing out of life.

The earnestness of Cebes seemed to please Socrates. Here, said he, turning to us, is a man who is always inquiring, and is not to be convinced all in a moment, nor by every argument.

And in this case, added Simmias, his objection does appear to me to have some force. For what can be the meaning of a truly wise man wanting to fly away and lightly leave a master who is better than himself? And I rather imagine that Cebes is referring to you; he thinks that you are too ready to leave us, and too ready to leave the gods who, as you acknowledge, are our good rulers.

Yes, replied Socrates; there is reason in that. And this indictment you think that I ought to answer as if I were in court?

That is what we should like, said Simmias.

Then I must try to make a better impression upon you than I did when defending myself before the judges. For I am quite ready to acknowledge, Simmias and Cebes, that I ought to be grieved at death, if I were not persuaded that I am going to other gods who are wise and good (of this I am as certain as I can be of anything of the sort) and to men departed (though I am not so certain of this), who are better than those whom I leave behind; and therefore I do not grieve as I might have done, for I have good hope that there is yet something remaining for the dead, and, as has been said of old, some far better thing for the good than for the evil.

But do you mean to take away your thoughts with you, Socrates? said Simmias. Will you not communicate them to us?—the benefit is one in which we too may hope to share. Moreover, if you succeed in convincing us, that will be an answer to the charge against yourself.

I will do my best, replied Socrates. But you must first let me hear what Crito wants; he was going to say something to me.

Only this, Socrates, replied Crito: the attendant who is to give you the poison has been telling me that you are not to talk much, and he wants me to let you know this; for that by talking heat is increased, and this interferes with the action of the poison; those who excite themselves are sometimes obliged to drink the poison two or three times.

Then, said Socrates, let him mind his business and be prepared to give the poison two or three times, if necessary; that is all.

I was almost certain that you would say that, replied Crito; but I was obliged to satisfy him.

Never mind him, he said.

And now I will make answer to you, O my judges, and show that he who has lived as a true philosopher has reason to be of good cheer when he is about to die, and that after death he may hope to receive the greatest good in the other world. And how this may be, Simmias and Cebes, I will endeavor to explain. For I deem that the true disciple of philosophy is likely to be misunder-

stood by other men; they do not perceive that he is ever pursuing death and dying; and if this is true, why, having had the desire of death all his life long, should he repine at the arrival of that which he has been always pursuing and desiring?

Simmias laughed and said: Though not in a laughing humor, I swear that I cannot help laughing when I think what the wicked world will say when they hear this. They will say that this is very true, and our people at home will agree with them in saying that the life which philosophers desire is truly death, and that they have found them out to be deserving of the death which they desire.

And they are right, Simmias, in saying this, with the exception of the words "They have found them out"; for they have not found out what is the nature of this death which the true philosopher desires, or how he deserves or desires death. But let us leave them and have a word with ourselves: Do we believe that there is such a thing as death?

To be sure, replied Simmias.

And is this anything but the separation of soul and body? And being dead is the attainment of this separation; when the soul exists in herself, and is parted from the body and the body is parted from the soul—that is death?

Exactly: that and nothing else, he replied.

And what do you say of another question, my friend, about which I should like to have your opinion, and the answer to which will probably throw light on our present inquiry: Do you think that the philosopher ought to care about the pleasures—if they are to be called pleasures—of eating and drinking?

Certainly not, answered Simmias.

And what do you say of the pleasures of love—should he care about them?

By no means.

And will he think much of the other ways of indulging the body—for example, the acquisition of costly raiment, or sandals, or other adornments of the body? Instead of caring about them, does he not rather despise anything more than nature needs? What do you say?

I should say the true philosopher would despise them.

Would you not say that he is entirely concerned with the soul and not with the body? He would like, as far as he can, to be quit of the body and turn to the soul.

That is true.

In matters of this sort philosophers, above all other men, may be observed in every sort of way to dissever the soul from the body.

That is true.

Whereas, Simmias, the rest of the world are of opinion that a life which has no bodily pleasures and no part in them is not worth having; but that he who thinks nothing of bodily pleasures is almost as though he were dead.

That is quite true.

What again shall we say of the actual acquirement of knowledge?—is the body, if invited to share in the inquiry, a hinderer or a helper? I mean to say, have sight and hearing any truth in them? Are they not, as the poets are always telling us, inaccurate witnesses? and yet, if even they are inaccurate and indistinct, what is to be said of the other senses?—for you will allow that they are the best of them?

Certainly, he replied.

Then when does the soul attain truth?—for in attempting to consider anything in company with the body she is obviously deceived.

Yes, that is true.

Then must not existence be revealed to her in thought, if at all?

Yes.

And thought is best when the mind is gathered into herself and none of these things trouble her—neither sounds nor sights nor pain nor any pleasure—when she has as little as possible to do with the body, and has no bodily sense or feeling, but is aspiring after being?

That is true.

And in this the philosopher dishonors the body; his soul runs away from the body and desires to be alone and by herself?

That is true.

Well, but there is another thing, Simmias: Is there or is there not an absolute justice?

Assuredly there is.

And an absolute beauty and absolute good?

Of course.

But did you ever behold any of them with your eyes?

Certainly not.

Or did you ever reach them with any other bodily sense? (and I speak not of these alone, but of absolute greatness, and health, and strength, and of the essence or true nature of everything). Has the reality of them ever been perceived by you through the bodily organs? or rather, is not the nearest approach to the knowledge of their several natures made by him who so orders his intellectual vision as to have the most exact conception of the essence of that which he considers?

Certainly.

And he attains to the knowledge of them in their highest purity who goes to each of them with the mind alone, not allowing when in the act of thought the intrusion or introduction of sight or any other sense in the company of reason, but with the very light of the mind in her clearness penetrates into the very fight of truth in each; he has got rid, as far as he can, of eyes and ears and of the whole body, which he conceives of only as a disturbing element, hindering the soul from the acquisition of knowledge when in company with her—is not this the sort of man who, if ever man did, is likely to attain the knowledge of existence?

There is admirable truth in that, Socrates, replied Simmias.

And when they consider all this, must not true philosophers make a reflection, of which they will speak to one another in such words as these: We have found, they will say, a path of speculation which seems to bring us and the argument to the conclusion that while we are in the body, and while the soul is mingled with this mass of evil, our desire will not be satisfied, and our desire is of the truth. For the body is a source of endless trouble to us by reason of the mere requirement of food; and also is liable to diseases which overtake and impede us in the search after truth: and by filling us so full of loves, and lusts, and fears, and fancies, and idols, and every sort of folly, prevents our ever having, as people say, so much as a thought. For whence come wars, and fightings, and factions? whence but from the body and the lusts of the body? For wars are occasioned by the love of money, and money has to be acquired for the sake and in the service of the body; and in consequence of all these things the time which ought to be given to philosophy is lost. Moreover, if there is time and an inclination toward philosophy, yet the body introduces a turmoil and confusion and fear into the course of speculation, and hinders us from seeing the truth: and all experience shows that if we would have pure knowledge of anything we must be quit of the body, and the soul in herself must behold all things in themselves: then I suppose that we shall attain that which we desire, and of which we say that we are lovers, and that is wisdom, not while we live, but after death, as the argument shows; for if while in company with the body the soul cannot have pure knowledge, one of two things seems to follow—either knowledge is not to be attained at all, or, if at all, after death. For then, and not till then, the soul will be in herself alone and without the body. In this present life, I reckon that we make the nearest approach to knowledge when we have the least possible concern or interest in the body, and are not saturated with the bodily nature, but remain pure until the hour when God himself is pleased to release us. And then the foolishness of the body will be cleared away and we shall be pure and hold converse with other pure souls, and know of ourselves the clear light everywhere; and this is surely the light of truth. For no impure thing is allowed to approach the pure. These are the sort of words, Simmias, which the true lovers of wisdom cannot help saying to one another, and thinking. You will agree with me in that?

Certainly, Socrates.

But if this is true, O my friend, then there is great hope that, going whither I go, I shall there be satisfied with that which has been the chief concern of you and me in our past lives. And now that the hour of departure is appointed to me, this is the hope with which I depart, and not I only, but every man who believes that he has his mind purified.

Certainly, replied Simmias.

And what is purification but the separation of the soul from the body, as I was saying before; the habit of the soul gathering and collecting herself into herself, out of all the courses of the body; the dwelling in her own place alone, as in another life, so also in this, as far as she can; the release of the soul from the chains of the body?

Very true, he said.

And what is that which is termed death, but this very separation and release of the soul from the body?

To be sure, he said.

And the true philosophers, and they only, study and are eager to release the soul. Is not the separation and release of the soul from the body their especial study?

That is true.

And as I was saying at first, there would be a ridiculous contradiction in men studying to live as nearly as they can in a state of death, and yet repining when death comes.

Certainly.

Then, Simmias, as the true philosophers are ever studying death, to them, of all men, death is the least terrible. Look at the matter in this way: how inconsistent of them to have been always enemies of the body, and wanting to have the soul alone, and when this is granted to them, to be trembling and repining; instead of rejoicing at their departing to that place where, when they arrive, they hope to gain that which in life they loved (and this was wisdom), and at the same time to be rid of the company of their enemy. Many a man has been willing to go to the world below in the hope of seeing there an earthly love, or wife, or son, and conversing with them. And will he who is a true lover of wisdom, and is persuaded in like manner that only in the world below he can worthily enjoy her, still repine at death? Will he not depart with joy? Surely he will, my friend, if he be a true philosopher. For he will have a firm conviction that there only, and nowhere else, he can find wisdom in her purity. And if this be true, he would be very absurd, as I was saying, if he were to fear death.

He would, indeed, replied Simmias.

And when you see a man who is repining at the approach of death, is not his reluctance a sufficient proof that he is not a lover of wisdom, but a lover of the body, and probably at the same time a lover of either money or power, or both?

That is very true, he replied.

There is a virtue, Simmias, which is named courage. Is not that a special attribute of the philosopher?

Certainly.

Again, there is temperance. Is not the calm, and control, and disdain of the passions which even the many call temperance, a quality belonging only to those who despise the body and live in philosophy?

That is not to be denied.

For the courage and temperance of other men, if you will consider them, are really a contradiction.

How is that, Socrates?

Well, he said, you are aware that death is regarded by men in general as a great evil.

That is true, he said.

And do not courageous men endure death because they are afraid of yet greater evils?

That is true.

Then all but the philosophers are courageous only from fear, and because they are afraid; and yet that a man should be courageous from fear, and because he is a coward, is surely a strange thing.

Very true.

And are not the temperate exactly in the same case? They are temperate because they are intemperate—which may seem to be a contradiction, but is nevertheless the sort of thing which happens with this foolish temperance. For there are pleasures which they must have, and are afraid of losing; and therefore they abstain from one class of pleasures because they are overcome by another: and whereas intemperance is defined as "being under the dominion of pleasure," they overcome only because they are overcome by pleasure. And that is what I mean by saying that they are temperate through intemperance.

That appears to be true.

Yet the exchange of one fear or pleasure or pain for another fear or pleasure or pain, which are measured like coins, the greater with the less, is not the exchange of virtue. O my dear Simmias, is there not one true coin for which all things ought to exchange?—and that is wisdom; and only in exchange for this, and in company with this, is anything truly bought or sold, whether courage or temperance or justice. And is not all true virtue the companion of wisdom, no matter what fears or pleasures or other similar goods or evils may or may not attend her? But the virtue which is made up of these goods, when they are severed from wisdom and exchanged with one another, is a shadow of virtue only, nor is there any freedom or health or truth in her; but in the true exchange there is a purging away of all these things, and temperance, and justice, and courage, and wisdom herself are a purgation of them. And I conceive that the founders of the mysteries had a real meaning and were not mere triflers when they intimated in a figure long ago that he who passes unsanctified and uninitiated into the world below will live in a slough, but that he who arrives there after initiation and purification will dwell with the gods.

For "many," as they say in the mysteries, "are the thyrsus bearers, but few are the mystics,"—meaning, as I interpret the words, the true philosophers. In the number of whom I have been seeking, according to my ability, to find a place during my whole life; whether I have sought in a right way or not, and whether I have succeeded or not, I shall truly know in a little while, if God will, when I myself arrive in the other world: that is my belief. And now, Simmias and Cebes, I have answered those who charge me with not grieving or repining at parting from you and my masters in this world; and I am right in not repining, for I believe that I shall find other masters and friends who are as good in the world below. But all men cannot believe this, and I shall be glad if my words have any more success with you than with the judges of the Athenians.

Cebes answered: I agree, Socrates, in the greater part of what you say. But in what relates to the soul, men are apt to be incredulous; they fear that when she leaves the body her place may be nowhere, and that on the very day of death she may be destroyed and perish—immediately on her release from the body, issuing forth like smoke or air and vanishing away into nothingness. For if she could only hold together and be herself after she was released from the evils of the body, there would be good reason to hope, Socrates, that what you say is true. But much persuasion and many arguments are required in order to prove that when the man is dead the soul yet exists, and has any force of intelligence.

True, Cebes, said Socrates; and shall I suggest that we talk a little of the probabilities of these things?

I am sure, said Cebes, that I should greatly like to know your opinion about them.

I reckon, said Socrates, that no one who heard me now, not even if he were one of my old enemies, the comic poets, could accuse me of idle talking about matters in which I have no concern. Let us, then, if you please, proceed with the inquiry.

Whether the souls of men after death are or are not in the world below, is a question which may be argued in this manner: The ancient doctrine of which I have been speaking affirms that they go from this into the other world, and return hither, and are born from the dead. Now if this be true, and the living come from the dead, then our souls must be in the other world, for if not, how could they be born again? And this would be conclusive, if there were any real evidence that the living are only born from the dead; but if there is no evidence of this, then other arguments will have to be adduced.

That is very true, replied Cebes.

Then let us consider this question, not in relation to man only, but in relation to animals generally, and to plants, and to everything of which there is generation, and the proof will be easier. Are not all things which have opposites generated out of their opposites? I mean such things as good and evil, just and unjust—and there are innumerable other opposites which are generated out of opposites. And I want to show that this holds universally of all opposites; I mean to say, for example, that anything which becomes greater must become greater after being less.

True.

And that which becomes less must have been once greater and then become less.

Yes.

And the weaker is generated from the stronger, and the swifter from the slower.

Very true.

And the worse is from the better, and the more just is from the more unjust.

Of course.

And is this true of all opposites? and are we convinced that all of them are generated out of opposites?

Yes.

And in this universal opposition of all things, are there not also two intermediate processes which are ever going on, from one to the other, and back again; where there is a greater and a less there is also an intermediate process of increase and diminution, and that which grows is said to wax, and that which decays to wane?

Yes, he said.

And there are many other processes, such as division and composition, cooling and heating, which equally involve a passage into and out of one another. And this holds of all opposites, even though not always expressed in words—they are generated out of one another, and there is a passing or process from one to the other of them?

Very true, he replied.

Well, and is there not an opposite of life, as sleep is the opposite of waking?

True, he said.

And what is that?

Death, he answered.

And these, then, are generated, if they are opposites, the one from the other, and have there their two intermediate processes also?

Of course.

Now, said Socrates, I will analyze one of the two pairs of opposites which I have mentioned to you, and also its intermediate processes, and you shall analyze the other to me. The state of sleep is opposed to the state of waking, and out of sleeping waking is generated, and out of waking, sleeping, and the process of generation is in the one case falling asleep, and in the other waking up. Are you agreed about that?

Quite agreed.

Then suppose that you analyze life and death to me in the same manner. Is not death opposed to life?

Yes.

And they are generated one from the other?

Yes.

What is generated from life?

Death.

And what from death?

I can only say in answer—life.

Then the living, whether things or persons, Cebes, are generated from the dead?

That is clear, he replied.

Then the inference is, that our souls are in the world below?

That is true.

And one of the two processes or generations is visible—for surely the act of dying is visible?

Surely, he said.

And may not the other be inferred as the complement of nature, who is not to be supposed to go on one leg only? And if not, a corresponding process of generation in death must also be assigned to her?

Certainly, he replied.

And what is that process?

Revival.

And revival, if there be such a thing, is the birth of the dead into the world of the living?

Quite true.

Then there is a new way in which we arrive at the inference that the living come from the dead, just as the dead come from the living; and if this is true, then the souls of the dead must be in some place out of which they come again. And this, as I think, has been satisfactorily proved.

Yes, Socrates, he said; all this seems to flow necessarily out of our previous admissions.

And that these admissions are not unfair, Cebes, he said, may be shown, as I think, in this way: If generation were in a straight line only, and there were no compensation or circle in nature, no turn or return into one another, then you know that all things would at last have the same form and pass into the same state, and there would be no more generation of them.

What do you mean? he said.

A simple thing enough, which I will illustrate by the case of sleep, he replied. You know that if there were no compensation of sleeping and waking, the story of the sleeping Endymion would in the end have no meaning, because all other things would be asleep, too, and he would not be thought of. Or if there were composition only, and no division of substances, then the chaos of Anaxagoras would come again. And in like manner, my dear Cebes, if all things which partook of life were to die, and after they were dead remained in the form of death, and did not come to life again, all would at last die, and nothing would be alive—how could this be otherwise? For if the living spring from any others who are not the dead, and they die, must not all things at last be swallowed up in death?

There is no escape from that, Socrates, said Cebes; and I think that what you say is entirely true.

Yes, he said, Cebes, I entirely think so, too; and we are not walking in a vain imagination; but I am confident in the belief that there truly is such a thing as living again, and that the living spring from the dead, and that the souls of the dead are in existence, and that the good souls have a better portion than the evil.

Cebes added: Your favorite doctrine, Socrates, that knowledge is simply recollection, if true, also necessarily implies a previous time in which we learned that which we now recollect. But this would be impossible unless our soul was in some place before existing in the human form; here, then, is another argument of the soul's immortality.

But tell me, Cebes, said Simmias, interposing, what proofs are given of this doctrine of recollection? I am not very sure at this moment that I remember them.

One excellent proof, said Cebes, is afforded by questions. If you put a question to a person in a right way, he will give a true answer of himself; but how could he do this unless there were knowledge and right reason already in him? And this is most clearly shown when he is taken to a diagram or to anything of that sort.

But if, said Socrates, you are still incredulous, Simmias, I would ask you whether you may not agree with me when you look at the matter in another way; I mean, if you are still incredulous as to whether knowledge is recollection.

Incredulous, I am not, said Simmias; but I want to have this doctrine of recollection brought to my own recollection, and, from what Cebes has said, I am beginning to recollect and be convinced; but I should still like to hear what more you have to say.

This is what I would say, he replied: We should agree, if I am not mistaken, that what a man recollects he must have known at some previous time.

Very true.

And what is the nature of this recollection? And, in asking this, I mean to ask whether, when a person has already seen or heard or in any way perceived anything, and he knows not only that, but something else of which he has not the same, but another knowledge, we may not fairly say that he recollects that which comes into his mind. Are we agreed about that?

What do you mean?

I mean what I may illustrate by the following instance: The knowledge of a lyre is not the same as the knowledge of a man?

True.

And yet what is the feeling of lovers when they recognize a lyre, or a garment, or anything else which the beloved has been in the habit of using? Do not they, from knowing the lyre, form in the mind's eye an image of the youth to whom the lyre belongs? And this is recollection: and in the same way anyone who sees Simmias may remember Cebes; and there are endless other things of the same nature.

Yes, indeed, there are endless, replied Simmias.

And this sort of thing, he said, is recollection, and is most commonly a process of recovering that which has been forgotten through time and inattention.

Very true, he said.

Well; and may you not also from seeing the picture of a horse or a lyre remember a man? and from the picture of Simmias, you may be led to remember Cebes?

True.

Or you may also be led to the recollection of Simmias himself?

True, he said.

And in all these cases, the recollection may be derived from things either like or unlike?

That is true.

And when the recollection is derived from like things, then there is sure to be another question, which is, whether the likeness of that which is recollected is in any way defective or not.

Very true, he said.

And shall we proceed a step further, and affirm that there is such a thing as equality, not of wood with wood, or of stone with stone, but that, over and above this, there is equality in the abstract? Shall we affirm this?

Affirm, yes, and swear to it, replied Simmias, with all the confidence in life.

And do we know the nature of this abstract essence?

To be sure, he said.

And whence did we obtain this knowledge? Did we not see equalities of material things, such as pieces of wood and stones, and gather from them the idea of an equality which is different from them?—you will admit that? Or look at the matter again in this way: Do not the same pieces of wood or stone appear at one time equal, and at another time unequal?

That is certain.

But are real equals ever unequal? or is the idea of equality ever inequality?

That surely was never yet known, Socrates.

Then these (so-called) equals are not the same with the idea of equality?

I should say, clearly not, Socrates.

And yet from these equals, although differing from the idea of equality, you conceived and attained that idea?

Very true, he said.

Which might be like, or might be unlike them?

Yes.

But that makes no difference; whenever from seeing one thing you conceived another, whether like or unlike, there must surely have been an act of recollection?

Very true.

But what would you say of equal portions of wood and stone, or other material equals? and what is the impression produced by them? Are they equals in the same sense as absolute equality? or do they fall short of this in a measure?

Yes, he said, in a very great measure, too.

And must we not allow that when I or anyone look at any object, and perceive that the object aims at being some other thing, but falls short of, and cannot attain to it—he who makes this observation must have had previous knowledge of that to which, as he says, the other, although similar, was inferior?

Certainly.

And has not this been our case in the matter of equals and of absolute equality?

Precisely.

Then we must have known absolute equality previously to the time when we first saw the material equals, and reflected that all these apparent equals aim at this absolute equality, but fall short of it?

That is true.

And we recognize also that this absolute equality has only been known, and can only be known, through the medium of sight or touch, or of some other sense. And this I would affirm of all such conceptions.

Yes, Socrates, as far as the argument is concerned, one of them is the same as the other.

And from the senses, then, is derived the knowledge that all sensible things aim at an idea of equality of which they fall short—is not that true?

Yes.

Then before we began to see or hear or perceive in any way, we must have had a knowledge of absolute equality, or we could not have referred to that the equals which are derived from the senses—for to that they all aspire, and of that they fall short?

That, Socrates, is certainly to be inferred from the previous statements.

And did we not see and hear and acquire our other senses as soon as we were born?

Certainly.

Then we must have acquired the knowledge of the ideal equal at some time previous to this?

Yes.

That is to say, before we were born, I suppose?

True.

And if we acquired this knowledge before we were born, and were born having it, then we also knew before we were born and at the instant of birth not only equal or the greater or the less, but all other ideas; for we are not speaking only of equality absolute, but of beauty, goodness, justice, holiness, and all which we stamp with the name of essence in the dialectical process, when we ask and answer questions. Of all this we may certainly affirm that we acquired the knowledge before birth?

That is true.

But if, after having acquired, we have not forgotten that which we acquired, then we must always have been born with knowledge, and shall always continue to know as long as life lasts—for knowing is the acquiring and retaining knowledge and not forgetting. Is not forgetting, Simmias, just the losing of knowledge?

Quite true, Socrates.

But if the knowledge which we acquired before birth was lost by us at birth, and afterwards by the use of the senses we recovered that which we previously knew, will not that which we call learning be a process of recovering our knowledge, and may not this be rightly termed recollection by us?

Very true.

For this is clear, that when we perceived something, either by the help of sight or hearing, or some other sense, there was no difficulty in receiving from this a conception of some other thing like or unlike which had been forgotten and which was associated with this; and therefore, as I was saying, one of two alternatives follows: either we had this knowledge at birth, and continued to know through life; or, after birth, those who are said to learn only remember, and learning is recollection only.

Yes, that is quite true, Socrates.

And which alternative, Simmias, do you prefer? Had we the knowledge at our birth, or did we remember afterwards the things which we knew previously to our birth?

I cannot decide at the moment.

At any rate you can decide whether he who has knowledge ought or ought not to be able to give a reason for what he knows.

Certainly, he ought.

But do you think that every man is able to give a reason about these very matters of which we are speaking?

I wish that they could, Socrates, but I greatly fear that tomorrow at this time there will be no one able to give a reason worth having.

Then you are not of opinion, Simmias, that all men know these things?

Certainly not.

Then they are in process of recollecting that which they learned before.

Certainly.

But when did our souls acquire this knowledge?—not since we were born as men?

Certainly not.

And therefore previously?

Yes.

Then, Simmias, our souls must have existed before they were in the form of man—without bodies, and must have had intelligence.

Unless indeed you suppose, Socrates, that these notions were given us at the moment of birth; for this is the only time that remains.

Yes, my friend, but when did we lose them? for they are not in us when we are born—that is admitted. Did we lose them at the moment of receiving them, or at some other time?

No, Socrates, I perceive that I was unconsciously talking nonsense.

Then may we not say, Simmias, that if, as we are always repeating, there is an absolute beauty, and goodness, and essence in general, and to this, which is now discovered to be a previous condition of our being, we refer all our sensations, and with this compare them—assuming this to have a prior existence, then our souls must have had a prior existence, but if not, there would be no force in the argument? There can be no doubt that if these absolute ideas existed before we were born, then our souls must have existed before we were born, and if not the ideas, then not the souls.

Yes, Socrates; I am convinced that there is precisely the same necessity for the existence of the soul before birth, and of the essence of which you are speaking: and the argument arrives at a result which happily agrees with my own notion. For there is nothing which to my mind is so evident as that beauty, goodness, and other notions of which you were just now speaking have a most real and absolute existence; and I am satisfied with the proof.

Well, but is Cebes equally satisfied? for I must convince him too.

I think, said Simmias, that Cebes is satisfied: although he is the most incredulous of mortals, yet I believe that he is convinced of the existence of the soul before birth. But that after death the soul will continue to exist is not yet proven even to my own satisfaction. I cannot get rid of the feeling of the many to which Cebes was referring—the feeling that when the man dies the soul may be scattered, and that this may be the end of her. For admitting that she may be generated and created in some other place, and may have existed before entering the human body, why after having entered in and gone out again may she not herself be destroyed and come to an end?

Very true, Simmias, said Cebes; that our soul existed before we were born was the first half of the argument, and this appears to have been proven; that the soul will exist after death as well as before birth is the other half of which the proof is still wanting, and has to be supplied.

But that proof, Simmias and Cebes, has been already given, said Socrates, if you put the two arguments together—I mean this and the former one, in which we admitted that everything living is born of the dead. For if the soul existed before birth, and in coming to life and being born can be born only from death and dying, must she not after death continue to exist, since she has to be born again? surely the proof which you desire has been already furnished. Still I suspect that you and Simmias would be glad to probe the argument further; like children, you are haunted with a fear that when the soul leaves the body, the wind may really blow her away and scatter her; especially if a man should happen to die in stormy weather and not when the sky is calm.

Cebes answered with a smile: Then, Socrates, you must argue us out of our fears—and yet, strictly speaking, they are not our fears, but there is a child within us to whom death is a sort of hobgoblin; him too we must persuade not to be afraid when he is alone with him in the dark.

Socrates said: Let the voice of the charmer be applied daily until you have charmed him away.

And where shall we find a good charmer of our fears, Socrates, when you are gone?

Hellas, he replied, is a large place, Cebes, and has many good men, and there are barbarous races not a few: seek for him among them all, far and wide, sparing neither pains nor money; for there is no better way of using your money. And you must not forget to seek for him among yourselves too; for he is nowhere more likely to be found.

The search, replied Cebes, shall certainly be made. And now, if you please, let us return to the point of the argument at which we digressed.

By all means, replied Socrates; what else should I please?

Very good, he said.

Must we not, said Socrates, ask ourselves some question of this sort?—What is that which, as we imagine, is liable to be scattered away, and about which we fear? and what again is that about which we have no fear? And then we may proceed to inquire whether that which suffers dispersion is or is not of the nature of soul—our hopes and fears as to our own souls will turn upon that.

That is true, he said.

Now the compound or composite may be supposed to be naturally capable of being dissolved in like manner as of being compounded; but that which is uncompounded, and that only, must be, if anything is, indissoluble.

Yes; that is what I should imagine, said Cebes.

And the uncompounded may be assumed to be the same and unchanging, where the compound is always changing and never the same?

That I also think, he said.

Then now let us return to the previous discussion. Is that idea or essence, which in the dialectical process we define as essence of true existence—whether essence of equality, beauty, or anything else: are these essences, I say, liable at times to some degree of change? or are they each of them always what they are, having the same simple, self-existent and unchanging forms, and not admitting of variation at all, or in any way, or at any time?

They must be always the same, Socrates, replied Cebes.

And what would you say of the many beautiful—whether men or horses or garments or any other things which may be called equal or beautiful—are they all unchanging and the same always, or quite the reverse? May they not rather be described as almost always changing and hardly ever the same either with themselves or with one another?

The latter, replied Cebes; they are always in a state of change.

And these you can touch and see and perceive with the senses, but the unchanging things you can only perceive with the mind—they are invisible and are not seen?

That is very true, he said.

Well, then, he added, let us suppose that there are two sorts of existences, one seen, the other unseen.

Let us suppose them.

The seen is the changing, and the unseen is the unchanging.

That may be also supposed.

And, further, is not one part of us body, and the rest of us soul?

To be sure.

And to which class may we say that the body is more alike and akin?

Clearly to the seen: no one can doubt that.

And is the soul seen or not seen?

Not by man, Socrates.

And by "seen" and "not seen" is meant by us that which is or is not visible to the eye of man?

Yes, to the eye of man.

And what do we say of the soul? is that seen or not seen?

Not seen.

Unseen then?

Yes.

Then the soul is more like to the unseen, and the body to the seen?

That is most certain, Socrates.

And were we not saying long ago that the soul when using the body as an instrument of perception, that is to say, when using the sense of sight or hearing or some other sense (for the meaning of perceiving through the body is per-

ceiving through the senses)—were we not saying that the soul too is then dragged by the body into the region of the changeable, and wanders and is confused; the world spins round her, and she is like a drunkard when under their influence?

Very true.

But when returning into herself she reflects; then she passes into the realm of purity, and eternity, and immortality, and unchangeableness, which are her kindred, and with them she ever lives, when she is by herself and is not let or hindered; then she ceases from her erring ways, and being in communion with the unchanging is unchanging. And this state of the soul is called wisdom?

That is well and truly said, Socrates, he replied.

And to which class is the soul more nearly alike and akin, as far as may be inferred from this argument, as well as from the preceding one?

I think, Socrates, that, in the opinion of everyone who follows the argument, the soul will be infinitely more like the unchangeable; even the most stupid person will not deny that.

And the body is more like the changing?

Yes.

Yet once more consider the matter in this light: When the soul and the body are united, then nature orders the soul to rule and govern, and the body to obey and serve.

Now which of these two functions is akin to the divine? and which to the mortal? Does not the divine appear to you to be that which naturally orders and rules, and the mortal that which is subject and servant?

True.

And which does the soul resemble?

The soul resembles the divine and the body the mortal—there can be no doubt of that, Socrates.

Then reflect, Cebes: is not the conclusion of the whole matter this?—that the soul is in the very likeness of the divine, and immortal, and intelligible, and uniform, and indissoluble, and unchangeable; and the body is in the very likeness of the human, and mortal, and unintelligible, and multiform, and dissoluble, and changeable. Can this, my dear Cebes, be denied?

No, indeed.

But if this is true, then is not the body liable to speedy dissolution? and is not the soul almost or altogether indissoluble?

Certainly.

And do you further observe, that after a man is dead, the body, which is the visible part of man, and has a visible framework, which is called a corpse, and which would naturally be dissolved and decomposed and dissipated, is not dissolved or decomposed at once, but may remain for a good while, if the constitution be sound at the time of death, and the season of the year favorable? For the body when shrunk and embalmed, as is the custom in Egypt, may remain almost entire through infinite ages; and even in decay, still there are some portions, such as the bones and ligaments, which are practically indestructible. You allow that?

Yes.

And are we to suppose that the soul, which is invisible, in passing to the true Hades, which like her is invisible, and pure, and noble, and on her way to the good and wise God, whether, if God will, my soul is also soon to go—that the soul, I repeat, if this be her nature and origin, is blown away and perishes immediately on quitting the body as the many say? That can never be, dear Simmias and Cebes. The truth rather is that the soul which is pure at departing draws after her no bodily taint, having never voluntarily had connection with the body, which she is ever avoiding, herself gathered into herself (for such abstraction has been the study of her life). And what does this mean but that she has been a true disciple of philosophy and has practised how to die easily? And is not philosophy the practice of death?

Certainly.

That soul, I say, herself invisible, departs to the invisible world to the divine and immortal and rational: thither arriving, she lives in bliss and is released from the error and folly of men, their fears and wild passions and all other human ills, and forever dwells, as they say of the initiated, in company with the gods. Is not this true, Cebes?

Yes, said Cebes, beyond a doubt.

. . .

Briefly, the sum of your objection is as follows: You want to have proven to you that the soul is imperishable and immortal, and you think that the philosopher who is confident in death has but a vain and foolish confidence, if he thinks that he will fare better than one who has led another sort of life, in the world below, unless he can prove this; and you say that the demonstration of the strength and divinity of the soul, and of her existence prior to our becoming men, does not necessarily imply her immortality. Granting that the soul is longlived, and has known and done much in a former state, still she is not on that account immortal; and her entrance into the human form may be a sort of disease which is the beginning of dissolution, and may at last, after the toils of life are over, end in that which is called death. And whether the soul enters into the body once only or many times, that, as you would say, makes no difference in the fears of individuals. For any man, who is not devoid of natural feeling, has reason to fear, if he has no knowledge or proof of the soul's immortality. That is what I suppose you to say, Cebes, which I designedly repeat, in order that nothing may escape us, and that you may, if you wish, add or subtract anything.

But, said Cebes, as far as I can see at present, I have nothing to add or subtract; you have expressed my meaning.

Socrates paused awhile, and seemed to be absorbed in reflection. At length he said: This is a very serious inquiry which you are raising, Cebes, involving the whole question of generation and corruption, about which I will, if you like, give you my own experience; and you can apply this, if you think that anything which I say will avail towards the solution of your difficulty.

I should very much like, said Cebes, to hear what you have to say.

Then I will tell you, said Socrates. When I was young, Cebes, I had a prodigious desire to know that department of philosophy which is called Natural Science; this appeared to me to have lofty aims, as being the science which has to do with the causes of things, and which teaches why a thing is, and is created and destroyed; and I was always agitating myself with the consideration of such questions as these: Is the growth of animals the result of some decay which the hot and cold principle contracts, as some have said? Is the blood the element with which we think, or the air, or the fire? or perhaps nothing of this sort—but the brain may be the originating power of the perceptions of hearing and sight and smell, and memory and opinion may come from them, and science may be based on memory and opinion when no longer in motion, but at rest. And then I went on to examine the decay of them, and then to the things of heaven and earth, and at last I concluded that I was wholly incapable of these inquiries, as I will satisfactorily prove to you. For I was fascinated by them to such a degree that my eyes grew blind to things that I had seemed to myself, and also to others, to know quite well; and I forgot what I had before thought to be self-evident, that the growth of man is the result of eating and drinking; for when by the digestion of food flesh is added to flesh and bone to bone, and whenever there is an aggregation of congenial elements, the lesser bulk becomes larger and the small man greater. Was not that a reasonable notion?

Yes, said Cebes, I think so.

Well; but let me tell you something more. There was a time when I thought that I understood the meaning of greater and less pretty well; and when I saw a great man standing by a little one I fancied that one was taller than the other by a head; or one horse would appear to be greater than another horse: and still more clearly did I seem to perceive that ten is two more than eight, and that two cubits are more than one, because two is twice one.

And what is now your notion of such matters? said Cebes.

I should be far enough from imagining, he replied, that I knew the cause of any of them, indeed I should, for I cannot satisfy myself that when one is added to one, the one to which the addition is made becomes two, or that the two units added together make two by reason of the addition. For I cannot understand how, when separated from the other, each of them was one and not two, and now, when they are brought together, the mere juxtaposition of them can be the cause of their becoming two: nor can I understand how the division of one is the way to make two; for then a different cause would produce the same effect—as in the former instance the addition and juxtaposition of one to one was the cause of two, in this the separation and subtraction of one from the other would be the cause. Nor am I any longer satisfied that I understand the reason why one or anything else either is generated or destroyed or is at all, but I have in my mind some

confused notion of another method, and can never admit this.

Then I heard someone who had a book of Anaxagoras, as he said, out of which he read that mind was the disposer and cause of all, and I was quite delighted at the notion of this, which appeared admirable, and I said to myself: If mind is the disposer, mind will dispose all for the best, and put each particular in the best place; and I argued that if anyone desired to find out the cause of the generation or destruction or existence of anything, he must find out what state of being or suffering or doing was best for that thing, and therefore a man had only to consider the best for himself and others, and then he would also know the worse, for that the same science comprised both. And I rejoiced to think that I had found in Anaxagoras a teacher of the causes of existence such as I desired, and I imagined that he would tell me first whether the earth is flat or round; and then he would further explain the cause and the necessity of this, and would teach me the nature of the best and show that this was best; and if he said that the earth was in the centre, he would explain that this position was the best, and I should be satisfied if this were shown to me, and not want any other sort of cause. And I thought that I would then go and ask him about the sun and moon and stars, and that he would explain to me their comparative swiftness, and their returnings and various states, and how their several affections, active and passive, were all for the best. For I could not imagine that when he spoke of mind as the disposer of them, he would give any other account of their being as they are, except that this was best; and I thought when he had explained to me in detail the cause of each and the cause of all, he would go on to explain to me what was best for each and what was best for all. I had hopes which I would not have sold for much, and I seized the books and read them as fast as I could in my eagerness to know the better and the worse.

What hopes I had formed, and how grievously was I disappointed! As I proceeded, I found my philosopher altogether forsaking mind or any other principle of order, but having recourse to air, and ether, and water, and other eccentricities. I might compare him to a person who began by maintaining generally that mind is the cause of the actions of Socrates, but who, when he endeavored to explain the causes of my several actions in detail, went on to show that I sit here because my body is made up of bones and muscles; and the bones, as he would say, are hard and have ligaments which divide them, and the muscles are elastic, and they cover the bones, which have also a covering or environment of flesh and skin which contains them; and as the bones are lifted at their joints by the contraction or relaxation of the muscles, I am able to bend my limbs, and this is why I am sitting here in a curved posture: that is what he would say, and he would have a similar explanation of my talking to you, which he would attribute to sound, and air, and hearing, and he would assign ten thousand other causes of the same sort, forgetting to mention the true cause, which is that the Athenians have thought fit to condemn me, and accordingly I have thought it better and more right to remain here and undergo my sentence; for I am inclined to think that these muscles and bones of mine would have gone off to Megara or Boeotia—by the dog of Egypt they would, if they had been guided only by their own idea of what was best, and if I had not chosen as the better and nobler part, instead of playing truant and running away, to undergo any punishment which the State inflicts. There is surely a strange confusion of causes and conditions in all this. It may be said, indeed, that without bones and muscles and the other parts of the body I cannot execute my purposes. But to say that I do as I do because of them, and that this is the way in which mind acts, and not from the choice of the best, is a very careless and idle mode of speaking. I wonder that they cannot distinguish the cause from the condition, which the many, feeling about in the dark, are always mistaking and misnaming. And thus one man makes a vortex all round and steadies the earth by the heaven; another gives the air as a support to the earth, which is a sort of broad trough. Any power which in disposing them as they are disposes them for the best never enters into their minds, nor do they imagine that there is any superhuman strength in that; they rather expect to find another Atlas of the world who is stronger and more everlasting and more containing than the good is, and are clearly of opinion that the obligatory and containing power of the good is as nothing; and yet this is the principle which I would fain learn if anyone would teach me. But as I have

failed either to discover myself or to learn of anyone else, the nature of the best, I will exhibit to you, if you like, what I have found to be the second best mode of inquiring into the cause.

I should very much like to hear that, he replied.

Socrates proceeded: I thought that as I had failed in the contemplation of true existence, I ought to be careful that I did not lose the eye of my soul; as people may injure their bodily eye by observing and gazing on the sun during an eclipse, unless they take the precaution of only looking at the image reflected in the water, or in some similar medium. That occurred to me, and I was afraid that my soul might be blinded altogether if I looked at things with my eyes or tried by the help of the senses to apprehend them. And I thought that I had better have recourse to ideas, and seek in them the truth of existence. I dare say that the simile is not perfect—for I am very far from admitting that he who contemplates existence through the medium of ideas, sees them only "through a glass darkly," any more than he who sees them in their working and effects. However, this was the method which I adopted: I first assumed some principle which I judged to be the strongest, and then I affirmed as true whatever seemed to agree with this, whether relating to the cause or to anything else; and that which disagreed I regarded as untrue. But I should like to explain my meaning clearly, as I do not think that you understand me.

No, indeed, replied Cebes, not very well.

There is nothing new, he said, in what I am about to tell you; but only what I have been always and everywhere repeating in the previous discussion and on other occasions: I want to show you the nature of that cause which has occupied my thoughts, and I shall have to go back to those familiar words which are in the mouth of everyone, and first of all assume that there is an absolute beauty and goodness and greatness, and the like; grant me this, and I hope to be able to show you the nature of the cause, and to prove the immortality of the soul.

Cebes said: You may proceed at once with the proof, as I readily grant you this.

Well, he said, then I should like to know whether you agree with me in the next step; for I cannot help thinking that if there be anything beautiful other than absolute beauty, that can only be beautiful in as far as it partakes of absolute beauty—and this I should say of everything. Do you agree in this notion of the cause?

Yes, he said, I agree.

He proceeded: I know nothing and can understand nothing of any other of those wise causes which are alleged; and if a person says to me that the bloom of color, or form, or anything else of that sort is a source of beauty, I leave all that, which is only confusing to me, and simply and singly, and perhaps foolishly, hold and am assured in my own mind that nothing makes a thing beautiful but the presence and participation of beauty in whatever way or manner obtained; for as to the manner I am uncertain, but I stoutly contend that by beauty all beautiful things become beautiful. That appears to me to be the only safe answer that I can give, either to myself or to any other, and to that I cling, in the persuasion that I shall never be overthrown, and that I may safely answer to myself or any other that by beauty beautiful things become beautiful. Do you not agree to that?

Yes, I agree.

And that by greatness only great things become great and greater, and by smallness the less becomes less.

True.

Then if a person remarks that A is taller by a head than B, and B less by a head than A, you would refuse to admit this, and would stoutly contend that what you mean is only that the greater is greater by, and by reason of, greatness, and the less is less only by, or by reason of, smallness; and thus you would avoid the danger of saying that the greater is greater and the less by the measure of the head, which is the same in both, and would also avoid the monstrous absurdity of supposing that the greater man is greater by reason of the head, which is small. Would you not be afraid of that?

Indeed, I should, said Cebes, laughing.

In like manner you would be afraid to say that ten exceeded eight by, and by reason of, two; but would say by, and by reason of, number; or that two cubits exceed one cubit not by a half, but by magnitude?—that is what you would say, for there is the same danger in both cases.

Very true, he said.

Again, would you not be cautious of affirming that the addition of one to one, or the division of one, is the cause of two? And you would loudly asseverate that you know of no way in which anything comes into existence except by participation in its own proper essence, and consequently, as far as you know, the only cause of two is the participation in duality; that is the way to make two, and the participation in one is the way to make one. You would say: I will let alone puzzles of division and addition—wiser heads than mine may answer them; inexperienced as I am, and ready to start, as the proverb says, at my own shadow, I cannot afford to give up the sure ground of a principle. And if anyone assails you there, you would not mind him, or answer him until you had seen whether the consequences which follow agree with one another or not, and when you are further required to give an explanation of this principle, you would go on to assume a higher principle, and the best of the higher ones, until you found a resting-place; but you would not refuse the principle and the consequences in your reasoning like the Eristics—at least if you wanted to discover real existence. Not that this confusion signifies to them who never care or think about the matter at all, for they have the wit to be well pleased with themselves, however great may be the turmoil of their ideas. But you, if you are a philosopher, will, I believe, do as I say.

What you say is most true, said Simmias and Cebes, both speaking at once.

ECH.: Yes, Phaedo; and I don't wonder at their assenting. Anyone who has the least sense will acknowledge the wonderful clearness of Socrates' reasoning.

PHAED.: Certainly, Echecrates; and that was the feeling of the whole company at the time.

ECH.: Yes, and equally of ourselves, who were not of the company, and are now listening to your recital. But what followed?

PHAED.: After all this was admitted, and they had agreed about the existence of ideas and the participation in them of the other things which derive their names from them, Socrates, if I remember rightly, said:

This is your way of speaking; and yet when you say that Simmias is greater than Socrates and less than Phaedo, do you not predicate of Simmias both greatness and smallness?

Yes, I do.

But still you allow that Simmias does not really exceed Socrates, as the words may seem to imply, because he is Simmias, but by reason of the size which he has; just as Simmias does not exceed Socrates because he is Simmias, any more than because Socrates is Socrates, but because he has smallness when compared with the greatness of Simmias?

True.

And if Phaedo exceeds him in size, this is not because Phaedo is Phaedo, but because Phaedo has greatness relatively to Simmias, who is comparatively smaller?

That is true.

And therefore Simmias is said to be great, and is also said to be small, because he is in a mean between them, exceeding the smallness of the one by his greatness, and allowing the greatness of the other to exceed his smallness. He added, laughing, I am speaking like a book, but I believe that what I am saying is true.

Simmias assented to this.

The reason why I say this is that I want you to agree with me in thinking, not only that absolute greatness will never be great and also small, but that greatness in us or in the concrete will never admit the small or admit of being exceeded: instead of this, one of two things will happen—either the greater will fly or retire before the opposite, which is the less, or at the advance of the less will cease to exist; but will not, if allowing or admitting smallness, be changed by that; even as I, having received and admitted smallness when compared with Simmias, remain just as I was, and am the same small person. And as the idea of greatness cannot condescend ever to be or become small, in like manner the smallness in us cannot be or become great; nor can any other opposite which remains the same ever be or become its own opposite, but either passes away or perishes in the change.

That, replied Cebes, is quite my notion.

One of the company, though I do not exactly remember which of them, on hearing this, said: By Heaven, is not this the direct contrary of what was admitted before—that out of the greater came the less and out of the less the greater, and that opposites are simply generated from opposites; whereas now this seems to be utterly denied.

Socrates inclined his head to the speaker and listened. I like your courage, he said, in reminding us of this. But you do not observe that there is a difference in the two cases. For then we were speaking of opposites in the concrete, and now of the essential opposite which, as is affirmed, neither in us nor in nature can ever be at variance with itself: then, my friend, we were speaking of things in which opposites are inherent and which are called after them, but now about the opposites which are inherent in them and which give their name to them; these essential opposites will never, as we maintain, admit of generation into or out of one another. At the same time, turning to Cebes, he said: Were you at all disconcerted, Cebes, at our friend's objection?

That was not my feeling, said Cebes; and yet I cannot deny that I am apt to be disconcerted.

Then we are agreed after all, said Socrates, that the opposite will never in any case be opposed to itself?

To that we are quite agreed, he replied.

Yet once more let me ask you to consider the question from another point of view, and see whether you agree with me: There is a thing which you term heat, and another thing which you term cold?

Certainly.

But are they the same as fire and snow?

Most assuredly not.

Heat is not the same as fire, nor is cold the same as snow?

No.

And yet you will surely admit, that when snow, as before said, is under the influence of heat, they will not remain snow and heat; but at the advance of the heat the snow will either retire or perish?

Very true, he replied.

And the fire too at the advance of the cold will either retire or perish; and when the fire is under the influence of the cold, they will not remain, as before, fire and cold.

That is true, he said.

And in some cases the name of the idea is not confined to the idea; but anything else which, not being the idea, exists only in the form of the idea, may also lay claim to it. I will try to make this clearer by an example: The odd number is always called by the name of odd?

Very true.

But is this the only thing which is called odd? Are there not other things which have their own name, and yet are called odd, because, although not the same as oddness, they are never without oddness?—that is what I mean to ask—whether numbers such as the number three are not of the class of odd. And there are many other examples: would you not say, for example, that three may be called by its proper name, and also be called odd, which is not the same with three? and this may be said not only of three but also of five, and every alternate number—each of them without being oddness is odd, and in the same way two and four, and the whole series of alternate numbers, has every number even, without being evenness. Do you admit that?

Yes, he said, how can I deny that?

Then now mark the point at which I am aiming: not only do essential opposites exclude one another, but also concrete things, which, although not in themselves opposed, contain opposites; these, I say, also reject the idea which is opposed to that which is contained in them, and at the advance of that they either perish or withdraw. There is the number three for example; will not that endure annihilation or anything sooner than be converted into an even number, remaining three?

Very true, said Cebes.

And yet, he said, the number two is certainly not opposed to the number three?

It is not.

Then not only do opposite ideas repel the advance of one another, but also there are other things which repel the approach of opposites.

That is quite true, he said.

Suppose, he said, that we endeavor, if possible, to determine what these are.

By all means.

Are they not, Cebes, such as compel the things of which they have possession, not only to take their own form, but also the form of some opposite?

What do you mean?

I mean, as I was just now saying, and have no need to repeat to you, that those things which are possessed by the number three must not only be three in number, but must also be odd.

Quite true.

And on this oddness, of which the number three has the impress, the opposite idea will never intrude?

No.

And this impress was given by the odd principle?

Yes.

And to the odd is opposed the even?

True.

Then the idea of the even number will never arrive at three?

No.

Then three has no part in the even?

None.

Then the triad or number three is uneven?

Very true.

To return then to my distinction of natures which are not opposites, and yet do not admit opposites: as, in this instance, three, although not opposed to the even, does not any the more admit of the even, but always brings the opposite into play on the other side; or as two does not receive the odd, or fire the cold—from these examples (and there are many more of them) perhaps you may be able to arrive at the general conclusion that not only opposites will not receive opposites, but also that nothing which brings the opposite will admit the opposite of that which it brings in that to which it is brought. And here let me recapitulate—for there is no harm in repetition. The number five will not admit the nature of the even, any more than ten, which is the double of five, will admit the nature of the odd—the double, though not strictly opposed to the odd, rejects the odd altogether. Nor again will parts in the ratio 3:2, nor any fraction in which there is a half, nor again in which there is a third, admit the notion of the whole, although they are not opposed to the whole. You will agree to that?

Yes, he said, I entirely agree and go along with you in that.

And now, he said, I think that I may begin again; and to the question which I am about to ask I will beg you to give not the old safe answer, but another, of which I will offer you an example; and I hope that you will find in what has been just said another foundation which is as safe. I mean that if anyone asks you "what that is, the inherence of which makes the body hot," you will reply not heat (this is what I call the safe and stupid answer), but fire, a far better answer, which we are now in a condition to give. Or if anyone asks you "'why a body is diseased," you will not say from disease, but from fever; and instead of saying that oddness is the cause of odd numbers, you will say that the monad is the cause of them: and so of things in general, as I dare say that you will understand sufficiently without my adducing any further examples.

Yes, he said, I quite understand you.

Tell me, then, what is that the inherence of which will render the body alive?

The soul, he replied.

And is this always the case?

Yes, he said, of course.

Then whatever the soul possesses, to that she comes bearing life?

Yes, certainly.

And is there any opposite to life?

There is, he said.

And what is that?

Death.

Then the soul, as has been acknowledged, will never receive the opposite of what she brings. And now, he said, what did we call that principle which repels the even?

The odd.

And that principle which repels the musical, or the just?

The unmusical, he said, and the unjust.

And what do we call the principle which does not admit of death?

The immortal, he said.

And does the soul admit of death?

No.

Then the soul is immortal?

Yes, he said.

And may we say that this is proven?

Yes, abundantly proven, Socrates, he replied.

And supposing that the odd were imperishable, must not three be imperishable?

Of course.

And if that which is cold were imperishable, when the warm principle came attacking the snow, must not the snow have retired whole and unmelted—for it could never have perished, nor could it have remained and admitted the heat?

True, he said.

Again, if the uncooling or warm principle were imperishable, the fire when assailed by cold would not have perished or have been extinguished, but would have gone away unaffected?

Certainly, he said.

And the same may be said of the immortal: if the immortal is also imperishable, the soul when attacked by death cannot perish; for the preceding argument shows that the soul will not admit of death, or ever be dead, any more than three or the odd number will admit of the even, or fire or the heat in the fire, of the cold. Yet a person may say: "But although the odd will not become even at the approach of the even, why may not the odd perish and the even take the place of the odd?" Now to him who makes this objection, we cannot answer that the odd principle is imperishable; for this has not been acknowledged, but if this had been acknowledged, there would have been no difficulty in contending that at the approach of the even the odd principle and the number three took up their departure; and the same argument would have held good of fire and heat and any other thing.

Very true.

And the same may be said of the immortal: if the immortal is also imperishable, then the soul will be imperishable as well as immortal; but if not, some other proof of her imperishableness will have to be given.

No other proof is needed, he said; for if the immortal, being eternal, is liable to perish, then nothing is imperishable.

Yes, replied Socrates, all men will agree that God, and the essential form of life, and the immortal in general, will never perish.

Yes, all men, he said—that is true; and what is more, gods, if I am not mistaken, as well as men.

Seeing then that the immortal is indestructible, must not the soul, if she is immortal, be also imperishable?

Most certainly.

Then when death attacks a man, the mortal portion of him may be supposed to die, but the immortal goes out of the way of death and is preserved safe and sound?

True.

Then, Cebes, beyond question the soul is immortal and imperishable, and our souls will truly exist in another world!

I am convinced, Socrates, said Cebes, and have nothing more to object; but if my friend Simmias, or anyone else, has any further objection, he had better speak out, and not keep silence, since I do not know how there can ever be a more fitting time to which he can defer the discussion, if there is anything which he wants to say or have said.

But I have nothing more to say, replied Simmias; nor do I see any room for uncertainty, except that which arises necessarily out of the greatness of the subject and the feebleness of man, and which I cannot help feeling.

Yes, Simmias, replied Socrates, that is well said: and more than that, first principles, even if they appear certain, should be carefully considered; and when they are satisfactorily ascertained, then, with a sort of hesitating confidence in human reason, you may, I think, follow the course of the argument; and if this is clear, there will be no need for any further inquiry.

That, he said, is true. . . .

12. *On Substance*

ARISTOTLE

Aristotle entered Plato's Academy when he was seventeen and remained there as a student and then teacher for twenty years. Naturally, Plato had an enormous influence on Aristotle's thought, but like the brilliant student he was, Aristotle came to repudiate some central theses of his teacher. For Aristotle, ordinary individual things (what he calls "primary substances") are fundamental realities—not Plato's Forms.

Plato's distinction between an individual thing and its qualities is essential to his account of change, but he has little confidence that changing things can be known the way the Forms can. Aristotle, on the other hand, says a great deal about particular things. In the *Categories*, Aristotle approaches the question What is a substance? through a consideration of the role that words referring to individual things play in ordinary language. Thus, he distinguishes between primary substances (this man, this horse), which are subjects but never predicates, and secondary substances (man, horse), which can be predicated of a subject. He further claims the most distinctive mark of primary substance is that "while remaining numerically one and the same, it is capable of admitting contrary qualities." In *On Generation and Corruption*, Aristotle explains the difference between a substance coming to be (or ceasing to be) and its coming to have different qualities. In *Metaphysics Z*, he analyzes substances in a way that sheds light on questions about their identity.

Categories

Things are said to be named 'equivocally' when, though they have a common name, the definition corresponding with the name differs for each. Thus, a real man and a figure in a picture can both lay claim to the name 'animal'; yet these are equivocally so named, for, though they have a common name, the definition corresponding with

From *The Basic Works of Aristotle* (1941), edited by Richard McKeon, pp. 7–14, 45–48, 484–485, 783–795, 964–969. Reprinted by permission of Oxford University Press.

the name differs for each. For should any one define in what sense each is an animal, his definition in the one case will be appropriate to that case only.

On the other hand, things are said to be named 'univocally' which have both the name and the definition answering to the name in common. A man and an ox are both 'animal', and these are univocally so named, inasmuch as not only the name, but also the definition, is the same in both cases: for if a man should state in what sense each is an animal, the statement in the one case would be identical with that in the other.

Things are said to be named 'derivatively', which derive their name from some other name, but differ from it in termination. Thus the grammarian derives his name from the word 'grammar', and the courageous man from the word 'courage'.

Forms of speech are either simple or composite. Examples of the latter are such expressions as 'the man runs', 'the man wins'; of the former 'man', 'ox', 'runs', 'wins'.

Of things themselves some are predicable of a subject, and are never present in a subject. Thus 'man' is predicable of the individual man, and is never present in a subject.

By being 'present in a subject' I do not mean present as parts are present in a whole, but being incapable of existence apart from the said subject.

Some things, again, are present in a subject, but are never predicable of a subject. For instance, a certain point of grammatical knowledge is present in the mind, but is not predicable of any subject; or again, a certain whiteness may be present in the body (for colour requires a material basis), yet it is never predicable of anything.

Other things, again, are both predicable of a subject and present in a subject. Thus while knowledge is present in the human mind, it is predicable of grammar.

There is, lastly, a class of things which are neither present in a subject nor predicable of a subject, such as the individual man or the individual horse. But, to speak more generally, that which is individual and has the character of a unit is never predicable of a subject. Yet in some cases there is nothing to prevent such being present in a subject. Thus a certain point of grammatical knowledge is present in a subject.

When one thing is predicated of another, all that which is predicable of the predicate will be predicable also of the subject. Thus 'man' is predicated of the individual man; but 'animal' is predicated of 'man'; it will, therefore, be predicable of the individual man also: for the individual man is both 'man' and 'animal'.

If genera are different and coordinate, their differentiae are themselves different in kind. Take as an instance the genus 'animal' and the genus 'knowledge'. 'With feet', 'two-footed', 'winged', 'aquatic', are differentiae of 'animal'; the species of knowledge are not distinguished by the same differentiae. One species of knowledge does not differ from another in being 'two-footed'.

But where one genus is subordinate to another, there is nothing to prevent their having the same differentiae: for the greater class is predicated of the lesser, so that all the differentiae of the predicate will be differentiae also of the subject.

Expressions which are in no way composite signify substance, quantity, quality, relation, place, time, position, state, action, or affection. To sketch my meaning roughly, examples of substance are 'man' or 'the horse', of quantity, such terms as 'two cubits long' or 'three cubits long', of quality, such attributes as 'white', 'grammatical'. 'Double', 'half', 'greater', fall under the category of relation; 'in the market place', 'in the Lyceum', under that of place; 'yesterday', 'last year', under that of time. 'Lying', 'sitting', are terms indicating position; 'shod', 'armed', state; 'to lance', 'to cauterize', action; 'to be lanced', 'to be cauterized', affection.

No one of these terms, in and by itself, involves an affirmation; it is by the combination of such terms that positive or negative statements arise. For every assertion must, as is admitted, be either true or false, whereas expressions which are not in any way composite, such as 'man', 'white', 'runs', 'wins', cannot be either true or false.

Substance, in the truest and primary and most definite sense of the word, is that which is neither predicable of a subject nor present in a subject; for instance, the individual man or horse. But in a secondary sense those things are called substances within which, as species, the primary substances are included; also those which, as genera, include the species. For instance, the individual man is included in the species 'man', and the genus to which the species belongs is 'animal'; these, there-fore—that is to say, the species 'man' and the genus 'animal'—are termed secondary substances.

It is plain from what has been said that both the name and the definition of the predicate must be predicable of the subject. For instance, 'man' is predicated of the individual man. Now in this case the name of the species 'man' is applied to the individual, for we use the term 'man' in describing the individual; and the definition of 'man' will also be predicated of the individual man, for the indi-vidual man is both man and animal. Thus, both the name and the definition of the species are predicable of the individual.

With regard, on the other hand, to those things which are present in a subject, it is generally the case that neither their name nor their defini-tion is predicable of that in which they are present. Though, however, the definition is never predica-ble, there is nothing in certain cases to prevent the name being used. For instance, 'white' being pres-ent in a body is predicated of that in which it is present, for a body is called white: the definition, however, of the colour 'white' is never predicable of the body.

Everything except primary substances is either predicable of a primary substance or present in a primary substance. This becomes evident by refer-ence to particular instances which occur. 'Animal' is predicated of the species 'man', therefore of the individual man, for if there were no individual man of whom it could be predicated, it could not be predicated of the species 'man' at all. Again, colour is present in body, therefore in individual bodies, for if there were no individual body in which it was present, it could not be present in body at all. Thus everything except primary sub-stances is either predicated of primary substances, or is present in them, and if these last did not exist, it would be impossible for anything else to exist.

Of secondary substances, the species is more truly substance than the genus, being more nearly related to primary substance. For if any one should render an account of what a primary sub-stance is, he would render a more instructive account, and one more proper to the subject, by stating the species than by stating the genus. Thus, he would give a more instructive account of an individual man by stating that he was man than by stating that he was animal, for the former

description is peculiar to the individual in a greater degree, while the latter is too general. Again, the man who gives an account of the nature of an individual tree will give a more instructive account by mentioning the species 'tree' than by mentioning the genus 'plant'.

Moreover, primary substances are most prop-erly called substances in virtue of the fact that they are the entities which underlie everything else, and that everything else is either predicated of them or present in them. Now the same relation which subsists between primary substance and everything else subsists also between the species and the genus: for the species is to the genus as subject is to predicate, since the genus is predicated of the species, whereas the species cannot be predicated of the genus. Thus we have a second ground for asserting that the species is more truly substance than the genus.

Of species themselves, except in the case of such as are genera, no one is more truly substance than another. We should not give a more appro-priate account of the individual man by stating the species to which he belonged, than we should of an individual horse by adopting the same method of definition. In the same way, of primary sub-stances, no one is more truly substance than another; an individual man is not more truly sub-stance than an individual ox.

It is, then, with good reason that of all that remains, when we exclude primary substances, we concede to species and genera alone the name 'secondary substance', for these alone of all the predicates convey a knowledge of primary sub-stance. For it is by stating the species or the genus that we appropriately define any individual man; and we shall make our definition more exact by stating the former than by stating the latter. All other things that we state, such as that he is white, that he runs, and so on, are irrelevant to the defi-nition. Thus it is just that these alone, apart from primary substances, should be called substances.

Further, primary substances are most properly so called, because they underlie and are the sub-jects of everything else. Now the same relation that subsists between primary substance and every-thing else subsists also between the species and the genus to which the primary substance belongs, on the one hand, and every attribute which is not included within these, on the other. For these are the subjects of all such. If we call an individual man 'skilled in grammar', the predicate is applicable also to the species and to the genus to which he belongs. This law holds good in all cases.

It is a common characteristic of all substance that it is never present in a subject. For primary substance is neither present in a subject nor predicated of a subject; while, with regard to secondary substances, it is clear from the following arguments (apart from others) that they are not present in a subject. For 'man' is predicated of the individual man, but is not present in any subject: for manhood is not present in the individual man. In the same way, 'animal' is also predicated of the individual man, but is not present in him. Again, when a thing is present in a subject, though the name may quite well be applied to that in which it is present, the definition cannot be applied. Yet of secondary substances, not only the name, but also the definition, applies to the subject: we should use both the definition of the species and that of the genus with reference to the individual man. Thus substance cannot be present in a subject.

Yet this is not peculiar to substance, for it is also the case that differentiae cannot be present in subjects. The characteristics 'terrestrial' and 'two-footed' are predicated of the species 'man', but not present in it. For they are not *in* man. Moreover, the definition of the differentia may be predicated of that of which the differentia itself is predicated. For instance, if the characteristic 'terrestrial' is predicated of the species 'man', the definition also of that characteristic may be used to form the predicate of the species 'man': for 'man' is terrestrial.

The fact that the parts of substances appear to be present in the whole, as in a subject, should not make us apprehensive lest we should have to admit that such parts are not substances: for in explaining the phrase 'being present in a subject', we stated that we meant 'otherwise than as parts of a whole'.

It is the mark of substances and of differentiae that, in all propositions of which they form the predicate, they are predicated univocally. For all such propositions have for their subject either the individual or the species. It is true that, inasmuch as primary substance is not predicable of anything, it can never form the predicate of any proposition.

But of secondary substances, the species is predicated of the individual, the genus both of the species and of the individual. Similarly the differentiae are predicated of the species and of the individuals. Moreover, the definition of the species and that of the genus are applicable to the primary substance, and that of the genus to the species. For all that is predicated of the predicate will be predicated also of the subject. Similarly, the definition of the differentiae will be applicable to the species and to the individuals. But it was stated above that the word 'univocal' was applied to those things which had both name and definition in common. It is, therefore, established that in every proposition, of which either substance or a differentia forms the predicate, these are predicated univocally.

All substance appears to signify that which is individual. In the case of primary substance this is indisputably true, for the thing is a unit. In the case of secondary substances, when we speak, for instance, of 'man' or 'animal', our form of speech gives the impression that we are here also indicating that which is individual, but the impression is not strictly true; for a secondary substance is not an individual, but a class with a certain qualification; for it is not one and single as a primary substance is; the words 'man', 'animal', are predicable of more than one subject.

Yet species and genus do not merely indicate quality, like the term 'white'; 'white' indicates quality and nothing further, but species and genus determine the quality with reference to a substance: they signify substance qualitatively differentiated. The determinate qualification covers a larger field in the case of the genus than in that of the species: he who uses the word 'animal' is herein using a word of wider extension than he who uses the word 'man'.

Another mark of substance is that it has no contrary. What could be the contrary of any primary substance, such as the individual man or animal? It has none. Nor can the species or the genus have a contrary. Yet this characteristic is not peculiar to substance, but is true of many other things, such as quantity. There is nothing that forms the contrary of 'two cubits long' or of 'three cubits long', or of 'ten', or of any such term. A man may contend that 'much' is the contrary of 'little', or 'great' of 'small', but of definite quantitative terms no contrary exists.

Substance, again, does not appear to admit of variation of degree. I do not mean by this that one substance cannot be more or less truly substance than another, for it has already been stated that this is the case; but that no single substance admits of varying degrees within itself. For instance, one particular substance, 'man', cannot be more or less man either than himself at some other time or than some other man. One man cannot be more man than another, as that which is white may be more or less white than some other white object, or as that which is beautiful may be more or less beautiful than some other beautiful object. The same quality, moreover, is said to subsist in a thing in varying degrees at different times. A body, being white, is said to be whiter at one time than it was before, or, being warm, is said to be warmer or less warm than at some other time. But substance is not said to be more or less that which it is: a man is not more truly a man at one time than he was before, nor is anything, if it is substance, more or less what it is. Substance, then, does not admit of variation of degree.

The most distinctive mark of substance appears to be that, while remaining numerically one and the same, it is capable of admitting contrary qualities. From among things other than substance, we should find ourselves unable to bring forward any which possessed this mark. Thus, one and the same colour cannot be white and black. Nor can the same one action be good and bad: this law holds good with everything that is not substance. But one and the self-same substance, while retaining its identity, is yet capable of admitting contrary qualities. The same individual person is at one time white, at another black, at one time warm, at another cold, at one time good, at another bad. This capacity is found nowhere else, though it might be maintained that a statement or opinion was an exception to the rule. The same statement, it is agreed, can be both true and false. For if the statement 'he is sitting' is true, yet, when the person in question has risen, the same statement will be false. The same applies to opinions. For if any one thinks truly that a person is sitting, yet, when that person has risen, this same opinion, if still held, will be false. Yet although this exception may be allowed, there is, nevertheless, a difference in the manner in which the thing takes place. It is by themselves changing that substances admit contrary qualities. It is thus that that which was hot becomes cold, for it has entered into a different state. Similarly that which was white becomes black, and that which was bad good, by a process of change; and in the same way in all other cases it is by changing that substances are capable of admitting contrary qualities. But statements and opinions themselves remain unaltered in all respects: it is by the alteration in the facts of the case that the contrary quality comes to be theirs. The statement 'he is sitting' remains unaltered, but it is at one time true, at another false, according to circumstances. What has been said of statements applies also to opinions. Thus, in respect of the manner in which the thing takes place, it is the peculiar mark of substance that it should be capable of admitting contrary qualities; for it is by itself changing that it does so.

If, then, a man should make this exception and contend that statements and opinions are capable of admitting contrary qualities, his contention is unsound. For statements and opinions are said to have this capacity, not because they themselves undergo modification, but because this modification occurs in the case of something else. The truth or falsity of a statement depends on facts, and not on any power on the part of the statement itself of admitting contrary qualities. In short, there is nothing which can alter the nature of statements and opinions. As, then, no change takes place in themselves, these cannot be said to be capable of admitting contrary qualities.

But it is by reason of the modification which takes place within the substance itself that a substance is said to be capable of admitting contrary qualities; for a substance admits within itself either disease or health, whiteness or blackness. It is in this sense that it is said to be capable of admitting contrary qualities.

To sum up, it is a distinctive mark of substance, that, while remaining numerically one and the same, it is capable of admitting contrary qualities, the modification taking place through a change in the substance itself.

Let these remarks suffice on the subject of substance.

On Generation and Corruption

So much, then, on these topics. Next we must state what the difference is between coming-to-be and 'alteration'—for we maintain that these changes are distinct from one another.

Since, then, we must distinguish (*a*) the *substratum,* and (*b*) the property whose nature it is to be predicated of the *substratum;* and since change of each of these occurs; there is 'alteration' when the *substratum* is perceptible and persists, but changes in its own properties, the properties in question being opposed to one another either as contraries or as intermediates. The body, e.g., although persisting as the same body, is now healthy and now ill; and the bronze is now spherical and at another time angular, and yet remains the same bronze. But when nothing perceptible persists in its identity as a *substratum,* and the thing changes as a whole (when e.g., the seed as a whole is converted into blood, or water into air, or air as a whole into water), such an occurrence is no longer 'alteration'. It is a coming-to-be of one substance and a passing-away of the other—especially if the change proceeds from an imperceptible something to something perceptible (either to touch or to all the senses), as when water comes-to-be out of, or passes-away into, air: for air is pretty well imperceptible. If, however, in such cases, any property (being one of a pair of contraries) persists, in the thing that has come-to-be, the same as it was in the thing which has passed-away—if, e.g., when water comes-to-be out of air, both are transparent or cold—the *second* thing, into which the *first* changes, must not be a property of this persistent identical something. Otherwise the change will be 'alteration'.

Suppose, e.g., that *the musical man* passed-away and *an unmusical man* came-to-be, and that *the man* persists as something identical. Now, if 'musicalness and unmusicalness' had not been a property essentially inhering in man, these changes would have been a coming-to-be of unmusicalness and a passing-away of musicalness: but in fact 'musicalness and unmusicalness' are a property of the persistent identity, viz. man. (Hence, as regards *man*, these changes are 'modifications'; though, as regards *musical man* and *unmusical*

man, they are a passing-away and a coming-to-be.) Consequently such changes are 'alteration'.

When the change from contrary to contrary is *in quantity,* it is 'growth and diminution'; when it is *in place,* it is 'motion'; when it is in property, i.e., *in quality,* it is 'alteration'; but when nothing persists, of which the resultant is a property (or an 'accident' in any sense of the term), it is 'coming-to-be', and the converse change is 'passing-away'.

'Matter', in the most proper sense of the term is to be identified with the *substratum* which is receptive of coming-to-be and passing-away: but the *substratum* of the remaining kinds of change is also, in a certain sense, 'matter', because all these *substrata* are receptive of 'contrarieties' of some kind. So much, then, as an answer to the questions (i) whether coming-to-be 'is' or 'is not'—i.e., what are the precise conditions of its occurrence—and (ii) what 'alteration' is; but we have still to treat of growth.

Metaphysics Z

There are several senses in which a thing may be said to 'be', as we pointed out previously in our book on the various senses of words; for in one sense the 'being' meant is 'what a thing is' or a 'this', and in another sense it means a quality or quantity or one of the other things that are predicated as these are. While 'being' has all these senses, obviously that which 'is' primarily is the 'what', which indicates the substance of the thing. For when we say of what quality a thing is, we say that it is good or bad, not that it is three cubits long or that it is a man; but when we say *what* it is, we do not say 'white' or 'hot' or 'three cubits long', but 'a man' or 'a god'. And all other things are said to be because they are, some of them, quantities of that which *is* in this primary sense, others qualities of it, others affections of it, and others some other determination of it. And so one might even raise the question whether the words 'to walk', 'to be healthy', 'to sit' imply that each of these things is existent, and similarly in any other case of this sort; for none of them is either self-subsistent or capable of being separated from substance, but rather, if anything, it is that which walks or sits or is healthy that is an existent thing.

Now these are seen to be more real because there is something definite which underlies them (i.e., the substance or individual), which is implied in such a predicate; for we never use the word 'good' or 'sitting' without implying this. Clearly then it is in virtue of this category that each of the others also *is*. Therefore that which is primarily, i.e., not in a qualified sense but without qualification, must be substance.

Now there are several senses in which a thing is said to be first; yet substance is first in every sense—(1) in definition, (2) in order of knowledge, (3) in time. For (3) of the other categories none can exist independently, but only substance. And (1) in definition also this is first; for in the definition of each term the definition of its substance must be present. And (2) we think we know each thing most fully, when we know what it is, e.g., what man is or what fire is, rather than when we know its quality, its quantity, or its place; since we know each of these predicates also, only when we know *what* the quantity or the quality *is*.

And indeed the question which was raised of old and is raised now and always, and is always the subject of doubt, viz. what being is, is just the question, what is substance? For it is this that some assert to be one, others more than one, and that some assert to be limited in number, others unlimited. And so we also must consider chiefly and primarily and almost exclusively what that is which *is* in *this* sense.

Substance is thought to belong most obviously to bodies; and so we say that not only animals and plants and their parts are substances, but also natural bodies such as fire and water and earth and everything of the sort, and all things that are either parts of these or composed of these (either of parts or of the whole bodies), e.g., the physical universe and its parts, stars and moon and sun. But whether these alone are substances, or there are also others, or only some of these, or others as well, or none of these but only some other things, are substances, must be considered. Some think the limits of body, i.e., surface, line, point, and unit, are substances, and more so than body or the solid.

Further, some do not think there is anything substantial besides sensible things, but others think there are eternal substances which are more in number and more real; e.g., Plato posited two kinds of substance—the Forms and the objects of mathe-matics—as well as a third kind, viz. the substance of sensible bodies. And Speusippus made still more kinds of substance, beginning with the One, and assuming principles for each kind of substance, one for numbers, another for spatial magnitudes, and then another for the soul; and by going on in this way he multiplies the kinds of substance. And some say Forms and numbers have the same nature, and the other things come after them—lines and planes—until we come to the substance of the material universe and to sensible bodies.

Regarding these matters, then, we must inquire which of the common statements are right and which are not right, and what substances there are, and whether there are or are not any besides sensible substances, and how sensible substances exist, and whether there is a substance capable of separate existence (and if so why and how) or no such substance, apart from sensible substances; and we must first sketch the nature of substance.

The word 'substance' is applied, if not in more senses, still at least to four main objects; for both the essence and the universal and the genus are thought to be the substance of each thing, and fourthly the substratum. Now the substratum is that of which everything else is predicated, while it is itself not predicated of anything else. And so we must first determine the nature of this; for that which underlies a thing primarily is thought to be in the truest sense its substance. And in one sense matter is said to be of the nature of substratum, in another, shape, and in a third, the compound of these. (By the matter I mean, for instance, the bronze, by the shape the pattern of its form, and by the compound of these the statue, the concrete whole.) Therefore if the form is prior to the matter and more real, it will be prior also to the compound of both, for the same reason.

We have now outlined the nature of substance, showing that it is that which is not predicated of a stratum, but of which all else is predicated. But we must not merely state the matter thus; for this is not enough. The statement itself is obscure, and further, on this view, *matter* becomes substance. For if this is not substance, it baffles us to say what else is. When all else is stripped off evidently nothing but matter remains. For while the rest are affections, products, and potencies of bodies, length, breadth, and depth are quantities and not substances (for a quantity is not a substance), but the substance is rather that to which these belong primarily. But when length and breadth and depth are taken away we see nothing left unless there is something that is bounded by these; so that to those who consider the question thus matter alone must seem to be substance. By matter I mean that which in itself is neither a particular thing nor of a certain quantity nor assigned to any other of the categories by which being is determined. For there is something of which each of these is predicated, whose being is different from that of each of the predicates (for the predicates other than substance are predicated of substance, while substance is predicated of matter). Therefore the ultimate substratum is of itself neither a particular thing nor of a particular quantity nor otherwise positively characterized; nor yet is it the negations of these, for negations also will belong to it only by accident.

If we adopt this point of view, then, it follows that matter is substance. But this is impossible; for both separability and 'thisness' are thought to belong chiefly to substance. And so form and the compound of form and matter would be thought to be substance, rather than matter. The substance compounded of both, i.e., of matter and shape, may be dismissed; for it is posterior and its nature is obvious. And matter also is in a sense manifest. But we must inquire into the third kind of substance; for this is the most perplexing.

Some of the sensible substances are generally admitted to be substances, so that we must look first among these. For it is an advantage to advance to that which is more knowable. For learning proceeds for all in this way—through that which is less knowable by nature to that which is more knowable; and just as in conduct our task is to start from what is good for each and make what is without qualification good for each, so it is our task to start from what is more knowable to oneself and make what is knowable by nature knowable to oneself. Now what is knowable and primary for particular sets of people is often knowable to a very small extent, and has little or nothing of reality. But yet one must start from that which is barely knowable but knowable to oneself, and try to know what is knowable without qualification, passing, as has been said, by way of those very things which one does know.

Since at the start we distinguished the various marks by which we determine substance, and one of these was thought to be the essence, we must investigate this. And first let us make some linguistic remarks about it. The essence of each thing is what it is said to be *propter se*. For being you is not being musical, since you are not by your very nature musical. What, then, you are by your very nature is your essence.

Nor yet is the whole of this the essence of a thing; not that which is *propter se* as white is to a surface, because being a surface is not *identical* with being white. But again the combination of both—'being a white surface'—is not the essence of surface, because 'surface' itself is added. The formula, therefore, in which the term itself is not present but its meaning is expressed, this is the formula of the essence of each thing. Therefore if to be a white surface is to be a smooth surface, to be white and to be smooth are one and the same.

But since there are also compounds answering to the other categories (for there is a substratum for each category, e.g., for quality, quantity, time, place, and motion), we must inquire whether there is a formula of the essence of each of them, i.e., whether to these compounds also there belongs an essence, e.g., to 'white man'. Let the compound be denoted by 'cloak'. What is the essence of cloak? But, it may be said, this also is not a *propter se* expression. We reply that there are just two ways in which a predicate may fail to be true of a subject *propter se*, and one of these results from the addition, and the other from the omission, of a determinant. *One* kind of predicate is not *propter se* because the term that is being defined is combined with another determinant, e.g., if in defining the essence of white one were to state the formula of white *man;* the *other* because in the subject another determinant is combined with that which is expressed in the formula, e.g., of 'cloak' meant 'white man', and one were to define cloak as white; white man is white indeed, but its essence is not to be white.

But is being-a-cloak an essence at all? Probably not. For the essence is precisely what something *is;* but when an attribute is asserted of a subject other than itself, the complex is not precisely what some 'this' *is,* e.g., white man is not precisely what some 'this' *is,* since thisness belongs only to substances. Therefore there is an essence only of those things whose formula is a definition. But we have a definition not where we have a word and a formula identical in meaning (for in that case all formulae or sets of words would be definitions; for there will be some name for any set of words whatever, so that even the *Iliad* will be a definition), but where there is a formula of something primary; and primary things are those which do not imply the predication of one element in them of another element. Nothing, then, which is not a species of a genus will have an *essence*—only species will have it, for these are thought to imply not merely that the subject participates in the attribute and has it as an affection, or has it by accident; but for everything else as well, if it has a name, there will be a *formula of its meaning*—viz., that this attribute belongs to this subject; or instead of a simple formula we shall be able to give a more accurate one; but there will be no definition nor essence.

Or has 'definition', like 'what a thing is', several meanings? 'What a thing is' in one sense means substance and **the** 'this', in another one or other of the predicates, quantity, quality, and the like. For as 'is' belongs to all things, not however in the same sense, but to one sort of thing primarily and to others in a secondary way, so too 'what a thing is' belongs in the simple sense to substance, but in a limited sense to the other categories. For even of a quality we might ask what it is, so that quality also is a 'what a thing is'—not in the simple sense, however, but just as, in the case of that which is not, some say, emphasizing the linguistic form, that that which is not *is*—not *is* simply, but *is* nonexistent; so too with quality.

We must no doubt inquire how we should express ourselves on each point, but certainly not more than how the facts actually stand. And so now also, since it is evident what language we use, essence will belong, just as 'what a thing is' does, primarily and in the simple sense to substance, and in a secondary way to the other categories also— not essence in the simple sense, but the essence of a quality or of a quantity. For it must be either by an equivocation that we say these *are,* or by adding to and taking from the meaning of 'are' (in the way in which that which is not known may be said to be known)—the truth being that we use the word neither ambiguously nor in the same sense, but just as we apply the word 'medical' by virtue

of a *reference* to one and the same thing, not *meaning* one and the same thing, nor yet speaking ambiguously; for a patient and an operation and an instrument are called medical neither by an ambiguity nor with a single meaning, but with reference to a common end. But it does not matter at all in which of the two ways one likes to describe the facts; this is evident, that definition and essence in the primary and simple sense belong to substances. Still they belong to other things as well, only not in the primary sense. For if we suppose this it does not follow that there is a definition of every word which means the same as any formula; it must mean the same as a particular kind of formula; and this condition is satisfied if it is a formula of something which is one, not by continuity like the *Iliad* or the things that are one by being bound together, but in one of the main senses of 'one', which answer to the senses of 'is'; now 'that which is' in one sense denotes a 'this', in another a quantity, in another a quality. And so there can be a formula or definition even of white man, but not in the sense in which there is a definition either of white or of a substance.

It is a difficult question, if one denies that a formula with an added determinant is a definition, whether any of the terms that are not simple but coupled will be definable. For we *must* explain them by adding a determinant. E.g., there is the nose, and concavity, and snubness, which is compounded out of the two by the presence of the one in the other, and it is not by *accident* that the nose has the attribute either of concavity or of snubness, but in virtue of its nature; nor do they attach to it as whiteness does to Callias, or to man (because Callias, who happens to be a man, is white), but as 'male' attaches to animal and 'equal' to quantity, and as all so-called 'attributes *propter se*' attach to their subjects. And such attributes are those in which is involved either the *formula* or the *name* of the subject of the particular attribute, and which cannot be explained without this; e.g., white can be explained apart from man, but not female apart from animal. Therefore there is either no essence and definition of any of these things, or if there is, it is in another sense, as we have said.

But there is also a second difficulty about them. For if snub nose and concave nose are the same thing, snub and concave will be the same thing; but if snub and concave are not the same (because it is impossible to speak of snubness apart from the thing of which it is an attribute *propter se,* for snubness is concavity-*in-a-nose*), either it is impossible to say 'snub nose' or the same thing will have been said twice, concave-nose nose; for snub nose will be concave-nose nose. And so it is absurd that such things should have an essence; if they have, there will be an infinite regress; for in snub-nose nose yet another 'nose' will be involved.

Clearly, then, only substance is definable. For if the other categories also are definable, it must be by addition of a determinant, e.g., the qualitative is defined thus, and so is the odd, for it cannot be defined apart from number; nor can female be defined apart from animal. (When I say 'by addition' I mean the expression in which it turns out that we are saying the same thing twice, as in these instances.) And if this is true, coupled terms also, like 'odd number', will not be definable (but this escapes our notice because our formulae are not accurate). But if these also are definable, either it is in some other way or, as we said, definition and essence must be said to have more than one sense. Therefore in one sense nothing will have a definition and nothing will have an essence, except substances, but in another sense other things will have them. Clearly, then, definition is the formula of the essence, and essence belongs to substances either alone or chiefly and primarily and in the unqualified sense.

We must inquire whether each thing and its essence are the same or different. This is of some use for the inquiry concerning substance; for each thing is thought to be not different from its substance, and the essence is said to be the substance of each thing.

Now in the case of accidental unities the two would be generally thought to be different, e.g., white man would be thought to be different from the essence of white man. For if they are the same, the essence of man and that of white man are also the same; for a man and a white man are the same thing, as people say, so that the essence of white man and that of man would be also the same. But perhaps it does not follow that the essence of accidental unities should be the same as that of the simple terms. For the extreme terms are not in the same way identical with the middle term. But perhaps *this* might be thought to follow, that the extreme

terms, the accidents, should turn out to be the same, e.g., the essence of white and that of musical; but this is not actually thought to be the case.

But in the case of so-called self-subsistent things, is a thing necessarily the same as its essence? E.g., if there are some substances which have no other substances nor entities prior to them—substances such as some assert the Ideas to be?—If the essence of good is to be different from good-itself, and the essence of animal from animal-itself, and the essence of being from being-itself, there will, firstly, be other substances and entities and Ideas besides those which are asserted, and, secondly, these others will be prior substances, if essence is substance. And if the posterior substances and the prior are severed from each other (*a*) there will be no knowledge of the former, and (*b*) the latter will have no being. (By 'severed' I mean, if the good-itself has not the essence of good, and the latter has not the property of being good.) For (*a*) there is knowledge of each thing only when we know its essence. And (*b*) the case is the same for other things as for the good; so that if the essence of good is not good, neither is the essence of reality real, nor the essence of unity one. And all essences alike exist or none of them does; so that if the essence of reality is not real, neither is any of the others. Again, that to which the essence of good does not belong is not good.—The good, then, must be one with the essence of good, and the beautiful with the essence of beauty, and so with all things which do not depend on something else but are self-subsistent and primary. For it is enough if they are this, even if they are not Forms; or rather, perhaps, even if they *are* Forms. (At the same time it is clear that if there are Ideas such as some people say there are, it will not be substratum that is substance; for these must be substances, but not predicable of a substratum; for if they were they would exist only by being participated in.)

Each thing itself, then, and its essence are one and the same in no merely accidental way, as is evident both from the preceding arguments and because to *know* each thing, at least, is just to know its essence, so that even by the exhibition of instances it becomes clear that both must be one.

(But of an accidental term, e.g., 'the musical' or 'the white', since it has two meanings, it is not true to say that it itself is identical with its essence;

for both that to which the accidental quality belongs, and the accidental quality, are white, so that in a sense the accident and its essence are the same, and in a sense they are not; for the essence of white is not the same as the man or the white man, but it is the same as the attribute white.)

The absurdity of the separation would appear also if one were to assign a name to each of the essences; for there would be yet another essence besides the original one, e.g., to the essence of horse there will belong a second essence. Yet why should not some things be their essences from the start, since essence is substance? But indeed not only are a thing and its essence one, but the formula of them is also the same, as is clear even from what has been said; for it is not by accident that the essence of one, and the one, are one. Further, if they are to be different, the process will go on to infinity; for we shall have (1) the essence of one, and (2) the one, so that to terms of the former kind the same argument will be applicable.

Clearly, then, each primary and self-subsistent thing is one and the same as its essence. The sophistical objections to this position, and the question whether Socrates and to be Socrates are the same thing, are obviously answered by the same solution; for there is no difference either in the standpoint from which the question would be asked, or in that from which one could answer it successfully. We have explained, then, in what sense each thing is the same as its essence and in which sense it is not.

Of things that come to be, some come to be by nature, some by art, some spontaneously. Now everything that comes to be comes to be by the agency of something and from something and comes to be something. And the something which I say it comes to be may be found in any category; it may come to be either a 'this' or of some size or of some quality or somewhere.

Now natural comings to be are the comings to be of those things which come to be by nature; and that out of which they come to be is what we call matter; and that by which they come to be is something which exists naturally; and the something which they come to be is a man or a plant or one of the things of this kind, which we say are substances if anything is—all things produced either by nature or by art have matter; for each of

them is capable both of being and of not being, and this capacity is the matter in each—and, in general, both that from which they are produced is nature, and the type according to which they are produced is nature (for that which is produced, e.g., a plant or an animal, has a nature), and so is that by which they are produced—the so-called 'formal' nature, which is specifically the same (though this is in another individual); for man begets man.

Thus, then, are natural products produced; all other productions are called 'makings'. And all makings proceed either from art or from a faculty or from thought. Some of them happen also spontaneously or by luck just as natural products sometimes do; for there also the same things sometimes are produced without seed as well as from seed. Concerning these cases, then, we must inquire later, but from art proceed the things of which the form is in the soul of the artist. (By form I mean the essence of each thing and its primary substance.) For even contraries have in a sense the same form; for the substance of a privation is the opposite substance, e.g., health is the substance of disease (for disease is the absence of health); and health is the formula in the soul or the knowledge of it. The healthy subject is produced as the result of the following train of thought: since *this* is health, if the subject is to be healthy *this* must first be present, e.g., a uniform state of body, and if this is to be present, there must be heat; and the physician goes on thinking thus until he reduces the matter to a final something which he himself can produce. Then the process from this point onward, i.e., the process towards health, is called a 'making'. Therefore it follows that in a sense health comes from health and house from house, that with matter from that without matter; for the medical art and the building art are the form of health and of the house, and when I speak of substance without matter I mean essence.

Of the productions or processes one part is called thinking and the other making—that which proceeds from the starting-point and the form is thinking, and that which proceeds from the final step of the thinking is making. And each of the other, intermediate, things is produced in the same way. I mean, for instance, if the subject is to be healthy his bodily state must be made uniform. What then does being made uniform imply? This or that. And this depends on his being made warm. What does this imply? Something else. And this something is present potentially; and what is present potentially is already in the physician's power.

The active principle then and the starting-point for the process of becoming healthy is, if it happens by art, the form in the soul, and if spontaneously, it is that, whatever it is, which starts the making, for the man who makes by art, as in healing the starting-point is perhaps the production of warmth (and this the physician produces by rubbing). Warmth in the body, then, is either a part of health or is followed (either directly or through several intermediate steps) by something similar which is a part of health; and this, viz. that which produces the part of health, is the limiting-point—and so too with a house (the stones are the limiting-point here) and in all other cases.

Therefore, as the saying goes, it is impossible that anything should be produced if there were nothing existing before. Obviously then some part of the result will pre-exist of necessity; for the matter is a part; for this is present in the process and it is this that becomes something. But is the matter an element even in the *formula?* We certainly describe in both ways what brazen circles are; we describe both the matter by saying it is brass, and the form by saying that it is such and such a figure; and figure is the proximate genus in which it is placed. The brazen circle, then, has its matter *in its formula.*

As for that out of which as matter they are produced, some things are said, when they have been produced, to be not that but 'that-en'; e.g., the statue is not gold but golden. And a healthy man is not said to be that from which he has come. The reason is that though a thing comes both from its privation and from its substratum, which we call its matter (e.g., what becomes healthy is both a man and an invalid), it is said to come rather from its privation (e.g., it is from an invalid rather than from a man that a healthy subject is produced). And so the healthy subject is not said to *be* an invalid, but to be a man, and the man is said to be healthy. But as for the things whose privation is obscure and nameless, e.g., in brass the privation of a particular shape or in bricks and timber the privation of arrangement as a house, the thing is thought to be produced *from* these materials, as in the former case the healthy man is produced *from* an invalid. And so, as there also a thing

is not said to be that from which it comes, here the statue is not said to be wood but is said by a verbal change to be wooden, not brass but brazen, not gold but golden, and the house is said to be not bricks but bricken (though we should not say without qualification, if we looked at the matter carefully, even that a statue is produced from wood or a house from bricks, because coming to be implies change in that from which a thing comes to be, and not permanence). It is for this reason, then, that we use this way of speaking.

Since anything which is produced is produced by something (and this I call the starting-point of the production), and from something (and let this be taken to be not the privation but the matter; for the meaning we attach to this has already been explained), and since something is produced (and this is either a sphere or a circle or whatever else it may chance to be), just as we do not make the substratum (the brass), so we do not make the sphere, except incidentally, because the brazen sphere is a sphere and we make the former. For to make a 'this' is to make a 'this' out of the substratum in the full sense of the word. (I mean that to make the brass round is not to make the round or the sphere, but something else, i.e., to produce this form in something different from itself. For if we make the form, we must make it out of something else; for this was assumed. E.g., we make a brazen sphere; and that in the sense that out of this, which is brass, we make this other, which is a sphere.) If, then, we also make the substratum itself, clearly we shall make it in the same way, and the processes of making will regress to infinity. Obviously then the form also, or whatever we ought to call the shape present in the sensible thing, is not produced, nor is there any production of it, nor is the essence produced; for this is that which is made to be in something else either by art or by nature or by some faculty. But that there is a *brazen sphere,* this we make. For we make it out of brass and the sphere; we bring the form into this particular matter, and the result is a brazen sphere. But if the essence of sphere in general is to be produced, something must be produced out of something. For the product will always have to be divisible, and one part must be this and another that; I mean the one must be matter and the other form. If then, a sphere is 'the figure whose circumference is at all points equidistant from the centre', part of this will be the medium in which the thing made will be, and part will be in that medium, and the whole will be the thing produced, which corresponds to the brazen sphere. It is obvious, then, from what has been said, that that which is spoken of as form or substance is not produced, but the concrete thing which gets its name from this is produced, and that in everything which is generated matter is present, and one part of the thing is matter and the other form.

Is there, then, a sphere apart from the individual spheres or a house apart from the bricks? Rather we may say that no 'this' would ever have been coming to be, if this had been so, but that the 'form' means the 'such', and is not a 'this'—a definite thing; but the artist makes, or the father begets a 'such' out of a 'this'; and when it has been begotten, it is a 'this such'. And the whole 'this', Callias or Socrates, is analogous to 'this brazen sphere', but man and animal to 'brazen sphere' in general. Obviously, then, the cause which consists of the Forms (taken in the sense in which some maintain the existence of the Forms, i.e., if they are something apart from the individuals) is use-less, at least with regard to comings-to-be and to substances; and the Forms need not, for this reason at least, be self-subsistent substances. In some cases indeed it is even obvious that the begetter is of the same kind as the begotten (not, however, the *same* nor one in number, but in form), i.e., in the case of natural products (for man begets man), unless something happens contrary to nature, e.g., the production of a mule by a horse. (And even these cases are similar; for that which would be found to be common to horse and ass, the genus next above them, has not received a name, but it would doubtless be both, in fact something like a mule.) Obviously, therefore, it is quite unnecessary to set up a Form as a pattern (for we should have looked for Forms in these cases if in any; for these are substances if anything is so); the begetter is adequate to the making of the product and to the causing of the form in the matter. And when we have the whole, such and such a form in this flesh and in these bones, this is Callias or Socrates; and they are different in virtue of their matter (for that is different), but the same in form; for their form is indivisible.

13. Of Identity and Diversity

THOMAS HOBBES

Thomas Hobbes (1588–1679) was an English philosopher who attempted to extend mechanistic explanations to people and society. Impressed by the new physics of the Scientific Revolution, he tried to view everything in terms of material bodies and their interactions. As a nominalist, he believed meanings are just a matter of the interactions among particular signs. He attempted to diagnose many traditional philosophical problems as stemming from a misunderstanding of meaning (and for this reason some have wanted to call him the first "analytic" philosopher). His discussion of an ancient puzzle about identity—the ship of Theseus puzzle, in which a ship's parts are gradually replaced while the old parts are reassembled—is an example of his concern about clarity. Which ship qualifies as the *same* ship? Hobbes insisted that one specify "by what name [sign]" the ship is called. In other words, is one asking about the same matter, about the same form, or about the same aggregate of parts? For persons, he indicated that the same form is usually what one is interested in. Later philosophers, however, worry that analogs of the ship of Theseus puzzle that apply to persons may require a different solution. (See Chapter 17, Chisholm's "Problems of Identity.")

1. *What it is for one thing to differ from another.*
Hitherto I have spoken of body simply, and accidents common to all bodies, *as magnitude, motion, rest, action, passion, power, possible, etc.;* and I should now descend to those accidents by which one body is distinguished from another, but that it is first to be declared what it is to be *distinct* and *not distinct,* namely, what are the SAME and DIFFERENT; for this also is common to all bodies, that they may be distinguished and differenced from one another. Now, two bodies are said to *differ* from one another, when something may be said of one of them, which cannot be said of the other at the same time.

2. *To differ in number, magnitude, species, and genus, what.* And, first of all, it is manifest that no two bodies are the *same;* for seeing they are two, they are in two places at the same time; as that, which is the *same,* is at the same time in one and the same place. All bodies therefore differ from one another in *number,* namely, as one and another; so that the *same* and *different in number,* are names opposed to one another by contradiction.

In *magnitude* bodies differ when one is greater than another, as *a cubit long,* and *two cubits long,* of *two pound weight,* and of *three pound weight.* And to these, *equals* are opposed.

Bodies, which differ more than in magnitude, are called *unlike;* and those, which differ only in magnitude, *like.* Also, of unlike bodies, some are said to differ in the *species,* others in the *genus;* in the *species,* when their difference is perceived by one and the same sense, as *white* and *black;* and in the *genus,* when their difference is not perceived but by divers senses, as *white* and *hot.*

3. *What is relation, proportion, and relatives.*
And the *likeness,* or *unlikeness, equality,* or *inequality* of one body to another, is called their RELATION; and the bodies themselves *relatives* or *correlatives; Aristotle* calls them τὰ πρὸς τί; the first whereof is usually named the *antecedent,* and the second the *consequent;* and the *relation* of the antecedent to the consequent, according to magnitude, namely, the equality, the excess or defect thereof, is called the PROPORTION of the antecedent to the consequent; so that *proportion* is nothing but the equality or inequality of the mag-

nitude of the antecedent compared to the magnitude of the consequent by their difference only, or compared also with their difference. For example, the *proportion* of three to two consists only in this, that three *exceeds* two by unity; and the proportion of two to five in this, that two, compared with five, is *deficient* of it by three, either simply, or compared with the numbers different; and therefore in proportion of unequals, the proportion of the less to the greater, is called DEFECT; and that of the greater to the less, EXCESS.

4. *Proportionals, what.* Besides, of unequals, some are more, some less, and some equally unequal; so that there is *proportion of proportions,* as well as of *magnitudes;* namely, where two unequals have relation to two other unequals; as, when the inequality which is between 2 and 3, is compared with the inequality which is between 4 and 5. In which comparison there are always four magnitudes; or, which is all one, if there be but three, the middlemost is twice numbered; and if the proportion of the first to the second, be equal to the proportion of the third to the fourth, then the four are said to be *proportionals;* otherwise they are not proportionals.

5. *The proportion of magnitudes to one another, wherein it consists.* The proportion of the antecedent to the consequent consists in their difference, not only simply taken, but also as compared with one of the relatives; that is, either in that part of the greater, by which it exceeds the less, or in the remainder, after the less is taken out of the greater; as the proportion of two to five consists in the three by which five exceeds two, not in three simply only, but also as compared with five or two. For though there be the same difference between two and five, which is between nine and twelve, namely three, yet there is not the same inequality; and therefore the proportion of two to five is not in all relation the same with that of nine to twelve, but only in that which is called arithmetical.

6. *Relation is no new accident, but one of those that were in the relative, before the relation or comparison was made. Also the causes of accidents in correlatives are the cause of relation.* But we must not so think of relation, as if it were an accident differing from all the other accidents of the relative; but one of them, namely, that by which the comparison is made. For example, the likeness of one *white* to another *white,* or its unlikeness to

From Hobbes's *Elements of Philosophy,* Section I, Part II, Chapter 11, first published in 1839.

black, is the same accident with its *whiteness;* and *equality* and *inequality,* the same accident with the *magnitude* of the thing compared, though under another name: for that which is called *white* or *great,* when it is not compared with something else, the same when it is compared, is called *like* or *unlike, equal* or *unequal.* And from this it follows that the causes of the accidents, which are in relatives, are the causes also of *likeness, unlikeness, equality* and *inequality;* namely, that he, that makes two unequal bodies, makes also their inequality; and he, that makes a rule and an action, makes also, if the action be congruous to the rule, their congruity; if incongruous, their incongruity. And thus much concerning *comparison* of one body with another.

7. *Of the beginning of individuation.* But the same body may at different times be compared with itself. And from hence springs a great controversy among philosophers about the *beginning of individuation,* namely, in what sense it may be conceived that a body is at one time the same, at another time not the same it was formerly. For example, whether a man grown old be the same man he was whilst he was young, or another man; or whether a city be in different ages the same, or another city. Some place *individuity* in the unity of *matter;* others, in the unity of *form;* and one says it consists in the unity of the *aggregate of all the accidents together.* For *matter,* it is pleaded that a lump of wax, whether it be spherical or cubical, is the same wax, because the same matter. For *form,* that when a man is grown from an infant to be an old man, though his matter be changed, yet he is still the same numerical man; for that *identity,* which cannot be attributed to the matter, ought probably to be ascribed to the form. For the *aggregate of accidents,* no instance can be made; but because, when any new accident is generated, a new name is commonly imposed on the thing, therefore he, that assigned this cause of *individuity,* thought the thing itself also was become another thing. According to the first opinion, he that sins, and he that is punished, should not be the same man, by reason of the perpetual flux and change of man's body; nor should the city, which makes laws in one age and abrogates them in another, be the same city; which were to confound all civil rights. According to the second opinion, two bodies existing both at once, would be one

and the same numerical body. For if, for example, that ship of Theseus, concerning the difference whereof made by continual reparation in taking out the old planks and putting in new, the sophisters of Athens were wont to dispute, were, after all the planks were changed, the same numerical ship it was at the beginning; and if some man had kept the old planks as they were taken out, and by putting them afterwards together in the same order, had again made a ship of them, this, without doubt, had also been the same numerical ship with that which was at the beginning; and so there would have been two ships numerically the same, which is absurd. But, according to the third opinion, nothing would be the same it was; so that a man standing would not be the same he was sitting; nor the water, which is in the vessel, the same with that which is poured out of it. Wherefore the beginning of *individuation* is not always to be taken either from matter alone, or from form alone.

But we must consider by what name anything is called, when we inquire concerning the *identity* of it. For it is one thing to ask concerning Socrates, whether he be the same man, and another to ask whether he be the same body; for his body, when he is old, cannot be the same it was when he was an infant, by reason of the difference of magnitude; for one body has always one and the same magnitude; yet, nevertheless, he may be the same man. And therefore, whensoever the name, by which it is asked whether a thing be the same it was, is given it for the matter only, then, if the matter be the same, the thing also is *individually* the same; as the water, which was in the sea, is the same which is afterwards in the cloud; and any body is the same, whether the parts of it be put together, or dispersed; or whether it be congealed, or dissolved. Also, if the name be given for such form as is the beginning of motion, then, as long as that motion remains, it will be the same *individual* thing; as that man will be always the same, whose actions and thoughts proceed all from the same beginning of motion, namely, that which was in his generation; and that will be the same river which flows from one and the same fountain, whether the same water, or other water, or something else than water, flow from thence; and that the same city, whose acts proceed continually from the same institution, whether the men be the same or no. Lastly, if the name be given for some accident, then the *identity* of the thing will depend upon the matter; for, by the taking away and supplying of matter, the accidents that were, are destroyed, and other new ones are generated, which cannot be the same numerically; so that a ship, which signifies matter so figured, will be the same as long as the matter remains the same; but if no part of the matter be the same, then it is numerically another ship; and if part of the matter remain and part be changed, then the ship will be partly the same, and partly not the same.

14. Of *Identity and Diversity*

JOHN LOCKE

John Locke (1632–1704) is considered an empiricist because of his commitment to the doctrine that all knowledge (ideas) about the world is based on sensory experience and introspection. The selection below is from Locke's most important work, *Essay Concerning Human Understanding*. Like Hobbes, Locke maintains that questions of identity can be answered only by specifying the *kind* of thing we are inquiring about. Thus, he gives different accounts of the identity of inanimate substances, living things, and persons. Furthermore, Locke uses a thought experiment or "puzzle case" to support his conception of personal identity. Locke considers the possibility of a prince having his consciousness transferred to a cobbler's body and vice versa. He uses this case, variations of which have become common fare in recent discussions of personal identity, to lend support to his thesis that memory, not bodily identity, is constitutive of personal identity. Another innovative feature of Locke's view is his attempt to analyze personal identity in terms of a *relation* (memory) between diverse things and not in terms of a continuing underlying substance or Platonic soul. Much of the current discussion of personal identity consists of criticisms and modifications of Locke's views. (See, for example, the selection by Parfit, Chapter 20.)

1. *Wherein Identity Consists.* Another occasion the mind often takes of comparing, is the very being of things; when, considering anything as existing at any determined time and place, we compare it with itself existing at another time, and thereon form the ideas of identity and diversity. When we see anything to be in any place in any instant of time, we are sure (be it what it will) that it is that very thing, and not another, which at that same time exists in another place, how like and undistinguishable soever it may be in all other respects: and in this consists identity, when the ideas it is attributed to vary not at all from what they were that moment wherein we consider their former existence, and to which we compare the present. For we never finding, nor conceiving it possible, that two things of the same kind should exist in the same place at the same time, we rightly conclude, that, whatever exists anywhere at any time, excludes all of the same kind, and is there itself alone. When therefore we demand whether anything be the same or no, it refers always to something that existed such a time in such a place,

From Locke's *Essay Concerning Human Understanding,* 2nd ed., Chapter 27, first published in 1694.

which it was certain at that instant was the same with itself, and no other. From whence it follows, that one thing cannot have two beginnings of existence, nor two things one beginning; it being impossible for two things of the same kind to be or exist in the same instant, in the very same place, or one and the same thing in different places. That, therefore, that had one beginning, is the same thing; and that which had a different beginning in time and place from that, is not the same, but diverse. That which had made the difficulty about this relation has been the little care and attention used in having precise notions of the things to which it is attributed.

2. *Identity of Substances.* We have the ideas but of three sorts of substances: (1) God, (2) finite intelligences, (3) bodies. First, God is without beginning, eternal, unalterable, and everywhere; and therefore concerning his identity there can be no doubt. Secondly, finite spirits having had each its determinate time and place of beginning to exist, the relation to that time and place will always determine to each of them its identity, as long as it exists. Thirdly, the same will hold of every particle of matter, to which no addition or subtraction of matter being made, it is the same. For, though these three sorts of substances, as we term them, do not exclude one another out of the same place, yet we cannot conceive but that they must necessarily each of them exclude any of the same kind out of the same place; or else the notions and names of identity and diversity would be in vain, and there could be no such distinctions of substances, or anything else one from another. For example: could two bodies be in the same place at the same time, then those two parcels of matter must be one and the same, take them great or little; nay, all bodies must be one and the same. For, by the same reason that two particles of matter may be in one place, all bodies may be in one place; which, when it can be supposed, takes away the distinction of identity and diversity of one and more, and renders it ridiculous. But it being a contradiction that two or more should be one, identity and diversity are relations and ways of comparing well founded, and of use to the understanding.

Identity of Modes. All other things being but modes or relations ultimately terminated in substances, the identity and diversity of each particular existence of them too will be by the same way determined: only as to things whose existence is in succession, such as are the actions of finite beings, v.g., motion and thought, both which consist in a continued train of succession: concerning their diversity there can be no question; because each perishing the moment it begins, they cannot exist in different times, or in different places, as permanent beings can at different times exist in distant places; and therefore no motion or thought, considered as at different times, can be the same, each part thereof having a different beginning of existence.

3. *Principium Individuationis.* From what has been said, it is easy to discover what is so much inquired after, the *principium individuationis;* and that, it is plain, is existence itself, which determines a being of any sort to a particular time and place, incommunicable to two beings of the same kind. This, though it seems easier to conceive in simple substances or modes, yet, when reflected on, is not more difficult in compound ones, if care be taken to what it is applied: v.g., let us suppose an atom, i.e., a continued body under one immutable superfices, existing in a determined time and place; it is evident, that considered in any instant of its existence, it is in that instant the same with itself. For, being at that instant what it is, and nothing else, it is the same, and so must continue as long as its existence is continued; for so long it will be the same, and no other. In like manner, if two or more atoms be joined together into the same mass, every one of those atoms will be the same, by the foregoing rule: and whilst they exist united together, the mass, consisting of the same atoms, must be the same mass, or the same body, let the parts be ever so differently jumbled. But if one of these atoms be taken away, or one new one added, it is no longer the same mass or the same body. In the state of living creatures, their identity depends not on a mass of the same particles, but on something else. For in them the variation of great parcels of matter alters not the identity: an oak growing from a plant to a great tree, and then lopped, is still the same oak; and a colt grown up to a horse, sometimes fat, sometimes lean, is all the while the same horse: though, in both these cases, there may be a manifest change of the parts; so that truly they are not either of them the same masses of matter, though they be truly one of them the same oak, and the other the same horse. The reason whereof is, that, in these two cases, a mass of matter, and a living body, identity is not applied to the same thing.

4. *Identity of Vegetables.* We must therefore consider wherein an oak differs from a mass of matter, and that seems to me to be in this, that the one is only the cohesion of particles of matter any how united, the other such a disposition of them as constitutes the parts of an oak; and such an organization of those parts as is fit to receive and distribute nourishment, so as to continue and frame the wood, bark, and leaves, etc., of an oak, in which consists the vegetable life. That being then one plant which has such an organization of parts in one coherent body, partaking of one common life, it continues to be the same plant as long as it partakes of the same life, though that life be communicated to new particles of matter vitally united to the living plant, in a like continued organization comformable to that sort of plants. For this organization being at any one instant in any one collection of matter, is in that particular concrete distinguished from all other, and is that individual life, which existing constantly from that moment both forwards and backwards, in the same continuity of insensibly succeeding parts united to the living body of the plant, it has that identity which makes the same plant, and all the parts of it, parts of the same plant, during all the time that they exist united in that continued organization, which is fit to convey that common life to all the parts so united.

5. *Identity of Animals.* The case is not so much different in brutes, but that any one may hence see what makes an animal and continues it the same. Something we have like this in machines, and may serve to illustrate it. For example, what is a watch? It is plain it is nothing but a fit organization or construction of parts to a certain end, which, when a sufficient force is added to it, it is capable to attain. If we would suppose this machine one continued body, all whose organized parts were repaired, increased, or diminished by a constant addition or separation of insensible parts, with one common life, we should have something very much like the body of an animal; with this difference, that, in an animal the fitness of the organization, and the motion wherein life consists, begin together, the motion coming from within; but in machines, the force coming sensibly from without, often away when the organ is in order, and well fitted to receive it.

6. *The Identity of Man.* This also shows wherein the identity of the same man consists; viz., in nothing but a participation of the same continued life, by constantly fleeting particles of matter, in succession vitally united to the same organized body. He that shall place the identity of man in anything else, but like that of other animals, in one fitly organized body, taken in any one instant, and from these continued, under one organization of life, in several successively fleeting particles of matter united to it, will find it hard to make an embryo, one of years, mad and sober, the same man, by any supposition, that will not make it possible for Seth, Ismael, Socrates, Pilate, St. Austin, and Caesar Borgia, to be the same man. For, if the identity of soul alone makes the same man, and there be nothing in the nature of matter why the same individual spirit may not be united to different bodies, it will be possible that those men living in distant ages, and of different tempers, may have been the same man: which way of speaking must be, from a very strange use of the word man, applied to an idea, out of which body and shape are excluded. And that way of speaking would agree yet worse with the notions of those philosophers who allow of transmigration, and are of opinion that the souls of men may, for their miscarriages, be detruded into the bodies of beasts, as fit habitations, with organs suited to the satisfaction of their brutal inclinations. But yet I think nobody, could he be sure that the soul of Heliogabalus were in one of his hogs, would yet say that hog were a man or Heliogabalus.

7. *Identity Suited to the Idea.* It is not therefore unity of substance that comprehends all sorts of identity, or will determine it in every case; but to conceive and judge of it aright, we must consider what idea the word it is applied to stands for: it being one thing to be the same substance, another the same man, and a third the same person, if person, man, and substance, are three names standing for three different ideas; for such as is the idea belonging to that name, such must be the identity; which, if it had been a little more carefully attended to, would possibly have prevented a great deal of that confusion which often occurs about this matter, with no small seeming difficulties, especially concerning personal identity, which therefore we shall in the next place a little consider.

8. *Same Man.* An animal is living organized body; and consequently the same animal, as we have observed, is the same continued life communicated to different particles of matter, as they happen successively to be united to that organized living body. And whatever is talked of other definitions, ingenious observation puts it past doubt, that the idea in our minds, of which the sound man in our mouths is the sign, is nothing else but of an animal of such a certain form: since I think I may be confident, that, whoever should see a creature of his own shape or make, though it had no more reason all its life than a cat or a parrot, would call him still a man; or whoever should hear a cat or a parrot discourse, reason, and philosophize, would call or think it nothing but a cat or a parrot; and say, the one was a dull irrational man, and the other a very intelligent rational parrot. A relation we have in an author of great note, is sufficient to countenance the supposition of a rational parrot. His words are:

> I had a mind to know, from Prince Maurice's own mouth, the account of a common, but much credited story, that I had heard so often from many others, of an old parrot he had in Brazil, during his government there, that spoke, and asked, and answered common questions, like a reasonable creature: so that those of his train there generally concluded it to be witchery or possession; and one of his chaplains, who lived long afterwards in Holland, would never from that time endure a parrot, but said they all had a devil in them. I had heard many particulars of this story, and assevered by people hard to be discredited, which made me ask Prince Maurice what there was of it. He said, with his usual plainness and dryness in talk, there was something true, but a great deal false of what had been reported. I desired to know of him what there was of the first. He told me short and coldly, that he had heard of such an old parrot when he had been at Brazil; and though he believed nothing of it, and it was a good way off, yet he had so much curiosity as to send for it: that it was a very great and a very old one;

> and when it came first into the room where the prince was, with a great many Dutchmen about him, it said presently, What a company of white men are here! They asked it, what it thought that man was, pointing to the prince. It answered, Some General or other. When they brought it close to him, he asked it, D'ou venez-vous? It answered, De Marinnan. The Prince, A qui estes-vous? The parrot, A un Portugais. The Prince, Que fais-tu là? Je garde les poulles. The Prince laughed, and said, Vous gardez les poulles? The parrot answered, Oui, moi, et je sçai bein faire; and made the chuck four or five times that people use to make to chickens when they call them. I set down the words of this worthy dialogue in French, just as Prince Maurice said them to me. I asked him in what language the parrot spoke, and he said in Brazilian. I asked whether he understood Brazilian; he said no: but he had taken care to have two interpreters by him, the one a Dutchman that spoke Brazilian, and the other a Brazilian that spoke Dutch; that he asked them separately and privately, and both of them agreed in telling him just the same thing that the parrot had said. I could not but tell this odd story, because it is so much out of the way, and from the first hand, and what may pass for a good one; for I dare say this prince at least believed himself in all he told me, having ever passed for a very honest and pious man: I leave it to naturalists to reason, and to other men to believe, as they please upon it; however, it is not, perhaps, amiss to relieve or enliven a busy scene sometimes with such digressions, whether to the purpose or no.

Same Man. I have taken care that the reader should have the story at large in the author's own words, because he seems to me not to have thought it incredible; for it cannot be imagined that so able a man as he, who had sufficiency enough to warrant all the testimonies he gives of himself, should take so much pains, in a place where it had nothing to do, to pin so close not only on a man whom he mentions as his friend, but on a prince in whom he acknowledges very great honesty and piety, a story which, if he himself thought incredible, he could not but also think ridiculous. The prince, it is plain, who vouches this story, and our author, who relates it from him, both of them call this talker a parrot: and I ask any one else who thinks such a story fit to be told, whether—if this parrot, and all of its kind, had always talked, as we have a prince's word for it this one did—whether, I say, they would not have passed for a race of rational animals; but yet, whether, for all that, they would have been allowed to be men, and not parrots? For I presume it is not the idea of a thinking or rational being alone that makes the idea of a man in most people's sense, but of a body, so and so shaped, joined to it; and if that be the idea of a man, the same successive body not shifted all at once, must, as well as the same immaterial spirit, go to the making of the same man.

9. *Personal Identity.* This being premised, to find wherein personal identity consists, we must consider what person stands for; which, I think, is a thinking intelligent being, that has reason and reflection, and can consider itself as itself, the same thinking thing, in different times and places; which it does only by that consciousness which is inseparable from thinking, and, as it seems to me, essential to it: it being impossible for any one to perceive without perceiving that he does perceive. When we see, hear, smell, taste, feel, meditate, or will anything, we know that we do so. Thus it is always as to our present sensations and perceptions: and by this every one is to himself that which he calls self; it not being considered, in this case, whether the same self be continued in the same or divers substances. For, since consciousness always accompanies thinking, and it is that which makes every one to be what he calls self, and thereby distinguishes himself from all other thinking things: in this alone consists personal identity, i.e., the sameness of a rational being; and as far as this consciousness can be extended backwards to any past action or thought, so far reaches the identity of that person; it is the same self now it was then; and it is by the same self with this present one that now reflects on it, that that action was done.

10. *Consciousness Makes Personal Identity.* But it is further inquired, whether it be the same identical substance? This, few would think they had reason to doubt of, if these perceptions, with their consciousness, always remained present in the mind, whereby the same thinking thing would be always consciously present, and, as would be thought, evidently the same to itself. But that which seems to make the difficulty is this, that this consciousness being interrupted always by forgetfulness, there being no moment of our lives wherein we have the whole train of all our past actions before our eyes in one view, but even the best memories losing the sight of one part whilst they are viewing another; and we sometimes, and that the greatest part of our lives, not reflecting on our past selves, being intent on our present thoughts, and in sound sleep having no thoughts at all, or at least none with that consciousness which remarks our waking thoughts; I say, in all these cases, our consciousness being interrupted, and we losing the sight of our past selves, doubts are raised whether we are the same thinking thing, i.e., the same substance or no. Which, however reasonable or unreasonable, concerns not personal identity at all: the question being, what makes the same person, and not whether it be the same identical substance, which always thinks in the same person; which, in this case, matters not at all: different substances, by the same consciousness (where they do partake in it) being united into one person, as well as different bodies by the same life are united into one animal, whose identity is preserved in that change of substances by the unity of one continued life. For it being the same consciousness that makes a man be himself to himself, personal identity depends on that only, whether it be annexed solely to one individual substance, or can be continued in a succession of several substances. For as far as any intelligent being can repeat the idea of any past action with the same consciousness it had of it at first, and with the same consciousness it has of any present action; so far it is the same personal self. For it is by the consciousness it has of its present thoughts and actions, that it is self to itself now, and so will be the same self, as far as the same consciousness can extend to actions past or to come; and would be by distance of time, or change of substance, no more two persons, than a man be two men by wearing other clothes today than he did yesterday, with a long or a short sleep between: the same consciousness uniting those distant actions into the same person, whatever substances contributed to their production.

11. *Personal Identity in Change of Substances.* That this is so, we have some kind of evidence in our very bodies, all whose particles, whilst vitally united to this same thinking conscious self, so that we feel when they are touched, and are affected by, and conscious of good or harm that happens to them, are a part of ourselves; i.e., of our thinking conscious self. Thus, the limbs of his body are to every one a part of himself; he sympathizes and is concerned for them. Cut off a hand, and thereby separate it from that consciousness he had of its heat, cold, and other affections, and it is then no longer a part of that which is himself, any more than the remotest part of matter. Thus, we see the substance whereof personal self consisted at one time may be varied at another, without the change of personal identity; there being no question about the same person, though the limbs which but now were a part of it, be cut off.

12. But the question is, "Whether, if the same substance, which thinks, be changed, it can be the same person; or, remaining the same, it can be different persons?"

Whether in the Change of Thinking Substances. And to this I answer: First, This can be no question at all to those who place thought in a purely material animal constitution, void of an immaterial substance. For, whether their supposition be true or no, it is plain they conceive personal identity preserved in something else than identity of substance; as animal identity is preserved in identity of life, and not of substance. And therefore those who place thinking in an immaterial substance only, before they can come to deal with these men, must show why personal identity cannot be preserved in the change of immaterial substances, or variety of particular immaterial substances, as well as animal identity is preserved in the change of material substances, or variety of particular bodies: unless they will say, it is one immaterial spirit that makes the same life in brutes, as it is one immaterial spirit that makes the same person in men; which the Cartesians at least will not admit, for fear of making brutes thinking things too.

13. But next, as to the first part of the question, "Whether, if the same thinking substance (supposing immaterial substances only to think) be changed, it can be the same person?" I answer, that cannot be resolved, but by those who know what kind of substances they are that do think, and

whether the consciousness of past actions can be transferred from one thinking substance to another. I grant, were the same consciousness the same individual action, it could not: but it being a present representation of a past action, why it may not be possible that that may be represented to the mind to have been, which really never was, will remain to be shown. And therefore how far the consciousness of past actions is annexed to any individual agent, so that another cannot possibly have it, will be hard for us to determine, till we know what kind of action it is that cannot be done without a reflex act of perception accompanying it, and how performed by thinking substances, who cannot think without being conscious of it. But that which we call the same consciousness, not being the same individual act, why one intellectual substance may not have represented to it, as done by itself, what it never did, and was perhaps done by some other agent; why, I say, such a representation may not possibly be without reality of matter of fact, as well as several representations in dreams are, which yet whilst dreaming we take for true, will be difficult to conclude from the nature of things. And that it never is so, will by us, till we have clearer views of the nature of thinking substances, be best resolved into the goodness of God, who, as far as the happiness or misery of any of his sensible creatures is concerned in it, will not, by a fatal error of theirs, transfer from one to another that consciousness which draws reward or punishment with it. How far this may be an argument against those who would place thinking in a system of fleeting animal spirits, I leave to be considered. But yet, to return to the question before us, it must be allowed, that, if the same consciousness (which, as has been shown, is quite a different thing from the same numerical figure or motion in body) can be transferred from one thinking substance to another, it will be possible that two thinking substances may make but one person. For the same consciousness being preserved, whether in the same or different substances, the personal identity is preserved.

14. As to the second part of the question, "Whether the same immaterial substance remaining, there may be two distinct person?" which question seems to me to be built on this, whether the same immaterial being, being conscious of the action of its past duration, may be wholly stripped of all the consciousness of its past existence, and lose it beyond the power of ever retrieving it again; and so as it were beginning a new account from a new period, have a consciousness that cannot reach beyond this new state. All those who hold pre-existence are evidently of this mind, since they allow the soul to have no remaining consciousness of what it did in that pre-existent state, either wholly separate from body, or informing any other body; and if they should not, it is plain experience would be against them. So that personal identity reaching no further than consciousness reaches, a pre-existent spirit not having continued so many ages in a state of silence, must needs make different persons. Suppose a Christian Platonist or a Pythagorean should, upon God's having ended all his works of creation the seventh day, think his soul hath existed ever since; and would imagine it has revolved in several human bodies, as I once met with one, who was persuaded his had been the soul of Socrates; (how reasonably I will not dispute; this I know, that in the post he filled, which was no inconsiderable one, he passed for a very rational man, and the press has shown that he wanted not parts or learning); would any one say, that he, being not conscious of any of Socrates' actions or thoughts, could be the same person with Socrates? Let any one reflect upon himself, and conclude that he has in himself an immaterial spirit, which is that which thinks in him, and, in the constant change of his body keeps him the same: and is that which he calls himself: let him also suppose it to be the same soul that was in Nestor or Thersites, at the siege of Troy (for souls being, as far as we know anything of them, in their nature indifferent to any parcel of matter, the supposition has no apparent absurdity in it), which it may have been, as well as it is now the soul of any other man: but he now having no consciousness of any of the actions either of Nestor or Thersites, does or can he conceive himself the same person with either of them? Can he be concerned in either of their actions? attribute them to himself, or think them his own, more than the actions of any other men that ever existed? So that this consciousness not reaching to any of the actions of either of those men, he is no more one self with either of them, than if the soul or immaterial spirit that now informs him had been created, and began to exist, when it began to inform his present body, though

it were ever so true, that the same spirit that informed Nestor's or Thersites' body were numerically the same that now informs his. For this would no more make him the same person with Nestor, than if some of the particles of matter that were once a part of Nestor, were now a part of this man; the same immaterial substance, without the same consciousness, no more making the same person by being united to any body, than the same particle of matter, without consciousness united to any body, makes the same person. But let him once find himself conscious of any of the actions of Nestor, he then finds himself the same person with Nestor.

15. And thus may we be able, without any difficulty, to conceive the same person at the resurrection, though in a body not exactly in make or parts the same which he had here, the same consciousness going along with the soul that inhabits it. But yet the soul alone, in the change of bodies, would scarce to any one but to him that makes the soul the man, be enough to make the same man. "For should the soul of a prince, carrying with it the consciousness of the prince's past life, enter and inform the body of a cobbler, as soon as deserted by his own soul, every one sees he would be the same person with the prince," accountable only for the prince's actions: but who would say it was the same man? The body too goes to the making the man, and would, I guess, to everybody determine the man in this case; wherein the soul, with all its princely thoughts about it, would not make another man: but he would be the same cobbler to every one besides himself. I know that, in the ordinary way of speaking, the same person, and the same man, stand for one and the same thing. And indeed every one will always have a liberty to speak as he pleases, and to apply what articulate sounds to what ideas he thinks fit, and change them as often as he pleases. But yet, when we will inquire what makes the same spirit, man, or person, we must fix the ideas of spirit, man, or person in our minds, and having resolved with ourselves what we mean by them, it will not be hard to determine in either of them, or the like, when it is the same, and when not.

16. *Consciousness Makes the Same Person.* But though the same immaterial substance or soul does not alone, wherever it be, and in whatsoever state, make the same man; yet it is plain, consciousness, as far as ever it can be extended, should it be to ages past, unites existences and actions, very remote in time into the same person, as well as it does the existences and actions of the immediately preceding moment: so that whatever has the consciousness of present and past actions, is the same person to whom they both belong. Had I the same consciousness that I saw the ark and Noah's flood, as that I saw an overflowing of the Thames last winter, or as that I write now; I could no more doubt that I who write this now, that saw the Thames overflowed last winter, and that viewed the flood at the general deluge, was the same self, place that self in what substance you please, than that I who write this am the same myself now whilst I write (whether I consist of all the same substance, material or immaterial, or no) that I was yesterday; for as to this point of being the same self, it matters not whether this present self be made up of the same or other substances; I being as much concerned, and as justly accountable for any action that was done a thousand years since, appropriated to me now by this self-consciousness, as I am for what I did the last moment.

17. *Self Depends on Consciousness.* Self is that conscious thinking thing, whatever substance made up of (whether spiritual or material, simple or compounded, it matters not), which is sensible or conscious of pleasure and pain, capable of happiness or misery, and so is concerned for itself, as far as that consciousness extends. Thus every one finds, that whilst comprehended under that consciousness, the little finger is as much a part of himself as what is most so. Upon separation of this little finger, should this consciousness go along with the little finger, and leave the rest of the body, it is evident the little finger would be the person, the same person, and self then would have nothing to do with the rest of the body. As in this case it is the consciousness that goes along with the substance, when one part is separate from another, which makes the same person, and constitutes this inseparable self; so it is in reference to substances remote in time. That with which the consciousness of this present thinking thing can join itself, makes the same person, and is one self with it, and with nothing else; and so attributes to itself, and owns all the actions of that thing as its own, as far as that consciousness reaches, and no further; as every one who reflects will perceive.

18. *Objects of Reward and Punishment.* In this personal identity is founded all the right and justice of reward and punishment; happiness and misery being that for which every one is concerned for himself, and not mattering what becomes of any substance not joined to, or affected with that consciousness. For as it is evident in the instance I gave but now, if the consciousness went along with the little finger when it was cut off, that would be the same self which was concerned for the whole body yesterday, as making part of itself, whose actions then it cannot but admit as its own now. Though, if the same body should still live, and immediately from the separation of the little finger have its own peculiar consciousness, whereof the little finger knew nothing; it would not at all be concerned for it, as a part of itself, or could own any of its actions, or have any of them imputed to him.

19. This may show us wherein personal identity consists: not in the identity of substance, but, as I have said, in the identity of consciousness; wherein if Socrates and the present mayor of Queenborough agree, they are the same person: if the same Socrates waking and sleeping do not partake of the same consciousness, Socrates waking and sleeping is not the same person. And to punish Socrates waking for what sleeping Socrates thought, and waking Socrates was never conscious of, would be no more of right, than to punish one twin for what his brother-twin did, whereof he knew nothing, because their outsides were so like, that they could not be distinguished; for such twins have been seen.

20. But yet possibly it will still be objected, suppose I wholly lose the memory of some parts of my life, beyond a possibility of retrieving them, so that perhaps I shall never be conscious of them again; yet am I not the same person that did those actions, had those thoughts that I once was conscious of, though I have now forgot them? To which I answer, that we must here take notice what the word I is applied to; which, in this case, is the man only. And the same man being presumed to be the same person, I is easily here supposed to stand also for the same person. But if it be possible for the same man to have distinct incommunicable consciousness at different times, it is past doubt the same man would at different times make different persons; which, we see, is the sense of mankind in the solemnest declaration of their opinions; human laws not punishing the mad man for the sober man's actions, nor the sober man for what the mad man did, thereby making them two persons: which is somewhat explained by our way of speaking in English, when we say such an one is not himself, or is beside himself; in which phrases it is insinuated, as if those who now, or at least first used them, thought that self was changed, the selfsame person was no longer in that man.

21. *Difference Between Identity of Man and Person.* But yet it is hard to conceive that Socrates, the same individual man, should be two persons. To help us a little in this, we must consider what is meant by Socrates, or the same individual man.

First, it must be either the same individual, immaterial, thinking substance; in short, the same numerical soul, and nothing else.

Secondly, or the same animal, without any regard to an immaterial soul.

Thirdly, or the same immaterial spirit united to the same animal.

Now, take which of these suppositions you please, it is impossible to make personal identity to consist in anything but consciousness, or reach any further than that does.

For, by the first of them, it must be allowed possible that a man born of different women, and in distant times, may be the same man. A way of speaking, which whoever admits, must allow it possible for the same man to be two distinct persons, as any two that have lived in different ages, without the knowledge of one another's thoughts.

By the second and third, Socrates, in this life and after it, cannot be the same man any way, but by the same consciousness; and so making human identity to consist in the same thing wherein we place personal identity, there will be no difficulty to allow the same man to be the same person. But then they who place human identity in consciousness only, and not in something else, must consider how they will make the infant Socrates the same man with Socrates after the resurrection. But whatsoever to some men makes a man, and consequently the same individual man, wherein perhaps few are agreed, personal identity can by us be placed in nothing but consciousness (which is that alone which makes what we call self), without involving us in great absurdities.

22. But is not a man drunk and sober the same person? Why else is he punished for the fact he commits when drunk, though he be never afterwards conscious of it? Just as much the same person as a man that walks, and does other things in his sleep, is the same person, and is answerable for any mischief he shall do in it. Human laws punish both, with a justice suitable to their way of knowledge; because, in these cases, they cannot distinguish certainly what is real, what counterfeit: and so the ignorance in drunkenness or sleep is not admitted as a plea. For, though punishment be annexed to personality, and personality to consciousness, and the drunkard perhaps be not conscious of what he did, yet human judicatures justly punish him, because the fact is proved against him, but want of consciousness cannot be proved for him. But in the great day, wherein the secrets of all hearts shall be laid open, it may be reasonable to think, no one shall be made to answer for what he knows nothing of; but shall receive his doom, his conscience accusing or excusing him.

23. *Consciousness Alone Makes Self.* Nothing but consciousness can unite remote existences into the same person: the identity of substance will not do it; for whatever substance there is, however framed, without consciousness there is no person: and a carcass may be a person, as well as any sort of substance be so without consciousness.

Could we suppose two distinct incommunicable consciousnesses acting the same body, the one constantly by day, the other by night; and, on the other side, the same consciousness, acting by intervals, two distinct bodies; I ask, in the first case, whether the day and the night man would not be two as distinct persons as Socrates and Plato? And whether, in the second case, there would not be one person in two distinct bodies, as much as one man is the same in two distinct clothings? Nor is it at all material to say, that this same, and this distinct consciousness, in the cases above mentioned, is owing to the same and distinct immaterial substances, bringing it with them to those bodies; which, whether true or no, alters not the case; since it is evident the personal identity would equally be determined by the consciousness, whether that consciousness were annexed to some individual immaterial substance or no. For, granting that the thinking substance in man must be necessarily supposed immaterial, it is evident that immaterial thinking thing may sometimes part with its past consciousness, and be restored to it again, as appears in the forgetfulness men often have of their past actions: and the mind many times recovers the memory of a past consciousness, which it had lost for twenty years together. Make these intervals of memory and forgetfulness to take their turns regularly by day and night, and you have two persons with the same immaterial spirit, as much as in the former instance two persons with the same body. So that self is not determined by identity or diversity of substance, which it cannot be sure of, but only by identity of consciousness.

24. Indeed it may conceive the substance whereof it is now made up to have existed formerly, united in the same conscious being; but, consciousness removed, that substance is no more itself, or makes no more a part of it, than any other substance; as is evident in the instance we have already given of a limb cut off, of whose heat, or cold, or other affections, having no longer any consciousness, it is no more of a man's self, than any other matter of the universe. In like manner it will be in reference to any immaterial substance, which is void of that consciousness whereby I am myself to myself: if there be any part of its existence which I cannot upon recollection join with that present consciousness, whereby I am now myself, it is in that part of its existence no more myself, than any other immaterial being. For whatsoever any substance has thought or done, which I cannot recollect, and by my consciousness make my own thought and action, it will no more belong to me, whether a part of me thought or did it, than if it had been thought or done by any other immaterial being anywhere existing.

25. I agree, the more probable opinion is, that this consciousness is annexed to, and the affection of, one individual immaterial substance.

But let men, according to their diverse hypotheses, resolve of that as they please; this very intelligent being, sensible of happiness or misery, must grant that there is something that is himself that he is concerned for, and would have happy; that this self has existed in a continued duration more than one instant, and therefore it is possible may exist, as it has done, months and years to come, without any certain bounds to be set to its duration; and may be the same self by the same consciousness continued on for the future. And

thus, by this consciousness, he finds himself to be the same self which did such and such an action some years since, by which he comes to be happy or miserable now. In all which account of self, the same numerical substance is not considered as making the same self; but the same continued consciousness, in which several substances may have been united, and again separated from it; which, whilst they continued in a vital union with that wherein this consciousness then resided, made a part of that same self. Thus any part of our bodies vitally united to that which is conscious in us, makes a part of ourselves: but upon separation from the vital union by which that consciousness is communicated, that which a moment since was part of ourselves, is now no more so than a part of another man's self is a part of me: and it is not impossible but in a little time may become a real part of another person. And so we have the same numerical substance become a part of two different persons; and the same person preserved under the change of various substances. Could we suppose any spirit wholly stripped of all its memory or consciousness of past actions, as we find our minds always are of a great part of ours, and sometimes of them all; the union or separation of such a spiritual substance would make no variation of personal identity, and more than that of any particle of matter does. Any substance vitally united to the present thinking being, is a part of that very same self which now is; anything united to it by a consciousness of former actions, makes also a part of the same self, which is the same both then and now.

26. *Person a Forensic Term*. Person, as I take it, is the name for this self. Wherever a man finds what he calls himself there, I think, another may say is the same person. It is a forensic term, appropriating actions and their merit; and so belongs only to intelligent agents capable of a law, and happiness, and misery. This personality extends itself beyond present existence to what is past, only by consciousness, whereby it becomes concerned and accountable, owns and imputes to itself past actions, just upon the same ground and for the same reason that it does the present. All which is founded in a concern for happiness, the unavoidable concomitant of consciousness; that which is conscious of pleasure and pain, desiring that that self that is conscious should be happy. And therefore whatever past actions it cannot reconcile or appropriate to that present self by consciousness, it can be no more concerned in, than if they had never been done; and to receive pleasure or pain, i.e., reward or punishment, on the account of any such action, is all one as to be made happy or miserable in its first being, without any demerit at all: for supposing a man punished now for what he had done in another life, whereof he could be made to have no consciousness at all, what difference is there between that punishment, and being created miserable? And therefore, conformable to this, the apostle tells us, that, at the great day, when every one shall "receive according to his doings, the secrets of all hearts shall be laid open." The sentence shall be justified by the consciousness all persons shall have, that they themselves, in what bodies soever they appear, or what substances soever that consciousness adheres to, are the same that committed those actions, and deserve that punishment for them.

27. I am apt enough to think I have, in treating of this subject, made some suppositions that will look strange to some readers, and possibly they are so in themselves. But yet, I think they are such as are pardonable, in this ignorance we are in of the nature of that thinking thing that is in us, and which we look on as ourselves. Did we know what it was, or how it was tied to a certain system of fleeting animal spirits; or whether it could or could not perform its operations of thinking and memory out of a body organized as ours is: and whether it has pleased God, that no one such spirit shall ever be united to any one but such body, upon the right constitution of whose organs its memory should depend; we might see the absurdity of some of these suppositions I have made. But, taking as we ordinarily now do, (in the dark concerning these matters,) the soul of a man for an immaterial substance, independent from matter, and indifferent alike to it all, there can, from the nature of things, be no absurdity at all to suppose that the same soul may at different times be united to different bodies, and with them make up for

that time one man, as well as we suppose a part of a sheep's body yesterday should be a part of a man's body tomorrow, and in that union make a vital part of Meliboeus himself, as well as it did of his ram.

28. *The Difficulty from Ill Use of Names.* To conclude: Whatever substance begins to exist, it must, during its existence, necessarily be the same: whatever compositions of substances begin to exist, during the union of those substances the concrete must be the same; whatsoever mode begins to exist, during its existence it is the same; and so if the composition be of distinct substances and different modes, the same rule holds: whereby it will appear, that the difficulty or obscurity that has been about this matter rather rises from the names ill used, than from any obscurity in things themselves. For whatever makes the specific idea to which the name is applied, if that idea be steadily kept to, the distinction of anything into the same, and divers, will easily be conceived, and there can arise no doubt about it.

29. *Continued Existence Makes Identity.* For, supposing a rational spirit be the idea of a man, it is easy to know what is the same man, viz., the same spirit, whether separate or in a body, will be the same man. Supposing a rational spirit vitally united to a body of a certain conformation of parts to make a man, whilst that rational spirit, with that vital conformation of parts, though continued in a fleeting successive body, remain, it will be the same man. But if to any one the idea of a man be but the vital union of parts in a certain shape, as long as that vital union and shape remain in a concrete no otherwise the same, but by a continued succession of fleeting particles, it will be the same man. For, whatever be the composition whereof the complex idea is made, whenever existence makes it one particular thing under any denomination, the same existence continued, preserves it the same individual under the same denomination.

15. Of Identity and Of Mr. Locke's Theory of Personal Identity

THOMAS REID

Thomas Reid (1710–1796), the founder of the Scottish School of Common Sense, was born in Aberdeen. He was an insightful, albeit critical, interpreter of the empiricists and a staunch defender of the view that the mind and the body are two different substances (mind-body dualism). In the first selection, Reid maintains that the idea or concept of identity is univocal and involves "continued, uninterrupted existence." Since physical objects are continually changing their parts, they do not, according to the strict and philosophical sense of the term, have strict identity through time. A person, on the other hand, is a simple indivisible substance that remains, in the strict and philosophical sense, identical through time. In the second selection, Reid raises several objections to Locke's views on personal identity.

Of Identity

The conviction which every man has of his identity, as far back as his memory reaches, needs no aid of philosophy to strengthen it; and no philosophy can weaken it, without first producing some degree of insanity.

The philosopher, however, may very properly consider this conviction as a phenomenon of human nature worthy of his attention. If he can discover its cause, an addition is made to his stock of knowledge; if not, it must be held as a part of our original constitution, or an effect of that constitution produced in a manner unknown to us.

We may observe, first of all, that this conviction is indispensably necessary to all exercise of reason. The operations of reason, whether in action or in speculation, are made up of successive parts. The antecedent are the foundation of the consequent, and, without the conviction that the antecedent have been seen or done by me, I could have no reason to proceed to the consequent, in any speculation, or in any active project whatever.

There can be no memory of what is past without the conviction that we existed at the time remembered. There may be good arguments to

From Reid's *Essays on the Intellectual Powers of Man,* first published in 1785. "Of Identity" is Essay III, Chapter 4; "Of Mr. Locke's Account of Our Personal Identity" is Essay III, Chapter 6.

convince me that I existed before the earliest thing I can remember; but to suppose that my memory reaches a moment farther back than my belief and conviction of my existence, is a contradiction.

The moment a man loses this conviction, as if he had drunk the water of Lethe, past things are done away; and, in his own belief, he then begins to exist. Whatever was thought, or said, or done, or suffered before that period, may belong to some other person; but he can never impute it to himself, or take any subsequent step that supposes it to be his doing.

From this it is evident that we must have the conviction of our own continued existence and identity, as soon as we are capable of thinking or doing anything, on account of what we have thought, or done, or suffered before; that is, as soon as we are reasonable creatures.

That we may form as distinct a notion as we are able of this phenomenon of the human mind, it is proper to consider what is meant by identity in general, what by our own personal identity, and how we are led into that invincible belief and conviction which every man has of his own personal identity, as far as his memory reaches.

Identity in general I take to be a relation between a thing which is known to exist at one time, and a thing which is known to have existed at another time. If you ask whether they are one and the same, or two different things, every man of common sense understands the meaning of your question perfectly. Whence we may infer with certainty, that every man of common sense has a clear and distinct notion of identity.

If you ask a definition of identity, I confess I can give none; it is too simple a notion to admit of logical definition: I can say it is a relation, but I cannot find words to express the specific difference between this and other relations, though I am in no danger of confounding it with any other. I can say that diversity is a contrary relation, and that similitude and dissimilitude are another couple of contrary relations, which every man easily distinguishes in his conception from identity and diversity.

I see evidently that identity supposes an uninterrupted continuance of existence. That which has ceased to exist cannot be the same with that which afterwards begins to exist; for this would be to suppose a being to exist after it ceased to exist, and to have had existence before it was produced, which are manifest contradictions. Continued uninterrupted existence is therefore necessarily implied in identity.

Hence we may infer, that identity cannot, in its proper sense, be applied to our pains, our pleasures, our thoughts, or any operation of our minds. The pain felt this day is not the same individual pain which I felt yesterday, though they may be *similar* in kind and degree, and have the same cause. The same may be said of every feeling, and of every operation of mind. They are all successive in their nature, like time itself, no two moments of which can be the same moment.

It is otherwise with the parts of absolute space. They always are, and were, and will be the same. So far, I think, we proceed upon clear ground in fixing the notion of identity in general.

It is perhaps more difficult to ascertain with precision the meaning of personality; but it is not necessary in the present subject: it is sufficient for our purpose to observe, that all mankind place their personality in something that cannot be divided, or consist of parts.

A part of a person is a manifest absurdity. When a man loses his estate, his health, his strength, he is still the same person, and has lost nothing of his personality. If he has a leg or an arm cut off, he is the same person he was before. The amputated member is no part of his person, otherwise it would have a right to a part of his estate, and be liable for a part of his engagements. It would be entitled to a share of his merit and demerit, which is manifestly absurd. A person is something indivisible, and is what Leibnitz calls a *monad*.

My personal identity, therefore, implies the continued existence of that indivisible thing which I call *myself*. Whatever this self may be, it is something which thinks, and deliberates, and resolves, and acts, and suffers. I am not thought, I am not action, I am not feeling; I am something that thinks, and acts, and suffers. My thoughts, and actions, and feelings, change every moment; they have no continued, but a successive, existence; but that *self*, or *I*, to which they belong, is permanent, and has the same relation to all the succeeding thoughts, actions, and feelings which I call mine.

Such are the notions that I have of my personal identity. But perhaps it may be said, this may all be fancy without reality. How do you know—what evidence have you—that there is such a permanent self which has a claim to all the thoughts, actions, and feelings which you call yours?

To this I answer, that the proper evidence I have of all this is remembrance. I remember that twenty years ago I conversed with such a person; I remember several things that passed in that conversation: my memory testifies, not only that this was done, but that it was done by me who now remember it. If it was done by me, I must have existed at that time, and continued to exist from that time to the present: if the identical person whom I call myself had not a part in that conversation, my memory is fallacious; it gives a distinct and positive testimony of what is not true. Every man in his senses believes what he distinctly remembers, and every thing he remembers convinces him that he existed at the time remembered.

Although memory gives the most irresistible evidence of my being the identical person that did such a thing, at such a time, I may have other good evidence of things which befell me, and which I do not remember: I know who bare me, and suckled me, but I do not remember these events.

It may here be observed (though the observation would have been unnecessary, if some great philosophers had not contradicted it), that it is not my remembering any action of mine that makes me to be the person who did it. This remembrance makes me to know assuredly that I did it; but I might have done it, though I did not remember it. That relation to me, which is expressed by saying that I did it, would be the same, though I had not the least remembrance of it. To say that my remembering that I did such a thing, or, as some choose to express it, my being conscious that I did it, makes me to have done it, appears to me as great an absurdity as it would be to say, that my belief that the world was created made it to be created.

When we pass judgment on the identity of other persons than ourselves, we proceed upon other grounds, and determine from a variety of circumstances, which sometimes produce the firmest assurance, and sometimes leave room for doubt. The identity of persons has often furnished matter of serious litigation before tribunals of justice. But no man of a sound mind ever doubted of his own identity, as far as he distinctly remembered.

The identity of a person is a perfect identity: wherever it is real, it admits of no degrees; and it is impossible that a person should be in part the same, and in part different; because a person is a *monad,* and is not divisible into parts. The evidence of identity in other persons than ourselves does indeed admit of all degrees, from what we account certainty, to the least degree of probability. But still it is true, that the same person is perfectly the same, and cannot be so in part, or in some degree only.

For this cause, I have first considered personal identity, as that which is perfect in its kind, and the natural measure of that which is imperfect.

We probably at first derive our notion of identity from that natural conviction which every man has from the dawn of reason of his own identity and continued existence. The operations of our minds are all successive, and have no continued existence. But the thinking being has a continued existence, and we have an invincible belief, that it remains the same when all its thoughts and operations change.

Our judgments of the identity of objects of sense seem to be formed much upon the same grounds as judgments of the identity of other persons than ourselves.

Wherever we observe great similarity, we are apt to presume identity, if no reason appears to the contrary. Two objects ever so like, when they are perceived at the same time, cannot be the same; but if they are presented to our senses at different times, we are apt to think them the same, merely from their similarity.

Whether this be a natural prejudice, or from whatever cause it proceeds, it certainly appears in children from infancy; and when we grow up, it is confirmed in most instances by experience: for we rarely find two individuals of the same species that are not distinguishable by obvious differences.

A man challenges a thief whom he finds in possession of his horse or his watch, only on similarity. When the watchmaker swears that he sold this watch to such a person, his testimony is grounded on similarity. The testimony of witnesses to the identity of a person is commonly grounded on no other evidence.

Thus it appears, that the evidence we have of our own identity, as far back as we remember, is totally of a different kind from the evidence we have of the identity of other persons, or of objects of sense. The first is grounded on memory, and gives undoubted certainty. The last is grounded on similarity, and on other circumstances, which in many cases are not so decisive as to leave no room for doubt.

It may likewise be observed, that the identity of objects of sense is never perfect. All bodies, as they consist of innumerable parts that may be disjoined from them by a great variety of causes, are subject to continual changes of their substance, increasing, diminishing, changing insensibly. When such alterations are gradual, because language could not afford a different name for every different state of such a changeable being, it retains the same name, and is considered as the same thing. Thus we say of an old regiment, that it did such a thing a century ago, though there now is not a man alive who then belonged to it. We say a tree is the same in the seed-bed and in the forest. A ship of war, which has successively changed her anchors, her tackle, her sails, her masts, her planks, and her timbers, while she keeps the same name, is the same.

The identity, therefore, which we ascribe to bodies, whether natural or artificial, is not perfect identity; it is rather something which, for the conveniency of speech, we call identity. It admits of a great change of the subject, providing the change be gradual; sometimes, even of a total change. And the changes which in common language are made consistent with identity differ from those that are thought to destroy it, not in kind, but in number and degree. It has no fixed nature when applied to bodies; and questions about the identity of a body are very often questions about words. But identity, when applied to persons, has no ambiguity, and admits not of degrees, or of more and less. It is the foundation of all rights and obligations, and of all accountableness; and the notion of it is fixed and precise.

Of Mr. Locke's Account of Our Personal Identity

In a long chapter upon Identity and Diversity, Mr. Locke has made many ingenious and just observations, and some which I think cannot be defended. I shall only take notice of the account he gives of our own personal identity. His doctrine upon this subject has been censured by Bishop Butler, in a short essay subjoined to his *Analogy,* with whose sentiments I perfectly agree.

Identity, as was observed, supposes the continued existence of the being of which it is affirmed, and therefore can be applied only to things which have a continued existence. While any being continues to exist, it is the same being; but two beings which have a different beginning or a different ending of their existence cannot possibly be the same. To this, I think, Mr. Locke agrees.

He observes, very justly, that, to know what is meant by the same person, we must consider what the word *person* stands for; and he defines a person to be an intelligent being, endowed with reason and with consciousness, which last he thinks inseparable from thought.

From this definition of a person, it must necessarily follow, that, while the intelligent being continues to exist and to be intelligent, it must be the same person. To say that the intelligent being is the person, and yet that the person ceases to exist while the intelligent being continues, or that the person continues while the intelligent being ceases to exist, is to my apprehension a manifest contradiction.

One would think that the definition of a person should perfectly ascertain the nature of personal identity, or wherein it consists, though it

might still be a question how we come to know and be assured of our personal identity.

Mr. Locke tells us, however, "that personal identity, that is, the sameness of a rational being, consists in consciousness alone, and, as far as this consciousness can be extended backwards to any past action or thought, so far reaches the identity of that person. So that whatever has the consciousness of present and past actions is the same person to whom they belong."

This doctrine has some strange consequences, which the author was aware of. Such as, that if the same consciousness can be transferred from one intelligent being to another, which he thinks we cannot show to be impossible, *then two or twenty intelligent beings may be the same person.* And if the intelligent being may lose the consciousness of the actions done by him, which surely is possible, then he is not the person that did those actions; so that *one intelligent being may be two or twenty different persons,* if he shall so often lose the consciousness of his former actions.

There is another consequence of this doctrine, which follows no less necessarily, though Mr. Locke probably did not see it. It is, *that a man may be, and at the same time not be, the person that did a particular action.*

Suppose a brave officer to have been flogged when a boy at school for robbing an orchard, to have taken a standard from the enemy in his first campaign, and to have been made a general in advanced life; suppose, also, which must be admitted to be possible, that, when he took the standard, he was conscious of his having been flogged at school, and that, when made a general, he was conscious of his taking the standard, but had absolutely lost the consciousness of his flogging.

These things being supposed, it follows, from Mr. Locke's doctrine, that he who was flogged at school is the same person who took the standard, and that he who took the standard is the same person who was made a general. Whence it follows, if there be any truth in logic, that the general is the same person with him who was flogged at school. But the general's consciousness does not reach so far back as his flogging; therefore, according to Mr. Locke's doctrine, he is not the person who was flogged. Therefore the general is, and at the same time is not, the same person with him who was flogged at school.

Leaving the consequences of this doctrine to those who have leisure to trace them, we may observe, with regard to the doctrine itself:

First, that Mr. Locke attributes to consciousness the conviction we have of our past actions, as if a man may now be conscious of what he did twenty years ago. It is impossible to understand the meaning of this, unless by consciousness be meant memory, the only faculty by which we have an immediate knowledge of our past actions.

Sometimes, in popular discourse, a man says he is conscious that he did such a thing, meaning that he distinctly remembers that he did it. It is unnecessary, in common discourse, to fix accurately the limits between consciousness and memory. This was formerly shown to be the case with regard to sense and memory: and therefore distinct remembrance is sometimes called sense, sometimes consciousness, without any inconvenience.

But this ought to be avoided in philosophy, otherwise we confound the different powers of the mind, and ascribe to one what really belongs to another. If a man can be conscious of what he did twenty years or twenty minutes ago, there is no use for memory, nor ought we to allow that there is any such faculty. The faculties of consciousness and memory are chiefly distinguished by this, that the first is an immediate knowledge of the present, the second an immediate knowledge of the past.

When, therefore, Mr. Locke's notion of personal identity is properly expressed, it is, that personal identity consists in distinct remembrance; for, even in the popular sense, to say that I am conscious of a past action means nothing else than that I distinctly remember that I did it.

Secondly, it may be observed, that, in this doctrine, not only is consciousness confounded with memory, but, which is still more strange, personal identity is confounded with the evidence which we have of our personal identity.

It is very true, that my remembrance that I did such a thing is the evidence I have that I am the identical person who did it. And this, I am apt to think, Mr. Locke meant. But to say that my remembrance that I did such a thing, or my consciousness, makes me the person who did it, is, in my apprehension, an absurdity too gross to be entertained by any man who attends to the meaning of it; for it is to attribute to memory or consciousness a strange magical power of producing

its object, though that object must have existed before the memory or consciousness which produced it.

Consciousness is the testimony of one faculty; memory is the testimony of another faculty; and to say that the testimony is the cause of the thing testified, this surely is absurd, if any thing be, and could not have been said by Mr. Locke, if he had not confounded the testimony with the thing testified.

When a horse that was stolen is found and claimed by the owner, the only evidence he can have, or that a judge or witnesses can have, that this is the very identical horse which was his property, is similitude. But would it not be ridiculous from this to infer that the identity of a horse consists in similitude only? The only evidence I have that I am the identical person who did such actions is, that I remember distinctly I did them; or, as Mr. Locke expresses it, I am conscious I did them. To infer from this, that personal identity consists in consciousness, is an argument which, if it had any force, would prove the identity of a stolen horse to consist solely in similitude.

Thirdly, is it not strange that the sameness or identity of a person should consist in a thing which is continually changing, and is not any two minutes the same?

Our consciousness, our memory, and every operation of the mind, are still flowing like the water of a river, or like time itself. The consciousness I have this moment can no more be the same consciousness I had last moment, than this moment can be the last moment. Identity can only be affirmed of things which have a continued existence. Consciousness, and every kind of thought, are transient and momentary, and have no continued existence; and, therefore, if personal identity consisted in consciousness, it would certainly follow, that no man is the same person any two moments of his life; and as the right and justice of reward and punishment are founded on personal identity, no man could be responsible for his actions.

But though I take this to be the unavoidable consequence of Mr. Locke's doctrine concerning personal identity, and though some persons may have liked the doctrine the better on this account, I am far from imputing any thing of this kind to Mr. Locke. He was too good a man not to have rejected with abhorrence a doctrine which he believed to draw this consequence after it.

Fourthly, there are many expressions used by Mr. Locke, in speaking of personal identity, which to me are altogether unintelligible, unless we suppose that he confounded that sameness or identity which we ascribe to an individual with the identity which, in common discourse, is often ascribed to many individuals of the same species.

When we say that pain and pleasure, consciousness and memory, are the same in all men, this sameness can only mean similarity, or sameness of kind. That the pain of one man can be the same individual pain with that of another man is no less impossible, than that one man should be another man: the pain felt by me yesterday can no more be the pain I feel today, than yesterday can be this day; and the same thing may be said of every passion and of every operation of the mind. The same kind or species of operation may be in different men, or in the same man at different times; but it is impossible that the same individual operation should be in different men, or in the same man at different times.

When Mr. Locke, therefore, speaks of "the same consciousness being continued through a succession of different substances"; when he speaks of "repeating the idea of a past action, with the same consciousness we had of it at the first," and of "the same consciousness extending to actions past and to come"; these expressions are to me unintelligible, unless he means not the same individual consciousness, but a consciousness that is similar, or of the same kind.

If our personal identity consists in consciousness, as this consciousness cannot be the same individually any two moments, but only of the same kind, it would follow, that we are not for any two moments the same individual persons, but the same kind of persons.

As our consciousness sometimes ceases to exist, as in sound sleep, our personal identity must cease with it. Mr. Locke allows, that the same thing cannot have two beginnings of existence, so that our identity would be irrecoverably gone every time we ceased to think, if it was but for a moment.

16. On Identity and Personal Identity

DAVID HUME

David Hume (1711–1776), a Scottish philosopher and historian, was born in Edinburgh. His philosophy was based on the empiricist dictum that all ideas are copies of prior impressions (experiences). He recommended skepticism about many metaphysical topics (see his selection in Part V). What follows are three excerpts from Hume's *Treatise of Human Nature.* In the first on identity, Hume elucidates a view that accords well with Reid's position, since for Hume identity involves an "invariable uninterrupted existence." Where he differs from Reid is in maintaining that neither persons nor non-persons have a perfect identity through change. In the second, after rejecting the view of the self as a substance (see Plato and Reid in previous readings and Descartes in Part III), Hume offers his own account of the self as a bundle of perceptions, that is, thoughts, feelings, and experiences. In the third selection, he gives up hope of ever achieving an adequate account of the relation that would tie the successive perceptions into a *single* self.

On Identity[1]

First, as to the principle of individuation; we may observe, that the view of any one object is not sufficient to convey the idea of identity. For in that proposition, *an object is the same with itself,* if the idea express'd by the word, *object,* were no ways distinguish'd from that meant by *itself;* we really shou'd mean nothing, nor wou'd the proposition contain a predicate and a subject, which however are imply'd in this affirmation. One single object conveys the idea of unity, not that of identity.

On the other hand, a multiplicity of objects can never convey this idea, however resembling they may be suppos'd. The mind always pronounces the one not to be the other, and considers them as forming two, three, or any determinate number of objects, whose existences are entirely distinct and independent.

Since then both number and unity are incompatible with the relation of identity, it must lie in something that is neither of them. But to tell the truth, at first sight this seems utterly impossible. Betwixt unity and number there can be no medium; no more than betwixt existence and non-existence. After one object is suppos'd to exist, we must either suppose another also to exist; in which case we have the idea of number: Or we must suppose it not to exist; in which case the first object remains at unity.

To remove this difficulty, let us have recourse to the idea of time or duration. I have already observ'd,[2] that time, in a strict sense, implies succession, and that when we apply its idea to any unchangeable object, 'tis only by a fiction of the imagination, by which the unchangeable object is suppos'd to participate of the changes of the co-existent objects, and in particular of that of our perceptions. The fiction of the imagination almost universally takes place; and 'tis by means of it, that a single object, plac'd before us, and survey'd for any time without our discovering in it any interruption or variation, is able to give us a notion of identity. For when we consider any two points of this time, we may place them in different lights: We may either survey them at the very same instant; in which case they give us the idea of number, both by themselves and by the object; which must be multiply'd, in order to be conceiv'd at once, as existent in these two different points of time: Or on the other hand, we may trace the succession of time by a like succession of ideas, and conceiving first one moment, along with the object then existent, imagine afterwards a change in the time without any *variation* or *interruption* in the object; in which case it gives us the idea of unity. Here then is an idea, which is a medium betwixt unity and number; or more properly speaking, is either of them, according to the view, in which we take it: And this idea we call that of identity. We cannot, in any propriety of speech, say, that an object is the same with itself, unless we mean, that the object existent at one time is the same with itself existent at another. By this means we make a difference, betwixt the idea meant by the word, *object,* and that meant by *itself,* without going the length of number, and at the same time without restraining ourselves to a strict and absolute unity.

Thus the principle of individuation is nothing but the *invariableness* and *uninterruptedness* of any object, thro' a suppos'd variation of time, by which the mind can trace it in the different periods of its existence, without any break of the view, and without being oblig'd to form the idea of multiplicity or number.

Of Personal Identity[3]

There are some philosophers, who imagine we are every moment intimately conscious of what we call our *self;* that we feel its existence and its continuance in existence; and are certain, beyond the evidence of a demonstration, both of its perfect identity and simplicity. The strongest sensation, the most violent passion, say they, instead of distracting us from this view, only fix it the more intensely, and make us consider their influence on *self* either by their pain or pleasure. To attempt a farther proof of this were to weaken its evidence; since no proof can be deriv'd from any fact, of which we are so intimately conscious; nor is there any thing, of which we can be certain, if we doubt of this.

Unluckily all these positive assertions are contrary to that very experience, which is pleaded for them, nor have we any idea of *self,* after the manner it is here explain'd. For from what impression cou'd this idea be deriv'd? This question 'tis impossible to answer without a manifest contradiction and absurdity; and yet 'tis a question, which must necessarily be answer'd, if we wou'd have the idea of self pass for clear and intelligible. It must be some one impression, that gives rise to every real idea. But self or person is not any one impression, but that to which our several impressions and ideas are suppos'd to have a reference. If any impression gives rise to the idea of self, that impression must continue invariably the same, thro' the whole course of our lives; since self is suppos'd to exist after that manner. But there is no impression constant and invariable. Pain and pleasure, grief and joy, passions and sensations succeed each other, and never all exist at the same time. It cannot, therefore, be from any of these impressions, or from any other, that the idea of self is deriv'd; and consequently there is no such idea.

But farther, what must become of all our particular perceptions upon this hypothesis? All these are different, and distinguishable, and separable from each other, and may be separately consider'd, and may exist separately, and have no need of any thing to support their existence. After what manner, therefore, do they belong to self; and how are they connected with it? For my part, when I enter most intimately into what I call *myself*, I always stumble on some particular perception or other, of heat or cold, light or shade, love or hatred, pain or pleasure. I never can catch *myself* at any time without a perception, and never can observe any thing but the perception. When my perceptions are remov'd for any time, as by sound sleep; so long am I insensible of *myself*, and may truly be said not to exist. And were all my perceptions remov'd by death, and cou'd I neither think, nor feel, nor see, nor love, nor hate after the dissolution of my body, I shou'd be entirely annihilated, nor do I conceive what is farther requisite to make me a perfect non-entity. If any one upon serious and unprejudic'd reflexion, thinks he has a different notion of *himself*, I must confess I can reason no longer with him. All I can allow him is, that he may be in the right as well as I, and that we are essentially different in this particular. He may, perhaps, perceive something simple and continu'd, which he calls *himself*; tho' I am certain there is no such principle in me.

But setting aside some metaphysicians of this kind, I may venture to affirm the rest of mankind, that they are nothing but a bundle or collection of different perceptions, which succeed each other with an inconceivable rapidity, and are in a perpetual flux and movement. Our eyes cannot turn in their sockets without varying our perceptions. Our thought is still more variable than our sight; and all our other senses and faculties contribute to this change; nor is there any single power of the soul, which remains unalterably the same, perhaps for one moment. The mind is a kind of theatre, where several perceptions successively make their appearance; pass, re-pass, glide away, and mingle in an infinite variety of postures and situations. There is properly no *simplicity* in it at one time, nor *identity* in different; whatever natural propension we may have to imagine that simplicity and identity. The comparison of the theatre must not mislead us. They are the successive perceptions only, that constitute the mind; nor have we the most distant notion of the place, where these scenes are represented, or of the materials, of which it is compos'd.

What then gives us so great a propension to ascribe an identity to these successive perceptions, and to suppose ourselves possest of an invariable and uninterrupted existence thro' the whole course of our lives? In order to answer this question, we must distinguish betwixt personal identity, as it regards our thought or imagination, and as it regards our passions or the concern we take in ourselves. The first is our present subject; and to explain it perfectly we must take the matter pretty deep, and account for that identity, which we attribute to plants and animals: there being a great analogy betwixt it, and the identity of a self or person.

We have a distinct idea of an object, that remains invariable and uninterrupted thro' a suppos'd variation of time; and this idea we call that of *identity* or *sameness*. We have also a distinct idea of several different objects existing in succession, and connected together by a close relation; and this to an accurate view affords as perfect a notion of *diversity*, as if there was no manner of relation among the objects. But tho' these two ideas of identity, and a succession of related objects be in themselves perfectly distinct, and even contrary, yet 'tis certain, that in our common way of thinking they are generally confounded with each other. That action of the imagination, by which we consider the uninterrupted and invariable object, and that by which we reflect on the succession of related objects, are almost the same to the feeling, nor is there much more effort of thought requir'd in the latter case than in the former. The relation facilitates the transition of the mind from one object to another, and renders its passage as smooth as if it contemplated one continu'd object. This resemblance is the cause of the confusion and mistake, and makes us substitute the notion of identity, instead of that of related objects. However at one instant we may consider the related succession as variable or interrupted, we are sure the next to ascribe to it a perfect identity, and regard it as invariable and uninterrupted. Our propensity to this mistake is so great from the resemblance above-mention'd, that we fall into it before we are aware; and tho' we incessantly correct ourselves by reflexion, and return to a more accurate method of thinking, yet we cannot long sustain our philosophy, or take off this bias from the imagination. Our last resource is to yield to it, and boldly assert that these different related objects are in effect the same, however interrupted and variable. In order to justify to ourselves this absurdity, we often feign some new and unintelligible principle, that connects the objects together, and prevents their interruption or variation. Thus we feign the continu'd existence of the perceptions of our senses, to remove the interruption; and run into the notion of a *soul*, and *self*, and *substance*, to disguise the variation. But we may farther observe, that where we do not give rise to such a fiction, our propension to confound identity with relation is so great, that we are apt to imagine⁴ something unknown and mysterious, connecting the parts, beside their relation; and this I take to be the case with regard to the identity we ascribe to plants and vegetables. And even when this does not take place, we still feel a propensity to confound these ideas, tho' we are not able fully to satisfy ourselves in that particular, nor find any thing invariable and uninterrupted to justify our notion of identity.

Thus the controversy concerning identity is not merely a dispute of words. For when we attribute identity, in an improper sense, to variable or interrupted objects, our mistake is not confin'd to the expression, but is commonly attended with a fiction, either of something invariable and uninterrupted, or of something mysterious and inexplicable, or at least with a propensity to such fictions. What will suffice to prove this hypothesis to the satisfaction of every fair enquirer, is to shew from daily experience and observation, that the objects, which are variable or interrupted, and yet are suppos'd to continue the same, are such only as consist of a succession of parts, connected together by resemblance, contiguity, or causation. For as such a succession answers evidently to our notion of diversity, it can only be by mistake we ascribe to it an identity; and as the relation of parts, which leads us into this mistake, is really nothing but a quality, which produces an association of ideas, and an easy transition of the imagination from one to another, it can only be from the resemblance, which this act of the mind bears to that, by which we contemplate one continu'd object, that the error arises. Our chief business, then, must be to prove, that all objects, to which we ascribe identity, without observing their invariableness and uninterruptedness, are such as consist of a succession of related objects.

In order to this, suppose any mass of matter, of which the parts are contiguous and connected, to be plac'd before us; 'tis plain we must attribute a perfect identity to this mass, provided all the parts continue uninterruptedly and invariably the same, whatever motion or change of place we may observe either in the whole or in any of the parts. But supposing some very *small* or *inconsiderable* part to be added to the mass, or subtracted from it; tho' this absolutely destroys the identity of the whole, strictly speaking; yet as we seldom think so accurately, we scruple not to pronounce a mass of matter the same, where we find so trivial an alteration. The passage of the thought from the object before the change to the object after it, is so smooth and easy, that we scarce perceive the transition, and are apt to imagine that 'tis nothing but a continu'd survey of the same object.

There is a very remarkable circumstance, that attends this experiment; which is, that tho' the change of any considerable part in a mass of matter destroys the identity of the whole, yet we must measure the greatness of the part, not absolutely, but by its *proportion* to the whole. The addition or diminution of a mountain wou'd not be sufficient to produce a diversity in a planet; tho' the change of a very few inches wou'd be able to destroy the identity of some bodies. 'Twill be impossible to account for this, but by reflecting that objects operate upon the mind, and break or interrupt the continuity of its actions not according to their real greatness, but according to their proportion to each other: And therefore, since this interruption makes an object cease to appear the same, it must be the uninterrupted progress of the thought, which constitutes the imperfect identity.

This may be confirm'd by another phœnomenon. A change in any considerable part of a body destroys its identity; but 'tis remarkable, that where the change is produc'd *gradually* and *insensibly* we are less apt to ascribe to it the same effect. The reason can plainly be no other, than that the mind, in following the successive changes of the body, feels an easy passage from the surveying its condition in one moment to the viewing of it in another, and at no particular time perceives any interruption in its actions. From which continu'd perception, it ascribes a continu'd existence and identity to the object.

But whatever precaution we may use in introducing the changes gradually, and making them proportionable to the whole, 'tis certain, that where the changes are at last observ'd to become considerable, we make a scruple of ascribing identity to such different objects. There is, however, another artifice, by which we may induce the imagination to advance a step farther; and that is, by producing a reference of the parts to each other, and a combination to some *common end* or purpose. A ship, of which a considerable part has been chang'd by frequent reparations, is still consider'd as the same; nor does the difference of the materials hinder us from ascribing an identity to it. The common end, in which the parts conspire, is the same under all their variations, and affords an easy transition of the imagination from one situation of the body to another.

But this is still more remarkable, when we add a *sympathy* of parts to their *common end,* and suppose that they bear to each other, the reciprocal relation of cause and effect in all their actions and operations. This is the case with all animals and vegetables; where not only the several parts have a reference to some general purpose, but also a mutual dependance on, and connexion with each other. The effect of so strong a relation is, that tho' every one must allow, that in a very few years both vegetables and animals endure a *total* change, yet we still attribute identity to them, while their form, size, and substance are entirely alter'd. An oak, that grows from a small plant to a large tree, is still the same oak; tho' there be not one particle of matter, or figure of its parts the same. An infant becomes a man, and is sometimes fat, sometimes lean, without any change in his identity.

We may also consider the two following phœnomena, which are remarkable in their kind. The first is, that tho' we commonly be able to distinguish pretty exactly betwixt numerical and specific identity, yet it sometimes happens, that we confound them, and in our thinking and reasoning employ the one for the other. Thus a man, who hears a noise, that is frequently interrupted and renew'd, says, it is still the same noise; tho' 'tis evident the sounds have only a specific identity or resemblance, and there is nothing numerically the same, but the cause, which produc'd them. In like manner it may be said without breach of the propriety of language, that such a church, which was formerly of brick, fell to ruin, and that the parish rebuilt the same church of free-stone, and according to modern architecture. Here neither the form nor materials are the same, nor is there any thing common to the two objects, but their relation to the inhabitants of the parish; and yet this alone is sufficient to make us denominate them the same. But we must observe, that in these cases the first object is in a manner annihilated before the second comes into existence; by which means, we are never presented in any one point of time with the idea of difference and multiplicity; and for that reason are less scrupulous in calling them the same.

Secondly, We may remark, that tho' in a succession of related objects, it be in a manner requisite, that the change of parts be not sudden nor entire, in order to preserve the identity, yet where the objects are in their nature changeable and inconstant, we admit of a more sudden transition, than wou'd otherwise be consistent with that relation. Thus as the nature of a river consists in the motion and change of parts; tho' in less than four and twenty hours these be totally alter'd; this hinders not the river from continuing the same during several ages. What is natural and essential to any thing is, in a manner, expected; and what is expected makes less impression, and appears of less moment, than what is unusual and extraordinary. A considerable change of the former kind seems really less to the imagination, than the most trivial alteration of the latter; and by breaking less the continuity of the thought, has less influence in destroying the identity.

We now proceed to explain the nature of *personal identity*, which has become so great a question in philosophy, especially of late years in *England,* where all the abstruser sciences are study'd with a peculiar ardour and application. And here 'tis evident, the same method of reasoning must be continu'd, which has so successfully explain'd the identity of plants, and animals, and ships, and houses, and of all the compounded and changeable productions either of art or nature. The identity, which we ascribe to the mind of man, is only a fictitious one, and of a like kind with that which we ascribe to vegetables and animal bodies. It cannot, therefore, have a different origin, but must proceed from a like operation of the imagination upon like objects.

But lest this argument shou'd not convince the reader; tho' in my opinion perfectly decisive; let him weigh the following reasoning, which is still closer and more immediate. 'Tis evident, that the identity, which we attribute to the human mind, however perfect we may imagine it to be, is not able to run the several different perceptions into one, and make them lose their characters of distinction and difference, which are essential to them. 'Tis still true, that every distinct perception, which enters into the composition of the mind, is a distinct existence, and is different, and distinguishable, and separable from every other perception, either contemporary or successive. But, as, notwithstanding this distinction and separability, we suppose the whole train of perceptions to be united by identity, a question naturally arises concerning this relation of identity; whether it be something that really binds our several perceptions together, or only associates their ideas in the imagination. That is, in other words, whether in pronouncing concerning the identity of a person, we observe some real bond among his perceptions, or

only feel one among the ideas we form of them. This question we might easily decide, if we wou'd recollect what has been already prov'd at large, that the understanding never observes any real connexion among objects, and that even the union of cause and effect, when strictly examin'd, resolves itself into a customary association of ideas. For from thence it evidently follows, that identity is nothing really belonging to these different perceptions, and uniting them together; but is merely a quality, which we attribute to them, because of the union of their ideas in the imagination, when we reflect upon them. Now the only qualities, which can give ideas an union in the imagination, are these three relations above-mention'd. These are the uniting principles in the ideal world, and without them every distinct object is separable by the mind, and may be separately consider'd, and appears not to have any more connexion with any other object, than if disjoin'd by the greatest difference and remoteness. 'Tis, therefore, on some of these three relations of resemblance, contiguity and causation, that identity depends; and as the very essence of these relations consists in their producing an easy transition of ideas; it follows, that our notions of personal identity, proceed entirely from the smooth and uninterrupted progress of the thought along a train of connected ideas, according to the principles above-explain'd.

The only question, therefore, which remains, is, by what relations this uninterrupted progress of our thought is produc'd, when we consider the successive existence of a mind or thinking person. And here 'tis evident we must confine ourselves to resemblance and causation, and must drop contiguity, which has little or no influence in the present case.

To begin with *resemblance;* suppose we cou'd see clearly into the breast of another, and observe that succession of preceptions, which constitutes his mind or thinking principle, and suppose that he always preserves the memory of a considerable part of past perceptions; 'tis evident that nothing cou'd more contribute to the bestowing a relation on this succession amidst all its variations. For what is the memory but a faculty, by which we raise up the images of past perceptions? And as an image necessarily resembles its object, must not the frequent placing of these resembling perceptions in the chain of thought, convey the imagination more easily from one link to another, and make the whole seem like the continuance of one object? In this particular, then, the memory not only discovers the identity, but also contributes to its production, by producing the relation of resemblance among the perceptions. The case is the same whether we consider ourselves or others.

As to *causation;* we may observe, that the true idea of the human mind, is to consider it as a system of different perceptions or different existences, which are link'd together by the relation of cause and effect, and mutually produce, destroy, influence, and modify each other. Our impressions give rise to their correspondent ideas; and these ideas in their turn produce other impressions. One thought chases another, and draws after it a third, by which it is expell'd in its turn. In this respect, I cannot compare the soul more properly to any thing than to a republic or commonwealth, in which the several members are united by the reciprocal ties of government and subordination, and give rise to other persons, who propagate the same republic in the incessant changes of its parts. And as the same individual republic may not only change its members, but also its laws and constitutions; in like manner the same person may vary his character and disposition, as well as his impressions and ideas, without losing his identity. Whatever changes he endures, his several parts are still connected by the relation of causation. And in this view our identity with regard to the passions serves to corroborate that with regard to the imagination, by the making our distant perceptions influence each other, and by giving us a present concern for our past or future pains and pleasures.

As memory alone acquaints us with the continuance and extent of this succession of perceptions, 'tis to be considered, upon that account chiefly, as the source of personal identity. Had we no memory, we never shou'd have any notion of causation, nor consequently of that chain of causes and effects, which constitute our self or person. But having once acquir'd this notion of causation from the memory, we can extend the same chain of causes, and consequently the identity of our persons beyond our memory, and can comprehend times, and circumstances, and actions, which we have entirely forgot, but suppose in general to

have existed. For how few of our past actions are there, of which we have any memory? Who can tell me, for instance, what were his thoughts and actions on the first of January 1715, the 11th of March 1719, and the 3d of August 1733? Or will he affirm, because he has entirely forgot the incidents of these days, that the present self is not the same person with the self of that time; and by that means overturn all the most establish'd notions of personal identity? In this view, therefore, memory does not so much *produce* as *discover* personal identity, by shewing us the relation of cause and effect among our different perceptions. 'Twill be incumbent on those, who affirm that memory produces entirely our personal identity, to give a reason why we can thus extend our identity beyond our memory.

The whole of this doctrine leads us to a conclusion, which is of great importance in the present affair, viz., that all the nice and subtile questions concerning personal identity can never possibly be decided, and are to be regarded rather as grammatical than as philosophical difficulties. Identity depends on the relations of ideas; and these relations produce identity, by means of that easy transition they occasion. But as the relations, and the easiness of the transition may diminish by insensible degrees, we have no just standard, by which we can decide any dispute concerning the time, when they acquire or lose a title to the name of identity. All the disputes concerning the identity of connected objects are merely verbal, except so far as the relation of parts gives rise to some fiction or imaginary principle of union, as we have already observ'd.

What I have said concerning the first origin and the uncertainty of our notion of identity, as apply'd to the human mind, may be extended with little or no variation to that of *simplicity.* An object, whose different co-existent parts are bound together by a close relation, operates upon the imagination after much the same manner as one perfectly simple and indivisible, and requires not a much greater stretch of thought in order to its conception. From this similarity of operation we attribute a simplicity to it, and feign a principle of union as the support of this simplicity, and the center of all the different parts and qualities of the object.

Appendix[5]

I had entertain'd some hopes, that however deficient our theory of the intellectual world might be, it wou'd be free from those contradictions, and absurdities, which seem to attend every explication, that human reason can give of the material world. But upon a more strict review of the section concerning *personal identity*, I find myself involv'd in such a labyrinth, that, I must confess, I neither know how to correct my former opinions, nor how to render them consistent. If this be not a good *general* reason for scepticism, 'tis at least a sufficient one (if I were not already abundantly supplied) for me to entertain a diffidence and modesty in all my decisions. I shall propose the arguments on both sides, beginning with those that induc'd me to deny the strict and proper identity and simplicity of a self or thinking being.

When we talk of *self* or *substance*, we must have an idea annex'd to these terms, otherwise they are altogether unintelligible. Every idea is deriv'd from preceding impressions; and we have no impression of self or substance, as something simple and individual. We have, therefore, no idea of them in that sense.

Whatever is distinct, is distinguishable; and whatever is distinguishable, is separable by the thought or imagination. All perceptions are distinct. They are, therefore, distinguishable, and separable, and may be conceiv'd as separately existent, and may exist separately, without any contradiction or absurdity.

When I view this table and that chimney, nothing is present to me but particular perceptions, which are of a like nature with all the other perceptions. This is the doctrine of philosophers. But this table, which is present to me, and that chimney, may and do exist separately. This is the doctrine of the vulgar, and implies no contradiction. There is no contradiction, therefore, in extending the same doctrine to all the perceptions.

In general, the following reasoning seems satisfactory. All ideas are borrow'd from preceding perceptions. Our ideas of objects, therefore, are deriv'd from that source. Consequently no proposition can be intelligible or consistent with regard to objects, which is not so with regard to percep-

tions. But 'tis intelligible and consistent to say, that objects exist distinct and independent, without any common *simple* substance or subject of inhesion. This proposition, therefore, can never be absurd with regard to perceptions.

When I turn my reflexion on *myself*, I never can perceive this *self* without some one or more perceptions; nor can I ever perceive any thing but the perceptions. 'Tis the composition of these, therefore, which forms the self.

We can conceive a thinking being to have either many or few perceptions. Suppose the mind to be reduc'd even below the life of an oyster. Suppose it to have only one perception, as of thirst or hunger. Consider it in that situation. Do you conceive any thing but merely that perception? Have you any notion of *self* or *substance*? If not, the addition of other perceptions can never give you that notion.

The annihilation, which some people suppose to follow upon death, and which entirely destroys this self, is nothing but an extinction of all particular perceptions; love and hatred, pain and pleasure, thought and sensation. These therefore must be the same with self; since the one cannot survive the other.

Is *self* the same with *substance*? If it be, how can that question have place, concerning the subsistence of self, under a change of substance? If they be distinct, what is the difference betwixt them? For my part, I have a notion of neither, when conceiv'd distinct from particular perceptions.

Philosophers begin to be reconcil'd to the principle, *that we have no idea of external substance, distinct from the ideas of particular qualities*. This must pave the way for a like principle with regard to the mind, *that we have no notion of it, distinct from the particular perceptions.*

So far I seem to be attended with sufficient evidence. But having thus loosen'd all our particular perceptions, when[6] I proceed to explain the principle of connexion, which binds them together, and makes us attribute to them a real simplicity and identity; I am sensible, that my account is very defective, and that nothing but the seeming evidence of the precedent reasonings cou'd have induc'd me to receive it. If perceptions are distinct existences, they form a whole only by being connected together. But no connexions among distinct existences are ever discoverable by human understanding. We only *feel* a connexion or determination of the thought, to pass from one object to another. It follows, therefore, that the thought alone finds personal identity, when reflecting on the train of past perceptions, that compose a mind, the ideas of them are felt to be connected together, and naturally introduce each other. However extraordinary this conclusion may seem, it need not surprise us. Most philosophers seem inclin'd to think, that personal identity *arises* from consciousness; and consciousness is nothing but a reflected thought or perception. The present philosophy, therefore, has so far a promising aspect. But all my hopes vanish, when I come to explain the principles, that unite our successive perceptions in our thought or consciousness. I cannot discover any theory, which gives me satisfaction on this head.

In short there are two principles, which I cannot render consistent; nor is it in my power to renounce either of them, viz., *that all our distinct perceptions are distinct existences*, and *that the mind never perceives any real connexion among distinct existences*. Did our perceptions either inhere in something simple and individual, or did the mind perceive some real connexion among them,

there wou'd be no difficulty in the case. For my part, I must plead the privilege of a sceptic, and confess, that this difficulty is too hard for my understanding. I pretend not, however, to pronounce it absolutely insuperable. Others, perhaps, or myself, upon more mature reflexions, may discover some hypothesis, that will reconcile those contradictions.

Endnotes

[1]This selection is a part of "Of Skepticism with Regard to the Senses," which is section 2 of Part IV of Book I of Hume's *Treatise of Human Nature,* first published in 1739.

[2]Sect. 5, Part II, Book I, *Treatise of Human Nature.*

[3]This selection is section 6 of Part IV of Book I of Hume's *Treatise of Human Nature,* first published in 1739.

[4]Hume notes: "If the reader is desirous to see how a great genius may be influenc'd by these seemingly trivial principles of the imagination, as well as the mere vulgar, let him read my Lord Shaftsbury's reasonings concerning the uniting principle of the universe, and the identity of plants and animals. See his *Moralists* or *Philosophical rhapsody.*"

[5]This selection is from the appendix Hume attached to the first edition of Book III of his *Treatise of Human Nature,* which was first published in 1740.

[6]Book I.

---

17. *Problems of Identity*

RODERICK M. CHISHOLM

Roderick Chisholm (1916–1999) was a professor of philosophy at Brown University. In "Problems of Identity," Chisholm attempts to show why many of the traditional metaphysical approaches to identity (e.g., Hobbes') will not work for persons. Basically, he defends Reid's intuition that personal identity requires the persistence of some "unity." But unlike Hume, Chisholm claims to find some experienced basis for personal identity. Referring to the work of Brentano (see his essay in Part III), Chisholm suggests the complex diversity of experience (for example, seeing and hearing something at the same time) demands that the different components of the experience be united in the experience of a single self. Similarly, Chisholm claims it must be the same self that can have different experiences at different times. In the course of his discussion, Chisholm considers and rejects the "doctrine of temporal parts." This view, which is congenial to the tenseless analysis of time (see Part I), analyses change and identity in terms of the relations among the temporal parts of an object's history (see the following article by Armstrong). Chisholm feels this kind of analysis is contrary to experience and not needed to account for the fact that the same object can have different properties at different times.

Identity and Persistence

I shall discuss what is, for me at least, an extraordinarily difficult and puzzling topic: that of persistence, or identity through time. I have discussed this topic on other occasions when, I regret to say, I have been even more confused than I am now. But I find that other philosophers are confused too. I think I have made some progress. And so I feel justified, therefore, in taking up the topic once again.

I will begin by formulating three different puzzles, Puzzle A, Puzzle B, and Puzzle C, and by describing a uniform way of treating all three puzzles. The treatment in question is reasonably plausible in connection with Puzzle A, which has to do with identity through space. It is fairly plausible in connection with Puzzle B, which has to do with the identity of a familiar type of physical thing through time. But, I will try to suggest, the treatment is entirely implausible in connection with Puzzle C, which has to do with the identity of persons through time. I will also try to suggest that by contemplating the nature of a person, or, better, by contemplating upon the nature of *oneself*, we will be led to a more adequate view of the nature of persistence, or identity through time. My approach to these questions is very much like that of Leibniz, Bishop Butler, and Thomas Reid.[1]

We begin, then, with Puzzle A. We will depict, somewhat schematically, a dispute about the identity of roads. In the northern part of the city, there is a road composed of two parts: *A*, which is the

```
        AB
        CD
    EF      GH
    IJ      KL
```

south-bound lane, and *B*, which is the north-bound lane. Proceeding down the south-bound lane, we come to another area where the road is composed, in a similar way, of *C* and *D*. Then we arrive at a fork in the road: one can go in a southeasterly direction through *GH* to *KL*, or one can go in a southwesterly direction through *EF* to *IJ*. The road from *AB* to *IJ* is called "Elm Street" and the road from *AB* to *KL* is called "Route 42." Elm Street has been in approximately the same place for more than 100 years, while Route 42 is less than 10 years old. But Route 42 is a three-lane highway with the same kind of topping from one end to the other, while Elm Street switches at the fork from tar to concrete and from three lanes to two. We can imagine now that a dispute could develop over the question: "If you start out at *AB* and stay on the same road, will you end up at *IJ* or at *KL*?" The Elm Street faction insists that you will end up at *IJ* and the Route 42 group insists that it will be at *KL*. They consult a metaphysician and he gives them this advice:

"Your dispute has to do with the following six objects among others: (1) the northern stretch of road *AB;* (2) the southwestern stretch *IJ;* (3) the southeastern stretch *KL;* (4) a road which begins at *AB* and ends at *IJ*, that is, Elm Street; (5) a road which begins at *AB* and ends up at *KL,* that is, Route 42; and (6) a Y-shaped object with *AB* as its handle and *IJ* and *KL* as the ends of its forks. These objects overlap in various ways but they are six different things. *IJ* is not identical with *KL;* neither of these is identical with *AB* or with Elm Street or with Route 42 or with the Y-shaped object; and Elm Street, Route 42, and the Y-shaped object are different things despite their overlap. These six different things are equally respectable ontologically. No one of them is any less genuine an entity than any of the others.

"Now there is no dispute about any observational data. You have agreed about what it is that is called 'Elm Street', about what it is that is called 'Route 42', about the number of lanes in the various places, and about what parts are composed of what. Your dispute, then, has to do with criteria for *constituting the same road* or, as we may also put it, with criteria for applying the expression '*x* constitutes the same road as does *y*'. Both groups should be able to see that the members of the other side have correctly *applied* the criterion they happen to be using. That is to say, given the criterion of the Elm Street faction, it would be true to say that if you start at *AB* and continue on the same road you will end up at *IJ*. And given the criterion of the Route 42 group, it would be true to say that you would end up instead at *KL*. It's just a matter, therefore, of your employing conflicting criteria. You have different standards for applying such expressions as 'the same road' and '*x* constitutes the same road as does *y*'.

"I realize you may be inclined to say that you have the 'right' criterion and that the other people have the 'wrong' one. But think more carefully and try to see just what it is you would be trying to express if you talk that way. For once you see what it is, we can call in other experts—in all probability nonphilosophers this time—and they will settle the dispute for you.

"Thus if you think you are using the expression 'the same road' the way the majority of people do or the way the traffic experts of our culture circle or some other more select group uses it and if you think the other group is not using the expression that way, then we can call in the linguists. They can work up questionnaires and conduct surveys and, it may be hoped, you will soon find out who is right. Or perhaps your concern is not with the ways in which other people may happen to use 'the same road'. You may think only that your way of using it is the most convenient one. If you think, say, that we can handle traffic problems more efficiently by using the expression your way than by using it the other way, then the traffic experts and psychologists should be able to help. Or if you think that your use is the better one for promoting some other kind of good, there will be some expert who will know better than any of us.

"Finally, keep in mind that if people had quite different interests from those that any of us now happen to have and if we had been brought up to play some language game very different from this one, there might be no temptation at all to use *either* of the present criteria. If you were grasshop-

pers, for example, you might be arguing whether the road from *C* to *K* goes through *E* or goes through *I*."

I think now we can leave the dispute about the road. As philosophers, surely, we have little or no interest in the outcome. I hope we can agree that, in this instance, the metaphysician's advice is fairly reasonable and that there is little more to be said.

But let us now consider what happens when he applies a similar treatment to two analogous problems having to do with identity or persistence through time. I will formulate Puzzle B and Puzzle C. It may be tempting to follow the metaphysician in his treatment of Puzzle B, but something is clearly wrong, I think, with his treatment of Puzzle C. I suggest that, it is not until we have seen what is wrong with his treatment of Puzzle C, that we can really appreciate the problem of identity through time.

Puzzle B is a version of the ancient problem of the Ship of Theseus. We now consider a dispute that might arise about the identity of ships through time. The ship when it first set sail was composed of two parts *A* and *B*. Parts of parts were replaced and at a later point in its history it was composed of *C* and *D* where previously it had been composed of *A* and *B*. At a certain point it underwent fission and went off, so to speak, in two different directions—one ship being composed of *E* and *F* going off toward the southwest and another ship being composed of *G* and *H* going off toward the southeast. The ship that went southwest ended up being composed of *I* and *J* and the one that went southeast

$$
\begin{array}{cc}
AB & \\
CD & \\
EF & GH \\
IJ & KL \\
\end{array}
$$

being composed of *K* and *L*. This time the question arises: "Had you boarded *AB* when it first set sail and remained on the same ship, would you now be on the southwesterly *IJ* or on the southeasterly *KL*?" The *IJ* faction may point out that, if you end up on *IJ*, you will have remained throughout on a wooden ship called *Theseus* and that, if you end up on *KL*, you will now be on an aluminum ship called *The East Coast Ferry*. The *KL* group may point out, to the contrary, that if you end up on *KL*, you will have remained throughout on a ship having the same daily schedule, the same crew, and the same traditions and that, if you end up on *IJ,* you will be on a weekend cruise ship having an amateur crew and nothing worth calling a tradition. Being impressed by the way in which our metaphysician handled the problem of the roads, the two parties turn to him for advice. And this is what he tells them:

"There is no difference in principle between the present problem and the problem of the roads. For just as an object that is extended through space at a given time has, for each portion of space that it occupies, *a spatial part* that is unique to that portion of space at that time, so, too, any object that persists through a period of time has, for each subperiod of time during which it exists, *a temporal part* that is unique to that subperiod of time.

"Taking our cue from the problem of the roads, we see that in this case, too, there are six objects which are of special concern. Just as a road that extends through space has different spatial parts at the different places at which it exists, a ship that persists through time has different temporal parts at the different times at which it exists. So we may distinguish (1) the earlier temporal part *AB;* (2) the present southwestern part *IJ;* (3) the present southeastern part *KL;* (4) that temporally extended object now called the *Theseus* with the early part *AB,* the later part *IJ,* and *CD* and *EF* falling in between; (5) that temporally extended object now called *The East Coast Ferry* with the early part *AB,* the later part *KL,* and *CD* and *GH* falling in between; and (6), what you may not have noticed, a Y-shaped temporal object with *AB* as its root and *IJ* and *KL* as the ends of its forks. As in the previous case, these are different things despite their overlap and they are all on a par ontologically.

"There is no dispute about any of the observational data. You are in agreement about crews, schedules, stuff, and traditions, and about what things are called what. Your dispute has to do with *criteria* for constituting the same ship, or, as we may now also put it, with criteria for applying the expression '*x* constitutes the same ship as does *y*'. The members of each faction have correctly applied their own criteria. If you are inclined to say that your criterion is the right one and that the other one is the wrong one, reflect a little further and I'm sure we can find some nonphilosophical expert who can help you settle the question. Do

you think, for example, that you are using 'the same ship' the way the majority of people do or the way the nautical people do? The linguists can check on that for you. Or do you think you are using it the way it's used in the courts? Then we can call in the lawyers. Or do you think that your way of using it is the most convenient one given your purposes or given the purposes of most people? State as clearly as you can what the purposes in question are and then we can find an expert who will help you out.

"Keep in mind that, if people had quite different interests and played a different language game, then there might be no temptation to use either of the present criteria. After all there are still other temporal objects involved here: for example, the temporally scattered object made up of *A, F,* and *L,* the one made up of *C, H,* and *J,* and so on. Some one of those might be what you would call a ship—if *you* were a different type of temporal object."

Let us not pause to evaluate this advice. For our interest in Puzzle B and its treatment is only transitional. I have spelled out the account only to prepare us for Puzzle C.

Puzzle C: Mr. Jones has learned somehow that he is about to undergo fission. Or, more accurately, he has learned that his body will undergo fission. It is now made up of parts *A* and *B.* Presently it will be made up of *C* and *D.* Then there will be fission; one body will go off as *EF* and end up as *IJ,* and the other will go off as *GH* and end up as *KL.* Then there will be the two men, *IJ* and *KL.* Or, to be more cautious, there will be a man who has *IJ* as his body and there will be a man who has *KL* as his body.

$$
\begin{array}{cc}
AB & \\
CD & \\
EF & GH \\
IJ & KL
\end{array}
$$

Mr. Jones knows that the man who ends up with *IJ* will have the distinctive physical characteristics—brain waves, fingerprints, and all the rest—that he, Mr. Jones, now has, and that the man who ends up as *KL* will not. He also knows that the inner parts of *IJ* will have evolved in the usual manner from the inner parts he has now, that is, from the inner parts of *AB,* whereas a number of the crucial organs within *KL* will have been transplanted from outside. But he knows further that the man who has *KL* as his body will have the memories, or a significant part of the memories, that he, Mr. Jones, now has, and what is more that the man will remember doing things that only Mr. Jones has ever done. Or perhaps we should say, more cautiously, that the man will *seem* to himself to remember—will *think he remembers*—having done those things. And the memory, or ostensible memory, will be extraordinarily accurate in points of detail. Mr. Jones now puts this question: "Will I be the one who ends up as *IJ* or will I be the one who ends up as *KL?*"

It has been said that there are "two main competing answers" to the question "What are the criteria for the identity of a person through time?" One of these is that "the criterion of the identity of a person is the identity of the body that he has." And the other is that "the criterion of the identity of a person is the set of memories which he has."[2] We will suppose that, according to the first of these criteria ("the bodily criterion") the man who has *IJ* as his body is the same person as Mr. Jones; and according to the second of these criteria ("the memory criterion") the man who has *KL* as his body is the same person as Mr. Jones.

To make sure that Mr. Jones's interest in the question is not purely theoretical, let us suppose further that he has the following information: Though both men will languish during their final phases, the *IJ* and the *KL* phases, the man who ends up as *KL* will lead the most wretched of lives during his *GH* phase, and the man who ends up as *IJ* will lead a life of great happiness and value during his *EF* phase. And so Mr. Jones asks with some concern: "Which one am I going to be?"

The approach of the metaphysician should now be familiar. He will note that, for each portion of space that Mr. Jones's body now occupies there is a spatial part of Mr. Jones's body that is now unique to that portion of space. He will then point out that, for any period of time during which Mr. Jones will have existed, there is a *temporal part* of Mr. Jones that is unique to that period of time. Turning to the problem at hand, he will distinguish the following things among others: *AB; IJ; KL;* the thing that begins as *AB* and ends as *LJ;* the thing that begins as *AB* and ends as *KL;* and the Y-shaped object that begins as *AB* and ends as *IJ* in one place and *KL* in another.

He will note that Mr. Jones is raising a question about criteria: "Is 'the memory criterion' or 'the bodily criterion' the correct criterion of what it is for someone at one time to constitute the same person as does someone at some other time?" He will point out to Mr. Jones that, in asking which is the correct criterion, he is in fact concerned with some more specific question. If he is asking how the majority of people, or how certain people, use the expression "same person," he should consult the linguists. If he is asking how the courts would deal with the question, he should look up the law books. And if he is asking, with respect to certain definite ends, what linguistic uses would best promote those ends, there will be authorities who can give him at least a probable answer. (*We* might remind Mr. Jones, however, that if he asks these empirical authorities how *he,* Mr. Jones, could best promote certain ends after the fission has taken place, then he should look very carefully at the answer.)

As before, the metaphysician will conclude with some general advice: "Keep in mind that, if people had quite different interests and played a different language game, there might be no temptation to use either the bodily criterion or the memory criterion. After all, there are still other temporal objects involved in your problem. With different interests and a different makeup, you might be more concerned with two of *them* instead of with the two that you happen to have singled out. You claim to know that the *EF* phase is going to be good and that the *GH* phase is going to be bad. You haven't noticed, apparently, that there is more than one person who will go through the *EF* phase and more than one person who will go through the *GH* phase. What other persons? For example, there is the one that goes from *AB* to *EF* to *KL,* and then there is the one that goes from *CD* through *GH* to *IJ.* If you had a different makeup, you might wish you were one of *those* and hope you're not the other."

If Mr. Jones is at all reasonable, he will feel at this point that something has gone wrong. However many persons the problem involves, if there is a person who starts out as *AB*, goes through *CD* and *EF* to *IJ*, there is not also *another* person who starts out as *AB*, goes through *EF*, and ends up as *KL*. And if there is a person who starts out as *AB*, goes through *CD* and *GH* to *KL,* there is not *another* person who goes through *GH* and ends up as *IJ*. (It would hardly be just to punish *two* persons for the sins that someone committed during the *GH* phase.) And, what is more important, after Mr. Jones has consulted the various empirical authorities, he will still wonder whether he has an answer to his question: "Which one am I going to be?"

Where did the metaphysician go wrong?

Going back for a moment to Route 42 in Puzzle A, consider what is involved when we say there is a Buick and an Oldsmobile on the road, the former a mile behind the latter. We are saying, of course, that there exists an *x*, namely, Route 42, which is such that a Buick is on *x* and an Oldsmobile is on *x*, a mile in front of the Buick. But this is to say that there is a *y* and a *z* which are distinct from *x* and from each other and which are such that the Buick is on *y* and not on *z* and the Oldsmobile is on *z* and not on *y*. And so we are referring to *three* different things in addition to the Oldsmobile and the Buick. We are referring, first, to Route 42 which both the Oldsmobile and the Buick are on; we are referring, secondly, to that portion of Route 42 which the Oldsmobile but not the Buick is on; and we are referring, thirdly, to that portion of Route 42 which the Buick but not the Oldsmobile is on. Our metaphysician assumes that temporal differences are analogous.

What is involved when we say that a ship had been red and then subsequently became blue? According to our metaphysician we are, once again, referring to three different things. We are saying, of course, that there was an *x*, namely, the ship, which was such that *x* was red and then *x* became blue. And this, according to our metaphysician, is to say that there was a *y* and a *z*, each distinct from *x* and from each other, which were such that *y* was red and not blue and *z* was blue and not red. In addition to the ship, there was that "temporal part" of it which was red and that other "temporal part" of it which was blue.

It is very important to note that, according to the metaphysician, his thesis will be true whether or not any of the parts of the ship are ever replaced—or, more exactly, it will be true whether or not anything occurs that would *ordinarily* be described as replacement of the parts of the ship. Let the ship be such that we could describe it in our ordinary language by saying it has kept all its parts intactly, down to the smallest particles. Our metaphysician will nevertheless say that that temporal part of the ship which is red is other than that temporal part of the ship which is blue and that each of these is other than the ship itself.

And he maintains a similar thesis with respect to Puzzle C. Consider now the man who began with the body made up of *A* and *B* and ended up with *I* and *J*. What is involved in saying that he is sad one day and happy the next? Again, there will be an *x*, the man, such that *x* is sad and subsequently *x* is happy. And to say this, according to our metaphysician, is to say that there is also a *y* and a *z* each distinct from *x* and from each other and such that *y* is sad and *z* is happy. But is this true?

It may be instructive to compare the doctrine of our metaphysician with what Jonathan Edwards says in defense of the doctrine of original sin. Edwards is concerned with the question whether it is just to impute to you and me the sins that were committed by Adam. And he wishes to show that it is *as* just to attribute Adam's sins to us now as it is to attribute any *other* past sins to us now.

He appeals to the doctrine, which he accepts, that God not only created the world *ex nihilo* but constantly preserves or upholds the things which he creates. Without God's continued preservation of the world, all created things would fall into nothingness. Now Edwards says that "God's upholding created substance, or causing its existence in each successive moment, is altogether equivalent to an immediate *production out of nothing,* at each moment." In preserving the table in its being a moment from now, God will get no help from the table. It isn't as though the table will be there waiting to be upheld. If it were there waiting to be upheld, if it were available to God and ready for preservation, he would not *need* to uphold or preserve it. God does not uphold the table by making use of matter that is left over from an earlier moment. Edwards compares the persistence of such things as the table with that of the reflection or image on the surface of a mirror. "The image that exists this moment, is not at all *derived* from the image which existed the last preceding moment. . . . If the succession of new *rays* be intercepted, by something interposed between the object and the glass, the image immediately ceases; the *past existence* of the image has no influence to uphold it, so much as for one moment.

Which shows that the image is altogether completely remade every moment; and strictly speaking, is in no part numerically the same with that which existed in the moment preceding. And truly so the matter must be with the *bodies* themselves, as well as their images. They also cannot be the same, with an absolute identity, but must be wholly renewed every moment. . . ." Edwards summarizes his doctrine of preservation this way: "If the existence of created *substance,* in each successive moment, be wholly the effect of God's immediate power, in *that* moment, without any dependence on prior existence, as much as the first creation out of *nothing,* then what exists at this moment, by this power, is a *new effect,* and simply and absolutely considered, not the same with any past existence. . . ."[3]

This conception of persisting physical things, though not its theological basis, is also defended by a number of contemporary philosophers. It may be found, for example, in the axiom system concerning things and their parts that is developed in Carnap's *Introduction to Symbolic Logic.*[4] Carnap's system is derived from the systems developed by J. H. Woodger and Alfred Tarski, in Woodger's *The Axiomatic Method in Biology.*[5] These authors say that, for every moment at which a thing exists there is a set of momentary parts of the thing; none of these parts exists at any other moment; and the thing itself is the sum of its momentary parts.[6]

The thing that constitutes you now, according to this view, is diverse from the things that have constituted you at any other moment, just as you are diverse from every other person who exists now. But God, according to Jonathan Edwards, can contemplate a collection of objects existing at different times and "treat them as one." He can take a collection of various individuals existing at different times and think of them as all constituting a single individual. Edwards appeals to a doctrine of truth by divine convention; he says that God *"makes truth* in affairs of this nature." Like our metaphysician, God could regard temporally scattered individuals—you this year, me last year, and General De Gaulle the year before that—as comprising a single individual. And then he could justly punish you this year and me last year for the sins that General De Gaulle committed the year before that. And so, Edwards concludes, "No solid reason can be given, why

God . . . may not establish a constitution whereby the natural posterity of Adam . . . should be treated as *one* with him, for the derivation, either of righteousness, and communion in rewards, or of the loss of righteousness, and consequent corruption and guilt."

Like our metaphysician, Edwards is impressed by what he takes to be the analogy between space and time. To persuade his reader that God could reasonably regard Adam's posterity as being one with Adam, he asserts that there would be no problem at all if Adam's posterity *coexisted* with Adam. If Adam's posterity had "somehow *grown out of him,* and yet remained *contiguous* and literally *united to him,* as the branches to a tree, or the members of the body to the head; and had all, before the fall, existed together at the *same time,* though in *different places,* as the head and members are in different places," surely then, Edwards says, God could treat the whole collection as "one moral whole" with each of us as its parts. And if a collection of persons existing in different places can be thought of as a single moral whole, why not also a collection of persons existing at different times?

What are we to say of all this? What Jonathan Edwards and our metaphysician have left out, if I am not mistaken, is what has traditionally been called the *unity* of every real thing. Leibniz said that we acquire this notion of unity by reflecting upon our own nature.[7] I suggest that this is so and that if we reflect "upon our own nature," we will see what is wrong with the Edwardian doctrine and with the solution to Puzzle C.

Edwards was even mistaken in his spatial figure. If we think of Adam's posterity as growing out of Adam's body, with me here and you there and Adam some place in between, we cannot properly regard the resulting whole as "a moral unity." Though there may be just one body involved there will be irreducibly many persons if one of them is me, another you, and a third Adam.

Let me quote to you from the chapter "On the Unity of Consciousness" from Franz Brentano's *Psychologie vom empirischen Standpunkt.* Brentano asks whether when we consider our own consciousness at any moment we find a real unified whole or a bare multiplicity—what he called a mere *collectivum* and not a unity or unitary whole. Suppose you find yourself hearing a certain sound and seeing a certain color, as you do now, and you realize that these are two different experiences. Could one conceivably say that the thing that is doing the seeing is *other* than the thing that is doing the hearing? "If the presentation of the color is to be ascribed to one thing and the presentation of the sound to another, is the presentation of the difference to be ascribed to the one, or to the other, or to both together, or to a third thing?" If one thing is doing the hearing and another thing is doing the seeing, how would either of *those* things become aware of the fact that there are two different experiences going on, one the hearing and the other the seeing? It wouldn't do, Brentano says, to attribute the perception of the difference to some *third* thing—some thing other than the thing that's doing the seeing and other than the thing that's doing the hearing. Should we ascribe the perception of the difference then to the *two* different things—to the seer and to the hearer? "This, too, would be ridiculous. It would be as though one were to say that, although neither a blind man nor a deaf man can perceive the difference between a color and a tone, the two of them can perceive it together when the one sees and the other hears. . . . When we combine the activities of the blind man and the deaf man, we have only a *collectivum,* not a real unitary thing [*immer nur ein Kollektiv, niemals ein einheitliches wirkliches Ding*]. Whether the blind man and the deaf man are close together or far apart makes no difference. It wouldn't make any difference whether they lived in the same house, or whether they were Siamese twins, or whether they had developed even more inseparably together. It is only when the color and the sound are presented to one and the same individual thing, that it is thinkable that they may be compared with each other."[8]

In short, when you see and hear something at the same time, the experience cannot be adequately described by saying "There exists an x and a y such that x sees something, y hears something, and x is other than y." We can use just one personal variable ("There exists an x such that x sees something and x also hears it") or if we use two ("There exists an x such that x hears something and there exists a y such that y hears it"), then we must add that their values are one and the same ("x is identical with y").

Brentano discussed the kind of unity that is involved when we are aware of ourselves as having two different experiences, seeing and hearing, at the same time. Let us now consider, analogously,

the kind of unity that is involved when we are aware of ourselves as having different experiences throughout an interval of time. This is what happens when, as now, you are listening to someone talking, or what happens when you are listening to a melody. But consider an experience of even shorter duration: one hears the birdcall "Bob White." The experience might be described by saying "There exists an x such that x hears 'Bob' and x hears 'White'." 'But we want to make sure we are not talking about the experience wherein one hears two sounds at once—'Bob' from one bird and 'White' from another. And so we might say "There exists an x and two times, t^1 *and* t^2, such that t^2 is later than t^1, and such that x hears 'Bob' at t^1 and x hears 'White' at t^2." If we are not to reify times, we will put the matter another way, perhaps as "There exists an x such that x hears 'Bob' *before* x hears 'White' or as "There exists an x such that x hears 'Bob' *and then* x hears 'White'." But we are not now concerned with what is philosophically the best way to describe the passage of time. Our present concern is with the variable 'x' and the thing that it refers to.

We will say, then, "There exists an x such that x hears 'Bob' and then x hears 'White'." Jonathan Edwards and our metaphysician would say that the experience could be adequately described by using two variables: "There exists a y and a z such that y hears 'Bob' and z hears 'White'." But the latter sentence is *not* adequate to the experience in question. The man who has the experience knows not only (1) that there is someone who hears 'Bob' and someone who hears 'White'. He also knows (2) that the one who hears 'Bob' is *identical with* the one who hears 'White'. And, what is crucial to the present problem, he knows (3) that his experience of hearing 'Bob' and his experience of hearing 'White' were not *also* had by two other things, each distinct from himself and from each other.

What are we to say, then, of the doctrine of "temporal parts," of the doctrine according to which, for every period of time during which an individual thing exists, there is a temporal part of that thing which is unique to that period of time? We can point out, as I have tried to do, that it is not adequate to the experience we have of ourselves. We can also point out that the doctrine multiplies entities beyond necessity. And, finally, we can criticize the case *for* the doctrine of temporal parts.

What is this case? It is based, presumably, upon the assumption that whatever may be said about spatial continuity and identity may also be said, *mutatis mutandis,* about temporal continuity and identity. If this assumption is correct, then the doctrine of temporal parts would seem to be true. We may say, as our metaphysician did: "Just as an object that is extended through space at a given time has, for each portion of space that it occupies, a *spatial part* that is unique to that portion of space at that time, so, too, any object that persists through a period of time has, for each subperiod of time during which it exists, a *temporal part* that is unique to that subperiod of time." But is it correct to assume that whatever may be said about spatial continuity and identity may also be said, *mutatis mutandis,* about temporal continuity and identity? I would say that there is a fundamental *disanalogy* between space and time.

The disanalogy may be suggested by saying simply: "One and the same thing cannot be in two different places at one and the same time. But one and the same thing can be at two different times in one and the same place." Let us put the point of disanalogy, however, somewhat more precisely.

When we say, "A thing cannot be in two different places at one and the same time," we mean that it is not possible for *all* the parts of the thing to be in one of the places at that one time and *also* to be in the other of the places at that same time. It *is* possible, of course, for *some* part of the thing to be in place at a certain time and *another* part of the thing to be in another place at that time. And to remove a possible ambiguity in the expression "all the parts of a thing," let us spell it out to "all the parts that the thing ever will have had."

Instead of saying simply, "a thing cannot be in two different places at one and the same time," let us say this: "It is *not* possible for there to be a thing which is such that all the parts it ever will have had are in one place at one time and also in another place at that same time." And instead of saying "a thing can be at two different times in one and the same place," let us say this: "It *is* possible for there to be a thing which is such that all the parts it ever will have had are in one place at one time and also in that same place at another time."

It seems to me to be clear that each of these two theses is true and therefore that there is a fundamental disanalogy between space and time. And

so if the case *for* the doctrine of temporal parts presupposes that there is no such disanalogy, then the case is inadequate. (We may, of course, appeal to the doctrine of temporal parts in order to *defend* the view that there is no such disanalogy. We may use it, in particular, to criticize the second of the two theses I set forth above, the thesis according to which it is possible for there to be a thing which is such that all the parts it ever will have had are in one place at one time and also in that same place at another time. But what, then, is the case *for* the doctrine of temporal parts?)

The doctrine of temporal parts is sometimes invoked as a solution to this type of puzzle. "(i) Johnson was President five years ago but is not President now. Therefore (ii) something can be truly said of the Johnson of five years ago that cannot be truly said of the Johnson of now. Hence (iii) the Johnson of five years ago is other than the Johnson of now. How, then, are they related?" The proposed solution is "they are different temporal parts of the same person." But it is simpler just to note that (ii) is false. *Nothing* can truly be said of the Johnson of five years ago that cannot be truly said of the Johnson of now. The Johnson of now, like the Johnson of five years ago, *was* President five years ago, and the Johnson of five years ago, like the Johnson of now, is *not* President now. But if (ii) is false, then the derivation of (iii) is invalid. And so the puzzle disappears.

Mr. Jones's problem, the problem of Puzzle C, is much more difficult than our metaphysician thought it was. I fear that we cannot help him either, but we may point out, in conclusion, certain considerations which would be relevant to the solution of his problem.

Let us say that an "Edwardian object" is an individual thing such that, for any two different moments at which it exists, there is a set of things making it up at the one moment and another set of things making it up at the other moment and the two sets of things have no members in common. According to Jonathan Edwards and to the doctrine of temporal parts, *every* individual thing is Edwardian. I have suggested that some things that persist through time, namely, we ourselves, are *not* Edwardian. Some persisting things have a kind of *unity* through time that Edwardian objects, if there *are* any Edwardian objects, do not have.[9] How are we to characterize this unity?

We might characterize it by reference to "intact persistence." Let us say that a thing "persists intactly" if it has continued, uninterrupted existence through a period of time and if, at any moment of its existence, it has precisely the same parts it has at any other moment of its existence. Thus a thing that persists intactly would exist at least two different times; for any two times during which it exists, it also exists at any time between those times; and at no time during which it exists does it have any part it does not have at any other time during which it exists. We might now define a "primary thing" as a thing that persists intactly during every moment of its existence. The simplest type of unity through time, then, would be that possessed by primary things. Other types of unity could then be described by reference to it.

It is tempting to say, in Leibnizian fashion: "There are things. Therefore there are primary things." But a somewhat more modest thesis would be this: Every extended period of time, however short, is such that some primary thing exists during some part of that time. I would suggest that it is only by presupposing this thesis that we can make sense of the identity or persistence of any individual thing through time.

So far as Mr. Jones's problem is concerned, we may note that it is at least possible that persons are primary things and hence that Mr. Jones is a primary thing. This would mean, of course, that we could not identify Mr. Jones with that object that persists without remaining intact which is his body. But for all anyone knows he might be identical with some physical thing which is a *part* of that body. We should also note that it is logically possible for a primary thing to persist from one time to another without there being any *criterion* by means of which anyone who had identified it at the earlier time could also identify it at the later time. Hence if Mr. Jones is a primary thing, it is possible that *he* will be the one who has bodily parts *IJ* even though neither he nor anyone else will ever know, or even have good reason to believe, that the man who now has bodily parts *AB* is also the man who will have bodily parts *IJ*.[10]

Endnotes

[1]See Leibniz' *New Essays Concerning Human Understanding*, Book II, Chapter XXVII ("What Identity or Diversity Is"); Bishop Butler's dissertation "Of Personal Identity"; and Thomas Reid, *Essays on the Intellectual Powers of Man*, Essay III, Chapters IV and VI. I have discussed these questions in "The Loose and Popular and the Strict and Philosophical Senses of Identity," in Norman S. Care and Robert H. Grimm, eds., *Perception and Personal Identity* (Cleveland: The Press of Western Reserve University, 1969); and in "Identity Through Time," in Howard Keifer and Milton K. Munitz, eds., *Language, Belief, and Metaphysics* (Albany: State University of New York Press, 1970).

[2]See Terence Penelhum's article, "Personal Identity," in *The Encyclopedia of Philosophy*, ed. Paul Edwards (New York: Macmillan, 1967), Vol. VI.

[3]The quotations are from Edwards' *Doctrine of Original Sin Defended* (1758), Part IV, Chapter II.

[4]Rudolf Carnap, *Introduction to Symbolic Logic* (New York: Dover Publications, 1958), p. 213 ff.

[5]J. H. Woodger, *The Axiomatic Method in Biology* (Cambridge: Cambridge University Press, 1937); see especially pp. 55–63, and Appendix E by Alfred Tarski (pp. 161–172).

[6]A thing a is said to be the *sum* of a class F, provided only every member of the class F is a part of a, and every part of a has a part in common with some member of the class. If, as these authors postulate, every nonempty class has a sum, there would be, for example, an *individual thing* which is the sum of the class of men: Every man would be a part of this collective man and every part of this collective man would share a part with some individual man. The same would hold for that class the only members of which are this man and that horse. An opposing view is that of Boethius: A man and a horse are not one thing. See D. P. Henry, *The Logic of Saint Anselm* (Oxford: The Clarendon Press, 1967), p. 56.

[7] *New Essays Concerning Human Understanding*, Book II, Ch. 1, sec. 8.

[8]Franz Brentano, *Psychologie vom empirischen Standpunkt*, Vol. 1 (Leipzig: Felix Meiner, 1924), pp. 226–227.

[9]I have attributed to Carnap the view that every individual thing is Edwardian; see Carnap, *op. cit.*, p. 213 ff. I should note, however, that he is quite aware of what I have called the problem of the unity of a persisting thing through time. He is aware, for example, that such an object as the one that is composed of my temporal parts of this year, yours of last year, and General De Gaulle's of the year before that does not have the type of unity through time that other objects do. To secure the latter type of unity he introduces the concept of *genidentity*. "Following Kurt Lewin, we say that world-points [temporal slices] of *the same particle* are *genidentical*"; *op. cit.*, p. 198. (I have italicized "the same particle.") But if we do not multiply entities by assuming that every concrete individual is Edwardian, we need not multiply relations by supposing that there is a concept of *genidentity* in addition to that of identity, or persistence through time.

[10]Compare Sydney S. Shoemaker, "Comments," and Roderick M. Chisholm, "Reply," in *Perception and Personal Identity*, Norman S. Care and Robert H. Grimm, eds. (Cleveland: The Press of Case Western Reserve University, 1969).

18. *Identity through Time*

DAVID M. ARMSTRONG

In this article, David M. Armstrong, emeritus professor of philosophy at the University of Sydney, distinguishes what he calls the "identity analysis" and the "relational analysis" of identity through time. These analyses provide different answers to the question In virtue of what are X and Y stages (or phases) of one and the same object P? Armstrong attempts to defend a relational analysis, according to which the identity of a thing is composed of suitably related temporal parts. He appeals to *causality* as the glue that unites the diverse parts into a single whole.

Some philosophers in their work are led on to ever greater complexity; others seek simplicity and clarity of argument and vision. Each type of mind serves to check the shortcomings of the other. In our age philosophy is more professionalized than ever before, so as a result the first sort of mind is in the ascendant. All the more important, therefore, is the role of those who will not let their thought be dissipated in endless ramifications. Richard Taylor's particular intellectual contribution has been to discover, or to restate, simple and direct, yet profound and forceful, arguments which lead to important conclusions about major philosophical issues. He has done this in a way which involves no sacrifice of contemporary standards of rigor and exactness.

Identity through Time: The Identity and the Relational View

Two views may be taken of the identity of particulars through time. We may call them the identity view and the relational view. Many, but not all, contemporary analytical philosophers accept the relational view. So do I. Recently, however, as a result of working on the problem of universals, I

From Peter van Inwagen, ed., *Time and Cause: Essays Presented to Richard Taylor*, pp. 67–78. Copyright © 1980 by D. Reidel Publishing Company. Reprinted by permission of Kluwer Academic Publishers.

have come to have more sympathy with the identity view. I still think it is false, but I do not think, as I used to think, that it is nonsense. In this paper I want to consider again the dispute between the two views.

It is to be understood that neither of these views challenges the truism that if X and Y are different phases of an object, P, then they are phases of one identical thing. The identity and the relational views are, rather, different philosophical analyses of the situations referred to in the previous sentence. I oppose an "identity" to a "relational" view because I believe that identity is not a genuine relation. If this is an incorrect belief, however, for our present purposes it means no more than that my terminology is ill-chosen.

I begin by trying to characterize the relational view. If we consider nonoverlapping phases in the history of the same particular, P, then, according to the relational view, such phases are in no way identical. What we have is simply a particular case of different *parts* of the same thing. They are temporal parts rather than spatial parts, but the adjectives 'temporal' and 'spatial' do not modify the meaning of the word 'parts.' These parts, themselves particulars, are related in various ways to each other and to further particulars. The holding of some of these relations *constitutes* what it is for the parts to be different temporal parts of P.

Consider, by way of comparison, nonoverlapping spatial parts of P at a certain instant of time. Very few philosophers would want to argue that such spatial parts are in any way identical with each other. These parts, themselves particulars, are related in various ways, to each other and to further particulars. The holding of some of these relations *constitutes* what it is for the parts to be different spatial parts of *P*. Just what these constituting relations are will depend upon what sort of thing *P* is. The relations between the handle of a cup and the rest of the cup which make the two particulars into a cup are rather different from the relations which make the soldiers of an army into an army. But the unity of *P* at a time seems secured simply by uniting relations between *P*'s spatial parts at that time, or, in some cases, their relations to some further particular or particulars.

If we accept this view about the spatial case, it is natural to conclude that the temporal parts, that is, the phases, of *P* are also united to form *P* by nothing more than relations.

Nevertheless, we do have a sense that nonoverlapping phases of the history of the one particular are not mere different parts of the same particular, but are actually *identical* with each other in some deeper way. It is the same thing which existed yesterday and today, we are inclined to think, in a way that the different spatial parts of the same thing are not identical with each other in any way. We do have some intuitive sense that a relational analysis of identity through time is false and that an identity theory is true.

Is this feeling just nonsense, nonsense which, perhaps, appeals to us because of our deep emotional interest in the continuing of ourselves and other things which we cherish? I think that Hume thought it was nonsense, although he recognized that it was nonsense to which we are instinctively attracted. He spoke of the way in which we 'feign' an identity between the different phases of the same thing.[1]

A strong argument can be advanced in support of Hume's view that the identity account of identity through time is nonsense. Consider again two nonoverlapping phases of the particular *P*. However intimately they may be related, it seems impossible to deny that they are two wholly distinct particulars. This becomes clear when we consider that we can attribute properties and relations to both phases, and that these properties and relations may be different from (and even incompatible with) each other. *P* may be at one temperature during the first phase, another temperature during the second. Things which differ in their properties are different things. But if the two phases are different things, then they are not the same thing.

I think that this argument does show that non-overlapping phases of the same particular are distinct particulars. What it fails to show, however, is that they are *wholly* distinct particulars. It leaves open the possibility that they are distinct, but not wholly distinct.

In thinking about identity there is a tendency for one's thought to be dominated by the two extreme cases. These cases may be illustrated by the complete identity of the morning star with the evening star, on the one hand, and the complete non-identity of the morning star with the Red Planet, on the other. But we need to remember that there are intermediate cases: for instance, terraced houses which have a party wall in common, or unseparated Siamese twins. Another sort of case is that where phases of the same particular overlap but do not coincide completely. Wherever things overlap or stand as part to whole we have merely partial identity.

But what is the relevance of all this to the case, which we are considering, of *nonoverlapping* phases of a particular? The answer is that, given certain further assumptions, even different particulars of this sort may be partially identical. Suppose, in particular, that one rejects nominalism, the doctrine that nothing exists which is not a particular. Suppose that, as I do, one accepts the objective reality of (instantiated) universals. Suppose one holds that different particulars may have the very same, the *identical*, property, for instance, the same mass. One is then committed to saying that such particulars are (at least partially) identical in nature. And if identity is a univocal notion, as I believe it is, partial identity of nature entails partial identity.

To think along these lines is to have one's ideas about the complete nonidentity of nonoverlapping particulars shaken up in a fruitful way. But it is hardly to accept that nonoverlapping phases of the same particular could be identical *as particulars*.

To understand this latter possibility we need to consider what a particular is. The view which I accept is the orthodox view among those who are realists, that is, are believers in universals. A particular is, essentially, a particular-having-certain-properties-and-relations. Its particularity is distinguishable but not separable from its properties and relations. Following Scotus, we can say that it involves both thisness and nature, or with Aristotle that it is a this-such.

Against the background of this view we can now characterize the identity analysis of the identity of particulars through time. We may note as a preliminary that identity analyses are normally restricted to certain favored particulars, such as atoms and spiritual substances.[2] Suppose that X and Y are nonoverlapping phases of a particular P. X and Y are particulars themselves, particulars having certain properties and relations. The identity view is that the particularity or thisness of X is identical with the particularity or thisness of Y. The relational view is that they are distinct.

My present inclination is to say that both identity and relational analyses are intelligible hypotheses. I reject the identity analysis, looking rather to relations between different phases to secure the unity of a particular over time. But I do not think that the identity view can be rejected as illogical. If it is to be rejected, then I think it must be rejected for Occamist reasons. The different phases exist, and so do their relations. These phases so related, it seems, are sufficient to secure identity through time for all particulars.

Locke on Identity through Time

I suggest, then, that the identity view of identity through time is not illogical. The question is rather whether it is a postulation which is fruitful, or expedient, or which we are compelled, to make. I shall try now to illuminate the difficulties faced by an identity theory by a discussion of Locke's views.[3] Locke, I believe, accepted the identity view, at any rate for certain sorts of entity. I think that this is what he meant when he spoke of "identity of substance": ". . . whatever substance begins to exist, it must, during its existence, necessarily be the same".[4] Such identity appears to be one of the notions involved in the Lockean notion of a *substratum* which underlies and supports the properties and relations of things. Among other things, the substratum is that which is identical in the different phases of a thing's existence. However, this function does not seem to be an essential part of the doctrine of substratum. It is possible to have a less rich conception of substratum which could be combined with a relational theory of identity through time. Contrariwise, it would be possible to take an identity view and yet reject the notion of an underlying substratum. Locke's substratum, however, both underlies properties and relations and is also identical through different phases. It is the latter function only which we are interested in here.

But there is a difficulty for the identity view, a difficulty of which Locke is well aware:

> . . . if two or more atoms be joined together into the same mass, every one of those atoms will be the same, . . . and whilst they exist united together, the mass, consisting of the same atoms, must be the same mass, or the same body, let the parts be never so differently jumbled. *But if one of these atoms be taken away, or one new one added, it is no longer the same mass or the same body.*[5]

From the perspective of a relational view of identity through time this can only seem to be extreme pedantry. For the relational theorist is not saddled with any very strict rules as to what will constitute 'the very same thing at a later time'. The rules may differ for different sorts of things. But Locke has less room for maneuver. On the basis of the science of his day Locke assumes, as we still assume, that ordinary physical objects are made up of atoms. Further he adopts an identity view of their identity through time. (Unlike our atoms, they are physically indivisible.) Now suppose that an ordinary physical object loses a few atoms and gains others over a period of time. The atoms which it loses continue their career elsewhere. What object at the latter time is identical with the object at the earlier time? For an identity theorist the best candidate *must be* the collection of the original atoms with which the object started out, in however scattered a state those atoms are at the later time. There the identity is complete. By comparison, the collection of atoms actually adhering together is only *partially* identical with the original collection. This, I believe, is why Locke wrote as he did in Section 4. The difficulty he is in is a difficulty only for one who holds an identity view. This in turn is evidence that, with respect to atoms, Locke did hold an identity view.

The situation is still more paradoxical for Locke in cases of objects all of whose matter is replaced over a period of time, as is said to occur in the case of the human body. Since the body in its later state does not contain a single one of the original atoms, it cannot even be partially identical with the body in its earlier state. They are two completely different substances.

What is Locke to do? He is well aware of this problem faced by an identity theory. He wants to give a nonskeptical account of identity through time for human and animal bodies, trees and so on. One solution for him would be to fall back on a relational analysis for such objects. And, indeed, when it comes to giving an account of *personal* identity Locke does embrace a relational analysis. In the case of the bodies of animals and men, however, his view appears to be different. He says of the bodies of animals that ". . . animal identity is preserved in identity of *life* and not of substance."[6] What is meant by "identity of life"? Locke, I believe, thinks of life here as a certain property which the animal possesses. In particular, it is a structural property, a way in which the (spatial) parts of the animal are related and organized.[7] Locke calls such a property a "mode", and, when summing up his position, after having said that ". . . whatever substance begins to exist, it must, during its existence, necessarily be the same; . . ." he also says that ". . . whatsoever mode begins to exist, during its existence it is the same."[8]

I think that what he is suggesting here is an identity theory for properties as well as substances. Suppose that particular a has property L at t_1 and that b has L at t_2. Suppose, also, that a and b are not even partially 'identical in substance.' It may nevertheless be the case that L at t_1 is identical with L at t_2. If so, then it can be said that a and b, although not different phases of the same *substance*, are different phases in the existence of the same L. Suppose L to be the property of *being a living thing*. Then a at t_1 and b at t_2 are different phases in the existence of the same living thing. It might have been a caterpillar at t_1 and a butterfly at t_2.

It seems that a restriction will have to be put upon the sort of property which L is. It will have to be the sort of property which 'divides its instantiations' so that, at a given time, there is a certain definite number, finite or infinite, of instances of L in the universe. But, given this restriction to the

sort of property L is, may not Locke postulate such an identity to account for the identity through time of such things as oaks?

There is, however, a difficulty which Locke must face here. If L is a property, and a property is a universal, then it is all too easy for L to be identical with itself at different times. For it is the same property wherever it is instantiated. This has the consequence, contrary to what Locke requires, that no special identity is set up between L, the property of a at t_1, and L, the property of b at t_2.

What this makes clear is that the conception of a property which Locke requires if he is to make good his notion of property identity through time is not that of a property as a universal but that of a property-instance. Certain philosophers, G. F. Stout was a prominent Anglo-Saxon example, hold that where two billiard balls are red or are spherical each of the balls has its own redness or sphericity. These properties are not universals, but are as particular as the billiard balls themselves. This position may or may not be combined with the admission that these particular properties themselves have universal properties ('This redness is red').

Let it now be given that the L-ness of a at t_1 and the L-ness of b at t_2 are particulars. Might they not be different phases of the same property-instance? And might we not give an identity rather than a relational account of what makes the two phases phases of the same property-instance? It is difficult to see how the distinction between particularity and nature could be drawn in the case of property-instances. But perhaps it could be said that the different phases in the existence of a property-instance are not numerically diverse, as a relational theorist would assert, but are instead completely identical.

When Locke asserts that "whatsoever mode begins to exist, during its existence it is the same", he appears to be asserting that we must give an identity analysis of the situation. I do not see that an identity analysis is required, but granted the conception of a property-instance, it seems to be a possible analysis.

Whether or not Locke explicitly holds to the notion of property-instance, I do not know. But it may be noted that it would fit in well with his general position. Locke talks freely of modes and qualities. Yet at the same time he is an explicit nominalist, holding that everything there is is a particular. If he is to be consistent, then he should hold that modes and qualities are particulars. And we have seen that this doctrine is required if he is to have any show of maintaining his doctrine of the identity of modes over time.

Locke's building, however, is only as strong as its foundations. And here I am given pause. It would take me too far afield to argue the matter in detail, but I am convinced that the notion of a property-instance turns out in the end to be an incoherent one. The idea of property is the idea of a nature, a nature which is different for different properties. I do not think that we can make any sense of the notion of nature unless we conceive of properties as universals. If this is correct, then Locke's ingenious attempt to supplement his identity view of the identity of substances through time with an identity view of the identity of modes through time, does not succeed.

T*he* R*elational* V*iew* D*efended*

Relational theorists are inclined to argue that identity theories of identity through time are unintelligible. I have argued, however, that identity views are in good logical order. Perhaps postulating such identities is to fall into an abyss of nonsense but I cannot at present see that this is so. I have argued that Locke's notion of the identity of modes through time rests upon the notion of a property-instance, and the latter notion, I believe, is an untenable one. But if property-instances are acceptable, as I think they are not, then perhaps an identity theorist can even deal with the identity through time of things which 'change their substance' during that time.

But to show that the identity theory is in good logical order is not to show that we should adopt it. We can distinguish between, and refer to, different phases in the existence of the same particular. Since the different phases will, in general at least, have different properties, we must recognize them as different particulars. Such difference is compatible with partial identity, and to the extent that particulars have common properties they are partially identical. But why should we say that different phases of a particular are identical in their

particularity? It is clear from our discussion of Locke's difficulties that, at best, it is plausible to say this only of certain favored individuals which do not change their substance, such as Newtonian atoms. But even in such a case it seems that unity can be secured for the enduring individual simply by relations between the phases. To extend the relational analysis to all enduring particulars is therefore economy of theory.

As already mentioned, one very powerful intellectual motive here is our unwillingness to contemplate an identity view with respect to the different spatial parts of the same thing. As Hume points out in his satirical way, in spatial cases we find the scholastic maxim, *"totum in toto, et totum in qualibet parte"* [the whole in the whole and in each part], quite unacceptable.[9] I should still want to argue, against Hume, that this identity view is, or can be presented as, an intelligible hypothesis. But surely an adequate account of spatial unities can be given without appealing to anything except the relations which the spatial parts of the object, be it nation, plant, animal, or stone, bear to each other? Any other account seems to be extravagance. But if a relational account is possible in the case of spatial unities, that is surely a strong reason for thinking that a similar account can be given of the different *phases* of the same thing. To deny the parallel is to set up a very dubious distinction between space and time.

I note here in passing that it has been a major theme in Richard Taylor's metaphysical reflection to reject various asymmetries between space and time. In this particular case, to combine an identity view of identity through time with a relational view of identity across space seems even to involve scientific difficulty. For how is the combination to be effected if the simultaneity of spatially separated things is a relative rather than an absolute notion (a three-termed rather than a two-termed relation)?

If we are looking for relations to bind together the spatial parts of a thing so that it constitutes a thing of a certain sort, then, in general, we must appeal to different relations in the case of different sorts of things. But there is one relation which seems to be of quite peculiar importance in the case of the spatial parts. It is causation. In the case of solid objects, and particularly in the case of organisms, reciprocal causal relations between the spatial parts are all-important. By contrast, in the case of identity through time it is fashionable to set great store by spatiotemporal continuity. Again, however, I believe that we ought to set greater store by causal relations.

Hume was well aware of the importance of causality for relational accounts of identity through time. Ironically, it is probably the ontological downgrading of causality involved in Humean analyses of causality which has brought about the modern neglect of causal relation as a cement for different phases of the same thing. In the case of spatial parts the causal relation stares us in the face, so that it cannot be ignored.

I reject all Humean analyses of the causal relation. I do accept the Humean view that causal connection is a species of nomic connection. But I reject the view that nomic connection is nothing more than a regularity. In my view it is a regularity determined by a relation between universals. Causal connection *so conceived* seems capable of welding different phases of the same particular much more closely together than mere spatiotemporal continuity.

We do not normally speak of an earlier phase of an object as being the cause of a succeeding phase. But, in general at least, the earlier phase will be one of the nomically necessary conditions for the existence of the latter phase. Quite often, it will be absolutely nomically necessary. For instance, there is no known method, at least, of creating an adult human being except by creating an embryo and letting it develop under appropriate conditions. Embryonic and childhood phases appear, at least, to be absolutely nomically necessary for the existence of adult phases. But even where there is no such absolute nomical necessity, the earlier phases of an object may still be nomically necessary for later phases in a given particular situation. Given the concrete situation, the recent existence of this desk I write on is nomically necessary for the current existence of this desk. For consider the concrete situation which obtained in this room a few minutes ago, but subtract from it the desk. It is nomically impossible that in that situation a desk should come to be in my room now having the same properties as the original desk. In all probability, it is nomically impossible that in that situation a desk should come to be in my room now having rather similar properties to my desk.

So we seem justified in saying that, for the vast majority of cases at least, preceding phases of a thing are a necessary part of the total cause which brings the succeeding phases to be. The succeeding phases are got by way of the preceding phases, even if for many things (plants and animals especially) much cooperation from the environment is also needed. All this paves the way for the suggestion that, for most sorts of things at least, this causal relation between phases is a logically necessary condition for the *identity* of that thing through time.

The suggestion may be supported by considering a case where the usually suggested marks of identity through time, such as spatiotemporal continuity, are present but it is given that there is no causal connection between an earlier and a later 'phase'. (I call this method of arguing for a logically necessary condition 'the method of subtraction'.) Suppose, then, that there are two very powerful deities, each able to annihilate and create, who operate quite independently of each other. The first deity decides to annihilate Richard Taylor and does so at place p, time t. The second deity has not been watching what was happening. He decides to create a man at p and t. By a coincidence which can only be described as cosmic, he decides to give this man exactly the same physical and mental characteristics that Taylor had at p and t. Life goes on as usual.

The question is 'Did Taylor survive?'; 'Is Taylor$_2$ identical with Taylor$_1$?' I hope that the reader will agree with my intuition that he did not and is not. It is true, of course, that everybody earthly, including Taylor$_2$, will take for granted (because they will not even raise the question) that Taylor$_2$ is Taylor$_1$. But I think that that only shows that, given the right stage setting, it is logically possible that we should be deceived about anything at all, including Taylor about Taylor's identity.

We may note, incidentally, that a spatiotemporal gap seems quite unimportant provided the proper causal connection is present. If Taylor$_1$ appears to be annihilated at t_1 and p_1, and Taylor$_2$ comes into existence at t_2 and p_2 as, or much as, Taylor$_1$ was at t_1 and p_1, and if further the coming-to-be of Taylor$_2$ stands in a suitable causal relation to Taylor$_1$, then Taylor$_2$ would appear to be simply a later phase of the existence of Taylor$_1$. (It will be noticed that I say 'suitable' causal relation. I am far from thinking that I have adequately character-ized the particular nature of the causal relation which holds between different phases of the same thing.) Spatiotemporal continuity of phases of things appears to be a mere result of, an observable sign of, the existence of a certain sort of causal relation between the phases.

I will finish this paper by considering another imaginary case which I think brings out quite strongly the attraction of an identity view of iden-tity through time. But I will then argue that the puzzle which it creates for the relational view can be resolved by an appeal to causation.

In general, we can distinguish between a spherical object rotating on its own axis and that same object stationary. Consider, however, an exactly spherical object of completely homoge-neous material containing no empty space at all. (Perhaps the situation is no more than logically possible.) Can a relational theory make the dis-tinction between such a sphere stationary and the same sphere rotating on its own axis? Let it be granted that there is no way of telling whether rotation is occurring or not. It seems natural still to say that it might rotate or not rotate.

However, the difficulty for a relational theory of identity through time is that if the sphere is con-sidered at any instant, its nature, including its rela-tions to other things, appears to be exactly the same whether the sphere is rotating or not. But if the nature of the sphere supposedly stationary and the nature of the sphere supposedly rotating are the same at every instant, then it seems that, contrary to intuition, no distinction can be drawn between the sphere stationary and the sphere rotating.

It is here that the identity view becomes attrac-tive, as enabling us to draw the distinction. Suppose that the sphere is not rotating. Consider, then, the eastern portion of the sphere from t_1 to t_2. The phases of the eastern portion will not merely remain identical in nature (as they would if the sphere were rotating), but will at all times be phases of the very same thing, in the sense which an identity analysis would yield. If, however, the sphere starts to rotate, then such an identity of the eastern portion will not be maintained except at the instants when the sphere has made exactly N revolutions, for any whole number N. On the relational analysis, how-ever, it seems that there is no difference between the stationary and the rotating sphere.

But I suggest that a relational view can appeal to causality here as a means of differentiating the two cases, though it will certainly have to be causal-ity conceived of in a non-Humean manner. If the sphere is stationary, then the phases of the eastern portion from t_1 to t_2 will bear to each other that particular causal relationship which is required for phases of the same thing to constitute phases of the same thing. In particular, the existence of the ear-lier phases will be nomically required for the exis-tence of the later phases in a way which will not be so for different temporal phases of spatially separate portions of the sphere. If the sphere is rotating, the causal relations will at once be different.

The point may be brought out by considering the sphere with a segment removed. If the sphere is stationary, the empty segment stays stationary, because nothing comes from nothing. If the sphere rotates, then the empty segment moves round for exactly the same reason. The hypothesis that the sphere is really stationary but that the empty segment moves round is logically possible. But it demands annihilations and creations at every moment of revolution which we believe to be nomically impossible.

So I suggest that we should continue to favor a relational account of identity through time, appealing in particular to the relation of causality between the successive phases. Causality does seem to furnish a powerful enough cement to bond together different phases of the same thing. Only *if* this program encounters insuperable diffi-culties need we consider falling back upon an iden-tity analysis.

Endnotes

[1] *A Treatise of Human Nature* 1. 4. 2, 6, ed. by L. A. Selby-Bigge, Oxford University Press, London, 1888, pp. 187–218, 251–263.

[2] One contemporary philosopher who appears to accept an identity analysis of identity through time, at any rate with respect to the *self*, is Roderick Chisholm. See Section 1 of his 'Problems of Identity' in *Identity and Individuation,* ed. by Milton K. Munitz, New York University Press, 1971, pp. 3–30.

[3] Presented in his rich though difficult Chap. 27 ('Of Identity and Diversity') in Book 2 of *An Essay Concerning Human Understanding,* 2 vols., ed. by A. C. Fraser, Oxford University Press, Oxford, 1894, Vol. 1, pp. 439–470.

[4] *Essay* 2. 27. 28; Fraser edition, Vol. 1, p. 469.

[5] *Essay* 2. 27. 4; Fraser edition, Vol. 1, pp. 442; emphasis added.

[6] *Essay* 2. 27. 12; Fraser edition, Vol. 1, p. 453; emphasis added.

[7] Section 5 may be quoted here (Fraser, Vol. 1, p. 443): "We must therefore consider wherein an oak differs from a mass of matter, and that seems to me to be in this, that the one is only the cohesion of particles of matter any how united, the other such a disposition of them as constitutes the parts of an oak; and such an organization of those parts as is fit to receive and distribute nourishment, so as to continue and frame the wood, bark, and leaves, etc., of an oak, in which consists the vegetable life. That being then one plant which has such an organization of parts in one coherent body, partaking of one common life, it continues to be the same plant as long as it partakes of the same life, though that life be communicated to new particles of matter vitally united to the living plant."

[8] *Essay* 2. 27. 28; Fraser, Vol. 1, p. 469.

[9] *Treatise* 1. 4. 5; Selby-Bigge edition, p. 238.

---

19. *The Third Night: The Bodily Theory of Personal Identity*

JOHN PERRY

John Perry is the Henry Waldgrave Stuart Professor of Philosophy at Stanford University. His book *A Dialogue on Personal Identity and Immortality* is an excellent contemporary introduction to these topics. In the part reprinted here the dialogue participants discuss the philosophical significance of a "body transplant" where the healthy brain is removed from a dead person's body and placed in a healthy body of someone who has just had a stroke. This familiar Lockean puzzle case leads to a defense of the bodily criterion of personal identity on the one hand and a consideration of a new issue on the other. The new issue that is raised concerns the importance of identity. The psychological criterion is thought to better able to explain the importance or special concern we attach to our own future selves because those selves share or continue the psychological characteristics that we presently possess. Gretchen Weirob, who is sympathetic with the bodily view questions this line of reasoning by arguing that since the possibility of "brain rejuvenation" or the creation of duplicate brains requires the psychological criterion to appeal to brain identity to preserve personal identity, the psychological criterion cannot explain the special importance we attach to our own identity. The dialogue ends with the provocative suggestion, explored in detail in the selection by Derek Parfit, that even if a body transplant or brain rejuvenation does not preserve identity that might not matter since it is not personal identity that matters in questions of survival, but psychological continuity.

WEIROB: Well, Sam, are you here for a third attempt to convince me of the possibility of survival?

From John Perry, *A Dialogue on Personal Identity and Immortality* (Indianapolis, IN and Cambridge, Mass: Hackett, 1979), pp. 37–49. Reprinted by permission of Hackett Publishing Company. All rights reserved.

MILLER: No, I have given up. I suggest we talk about fishing or football or something unrelated to your imminent demise. You will outwit any straightforward attempts to comfort you, but perhaps I can at least divert your mind.

COHEN: But before we start on fishing—although I don't have any particular brief for survival—there is one point in our discussion of the last two evenings that still bothers me. Would you mind discussing for a while the notion of personal identity itself, without worrying about the more difficult case of survival after death?

WEIROB: I would enjoy it. What point bothers you?

COHEN: Your position seems to be that personal identity amounts to identity of a human body, nothing more, nothing less. A person is just a live human body, or more precisely, I suppose, a human body that is alive and has certain capacities—consciousness and perhaps rationality. Is that right?

WEIROB: Yes, it seems that simple to me.

COHEN: But I think there has actually been an episode which disproves that. I am thinking of the strange case of Julia North, which occurred in California a few months ago. Surely you remember it.

WEIROB: Yes, only too well. But you had better explain it to Sam, for I'll wager he has not heard of it.

COHEN: Not heard of Julia North? But the case was all over the headlines.

MILLER: Well, Gretchen is right. I know nothing of it. She knows that I only read the sports page.

COHEN: You only read the sports page!

WEIROB: It's an expression of his unconcern with earthly matters.

MILLER: Well, that's not quite fair, Gretchen. It's a matter of preference. I much prefer to spend what time I have for reading in reading about the eighteenth century, rather than the drab and miserable century into which I had the misfortune to be born. It was really a much more civilized century, you know. But let's not dwell on my peculiar habits. Tell me about Julia North.

COHEN: Very well. Julia North was a young woman who was run over by a streetcar while saving the life of a young child who wandered onto the tracks. The child's mother, one Mary Frances Beaudine, had a stroke while watching the horrible scene. Julia's healthy brain and wasted body, and Mary Frances' healthy body and wasted brain,

were transported to a hospital where a brilliant neurosurgeon, Dr. Matthews, was in residence. He had worked out a procedure for what he called a "body transplant." He removed the brain from Julia's head and placed it in Mary Frances', splicing the nerves, and so forth, using techniques not available until quite recently. The survivor of all this was obviously Julia, as everyone agreed—except, unfortunately, Mary Frances' husband. His shortsightedness and lack of imagination led to great complications and drama, and made the case more famous in the history of crime than in the history of medicine. I shall not go into the details of this sorry aspect of the case—they are well reported in a book by Barbara Harris called *Who is Julia?*, in case you are interested.

MILLER: Fascinating!

COHEN: Well, the relevance of this case is obvious. Julia North had one body up until the time of the accident, and another body after the operation. So one person had two bodies. So a person cannot be simply *identified* with a human body. So something must be wrong with your view, Gretchen. What do you say to this?

WEIROB: I'll say to you just what I said to Dr. Matthews—

COHEN: You have spoken with Dr. Matthews?

WEIROB: Yes. He contacted me shortly after my accident. My physician had phoned him up about my case. Matthews said he could perform the same operation for me he did for Julia North. I refused.

COHEN: You refused! But Gretchen, why—?

MILLER: Gretchen, I *am* shocked. Your decision practically amounts to suicide! You passed up an opportunity to continue living? Why on earth—

WEIROB: Hold on, hold on. You are both making an assumption I reject. If the case of Julia North amounts to a counterexample to my view that a person is just a live human body, and if my refusal to submit to this procedure amounts to suicide, then the survivor of such an operation must be reckoned as the same person as the brain donor. That is, the survivor of Julia North's operation must have been Julia, and the survivor of the operation on me would have to be me. This is the assumption you both make in criticizing me. But I reject it. I think Jack Beaudine was right. The survivor of the operation involving Julia North's brain was Mary Frances Beaudine, and the survivor of the operation using my brain would not have been me.

MILLER: Gretchen, how on earth can you say that? Will you not give up your view that personal identity is just bodily identity, no matter how clear the counter-example? I really think you simply have an irrational attachment to the lump of material that is your body.

COHEN: Yes, Gretchen, I agree with Sam. You are being preposterous! The survivor of Julia North's operation had no idea who Mary Frances Beaudine was. She remembered being Julia—

WEIROB: She *seemed* to remember being Julia. Have you forgotten so quickly the importance of this distinction? In my opinion, the effect of the operation was that Mary Frances Beaudine survived deluded, thinking she was someone else.

COHEN: But as you know, the case was litigated. It went to the Supreme Court. They said that the survivor was Julia.

WEIROB: That argument is unworthy of you, Dave. Is the Supreme Court infallible?

COHEN: No, it isn't. But I don't think it's such a stupid point.

Look at it this way, Gretchen. This is a case in which two criteria we use to make judgments of identity conflict. Usually we expect personal identity to involve both bodily identity and psychological continuity. That is, we expect that if we have the same body, then the beliefs, memories, character traits, and the like also will be enormously similar. In this case, these two criteria which usually coincide do not. If we choose one criterion, we say that the survivor is Mary Frances Beaudine and she has undergone drastic psychological changes. If we choose the other, we say that Julia has survived with a new body. We have to choose which criterion is more important. It's a matter of choice of how to use our language, how to extend the concept "same person" to a new situation. The overwhelming majority of people involved in the case took the survivor to be Julia. That is, society chose to use the concept one way rather than the other. The Supreme Court is *not* beside the point. One of their functions is to settle just how old concepts shall be applied to new circumstances—how "free-

dom of the press" is to be understood when applied to movies or television, whose existence was not forseen when the concept was shaped, or to say whether "murder" is to include the abortion of a fetus. They are fallible on points of fact, but they are the final authority on the development of certain important concepts used in law. The notion of *person* is such a concept.

WEIROB: You think that who the survivor was, was a matter of convention, of how we choose to use language?

COHEN: Yes.

WEIROB: I can show the preposterousness of all that with an example.

Let us suppose that I agree to the operation. I lie in bed, expecting my continued existence, anticipating the feelings and thoughts I shall have upon awakening after the operation. Dr. Matthews enters and asks me to take several aspirin, so as not to have a headache when I awake. I protest that aspirin upsets my stomach; he asks whether I would rather have a terrible headache tomorrow or a mild stomachache now, and I agree that it would be reasonable to take them.

Let us suppose that you enter at this point, with bad news. The Supreme Court has changed its mind! So the survivor will not be me. So, I say, "Oh, then I will not take the aspirin, for it's not me that will have a headache, but someone else. Why should I endure a stomachache, however mild, for the comfort of someone else? After all, I am already donating my brain to that person."

Now this is clearly absurd. If I were correct, in the first place, to anticipate having the sensations and thoughts that the survivor is to have the next day, the decision of nine old men a thousand or so miles away wouldn't make me wrong. And if I was wrong to so anticipate, their decision couldn't make me right. How can the correctness of my anticipation of survival be a matter of the way we use our words? If it is not such a matter, then my identity is not either. My identity with the survivor, my survival, is a question of fact, not of convention.

COHEN: Your example is persuasive. I admit I am befuddled. On the one hand, I cannot see how the matter can be other than I have described. When we know all the facts what can remain to be decided but how we are to describe them, how we are to use our language? And yet I can see that it seems absurd to suppose that the correctness or incorrectness of anticipation of future experience is a matter for convention to decide.

MILLER: Well, I didn't think the business about convention was very plausible anyway. But I should like to return you to the main question, Gretchen. Fact or convention, it still remains. Why will you not admit that the survivor of this operation would be you?

WEIROB: Well, *you* tell *me*, why you think she would be me?

MILLER: I can appeal to the theory I developed last night. You argued that the idea that personal identity consists in memory would not guarantee the possibility of survival after death. But you said nothing to shake its plausibility as an account of personal identity. It has enormous advantage, remember of making sense of our ability to judge our own identity, without examination of our bodies. I should argue that it is the correctness of this theory that explains the *almost* universal willingness to say that the survivor of Julia's operation was Julia. We need not deliberate over how to extend our concept, we need only apply the concept we already have. Memory is sufficient for identity and bodily identity is *not* necessary for it. The survivor remembered Julia's thoughts and actions, and so was Julia. Would you but submit to the operation, the survivor would remember your thoughts and actions, would remember this very conversation we are now having, and would be you.

COHEN: Yes, I now agree completely with Sam: The theory that personal identity is to be analyzed in terms of memory is correct, and according to it you will survive if you submit to the operation.

Let me add another argument against your view and in favor of the memory theory. You have emphasized that identity is the condition of *anticipation*. That means, among other things, that we have a particular concern for that person in the future whom we take to be ourselves. If I were told that any of the three of us were to suffer pain tomorrow, I should be sad. But if it were you or Sam that were to be hurt, my concern would be altruistic or unselfish. That is because I would not anticipate having the painful experience myself.

Here I do no more than repeat points you have made earlier in our conversations.

Now what is there about mere sameness of body that makes sense of this asymmetry, between the way we look at our own futures, and the way we look at the futures of others? In other words, why is the identity of your body—that mere lump of matter, as Sam put it—of such great importance? Why care so much about it?

WEIROB: You say, and I surely agree, that identity of person is a very special relationship—so special as perhaps not even happily called a relationship at all. And you say that since my theory is that identity of person is identity of body, I should be able to explain the importance of the one in terms of the importance of the other.

I'm not sure I can do that. But does the theory that personal identity consists in memory fare better on this score?

COHEN: Well, I think it does. Those properties of persons which make persons of such great value, and mark their individuality, and make one person so special to his friends and loved ones, are ultimately psychological or mental. One's character, personality, beliefs, attitudes, convictions—they are what make every person so unique and special. A skinny Gretchen would be a shock to us all, but not a Gretchen diminished in any important way. But a Gretchen who was not witty, or not gruff, or not as honest to the path an argument takes as is humanly possible—those would be fundamental changes. Is it any wonder that the survivor of that California fiasco was reckoned as Julia North? Would it make sense to take her to be Mary Jane Beaudine, when she had none of her beliefs or attitudes or memories?

Now if such properties are what is of importance about a person to others, is it not reasonable that they are the basis of one's importance to oneself? And these are just the properties that personal identity preserves when it is taken to consist in links of memory. Do we not have, in this idea, at least the beginning of an explanation of the importance of identity?

WEIROB: So on two counts you favor the memory theory. First, you say it explains how it is possible to judge as to one's own identity, without having to examine one's body. Second, you say it explains the importance of personal identity.

COHEN: Now surely you must agree the memory theory is correct. Do you agree? There may be still time to contact Dr. Matthews—

WEIROB: Hold on, hold on. Try to relax and enjoy the argument. I am. Quit trying to save my life and worry about saving your theory—for I'm still not persuaded. Granted the survivor will *think* she is me, will *seem* to remember thinking my thoughts. But recall the importance of distinguishing between real and merely apparent memory—

COHEN: But *you* recall that this distinction is to be made on the basis of whether the apparent memories were or were not caused by the prior experiences in the appropriate way. The survivor will not seem to remember your thoughts because of hypnosis or by coincidence or overweening imagination. She will seem to remember them because the traces those experiences left on your brain now activate her mind in the usual way. She will seem to remember them because she does remember them, and will be you.

WEIROB: You are very empathic, and I'm feeling rather weak. I'm not sure there is time left to untangle all of this. But there is never an advantage to hurrying when doing philosophy. So let's go over this slowly.

We all agree that the fact that the survivor of this strange operation Dr. Matthews proposes would *seem* to remember doing what I have done. Let us even suppose she would take herself to be me, claim to be Gretchen Weirob—and have no idea who else she might be. (We are then assuming that she differs from me in one aspect—her theory of personal identity. But that does not show her not to be me, for I could change my mind by then.) We all first agree that this much does not make her me. For this could all be true of someone suffering a delusion, or a subject of hypnosis.

COHEN: Yes, this is all agreed.

WEIROB: But now you think that some *future* condition is satisfied, which makes her apparent memories *real* memories. Now what exactly is this future condition?

COHEN: Well, that the same brain was involved in the perception of the events, and their later *memory*. Thus we have here a causal chain of just the same sort as when only a single body is involved. That is, perceptions when the event occurs leave a trace in the brain, which is later responsible for the content of the memory. And we agreed, did we not, that apparent memory, caused in the right way, is real memory?

WEIROB: Now is it absolutely crucial that the same brain is involved?

COHEN: What do you mean?

WEIROB: Let me explain again by reference to Dr. Matthews. In our conversation he explained a new procedure on which he was working, called a *brain rejuvenation*. By this process, which is not yet available—only the feasibility of developing it is being studied—a new brain could be made which is an exact duplicate of my brain—that is, an exact duplicate in terms of psychologically relevant states. It might not duplicate all the properties of my brain—for example, the blood vessels in the new brain might be stronger than in the old brain.

MILLER: What is the point of developing such a macabre technique?

WEIROB: Dr. Matthews' idea is that when weaknesses which might lead to stroke or other brain injury are noted, a healthy duplicate could be made to replace the original, forestalling the problem.

Now Dave, suppose my problem were not with my liver and kidneys and such, but with my brain. Would you recommend such an operation as to my benefit?

COHEN: You mean, do I think the survivor of such an operation would be you?

WEIROB: Exactly. You may assume that Dr. Matthews' technique works perfectly so the causal process involved is no less reliable than that involved in ordinary memory.

COHEN: Then I would say it was you— No! Wait! No, it wouldn't be you—absolutely not.

MILLER: But why the sudden reversal? It seems to me it would be her. Indeed, I should try such an operation myself, if it would clear up my dizzy spells and leave me otherwise unaffected.

COHEN: No, don't you see, she is leading us into a false trap. If we say it *is* her, then she will say, "then what if he makes two duplicates, or three or ten? They can't all be me, they all have an equal claim, so none will be me." It would be the argument of last night, reapplied on earth. So the answer is no, absolutely not, it wouldn't be you. Duplication of brain does not preserve identity. Identity of the person requires identity of the brain.

MILLER: Quite right.

WEIROB: Now let me see if I have managed to understand your theory, for my powers of concentration seem to be fading. Suppose we have two bodies, A and B. My brain is put into A, a duplicate into B. The survivor of this, call them "A-Gretchen" and "B-Gretchen," both seem to remember giving this very speech. Both are in this state of seeming to remember, as the last stage in an information-preserving causal chain, initiated by my giving this speech. Both have my character, personality, beliefs, and the like. But one is *really* remembering. the other is not. A-Gretchen is really me, B-Gretchen is not.

COHEN: Precisely. Is this incoherent?

WEIROB: No, I guess there is nothing incoherent about it. But look what has happened to the advantages you claimed for the memory theory.

First, you said, it explains how I can know who I am without opening my eyes and recognizing my body. But on your theory Gretchen-A and Gretchen-B cannot know who they are even if they do open their eyes and examine their bodies. How is Gretchen-A to know whether she has the original brain and is who she seems to be, or has the duplicate and is a new person, only a few minutes old, and with no memories but mere delusions? If the hospital kept careless records, or the surgeon thought it was of no great importance to keep track of who got the original and who got the duplicate, she might never know who she was. By making identity of person turn into identity of brain, your theory makes the ease with which I can determine who I am not less but more mysterious than my theory.

Second, you said, your theory explains why my concern for Gretchen-A, who is me whether she knows it or not, would be selfish, and my anticipation of her experience correct while my concern for Gretchen-B with her duplicated brain would be unselfish, and my anticipation of having her experiences incorrect. And it explains this, you said, because by insisting on the links of memory, we preserve in personal identity more psychologi-

cal characteristics which are the most important features of a person.

But Gretchen-A and Gretchen-B are psychologically indiscernible. Though they will go their separate ways, at the moment of awakening they could well be exactly similar in every psychological respect. In terms of character and belief and the contents of their minds, Gretchen-A is no more like me than Gretchen-B. So there is nothing in your theory after all to explain why anticipation is appropriate when we have identity and not otherwise.

You said, Sam, that I had an irrational attachment for this unworthy material object, my body. But you too are as irrationally attached to your brain. I have never seen my brain. I should have easily given it up for a rejuvenated version, had that been the choice with which I was faced. I have never seen it, never felt it, and have no attachment to it. But my body? That seems to me all that I am. I see no point in trying to evade its fate, even if there were still time.

But perhaps I miss the merit of your arguments. I am tired, and perhaps my poor brain, feeling slighted, has begun to desert me—

COHEN: Oh, don't worry, Gretchen, you are still clever. Again you have left me befuddled. I don't know what to say. But answer me this. Suppose you are right and we are wrong. But suppose these arguments had not occurred to you, and, sharing in our error, you had agreed to the operation. You anticipate the operation until it happens, thinking you will survive. You are happy. The survivor takes herself to be you, and thinks she made a decision before the operation which has now turned out to be right. She is happy. Your friends are happy. Who would be worse off, either before or after the operation?

Suppose even that you realize identity would not be preserved by such an operation, but have it done anyway, and as the time for the operation approaches, you go ahead and anticipate the experiences of the survivor. Where exactly is the mistake? Do you really have any less reason to care for the survivor than for yourself? Can mere identity of body, the lack of which alone keeps you from being her, mean that much? Perhaps we were wrong, after all, in focusing on identity as the necessary condition of anticipation—

MILLER: Dave, it's too late.

20. *Personal Identity*¹

DEREK PARFIT

In this selection, Derek Parfit, senior research fellow at All Souls College, Oxford, attempts to show how a sophisticated but essentially Lockean view of personal identity against the objections of Reid and Williams. Parfit's view is richer than Locke's since it includes, in addition to memory, a person's character (for example, beliefs, intentions, goals, and ambitions) as pertinent to the relations that unite different stages of one life. Parfit guards against Williams's duplication argument by maintaining that personal identity requires *non-branching* psychological continuity. Thus, in a duplication where two people are psychologically continuous with an earlier pre-duplicated person, *neither* of the resulting people would be identical to the original. But in the end, according to Parfit, psychological connections and continuities, whether one-one or one-many, are what matter when discussing questions of survival and responsibility. The views expressed in "Personal Identity" have been elaborated in Part III of Parfit's much discussed book, *Reasons and Persons.*

We can, I think, describe cases in which, though we know the answer to every other question, we have no idea how to answer a question about personal identity. These cases are not covered by the criteria of personal identity that we actually use.

Do they present a problem?

It might be thought that they do not, because they could never occur. I suspect that some of them could. (Some, for instance, might become scientifically possible.) But I shall claim that even if they did they would present no problem.

My targets are two beliefs: one about the nature of personal identity, the other about its importance.

The first is that in these cases the question about identity must have an answer.

No one thinks this about, say, nations or machines. Our criteria for the identity of these do not cover certain cases. No one thinks that in these cases the questions "Is it the same nation?" or "Is it the same machine?" must have answers.

Some people believe that in this respect they are different. They agree that our criteria of per-

From Derek Parfit, "Personal Identity," *Philosophical Review,* 80 (1971): 3–27. Copyright © 1971 Cornell University. Reprinted by permission of the publisher and the author.

sonal identity do not cover certain cases, but they believe that the nature of their own identity through time is, somehow, such as to guarantee that in these cases questions about their identity must have answers. This belief might be expressed as follows: "Whatever happens between now and any future time, either I shall still exist, or I shall not. Any future experience will either be *my* experience, or it will not."

This first belief—in the special nature of personal identity—has, I think, certain effects. It makes people assume that the principle of self-interest is more rationally compelling than any moral principle. And it makes them more depressed by the thought of aging and of death.

I cannot see how to disprove this first belief. I shall describe a problem case. But this can only make it seem implausible.

Another approach might be this. We might suggest that one cause of the belief is the projection of our emotions. When we imagine ourselves in a problem case, we do feel that the question "Would it be me?" must have an answer. But what we take to be a bafflement about a further fact may be only the bafflement of our concern.

It shall not pursue this suggestion here. But one cause of our concern is the belief which is my second target. This is that unless the question about identity has an answer, we cannot answer certain important questions (questions about such matters as survival, memory, and responsibility).

Against this second belief my claim will be this. Certain important questions do presuppose a question about personal identity. But they can be freed of this presupposition. And when they are, the question about identity has no importance.

I.

We can start by considering the much discussed case of the man who, like an amoeba, divides.[2]

Wiggins has recently dramatized this case.[3] He first referred to the operation imagined by Shoemaker.[4] We suppose that my brain is transplanted into someone else's (brainless) body, and that the resulting person has my character and apparent memories of my life. Most of us would agree, after thought, that the resulting person is me. I shall here assume such agreement.[5]

Wiggins then imagined his own operation. My brain is divided, and each half is housed in a new body. Both resulting people have my character and apparent memories of my life.

What happens to me? There seem only three possibilities: (1) I do not survive; (2) I survive as one of the two people; (3) I survive as both.

The trouble with (1) is this. We agreed that I could survive if my brain were successfully transplanted. And people have in fact survived with half their brains destroyed. It seems to follow that I could survive if half my brain were successfully transplanted and the other half were destroyed. But if this is so, how could I *not* survive if the other half were also successfully transplanted? How could a double success be a failure?

We can move to the second description. Perhaps one success is the maximum score. Perhaps I shall be one of the resulting people.

The trouble here is that in Wiggins' case each half of my brain is exactly similar, and so, to start with, is each resulting person. So how can I survive as only one of the two people? What can make me one of them rather than the other?

It seems clear that both of these descriptions—that I do not survive, and that I survive as

one of the people—are highly implausible. Those who have accepted them must have assumed that they were the only possible descriptions.

What about our third description: that I survive as both people?

It might be said, "If 'survive' implies identity, this description makes no sense—you cannot be two people. If it does not, the description is irrelevant to a problem about identity."

I shall later deny the second of these remarks. But there are ways of denying the first. We might say, "What we have called 'the two resulting people' are not two people. They are one person. I do survive Wiggins' operation. Its effect is to give me two bodies and a divided mind."

It would shorten my argument if this were absurd. But I do not think it is. It is worth showing why.

We can, I suggest, imagine a divided mind. We can imagine a man having two simultaneous experiences, in having each of which he is unaware of having the other.

We may not even need to imagine this. Certain actual cases, to which Wiggins referred, seem to be best described in these terms. These involve the cutting of the bridge between the hemispheres of the brain. The aim was to cure epilepsy. But the result appears to be, in the surgeon's words, the creation of "two separate spheres of consciousness,"[6] each of which controls one half of the patient's body. What is experienced in each is, presumably, experienced by the patient.

There are certain complications in these actual cases. So let us imagine a simpler case.

Suppose that the bridge between my hemispheres is brought under my voluntary control. This would enable me to disconnect my hemispheres as easily as if I were blinking. By doing this I would divide my mind. And we can suppose that when my mind is divided I can, in each half, bring about reunion.

This ability would have obvious uses. To give an example: I am near the end of a math exam, and see two ways of tackling the last problem. I decide to divide my mind, to work, with each half, at one of two calculations, and then to reunite my mind and write a fair copy of the best result.

What shall I experience?

When I disconnect my hemispheres, my consciousness divides into two streams. But this division is not something that I experience. Each of my two streams of consciousness seems to have been straightforwardly continuous with my one stream of consciousness up to the moment of division. The only changes in each stream are the disappearance of half my visual field and the loss of sensation in, and control over, half my body.

Consider my experiences in what we can call my "right-handed" stream. I remember that I assigned my right hand to longer calculation. This I now begin. In working at this calculation I can see, from the movements of my left hand, that I am also working at the other. But I am not aware of working at the other. So I might, in my right-handed stream, wonder how, in my left-handed stream, I am getting on.

My work is now over, I am about to reunite my mind. What should I, in each stream, expect? Simply that I shall suddenly seem to remember just having thought out two calculations, in thinking out each of which I was not aware of thinking out the other. This, I submit, we can imagine. And if my mind was divided, these memories are correct.

In describing this episode, I assumed that there were two series of thoughts, and that they were both mine. If my two hands visibly wrote out two calculations, and if I claimed to remember two corresponding series of thoughts, this is surely what we should want to say.

If it is, then a person's mental history need not be like a canal, with only one channel. It could be like a river, with islands, and with separate streams.

To apply this to Wiggins' operation: we mentioned the view that it gives me two bodies and a divided mind. We cannot now call this absurd. But it is, I think, unsatisfactory.

There were two features of the case of the exam that made us want to say that only one person was involved. The mind was soon reunited, and there was only one body. If a mind was permanently divided and its halves developed in different ways, the point of speaking of one person would start to disappear. Wiggins' case, where there are also two bodies, seems to be over the borderline. After I have had his operation, the two "products" each have all the attributes of a person. They could live at opposite ends of the earth. (If they later met, they might even fail to recognize each other.) It would become intolerable to deny that they were different people.

Suppose we admit that they are different people. Could we still claim that I survived as both, using "survive" to imply identity?

We could. For we might suggest that two people could compose a third. We might say, "I do survive Wiggins' operation as two people. They can be different people, and yet be me, in just the way in which the Pope's three crowns are one crown."[7]

This is a possible way of giving sense to the claim that I survive as two different people, using "survive" to imply identity. But it keeps the language of identity only by changing the concept of a person. And there are obvious objections to this change.[8]

The alternative, for which I shall argue, is to give up the language of identity. We can suggest that I survive as two different people without implying that I am these people.

When I first mentioned this alternative, I mentioned this objection: "If your new way of talking does not imply identity, it cannot solve our problem. For that is about identity. The problem is that all the possible answers to the question about identity are highly implausible."

We can now answer this objection.

We can start by reminding ourselves that this is an objection only if we have one or both of the beliefs which I mentioned at the start of this paper.

The first was the belief that to any question about personal identity, in any describable case, there must be a true answer. For those with this belief, Wiggins' case is doubly perplexing. If all the possible answers are implausible, it is hard to decide which of them is true, and hard even to keep the belief that one of them must be true. If we give up this belief, as I think we should, these problems disappear. We shall then regard the case as like many others in which, for quite unpuzzling reasons, there *is* no answer to a question about identity. (Consider "Was England the same nation after 1066?")

Wiggins' case makes the first belief implausible. It also makes it trivial. For it undermines the second belief. This was the belief that important questions turn upon the question about identity. (It is worth pointing out that those who have only this second belief do not think that there must *be* an answer to this question, but rather that we must decide upon an answer.)

Against this second belief my claim is this. Certain questions do presuppose a question about personal identity. And because these questions *are* important, Wiggins' case does present a problem. But we cannot solve this problem by answering the question about identity. We can solve this problem only by taking these important questions and prizing them apart from the question about identity. After we have done this, the question about identity (though we might for the sake of neatness decide it) has no further interest.

Because there are several questions which presuppose identity, this claim will take some time to fill out.

We can first return to the question of survival. This is a special case, for survival does not so much presuppose the retaining of identity as seem equivalent to it. It is thus the general relation which we need to prize apart from identity. We can then consider particular relations, such as those involved in memory and intention.

"Will I survive?" seems, I said, equivalent to "Will there be some person alive who is the same person as me?"

If we treat these questions as equivalent, then the least unsatisfactory description of Wiggins' case is, I think, that I survive with two bodies and a divided mind.

Several writers have chosen to say that I am neither of the resulting people. Given our equivalence, this implies that I do not survive, and hence, presumably, that even if Wiggins' operation is not literally death, I ought, since I will not survive it, to regard it *as* death. But this seemed absurd.

It is worth repeating why. An emotion or attitude can be criticized for resting on a false belief, or for being inconsistent. A man who regarded Wiggins' operation as death must, I suggest, be open to one of these criticisms.

He might believe that his relation to each of the resulting people fails to contain some element which is contained in survival. But how can this be true? We agreed that he *would* survive if he stood in this very same relation to only *one* of the resulting people. So it cannot be the nature of this relation which makes it fail, in Wiggins' case, to be survival. It can only be its duplication.

Suppose that our man accepts this, but still regards division as death. His reaction would now seem wildly inconsistent. He would be like a man who, when told of a drug that could double his years of life, regarded the taking of this drug as death. The only difference in this case of division is that the extra years are to run concurrently. This is an interesting difference. But it cannot mean that there are *no* years to run.

I have argued this for those who think that there must, in Wiggins' case, be a true answer to the question about identity. For them, we might add, "Perhaps the original person does lose his identity. But there may be other ways to do this than to die. One other way might be to multiply. To regard these as the same is to confuse nought with two."

For those who think that the question of identity is up for decision, it would be clearly absurd to regard Wiggins' operation as death. These people would have to think, "We could have chosen to say that I should be one of the resulting people. If we had, I should not have regarded it as death. But since we have chosen to say that I am neither person, I *do*." This is hard even to understand.[9]

My first conclusion, then, is this. The relation of the original person to each of the resulting people contains all that interests us—all that matters—in any ordinary case of survival. This is why we need a sense in which one person can survive as two.[10]

One of my aims in the rest of this paper will be to suggest such a sense. But we can first make some general remarks.

II.

Identity is a one-one relation. Wiggins' case serves to show that what matters in survival need not be one-one.

Wiggins' case is of course unlikely to occur. The relations which matter are, in fact, one-one. It is because they are that we can imply the holding of these relations by using the language of identity.

This use of language is convenient. But it can lead us astray. We may assume that what matters *is* identity and, hence, has the properties of identity.

In the case of the property of being one-one, this mistake is not serious. For what matters is in fact one-one. But in the case of another property, the mistake *is* serious. Identity is all-or-nothing. Most of the relations which matter in survival are, in fact, relations of degree. If we ignore this, we shall be led into quite ill-grounded attitudes and beliefs.

The claim that I have just made—that most of what matters are relations of degree—I have yet to support. Wiggins' case shows only that these relations need not be one-one. The merit of the case is not that it shows this in particular, but that it makes the first break between what matters and identity. The belief that identity *is* what matters is hard to overcome. This is shown in most discussions of the problem cases which actually occur: cases, say, of amnesia or of brain damage. Once Wiggins' case has made one breach in this belief, the rest should be easier to remove.[11]

To turn to a recent debate: most of the relations which matter can be provisionally referred to under the heading "psychological continuity" (which includes causal continuity). My claim is thus that we use the language of personal identity in order to imply such continuity. This is close to the view that psychological continuity provides a criterion of identity.

Williams has attacked this view with the following argument. Identity is a one-one relation. So any criterion of identity must appeal to a relation which is logically one-one. Psychological continuity is not logically one-one. So it cannot provide a criterion.[12]

Some writers have replied that it is enough if the relation appealed to is always in fact one-one.[13]

I suggest a slightly different reply. Psychological continuity is a ground for speaking of identity when it is one-one.

If psychological continuity took a one-many or branching form, we should need, I have argued, to abandon the language of identity. So this possibility would not count against this view.

We can make a stronger claim. This possibility would count in its favor.

The view might be defended as follows. Judgments of personal identity have great importance. What gives them their importance is the fact that they imply psychological continuity. This is why, whenever there is such continuity, we ought, if we can, to imply it by making a judgment of identity.

If psychological continuity took a branching form, no coherent set of judgments of identity could correspond to, and thus be used to imply, the branching form of this relation. But what we ought to do, in such a case, is take the importance which would attach to a judgment of identity and attach this importance directly to each limb of the branching relation. So this case helps to show that judgments of personal identity do derive their importance from the fact that they imply psychological continuity. It helps to show that when we can, usefully, speak of identity, this relation is our ground.

This argument appeals to a principle which Williams put forward.[14] The principle is that an important judgment should be asserted and denied only on importantly different grounds.

Williams applied this principle to a case in which one man is psychologically continuous with the dead Guy Fawkes, and a case in which two men are. His argument was this. If we treat psychological continuity as a sufficient ground for speaking of identity, we shall say that the one man is Guy Fawkes. But we could not say that the two men are, although we should have the same ground. This disobeys the principle. The remedy is to deny that the one man is Guy Fawkes, to insist that sameness of the body is necessary for identity.

Williams' principle can yield a different answer. Suppose we regard psychological continuity as more important than sameness of the body.[15] And suppose that the one man really is psychologically (and causally) continuous with Guy Fawkes. If he is, it would disobey the principle to deny that he is Guy Fawkes, for we have the same important ground as in a normal case of identity. In the case of the two men, we again have the same important ground. So we ought to take the importance from the judgment of identity and attach it directly to this ground. We ought to say, as in Wiggins' case, that each limb of the branching relation is as good as survival. This obeys the principle.

To sum up these remarks: even if psychological continuity is neither logically, nor always in fact, one-one, it can provide a criterion of identity. For this can appeal to the relation of *non-branching* psychological continuity, which is logically one-one.[16]

The criterion might be sketched as follows. "X and Y are the same person if they are psychologically continuous and there is no person who is contemporary with either and psychologically continuous with the other." We should need to explain what we mean by "psychologically continuous" and say how much continuity the criterion requires. We should then, I think, have described a sufficient condition for speaking of identity.[17]

We need to say something more. If we admit that psychological continuity might not be one-one, we need to say what we ought to do if it were not one-one. Otherwise our account would be open to the objections that it is incomplete and arbitrary.[18]

I have suggested that if psychological continuity took a branching form, we ought to speak in a new way, regarding what we describe as having the same significance as identity. This answers these objections.[19]

We can now return to our discussion. We have three remaining aims. One is to suggest a sense of "survive" which does not imply identity. Another is to show that most of what matters in survival are relations of degree. A third is to show that none of these relations needs to be described in a way that presupposes identity.

We can take these aims in the reverse order.

III.

The most important particular relation is that involved in memory. This is because it is so easy to believe that its description must refer to identity.[20] This belief about memory is an important cause of the view that personal identity has a special nature. But it has been well discussed by Shoemaker[21] and by Wiggins.[22] So we can be brief.

It may be a logical truth that we can only remember our own experiences. But we can frame a new concept for which this is not a logical truth. Let us call this "q-memory."

To sketch a definition[23] I am q-remembering an experience if (1) I have a belief about a past experience which seems in itself like a memory belief, (2) someone did have such an experience, and (3) my belief is dependent upon this experi-

ence in the same way (whatever that is) in which a memory of an experience is dependent upon it.

According to (1) q-memories seem like memories. So I q-remember *having* experiences.

This may seem to make q-memory presuppose identity. One might say, "My apparent memory of *having* an experience is an apparent memory of *my* having an experience. So how could I q-remember my having other people's experiences?"

This objection rests on a mistake. When I seem to remember an experience, I do indeed seem to remember *having* it.[24] But it cannot be a part of what I seem to remember about this experience that I, the person who now seems to remember it, am the person who had this experience.[25] That I am is something that I automatically assume. (My apparent memories sometimes come to me simply as the belief that *I* had a certain experience.) But it is something that I am justified in assuming only because I do not in fact have q-memories of other people's experiences.

Suppose that I did start to have such q-memories. If I did, I should cease to assume that my apparent memories must be about my own experiences. I should come to assess an apparent memory by asking two questions: (1) Does it tell me about a past experience? (2) If so, whose?

Moreover (and this is a crucial point) my apparent memories would now come to me *as q-memories*. Consider those of my apparent memories which do come to me simply as beliefs about my past: for example, "I did that." If I knew that I could q-remember other people's experiences, these beliefs would come to me in a more guarded form: for example, "Someone—probably I—did that." I might have to work out who it was.

I have suggested that the concept of q-memory is coherent. Wiggins' case provides an illustration. The resulting people, in his case, both have apparent memories of living the life of the original person. If they agree that they are not this person, they will have to regard these as only q-memories. And when they are asked a question like "Have you heard this music before?" they might have to answer "I am sure that I q-remember hearing it. But I am not sure whether I remember hearing it. I am not sure whether it was I who heard it, or the original person."

We can next point out that on our definition every memory is also a q-memory. Memories are, simply, q-memories of one's own experiences. Since this is so, we could afford now to drop the concept of memory and use in its place the wider concept q-memory. If we did, we should describe the relation between an experience and what we now call a "memory" of this experience in a way which does not presuppose that they are had by the same person.[26]

This way of describing this relation has certain merits. It vindicates the "memory criterion" of personal identity against the charge of circularity.[27] And it might, I think, help with the problem of other minds.

But we must move on. We can next take the relation between an intention and a later action. It may be a logical truth that we can intend to perform only our own actions. But intentions can be redescribed as q-intentions. And one person could q-intend to perform another person's actions.

Wiggins' case again provides the illustration. We are supposing that neither of the resulting people is the original person. If so, we shall have to agree that the original person can, before the operation, q-intend to perform their actions. He might, for example, q-intend, as one of them, to continue his present career, and, as the other, to try something new[28] (I say "q-intend *as* one of them" because the phrase "q-intend that one of them" would not convey the directness of the relation which is involved. If I intend that someone else should do something, I cannot get him to do it simply by forming this intention. But if I am the original person, and he is one of the resulting people, I can.)

The phrase "q-intend *as* one of them" reminds us that we need a sense in which one person can survive as two. But we can first point out that the concepts of q-memory and q-intention give us our model for the others that we need: thus, a man who can q-remember could q-recognize, and be a q-witness of, what he has never seen; and a man who can q-intend could have q-ambitions, make q-promises, and be q-responsible for.

To put this claim in general terms: many different relations are included within, or are a consequence of, psychological continuity. We describe these relations in ways which presuppose the continued existence of one person. But we could describe them in new ways which do not.

This suggests a bolder claim. It might be possible to think of experiences in a wholly "impersonal" way. I shall not develop this claim here. What I shall try to describe is a way of thinking of our own identity through time which is more flexible, and less misleading, than the way in which we now think.

This way of thinking will allow for a sense in which one person can survive as two. A more important feature is that it treats survival as a matter of degree.

IV.

We must first show the need for this second feature. I shall use two imaginary examples.

The first is the converse of Wiggins' case: fusion. Just as division serves to show that what matters in survival need not be one-one, so fusion serves to show that it can be a question of degree.

Physically, fusion is easy to describe. Two people come together. While they are unconscious, their two bodies grow into one. One person then wakes up.

The psychology of fusion is more complex. One detail we have already dealt with in the case of the exam. When my mind was reunited, I remembered just having thought out two calculations. The one person who results from a fusion can, similarly, q-remember living the lives of the two original people. None of their q-memories need be lost.

But some things must be lost. For any two people who fuse together will have different characteristics, different desires, and different intentions. How can these be combined?

We might suggest the following. Some of these will be compatible. These can coexist in the one resulting person. Some will be incompatible. These, if of equal strength, can cancel out, and if of different strengths, the stronger can be made weaker. And all these effects might be predictable.

To give examples—first, of compatibility: I like Palladio and intend to visit Venice. I am about to fuse with a person who likes Giotto and intends to visit Padua. I can know that the one person we shall become will have both tastes and both intentions. Second, of incompatibility: I hate red hair, and always vote Labour. The other person loves red hair, and always votes Conservative. I can know that the one person we shall become will be indifferent to red hair, and a floating voter.

If we were about to undergo a fusion of this kind, would we regard it as death?

Some of us might. This is less absurd than regarding division as death. For after my division the two resulting people will be in every way like me, while after my fusion the one resulting person will not be wholly similar. This makes it easier to say, when faced with fusion, "I shall not survive," thus continuing to regard survival as a matter of all-or-nothing.

This reaction is less absurd. But here are two analogies which tell against it.

First, fusion would involve the changing of some of our characteristics and some of our desires. But only the very self-satisfied would think of this as death. Many people welcome treatments with these effects.

Second, someone who is about to fuse can have, beforehand, just as much "intentional control" over the actions of the resulting individual as someone who is about to marry can have, beforehand, over the actions of the resulting couple. And the choice of a partner for fusion can be just as well considered as the choice of a marriage partner. The two original people can make sure (perhaps by "trial fusion") that they do have compatible characters, desires, and intentions.

I have suggested that fusion, while not clearly survival, is not clearly failure to survive, and hence that what matters in survival can have degrees.

To reinforce this claim we can now turn to a second example. This is provided by certain imaginary beings. These beings are just like ourselves except that they reproduce by a process of natural division.

We can illustrate the histories of these imagined beings with the aid of a diagram (Figure 1). The lines on the diagram represent the spatiotemporal paths which would be traced out by the bodies of these beings. We can call each single line (like the double line) a "branch"; and we can call the whole structure a "tree." And let us suppose that each "branch" corresponds to what is thought

of as the life of one individual. These individuals are referred to as "A," "B+1," and so forth.

Now, each single division is an instance of Wiggins' case. So A's relation to both B+1 and B+2 is just as good as survival. But what of A's relation to B+30?

I said earlier that what matters in survival could be provisionally referred to as "psychological continuity." I must now distinguish this relation from another, which I shall call "psychological connectedness."

Let us say that the relation between a q-memory and the experience q-remembered is a "direct" relation. Another "direct" relation is that which holds between a q-intention and the q-intended action. A third is that which holds between different expressions of some lasting q-characteristic.

"Psychological connectedness," as I define it, requires the holding of these direct psychological relations. "Connectedness" is not transitive, since these relations are not transitive. Thus, if X q-remembers most of Y' life, and Y q-remembers most of Z's life, it does not follow that X q-remembers most of Z's life. And if X carries out the q-intentions of Y, and Y carries out the q-intentions of Z, it does not follow that X carries out the q-intentions of Z.

"Psychological continuity," in contrast, only requires overlapping chains of direct psychological relations. So "continuity" is transitive.

To return to our diagram. A is psychologically continuous with B+30. There are between the two continuous chains of overlapping relations. Thus, A has q-intentional control over B+2, B+2 has q-intentional control over B+6, and so on up to B+30.

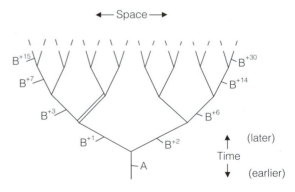

Figure 1

Or B^{+30} can q-remember the life of B^{+14}, B^{+14} can q-remember the life of B^{+6}, and so on back to A.[29]

A, however, need *not* be psychologically connected to B^{+30}. Connectedness requires direct relations. And if these beings are like us, A cannot stand in such relations to every individual in his indefinitely long "tree." Q-memories will weaken with the passage of time, and then fade away. Q-ambitions, once fulfilled, will be replaced by others. Q-characteristics will gradually change. In general, A stands in fewer and fewer direct psychological relations to an individual in his "tree" the more remote that individual is. And if the individual is (like B^{+30}) sufficiently remote, there may be between the two *no* direct psychological relations.

Now that we have distinguished the general relations of psychological continuity and psychological connectedness, I suggest that connectedness is a more important element in survival. As a claim about our own survival, this would need more arguments than I have space to give. But it seems clearly true for my imagined beings. A is as close psychologically to B^{+1} as I today am to myself tomorrow. A is as distant from B^{+30} as I am from my great-great-grandson.

Even if connectedness is not more important than continuity, the fact that one of these is a relation of degree is enough to show that what matters in survival can have degrees. And in any case the two relations are quite different. So our imagined beings would need a way of thinking in which this difference is recognized.

V.

What I propose is this.

First, A can think of any individual, anywhere in his "tree," as "a descendant self." This phrase implies psychological continuity. Similarly, any later individual can think of any earlier individual on the single path[30] which connects him to A as "an ancestral self."

Since psychological continuity is transitive, "being an ancestral self of" and "being a descendant self of " are also transitive.

To imply psychological connectedness I suggest the phrases "one of my future selves" and "one of my past selves."

These are the phrases with which we can describe Wiggins' case. For having past and future selves is, what we needed, a way of continuing to exist which does not imply identity through time. The original person does, in this sense, survive Wiggins' operation: the two resulting people are his later selves. And they can each refer to him as "my past self." (They can share a past self without being the same self as each other.)

Since psychological connectedness is not transitive, and is a matter of degree, the relations "being a past self of" and "being a future self of" should themselves be treated as relations of degree. We allow for this series of descriptions: "my most recent self," "one of my earlier selves," "one of my distant selves," "hardly one of *my* past selves (I can only q-remember a few of his experiences)," and, finally, "not in any way one of *my* past selves—just an ancestral self."

This way of thinking would clearly suit our first imagined beings. But let us now turn to a second kind of being. These reproduce by fusion as well as by division.[31] And let us suppose that they fuse every autumn and divide every spring. This yields the following diagram:

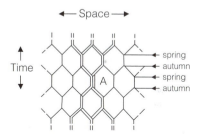

Figure 2

If A is the individual whose life is represented by the three-lined "branch," the two-lined "tree" represents those lives which are psychologically continuous with A's life. (It can be seen that each individual has his own "tree," which overlaps with many others.)

For the imagined beings in this second world, the phrases "an ancestral self" and "a descendant self" would cover too much to be of much use. (There may well be pairs of dates such that every individual who ever lived before the first date was an ancestral self of every individual who ever will live after the second date.) Conversely, since the lives of each individual last for only half a year, the word "I" would cover too little to do all of the work which it does for us. So part of this work would have to be done, for these second beings, by talk about past and future selves.

We can now point out a theoretical flaw in our proposed way of thinking. The phrase "a past self of" implies psychological connectedness. Being a past self of is treated as a relation of degree, so that this phrase can be used to imply the varying degrees of psychological connectedness. But this phrase can imply only the degrees of connectedness between different lives. It cannot be used within a single life. And our way of delimiting successive lives does not refer to the degrees of psychological connectedness. Hence there is no guarantee that this phrase, "a past self of," could be used whenever it was needed. There is no guarantee that psychological connectedness will not vary in degree within a single life.

This flaw would not concern our imagined beings. For they divide and unite so frequently, and their lives are in consequence so short, that within a single life psychological connectedness would always stand at a maximum.

But let us look, finally, at a third kind of being.

In this world there is neither division nor union. There are a number of everlasting bodies, which gradually change in appearance. And direct psychological relations, as before, hold only over limited periods of time. This can be illustrated with a third diagram (Figure 3). In this diagram

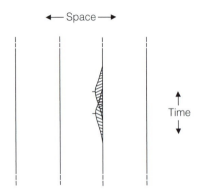

Figure 3

the two shadings represent the degrees of psychological connectedness to their two central points.

These beings could not use the way of thinking that we have proposed. Since there is no branching of psychological continuity, they would have to regard themselves as immortal. It might be said that this is what they are. But there is, I suggest, a better description.

Our beings would have one reason for thinking of themselves as immortal. The parts of each "line" are all psychologically continuous. But the parts of each "line" are not all psychologically connected. Direct psychological relations hold only between those parts which are close to each other in time. This gives our beings a reason for *not* thinking of each "line" as corresponding to one single life. For if they did, they would have no way of implying these direct relations. When a speaker says, for example, "I spent a period doing such and such," his hearers would not be entitled to assume that the speaker has any memories of this period, that his character then and now are in any way similar, that he is now carrying out any of the plans or intentions which he then had, and so forth. Because the word "I" would carry none of these implications, it would not have for these "immortal" beings the usefulness which it has for us.[32]

To gain a better way of thinking, we must revise the way of thinking that we proposed above. The revision is this. The distinction between successive selves can be made by reference, not to the branching psychological continuity, but to the degrees of psychological connectedness. Since this connectedness is a matter of degree, the drawing of these distinctions can be left to the choice of the speaker and be allowed to vary from context to context.

On this way of thinking, the word "I" can be used to imply the greatest degree of psychological connectedness. When the connections are reduced, when there has been any marked change of character or style of life, or any marked loss of memory, our imagined beings would say, "It was not I who did that, but an earlier self." They could then describe in what ways, and to what degree, they are related to this earlier self.

This revised way of thinking would suit not only our "immortal" beings. It is also the way in which we ourselves could think about our lives. And it is, I suggest, surprisingly natural.

One of its features, the distinction between successive selves, has already been used by several writers. To give an example, from Proust: "We are incapable, while we are in love, of acting as fit predecessors of the next persons who, when we are in love no longer, we shall presently have become. . . ."[33]

Although Proust distinguished between successive selves, he still thought of one person as being these different selves. This we would not do on the way of thinking that I propose. If I say, "It will not be me, but one of my future selves," I do not imply that I will be that future self. He is one of my later selves, and I am one of his earlier selves. There is no underlying person who we both are.

To point out another feature of this way of thinking. When I say, "There is no person who we both are," I am only giving my decision. Another person could say, "It will be you," thus deciding differently. There is no question of either of these decisions being a mistake. Whether to say "I," or "one of my future selves," or "a descendant self" is entirely a matter of choice. The matter of fact, which must be agreed, is only whether the disjunction applies. (The question "Are X and Y the same person?" thus becomes "Is X *at least* an ancestral [or descendant] self of Y?")

VI.

I have tried to show that what matters in the continued existence of a person are, for the most part, relations of degree. And I have proposed a way of thinking in which this would be recognized.

I shall end by suggesting two consequences and asking one question.

It is sometimes thought to be especially rational to act in our own best interests. But I suggest that the principle of self-interest has no force. There are only two genuine competitors in this particular field. One is the principle of biased rationality: do what will best achieve what you actually want. The other is the principle of impartiality: do what is in the best interests of everyone concerned.

The apparent force of the principle of self-interest derives, I think, from these two other principles.

The principle of self-interest is normally supported by the principle of biased rationality. This is because most people care about their own future interests.

Suppose that this prop is lacking. Suppose that a man does not care what happens to him in, say, the more distant future. To such a man, the principle of self-interest can only be propped up by an appeal to the principle of impartiality. We must say, "Even if you don't care, you ought to take what happens to you then equally into account." But for this, as a special claim, there seem to me no good arguments. It can only be supported as part of the general claim, "You ought to take what happens to everyone equally into account."[34]

The special claim tells a man to grant an *equal* weight to all the parts of his future. The argument for this can only be that all the parts of his future are *equally* parts of *his* future. This is true. But it is a truth too superficial to bear the weight of the argument. (To give an analogy: The unity of a nation is, in its nature, a matter of degree. It is therefore only a superficial truth that all of a man's compatriots are *equally* his compatriots. This truth cannot support a good argument for nationalism.)[35]

I have suggested that the principle of self-interest has no strength of its own. If this is so, there is no special problem in the fact that what we ought to do can be against our interests. There is only the general problem that it may not be what we want to do.

The second consequence which I shall mention is implied in the first. Egoism, the fear not of near but of distant death, the regret that so much of one's *only* life should have gone by—these are not, I think, wholly natural or instinctive. They are all strengthened by the beliefs about personal identity which I have been attacking. If we give up these beliefs, they should be weakened.

My final question is this. These emotions are bad, and if we weaken them we gain. But can we achieve this gain without, say, also weakening loyalty to, or love of, other particular selves? As Hume warned, the "refined reflections which philosophy suggests . . . cannot diminish . . . our vicious passions . . . without diminishing . . . such as are virtuous. They are . . . applicable to all our affections. In vain do we hope to direct their influence only to one side."[36]

That hope *is* vain. But Hume had another: that more of what is bad depends upon false belief. This is also my hope.[37]

Endnotes

[1]I have been helped in writing this by D. Wiggins, D. F. Pears, P. F. Strawson, A. J. Ayer, M. Woods, N. Newman, and (through his publications) S. Shoemaker.

[2]Implicit in John Locke, *Essay Concerning Human Understanding,* ed. by John W. Yolton, vol. 2, chap. 27, sec. 18 (London, 1961) and discussed by (among others) A. N. Prior in "Opposite Number," *Review of Metaphysics,* 11 (1957–1958), and "Time, Existence and Identity," *Proceedings of the Aristotelian Society,* vol. 57 (1965–1966); J. Bennett in "The Simplicity of the Soul," *Journal of Philosophy,* vol. 64 (1967); and R. Chisholm and S. Shoemaker in "The Loose and Popular and the Strict and the Philosophical Senses of Identity," in *Perception and Personal Identity: Proceeding of the 1967 Oberlin Colloquium in Philosophy,* ed. Norman Care and Robert H. Grimm (Cleveland, 1967).

[3]David Wiggins, *Identity and Spatio-Temporal Continuity* (Oxford, 1967), p. 50.

[4]Sydney S. Shoemaker, *Self-Knowledge and Self-Identity* (Ithaca, N.Y., 1963), p. 22.

[5]Those who would disagree are not making a mistake. For them my argument would need a different case. There must be some multiple transplant, faced with which these people would both find it hard to believe that there must be an answer to the question about personal identity, and be able to be shown that nothing of importance turns upon this question.

[6]R. W. Sperry, in *Brain and Conscious Experience,* ed. J. C. Eccles (New York, 1966), p. 299.

[7]Cf. David Wiggins, *op. cit,* p. 40.

[8]Suppose the resulting people fight a duel. Are there three people fighting, one on each side, and one on both? And suppose one of the bullets kills. Are there two acts, one murder and one suicide? How many people are left alive? One? Two? (We could hardly say, "One and a half.") We could talk in this way. But instead of saying that the resulting people are the original person—so that the pair is a trio—it would be far simpler to treat them as a pair, and describe their relation to the original person in some new way. (I owe this suggested way of talking, and the objections to it, to Michael Woods.)

[9]Cf. Sydney Shoemaker, in *Perception and Personal Identity,* p. 54.

[10]Cf. David Wiggins, *op. cit.*

[11]Bernard Williams' "The Self and the Future," *Philosophical Review,* 79 (1970), 161–180, is relevant here. He asks the question "Shall I survive?" in a range of problem cases, and he shows how natural it is to believe (1) that this question must have an answer, (2) that the answer must be all-or-nothing, and (3) that there is a "risk" of our reaching the wrong answer. Because these beliefs are so natural, we should need in undermining them to discuss their causes. These, I think, can be found in the ways in which we misinterpret what it is to remember and to anticipate (cf. Williams' "Imagination and the Self," *Proceedings of the British Academy,* 52 [1966], 105–124); and also in the way in which certain features of our egoistic concern—e.g., that it is simple, and applies to all imaginable cases—are "projected" onto its object. (For another relevant discussion, see Terence Penelhum's *Survival and Disembodied Existence* [London, 1970], final chapters.)

[12]"Personal Identity and Individuation," *Proceedings of the Aristotelian Society,* 57 (1956–1957), 229–253; also *Analysis,* 21 (1960–1961), 43–48.

[13]J. M. Shorter, "More about Bodily Continuity and Personal Identity," *Analysis,* 22 (1961–1962), 79–85; and Mrs. J. M. R. Jack (unpublished), who requires that this truth be embedded in a causal theory.

[14]*Analysis,* 21 (1960–1961), 44.

[15]For the reasons given by A. M. Quinton in "The Soul," *Journal of Philosophy,* 59 (1962), 393–409.

[16]Cf. S. Shoemaker, "Persons and Their Pasts," *American Philosophical Quarterly,* 7 (1970), 269; and "Wiggins on Identity," *Philosophical Review,* 79 (1970), 542.

[17]But not a necessary condition, for in the absence of psychological continuity bodily identity might be sufficient.

[18]Cf. Bernard Williams, "Personal Identity and Individuation," *Proceedings of the Aristotelian Society,* 57 (1956–1957), 240–241, and *Analysis,* 21 (1960–1961), 44; and also Wiggins, *op. cit.,* p. 38: "if coincidence under [the concept] *f* is to be *genuinely* sufficient we must not withhold identity . . . simply because transitivity is threatened."

[19]Williams produced another objection to the "psychological criterion," that it makes it hard to explain the difference between the concepts of identity and exact similarity (*Analysis,* 21 [1960–1961], 48). But if we include the requirement of causal continuity we avoid this objection (and one of those produced by Wiggins in his note 47).

[20]Those philosophers who have held this belief, from Butler onward, are too numerous to cite.

[21]*Op. cit.*

[22]In a paper on Butler's objection to Locke (not yet published).

[23]I here follow Shoemaker's "quasi-memory." Cf. also Penelhum's "retrocognition," in his article on "Personal Identity," in the *Encyclopedia of Philosophy,* ed. Paul Edwards.

[24]As Shoemaker put it, I seem to remember the experience "from the inside" (*op. cit.*).

[25]This is what so many writers have overlooked. Cf. Thomas Reid: "My memory testifies not only that this was done, but that it was done by me who now remember it" ("Of Identity," in *Essays on the Intellectual Powers of Man,* ed. A. D. Woozley [London, 1941], p. 203). This mistake is discussed by A. B. Palma in "Memory and Personal Identity," *Australasian Journal of Philosophy,* 42 (1964), 57.

26It is not logically necessary that we only *q*-remember our own experiences. But it might be necessary on other grounds. This possibility is intriguingly explored by Shoemaker in his "Persons and Their Pasts" (*op. cit.*). He shows that *q*-memories can provide a knowledge of the world only if the observations which are *q*-remembered trace out fairly continuous spatiotemporal paths. If the observations which are *q*-remembered traced out a network of frequently interlocking paths, they could not, I think, be usefully ascribed to persisting observers, but would have to be referred to in some more complex way. But in fact the observations which are *q*-remembered trace out single separate paths; so we can ascribe them to ourselves. In other words, it is epistemologically necessary that the observations which are *q*-remembered should satisfy a certain general condition, one particular form of which allows them to be usefully self-ascribed.

27Cf. Wiggins' paper on Butler's objection to Locke.

28There are complications here. He could form *divergent q*-intentions only if he could distinguish, in advance, between the resulting people (e.g., as "the left-hander" and "the right-hander"). And he could be confident that such divergent *q*-intentions would be carried out only if he had reason to believe that neither of the resulting people would change their (inherited) mind. Suppose he was torn between duty and desire. He could not solve this dilemma by *q*-intending, as one of the resulting people, to do his duty, and, as the other, to do what he desires. For the one he *q*-intended to do his duty would face the same dilemma.

29The chain of continuity must run in one direction of time. B^{+2} is not, in the sense I intend, psychologically continuous with B^{+1}.

30Cf. David Wiggins, *op. cit.*

31Cf. Sydney Shoemaker in "Persons and Their Pasts," *op. cit.*

32Cf. Austin Duncan Jones, "Man's Mortality," *Analysis*, 28 (1967–1968), 65–70.

33*Within a Budding Grove* (London, 1949), I, 226 (my own translation).

34Cf. Thomas Nagel's *The Possibility of Altruism* (Oxford, 1970), in which the special claim is in effect defended as part of the general claim.

35The unity of a nation we seldom take for more than what it is. This is partly because we often think of nations, not as units, but in a more complex way. If we thought of ourselves in the way that I proposed, we might be less likely to take our own identity for more than what it is. We are, for example, sometimes told, "It is irrational to act against your own interests. After all, it will be you who will regret it." To this we could reply, "No, not me. Not even one of my future selves. Just a descendant self."

36"The Sceptic," in "Essays Moral, Political and Literary," *Humes's Moral and Political Philosophy* (New York, 1959), p. 349.

37(Footnote added in 1976.) Of the many things which I now regret in this paper, I shall briefly mention three. (1) Talk about 'successive selves' is only a *façon de parler;* taken as anything more it can be misleading. (2) I should not have claimed that connectedness was more important than continuity. I now think that neither relation can be shown to be more important than the other. (3) The real issue seems to me now this. Does personal identity just consist in bodily and psychological continuity, or is it a further fact, independent of the facts about these continuities? Our reactions to the 'problem cases' show, I think, that we believe the latter. And we seem inclined to believe that this further fact is peculiarly deep, and is all-or-nothing—we believe that in any describable case it must hold either completely or not at all. My main claim is the *denial of this further fact.* This is what may make a difference. (No one needs to be told that psychological continuity is, in part, a matter of degree.) For some further remarks, see 'On "The Importance of Self-identity," ' *Journal of Philosophy*, 21 Oct. 1971, 'Later Selves and Moral Principles,' in *Philosophy and Personal Relations,* ed. Alan Montefiore (Routledge & Kegan Paul, 1973), and 'Lewis, Perry, and What Matters', in *The Identities of Persons,* ed. Amelie Rorty (University of California Press, 1976).

21. *Friends and Future Selves*

JENNIFER E. WHITING

One question raised by the selection by Perry is: What accounts for the difference between special concern—the selfish concern—we have about our own future selves, and the altruistic concern we have for another? In "Friends and Future Selves," Jennifer Whiting argues, generally, that belief in the numerical identity of our present and future selves is irrelevant to the justification of concern for future selves, and more specifically, that belonging to the same soul is not necessary or sufficient to justify the sort of concern that we have for our future selves. In a more positive vein she argues that psychological continuity is similar to friendship and since concern for our friends is a component of the friendship relation, concern for our future selves is a component of psychological continuity. As Whiting develops her view, part of what makes a future self *myself,* indeed the very existence of *my* future self, is my concern for it. Jennifer Whiting is a professor of philosophy at the University of Toronto.

Most of us believe that we have reasons to care about out own future selves and that these reasons differ, either in degree or in kind, from the reasons we have to act on behalf of one another. It is often assumed that an adequate account of personal identity should be able to explain—and perhaps also to justify—the sort of concern we have for our future selves. And this is thought to pose a special problem for psychological continuity accounts of personal identity—that is, for accounts which treat personal identity through time as consisting in some sort of continuity of experience rather than in the persistence of an irreducible subject such as an immaterial soul or a bare Cartesian ego. It is supposed to be obvious that I have special reasons to care about my future self if she has my immaterial soul in a way in which it is not obvious that I have special reasons to care about her if all she is is someone whose experiences are connected in certain ways to my present ones.

But this is far from obvious to me. In fact, my intuitions run the opposite way. I believe that I have special reasons to care about my future self if her experiences are connected in certain important ways to my present ones—if, for example, she will recall and carry out some of my present but future-directed intentions. And I doubt that I have any more reason to care about her than about anyone else, if her experiences are related to mine only in the sense that they belong to the same immaterial soul. But that may be because I assume that my soul—if I've got one—is no different from anyone else's except in so far as it has my experiences, memories, intentions and so on. Without these things, my soul is nothing to me.

What follows is a defense of these intuitions—or at least of one of them. My primary aim is to argue that psychological continuity accounts of personal identity can explain, and in some sense justify, the sort of concern that each of us has for her own future selves. I will not argue that I have no reason to care about my future self if her experiences are related to mine only in the sense that they belong to the same immaterial soul. I simply want to show that their belonging to the same soul is *not necessary* to justify the sort of concern that we have for our future selves. But once we see why sameness of soul is not necessary to justify such concern, I think we will also come to doubt that it is suffi-

From Jennifer E. Whiting, "Friends and Future Selves," *The Philosophical Review* 95 (1986): 547–80. Copyright © 1986 Cornell University. Reprinted by permission of the publisher and the author.

cient. My general view is that the numerical identity of our present and future selves, for which sameness of soul has often been thought necessary, is irrelevant to the justification of concern for our future selves.

I.

Let me begin with a word about psychological continuity accounts of personal identity and why concern for our future selves is supposed to pose a special problem for them. Psychological continuity accounts analyze personal identity in terms of the psychological relations among experiences themselves and without relating these experiences to any further underlying subjects—and in particular, without relating these experiences to irreducible or unanalyzable subjects which are either unchanging or indivisible. On a psychological continuity account, what makes some future self to be me—or to be my future self—is the fact that her experiences are related in certain ways to my present ones and not the fact that each of our experiences belongs to some further and irreducible subject such as an immaterial soul or a Cartesian ego.[1]

Many people object that if a psychological continuity account of personal identity is correct, then my present self has no reason to care about my future selves. This objection has recently been dubbed "the Extreme Claim."[2] But the name may mislead, for it is applied to a number of claims, some of which are not so extreme. First, there are strong and weak versions of the Extreme Claim. The *strong* versions claim that it is *irrational* to have a certain sort of concern for our future selves. The *weak* versions claim only that such concern is *not rationally* required. Second, there are absolute and comparative versions of the Extreme Claim. The *absolute* versions claim that my present self has no reason to care about my future selves. The *comparative* versions claim that my present self has no more reason to care about my future selves than about anyone else. The comparative versions are sometimes expressed in non-comparative form as claiming that I have no *special* reasons to care about my own future selves.[3] It is important to be aware of the homonymy of the Extreme Claim. For lack of

such awareness has caused much confusion and arguments which support one version have often been taken to support others. So I'll continue to talk of "the Extreme Claim," but with this warning: I'm talking about a family of claims. When I'm talking selectively about specific versions of the Extreme Claim, I'll try to make that clear.

Arguments of two types are generally offered for the Extreme Claim. The first and traditional argument for the Extreme Claim rests on the view that without unanalyzable subjects which are either indivisible or unchanging, psychological accounts are committed to the numerical distinctness of our present and future selves. The argument, suggested first by Butler and later by Sidgwick, is roughly that given this numerical distinctness, my present self has no more reason to care about my own future selves than about any other numerically distinct selves.[4] This argument supports only comparative versions of the Extreme Claim. The idea is that psychological accounts, in abandoning the numerical identity of our present and future selves, leave the reasons we have for caring about our own future selves no different in kind from those we have for caring about others. This is not to say that psychological accounts leave us no reasons at all to care about our own future selves, but only that they leave us no special reasons to care about our own future selves as opposed to anyone else.

Butler and Sidgwick reject this conclusion; they reject psychological accounts of personal identity and believe that we do have special reasons to care about our own future selves. The specialness of these reasons seems to depend on the view that benefits to our future selves in some sense compensate for burdens imposed on our present selves in a way in which benefits to others do not compensate for burdens imposed on us.[5] So their argument for the Extreme Claim can be filled out more precisely as follows:

(1) Special concern presupposes compensation—that is, A is justified in having special concern for B only if B's benefits compensate for A's burdens.

(2) Compensation presupposes the numerical identity of the burdened and the beneficiary—that is, the identity of the subject and the object of concern.

(3) Therefore, special concern presupposes the numerical identity of the subject and the object of concern.

(4) On the psychological continuity account of personal identity, our present and future selves are numerically distinct.

(5) Therefore, on the psychological account, benefits to our future selves cannot compensate for burdens imposed on our present selves.

(6) Therefore, on the psychological account, special concern for our future selves is not justified.

The second argument for the Extreme Claim is more general than the first. For it is supposed to support both absolute and comparative versions of that claim. This argument rests on the view that psychological continuity is not a relation which justifies concern. So if psychological continuity is all that personal identity consists in, then personal identity does not justify concern; if what it is for some future self to be me is simply for her experiences to be psychologically related in certain ways to my present ones, then my present self has no reason—or no special reason—to care about my future selves.[6]

But this argument is simply a special case of a general argument which can be used against *any* account of personal identity. Of any candidate for what constitutes such identity—for example, bodily continuity or sameness of immaterial soul—we can always ask how that candidate justifies concern. And it's not clear that any account has a very satisfactory answer. Even those who think that sameness of irreducible subject justifies concern in a way that psychological continuity (does not, end up saying things like, "the only tolerable answer to the question 'Why fear that future pain?' is that it is, unanalyzably, mine."[7] It has always mystified me how reasons for concern are lost in the move from a pain's being unanalyzably mine to its being analyzably mine.

In what follows, I defend the view that these arguments rest on the false supposition that concern for our future selves must be separable from personal identity and something for which such identity provides independent and antecedent justification. I will argue that concern for our future selves is a component of psychological continuity and so, according to the psychological criterion, a component of personal identity. In this respect, psychological accounts may actually be better able than others to reply to the second argument. For psychological accounts can take concern for our future selves to be necessary for personal identity in a way in which other accounts cannot. This also strikes against the first argument; on psychological accounts, concern for our future selves is necessary if we're to be persons in a way in which concern for others is not.

II.

Many psychological continuity theorists deny even comparative versions of the Extreme Claim. They believe that we do have special reasons for caring about those future selves which are psychologically continuous with our present selves—reasons we do not have for caring about selves, whether present or future, which are not so continuous with us. Their standard response to the first argument has been to deny premise (4)—that is, to deny that psychological continuity theories are committed to the numerical distinctness of our present and future selves.[8] On their view, talk of my past, present and future selves is simply talk of one and the same persisting thing—namely, me—as I exist at different times and no more commits us to the existence of numerically distinct objects than does talk of my public and private lives;[9] what makes my past and future selves to be me—that is, what makes them parts of numerically the same person as my present self—is just the fact that their experiences are related in certain ways to my present ones and not that they belong to numerically the same unanalyzable subject.

These psychological continuity theorists agree with Sidgwick and Butler that the sort of concern we have for our own future selves presupposes the numerical identity of the subject and the object of concern. But they disagree with Sidgwick and Butler about what constitutes that identity. For they deny that the numerical identity of our present and future selves requires the persistence of an irreducible subject. On their view, psychological continuity—or rather, *non-branching* psychological continuity—is sufficient for the numerical identity of our present and future selves.[10] On this view, whether or not my present stage is part of numerically the same person as my future stages will depend on whether or not it is psychologically continuous with only one stage existing at any future time. For if it is continuous with two or more simultaneously existing stages, then it cannot (without violating the transitivity of identity) be part of numerically the same person as either of those stages.

The main objection to non-branching psychological continuity theories has been that they violate the necessity of identity. Imagine a case in which my present self is psychologically continuous with only one future person stage at any given time, but only because the attempted transplant of the left half of my brain fails and only the right half—call her "Righty"—survives. It is often objected that in this case, the non-branching psychological continuity theorist is forced to say that although my present and future selves are in fact parts of numerically the same person, they would not have been had the attempted half-brain transplant been successful and Lefty also survived.[11] This seems to involve saying that although Righty is identical with me, she might not have been. But that violates the necessity of identity. This objection is supposed to show that only an indivisible subject—that is, one which *cannot* divide and so remains necessarily the same at different times—will secure the numerical identity of my present and future selves.

Shoemaker argues that this objection fails because it assumes that "Righty" refers to the same individual both in the world where Lefty survives and in the world where Lefty does not.[12] But this is like supposing that "the 42nd President of the United States" refers to the same individual both in the world in which Reagan won the 1984 election and in the world in which Mondale won that election. For on the non-branching psychological criterion, "Righty" does not refer to the same individual in both worlds. In the world in which the operation fails and only Righty survives, Righty *is* me. But in the world in which the operation succeeds and Lefty also survives neither I nor the person called "Righty" in the other world survive and someone else is now called "Righty."

Of course, Shoemaker's claims about transworld identity assume the non-branching psychological criterion and so would not convince the opponent who thinks that indivisible and unanalyzable subjects are necessary for the numerical identity of our present and future selves. Similarly, this opponent's claims about transworld identity assume his own criterion and so would fail to move the non-branching psychological continuity theorist. In this sense, the necessity of identity objection leads to stalemate. But Shoemaker's argument does seem to show that the psychological continuity theorist can, within his own theory, defend the necessity of identity.

This allows the psychological continuity theorist to deny that he is committed to the numerical distinctness of our present and future selves and so, to deny premise (4) of the first argument for the Extreme Claim. He can thus claim that non-branching psychological continuity secures that numerical identity which is necessary to justify special concern for our own future selves.

III.

Nevertheless, the psychological continuity theorist should not be content with this way out of the Extreme Claim. For even if he is entitled to claim the numerical identity of our present and future selves, the assumption that such identity is necessary to justify the sort of concern we have for our own future selves is going to run him into trouble. For that assumption seems to commit him to the following counterintuitive beliefs about the case of my attempted but unsuccessful fission where only Righty survives: (a) that benefits to Righty do compensate for burdens imposed on my present self and so I have special reasons to care about Righty even though "Righty's" benefits would not have compensated for my present burdens and I would not have had special reasons to care about her if the operation had been successful and Lefty had also survived; (b) that when Righty is in pain it will be me (that is, numerically the same person as my present self) who is in pain and so I have special reasons to fear and prevent her pain even though "Righty's" pain would not be mine and I would have no special (as opposed to merely altruistic) reasons to fear and to prevent her pain if the operation had been successful and Lefty had also survived.

The problem here is that the non-branching psychological continuity theorist who assumes that the sort of concern we have for our own future selves depends on numerical identity seems forced to make that concern depend on something as trivial and extrinsic as the absence of a competitor. Both in the case where Lefty survives and in the case where she does not, my present self stands in exactly the same intrinsic relations of bodily and psychological continuity to the person called "Righty."[13] But in one case I am supposed to have special reasons for caring about that person which I do not have in the other. And this seems implausible, even if we prefer that Lefty not survive because we attach some independent value to our uniqueness. This suggests that the psychological continuity theorist should abandon (3)—the claim that numerical identity is necessary to justify the sort of concern we have for our own future selves. For that claim lands him in the dilemma of having either to accept the Extreme Claim or to say that such concern depends on something as trivial and extrinsic as the absence of a competitor and to embrace the counterintuitive consequences.[14]

Reflection on the possibility of psychological fission has led some psychological continuity theorists to *conclude* that what justifies concern for our future selves is not identity *per se*, but rather the psychological continuity which, when non-branching, constitutes such identity.[15] Because psychological continuity coincides with identity in the actual world—that is, because we have not encountered actual cases of branching psychological continuity—they think we have mistakenly assumed that it is identity rather than psychological continuity which justifies the sort of concern we have for our own future selves. But had our experience been different, we would not have made this assumption.

This may be true, but it will not convince a hard-core Extreme Claimant who believes that identity is the *only* relation which justifies such concern. He will object that the psychological continuity theorist cannot avoid the foregoing dilemma simply by denying that the sort of concern we have for our own future selves presup-

poses the identity of the subject and the object of concern. Nor will it convince someone who believes simply that psychological continuity is not a relation which can justify concern—that is, someone who accepts the second argument for the Extreme Claim. He will object that the psychological continuity theorist must show how psychological continuity justifies such concern.

In support of the claim that concern for our future selves does not presuppose identity, the psychological continuity theorist can point out that most of us do not think that identity is the *only* relation which justifies concern. Nor is it the only relation which justifies special concern. We ordinarily take ourselves to be justified in having special concern for other persons to whom we stand in certain special relations—for example, our parents and children, friends and lovers.[16] This suggests that the psychological continuity theorist might take friendship as a model for how psychological continuity can justify concern. If he can show that psychological continuity is similar to friendship in those respects in which friendship justifies concern in the absence of identity, then he may be able to claim that psychological continuity justifies concern in much the same way.[17]

If we believe that at least part of what justifies concern for our friends is the fact that we and they have common experiences, shared desires, interests and values and that our interaction with one another causally affects the formation of these desires, interests and values, then it is plausible to claim that psychological continuity is analogous to friendship in those respects in which friendship justifies concern. For the memory-connectedness and anticipation of future experience which are partially constitutive of psychological continuity make it plausible to claim that we and our future selves have common experiences. And the continuity of character which partially constitutes psychological continuity consists in certain causal relations between the formation of our desires, interests and values and the desires, interests and values of our future selves. Because their characters are causally affected by ours in this way, they generally share at least some of our desires, interests and values with us.

It is less obvious that this causal interaction is reciprocal—that is, that the desires, interests and values of our future selves affect the formation of ours. But even here I think it is plausible to say that by taking their predicted desires and interests into account, we can allow the desires and interests of our future selves to affect those of our present selves. Suppose, for example, that my present self is faced with a difficult choice between pursuing an academic career and playing professional squash. Even if she now prefers squash but believes that her future selves will soon he bored with it or too old to play, she may take their predicted desires and interests into account and choose the longer term but less immediately satisfying rewards of an academic career instead. But then again she may not; she may regard acting in the interest of her future selves as something which is justified, but not rationally required.

The important point here is that my present self needn't base her reasoning on the belief that *she* will maximize *her own* long term benefits by acting on behalf of her future selves. She may instead regard her future selves and benefits to them in much the same way that she regards her friends and benefits to them. Because she cares about them as she does—and for whatever, if any, reasons—she regards certain benefits to them as capable of compensating for burdens imposed on her. In cases where the desires and interests of her future selves conflict with her desires and interests, the adjudication of interests will proceed in much the same way as it proceeds in the case of friendship. In that case, we do not think it is always unreasonable to set aside our own interests for the sake of our friends and we may even think that there are times when friendship actually requires us to do so.[18]

The difficult cases are those where our friends and future selves have desires or interests which express values that conflict with those we now believe to be justified—for example, their desires to join the Ku Klux Klan or the Moral Majority. Here we may do what we can to change their (predicted) desires and interests, but at some point we may simply say that their desires are so morally outrageous that our concern for them is no longer justified. I don't see what is wrong with that. It certainly does not show that our general concern is not ordinarily justified, which is all I'm really after.[19]

IV.

Here someone might object that the sort of concern we have for our own future selves is special in a different sense from that in which concern for our friends is special; and so, that we cannot use the special sort of concern we have for our friends to show that the special sort of concern we have for our own future selves does not presuppose numerical identity. But if we think that what makes concern for our future selves special is the fact that benefits to them somehow compensate for burdens imposed on our present selves *and* that there is a sense in which benefits to our friends and loved ones can compensate for our losses in a way in which benefits to strangers do not, then we can claim that what makes our concern special—namely, compensation—is the same in both cases.[20]

The idea is that we should avoid (3) by denying (2)—that compensation presupposes numerical identity—rather than by denying (1)—that special concern presupposes compensation. And this seems reasonable; many of us do think that benefits to our friends and loved ones can compensate for our burdens in a way in which benefits to strangers do not. But the important point for now is that such compensation seems to depend on our attitudes towards these friends and loved ones. It's because we care about them as we do that benefits to them can compensate for our burdens; if we didn't care, such compensation would not occur. My present suggestion is that the same goes for our future selves; benefits to them can compensate for burdens imposed on our present selves, if our present selves care about them in ways analogous to those in which we care for our friends. And this is true, whether or not our future selves are numerically identical with us.

V.

Because we generally take concern for our friends as a component of the friendship relation—that is, as part of what it is to be a friend—the psychological continuity theorist might support the friendship analogy by arguing that concern for our future selves is a component of psychological continuity.

The first step is to notice that among the components of psychological continuity are desires. Without desires, we would not form intentions to act in certain ways and so would be deprived of the connections between our intentions and actions, connections which we take to be partially constitutive of psychological continuity. Without desires, psychological continuity would be reduced to mere memory-connectedness and our existence would be primarily passive and oriented toward the past and present, rather than the future.[21] We would cease to be agents, and perhaps also to be persons. For I take it that agency—or at least the capacity for agency—is central to personhood.

The second step is to notice that desires are essentially future-directed—that is, that desires generally take as their objects future states of affairs even if those states of affairs lie only moments into the future. To see this, suppose that desires were not future-directed and that the objects of desires were primarily present or past states of affairs—for example, that I *now* be out running (instead of writing this paper) or that Reagan had not won the 1984 Presidential election. In this case, desires would not be causally related to actions in the way that we ordinarily take them to be. And even if we can have *some* desires for present objects—desires which do not affect our actions—I doubt that these can be the central cases of desire. Our concept of desire seems to be essentially related to that of action in ways such that desires are essentially future directed.[22]

At this point it is important to distinguish two types of desire—personal and impersonal—and to notice that many of the desires which in fact constitute psychological continuity are personal. I take a personal desire to be one whose object *essentially* includes its subject's being in certain states or doing certain things—for example, my desire that *I* write this paper, that *I* win an Olympic medal or that *I* care for my children.[23] An impersonal desire is then one whose object does not essentially include its subject's being in certain states or doing certain things—for example, my desire that this be written (by someone or other), that Carl Lewis win four Olympic medals, or that these children (who happen to be mine) be cared for.[24]

Here it is important to notice that the psychological continuity theorist need not distinguish personal from impersonal desires by appeal to numerical identity; he can instead distinguish them by appeal to psychological continuity. Personal desires will then take objects which essentially include states or actions of subjects who are psychologically continuous (and perhaps also identical) with the present subjects of those desires.[25] This leaves open the possibility that I should have personal desires for the future satisfactions of two distinct subjects, each of whom is psychologically continuous with me but not with the other; and so, that I should have personal desires for the satisfaction of subjects with whom I am not numerically identical. And this is precisely the possibility which our psychological continuity theorist seeks to allow. He claims that properly understood, personal desires for future satisfactions needn't rest on the (potentially) false supposition that the person receiving those satisfactions will be numerically identical with the present subject of those desires.

It is clear that most of us do have both personal and impersonal desires. I think it is also clear that in most cases, personal desires have greater effects on our intentions and *ipso facto* on our actions than do impersonal ones. So many of the desires which constitute psychological continuity (via intention-connectedness) are in fact personal.

This is important because personal desires may be taken as "primitive forms of concern" for our future selves.[26] They exhibit a concern on the part of our present selves that our future selves be doing or experiencing certain things. This concern seems in principle no different from that involved in desires for immediate satisfactions—that is, satisfactions lying only instants into the future such as my desire that the subject of this desire now (that is, in the next few moments) be writing this paragraph or my desire that the subject of this pain now (that is, in the next few moments) be free of it.[27] If we are willing to count such desires for immediate satisfactions as primitive forms of concern for the subjects of those desires—that is, as primitive forms of concern for our present selves—then we ought to be willing to count personal desires for future satisfaction as primitive forms of concern for our future selves.[28]

Such concern is primitive in two ways. First, it does not depend on any general conception of, or concern for, the welfare of its object. It is simply a desire that someone do or experience a certain thing. In this sense we can have primitive concern for others; I see a stranger crossing a busy street or auditioning for the ballet and I come to desire that he succeed.

Second, such concern is primitive in so far as general concern for a person derives from it. This is largely a matter of psychological fact. We do not ordinarily come to have desires that others do and experience certain things as a result of having a general concern for their welfare. Usually it is the other way around; our general concern for a person grows out of primitive concerns that she do and experience particular things. This is clear in the case of friendship, which often begins when we share particular interests with others. Take, for example, a case where I share an interest in squash with one of my teammates. We practice together daily and coach one another between games at tournaments, each desiring that the other win her match. As time goes on, I learn about her other interests; I learn, for example, about her children and about the book she's writing, and come to care about these things too. As our friendship develops, I come to have a general concern for her—that is, a second order concern that her first order desires and interests in general be satisfied. My current suggestion is that general concern for my future selves can, in much the same way, grow out of primitive concerns that they do and experience particular things.

Here it is important to notice that these primitive forms of concern for my future selves no more presuppose numerical identity than do the personal desires with which they are identified; if I know that there will tomorrow be two persons each of whom is psychologically continuous with me, I can desire that each of them do and experience certain things, perhaps even different things. These desires will be personal provided that I desire these subjects to do and experience these things under descriptions making use of first person indexicals—under descriptions such as "someone psychologically continuous with *me* in these ways having this experience." So I can have personal desires for the future satisfactions of subjects with whom I am not numerically identical and these desires are primitive forms of concern for those subjects—that is, primitive forms of concern for my future selves. Since

such desires are components of psychological continuity, it looks as though primitive forms of concern for our future selves are likewise components of psychological continuity.

But once again, I'm talking only about what in fact constitutes psychological continuity in most cases. I have not argued that these personal desires or primitive forms of concern for our future selves are justified or rationally required. The important point for now is simply that most actual cases of psychological continuity include primitive forms of concern for our future selves. So concern for our future selves is in fact a component of the psychological continuity which, assuming the psychological criterion, makes those future selves ours. In this sense, we make our future selves by coming to care about them in much the same way that we make friends by coming to care about others.

VI.

It has been objected that my analogy between making friends and making future selves is "suspiciously like a rather outrageous pun," but I intend it to be taken seriously. The objection is that making friends and making future selves are disanalogous in the following way. With friends, there is someone who exists independently of my concern for her on whom I simply confer the status of being my friend as I come to care. But with future selves, there is no one existing independently of my concern for her on whom I simply confer the status of being my future self as I come to care. There is a very literal sense in which I make my future selves and in which I do not make my friends.

In one sense I agree and take this objection to support my fundamental point that as a matter of fact, our concern for our future selves is causally relevant to the very existence of those selves. Without such concern, psychological continuity disintegrates, taking with it our selves. But in another sense, I do not agree. There are other components of psychological continuity besides concern, and some of these—for example, memory-connectedness and the continuity of impersonal beliefs and intentions—may allow us to predict that there will in the future be subjects who are psychologically continuous with us in ways which are relatively independent of our concern for them. And in coming to care about these subjects, we can confer on them the status of future selves in much the same way that we confer on others the status of friends.

The idea here is that there are thinner and thicker varieties of psychological continuity which may obtain between me and a future subject, not all of which are sufficient for that subject's being my future self. Suppose, for example, that there is a series of future subjects who have memories of my experiences but whose desires, beliefs and values are controlled largely by external forces or random events; they regularly undergo radical and random changes of character and no amount of activity or concern on my part will have much effect on their projects and commitments. In this case, it seems reasonable for me to deny that these future subjects (who are psychologically continuous with me in the thin sense afforded by memory-connectedness) are my future *selves*.[29]

If we think that overlapping chains of intention-connectedness between me and some future subject are necessary for that subject's being my future self, then we can see how my coming to care about future subjects who are psychologically continuous with me in a thin sense may confer on those subjects the status of being my future selves; my caring about them may be causally relevant to their being intention-connected with me. This is especially clear, if personal desires are primitive forms of concern for our future selves; for these personal desires are components of the intention-connectedness which I've just suggested is part of what makes those future subjects to be my future selves.

Here, however, it is important to ask whether personal desires are necessary components of the sort of intention-connectedness we think necessary for some future subject to be my future self. Suppose, for example, that there is a future subject intention-connected with me, but only via intentions based on impersonal desires—that is, a subject whose intentions are partially affected by my present but strictly impersonal desires and who has no personal desires or intentions of her own; she, like me, desires that this paper be written, that Carl Lewis win four Olympic medals and that these children (who happen to be mine) be cared for and she intends to do what she can to bring about the objects of those desires. If such

intention-connectedness is sufficient for that subject's being my future self then it looks as though my primitive concern for a future subject is not necessary for that subject to be my future self.[30]

I'm not sure what to say about such "impersonal agents," but there is a case to be made for denying that they are persons. They must, of course, have a thick enough notion of themselves to enable them to form intentions for themselves (or their immediate successors) to do things, but they seem to regard their own actions simply as instruments for bringing about states of affairs whose value is supposed to be entirely independent of them in the sense that these states of affairs could in principle he brought about by other means instead. These agents attach no independent value to *their* doing certain things or to *their* being in certain states—for example, to *their* writing these papers or to *their* caring for these children. Because they attach no independent value to their own states and actions, these agents seem to have no conception of their own welfare. So if we think that having some conception of one's own welfare and attaching some independent value to one's own states and actions are necessary for personhood, then it seems reasonable to deny that these agents are persons.

It is, of course, controversial to claim that having some conception of one's own welfare and attaching some independent value to one's own states and actions are logically required for personhood; although I think this claim defensible, I cannot now defend it. But even if it turns out that this claim is false, there may still be a sense in which having personal desires is necessary for personhood. For even if impersonal agency is logically possible, it may not be practically possible—at least not for most mortals. Complete selflessness of the sort associated with sainthood is rarely, if ever, achieved.[31] In this sense, it looks as though having at least some personal desires—and so, at least some primitive concern for one's future selves—is practically necessary for the sort of intention-connectedness which, assuming a psychological criterion, constitutes personal identity.

Once again, this allows us to recognize that there will in the future be subjects—though not necessarily selves—who are psychologically connected with us in the thin senses afforded by memory-connectedness and the continuity of impersonal intentions, subjects on whom we can confer the status of future selves by coming to care about them in much the same way that we confer on others the status of friends by coming to care about them. So the analogy between making friends and making future selves holds.

VII.

The friendship analogy is important because it reveals what I believe to be a false supposition of many contemporary attempts to justify concern for our future selves. There is a tendency to suppose that the relationship between our present and future selves is one thing, and our concern for them another, and that what we want to know is whether this relationship is one which justifies concern for them or not. But the friendship analogy challenges this supposition.

My relationship to my friend is not one thing and my concern for her another. My being concerned about her is part of what it is for me to be her friend—that is, part of what it is for me to stand in the relation of friendship to her. So my concern for her—and hers for me—are components of our relationship. Similarly, in the case of love. Part of what it is for me to love someone is for me to be concerned about her welfare. I do not ask myself whether I love someone—or whether someone is my friend—and then upon discovering that the answer is "yes," conclude that I stand in a relation to her such that I am justified in being specially concerned about her. It's because I care about her that she is my friend or loved one.

The same goes for our future selves. Our relationship to them is not one thing and our concern for them another. Part of what it is for some future self to be my future self is for me to be concerned about her in certain ways—for me to have desires that she do and experience certain things.[32] On this view, concern for our future selves is one of the components of psychological continuity and not something for which psychological continuity provides independent and antecedent justification.

Now this may seem odd. We ordinarily think that our relationship to our future selves is one thing and our concern for them another, and that it is our belief that some future selves will be our own

which explains, and perhaps also justifies our being concerned about them rather than about some other future selves. But if our concern for them is part of what makes them to be our future selves in the first place, then we cannot appeal to the fact that some future selves will be ours in order to explain or to justify our concern for them. For it's only if we care about them in the first place—or about selves which care either directly or indirectly about them—that they will be our future selves.

The deep worry here is that it is circular to say that I have reasons to care about my future selves because they are my future selves, if what makes them my future selves is even partly the fact that I care about them in the first place. For then we seem to be saying that I have reasons to care about my future selves because I care about them in the first place. But this seems to me to be no more worrisome than saying that I have reasons to care about my friends because they are my friends, when what makes them my friends is the fact that I care about them in the first place—no more worrisome, that is, than saying that I have reasons to care about my friends because I care about them in the first place.

Here it's worth pausing to note that there are two common attitudes toward the sort of concern involved in friendship. Some people believe that such concern is something we simply come to have and not something which demands initial justification. Initially at least, they believe that friendship is something to be explained and not justified. Others believe that the sort of concern involved in friendship may initially be justified by certain features of the persons about whom we come to care. We may approve of someone's character or of her projects and commitments and so think her worthy of our concern.[33] But whether or not they think that the initial concern involved in friendship is justified, most people think that once such concern is in place and someone has become my friend, further concern is justified; I then have reasons to care for her which I did not previously have and which I would not now have had I never come to care in the first place. And I then have reasons to care for her which I do not have to care for other perhaps equally deserving persons about whom I never came to care.

These two attitudes show that the analogy between friendship and psychological continuity can be developed in different ways. We may take the sort of concern involved in psychological continuity to be something we simply come to have and not something which demands initial justification. Or we may take such concern to be something which is initially justified by certain (predicted) features of our future selves. But in either case we can claim that once such concern is in place and someone has become my future self, further concern is justified; I then have reasons to care about her which I did not previously have and which I would not now have had I never come to care about her in the first place.[34] And I then have reasons to care about her which I do not have for caring about other and perhaps equally deserving persons about whom I never came to care.

Now it seems to me that the worry about circularity runs deeper on the first view than on the second. If we deny that there is anything which justifies our initial concern and take such concern as providing us with further reasons for concern, then it looks as though we really do have reasons to care, if at all, only because we care in the first place. But insofar as we are willing to allow this in the case of concern for our friends, we should also be willing to allow it of concern for our future selves. There is, however, a way out of this circularity if we adopt the second attitude and allow that some initial concern for others can be justified.

The idea here is that our prospective friends and future selves may have characters we admire or projects and desires of which we approve—that is, characters, projects and desires which we regard as making them worthy of our concern. Initially, we may even care more about their projects and commitments than we do about them. We may recognize this or that particular project or desire of theirs as worth supporting and come eventually to care generally about them, qua pursuers of certain ends, as a result of caring about and recognizing as worthwhile, their particular projects and desires. Appealing to these particular projects and desires seems to me to be the closest we can come to giving reasons to care in the first place and so, the best we can do to answer the circularity objection. The particular projects and desires of other and future selves are features of those selves which, at least initially, are relatively independent of our relationship to them and may provide us with some initial reasons to care—that is, to make them our friends and future selves. But once we do

care—that is, once they have become our friends and future selves—our relationship to them provides us with additional reasons for concern.

VIII.

So far, I've been recommending that we assimilate the justification of concern for our future selves to that of concern for our friends.[35] Although I've allowed that we may adopt the first attitude toward friendship, and claim that concern for our future selves demands no more in the way of initial justification than does concern for our friends, I prefer the second view which allows some initial justification of concern for our friends. But in either case, there is a problem about how concern for our future selves is supposed to be special.

If we believe that concern for our friends is something we simply come to have and not something which demands initial justification then we are likely to think that concern for others is not rationally required but something which, if we happen to have it, is not unreasonable. Similarly, we will think that concern for our future selves is reasonable if we happen to have it, but not something we are rationally required to have. And insofar as this commits us to saying that concern for our future selves is not rationally required, it seems to be a weak version of the Extreme Claim.

But even if we think that concern for our friends can initially be justified by certain of their features, we are not likely to claim that such concern is rationally required. For one thing, many more people than I have the energy and resources to care about may have features which would justify my caring about them; and it seems to be true of each that it would be reasonable, though not rationally required, for me to care about her. And the same may be said of my future selves, especially if what justifies my concern for them is the same as what justifies my concern for others. If, for example, it is the fact that some future self has a character or projects and desires of which I approve, which provides me with initial reasons to care about her, then these reasons are independent not only of numerical identity, but also of psychological continuity. So they are independent of whether or not she is my future self. Even if her having a character or projects and desires of which I approve is the result of her being psychologically continuous with me, she or someone else could have that character or those projects and desires without being psychologically continuous with me; and in that case, my initial reasons to care about these other selves would seem to be the same as those for caring about my future selves. So if we think that concern for these other selves is justified but not rationally required, we ought to say the same of concern for our future selves. Once again, assimilating the justification of concern for our future selves to that of concern for our friends seems to commit us to a weak version of the Extreme Claim.

Now I am willing to allow a sense in which the Extreme Claim is true and concern for our future selves not rationally required. Buddhists apparently accept a strong version of the Extreme Claim. They believe that concern for our future selves is irrational—irrational in the Humean sense that it is based on a false belief in the existence of the self. They believe that our personal desires and attachments are simply manifestations of this false belief and that it is only by giving up these desires and attachments (and with them our belief in the self) that we will reach *nirvana*.[36]

Now I agree—and this is partly my point—that if we give up these desires and attachments, there will be no selves or persons left to believe in. For these desires and attachments and their attendant belief in the self are causally relevant to the very existence of that self. It is partly by having desires, and so coming to think of ourselves as temporally extended creatures, that we come to be selves or persons in the first place. So there are no selves or persons apart from our having certain beliefs and attitudes. But this does not mean that when we have these beliefs and attitudes, they are false. For these beliefs and attitudes are, in a sense, self-insuring.

Nevertheless, I do not think we can argue against the Buddhist who has renounced desire altogether that personal desires and attachments are rationally required.[37] We cannot show that it is worse *for him* not to have desires and the sort of concern for the self which goes along with them. For if it is possible to renounce desire and attachments altogether then there is no self there of whom it is true to say that *it* would be better off, if it cared about itself. In this sense, I am willing to

concede that some weak version of the Extreme Claim is true, and that it is not rationally required to have the sort of desires I've argued are primitive forms of concern for our future selves. But here it is important to notice that although such desires are not rationally required in this sense, they are necessary if persons are to exist. That was the point of arguing that such desires are components of the psychological continuity which—assuming a psychological criterion—constitutes personal identity. The price we have to pay for giving up such desires—namely, our selves or persons—is one the Buddhist is willing to pay, but which, I suspect, many of us are not.

Once we acknowledge that primitive forms of concern for our future selves are necessary components of personal identity, we can see how concern for our own future selves is special in a way in which concern for others is not; concern for our own future selves is necessary for our own existence and persistence in a way in which concern for others is not.[38] A creature who lacks such concern will fail (or cease) to be a person. So we can say that concern for our own future selves is required, if we are to be persons, in a way in which concern for others is not. In this sense, the Extreme Claim is false and we have special reasons to care about our own future selves.

IX.

Although I've argued that concern for our own future selves is special in so far as it is required if we are to be persons, it is important to keep in mind that there is another sense in which concern for our own future selves is not so special. In assimilating the justification of concern for our own future selves to that of concern for our friends, I'm allowing that concern for our future selves is no different in kind from our concern for others—or at least not from our concern for those persons to whom we stand in certain special relationships such as those of love and friendship. This yields a sense in which the Extreme Claim is true.

Suppose that there is a threshold level of concern for one's own future selves such that below this threshold, the sort of psychological continuity which constitutes personal identity does not occur.

We might then say that once an agent reaches and sustains this level of concern, comparative versions of the Extreme Claim are true of him in one sense and false in another. They are false, if they claim that he has no more reason to care about his own future selves than he has to care about any arbitrary individual. For his future selves, unlike arbitrary individuals, stand to him in special relations which are supposed to justify concern.

Nevertheless, there may be *some* other selves of whom it is true to say that our agent has no more reason to care about his future selves than about them. The reasons he has for caring about his future selves are the same in kind as those he has for caring about his friends and loved ones and so our agent can weigh these reasons against one another in cases where the interests of his future selves conflict with those of his friends and loved ones. And once he has reached the threshold of personal concern, he is not rationally required to give preferential treatment to his future selves. He may, in fact, care more about a very close friend or loved one than he does about his future selves and so, choose to benefit her at their expense. Parents often do this sort of thing for their children, and we do not ordinarily think it irrational. The story I've been telling suggests why not; we think that benefits to our loved ones compensate for our burdens in much the same way that benefits to our future selves do. So once someone reaches the threshold of personal concern, a comparative version of the Extreme Claim may be trite with respect to his close friends and loved ones; he may be no more rationally required to care about his future selves than he is to care about these friends and loved ones.

X.

Before concluding, I'd like to compare my account of how the psychological continuity theorist can defend concern for our future selves to Perry's alternative account. I choose his account for two reasons. First, it is the strongest published alternative. And second, Perry's account is fundamentally opposed to mine. Perry takes non-private projects (which are roughly what I've been calling "impersonal" projects) as primary and attempts to derive concern for our future selves from them. I take personal projects (which are roughly what Perry calls "private" projects) as primary and regard them as primitive and non-derivative forms of concern for our future selves.[39]

Perry believes that the only compelling justification for private projects is derivative; we have certain non-private projects and believe that our future selves are the persons most likely to succeed in carrying them out. He thinks, for example, that the only compelling justification for having the private project that *I* care for my children is that I have the relevant non-private project that my children be cared for and empirical reasons for believing that my future selves are the persons most likely to care for them. In cases where our future selves are not in fact the persons most likely to carry out our non-private projects, Perry thinks we have no more reason to care about them than about anyone else—except for those who are more likely than they to carry out our non-private projects.[40] Perry thinks that "unsupported" private projects, by which he seems to mean private projects not supported by the belief that one's own future selves will be most likely to carry them out, are irrational "not in the sense that they are self-contradictory" but rather in the sense explained by Brandt that they "would not survive . . . in the vivid awareness of knowable propositions."[41] Perry claims that it would not be irrational to fail to have unsupported private projects.

Now perhaps it is not irrational to fail to have unsupported private projects in the same way that the Buddha's position is not irrational. But I do not think it is irrational to have unsupported private projects in the way that Perry thinks it is. Even if we concede, as I think we must, that there are cases in which it is more important for a non-private project to succeed than for the private projects deriving from it to succeed, it does not follow that we attach no independent value to the egocentric components of our private projects. For example, even if we think that it is more important that our children be cared for than that *we* care for them—or that it is more important that a cure for cancer be discovered than that *we* discover it—this does not mean that we attach no independent value to our doing these things for ourselves. Many people insist on making into private projects, non-private projects which they know perfectly well that others are better qualified and just as likely to do.

Furthermore, it is clear that we do not acquire our private projects by looking around the world and asking ourselves what we would like to happen, and then asking which of these things is not likely to happen if we ourselves do not take action. There are many things which other people would be quite happy to do and which we compete with them for the opportunity to do. The fact that someone else will win that gold medal or write this paper if I don't—or that someone else will care for my children if I don't—doesn't make me drop these projects and start looking around for other projects which will go unfulfilled unless I take action.

Now Perry may object that these observations are irrelevant since they can be explained by the fact that all or most of us have false beliefs about ourselves and our relationships to the success of our projects. But I think that we have many projects which are irreducibly private and which make our own and other people's lives worth caring about. (These are what I've been calling "personal" projects.) My project of learning to play Beethoven piano sonatas is not entirely derivative from the non-private project that Beethoven sonatas be performed. This project will not disappear, if I learn that plenty of others will perform Beethoven sonatas much more proficiently than I will. Nor is my private project of playing squash entirely derivative from the desire that squash be played. And even in the more difficult cases where the non-private component seems most important—for example, in the case of my project that I care for any children or that I fight for justice in the world—I don't think the impersonalist story succeeds. For I doubt that my children (or anyone else's) would be worth caring for—or that justice would amount to anything—in a world in which people did not have irreducibly private projects and irreducibly private desires and attachments.

This is a familiar point, which applies both to other-directed concern and to self concern. Williams applies it to other-directed concern when he observes that without first-order projects, "the general utilitarian project would have nothing to work on, and would be vacuous."[42] The *locus classicus* of the application to self-concern is in Butler, who claims that

the very idea of interest or happiness consists in this, that an appetite or affection enjoys its object. It is not because we love ourselves that we find delight in such and such objects, but because we have particular affections towards them. Take away these affections and you leave self-love absolutely nothing at all to employ itself about.[43]

Butler's point, that a world without particular affections is monthly impoverished, applies to Perry's world without irreducibly private (or what I've been calling "personal") projects. Our particular affections and personal projects are the stuff of which our general concerns, both for ourselves and others, are made.

I've been arguing that these particular affections and personal projects are components of the psychological continuity which—assuming a psychological criterion—constitutes personal identity. They are primitive forms of self-concern which are built into psychological continuity and from which our more general concern derives. I'd like to conclude by taking Butler's point a step beyond Butler. It is not because we love ourselves that we have these particular affections, but because we have these affections that we have selves to love; take away these particular affections and you leave *no selves*—and so, nothing for self-love or other-love to employ itself about. There is an element of irony that the major premise of Butler's argument against psychological hedonism should come in so handy in defending concern for our future selves against his own attack.[44]

Endnotes

[1]Because the present objection to psychological accounts usually comes from those who hold the Simple View—that is, the view that personal identity is simple and unanalyzable—I choose to focus on this contrast and to ignore versions of the bodily criterion. Psychological accounts need not deny the existence of underlying subjects; they simply deny that such subjects must be irreducible, indivisible or, as some proponents of the Simple View (perhaps as a result of confusion) believe, unchanging. The "Simple View" terminology is taken front Derek Parfit, "Later Selves and Moral Principles," in *Philosophy and Personal Relations*, ed. A. Montefiore (London: Routledge and Kegan Paul, 1973), p. 138. For accounts of the Simple View, see Richard Swinburne in S. Shoemaker and R. Swinburne, *Personal Identity* (Oxford: Basil Blackwell, 1984), pp. 19–21; and Geoffrey Madell, *The Identity of*

the Self (Edinburgh: Edinburgh University Press 1981), pp. 4–6.

²See Derek Parfit, *Reasons and Persons* (Oxford: Oxford University Press, 1984), pp. 307–312.

³So there are at least four versions of the Extreme Claim—the strong absolute (that it is irrational to care about one's future selves); the weak absolute (that it is not rationally required to care about one's future selves); the strong comparative (that it is irrational to care more about one's future selves than about anyone else); and the weak comparative (that it is not rationally required to care more about one's future selves than about anyone else).

⁴Sidgwick, in *The Methods of Ethics* (London: Macmillan, 1907), p. 419, asks why, if Hume's psychological account of personal identity is correct, "should one part of the series of feelings into which the Ego is resolved be concerned with another part of the same series, any more than with any other series?" (It is not clear that Sidgwick thinks his objection applies to all versions of the psychological criterion; he addresses it to Hume and "those who adopt the view of the *extreme* school of empirical psychologists.") In "Of Personal Identity," the first appendix to *The Analogy of Religion* (1736), reprinted in John Perry, ed., *Personal Identity* (Berkeley: University of California Press, 1975), pp. 99–105, Butler claims that if Locke's psychological account of personal identity is correct, then "it is a fallacy . . . to imagine . . . our present self will be interested in what will befall us tomorrow; since our present self is not, in reality, the same with the self of yesterday, but another self or person coming in its room, and mistaken for it; to which another self will succeed tomorrow. . . . If the self or person of today, and that of tomorrow, are not the same, but only like persons, the person of today is really no more interested in what will befall the person of tomorrow, than in what will befall any other person." (See p. 102 in Perry.) Although Butler begins by stating the Extreme Claim non-comparatively, he immediately repeats it (as Sidgwick states it) in comparative form and this is all that their arguments, taken by themselves, warrant. Of course, the comparative version is compatible with the non-comparative one, if it turns out that altruistic concern is not justified. But it is important to realize that we need additional premises to get that conclusion.

⁵See Parfit, *Reasons and Persons*, p. 337; and Milton Wachsberg, *Personal Identity, The Nature of Persons, and Ethical Theory*, Ph.D. thesis, Princeton University, 1983, Chapter Two. Sidgwick and Butler do not explicitly mention compensation, but I believe that their arguments make the best sense if interpreted in this way. And even if this is not exactly what they had in mind, the argument supplied above is one plausible argument for the Extreme Claim.

⁶See John Perry, "The Importance of Being Identical," in *The Identities of Persons*, ed., A. Rorty (Berkeley: University of California Press, 1976), pp. 67–68.

⁷Madell, P. 112.

⁸See Wachsberg, pp. 68–69; and Perry, "The Importance of Being Identical," p. 68.

⁹See David Wiggins, "Locke, Butler and the Stream of Consciousness," in Rorty ed., pp. 169–170, notes 9 and 11.

¹⁰Because psychological continuity seems to be capable of branching and so is potentially a one-many relation whereas identity is always and necessarily a one-one relation, psychological continuity theorists often add a non-branching clause to their claim that what makes two person stages to be stages of numerically the same person is the fact that they stand in the relation of psychological continuity to one another; numerical identity requires that the stages stand in the relation of *non-branching* psychological continuity to one another. See Sydney Shoemaker in Shoemaker and Swinburne, p. 90; and in "Persons and Their Pasts," *American Philosophical Quarterly* 7 (1970), p. 279. For discussion of the ways in which psychological continuity might branch, see David Wiggins, *Identity and Spatio-Temporal Continuity* (Oxford: Basil Blackwell, 1967), p. 50; Derek Parfit, "Personal Identity," *The Philosophical Review* 80 (1971), pp. 3–27, (reprinted in Perry, *Personal Identity*, pp. 199–223) and *Reasons and Persons*, Chapter 12.

¹¹See R. C. Swinburne, "Personal Identity," *Proceedings of the Aristotelian Society* (1973–74), pp. 236–237; Shoemaker and Swinburne, pp. 14–19.

¹²See Shoemaker and Swinburne, pp. 114–118; see also Nathan Salmon, *Reference and Essence* (Princeton: Princeton University Press, 1981), Appendix I; and Hugh Chandler, "Rigid Designation," *The Journal of Philosophy* 72 (1975), pp. 363–369.

¹³Here, I'm assuming that the Simple View (see note 1) is false. It's also important to notice that "Righty" may have different referents in the two cases, even though the intrinsic relations are the same.

¹⁴Paul Hoffman has suggested to me that there are third person cases in which we think that our concern may legitimately depend on the absence of competitors. Take, for example, the case of someone who is justified in having a certain sort of special concern for her second husband, but only because her first husband has died or left. This suggests that the psychological continuity theorist might defend his view by allowing that first person concern can also depend on the absence of competitors. Furthermore, he might allow that the presence or absence of a competitor is relevant whether or not he believes numerical identity to be at stake. In other words, he might think that we have special reasons to care about the future persons psychologically closest to us and which future persons are psychologically closest to us will be determined by the presence or absence of competitors. This point is made clearly by Robert Nozick in defense of his "closest continuer theory" in *Philosophical Explanations* (Cambridge Harvard University Press, 1981), pp. 27–39.

¹⁵Because they assume that concern is justified in the normal, non-branching case and believe *both* that there are exactly the same intrinsic reasons for concern in the branching case *and* that concern cannot depend on something as trivial and extrinsic as the absence of a competitor, they conclude that concern must be justified in the branching case too. (See Shoemaker in Shoemaker and Swinburne, p. 121; and Parfit "Personal Identity," pp. 205–206 (in the Perry reprint), and *Reasons and Persons* pp. 261–264). But this argument will not work against the

Extreme Claimant who denies that concern is justified in the normal non-branching case.

[16]In an earlier draft of this paper, there was a note here thanking Derek Parfit for *first* calling this point to my attention! What I meant was to thank him for *reminding* me of the relevance of this obvious (but often neglected) point.

[17]It is crucial to note that I'm requiring only that psychological continuity be analogous to friendship *in those respects in which friendship justifies concern,* and not in all respects. For the most typical reaction among those presented with my view has been to cite respects in which psychological continuity and friendship are disanalogous. Now I agree that there are some respects in which friendship and psychological continuity are disanalogous, but as long as they are analogous in those respects in which friendship justifies concern I don't think that this affects my central point that concern for our future selves can be justified in the same way as concern for our friends. The main function of the analogy is simply to show that the same kind of justification can be applied in both cases.

[18]I do not mean to suggest a sharp or exclusive distinction between my interests and the interests of my friends. There seems to be an important sense in which genuine friendship requires me to regard my friend's interests as my own. And I do not think that potential conflicts between my friend's interests and my other interests (that is, my interests in addition to my interest in her) should create any more problem than that created by potential conflicts between my other more self-confined interests—for example, than that between my desires to become a championship athlete and to become an accomplished musician. Where my friend's interests conflict with my other interests, I can regard that as a conflict of *my* interests—that is, as a conflict between my interests in her and my other interests.

[19]This may seem even less of a problem if we consider that even our present selves may suffer conflicts of values. On this issue, see Parfit, *Reasons and Persons,* pp. 153–156; and Thomas Nagel, *The Possibility of Altruism* (Princeton: Princeton University Press, 1970), pp. 73–74. Here, I might note that self-hatred is not necessarily an obstacle to my view. Self-hatred is often a product of an agent's desires to act in ways which she regards as morally or otherwise valuable and these desires are, on my view, forms of self-concern.

[20]Here, as elsewhere, it is important to notice how the belief that what makes concern for our own future selves special is (different from what makes concern for friends and loved ones special may rest on false—or at least disputed—beliefs about the nature of personal identity. For more on the way in which concern for our future selves is special, see Sections VIII–IX below.

[21]I believe that the emphasis on memory-connectedness in contemporary discussions of personal identity is unfortunate. For I think that we value memory largely—though not entirely—because it enables us to form a conception of ourselves as temporally extended creatures, a conception without which we would not be agents.

[22]This point is most obvious if we adopt a functionalist account of desire according to which desires are *defined* in terms of their causal relations to, among other things, our

beliefs and actions. But nothing in my argument depends on adopting a functionalist account.

[23]Here, it is necessary that I desire these states of affairs under descriptions which make use of a first person indexical; otherwise, my being in certain states and doing certain things is desired only accidentally—as for example, in the case where I desire that the person (whoever it is) most likely to discover a cure for cancer receive a certain research grant and I happen to be that person. In this case, there is a sense in which I desire that I get the grant. But my desire is impersonal because I desire this not under the description "my getting the grant," but rather under the description "the person most likely to discover a cure getting the grant." This desire is impersonal because its object does not *essentially* include its subject's being in certain states or doing certain things. Here, it's worth noting that personal desires needn't be desires for the agent's self-interest narrowly conceived. I can, for example, have personal desires that *I* discover a cure for cancer, that *I* care for my children and so on. All that is required here is that I attach some independent and non-instrumental value to its being me who does these things and this is true even if my primary reason for wanting to do them is that I believe that it is a good thing, impersonally, that they be done—done, that is, by someone or other. (This is an important difference between what I call "personal" and what Perry calls "private." See Section X and note 39 below.)

[24]We can distinguish three ways in which I might desire that I do something: (1) My desire might be *entirely derivative from an impersonal desire* that the thing be done—as for example, in the case where I have an impersonal desire that the person most qualified to discover a cure for cancer get a certain grant and use it for cancer research and I happen to be that person. If, as a result, I desire to get the grant and do the research, but attach no independent value to its being me who does it, then my desire is entirely derivative from my impersonal desire that a cure be discovered. (2) My desire might be *partially derivative from an impersonal desire*—as, for example, in the case where I want to do something primarily because I believe that doing it will bring about some impersonally valuable result, but where I attach some independent value to its being *me* who does it (perhaps because I want to be the sort of person who acts on impersonal values or for some other reason). (3) My desire might be *non-derivative*—as, for example, in the case where I just want to do it. Now my account of the distinction between personal and impersonal desires classifies desires of type (1) as impersonal, even though many would call them "personal." This is partly for convenience of exposition. My general argument is that personal desires and projects are primitive forms of self-concern and so, to the extent that personal desires and projects are necessary for psychological continuity of the sort we take to be constitutive of personal identity, primitive forms of self-concern are necessary for such continuity. Since I'm not convinced that desires and projects entirely derivative from impersonal ones are primitive forms of self-concern, the argument cannot be stated in this way, if these entirely derivative desires and projects are included among personal desires and projects. So I prefer to group these entirely derivative desires and projects with impersonal ones and to deal with them sepa-

rately. This allows me to distinguish more sharply a problem which arises whichever way I state the case—that is, the problem of impersonal agency discussed in Section VI. Were I to classify entirely derivative desires and projects as personal, this would have to be stated as a case of personal desires which do not seem to be primitive forms of self-concern and what I would have to show is that an agent with entirely derivative personal desires would not exhibit the sort of psychological continuity which we take to be necessary for personhood.

[25]Note that desiring a state of affairs under the description "someone psychologically continuous with *me* doing x" satisfies the criterion for having a personal desire; that state of affairs is desired under a description containing a first person indexical.

[26]I am indebted to Sydney Shoemaker for the expression "primitive forms of self-concern." For his view, see Shoemaker and Swinburne, p. 121.

[27]Since I'm arguing that these desires are among the components of the sort of psychological continuity constitutive of personal identity, it is important that the content of these desires can be described without reference to the identity of the subject whose identity they are being used to establish. That's why I've said that they are desires that the subject of this desire (or someone psychologically continuous with the subject of this desire) does or experiences something rather than desires that *I* do or experience something. The worry here is parallel to the worry that taking memory as a criterion of personal identity is circular; I'm suggesting that this worry be handled in roughly the same way as Shoemaker has handled the parallel worry about the memory criterion. See Shoemaker and Swinburne, pp. 81–86.

[28]It is difficult to deny that such primitive forms of concern are justified, without claiming that having desires is in general unjustified. And it's hard to see how the Extreme Claimant can draw a non-arbitrary line somewhere between the specious present and the future and claim that desires for objects which fall on the other side of that line are unjustified in a way in which desires falling on this side of the line are not.

[29]This seems at least as reasonable as it would be for me to disclaim ownership of *present* actions lying entirely outside of my control. Here we may even want to deny that some future subject is *a* future self, if it is merely passive and without intentions of its own. But even if we allow that it is *a* future self on the ground that it has intentions and the capacity for agency, we may deny that it is *my* future self if its character and intention, are not causally related in certain ways to my present ones. (I assume that beliefs can be causally related to one another and to actions in the relevant ways. There are deep issues here about agency, freedom and responsibility, issues which I cannot now discuss.)

[30]Here I'm imagining a creature who has no personal desires rather than one who has personal desires, but always chooses to act on impersonal motives instead. It's not clear to me that such an agent's motivating states are really desires. Perhaps they should be called "impersonal motives" instead. In any case, impersonal agency seems to require an extreme externalism about reasons for action.

[31]The fact that this state is called "selflessness" may itself provide some support for my point.

[32]Something like this is suggested by Shoemaker who says that "having a special regard for the welfare of a future self is *part* of what it *is* to regard that self as oneself." Shoemaker compares this suggestion to Wittgenstein's claim that part of what it is to "believe" that others have souls is to have certain attitudes toward them. (See Shoemaker's reply to Chisholm in Norman S. Care and Robert H. Grimm, eds., *Perception and Personal Identity* (Cleveland: Press of Case Western Reserve University, 1969), p. 119.) The main difference between Shoemaker's position and mine is that he claims only that having special concern for some future self is part of what it is to regard that future self as one's own, whereas I claim that having special concern for some future self is part of what makes that future self one's own.

[33]Here I have in mind something like the account of character or virtue friendship developed by Aristotle in *Nicomachean Ethics* VIII–IX. It is clear that the features which justify concern and friendship may underdetermine those relations in the sense that many more people may have features which would justify our concern and friendship than we can possibly befriend and that at some point, contingent and non justifying factors will have to enter into determining which of the many deserving candidates we in fact befriend. But the fact that such things enter in here does not undermine the claim that there are features which justify concern for a certain sort of person and so, for this or that particular person of that sort.

[34]I realize that the locution "once someone has become my future self" is somewhat odd, but I hope that Section VI's account of making future selves will serve to explain how it is being used.

[35]Although I've argued only for assimilating the *justification* of concern for our future selves to the *justification* of concern for our friends, someone who denied the numerical identity of our present and future selves might argue that our future selves just are friends. This would amount to turning Aristotle's claim that "a friend is another self" (*Nicomachean Ethics* 1166a33, 1170b6) on its head and claiming that our future selves are other friends. But nothing in my argument requires this additional move. For a discussion of Aristotle's view of the friend as another self, see Elijah Millgram, "Aristotle on Making Other Selves," *Canadian Journal of Philosophy,* forthcoming.

[36]See Steven Collins, *Selfless Persons* (Cambridge: Cambridge University Press, 1982), Part II.

[37]There is a problem here about whether it is *possible* to live without personal desires and attachments—a problem analogous to that of whether the skeptic can live a life without belief. See David Hume, *An Enquiry Concerning Human Understanding,* Section XII, 128. The same sort of problem arises about the impersonal agents discussed in Section VI.

[38]Here someone might defend comparative versions of the Extreme Claim by arguing that a creature entirely lacking in concern for anyone not a person.

[39]Perry, "The Importance of Being Identical," pp. 78–81. Perry's distinction between private and non-private pro-

jects coincides roughly with my distinction between personal and impersonal projects and desires. The main difference seems to be that he is willing to call "private," projects which are entirely derivative from non-private projects, whereas I say that projects which are entirely derivative from impersonal projects are themselves impersonal. See note 24. Another important difference is that Perry thinks that there is no justification for having what I call "personal" projects—that is, projects which are not entirely derivative from impersonal ones, in the sense that they attach some independent value to its being *me* who carries them out. (Perry calls these "unsupported private projects.") The result is that Perry is advocating something like the impersonal agency discussed in Section VI.

[40]This seems to be a sense in which Perry accepts the Extreme Claim.

[41]Perry, p. 80; the quote from Brandt is from "Rational Desires," *Proceedings and Addresses of the American Philosophical Association* XLII (1969–1970), p. 46.

[42]J. C. Smart and Bernard Williams, *Utilitarianism: For and Against* (Cambridge: Cambridge University Press, 1973), p. 110.

[43]Joseph Butler, Preface to *Fifteen Sermons,* Section 383.

[44]My first and deepest debt is to Sydney Shoemaker, for all that I've learned from his written work and from discussions with him. Thanks are due to many others including David Brink, Leon Galis, Bill Haines, Richard Kraut, Robert Nozick, Derek Parfit, John Rawls, Henry Richardson, Steve Rieber, Marya Schechtman—and especially, Paul Hoffman and Terry Irwin. I'd like to thank Elijah Millgram for his special concern.

22. *The Self as Private Object*

THOMAS NAGEL

According to Thomas Nagel, professor of philosophy at New York University, the concept of the self is essentially a psychological concept. It is the concept of a *subject* that has various mental states and is aware of the world from a particular (first-person) point of view. He sides with Locke against Reid in maintaining that one can conceive of the same self as having a different soul from time to time. But he also sides with Reid in maintaining that psychological discontinuity is compatible with sameness of self. Thus, he finds no solution to the problem of personal identity in either the persistent unity view of Reid or Chisholm, or the psychological continuity theories of Locke and Parfit. Nagel's own gambit is to treat the self as "whatever persisting individual in the objective order underlies the subjective continuities of that mental life that I call mine." Essentially, he believes the entity that fills that criterion is the brain, and so he maintains that one is essentially one's brain.

The concept of the self seems suspiciously pure—too pure—when we look at it from inside. The self is the ultimate private object, apparently lacking logical connections to anything else, mental or physical. When I consider my own individual life from inside, it seems that my existence in the future or the past—the existence of the same 'I' as this one—depends on nothing but itself. To capture my own existence it seems enough to use the word "I", whose meaning is entirely revealed on any occasion of its use. "I know what I mean by 'I.' I mean *this!*" (as one might think that the concept of a phenomenological quality like sweetness is fully captured in the thought "the same as *this*").

My nature then appears to be at least conceptually independent not only of bodily continuity but also of all other subjective mental conditions, such as memory and psychological similarity. It can seem, in this frame of mind, that whether a past or future mental state is mine or not is a fact

From Thomas Nagel, *The View from Nowhere* (Oxford University Press, 1986), pp. 32–45. Copyright © 1986 by Thomas Nagel. Reprinted by permission of Oxford University Press.

not analyzable in terms of any relations of continuity, psychological or physical, between that state and my present state. The migration of the self from one body to another seems conceivable, even if it is not in fact possible. So does the persistence of the self over a total break in psychological continuity—as in the fantasy of reincarnation without memory. If all these things really are possible, I certainly can't be an organism: I must be a pure, featureless mental receptacle.

The apparently strict, perfect, and unanalyzable identity of self has tempted some to objectify its existence by postulating a similarly disconnected soul designed expressly for the purpose, and otherwise characterized negatively. But such a thing seems inadequate to bear the weight of personal identity, which seems to escape all attempts to define it. We can see this in the classical debates about personal identity between Locke on the one hand and Reid and Butler on the other. Both sides seem to be right in their rejection of the other side, but wrong in their positive theories.

Locke seems right in asserting that a divergence of same self from either same soul or same body is conceivable. This reflects the truth that the self cannot be defined as a kind of object, either physical or nonphysical, but must be understood as same subjective consciousness. What Locke claimed was that if a soul were postulated as the individual that gave identity to the self, it would drop out as irrelevant to the actual operation of that idea. Kant makes a similar point in the third paralogism.

On the other hand, Butler and Reid seem right in arguing that sameness of self cannot be adequately defined in terms of memory continuity. And even more sophisticated analyses in terms of qualitative psychological continuity seem not to capture the essence of the idea of same consciousness, which seems to be something additional and not complex at all. Discontinuity in the self seems compatible with any amount of continuity in psychological content, and vice versa. But Reid and Butler are wrong in thinking that a nonphysical substance is therefore what the self must be. That after all is just another occupant of the objective order. An individual consciousness may depend for its existence on either a body or a soul, but its identity is essentially that of a psychological subject, and not equivalent to anything else—not even anything else psychological.

At the same time it seems to be something determinate and nonconventional. That is, the question with regard to any future experience, "Will it be mine or not?" seems to require a definite yes or no answer. And the answer must be determined by the facts, and not by an externally motivated and optional decision about how a word is to be used or how it is convenient to cut up the world into pieces (as might be possible with 'same nation', 'same restaurant', or 'same automobile').

This seems to leave us with the conclusion that being mine is an irreducible, unanalyzable characteristic of all my mental states, and that it has no essential connection with anything in the objective order or any connection among those states over time.[1] Even if it is causally dependent on something else, such as the continued existence of my brain, there is no way of finding this out on the basis of the idea of the self. The question of whether a future experience will be mine or not demands a definite answer without providing any way of determining what that answer is, even if all other facts are known.

There must be something wrong with this picture, but it is not easy to say what or to suggest a better one that admits essential connections between personal identity and anything else. Like other psychological concepts, the ordinary concept of the self breeds philosophical illusions that are difficult to resist without falling into errors that are at least as bad, and often shallower.

The apparent impossibility of identifying or essentially connecting the self with anything comes from the Cartesian conviction that its nature is fully revealed to introspection, and that our immediate subjective conception of the thing in our own case contains everything essential to it, if only we could extract it. But it turns out that we can extract nothing, not even a Cartesian soul. And the very bareness and apparent completeness of the concept leaves no room for the discovery that it refers to something that has other essential features which would figure in a richer account of what I really am. Identification of myself with an objectively persisting thing of whatever kind seems to be excluded in advance.

The first step in resisting this conclusion is to deny that the concept of myself, or any other psychological concept, is or could be as purely subjective as the Cartesian assumption takes it to be. As I said earlier, picking up a famous point of Wittgenstein's, even subjective concepts have their appropriate objectivity. I [have] discussed the possibility of extending the idea of mental objectivity to cover more than the range of mental phenomena with which we are subjectively familiar, but here I want to concentrate on the more limited objectivity that characterizes even those ordinary mental concepts, including personal identity, which we can all apply in the first person to ourselves.

Some of the more radical experiments of imagination that lead to the apparent detachment of the self from everything else result from delusions of conceptual power. It is an error, though a natural one, to think that a psychological concept like personal identity can be understood through an examination of my first-person concept of self, apart from the more general concept of 'someone' of which it is the essence of 'I' to be the first-person form. I would add only that the full conditions of personal identity cannot be extracted from the concept of a person at all: they cannot be arrived at a priori.

The concept of 'someone' is not a generalization of the concept of 'I'. Neither can exist without the other, and neither is prior to the other. To possess the concept of a subject of consciousness an individual must be able in certain circumstances to identify himself and the states he is in without external observation. But these identifications must correspond by and large to those that can be made on the basis of external observation, both by others and by the individual himself. In this respect 'I' is like other psychological concepts, which are applicable to states of which their subjects can be aware without the observational evidence used by others to ascribe those states to them.

As with other concepts, however, we cannot immediately infer the nature of the thing referred to from the conditions of our possession of the concept. Just as adrenalin would exist even if no one had ever thought about it, so conscious mental states and persisting selves could exist even if the concepts didn't. Given that we have these concepts, we apply them to other beings, actual and possible, who lack them. The natural (and treacherous) question then becomes, what *are* these things, apart from the concepts which enable us to refer to them? In particular, what is this self which I can reidentify without the observational evidence used by others to reidentify it? The problem, with regard to the self as with regard to sensations, is how to avoid the error of false objectification, or objectification of the wrong form, of something that does not conform to the physical conception of objective reality.

There must be a notion of objectivity which applies to the self, to phenomenological qualities, and to other mental categories, for it is clear that the idea of a mistake with regard to my own personal identity, or with regard to the phenomenological quality of an experience, makes sense. I may falsely remember making a witty remark that in fact was made in my presence by someone else, I may think falsely that the way something tastes to me now is the same as it tasted to me yesterday; I may think that I am someone I am not. There is a distinction between appearance and reality in this domain as elsewhere. Only the objectivity underlying this distinction must be understood as objectivity with regard to something subjective—mental rather than physical objectivity.

In the case of sensation, the reality is itself a form of appearance, and the distinction one between real appearance and apparent appearance. This cannot be captured by something which is just like an ordinary object or physical property, except that it is visible to only one person. But the correct account of it is extremely difficult, because the conditions of objectivity in the application of psychological concepts do not enter noticeably into each application of those concepts, especially in the first person. They are hidden, because the concepts seem perfectly simple.

When a mental concept seems simple and unanalyzable, there is a philosophical temptation to interpret it as referring to a privately accessible something, which the subjective appearance of the self, or of phenomenological sameness, is the appearance *of*. I believe Wittgenstein in the *Investigations* has made a convincing case that if we construe mental concepts this way, the private something drops out as irrelevant, which shows that there is something wrong with the construal (secs. 200–300, approximately). His argument was offered with respect to sensations: it was designed to show that sensation terms were not the names of private features or objects of experience such as sense data were supposed to be. Similarity or difference of sensations is similarity or difference of sensory appearances, not of something that appears.

The argument is in part a *reductio:* Even if every sensation were the perception of a private object or feature, the sensation would be not the thing itself but its appearing to us in a certain way. Even if the thing changed, the sensation would be the same if it appeared the same. Thus the object drops out as irrelevant to the operation of the concept. (This need not imply incorrigibility with regard to our sensations, since there can be divergence between an appearance and our beliefs about it. It is the appearance itself to which the sensation term refers.)

The other aspect of the argument—the general private language argument—is too complex to discuss adequately here. Wittgenstein claims that there could be no concept of a necessarily private object of experience—that is, a type of thing that was in principle detectable by only one person— since no distinction could exist between the correct and incorrect sincere application of such a concept: adherence to or deviation from the rule for its application by its sole user. All concepts, including concepts of how things appear to us, must admit this distinction. The rule for their use cannot collapse into the individual user's sincere application of them. Otherwise there is nothing he is *saying about* a thing in applying the term to it. To mean something by a term I must be able to make sense of the possibility that my actual use of the term has deviated from that meaning without my knowing it. Otherwise my use doesn't bring with it any meaning apart from itself.

Wittgenstein believes that psychological concepts meet the condition of being governed by objective rules, in virtue of the connection between first-person and third-person ascription. That is the sort of objectivity appropriate to what is essentially subjective.

Whether or not we accept his positive account, with its famous obscurity and reticence, I believe his point that mental concepts are sui generis is correct. They refer not to private objects like souls and sense data but to subjective points of view and their modifications—even though the range of mental phenomena is not limited to those we ourselves can identify subjectively. The question is how to apply to the problem of personal identity this general idea that mental concepts do not refer to logically private objects of awareness.

Personal Identity and Reference

Identity is not similarity. The conditions of objectivity for sensations cannot be directly transferred to the self, because being mine is not a phenomenological quality of my experiences and, as with other types of thing, qualitative similarity is here neither a necessary nor a sufficient condition of numerical identity. Still, some sort of objectivity must characterize the identity of the self, otherwise the subjective question whether a future experience will be mine or not will be contentless: *nothing* will make an answer right or wrong. What kind of objectivity can this be?

There are two possible types of answer. One explains the identity of the self in terms of other psychological concepts, thus making its objectivity parasitic on theirs. This is the family of explanations of personal identity in terms of some form or other of psychological continuity—psychological continuity broadly conceived to include action, emotion, and intention as well as thought, memory, and perception. The other type of answer treats personal identity as an independent psychological concept, so that the self is something that underlies the psychological continuities where they exist but has no necessary or sufficient conditions specifiable in terms of them.

This second type of answer is what I shall defend. I believe that whatever we are told about continuity of mental content between two stages of experience, the issue logically remains open whether they have the same subject or not. In addition, it is clearly part of the idea of my identity that I could have led a completely different mental life, from birth. This would have happened, for example, if I had been adopted at birth and brought up in Argentina. The question is how this idea of the same subject can meet the conditions of objectivity appropriate for a psychological concept: how it can express an identity that is subjective (not merely biological) but at the same time admits the distinction between correct and incorrect self-identification.

Even if such a thing cannot be defined in terms of psychological continuities, it will be closely connected with them. Most of my self-reidentifications, and most reidentifications of me by others, refer to stages linked to the present directly or indirectly by memory, intention, and so forth. But here as elsewhere the reality can diverge from the evidence. The idea of myself is the idea of something to which memory and externally observable continuity of mental life stand in an evidential relation—something which can at one time subjectively reidentify itself in memory, expectation, and intention, and can be observationally reidentified as the same person by others, but which *is* something in its own right. In other words, I am rejecting the view that the person is merely the grammatical or logical subject of mental and physical predicates ascribed on the usual grounds. Those grounds provide only evidence of personal identity, rather than criteria of it.

The question is whether this reach of the concept beyond the introspective and observational evidence and the correlation between them permits us to interpret it as referring to something with still further features—something with a nature of its own. If so, then those features can supply further conditions of personal identity which may determine an answer to the question whether someone will be me, in cases where the usual psychological evidence leaves the question unsettled. The idea is that the ordinary conditions of application of the concept point to something further to which the concept refers but whose essence it does not capture.

This is possible only on the assumption that the concept of the self does not tell us fully what kind of things we are. But that assumption seems to me to be true. Our idea of ourselves is one whose exact extension is determined in part by things we don't necessarily know simply in virtue of, or as a condition of, having the concept: our true nature and the principle of our identity may be partly hidden from us. This is a familiar enough situation with regard to other concepts. It is obviously true of definite descriptions, and Kripke and Putnam have argued that it is also true of proper names and natural kind terms,

even if they cannot be analyzed as definite descriptions in disguise.[2] But it is harder to accept with respect to the self, because of the apparent subjective completeness of that idea. It does not immediately seem, like the concept of 'gold' or the concept of 'cat' or the concept of 'Cicero', to have any blank space which can be filled in by discoveries as to the true internal constitution of the thing. Nothing seems to correspond here to our general idea of a kind of substance or a kind of living creature whose complete nature we do not know. The idea of the self seems not to be a partial specification of anything.

In general, when a term refers to something whose real nature is not fully captured by the subjective conditions for the term's application, those conditions will nevertheless dictate what kind of thing it is about the world that determines the real nature of the referent. Thus before the development of chemistry, gold already referred to a type of metal, and this determined which kinds of further discoveries about its material composition would reveal the true nature of gold. Specifically it determined that certain common observable properties of gold would have to be explained by its true nature, and that the explanation would have to be uniform for different samples of gold, in terms of something of which they were all composed.

What might perform the function of the idea of a 'type of metal,' or 'type of material substance' in the case of ourselves? Subjects of experience are not like anything else. While they do have observable properties, the most important thing about them is that they are subjects, and it is their subjective mental properties that must be explained if we are to be able to identify them with anything in the objective order. As with gold, there is also an implication of generality—that the self in my case is something of the same kind as it is for other persons.

I suggest that the concept of the self is open to objective "completion" provided something can be found which straddles the subjective-objective gap. That is, the concept contains the possibility that it refers to something with further objective essential features beyond those included in the psychological concept itself—something whose objective persistence is among the necessary conditions of personal identity—but only if this objectively describable referent is in a strong sense the basis for those subjective features that typify the persistent self.

This is where dual aspect theory comes in. The concept of the self does not of course imply the truth of dual aspect theory. The concept implies only that if it refers at all, it must refer to something essentially subjective, often identifiable nonobservationally in the first person and observationally in the third, which is the persisting locus of mental states and activities and the vehicle for carrying forward familiar psychological continuities when they occur. So far as the *concept* is concerned, this might turn out to be any of a number of things or there might be no such thing. But if dual aspect theory is correct, then it is as a matter of fact the intact brain—customarily found in a living animal of a certain kind but not in principle inseparable from it. I could lose everything but my functioning brain and still be me, and it might even be possible by some monstrosity of genetic engineering to produce a brain that had never been part of an animal but was nevertheless an individual subject.

Let me repeat that this is not offered as an analysis of the concept of the self but as an empirical hypothesis about its true nature. My concept of myself contains the blank space for such an objective completion, but does not fill it in. I am whatever persisting individual in the objective order underlies the subjective continuities of that mental life that I call mine. But a type of objective identity can settle questions about the identity of the self only if the thing in question is both the bearer of mental states and the cause of their continuity when there is continuity. If my brain meets these conditions then the core of the self—what is essential to my existence—is my functioning brain. As things are, the rest of my body is integrally attached to it and is also part of me, so I am not just my brain: I weigh more than three pounds, am more than six inches high, have a skeleton, etc. But the brain is the only part of me whose destruction I could not possibly survive. The brain, but not the rest of the animal, is essential to the self.

Let me express this with mild exaggeration as the hypothesis that I am my brain, and let me leave aside for now problems that could be raised about what counts as the same brain (for example, about its dependence on the sameness of the organism). On the evidence, the intact brain seems to be responsible for the maintenance of memory and other psychological continuities and for the unity of consciousness. If in addition the mental states are themselves states of the brain, which is therefore not just a physical system, then the brain is a serious candidate for being the self—even though, as I shall admit, it does not meet all the intuitive conditions on the idea of the self.

What I am is whatever is in fact the seat of the person TN's experiences and his capacity to identify and reidentify himself and his mental states, in memory, experience, and thought, without relying on the sort of observational evidence that others must use to understand him. That I am a person requires that I have this capacity, but not that I know what makes it possible. In fact, I do not know in any detail what is responsible for it, and others need not know it either in order to know that I am a person. So far as their concept of me and my conception of myself as a self are concerned, the possibility of my subjective identification of myself could depend on a soul, or on the activity of a part of my brain, or on something else that I can't even imagine. If it depended on a soul, then my identity would be the identity of that soul, so long as the soul persisted in the condition which, when it occupies TN, allows it to undergo TN's experiences and enables TN to identify himself and his states subjectively. If it could persist thus after the death of the body, I could exist after death. (Perhaps I could even exist without memory of my present life.)

If, on the other hand, my mental life depends entirely on certain states and activities of my brain, and if some form of dual aspect theory is correct, then that brain in those states (not just in its physical states) is what I am, and my survival of the destruction of my brain is not conceivable. However, I may not know that it is not conceivable, because I may not know the conditions of my own identity. That knowledge is not provided by my subjective idea of myself. It is not provided by the idea others have of me either. Something is left open by the idea which has to be discovered.

The point is a familiar one, taken from Kripke's views about reference. The essence of what a term refers to depends on what the world is actually like, and not just on what we have to know in order to use and understand the term. I may understand and be able to apply the term "gold" without knowing what gold really is—what physical and chemical conditions anything must meet to be gold. My prescientific idea of gold, including my knowledge of the perceptible features by which I identify samples of it, includes a blank space to be filled in by empirical discoveries about its intrinsic nature. Similarly I may understand and be able to apply the term "I" to myself without knowing what I really am. In Kripke's phrase, what I use to *fix the reference* of the term does not tell me everything about the nature of the referent.

This can give rise to those illusions, discussed earlier, concerning the detachability of the self from everything else. Since I do not know what I really am, it seems possible so far as what I *do* know is concerned—epistemically possible—that I may really be any of a variety of things (soul, brain, etc.) that could underlie my capacity for subjective self-identification. Various accounts of my real nature, and therefore various conditions of my identity over time, are compatible with my concept of myself as a self, for that concept leaves open the real nature of what it refers to. This is equally true of other people's concept of me as a self, since it is true of the concept of a self or continuing subject of consciousness in general.

Now this may lead me to think I can imagine myself surviving the death of my brain even if that is not in fact imaginable. On the other hand, it may equally well lead me to think I can imagine myself surviving the destruction of my soul—or anything else. What I imagine may be possible so far as what I know about my nature is concerned, but may not be possible so far as my actual nature is concerned. In that case I will not have imagined *myself* surviving the death of my brain, but will merely have confused epistemic with metaphysical possibility. In trying to conceive of my survival after the destruction of my brain, I will not succeed in referring to myself in such a situation if I am in fact my brain. Even if I conceive of a soul with the appropriate memories surviving the death of my body, that will not be to conceive of myself surviving, if in fact I am not a soul.[3]

It is the mistake of thinking that my concept of myself alone can reveal the objective conditions of my identity that leads to the giddy sense that personal identity is totally independent of everything else, so that it might even be possible for you

and me to switch selves although *nothing* else changed, either physically or psychologically, or in any other respect. Adding in the third person and second person conditions of application of the concept doesn't complete the specification of its reference either, though. The fact that I can reidentify persons by looking at them, tracing their movements, and listening to what they say does not mean that I know their true nature. I do not know it (though I may conjecture about it), unless I know not only what makes them the organisms they are, but also what makes them capable of subjective, nonobservational self-knowledge extending over time. Without this information, the concept of personal identity will not tell me what I am or what they are.

Parfit

This approach to personal identity is not without its problems. If what we are depends not only on our concept of ourselves but on the world, the possibility arises that nothing in the world satisfies the concept perfectly. The best candidate may be in various ways defective.

To what extent could it turn out that our true nature diverges from our intuitive conception of ourselves? More specifically, does the hypothesis that I am my brain require the abandonment of central features of my conception of myself; and if so, does this cast doubt on the hypothesis? If the best candidate for what I am is my brain, the best candidate may not be good enough; in that case the proper conclusion would be that the self which we intuitively take ourselves to be does not exist at all.

The problems I have in mind are those which have led Derek Parfit to conclude that the most natural prereflective concept of the self does not apply to us. To say that I am, as a matter of fact rather than of definition, essentially my brain does not solve those acute puzzles he has posed, concerning the apparent unique simplicity and indivisibility of the self.

Parfit begins by describing a natural conception of the self which he calls the Simple View.[4] This says that nothing can be me unless (a) it determines a completely definite answer to the question whether any given experience—past, present, or future—is mine or not (the all-or-nothing condition); and (b) it excludes the possibility that two experiences both of which are mine should occur in subjects that are not identical with each other (the one-one condition). Subjectively, these seem like nonnegotiably essential features of myself.

But the brain is a complex organ, neither simple nor indivisible. While there are no examples of gradual replacement of its cells over time, for example by grafting, there are the famous examples of its division by commissurotomy, with striking psychological effects.[5] As Parfit points out, if my survival depends on the continued functioning of my brain, it seems that I might be able to survive as two distinct selves, not identical with each other, and this would violate the one-one condition. Similarly, he has observed, if the cells of my brain could be gradually replaced, with accompanying gradual transformation of my personality and memories, then a future experience might belong to someone about whom there was *no answer* to the question whether he was me or not, and this would violate the all-or-nothing condition.

Parfit himself concludes that the conditions of the ordinary concept of personal identity cannot be met if such things are possible. Our ordinary concept is so tied to the Simple View that it can actually apply only if the mental life of each of us has a subject that makes such things impossible—something like a simple, indivisible soul. If, as appears to be the case, the subject of our mental lives is a complex, divisible brain, then it is not a suitable bearer of the identity of the self, and we should adopt instead a more complex view of our own nature. His suggestion is that we should withdraw our special self-interested concern from the identity of the organ that underlies our mental lives, and be concerned instead about the psychological continuities themselves, however they are produced, which may hold to different degrees and need not be one-one.

I believe, however, that the actual cause is what matters—even if it doesn't satisfy the conditions of the Simple View. This would be one of those cases where some of our most important beliefs about the referent of one of our concepts may be false, without its following that there is no such thing. In ordinary circumstances, the brain satisfies the one-one and all-or-nothing conditions, but it does not do so necessarily. Nevertheless, it seems to me to be something without which I could not survive—so that if a physically distinct replica of me were produced who was psychologically continuous with me though my brain had been destroyed, it would not be me and its survival would not be as good (for me) as my survival. This assumes that there can be an empirically discoverable answer to the question what I in fact am which falsifies some of my fundamental beliefs about what kind of thing I am.[6]

The difficult issue is whether the answer I propose falsifies such fundamental beliefs that it is disqualified. The brain does not guarantee an absolutely definite and unique answer to the question whether any of the centers of consciousness existing at some past or future time are mine or not. The possibility of its being split or partially replaced implies this. It is therefore hard to internalize a conception of myself as identical with my brain: if I am told that my brain is about to be split, and that the left half will be miserable and the right half euphoric, there is no form that my subjective expectations can take, because my idea of myself doesn't allow for divisibility—nor do the emotions of expectation, fear, and hope.

It might be asked, if I am prepared to abandon the Simple View over such resistance, why not go all the way with Parfit and abandon the identification of the self with the typical underlying cause of the mental life—regarding psychological continuity, however maintained, as what is really important? What is the advantage of continuing to identify myself with a *thing* whose survival need be neither one-one nor all-or-nothing? Why isn't it enough to identify myself as a person in the weaker sense in which this is the subject of mental predicates but not a separately existing thing—more like a nation than a Cartesian ego?

I don't really have an answer to this, except the question-begging answer that one of the conditions that the self should meet if possible is that it be something in which the flow of consciousness and the beliefs, desires, intentions, and character traits that I have all take place—something beneath the contents of consciousness, which might even survive a radical break in the continuity of consciousness. If there were no such thing, then the idea of personal identity would be an illusion, but we are not in that situation. Even if nothing can be found to fill this role which satisfies the condition of the Simple View, the brain with its problematic conditions of identity in certain cases is still better than nothing. And it is a possible hypothesis that I am my brain, since it is not ruled out by the apparent subjective conceivability of my moving to a different brain. That seems conceivable, to the extent that it does, only so far as what my incomplete concept of myself tells me; and that isn't a reliable basis for deciding what is possible. If a dual aspect theory is correct, then it is not possible for my mental life to go on in a different brain.[7]

Endnotes

[1]The conclusion is accepted by Madell [*The Identity of the Self*, Edinburgh University Press, 1983]. What unites all my experiences, he says, is simply that they all have the irreducible and unanalyzable property of "mineness."

[2]Kripke [*Naming and Necessity*, Harvard University Press, 1980]; Putnam ["The Meaning of 'Meaning,' " *Mind, Language, and Reality: Philosophical Papers,* Vol 2, Cambridge University Press, 1975]; see Searle [*Intentionality*, Cambridge University Press, 1983] for an argument that this view doesn't involve as big a departure from the Fregean tradition of analysis of sense and reference as is often supposed.

[3]Cf. Williams ["Imagination and the Self," *Proceedings of the British Academy*, 1966, p. 44]: "At least with regard to the self, the imagination is too tricky a thing to provide a reliable road to the comprehension of what is logically possible."

[4]This term appears in Parfit ["Later Selves and Moral Principles," in A. Montefiore, ed., *Philosophy and Personal Relations,* London, Routledge & Kegan Paul, 1973], and I shall use it for convenience here, even though in the much more elaborate treatment of Parfit [*Reasons and Persons,* Oxford University Press, 1984], several different non-reductionist views are distinguished. See p. 210, for example.

[5]Parfit [*Reasons and Persons,* sec. 87]. I have discussed these cases in Nagel ["Brain Bisection and the Unity of Consciousness," *Synthese,* 1971].

[6]My position is rather like Mackie's, except that he recommends it as a conceptual reform, inconsistent with our present concept of personal identity. He also thinks that further reform might be in order if it turned out that we could produce exact physical and psychological replicas of people: then even brain identity could be dropped as a condition of personal identity. See Mackie [*Problems from Locke,* Oxford University Press, 1976], pp. 201–3.

[7]I have not begun to do justice here to the Proustian exhaustiveness of Parfit's arguments. Among other things, he comments on some remarks in an earlier draft of the present chapter which I have since abandoned—having to do with possible "series-persons" whose bodies are destroyed and replicated regularly. I said there that they could reasonably regard replication as survival, though we could not. Parfit replies that we can choose what type of beings to think of ourselves as—and he defines "Phoenix Parfit" as the individual he is who *would* survive replication. This is an ingenious suggestion, but there must be some objective limits to the freedom to reconstruct oneself, or it will become hollow. I can't defeat death by identifying myself as "Proteus Nagel", the being who survives if *anyone* survives. "Phoenix Parfit" seems to me also an abuse, though clearly a lesser one, of the privilege of choosing one's own identity.

But I also think now that the series-persons themselves, if they were of human origin, might simply be deluded to think they survive replication—and that like us, they would not be entitled to the "Phoenix" concept of themselves.

Further Reading

Ayer, A. J., *The Concept of a Person and Other Essays* (New York: Macmillan, 1964).

Ayers, M., *Locke, Volume II: Ontology* (London: Routledge, 1991).

Baker, L. R., *Persons and Bodies: A Constitution View* (New York: Cambridge University Press, 2000).

Brennan, A., *Conditions of Identity* (New York: Oxford University Press, 1988).

Brody, B., *Identity and Essence* (Princeton: Princeton University Press, 1980).

Butchvarov, P., *Being Qua Being* (Bloomington: Indiana University Press, 1979).

Care, N., and Grimm, R. H., eds., *Perception and Personal Identity* (Cleveland: Ohio University Press, 1969).

Carruthers, P., *Introducing Persons* (London: Routledge, 1989).

Chisholm, R. D., *Person and Object* (Chicago: Open Court, 1976).

Cockburn, D., ed., *Human Beings* (Cambridge: Cambridge University Press, 1991).

Flew, A., ed., *Body, Mind and Death* (New York: Macmillan, 1964).

Flew, A., *The Logic of Mortality: On Personal Identity* (Oxford: Blackwell, 1987).

Heller, M., *The Ontology of Physical Objects* (Cambridge: Cambridge University Press, 1990).

Hirsch, E., *The Concept of Identity* (New York: Oxford University Press, 1982).

Hudson, H., *A Materialist Metaphysics of the Human Person* (Ithaca, N.Y.: Cornell University Press, 2001).

Lewis, D., *On the Plurality of Worlds* (Oxford: Blackwell, 1986).

Lewis, H. D., *The Elusive Self* (London: Macmillan, 1982).

Loux, M., *Substance and Attribute* (Dördrecht: D. Reidel, 1978).

Mackie, J., *Problems from Locke,* Chapter 6 (New York: Oxford University Press, 1976).

Madell, G., *The Identity of the Self* (Edinburgh: Edinburgh University Press, 1981).

Marks, C. E., *Commissurotomy, Consciousness, and Unity of Mind* (Cambridge, Mass.: MIT Press, 1986).

Noonan, H., ed., *Identity* (Aldershot, UK: Ashgate Publishing, Ltd., 1993).

Noonan, H., *Personal Identity* (New York: Routledge & Kegan Paul, 1989).

Nozick, R., *Philosophical Explanations,* Chapter I (Cambridge, Mass.: Harvard University Press, 1981).

Olson, E., *The Human Animal: Personal Identity without Psychology* (Oxford: Oxford University Press, 1997).

Peacocke, A., and Gillett, G., eds. *Persons and Personality* (Oxford: Blackwell, 1987).

Penelhum, T., *Survival and Disembodied Existence* (London: Routledge & Kegan Paul, 1970).

Perry, J., *A Dialogue on Personal Identity and Immortality* (Indianapolis: Hackett, 1978).

Perry, J., ed., *Personal Identity* (Berkeley: University of California Press, 1976).

Rorty, A., ed., *The Identities of Persons* (Berkeley: University of California Press, 1976).

Schechtman, M., *The Constitution of Selves* (Ithaca, N.Y.: Cornell University Press, 1996).

Shalom, A., *The Body/Mind Conceptual Framework and the Problem of Personal Identity: Some Theories in Philosophy, Psychoanalysis and Neurology* (Atlantic Highlands, N.J.: Humanities Press International, 1985).

Shoemaker, S., *Self-Knowledge and Self-Identity* (Ithaca, N.Y.: Cornell University Press, 1963).

Shoemaker, S., *Identity, Cause and Mind* (Cambridge: Cambridge University Press, 1984).

Shoemaker, S., and Swinburne, R. G., *Personal Identity* (Oxford: Blackwell, 1984).

Strawson, P. F., *Individuals* (London: Methuen, 1959).

Swinburne, R. G., *The Evolution of the Soul* (Oxford: Oxford Clarendon Press, 1986).

Van Inwagen, P., *Material Beings* (Ithaca, N.Y.: Cornell University Press, 1990).

Van Inwagen, P., *Ontology, Identity, Modality* (Cambridge: Cambridge University Press, 2001).

Vesey, G., *Personal Identity* (New York: Macmillan, 1974).

Wiggins, D., *Identity and Spatio-Temporal Continuity* (Oxford: Blackwell, 1967).

Wiggins, D., *Sameness and Substance Renewed* (Cambridge: Cambridge University Press, 1990).

Wilkes, K., *Real People* (Cambridge: Cambridge University Press, 1989).

Williams, B., *Problems of the Self* (Cambridge: Cambridge University Press, 1973).

Wittgenstein, L., *The Blue and Brown Books* (Oxford: Blackwell, 1958).

Wollheim, R., *The Thread of Life* (Cambridge, Mass.: Harvard University Press, 1984).

Part III

Mind

What are persons? In Part II, this question was raised in the context of wondering what constituted the *identity* of a person through change. Most answers assume a person is a conscious, thinking being (or a being able to be conscious). In other words, it is assumed a person has a *mind*. Though one can be certain one is conscious, at least when thinking about thinking, the *nature* of consciousness has often struck philosophers as most puzzling. Minds are quite different from rocks or trees, but how exactly should the differences be described and understood? When philosophers ask this question they are often wondering whether an explanation of mental phenomena must posit basic kinds of entities that are very different from the basic entities used to explain the rest of nature. For example, are minds so different from rocks and trees that they cannot be understood to be arrangements of matter and energy in the way rocks and trees are so understood?

Debates about the nature of mind often center on what is called the mind-body problem. Is the mind some part or aspect of the body? Are mental phenomena in the brain? Are they some process in the nervous system? Mental life involves a variety of feelings, qualitative perceptions, and an ability to grasp meaning. Assuming one's body is made of physical stuff (namely, collections of molecules), how can all these mental phenomena be just the electrochemical activity of molecules in one's head?

Some philosophers claim they cannot be, so they argue that the mind is not physical. They believe it is something altogether different from the body as it is understood by science. Other philosophers, however, are impressed by the underlying unity of nature as revealed in science, and they argue that mental phenomena can in some way be identified with, or reduced to, physical phenomena.

Formulated in this way, the mind-body problem is a relatively recent problem. It came into sharp focus in the context of the development of modern science. It was not until the seventeenth century (during the Scientific Revolution) that physics held out the real promise of developing a complete theory of nature in terms of the mechanical properties of matter. In the seventeenth century, while contributing to the advancement of mechanistic physics, Descartes nevertheless argued that minds are distinct things, quite different from material bodies. Descartes's dualistic views, expressed in his second and sixth *Meditations,* mark the beginning of the modern mind-body problem.

Prior to the rise of mechanistic physics, it was common to try to explain the behavior of all things using either persons or organisms as explanatory models. For example, ancient myths viewed natural objects and forces anthropomorphically. Minds were everywhere, so to speak, directing all action—from storms to the movement of the stars. Minds and willful actions were not viewed as needing to be explained in terms of something better understood. Even when people began to abandon explicitly anthropomorphic explanations, their conceptions of the elements (including matter) often remained more organic than mechanical. Aristotle, for example, thought things made of earth (for example, rocks) tended to move toward the center of the universe because they have in them the potential for such directed movement, just as an acorn has in it the potential to become an oak tree.

Though versions of the mind-body problem that are inspired by developments in science may be comparatively recent, nonetheless, arguments about the nature of mind frequently rely on views of the mind or soul that were articulated long ago. The ancient Greek idea of the soul (or *psyche*) was that it is whatever is responsible for life, and mind was regarded as a part or aspect of the soul. Some philosophers tried to identify soul with something elemental like air (breath) or fire (the heat of the body). Sometimes it was imagined that the soul might journey from the body and continue to be conscious, but this did not mean the soul was not a part of (or like) the rest of nature. It was Plato who voiced the idea that the soul might be totally different from things in nature, and this was, in part, because he was skeptical about the reality of the temporal world of changing things. The excerpt in Part II from Plato's *Phaedo* should also be read in conjunction with the selections in Part III. In the *Phaedo,* Plato argues that the soul is eternal and separable from the chaotic flux of ordinary things.

Aristotle offered what was, perhaps, the most influential analysis of soul prior to Descartes. Aristotle thought the soul was just the form (in his technical sense of "form") of a living body, and he rejected Plato's belief that forms could exist separately from matter. Aristotle's analyses of thinking and perceiving (as aspects of the soul) are subtle, and they incorporate much of the scientific opinion of his time. Yet, they have a down-to-earth quality that has made Aristotle's views attractive to people who find Plato's world of transcendent forms too removed from experience. (For example, the traditional Christian conception of personal immortality has often been interpreted as requiring resurrection of the body, and this is more Aristotelian than Platonic.)

The writings in Part III that follow the selections from Aristotle and Descartes were chosen because they highlight contemporary issues pertinent to the mind-body problem and illustrate recent philosophical strategies for dealing with them. What exactly are the properties of mental phenomena that make it seem that mind cannot be understood in physical terms? The readings cover at least three features that have been at the center of recent controversies: (1) the intentionality (or aboutness) of mental states; (2) the qualitative features of sensations; and (3) the subjectivity of consciousness. The selections also represent four strategies: (1) nonreductionism (Brentano and Nagel); (2) identity theories (Armstrong); (3) functionalism (Dennett and Putnam); and (4) eliminative materialism (Churchland).

Since the first edition of this anthology there has been an explosion of empirical research focused on the mind, and this research has taken place in many fields: cognitive science, neuroscience, ethology, and more. Rather than try to survey the many important philosophical issues raised by all this work, the editors have added selections relevant to old concerns about intentionality and dualism that nevertheless give a glimpse of philosophers taking part in or reacting to this empirical work. The selections by Ruth Garrett Millikan, John Searle, and Patricia Smith Churchland fall in this category. It should also be noted that the last selection in Part I by John Perry, "Time, Consciousness, and the Knowledge Argument," is also pertinent to the issues in Part III (especially those raised by Nagel and Jackson).

23. *On the Soul*

ARISTOTLE

The ancient Greeks viewed the soul as the principle, or cause, of life, but they disagreed about its nature. Some speculated it was something elemental, like fire or air. Is it what leaves the body at death (like heat or breath)? What implications does the absence or departure of the soul have for questions about personal immortality? In the *Phaedo* selections in Part II, Plato argues that the soul is eternal and cannot die. Plato maintains that the soul can exist apart from the body; and, in thus being eternal and separable from matter, it is akin to (and can know) ideal Forms. In "On the Soul," Aristotle examines and rejects the views of his predecessors. Aristotle does not posit soul as a separate entity. Instead, it is just the form or actuality of a material body having the potential for life. For Aristotle, describing the form and function (or "formal" and "final causes") of things was part of a systematic explanation of their nature. As an aspect of being alive, living things are more or less capable of sensation, perception, and thought. Thus, the investigation of the soul (or the forms of living things) leads Aristotle to an analysis of perceiving and thinking. In "On the Soul," Aristotle explores the idea that perceiving occurs when some of the forms of the objects of perception come to be embodied in the different material of a person's sensory or cognitive faculties. Though Aristotle's general position is that souls cannot exist without being embodied, there are passages hinting he entertained the idea that the thinking part of the soul might, in some sense, be able to do so. (For Aristotle's disagreement with Plato about the existence of Forms apart from matter and about their explanatory power, the reader should study Book I of Aristotle's *Metaphysics*.)

Book I

Holding as we do that, while knowledge of any kind is a thing to be honoured and prized, one kind of it may, either by reason of its greater exactness or of a higher dignity and greater wonderfulness in its objects, be more honourable and precious than another, on both accounts we should naturally be led to place in the front rank the study of the soul. The knowledge of the soul admittedly contributes greatly to the advance of truth in general, and, above all, to our under-

From Jonathan Barnes, ed., *Complete Works of Aristotle: The Revised Oxford Translations*. Bollingen Series 71, J. A. Smith, trans. Copyright © 1984 Jowett Copyright Trustees. Excerpt, pp. 642–687. Reprinted with permission of Princeton University Press.

standing of Nature, for the soul is in some sense the principle of animal life. Our aim is to grasp and understand, first its essential nature, and secondly its properties; of these some are thought to be affections proper to the soul itself, while others are considered to attach to the animal owing to the presence of soul.

To attain any knowledge about the soul is one of the most difficult things in the world. As the form of question which here presents itself, viz., the question 'What is it?' recurs in other fields, it might be supposed that there was some single method of inquiry applicable to all objects whose essential nature we are endeavouring to ascertain (as there *is* for incidental properties the single method of demonstration); in that case what we should have to seek for would be this unique method. But if there is no such single and general method for solving the question of essence, our task becomes still more difficult; in the case of each different subject we shall have to determine the appropriate process of investigation. If to this there be a clear answer, e.g., that the process is demonstration or division, or some other known method, many difficulties and hesitations still beset us—with what facts shall we begin the inquiry? For the facts which form the starting-points in different subjects must be different, as e.g., in the case of numbers and surfaces.

First, no doubt, it is necessary to determine in which of the *summa genera* soul lies, what it *is;* is it 'a this-somewhat', a substance, or is it a quale or a quantum, or some other of the remaining kinds of predicates which we have distinguished? Further, does soul belong to the class of potential existents, or is it not rather an actuality? Our answer to this question is of the greatest importance.

We must consider also whether soul is divisible or is without parts, and whether it is everywhere homogeneous or not; and if not homogeneous, whether its various forms are different specifically or generically: up to the present time those who have discussed and investigated soul seem to have confined themselves to the human soul. We must be careful not to ignore the question whether soul can be defined in a single account, as is the case with animal, or whether we must not give a separate account for each sort of it, as we do for horse, dog, man, god (in the latter case the universal, animal—and so too every other common predicate—is either nothing or posterior). Further, if what exists is not a plurality of souls, but a plurality of parts of one soul, which ought we to investigate first, the whole soul or its parts? It is also a difficult problem to decide which of these parts are in nature distinct from one another. Again, which ought we to investigate first, these parts or their functions, mind or thinking, the faculty or the act of sensation, and so on? If the investigation of the functions precedes that of the parts, the further question suggests itself: ought we not before either to consider the correlative objects, e.g., of sense or thought? It seems not only useful for the discovery of the causes of the incidental properties of substances to be acquainted with the essential nature of those substances (as in mathematics it is useful for the understanding of the property of the equality of the interior angles of a triangle to two right angles to know the essential nature of the straight and the curved or of the line and the plane) but also conversely, for the knowledge of the essential nature of a substance is largely promoted by an acquaintance with its properties: for, when we are able to give an account conformable to experience of all or most of the properties of a substance, we shall be in the most favourable position to say something worth saying about the essential nature of that subject; in all demonstration a definition of the essence is required as a starting-point, so that definitions which do not enable us to discover the incidental properties, or which fail to facilitate even a conjecture about them, must obviously, one and all, be dialectical and futile.

A further problem presented by the affections of soul is this: are they all affections of the complex of body and soul, or is there any one among them peculiar to the soul by itself? To determine this is indispensable but difficult. If we consider the majority of them, there seems to be no case in which the soul can act or be acted upon without involving the body; e.g., anger, courage, appetite, and sensation generally. Thinking seems the most probable exception; but if this too proves to be a form of imagination or to be impossible without imagination, it too requires a body as a condition of its existence. If there is any way of acting or being acted upon proper to soul, soul will be capable of separate existence; if there is none, its separate existence is impossible. In the latter case, it will be like what is straight, which has many properties arising from the straightness in it, e.g., that of touching a bronze sphere at a point, though straightness divorced from the other constituents of the straight thing cannot touch it in this way; it cannot be so divorced at all, since it is always found in a body. It seems that all the affections of soul involve a body—passion, gentleness, fear, pity, courage, joy, loving, and hating; in all these there is a concurrent affection of the body. In support of this we may point to the fact that, while sometimes on the occasion of violent and striking occurrences there is no excitement or fear felt, on others faint and feeble stimulations produce these emotions, viz., when the body is already in a state of tension resembling its condition when we are angry. Here is a still clearer case: in the absence of any external cause of terror we find ourselves experiencing the feelings of a man in terror. From all this it is obvious that the affections of soul are enmattered accounts.

Consequently their definitions ought to correspond, e.g., anger should be defined as a certain mode of movement of such and such a body (or part or faculty of a body) by this or that cause and for this or that end. That is precisely why the study of the soul—either every soul or souls of this sort—must fall within the science of nature. Hence a physicist would define an affection of soul differently from a dialectician; the latter would define e.g., anger as the appetite for returning pain for pain, or something like that, while the former would define it as a boiling of the blood or warm substance surrounding the heart. The one assigns the material conditions, the other the form or account; for what he states is the account of the fact, though for its actual existence there must be embodiment of it in a material such as is described by the other. Thus the essence of a house is assigned in such an account as 'a shelter against destruction by wind, rain, and heat'; the physicist would describe it as 'stones, bricks, and timbers'; but there is a third possible description which would say that it was that form in that material with that purpose or end. Which, then, among these is entitled to be regarded as the genuine physicist? The one who confines himself to the material, or the one who restricts himself to the account alone? Is it not rather the one who combines both? If this is so, how are we to characterize the other two? Must we not say that there is no type of thinker who concerns himself with those qualities or attributes of the material which are in fact inseparable from the material, and without attempting even in thought to separate them? The physicist is he who concerns himself with all the properties active and passive of bodies or materials thus or thus defined; attributes not considered as being of this character he leaves to others, in certain cases it may be to a specialist, e.g., a carpenter or a physician, in others (*a*) where they are inseparable in fact, but are separable from any particular kind of body by an effort of abstraction, to the mathematician, (*b*) where they are separate, to the First Philosopher. But we must return from this digression, and repeat that the affections of soul, insofar as they are such as passion and fear, are inseparable from the natural matter of animals in this way and not in the same way as a line or surface.

For our study of soul it is necessary, while formulating the problems of which in our further advance we are to find the solutions, to call into council the views of those of our predecessors who have declared any opinion on this subject, in order that we may profit by whatever is sound in their suggestions and avoid their errors.

The starting-point of our inquiry is an exposition of those characteristics which have chiefly been held to belong to soul in its very nature. Two characteristic marks have above all others been recognized as distinguishing that which has soul in it from that which has not—movement and sensation. It may be said that these two are what our predecessors have fixed upon as characteristic of soul.

Some say that what originates movement is both pre-eminently and primarily soul; believing that what is not itself moved cannot originate movement in another, they arrived at the view that soul belongs to the class of things in movement. This is what led Democritus to say that soul is a sort of fire or hot substance; his 'forms' or atoms are infinite in number; those which are spherical he calls fire and soul, and compares them to the motes in the air which we see in shafts of light coming through windows; the mixture of seeds of all sorts he calls the elements of the whole of nature (Leucippus gives a similar account); the spherical atoms are identified with soul because atoms of that shape are most adapted to permeate everywhere, and to set all the others moving by being themselves in movement. This implies the view that soul is identical with what produces movement in animals. That is why, further, they regard respiration as the characteristic mark of life; as the environment compresses the bodies of animals, and tends to extrude those atoms which impart movement to them, because they themselves are never at rest, there must be a reinforcement of these by similar atoms coming in from without in the act of respiration; for they prevent the extrusion of those which are already within by counteracting the compressing and consolidating force of the environment; and animals continue to live only so long as they are able to maintain this resistance.

The doctrine of the Pythagoreans seems to rest upon the same ideas; some of them declared the motes in air, others what moved them, to be soul. These motes were referred to because they are seen always in movement, even in a complete calm.

The same tendency is shown by those who define soul as that which moves itself; all these seem to hold the view that movement is what is closest to the nature of soul, and that while all else is moved by soul, it alone moves itself. This belief arises from their never seeing anything originating movement which is not first itself moved.

Similarly also Anaxagoras (and whoever agrees with him in saying that thought set the whole in movement) declares the moving cause of things to be soul. His position must, however, be distinguished from that of Democritus. Democritus roundly identifies soul and mind, for he identifies what appears with what is true—that is why he commends Homer for the phrase 'Hector lay with thought distraught'; he does not employ mind as a special faculty dealing with truth, but identifies soul with thought. What Anaxagoras says about them is less clear; in many places he tells us that the cause of beauty and order is thought, elsewhere that it is soul; it is found, he says, in all animals, great and small, high and low, but thought (in the sense of intelligence) appears not to belong alike to all animals, and indeed not even to all human beings.

All those, then, who had special regard to the fact that what has soul in it is moved, adopted the view that soul is to be identified with what is eminently originative of movement. All, on the other hand, who looked to the fact that what has soul in it knows or perceives what is, identify soul with the principle or principles of Nature, according as they admit several such principles or one only. Thus Empedocles declares that it is formed out of all his elements, each of them also being his soul; his words are:

For 'tis by Earth we see Earth, by Water Water,
By Ether Ether divine, by Fire destructive Fire,
By Love Love, and Hate by cruel Hate.

In the same way Plato in the *Timaeus* fashions the soul out of his elements; for like, he holds, is known by like, and things are formed out of the principles or elements. Similarly also in the lectures 'On Philosophy' it was set forth that the Animal-itself is compounded of the Idea itself of the One together with the primary length, breadth, and depth, everything else being similarly constituted. Again he puts his view in yet other terms: Mind is the monad, science or knowledge the dyad (because it goes undeviatingly from one point to another), opinion the number of the plane, sensation the number of the solid; the numbers are by him expressly identified with the Forms themselves or principles, and are formed out of the elements; now things are apprehended either by mind or science or opinion or sensation, and these same numbers are the Forms of things.

Some thinkers, accepting both premises, viz., that the soul is both originative of movement and cognitive, have compounded it of both and declared the soul to be a self-moving number.

As to the nature and number of the first principles opinions differ. The difference is greatest between those who regard them as corporeal and those who regard them as incorporeal, and from both dissent those who make a blend and draw their principles from both sources. The number of principles is also in dispute; some admit one only, others assert several. There is a consequent diversity in their several accounts of soul; they assume, naturally enough, that what is in its own nature originative of movement must be among what is primordial. That has led some to regard it as fire, for fire is the subtlest of the elements and nearest to incorporeality; further, in the primary sense, fire both is moved and originates movement in all the others.

Democritus has expressed himself more ingeniously than the rest on the grounds for ascribing each of these two characters to soul; soul and thought are, he says, one and the same thing, and this thing must be one of the primary and indivisible bodies, and its power of originating movement must be due to its fineness of grain and the shape of its atoms; he says that of all the shapes the spherical is the most mobile, and that this is the shape of the particles of both fire and thought.

Each of the elements has thus found its partisan, except earth—earth has found no supporter unless we count as such those who have declared soul to be, or to be compounded of, *all* the elements. All, then, it may be said, characterize the soul by three marks. Movement, Sensation, Incorporeality, and each of these is traced back to the first principles. That is why (with one exception) all those who define the soul by its power of knowing make it either an element or constructed out of the elements. The language they all use is similar; like, they say, is known by like; as the soul knows everything, they construct it out of all the principles. Hence all those who admit but one cause or element, make the soul also one (e.g., fire or air), while those who admit a multiplicity of principles make the soul also multiple. The exception is Anaxagoras; he alone says that thought is impassible and has nothing in common with anything else. But, if this is so, how or in virtue of what cause can it know? That Anaxagoras has not explained, nor can any answer be inferred from his words. All who acknowledge pairs of opposites among their principles, construct the soul also out of these contraries, while those who admit as principles only one contrary of each pair, e.g., either hot or cold, likewise make the soul some one of these. That is why they allow themselves to be guided by the names; those who identify soul with the hot argue that to live is derived from to boil, while those who identify it with the cold say that soul (φυχή) is so called from the process of respiration and refrigeration.

Such are the traditional opinions concerning soul, together with the grounds on which they are maintained. . . .

The view we have just been examining, in company with most theories about the soul, involves the following absurdity: they all join the soul to a body, or place it in a body, without adding any specification of the reason of their union, or of the bodily conditions required for it. Yet such explanation can scarcely be omitted; for some community of nature is presupposed by the fact that the one acts and the other is acted upon, the one moves and the other is moved; but it is not the case that *any* two things are related to one another in these ways. All, however, that these thinkers do is to describe the specific characteristics of the soul; they do not try to determine anything about the body which is to contain it, as if it were possible, as in the Pythagorean myths, that any soul could be clothed in any body—an absurd view, for each body seems to have a form and shape of its own. It is as absurd as to say that the art of carpentry could embody itself in flutes; each art must use its tools, each soul its body.

There is yet another opinion about soul, which has commended itself to many as no less probable than any of those we have hitherto mentioned, and has rendered public account of itself in the court of popular discussion. Its supporters say that the soul is a kind of harmony; for harmony is a blend or composition of contraries, and the body is compounded out of contraries. Harmony, however, is a certain proportion or composition of the constituents blended, and soul can be neither the one nor the other of these. Further, the power of originating movement cannot belong to a harmony, while all concur in regarding this pretty well as a principal attribute of soul. It is more appropriate to call health (or generally one of the good states of the body) a harmony than to predicate it of the soul. The absurdity becomes most apparent when we try to attribute the active and passive affections of the soul to a harmony—it is difficult to harmonize them. Further, in using the word 'harmony' we have one or other of two cases in mind: the most proper sense is in relation to magnitudes which have motion and position, where harmony means their being compounded and harmonized in such a manner as to prevent the introduction of anything homogeneous; and the derived sense is that in which it means the ratio between the constituents so blended; in neither of these senses is it plausible to predicate it of soul. That soul is a harmony in the sense of the composition of the parts of the body is a view easily refutable; for there are many and various compoundings of the parts; of what is thought or the sensitive or the appetitive faculty the composition? And what *is* the composition which constitutes each of them? It is equally absurd to identify the soul with the ratio of the mixture; for the mixture of the elements which makes flesh has a different ratio from that which makes bone. The consequence of this view will therefore be that distributed throughout the whole body there will be many souls, since every one of the bodily parts is a mixture of the elements, and the ratio of mixture is in each case a harmony, i.e., a soul.

From Empedocles at any rate we might demand an answer to the following question—for he says that each of the parts of the body is what it is in virtue of a ratio between the elements: is the soul identical with this ratio, or is it not rather something over and above this which is formed in the parts? Is love the cause of any and every mixture, or only of those that are in the right ratio? Is love this ratio itself, or is love something over and above this? Such are the problems raised by this account. But, on the other hand, if the soul is different from the mixture, why does it disappear at one and the same moment with that relation between the elements which constitutes flesh or the other parts of the animal body? Further, if the soul is not identical with the ratio of mixture, and it is consequently not the case that each of the parts has a soul, what is that which perishes when the soul quits the body?

That the soul cannot either be a harmony, or be moved in a circle, is clear from what we have said. Yet that it can be moved incidentally is, as we said above, possible, and even that it can move itself, i.e., in the sense that *the vehicle* in which it is can be moved, and moved by it; in no other sense can the soul be moved in space.

More legitimate doubts might remain as to its movement in view of the following facts. We speak of the soul as being pained or pleased, being bold or fearful, being angry, perceiving, thinking. All these are regarded as modes of movement, and hence it might be inferred that the soul is moved. This, however, does not necessarily follow. We may admit to the full that being pained or pleased, or thinking, are movements (each of them a being moved), and that the movement is originated by the soul. For example we may regard anger or fear as such and such movements of the heart, and thinking as such and such another movement of that organ, or of some other; these modifications may arise either from changes of place in certain parts or from qualitative alterations (the special nature of the parts and the special modes of their changes being for our present purpose irrelevant). Yet to say that it is the soul which is angry is as if we were to say that it is the soul that weaves or builds houses. It is doubtless better to avoid saying that the soul pities or learns or thinks, and rather to say that it is the man who does this with

his soul. What we mean is not that the movement is in the soul, but that sometimes it terminates in the soul and sometimes starts from it, sensation e.g., coming from without, and reminiscence starting from the soul and terminating with the movements or states of rest in the sense organs.

But thought seems to be an independent substance implanted within us and to be incapable of being destroyed. If it could be destroyed at all, it would be under the blunting influence of old age. What really happens is, however, exactly parallel to what happens in the case of the sense organs; if the old man could recover the proper kind of eye, he would see just as well as the young man. The incapacity of old age is due to an affection not of the soul but of its vehicle, as occurs in drunkenness or disease. Thus it is that thinking and reflecting decline through the decay of some other inward part and are themselves impassible. Thinking, loving, and hating are affections not of thought, but of that which has thought, so far as it has it. That is why, when this vehicle decays, memory and love cease; they were activities not of thought, but of the composite which has perished; thought is, no doubt, something more divine and impassible. That the soul cannot be moved is therefore clear from what we have said, and if it cannot be moved at all, manifestly it cannot be moved by itself. . . .

Such are the three ways in which soul has traditionally been defined: one group of thinkers declared it to be that which is most originative of movement because it moves itself, another group to be the subtlest and most incorporeal of all kinds of body. We have now sufficiently set forth the difficulties and inconsistencies to which these theories are exposed. It remains now to examine the doctrine that soul is composed of the elements.

The reason assigned for this doctrine is that thus the soul may perceive and come to know everything that is; but the theory necessarily involves itself in many impossibilities. Its upholders assume that like is known by like, as though they were assuming that the soul is identical with the objects. But the elements are not the only things; there are many others, or, more exactly, an infinite number of others, formed out of the elements. Let us admit that the soul knows and perceives the elements out of which each of these composites is made up; but by what means will it know or perceive the composite whole, e.g., what god, man, flesh, bone (or any other compound) is? For each *is,* not merely the elements of which it is composed, but those elements combined in a determinate mode or ratio, as Empedocles himself says of bone,

> The kindly Earth in its broad-bosomed moulds
> Won of clear Water two parts out of eight
> And four of Fire; and so white bones were formed.

Nothing, therefore, will be gained by the presence of the elements of the soul, unless there be also present there the ratios and the composition. Each element will indeed know its like, but there will be no knowledge of bone or man, unless they too are present in it. The impossibility of this needs no pointing out; for who would suggest that a stone or a man is in the soul? The same applies to the good and the not-good, and so on.

Further, things are said to be in many ways: 'be' signifies of a 'this' or substance, or a quantum, or a quale, or any other of the kinds of predicates we have distinguished. Does the soul consist of all of these or not? It does not appear that all have common elements. Is the soul formed out of those elements alone which enter into substances? If so, how will it be able to know each of the other kinds of thing? Will it be said that each kind of thing has elements or principles of its own, and that the soul is formed out of these? In that case, the soul must be a quantum *and* a quale *and* a substance. But all that can be made out of the elements of a quantum is a quantum, not a substance. These (and others like them) are the consequences of the view that the soul is composed of all the elements. . . .

From what has been said it is now clear that knowing as an attribute of soul cannot be explained by soul's being composed of the elements, and that it is neither sound nor true to speak of soul as moved. But since knowing, perceiving, opining, and further desiring, wishing, and generally all other modes of appetition, belong to soul, and the local movements of animals, and growth, maturity, and decay are produced by the soul, we must ask whether each of these is an attribute of the soul as a whole, i.e., whether it is with the whole soul we think, perceive, move ourselves, act or are acted upon, or whether each of them requires a different part of the soul? So too with regard to life. Does it depend on one of the parts of soul? Or is it dependent on more than one? Or on all? Or has it some quite other cause?

Some hold that the soul is divisible, and that we think with one part and desire with another. If, then, its nature admits of its being divided, what can it be that holds the parts together? Surely not the body; on the contrary it seems rather to be the soul that holds the body together; at any rate when the soul departs the body disintegrates and decays. If, then, there is something else which makes the soul one, this would have the best right to the name of soul, and we shall have to repeat for it the question: Is *it* one or multipartite? If it is one, why not at once admit that *the soul* is one? If it has parts, once more the question must be put: What holds *its* parts together, and so *ad infinitum*?

The question might also be raised about the parts of the soul: What is the separate role of each in relation to the body? For, if the whole soul holds together the whole body, we should expect each part of the soul to hold together a part of the body. But this seems an impossibility; it is difficult even to imagine what sort of bodily part thought will hold together, or how it will do this.

It is a fact of observation that plants and certain insects go on living when divided into segments; this means that each of the segments has a soul in it identical in species, though not numerically; for both of the segments for a time possess the power of sensation and local movement. That this does not last is not surprising, for they no longer possess the organs necessary for self-maintenance. But, all the same, in each of the parts there are present all the parts of soul, and the souls so present are homogeneous with one another and with the whole—the several parts of the soul being inseparable from one another, although the whole soul is divisible. It seems that the principle found in plants is also a kind of soul; for this is the only principle which is common to both animals and plants; and this exists in isolation from the principle of sensation, though there is nothing which has the latter without the former.

Book II

Let the foregoing suffice as our account of the views concerning the soul which have been handed on by our predecessors; let us now make as it were a completely fresh start, endeavouring to answer the question, What is soul? i.e., to formulate the most general possible account of it.

We say that substance is one kind of what is, and that in several senses: in the sense of matter or that which in itself is not a this, and in the sense of form or essence, which is that precisely in virtue of which a thing is called a this, and thirdly in the sense of that which is compounded of both. Now matter is potentiality, form actuality; and actuality is of two kinds, one as e.g., knowledge, the other as e.g., reflecting.

Among substances are by general consent reckoned bodies and especially natural bodies; for they are the principles of all other bodies. Of natural bodies some have life in them, others not; by life we mean self-nutrition and growth and decay. It follows that every natural body which has life in it is a substance in the sense of a composite.

Now given that there are bodies of such and such a kind, viz., having life, the soul cannot be a body; for the body is the subject or matter, not what is attributed to it. Hence the soul must be a substance in the sense of the form of a natural body having life potentially within it. But substance is actuality, and thus soul is the actuality of a body as above characterized. Now there are two kinds of actuality corresponding to knowledge and to reflecting. It is obvious that the soul is an actuality like knowledge; for both sleeping and waking presuppose the existence of soul, and of these waking corresponds to reflecting, sleeping to knowledge possessed but not employed, and knowledge of something is temporally prior.

That is why the soul is an actuality of the first kind of a natural body having life potentially in it. The body so described is a body which is organized. The parts of plants in spite of their extreme simplicity are organs; e.g., the leaf serves to shelter the pericarp, the pericarp to shelter the fruit, while the roots of plants are analogous to the mouth of animals, both serving for the absorption of food. If, then, we have to give a general formula applicable to all kinds of soul, we must describe it as an actuality of the first kind of a natural organized body. That is why we can dismiss as unnecessary the question whether the soul and the body are one: it is as though we were to ask whether the wax and its shape are one, or generally the matter of a thing and that of which it is the matter. Unity has many senses (as many as 'is' has), but the proper one is that of actuality.

We have now given a general answer to the question, What is soul? It is substance in the sense which corresponds to the account of a thing. That means that it is what it is to be for a body of the character just assigned. Suppose that a tool, e.g., an axe, were a *natural* body, then being an axe would have been its essence, and so its soul; if this disappeared from it, it would have ceased to be an axe, except in name. As it is, it is an axe; for it is not of a body of that sort that what it is to be, i.e., its account, is a soul, but of a natural body of a particular kind, viz., one having in itself the power of setting itself in movement and arresting itself. Next, apply this doctrine in the case of the parts of the living body. Suppose that the eye were an animal—sight would have been its soul, for sight is the substance of the eye which corresponds to the account, the eye being merely the matter of seeing; when seeing is removed the eye is no longer an eye, except in name—no more than the eye of a statue or of a painted figure. We must now extend our consideration from the parts to the whole living body; for what the part is to the part, that the whole faculty of sense is to the whole sensitive body as such.

We must not understand by that which is potentially capable of living what has lost the soul it had, but only what still retains it; but seeds and fruits are bodies which are potentially of that sort. Consequently, while waking is actuality in a sense corresponding to the cutting and the seeing, the soul is actuality in the sense corresponding to sight and the power in the tool; the body corresponds to what is in potentiality; as the pupil *plus* the power of sight constitutes the eye, so the soul *plus* the body constitutes the animal.

From this it is clear that the soul is inseparable from its body, or at any rate that certain parts of it are (if it has parts)—for the actuality of some of them is the actuality of the parts themselves. Yet some may be separable because they are not the actualities of any body at all. Further, we have no light on the problem whether the soul may not be the actuality of its body in the sense in which the sailor is the actuality of the ship.

This must suffice as our sketch or outline of the nature of soul.

Since what is clear and more familiar in account emerges from what in itself is confused but more observable by us, we must reconsider our results from this point of view. For it is not enough for a definitional account to express as most now do the mere fact; it must include and exhibit the cause also. At present definitions are given in a form analogous to the conclusion of an argument; e.g., What is squaring? The construction of an equilateral rectangle equal to a given oblong red-angle. Such a definition is in form equivalent to a conclusion. One that tells us that squaring is the discovery of a mean proportional discloses the cause of what is defined.

We resume our inquiry from a fresh starting-point by calling attention to the fact that what has soul in it differs from what has not in that the former displays life. Now this word has more than one sense, and provided any one alone of these is found in a thing we say that thing is living—viz., thinking or perception or local movement and rest, or movement in the sense of nutrition, decay and growth. Hence we think of plants also as living, for they are observed to possess in themselves an originative power through which they increase or decrease in all spatial directions; they do not grow up but not down—they grow alike in both, indeed in all, directions; and that holds for everything which is constantly nourished and continues to live, so long as it can absorb nutriment.

This power of self-nutrition can be separated from the other powers mentioned, but not they from it—in mortal beings at least. The fact is obvious in plants; for it is the only psychic power they possess.

This is the originative power the possession of which leads us to speak of things as *living* at all, but it is the possession of sensation that leads us for the first time to speak of living things as *ani-*

mals; for even those beings which possess no power of local movement but do possess the power of sensation we call animals and not merely living things.

The primary form of sense is touch, which belongs to all animals. Just as the power of self-nutrition can be separated from touch and sensation generally, so touch can be separated from all other forms of sense. (By the power of self-nutrition we mean that part of the soul which is common to plants and animals: all animals whatsoever are observed to have the sense of touch.) What the explanation of these two facts is, we must discuss later. At present we must confine ourselves to saying that soul is the source of these phenomena and is characterized by them, viz., by the powers of self-nutrition, sensation, thinking, and movement.

Is each of these a soul or a part of a soul? And if a part, a part merely distinguishable by definition or a part distinct in local situation as well? In the case of certain of these powers, the answers to these questions are easy, in the case of others we are puzzled what to say. Just as in the case of plants which when divided are observed to continue to live though separated from one another (thus showing that in *their* case the soul of each individual plant was actually one, potentially many), so we notice a similar result in other varieties of soul, e.g., in insects which have been cut in two; each of the segments possesses both sensation and local movement; and if sensation, necessarily also imagination and appetition; for, where there is sensation, there is also pleasure and pain, and, where these, necessarily also desire.

We have no evidence as yet about thought or the power of reflexion; it seems to be a different kind of soul, differing as what is eternal from what is perishable; it alone is capable of being separated. All the other parts of soul, it is evident from what we have said, are, in spite of certain statements to the contrary, incapable of separate existence though, of course, distinguishable by definition. If opining is distinct from perceiving, to be capable of opining and to be capable of perceiving must be distinct, and so with all the other forms of living above enumerated. Further, some animals possess all these parts of soul, some certain of them only, others one only (this is what enables us to classify animals); the cause must be considered later. A similar arrangement is found also within the field of the senses; some classes of animals have all the senses, some only certain of them, others only one, the most indispensable, touch.

Since the expression 'that whereby we live and perceive' has two meanings, just like the expression 'that whereby we know'—that may mean either knowledge or the soul, for we can speak of knowing *by* either, and similarly that whereby we are in health may be either health or the body or some part of the body; and since of these knowledge or health is a form, essence, or account, or if we so express it an activity of a recipient matter—knowledge of what is capable of knowing, health of what is capable of being made healthy (for the activity of that which is capable of originating change seems to take place in what is changed or altered); further, since it is the soul by which primarily we live, perceive, and think:—it follows that the soul must be an account and essence, not matter or a subject. For, as we said, the word substance has three meanings—form, matter, and the complex of both—and of these matter is potentiality, form actuality. Since then the complex here is the living thing, the body cannot be the actuality of the soul; it is the soul which is the actuality of a certain kind of body. Hence the rightness of the view that the soul cannot be without a body, while it cannot *be* a body; it is not a body but something relative to a body. That is why it is *in* a body, and a body of a definite kind. It was a mistake, therefore, to do as former thinkers did, merely to fit it into a body without adding a definite specification of the kind or character of that body, although evidently one chance thing will not receive another. It comes about as reason requires: the actuality of any given thing can only be realized in what is already potentially that thing, i.e., in a matter of its own appropriate to it. From all this it is plain that soul is an actuality or account of something that possesses a potentiality of being such. . . .

The soul is the cause or source of the living body. The terms cause and source have many senses. But the soul is the cause of its body alike in all three senses which we explicitly recognize. It is the source of movement, it is the end, it is the essence of the whole living body.

That it is the last, is clear; for in everything the essence is identical with the cause of its being, and here, in the case of living things, their being is to live, and of their being and their living the soul in them is the cause or source. Further, the actuality of whatever is potential is identical with its account.

It is manifest that the soul is also the final cause. For nature, like thought, always does whatever it does for the sake of something, which something is its end. To that something corresponds in the case of animals the soul and in this it follows the order of nature; all natural bodies are organs of the soul. This is true of those that enter into the constitution of plants as well as of those which enter into that of animals. This shows that that for the sake of which they are is soul. That for the sake of which has two senses, viz., the end to achieve which, and the being in whose interest, anything is or is done.

The soul is also the cause of the living body as the original source of local movement. The power of locomotion is not found, however, in all living things. But change of quality and change of quantity are also due to the soul. Sensation is held to be a qualitative alteration, and nothing except what has soul in it is capable of sensation. The same holds of growth and decay; nothing grows or decays naturally except what feeds itself, and nothing feeds itself except what has a share in life in it. . . .

In dealing with each of the senses we shall have first to speak of the objects which are perceptible by each. The term 'object of sense' covers three kinds of objects, two kinds of which we call perceptible in themselves, while the remaining one is only incidentally perceptible. Of the first two kinds one consists of what is special to a single sense, the other of what is common to any and all of the senses. I call by the name of special object of this or that sense that which cannot be perceived by any other sense than that one and in respect of which no error is possible; in this sense colour is the special object of sight, sound of hearing, flavour of taste. Touch, indeed, discriminates more than one set of different qualities. Each sense has one kind of object which it discerns, and never errs in reporting that what is before it is colour or sound (though it may err as to what it is that is coloured or where that is, or what it is that is sounding or where that is). Such objects are what we call the special objects of this or that sense.

Common sensibles are movement, rest, number, figure, magnitude; these are not special to any one sense, but are common to all. There are at any rate certain kinds of movement which are perceptible both by touch and by sight.

We speak of an incidental object of sense where e.g., the white object which we see is the son of Diares; here because being the son of Diares is incidental to the white which is perceived, we speak of the son of Diares as being incidentally perceived. That is why it in no way as such affects the senses. Of the things perceptible in themselves, the special objects are properly called perceptible and it is to them that in the nature of things the structure of each several sense is adapted. [Omitted Chapters 7–11 deal with how the senses might work.]

Generally, about all perception, we can say that a sense is what has the power of receiving into itself the sensible forms of things without the matter, in the way in which a piece of wax takes on the impress of a signet-ring without the iron or gold; what produces the impression is a signet of bronze or gold, but not *qua* bronze or gold; in a similar way the sense is affected by what is coloured or flavoured or sounding not insofar as each is what it is, but insofar as it is of such and such a sort and according to its form.

A primary sense-organ is that in which such a power is seated. The sense and its organ are the same in fact, but their essence is not the same. What perceives is, of course, a spatial magnitude, but we must not admit that either the having the power to perceive or the sense itself is a magnitude; what they are is a certain form or power in a magnitude. This enables us to explain why excesses in objects of sense destroy the organs of sense; if the movement set up by an object is too strong for the organ, the form which is its sensory power is disturbed; it is precisely as concord and tone are destroyed by too violently twanging the strings of a lyre. This explains also why plants cannot perceive, in spite of their having a portion of soul in them and being affected by tangible objects themselves; for their temperature can be lowered or raised. The explanation is that they have no mean, and so no principle in them capable of taking on the forms of sensible objects but are affected together with their matter.

Book III

. . . There are two distinctive peculiarities by reference to which we characterize the soul—(1) local movement and (2) thinking, understanding, and perceiving. Thinking and understanding are regarded as akin to a form of perceiving; for in the one as well as the other the soul discriminates and is cognizant of something which is. Indeed the ancients go so far as to identify thinking and perceiving; e.g., Empedocles says 'For 'tis in respect of what is present that man's wit is increased', and again 'Whence it befalls them from time to time to think diverse thoughts', and Homer's phrase, 'For suchlike is man's mind' means the same. They all look upon thinking as a bodily process like perceiving, and hold that like is understood as well as perceived by like, as I explained at the beginning of our discussion. Yet they ought at the same time to have accounted for error also; for it is more intimately connected with animal existence and the soul continues longer in the state of error. They cannot escape the dilemma: either whatever seems is true (and there are some who accept this) or error is contact with the unlike: for that is the opposite of the knowing of like by like.

But it seems that error as well as knowledge in respect to contraries is one and the same.

That perceiving and understanding are not identical is therefore obvious; for the former is universal in the animal world, the latter is found in only a small division of it. Further, thinking is also distinct from perceiving—I mean that in which we find rightness and wrongness—rightness in understanding, knowledge, true opinion, wrongness in their opposites; for perception of the special objects of sense is always free from error, and is found in all animals, while it is possible to think falsely as well as truly, and thought is found only where there is discourse of reason. For imagination is different from either perceiving or discursive thinking, though it is not found without sensation, or judgement without it. That this activity is not the same kind of thinking as judgement is obvious. For imagining lies within our own power whenever we wish (e.g., we can call up a picture, as in the practice of mnemonics by the use of mental images), but in forming opinions we are not free: we cannot escape the alternative of falsehood or truth. Further, when we think something to be fearful or threatening, emotion is immediately produced, and so too with what is encouraging; but when we merely imagine we remain as unaffected as persons who are looking at a painting of some dreadful or encouraging scene. Again within the field of judgement itself we find varieties—knowledge, opinion, understanding, and their opposites; of the differences between these I must speak elsewhere.

Thinking is different from perceiving and is held to be in part imagination, in part judgement: we must therefore first mark off the sphere of imagination and then speak of judgement. If then imagination is that in virtue of which an image arises for us, excluding metaphorical uses of the term, is it a single faculty or disposition relative to images, in virtue of which we discriminate and are either in error or not? The faculties in virtue of which we do this are sense, opinion, knowledge, thought.

Turning now to the part of the soul with which the soul knows and (whether this is separable from the others in definition only, or spatially as well) we have to inquire what differentiates this part, and how thinking can take place.

If thinking is like perceiving, it must be either a process in which the soul is acted upon by what is capable of being thought, or a process different from but analogous to that. The thinking part of the soul must therefore be, while impassible, capable of receiving the form of an object; that is, must be potentially identical in character with its object without being the object. Thought must be related to what is thinkable, as sense is to what is sensible.

Therefore, since everything is a possible object of thought, mind in order, as Anaxagoras says, to dominate, that is, to know, must be pure from all admixture; for the co-presence of what is alien to its nature is a hindrance and a block: it follows that it can have no nature of its own, other than that of having a certain capacity. Thus that in the soul which is called thought (by thought I mean that whereby the soul thinks and judges) is, before it thinks, not actually any real thing. For this reason it cannot reasonably be regarded as blended with the body: if so, it would acquire some quality, e.g., warmth or cold, or even have an organ like the sensitive faculty: as it is, it has

none. It was a good idea to call the soul 'the place of forms,' though this description holds only of the thinking soul, and even this is the forms only potentially, not actually.

Observation of the sense-organs and their employment reveals a distinction between the impassibility of the sensitive faculty and that of the faculty of thought. After strong stimulation of a sense we are less able to exercise it than before, as e.g., in the case of a loud sound we cannot hear easily immediately after, or in the case of a bright colour or a powerful odour we cannot see or smell, but in the case of thought thinking about an object that is highly thinkable renders it more and not less able afterwards to think of objects that are less thinkable: the reason is that while the faculty of sensation is dependent upon the body, thought is separable from it.

When thought has become each thing in the way in which a man who actually knows is said to do so (this happens when he is now able to exercise the power on his own initiative), its condition is still one of potentiality, but in a different sense from the potentiality which preceded the acquisition of knowledge by learning or discovery; and thought is then able to think of itself.

Since we can distinguish between a magnitude and what it is to be a magnitude, and between water and what it is to be water, and so in many other cases (though not in all; for in certain cases the thing and its form are identical), flesh and what it is to be flesh are discriminated either by different faculties, or by the same faculty in two different states; for flesh necessarily involves matter and is like what is snub-nosed, a *this* in a *this*. Now it is by means of the sensitive faculty that we discriminate the hot and the cold, i.e., the factors which combined in a certain ratio constitute flesh: the essential character of flesh is apprehended by something different either wholly separate from the sensitive faculty or related to it as a bent line to the same line when it has been straightened out.

Again in the case of abstract objects what is straight is analogous to what is snub-nosed; for it necessarily implies a continuum: its constitutive essence is different, if we may distinguish between straightness and what is straight: let us take it to be twoness. It must be apprehended, therefore, by a different power or by the same power in a different state. To sum up, in so far as the realities it knows are capable of being separated from their matter, so it is also with the powers of thought.

The problem might be suggested: if thinking is a passive affection, then if thought is simple and impassible and has nothing in common with anything else, as Anaxagoras says, how can it come to think at all? For interaction between two factors is held to require a precedent community of nature between the factors. Again it might be asked, is thought a possible object of thought to itself? For if thought is thinkable *per se* and what is thinkable is in kind one and the same, then either thought will belong to everything, or it will contain some element common to it with all other realities which makes them all thinkable.

Have not we already disposed of the difficulty about interaction involving a common element, when we said that thought is in a sense potentially whatever is thinkable, though actually it is nothing until it has thought? What it thinks must be in it just as characters may be said to be on a writing-table on which as yet nothing actually stands written: this is exactly what happens with thought.

Thought is itself thinkable in exactly the same way as its objects are. For in the case of objects which involve no matter, what thinks and what is thought are identical; for speculative knowledge and its object are identical. (Why thought is not always thinking we must consider later.) In the case of those which contain matter each of the objects of thought is only potentially present. It follows that while they will not have thought in them (for thought is a potentiality of them only in so far as they are capable of being disengaged from matter) thought may yet be thinkable.

Since in every class of things, as in nature as a whole, we find two factors involved, a matter which is potentially all the particulars included in the class, a cause which is productive in the sense that it makes them all (the latter standing to the former, as e.g., an art to its material), these distinct elements must likewise be found within the soul.

And in fact thought, as we have described it, is what it is by virtue of becoming all things, while there is another which is what it is by virtue of making all things: this is a sort of positive state like light; for in a sense light makes potential colours into actual colours.

Thought in this sense of it is separable, impassible, unmixed, since it is in its essential nature activity (for always the active is superior to the passive factor, the originating force to the matter).

Actual knowledge is identical with its object: in the individual, potential knowledge is in time prior to actual knowledge, but absolutely it is not prior even in time. It does not sometimes think and sometimes not think. When separated it is alone just what it is, and this above is immortal and eternal (we do not remember because, while this is impossible, passive thought is perishable); and without this nothing thinks.

Let us now summarize our results about soul, and repeat that the soul is in a way all existing things; for existing things are either sensible or thinkable, and knowledge is in a way what is knowable, and sensation is in a way what is sensible: in *what* way we must inquire.

Knowledge and sensation are divided to correspond with the realities, potential knowledge and sensation answering to potentialities, actual knowledge and sensation to actualities. Within the soul the faculties of knowledge and sensation are *potentially* these objects, the one what is knowable, the other what is sensible. They must be either the things themselves or their forms. The former alternative is of course impossible: it is not the stone which is present in the soul but its form.

It follows that the soul is analogous to the hand; for as the hand is a tool of tools, so thought is the form of forms and sense the form of sensible things.

Since it seems that there is nothing outside and separate in existence from sensible spatial magnitudes, the objects of thought are in the sensible forms, viz., both the abstract objects and all the states and affections of sensible things. Hence no one can learn or understand anything in the absence of sense, and when the mind is actively aware of anything it is necessarily aware of it along with an image; for images are like sensuous contents except in that they contain no matter.

Imagination is different from assertion and denial; for what is true or false involves a synthesis of thoughts. In what will the primary thoughts differ from images? Must we not say that neither these nor even our other thoughts are images, though they necessarily involve them?

24. *Meditations on First Philosophy*

RENÉ DESCARTES

René Descartes (1596–1650), French mathematician and philosopher, is commonly called the father of modern philosophy. He lived during a time of great intellectual upheaval. In 1543, Copernicus published his radical, non-Aristotelian view that the earth rotates on its axis and revolves around the sun. Galileo was supporting the Copernican theory by attacking Aristotle's physics. His famous slogan said that God wrote the book of nature in the language of mathematics, and the picture of nature that was to emerge during the Scientific Revolution was a picture that increasingly emphasized the mechanistic causality of matter in motion. Descartes took part in this revolution by, for example, inventing analytic geometry and proposing mechanistic models of planetary motion and for the operation of the nervous system. The new scientific ideas were controversial, and they became mixed with disputes in religion. The Protestant Reformation was attacking the authority of the Roman Catholic Church on theological matters; and by 1633, the church (through the Inquisition) tried to suppress Galileo's work by banning it and by putting him under house arrest. It is against this background of doubt and dispute that Descartes tried to find a new foundation for philosophy.

In *Meditations on First Philosophy,* Descartes proposes to base knowledge of nature and God on a foundation of indubitable beliefs about thinking: one can be certain one is thinking, and some of one's ideas reveal the essences of things. As a by-product of his theory of knowledge, Descartes posed the modern mind-body problem: he claims an examination of the ideas of mind and body show that they must be metaphysically distinct substances.

Are Descartes' arguments in support of mind-body dualism correct? If so, how do mind and body interact? If not, how can the apparently incompatible properties of mind and body be explained or accommodated in a comprehensive metaphysics?

Meditation II.

Of the Nature of the Human Mind; and That It Is More Easily Known than the Body.

The Meditation of yesterday has filled my mind with so many doubts, that it is no longer in my power to forget them. Nor do I see, meanwhile, any principle on which they can be resolved; and, just as if I had fallen all of a sudden into very deep water, I am so greatly disconcerted as to be unable either to plant my feet firmly on the bottom or sustain myself by swimming on the surface. I will, nevertheless, make an effort, and try anew the same path on which I had entered yesterday, that is, proceed by casting aside all that admits of the slightest doubt, not less than if I had discovered it to be absolutely false; and I will continue always in this track until I shall find something that is certain, or at least, if I can do nothing more, until I shall know with certainty that there is nothing certain. Archimedes, that he might transport the entire globe from the place it occupied to another, demanded only a point that was firm and immovable; so, also, I shall be entitled to entertain the highest expectations, if I am fortunate enough to discover only one thing that is certain and indubitable.

From René Descartes, *Meditations on First Philosophy.* Translated by John Veitch, 1901. First published in 1641.

I suppose, accordingly, that all the things which I see are false (fictitious); I believe that none of those objects which my fallacious memory represents ever existed; I suppose that I possess no senses; I believe that body, figure, extension, motion, and place are merely fictions of my mind. What is there, then, that can be esteemed true? Perhaps this only, that there is absolutely nothing certain.

But how do I know that there is not something different altogether from the objects I have now enumerated, of which it is impossible to entertain the slightest doubt? Is there not a God, or some being, by whatever name I may designate him, who causes these thoughts to arise in my mind? But why suppose such a being, for it may be I myself am capable of producing them? Am I, then, at least not something? But I before denied that I possessed senses or a body; I hesitate, however, for what follows from that? Am I so dependent on the body and the senses that without these I cannot exist? But I had the persuasion that there was absolutely nothing in the world, that there was no sky and no earth, neither minds nor bodies; was I not, therefore, at the same time, persuaded that I did not exist? Far from it; I assuredly existed, since I was persuaded. But there is I know not what being, who is possessed at once of the highest power and the deepest cunning, who is constantly employing all his ingenuity in deceiving me. Doubtless, then, I exist, since I am deceived; and, let him deceive me as he may, he can never bring it about that I am nothing, so long as I shall be conscious that I am something. So that it must, in fine, be maintained, all things being maturely and carefully considered, that this proposition (*pronunciatum*) I am, I exist, is necessarily true each time it is expressed by me, or conceived in my mind.

But I do not yet know with sufficient clearness what I am, though assured that I am; and hence, in the next place, I must take care, lest perchance I inconsiderately substitute some other object in room of what is properly myself, and thus wander from truth, even in that knowledge (cognition) which I hold to be of all others the most certain and evident. For this reason, I will now consider anew what I formerly believed myself to be, before I entered on the present train of thought; and of my previous opinion I will retrench all that can in the least be invalidated by the grounds of doubt I have adduced, in order that there may at length remain nothing but what is certain and indubitable. What then did I formerly think I was? Undoubtedly I judged that I was a man. But what is a man? Shall I say a rational animal? Assuredly not; for it would be necessary forthwith to inquire into what is meant by animal, and what by rational, and thus, from a single question, I should insensibly glide into others, and these more difficult than the first; nor do I now possess enough of leisure to warrant me in wasting my time amid subtleties of this sort. I prefer here to attend to the thoughts that sprung up of themselves in my mind, and were inspired by my own nature alone, when I applied myself to the consideration of what I was. In the first place, then, I thought that I possessed a countenance, hands, arms, and all the fabric of members that appears in a corpse, and which I called by the name of body. It further occurred to me that I was nourished, that I walked, perceived, and thought, and all those actions I referred to the soul; but what the soul itself was I either did not stay to consider, or, if I did, I imagined that it was something extremely rare and subtile, like wind, or flame, or ether, spread through my grosser parts. As regarded the body, I did not even doubt of its nature, but thought I distinctly knew it, and if I had wished to describe it according to the notions I then entertained, I should have explained myself in this manner: By body I understand all that can be terminated by a certain figure; that can be comprised in a certain place, and so fill a certain space as therefrom to exclude every other body; that can be perceived either by touch, sight, hearing, taste, or smell; that can be moved in different ways, not indeed of itself, but by something foreign to it by which it is touched [and from which it receives the impression]; for the power of self-motion, as likewise that of perceiving and thinking, I held as by no means pertaining to the nature of body; on the contrary, I was somewhat astonished to find such faculties existing in some bodies.

But [as to myself, what can I now say that I am], since I suppose there exists an extremely powerful, and, if I may so speak, malignant being, whose whole endeavors are directed toward deceiving me? Can I affirm that I possess any one of all those attributes of which I have lately spoken as belonging to the nature of body? After attentively considering them in my own mind, I find none of them that can properly be said to belong to myself. To recount them were idle and tedious. Let us pass, then, to the attributes of the soul. The first mentioned were the powers of nutrition and walking; but, if it be true that I have no body, it is true likewise that I am capable neither of walking nor of being nourished. Perception is another attribute of the soul; but perception too is impossible without the body; besides, I have frequently, during sleep, believed that I perceived objects which I afterward observed I did not in reality perceive. Thinking is another attribute of the soul; and here I discover what properly belongs to myself. This alone is inseparable from me. I am—I exist: this is certain; but how often? As often as I think; for perhaps it would even happen, if I should wholly cease to think, that I should at the same time altogether cease to be. I now admit nothing that is not necessarily true. I am therefore, precisely speaking, only a thinking thing, that is, a mind (*mens sive animus*), understanding, or reason, terms whose signification was before unknown to me. I am, however, a real thing, and really existent; but what thing? The answer was, a thinking thing. The question now arises, am I aught besides? I will stimulate my imagination with a view to discover whether I am still something more than a thinking being. Now it is plain I am not the assemblage of members called the human body; I am not a thin and penetrating air diffused through all these members, or wind, or flame, or vapor, or breath, or any of all the things I can imagine; for I supposed that all these were not, and, without changing the supposition, I find that I still feel assured of my existence.

But it is true, perhaps, that those very things which I suppose to be non-existent, because they are unknown to me, are not in truth different from myself whom I know. This is a point I cannot determine, and do not now enter into any dispute regarding it. I can only judge of things that are known to me: I am conscious that I exist, and I who know that I exist inquire into what I am. It is, however, perfectly certain that the knowledge of my existence, thus precisely taken, is not dependent on things, the existence of which is as yet unknown to me: and consequently it is not dependent on any of the things I can feign in imagination. Moreover, the phrase itself, I frame an image (*efffingo*), reminds me of my error; for I should in truth frame one if I were to imagine myself to be anything, since to imagine is nothing more than to contemplate the figure or image of a corporeal thing; but I already know that I exist, and that it is possible at the same time that all those images, and in general all that relates to the nature of body, are merely dreams [or chimeras]. From this I discover that it is not more reasonable to say, I will excite my imagination that I may know more distinctly what I am, than to express myself as follows: I am now awake, and perceive something real; but because my perception is not sufficiently clear, I will of express purpose go to sleep that my dreams may represent to me the object of my perception with more truth and clearness. And, therefore, I know that nothing of all that I can embrace in imagination belongs to the knowledge which I have of myself, and that there is need to recall with the utmost care the mind from this mode of thinking, that it may be able to know its own nature with perfect distinctness.

But what, then, am I? A thinking thing, it has been said. But what is a thinking thing? It is a thing that doubts, understands, [conceives], affirms, denies, wills, refuses; that imagines also, and perceives. Assuredly it is not little, if all these properties belong to my nature. But why should they not belong to it? Am I not that very being who now doubts of almost everything; who, for all that, understands and conceives certain things; who affirms one alone as true, and denies the others; who desires to know more of them, and does not wish to be deceived; who imagines many things, sometimes even despite his will; and is likewise percipient of many, as if through the medium of the senses. Is there nothing of all this as true as that I am, even although I should be always dreaming, and although he who gave me being employed all his ingenuity to deceive me? Is there also any one of these attributes that can be properly distinguished from my thought, or that can be said to be separate from myself? For it is of itself so evident that it is I who doubt, I who understand, and I who desire, that it is here unnecessary to add anything by way of rendering it more clear. And I am as certainly the same being who imagines; for although it may be (as I before supposed) that nothing I imagine is true, still the power of imagination does not cease really to exist in me and to form part of my thought. In fine, I am the same being who perceives, that is, who apprehends certain objects as by the organs of sense, since, in truth, I see light, hear a noise, and feel heat. But it will be said that these presentations are false, and that I am dreaming. Let it be so. At all events it is certain that I seem to see light, hear a noise, and feel heat; this cannot be false, and this is what in me is properly called perceiving (*sentire*), which is nothing else than thinking. From this I begin to know what I am with somewhat greater clearness and distinctness than heretofore.

But, nevertheless, it still seems to me, and I cannot help believing, that corporeal things, whose images are formed by thought [which fall under the senses], and are examined by the same, are known with much greater distinctness than that I know not what part of myself which is not imaginable; although, in truth, it may seem strange to say that I know and comprehend with greater distinctness things whose existence appears to me doubtful, that are unknown, and do not belong to me, than others of whose reality I am persuaded, that are known to me, and appertain to my proper nature; in a word, than myself. But I see clearly what is the state of the case. My mind is apt to wander, and will not yet submit to be restrained within the limits of truth. Let us therefore leave the mind to itself once more, and, according to it every kind of liberty [permit it to consider the objects that appear to it from without], in order that, having afterward withdrawn it from these gently and opportunely [and fixed it on the consideration of its being and the properties it finds in itself], it may then be the more easily controlled.

Let us now accordingly consider the objects that are commonly thought to be [the most easily, and likewise] the most distinctly known, viz, the bodies we touch and see; not, indeed, bodies in general, for these general notions are usually somewhat more confused, but one body in particular. Take, for example, this piece of wax; it is quite fresh, having been but recently taken from the beehive; it has not yet lost the sweetness of the honey it contained; it still retains somewhat of the odor of the flowers from which it was gathered; its color, figure, size, are apparent (to the sight); it is hard, cold, easily handled; and sounds when struck upon with the finger. In fine, all that contributes to make a body as distinctly known as possible, is

found in the one before us. But, while I am speaking, let it be placed near the fire—what remained of the taste exhales, the smell evaporates, the color changes, its figure is destroyed, its size increases, it becomes liquid, it grows hot, it can hardly be handled, and, although struck upon, it emits no sound. Does the same wax still remain after this change? It must be admitted that it does remain; no one doubts it, or judges otherwise. What, then, was it I knew with so much distinctness in the piece of wax? Assuredly, it could be nothing of all that I observed by means of the senses, since all the things that fell under taste, smell, sight, touch, and hearing are changed, and yet the same wax remains. It was perhaps what I now think, viz, that this wax was neither the sweetness of honey, the pleasant odor of flowers, the whiteness, the figure, nor the sound, but only a body that a little before appeared to me conspicuous under these forms, and which is now perceived under others. But, to speak precisely, what is it that I imagine when I think of it in this way? Let it be attentively considered, and, retrenching all that does not belong to the wax, let us see what remains. There certainly remains nothing, except something extended, flexible, and movable. But what is meant by flexible and movable? Is it not that I imagine that the piece of wax, being round, is capable of becoming square, or of passing from a square into a triangular figure? Assuredly such is not the case, because I conceive that it admits of an infinity of similar changes; and I am, moreover, unable to compass this infinity by imagination, and consequently this conception which I have of the wax is not the product of the faculty of imagination. But what now is this extension? Is it not also unknown? for it becomes greater when the wax is melted, greater when it is boiled, and greater still when the heat increases; and I should not conceive [clearly and] according to truth, the wax as it is, if I did not suppose that the piece we are considering admitted even of a wider variety of extension than I ever imagined, I must, therefore, admit that I cannot even comprehend by imagination what the piece of wax is, and that it is the mind alone (*mens*, Lat., *entendement*, F.) which perceives it. I speak of one piece in particular; for as to wax in general, this is still more evident. But what is the piece of wax that can be perceived only by the [understanding or] mind? It is certainly the same which I see, touch, imagine; and, in fine, it is the same which, from the beginning, I believed it to be. But (and this it is of moment to observe) the perception of it is neither an act of sight, of touch, nor of imagination, and never was either of these, though it might formerly seem so, but is simply an intuition (*inspectio*) of the mind, which may be imperfect and confused, as it formerly was, or very clear and distinct, as it is at present, according as the attention is more or less directed to the elements which it contains, and of which it is composed.

But, meanwhile, I feel greatly astonished when I observe [the weakness of my mind, and] its proneness to error. For although, without at all giving expression to what I think, I consider all this in my own mind, words yet occasionally impede my progress, and I am almost led into error by the terms of ordinary language. We say, for example, that we see the same wax when it is before us, and not that we judge it to be the same from its retaining the same color and figure: whence I should forthwith be disposed to conclude that the wax is known by the act of sight, and not by the intuition of the mind alone, were it not for the analogous instance of human beings passing on in the street below, as observed from a window. In this case I do not fail to say that I see the men themselves, just as I say that I see the wax; and yet what do I see from the window beyond hats and cloaks that might cover artificial machines, whose motions might be determined by springs? But I judge that there are human beings from these appearances, and thus I comprehend, by the faculty of judgment alone which is in the mind, what I believed I saw with my eyes.

The man who makes it his aim to rise to knowledge superior to the common, ought to be ashamed to seek occasions of doubting from the vulgar forms of speech: instead, therefore, of doing this, I shall proceed with the matter in hand, and inquire whether I had a clearer and more perfect perception of the piece of wax when I first saw it, and when I thought I knew it by means of the external sense itself, or, at all events, by the common sense (*sensus communis*), as it is called, that is, by the imaginative faculty; or whether I rather apprehend it more clearly at present, after having examined with greater care, both what it is, and in what way it can be known. It would certainly be ridiculous to entertain any doubt on this point.

For what, in that first perception, was there distinct? What did I perceive which any animal might not have perceived? But when I distinguish the wax from its exterior forms, and when, as if I had stripped it of its vestments, I consider it quite naked, it is certain, although some error may still be found in my judgment, that I cannot, nevertheless, thus apprehend it without possessing a human mind.

But finally, what shall I say of the mind itself, that is, of myself? for as yet I do not admit that I am anything but mind. What, then! I who seem to possess so distinct an apprehension of the piece of wax, do I not know myself, both with greater truth and certitude, and also much more distinctly and clearly? For if I judge that the wax exists because I see it, it assuredly follows, much more evidently, that I myself am or exist, for the same reason: for it is possible that what I see may not in truth be wax, and that I do not even possess eyes with which to see anything; but it cannot be that when I see, or, which comes to the same thing, when I think I see, I myself who think am nothing. So likewise, if I judge that the wax exists because I touch it, it will still also follow that I am; and if I determine that my imagination, or any other cause, whatever it be, persuades me of the existence of the wax, I will still draw the same conclusion. And what is here remarked of the piece of wax, is applicable to all the other things that are external to me. And further, if the [notion or] perception of wax appeared to me more precise and distinct, after that not only sight and touch, but many other causes besides, rendered it manifest to my apprehension, with how much greater distinctness must I now know myself, since all the reasons that contribute to the knowledge of the nature of wax, or of any body whatever, manifest still better the nature of my mind? And there are besides so many other things in the mind itself that contribute to the illustration of its nature, that those dependent on the body, to which I have here referred, scarcely merit to be taken into account.

But, in conclusion, I find I have insensibly reverted to the point I desired; for, since it is now manifest to me that bodies themselves are not properly perceived by the senses nor by the faculty of imagination, but by the intellect alone; and since they are not perceived because they are seen and touched, but only because they are understood [or rightly comprehended by thought], I readily discover that there is nothing more easily or clearly apprehended than my own mind. But because it is difficult to rid one's self so promptly of an opinion to which one has been long accustomed, it will be desirable to tarry for some time at this stage, that, by long continued meditation, I may more deeply impress upon my memory this new knowledge.

• • •

Meditation VI.
Of the Existence of Material Things, and of the Real Distinction between the Mind and Body of Man.

There now only remains the inquiry as to whether material things exist. With regard to this question, I at least know with certainty that such things may exist, in as far as they constitute the object of the pure mathematics, since, regarding them in this aspect, I can conceive them clearly and distinctly. For there can be no doubt that God possesses the power of producing all the objects I am able distinctly to conceive, and I never considered anything impossible to him, unless when I experienced a contradiction in the attempt to conceive it aright. Further, the faculty of imagination which I possess, and of which I am conscious that I make use when I apply myself to the consideration of material things, is sufficient to persuade me of their existence: for, when I attentively consider what imagination is, I find that it is simply a certain application of the cognitive faculty (*facultas cognoscitiva*) to a body which is immediately present to it, and which therefore exists.

And to render this quite clear, I remark, in the first place, the difference that subsists between imagination and pure intellection [or conception]. For example, when I imagine a triangle I not only conceive (*intelligo*) that it is a figure comprehended by three lines, but at the same time also I look upon (*intueor*) these three lines as present by the power and internal application of my mind (*acie mentis*), and this is what I call imagining. But if I desire to think of a chiliogon, I indeed rightly conceive that it is a figure composed of a thousand

sides, as easily as I conceive that a triangle is a figure composed of only three sides; but I cannot imagine the thousand sides of a chiliogon as I do the three sides of a triangle, nor, so to speak, view them as present [with the eyes of my mind]. And although, in accordance with the habit I have of always imagining something when I think of corporeal things, it may happen that, in conceiving a chiliogon, I confusedly represent some figure to myself, yet it is quite evident that this is not a chiliogon, since it in no wise differs from that which I would represent to myself, if I were to think of a myriogon, or any other figure of many sides; nor would this representation be of any use in discovering and unfolding the properties that constitute the difference between a chiliogon and other polygons. But if the question turns on a pentagon, it is quite true that I can conceive its figure, as well as that of a chiliogon, without the aid of imagination; but I can likewise imagine it by applying the attention of my mind to its five sides, and at the same time to the area which they contain. Thus I observe that a special effort of mind is necessary to the act of imagination, which is not required to conceiving or understanding (*ad intelligendum*); and this special exertion of mind clearly shows the difference between imagination and pure intellection (*imaginatio et intellectio pura*). I remark, besides, that this power of imagination which I possess, in as far as it differs from the power of conceiving, is in no way necessary to my [nature or] essence, that is, to the essence of my mind; for although I did not possess it, I should still remain the same that I now am, from which it seems we may conclude that it depends on something different from the mind. And I easily understand that, if some body exists, with which my mind is so conjoined and united as to be able, as it were, to consider it when it chooses, it may thus imagine corporeal objects; so that this mode of thinking differs from pure intellection only in this respect, that the mind in conceiving turns in some way upon itself, and considers some one of the ideas it possesses within itself; but in imagining it turns toward the body, and contemplates in it some object conformed to the idea which it either of itself conceived or apprehended by sense. I easily understand, I say, that imagination may be thus formed, if it is true that there are bodies; and because I find no other obvious mode of explaining it, I thence, with probability, conjecture that they exist, but only with probability; and although I carefully examine all things, nevertheless I do not find that, from the distinct idea of corporeal nature I have in my imagination, I can necessarily infer the existence of any body.

But I am accustomed to imagine many other objects besides that corporeal nature which is the object of the pure mathematics, as, for example, colors, sounds, tastes, pain, and the like, although with less distinctness; and, inasmuch as I perceive these objects much better by the senses, through the medium of which and of memory, they seem to have reached the imagination, I believe that, in order the more advantageously to examine them, it is proper I should at the same time examine what sense-perception is, and inquire whether from those ideas that are apprehended by this mode of thinking (consciousness), I cannot obtain a certain proof of the existence of corporeal objects.

And, in the first place, I will recall to my mind the things I have hitherto held as true, because perceived by the senses, and the foundations upon which my belief in their truth rested; I will, in the second place, examine the reasons that afterward constrained me to doubt of them; and, finally, I will consider what of them I ought now to believe.

Firstly, then, I perceived that I had a head, hands, feet and other members composing that body which I considered as part, or perhaps even as the whole, of myself. I perceived further, that that body was placed among many others, by which it was capable of being affected in diverse ways, both beneficial and hurtful; and what was beneficial I remarked by a certain sensation of pleasure, and what was hurtful by a sensation of pain. And besides this pleasure and pain, I was likewise conscious of hunger, thirst, and other appetites, as well as certain corporeal inclinations toward joy, sadness, anger, and similar passions. And, out of myself, besides the extension, figure, and motions of bodies, I likewise perceived in them hardness, heat, and the other tactile qualities, and, in addition, light, colors, odors, tastes, and sounds, the variety of which gave me the means of distinguishing the sky, the earth, the sea, and generally all the other bodies, from one another. And certainly, considering the ideas of all these qualities, which were presented to my mind,

and which alone I properly and immediately perceived, it was not without reason that I thought I perceived certain objects wholly different from my thought, namely, bodies from which those ideas proceeded; for I was conscious that the ideas were presented to me without my consent being required, so that I could not perceive any object, however desirous I might be, unless it were present to the organ of sense; and it was wholly out of my power not to perceive it when it was thus present. And because the ideas I perceived by the senses were much more lively and clear, and even, in their own way, more distinct than any of those I could of myself frame by meditation, or which I found impressed on my memory, it seemed that they could not have proceeded from myself, and must therefore have been caused in me by some other objects; and as of those objects I had no knowledge beyond what the ideas themselves gave me, nothing was so likely to occur to my mind as the supposition that the objects were similar to the ideas which they caused. And because I recollected also that I had formerly trusted to the senses, rather than to reason, and that the ideas which I myself formed were not so clear as those I perceived by sense, and that they were even for the most part composed of parts of the latter, I was readily persuaded that I had no idea in my intellect which had not formerly passed through the senses. Nor was I altogether wrong in likewise believing that that body which, by a special right, I called my own, pertained to me more properly and strictly than any of the others; for in truth, I could never be separated from it as from other bodies; I felt in it and on account of it all my appetites and affections, and in fine I was affected in its parts by pain and the titillation of pleasure, and not in the parts of the other bodies that were separated from it. But when I inquired into the reason why, from this I know not what sensation of pain, sadness of mind should follow, and why from the sensation of pleasure, joy should arise, or why this indescribable twitching of the stomach, which I call hunger, should put me in mind of taking food, and the parchedness of the throat of drink, and so in other cases, I was unable to give any explanation, unless that I was so taught by nature; for there is assuredly no affinity, at least none that I am able to comprehend, between this irritation of the stomach and the desire of food, any more than between the perception of an object that causes pain and the consciousness of sadness which springs from the perception. And in the same way it seemed to me that all the other judgments I had formed regarding the objects of sense, were dictates of nature; because I remarked that those judgments were formed in me, before I had leisure to weigh and consider the reasons that might constrain me to form them.

But, afterward, a wide experience by degrees sapped the faith I had reposed in my senses; for I frequently observed that towers, which at a distance seemed round, appeared square, when more closely viewed, and that colossal figures, raised on the summits of these towers, looked like small statues, when viewed from the bottom of them; and, in other instances without number, I also discovered error in judgments founded on the external senses; and not only in those founded on the external, but even in those that rested on the internal senses; for is there aught more internal than pain? And yet I have sometimes been informed by parties whose arm or leg had been amputated, that they still occasionally seemed to feel pain in that part of the body which they had lost,—a circumstance that led me to think that I could not be quite certain even that any one of my members was affected when I felt pain in it. And to these grounds of doubt I shortly afterward also added two others of very wide generality: the first of them was that I believed I never perceived anything when awake which I could not occasionally think I also perceived when asleep, and as I do not believe that the ideas I seem to perceive in my sleep proceed from objects external to me, I did not any more observe any ground for believing this of such as I seem to perceive when awake; the second was that since I was as yet ignorant of the author of my being or at least supposed myself to be so, I saw nothing to prevent my having been so constituted by nature as that I should be deceived even in matters that appeared to me to possess the greatest truth. And, with respect to the grounds on which I had before been persuaded of the existence of sensible objects, I had no great difficulty in finding suitable answers to them; for as nature seemed to incline me to many things from which reason made me averse, I thought that I ought not to confide much in its teachings. And although the perceptions of the senses were not dependent on my will, I did not think that I ought on that ground to conclude that they proceeded from things different from myself, since perhaps there might be found in me some faculty, though hitherto unknown to me, which produced them.

But now that I begin to know myself better, and to discover more clearly the author of my being, I do not, indeed, think that I ought rashly to admit all which the senses seem to teach, nor, on the other hand, is it my conviction that I ought to doubt in general of their teachings.

And, firstly, because I know that all which I clearly and distinctly conceive can be produced by God exactly as I conceive it, it is sufficient that I am able clearly and distinctly to conceive one thing apart from another, in order to be certain that the one is different from the other, seeing they may at least be made to exist separately, by the omnipotence of God; and it matters not by what power this separation is made, in order to be compelled to judge them different; and, therefore, merely because I know with certitude that I exist, and because, in the meantime, I do not observe that aught necessarily belongs to my nature or essence beyond my being a thinking thing, I rightly conclude that my essence consists only in my being a thinking thing [or a substance whose whole essence or nature is merely thinking]. And although I may, or rather, as I will shortly say, although I certainly do possess a body with which I am very closely conjoined; nevertheless, because, on the one hand, I have a clear and distinct idea of myself, in as far as I am only a thinking and unextended thing, and as, on the other hand, I possess a distinct idea of body, in as far as it is only an extended and unthinking thing, it is certain that I, [that is, my mind, by which I am what I am], is entirely and truly distinct from my body, and may exist without it.

Moreover, I find in myself diverse faculties of thinking that have each their special mode: for example, I find I possess the faculties of imagining and perceiving, without which I can indeed clearly and distinctly conceive myself as entire, but I cannot reciprocally conceive them without conceiving myself, that is to say, without an intelligent substance in which they reside, for [in the notion we have of them, or to use the terms of the schools] in their formal concept, they comprise some sort of intellection; whence I perceive that they are distinct from myself as modes are from things. I remark likewise certain other faculties, as the power of changing place, of assuming diverse figures, and the like, that cannot be conceived and cannot therefore exist, any more than the preceding, apart from a substance in which they inhere. It is very evident, however, that these faculties, if they really exist, must belong to some corporeal or extended substance, since in their clear and distinct concept there is contained some sort of extension, but no intellection at all. Further, I cannot doubt but that there is in me a certain passive faculty of perception, that is, of receiving and taking knowledge of the ideas of sensible things; but this would be useless to me, if there did not also exist in me, or in some other thing, another active faculty capable of forming and producing those ideas. But this active faculty cannot be in me [in as far as I am but a thinking thing], seeing that it does not presuppose thought, and also that those ideas are frequently produced in my mind without my contributing to it in any way, and even frequently contrary to my will. This faculty must therefore exist in some substance different from me, in which all the objective reality of the ideas that are produced by this faculty is contained formally or eminently, as I before remarked; and this substance is either a body, that is to say, a corporeal nature in which is contained formally [and in effect] all that is objectively [and by representation] in those ideas; or it is God himself, or some other creature, of a rank superior to body, in which the same is contained eminently. But as God is no deceiver, it is manifest that he does not of himself and immediately communicate those ideas to me, nor even by the intervention of any creature in which their objective reality is not formally, but only eminently, contained. For as he has given me no faculty whereby I can discover this to be the case, but, on the contrary, a very strong inclination to believe that those ideas arise from corporeal objects, I do not see how he could be vindicated from the charge of deceit, if in truth they proceeded from any other source, or were produced by other causes than corporeal things: and accordingly it must be concluded, that corporeal objects exist. Nevertheless, they are not perhaps exactly such as we perceive by the senses, for their comprehension by the senses is, in many instances, very obscure and confused; but it is at least necessary to admit that all which I clearly and distinctly conceive as in them, that is, generally speaking all that is comprehended in the object of speculative geometry, really exists external to me.

But with respect to other things which are either only particular, as, for example, that the sun is of such a size and figure, etc., or are conceived with less clearness and distinctness, as light, sound, pain, and the like, although they are highly dubious and uncertain, nevertheless on the ground alone that God is no deceiver, and that consequently he has permitted no falsity in my opinions which he has not likewise given me a faculty of correcting, I think I may with safety conclude that I possess in myself the means of arriving at the truth. And, in the first place, it cannot be doubted that in each of the dictates of nature there is some truth: for by nature, considered in general, I now understand nothing more than God himself, or the order and disposition established by God in created things; and by my nature in particular I understand the assemblage of all that God has given me.

But there is nothing which that nature teaches me more expressly [or more sensibly] than that I have a body which is ill affected when I feel pain, and stands in need of food and drink when I experience the sensations of hunger and thirst, etc. And therefore I ought not to doubt but that there is some truth in these informations.

Nature likewise teaches me by these sensations of pain, hunger, thirst, etc., that I am not only lodged in my body as a pilot in a vessel, but that I am besides so intimately conjoined, and as it were intermixed with it, that my mind and body compose a certain unity. For if this were not the case, I should not feel pain when my body is hurt, seeing I am merely a thinking thing, but should perceive the wound by the understanding alone, just as a pilot perceives by sight when any part of his vessel is damaged; and when my body has need of food or drink, I should have a clear knowledge of this, and not be made aware of it by the confused sensations of hunger and thirst: for, in truth, all these sensations of hunger, thirst, pain, etc., are nothing more than certain confused modes of thinking, arising from the union and apparent fusion of mind and body.

Besides this, nature teaches me that my own body is surrounded by many other bodies, some of which I have to seek after, and others to shun. And indeed, as I perceive different sorts of colors, sounds, odors, tastes, heat, hardness, etc., I safely conclude that there are in the bodies from which the diverse perceptions of the senses proceed, certain varieties corresponding to them, although, perhaps, not in reality like them; and since, among these diverse perceptions of the senses, some are agreeable, and others disagreeable, there can be no doubt that my body, or rather my entire self, in as far as I am composed of body and mind, may be variously affected, both beneficially and hurtfully, by surrounding bodies.

But there are many other beliefs which though seemingly the teaching of nature, are not in reality so, but which obtained a place in my mind through a habit of judging inconsiderately of things. It may thus easily happen that such judgments shall contain error: thus, for example, the opinion I have that all space in which there is nothing to affect [or make an impression on] my senses is void: that in a hot body there is something in every respect similar to the idea of heat in my mind; that in a white or green body there is the same whiteness or greenness which I perceive; that in a bitter or sweet body there is the same taste, and so in other instances; that the stars, towers, and all distant bodies, are of the same size and figure as they appear to our eyes, etc. But that I may avoid everything like indistinctness of conception, I must accurately define what I properly understand by being taught by nature. For nature is here taken in a narrower sense than when it signifies the sum of all the things which God has given me; seeing that in that meaning the notion comprehends much that belongs only to the mind [to which I am not here to be understood as referring when I use the term nature]; as, for example, the notion I have of the truth, that what is done cannot be undone, and all the other truths I discern by the natural light [without the aid of the body]; and seeing that it comprehends likewise much besides that belongs only to body, and is not here any more contained under the name nature, as the quality of heaviness, and the like, of which I do not speak, the term being reserved exclusively to designate the things which God has given to me as a being composed of mind and body. But nature, taking the term in the sense explained, teaches me to shun what causes in me the sensation of pain,

and to pursue what affords me the sensation of pleasure, and other things of this sort; but I do not discover that it teaches me, in addition to this, from these diverse perceptions of the senses, to draw any conclusions respecting external objects without a previous [careful and mature] consideration of them by the mind: for it is, as appears to me, the office of the mind alone, and not of the composite whole of mind and body, to discern the truth in those matters. Thus, although the impression a star makes on my eye is not larger than that from the flame of a candle, I do not, nevertheless, experience any real or positive impulse determining me to believe that the star is not greater than the flame; the true account of the matter being merely that I have so judged from my youth without any rational ground. And, though on approaching the fire I feel heat, and even pain on approaching it too closely, I have, however, from this no ground for holding that something resembling the heat I feel is in the fire, any more than that there is something similar to the pain; all that I have ground for believing is, that there is something in it, whatever it may be, which excites in me those sensations of heat or pain. So also, although there are spaces in which I find nothing to excite and affect my senses, I must not therefore conclude that those spaces contain in them no body; for I see that in this, as in many other similar matters, I have been accustomed to pervert the order of nature, because these perceptions of the senses, although given me by nature merely to signify to my mind what things are beneficial and hurtful to the composite whole of which it is a part, and being sufficiently clear and distinct for that purpose, are nevertheless used by me as infallible rules by which to determine immediately the essence of the bodies that exist out of me, of which they can of course afford me only the most obscure and confused knowledge.

But I have already sufficiently considered how it happens that, notwithstanding the supreme goodness of God, there is falsity in my judgments. A difficulty, however, here presents itself, respecting the things which I am taught by nature must be pursued or avoided, and also respecting the internal sensations in which I seem to have occasionally detected error, [and thus to be directly deceived by nature]: thus, for example, I may be so deceived by the agreeable taste of some viand with which poison has been mixed, as to be induced to take the poison. In this case, however, nature may be excused, for it simply leads me to desire the viand for its agreeable taste, and not the poison, which is unknown to it; and thus we can infer nothing from this circumstance beyond that our nature is not omniscient; at which there is assuredly no ground for surprise, since, man being of a finite nature, his knowledge must likewise be of a limited perfection. But we also not unfrequently err in that to which we are directly impelled by nature, as is the case with invalids who desire drink or food that would be hurtful to them. It will here, perhaps, be alleged that the reason why such persons are deceived is that their nature is corrupted; but this leaves the difficulty untouched, for a sick man is not less really the creature of God than a man who is in full health; and therefore it is as repugnant to the goodness of God that the nature of the former should be deceitful as it is for that of the latter to be so. And as a clock, composed of wheels and counter weights, observes not the less accurately all the laws of nature when it is ill made, and points out the hours incorrectly, than when it satisfies the desire of the maker in every respect; so likewise if the body of man be considered as a kind of machine, so made up and composed of bones, nerves, muscles, veins, blood, and skin, that although there were in it no mind, it would still exhibit the same motions which it at present manifests involuntarily, and therefore without the aid of the mind, [and simply by the dispositions of its organs], I easily discern that it would also be as natural for such a body, supposing it dropsical, for example, to experience the parchedness of the throat that is usually accompanied in the mind by the sensation of thirst, and to be disposed by this parchedness to move its nerves and its other parts in the way required for drinking, and thus increase its malady and do itself harm, as it is natural for it, when it is not indisposed to be stimulated to drink for its good by a similar cause; and although looking to the use for which a clock was destined by its maker, I may say that it is deflected from its proper nature when it incorrectly indicates the hours, and on the same principle, considering the machine of the human body as having been formed by God for the sake of the motions which it usually manifests, although I may likewise have ground for

thinking that it does not follow the order of its nature when the throat is parched and drink does not tend to its preservation, nevertheless I yet plainly discern that this latter acceptation of the term nature is very different from the other: for this is nothing more than a certain denomination, depending entirely on my thought, and hence called extrinsic, by which I compare a sick man and an imperfectly constructed clock with the idea I have of a man in good health and a well made clock; while by the other acceptation of nature is understood something which is truly found in things, and therefore possessed of some truth.

But certainly, although in respect of a dropsical body, it is only by way of exterior denomination that we say its nature is corrupted, when, without requiring drink, the throat is parched; yet, in respect of the composite whole, that is, of the mind in its union with the body, it is not a pure denomination, but really an error of nature, for it to feel thirst when drink would be hurtful to it: and, accordingly, it still remains to be considered why it is that the goodness of God does not prevent the nature of man thus taken from being fallacious.

To commence this examination accordingly, I here remark, in the first place, that there is a vast difference between mind and body, in respect that body, from its nature, is always divisible, and that mind is entirely indivisible. For in truth, when I consider the mind, that is, when I consider myself in so far only as I am a thinking thing, I can distinguish in myself no parts, but I very clearly discern that I am somewhat absolutely one and entire; and although the whole mind seems to be united to the whole body, yet, when a foot, an arm, or any other part is cut off, I am conscious that nothing has been taken from my mind; nor can the faculties of willing, perceiving, conceiving, etc., properly be called its parts, for it is the same mind that is exercised [all entire] in willing, in perceiving, and in conceiving, etc. But quite the opposite holds in corporeal or extended things; for I cannot imagine any one of them [how small soever it may be], which I cannot easily sunder in thought, and which, therefore, I do not know to be divisible. This would be sufficient to teach me that the mind or soul of man is entirely different from the body, if I had not already been apprised of it on other grounds.

I remark, in the next place, that the mind does not immediately receive the impression from all the parts of the body, but only from the brain, or perhaps even from one small part of it, viz, that in which the common sense (*senses communis*) is said to be, which as often as it is affected in the same way gives rise to the same perception in the mind, although meanwhile the other parts of the body may be diversely disposed, as is proved by innumerable experiments, which it is unnecessary here to enumerate.

I remark, besides, that the nature of body is such that none of its parts can be moved by another part a little removed from the other, which cannot likewise be moved in the same way by any one of the parts that lie between those two, although the most remote part does not act at all. As, for example, in the cord A, B, C, D [which is in tension], if its last part D, be pulled, the first part A, will not be moved in a different way than it would be were one of the intermediate parts B or C to be pulled, and the last part D meanwhile to remain fixed. And in the same way, when I feel pain in the foot, the science of physics teaches me that this sensation is experienced by means of the nerves dispersed over the foot, which, extending like cords from it to the brain, when they are contracted in the foot, contract at the same time the inmost parts of the brain in which they have their origin, and excite in these parts a certain motion appointed by nature to cause in the mind a sensation of pain, as if existing in the foot; but as these nerves must pass through the tibia, the leg, the loins, the back, and neck, in order to reach the brain, it may happen that although their extremities in the foot are not affected, but only certain of their parts that pass through the loins or neck, the same movements, nevertheless, are excited in the brain by this motion as would have been caused there by a hurt received in the foot, and hence the mind will necessarily feel pain in the foot, just as if it had been hurt; and the same is true of all the other perceptions of our senses.

I remark, finally, that as each of the movements that are made in the part of the brain by which the mind is immediately affected, impresses it with but a single sensation, the most likely supposition in the circumstances is, that this movement causes the mind to experience, among all the sensations which it is capable of impressing upon it; that one which is the best fitted, and generally the most useful for the preservation of the human body when it is in full health. But experience shows us that all the perceptions which nature has given us are of such a kind as I have mentioned; and accordingly, there is nothing found in them that does not manifest the power and goodness of God. Thus, for example, when the nerves of the foot are violently or more than usually shaken, the motion passing through the medulla of the spine to the innermost parts of the brain affords a sign to the mind on which it experiences a sensation viz., of pain, as if it were in the foot, by which the mind is admonished and excited to do its utmost to remove the cause of it as dangerous and hurtful to the foot. It is true that God could have so constituted the nature of man as that the same motion in the brain would have informed the mind of something altogether different: the motion might, for example, have been the occasion on which the mind became conscious of itself, in so far as it is in the brain, or in so far as it is in some place intermediate between the foot and the brain, or, finally, the occasion on which it perceived some other object quite different, whatever that might be; but nothing of all this would have so well contributed to the preservation of the body as that which the mind actually feels. In the same way, when we stand in need of drink, there arises from this want a certain parchedness in the throat that moves its nerves, and by means of them the internal parts of the brain; and this movement affects the mind with the sensation of thirst, because there is nothing on that occasion which is more useful for us than to be made aware that we have need of drink for the preservation of our health; and so in other instances.

Whence it is quite manifest that, notwithstanding the sovereign goodness of God, the nature of man, in so far as it is composed of mind and body, cannot but be sometimes fallacious. For, if there is any cause which excites, not in the foot, but in some one of the parts of the nerves that stretch from the foot to the brain, or even in the brain itself, the same movement that is ordinarily created when the foot is ill affected, pain will be felt, as it were, in the foot, and the sense will thus be naturally deceived; for as the same movement in the brain can but impress the mind with the same sensation, and as this sensation is much more frequently excited by a cause which hurts the foot than by one acting in a different quarter, it is reasonable that it should lead the mind to feel pain in the foot rather than in any other part of the body. And if it sometimes happens that the parchedness of the throat does not arise, as is usual, from drink being necessary for the health of the body, but from quite the opposite cause, as is the case with the dropsical, yet it is much better that it should be deceitful in that instance, than if, on the contrary, it were continually fallacious when the body is well-disposed; and the same holds true in other cases.

And certainly this consideration is of great service, not only in enabling me to recognize the errors to which my nature is liable, but likewise in rendering it more easy to avoid or correct them: for, knowing that all my senses more usually indicate to me what is true than what is false, in matters relating to the advantage of the body, and being able almost always to make use of more than a single sense in examining the same object, and besides this, being able to use my memory in connecting present with past knowledge, and my understanding which has already discovered all the causes of my errors, I ought no longer to fear that falsity may be met with in what is daily presented to me by the senses. And I ought to reject all the doubts of those bygone days, as hyperbolical and ridiculous, especially the general uncertainty respecting sleep, which I could not distinguish from the waking state: for I now find a very marked difference between the two states, in respect that our memory can never connect our dreams with each other and with the course of life, in the way it is in the habit of doing with events that occur when we are awake. And, in truth, if some one, when I am awake, appeared to me all of a sudden and as suddenly disappeared, as do the images I see in sleep, so that I could not observe either whence he came or whither he went, I should not without reason esteem it either a specter or phantom formed in my brain, rather than a real man. But when I perceive objects with regard to which I can distinctly determine both the place whence they come, and that in which they are, and the time at which they appear to me, and when, without interruption, I can connect the perception I have of them with the whole of the other parts of my life, I am perfectly sure that what I thus perceive occurs while I am awake and not during sleep. And I ought not in the least degree to doubt of the truth of these presentations, if, after having called together all my senses, my memory, and my understanding for the purpose of examining them, no deliverance is given by any one of these faculties which is repugnant to that of any other: for since God is no deceiver, it necessarily follows that I am not herein deceived. But because the necessities of action frequently oblige us to come to a determination before we have had leisure for so careful an examination, it must be confessed that the life of man is frequently obnoxious to error with respect to individual objects; and we must, in conclusion, acknowledge the weakness of our nature.

25. *The Distinction between Mental and Physical Phenomena*

FRANZ BRENTANO

Descartes's confidence that ideas (that is, what is in the mind) can yield knowledge of reality beyond the mind was challenged by empiricists like Berkeley and Hume. Berkeley argued that the idea of matter as something existing independently of mind was incoherent, and he concluded that reality was entirely mental or mind-dependent (metaphysical idealism). Hume felt only sensory ideas (sense impressions) could provide knowledge about what exists, but he argued that these ideas could not adequately support beliefs about matter, causality, or even enduring minds (see Hume's essays in Part II and Part V). Thus, Hume advocated metaphysical skepticism. Yet, whether they were idealists, empiricists, or skeptics, eighteenth- and nineteenth-century philosophers tended to adopt Descartes' starting point: what is indubitable is something mental given in present consciousness. Compared to the phenomena of experience, concepts of matter remained philosophically problematic throughout the nineteenth century: Mill tried to construct things out of sensations, and Bergson and James tried to construct them out of the stream of experience (see Bergson's essay in Part I).

Franz Brentano (1838–1917) was a German philosopher and psychologist who taught at the University of Vienna. He believed psychologists and philosophers had become muddled in their talk about what is mental and what is physical. He attempted to clarify matters by rejecting part of Descartes's legacy: the assumption that consciousness is always just an inspection of mental entities (ideas, images, or sensations). It is this view that risks turning all phenomena into mental phenomena. As an alternative, Brentano recommends that we identify the mental as the "acts" that are "directed upon" (or about) objects (or, using Scholastic terminology, the mental is what can have "intentionally inexistent objects"). This characteristic of "mental acts" (like wanting a million dollars or believing in Santa Claus) later came to be called their "intentionality." (Note that "intentionality" in this sense is a technical term that should not be confused with "intentionally," or doing something purposely.)

Brentano's work has been influential and has led philosophers to debate the correct metaphysical analysis of mental acts and their objects. Through his student, Husserl, it helped spawn Phenomenology (the philosophical movement that recommends "reflection" on mental acts as a means to knowledge of the necessary structure of experience). And in claiming nothing physical is characterized by intentionality, it has challenged twentieth-century philosophers who want to show that the mind is, at bottom, something physical.

1.

The data of our consciousness make up a world which, taken in its entirety, falls into two great classes, the class of *physical* and the class of *mental* phenomena. . . .

The fact that neither unity nor complete clarity has yet been achieved regarding the line of demarcation between the two areas seems to make this all the more necessary. We have already had occasion to see how physical phenomena which appear in the imagination have been taken to be mental. But

From *Introduction to the Philosophy of Mind*, edited by Harold Morick, trans. D. Terrell (New York: Scott, Foresman and Company, 1970). Reprinted by permission of Humanities Press International, Inc., Atlantic Highlands, NJ.

there are many other cases of confusion as well. Even psychologists of considerable importance may find it difficult to vindicate themselves against the charge of self-contradiction. We occasionally encounter such assertions as that sensation and imagination are differentiated by the fact that one occurs as the result of a physical phenomenon, while the other is evoked, according to the laws of association, by means of a mental phenomenon. But along with this the same psychologists admit that what appears in sensation does not correspond to its efficient cause. Accordingly, it turns out that what they call physical phenomena never appear to us in actual fact, and that we have no presentation of them whatsoever; surely this is a strange way in which to misuse the term "phenomenon"! When affairs are in such a state, we can not refrain from taking a somewhat closer look at the problem.

2.

. . . Our object is the elucidation of the two terms: physical phenomenon—mental phenomenon. We wish to exclude misunderstanding and confusion in connection with them. And for this we needn't be concerned about the means used, if only they really serve to produce clarity.

Giving more general, superordinate definitions is not the only useful means that can be employed for such an end. Just as induction is contrasted with deduction in the sphere of demonstration, here definition by way of the specific, i.e., by way of an example, is contrasted with definition by means of the more general. And the former method will be more appropriate as long as the particular term is more intelligible than the general. Hence, it may be a more effective procedure to define the term "color" by saying that it designates the general class for red, blue, green, and yellow, than to choose to give an account of red—following the opposite procedure—as a particular species of color. Definition by way of particular cases will perform still more useful service in connection with terms, such as those involved in our case, which are not at all common in ordinary life, while the names of the particular phenomena comprehended under them are familiar enough. So let us start with an attempt to make our concepts clear by way of examples.

Every presentation (*Vorstellung*) of sensation or imagination offers an example of the mental phenomenon; and here I understand by presentation not that which is presented, but the act of presentation. Thus, hearing a sound, seeing a colored object, sensing warm or cold, and the comparable states of imagination as well, are examples of what I mean; but thinking of a general concept, provided such a thing does actually occur, is equally so. Furthermore, every judgment, every recollection, every expectation, every inference, every conviction or opinion, every doubt, is a mental phenomenon. And again, every emotion, joy, sorrow, fear, hope, pride, despair, anger, love, hate, desire, choice, intention, astonishment, wonder, contempt, etc., is such a phenomenon.

Examples of physical phenomena, on the other hand, are a color, a shape, a landscape, which I see; a musical chord, which I hear; heat, cold, odor, which I sense; as well as comparable images, which appear to me in my imagination.

These examples may suffice as concrete illustrations of the distinction between the two classes.

3.

Nevertheless, we will attempt to give a definition of the mental phenomenon in another, more unified way. For this, there is available a definition we have used before, when we said that by the term, mental phenomena, we designate presentations and, likewise, all those phenomena which are based on presentations. It scarcely requires notice that, once again, by presentation we understand here not what is presented but the presenting of it. This presentation forms the basis not merely of judgments, but also of desires, as well as of every other mental act. We cannot judge of anything, cannot desire anything, cannot hope for anything, or fear anything, if it is not presented. Hence, the definition which we gave embraces all of the examples just introduced and, in general, all of the phenomena belonging to this domain.

It is a sign of the immature state in which psychology finds itself that one can scarcely utter a single sentence about mental phenomena which would not be disputed by many. Still, the great majority agree with what we just said; presentations are the basis for the other mental phenomena. Thus, Herbart is quite correct in saying: "In every case of emotion, something, no matter how diversified and complicated, must be in consciousness as something presented; so that this particular presentation is included in this particular feeling. And every time we have a desire . . . [we] also have in our thoughts that which we desire." As we use the word "to present," "to be presented" comes to the same thing as "to appear." . . . Still, we may surely find that, as regards some kinds of sensual feelings of pleasure and displeasure, [some] actually hold the opinion that there is no presentation, even in our sense, on which they are based. We cannot deny a certain temptation in that direction, at least. This holds, for example, in regard to feelings which are caused by a cut or a burn. If someone is cut, then for the most part he has no further perception of touch; if he is burned, no further perception of heat; but pain alone seems to be present in the one case and the other.

Nonetheless, there is no doubt that even here the feeling is based on a presentation. In such cases we always have the presentation of a definite spatial location, which we ordinarily specify in relation to one or the other of the visible and palpable parts of our body. We say that our foot hurts, or our hand hurts, this or the other place on our body is in pain. In the first place, then, those who look on such a spatial presentation as something originally given by means of the neural stimulation itself will therefore be unable to deny that a presentation is the basis of this feeling. But others, too, cannot avoid making the same assumption. For we have within us not merely the presentation of a definite spatial location, but also that of a particular sensory quality, analogous to color, sound, and other so-called sensory qualities, a quality which belongs among the physical phenomena and which is definitely to be distinguished from the accompanying feeling. If we hear a pleasant, mild sound or a shrill one, a harmonious chord or a discord, it will occur to no one to identify the sound with the accompanying feeling of pleasure or pain. But, likewise, when a cut, a burn, or a tickle arouses a feeling of pain or pleasure in us, we must maintain in a similar manner the distinction between a physical phenomenon, which enters in as the object of outer perception, and a mental phenomenon of feeling, which accompanies its appearance, even though the superficial observer is rather inclined to confusion here. . . .

A further basis of the illusion is that the quality on which the feeling ensues, and the feeling itself, do not bear two distinct names. We call the physical phenomenon, which occurs along with the feeling of pain, itself pain in this case. We do not say that this or that phenomenon in the foot is experienced with pain so much as we say that pain is experienced in the foot. To be sure, this is an equivocation such as we find elsewhere, whenever things stand in a close relationship to each other. We call the body healthy, and in connection with it, the air, food, facial color, and so on, but plainly in different senses. In our case, a physical phenomenon itself is called pleasure or pain, after the feeling of pleasure or pain which accompanies its appearance, and here too the sense is modified. It is as if we should say of a harmonious sound that

it is a pleasure to us, because we experience a feeling of pleasure on its occurrence; or that the loss of a friend is a great sorrow to us. Experience shows that equivocation is one of the foremost hindrances to our knowledge of distinctions. It must necessarily be very much so here, where a danger of being deluded exists in and of itself, and the transference of the term was perhaps itself the result of a confusion. Hence, many psychologists were deceived, and further errors were tied up with this one. Many arrived at the false conclusion that the experiencing subject must be present at the place of the injured limb in which a painful phenomenon is localized in perception. For, insofar as they identified the phenomenon with the accompanying feeling of pain, they regarded it as a mental, not as a physical, phenomenon. And for just that reason, they believed its perception in the limb to be an inner, and consequently, an evident and infallible perception. But their opinion is contradicted by the fact that the same phenomena often appear in the same way after the limb has been amputated. Others accordingly argued rather to the opposite effect, skeptically opposing the self-evidence (*Evidenz*) of inner perception. This is all resolved, if one has learned to distinguish between the pain in the sense in which the term designates the apparent property of a part of our body and the feeling of pain which is tied up with sensing it. But if one has done this, then one is no longer inclined to hold that the feeling of sensory pain which one experiences on being injured is not based on any presentation.

We may, accordingly, regard it as an indubitably correct definition of mental phenomena that they are either presentations or (in the sense which has been explained) rest on presentations as their basis. In this we would thus have a second definition of the concept [of mental phenomena] which breaks down into fewer terms. Yet it is not entirely unified, since it presents mental phenomena as divided into two groups.

4.

The attempt has been made to give a perfectly unified definition which distinguishes all of the mental phenomena, as contrasted with the physical, by means of negation. All physical phenomena, it is said, manifest extension and definite spatial location, whether they are appearances to sight or another sense, or products of the imagination, which presents similar objects to us. The opposite, however, is true of mental phenomena; thinking, willing, and so on appear as unextended and without a situation in space.

According to this view, we would be in a position to characterize the physical phenomena easily and rigorously in contrast to the mental, if we were to say that they are those which appear extended and spatial. And, with the same exactitude, the mental phenomena would then be definable, as contrasted with the physical, as those which exhibit no extension or definite spatial location. One could call on Descartes and Spinoza in support of such a differentiation, but particularly on Kant, who declares space to be the form of intuition of outer sensation. . . .

But here, too, unanimity does not prevail among the psychologists, and for diverse reasons we often hear it denied that extension and the absence of extension are differentiating characteristics distinguishing physical and mental phenomena.

Many believe that the definition is false because not only mental, but also many physical phenomena, appear without extension. Thus, a large number of not unimportant psychologists teach that the phenomena of certain senses, or even of the senses in general, originally manifest themselves free of all extension and definite spatial character. This is very generally believed [to be true] of sounds and of the phenomena of smell. According to Berkeley, the same holds true of colors, and according to Platner, of the phenomena of the sense of touch. . . .

Others, as I have said, will reject the definition for contrary reasons. It is not so much the claim that all physical phenomena appear extended that arouses their opposition. It is the claim, rather, that all mental phenomena lack extension; according to them, certain mental phenomena also manifest themselves as extended. Aristotle appears to have been of this opinion when, in the first chapter of his treatise on sensation and the object of sense, he regards it as evident, immediately and without previous proof, that sense perception is the act of a physical organ. . . .

So we see that the stated distinction is assailed with regard to both physical and mental phenomena. Perhaps both points raised against it are equally unfounded.[1] Nevertheless, a further definition common to mental phenomena is still desirable in any case. For conflict over the question whether certain mental and physical phenomena appear extended or not shows at once that the alleged attribute does not suffice for a distinct differentiation; furthermore, for the mental phenomena it is negative only.

5.

What positive attribute will we now be able to advance? Or is there, perhaps, no positive definition at all which holds true of all mental phenomena generally?

A. Bain says that in fact there is none. Nonetheless, psychologists of an earlier period have already directed attention to a particular affinity and analogy which exists among all mental phenomena, while the physical do not share in it. Every mental phenomenon is characterized by what the scholastics of the Middle Ages called the intentional (and also mental)[2] inexistence (*Inexistenz*) of an object (*Gegenstand*), and what we could call, although in not entirely unambiguous terms, the reference to a content, a direction upon an object (by which we are not to understand a reality in this case), or an immanent objectivity. Each one includes something as object within itself, although not always in the same way. In presentation something is presented, in judgment something is affirmed or denied, in love [something is] loved, in hate [something] hated, in desire [something] desired, etc.[3]

This intentional inexistence is exclusively characteristic of mental phenomena. No physical phenomenon manifests anything similar. Consequently, we can define mental phenomena by saying that they are such phenomena as include an object intentionally within themselves.

But here, too, we come up against conflict and contradiction. And it is Hamilton in particular who denies the alleged property of a whole broad class of mental phenomena, namely, of all those which he designates as feelings, of pleasure and pain in their most diverse shades and varieties. He is in agreement with us concerning the phenomena of thinking and desire. Obviously, there would be no thinking without an object which is thought, no desire without an object which is desired. "In the phenomena of Feeling—the phenomena of Pleasure and Pain—on the contrary, consciousness does not place the mental modification or state before itself; it does not contemplate it apart—as separate from itself—but is, as it were, fused into one. The peculiarity of Feeling, therefore, is that there is nothing but what is subjectively subjective; there is no object different from self—no objectification of any mode of self." In the first case, there would be something there which, according to Hamilton's way of expression, is "objective"; in the second, something which is "objectively subjective," as in self-knowledge, whose object Hamilton therefore calls subject-object; Hamilton, in denying both with regard to feeling, most definitely denies any intentional inexistence to it.

However, what Hamilton says is surely not entirely correct. Certain feelings are unmistakably referred to objects, and language itself indicates these through the expressions it uses. We say that a person rejoices in or about something, that a person sorrows or grieves about something. And once again: that delights me, that pains me, that hurts me, and so on. Joy and sorrow, like affirmation and denial, love and hate, desire and aversion, distinctly ensue upon a presentation and are referred to what is presented in it.

At the utmost, one could be inclined to agree with Hamilton in *those* cases in which one succumbs most easily, as we saw before, to the illusion that feeling is not based on any presentation: the case of the pain which is aroused by a cut or burn, for example. But its basis is none other than the very temptation toward this hypothesis, which, as we saw, is erroneous. Moreover, even Hamilton recognizes with us the fact that, without exception, presentations form that basis of feelings, and consequently [do so] in these cases as well. Therefore, his denial that feelings have an object seems so much the more striking.

To be sure, one thing is to be granted. The object to which a feeling refers is not always an external object. Even when I hear a harmonious chord, the pleasure which I feel is not really a pleasure in the sound, but a pleasure in the hearing [of it]. Indeed, one might not be mistaken in saying that it even refers to itself in a certain way and, therefore, that what Hamilton asserts, namely, that the feeling is "fused into one" with its object, *does* occur more or less. But this is nothing which does not likewise hold true of many phenomena of presentation and knowledge, as we shall see in our study of inner consciousness. Nevertheless, in them there is still a mental inexistence, a subject-object, to speak Hamilton's language; and the same will therefore hold true of these feelings as well. Hamilton is mistaken when he says that, in them, everything is "subjectively subjective," an expression which is indeed really self-contradictory; for where we can no longer speak of an object, we can no longer speak of a subject either. Even when Hamilton spoke of a fusion-into-one of the feeling with the mental modification, he gave witness against himself if we consider the matter exactly. Every fusion is a unification of several things; and consequently the pictorial expression, which is intended to make us concretely aware of the distinctive character of feeling, still indicates a certain duality in the unity.

We may thus take it to be valid that the intentional inexistence of an object is a general distinguishing characteristic of mental phenomena, which differentiates this class of phenomena from the class of physical phenomena.

6.

It is a further general characteristic of all mental phenomena that they are perceived only in inner consciousness, while only outer perception is possible for the physical.

One could believe that such a definition says little, since it would seem more natural to take the opposite course, defining the act by reference to its object, and so defining inner perception, in contrast to all others, as perception of mental phenomena. But inner perception has still another characteristic, apart from the special nature of its object, which distinguishes it: namely, that immediate, infallible self-evidence, which pertains to it alone among all the cases in which we know objects of experience. Thus, if we say that mental phenomena are those which are grasped by means of inner perception, we have accordingly said that their perception is immediately evident.

Still more! Inner perception is not merely unique as immediately evident perception; it is really unique as perception (*Wahrmehmung*) in the strict sense of the word. We have seen that the phenomena of so-called outer perception can in no way be demonstrated to be true and real, even by means of indirect reasoning. Indeed, we have seen that anyone who placed confidence in them and took them to be what they presented themselves as being is misled by the way the phenomena hang together. Strictly speaking, so-called outer perception is thus not perception; and mental phenomena can accordingly be designated as the only ones of which perception in the strict sense of the word is possible.

Mental phenomena are also adequately characterized by means of this definition. It is not as if all mental phenomena are introspectively perceivable for everyone, and therefore that everything which a person cannot perceive he is to count among the physical phenomena. On the contrary, it is obvious, and was already expressly remarked by us earlier, that no mental phenomenon is perceived by more than a single individual; but on that occasion we also saw that every type of mental phenomenon is represented in the psychical life of every fully developed human being. For this reason, reference to the phenomena which constitute the realm of inner perception serves our purpose satisfactorily.

7.

We said that mental phenomena are the only ones of which a perception in the strict sense is possible. We could just as well say that they are the only phenomena to which actual, as well as intentional, existence pertains. Knowledge, joy, desire, exist actually; color, sound, heat, only phenomenally and intentionally.

There are philosophers who go so far as to say that it is self-evident that no actuality *could* correspond to a phenomenon such as we call a physical one. They maintain that anyone who assumes this and ascribes to physical phenomena any existence other than mental holds a view which is self-contradictory in itself. Bain, for example, says that some people have attempted to explain the phenomena of outer perception by the hypothesis of a material world, "in the first instance, detached from perception, and, afterwards, coming into perception, by operating upon the mind." "This view," he says, "involves a contradiction. The prevailing doctrine is that a tree is something in itself apart from all perception; that, by its luminous emanations, it impresses our mind and is then perceived; the perception being an effect, and the unperceived tree [i.e., the one which exists outside of perception] the cause. But the tree is known only through perception; what it may be anterior to, or independent of, perception, we cannot tell; we can think of it as perceived but not as unperceived. There is a manifest contradiction in the supposition; we are required at the same moment to perceive the thing and not to perceive it. We know the touch of iron, but we cannot know the touch apart from the touch."[4]

I must confess that I am not in a position to be convinced of the correctness of this argument. As certain as it is that a color only appears to us when it is an object of our presentation [*wenn wir sie vorstellen*], it is nevertheless not to be inferred from this that a color could not exist without being presented. Only if being persented were included as one factor in the color, just as a certain quality and intensity is included in it, would a color which is not presented signify a contradiction, since a whole without one of its parts is truly a contradiction. This, however, is obviously not the case. Otherwise it would be strictly inconceivable how the belief in the actual existence of the physical phenomenon outside of our presentation of it could have, not to say originated, but achieved the most general dissemination, been maintained with the utmost tenacity, and, indeed, even long been shared by thinkers of the first rank. If what Bain says were correct: "We can think of [a tree] as perceived, but not as unperceived. There is manifest contradiction in the supposition," then his further conclusion would surely no longer be subject to objection. But it is precisely this which is not to be granted. Bain explains his dictum by saying: "We are required at the same moment to perceive the thing and not to perceive it." But it is not true that this is required: For, in the first place, not every case of thinking is a perception; and further, even if this were the case, it would only follow that a person could only think of trees perceived by him, but not that he could only think of trees *as perceived by him*. To taste a white piece of sugar does not mean to taste a piece of sugar *as white*. The fallacy reveals itself quite distinctly when it is applied to mental phenomena. If one should say: "I cannot think of a mental phenomenon without thinking of it; and so I can only think of mental phenomena as thought by me; hence no mental phenomena exists outside of my thinking," this mode of inference would be exactly like the one Bain uses. Nonetheless, Bain himself will not deny that his individual mental life is not the only thing to which actual existence belongs. When Bain adds, "We know the touch of iron, but it is not possible that we should know the touch apart from the touch," he uses the word "touch," in the first place, obviously, in the sense of what is felt, and then in the sense of the feeling of it. These are different concepts even if they have the same name. Accordingly, only someone who permits himself to be deceived by the equivocation could make the concession of immediate evidence required by Bain.

It is not true, then, that the hypothesis that a physical phenomenon like those which exist intentionally in us exists outside of the mind in actuality includes a contradiction. It is only that, when we compare one with the other, conflicts are revealed, which show clearly that there is no actual existence corresponding to the intentional existence in this case. And even though this holds true in the first instance only as far as our experience extends, we will, nevertheless, make no mistake if we quite generally deny to physical phenomena any existence other than intentional existence.

• • •

——
——

9.

In conclusion, let us summarize the results of our comments on the distinction between physical and mental phenomena. First of all, we made ourselves concretely aware of the distinctive nature of the two classes by means of *examples*. We then defined mental phenomena as *presentations* and such phenomena which are *based upon presentations;* all the

rest belong to the physical. We next spoke of the attribute of *extension*, which was taken by psychologists to be a distinctive characteristic of all physical phenomena; all mental phenomena were supposed to lack it. The contention had not remained uncontested, however, and only later investigations could decide the issue; that in fact mental phenomena do invariably appear unextended was all that could be confirmed now. We next found *intentional inexistence*, the reference to something as an object, to be a distinguishing feature of all mental phenomena; no physical phenomenon manifests anything similar. We further defined mental phenomena as the exclusive *object of inner perception;* they alone are therefore perceived with immediate evidence; indeed, they alone are perceived in the strict sense of the word. And with this there was bound up the further definition, that they alone are phenomena which possess *actual* existence besides their intentional existence. Finally, we advanced it as a distinguishing [feature] that the mental phenomena which someone perceives *always* appear *as a unity* despite their variety, while the physical phenomena which he may perceive simultaneously are not all presented in the same way as partial phenomena within a single phenomenon.

There can be no doubt but that the characteristic which is more distinctive of mental phenomena than any of the others is intentional inexistence. We may now regard them as distinctly defined, over against the physical phenomena, by this, as well as by the other properties which were introduced.

The definitions of mental and physical phenomena which have been given cannot fail to throw a brighter light on our earlier definitions of mental science and physical science (*psychischer and Naturwissenschaft*): indeed, we said of the latter that it is the science of physical phenomena and of the former that it is the science of mental phenomena. It is now easy to see that both definitions implicitly include certain limitations.

This holds true principally of the definition of physical science. For it is not concerned with all physical phenomena; not with those of imagination, but only with those which appear in sensation. And it determines laws for these only insofar as they depend upon physical stimulation of the sense organs. We could express the scientific task of physical science precisely by saying that physical science is the science which attempts to explain the succession of physical phenomena which are normal and pure (not influenced by any particular psychological states and events) on the basis of the hypothesis [that they are the effect] of the stimulation of our sense organs by a world which is quasi-spatially *(raumähnlich)* extended in three dimensions and which proceeds quasi-temporally *(zeitähnlich)* in *one* direction.[5] Without giving any particulars concerning the absolute nature of this world, [physical science] is satisfied to ascribe to it powers which evoke the sensations and mutually influence each other in their working, and to determine the laws of coexistence and succession for these powers. In those laws, it then indirectly gives the laws governing the succession of the physical phenomena of sensation when, by means of scientific abstraction from concomitant psychological conditions, these are regarded as pure and as occurring in relation to a constant sensory capacity. Hence, "science of physical phenomena" must be interpreted in this somewhat complicated way, if it is made synonymous with physical science.[6]

We have seen, along the way, how the expression "physical phenomenon" is sometimes misused by being applied to the above-mentioned powers themselves. And, since the object of a science is naturally designated as the one for which it determines laws directly and explicitly, I believe I make no mistake in also assuming with respect to the definition of physical science as the science of physical phenomena that there is ordinarily bound up with this term the concept of powers belonging to a world which is quasi-spatially extended and which proceeds quasi-temporally, powers which evoke sensations by their effect on the sense organs and which reciprocally influence one another, and for which physical science investigates the laws of coexistence and succession. If one regards these powers as the object [of physical science], this also has the convenient feature that something which truly and actually exists appears as object of the science. This last would be just as attainable if we defined physical science as the science of sensations, implicitly adding the same limitation of which we just spoke. What made the expression "physical phenomenon" seem preferable was, probably, primarily the fact that the external causes of sensation were thought of as

corresponding to the physical phenomena appearing in it (whether this be in every respect, as was originally the case, or whether it be, as now, in respect at least to extension in three dimensions). From this, there also arose the otherwise inappropriate term, "outer perception." It is pertinent, however, that the act of sensation manifests, along with the intentional inexistence of the physical phenomenon, still other properties with which the physical scientist (*Naturforscher*) is not at all concerned, since sensation does not give through them similar information about the distinctive relationships of the external world.

With respect to the definition of psychology, it may be apparent in the first place that the concept of mental phenomena is to be broadened rather than narrowed. For the physical phenomena of imagination, at least, fall completely within its scope just as much as do mental phenomena, in the sense defined earlier; and those which appear in sensation can also not remain unconsidered in the theory of sensation. But it is obvious that they come into consideration only as the content of mental phenomena, when the characteristics of those phenomena are being described. And the same holds true of all mental phenomena which possess exclusively phenomenal existence. It is only mental phenomena in the sense of actual states which we shall have to regard as the true object of psychology. And it is exclusively with reference to them that we say psychology is the science of mental phenomena.

Endnotes

[1]The claim that even mental phenomena appear extended rests plainly on a confusion between physical and mental phenomena similar to the one we became convinced of above, when we established that even sensory feelings are necessarily based on a presentation.

[2]They also use the expression "to be in something objectively," which, if we should wish to make use of it now, could possibly be taken in just the opposite sense, as the designation of a real existence outside of the mind. Nevertheless, it reminds one of the expression "to be immanently objective," which we sometimes use in a similar sense, and in which the "immanently" is intended to exclude the misunderstanding that was to be feared.

[3]Aristotle has already spoken of this mental inherence. In his books on the soul, he says that what is experienced, insofar as it is experienced, is in the one experiencing it,

that sense contains what is experienced without its matter, that what is thought is in the thinking intellect. In Philo we likewise find the doctrine of mental existence and inexistence. In confusing this, however, with existence in the strict sense, he arrives at his doctrine of the Logos and Ideas, with its wealth of contradictions. The like holds true of the Neo-Platonists. Augustine touches on the same fact in his theory of the *Verbum mentis* and its internal origin. Anselm does so in his well-known ontological argument; and many have alleged the basis of his fallacy to be the fact that he regarded mental existence as if it were actual existence (see Ueberweg, *History of Philosophy,* Vol. II). Thomas Aquinas teaches that what is thought is intentionally in the one thinking, the object of love in the person loving, what is desired in the person desiring, and uses this for theological purposes. When the scripture speaks of an indwelling of the Holy Ghost, he explains this as an intentional indwelling by way of love. And he also seeks to find in intentional inexistence, in the cases of thinking and loving, a certain analogy for the mystery of the Trinity and the procession of the Word and Spirit.

[4]*Mental Science,* 3d ed., p. 198.

[5]On this point see Ueberweg (*System der Logik*), in whose analysis, to be sure, not everything is deserving of approval. He is mistaken particularly when he considers the external causes to be spatial instead of quasi-spatial, temporal instead of quasi-temporal.

[6]The interpretation would not be quite as Kant would have it; nevertheless, it approximates his interpretations as far as is feasible. In a certain sense, it comes closer to the viewpoint of Mill in his book against Hamilton, but still without agreeing with him in all the essential respects. What Mill calls permanent possibilities of sensations has a close relationship with what we call powers. The relationship to, as well as the most important departure from, Ueberweg's view was already touched upon in the preceding note.

26. *Intentional Systems*

DANIEL C. DENNETT

In the previous selection, Brentano claims that nothing physical exhibits intentionality, the feature of consciousness whereby mind is "directed upon an object." This thesis has been championed by dualists and idealists who want to deny that minds are really physical brains or aspects of the nervous system. Many twentieth-century philosophers, however, have been impressed by progress in science whereby things (like heat, genes, or molecules) turn out to be complex properties or configurations of basic physical entities, and they suspect that the mind, too, will turn out to be physical (see the following essay by Armstrong). Also, along with many psychologists, many philosophers doubt the mind has the ability to intuit (or to introspect) its own essence. For these philosophers, the challenge is to account for intentionality in a way that leaves the door open for a physicalist understanding of the mind. Dennett argues that it is useful in explanations of behavior to ascribe intentionality to a variety of systems, including physical ones. Similarly, physicalists have suggested, the attribution of intentionality to persons may not indicate the presence of a preternatural power of mind, but instead just be part of an explanation of behavior. Dennett, an American philosopher who teaches at Tufts University, further develops this strategy in his 1987 book, *The Intentional Stance.*

I wish to examine the concept of a system whose behavior can be—at least sometimes—explained and predicted by relying on ascriptions to the sys-

From *Journal of Philosophy 68,* No. 4 (February 1971): 87–101 and 106. Reprinted by permission of the author and the *Journal of Philosophy.*

tem of beliefs and desires (and hopes, fears, intentions, hunches, . . .). I will call such systems *intentional systems,* and such explanations and predictions intentional explanations and predictions, in virtue of the intentionality of the idioms of belief and desire (and hope, fear, intention, hunch, . . .).

I used to insist on capitalizing "intentional" wherever I meant to be using Brentano's notion of *intentionality,* in order to distinguish this technical term from its cousin, e.g., "an intentional shove," but the technical term is now in much greater currency, and since almost everyone else who uses the term seems content to risk this confusion, I have decided, with some trepidation, to abandon my typographical eccentricity. But let the uninitiated reader beware: "intentional" as it occurs here is *not* the familiar term of layman's English. For me, as for many recent authors, intentionality is primarily a feature of linguistic entities—idioms, contexts—and for my purposes here we can be satisfied that an idiom is intentional if substitution of codesignative terms do not preserve truth or if the "objects" of the idiom are not capturable in the usual way by quantifiers.

I.

The first point to make about intentional systems as I have just defined them is that a particular thing is an intentional system only in relation to the strategies of someone who is trying to explain and predict its behavior. What this amounts to can best be brought out by example. Consider the case of a chess-playing computer, and the different strategies or stances one might adopt as its opponent in trying to predict its moves. There are three different stances of interest to us. First there is the *design stance.* If one knows exactly how the computer is designed (including the impermanent part of its design: its program) one can predict its designed response to any move one makes by following the computation instructions of the program. One's prediction will come true provided only that the computer performs as designed—that is, without breakdown. Different varieties of design-stance predictions can be discerned, but all of them are alike in relying on the notion of *func-*

tion, which is purpose-relative or teleological. That is, a design of a system breaks it up into larger or smaller functional parts, and design-stance predictions are generated by assuming that each functional part will function properly. For instance, the radio engineer's schematic wiring diagrams have symbols for each resistor, capacitor, transistor, etc.—*each with its task to perform*—and he can give a design-stance prediction of the behavior of a circuit by assuming that each element performs its task. Thus one can make design-stance predictions of the computer's response at several different levels of abstraction, depending on whether one's design treats as smallest functional elements strategy-generators and consequence-testers, multipliers and dividers, or transistors and switches. (It should be noted that not all diagrams or pictures are designs in this sense, for a diagram may carry no information about the functions—intended or observed—of the elements it depicts.)

We generally adopt the design stance when making predictions about the behavior of mechanical objects, e.g., "As the typewriter carriage approaches the margin, a bell will ring (provided the machine is in working order)," and more simply, "Strike the match and it will light." We also often adopt this stance in predictions involving natural objects: "Heavy pruning will stimulate denser foliage and stronger limbs." The essential feature of the design stance is that we make predictions solely from knowledge or assumptions about the system's functional design, irrespective of the physical constitution or condition of the innards of the particular object.

Second, there is what we may call the *physical stance.* From this stance our predictions are based on the actual physical state of the particular object, and are worked out by applying whatever knowledge we have of the laws of nature. It is from this stance alone that we can predict the malfunction of systems (unless, as sometimes happens these days, a system is *designed* to malfunction after a certain time, in which case malfunctioning in one sense becomes a part of its proper functioning). Instances of predictions from the physical stance are common enough: "If you turn on the switch you'll get a nasty shock," and, "When the snows come that branch will break right off." One seldom adopts the physical stance in dealing with a computer just because the number of critical variables in the physical constitution of a computer would overwhelm the most prodigious calculator. Significantly, the physical stance is generally reserved for instances of breakdown, where the condition preventing normal operation is generalized and easily locatable, e.g., "Nothing will happen when you type in your questions, because it isn't plugged in," or, "It won't work with all that flood water in it." Attempting to give a physical account or prediction of the chess-playing computer would be a pointless and herculean labor, but it would work in principle. One could predict the response it would make in a chess game by tracing out the effects of the input energies all the way through the computer until once more type was pressed against paper and a response was printed. (Because of the digital nature of computers, quantum-level indeterminacies, if such there be, will cancel out rather than accumulate, unless of course a radium "randomizer" or other amplifier of quantum effects is built into the computer).

The best chess-playing computers these days are practically inaccessible to prediction from either the design stance or the physical stance; they have become too complex for even their own designers to view from the design stance. A man's best hope of defeating such a machine in a chess match is to predict its responses by figuring out as best he can what the best or most rational move would be, given the rules and goals of chess. That is, one assumes not only (1) that the machine will function as designed, but (2) that the design is optimal as well, that the computer will "choose" the most rational move. Predictions made on these assumptions may well fail if either assumption proves unwarranted in the particular case, but still this *means* of prediction may impress us as the most fruitful one to adopt in dealing with a particular system. Put another way, when one can no longer hope to beat the machine by utilizing one's knowledge of physics or programming to anticipate its responses, one may still be able to avoid defeat by treating the machine rather like an intelligent human opponent.

We must look more closely at this strategy. A prediction relying on the assumption of the system's rationality is relative to a number of things. First, rationality here so far means nothing more than optimal design relative to a goal or optimally weighted hierarchy of goals (checkmate, winning pieces, defense, etc., in the case of chess) and a set of constraints (the rules and starting position). Prediction itself is, moreover, relative to the nature and extent of the information the system has at the time about the field of endeavor. The question one asks in framing a prediction of this sort is: What is the most rational thing for the computer to do, given goals $x,y,z, \ldots$, constraints $a,b,c, \ldots$ and information (including misinformation, if any) about the present state of affairs $p,q,r, \ldots$? In predicting the computer's response to my chess move, my assessment of the computer's most rational move may depend, for instance, not only on my assumption that the computer has information about the present disposition of all the pieces, but also on whether I believe the computer has information about my inability to see four moves ahead, the relative powers of knights and bishops, and my weakness for knight-bishop exchanges. In the end I may not be able to frame a very good prediction, if I am unable to determine with any accuracy what information and goals the computer has, or if the information and goals I take to be given do not dictate any one best move, or if I simply am not so good as the computer is at generating an optimal move from this given. Such predictions then are very precarious; not only are they relative to a set of postulates about goals, constraints, and information, and not only do they hinge on determining an optimal response in situations where we may have no clear criteria for what is optimal, but also they are vulnerable to short-circuit falsifications that are in principle unpredictable from this stance. Just as design-stance predictions are vulnerable to malfunctions (by depending on the assumption of no malfunction), so these predictions are vulnerable to design weaknesses and lapses (by depending on the assumption of optimal design). It is a measure of the success of contemporary program designers that these precarious predictions turn out to be true with enough regularity to make the method useful.

The denouement of this extended example should now be obvious: this third stance, with its assumption of rationality, is the *intentional stance;* the predictions one makes from it are intentional predictions; one is viewing the computer as an intentional system. One predicts behavior in such a case by ascribing to the system *the possession of certain information* and supposing it to be *directed by certain goals,* and then by working out the most reasonable or appropriate action on the basis of these ascriptions and suppositions. It is a small step to calling the information possessed the computer's *beliefs,* its goals and subgoals its *desires.* What I mean by saying that this is a small step, is that the notion of possession of information or misinformation is just as intentional a notion as that of belief. The "possession" at issue is hardly the bland and innocent notion of storage one might suppose; it is, and must be, "epistemic possession"—an analogue of belief. Consider: the Frenchman who possesses the *Encyclopedia Britannica* but knows no English might be said to "possess" the information in it, but if there is such a sense of possession, it is not strong enough to serve as the sort of possession the computer must be supposed to enjoy, relative to the information it *uses* in "choosing" a chess move. In a similar way, the goals of a goal-directed computer must be specified intentionally, just like desires.

Lingering doubts about whether the chess-playing computer *really* has beliefs and desires are misplaced; for the definition of intentional systems I have given does not say that intentional systems *really* have beliefs and desires, but that one can explain and predict their behavior by *ascribing* beliefs and desires to them, and whether one calls what one ascribes to the computer beliefs or belief-analogues or information complexes or intentional whatnots makes no difference to the nature of the calculation one makes on the basis of the ascriptions. One will arrive at the same predictions whether one forthrightly thinks in terms of the computer's beliefs and desires, or in terms of the computer's information-store and goal-specifications. The inescapable and interesting fact is that for the best chess-playing computers of today, intentional explanation and prediction of their behavior is not only common, but works when no other sort of prediction of their behavior is manageable. We do quite successfully treat these computers as intentional systems, and we do this independently of any considerations about what substance they are composed of, their origin, their position or lack of position in the community of moral agents, their consciousness or self-consciousness, or the determinacy or indeterminacy of their operations. The decision to adopt the strategy is pragmatic, and is not intrinsically right or wrong. One can always refuse to adopt the intentional stance toward the computer, and accept its checkmates. One can switch stances at will without involving oneself in any inconsistencies or inhumanities, adopting the intentional stance in one's role as opponent, the design stance in one's role as redesigner, and the physical stance in one's role as repairman.

This celebration of our chess-playing computer is not intended to imply that it is a completely adequate model or simulation of Mind, or intelligent human or animal activity; nor am I saying that the attitude we adopt toward this computer is precisely the same that we adopt toward a creature we deem to be conscious and rational. All that has been claimed is that on occasion, a purely physical system can be so complex, and yet so organized, that we find it convenient, explanatory, pragmatically necessary for prediction, to treat it as if it had beliefs and desires and was rational. The chess-playing computer is just that, a machine for playing chess, which no man or animal is; and hence its "rationality" is pinched and artificial.

Perhaps we could straightforwardly expand the chess-playing computer into a more faithful model of human rationality, and perhaps not. I prefer to pursue a more fundamental line of inquiry first.

When should we expect the tactic of adopting the intentional stance to pay off? Whenever we have reason to suppose the assumption of optimal design is warranted, and doubt the practicality of prediction from the design or physical stance. Suppose we travel to a distant planet and find it inhabited by things moving about its surface, multiplying, decaying, apparently reacting to events in the environment, but otherwise as unlike human beings as you please. Can we make intentional predictions and explanations of their behavior? If we have reason to suppose that a process of natural selection has been in effect, then we can be assured that the populations we observe have been selected in virtue of their design: they will respond to at least some of the more common event-types in this environment in ways that are normally appropriate—that is, conducive to propagation of the species.[1] Once we have tentatively identified the perils and succors of the environment (relative to the constitution of the inhabitants, not ours), we shall be able to estimate which goals and which weighting of goals will be optimal relative to the creatures' *needs* (for survival and propagation), which sorts of information about the environment will be *useful* in guiding goal-directed activity, and which activities will be appropriate given the environmental circumstances. Having doped out these conditions (which will always be subject to revision) we can proceed at once to ascribe beliefs and desires to the creatures. Their behavior will "manifest" their beliefs by being seen as the actions which, given the creatures' desires, would be appropriate to such beliefs as would be appropriate to the environmental stimulation. Desires, in turn, will be "manifested" in behavior as those appropriate desires (given the needs of the creature) to which the actions of the creature would be appropriate, given the creature's beliefs. The circularity of these interlocking specifications is no accident. Ascriptions of beliefs and desires must be interdependent, and the only points of anchorage are the demonstrable needs for survival, the regularities of behavior, and the assumption, grounded in faith in natural selection, of optimal design. Once one has ascribed beliefs and desires, however, one can at once set about predicting behavior on their basis, and if evolution has done its job—as it must over the long run—our predictions will be reliable enough to be useful.

It might at first seem that this tactic unjustifiably imposes human categories and attributes (belief, desire, and so forth) on these alien entities. It is a sort of anthropomorphizing, to be sure, but it is conceptually innocent anthropomorphizing. We do not have to suppose these creatures share with us any peculiarly human inclinations, attitudes, hopes, foibles, pleasures, or outlooks; their actions may not include running, jumping, hiding, eating, sleeping, listening, or copulating. All we transport from our world to theirs are the categories of rationality, perception (information input by some "sense" modality or modalities—perhaps radar or cosmic radiation), and action. The question of whether we can expect them to share any of our beliefs or desires is tricky, but there are a few points that can be made at this time; in virtue of their rationality they can be supposed to share our belief in logical truths,[2] and we cannot suppose that they normally desire their own destruction, for instance.

II.

When one deals with a system—be it man, machine, or alien creature—by explaining and predicting its behavior by citing its beliefs and desires, one has what might be called a "theory of behavior" for the system. Let us see how such intentional theories of behavior relate to other putative theories of behavior.

One fact so obvious that it is easily overlooked is that our "common-sense" explanations and predictions of the behavior of both men and animals are intentional. We start by assuming rationality. We do not *expect* new acquaintances to react irrationally to particular topics or eventualities, but when they do we learn to adjust our strategies accordingly, just as, with a chess-playing computer, one sets out with a high regard for its rationality and adjusts one's estimate downward wherever performance reveals flaws. The presumption of rationality is so strongly entrenched in our inference habits that when our predictions prove false, we at first cast about for adjustments in the information-possession conditions (he must not have heard, he must not know English, he must not have seen x, been aware that y, etc.) or goal weightings, before questioning the rationality of the system as a whole. In extreme cases personalities may prove to be so unpredictable from the intentional stance that we abandon it, and if we have accumulated a lot of evidence in the meanwhile about the nature of response patterns in the individual, we may find that a species of design stance can be effectively adopted. This is the fundamentally different attitude we occasionally adopt toward the insane. To watch an asylum attendant manipulate an obsessively countersuggestive patient, for instance, is to watch something radically unlike normal interpersonal relations.

Our prediction of animal behavior by "common sense" is also intentional. Whether or not sentimental folk go overboard when they talk to their dogs or fill their cats' heads with schemes and worries, even the most hardboiled among us predict animals' behavior intentionally. If we observe a mouse in a situation where it can see a cat waiting at one mousehole and cheese at another, we know which way the mouse will go, providing it is not deranged; our prediction is not based on our familiarity with maze-experiments or any assumptions about the sort of special training the mouse has been through. We suppose the mouse can see the cat and the cheese, and hence has beliefs (belief-analogues, intentional whatnots) to the effect that there is a cat to the left, cheese to the right, and we ascribe to the mouse also the desire to eat the cheese and the desire to avoid the cat (subsumed, appropriately enough, under the more general desires to eat and to avoid peril); so we predict that the mouse will do what is appropriate to such beliefs and desires, namely, go to the right in order to get the cheese and avoid the cat. Whatever academic allegiances or theoretical predilections we may have, we would be astonished if, in the general run, mice and other animals falsified such intentional predictions of their behavior. Indeed, experimental psychologists of every school would have a hard time devising experimental situations to support their various theories without the help of their intentional expectations of how the test animals will respond to circumstances.

Earlier I alleged that even creatures from another planet would share with us our beliefs in logical truths; light can be shed on this claim by asking whether mice and other animals, in virtue of being intentional systems, also believe the truths of logic. There is something bizarre in the picture of a dog or mouse cogitating a list of tautologies, but we can avoid that picture. The assumption that something is an intentional system is the assumption that it is rational; that is, one gets nowhere with the assumption that entity x has beliefs $p,q,r, \ldots$ unless one also supposes that x believes what follows from $p,q,r, \ldots$; otherwise there is no way of ruling out the prediction that x will, in the face of its beliefs $p,q,r, \ldots$ do something utterly stupid, and, if we cannot rule out *that* prediction, we will have acquired no predictive power at all. So whether or not the animal is said to *believe* the *truths* of logic, it must be supposed to *follow* the *rules* of logic. Surely our mouse follows or believes in *modus ponens,* for we ascribed to it the beliefs: (a) *there is a cat to the left,* and (b) *if there is a cat to the left, I had better not go left,* and our prediction relied on the mouse's ability to get to the conclusion. In general there is a trade-off between rules and truths; we can suppose x to have an inference rule taking A to B or

we can give x the belief in the "theorem"; *if A then B.* As far as our predictions are concerned, we are free to ascribe to the mouse either a few inference rules and belief in many logical propositions, or many inference rules and few if any logical beliefs.[3] We can even take a patently nonlogical belief like (b) and recast it as an inference rule taking (a) to the desired conclusion.

Will all logical truths appear among the beliefs of any intentional system? If the system were ideally or perfectly 'rational, all logical truths would appear, but any actual intentional system will be imperfect, and so not all logical truths must be ascribed as beliefs to any system. Moreover, not all the inference rules of an actual intentional system may be valid; not all its inference-licensing beliefs may be truths of logic. Experience may indicate where the shortcomings lie in any particular system. If we found an imperfectly rational creature whose allegiance to *modus ponens,* say, varied with the subject matter, we could characterize that by excluding *modus ponens* as a rule and ascribing in its stead a set of nonlogical inference rules covering the *modus ponens* step for each subject matter where the rule was followed. Not surprisingly, as we discover more and more imperfections (as we banish more and more logical truths from the creature's beliefs), our efforts at intentional prediction become more and more cumbersome and undecidable, for we can no longer count on the beliefs, desires, and actions going together that *ought* to go together. Eventually we end up, following this process, by predicting from the design stance; we end up, that is, dropping the assumption of rationality.[4]

This migration from common-sense intentional explanations and predictions to more reliable design-stance explanations and predictions that is forced on us when we discover that our subjects are imperfectly rational is, independently of any such discovery, the proper direction for theory builders to take whenever possible. In the end, we want to be able to explain the intelligence of man, or beast, in terms of his design, and this in turn in terms of the natural selection of this design; so whenever we stop in our explanations at the intentional level we have left over an unexplained instance of intelligence or rationality. This comes out vividly if we look at theory building from the vantage point of economics.

Any time a theory builder proposes to call any event, state, structure, etc., in any system (say the brain of an organism) a *signal* or *message* or *command* or otherwise endows it with content, he *takes out a loan* of intelligence. He implicitly posits along with his signals, messages, or commands, something that can serve as a signal-*reader, message-understander,* or *commander,* else his "signals" will be for naught, will decay unreceived, uncomprehended. This loan must be repaid eventually by finding and analyzing away these readers or comprehenders; for, failing this, the theory will have among its elements unanalyzed man-analogues endowed with enough intelligence to read the signals, etc., and thus the theory will *postpone* answering the major question: what makes for intelligence? The intentionality of all such talk of signals and commands reminds us that rationality is being taken for granted, and in this way shows us where a theory is incomplete. It is this feature that, to my mind, puts a premium on the yet unfinished task of devising a rigorous definition of intentionality, for if we can lay claim to a purely formal criterion of intentional discourse, we will have what amounts to a medium of exchange for assessing theories of behavior. Intentionality *abstracts* from the inessential details of the various forms intelligence-loans can take (e.g., signal-readers, volition-emitters, librarians in the corridors of memory, egos and superegos) and serves as a reliable means of detecting exactly where a theory is *in the red* relative to the task of explaining intelligence; wherever a theory relies on a formulation bearing the logical marks of intentionality, there a little man is concealed.

This insufficiency of intentional explanation from the point of view of psychology has been widely felt and as widely misconceived. The most influential misgivings, expressed in the behaviorism of Skinner and Quine, can be succinctly characterized in terms of our economic metaphor. Skinner's and Quine's adamant prohibitions of intentional idioms at all levels of theory is the analogue of rock-ribbed New England conservatism: no deficit spending when building a theory! In Quine's case, the abhorrence of loans is due mainly to his fear that they can never be repaid, whereas Skinner stresses rather that what is bor-

rowed is worthless to begin with. Skinner's suspicion is that intentionally couched claims are empirically vacuous, in the sense that they are altogether too easy to accommodate to the data, like the *virtus dormitiva* Molière's doctor ascribes to the sleeping powder. Questions can be begged on a temporary basis, however, permitting a mode of prediction and explanation not totally vacuous. Consider the following intentional prediction: if I were to ask a thousand American mathematicians how much seven times five is, more than nine hundred would respond by saying that it was thirty-five. (I have allowed for a few to mis-hear my question, a few others to be obstreperous, a few to make slips of the tongue.) If you doubt the prediction, you can test it; I would bet good money on it. It seems to have empirical content because it can, in a fashion, be tested, and yet it is unsatisfactory as a prediction of an empirical theory of psychology. It works, of course, because of the contingent, empirical—but evolution-guaranteed—fact that men in general are well enough designed both to get the answer right and to want to get it right. It will hold with as few exceptions for any group of Martians with whom we are able to converse, for it is not a prediction just of *human* psychology, but of the "psychology" of intentional systems generally.

Deciding on the basis of available empirical evidence that something is a piece of copper or a lichen permits one to make predictions based on the empirical theories dealing with copper and lichens, but deciding on the basis of available evidence that something is (may be treated as) an intentional system permits predictions having a normative or logical basis rather than an empirical one, and hence the success of an intentional prediction, based as it is on no particular picture of the system's design, cannot be construed to confirm or disconfirm any particular pictures of the system's design.

Skinner's reaction to this has been to try to frame predictions purely in non-intentional language, by predicting bodily responses to physical stimuli, but to date this has not provided him with the alternative mode of prediction and explanation he has sought, as perhaps an extremely cursory review can indicate. To provide a setting for non-intentional prediction of behavior, he invented the

Skinner box, in which the rewarded behavior of the occupant—say, a rat—is a highly restricted and stereotypic bodily motion—usually pressing a bar with the front paws.

The claim that is then made is that once the animal has been trained, a law-like relationship is discovered to hold between non-intentionally characterized events: controlling stimuli and bar-pressing responses. A regularity is discovered to hold, to be sure, but the fact that it is between non-intentionally defined events is due to a property of the Skinner box and not of the occupant. For let us turn our prediction about mathematicians into a Skinnerian prediction: strap a mathematician in a Skinner box so he can move only his head; display in front of him a card on which appear the marks: "How much is seven times five?"; move into the range of his head-motions two buttons, over one of which is the mark "35" and over the other "34"; place electrodes on the soles of his feet and give him a few quick shocks; the controlling stimulus is then to be the sound: "Answer now!" I predict that in a statistically significant number of cases, even *before* training trials to condition the man to press button "35" with his forehead, he will do this when given the controlling stimulus. Is this a satisfactory scientific prediction just because it eschews the intentional vocabulary? No, it is an intentional prediction disguised by so restricting the environment that only one bodily motion is available to fulfill the intentional *action* that anyone would prescribe as appropriate to the circumstances of perception, belief, desire. That it is action, not merely motion, that is predicted can also be seen in the case of subjects less intelligent than mathematicians. Suppose a mouse were trained, in a Skinner box with a food reward, to take exactly four steps forward and press a bar with its nose; if Skinner's laws truly held between stimuli and responses defined in terms of bodily motion, were we to move the bar an inch farther away, so four steps did not reach it, Skinner would have to predict that the mouse would jab its nose into the empty air rather than take a fifth step.

A variation of Skinnerian theory designed to meet this objection acknowledges that the trained response one predicts is not truly captured in a description of skeletal motion alone, but rather in a description of an environmental effect achieved: the bar going down, the "35" button being depressed. This will also not do. Suppose we could in fact train a man or animal to achieve an environmental effect, as this theory proposes. Suppose, for instance, we train a man to push a button under the longer of two displays, such as drawings or simple designs, that is, we reward him when he pushes the button under the longer of two pictures of pencils, or cigars, etc. The miraculous consequence of this theory, were it correct, would be that if, after training him on simple views, we were to present him with the Müller-Lyer arrowhead illusion, he would be immune to it, for *ex hypothesi* he has been trained to achieve an *actual* environmental effect (choosing the display that *is* longer), not a *perceived* or *believed* environmental effect (choosing the display that *seems* longer). The reliable prediction, again, is the intentional one.[5]

Skinner's experimental design is supposed to eliminate the intentional, but it merely masks it. Skinner's non-intentional predictions work to the extent they do, not because Skinner has truly found non-intentional behavioral laws, but because the highly reliable intentional predictions underlying his experimental situations (the rat desires food and believes it will get food by pressing the bar—something for which it has been given good evidence—so it will press the bar) are disguised by leaving virtually no room in the environment for more than one bodily motion to be the appropriate action and by leaving virtually no room in the environment for discrepancy to arise between the subject's beliefs and the reality.

Where, then, should we look for a satisfactory theory of behavior? Intentional theory is vacuous as psychology because it presupposes and does not explain rationality or intelligence. The apparent successes of Skinnerian behaviorism, however, rely on hidden intentional predictions. Skinner is right in recognizing that intentionality can be no *foundation* for psychology, and right also to look for purely mechanistic regularities in the activities of his subjects, but there is little reason to suppose they will lie on the surface in gross behavior—except, as we have seen, when we put an artificial straitjacket on an intentional regularity. Rather, we will find whatever mechanistic regularities there are in the functioning of internal systems whose design approaches the optimal (relative to some ends). In seeking knowledge of internal design our most promising tactic is to take out intelligence-loans, endow peripheral and internal events with content, and then look for mechanisms that will function appropriately with such "messages" so that we can pay back the loans. This tactic is hardly untried. Research in artificial intelligence, which has produced, among other things, the chess-playing computer, proceeds by working from an intentionally characterized problem (how to get the computer to consider the right sorts of information, make the right decisions) to a design-stance solution—an approximation of optimal design. Psychophysicists and neurophysiologists who routinely describe events in terms of the transmission of information within the nervous system are similarly borrowing intentional capital—even if they are often inclined to ignore or disavow their debts.

Finally, it should not be supposed that, just because intentional theory is vacuous as psychology, in virtue of its assumption of rationality, it is vacuous from all points of view. Game theory, for example, is inescapably intentional, but as a formal normative theory and not a psychology this is nothing amiss. Game-theoretical predictions applied to human subjects achieve their accuracy in virtue of the evolutionary guarantee that man is well designed as a game player, a special case of rationality. Similarly, economics, the social science of greatest predictive power today, is not a psychological theory and presupposes what psychology must explain. Economic explanation and prediction is intentional (although some is disguised) and succeeds to the extent that it does because individual men are in general good approximations of the optimal operator in the marketplace.

III.

The concept of an intentional system is a relatively uncluttered and unmetaphysical notion, abstracted as it is from questions of the composition, constitution, consciousness, morality, or divinity of the entities falling under it. Thus, for example, it is much easier to decide whether a machine can be an intentional system than it is to decide whether a machine can *really* think, or be conscious, or morally responsible. This simplicity makes it ideal as a source of order and organization in philosophical analyses of "mental" concepts. Whatever else a person might be—embodied mind or soul, self-conscious moral agent, "emergent" form of intelligence—he is an intentional system, and whatever follows just from being an intentional system is thus true of a person. It is interesting to see just how much of what we hold to be the case about persons or their minds follows directly from their being intentional systems. To revert for a moment to the economic metaphor, the guiding or challenging question that defines work in the philosophy of mind is this: are there mental treasures that cannot be purchased with intentional coin? If not, a considerable unification of science can be foreseen in outline. Of special importance for such an examination is the subclass of intentional systems that have language, that can communicate; for these provide a framework for a theory of consciousness. . . .

What will be true of human believers just in virtue of their being intentional systems with the capacity to communicate?

Just as not all intentional systems currently known to us can fly or swim, so not all intentional systems can talk, but those which can do this raise special problems and opportunities when we come to ascribe beliefs and desires to them. That is a massive understatement; without the talking intentional systems, of course, there would be no ascribing beliefs, no theorizing, no assuming rationality, no predicting. The capacity for language is without doubt the crowning achievement of evolution, an achievement that feeds on itself to produce ever more versatile and subtle rational systems, but still it can be looked at as an adaptation which is subject to the same conditions of environmental utility as any other behavioral talent. When it is looked at in this way several striking facts emerge. One of the most pervasive features of evolutionary histories is the interdependence of distinct organs and capacities in a species. Advanced eyes and other distance receptors are of no utility to an organism unless it develops advanced means of locomotion; the talents of a predator will not accrue to a species that does not evolve a carnivore's digestive system. The capacities of belief and communication have prerequisites of their own. We have already seen that there is no point in ascribing beliefs to a system unless the beliefs ascribed are in general appropriate to the environment, and the system responds appropriately to the beliefs. An eccentric expression of this would be: the capacity to believe would have no survival value unless it were a capacity to believe truths. What is eccentric and potentially misleading about this is that it hints at the picture of a species "trying on" a faculty giving rise to beliefs most of which were false, having its inutility demonstrated, and abandoning it. A species might "experiment" by mutation in any number of inefficacious systems, but none of these systems would deserve to be called belief systems precisely because of their defects, their nonrationality, and hence a false belief system is a conceptual impossibility. To borrow an example from a short story by MacDonald Harris, a soluble fish is an evolutionary impossibility, but a system for false beliefs cannot even be given a coherent description. The same evolutionary bias in favor of truth prunes the capacity to communicate as it develops; a capacity for false communication would not be a capacity for communication at all, but just an emission proclivity of no systematic value to the species. The faculty of communication would not gain ground in evolution unless it was by and large the faculty of transmitting true beliefs, which means only: the faculty of altering other members of the species in the direction of more optimal design. . . .

The concept of an intentional system explicated in these pages is made to bear a heavy load. It has been used here to form a bridge connecting the intentional domain (which includes our "common-sense" world of persons and actions, game theory, and the "neural signals" of the biologist) to the non-intentional domain of the physical sciences. That is a lot to expect of one concept, but nothing less than Brentano himself expected when, in a day of less fragmented science, he proposed intentionality as the mark that sunders the universe in the most fundamental way: dividing the mental from the physical.

Endnotes

[1]Note that what is *directly* selected, the gene, is a diagram and not a design; it is selected, however, because it happens to ensure that its bearer has a certain (functional) design. This was pointed out to me by Woodruff.

[2]Cf. Quine's argument about the necessity of "discovering" our logical connectives in any language we can translate in *Word and Object* (Cambridge, Mass.: MIT, 1960), Section 13. More will be said in defense of this below.

[3]Accepting the argument of Lewis Carroll, in "What the Tortoise Said to Achilles," *Mind* (1895), reprinted in I. M. Copi and J. A. Gould, *Readings on Logic* (New York: MacMillan, 1964), we cannot allow all the rules for a system to be replaced by beliefs, for this would generate an infinite and unproductive nesting of distinct beliefs about what can be inferred from what.

[4]This paragraph owes much to discussion with John Vickers, whose paper "Judgment and Belief," in K. Lambert, *The Logical Way of Doing Things* (New Haven, Conn.: Yale, 1969), goes beyond the remarks here by considering the problems of the relative strength or weighting of beliefs and desires.

[5]R. L. Gregory, *Eye and Brain* (London: World University Library, 1966): p. 137, reports that pigeons and fish given just this training are, not surprisingly, susceptible to visual illusions of length.

27. *Biosemantics*

RUTH GARRETT MILLIKAN

If mental states are states of organisms, and if organisms are, at bottom, complex natural (physical) systems, then how exactly can such states have content? How can they be representings of things that exist and, sometimes, representings of things that do not exist? Here Ruth Garrett Millikan goes beyond causal accounts of content that focus on the typical production of mental states. She suggests that a theory of the nature of mental contents must involve understanding the "proper functioning" of representations in the activities of organisms. She links such proper functioning to natural selection: humans, for example, have evolved to be "learning organisms" whose representings can "cut to the very bone of the ontological structure of the world." Professor Millikan is a professor of philosophy at the University of Connecticut Storrs.

Causal or informational theories of the semantic content of mental states which have had an eye on the problem of false representations have characteristically begun with something like this intuition. There are some circumstances under which an inner representation has its represented as a necessary and/or sufficient cause or condition of production. That is how the content of the representation is fixed. False representations are to be explained as tokens that are produced under other circumstances. The challenge, then, is to tell what defines certain circumstances as the content-fixing ones.

I.

Note that the answer cannot be just that these circumstances are *statistically* normal conditions. To gather such statistics, one would need to delimit a reference class of occasions, know how to count its members, and specify description categories. It would not do, for example, just to average over conditions-in-the-universe-any-place-any-time. Nor is it given how to carve out relevant description categories for conditions on occasions. Is it

"average" in the summer for it to be (precisely) between 80° and 80.5° Fahrenheit with humidity 87%? And are average conditions those which obtain on at least 50% of the occasions, or is it 90%? Depending on how one sets these parameters, radically different conditions are "statistically normal." But the notion of semantic content clearly is not relative, in this manner, to arbitrary parameters. The content-fixing circumstances must be *nonarbitrarily* determined.

A number of recent writers have made an appeal to teleology here, specifically to conditions of normal function or well-functioning of the systems that produce inner representations. Where the represented is R and its representation is "R," under conditions of well-functioning, we might suppose, only Rs can or are likely to produce "Rs." Or perhaps "R" is a representation of R just in case the system was designed to react to Rs by producing "Rs." But this sort of move yields too many representations. Every state of every functional system has normal causes, things that it is a response to in accordance with design. These causes may be proximate or remote, and many are disjunctive. Thus, a proximate normal cause of dilation of the skin capillaries is certain substances in the blood, more remote causes include muscular effort, sunburn, and being in an overheated environment. To each of these causes the vascular system responds by design, yet the response (a red face), though it may

From Ruth Garrett Millikan, "Biosemantics," originally published in the *Journal of Philosophy* 86, No. 6 (June 1989): 281–97. Reprinted by permission of the author and the *Journal of Philosophy*.

be a natural sign of burn or exertion or overheating, certainly is not a representation of that. If not every state of a system represents its normal causes, which are the states that do?

Jerry Fodor[1] has said that, whereas the content of an inner representation is determined by some sort of causal story, its status *as* a representation is determined by the functional organization of the part of the system which uses it. There is such a thing, it seems, as behaving like a representation without behaving like a representation of anything in particular. What the thing is a representation of is then determined by its cause under content-fixing conditions. It would be interesting to have the character of universal I-am-a-representation behavior spelled out for us. Yet, as Fodor well knows, there would still be the problem of demonstrating that there was only one normal cause per representation type.

A number of writers, including Dennis Stampe,[2] Fred Dretske,[3] and Mohan Matthen,[4] have suggested that what is different about effects that are representations is that their function is, precisely, to represent, "indicate," or "detect." For example, Matthen says of (fullfledged) perceptual states that they are "state[s] that [have] the function of *detecting* the presence of things of a certain type . . ." (*ibid.*, p. 20). It does not help to be told that inner representations are things that have representing (indicating, detecting) as their function, however, unless we are also told what kind of activity representing (indicating, detecting) is. Matthen does not tell us how to naturalize the notion "detecting." If "detecting" is a function of a representational state, it must be something that the state effects or produces. For example, it cannot be the function of a state to have been produced in response to something. Or does Matthen mean that it is not the representational states themselves, but the part of the system which produces them, which has the function of detecting? It has the function, say, of producing states that correspond to or covary with something in the outside world? But, unfortunately, not every device whose job description includes producing items that vary with the world is a representation producer. The devices in me that produce calluses are supposed to vary their placement according to where the friction is, but calluses are not representations. The pigment arrangers in the skin of a chameleon, the function of which is to vary the chameleon's color with what it sits on, are not representation producers.

Stampe and Dretske do address the question what representing or (Dretske) "detecting" is. Each brings in his own description of what a natural sign or natural representation is, then assimilates *having the function of representing R* to being a natural sign or representer of *R* when the system functions normally. Now, the production of natural signs is undoubtedly an accidental side effect of normal operation of many systems. From my red face you can tell that either I have been exerting myself, or I have been in the heat, or I am burned. But the production of an accidental side effect, no matter how regular, is not one of a system's functions; that goes by definition. More damaging, however, it simply is not true that representations must carry natural information. Consider the signals with which various animals signal danger. Nature knows that it is better to err on the side of caution, and it is likely that many of these signs occur more often in the absence than in the presence of any real danger. Certainly there is nothing incoherent in the idea that this might be so, hence that many of these signals do not carry natural information concerning the dangers they signal.

II.

I fully agree, however, that an appeal to teleology, to function, is what is needed to fly a naturalist theory of content. Moreover, what makes a thing into an inner representation is, near enough, that its function is to represent. But, I shall argue, the way to unpack this insight is to focus on representation *consumption*, rather than representation production. It is the devices that *use* representations which determine these to be representations and, at the same time (contra Fodor), determine their content. If it really is the function of an inner representation to indicate its represented, clearly it is not just a natural sign, a sign that you or I looking on might interpret. It must be one that functions as a sign or representation *for the system itself*. What is it then for a system to use a representation *as* a representation?

The conception of function on which I shall rely was defined in my *Language, Thought, and Other Biological Categories*[5] and defended in "In Defense of Proper Functions"[6] under the label "proper function." Proper functions are determined by the histories of the items possessing them; functions that were "selected for" are paradigm cases.[7] The notions "function" and "design" should not be read, however, as referring only to origin. Natural selection does not slack after the emergence of a structure but actively preserves it by acting against the later emergence of less fit structures. And structures can be preserved due to performance of new functions unrelated to the forces that originally shaped them. Such functions are "proper functions," too, and are "performed in accordance with design."

The notion "design" should not be read— and this is very important—as a reference to innateness. A system may have been designed to be altered by its experience, perhaps to learn from its experience in a prescribed manner. Doing what it has learned to do in this manner is then "behaving in accordance with design" or "functioning properly."[8]

My term "normal" should be read normatively, historically, and relative to specific function. In the first instance, "normal" applies to explanations. A "normal explanation" explains the performance of a particular function, telling how it was (typically) historically performed on those (perhaps rare) occasions when it was properly performed. Normal explanations do not tell, say, why it has been common for a function to be performed; they are not statistical explanations. They cover only past times of actual performance, showing how these performances were entailed by natural law, given certain conditions, coupled with the dispositions and structures of the relevant functional devices.[9] In the second instance, "normal" applies to conditions. A "normal condition for performance of a function" is a condition, the presence of which must be mentioned in giving a full normal explanation for performance of that function. Other functions of the same organism or system may have other normal conditions. For example, normal conditions for discriminating colors are not the same as normal conditions for discriminating tastes, and normal conditions for seeing very large objects are not the same as for seeing very small ones. It follows that "normal conditions" must not be read as having anything to do with what is typical or average or even, in many cases, at all common. First, many functions are performed only rarely. For example, very few wild seeds land in conditions normal for their growth and development, and the protective colorings of caterpillars seldom actually succeed in preventing them from being eaten. Indeed, normal conditions might almost better be called "historically optimal" conditions. (If normal conditions for proper functioning, hence survival and proliferation, were a statistical norm, imagine how many rabbits there would be in the world.) Second, many proper functions only need to be performed under rare conditions. Consider, for example, the vomiting reflex, the function of which is to prevent (further) toxification of the body. A normal condition for performance of this function is presence, specifically of poison in the stomach, for (I am guessing) it is only under that condition that this reflex has historically had beneficial effects. But poison in the stomach certainly is not an average condition. (Nor, of course, is it a normal condition for other functions of the digestive system.[10])

If it is actually one of a system's functions to produce representations, as we have said, these representations must function as representations for the system itself. Let us view the system, then, as divided into two parts or two aspects, one of which produces representations for the other to consume. What we need to look at is the consumer part, at what it is to use a thing *as* a representation. Indeed, a good look at the consumer part of the system ought to be all that is needed to determine not only representational status but representational content. We argue this as follows. First, the part of the system which consumes representations must understand the representations proffered to it. Suppose, for example, that there were abundant "natural information" (in Dretske's[11] sense) contained in numerous natural signs all present in a certain state of a system. This information could still not serve the system *as* information, unless the signs were understood by the system, and, furthermore, understood as bearers of whatever specific information they, in fact, do bear. (Contrast Fodor's notion that something could function like a representation without functioning like a representation of anything in particular.) So there must be something about the consumer that *constitutes* its taking the signs to indicate, say, *p*, *q*, and *r* rather than *s*, *t*, and *u*. But, if we know what constitutes the consumer's *taking* a sign to indicate *p*, what *q*, what *r*, etc., then, granted that the consumer's takings are in some way systematically derived from the structures of the signs so taken, we can construct a semantics for the consumer's language. Anything the signs may indicate qua natural signs or natural information carriers then drops out as entirely irrelevant; the representation-producing side of the system had better pay undivided attention to the language of its consumer. The sign producer's function will be to produce signs that are true *as the consumer reads the language.*

The problem for the naturalist bent on describing intentionality, then, does not concern representation production at all. Although a representation always is something that is produced by a system whose proper function is to make that representation correspond by rule to the world, what the rule of correspondence is, what gives definition to this function, is determined entirely by the representation's consumers.

For a system to use an inner item as a representation, I propose, is for the following two conditions to be met. First, unless the representation accords, *so* (by a certain rule), with a represented, the consumer's normal use of, or response to, the representation will not be able to fulfill all of the consumer's proper functions in so responding—not, at least, in accordance with a normal explanation. (Of course, it might still fulfill these functions by freak accident, but not in the historically normal way.) Putting this more formally, that the representation and the represented accord with one another, so, is a normal condition for proper functioning of the consumer device as it reacts to the representation.[12] Note that the proposal is not that the content of the representation rests on the function of the representation or of the consumer, on what these do. The idea is not that there is such a thing as behaving like a representation of *X* or as being treated like a representation of *X*. The content hangs only on there being a certain condition that would be *normal* for performance of the consumer's functions—namely, that a certain correspondence relation hold between sign and world—whatever those functions may happen to be. For example, suppose the semantic rules for my belief representations are determined by the fact that belief tokens in me will aid the devices that use them to perform certain of their tasks in accordance with a normal explanation for success only under the condition that the forms or "shapes" of these belief tokens correspond, in accordance with said rules, to conditions in the world. Just what these user tasks are need not be mentioned.[13]

Second, represented conditions are conditions that vary, depending on the *form* of the representation, in accordance with specifiable correspondence rules that give the semantics for the relevant *system* of representation. More precisely, representations always admit of significant transformations (in the mathematical sense), which accord with transformations of their corresponding representeds, thus displaying significant articulation into variant and invariant aspects. If an item considered as compounded of certain variant and invariant aspects can be said to be "composed" of these, then we can also say that every representation is, as such, a member of a representational system having a "compositional semantics." For it is not that the represented condition is itself a normal condition for proper operation of the representation consumer. A certain correspondence between the representation and the world is what is normal. Coordinately, there is no such thing as a representation consumer that can understand only one representation. There are always other representations, composed other ways, saying other things, which it could have understood as well, in accordance with the same principles of operation. A couple of very elementary examples should make this clear.[14]

First, consider beavers, who splash the water smartly with their tails to signal danger. This instinctive behavior has the function of causing other beavers to take cover. The splash means danger, because only when it corresponds to danger does the instinctive response to the splash on the part of the interpreter beavers, the consumers, serve a purpose. If there is no danger present, the interpreter beavers interrupt their activities uselessly. Hence, that the splash corresponds to danger is a normal condition for proper functioning of the interpreter beavers' instinctive reaction to the splash. (It does not follow, of course, that it is a usual condition. Beavers being skittish, most beaver splashes possibly occur in response to things not in fact endangering the beaver.) In the beaver splash semantic system, the time and place of the splash varies with, "corresponds to," the time and place of danger. The representation is articulate: properly speaking, it is not a splash but a splash-at-a-time-and-a-place. Other representations in the same system, splashes at other times and places, indicate other danger locations.

Second, consider honey bees, which perform "dances" to indicate the location of sources of nectar they have discovered. Variations in the tempo of the dance and in the angle of its long axis vary with the distance and direction of the nectar. The interpreter mechanisms in the watching bees—these are the representation consumers—will not perform their full proper functions of aiding the process of nectar collection in accordance with a normal explanation, unless the location of nectar corresponds correctly to the dance. So, the dances are representations of the location of nectar. The full representation here is a dance-at-a-time-in-a-place-at-a-tempo-with-an-orientation.

Notice that, on this account, it is not necessary to assume that most representations are true. Many biological devices perform their proper functions not on the average, but just often enough. The protective coloring of the juveniles of many animal species, for example, is an adaptation passed on because *occasionally* it prevents a juvenile from being eaten, though most of the juveniles of these species get eaten anyway. Similarly, it is conceivable that the devices that fix human beliefs fix true ones not on the average, but just often enough. If the true beliefs are functional and the false beliefs are, for the most part, no worse than having an empty mind, then even very fallible belief-fixing devices might be better than no belief-fixing devices at all. These devices might even be, in a sense, "designed to deliver some falsehoods." Perhaps, given the difficulty of designing highly accurate belief-fixing mechanisms, it is actually advantageous to fix too many beliefs, letting some of these be false, rather than fix too few beliefs. Coordinately, perhaps our belief-consuming mechanisms are carefully designed to tolerate a large proportion of false

beliefs. It would not follow, of course, that the belief consumers are designed to *use* false beliefs, certainly not that false beliefs can serve all of the functions that true ones can. Indeed, surely if none of the mechanisms that used beliefs ever cared at all how or whether these beliefs corresponded to anything in the world, beliefs would not be functioning as representations, but in some other capacity.

Shifting our focus from producing devices to consuming devices in our search for naturalized semantic content is important. But the shift from the *function* of consumers to *normal conditions* for proper operation is equally important. Matthen, for example, characterizes what he calls a "quasi-perceptual state" as, roughly, one whose job is to cause the system to do what it must do to perform its function, given that it is in certain circumstances, which are what it represents. Matthen is thus looking pretty squarely at the representation consumers, but at what it is the representation's job to get these consumers to do, rather than at normal conditions for their proper operation. As a result, Matthen now retreats. The description he has given of quasi-perceptual states, he says, cannot cover "real perception such as that which we humans experience. Quite simply, there is no such thing as *the* proper response, or even a range of functionally appropriate responses, to what perception tells us" (*op. cit.*, p. 20).[15] On the contrary, representational content rests not on univocity of consumer function but on sameness of normal conditions for those functions. The same percept of the world may be used to guide any of very many and diverse activities, practical or theoretical. What stays the same is that the percept must correspond to environmental configurations in accordance with the same correspondence rules for each of these activities. For example, if the position of the chair in the room does not correspond, so, to my visual representation of its position, that will hinder me equally in my attempts to avoid the chair when passing through the room, to move the chair, to sit in it, to remove the cat from it, to make judgments about it, etc. Similarly, my belief that New York is large may be turned to any of diverse purposes, but those which require it to be a *representation* require also that New York indeed be large if these purposes are to succeed in accordance with a normal explanation for functioning of my cognitive systems.

III.

We have just cleanly bypassed the whole genre of causal/informational accounts of mental content. To illustrate this, we consider an example of Dretske's. Dretske tells of a certain species of northern hemisphere bacteria which orient themselves away from toxic oxygen-rich surface water by attending to their magnetosomes, tiny inner magnets, which pull toward the magnetic north pole, hence pull down (*ibid.*). (Southern hemisphere bacteria have their magnetosomes reversed.) The function of the magnetosome thus appears to be to effect that the bacterium moves into oxygen-free water. Correlatively, intuition tells us that what the pull of the magnetosome represents is the whereabouts of oxygen-free water. The direction of oxygen-free water is not, however, a factor in *causing* the direction of pull of the magnetosome. And the most reliable natural information that the magnetosome carries is surely not about oxygen-free water but about distal and proximal causes of the pull, about the direction of geomagnetic or better, just plain magnetic, north. One can, after all, easily deflect the magnetosome away from the direction of lesser oxygen merely by holding a bar magnet overhead. Moreover, it is surely a function of the magnetosome to respond to that magnetic field, that is part of its normal mechanism of operation, whereas responding to oxygen density is not. None of this makes any sense on a causal or informational approach.

But on the biosemantic theory it does make sense. What the magnetosome represents is only what its *consumers* require that it correspond to in order to perform *their* tasks. Ignore, then, how the representation (a pull-in-a-direction-at-a-time) is normally produced. Concentrate, instead, on how the systems that react to the representation work, on what these systems need in order to do their job. What they need is only that the pull be in the direction of oxygen-free water at the time. For example, they care not at all how it came about that the pull is in that direction; the magnetosome

that points toward oxygen-free water quite by accident and not in accordance with any normal explanation will do just as well as one that points that way for the normal reasons. (As Socrates concedes in the *Meno*, true opinion is just as good as knowledge so long as it stays put.) What the magnetosome represents then is univocal; it represents only the direction of oxygen-free water. For that is the only thing that corresponds (by a compositional rule) to it, the absence of which would matter—the absence of which would disrupt the function of those mechanisms which rely on the magnetosome for guidance.

It is worth noting that what is represented by the magnetosome is not proximal but distal; no proximal stimulus is represented at all. Nor, of course, does the bacterium perform an inference from the existence of the proximal stimulus (the magnetic field) to the existence of the represented. These are good results for a theory of content to have, for otherwise one needs to introduce a derivative theory of content for mental representations that do not refer, say, to sensory stimulations, and also a foundationalist account of belief fixation. Note also that, on the present view, representations manufactured in identical ways by different species of animal might have different contents. Thus, a certain kind of small swift image on the toad's retina, manufactured by his eye lens, represents a bug, for that is what it must correspond to if the reflex it (invariably) triggers is to perform its proper functions normally, while exactly the same kind of small swift image on the retina of a male hoverfly, manufactured, let us suppose, by a nearly identical lens, represents a passing female hoverfly, for that is what it must correspond to if the female-chasing reflex it (invariably) triggers is to perform its proper functions normally. Turning the coin over, representations with the same content may be normally manufactured in a diversity of ways, even in the same species. How many different ways do you have, for example, of telling a lemon or your spouse? Nor is it necessary that any of the ways one has of manufacturing a given representation be especially reliable ways in order for the representation to have determinate content. These various results cut the biosemantic approach off from all varieties of verificationism and foundationalism with a clean, sharp knife.

IV.

But perhaps it will be thought that belief fixation and consumption are not biologically proper activities, hence that there are no normal explanations, in our defined sense, for proper performances of human beliefs. Unlike bee dances, which are all variations on the same simple theme, beliefs in dinosaurs, in quarks, and in the instability of the dollar are recent, novel, and innumerably diverse, as are their possible uses. How could there be anything *biologically* normal or abnormal about the details of the consumption of such beliefs?

But what an organism does in accordance with evolutionary design can be very novel and surprising, for the more complex of nature's creatures are designed to learn. Unlike evolutionary adaptation, learning is not accomplished by *random* generate-and-test procedures. Even when learning involves trial and error (probably the exception rather than the rule), there are principles in accordance with which responses are selected by the system to try, and there are specific principles of generalization and discrimination, etc., which have been built into the system by natural selection. How these principles normally work, that is, how they work given normal (i.e., historically optimal) environments, to produce changes in the learner's nervous system which will effect the furthering of ends of the system has, of course, an explanation—the normal explanation for proper performance of the learning mechanism and of the states of the nervous system it produces.

Using a worn-out comparison, there is an infinity of functions which a modern computer mainframe is capable of performing, depending upon its input and on the program it is running. Each of these things it can do, so long as it is not damaged or broken, "in accordance with design," and to each of these capacities there corresponds an explanation of how it would be activated or fulfilled normally. The human's mainframe takes, roughly, stimulations of the afferent nerves as input, both to program and to run it.[16] It responds, in part, by developing concepts, by acquiring beliefs and desires in accordance with these concepts, by engaging in practical inference leading ultimately to action. Each of these activi-

ties may, of course, involve circumscribed sorts of trial and error learning. When conditions are optimal, all this aids survival and proliferation in accordance with an historically normal explanation—one of high generality, of course. When conditions are not optimal, it may yield, among other things, empty or confused concepts, biologically useless desires, and false beliefs. But, even when the desires are biologically useless (though probably not when the concepts expressed in them are empty or confused), there are still biologically normal ways for them to get fulfilled, the most obvious of which require reliance on true beliefs.[17]

Yet how do we know that our contemporary ways of forming concepts, desires, and beliefs do occur in accordance with evolutionary design? Fodor, for example, is ready with the labels "pop Darwinism" and "naive adaptationism" to abuse anyone who supposes that our cognitive systems were actually selected for their belief and desire using capacities.[18] Clearly, to believe that every structure must have a function would be naive. Nor is it wise uncritically to adopt hypotheses about the functions of structures when these functions are obscure. It does not follow that we should balk at the sort of adaptationist who, having found a highly complex structure that quite evidently is currently and effectively performing a highly complex and obviously indispensable function, then concludes, *ceteris paribus,* that this function has been the most recent historical task stabilizing the structure. To suspect that the brain has not been preserved for thinking with or that the eye has not been preserved for seeing with—to suspect this, moreover, in the absence of any alternative hypotheses about causes of the stability of these structures—would be totally irresponsible. Consider: nearly every human behavior is bound up with intentional action. Are we really to suppose that the degree to which our behaviors help to fulfill intentions, and the degree to which intentions result from logically related desires plus beliefs, is a sheer coincidence—that these patterns are irrelevant to survival and proliferation or, though relevant, have had no stabilizing effect on the gene pool? But the only alternative to biological design, in our sense of "design", is sheer coincidence, freak accident—unless there is a ghost running the machine!

Indeed, it is reasonable to suppose that the brain structures we have recently been using in developing space technology and elementary particle physics have been operating in accordance with the very same general principles as when prehistoric man used them for more primitive ventures. They are no more performing new and different functions or operating in accordance with new and different principles nowadays than are the eyes when what they see is television screens and space shuttles. Compare: the wheel was invented for the purpose of rolling ox carts, and did not come into its own (pulleys, gears, etc.) for several thousand years thereafter, during the industrial revolution. Similarly, it is reasonable that the cognitive structures with which man is endowed were originally nature's solution to some very simple demands made by man's evolutionary niche. But the solution nature stumbled on was elegant, supremely general, and powerful, indeed; I believe it was a solution that cut to the very bone of the ontological structure of the world. That solution involved the introduction of representations, inner and/or outer, having a subject/predicate structure, and subject to a negation transformation. (Why I believe that that particular development was so radical and so powerful has been explained in depth in LTOBC, chapters 14–19. But see also section V.6. . . .)

———

V.

One last worry about our sort of position is voiced by Daniel Dennett[19] and discussed at length by Fodor.[20] Is it really plausible that bacteria and paramecia, or even birds and bees, have inner representations in the same sense that we do? Am I really prepared to say that these creatures, too, have mental states, that they think? I am not prepared to say that. On the contrary, the representations that they have must differ from human beliefs in at least six very fundamental ways.[21]

(1) *Self-representing Elements.* The representations that the magnetosome produces have three significant variables, each of which refers to itself. The time of the pull refers to the time of the oxygen-free water, the locale of the pull refers to the locale of the oxygen-free water, and the direction of pull refers to the direction of oxygen-free water. The beaver's splash has two self-referring variables: a splash at a certain time and place indicates that there is danger at that same time and place. (There is nothing necessary about this. It might have meant that there would be danger at the nearest beaver dam in five minutes.) Compare the standard color coding on the outsides of colored markers: each color stands for itself. True, it may be that sophisticated indexical representations such as percepts and indexical beliefs also have their time or place or both as significant self-representing elements, but they also have other significant variables that are not self-representing. The magnetosome does not.

(2) *Storing Representations.* Any representation the time or place of which is a significant variable obviously cannot be stored away, carried about with the organism for use on future occasions. Most beliefs are representations that can be stored away. Clearly this is an important difference.

(3) *Indicative and Imperative Representations.* The theory I have sketched here of the content of inner representations applies only to indicative representations, representations which are supposed to be determined by the facts, which tell what is the case. It does not apply to imperative representations, representations which are supposed to determine the facts, which tell the interpreter what to do. Neither do causal-informational theories of content apply to the contents of imperative representations. True, some philosophers seem to have assumed that having defined the content of various mental symbols by reference to what causes them to enter the "belief box," then when one finds these same symbols in, say, the "desire box" or the "intention box," one already knows what they mean. But how do we know that the desire box or the intention box use the same representational system as the belief box? To answer that question we would have to know what constitutes a desire box's or an intention box's using one representational system rather than another which, turned around, is the very question at issue. In LTOBC and "Thoughts Without Laws; Cognitive Science With Content,"[22] I developed a parallel theory of the content of imperative representations. Very roughly, one of the proper functions of the consumer system for an imperative representation is to help *produce* a

correspondence between the representation and the world. (Of course, this proper function often is not performed.) I also argued that desires and intentions are imperative representations.

Consider, then, the beaver's splash. It tells that there is danger here now. Or why not say, instead, that it tells other nearby beavers what to do now, namely, to seek cover? Consider the magnetosome. It tells which is the direction of oxygen-free water. Or why not say, instead, that it tells the bacterium which way to go? Simple animal signals are invariably both indicative and imperative. Even the dance of the honey bee, which is certainly no simple signal, is both indicative and imperative. It tells the worker bees where the nectar is; equally, it tells them where to go. The step from these primitive representations to human beliefs is an enormous one, for it involves the separation of indicative from imperative functions of the representational system. Representations that are undifferentiated between indicative and imperative connect states of affairs directly to actions, to specific things to be done in the face of those states of affairs. Human beliefs are not tied directly to actions. Unless combined with appropriate desires, human beliefs are impotent. And human desires are equally impotent unless combined with suitable beliefs.[23]

(4) *Inference.* As indicative and imperative functions are separated in the central inner representational systems of humans, they need to be reintegrated. Thus, humans engage in practical inference, combining beliefs and desires in novel ways to yield first intentions and then action. Humans also combine beliefs with beliefs to yield new beliefs. Surely nothing remotely like this takes place inside the bacterium.

(5) *Acts of Identifying.* Mediate inferences always turn on something like a middle term, which must have the same representational value in both premises for the inference to go through. Indeed, the representation consumers in us perform many functions that require them to use two or more overlapping representations together, and in such a manner that, unless the representeds corresponding to these indeed have a common element, these functions will not be properly performed. Put informally, the consumer device *takes* these represented elements to be the same, thus identifying their representational values. Suppose, for example, that you intend to speak to Henry about something. In order to carry out this intention you must, when the time comes, be able to recognize Henry in perception as the person to whom you intend to speak. You must identify Henry as represented in perception with Henry as represented in your intention. Activities that involve the coordinated use of representations from different sensory modalities, as in the case of eye-hand coordination, visual-tactile coordination, also require that certain objects, contours, places, or directions, etc., be identified as the same through the two modalities. Now, the foundation upon which modern representational theories of thought are built depends upon a denial that what is thought of is ever placed before a naked mind. Clearly, we can never know what an inner representation represents by a direct comparison of representation to represented. Rather, acts of identifying are our ways of "knowing what our representations represent." The bacterium is quite incapable of knowing, in this sense, what its representations are about. This might be a reason to say that it does not understand its own representations, not really.

(6) *Negation and Propositional Content.* The representational system to which the magnetosome pull belongs does not contain negation. Indeed, it does not even contain contrary representations, for the magnetosome cannot pull in two directions at once. Similarly, if two beavers splash at different times or places, or if two bees dance different dances at the same time, it may well be that there is indeed beaver danger two times or two places and that there is indeed nectar in two different locations.[24] Without contrariety, no conflict, of course and more specifically, no contradiction. If the law of non-contradiction plays as significant a role in the development of human concepts and knowledge as has traditionally been supposed, this is a large difference between us and the bacterium indeed.[25] In LTOBC, I argued that negation, hence explicit contradiction, is dependent upon subject-predicate, that is, propositional, structure and vice versa. Thus, representations that are simpler also do not have propositional content.

In sum, these six differences between our representations and those of the bacterium, or Fodor's paramecia, ought to be enough amply to secure our superiority, to make us feel comfortably more endowed with mind.

Endnotes

[1]"Banish Discontent," in Jeremy Butterfield, ed., *Language, Mind and Logic* (New York: Cambridge, 1986), pp. 1–23; *Psychosemantics: The Problem of Meaning in the Philosophy of Mind* (Cambridge: MIT, 1987).

[2]"Toward a Causal Theory of Representation," in Peter French, Theodore Uehling Jr., Howard Wettstein, eds., *Contemporary Perspectives in the Philosophy of Language* (Minneapolis: Minnesota UP, 1979), pp. 81–102.

[3]"Misrepresentation," in Radu Bogdan, ed., *Belief Form, Content, and Function* (New York: Oxford, 1986), pp. 17–36.

[4]"Biological Functions and Perceptual Content," this JOURNAL, LXXXV, 1 (January 1988):5–27.

[5]Cambridge: MIT, 1984 (hereafter LTOBC).

[6]*Philosophy of Science*, LVI, 2 (June 1989): 288–302.

[7]An odd custom exists of identifying this sort of view with Larry Wright, who does not hold it. See my "In Defense of Proper Functions." Natural selection is not the only source of proper functions. See LTOBC, chs. 1 and 2.

[8]See LTOBC; and "Truth Rules, Hoverflies, and the Kripke-Wittgenstein Paradox," *The Philosophical Review* (forthcoming).

[9]This last clarification is offered to aid Fodor ("On There Not Being an Evolutionary Theory of Content" [hereafter NETC], forthcoming), who uses my term 'Normal' (here I am not capitalizing it but the idea has not changed) in a multiply confused way, making a parody of my views on representation. In this connection, see also fns. 13 and 17.

[10]"Normal explanation" and "normal condition for performance of a function," along with "proper function," are defined with considerable detail in LTOBC. The reader may wish, in particular, to consult the discussion of normal explanations for performance of "adapted and derived proper functions" in ch. 2, for these functions cover the functions of states of the nervous system which result in part from learning, such as states of human belief and desire.

[11]*Knowledge and the Flow of Information* (Cambridge: MIT, 1981).

[12]Strictly, this normal condition must derive from a "most proximate normal explanation" of the consumer's proper functioning. See LTOBC, ch. 6, where a more precise account of what I am here calling "representations" is given under the heading "intentional icons."

[13]In this particular case, one task is, surely, contributing, in conformity with certain general principles or rules, to practical inference processes, hence to the fulfillment of current desires. So, if you like, all beliefs have the *same* proper function. Or, since the rules or principles that govern practical inference dictate that a belief's "shape" determines what other inner representations it may properly be combined with to form what products, we could say that each belief has a *different* range of proper functions. Take your pick. Cf. Fodor, "Information and Representation," in Philip Hanson, ed., *Information, Language, and Cognition* (Vancouver: British Columbia UP, 1989); and NETC.

[14]These examples are of representations that are not "inner" but out in the open. As in the case of inner representations, however, they are produced and consumed by mechanisms designed to cooperate with one another; each such representation stands intermediate between two parts of a single biological system.

[15]Dretske (in "Misrepresentation," p. 28) and David Papineau [in *Reality and Representation* (New York: Blackwell, 1987), p. 67ff] have similar concerns.

[16]This is a broad metaphor. I am not advocating computationalism.

[17]A word of caution. The normal conditions for a desire's fulfillment are not necessarily fulfillable conditions. In general, normal conditions for fulfillment of a function are not quite the same as conditions which, when you add them and stir, always effect proper function, because they may well be impossible conditions. For example, Fodor, in "Information and Representation" and NETC, has questioned me about the normal conditions under which his desire that it should rain tomorrow will perform its proper function of *getting* it to rain. Now, the biologically normal way for such a desire to be fulfilled is exactly the same as for any other desire: one has or acquires true beliefs about how to effect the fulfillment of the desire and acts on them. Biologically normal conditions for fulfillment of the desire for rain thus include the condition that one has true beliefs about how to make it rain. Clearly this is an example in which the biological norm fails to accord with the statistical norm: most desires about the weather are fulfilled, if at all, by biological accident. It may even be that the laws of nature, coupled with my situation, prohibit my having any true beliefs about how to make it rain; the needed general condition cannot be realized in the particular case. Similarly, normal conditions for proper function of beliefs in impossible things are, of course, impossible conditions: these beliefs are such that they cannot correspond, in accordance with the rules of mentalese, to conditions in the world.

[18]*Psychosemantics* and NETC.

[19]*Brainstorms* (Montgomery, VT: Bradford Books, 1978).

[20]"Why Paramecia Don't Have Mental Representations," in P. French, T. Uehling Jr., and H. Wettstein, eds., *Midwest Studies in Philosophy*, x (Minneapolis: Minnesota UP, 1986), pp. 3–23.

[21]Accordingly, in LTOBC I did not call these primitive forms "representations" but "intentional signals" and, for items like bee dances, "intentional icons," reserving the term "representation" for those icons, the representational values of which must be identified if their consumers are to function properly—see V.5. . . .

[22]*The Philosophical Review*, XLV, 1 (1986):47–80.

[23]Possibly human intentions are in both indicative and imperative mood, however, functioning simultaneously to represent settled facts about one's future and to direct one's action.

[24]On the other hand, the bees cannot go two places at once.

[25]In LTOBC, I defend the position that the law of non-contradiction plays a crucial role in allowing us to develop new methods of mapping the world with representations.

28. *The Nature of Mind*

DAVID M. ARMSTRONG

During the middle third of the twentieth century, many philosophers who rejected dualism were influenced by some form of behaviorism. In 1913, the psychologist J. B. Watson had begun to argue that psychology could ignore consciousness and should not rely on introspection. For some, behaviorism was primarily a methodological recommendation: one should investigate psychological phenomena by studying behavior. For others, behaviorism was a metaphysical thesis: behavior is all there is to psychological phenomena. It eventually became clear that metaphysical behaviorism faced serious problems. It proved impossible to classify behavior as belonging to interesting psychological categories without making some use of "mentalistic" concepts. And it proved fruitful to posit "inner" states as causes of behavior and as the basis of tendencies to behave. Some philosophers who still wanted to reject dualism proposed identity theories: mental states are neurophysiological states that cause behavior. Armstrong, an Australian philosopher who teaches at the University of Sydney, proposed a version of the identity theory that attempts to specify mental states in terms of their causal or functional character.

Men have minds, that is to say, they perceive, they have sensations, emotions, beliefs, thoughts, purposes, and desires.[1] What is it to have a mind? What is it to perceive, to feel emotion, to hold a belief, or to have a purpose? In common with many other modern philosophers, I think that the best clue we have to the nature of mind is furnished by the discoveries and hypotheses of modern science concerning the nature of man.

What does modern science have to say about the nature of man? There are, of course, all sorts of disagreements and divergencies in the views of individual scientists. But I think it is true to say that one view is steadily gaining ground, so that it bids fair to become established scientific doctrine. This is the view that we can give a complete account of man *in purely physico-chemical terms.* This view has received a tremendous impetus in the last decade from the new subject of molecular biology, a subject which promises to unravel the physical and chemical mechanisms which lie at the basis of life. Before that time, it received great encouragement from pioneering work in neurophysiology pointing to the likelihood of a purely electro-chemical account of the working of the brain. I think it is fair to say that those scientists who still reject the physico-chemical account of man do so primarily for philosophical, or moral, or religious reasons, and only secondarily, and half-heartedly, for reasons of scientific detail. This is not to say that in the future new evidence and new problems may not come to light which will force science to reconsider the physico-chemical view of man. But at present, the drift of scientific thought is clearly set towards the physico-chemical hypothesis. And we have nothing better to go on than the present.

For me, then, and for many philosophers who think like me, the moral is clear. We must try to work out an account of the nature of mind which is compatible with the view that man is nothing but a physico-chemical mechanism.

And in this paper I shall be concerned to do just this: to sketch (in barest outline) what may be called a Materialist or Physicalist account of the mind.

But before doing this I should like to go back and consider a criticism of my position which must inevitably occur to some. What reason have I, it may be asked, for taking my stand on science? Even granting that I am right about what is the currently dominant scientific view of man, why should we concede science a special authority to decide questions about the nature of man? What of the authority of philosophy, of religion, of morality, or even of literature and art? Why do I set the authority of science above all these? Why this 'scientism'?

It seems to me that the answer to this question is very simple. If we consider the search for truth, in all its fields, we find that it is only in science that men versed in their subject can, after investigation that is more or less prolonged, and which may in some cases extend beyond a single human lifetime, reach substantial agreement about what is the case. It is only as a result of scientific investigation that we ever seem to reach an intellectual consensus about controversial matters.

In the Epistle Dedicatory to his *De Corpore*, Hobbes wrote of William Harvey, the discoverer of the circulation of the blood, that he was 'the only man I know, that conquering envy, hath established a new doctrine in his lifetime'.

Before Copernicus, Galileo and Harvey, Hobbes remarks, 'There was nothing certain in natural philosophy.' And, we might add, with the exception of mathematics, there was nothing certain in any other learned discipline.

These remarks of Hobbes are incredibly revealing. They show us what a watershed in the intellectual history of the human race the seventeenth century was. Before that time inquiry proceeded, as it were, in the dark. Men could not hope to see their doctrine *established*, that is to say, accepted by the vast majority of those properly versed in the subject under discussion. There was no intellectual consensus. Since that time, it has become a commonplace to see new doctrines, sometimes of the most far-reaching kind, established to the satisfaction of the learned, often within the lifetime of their first proponents. Science has provided us with a method of deciding disputed questions. This is not to say, of course, that the consensus of those who are learned and competent in a subject cannot be mistaken. Of course such a consensus can be mistaken.

Sometimes it has been mistaken. But, granting fallibility, what better authority have we than such a consensus?

Now this is of the utmost importance. For in philosophy, in religion, in such disciplines as literary criticism, in moral questions in so far as they are thought to be matters of truth and falsity, there has been a notable failure to achieve an intellectual consensus about disputed questions among the learned. Must we not then attach a peculiar authority to the discipline that can achieve a consensus? And if it presents us with a certain vision of the nature of man, is this not a powerful reason for accepting that vision?

I will not take up here the deeper question *why* it is that the methods of science have enabled us to achieve an intellectual consensus about so many disputed matters. That question, I think, could receive no brief or uncontroversial answer. I am resting my argument on the simple and uncontroversial fact that, as a result of scientific investigation, such a consensus has been achieved.

It may be replied—it often is replied—that while science is all very well in its own sphere—the sphere of the physical, perhaps—there are matters of fact on which it is not competent to pronounce. And among such matters, it may be claimed, is the question what is the whole nature of man. But I cannot see that this reply has much force. Science has provided us with an island of truths, or, perhaps one should say, a raft of truths, to bear us up on the sea of our disputatious ignorance. There may have to be revisions and refinements, new results may set old findings in a new perspective, but what science has given us will not be altogether superseded. Must we not therefore appeal to these relative certainties for guidance when we come to consider uncertainties elsewhere? Perhaps science cannot help us to decide whether or not there is a God, whether or not human beings have immortal souls, or whether or not the will is free. But if science cannot assist us, what can? I conclude that it is the scientific vision of man, and not the philosophical or religious or artistic or moral vision of man, that is the best clue we have to the nature of man. And it is rational to argue from the best evidence we have.

Having in this way attempted to justify my procedure, I turn back to my subject: the attempt to work out an account of mind, or, if you prefer, of mental process, within the framework of the physico-chemical, or, as we may call it, the Materialist view of man.

Now there is one account of mental process that is at once attractive to any philosopher sympathetic to a Materialist view of man: this is Behaviourism. Formulated originally by a psychologist, J. B. Watson, it attracted widespread interest and considerable support from scientifically oriented philosophers. Traditional philosophy had tended to think of the mind as a rather mysterious inward arena that lay behind, and was responsible for, the outward or physical behaviour of our bodies. Descartes thought of this inner arena as a *spiritual substance,* and it was this conception of the mind as spiritual object that Gilbert Ryle attacked, apparently in the interest of Behaviourism, in his important book *The Concept of Mind*. He ridiculed the Cartesian view as the dogma of 'the ghost in the machine'. The mind was not something behind the behaviour of the body, it was simply part of that physical behaviour. My anger with you is not some modification of a spiritual substance which somehow brings about aggressive behaviour; rather it is the aggressive behaviour itself; my addressing strong words to you, striking you, turning my back on you, and so on. Thought is not an inner process that lies behind, and brings about, the words I speak and write: it is my speaking and writing. The mind is not an inner arena, it is outward act.

It is clear that such a view of mind fits in very well with a completely Materialistic or Physicalist view of man. If there is no need to draw a distinction between mental processes and their expression in physical behaviour, but if instead the mental processes are identified with their so-called 'expressions,' then the existence of mind stands in no conflict with the view that man is nothing but a physico-chemical mechanism.

However, the version of Behaviourism that I have just sketched is a very crude version, and its crudity lays it open to obvious objections. One obvious difficulty is that it is our common experience that there can be mental processes going on although there is no behaviour occurring that could possibly be treated as expressions of these processes. A man may be angry, but give no bodily sign; he may think, but say or do nothing at all.

In my view, the most plausible attempt to refine Behaviourism with a view to meeting this objection was made by introducing the notion of *a disposition to behave.* (Dispositions to behave play a particularly important part in Ryle's account of the mind.) Let us consider the general notion of disposition first. Brittleness is a disposition, a disposition possessed by materials like glass. Brittle materials are those which, when subjected to relatively small forces, break or shatter easily. But breaking and shattering easily is not brittleness, rather it is the *manifestation* of brittleness. Brittleness itself is the tendency or liability of the material to break or shatter easily. A piece of glass may never shatter or break throughout its whole history, but it is still the case that it is brittle: it is liable to shatter or break if dropped quite a small way or hit quite lightly. Now a disposition to *behave* is simply a tendency or liability of a person to behave in a certain way under certain circumstances. The brittleness of glass is a disposition that the glass retains throughout its history, but clearly there could also be dispositions that come and go. The dispositions to behave that are of interest to the Behaviourist are, for the most part, of this temporary character.

Now how did Ryle and others use the notion of a disposition to behave to meet the obvious objection to Behaviourism that there can be mental processes going on although the subject is engaging in no relevant behaviour? Their strategy was to argue that in such cases, although the subject was not behaving in any relevant way, he or she was *disposed* to behave in some relevant way. The glass does not shatter, but it is still brittle. The man does not behave, but he does have a disposition to behave. We can say he thinks although he does not speak or act because at that time he was disposed to speak or act in a certain way. *If* he had been asked, perhaps, he would have spoken or acted. We can say he is angry although he does not behave angrily, because he is disposed so to behave. *If* only one more word had been addressed to him, he would have burst out. And so on. In this way it was hoped that Behaviourism could be squared with the obvious facts.

It is very important to see just how these thinkers conceived of dispositions. I quote from Ryle:

To possess a dispositional property *is not to be in a particular state, or to undergo a particular change;* it is to be bound or liable to be in a particular state, or to undergo a particular change, when a particular condition is realised. (*The Concept of Mind*, p. 43, my italics.)

So to explain the breaking of a lightly struck glass on a particular occasion by saying it was brittle is, on this view of dispositions, simply to say that the glass broke because it is the sort of thing that regularly breaks when quite lightly struck. The breaking was the normal behaviour, or not abnormal behaviour, of such a thing. The brittleness is not to be conceived of as a *cause* for the breakage, or even, more vaguely, a *factor* in bringing about the breaking. Brittleness is just the fact that things of that sort break easily.

But although in this way the Behaviourists did something to deal with the objection that mental processes can occur in the absence of behaviour, it seems clear, now that the shouting and the dust have died, that they did not do enough. When I think, but my thoughts do not issue in any action, it seems as obvious as anything is obvious that there is something actually going on in me which constitutes my thought. It is not simply that I would speak or act if some conditions that are unfulfilled were to be fulfilled. Something is currently going on, in the strongest and most literal sense of 'going on', and this something is my thought. Rylean Behaviourism denies this, and so it is unsatisfactory as a theory of mind. Yet I know of no version of Behaviourism that is more satisfactory. The moral for those of us who wish to take a purely physicalistic view of man is that we must look for some other account of the nature of mind and of mental processes.

But perhaps we need not grieve too deeply about the failure of Behaviourism to produce a satisfactory theory of mind. Behaviourism is a profoundly unnatural account of mental processes. If somebody speaks and acts in certain ways it is natural to speak of this speech and action as the *expression* of his thought. It is not at all natural to speak of his speech and action as identical with his thought. We naturally think of the thought as something quite distinct from the speech and action which, under suitable circumstances, brings the speech and action about. Thoughts are not to

be identified with behaviour, we think, they lie behind behaviour. A man's behaviour constitutes the *reason* we have for attributing certain mental processes to him, but the behaviour cannot be identified with the mental processes.

This suggests a very interesting line of thought about the mind. Behaviourism is certainly wrong, but perhaps it is not altogether wrong. Perhaps the Behaviourists are wrong in identifying the mind and mental occurrences with behaviour, but perhaps they are right in thinking that our notion of a mind and of individual mental states is *logically tied to behaviour*. For perhaps what we mean by a mental state is some state of the person which, under suitable circumstances, *brings about* a certain range of behaviour. Perhaps mind can be defined not as behaviour, but rather as the inner *cause* of certain behaviour. Thought is not speech under suitable circumstances, rather it is something within the person which, in suitable circumstances, brings about speech. And, in fact, I believe that this is the true account, or, at any rate, a true first account, of what we mean by a mental state.

How does this line of thought link up with a purely physicalist view of man? The position is, I think, that while it does not make such a physicalist view inevitable, it does make it *possible*. It does not entail, but it is compatible with, a purely physicalist view of man. For if our notion of the mind and mental states is nothing but that of a cause within the person of certain ranges of behaviour, then it becomes a scientific question, and not a question of logical analysis, what in fact the intrinsic nature of that cause is. The cause might be, as Descartes thought it was, a spiritual substance working through the pineal gland to produce the complex bodily behaviour of which men are capable. It might be breath, or specially smooth and mobile atoms dispersed throughout the body; it might be many other things. But in fact the verdict of modern science seems to be that the sole cause of mind-betokening behaviour in man and the higher animals is the physico-chemical workings of the central nervous system. And so, assuming we have correctly characterised our concept of a mental state as nothing but the cause of certain sorts of behaviour, then we can identify these mental states with purely physical states of the central nervous system.

At this point we may stop and go back to the Behaviourists' dispositions. We saw that, according to them, the brittleness of glass or, to take another example, the elasticity of rubber, is not a state of the glass or the rubber, but is simply the fact that things of that sort behave in the way they do. But now let us consider how a scientist would think about brittleness or elasticity. Faced with the phenomenon of breakage under relatively small impacts, or the phenomenon of stretching when a force is applied followed by contraction when the force is removed, he will assume that there is some current *state* of the glass or the rubber which is responsible for the characteristic behaviour of samples of these two materials. At the beginning he will not know what this state is, but he will endeavour to find out, and he may succeed in finding out. And when he has found out he will very likely make remarks of this sort: 'We have discovered that the brittleness of glass is in fact a certain sort of pattern in the molecules of the glass.' That is to say, he will *identify* brittleness with the state of the glass that is responsible for the liability of the glass to break. For him, a disposition of an object is a state of the object. What makes the state a state of brittleness is the fact that it gives rise to the characteristic manifestations of brittleness. But the disposition itself is distinct from its manifestations: it is the state of the glass that gives rise to these manifestations in suitable circumstances.

You will see that this way of looking at dispositions is very different from that of Ryle and the Behaviourists. The great difference is this: If we treat dispositions as actual states, as I have suggested that scientists do, even if states whose intrinsic nature may yet have to be discovered, then we can say that dispositions are actual *causes,* or causal factors, which, in suitable circumstances, actually bring about those happenings which are the manifestations of the disposition. A certain molecular constitution of glass which constitutes its brittleness is actually *responsible* for the fact that, when the glass is truck, it breaks.

Now I shall not argue the matter here, because the detail of the argument is technical and difficult,[2] but I believe that the view of dispositions as states, which is the view that is natural to science, is the correct one. I believe it can be shown quite strictly that, to the extent that we admit the notion of dispositions at all, we are committed to the view that they are actual *states* of the object that has the disposition. I may add that I think that the same holds for the closely connected notions of capacities and powers. Here I will simply assume this step in my argument.

But perhaps it can be seen that the rejection of the idea that mind is simply a certain range of man's behaviour in favour of the view that mind is rather the inner *cause* of that range of man's behaviour is bound up with the rejection of the Rylean view of dispositions in favour of one that treats disposition as states of objects and so as having actual causal power. The Behaviourists were wrong to identify the mind with behaviour. They were not so far off the mark when they tried to deal with cases where mental happenings occur in the absence of behaviour by saying that these are dispositions to behave. But in order to reach a correct view, I am suggesting, they would have to conceive of these dispositions as actual *states* of the person who has the disposition, states that have actual power to bring about behaviour in suitable circumstances. But to do this is to abandon the central inspiration of Behaviourism: that in talking about the mind we do not have to go behind outward behaviour to inner states.

And so two separate but interlocking lines of thought have pushed me in the same direction. The first line of thought is that it goes profoundly against the grain to think of the mind as behaviour. The mind is, rather, that which stands behind and brings about our complex behaviour. The second line of thought is that the Behaviourists' dispositions, properly conceived, are really states that underlie behaviour, and, under suitable circumstances, bring about behaviour. Putting these two together, we reach the conception of a mental state as *a state of the person apt for producing certain ranges of behaviour*. This formula: a mental state is a state of the person apt for producing certain ranges of behaviour, I believe to be a very illuminating way of looking at the concept of a mental state. I have found it very fruitful in the search for detailed logical analyses of the individual mental concepts.

Now, I do not think that Hegel's dialectic has much to tell us about the nature of reality. But I think that human thought often moves in a dialectical way, from thesis to antithesis and then to the synthesis. Perhaps thought about the mind is a case in point. I have already said that classical philosophy tended to think of the mind as an inner arena of some sort. This we may call the Thesis. Behaviourism moved to the opposite extreme: the mind was seen as outward behaviour. This is the Antithesis. My proposed Synthesis is that the mind is properly conceived as an inner principle, but a principle that is identified in terms of the outward behaviour it is apt for bringing about. This way of looking at the mind and mental states does not itself entail a Materialist or Physicalist view of man, for nothing is said in this analysis about the intrinsic nature of these mental states. But if we have, as I have asserted that we do have, general scientific grounds for thinking that man is nothing but a physical mechanism, we can go on to argue that the mental states are in fact nothing but physical states of the central nervous system.

Along these lines, then, I would look for an account of the mind that is compatible with a purely Materialist theory of man. I have tried to carry out this programme in detail in *A Materialist Theory of the Mind*. There are, as may be imagined, all sorts of powerful objections that can be made to this view. But in the rest of this paper I propose to do only one thing. I will develop one very important objection to my view of the mind—an objection felt by many philosophers—and then try to show how the objection should be met.

The view that our notion of mind is nothing but that of an inner principle apt for bringing about certain sorts of behaviour may be thought to share a certain weakness with Behaviourism. Modern philosophers have put the point about Behaviourism by saying that although Behaviourism may be a satisfactory account of the mind from an *other-person point of view,* it will not do as a *first-person* account. To explain. In our encounters with other people, all we ever observe is their behaviour: their actions, their speech, and so on. And so, if we simply consider other people, Behaviourism might seem to do full justice to the facts. But the trouble about Behaviourism is that it seems so unsatisfactory as applied to our *own* case. In our own case, we seem to be aware of so much more than mere behaviour.

Suppose that now we conceive of the mind as an inner principle apt for bringing about certain sorts of behaviour. This again fits the other-person cases very well. Bodily behaviour of a very sophisticated sort is observed, quite different from the behaviour that ordinary physical objects display. It is inferred that this behaviour must spring from a very special sort of inner cause in the object that exhibits this behaviour. This inner cause is christened 'the mind', and those who take a physicalist view of man argue that it is simply the central nervous system of the body observed. Compare this with the case of glass. Certain characteristic behaviour is observed: the breaking and shattering of the material when acted upon by relatively small forces. A special inner state of the glass is postulated to explain this behaviour. Those who take a purely physicalist view of glass then argue that this state is a *natural* state of the glass. It is, perhaps, an arrangement of its molecules, and not, say, the peculiarly malevolent disposition of the demons that dwell in glass.

But when we turn to our own case, the position may seem less plausible. We are conscious, we have experiences. Now can we say that to be conscious, to have experiences, is simply for something to go on within us apt for the causing of certain sorts of behaviour? Such an account does not seem to do any justice to the phenomena. And so it seems that our account of the mind, like Behaviourism, will fail to do justice to the first-person case.

In order to understand the objection better it may be helpful to consider a particular case. If you have driven for a very long distance without a break, you may have had experience of a curious state of automatism, which can occur in these conditions. One can suddenly 'come to' and realise that one has driven for long distances without being aware of what one was doing, or indeed, without being aware of anything. One has kept the car on the road, used the brake and the clutch perhaps, yet all without any awareness of what one was doing.

Now, if we consider this case it is obvious that *in some sense* mental processes are still going on when one is in such an automatic state. Unless one's will was still operating in some way, and unless one was still perceiving in some way, the car would not still be on the road. Yet, of course, *something* mental is lacking. Now, I think, when it is alleged that an account of mind as an inner principle apt for the production of certain sorts of behaviour leaves out consciousness or experience, what is alleged to have been left out is just whatever is missing in the automatic driving case. It is conceded that an account of mental processes as states of the person apt for the production of certain sorts of behaviour may very possibly be adequate to deal with such cases as that of automatic driving. It may be adequate to deal with most of the mental processes of animals, who perhaps spend a good deal of their lives in this state of automatism. But, it is contended, it cannot deal with the conciousness that we normally enjoy.

I will now try to sketch an answer to this important and powerful objection. Let us begin in an apparently unlikely place, and consider the way that an account of mental processes of the sort I am giving would deal with *sense-perception*.

Now psychologists, in particular, have long realised that there is a very close logical tie between sense-perception and *selective behaviour*. Suppose we want to decide whether an animal can perceive the difference between red and green. We might give the animal a choice between two pathways, over one of which a red light shines and over the other of which a green light shines. If the animal happens by chance to choose the green pathway we reward it; if it happens to choose the other pathway we do not reward it. If, after some trials, the animal systematically takes the green-lighted pathway, and if we become assured that the only relevant differences in the two pathways are the differences in the colour of the lights, we are entitled to say that the animal can see this colour difference. Using its eyes, it selects between red-lighted and green-lighted pathways. So we say it can see the difference between red and green.

Now a Behaviourist would be tempted to say that the animal's regularly selecting the green-lighted pathway *was* its perception of the colour difference. But this is unsatisfactory, because we all want to say that perception is something that goes on within the person or animal—within its mind—although, of course, this mental event is normally *caused* by the operation of the environment upon the organism. Suppose, however, that we speak instead of *capacities* for selective behaviour towards the current environment, and suppose we think of these capacities, like dispositions, as actual inner states of the organism. We can then think of the animal's perception as a state within the animal apt, if the animal is so impelled, for selective

behaviour between the red- and green-lighted pathways.

In general, we can think of perceptions as inner states or events apt for the production of certain sorts of selective behaviour towards our environment. To perceive is like acquiring a key to a door. You do not have to use the key: you can put it in your pocket and never bother about the door. But if you do want to open the door the key may be essential. The blind man is a man who does not acquire certain keys, and, as a result, is not able to operate in his environment in the way that somebody who has his sight can operate. It seems, then, a very promising view to take of perceptions that they are inner states defined by the sorts of selective behaviour that they enable the perceiver to exhibit, if so impelled.

Now how is this discussion of perception related to the question of consciousness or experience, the sort of thing that the driver who is in a state of automatism has not got, but which we normally do have? Simply this. My proposal is that consciousness, in this sense of the word, is nothing but *perception or awareness of the state of our own mind*. The driver in a state of automatism perceives, or is aware of, the road. If he did not, the car would be in a ditch. But he is not currently aware of his awareness of the road. He perceives the road, but he does not perceive his perceiving, or anything else that is going on in his mind. He is not, as we normally are, conscious of what is going on in his mind.

And so I conceive of consciousness or experience, in this sense of the words, in the way that Locke and Kant conceived it, as like perception. Kant, in a striking phrase, spoke of 'inner sense'. We cannot directly observe the minds of others, but each of us has the power to observe directly our own minds, and 'perceive' what is going on there. The driver in the automatic state is one whose 'inner eye' is shut: who is not currently aware of what is going on in his own mind.

Now if this account is along the right lines, why should we not give an account of this inner observation along the same lines as we have already given of perception? Why should we not conceive of it as an inner state, a state in this case directed towards other inner states and not to the environment, which enables us, if we are so impelled, to behave in a selective way *towards our own states of mind?* One who is aware, or conscious, of his thoughts or his emotions is one who has the capacity to make discriminations between his different mental states. His capacity might be exhibited in words. He might say that he was in an angry state of mind when, and only when, he *was* in an angry state of mind. But such verbal behaviour would be the mere *expression* or *result* of the awareness. The awareness itself would be an inner state: the sort of inner state that gave the man a capacity for such behavioural expressions.

So I have argued that consciousness of our own mental state may be assimilated to *perception* of our own mental state, and that, like other perceptions, it may then be conceived of as an inner state or event giving a capacity for selective behavior, in this case selective behaviour towards our own mental state. All this is meant to be simply a logical analysis of consciousness, and none of it entails, although it does not rule out, a purely physicalist account of what these inner states are. But if we are convinced, on general scientific grounds, that a purely physical account of man is likely to be the true one, then there seems to be no bar to our identifying these inner states with purely physical states of the central nervous system. And so consciousness of our own mental state becomes simply the scanning of one part of our central nervous system by another. Consciousness is a self-scanning mechanism in the central nervous system.

As I have emphasised before, I have done no more than sketch a programme for a philosophy of mind. There are all sorts of expansions and elucidations to be made, and all sorts of doubts and difficulties to be stated and overcome. But I hope I have done enough to show that a purely physicalist theory of the mind is an exciting and plausible intellectual option.

Endnotes

[1]Inaugural lecture of the Challis Professor of Philosophy at the University of Sydney (1965); slightly amended (1968).

[2]It is presented in my book *A Materialist Theory of the Mind* (1968) ch. 6, sec. VI.

29. *Philosophy and Our Mental Life*

HILARY PUTNAM

In the previous selection, Armstrong proposed that mental states be understood as functionally (or causally) described states of the central nervous system. In the philosophy of mind, "functionalism" has come to refer to the view that mental entities are functional states. Many philosophers who find dualism implausible are attracted to some variety of functionalism because, like Armstrong, they want to identify mental states with the physical states that play a functional role. Interest in functionalism has also been influenced by computer science. In understanding computers, it often suffices to describe their states functionally (that is, in terms of their program or software) without making any reference to their specific physical nature (their hardware). In "Philosophy and Our Mental Life," Hilary Putnam claims functionalism should free us from worrying about whether or not our mental states are physical. He claims it is the functional character of psychological states—not what they are embodied in—that leads to understanding the nature and autonomy of our mental lives. Putnam teaches philosophy at Harvard University.

The question which troubles laymen, and which has long troubled philosophers, even if it is somewhat disguised by today's analytic style of writing philosophy, is this: are we made of matter or soul-stuff?[1] To put it as bluntly as possible, are we just material beings, or are we 'something more'? In this paper, I will argue as strongly as possible that this whole question rests on false assumptions. My purpose is not to dismiss the question, however, so much as to speak to the real concern which is behind the question. The real concern is, I believe, with the autonomy of our mental life.

People are worried that we may be debunked, that our behavior may be exposed as really explained by something mechanical. Not, to be sure, mechanical in the old sense of cogs and pulleys, but in the newer sense of electricity and magnetism and quantum chemistry and so forth. In this paper, part of what I want to do is to argue that this can't happen. Mentality is a real and autonomous feature of our world.

But even more important, at least in my feeling, is the fact that this whole question has nothing to do with our substance. Strange as it may seem to common sense and to sophisticated intuition alike, the question of the autonomy of our mental life does not hinge on and has nothing to do with that all too popular, all too old question about matter or soul-stuff. We could be made of Swiss cheese and it wouldn't matter.

Failure to see this, stubborn insistence on formulating the question as *matter or soul*, utterly prevents progress on these questions. Conversely, once we see that our substance is not the issue, I do not see how we can help but make progress.

The concept which is key to unravelling the mysteries in the philosophy of mind, I think, is the concept of *functional isomorphism*. Two systems are functionally isomorphic if *there is a correspondence between the states of one and the states of the other that preserves functional relations*. To start with computing machine examples, if the functional relations are just sequence relations, e.g., *state A is always followed by state B*, then, for F to be a functional isomorphism, it must be the case

that state A is followed by state B in system 1 if and only if state F(A) is followed by state F(B) in system 2. If the functional relations are, say, data or printout relations, e.g., *when symbol S is scanned on the tape, system 1 goes into state A*, these must be preserved. *When symbol S is scanned on the tape, system 2 goes into state F(A)*, if F is a functional isomorphism between system 1 and system 2. More generally, if T is a correct theory of the functioning of system 1, at the functional or psychological level, then an isomorphism between system 1 and system 2 must map each property and relation defined in system 2 in such a way that T comes out true when all references to system 1 are replaced by references to system 2, and all property and relation symbols in T are reinterpreted according to the mapping.

The difficulty with the notion of functional isomorphism is that it *presupposes the notion of a thing's being a functional or psychological description*. It is for this reason that, in various papers on this subject, I introduced and explained the notion in terms of Turing machines. And I felt constrained, therefore, to defend the thesis that *we* are Turing machines. Turing machines come, so to speak, with a normal form for their functional description, the so-called machine table—a standard style of program. But it does not seem fatally sloppy to me, although it is sloppy, if we apply the notion of functional isomorphism to systems for which we have no detailed idea at present what the normal form description would look like—systems like ourselves. The point is that even if we don't have any idea what a comprehensive psychological theory would look like, I claim that we know enough (and here analogies from computing machines, economic systems, games and so forth are helpful) to point out illuminating differences between any possible psychological theory of a human being, or even a functional description of a computing machine or an economic system, and a physical or chemical description. Indeed, Dennett and Fodor have done a great deal along these lines in recent books.

This brings me back to the question of *copper, cheese, or soul*. One point we can make immediately as soon as we have the basic concept of functional isomorphism is this: two systems can have quite different constitutions and be functionally isomorphic. For example, a computer made of electrical

From Hilary Putnam, *Philosophical Papers, Vol. II: Mind, Language, and Reality*, pp. 291–303. Copyright © 1975 by Cambridge University Press. Reprinted by permission of Cambridge University Press.

components can be isomorphic to one made of cogs and wheels. In other words, for each state in the first computer there is a corresponding state in the other, and, as we said before, the sequential relations are the same—if state S is followed by state B in the case of the electronic computer, state A would be followed by state B in the case of the computer made of cogs and wheels, and it doesn't matter at all that the *physical realizations* of those states are totally different. So a computer made of electrical components can be isomorphic to one made of cogs and wheels or to human clerks using paper and pencil. A computer made of one sort of wire, say copper wire, or one sort of relay, etc. will be in a different physical and chemical state when it computes than a computer made of a different sort of wire and relay. But the functional description may be the same.

We can extend this point still further. Assume that one thesis of materialism (I shall call it the 'first thesis') is correct, and we are, as wholes, just material systems obeying physical laws. Then the second thesis of classical materialism cannot be correct—namely, our mental states, e.g., *thinking about next summer's vacation,* cannot be *identical* with any physical or chemical states. For it is clear from what we already know about computers etc., that whatever the program of the brain may be, it must be physically possible, though not necessarily feasible, to produce something with that same program but quite a different physical and chemical constitution. Then to identify the state in question with its physical or chemical realization would be quite absurd, given that that realization is in a sense quite accidental, from the point of view of psychology, anyway (which is the relevant science).[2] It is as if we met Martians and discovered that they were in all functional respects isomorphic to us, but we refused to admit that they could feel pain because their C fibers were different.

Now, imagine two possible universes, perhaps 'parallel worlds,' in the science fiction sense, in one of which people have good old fashioned souls, operating through pineal glands, perhaps, and in the other of which they have complicated brains. And suppose that the souls in the soul world are functionally isomorphic to the brains in the brain world. Is there any more sense to attaching importance to this difference than to the dif-ference between copper wires and some other wires in the computer? Does it matter that the soul people have, so to speak, immaterial brains, and that the brain people have material souls? What matters is the common structure, the theory T of which we are, alas, in deep ignorance, and not the hardware, be it ever so etheral.

One may raise various objections to what I have said. I shall try to reply to some of them.

One might, for example, say that if the souls of the soul people are isomorphic to the brains of the brain people, then their souls must be automata-like, and that's not the sort of soul we are interested in. 'All your argument really shows is that there is no need to distinguish between a brain and an automaton-like soul.' But what precisely does that objection come to?

I think there are two ways of understanding it. It might come to the claim that the notion of functional organization or functional isomorphism only makes sense for automata. But that is totally false. Sloppy as our notions are at present, we at least know this much, that the notion of functional organization applies to anything to which the notion of a psychological theory applies. I explained the most general notion of functional isomorphism by saying that two systems are functionally isomorphic if there is an isomorphism that makes both of them models for the same psychological theory. (That is stronger than just saying that they are both models for the same psychological theory—they are isomorphic realizations of the same abstract structure.) To say that real old fashioned souls would not be in the domain of definition of the concept of functional organization or of the concept of functional isomorphisms would be to take the position that whatever we mean by the soul, it is something for which there can be no theory. That seems pure obscurantism. I will assume, henceforth, that it is not built into the notion of mind or soul or whatever that it is unintelligible or that there couldn't be a theory of it.

Secondly, someone might say more seriously that even if there is a theory of the soul or mind, the soul, at least in the full, rich old fashioned sense, is supposed to have powers that no mechanical system could have. In the latter part of this chapter I shall consider this claim.

If it is built into one's notions of the soul that the soul can do things that violate the laws of physics, then I admit I am stumped. There cannot be a soul which is isomorphic to a brain, if the soul can read the future clairvoyantly, in a way that is not in any way explainable by physical law. On the other hand, if one is interested in more modest forms of magic like telepathy, it seems to me that there is no reason in principle why we couldn't construct a device which would project subvocalized thoughts from one brain to another. As to reincarnation, if we are, as I am urging, a certain kind of functional structure (my identity is, as it were, my functional structure), there seems to be in principle no reason why that could not be reproduced after a thousand years or a million years or a billion years. Resurrection: as you know, Christians believe in resurrection in the flesh, which completely bypasses the need for an immaterial vehicle. So even if one is interested in those questions (and they are not my concern in this paper, although I am concerned to speak to people who have those concerns), even then one doesn't need an immaterial brain or soul-stuff.

So if I am right, and the question of matter or soul-stuff is really irrelevant to any question of philosophical or religious significance, why so much attention to it, why so much heat? The crux of the matter seems to be that both the Diderots of this world and the Descartes of this world have agreed that if we are matter, then there is a physical explanation for how we behave, disappointing or exciting. I think the traditional dualist says *'wouldn't it be terrible if we turned out to be just matter, for then there is a physical explanation for everything we do'*. And the traditional materialist says *'if we are just matter, then there is a physical explanation for everything we do. Isn't that exciting!'* (It is like the distinction between the optimist and the pessimist: an optimist is a person who says 'this is the best of all possible worlds'; and a pessimist is a person who says 'you're right'.)[3]

I think they are both wrong. I think Diderot and Descartes were both wrong in assuming that if we are matter, or our souls are material, then there is a physical explanation for our behavior.

Let me try to illustrate what I mean by a very simple analogy. Suppose we have a very simple physical system—a board in which there are two holes, a circle one inch in diameter and a square

one inch high, and a cubical peg one-sixteenth of an inch less than one inch high. We have the following very simple fact to explain: *the peg passes through the square hole, and it does not pass through the round hole.*

In explanation of this, one might attempt the following. One might say that the peg is, after all, a cloud or, better, a rigid lattice of atoms. One might even attempt to give a description of that lattice, compute its electrical potential energy, worry about why it does not collapse, produce some quantum mechanics to explain why it is stable, etc. The board is also a lattice of atoms. I will call the peg 'system *A*,' and the holes 'region 1' and 'region 2.' One could compute all possible trajectories of system *A* (there are, by the way, very serious questions about these computations, their effectiveness, feasibility, and so on, but let us assume this), and perhaps one could deduce from just the laws of particle mechanics or quantum electrodynamics that system *A* never passes through region 1, but that there is at least one trajectory which enables it to pass through region 2. Is this an explanation of the fact that the peg passes through the square hole and not the round hole?

Very often we are told that if something is made of matter, its behavior must have a physical explanation. And the argument is that if it is made of matter (and we make a lot of assumptions), then there should be a deduction of its behavior from its material structure. *What makes you call this deduction an explanation?*

On the other hand, if you are not 'hipped' on the idea that *the* explanation must be at the level of the ultimate constituents, and that in fact the explanation might have the property that *the ultimate constituents don't matter*, that *only the higher level structure matters*, then there is a very simple explanation here. The explanation is that the board is rigid, the peg is rigid, and as a matter of geometrical fact, the round hole is smaller than the peg, the square hole is bigger than the cross-section of the peg. The peg passes through the hole that is large enough to take its cross-section, and does not pass through the hole that is too small to take its cross-section. That is a correct explanation whether the peg consists of molecules, or continuous rigid substance, or whatever. (If one wanted to amplify the explanation, one might point out the geometrical fact that a square one inch high is bigger than a circle one inch across.)

Now, one can say that in this explanation certain *relevant structural features of the situation* are brought out. The geometrical features are brought out. It is *relevant* that a square one inch high is bigger than a circle one inch around. And the relationship between the size and shape of the peg and the size and shape of the holes is *relevant*. It is relevant that both the board and the peg are *rigid* under transportation. And nothing else is relevant. The same explanation will go in any world (whatever the microstructure) in which those *higher level structural features* are present. In that sense *this explanation is autonomous.*

People have argued that I am wrong to say that the microstructural deduction is not an explanation. I think that in terms of the *purposes for which we use the notion of explanation,* it is not an explanation. If you want to, let us say that the deduction *is* an explanation, it is just a terrible explanation, and why look for terrible explanations when good ones are available?

Goodness is not a subjective matter. Even if one agrees with the positivists who saddled us with the notion of explanation as deduction from laws, one of the things we do in science is to look for laws. Explanation is superior not just subjectively, but *methodologically,* in terms of facilitating the aims of scientific inquiry, if it brings out relevant laws. An explanation is superior if it is more general.

Just taking those two features, and there are many many more one could think of, compare the explanation at the higher level of this phenomenon with the atomic explanation. The explanation at the higher level brings out the relevant geometrical relationships. The lower level explanation conceals those laws. Also notice that the higher level explanation applies to a much more interesting class of systems (of course that has to do with what we are interested in).

The fact is that we are much more interested in generalizing to other structures which are rigid and have various geometrical relations, than we are in generalizing to *the next peg that has exactly this molecular structure,* for the very good reason that there is not going to *be* a next peg that has exactly this molecular structure. So in terms of real life dis-

ciplines, real life ways of slicing up scientific problems, the higher level explanation is far more general, which is why it is *explanatory.*

We were only able to deduce a statement which is lawful at the *higher* level, that the peg goes through the hole which is larger than the cross-section of the peg. When we try to deduce the possible trajectories of 'system *A*' from statements about the individual atoms, we use premises which are totally accidental—this atom is here, this carbon atom is there, and so forth. And that is one reason that it is very misleading to talk about a reduction of a science like economics to the level of the elementary particles making up the players of the economic game. In fact, their motions—buying this, selling that, arriving at an equilibrium price—these motions cannot be deduced from just the equations of motion. Otherwise they would be *physically necessitated,* not *economically necessitated,* to arrive at an equilibrium price. They play that game because they are particular systems with particular boundary conditions which are totally accidental from the point of view of physics. This means that the derivation of the laws of economics from *just* the laws of physics is *in principle* impossible. The derivation of the laws of economics from the laws of physics and *accidental statements about which particles were where when* by a Laplacian supermind might be in principle possible, but why want it? A few chapters of, e.g., von Neumann, will tell one far more about regularities at the level of economic structure than such a deduction ever could.

The conclusion I want to draw from this is that we do have the kind of autonomy that we are looking for in the mental realm. Whatever our mental functioning may be, there seems to be no serious reason to believe that it is *explainable* by our physics and chemistry. And what we are interested in is not: given that we consist of such and such particles, could someone have predicted that we would have this mental functioning? because such a prediction is not *explanatory,* however great a feat it may be. What we are interested in is: can we say at this autonomous level that since we have this sort of structure, this sort of program, it follows that we will be able to learn this, we will tend to like that, and so on? These are the problems of mental life—the description of this autonomous level of mental functioning—and that is what is to be discovered.

In previous papers, I have argued for the hypothesis that (1) a whole human being is a Turing machine, and (2) that psychological states of a human being are Turing machine states or disjunctions of Turing machine states. In this section I want to argue that this point of view was essentially wrong, and that I was too much in the grip of the reductionist outlook.

Let me begin with a technical difficulty. A *state* of a Turing machine is described in such a way that a Turing machine can be in exactly one state at a time. Moreover, memory and learning are not represented in the Turing machine model as acquisition of new states, but as acquisition of new information printed on the machine's tape. Thus, if human beings have any states at all which resemble Turing machine states, those states must (1) be states the human can be in at any time, independently of learning and memory; and (2) be *total* instantaneous states of the human being— states which determine, together with learning and memory, what the next state will be, as well as totally specifying the present condition of the human being ('totally' from the standpoint of psychological theory, that means).

These characteristics establish that *no* psychological state in any customary sense can be a Turing machine state. Take a particular kind of pain to be a 'psychological state'. If I *am* a Turing machine, then my present 'state' must determine not only whether or not I am having that particular kind of pain, but also whether or not I am about to say 'three', whether or not I am hearing a shrill whine, etc. So the psychological state in question (the pain) is not the same as my 'state' in the sense of *machine state,* although it is possible (so far) that my machine state *determines* my psychological state. Moreover, *no* psychological theory would pretend that having a pain of a particular kind, being about to say 'three,' or hearing a shrill whine, etc., all belong to *one* psychological state, although there could well be a machine state characterized by the fact that I was in it only when simultaneously having that pain, being about to say 'three', hearing a shrill whine, etc. So, even if I am a Turing machine, my machine states are *not* the same as my psychological states. My description *qua* Turing machine (machine table) and my description *qua* human being (*via* a psychological theory) are descriptions at two totally different levels of organization.

So far it is still possible that a psychological state is a large disjunction (practically speaking, an almost infinite disjunction) of machine states, although no *single* machine state is a psychological state. But this is very unlikely when we move away from states like 'pain' (which are almost *biological*) to states like 'jealousy' or 'love' or 'competitiveness'. Being jealous is certainly not an *instantaneous* state, and it depends on a great deal of information and on many learned facts and habits. But Turing machine states are instantaneous and are independent of learning and memory. That is, learning and memory may cause a Turing machine to go into a state, but the identity of the state does not depend on learning and memory, whereas, no matter what state I am in, identifying that state as 'being jealous of X's regard for Y' involves specifying that I have learned that X and Y are persons and a good deal about social relations among persons. Thus jealousy can neither be a machine state nor a disjunction of machine states.

One might attempt to modify the theory by saying that being jealous = either being in State A and having tape c_1 *or* being in State A and having tape c_2 *or* . . . being in State B and having tape d_1 *or* being in State B and having tape d_2 . . . *or* being in State Z and having tape y_1 . . . *or* being in State Z and having tape y_n—i.e., define a psychological state as a disjunction, the individual disjuncts being not Turing machine states, as before, but conjunctions of a machine state and a tape (i.e., a total description of the content of the memory bank). Besides the fact that such a description would be literally infinite, the theory is now without content, for the original purpose was to use the machine table as a model of a psychological theory, whereas it is now clear that the machine table description, although different from the description at the elementary particle level, is as removed from the description *via* a psychological theory as the physicochemical description is.

What is the importance of machines in the philosophy of mind? I think that machines have both a positive and a negative importance. The positive importance of machines was that it was in connection with machines, computing machines in particular, that the notion of functional organization first appeared. Machines forced us to distinguish between an abstract structure and its concrete realization. Not that that distinction came into the world for the first time with machines. But in the case of computing machines, we could not avoid rubbing our noses against the fact that what we had to count as to all intents and purposes the same structure could be realized in a bewildering variety of different ways; that the important properties were not physical-chemical. That the machines made us catch on to the idea of functional organization is extremely important. The negative importance of machines, however, is that they tempt us to oversimplification. The notion of functional organization became clear to us through systems with a very restricted, very specific functional organization. So the temptation is present to assume that we must have that restricted and specific kind of functional organization.

Now I want to consider an example—an example which may seem remote from what we have been talking about, but which may help. This is not an example from the philosophy of mind at all. Consider the following fact. The earth does not go around the sun in a circle, as was once believed, it goes around the sun in an ellipse, with the sun at one of the foci, not in the center of the ellipse. Yet one statement which would hold true if the orbit was a circle and the sun was at the centre still holds true, surprisingly. That is the following statement: the radius vector from the sun to the earth sweeps out equal areas in equal times. If the orbit were a circle, and the earth were moving with a constant velocity, that would be trivial. But the orbit is not a circle. Also the velocity is not constant—when the earth is farthest away from the sun, it is going most slowly, when it is closest to the sun, it is going fastest. The earth is speeding up and slowing down. But the earth's radius vector sweeps out equal areas in equal times.[4] Newton deduced that law in his *Principia*, and his deduction shows that the only thing on which that law depends is that the force acting on the earth is in the direction of the sun. That is absolutely the only fact one needs to deduce that law. Mathematically it is equiva-

lent to that law.[5] That is all well and good when the gravitational law is that every body attracts every other body according to an inverse square law, because then there is always a force on the earth in the direction of the sun. If we assume that we can neglect all the other bodies, that their influence is slight, then that is all we need, and we can use Newton's proof, or a more modern, simpler proof.

But today we have very complicated laws of gravitation. First of all, we say what is really going is that the world lines of freely falling bodies in space-time are geodesics. And the geometry is determined by the mass-energy tensor, and the ankle bone is connected to the leg bone, etc. So, one might ask, how would a modern relativity theorist explain Kepler's law? He would explain it very simply. *Kepler's laws are true because Newton's laws are approximately true.* And, in fact, an attempt to replace that argument by a deduction of Kepler's laws from the field equations would be regarded as almost as ridiculous (but not quite) as trying to deduce that the peg will go through one hole and not the other from the positions and velocities of the individual atoms.

I want to draw the philosophical conclusion that Newton's laws *have a kind of reality in our world* even though they are not *true*. The point is that it will be necessary to appeal to Newton's laws in order to explain Kepler's laws. Methodologically, I can make that claim at least plausible. One remark—due to Alan Garfinkel—is that *a good explanation is invariant under small perturbations of the assumptions.* One problem with deducing Kepler's laws from the gravitational field equations is that if we do it, tomorrow the gravitational field equations are likely to be different. Whereas the explanation which consists in showing that whichever equation we have implies Newton's equation to a first approximation is invariant under even moderate perturbations, quite big perturbations, of the assumptions. One might say that every explanation of Kepler's laws 'passes through' Newton's laws.

Let me come back to the philosophy of mind, now. If we assume a thorough atomic structure of matter, quantization and so forth, then, at first blush, it looks as if *continuities* cannot be relevant to our brain functioning. Mustn't it all be discrete? Physics says that the deepest level is discrete.

There are two problems with this argument. One is that there are continuities even in quantum mechanics, as well as discontinuities. But ignore that, suppose quantum mechanics were a thoroughly discrete theory.

The other problem is that if that were a good argument, it would be an argument against the utilizability of the model of air as a continuous liquid, which is the model on which aeroplane wings are constructed, at least if they are to fly at anything less than supersonic speeds. There are two points: one is that a discontinuous structure, a discrete structure, can approximate a continuous structure. The discontinuities may be irrelevant, just as in the case of the peg and the board. The fact that the peg and the board are not continuous solids is irrelevant. One can say that the peg and the board only approximate perfectly rigid continuous solids. But if the error in the approximation is irrelevant to the level of description, so what? It is not just that discrete systems can approximate continuous systems; the fact is that the system may behave in the way it does *because* a continuous system would behave in such and such a way, and the system approximates a continuous system.

This is not a Newtonian world. Tough. Kepler's law comes out true because the sun-earth system approximates a Newtonian system. And the error in the approximation is quite irrelevant at that level.

This analogy is not perfect because physicists are interested in laws to which the error in the approximation is relevant. It seems to me that in the psychological case the analogy is even better, that continuous models (for example, Hull's model for rote learning which used a continuous potential) could perfectly well be correct, whatever the ultimate structure of the brain is. We cannot deduce that a digital model has to be the correct model from the fact that ultimately there are neurons. The brain may work the way it does because it approximates some system whose laws are best conceptualized in terms of continuous mathematics. What is more, the errors in that approximation may be irrelevant at the level of psychology.

What I have said about *continuity* goes as well for many other things. Let us come back to the question of the soul people and the brain people, and the isomorphism between the souls in one world and the brains in the other. One objection was, if there is a functional isomorphism between souls and brains, wouldn't the souls have to be rather simple? The answer is no. Because brains can be essentially infinitely complex. A system with as many degrees of freedom as the brain can imitate to within the accuracy relevant to psychological theory any structure one can hope to describe. It might be, so to speak, that the ultimate physics of the soul will be quite different from the ultimate physics of the brain, but that at the level we are interested in, the level of functional organization, the same description might go for both. And also that that description might be formally incompatible with the actual physics of the brain, in the way that the description of the air flowing around an aeroplane wing as a continuous incompressible liquid is *formally incompatible with the actual structure of the air*.

Let me close by saying that these examples support the idea that our substance, what we are made of, places almost no first order restrictions on our form. And that what we are really interested in, as Aristotle saw,[6] is form and not matter. *What is our intellectual form?* is the question, not what the matter is. And whatever our substance may be, soul-stuff, or matter or Swiss cheese, it is not going to place any interesting first order restrictions on the answer to this question. It may, of course, place interesting higher order restrictions. Small effects may have to be explained in terms of the actual physics of the brain. But when we are not even at the level of an *idealized* description of the functional organization of the brain, to talk about the importance of small perturbations seems decidedly premature. My conclusion is that we have what we always wanted—an autonomous mental life. And we need no mysteries, no ghostly agents, no *élan vital* to have it.

Endnotes

[1]This paper was presented as a part of a Foerster symposium on 'Computers and the Mind' at the University of California (Berkeley) in October, 1973. I am indebted to Alan Garfinkel for comments on earlier versions of this paper.

[2]Even if it were not physically possible to realize human psychology in a creature made of anything but the usual protoplasm, DNA, etc., it would still not be correct to say

that psychological states are identical with their physical realizations. For, as will be argued below, such an identification has no *explanatory* value *in psychology*.

[3]Joke Credit: Joseph Weizenbaum.

[4]This is one of Kepler's laws.

[5]Provided that the two bodies—the sun and the earth—are the whole universe. If there are other forces, then, of course, Kepler's law cannot be *exactly* correct.

[6]E.g., Aristotle says: '. . . we can wholly dismiss as unnecessary the question whether the soul and the body are one: it is as meaningless to ask whether the wax and the shape given to it by the stamp are one, or generally the matter of a thing and that of which it is the matter.' (See *De Anima*, 412 a6–b9.)

---

30. *What Is It Like to Be a Bat?*

THOMAS NAGEL

Science attempts to understand the world objectively—in a way that abstracts from, and does not depend on, the peculiarities of a subjective point of view. During the rise of the mechanistic view of nature in the Scientific Revolution, discovering mathematical relations among material things became a paradigm of objective understanding. On the other hand, things like appearances, sensations, and feelings were considered subjective and relegated to the mind—the mind viewed dualistically as a dualistic container or stage for the phenomenal world. Contemporary physicalists and functionalists who want to understand mind objectively must find some way to analyze or dismiss such ostensibly nonphysical entities. In "What Is It Like to Be a Bat?" Thomas Nagel claims the objective strategies of physical science cannot capture the subjective points of view of conscious creatures, and he argues that to leave them out of an account of mind means the physicalist and functionalist theories are incomplete. Nagel is a member of the Philosophy Department at New York University. He further develops his point of view in his 1986 book, *The View from Nowhere*.

Consciousness is what makes the mind-body problem really intractable. Perhaps that is why current discussions of the problem give it little attention or get it obviously wrong. The recent wave of reductionist euphoria has produced several analyses of mental phenomena and mental concepts designed to explain the possibility of some variety of materialism, psychophysical identification, or reduction.[1] But the problems dealt with are those common to this type of reduction and other types, and what makes the mind-body problem unique, and unlike the water-H_2O problem or the Turing machine–IBM machine problem or the lightning-electrical discharge problem or the gene-DNA problem or the oak tree–hydrocarbon problem, is ignored.

Every reductionist has his favorite analogy from modern science. It is most unlikely that any of these unrelated examples of successful reduction will shed light on the relation of mind to brain. But philosophers share the general human weakness for explanations of what is incomprehensible

From Thomas Nagel, "What Is It Like to Be a Bat?" *Philosophical Review* 83 (1974): 435–50. Reprinted by permission of the author.

in terms suited for what is familiar and well under-stood, though entirely different. This has led to the acceptance of implausible accounts of the mental largely because they would permit familiar kinds of reduction. I shall try to explain why the usual examples do not help us to understand the relation between mind and body—why, indeed, we have at present no conception of what an explanation of the physical nature of a mental phenomenon would be. Without consciousness the mind-body problem would be much less interesting. With consciousness it seems hopeless. The most important and characteristic feature of conscious mental phenomena is very poorly understood. Most reductionist theories do not even try to explain it. And careful examination will show that no currently available concept of reduction is applicable to it. Perhaps a new theoretical form can be devised for the purpose, but such a solution, if it exists, lies in the distant intellectual future.

Conscious experience is a widespread phenomenon. It occurs at many levels of animal life, though we cannot be sure of its presence in the simpler organisms, and it is very difficult to say in general what provides evidence of it. (Some extremists have been prepared to deny it even of mammals other than man.) No doubt it occurs in countless forms totally unimaginable to us, on other planets in other solar systems throughout the universe. But no matter how the form may vary, the fact that an organism has conscious experience *at all* means, basically, that there is something it is like to *be* that organism. There may be further implications about the form of the experience; there may even (though I doubt it) be implications about the behavior of the organism. But fundamentally an organism has conscious mental states if and only if there is something that it is like to *be* that organism—something it is like *for* the organism.

We may call this the subjective character of experience. It is not captured by any of the familiar, recently devised reductive analyses of the mental, for all of them are logically compatible with its absence. It is not analyzable in terms of any explanatory system of functional states, or intentional states, since these could be ascribed to robots or automata that behaved like people though they experienced nothing.[2] It is not analyzable in terms of the causal role of experiences in relation to typical human behavior—for similar

reasons.[3] I do not deny that conscious mental states and events cause behavior, nor that they may be given functional characterizations. I deny only that this kind of thing exhausts their analysis. Any reductionist program has to be based on an analysis of what is to be reduced. If the analysis leaves something out, the problem will be falsely posed. It is useless to base the defense of materialism on any analysis of mental phenomena that fails to deal explicitly with their subjective character. For there is no reason to suppose that a reduction which seems plausible when no attempt is made to account for consciousness can be extended to include consciousness. Without some idea, therefore, of what the subjective character of experience is, we cannot know what is required of a physicalist theory.

While an account of the physical basis of mind must explain many things, this appears to be the most difficult. It is impossible to exclude the phenomenological features of experience from a reduction in the same way that one excludes the phenomenal features of an ordinary substance from a physical or chemical reduction of it—namely, by explaining them as effects on the minds of human observers.[4] If physicalism is to be defended, the phenomenological features must themselves be given a physical account. But when we examine their subjective character it seems that such a result is impossible. The reason is that every subjective phenomenon is essentially connected with a single point of view, and it seems inevitable that an objective, physical theory will abandon that point of view.

Let me first try to state the issue somewhat more fully than by referring to the relation between the subjective and the objective, or between the *pour-soi* and the *en-soi*. This is far from easy. Facts about what it is like to be an *X* are very peculiar, so peculiar that some may be inclined to doubt their reality, or the significance of claims about them. To illustrate the connection between subjectivity and a point of view, and to make evident the importance of subjective features, it will help to explore the matter in relation to an example that brings out clearly the divergence between the two types of conception, subjective and objective.

I assume we all believe that bats have experience. After all, they are mammals, and there is no more doubt that they have experience than that mice or pigeons or whales have experience. I have chosen bats instead of wasps or flounders because if one travels too far down the phylogenetic tree, people gradually shed their faith that there is experience there at all. Bats, although more closely related to us than those other species, nevertheless present a range of activity and a sensory apparatus so different from ours that the problem I want to pose is exceptionally vivid (though it certainly could be raised with other species). Even without the benefit of philosophical reflection, anyone who has spent some time in an enclosed space with an excited bat knows what it is to encounter a fundamentally *alien* form of life.

I have said that the essence of the belief that bats have experience is that there is something that it is like to be a bat. Now we know that most bats (the microchiroptera, to be precise) perceive the external world primarily by sonar, or echolocation, detecting the reflections, from objects within range, of their own rapid, subtly modulated, high-frequency shrieks. Their brains are designed to correlate the outgoing impulses with the subsequent echoes, and the information thus acquired enables bats to make precise discriminations of distance, size, shape, motion, and texture comparable to those we make by vision. But bat sonar, though clearly a form of perception, is not similar in its operation to any sense that we possess, and there is no reason to suppose that it is subjectively like anything we can experience or imagine. This appears to create difficulties for the notion of what it is like to be a bat. We must consider whether any method will permit us to extrapolate to the inner life of the bat from our own case,[5] and if not, what alternative methods there may be for understanding the notion.

Our own experience provides the basic material for our imagination, whose range is therefore limited. It will not help to try to imagine that one has webbing on one's arms, which enables one to fly around at dusk and dawn catching insects in one's mouth; that one has very poor vision, and perceives the surrounding world by a system of reflected high-frequency sound signals; and that one spends the day hanging upside down by one's feet in an attic. In so far as I can imagine this (which is not very far), it tells me only what it would be like for *me* to behave as a bat behaves.

But that is not the question. I want to know what it is like for a *bat* to be a bat. Yet if I try to imagine this, I am restricted to the resources of my own mind, and those resources are inadequate to the task. I cannot perform it either by imagining additions to my present experience, or by imagining segments gradually subtracted from it, or by imagining some combination of additions, subtractions, and modifications.

To the extent that I could look and behave like a wasp or a bat without changing my fundamental structure, my experiences would not be anything like the experiences of those animals. On the other hand, it is doubtful that any meaning can be attached to the supposition that I should possess the internal neurophysiological constitution of a bat. Even if I could by gradual degrees be transformed into a bat, nothing in my present constitution enables me to imagine what the experiences of such a future stage of myself thus metamorphosed would be like. The best evidence would come from the experiences of bats, if we only knew what they were like.

So if extrapolation from our own case is involved in the idea of what it is like to be a bat, the extrapolation must be incompletable. We cannot form more than a schematic conception of what it *is* like. For example, we may ascribe general *types* of experience on the basis of the animal's structure and behavior. Thus we describe bat sonar as a form of three-dimensional forward perception; we believe that bats feel some versions of pain, fear, hunger, and lust, and that they have other, more familiar types of perception besides sonar. But we believe that these experiences also have in each case a specific subjective character, which it is beyond our ability to conceive. And if there is conscious life elsewhere in the universe, it is likely that some of it will not be describable even in the most general experiential terms available to us.[6] (The problem is not confined to exotic cases, however, for it exists between one person and another. The subjective character of the experience of a person deaf and blind from birth is not accessible to me, for example, nor presumably is mine to him. This does not prevent us each from believing that the other's experience has such a subjective character.)

If anyone is inclined to deny that we can believe in the existence of facts like this whose exact nature we cannot possibly conceive, he should reflect that in contemplating the bats we are in much the same position that intelligent bats or Martians[7] would occupy if they tried to form a conception of what it was like to be us. The structure of their own minds might make it impossible for them to succeed, but we know they would be wrong to conclude that there is not anything precise that it is like to be us: that only certain general types of mental state could be ascribed to us (perhaps perception and appetite would be concepts common to us both; perhaps not). We know they would be wrong to draw such a skeptical conclusion because we know what it is like to be us. And we know that while it includes an enormous amount of variation and complexity, and while we do not possess the vocabulary to describe it adequately, its subjective character is highly specific, and in some respects describable in terms that can be understood only by creatures like us. The fact that we cannot expect ever to accommodate in our language a detailed description of Martian or bat phenomenology should not lead us to dismiss as meaningless the claim that bats and Martians have experiences fully comparable in richness of detail to our own. It would be fine if someone were to develop concepts and a theory that enabled us to think about those things; but such an understanding may be permanently denied to us by the limits of our nature. And to deny the reality or logical significance of what we can never describe or understand is the crudest form of cognitive dissonance.

This brings us to the edge of a topic that requires much more discussion than I can give it here: namely, the relation between facts on the one hand and conceptual schemes or systems of representation on the other. My realism about the subjective domain in all its forms implies a belief in the existence of facts beyond the reach of human concepts. Certainly it is possible for a human being to believe that there are facts which humans never *will* possess the requisite concepts to represent or comprehend. Indeed, it would be foolish to doubt this, given the finiteness of humanity's expectations. After all, there would have been transfinite numbers even if everyone had been wiped out by the Black Death before Cantor discovered them. But one might also believe that there are facts which *could* not ever be represented or comprehended by human beings, even if the species lasted forever—simply because our structure does not

permit us to operate with concepts of the requisite type. This impossibility might even be observed by other beings, but it is not clear that the existence of such beings, or the possibility of their existence, is a precondition of the significance of the hypothesis that there are humanly inaccessible facts. (After all, the nature of beings with access to humanly inaccessible facts is presumably itself a humanly inaccessible fact.) Reflection on what it is like to be a bat seems to lead us, therefore, to the conclusion that there are facts that do not consist in the truth of propositions expressible in a human language. We can be compelled to recognize the existence of such facts without being able to state or comprehend them.

I shall not pursue this subject, however. Its bearing on the topic before us (namely, the mind-body problem) is that it enables us to make a general observation about the subjective character of experience. Whatever may be the status of facts about what it is like to be a human being, or a bat, or a Martian, these appear to be facts that embody a particular point of view.

I am not adverting here to the alleged privacy of experience to its possessor. The point of view in question is not one accessible only to a single individual. Rather it is a *type*. It is often possible to take up a point of view other than one's own, so the comprehension of such facts is not limited to one's own case. There is a sense in which phenomenological facts are perfectly objective: one person can know or say of another what the quality of the other's experience is. They are subjective, however, in the sense that even this objective ascription of experience is possible only for someone sufficiently similar to the object of ascription to be able to adopt his point of view—to understand the ascription in the first person as well as in the third, so to speak. The more different from oneself the other experiencer is, the less success one can expect with this enterprise. In our own case we occupy the relevant point of view, but we will have as much difficulty understanding our own experience properly if we approach it from another point of view as we would if we tried to understand the experience of another species without taking up its point of view.[8]

This bears directly on the mind-body problem. For if the facts of experience—facts about what it is like *for* the experiencing organism—are accessible only from one point of view, then it is a mystery how the true character of experiences could be revealed in the physical operation of that organism. The latter is a domain of objective facts *par excellence*—the kind that can be observed and understood from many points of view and by individuals with differing perceptual systems. There are no comparable imaginative obstacles to the acquisition of knowledge about bat neurophysiology by human scientists, and intelligent bats or Martians might learn more about the human brain than we ever will.

This is not by itself an argument against reduction. A Martian scientist with no understanding of visual perception could understand the rainbow, or lightning, or clouds as physical phenomena, though he would never be able to understand the human concepts of rainbow, lightning, or cloud, or the place these things occupy in our phenomenal world. The objective nature of the things picked out by these concepts could be apprehended by him because, although the concepts themselves are connected with a particular point of view and a particular visual phenomenology, the things apprehended from that point of view are not: they are observable from the point of view but external to it; hence they can be comprehended from other points of view also, either by the same organisms or by others. Lightning has an objective character that is not exhausted by its visual appearance, and this can be investigated by a Martian without vision. To be precise, it has a *more* objective character than is revealed in its visual appearance. In speaking of the move from subjective to objective characterization, I wish to remain noncommittal about the existence of an end point, the completely objective intrinsic nature of the thing, which one might or might not be able to reach. It may be more accurate to think of objectivity as a direction in which the understanding can travel. And in understanding a phenomenon like lightning, it is legitimate to go as far away as one can from a strictly human viewpoint.[9]

In the case of experience, on the other hand, the connection with a particular point of view seems much closer. It is difficult to understand what could be meant by the *objective* character of an experience, apart from the particular point of view from which its subject apprehends it. After all, what would be left of what it was like to be a bat if one removed the viewpoint of the bat? But if experience does not have, in addition to its subjective character, an objective nature that can be apprehended from many different points of view, then how can it be supposed that a Martian investigating my brain might be observing physical processes which were my mental processes (as he might observe physical processes which were bolts of lightning), only from a different point of view? How, for that matter, could a human physiologist observe them from another point of view?[10]

We appear to be faced with a general difficulty about psychophysical reduction. In other areas the process of reduction is a move in the direction of greater objectivity, toward a more accurate view of the real nature of things. This is accomplished by reducing our dependence on individual or species-specific points of view toward the object of investigation. We describe it not in terms of the impressions it makes on our senses, but in terms of its more general effects and of properties detectable by means other than the human senses. The less it depends on a specifically human viewpoint, the more objective is our description. It is possible to follow this path because although the concepts and ideas we employ in thinking about the external world are initially applied from a point of view that involves our perceptual apparatus, they are used by us to refer to things beyond themselves—toward which we *have* the phenomenal point of view. Therefore we can abandon it in favor of another, and still be thinking about the same things.

Experience itself, however, does not seem to fit the pattern. The idea of moving from appearance to reality seems to make no sense here. What is the analogue in this case to pursuing a more objective understanding of the same phenomena by abandoning the initial subjective viewpoint toward them in favor of another that is more objective but concerns the same thing? Certainly it *appears* unlikely that we will get closer to the real nature of human experience by leaving behind the particularity of our human point of view and striving for a description in terms accessible to beings that could not imagine what it was like to be us. If the subjective character of experience is fully comprehensible only from one point of view, then any shift to greater objectivity—that is, less attachment to a specific viewpoint—does not take us nearer to the real nature of the phenomenon: it takes us farther away from it.

In a sense, the seeds of this objection to the reducibility of experience are already detectable in successful cases of reduction; for in discovering sound to be, in reality, a wave phenomenon in air or other media, we leave behind one viewpoint to take up another, and the auditory, human or animal viewpoint that we leave behind remains unreduced. Members of radically different species may both understand the same physical events in objective terms, and this does not require that they understand the phenomenal forms in which those events appear to the senses of members of the other species. Thus it is a condition of their referring to a common reality that their more particular viewpoints are not part of the common reality that they both apprehend. The reduction can succeed only if the species-specific viewpoint is omitted from what is to be reduced.

But while we are right to leave this point of view aside in seeking a fuller understanding of the external world, we cannot ignore it permanently, since it is the essence of the internal world, and not merely a point of view on it. Most of the neobehaviorism of recent philosophical psychology results from the effort to substitute an objective concept of mind for the real thing, in order to have nothing left over which cannot be reduced. If we acknowledge that a physical theory of mind must account for the subjective character of experience, we must admit that no presently available conception gives us a clue how this could be done. The problem is unique. If mental processes are indeed physical processes, then there is something it is like, intrinsically,[11] to undergo certain physical processes. What it is for such a thing to be the case remains a mystery.

What moral should be drawn from these reflections, and what should be done next? It would be a mistake to conclude that physicalism must be false. Nothing is proved by the inadequacy of physicalist hypotheses that assume a faulty objective analysis of mind. It would be truer to say that physicalism is a position we cannot understand because we do not at present have any conception of how it might be true. Perhaps it will be thought unreasonable to require such a conception as a condition of understanding. After all, it might be said, the meaning of physicalism is

clear enough: mental states are states of the body; mental events are physical events. We do not know *which* physical states and events they are, but that should not prevent us from understanding the hypothesis. What could be clearer than the words "is" and "are"?

But I believe it is precisely this apparent clarity of the word "is" that is deceptive. Usually, when we are told that X is Y we know *how* it is supposed to be true, but that depends on a conceptual or theoretical background and is not conveyed by the "is" alone. We know how both "X" and "Y" refer, and the kinds of things to which they refer, and we have a rough idea how the two referential paths might converge on a single thing, be it an object, a person, a process, an event, or whatever. But when the two terms of the identification are very disparate it may not be so clear how it could be true. We may not have even a rough idea of how the two referential paths could converge, or what kind of things they might converge on, and a theoretical framework may have to be supplied to enable us to understand this. Without the framework, an air of mysticism surrounds the identification.

This explains the magical flavor of popular presentations of fundamental scientific discoveries, given out as propositions to which one must subscribe without really understanding them. For example, people are now told at an early age that all matter is really energy. But despite the fact that they know what "is" means, most of them never form a conception of what makes this claim true, because they lack the theoretical background.

At the present time the status of physicalism is similar to that which the hypothesis that matter is energy would have had if uttered by a pre-Socratic philosopher. We do not have the beginnings of a conception of how it might be true. In order to understand the hypothesis that a mental event is a physical event, we require more than an understanding of the word "is." The idea of how a mental and a physical term might refer to the same thing is lacking, and the usual analogies with theoretical identification in other fields fail to supply it. They fail because if we construe the reference of mental terms to physical events on the usual model, we either get a reappearance of separate subjective events as the effects through which mental reference to physical events is secured, or else we get a false account of how mental terms refer (for example, a causal behaviorist one).

Strangely enough, we may have evidence for the truth of something we cannot really understand. Suppose a caterpillar is locked in a sterile safe by someone unfamiliar with insect metamorphosis, and weeks later the safe is reopened, revealing a butterfly. If the person knows that the safe has been shut the whole time, he has reason to believe that the butterfly is or was once the caterpillar, without having any idea in what sense this might be so. (One possibility is that the caterpillar contained a tiny winged parasite that devoured it and grew into the butterfly.)

It is conceivable that we are in such a position with regard to physicalism. Donald Davidson has argued that if mental events have physical causes and effects, they must have physical descriptions. He holds that we have reason to believe this even though we do not—and in fact *could* not—have a general psychophysical theory.[12] His argument applies to intentional mental events, but I think we also have some reason to believe that sensations are physical processes, without being in a position to understand how. Davidson's position is that certain physical events have irreducibly mental properties, and perhaps some view describable in this way is correct. But nothing of which we can now form a conception corresponds to it; nor have we any idea what a theory would be like that enabled us to conceive of it.[13]

Very little work has been done on the basic question (from which mention of the brain can be entirely omitted) whether any sense can be made of experiences' having an objective character at all. Does it make sense, in other words, to ask what my experiences are *really* like, as opposed to how they appear to me? We cannot genuinely understand the hypothesis that their nature is captured in a physical description unless we understand the more fundamental idea that they *have* an objective nature (or that objective processes can have a subjective nature).[14]

I should like to close with a speculative proposal. It may be possible to approach the gap between subjective and objective from another direction. Setting aside temporarily the relation between the mind and the brain, we can pursue a more objective understanding of the mental in its own right. At present we are completely unequipped to think about the subjective character of experience without relying on the imagination—without taking up the point of view of the experiential subject. This should be regarded as a challenge to form new concepts and devise a new method—an objective phenomenology not dependent on empathy or the imagination. Though presumably it would not capture everything, its goal would be to describe, at least in part, the subjective character of experiences in a form comprehensible to beings incapable of having those experiences.

We would have to develop such a phenomenology to describe the sonar experiences of bats; but it would also be possible to begin with humans. One might try, for example, to develop concepts that could be used to explain to a person blind from birth what it was like to see. One would reach a blank wall eventually, but it should be possible to devise a method of expressing in objective terms much more than we can at present, and with much greater precision. The loose intermodal analogies—for example, "Red is like the sound of a trumpet"—which crop up in discussions of this subject are of little use. That should be clear to anyone who has both heard a trumpet and seen red. But structural features of perception might be more accessible to objective description, even though something would be left out. And concepts alternative to those we learn in the first person may enable us to arrive at a kind of understanding even of our own experience which is denied us by the very ease of description and lack of distance that subjective concepts afford.

Apart from its own interest, a phenomenology that is in this sense objective may permit questions about the physical[15] basis of experience to assume a more intelligible form. Aspects of subjective experience that admitted this kind of objective description might be better candidates for objective explanations of a more familiar sort. But whether or not this guess is correct, it seems unlikely that any physical theory of mind can be contemplated until more thought has been given to the general problem of subjective and objective. Otherwise we cannot even pose the mind-body problem without sidestepping it.[16]

Endnotes

[1]Examples are J. J. C. Smart, *Philosophy and Scientific Realism* (London, 1963); David K. Lewis, "An Argument for the Identity Theory," *Journal of Philosophy,* 63 (1966), reprinted with addenda in David M. Rosenthal, *Materialism and the Mind-Body Problem* (Englewood Cliffs, N.J., 1971); Hilary Putnam, "Psychological Predicates" in Capitan and Merrill, *Art, Mind, and Religion* (Pittsburgh, 1967), reprinted in Rosenthal, op. cit., as "The Nature of Mental States"; D. M. Armstrong, *A Materialist Theory of the Mind* (London, 1968); D. C. Dennett, *Content and Consciousness* (London, 1969). I have expressed earlier doubts in "Armstrong on the Mind," *Philosophical Review,* 79 (1970), 394–403; "Brain Bisection and the Unity of Consciousness," *Synthese,* 22 (1971); and a review of Dennett, *Journal of Philosophy,* 69 (1972). See also Saul Kripke, "Naming and Necessity" in Davidson and Harman, *Semantics of Natural Language* (Dordrecht, 1972), esp. pp. 334–342; and M. T. Thornton, "Ostensive Terms and Materialism," *The Monist,* 56 (1972).

[2]Perhaps there could not actually be such robots. Perhaps anything complex enough to behave like a person would have experiences. But that, if true, is a fact which cannot be discovered merely by analyzing the concept of experience.

[3]It is not equivalent to that about which we are incorrigible, both because we are not incorrigible about experience and because experience is present in animals lacking language and thought, who have no beliefs at all about their experiences.

[4]Cf. Richard Rorty, "Mind-Body Identity, Privacy, and Categories," *The Review of Metaphysics,* 19 (1965), esp. 37–38.

[5]By "our own case" I do not mean just "my own case," but rather the mentalistic ideas that we apply unproblematically to ourselves and other human beings.

[6]Therefore the analogical form of the English expression "what it is *like*" is misleading. It does not mean "what (in our experience) it *resembles*," but rather "how it is for the subject himself."

[7]Any intelligent extraterrestrial beings totally different from us.

[8]It may be easier than I suppose to transcend interspecies barriers with the aid of the imagination. For example, blind people are able to detect objects near them by a form of sonar, using vocal clicks or taps of a cane. Perhaps if one knew what that was like, one could by extension imagine roughly what it was like to possess the much more refined sonar of a bat. The distance between oneself and other persons and other species can fall anywhere on a continuum. Even for other persons the understanding of what it is like to be them is only partial, and when one moves to species very different from oneself, a lesser degree of partial understanding may still be available. The imagination is remarkably flexible. My point, however, is not that we cannot *know* what it is like to be a bat. I am not raising that epistemological problem. My point is rather that even to form a *conception* of what it is like to be a bat (and a fortiori to know what it is like to be a bat) one must take up the bat's point of view. If one can take it up roughly, or partially, then one's conception will also be rough or partial. Or so it seems in our present state of understanding.

[9]The problem I am going to raise can therefore be posed even if the distinction between more subjective and more objective descriptions or viewpoints can itself be made only within a larger human point of view. I do not accept this kind of conceptual relativism, but it need not be refuted to make the point that psycho-physical reduction cannot be accommodated by the subjective-to-objective model familiar from other cases.

[10]The problem is not just that when I look at the "Mona Lisa," my visual experience has a certain quality, no trace of which is to be found by someone looking into my brain. For even if he did observe there a tiny image of the "Mona Lisa," he would have no reason to identify it with the experience.

[11]The relation would therefore not be a contingent one, like that of a cause and its distinct effect. It would be necessarily true that a certain physical state felt a certain way. Saul Kripke (op. cit.) argues that causal behaviorist and related analyses of the mental fail because they construe, e.g., "pain" as a merely contingent name of pains. The subjective character of an experience ("its immediate phenomenological quality" Kripke calls it [p. 340]) is the essential property left out by such analyses, and the one in virtue of which it is, necessarily, the experience it is. My view is closely related to his. Like Kripke, I find the hypothesis that a certain brain state should *necessarily* have a certain subjective character incomprehensible without further explanation. No such explanation emerges from theories which view the mind-brain relation as contingent, but perhaps there are other alternatives, not yet discovered.

A theory that explained how the mind-brain relation was necessary would still leave us with Kripke's problem of explaining why it nevertheless appears contingent. That difficulty seems to me surmountable, in the following way. We may imagine something by representing it to ourselves either perceptually, sympathetically, or symbolically. I shall not try to say how symbolic imagination works, but part of what happens in the other two cases is this. To imagine something perceptually, we put ourselves in a conscious state resembling the state we would be in if we perceived it. To imagine something sympathetically, we put ourselves in a conscious state resembling the thing itself. (This method can be used only to imagine mental events and states—our own or another's.) When we try to imagine a mental state occurring without its associated brain state, we first sympathetically imagine the occurrence of the mental state: that is, we put ourselves into a state that resembles it mentally. At the same time, we attempt to perceptually imagine the non-occurrence of the associated physical state, by putting ourselves into another state unconnected with the first: one resembling that which we would be in if we perceived the non-occurrence of the physical state. Where the imagination of physical features is perceptual and the imagination of mental features is sympathetic, it appears to us that we can imagine any experience occurring without its associated brain state, and vice versa. The relation between them will appear contingent even if it is necessary, because of the independence of the disparate types of imagination.

(Solipsism, incidentally, results if one misinterprets sympathetic imagination as if it worked like perceptual imagination: it then seems impossible to imagine any experience that is not one's own.)

[12]See "Mental Events" in Foster and Swanson, *Experience and Theory* (Amherst, 1970); though I don't understand the argument against psychophysical laws.

[13]Similar remarks apply to my paper "Physicalism," *Philosophical Review* 74 (1965), 339–356, reprinted with postscript in John O'Connor, *Modern Materialism* (New York, 1969).

[14]This question also lies at the heart of the problem of other minds, whose close connection with the mind-body problem is often overlooked. If one understood how subjective experience could have an objective nature, one would understand the existence of subjects other than oneself.

[15]I have not defined the term "physical." Obviously it does not apply just to what can be described by the concepts of contemporary physics, since we expect further developments. Some may think there is nothing to prevent mental phenomena from eventually being recognized as physical in their own right. But whatever else may be said of the physical, it has to be objective. So if our idea of the physical ever expands to include mental phenomena, it will have to assign them an objective character—whether or not this is done by analyzing them in terms of other phenomena already regarded as physical. It seems to me more likely, however, that mental-physical relations will eventually be expressed in a theory whose fundamental terms cannot be placed clearly in either category.

[16]I have read versions of this paper to a number of audiences, and am indebted to many people for their comments.

---

31. *Epiphenomenal Qualia*

FRANK JACKSON

Frank Jackson, professor of philosophy at Monash University, argues there are features of bodily sensations and perceptual experiences which no amount of physical information adequately describes. Jackson takes the existence of such "qualia" to show the incompleteness of physicalism. He goes on to defend qualia against the charge they might not be able to causally affect physical events—that is, they might be epiphenomena caused by physical entities.

It is undeniable that the physical, chemical and biological sciences have provided a great deal of information about the world we live in and about ourselves. I will use the label 'physical information' for this kind of information, and also for information that automatically comes along with it. For example, if a medical scientist tells me enough about the processes that go on in my nervous system, and about how they relate to happenings in the world around me, to what has happened in the past and is likely to happen in the future, to what happens to other similar and dissimilar organisms, and the like, he or she tells me—if I am clever enough to fit it together appropriately—about what is often called the functional role of those states in me (and in organisms in general in similar cases). This information, and its kin, I also label 'physical'.

I do not mean these sketchy remarks to constitute a definition of 'physical information', and of the correlative notions of physical property, process, and so on, but to indicate what I have in mind here. It is well known that there are problems with giving a precise definition of these notions, and so of the thesis of Physicalism that all

From *Philosophical Quarterly,* 1982, Vol. 32, pp. 127–136. Reprinted by permission of the author and Blackwell Publishing Ltd.

(correct) information is physical information.[1] But—unlike some—I take the question of definition to cut across the central problems I want to discuss in this paper.

I am what is sometimes known as a "qualia freak". I think that there are certain features of the bodily sensations especially, but also of certain perceptual experiences, which no amount of purely physical information includes. Tell me everything physical there is to tell about what is going on in a living brain, the kind of states, their functional role, their relation to what goes on at other times and in other brains, and so on and so forth, and be I as clever as can be in fitting it all together, you won't have told me about the hurtfulness of pains, the itchiness of itches, pangs of jealousy, or about the characteristic experience of tasting a lemon, smelling a rose, hearing a loud noise or seeing the sky.

There are many qualia freaks, and some of them say that their rejection of Physicalism is an unargued intuition.[2] I think that they are being unfair to themselves. They have the following argument. Nothing you could tell of a physical sort captures the smell of a rose, for instance. Therefore, Physicalism is false. By our lights this is a perfectly good argument. It is obviously not to the point to question its validity, and the premise is intuitively obviously true both to them and to me.

I must, however, admit that it is weak from a polemical point of view. There are, unfortunately for us, many who do not find the premise intuitively obvious. The task then is to present an argument whose premises are obvious to all, or at least to as many as possible. This I try to do in §I with what I will call "the Knowledge argument". In §II I contrast the Knowledge argument with the Modal argument and in §III with the "What is it like to be" argument. In §IV I tackle the question of the causal role of qualia. The major factor in stopping people from admitting qualia is the belief that they would have to be given a causal role with respect to the physical world and especially the brain;[3] and it is hard to do this without sounding like someone who believes in fairies. I seek in §IV to turn this objection by arguing that the view that qualia are epiphenomenal is a perfectly possible one.

I. *The Knowledge Argument for Qualia*

People vary considerably in their ability to discriminate colours. Suppose that in an experiment to catalogue this variation Fred is discovered. Fred has better colour vision than anyone else on record; he makes every discrimination that anyone has ever made, and moreover he makes one that we cannot even begin to make. Show him a batch of ripe tomatoes and he sorts them into two roughly equal groups and does so with complete consistency. That is, if you blindfold him, shuffle the tomatoes up, and then remove the blindfold and ask him to sort them out again, he sorts them into exactly the same two groups.

We ask Fred how he does it. He explains that all ripe tomatoes do not look the same colour to him, and in fact that this is true of a great many objects that we classify together as red. He sees two colours where we see one, and he has in consequence developed for his own use two words 'red$_1$' and 'red$_2$' to mark the difference. Perhaps he tells us that he has often tried to teach the difference between red$_1$ and red$_2$ to his friends but has got nowhere and has concluded that the rest of the world is red$_1$-red$_2$ colour-blind—or perhaps he has had partial success with his children, it doesn't matter. In any case he explains to us that it would be quite wrong to think that because 'red' appears in both 'red$_1$' and 'red$_2$' that the two colours are shades of the one colour. He only uses the common term 'red' to fit more easily into our restricted usage. To him red$_1$ and red$_2$ are as different from each other and all the other colours as yellow is from blue. And his discriminatory behaviour bears this out: he sorts red$_1$ from red$_2$ tomatoes with the greatest of ease in a wide variety of viewing circumstances. Moreover, an investigation of the physiological basis of Fred's exceptional ability reveals that Fred's optical system is able to separate out two groups of wave-lengths in the red spectrum as sharply as we are able to sort out yellow from blue.[4]

I think that we should admit that Fred can see, really see, at least one more colour than we can; red$_1$ is a different colour from red$_2$. We are to Fred as a totally red-green colour-blind person is to us. H. G. Wells' story "The Country of the Blind" is about a sighted person in a totally blind community.[5] This person never manages to convince them that he can see, that he has an extra sense. They ridicule this sense as quite inconceivable, and treat his capacity to avoid falling into ditches, to win fights and so on as precisely that capacity and nothing more. We would be making their mistake if we refused to allow that Fred can see one more colour than we can.

What kind of experience does Fred have when he sees red_1 and red_2? What is the new colour or colours like? We would dearly like to know but do not; and it seems that no amount of physical information about Fred's brain and optical system tells us. We find out perhaps that Fred's cones respond differentially to certain light waves in the red section of the spectrum that make no difference to ours (or perhaps he has an extra cone) and that this leads in Fred to a wider range of those brain states responsible for visual discriminatory behaviour. But none of this tells us what we really want to know about his colour experience. There is something about it we don't know. But we know, we may suppose, everything about Fred's body his behaviour and dispositions to behaviour and about his internal physiology, and everything about his history and relation to others that can be given in physical accounts of persons. We have all the physical information. Therefore, knowing all this is *not* knowing everything about Fred. It follows that Physicalism leaves something out.

To reinforce this conclusion, imagine that as a result of our investigations into the internal workings of Fred we find out how to make everyone's physiology like Fred's in the relevant respects; or perhaps Fred donates his body to science and on his death we are able to transplant his optical system into someone else—again the fine detail doesn't matter. The important point is that such a happening would create enormous interest. People would say, "At last we will know what it is like to see the extra colour, at last we will know how Fred has differed from us in the way he has struggled to tell us about for so long". Then it cannot be that we knew all along all about Fred. But *ex hypothesi* we did know all along everything about Fred that features in the physicalist scheme; hence the physicalist scheme leaves something out.

Put it this way. *After* the operation, we will know *more* about Fred and especially about his colour experiences. But beforehand we had all the physical information we could desire about his body and brain, and indeed everything that has ever featured in physicalist accounts of mind and consciousness. Hence there is more to know than all that. Hence Physicalism is incomplete.

Fred and the new colour(s) are of course essentially rhetorical devices. The same point can be made with normal people and familiar colours. Mary is a brilliant scientist who is, for whatever reason, forced to investigate the world from a black and white room *via* a black and white television monitor. She specialises in the neurophysiology of vision and acquires, let us suppose, all the physical information there is to obtain about what goes on when we see ripe tomatoes, or the sky, and use terms like 'red', 'blue', and so on. She discovers, for example, just which wave-length combinations from the sky stimulate the retina, and exactly how this produces *via* the central nervous system the contraction of the vocal chords and expulsion of air from the lungs that results in the uttering of the sentence "The sky is blue". (It can hardly be denied that it is in principle possible to obtain all this physical information from black and white television, otherwise the Open University would *of necessity* need to use colour television.)

What will happen when Mary is released from her black and white room or is given a colour television monitor? Will she *learn* anything or not? It seems just obvious that she will learn something about the world and our visual experience of it. But then it is inescapable that her previous knowledge was incomplete. But she had *all* the physical information. *Ergo* there is more to have than that, and Physicalism is false.

Clearly the same style of Knowledge argument could be deployed for taste, hearing, the bodily sensations and generally speaking for the various mental states which are said to have (as it is variously put) raw feels, phenomenal features or qualia. The conclusion in each case is that the qualia are left out of the physicalist story. And the polemical strength of the Knowledge argument is that it is so hard to deny the central claim that one can have all the physical information without having all the information there is to have.

II. *The Modal Argument*

By the Modal Argument I mean an argument of the following style.[6] Sceptics about other minds are not making a mistake in deductive logic, whatever else may be wrong with their position. No amount of physical information about another *logically entails* that he or she is conscious or feels anything at all. Consequently there is a possible world with organisms exactly like us in every physical respect (and remember that includes functional states, physical history, *et al.*) but which differ from us profoundly in that they have no conscious mental life at all. But then what is it that we have and they lack? Not anything physical *ex hypothesi*. In all physical regards we and they are exactly alike. Consequently there is more to us than the purely physical. Thus Physicalism is false.[7]

It is sometimes objected that the Modal argument misconceives Physicalism on the ground that that doctrine is advanced as a *contingent* truth.[8] But to say this is only to say that physicalists restrict their claim to *some* possible worlds, including especially ours; and the Modal argument is only directed against this lesser claim. If we in *our* world, let alone beings in any others, have features additional to those of our physical replicas in other possible worlds, then we have non-physical features or qualia.

The trouble rather with the Modal argument is that it rests on a disputable modal intuition. Disputable because it is disputed. Some sincerely deny that there can be physical replicas of us in other possible worlds which nevertheless lack consciousness. Moreover, at least one person who once had he intuition now has doubts.[9]

Head-counting may seem a poor approach to a discussion of the Modal argument. But frequently we can do no better when modal intuitions are in question, and remember our initial goal was to find the argument with the greatest polemical utility.

Of course, *qua* protagonists of the Knowledge argument we may well accept the modal intuition in question; but this will be a *consequence* of our heady having an argument to the conclusion that qualia are left out of the physicalist story, not our ground for that conclusion. Moreover, the matter is complicated by the possibility that the connection between matters physical and qualia is like that sometimes held to obtain between aesthetic qualities and natural ones. Two possible worlds which agree in all "natural" respects (including the experiences of sentient creatures) must agree in all aesthetic qualities also, but it is plausibly held that the aesthetic qualities cannot be reduced to the natural.

III. *The "What Is It Like to Be" Argument*

In "What is it like to be a bat?" Thomas Nagel argues that no amount of physical information can tell us what it is like to be a bat, and indeed that we, human beings, cannot imagine what it is like to be a bat.[10] His reason is that what this is like can only be understood from a bat's point of view, which is not our point of view and is not something capturable in physical terms which are essentially terms understandable equally from many points of view.

It is important to distinguish this argument from the Knowledge argument. When I complained that all the physical knowledge about Fred was not enough to tell us what his special colour experience was like, I was not complaining that we weren't finding out what it is like to *be* Fred. I was complaining that there is something *about* his experience, a property of it, of which we were left ignorant. And if and when we come to know what this property is we still will not know what it is like to *be* Fred, but we will know more *about* him. No amount of knowledge about Fred, be it physical or not, amounts to knowledge "from the inside" concerning Fred. We are not Fred. There is thus a whole set of items of knowledge expressed by forms of words like 'that it is *I myself* who is . . .' which Fred has and we simply cannot have because we are not him.[11]

When Fred sees the colour he alone can see, one thing he knows is the way his experience of it differs from his experience of seeing red and so on, *another* is that he himself is seeing it. Physicalist and qualia freaks alike should acknowledge that no amount of information of whatever kind that *others* have *about* Fred amounts to knowledge of the second. My complaint though concerned the first and was that the special quality of his experience is certainly a fact about it, and one which Physicalism leaves out because no amount of physical information told us what it is.

Nagel speaks as if the problem he is raising is one of extrapolating from knowledge of one experience to another, of imagining what an unfamiliar experience would be like on the basis of familiar ones. In terms of Hume's example, from knowledge of some shades of blue we can work out what it would be like to see other shades of blue. Nagel argues that the trouble with bats *et al.* is that they are too unlike us. It is hard to see an objection to Physicalism here. Physicalism makes no special claims about the imaginative or extrapolative powers of human beings, and it is hard to see why it need do so.[12]

Anyway, our Knowledge argument makes no assumptions on this point. If Physicalism were true, enough physical information about Fred would obviate any need to extrapolate or to perform special feats of imagination or understanding in order to know all about his special colour experience. *The information would already be in our possession.* But it clearly isn't. That was the nub of the argument.

IV. *The Bogey of Epiphenomenalism*

Is there any really *good* reason for refusing to countenance the idea that qualia are causally impotent with respect to the physical world? I will argue for the answer no, but in doing this I will say nothing about two views associated with the classical epiphenomenalist position. The first is that mental *states* are inefficacious with respect to the physical world. All I will be concerned to defend is that it is possible to hold that certain *properties* of certain mental states, namely those I've called qualia, are such that their possession or absence makes no difference to the physical world. The second is that the mental is *totally* causally inefficacious. For all I will say it may be that you have to hold that the instantiation of *qualia* makes a difference to *other mental states* though not to anything physical. Indeed general considerations to do with how you could come to be aware of the instantiation of qualia suggest such a position.[13]

Three reasons are standardly given for holding that a quale like the hurtfulness of a pain must be causally efficacious in the physical world, and so, for instance, that its instantiation must sometimes make a difference to what happens in the brain. None, I will argue, has any real force. (I am much indebted to Alec Hyslop and John Lucas for convincing me of this.)

(i) It is supposed to be just obvious that the hurtfulness of pain is partly responsible for the subject seeking to avoid pain, saying 'It hurts' and so on. But, to reverse Hume, anything can fail to cause anything. No matter how often *B* follows *A*, and no matter how initially obvious the causality of the connection seems, the hypothesis that *A* causes *B* can be overturned by an over-arching theory which shows the two as distinct effects of a common underlying causal process.

To the untutored the image on the screen of Lee Marvin's fist moving from left to right immediately followed by the image of John Wayne's head moving in the same general direction looks as causal as anything.[14] And of course throughout countless Westerns images similar to the first are followed by images similar to the second. All this counts for precisely nothing when we know the over-arching theory concerning how the relevant images are both effects of an underlying causal process involving the projector and the film. The epiphenomenalist can say exactly the same about the connection between, for example, hurtfulness and behaviour. It is simply a consequence of the fact that certain happenings in the brain cause both.

(ii) The second objection relates to Darwin's Theory of Evolution. According to natural selection the traits that evolve over time are those conducive to physical survival. We may assume that qualia evolved over time—we have them, the earliest forms of life do not—and so we should expect qualia to be conducive to survival. The objection is that they could hardly help us to survive if they do nothing to the physical world.

The appeal of this argument is undeniable, but there is a good reply to it. Polar bears have particularly thick, warm coats. The Theory of Evolution explains this (we suppose) by pointing out that having a thick, warm coat is conducive to survival in the Arctic. But having a thick coat goes along with having a heavy coat, and having a heavy coat is *not* conducive to survival. It slows the animal down.

Does this mean that we have refuted Darwin because we have found an evolved trait—having a heavy coat—which is not conducive to survival? Clearly not. Having a heavy coat is an unavoidable concomitant of having a warm coat (in the context, modern insulation was not available), and the advantages for survival of having a warm coat outweighed the disadvantages of having a heavy one. The point is that all we can extract from Darwin's theory is that we should expect any evolved characteristic to be *either* conducive to survival *or* a by-product of one that is so conducive. The epiphenomenalist holds that qualia fall into the latter category. They are a by-product of certain brain processes that are highly conducive to survival.

(iii) The third objection is based on a point about how we come to know about other minds. We know about other minds by knowing about other behaviour, at least in part. The nature of the inference is a matter of some controversy, but it is not a matter of controversy that it proceeds from behaviour. That is why we think that stones do not feel and dogs do feel. But, runs the objection, how can a person's behaviour provide any reason for believing he has qualia like mine, or indeed any qualia at all, unless this behaviour can be regarded as the *outcome* of the qualia. Man Friday's footprint was evidence of Man Friday because footprints are causal outcomes of feet attached to people. And an epiphenomenalist cannot regard behaviour, or indeed anything physical, as an outcome of qualia.

But consider my reading in *The Times* that Spurs won. This provides excellent evidence that *The Telegraph* has also reported that Spurs won, despite the fact that (I trust) *The Telegraph* does not get the results from *The Times*. They each send their own reporters to the game. *The Telegraph's* report is in no sense an outcome of *The Times'*, but the latter provides good evidence for the former nevertheless.

The reasoning involved can be reconstructed thus. I read in *The Times* that Spurs won. This gives me reason to think that Spurs won because I know that Spurs' winning is the most likely candidate to be what caused the report in *The Times*.

But I also know that Spurs' winning would have had many effects, including almost certainly a report in *The Telegraph*.

I am arguing from one effect back to its cause and out again to another effect. The fact that neither effect causes the other is irrelevant. Now the epiphenomenalist allows that qualia are effects of what goes on in the brain. Qualia cause nothing physical but are caused by something physical. Hence the epiphenomenalist can argue from the behaviour of others to the qualia of others by arguing from the behaviour of others back to its causes in the brains of others and out again to their qualia.

You may well feel for one reason or another that this is a more dubious chain of reasoning than its model in the case of newspaper reports. You are right. The problem of other minds is a major philosophical problem, the problem of other newspaper reports is not. But there is no special problem of Epiphenomenalism as opposed to, say, Interactionism here.

There is a very understandable response to the three replies I have just made. "All right, there is no knockdown refutation of the existence of epiphenomenal qualia. But the fact remains that they are an excrescence. They *do* nothing, they *explain* nothing, they serve merely to soothe the intuitions of dualists, and it is left a total mystery how they fit into the world view of science. In short we do not and cannot understand the how and why of them."

This is perfectly true; but is no objection to qualia, for it rests on an overly optimistic view of the human animal, and its powers. We are the products of Evolution. We understand and sense what we need to understand and sense in order to survive. Epiphenomenal qualia are totally irrelevant to survival. At no stage of our evolution did natural selection favour those who could make sense of how they are caused and the laws governing them, or in fact why they exist at all. And that is why we can't.

It is not sufficiently appreciated that Physicalism is an extremely optimistic view of our powers. If it is true, we have, in very broad outline admittedly, a grasp of our place in the scheme of things. Certain matters of sheer complexity defeat us—there are an awful lot of neurons—but in principle we have it all. But consider the antecedent probability that everything in the Universe be of a kind that is relevant in some way or other to the survival of *homo sapiens*. It is very low surely. But then one must admit that it is very likely that there is a part of the whole scheme of things, maybe a big part, which no amount of evolution will ever bring us near to knowledge about or understanding. For the simple reason that such knowledge and understanding is irrelevant to survival.

Physicalists typically emphasise that we are a part of nature on their view, which is fair enough. But if we are a part of nature, we are as nature has left us after however many years of evolution it is, and each step in that evolutionary progression has been a matter of chance constrained just by the need to preserve or increase survival value. The wonder is that we understand as much as we do, and there is no wonder that there should be matters which fall quite outside our comprehension. Perhaps exactly how epiphenomenal qualia fit into the scheme of things is one such.

This may seem an unduly pessimistic view of our capacity to articulate a truly comprehensive picture of our world and our place in it. But suppose we discovered living on the bottom of the deepest oceans a sort of sea slug which manifested intelligence. Perhaps survival in the conditions required rational powers. Despite their intelligence, these sea slugs have only a very restricted conception of the world by comparison with ours, the explanation for this being the nature of their immediate environment. Nevertheless they have developed sciences which work surprisingly well in these restricted terms. They also have philosophers, called slugists. Some call themselves tough-minded slugists, others confess to being soft-minded slugists.

The tough-minded slugists hold that the restricted terms (or ones pretty like them which may be introduced as their sciences progress) suffice in principle to describe everything without remainder. These tough-minded slugists admit in moments of weakness to a feeling that their theory leaves something out. They resist this feeling and their opponents, the soft-minded slugists, by pointing out—absolutely correctly—that no slugist has ever succeeded in spelling out how this mysterious residue fits into the highly successful view that their sciences have and are developing of how their world works.

Our sea slugs don't exist, but they might. And there might also exist super beings which stand to us as we stand to the sea slugs. We cannot adopt the perspective of these super beings, because we are not them, but the possibility of such a perspective is, I think, an antidote to excessive optimism.[15]

Endnotes

[1]See, e.g., D. H. Mellor, "Materialism and Phenomenal Qualities," *Aristotelian Society Supp. Vol.* 47 (1973), 107–19; and J. W. Cornman, *Materialism and Sensations* (New Haven and London, 1971).

[2]Particularly in discussion, but see, e.g., Keith Campbell, *Metaphysics* (Belmont, 1976), p. 67.

[3]See, e.g., D. C. Dennett, "Current Issues in the Philosophy of Mind," *American Philosophical Quarterly*, 15 (1978), 249–61.

[4]Put this, and similar simplifications below, in terms of Land's theory if you prefer. See, e.g., Edwin H. Land, "Experiments in Color Vision," *Scientific American*, 200 (5 May 1959), 84–99.

[5]H. G. Wells, *The Country of the Blind and Other Stories* (London, n.d.).

[6]See, e.g., Keith Campbell, *Body and Mind* (New York, 1970); and Robert Kirk, "Sentience and Behaviour," *Mind*, 83 (1974), 43–60.

[7]I have presented the argument in an inter-world rather than the more usual intra-world fashion to avoid inessential complications to do with supervenience, causal anomalies and the like.

[8]See, e.g., W. G. Lycan, "A New Lilliputian Argument Against Machine Functionalism," *Philosophical Studies*, 35 (1979), 279–87, p. 280; and Don Locke, "Zombies, Schizophrenics and Purely Physical Objects," *Mind*, 85 (1976), 97–9.

[9]See R. Kirk, "From Physical Explicability to Full-Blooded Materialism," *The Philosophical Quarterly*, 29 (1979), 229–37. See also the arguments against the modal intuition in, e.g., Sydney Shoemaker, "Functionalism and Qualia," *Philosophical Studies*, 27 (1975), 291–315.

[10]*The Philosophical Review*, 83 (1974), 435–50. Two things need to be said about this article. One is that, despite my dissociations to come, I am much indebted to it. The other is that the emphasis changes through the article, and by the end Nagel is objecting not so much to Physicalism as to all extant theories of mind for ignoring points of view, including those that admit (irreducible) qualia.

[11]Knowledge *de se* in the terms of David Lewis, "Attitudes De Dicto and De Se," *The Philosophical Review*, 88 (1979), 513–43.

[12]See Laurence Nemirow's comments on "What is it . . ." in his review of T. Nagel, *Mortal Questions*, in *The Philosophical Review*, 89 (1980), 473–7. I am indebted here in particular to a discussion with David Lewis.

[13]See my review of K. Campbell, *Body and Mind*, in *Australasian Journal of Philosophy*, 50 (1972), 77–80.

[14]Cf. Jean Piaget, "The Child's Conception of Physical Causality," reprinted in *The Essential Piaget* (London, 1977).

[15]I am indebted to Robert Pargetter for a number of comments and, despite his dissent, to §IV of Paul E. Meehl, "The Compleat Autocerebroscopist" in *Mind, Matter, and Method*, ed. Paul Feyerabend and Grover Maxwell (Minneapolis, 1966).

32. Reduction, Qualia, and the Direct Introspection of the Brain

PAUL M. CHURCHLAND

Dualists typically claim to know that the mind has properties that are not physical, and physicalists (like Armstrong) have often tried to identify those properties with physical ones. Some functionalists (like Putnam in "Philosophy and Our Mental Life") may be content to argue that mental properties are functional properties that could have (and in the human case probably do have) realization in systems of physical things. Recently, physicalists have explored another strategy, called "eliminative materialism." These philosophers contend that beliefs about the mind are shaped by learned systems of beliefs, or theories, and that the dualists' view of mind just expresses the beliefs of common sense—or so-called "folk psychology." But what if much of folk psychology is false and could be replaced by a better theory? Then, the eliminativists argue, there may be no need to try to *identify* mental states or properties with physical ones because, as traditionally conceived, they may not exist at all. In other words, new and better theories will *eliminate* them.

In this article, Paul Churchland, professor of philosophy at the University of California, San Diego, applies this strategy to beliefs about the qualitative features of sensations, taking as a focus the argument of Frank Jackson in the preceding selection, "Epiphenomenal Qualia." For more background, see Wilfrid Sellars's "Philosophy and the Scientific Image of Man" reprinted in Part VI of this book.

Do the phenomenological or qualitative features of our sensations constitute a permanent barrier to the reductive aspirations of any materialistic neuroscience? I here argue that they do not. Specifically, I wish to address the recent anti-reductionist arguments posed by Thomas Nagel,[1] Frank Jackson,[2] and Howard Robinson.[3] And I wish to explore the possibility of human subjective consciousness within a conceptual environment constituted by a matured and successful neuroscience.

If we are to deal sensibly with the issues here at stake, we must approach them with a general theory of scientific reduction already in hand, a

From Paul M. Churchland, *Journal of Philosophy*, 82, no. 1 (January 1985): 8–28. Reprinted by permission of the author and the *Journal of Philosophy*.

theory motivated by and adequate to the many instances and varieties of interconceptual reduction displayed *elsewhere* in our scientific history. With an independently based account of the nature and grounds of intertheoretic reduction, we can approach the specific case of subjective qualia, free from the myopia that results from trying to divine the proper conditions on reduction by simply staring long and hard at the problematic case at issue.

I. Intertheoretic Reduction

We may begin by remarking that the classical account of intertheoretic reduction[4] now appears to be importantly mistaken, though the repairs necessary are quickly and cleanly made. Suppressing niceties, we may state the original account as follows. A new and more comprehensive theory *reduces* an older theory just in case the new theory, when conjoined with appropriate correspondence rules, logically entails the principles of the older theory. (The point of the correspondence rules, or "bridge laws," is to connect the disparate ontologies of the two theories: often these are expressed as identity statements, such as *Temperature = $mv^2/2k$*.) Schematically,

$$T_N \text{ \& (Correspondence Rules)}$$

logically entails

$$T_O$$

Difficulties with this view begin with the observation that most reduced theories turn out to be, strictly speaking and in a variety of respects, *false*. (Real gases don't really obey $PV = \mu RT$, as in classical thermodynamics; the planets don't really move in ellipses, as in Keplerian astronomy; the acceleration of falling bodies isn't really uniform, as in Galilean dynamics; etc.) If reduction is *de*duction, modus tollens would thus require that the premises of the new reducing theories (statistical thermodynamics in the first case, Newtonian dynamics in the second and third) be somehow false as well, in contradiction to their assumed truth.

This complaint can be temporarily deflected by pointing out that the premises of a reduction must often include not just the new reducing theory but also some limiting assumptions or counterfactual boundary conditions (such as that the molecules of a gas enjoy only mechanical energy, or that the mass of the planets is negligible compared to the sun's, or that the distance any body falls is negligibly different from zero). Falsity in the reducing premises can thus be conceded, since it is safely confined to those limiting or counterfactual assumptions.

This defense will not deal with all cases of falsity, however, since in some cases the reduced theory is so radically false that some or all of its ontology must be rejected entirely, and the "correspondence rules" connecting that ontology to the newer ontology therefore display a problematic status. Newly conceived features cannot be identical with, nor even nomically connected with, old features, if the old features are illusory and uninstantiated. For example, relativistic mass is not identical with Newtonian mass, nor even coextensive with it, even at low velocities. Nevertheless, the reduction of Newtonian by Einsteinian mechanics is a paradigm of a successful reduction. For a second example, neither is caloric-fluid-pressure identical with, nor even coextensive with, mean molecular kinetic energy. But an overtly *fluid* thermodynamics (i.e., one committed to the existence of caloric) still finds a moderately impressive reduction within statistical thermodynamics. In sum, even theories with a *nonexistent* ontology can enjoy reduction, and this fact is problematic on the traditional account at issue.

What cases like these invite us to give up is the idea that what gets *de*duced in a reduction is the theory to be *re*duced. A more accurate, general, and illuminating schema for intertheoretic reduction is as follows:

$$T_N \text{ \& (Limiting Assumptions \& Boundary Conditions)}$$

logically entails

$$I_N \text{ [a set of theorems of (restricted) } T_N]$$
$$\text{e.g., } (x) (Ax . Bx)$$
$$(x) ((Bx \& Cx) . Dx)$$

which is relevantly isomorphic with

$$T_O \text{ (the older theory)}$$
$$e.g., (x) (Jx . Kx)$$
$$(x) ((Kx \& Lx) . Mx)$$

That is to say, a reduction consists in the deduction, within T_N, not of T_O itself, but rather of a roughly equipotent *image* of T_O, an image still expressed in the vocabulary proper to T_N. The correspondence rules play no part whatever in the *de*duction. They show up only later, and not necessarily as material-mode statements, but as mere ordered pairs: $<Ax, Jx>$, $<Bx, Kx>$, $<Cx, Lx>$, $<Dx, Mx>$. Their function is to indicate which term substitutions in the image I_N will yield the principles of T_O. The older theory, accordingly, is never deduced; it is just the target of a relevantly adequate *mimicry*. Construed in this way, a correspondence rule is entirely consistent with the assumption that the older predicate it encompasses has no extension whatever. This allows that a true theory might reduce even a substantially false theory.

The point of a reduction, according to this view, is to show that the new or more comprehensive theory contains explanatory and predictive resources that parallel, to a relevant degree of exactness, the explanatory and predictive resources of the reduced theory. The int*ra*-theoretic deduction (of I_N within T_N), and the int*er*-theoretic mapping (of T_O into I_N), constitute a fell-swoop demonstration that the older theory can be displaced wholesale by the new, without significant explanatory or predictive loss.[5]

Material-mode statements of identity can occasionally be made, of course. We do wish to assert that visible light = EM waves between .35 μm and .75 μm, that sound = atmospheric compression waves, that temperature = mean molecular KE, and that electric current = net motion of charged particles. But a correspondence rule does not itself make such a claim: at best, it records the fact that the new predicate applies in all those cases where its T_O-doppelganger predicate was normally *thought* to apply. On this view, full-fledged *identity* statements are licensed by the comparative *smoothness* of the relevant reduction (i.e., the limiting assumptions or boundary conditions on T_N are not wildly counterfactual, all or most of T_O's principles find close analogues in I_N, etc.). This

smoothness permits the comfortable assimilation of the old ontology within the new and thus allows the old theory to retain all or most of its ontological integrity. *It is smooth intertheoretic reductions that motivate and sustain statements of cross-theoretic identity, not the other way around.*

The preceding framework allows us to frame a useful conception of reduction for specific *properties*, as opposed to entire theories, and it allows us to frame a useful conception of the contrary notion of "emergent" properties. A property F, postulated by an older theory or conceptual framework T_O, is reduced to a property G in some new theory T_N just in case

1. T_N reduces T_O;

2. F and G are correspondence-rule paired in the reduction; and

3.   the reduction is sufficiently smooth to sustain the ontology of T_O, and thus to sustain the identity claim, "F-ness = G-ness."

Intuitively, and in the material mode, this means that F-ness reduces to G-ness just in case the "causal powers" of F-ness (as outlined in the laws of T_O) are a subset of the "causal powers" of G-ness (as outlined in the laws of T_N).

Finally, a property F will be said to be an *emergent* property (relative to T_N) just in case

1. F is definitely real and instantiated;

2. F is co-occurrent with some feature or complex circumstance recognized in T_N; but

3. F cannot be *reduced* to any property postulated by or definable within T_N.

Intuitively, this will happen when T_N does not have the resources adequate to define a property with all the "causal powers" possessed by F-ness. Claims about the emergence of certain properties are therefore claims about the relative poverty in the resources of certain aspirant theories.[6] Having outlined these notions, we shall turn to address substantive questions of emergence and irreducibility in a few moments.

Before we do so, several points about reduction need to be emphasized. The first is that, in arguing for the emergence of a given property F relative to some theory T_N, it is not sufficient to point out that the existence or appearance of F-

ness cannot be deduced from T_N. It is occasionally claimed, for example, that the objective features of warmth or blueness must be irreducibly emergent properties, since, however much one bends and squeezes the molecular theory concerning H_2O, one cannot deduce from it that water will be *blue,* but only that water will scatter electromagnetic radiation at such-and-such wavelengths. And however much one wrings from the mechanics of molecular motion, one cannot deduce from it that a roaring hearth will be warm, but only that its molecules will have such-and-such a mean kinetic energy and will collectively emit EM radiation at longish wavelengths.

These premises about nondeducibility are entirely true, but the conclusion against reducibility does not follow. It is a serious mistake even to make *in*direct deducibility (i.e., deducibility with the help of correspondence rules) a requirement on successful reduction, as we saw at the beginning of this section. And there are additional reasons why it would be even more foolish to insist on the much stronger condition of direct deducibility. For example, formal considerations alone guarantee that, for any predicate 'F' not already in the proprietary lexicon of the aspirant reducing theory T_N, no statements whatever involving 'F' (beyond tautologies and other trivial exceptions) will be deducible from T_N. The deducibility requirement would thus trivialize the notion of reduction by making it impossible for *any* conceptual framework to reduce any other, distinct conceptual framework. Even temperature—that paradigm of a successfully reduced property—would be rendered irreducible, since the term 'temperature' does not appear in the lexicon of statistical mechanics.

There is a further reason why the demand for direct deducibility is too strong. It is a historical accident that we humans currently use precisely the conceptual framework we do use. We might have used any one of an infinite number of other conceptual frameworks to describe the observable world, each one of which could have been roughly adequate to common experience and many of which would be roughly isomorphic (each in its different way) with some part of the correct account that a utopian theory will eventually provide. Accordingly, we can legitimately ask of a putatively correct theory of a given objective domain that it account for the phenomena in (= function successfully in) that domain. But we cannot insist that it also be able to predict how this, that, or the other conceptually idiosyncratic human culture is going to *conceive* of that domain. That would be to insist that the new theory do *predictive cultural anthropology* for us, as well as mechanics, or electromagnetic theory, or what have you. The demand that molecular theory directly entail *our* thermal or color concepts is evidently this same unreasonable demand.

All we can properly ask of a reducing theory is that it have the resources to conjure up a set of properties whose nomological powers/roles/features are systematic *analogues* of the powers/roles/features of the set of properties postulated by the old theory. Since both theories presume to describe the same empirical domain, these systematic nomological parallels constitute the best grounds there can be for concluding that both theories have managed to latch onto the *same* set of objective properties. The hypothesized identity of the properties at issue explains why I_N and T_O are taxonomically and nomically parallel: they are both at least partially correct accounts of the very same objective properties. I_N merely frames that account within a much more penetrating conceptual system—that of T_N.

Moreover, it is to be expected that existing conceptual frameworks will eventually be reduced or displaced by new and better ones, and those in turn by frameworks better still; for who will be so brash as to assert that the feeble conceptual achievements of our adolescent species comprise an exhaustive account of anything at all? If we put aside this conceit, then the only alternatives to intertheoretic reduction are epistemic stagnation or the outright elimination of old frameworks as wholly false and illusory.

II. *Theoretical Change and Perceptual Change*

Esoteric properties and arcane theoretical frameworks are not the only things that occasionally enjoy intertheoretic reduction. Observable properties and common-sense conceptual frameworks can also enjoy smooth reduction. Thus, being a middle-A sound is identical with being an oscillation in air pressure at 440 hz; being red is identical with having a certain triplet of electromagnetic reflectance efficiencies; being warm is identical with having a certain mean level of microscopically embodied energies, and so forth.

Moreover, the relevant reducing theory is capable of replacing the old framework not just in contexts of calculation and inference. *It should be appreciated that the reducing theory can displace the old framework in all its observational contexts as well.* Given the reality of the property identities just listed, it is quite open to us to begin framing our spontaneous perceptual reports in the language of the more sophisticated reducing theory. It is even desirable that we begin doing this, since the new vocabulary observes distinctions that are in fact within the discriminatory reach of our native perceptual systems, though those objective distinctions go unmarked and unnoticed from within the old framework. We can thus make more penetrating use of our native perceptual equipment. Such displacement is also desirable for a second reason: the greater inferential or computational power of the new conceptual framework. We can thus make better inferential *use* of our new perceptual judgments than we made of our old ones.

It is difficult to convey in words the vastness of such perceptual transformations and the naturalness of the new conceptual regime, once established. A nonscientific example may help to get the initial point across.

Consider the enormous increase in discriminatory skill that spans the gap between an untrained child's auditory apprehension of a symphony and the same person's apprehension. of the same symphony forty years later, heard in his capacity as conductor of the orchestra performing it. What was before a seamless voice is now a mosaic of distinguishable elements. What was before a dimly apprehended tune is now a rationally structured sequence of distinguishable and identifiable chords supporting an appropriately related melody line. The matured musician hears an entire world of structured detail, concerning which the child is both dumb and deaf.

Other modalities provide comparable examples. Consider the practiced and chemically sophisticated wine taster, for whom the "red wine" classification used by most of us divides into a network of fifteen or twenty distinguishable elements: ethanol, glycol, fructose, sucrose, tannin, acid, carbon dioxide, and so forth, whose relative concentrations he can estimate with accuracy.

Or consider the astronomer, for whom the speckled black dome of her youth has become a visible abyss, scattering nearby planets, yellow dwarf stars, blue and red giants, distant globular clusters, and even a remote galaxy or two, all discriminable as such and locatable in three-dimensional space with her unaided (repeat: *unaided*) eye.

In each of these cases, what is finally mastered is a conceptual framework—whether musical, chemical, or astronomical—a framework that embodies far more wisdom about the relevant sensory domain than is immediately apparent to untutored discrimination. Such frameworks are characteristically a cultural heritage, pieced together over many generations, and their mastery supplies a richness and penetration to our sensory lives that would be impossible in their absence.[7]

Our *introspective* lives are already the extensive beneficiaries of this phenomenon. The introspective discriminations we make are for the most part learned; they are acquired with practice and experience, often quite slowly. And the specific discriminations we learn to make are those it is useful for us to make. Generally, those are the discriminations that others are already making, the discriminations embodied in the psychological vocabulary of the language we learn. The conceptual framework for psychological states that is embedded in ordinary language is a modestly sophisticated theoretical achievement in its own right, and it shapes our matured introspection profoundly. If it embodied substantially *less* wisdom in its categories and connecting generalizations, our introspective apprehension of our internal states and activities would be much diminished, though our native discriminatory mechanisms remain the same. Correlatively, if folk psychology embodied substantially *more* wisdom about our inner nature than it actually does, our introspective discrimination and recognition could be very much *greater* than it is, though our native discriminatory mechanisms remain unchanged.

This brings me to the central positive suggestion of this paper. Consider now the possibility of learning to describe, conceive, and introspectively apprehend the teeming intricacies of our inner lives within the conceptual framework of a matured neuroscience, a neuroscience that successfully reduces, either smoothly or roughly, our common-sense folk psychology. Suppose we trained our native mechanisms to make a new and more detailed set of discriminations, a set that corresponded not to the primitive psychological taxonomy of ordinary language, but to some more penetrating taxonomy of states drawn from a completed neuroscience. And suppose we trained ourselves to respond to that reconfigured discriminative activity with judgments that were framed, as a matter of course, in the appropriate concepts from neuroscience.[8]

If the examples of the symphony conductor (who can hear the A$m7$ chords), the oenologist (who can see and taste the glycol), and the astronomer (who can see the temperature of a blue giant star) provide a fair parallel, then the enhancement in our introspective vision could approximate a revelation. Dopamine levels in the limbic system, the spiking frequencies in specific neural pathways, resonances in the nth layer of the occipital cortex, inhibitory feedback to the lateral geniculate nucleus, and countless other neurophysical niceties could be moved into the objective focus of our introspective discrimination, just as G$m7$ chords and Adim chords are moved into the objective focus of a trained musician's auditory discrimination. We will of course have to *learn* the conceptual framework of a matured neuroscience in order to pull this off. And we will have to *practice* its noninferential application. But that seems a small price to pay for the quantum leap in self-apprehension.

All of this suggests that there is no problem at all in conceiving the eventual reduction of mental states and properties to neurophysiological states and properties. A matured and successful neuroscience need only include, or prove able to define, a taxonomy of kinds with a set of embedding laws that faithfully mimics the taxonomy and causal generalizations of *folk* psychology. Whether future neuroscientific theories will prove able to do this is a wholly empirical question, not to be settled a priori. The evidence for a positive answer is substantial and familiar, centering on the growing explanatory success of the several neurosciences.

But there is negative evidence as well: I have even urged some of it myself ("Eliminative Materialism and the Propositional Attitudes," op. cit.). My negative arguments there center on the explanatory and predictive poverty of folk psychology, and they question whether it has the categorial integrity to *merit* the reductive preservation of its familiar ontology. That line suggests substantial revision or outright elimination as the eventual fate of our mentalistic ontology. The qualia-based arguments of Nagel, Jackson, and Robinson, however, take a quite different line. They find no fault with folk psychology. Their concern is with the explanatory and descriptive poverty of any possible *neuroscience,* and their line suggests that emergence is the correct story for our mentalistic ontology. Let us now examine their arguments.

III. *Thomas Nagel's Arguments*

For Thomas Nagel, it is the phenomological features of our experiences, the properties or *qualia* displayed by our sensations, that constitute a problem for the reductive aspirations of any materialistic neuroscience. In his classic position paper (op. cit.) I find three distinct arguments in support of the view that such properties will never find any plausible or adequate reduction within the framework of a matured neuroscience. All three arguments are beguiling, but all three, I shall argue, are unsound.

First Argument. What makes the proposed reduction of mental phenomena different from reductions elsewhere in science, says Nagel, is that

> It is impossible to exclude the phenomenological features of experience from a reduction, in the same way that one excludes the phenomenal features of an ordinary substance from a physical or chemical reduction of it—namely, by explaining them as effects on the minds of human observers.

The reason it is impossible to exclude them, continues Nagel, is that the phenomenological features are essential to experience and to the subjective point of view. But this is not what interests me about this argument. What interests me is the claim that reductions of various substances elsewhere in science *exclude the phenomenal features of the substance.*

This is simply false, and the point is extremely important. The phenomenal features at issue are those such as the objective redness of an apple, the warmth of a coffee cup, and the pitch of a sound. These properties are not excluded from our reductions. Redness, an objective phenomenal property of apples, is identical with a certain wave-length triplet of electromagnetic reflectance efficiencies. Warmth, an objective phenomenal property of objects, is identical with the mean level of the objects' microscopically embodied energies. Pitch, an objective phenomenal property of a sound, is identical with its oscillatory frequency. These electromagnetic and micromechanical properties, out there in the objective world, are genuine phenomenal properties. Despite widespread ignorance of their dynamical and microphysical details, it is these objective physical properties to which everyone's perceptual mechanisms are keyed.

The reductions whose existence Nagel denies are in fact so complete that one can already displace entirely large chunks of our common-sense vocabulary for observable properties and learn to frame one's perceptual judgments directly in terms of the reducing theory. The mean KE of the molecules in this room, for example, is currently about . . . 6.2×10^{-21} joules. The oscillatory frequency of this sound (I here whistle C one octave above middle C) is about 524 hz. And the three critical electromagnetic reflectance efficiencies (at .45, .53, and .63 μm) of this (white) piece of paper are all above 80 per cent. These microphysical and electromagnetic properties can be felt, heard, and seen, respectively. Our native sensory mechanisms can easily discriminate such properties, one from another, and their presence from their absence. They have been doing so for millennia. The "resolution" of these mechanisms is inadequate, of course, to reveal the microphysical details and the extended causal roles of the properties thus discriminated. But they are abundantly adequate to permit the reliable discrimination of the properties at issue.[9]

On this view, the standard perceptual properties are not "secondary" properties at all, in the standard sense which implies that they have no real existence save *inside* the minds of human observers. On the contrary, they are as objective as

you please, with a wide variety of objective causal properties. Moreover, it would be a mistake even to try to "kick the phenomenal properties inwards," since that would only postpone the problem of reckoning their place in nature. We would only confront them again later, as we address the place in nature of mental phenomena. And, as Nagel correctly points out, the relocation dodge is no longer open to us, once the problematic properties are already located within the mind.

Nagel concludes from this that subjective qualia are unique in being immune from the sort of reductions found elsewhere in science. I draw a very different conclusion. The *objective* qualia (redness, warmth, etc.) should never have been "kicked inwards to the minds of observers" in the first place. They should be confronted squarely, and they should be reduced where they stand: *out*side the human observer. As we saw, this can and has in fact been done. If objective phenomenal properties are so treated, then *subjective* qualia can be confronted with parallel forthrightness, and can be reduced where *they* stand: *in*side the human observer. So far then, the external and the internal case are not different: they are parallel after all.

Second Argument. A second argument urges the point that the intrinsic character of experiences, the qualia of sensations, are essentially accessible from only a single point of view, the subjective point of view of the experiencing subject. The properties of physical brain states, by contrast, are accessible from a variety of entirely objective points of view. We cannot hope adequately to account for the former, therefore, in terms of properties appropriate to the latter domain (cf. Nagel).

This somewhat diffuse argument appears to be an instance of the following argument:

1. The qualia of my sensations are directly known by me, by introspection, as elements of my conscious self.

2. The properties of my brain states are *not* directly known by me, by introspection, as elements of my conscious self.

∴**3.** The qualia of my sensations ≠ the properties of my brain states.

And perhaps there is a second argument here as well, a complement to the first:

1. The properties of my brain states are known-by-the-various-external-senses, as having such-and-such physical properties.

2. The qualia of my sensations are *not* known-by-the-various-external-senses, as having such-and-such physical properties.

∴**3.** The qualia of my sensations ≠ the properties of my brain states.

The argument form here is apparently

1. *Fa*

2. ~*Fb*

∴**3.** *a ≠ b*

Given Leibniz's law and the extensional nature of the property *F,* this is a valid argument form. But, in the examples at issue, *F* is obviously not an extensional property. The fallacy committed in both cases is amply illustrated in the following parallel arguments.

1. Hitler is widely recognized as a mass murderer.

2. Adolf Schicklgruber is *not* widely recognized as a mass murderer.

∴**3.** Hitler ≠ Adolf Schicklgruber.

or

1. Aspirin is known by John to be a pain reliever.

2. Acetylsalicylic acid is *not* known by John to be a pain reliever.

∴**3.** Aspirin ≠ acetylsalicylic acid.

or, to site an example very close to the case at issue,

1. Temperature is known by me, by tactile sensing, as a feature of material objects.

2. Mean molecular kinetic energy is *not* known by me, by tactile sensing, as a feature of material objects.

∴**3.** Temperature ≠ mean molecular kinetic energy.

The problem with all these arguments is that the "property" ascribed in premise 1 and withheld

in premise 2 consists only in the subject item's being *recognized, perceived,* or *known* as something, *under some specific description or other.* Such apprehension is not a genuine feature of the item itself, fit for divining identities, since one and the same subject may be successfully recognized under one description (e.g., "qualia of my mental state"), and yet fail to be recognized under another, equally accurate, coreferential description (e.g., "property of my brain state"). In logician's terms, the propositional function:

x is known (perceived, recognized) by me, as an *F*

is one of a large number of *intensional contexts* whose distinguishing feature is that they do not always retain the same truth value through substitution of a coreferential or coextensive term for whatever holds the place of 'x.' Accordingly, that such a context (i.e., the one at issue) should show a difference in truth value for two terms '*a*' and '*b*' (i.e., 'qualia of my sensations' and 'property of my brain-states') is therefore hardly grounds for concluding that '*a*' and '*b*' cannot be coreferential or coextensive terms![10]

This objection is decisive, I think, but it does not apply to a different version of the argument, which we must also consider. It may be urged that one's brain states are more than merely not (yet) known by introspection: they are not knowable by introspection under any circumstances. In correspondence, Thomas Nagel has advised me that what he wishes to defend is the following *modalized* version of the argument:

1. My mental states are knowable by me by introspection.

2. My brain states are *not* knowable by me by introspection.

∴**3.** My mental states ≠ my brain states.

Here Nagel will insist that being knowable-by-me-by-introspection is a genuine relational property of a thing and that this version of the argument is free of the intensional fallacy discussed above.

And so it is. But now the reductionist is in a position to insist that the argument contains a false premise: premise 2. At the very least, he can insist that (2) begs the question. For if mental states are indeed identical with brain states, then it is really brain states that we have been introspecting all along, though without appreciating their fine-grained nature. And if we can learn to think of and recognize those states under their familiar mentalistic descriptions—*as all of us have*—then we can certainly learn to think of and recognize them under their more pentrating neurophysiological descriptions. Brain states, that is, are indeed know*able* by introspection, and Nagel's argument commits the same error instanced below.

1. Temperature is knowable by tactile sensing.

2. Mean molecular kinetic energy is *not* knowable by tactile sensing.

∴3. Temperature ≠ mean molecular kinetic energy.

Here the conclusion is known to be false. Temperature is indeed mean molecular kinetic energy. Since the argument is valid, it must therefore have a false premise. Premise 2 is clearly the stinker. Just as one can learn to feel that the summer air is about 70°F, or 21°C, so one can learn to feel that the mean KE of its molecules is about 6.2×10^{-21} joules; for, whether we realize it or not, that is the property our native discriminatory mechanisms are keyed to. And if one can come to know, by feeling, the mean KE of atmospheric molecules, why is it unthinkable that one might come to know, by introspection, the states of one's brain? (What would that feel like? It would feel exactly the same as introspecting the states of one's mind, since they are one and the same states. One would simply employ a different and more penetrating conceptual framework in their description.)

One must be careful, in evaluating the plausibility of Nagel's second premise, to distinguish it from the second premise of the very first version of the argument, the version that commits the intensional fallacy. My guess is that Nagel has profited somewhat from the ambiguity here. For, in the first version, both premises are true. And in the second version, the argument is valid. Neither version, however, meets both conditions.

The matter of introspecting one's brain states will arise once more in the final section of this paper. For now, let us move on.

Third Argument. The last argument here is the one most widely associated with Nagel's paper. The leading example is the (mooted) character of the experiences enjoyed by an alien creature such as a bat. The claim is that, no matter how much one knew about the bat's neurophysiology and its interaction with the physical world, one could still not know, nor perhaps even imagine, what it is like to be a bat. Even total knowledge of the physical details still leaves something out. The lesson drawn is that the reductive aspirations of neurophysiology are doomed to dash themselves, unrealized, against the impenetrable keep of subjective qualia.

This argument is almost identical with an argument put forward in a recent paper by Frank Jackson.[11] Since Jackson's version deals directly with humans, I shall confront the problem as he formulates it.

IV. *Jackson's Knowledge Argument*

Imagine a brilliant neuroscientist named Mary, who has lived her entire life in a room that is rigorously controlled to display only various shades of black, white, and grey. She learns about the outside world by means of a black/white television monitor, and, being brilliant, she manages to transcend these obstacles. She becomes the world's greatest neuroscientist, all from within this room. In particular, she comes to know everything there is to know about the physical structure and activity of the brain and its visual system, of its actual and possible states.

But there would still be something she did *not* know, and could not even imagine, about the actual experiences of all the other people who live outside her black/white room, and about her possible experiences were she finally to leave her room: the nature of the experience of seeing a ripe tomato, what it is like to see red or have a sensation-of-red. Therefore, complete knowledge of the physical facts of visual perception and its related brain activity *still leaves something out*. Therefore, materialism cannot give an adequate reductionist account of all mental phenomena.

To give a conveniently tightened version of this argument:

1. Mary knows everything there is to know about brain states and their properties.

2. It is not the case that Mary knows everything there is to know about sensations and their properties.

Therefore, by Leibniz's law,

3. Sensations and their properties ≠ brain states and their properties.

It is tempting to insist that we here confront just another instance of the intensional fallacy discussed earlier, but Jackson's defenders[12] insist that 'knows *about*' is a perfectly transparent, entirely extensional context. Let us suppose that it is. We can, I think, find at least two other shortcomings in this sort of argument.

The First Shortcoming. This defect is simplicity itself. 'Knows about' may be transparent in both premises, but it is not *univocal* in both premises. (David Lewis[13] and Laurence Nemirow[14] have both raised this same objection, though their analysis of the ambiguity at issue differs from mine.) Jackson's argument is valid only if 'knows about' is univocal in both premises. But the kind of knowledge addressed in premise 1 seems pretty clearly to be different from the kind of knowledge addressed in (2). Knowledge in (1) seems to be a matter of having mastered a set of sentences or propositions, the kind one finds written in neuroscience texts, whereas knowledge in (2) seems to be a matter of having a representation of redness in some pre-linguistic or sublinguistic medium of representation for sensory variables, or to be a matter of being able to *make* certain sensory discriminations, or something along these lines.

Lewis and Nemirow plump for the "ability" analysis of the relevant sense of 'knows about', but they need not be so narrowly committed, and the complaint of equivocation need not be so narrowly based. As my alternative gloss illustrates, other analyses of 'knowledge by acquaintance' are possible, and the charge of equivocation will be sustained so long as the type of knowledge invoked in premise 1 is distinct from the type invoked in premise 2. Importantly, they do seem

very different, even in advance of a settled analysis of the latter.

In short, the difference between a person who knows all about the visual cortex but has never enjoyed a sensation of red, and a person who knows no neuroscience but knows well the sensation of red, may reside not in *what* is respectively known by each (brain states by the former, qualia by the latter), but rather in the different *type* of knowledge each has of *exactly the same thing*. The difference is in the manner of the knowing, not in the nature of the thing(s) known. If one replaces the ambiguous occurrences of 'knows about' in Jackson's argument with the two different expansions suggested above, the resulting argument is a clear non sequitur.

a. Mary has mastered the complete set of true propositions about people's brain states.

b. Mary does *not* have a representation of redness in her prelinguistic medium of representation for sensory variables.

Therefore, by Leibniz's law,

c. The redness sensation ≠ any brain state.

Premises a and b are compossible, even on a materialist view. But they do not entail (c).

In sum, there are pretty clearly more ways of "having knowledge" than having mastered a set of sentences. And nothing in materialism precludes this. The materialist can freely admit that one has "knowledge" of one's sensations in a way that is independent of the scientific theories one has learned. This does not mean that sensations are beyond the reach of physical science. *It just means that the brain uses more modes and media of representation than the simple storage of sentences.* And this proposition is pretty obviously true: almost certainly the brain uses a considerable variety of modes and media of representation, perhaps hundreds of them. Jackson's argument, and Nagel's, exploit this variety illegitimately: both arguments equivocate on 'knows about.'

This criticism is supported by the observation that, if Jackson's form of argument were sound, it would prove far too much. Suppose that Jackson were arguing, not against materialism, but against dualism: against the view that there exists a non-material substance—call it "ectoplasm"—whose hidden constitution and nomic intricacies ground all mental phenomena. Let our cloistered Mary be an "ectoplasmologist" this time, and let her know₁ everything there is to know about the ectoplasmic processes underlying vision. There would still be something she did not know₂: what it is like to see red. Dualism is therefore inadequate to account for all mental phenomena!

This argument is as plausible as Jackson's, and for the same reason: it exploits the same equivocation. But the truth is, such arguments show nothing, one way or the other, about how mental phenomena might be accounted for.

The Second Shortcoming. There is a further shortcoming with Jackson's argument, one of profound importance for understanding one of the most exciting consequences to be expected from a successful neuroscientific account of mind. I draw your attention to the assumption that even a utopian knowledge of neuroscience *must* leave Mary hopelessly in the dark about the subjective qualitative nature of sensations not-yet-enjoyed. It is true, of course, that no sentence of the form "x is a sensation-of-red" will be deducible from premises restricted to the language of neuroscience. But this is no point against the reducibility of phenomenological properties. As we saw in section I, direct deducibility is an intolerably strong demand on reduction, and if this is all the objection comes to, then there is no objection worth addressing. What the defender of emergent qualia must have in mind here, I think, is the claim that Mary could not even *imagine* what the relevant experience would be like, despite her exhaustive neuroscientific knowledge, and hence must still be missing certain crucial information.

This claim, however, is simply false. Given the truth of premise 1, premise 2 seems plausible to Jackson, Nagel, and Robinson only because none of these philosophers has adequately considered how much one might know if, as premise 1 asserts, one knew *everything* there is to know about the physical brain and nervous system. In particular, none of these philosophers has even begun to consider the changes in our introspective apprehension of our internal states that could follow upon a wholesale revision in our conceptual framework for our internal states.

The fact is, we can indeed imagine how neuroscientific information would give Mary detailed information about the qualia of various sensations. Recall our earlier discussion of the transformation of perception through the systematic reconceptualization of the relevant perceptual domain. In particular, suppose that Mary has learned to conceptualize her inner life, even in introspection, in terms of the completed neuroscience we are to imagine. So she does not identify her visual sensations crudely as "a sensation-of-black," "a sensation-of-grey," or "a sensation-of-white"; rather she identifies them more revealingly as various spiking frequencies in the *n*th layer of the occipital cortex (or whatever). If Mary has the relevant neuroscientific concepts for the sensational states at issue (viz., sensations-of-*red*), but has never yet been *in* those states, she may well be able to imagine being in the relevant cortical state, and imagine it with substantial success, even in advance of receiving external stimuli that would actually produce it.

One test of her ability in this regard would be to give her a stimulus that would (finally) produce in her the relevant state (viz., a spiking frequency of 90 hz in the gamma network: a "sensation-of-red" to us), and see whether she can identify it correctly *on introspective grounds alone,* as "a spiking frequency of 90 hz: the kind a tomato would cause." It does not seem to me to be impossible that she should succeed in this, and do so regularly on similar tests for other states, conceptualized clearly by her, but not previously enjoyed.

This may seem to some an outlandish suggestion, but the following will show that it is not. Musical chords are auditory phenomena that the young and unpracticed ear hears as undivided wholes, discriminable one from another, but without elements or internal structure. A musical education changes this, and one comes to hear chords as groups of discriminable notes. If one is sufficiently practiced to have absolute pitch, one can even name the notes of an apprehended chord. And the reverse is also true: if a set of notes is specified verbally, a trained pianist or guitarist can identify the chord and recall its sound in auditory imagination. Moreover, a really skilled individual can construct, in auditory imagination, the sound of a chord he may never have heard before, and certainly does not remember. Specify for him a relatively unusual one—an F#9th*add* 13th for example—and let him brood for a bit. Then play for him three or four chords, one of which is the target, and see whether he can pick it out as the sound that meets the description. Skilled musicians can do this. Why is a similar skill beyond all possibility for Mary?

"Ah," it is tempting to reply, "musicians can do this only because chords are audibly structured sets of elements. Sensations of color are not."

But neither did chords seem, initially, to be structured sets of elements. They also seemed to be undifferentiated wholes. Why should it be unthinkable that sensations of color possess a comparable internal structure, unnoticed so far, but awaiting our determined and informed inspection? Jackson's argument, to be successful, must rule this possibility out, and it is difficult to see how he can do this *a priori*. Especially since there has recently emerged excellent empirical evidence to suggest that *our sensations of color are indeed structured sets of elements.*

The retinex theory of color vision recently proposed by Edwin Land[15] represents any color apprehendable by the human visual system as being uniquely specified by its joint position along three vertices—its reflectance efficiencies at three critical wavelengths, those wavelengths to which the retina's triune cone system is selectively responsive. Since colors are apprehended by us, it is a good hypothesis that those three parameters are represented in our visual systems and that our sensations of color are in some direct way determined by them. Sensations of color may turn out literally to *be* three-element chords in some neural medium! In the face of all this, I do not see why it is even briefly plausible to insist that it is utterly impossible for a conceptually sophisticated Mary accurately to imagine, and subsequently to pick out, color sensations she has not previously enjoyed. We can already foresee how it might actually be done.

The preceding argument does not collapse the distinction (between knowledge-by-description and knowledge-by-acquaintance) urged earlier in the discussion of equivocation. But it does show that the "taxonomies" that reside in our prelinguistic media of representation can be profoundly shaped by the taxonomies that reside in the linguistic medium, especially if one has had long practice at the observational discrimination of items that answer to those linguistically embodied categories. This is just a further illustration of the plasticity of human perception.

I do not mean to suggest, of course, that there will be no limits to what Mary can imagine. Her brain is finite, and its specific anatomy will have specific limitations. For example, if a bat's brain includes computational machinery that the human brain simply lacks (which seems likely), then the subjective character of *some* of the bat's internal states may well be beyond human imagination. Clearly, however, the elusiveness of the bat's inner life here stems not from the metaphysical "emergence" of its internal qualia, but only from the finite capacities of our idiosyncratically human brains. Within those sheerly structural limitations, our imaginations may soar far beyond what Jackson, Nagel, and Robinson suspect, if we possess a neuroscientific conceptual framework that is at last adequate to the intricate phenomena at issue.

I suggest then, that those of us who prize the flux and content of our subjective phenomenological experience need not view the advance of materialistic neuroscience with fear and foreboding. Quite the contrary. The genuine arrival of a materialist kinematics and dynamics for psychological states and cognitive processes will constitute not a gloom in which our inner life is suppressed or eclipsed, but rather a dawning, in which its marvelous intricacies are finally *revealed*— most notably, if we apply ourselves, in direct self-conscious introspection.

Endnotes

[1] "What Is It Like to Be a Bat?" *Philosophical Review*, I., XXXXIII. 4 (October 1974): 435–450; page references to Nagel are to this paper.

[2] "Epiphenomenal Qualia," *Philosophical Quarterly*, XXXII. 127 (April 1982): 127–136.

[3] *Matter and Sense* (New York: Cambridge, 1982), p. 4.

[4] Ernest Nagel, *The Structures of Science* (New York: Harcourt, Brace & World, 1961), ch. 11.

[5] This sketch of intertheoretic reduction is drawn from my *Scientific Realism and the Plasticity of Mind* (New York: Cambridge, 1979), section 11. For a more detailed account see Clifford A. Hooker, "Towards a General Theory of Reduction," *Dialogue*, xx, 1, 2, 3 (March, June, September 1981): 38–59, 201–236, 496–529.

[6] A word of caution is perhaps in order here, since the expression 'emergent property' is often used in two dia-

metrically opposed senses. In scientific contexts, one frequently hears it used to apply to what might be called a "network property," a property that appears exactly when the elements of some substrate are suitably organized, a property that *consists* in the elements of that substrate standing in certain relations to one another, a set of relations that collectively sustain the set of causal powers ascribed to the "emergent" property. In this innocent sense of 'emergent,' there are a great many emergent properties, and quite probably the qualia of our sensations should be numbered among them. But in philosophical contexts one more often encounters a different sense of 'emergent,' one that implies that an "emergent" property does *not* consist in any collective or organizational feature of its substrate. The first sense positively implies reducibility; the second implies *ir*reducibility. It is emergence in the second sense that is at issue in this paper.

[7]The role of theory in perception, and the systematic enhancement of perception through theoretical progress, are examined at length in my *Scientific Realism and the Plasticity of Mind*, op. cit. secs. 1–6.

[8]I believe it was Paul K. Feyerabend and Richard Rorty who first identified and explored this suggestion. See Feyerabend, "Materialism and the Mind-Body Problem," *Review of Metaphysics*, XVIII.1, 65 (September 1963); 49–66: and Rorty, "Mind-Body Identity, Privacy, and Categories," ibid. XIX.1, 73 (September 1965): 24–54. This occurred in a theoretical environment prepared largely by Wilfrid Sellars in "Empiricism and the Philosophy of Mind," in Herbert Feigl and Michael Scriven, eds., *Minnesota Studies in the Philosophy of Mind*,

vol. I (Minneapolis: University of Minnesota Press, 1956): secs. 45–63. The idea has been explored more recently in my "Eliminative Materialism and the Propositional Attitudes," *Journal of Philosophy*, I.XXVIII, 2 (February 1981): 67–90.

[9]See again my *Scientific Realism and the Plasticity of Mind*, op. cit., specs. 2–6. See also Paul and Patricia Churchland, "Functionalism, Qualia, and Intentionality", *Philosophical Topics*, XII, 1 (October 1981): 121–145. Reprinted in J. I. Biro and R. W. Shahan, eds., in *Mind, Brain, and Function* (Norman: U. of Oklahoma Press, 1982): 121–145.

[10]I believe it was Richard Brandt and Jaegwon Kim who first identified this fallacy specifically in connection with the identity theory, in "The Logic of the Identity Theory," *Journal of Philosophy* 64, no. 7 (September 1967): 515–537.

[11]"Epiphenomenal Qualia," op. cit. Howard Robinson runs a very similar argument in *Matter and Sense*, op. cit., p. 4.

[12]See, for example, Keith Campbell, "Abstract Particulars and the Philosophy of Mind," *Australasian Journal of Philosophy*, LXI, 2 (June 1983): 129–141.

[13]"Postscript to "Mad Pain and Martian Pain," *Philosophical Papers*, vol. I (New York: Oxford, 1983).

[14]Review of Thomas Nagel, *Mortal Questions, Philosophical Review*, LXXXIX, 3 (July 1980): 473–477.

[15]"The Retinex Theory of Color Vision," *Scientific American* (December 1977): 108–128.

---

33. *Reductionism and the Irreducibility of Consciousness*

JOHN SEARLE

John Searle takes seriously the first-person perspective of philosophers like Nagel and Jackson, and he claims that consciousness is ontologically irreducible to the components of the nervous system. Though he claims that consciousness is "causally emergent" he attempts to analyze such emergence in a way that does not threaten our scientific worldview. In particular, he tries to explain why a causal understanding of mental states will not lead to a redefinition of the mental in terms of what its causes turn out to be. John Searle is Professor of Philosophy at the University of California, Berkeley.

The view of the relation between mind and body that I have been putting forward is sometimes called "reductionist," sometimes "antireductionist." It is often called "emergentism," and is gen-

From John Searle, "Reductionism and the Irreducibility of Consciousness" originally published as chapter 5 of his book, *The Rediscovery of the Mind* (Cambridge, MA: MIT Press, 1992), pp. 111–126. Reprinted by permission.

erally regarded as a form of "supervenience." I am not sure that any one of these attributions is at all clear, but a number of issues surround these mysterious terms, and . . . I will explore some of them.

I. *Emergent Properties*

Suppose we have a system, *S,* made up of elements *a, b, c* . . . For example, *S* might be a stone and the elements might be molecules. In general, there will be features of *S* that are not, or not necessarily, features of *a, b, c* . . . For example, *S* might weigh ten pounds, but the molecules individually do not weigh ten pounds. Let us call such features "system features." The shape and the weight of the stone are system features. Some system features can be deduced or figured out or calculated from the features of *a, b, c* . . . just from the way these are composed and arranged (and sometimes from their relations to the rest of the environment). Examples of these would be shape, weight, and velocity. But some other system features cannot be figured out just from the composition of the elements and environmental relations; they have to be explained in terms of the causal interactions among the elements. Let's call these "causally emergent system features." Solidity, liquidity, and transparency are examples of causally emergent system features.

On these definitions, consciousness is a causally emergent property of systems. It is an emergent feature of certain systems of neurons in the same way that solidity and liquidity are emergent features of systems of molecules. The existence of consciousness can be explained by the causal interactions between elements of the brain at the micro level, but consciousness cannot itself be deduced or calculated from the sheer physical structure of the neurons without some additional account of the causal relations between them.

This conception of causal emergence, call it "emergent1," has to be distinguished from a much more adventurous conception, call it "emergent2." A feature *F* is emergent2 iff [if and only if] *F* is emergent1 and *F* has causal powers that cannot be explained by the causal interactions of *a, b, c* . . . If consciousness were emergent2, then consciousness could cause things that could not be explained by the causal behavior of the neurons. The naive idea here is that consciousness gets squirted out by the behavior of the neurons in the brain, but once it has been squirted out, it then has a life of its own.

It should be obvious from the previous chapter that on my view consciousness is emergent1, but not emergent2. In fact, I cannot think of anything that is emergent2, and it seems unlikely that we will be able to find any features that are emergent2, because the existence of any such features would seem to violate even the weakest principle of the transitivity of causation.

II. *Reductionism*

Most discussions of reductionism are extremely confusing. Reductionism as an ideal seems to have been a feature of positivist philosophy of science, a philosophy now in many respects discredited. However, discussions of reductionism still survive, and the basic intuition that underlies the concept of reductionism seems to be the idea that certain things might be shown to be *nothing but* certain other sorts of things. Reductionism, then, leads to a peculiar form of the identity relation that we might as well call the "nothing-but" relation: in general, *A*'s can be reduced to *B*'s, iff *A*'s are nothing but *B*'s.

However, even within the nothing-but relation, people mean so many different things by the notion of "reduction" that we need to begin by making several distinctions. At the very outset it is important to be clear about what the relata of the relation are. What is its domain supposed to be: objects, properties, theories, or what? I find at least five different senses of "reduction"—or perhaps I should say five different kinds of reduction—in the theoretical literature, and I want to mention each of them so that we can see which are relevant to our discussion of the mind-body problem.

1. Ontological Reduction

The most important form of reduction is ontological reduction. It is the form in which objects of certain types can be shown to consist in nothing but objects of other types. For example, chairs are shown to be nothing but collections of molecules. This form is clearly important in the history of science. For example, material objects in general can be shown to be nothing but collections of molecules, genes can be shown to consist in nothing but DNA molecules. It seems to me this form of reduction is what the other forms are aiming at.

2. Property Ontological Reduction

This is a form of ontological reduction, but it concerns properties. For example, heat (of a gas) is nothing but the mean kinetic energy of molecule movements. Property reductions for properties corresponding to theoretical terms, such as "heat," "light," etc., are often a result of theoretical reductions.

3. Theoretical Reduction

Theoretical reductions are the favorite of theorists in the literature, but they seem to me rather rare in the actual practice of science, and it is perhaps not surprising that the same half dozen examples are given over and over in the standard textbooks. From the point of view of scientific explanation, theoretical reductions are mostly interesting if they enable us to carry out ontological reductions. In any case, theoretical reduction is primarily a relation between theories, where the laws of the reduced theory can (more or less) be deduced from the laws of the reducing theory. This demonstrates that the reduced theory is nothing but a special case of the reducing theory. The classical example that is usually given in textbooks is the reduction of the gas laws to the laws of statistical thermodynamics.

4. Logical or Definitional Reduction

This form of reduction used to be a great favorite among philosophers, but in recent decades it has fallen out of fashion. It is a relation between words and sentences, where words and sentences referring to one type of entity can be translated without any residue into those referring to another type of entity. For example, sentences about the average plumber in Berkeley are reducible to sentences about specific individual plumbers in Berkeley; sentences about numbers, according to one theory, can be translated into, and hence are reducible to, sentences about sets. Since the words and sentences are *logically* or *definitionally* reducible, the corresponding entities referred to by the words and sentences are *ontologically* reducible. For example, numbers are nothing but sets of sets.

5. Causal Reduction

This is a relation between any two types of things that can have causal powers, where the existence and a fortiori the causal powers of the reduced entity are shown to be entirely explainable in terms of the causal powers of the reducing phenomena. Thus, for example, some objects are solid and this has causal consequences: solid objects are impenetrable by other objects, they are resistant to pressure, etc. But these causal powers can be causally explained by the causal powers of vibratory movements of molecules in lattice structures.

Now when the views I have urged are accused of being reductionist—or sometimes insufficiently reductionist—which of these various senses do the accusers have in mind? I think that theoretical reduction and logical reduction are not intended. Apparently the question is whether the causal reductionism of my view leads—or fails to lead—to ontological reduction. I hold a view of mind/brain relations that is a form of causal reduction, as I have defined the notion: Mental features are caused by neurobiological processes. Does this imply ontological reduction?

In general in the history of science, successful causal reductions tend to lead to ontological reductions. Because where we have a successful causal reduction, we simply redefine the expression that denotes the reduced phenomena in such a way that the phenomena in question can now be identified with their causes. Thus, for example, color terms were once (tacitly) defined in terms of the subjective experience of color perceivers; for example, "red" was defined ostensively by pointing to examples, and then real red was defined as whatever seemed red to "normal" observers under "normal" conditions. But once we have a causal reduction of color phenomena to light reflectances, then, according to many thinkers, it becomes possible to redefine color expressions in terms of light reflectances. We thus carve off and eliminate the subjective experience of color from the "real" color. Real color has undergone a property ontological reduction to light reflectances. Similar remarks could be made about the reduction of heat to molecular motion, the reduction of solidity to molecular movements in lattice structures, and the reduction of sound to air waves. In each case, the causal reduction leads naturally to an ontological reduction by way of a redefinition of the expression that names the reduced phenomenon. Thus, to continue with the example of "red," once we know that the color experiences are caused by a certain sort of photon emission, we then redefine the word in terms of the specific features of the photon emission. "Red," according to some theorists, now refers to photon emissions of 600 nanometers. It thus follows trivially that the color red is nothing but photon emissions of 600 nanometers.

The general principle in such cases appears to be this: Once a property is seen to be *emergent1,* we automatically get a causal reduction, and that leads to an ontological reduction, by redefinition if necessary. The general trend in ontological reductions that have a scientific basis is toward greater generality, objectivity, and redefinition in terms of underlying causation.

So far so good. But now we come to an apparently shocking asymmetry. When we come to consciousness, we cannot perform the ontological reduction. Consciousness is a causally emergent property of the behavior of neurons, and so consciousness is causally reducible to the brain processes. But—and this is what seems so shocking—a perfect science of the brain would still not lead to an ontological reduction of consciousness in the way that our present science can reduce heat, solidity, color, or sound. It seems to many people whose opinions I respect that the irreducibility of consciousness is a primary reason why the mind-body problem continues to seem

so intractable. Dualists treat the irreducibility of consciousness as incontrovertible proof of the truth of dualism. Materialists insist that consciousness must be reducible to material reality, and that the price of denying the reducibility of consciousness would be the abandonment of our overall scientific world view.

I will briefly discuss two questions: First, I want to show why consciousness is irreducible, and second, I want to show why it does not make any difference at all to our scientific world view that it should be irreducible. It does not force us to property dualism or anything of the sort. It is a trivial consequence of certain more general phenomena.

III. *Why Consciousness Is an Irreducible Feature of Physical Reality*

There is a standard argument to show that consciousness is not reducible in the way that heat, etc., are. In different ways the argument occurs in the work of Thomas Nagel (1974), Saul Kripke (1971), and Frank Jackson (1982). I think the argument is decisive, though it is frequently misunderstood in ways that treat it as merely epistemic and not ontological. It is sometimes treated as an epistemic argument to the effect that, for example, the sort of third-person, objective knowledge we might possibly have of a bat's neurophysiology would still not include the first-person, subjective experience of what it feels like to be a bat. But for our present purposes, the point of the argument is ontological and not epistemic. It is a point about what real features exist in the world and not, except derivatively, about how we know about those features.

Here is how it goes: Consider what facts in the world make it the case that you are now in a certain conscious state such as pain. What fact in the world corresponds to your true statement, "I am now in pain"? Naively, there seem to be at least two sorts of facts. First and most important, there is the fact that you are now having certain unpleasant conscious sensations, and you are experiencing these sensations from your subjective, first-person point of view. It is these sensations that are constitutive of your present pain. But the pain is also caused by certain underlying neurophysiological processes consisting in large part of patterns of neuron firing in your thalamus and other regions of your brain. Now suppose we tried to reduce the subjective, conscious, first-person sensation of pain to the objective, third-person patterns of neuron firings. Suppose we tried to say the pain is really "nothing but" the patterns of neuron firings. Well, if we tried such an ontological reduction, the essential features of the pain would be left out. No description of the third-person, objective, physiological facts would convey the subjective, first-person character of the pain, simply because the first-person features are different from the third-person features. Nagel states this point by contrasting the objectivity of the third-person features with the what-it-is-like features of the subjective states of consciousness. Jackson states the same point by calling attention to the fact that someone who had a complete knowledge of the neurophysiology of a mental phenomenon such as pain would still not know what a pain was if he or she did not know what it felt like. Kripke makes the same point when he says that pains could not be identical with neurophysiological states such as neuron firings in the thalamus and elsewhere, because any such identity would have to be necessary, because both sides of the identity statement are rigid designators, and yet we know that the identity could not be necessary.[1] This fact has obvious epistemic consequences: my knowledge that I am in pain has a different sort of basis than my knowledge that you are in pain. But the antireductionist point of the argument is ontological and not epistemic.

So much for the antireductionist argument. It is ludicrously simple and quite decisive. An enormous amount of ink has been shed trying to answer it, but the answers are all so much wasted ink. But to many people it seems that such an argument paints us into a corner. To them it seems that if we accept that argument, we have abandoned our scientific world view and adopted property dualism. Indeed, they would ask, what is property dualism but the view that there are irreducible mental properties? In fact, doesn't Nagel accept property dualism and Jackson reject physicalism precisely because of this argument? And what is the point of scientific reduction if it stops

at the very door of the mind? So I now turn to the main point of this discussion.

IV. Why the Irreducibility of Consciousness Has No Deep Consequences

To understand fully why consciousness is irreducible, we have to consider in a little more detail the pattern of reduction that we found for perceivable properties such as heat, sound, color, solidity, liquidity, etc., and we have to show how the attempt to reduce consciousness differs from the other cases. In every case the ontological reduction was based on a prior causal reduction. We discovered that a surface feature of a phenomenon was caused by the behavior of the elements of an underlying microstructure. This is true both in the cases in which the reduced phenomenon was a matter of subjective appearances, such as the "secondary qualities" of heat or color; and in the cases of the "primary qualities" such as solidity, in which there was both an element of subjective appearance (solid things feel solid), and also many features independent of subjective appearances (solid things, e.g., are resistant to pressure and impenetrable by other solid objects). But in each case, for both the primary and secondary qualities, the point of the reduction was to carve off the surface features and redefine the original notion in terms of the causes that produce those surface features.

Thus, where the surface feature is a subjective appearance, we redefine the original notion in such a way as to exclude the appearance from its definition. For example, pretheoretically our notion of heat has something to do with perceived temperatures: Other things being equal, hot is what feels hot to us, cold is what feels cold. Similarly with colors: Red is what looks red to normal observers under normal conditions. But when we have a theory of what causes these and other phenomena, we discover that it is molecular movements causing sensations of heat and cold (as well as other phenomena such as increases in pressure), and light reflectances causing visual experiences of certain sorts (as well as other phenomena such as movements of light meters). We then *redefine* heat and color in terms of the underlying causes of both the subjective experiences and the other surface phenomena. And in the redefinition we eliminate any reference to the subjective appearances and other surface effects of the underlying causes. "Real" heat is now defined in terms of the kinetic energy of the molecular movements, and the subjective feel of heat that we get when we touch a hot object is now treated as just a subjective appearance caused by heat, as an effect of heat. It is no longer part of real heat. A similar distinction is made between real color and the subjective experience of color. The same pattern works for the primary qualities: Solidity is defined in terms of the vibratory movements of molecules in lattice structures, and objective, observer-independent features, such as impenetrability by other objects, are now seen as surface effects of the underlying reality. Such redefinitions are achieved by way of carving off all of the surface features of the phenomenon, whether subjective or objective, and treating them as effects of the real thing.

But now notice: The actual pattern of the facts in the world that correspond to statements about particular forms of heat such as specific temperatures are quite similar to the pattern of facts in the world that correspond to statements about particular forms of consciousness, such as pain. If I now say, "It's hot in this room," what are the facts? Well, first there is a set of "physical" facts involving the movement of molecules, and second there is a set of "mental" facts involving my subjective experience of heat, as caused by the impact of the moving air molecules on my nervous system. But similarly with pain. If I now say, "I am in pain," what are the facts? Well, first there is a set of "physical" facts involving my thalamus and other regions of the brain, and second there is a set of "mental" facts involving my subjective experience of pain. So why do we regard heat as reducible and pain as irreducible? The answer is that what interests us about heat is not the subjective appearance but the underlying physical causes. Once we get a causal reduction, we simply redefine the notion to enable us to get an ontological reduction. Once you know all the facts about heat—facts about molecule movements, impact on sensory nerve endings, subjective feelings, etc.—the reduction of heat to molecule movements involves no new *fact* whatever. It is simply a trivial consequence of the

redefinition. We don't first discover all the facts and then discover a new fact, the fact that heat is reducible; rather, we simply redefine heat so that the reduction follows from the definition. But this redefinition does not eliminate, and was not intended to eliminate, the subjective experiences of heat (or color, etc.) from the world. They exist the same as ever.

We might not have made the redefinition. Bishop Berkeley, for example, refused to accept such redefinitions. But it is easy to see why it is rational to make such redefinitions and accept their consequences: To get a greater understanding and control of reality, we want to know how it works causally, and we want our concepts to fit nature at its causal joints. We simply redefine phenomena with surface features in terms of the underlying causes. It then looks like a new discovery that heat is *nothing but* mean kinetic energy of molecule movement, and that if all subjective experiences disappeared from the world, real heat would still remain. But this is not a new discovery, it is a trivial consequence of a new definition. Such reductions do not show that heat, solidity, etc., do not really exist in the way that, for example, new knowledge showed that mermaids and unicorns do not exist.

Couldn't we say the same thing about consciousness? In the case of consciousness, we do have the distinction between the "physical" processes and the subjective "mental" experiences, so why can't consciousness be redefined in terms of the neurophysiological processes in the way that we redefined heat in terms of underlying physical processes? Well, of course, if we insisted on making the redefinition, we could. We could simply define, for example, "pain" as patterns of neuronal activity that cause subjective sensations of pain. And if such a redefinition took place, we would have achieved the same sort of reduction for pain that we have for heat. But of course, the reduction of pain to its physical reality still leaves the subjective experience of pain unreduced, just as the reduction of heat left the subjective experience of heat unreduced. Part of the point of the reductions was to carve off the subjective experiences and exclude them from the definition of the real phenomena, which are now defined in terms of those features that interest us most. But where the phenomena that interest us most are the subjective experiences themselves, there is no way to carve anything off. Part of the point of the reduction in the case of heat was to distinguish between the subjective appearance on the one hand and the underlying physical reality on the other. Indeed, it is a general feature of such reductions that the phenomenon is defined in terms of the "reality" and not in terms of the "appearance." But we can't make that sort of appearance-reality distinction for consciousness because consciousness consists in the appearances themselves. *Where appearance is concerned we cannot make the appearance-reality distinction because the appearance* is *the reality.*

For our present purposes, we can summarize this point by saying that consciousness is not reducible in the way that other phenomena are reducible, not because the pattern of facts in the real world involves anything special, but because the reduction of other phenomena depended in part on distinguishing between "objective physical reality," on the one hand, and mere "subjective appearance," on the other; and eliminating the appearance from the phenomena that have been reduced. But in the case of consciousness, its reality is the appearance; hence, the point of the reduction would be lost if we tried to carve off the appearance and simply defined consciousness in terms of the underlying physical reality. In general, the pattern of our reductions rests on rejecting the subjective epistemic basis for the presence of a property as part of the ultimate constituent of that property. We find out about heat or light by feeling and seeing, but we then define the phenomenon in a way that is independent of the epistemology. Consciousness is an exception to this pattern for a trivial reason. The reason, to repeat, is that the reductions that leave out the epistemic bases, the appearances, cannot work for the epistemic bases themselves. In such cases, the appearance is the reality.

But this shows that the irreducibility of consciousness is a trivial consequence of the pragmatics of our definitional practices. A trivial result such as this has only trivial consequences. It has no deep metaphysical consequences for the unity of our overall scientific world view. It does not show that consciousness is not part of the ultimate furniture of reality or cannot be a subject of scientific investigation or cannot be brought into our overall physical conception of the universe; it merely shows that in the way that we have decided to carry out reductions, consciousness, by definition, is excluded from a certain pattern of reduction. Consciousness fails to be reducible, not because of some mysterious feature, but simply because by definition it falls outside the pattern of reduction that we have chosen to use for pragmatic reasons. Pretheoretically, consciousness, like solidity, is a surface feature of certain physical systems. But unlike solidity, consciousness cannot be redefined in terms of an underlying microstructure, and the surface features then treated as mere effects of real consciousness, without losing the point of having the concept of consciousness in the first place.

So far, the argument of this chapter has been conducted, so to speak, from the point of view of the materialist. We can summarize the point I have been making as follows: The contrast between the reducibility of heat, color, solidity, etc., on the one hand, and the irreducibility of conscious states, on the other hand, does not reflect any distinction in the structure of reality, but a distinction in our definitional practices. We could put the same point from the point of view of the property dualist as follows: The apparent contrast between the irreducibility of consciousness and the reducibility of color, heat, solidity, etc., really was *only* apparent. We did not really eliminate the subjectivity of red, for example, when we reduced red to light reflectances; we simply stopped calling the subjective part "red." We did not eliminate any subjective phenomena whatever with these "reductions"; we simply stopped calling them by their old names. Whether we treat the irreducibility from the materialist or from the dualist point of view, we are still left with a universe that contains an irreducibly subjective physical component as a component of physical reality.

To conclude this part of the discussion, I want to make dear what I am saying and what I am not saying. I am not saying that consciousness is not a strange and wonderful phenomenon. I think, on the contrary, that we ought to be amazed by the fact that evolutionary processes produced nervous systems capable of causing and sustaining subjective conscious states. . . . [C]onsciousness is as empirically mysterious to us now as electromagnetism was previously, when people thought the universe must operate entirely on Newtonian principles. But I am saying that once the existence of (subjective, qualitative) consciousness is granted (and no sane person can deny its existence, though many pretend to do so), then there is nothing strange, wonderful, or mysterious about its *irreducibility*. Given its existence, its irreducibility is a trivial consequence of our definitional practices. Its irreducibility has no untoward scientific consequences whatever. Furthermore, when I speak of the irreducibility of consciousness, I am speaking of its *irreducibility according to standard patterns of reduction*. No one can rule out a priori the possibility of a major intellectual revolution that would give us a new— and at present unimaginable—conception of reduction, according to which consciousness would be reducible.

V. *Supervenience*

In recent years there has been a lot of heavy going about a relationship between properties called "supervenience" (e.g., Kim 1979, 1982; Haugeland 1982). It is frequently said in discussions in the philosophy of mind that the mental is supervenient on the physical. Intuitively, what is meant by this claim is that mental states are totally dependent on corresponding neurophysiological states in the sense that a difference in mental states would necessarily involve a corresponding difference in neurophysiological states. If, for example, I go from a state of being thirsty to a state of no longer being thirsty, then there must have been some change in my brain states corresponding to the change in my mental states.

On the account that I have been proposing, mental states are supervenient on neurophysiological states in the following respect: Type-identical neurophysiological causes would have type-identical mentalistic effects. Thus, to take the famous brain-in-the-vat example, if you had two brains that were type-identical down to the last molecule, then the causal basis of the mental would guarantee that they would have the same mental phenomena. On this characterization of the supervenience relation, the supervenience of the mental on the physical is marked by the fact that physical states are causally sufficient, though not necessarily causally neces-

sary, for the corresponding mental states. That is just another way of saying that as far as this definition of supervenience is concerned, sameness of neurophysiology guarantees sameness of mentality; but sameness of mentality does not guarantee sameness of neurophysiology.

It is worth emphasizing that this sort of supervenience is *causal* supervenience. Discussions of supervenience were originally introduced in connection with ethics, and the notion in question was not a causal notion. In the early writings of Moore (1922) and Hare (1952), the idea was that moral properties are supervenient on natural properties, that two objects cannot differ solely with respect to, for example, their goodness. If one object is better than another, there must be some other feature in virtue of which the former is better than the latter. But this notion of moral supervenience is not a causal notion. That is, the features of an object that make it good do not *cause* it to be good, they rather *constitute* its goodness. But in the case of mind/brain supervenience, the neural phenomena cause the mental phenomena.

So there are at least two notions of supervenience: a constitutive notion and a causal notion. I believe that only the causal notion is important for discussions of the mind-body problem. In this respect my account differs from the usual accounts of the supervenience of the mental on the physical. Thus Kim (1979, especially p. 45ff.) claims that we should not think of the relation of neural events to their supervening mental events as causal, and indeed he claims that supervening mental events have no causal status apart from their supervenience on neurophysiological events that have "a more direct causal role." "If this be epiphenomenalism, let us make the most of it," he says cheerfully (p. 47).

I disagree with both of these claims. It seems to me obvious from everything we know about the brain that macro mental phenomena are all caused by lower-level micro phenomena. There is nothing mysterious about such bottom-up causation; it is quite common in the physical world. Furthermore, the fact that the mental features are supervenient on neuronal features in no way diminishes their causal efficacy. The solidity of the piston is causally supervenient on its molecular structure, but this does not make solidity epiphenomenal and similarly, the causal supervenience of my present back pain on micro events in my brain does not make the pain epiphenomenal.

My conclusion is that once you recognize the existence of bottom-up, micro to macro forms of causation, the notion of supervenience no longer does any work in philosophy. The formal features of the relation are already present in the causal sufficiency of the micro-macro forms of causation. And the analogy with ethics is just a source of confusion. The relation of macro mental features of the brain to its micro neuronal features is totally unlike the relation of goodness to good-making features, and it is confusing to lump them together. As Wittgenstein says somewhere, "If you wrap up different kinds of furniture in enough wrapping paper, you can make them all look the same shape."

Endnote

[1]For further discussion of this point see chapter 2 [of *The Rediscovery of the Mind*].

---

34. Dualism and the Arguments against Neuroscientific Progress

PATRICIA SMITH CHURCHLAND

The last couple of decades have seen an explosion of empirical research about the mind in many fields, from neuroscience to cognitive science to the study of animal psychology and ethology. Philosophers' debates about the mind have often had their origin in issues concerning epistemology and theories of meaning. When philosophers (or scientists of like mind) draw attention to some problematic feature of consciousness they can often be taken as giving aid or comfort to some kind of dualism, as implying that the mind is so special it could never be explained as part of the natural world. A prominent exception is Patricia Smith Churchland, Chair of the Philosophy Department and UC President's Professor of Philosophy at the University of California, San Diego; she is also Adjunct Professor at the Salk Institute. In this selection she critically analyzes several recent arguments that are dualistic in spirit or attempt to "naysay" the significance of empirical research.

Life and Conscious Experience

At this stage of our knowledge, none of the functions—attention, short-term memory, being awake, perceiving, imagining—can plausibly be equated with consciousness, but we are learning more about consciousness, bit by little bit, as scientific progress is made on each of the topics. In

From Patricia Smith Churchland, "Dualism and the Arguments against Neuroscientific Progress," originally published as part of section 2 of chapter 5 of her book, *Brain-Wise: Studies in Neurophilosophy* (Cambridge, MA: MIT Press, 2002), pp. 171–193. Reprinted by permission. Footnotes and figures renumbered.

this respect, the virtues of the indirect approach to consciousness may be analogous to the virtues of the indirect approach to the problem of *what it is to be alive*. Just as identifying a micro-organizational correlate to being alive was not the winning strategy for the problem of life, so perhaps, by analogy, trying to identify a micro-organization correlate of consciousness *may* not be the winning strategy for the problem of awareness. But is the analogy between the problem of being alive and the problem of consciousness a *useful* analogy? Let's consider how it might be useful.

What is it for something to be alive? The fundamental answer is now available in college biology courses. Modern cell biology, molecular biology, physiology, and evolutionary biology have discovered so much that a *comprehensive, if not complete,* story can now be told. To be alive, cells need a cytoplasm containing structures such as mitochondria, to produce energy. They need the means of replication, such as DNA, along with microtubules to orchestrate cell division. They need protein-manufacturing apparatus, and so need ribosomes, enzymes, mRNA, tRNA, and DNA. They need specialized membranes, such as bilipid layers with specialized protein channels to admit certain molecules into the cell under specific conditions and to keep others out under certain conditions. They need endoplasmic reticulum for metabolic processes, lysosomes for digestion, and Golgi apparatus for sorting, finishing, and shipping cell products. The biochemistry segment of the course would talk about water, carbon compounds, amino acids, and proteins. The physiology segment of the course would discuss how tissues like muscle, and organs like kidneys, function. At the end of the course, one would have, at least in outline, the scientific account of what it is for something to be alive.

A biology professor winding down the course at the end of the year, might hear this complaint: "I now understand all *that,* but you still have not explained to us what *life itself* is." The reply is, roughly, that life is *all that.* You understand what it is for something to be alive when you understand the physical processes of metabolism, replication, protein building, and so forth. Once you know all that, there is no other phenomenon—*livingness itself*—to be explained. Certainly, there are many questions still unanswered concerning how cells work, but these are questions such as "How does a transmembrane protein get inserted?" not questions such as "How does the *life force* get into the cell?"

Unconvinced, someone might persist, noting that textbook explanations really involve the interactions of *dead stuff*—ribosomes, microtubules, etc.—but what he wants to know is what *living* (being alive) itself is, what the *essence* of life is. Surely, it may be contested, being alive cannot emerge from mere dead stuff, no matter how it is arranged and organized.

The assumption behind this persistent question was a seriously debated hypothesis in the not very distant past. By 1920, however, the assumption was already seriously behind the scientific

times. The assumption, known as vitalism, is that things are alive because they are infused with the "life force" or "vital spirit" or "urge." Vitalists are convinced that being alive cannot be a function of the dynamics and organization of dead molecules. Even as late as 1955, a few scientists still clung to the conviction that a nonphysical "urge" transforms a cell from a dead organization to a living organization.

Nevertheless, what modern biology has discovered is there is no vital spirit over and above a complex—*really* complex—organization of physical properties. The urge intuition takes a beating when the details of metabolism, protein production, membrane functions, and replication are understood. When you see how it all comes together, you see that no vital spirit is needed in the explanation. This is an example where *the nonexistence of something is established as highly probable, not through a single experiment demonstrating its nonexistence, but through acceptance of an explanatorily powerful framework that has no place for it.* The same thing happened to "impetus" as Newton's physics became accepted and . . . to "caloric fluid." This is not to say that the nonexistence of caloric fluid or vital spirit has been absolutely *proved,* but because these concepts play no explanatory role whatever in science, they are deemed to be outdated theoretical curiosities.

Those who pursue the scientific approach to consciousness believe that developments analogous to those in the biology of "life" will allow us to understand consciousness. That is, we are beginning to understand the neurobiology of sleep, dreaming, attention, perception, emotions, drives, moods, autobiographical memory, perceptual imagery, motor control, motor imagery, and self-representation. We are beginning to understand the neurobiology of what happens under various anesthetics, in a coma, in subthreshold perception, and in hallucinatory states. With more complete explanations of all, the nature of conscious phenomena should be understood, at least in a *general* way. Lots of detailed questions will remain, of course, but science is like that. What the research program envisions is that this understanding is an empirical possibility, not an empirical certainty.

If, having understood all those functions, someone were to persist, "But what about consciousness itself. Consciousness cannot come out of nonconscious physical stuff; no matter what its dynamics and organization," we shall have to respond more or less as we do now with the vitalists. We go back through the relevant science all over again. If the objection under consideration assumes that consciousness cannot be a brain function *because* consciousness is a soulish thing, science may be up against dogmatism, as it was with vitalism circa 1950.

Dualism . . . is not likely to be falsified by a single experiment or two showing the nonexistence of the soul. Rather, dualism is rendered improbable because the explanatory framework of psychology and neuroscience, though incomplete, and embedded within the larger framework of physics, chemistry, and evolutionary biology, is *much* more powerful than any dualist competitor. This could change, but so far the empirical evidence does not point that way.[1] As things stand, the concept of a nonphysical soul looks increasingly like an outdated theoretical curiosity.

Even granting that dualism is essentially moribund, a number of philosophers and scientists wish to argue that consciousness cannot *ever* be understood in terms of brain function. Even if dualism is false, they claim, neurobiological research on consciousness is a waste of time, and neurophilosophy is a snare and delusion. Although a host of such arguments exist, I shall analyze only those generally regarded as the strongest, the most widely held, or the most appealing.

Nine Naysaying Arguments[2]

A common argument consists in stressing what we *do not know,* and using this as a premise for concluding what we *cannot* know. Colin McGinn, for example, says that the problem of how the brain could generate consciousness is "miraculous, eerie, even faintly comic."[3] Finding the problem difficult, he concludes, "This is the kind of causal nexus we are precluded from ever understanding, given the way we have to form our concepts and develop our theories." He thinks that for us to understand the nature of consciousness is like a mouse understanding calculus. McGinn is by no means alone here. A number of contemporary thinkers believe they can already tell that the question is unanswerable—not just now, not just given what we know so far, but unanswerable *ever.* Zeno

Vendler chides the ambitions of neuroscience by saying that it is obvious from the nature of sensation, that our sensing selves "are in principle beyond what science can explain."[4] That we are trying to unravel the mystery is, in Vendler's view, a consequence of the overweening assumption that there are no questions science cannot answer. How can we respond to McGinn, Vendler, and other naysayers?

In each of the following subsections, I shall briefly entertain one naysaying objection and try to assess its cogency.[5]

I Cannot Imagine *How Science Could Explain Awareness!*

This is one of the most popular naysaying arguments, advanced frequently by philosophers and sometimes by scientists. What can be said in response?

In general, what substantive conclusions can be drawn when science has not advanced very far on a problem? Not much. One of the basic skills philosophers teach in logic is how to recognize and diagnose the range of nonformal fallacies that lurk under ostensibly appealing arguments: what it is to beg the question, what a non sequitur is, and so on. A prominent item in the fallacy roster is *argumentum ad ignorantiam*—argument from ignorance. The canonical version of this fallacy uses ignorance as the key premise from which a substantive conclusion is drawn. The canonical version looks like this:

We really do not understand much about a phenomenon *p.* (Science is largely ignorant about the nature of *p.*)
Therefore, we do know that

- *p* can never be explained, or

- nothing science could ever discover would deepen our understanding of *p,* or

- *p* can never be explained in terms of properties of kind *s.*

In its canonical version, the argument is obviously a fallacy: none of the proffered conclusions follow, not even a little. Surrounded with rhetorical flourishes, brow furrowing, and hand wringing, however, versions of this argument can hornswoggle the unwary.

From the fact that we do not know something, nothing very interesting follows—we just don't know. Nevertheless, the temptation to suspect that our ignorance is telling us something positive, something deep, something metaphysical or even radical, is ever-present. Perhaps we like to put our ignorance in a positive light, supposing that but for the awesome complexity of the phenomenon, we (smart as we are) *would* have knowledge. But there can be many reasons for not knowing, and the specialness of the phenomenon is, quite regularly, not the most significant reason. I am currently ignorant of what caused an unusual rapping noise in the woods last night. Can I conclude it must be something special, something unimaginable, something *alien, other-worldly?* Evidently not. For all I can tell now, it might merely have been a raccoon gnawing on the compost bin. Lack of evidence for something is just that: lack of evidence. It is not positive evidence for something else, let alone something of a spooky sort. That conclusion is not very thrilling, perhaps, but when ignorance is a premise, that is about all you can grind out of it.

Moreover, the mysteriousness of a problematic phenomenon is *not a fact about the phenomenon*. It is merely an epistemological fact about *us*. It is a fact about where we are in current science. It is a fact is about what we currently do and do not understand, about what, using the rest of our understanding, we can and cannot imagine. It is not a property of the problem itself.

It is sometimes assumed that there can be a valid transition from "We cannot *now* explain" to "We can *never* explain" if we have the help of a subsidiary premise, namely, "I cannot *imagine* how we could ever explain." But the subsidiary premise does not help, and this transition remains a straight-up application of argument from ignorance. Adding, "I cannot imagine explaining *p*" merely adds a psychological fact about the speaker, from which, again, nothing significant follows about the nature of the phenomenon in question.

Vitalists, we noted earlier, argued that life could be explained only by invoking a nonphysical kind of thing, a vital spirit; living things have it, dead things do not. A favored argument for vitalism ran as follows: I cannot *imagine* how you could get living things out of dead molecules. Out of bits of proteins, fats, sugars how could life itself emerge? It seemed obvious from the sheer mysteriousness of life that the problem could have no solution in biology or chemistry. We know now, of course, that this was all a shortsighted mistake.

Neuroscience is very much in its infancy. So if someone or other cannot imagine a certain kind of explanation of some brain phenomenon, it is not terribly significant. Aristotle could not imagine how a complex organism could come from a fertilized egg. Given early science (300 BC), it is no surprise that he could not imagine what it took many scientists hundreds of years to discover. I cannot imagine how ravens can solve a multistep problem in one trial, or how an organism integrates visual signals across time, or how the brain manages thermoregulation. But this is a (not very interesting) *psychological* fact about *me*. One could, of course, use various rhetorical devices to make it seem like an interesting fact about oneself, perhaps by emphasizing that it is a really, *really* hard problem, but if we are going to be sensible about this, it is clear that one's inability to imagine how thermoregulation works is, at bottom, pretty boring.

The "I cannot imagine" gambit suffers in another way. Being able to imagine an explanation for *p* is a highly open-ended and under-specified business. Given the poverty of delimiting conditions of the operation, you can pretty much rig the conclusion to go whichever way your heart desires. Logically, however, that flexibility is the kiss of death.

Suppose that someone claims that he *can* imagine the mechanisms for sensorimotor integration in the human brain but *cannot* imagine the mechanisms for consciousness. What exactly does this difference in imaginabiity amount to? Can he imagine the former in detail? No, because the details are not known. What, precisely, can he imagine? Suppose he answers that in a very general way he imagines that sensory neurons interact with interneurons that interact with motor neurons, and via these interactions, sensorimotor integration is achieved. Now if *that* is all it takes to be able to imagine, one might as well say that one *can* imagine the mechanisms underlying consciousness. Thus, "the interneurons do it." The point is this: if you want to contrast being *able* to imagine brain mechanisms for attention, short-term memory, planning, etc., with being *unable* to imagine mechanisms for consciousness, you have to do more than say that you can imagine neurons doing one but cannot imagine neurons doing the other. Otherwise, you simply beg the question.

There Could Be Zombies

This time the attack on neurobiological strategies derives from a so-called "thought experiment," which roughly goes as follows. (1) We can imagine a person, like us in all the aforementioned capacities (attention, short-term memory, verbal capacity, etc.), but lacking the *experience* of pain and the *experience* of seeing blue. That is, he would lack *qualia* (pronounce kwa-lee-a), i.e., the *qualitative* aspect of conscious experience, such as feeling pain or feeling dizzy, seeing colors, hearing a C-minor chord. This person would be *exactly* like us, save that he would be a *zombie*. He would even say things that we do, such as "I have a funny feeling in my tummy" as the airplane suddenly descends and, on a fine summer afternoon, "The sky is very blue today." The next premise of the argument says this: (2) If the scenario is *conceivable*, it is *logically possible*. The conclusion says, (3) Since a zombie is logically possible, then whatever consciousness is, it is *explanatorily independent* of brain activities. That is, even a complete explanation of every aspect of the human brain will not explain consciousness. This is because a true explanation *must* foreclose the logical possibility of there being a zombie. (Something akin to this was argued by Saul Kripke in the 1970s, by Joseph Levine in the 1980s, and again by David Chalmers in the 1990s.)

To most of us, this argument is puzzling, because many things are logically possible but not empirically possible, such as a 2-ton mouse or a spider that can play the flute. Why should we suppose that the logical possibility of a zombie tells us anything interesting about what research could be successful? After all, what neurophilosophy is really interested in is the actual empirical world and how it works. The reply depends on the pivotal claim about the standards for an explanation, namely, that *a proper explanation must foreclose logical possibilities.*

Assuming that this is the pivotal claim here, we need to recognize how absurdly strong a claim it is. Not only does it rule out explaining consciousness in terms of brain function, but it also rules out explaining consciousness in terms of *soul function* or *spooky-stuff function* or *quantum gravity* or *anything else* you might think of. So strong is the demand it places on successful explanation that no scientific explanation of any phenomenon has ever met it, or ever could meet it.

. . .[E]xplanatory reductions require that a new theory successfully reconstruct most of the features of the reduced phenomenon, as antecedently understood. But this falls far short of any *logical* entailments from the former to the latter such that *previously conceived possibilities* are now *logically impossible*. Good explanations rule out *empirical* possibilities, not logical possibilities. Historically speaking, no scientific reduction/integration has ever met such an absurdly strong requirement.

A further problem with *all* such "conceivability" arguments is that they want to draw an interesting conclusion about the nature of how things *really* are. *Nothing* interesting follows, however, from the fact that some particular human is, or is not, able to imagine something. That something *seems* possible does not thereby guarantee it *is* a genuine possibility in any interesting sense, so why should we think that the zombie idea *is* genuinely possible? To insist on its possibility on grounds that the premises are grammatical is to *confuse a real possibility with mere grammaticality.*

For the sake of argument, I have played along with the underlying assumption that we understand quite well the scope and limits of the domain of the logically possible. Nevertheless, this assumption is deeply flawed. Quine demonstrated in 1960 that such an assumption is actually just a bit of philosophical self-deception. A few hand-picked examples of what is and is not logically possible seem straightforward enough, but outside of these, all is fantasy, or group-think, or depends on self-serving definition. Not surprisingly, the especially controversial cases are those where philosophers want logical possibility to give them some real metaphysical leverage. And the argument at hand is very much a case in point. Standing back a bit, one does find something unconvincing in the idea that the conveniently elastic and philosophically concocted notion of logical possibility should dictate to neurobiology what it can and cannot discover—ever.

To see from a different perspective why the argument gets messed up, run an analogous zombie argument with respect to life. It says that we can imagine a planet where "deadbies" are things composed of cells with membranes, nuclei with DNA, the usual organelles, and so forth. Deadbies reproduce, digest, respire, metabolize, manufacture proteins, grow, and so forth, just as organisms on Earth do. Unlike us, however, deadbies are not *really* alive. This is a logical possibility. So life is *explanatorily independent* of biology.

Here too the premises are *possible* in the very weak sense that they are grammatical, but so far as we know, they do not state a *real* possibility. Here is another feeble thought experiment: imagine a planet where the velocity of molecules in a gas increases, but lo and behold, its temperature does not. Does this tell us that temperature is *explanatorily independent* of mean molecular kinetic energy? Certainly not. What does this tell us about the *actual* relation between mean molecule kinetic energy and temperature in a gas? Not a single thing.

I take the zombie argument to be a demonstration of the feebleness of the class of thought experiments that are factually isolated from the relevant science but nonetheless hope to draw a scientifically relevant conclusion.[6]

The Problem Is Too Hard

This objection is also very common, and is often advanced along with sundry other objections, both those discussed above and some from those given below. How valuable is it?

Can we tell how hard a problem is when we do not have a whole lot of science on the subject? To fill out the point, consider several lessons from the history of science. Before the turn of the twentieth century, people regarded as trivial the problem of explaining the precession of the perihelion of Mercury, that is, the fact that the elliptical orbit of Mercury constantly but slowly advances in the plane of its orbit. This movement was an annoying deviation from what Newton's Laws predict, but the problem was expected ultimately to sort itself out as more data came in. Essentially, it looked like an easy problem.

With the advantage of hindsight, we can see that the assessment was quite wrong: it took the Einsteinian revolution in physics to solve the problem of the precession of the perihelion of Mercury.

By contrast, the composition of the stars was thought to be a *really* hard problem. How could a sample ever be obtained? As soon as you try to get close enough to take a sample, you burn. But with the advent of spectral analysis, that turned out to be a readily solvable problem. When heated to incandescence, the elements turn out to have a kind of fingerprint, easily seen when light emitted from a source is passed through a prism.

Consider now a biological example. Before 1953, many people believed, on rather good grounds actually, that to address the copying problem (transmission of traits from parents to offspring), we would first have to solve the problem of how proteins fold, i.e., how a string of amino acids bends and twists so that it ends up having a highly specific shape unique to that protein. The copying problem was deemed a much harder problem than the problem of how a string of amino acids takes on the correct shape, and many scientists believed it was foolhardy to attack the copying problem directly. This was partly because it was generally believed that it would take something as complex as a protein to be the carrier of hereditary information. DNA, a mere acid, was considered too simple to qualify as a candidate.

As we all know now, the key to the copying problem lay in the base-pairing of DNA, and the copying problem was solved first. Humbling it is to realize that the problem of protein folding (secondary and tertiary folding) is *still* not solved.

What is the point of these stories? They illustrate the fallacy in arguments from ignorance. From the vantage point of ignorance, it is often very difficult to tell which problem will turn out to be more tractable than some other, and whether we have even conceptualized the problem in the best way. Consequently, our judgments about relative difficulty or ultimate tractability should be appropriately qualified and tentative. Guesswork has a useful place, of course, but it is best to distinguish between blind guesswork and educated guesswork, and between guesswork and confirmed fact. The philosophical lesson is this: when not much is known about a topic, don't take terribly seriously someone else's heartfelt conviction about what problems are scientifically tractable. Learn the science, do the science, and see what happens.

How Can I Know What You Experience?[7]

This worry takes several closely related forms, the oldest and most familiar of which is the so-called "inverted spectrum problem." The general worry is that the facts of anyone's phenomenal experience are always underdetermined by *any and all physical* facts, including all neurophysiological facts, that we might come to know about that person. (By *"p is underdetermined by q,"* philosophers mean that *p* cannot be strictly *deduced* from *q; q* may provide evidence for *p*. but not absolutely conclusive evidence.) Accordingly, the argument concludes, phenomenal facts must be distinct and independent facts in their own right, a class of facts that can never be explained in purely physical terms. This general argument finds specific expression in the following thought experiment.

Consider the possibility that you and I share the same range of visual color experiences, but in all those cases where I have the subjective experience of red (as when I look at a ripe tomato in broad daylight), you have the subjective experience of green, the experience that I get when I look at the lawn. Suppose, moreover, that these divergent color experiences are systematic: when I look at the rainbowlike spectrum projected by a prism, I see red on the left-hand side, fading progressively into orange, yellow, green, and blue as I look to the right, but in that same objective situation, you see blue on the left-hand side, fading progressively to green, yellow, orange, and red as you look to the right. In short, your internal spectrum of color experiences is mapped onto the external world in a fashion that is exactly the inverse of my own. But this internal difference is hidden by the fact that we apply our shared color *terms* to external objects in all of the same ways.

This, let us suppose, is entirely conceivable. But, continues the antiphysicalist argument, this possible inversion of our respective color qualia stubbornly *remains* perfectly conceivable no matter how much we might know about each others' brains, and no matter how similar we might be in our physical behavior, our physical constitution, and our internal neural activities. Our brains could be identical, and yet our conscious experiences could still diverge. The physical facts, apparently, do not "logically fix" the phenomenal facts, and so the phenomenal facts must be some kind of facts above and beyond the merely physical facts. Therefore, concludes the argument, we must look beyond the physical sciences for any explanation of phenomenal experiences. They evidently constitute a realm of nonphysical facts.

Is this argument compelling? To answer that, we must closely examine its logic. First, this argument too relies on what is and is not alleged to be imaginable/conceivable in order to generate support for its conclusion. The *key* premise asserts, "Our brains could be *identical* in every respect, but our qualia could *differ."* Not surprisingly, the "could" is the "could" of conceivability, not the "could" of "actually could." As noted in analysis of the zombie argument, that something is logically possible implies absolutely nothing about empirical or real possibility.[8]

If the key premise collapses, the argument collapses. Is perhaps the premise that our brains could be *identical* in every respect but our qualia could *differ* just *obviously* true, and hence not in need of any defense? Not at all. Given the weight of available empirical evidence showing that differences in conscious experience do in fact involve differences in brain activity, the premise cannot be sold as obviously true. For example, we know that if you decrease the activity in the neurons projecting from a decayed tooth to the brainstem, the pain disappears. If nothing is done, the pain persists. Direct stimulation of the hand area of the somatosensory cortex during surgery produces changes in sensations in the hand. We entirely lack any examples where we know the brain remains *exactly* the same but the conscious experience changes. If there is a causal relationship between neuronal activity and conscious experience, as there certainly seems to be, then the *falsity* of the key premise is exactly what one would predict.

Can the premise be defended by claiming that in the actual world there are known examples where brains are *identical* in every respect and our qualia do differ? That strategy would indeed begin to add real substance to the argument. Yet it is never adopted, for the simple reason that there are no examples, there is no factual evidence to bring to bear.

A distinct line of defense of the key premise asserts that the premise is true because qualitative experiences are *nonphysical properties*. Consequently, it is alleged, our brains could be *identical* in every respect but our qualia could *differ*. The weakness in this defense is that it invokes dualism, which, on independent grounds, appears to be highly improbable. Nevertheless, in a spirit of thoroughness, we shall explore this possibility in much greater detail below. . . .

A last ditch effort consists in defending the key premise on grounds that conscious experiences are not identifiable with any property of the nervous system. This move is ineffective because this very claim is what the argument is supposed to *show*, not what the argument gets to *assume*. If you defend the key premise by appeal to the very conclusion your argument is supposed to establish, the argument is utterly worthless—it simply runs in a circle. The illusion of progress can be conjured, however, especially if the defense of the key premise is left implicit and hence hidden from inspection. Incidentally, a variant on the circular argument consists in *defining* qualia as psychological states that are not identifiable with any pattern of neuronal activity. This is no better than simply arguing by restating the conclusion as a premise.

In sum, here is the logical fix the argument finds itself in. It cannot just help itself to the key premise "Our brains could be *identical* in every respect but our qualia could *differ*" on grounds that is it obviously true. The defense of the key

premise can, jointly or severally, take five forms (see table 1). Succinct criticism of these defenses is given in table 1.

The inverted-spectrum argument gets into trouble not because it envisages perceptual differences between subjects that are difficult to detect. The argument gets into trouble because it wants to crank out a very strong conclusion about the *nature of things* from essentially no facts; i.e., it wants to establish an a priori truth. It needs to persuade us that qualitative differences in experience are *undetectable;* not just undetectable given only behavioral data, but undetectable no matter what facts—behavioral, anatomical, physiological—are available.

Given the utter poverty of its cohort of defenses, dualism actually emerges as the strongest argument against a neurophysiological explanation of consciousness. At least the dualist has the option of launching an empirical argument for dualism. The empirically sensitive dualist will want to argue that if the facts prevent us from discovering whether one subject's color experiences are inverted with respect to those of another, then these facts constitute evidence in favor of dualism. In the next section, therefore, we shall take a closer look at the empirical possibility that one person's color experience might be systematically different from that of another, and whether we could indeed discover that this was so from the psychology and neuroscience of the visual system.

Table 1   Key premise: Our brains could be absolutely identical but our qualia could differ

Brief defense of the key premise	Brief criticism of the defense
It is conceivable.	So what?
It is empirically well supported.	Show us the data.
Dualism is true.	Dualism is improbable.
The conclusion is true, so the premise must be true.	Circular arguments are worthless.
By definition, qualia are independent of brain states.	Circular arguments are worthless.

What Happens If We Get More Empirical?

First, the argument, as stated above, betrays a much-too-simple conception of our actual color experiences.[9] The monochromatic linear spectrum produced by a prism presents only a small percentage of the visual color qualia enjoyed by normal human perceivers. That spectrum is missing brown, for example, and pink, and chartreuse, and sky blue, and jade green, and black and white too, for that matter. Indeed, it has been known for some time that the space of human color qualia is not one-dimensional, or even two-dimensional, but is fully three-dimensional. The Munsell color solid displays the structure of that fairly complex space. [Editors' note: We regret that we could not reproduce the original color plates in color in this text. Readers will find themselves in the predicament of Mary in Frank Jackson's "Epiphenomenal Qualia" (Chapter 31) when they try to understand the black and white versions of figures 5, 6, and 7.] Notice that every color discriminable by humans occupies a unique place within that space, a place fixed by the unique family of similarity and dissimilarity relations that it bears to all of the other colors that surround it, both near and far. Two distinct colors could not exchange their respective positions without thereby fouling up many of the similarity relations that structure the original space.

Notice also that the overall shape of this space is nonuniform. For whatever reasons, tying *equal distances* in this space to *equal increments of color discriminability* yields the decidedly nonspherical phenomenal space of figures 5 and 6. Most notably, yellow bulges out from the central axis and up towards the white pole, and at lower brightness levels, it fades to being indiscriminable from dark gray more swiftly than any other color. (In fact, this is roughly how Munsell pieced together his original model of our color space in the first place—by asking people to judge relative similarities and just barely discriminable color differences over a large sample of colored chips.) Additional experiments have shown that we can make finer discriminations among diverse external stimuli within the greenish, yellowish, and orangeish regions of our color space than we can in the blueish regions.

If we are going to perform a color-inversion thought experiment, then we need to imagine something a little more complex than the one-dimensional spectrum flip usually suggested. Specifically, we need to imagine that the subject of the proposed inversion has his phenomenal color solid either rotated (180°, say) or mirror-inverted relative to its normal family of causal connections to external stimuli—thus, the yellow part of his color space gets activated when he looks at the sky, the blue part of his color space gets activated when he looks at bananas, and so forth—*while all of the internal similarity relations of his three-dimensional color space remain exactly the same* (just as in the original thought experiment). Is there anything impossible or inconceivable about this scenario?

Not a thing. Such an inversion is perfectly conceivable. But we should notice that it would be behaviorally (that is, physically) *detectable* in short order. In comparison with normal humans, the inversion subject would be able to make more and finer discriminations than we can among external objects that we describe as various shades of blue, and he would suffer a relative discriminatory deficit among objects that we describe as various shades of red, yellow, orange, and green. (There are probably good evolutionary reasons why normal subjects make finer discriminations among the greens, for example, than among the blues. Birds, with a fourth cone type sensitive to wavelengths in the ultraviolet range, will make finer discriminations among the blues than *we* do.) Moreover, the inversion subject would locate the familiar color *boundaries* in different places. Some external objects that have different shades of the same color, according to us, will fall into entirely different color classes, according to him.

This follows from the refined and more accurate assumptions of our updated thought experiment, as specified at the top of this page. The inversion subject's objective perceptual capacities would be systematically different as well, in ways clearly predicted by the thought experiment, once it is properly performed. Evidently, it is *not true,* even on present scientific knowledge, let alone on all possible future knowledge, *that our color qualia could be differently connected to the external world without any physical or behavioral divergences to herald that phenomenal inversion.* The idea that our color qualia could be inverted, completely independently of any objectively detectable effects, had a superficial plausibility only because of our ignorance of the nonuniform structure of human phenomenal color space and the diversity in our discriminatory capacities, across the colors, that experiments have revealed. Repair that ignorance, as we have done, and the dualist must take his thought experiment back to the drawing board. That, you may be sure, the creative dualist will do.

Connecting Qualia and Neuronal Organization

But let us put the dualist aside for a moment, and ask the independently interesting questions, Why does human phenomenal color space have three dimensions? Why *those* three dimensions in particular? And why does it have the nonuniform shape that it does? What gives rise to the curious phenomenal arrangement of figure 5 in the first place?

Apparently, the shape of phenomenal color space arises quite naturally and inevitably from the physical organization and response profiles of the various neurons in the brain's visual pathways. The fundamentals of the story, according to vision researchers, are surprisingly simple and elegant. The story begins with the three types of light-sensitive *cone* cells scattered across the human retina. Unlike the *rod* cells, with which they are mixed, each cone type is preferentially sensitive to its own narrow band of wavelengths, as illustrated in figures 1 and 4. This allows the retina to do a crude *spectral analysis* of the mixture of various wavelengths entering the eye.

But this is only the first stage of color vision. The crucial stage is the next one. The cone cells in the retina make a set of excitatory and inhibitory synaptic connections, via the optic nerve, to a subsequent population of neurons in the lateral geniculate nucleus (LGN), as illustrated schematically in figure 2. That LGN population is also divided into three distinct kinds of cells, but their response properties are quite different from the cones that project to them. As you can see, the middle cell—labeled "green vs. red"—is the site of a constant tug-of-war between the excitatory signals received from the M-cones (roughly, the green part of the spectrum) and the inhibitory signals received from the L-cones (roughly, the red part of the spectrum). Its resulting activity is thus an ongoing

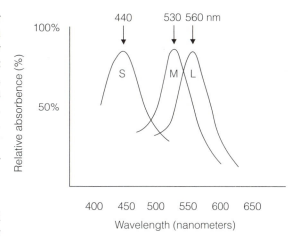

Figure 1 The neural-response curves for the three types of cones. Cones for short (S), medium (M), and long (L) wavelengths provide overlapping but differential responses to light of different wavelengths. These curves are defined by the absorption spectra of the three pigments found in normal cones.

measure of the relative *balance or ratio* of medium wavelengths over long wavelengths currently hitting the relevant part of the retina. (Notice, by the way, that the M- and L-cone curves in figures 1 and 4 overlap to a substantial degree. This means that our green-versus-red tug-of-war cell will be hypersensitive to small shifts, up or down, in the wavelength of monochromatic light in the spectral regions immediately to the right and left of the crossover point of the two curves.)

Similarly, the left-most cell—labeled "blue vs. yellow"—is the site of a tug-of-war between the excitatory signals from the S-cones (roughly, the blue part of the spectrum) and the inhibitory signals from both of the L- and M-cones (very roughly, the yellow part of the spectrum). Its activity reflects the balance of wavelengths from the shorter end of the spectrum over wavelengths from the medium and longer end. (Notice in figures 1 and 4, however, that in this case there is almost no crossover of the relevant curves. So our system will display no hypersensitive discriminations within this area of the spectrum.)

Finally, the right-most cell—labeled "white vs. black"—is the site of a tug-of-war between excitatory signals from all three types of retinal

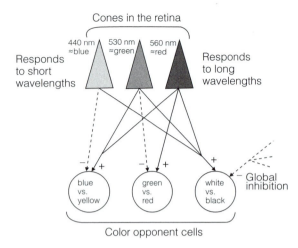

Cones in the retina

Responds to short wavelengths

Responds to long wavelengths

Global inhibition

Color opponent cells

Figure 2 A simplified diagram of neural circuits in opponent-process theory. Opponent responses are derived from the outputs of three classes of cones. Excitatory connections (+) are shown by solid lines, and inhibitory connections (–) are shown by broken lines.

cones (the L, M, and, to a lesser degree, the S cells) versus inhibitory signals averaged over the stimulus-levels reaching the retinal surface as a whole. The activity of that cell is thus a measure of how much *brighter or darker* is its local portion of the retina, compared to the brightness levels hitting the retina as a whole.

These three types of LGN cells—called "color opponent cells" for reasons that are obvious from the diagram—constitute a most interesting arena for the coding of information about the character of the light hitting any spot on the retina. The simultaneous activity levels of all three cell types constitute a three-dimensional comparative analysis of the peculiar wavelength structure of the light hitting any part of the retina to which they are connected. Not to waste words, this analysis constitutes the brain's initial representation of external color. In fact, we can graphically represent any particular neural representation of this sort as a single point in a three-dimensional space, a space whose three axes correspond to the possible activity levels of each of the three types of color-opponent cells.

When we do that, something quite arresting emerges. The range of *possible* coding triplets—that

is, the range of simultaneous activation-level patterns possible across the three kinds of color-opponent cells—does not include the entire volume of the three-dimensional cube portrayed in figure 7. The available range is constrained to an irregular central subvolume of that cube, as illustrated. This is because the three cell types have activation levels that are *not entirely independent* of each other, as can be seen from the wiring diagram of figure 2. The several corners of the coding cube are thus "off limits" to the trio of color-opponent cells.

More specifically, when one calculates what the actual *shape* of that interior volume will have to be (from the details of figures 1 and 7, from the relative numbers and influence of the three cone types, and from the specific overlap of their wavelength response profiles), that interior volume turns out to have the same shape, and to have its various parts associated with the *same* colors, as the original Munsell solid of figure 5. Most obviously, the yellow portion bulges out and up towards the white pole, and in and down towards the black pole. Moreover, equal increments of discriminability within the green, yellow, and orange regions of that neuronal activation space correspond to finer increments of external wavelength than do equal increments within the blue region, just as we found in our own discriminatory capacities.

To a first approximation, and at a rather abstract level, the mapping means we are looking at *the neuronal basis for our phenomenal color space.* The general characteristics of the neuronal basis for the existence, dimensionality, global shape, and chromatic orientation of our internal space for color qualia, as experimentally mapped out by Munsell and subsequent generations of visual psychologists, are discernible. In this *very general sense,* it is mildly tempting to hypothesize that we can discern the basic principles governing color qualia.

It is tempting to say this because, as you have just seen, the various possible coding triplets stand to each other in all of the same similarity/proximity relations that our color qualia stand to each other, and they stand in all of the same causal relations to stimulus objects in the external world, and they stand in all of the same causal relations to subsequent internal cognitive activities, such as believing or saying that the lawn is green. Now, in general, in science, if explanatory power is greatly enhanced by making a cross-level identification,

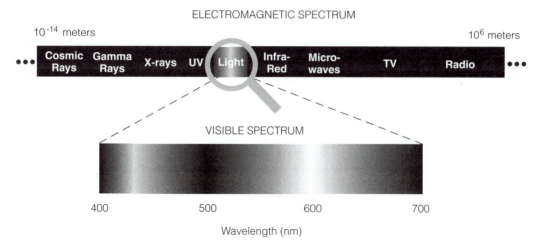

Figure 3 The electromagnetic spectrum. Radiant energy is characterized by its wavelength, which varies continuously from very small to very large. Visible light occupies the limited range from 400 to 700 nanometers (10^{-9} meters). It is the only form of electromagnetic radiation that people sense directly. (From Palmer 1999).

such as between light and electromagnetic radiation, or between temperature and mean molecular kinetic energy, then the identification looks like a reasonable bet.

In the case at hand, if we *hypothesize* that phenomenal color qualia are *identical with* coding triplets across our opponent cells, then the *systematic parallels in their causal and relational properties* are *explicable* rather than *coincidental*. The point is, the causal and relational properties displayed by qualia and by coding triplets will be systematically the same if the qualia and the coding triplets are *themselves* one and the same thing, in the same way that temperature and mean molecular kinetic energy, light and electromagnetic waves, and water and H_2O are one and the same thing.[10]

Is it possible that during inattention to color or even under anesthesia, perhaps, the coding triplets might be active, but no color qualities are experienced? Well, we do not know, but this is something we could find out. Additionally, it is safe to assume that there are many other events that must be taking place elsewhere, for example in the brainstem. To be a little more accurate, therefore, we should restate this *very provisional* hypothesis to say that the coding triplets are one component of a set of components that are *jointly sufficient* for color experience, and that there are a

host of background conditions, many of which remain to be discovered.

So, yes, the hypothesis is undoubtedly too simple to be correct. Nevertheless, my point is to emphasize the significance of the *fit* between the antecedently determined qualia profile and the neuronal-coding triplet profile. I should mention too that a range of other color perceptual phenomena, such as various color illusions, afterimages, and the various forms of color blindness, are also plausibly explained within this framework.[11] This expanding range of explanatory success lends credence to the reductive promise of the general approach; i.e., we have here the same sorts of evidential grounds and explanatory opportunities that standardly motivate reductive claims throughout science. And to that degree, we can get a grip on why materialism seems more plausible than dualism. For example, the task of the dualist's original thought experiment—to invert the qualia without changing anything physical or behavioral—is now one step harder yet to imagine. If the inversion is to preserve the metric of similarity and discriminability relations that structure our phenomenal qualia, then it will require wholesale changes in the synaptic connections that project to our various color-opponent cells, and/or major changes in the profile or location of the normal

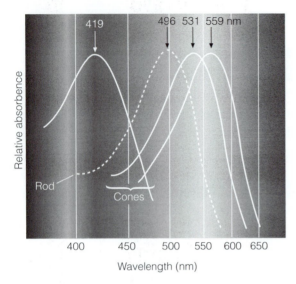

Figure 4 The absorption spectra of the four photopigments in the normal human retina. There are three types of cones, distinguished by three types of photopigments sensitive to light at distinct wavelengths. The sensitivity curve for rhodopsin, the photopigment in the rods, is also shown.

response profiles of our three cone-cell populations. It is these features of our nervous system, as we saw, that give rise to that nonuniform metric in the first place.

An inversion is still possible, to be sure, but if it were imposed, it would show up not just in the subject's color-discrimination behaviors (as we saw before); it would also show up in the form of *changed behavior in his cones* and/or massive physical adjustments to the *wiring* that connects his retinal cone cells to his LGN opponent-cells. Evidently, as our understanding of the brain's coding activities gradually expands, the claim that qualia might be inverted among us, without *any* behavioral or physical differences among us, looks less and less plausible.

The Dualist Tries Again

"Still," the Dualist might say, "it remains *conceivable*. We need only invert as well the *metric of the similarity/discriminability* relations, *in addition* to inverting the causal map of color qualia onto the external world, and the inversion will then require

no synaptic adjustments and it will lead to no differences in discriminatory behavior."

That is strictly true, although changing the global metric of the space of possible qualia raises the issue of whether we have thereby made a significant change in the nature of the qualia themselves. If every color in the original space now bears a *different* set of similarity and dissimilarity relations to every other color in the original space, are we still talking about the same family of colors that we started with? It is not clear that we are. But let us not insist on this point. Who are we to insist that *any one* of the features we have been discussing is *essential* to the nature of color qualia, and could not *conceivably* be switched around without compromising their identity? In the absence of any *settled* scientific understanding of what qualia really *are*, any such insistence would be premature and prejudicial. It is the job of unfolding research, in the fullness of time, to provide us with authoritative grounds for claims about the essential versus the accidental features of our color qualia.

The Dualist Is Hoist by His Own Petard

But if this is a lesson we materialists must learn to swallow, it is a lesson *no less obligatory for the dualist*. And for him it has an unwelcome edge to it, for the dualist's thought experiment, in all of its versions, depends on a preferential fixing of "how they present themselves to introspective judgment" as the *essential* feature of color qualia, while downgrading all other features of color qualia (and, as we saw, there are quite a few of them) as inessential contingencies, invertible without penalty at the drop of a thought experiment. But this very insistence is also premature and prejudicial, however much it may reflect the uncritical convictions of untutored common sense. The dualist *has no more right to that premise* than the functionalist has to "functional role" as *the* essential feature of color qualia, or the reductionist has to "family of similarity relations" as their essential feature. To insist on any one of these, *before* our science on the matter is completed, is to do science by *fiat* instead of by conceptual exploration and empirical evaluation.

Two points will drive this lesson home. The first is that the dualist himself can be victimized by an alternate instance of his own strategy, as follows.

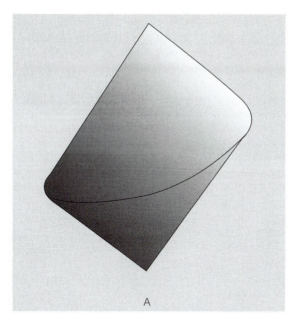 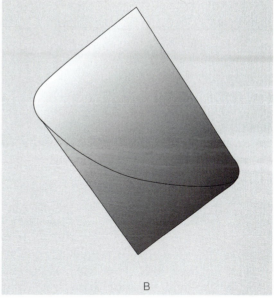

Figure 5 The color solid within color space. Each color is represented as a point within a three-dimensional space defined by the dimensions of hue, saturation, and lightness. This figure shows the outer surface of the color solid separately for the red side (A) and the green side (B). (From Palmer 1999).

Intrinsic-character-as-judged-by-introspection cannot be the defining feature of phenomenal qualia, since I can quite easily imagine that half the population suffers from "phenomenal judgment inversion syndrome," an undetectable malady whereby the faculty of judgment makes systematically inverted, and systematically *mistaken,* judgments about the identity of the phenomenal qualia had by the subject. Our judgmental take on our qualia, therefore, can hardly be definitive of their true nature. Accordingly, we shall have to dig even deeper still to find the identifying essence of color qualia. . . .

Though I am disinclined to defend this argument, its mere existence is instructive. Conceivability, it seems, is a two-edged sword.

To this it may be replied, perhaps in exasperation, "But qualia are *by definition* those things whose appearance *is* the reality!" As an observation about common usage, this claim may be strictly correct. But so were the following historical claims, famously uttered and with equal exasperation. "But atoms are by *definition* those things that cannot be split! (The Greek word "a-tom"

means not cuttable.) So you can forget about subatomic particles." Or equally fatuously, "But the Earth (*terra firma*) is by *definition* that-which-does-not-move! So you can forget about its revolving around the Sun."

These remarks illustrate the second major point. As Quine first argued, and many others have underscored since, *the meaning of words is not independent of beliefs about what those words apply to,* and also, *no claim is immune to revision or rejection in the face of sufficiently compelling new science.* If science discovers, as it did, that the Earth does in fact move, there is no point in trying to counteract the evidence by saying, "But by 'Earth' I mean, in part, the thing-that-does-not-move." This strategy is futile, for the plain and simple reason that whether the Earth moves or does not move depends on the *facts* of the matter. It does not depend on an existing dictionary entry plus human resolve to protect the dictionary from revision. In the present context, this means that the ultimate nature of phenomenal color qualia is something to be determined by empirical research, and not by preemptive linguistic analyses and thought experiments based

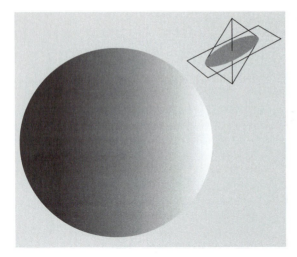

Figure 6 The color circle. This oblique section through the color solid shows the color circle, including the most saturated colors around its outer edge. Neutral gray is at the center, and the colors at various intermediate levels of saturation are located at intermediate positions. (From Palmer 1999).

on them. Thought experiments can be useful exploratory devices, but they have no authority in dictating empirical facts.

So Who Is Right?

None of this entails that the dualist hypothesis about the ultimate nature of color qualia is false. Despite the emptiness of the inverted-spectrum thought experiment as an *argument* for the truth of dualism, color qualia might still be a metaphysically basic feature of *some* nonphysical sort. What, then, will decide this issue?

The issue will be decided by the comparative virtues of the explanatory theories produced by both parties to the debate. You have seen, for what it is worth, what the physical sciences currently have to offer in the way of explaining human color experience: the opponent-cell activation-space theory of human color coding. You have seen some of the evidence for it and some of its explanatory prowess. Though far from proven, it plainly has at least some virtues. We can reopen the discussion when the dualist produces a competing

explanatory theory (a competing explanation of the shape of the Munsell color solid, for example), a theory with *comparable specificity, supporting evidence,* and *explanatory power*. In the end, the issue is scientific, and competing theories must be decided on their respective scientific merits. That is the ultimate lesson of this section.

Doesn't Neuroscience Leave Something Out?

Before moving on, it is useful to address one residual worry about the ability of any purely physical theory—such as the one just examined—to account for the qualitative character of our internal phenomenal experience. After all, knowing the theory of neural coding across various color-opponent cells doesn't tell me how to recognize, in *introspection,* a visual sensation as a sensation of red. And so, hasn't it thereby left something out? After all, I could be color blind, and thus phenomenally ignorant of that domain of experience. But learning the neuronal theory just outlined wouldn't help me one bit to repair that phenomenal ignorance.[12]

This last sentence is entirely true. To have the perceptual skill of discriminating and recognizing colors requires more than just knowledge of the theory of how our color-discriminating system works: it requires that the theory also be *true of* oneself. It requires that *one actually possess a functioning instance of the neuronal system that the theory describes*. A color-blind person doesn't have that system, and so he is doomed to be phenomenally ignorant where colors are concerned. Learning the theory of that missing system will be no help on that score.

But this doesn't mean there is anything inadequate about the *theory*, especially when that theory gives a detailed explanation of what *produces* the various forms of color blindness (the lack of one or more retinal-cone types, which leads to the partial or total loss of information reaching the several types of color-opponent cells), and especially when the theory tells you what to do to *repair* that discriminatory/representational deficit (namely, artificially induce the genetic expression of the missing cone type(s), and induce the growth of their missing synaptic connections with the LGN color-opponent cells).

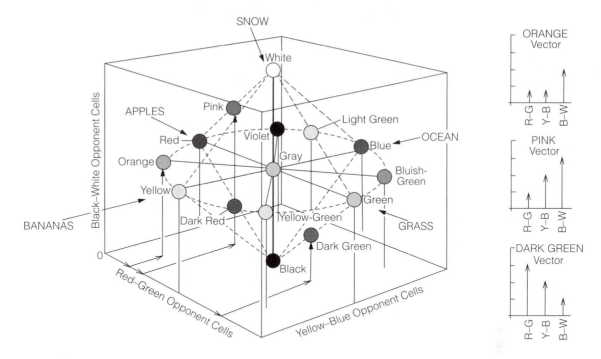

Figure 7 The vector space of opponent-cell coding, with some standard causal connections that it bears to the external world. Gray is roughly in the center of the space, white is at the top middle, and black at the bottom middle. The baseline activity for opponent cells is located midway along the opponent-cell-axis. Sample vectors—for orange, pink, and dark green—are displayed as histograms at the side. These vectors are traced within th ecolor space proper. Note the isomorphism with the phenomenological color space shown in figures 5 and 6, both in its internal relations and its external connections. (From P. M. Churchland and P. S. Churchland 1997).

The residual worry about leaving something out thus involves the confused expectation that having-a-certain-cognitive-skill (namely, being able to have and discriminate color qualia) should *result from* knowing-a-certain-theory (namely, the color-opponent-cell theory). But the two are quite different things, and simply knowing the latter (the theory) won't give you the former (the skill). However, if the theory at issue is *true of* you—if you actually *have* the neuronal system that the theory describes—then you will certainly have the skill at issue. You will be able to discriminate colors by spontaneous internal reaction to their intrinsic qualitative natures. That ability is what needed an explanation in the first place. And an explanation of that ability is precisely what the color-opponent theory provides.

It Is Ridiculous to Expect a Reduction from the Behavioral Level Directly to the Neuronal Level

This observation is sometimes used to support the conclusion that consciousness cannot be explained neurobiologically. The conclusion, however, just does not follow, and hence the argument is a non sequitur. Here is why.

Nervous systems appear to have many levels of organization, ranging in spatial scale from molecules such as serotonin, to dendritic spines, neurons, small networks, large networks, brain areas, and integrated systems. . . . Although it remains to be empirically determined what exactly are the functionally significant levels, it is unlikely that explanations of macro-effects such as face recognition will be explained directly in terms of the most microlevel. More likely, high-level network effects will be the outcome of smaller networks, and those effects in turn of the participating neurons and their interconnections, and those in turn of the properties of protein channels, neuromodulators, and neurotransmitters, and so forth. Emerging from efforts to understand these levels are a range of *midlevel concepts* applicable to mid-level neuronal organization and computation.

One misconception about the reductionist strategy interprets it as seeking a *direct* explanatory bridge between the highest level and the very lowest levels. This idea of "explanation-in-a-single-bound" does indeed stretch credulity, but neuroscientists are not remotely tempted by it. In contrast, the direct and indirect approaches predict that reductive explanations will proceed stepwise from highest to lowest, both agreeing, of course, that the research should proceed at all levels simultaneously. As more of the brain's organizational midlevels and their functions becomes known, a vocabulary suitable to those levels and functions will certainly develop.

Consciousness Is Not a Neural Effect but a Subatomic Effect

Roger Penrose, a Cambridge mathematician, and Stuart Hameroff, an Arizona researcher on anesthetics, also harbor reservations about explaining awareness neurobiologically, but are moved by rather different reasons (Penrose and Hameroff 1995). They believe the dynamic properties at the level of neurons and networks to be incapable of generating consciousness, regardless of the complexity. For Penrose and Hameroff, the key to consciousness lies in quantum events in tiny protein structures—microtubules—within neurons. Microtubules are in fact found in *all* cells. They have a number of functions, including mediating cell division. In neurons, they are used for the transport of proteins up and down the axon and the dendrites. So our question is this: why do Penrose and Hameroff believe that a subatomic phenomenon holds the secret? And second, why do they find microtubules a particularly likely

structure to mediate consciousness? I shall very briefly sketch their answers to these questions.

The answer to the first question is that Penrose believes the nature of mathematical understanding transcends the kind of computation that could conceivably by done by neurons and networks. As a demonstration of neuronal inadequacy, Penrose cites the Gödel Incompleteness Result, which concerns limitations to theorem-provability in axiom systems for arithmetic. What is needed to transcend these limitations, according to Penrose, are unique operations at the quantum level. Quantum gravity, were it to exist, could, he believes, do the trick. Granting that no adequate theory of quantum gravity exists, Penrose and Hameroff argue that microtubules are about the right size to support the envisioned quantum events, and they have the right sort of sensitivity to anesthetics to suggest that they do sustain consciousness (figure 8).

The details of Penrose and Hameroff's theory are highly technical, drawing on mathematics, physics, biochemistry, and neuroscience. Before investing time in mastering the details, most people want a measure of the theory's "figures of merit," as an engineer might put it.[13] Specifically, is there any hard evidence in support of the theory, is the theory testable, and if true, would the theory give a clear and cogent explanation of what it is supposed to explain? After all, there is no dearth of crackpot theories on every topic, from consciousness to sun spots. Making theories divulge their figures of merit is a minimal condition for further investment.

First, a brief interlude to glimpse the positive views Penrose has concerning the question of how humans understand mathematics. In 1989 he suggested as unblushing a Platonic solution as Plato himself proposed circa 400 BC: "Mathematical ideas have an existence of their own, and inhabit an ideal Platonic world, which is accessible via the intellect only. When one 'sees' a mathematical truth, one's consciousness breaks through into this world of ideas, and makes direct contact with it. . . . Mathematicians communicate . . . by each one having a *direct route to truth*" (1989, 428; Penrose's italics).

As a solution to questions in the epistemology of mathematics, Platonism is not remotely satisfactory. Given what we now know in biology, psy-

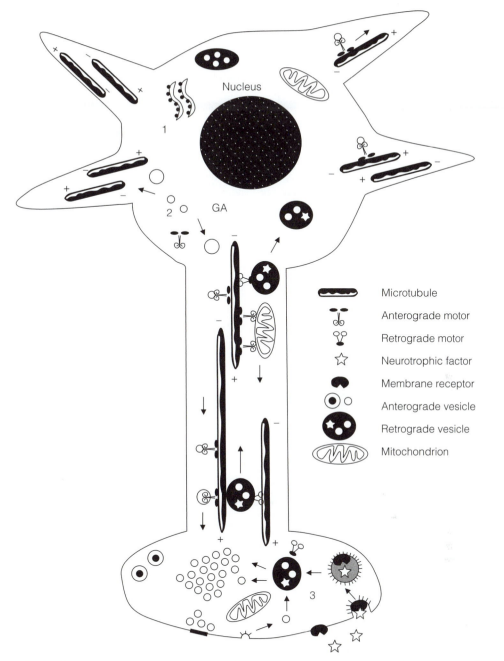

Legend:

— Microtubule

— Anterograde motor

— Retrograde motor

☆ Neurotrophic factor

— Membrane receptor

⊙ ○ Anterograde vesicle

● Retrograde vesicle

◯ Mitochondrion

Figure 8 This schematic diagram of a neuron and some of its organelles shows the position of long (100 μm) microtubules in the axon and the shorter microtubules in the dendrites. Axonal microtubules are oriented with the same polarity; dendritic microtubules have mixed polarity. The microtubules have a diameter of about 14 μm. Notice that the microtubules do not extend into the synaptic end bulb of the axon. Neurotransmitter is synthesized in the cell body by the endoplasmic reticulum (1), packaged by the Golgi apparatus (2), and transported down the axon or the dendrites by protein motors on the microtubule. The speed of anterograde transport is 100–400 mm per day. Vesicle proteins not sorted for reuse at the synapse are packaged into larger vesicles for transport back to the soma for recycling. Neurotrophic factors collected from intracellular space are also transported back to the cell body. The speed of retrograde transport is about 50–200 mm per day. (3) Mitochondria are the sites of the cell's energy production. (Based on Zigmond et al. 1999.)

chology, physics, and chemistry, the Platonic story of mathematical understanding is as much a fairy tale as the claim that Eve was created from Adam's rib. Far better to admit that we have no satisfactory solution than to adopt a "And God said Lo" solution.

Let us return now to evaluating the quantum-gravity-microtubule theory of conscious experience. The figures of merit are not encouraging. First, mathematical logicians generally disagree with Penrose on what the Gödel result implies for brain function. Additionally, the link between conscious experiences such as smelling cinnamon and the Gödel result is obscure, at best.[14]

Now, is there any significant evidential link between microtubules and awareness? Hameroff believes that microtubules are affected by hydrophobic anesthetics in a way that causes loss of consciousness. But there is no evidence that loss of consciousness under anesthesia depends on the envisaged changes in the microtubules, and only indirect evidence that anesthetics do in fact—as opposed to "could conceivably"—have *any* effect on microtubules. On the other hand, plenty of evidence points to proteins in the neuron membrane as the principal locus of action of hydrophobic anesthetics.[15]

Is there any hard evidence that the subatomic effect they cite, namely quantam coherence, happens in microtubules? *Only that it might.* Would not the presence of cytoplasmic ions in the microtubule pore disrupt this effect? *They might not.* Surely the effects of quantum coherence would be swamped by the millivolt signaling activity in the neuronal membrane? *They might not be.* Can the existence of quantum coherence in microtubules be tested experimentally? *For technical reasons, experiments on microtubules are performed in a dish (in vitro), rather than in the animal.* If tests under these conditions failed to show quantum coherence, would that be significant? *No, because microtubules might behave differently in the animal, where we cannot test for these effects.* Does any of this, supposing it to be true, help us explain such things as recall of past events, filling in of the blindspot, hallucinations, and attentional effects on sensory awareness? *Somehow, it might.*

The want of directly relevant data is frustrating enough, but the explanatory vacuum is catastrophic. Pixie dust in the synapses is about as explanatorily powerful as quantum coherence in the microtubules. Without at least a blueprint, outline, prospectus, or *something* showing how, if true, the theory could explain the various phenomena of conscious experience, Penrose and Hameroff have little to tempt us. None of this shows that Penrose and Hameroff are definitely wrong, only that their theory needs work. Whether it is worth additional work depends on how one assesses the theory's figures of merit.

Science Cannot Solve All Problems

Finally, consider Zeno Vendler's admonition: science cannot expect to solve all problems, answer all questions.[16] Let's agree with him—some questions may never be answered. What, we must inquire, is entailed by *this* problem—the problem of the neurobiology of consciousness? Absolutely nothing. Because significant progress has been made by neuroscience on many questions about the mind, it does look as though further progress is possible. We may at some point hit the wall, but so far, at least, no reason has emerged to indicate the wall has already been hit. What Vendler offers is not an argument, but off-the-shelf Faustian rhetoric.

Conclusions

The principal aim of this chapter has been to convey my sense of where things stand on the question of brain-based explanations for conscious phenomena. The chapter does not pretend to be a survey of all views, since there are an almost limitless number of those. Nor are all of them equally worth discussing. Of the theories I do discuss, some get better report cards than others. These judgments reflect my particular, and quite possibly mistaken, opinions concerning what is productive and important, what is logically compelling or a logical shell game.

The main philosophical argument submitted for uncompromised dissection concerns the "inverted spectrum" argument. In my experience, this particular problem is an unparalleled quagmire. Most of us are curious enough to want to get into it. We vaguely sense that there is *something* to it, though exactly what remains a bit foggy. We are reasonably confident that we can get to the crux of it and come away with a clearer understanding. In the end, however, we tend to find ourselves in an unholy jam, wondering how we got in the jam and how we can avoid embarrassing ourselves further. My goal was to lay bare the entire structure of the argument, following the various lines to their end, however tangled the path. If this works, readers should be able to identify the logical strengths or fallacies, and determine precisely what significance, if any, the argument has for neuroscientific attacks on the problems of conscious phenomena.

In addition to the inverted-spectrum argument, I considered a range of other philosophical arguments allegedly demonstrating the futility of looking to neuroscience for answers to questions about the nature of consciousness. Though each of the skeptical arguments considered boasts a considerable following, and for that reason alone must be dissected carefully, none is convincing once examined. Nor do they *collectively* create a credible skepticism even if *individually* they do not. That they are flawed does not, of course, show that neuroscience will in fact be successful in expanding our understanding of consciousness. It shows only that the skeptics' conclusions regarding the mere *possibility* are unconvincing. The most convincing answer to skepticism is, of course, explanatory progress in neuroscience.

Endnotes

[1]See also P. M. Churchland, 1987.

[2]Portions of this section are drawn from my 1996c paper.

[3]McGinn 1994, p. 99.

[4]Vendler 1994.

[5]Portions of what follows in the section are based on P. S. Churchland 1998.

[6]For an amusing but pointed discussion of this and related issues, see also Dennett 2001a.

[7]Pages 180–189 are closely based on P. M. Churchland and P. S. Churchland 1997 and also depend heavily on Palmer 1999.

[8]For this criticism, see P. M. Churchland 1996a and Perry 2001.

[9]On coding and models of color coding, see Lehky and Sejnowski 1999.

[10]See pp. 20–25 above.

[11]Palmer 1999.

[12]See Nagel 1994.

[13]For the details behind my reservations, see Grush and Churchland 1995 and the reply by Penrose and Hameroff (1995). See also Putnam 1994; Smullyan 1992; Maddy 1992, 1997. Pat Hayes and Ken Ford (1995) found Penrose's mathematical argument to be so outlandish that they awarded him the Simon Newcombe Award in 1995. They explain that Simon Newcombe (1835–1909) was a celebrated astronomer who insisted in various articles that manned flight was physically impossible.

[14]See Feferman 1996; Putnam 1994, 1995.

[15]Franks and Lieb 1994; Bowdle, Horita, and Kharasch 1994.

[16]Vendler 1994.

References

Bogen, J., and P. J. Vogel. 1965. Cerebral commissurotomy in man. *Bulletin of the Los Angeles Neurological Society* 27: 169–172.

Bornstein, R. F. 1992. Subliminal mere exposure effects. In R. F. Bornstein and T. S. Pittman, eds., *Perception without Awareness: Cognitive, Clinical, and Social Perspectives*, pp. 191–210. New York: Guilford.

Bourgeois, J.-P. 2001. Synaptogenesis in the neocortex of the newborn: the ultimate frontier of individuation? In C. A. Nelson and M. Luciana, eds., *Handbook of Developmental Cognitive Neuroscience*. Cambridge: MIT Press.

Bowdle, T. A., A. Horita, and E. D. Kharasch, eds. 1994. *The Pharmacologic Basis of Anesthesiology*. New York: Churchill Livingstone.

Boyer, Pascal. 2001. *Religion Explained*. New York: Basic Books.

Churchland, P. M. 1987. How parapsychology could become a science. *Inquiry* 30: 227–239. Reprinted in P. M. Churchland and P. S. Churchland 1998.

Churchland, P. M. 1996. The rediscovery of light. *Journal of Philosophy* 93: 211–228.

Churchland, P. M., and P. S. Churchland. 1997. Recent work on consciousness: philosophical, theoretical, and empirical. *Seminars in*

Neurology 17: 101–108. Reprinted in P. M. Churchland and P. S. Churchland 1998.

Churchland, P. M., and P. S. Churchland. 1998. *On the Contrary.* Cambridge: MIT Press.

Churchland, P. M., and P. S. Churchland. 2000. Foreword. In John von Neumann, *The Computer and the Brain,* 2nd ed. New Haven: Yale University Press.

Churchland, P. S. 1983. Consciousness: the transmutation of a concept. *Pacific Philosophical Quarterly* 64: 80–95.

Churchland, P. S. 1986. *Neurophilosophy: Towards a Unified Understanding of the Mind-Brain.* Cambridge: MIT Press.

Churchland, P. S. 1996a. Toward a neurobiology of the mind. In R. R. Llinás and P. S. Churchland, eds., *The Mind-Brain Continuum,* pp. 281–303. Cambridge: MIT Press.

Churchland, P. S. 1996b. Feeling reasons. In A. R. Damasio, H. Damasio, and Y. Christen, eds., *Decision-Making and the Brain,* pp. 181–199. Berlin: Springer-Verlag.

Churchland, P. S. 1996c. The hornswoggle problem. *Journal of Consciousness Studies* 3 (5–6): 402–408.

Churchland, P. S. 1997. Can neurobiology teach us anything about consciousness? In N. Block, O. Flanagan, and G. Güzeldere, eds., *The Nature of Consciousness: Philosophical Debates,* pp. 127–140. Cambridge: MIT Press.

Churchland, P. S. 1998. What should we expect from a theory of consciousness? In H. H. Jasper, L. Descarries, V. F. Castellucci, and S. Rossignol, eds., *Consciousness: At the Frontiers of Neuroscience.* Philadelphia: Lippincott-Raven.

Dennett, D. C. 1996. *Kinds of Minds: Towards an Understanding of Consciousness.* New York: Basic Books.

Dennett, D. C. 1998. *Brainchildren: Essays on Designing Minds.* Cambridge: MIT Press.

Dennett, D. C. 2001a. The Zombic Hunch: Extinction of an Intuition? In A. O'Hear, ed., *Philosophy at the New Millennium,* Royal

Institute of Philosophy, suppl. 48, pp. 27–43. Cambridge: Cambridge University Press.

Dennett, D. C. 2001b. Are we explaining consciousness yet? *Cognition* 79: 221–237.

Franks, N. P., and W. R. Lieb. 1994. Molecular and cellular mechanisms of general anaesthesia. *Nature* 367: 607–614.

Grush, R., and P. S. Churchland. 1995. Gaps in Penrose's toilings. *Journal of Consciousness Studies* 2: 10–29. Reprinted in P. M. Churchland and P. S. Churchland 1998.

Le Doux, J. 2002. *Synaptic Self.* New York: Viking Press.

Lehky, S. R., and T. J. Sejnowski. 1999. Seeing white: qualia in the context of decoding population codes. *Neural Computation* 11: 1261–1280.

Leibniz, G. W. 1989. *G. W. Leibniz: Philosophical Essays.* Translated by R. Ariew and D. Garber. Indianapolis: Hackett Publishing.

Leopold, D. A., and N. K. Logothetis. 1999. Multistable phenomena: changing views in perception. *Trends in Cognitive Sciences* 3: 154–264.

Leslie, A. M., and S. Keeble. 1987. Do sixth-month-old infants perceive causality? *Cognition* 25: 265–288.

MacLean, P. D. 1952. Some psychiatric implications of physiological studies on fronto-temporal portion of limbic system visceral brain. *Electrophysiological and Clinical Neurophysiology* 4: 407–418.

Maddy, P. 1992. *Realism in Mathematics.* Oxford: Clarendon Press.

Maddy, P. 1997. *Naturalism in Mathematics.* Oxford: Clarendon Press.

Makeig, S., T.-P. Jung, A. J. Bell, D. Ghahremani, and T. J. Sejnowski. 1997. Blind separation of auditory event-related brain responses into independent components. *Proceedings of the National Academy of Sciences, USA* 94: 10979–10984.

McGinn, C. 1994. Can we solve the mind-body problem? In R. Warner and T. Szubka, eds.,

The Mind-Body Problem: A Guide to the Current Debate, pp. 349–366. Oxford: Blackwell.

Murray, D. S. 1988. *A History of Western Pscyhology*. 2nd ed. Englewood Cliffs, N.J.: Prentice-Hall.

Nagel, T. 1994. Consciousness and objective reality. In R. Warner and T. Szubka, eds., *The Mind-Body Problem: A Guide to the Current Debate*, pp. 63–68. Oxford: Blackwell.

Necker, L. A. 1832. Observations on some remarkable phenomena seen in Switzerland: an optical phenomenon which occurs on viewing of a crystal or geometrical solid. *Philosophical Magazine* 3: 329–337.

Paine, T. 1794. *The Age of Reason: Being an Investigation of True and Fabulous Theology*. New York: Putnam's Sons, 1896.

Palmer, S. E. 1999. *Vision Science: Photons to Phenomenology*. Cambridge: MIT Press.

Panksepp, Jaak. 1998. *Affective Neuroscience*. New York: Oxford University Press.

Penrose, R. 1994. *Shadows of the Mind*. Oxford: Oxford University Press.

Penrose, R., and S. Hameroff. 1995. What "gaps"? Reply to Grush and Churchland. *Journal of Consciousness Studies* 2: 99–112.

Perry, J. 2001. *Knowledge, Possibility, and Consciousness*. Cambridge: MIT Press.

Persinger, Michael A. 1987. *Neuropsychological Bases of God Beliefs*. New York: Praeger.

Putnam, H. 1967. Psychological predicates. In W. H. Capitan and D. D. Merrill, eds., *Art, Mind, and Religion*, pp. 37–48. Pittsburgh: University of Pittsburgh Press.

Putnam, H. 1994. The best of all possible brains? Review of *Shadows of the Mind*, by R. Penrose. *New York Times Book Review*, November.

Pylyshyn, Z. 1984. *Computation and Cognition*. Cambridge: MIT Press.

Siegelmann, H. T., and E. D. Sontag. 1995. On the computational power of neural nets. *Journal of Computer and System Sciences* 50: 132–150.

Smullyan, R. 1992. *Gödel's Incompleteness Theorems*. Oxford: Oxford University Press.

Van Inwagen, P. 1975. The incompatibility of free will and determinism. *Philosophical Studies* 27: 185–199. Reprinted in G. Watson, ed., *Free Will*, pp. 46–58. Oxford: Oxford University Press, 1982.

Vendler, Z. 1994. The ineffable soul. In R. Warner and T. Szubka, eds., *The Mind-Body Problem: A Guide to the Current Debate*, pp. 317–328. Oxford: Blackwell.

Suggested Readings

Churchland, P. M. 1988. *Matter and Consciousness*. 2nd ed. Cambridge: MIT Press.

Churchland, P. M. 1995. *The Engine of Reason, The Seat of the Soul*. Cambridge: MIT Press.

Crick, F., and C. Koch. 2000. The unconscious homunculus. In T. Metzinger, ed., *Neural Correlates of Consciousness*, pp. 103–110. Cambridge: MIT Press.

Damasio, A. R. 1999. *The Feeling of What Happens*. New York: Harcourt Brace.

Dennett, D. C. 1991. *Consciousness Explained*. Boston: Little Brown.

Hobson, J. A. 1999. *Consciousness*. New York Scientific American Library.

Llinás, R. 2001. *I of the Vortex*. Cambridge: MIT Press.

Metzinger, T. 2003. *Being No One: The Self-Model Theory of Subjectivity*. Cambridge: MIT Press.

Palmer, S. E. 1999. *Vision Science: Photons to Phenomenology*. Cambridge: MIT Press. See especially chapter 13.

Parvizi, J., and A. R. Damasio. 2001. Consciousness and the brainstem. *Cognition* 79: 135–159.

Walsh, V., and A. Cowey. 2000. Transcranial magnetic stimulation and cognitive neuroscience. *Nature Reviews: Neuroscience* 1: 73–80.

Websites

BioMedNet Magazine:
    http://news.bmn.com/magazine

Comparative Mammalian Brain Collections:
    http://brainmuseum.org

Encyclopedia of Life Sciences:
    http://www.els.net

Higher Order Visual Areas:
    http://www.med.uwo.ca/physiology
    /courses/sensesweb/L3HigherVisual
    /l3v23.swf

The MIT Encyclopedia of the Cognitive
    Sciences: http://cognet.mit.edu/MITECS

Further Reading

Addis, L., *Natural Signs: A Theory of Intentionality* (Philadelphia: Temple University Press, 1989).

Armstrong, D. and Malcolm, N., *Consciousness and Causality* (Oxford: Blackwell, 1984).

Baker, L., *Saving Belief* (Princeton, N.J.: Princeton University Press, 1987).

Blackmore, S., *The Meme Machine* (New York: Oxford University Press, 1999).

Block, N., ed., *Readings in Philosophy of Psychology*, Vols. I and II (Cambridge: Harvard University Press, 1980).

Block, N., Flanagan, O. and Guzeldere G., eds., *The Nature of Consciousness* (Cambridge: MIT Press, 1997).

Borst, C., ed., *The Mind/Brain Identity Theory* (New York: St. Martin's Press, 1970).

Brandom, R., *Articulating Reasons* (Cambridge: Harvard University Press, 2000).

Brentano, F., *The Psychology of Aristotle* (Berkeley: University of California Press, 1977).

Broad, C., *The Mind and Its Place in Nature* (London: Routledge & Kegan Paul, 1925).

Chalmers, D., *The Conscious Mind* (New York: Oxford University Press, 1996).

Chalmers, D., ed., *Philosophy of Mind* (New York: Oxford University Press, 2002).

Churchland, P. M., *Scientific Realism and the Plasticity of Mind* (Cambridge: MIT Press, 1979).

Churchland, P. M., *Matter and Consciousness* (Cambridge: MIT Press, 1988).

Churchland, P. M., *The Engine of Reason, the Seat of the Soul* (Cambridge: MIT Press, 1995).

Churchland, P. S., *Neurophilosophy* (Cambridge: MIT Press, 1986).

Churchland, P. S., *Brain-Wise, Studies in Neurophilosophy* (Cambridge: MIT Press, 2002).

Clarke, A., *Being There: Putting Brain, Body and World Together Again* (Cambridge: MIT Press, 1996).

Cornman, J., *Materialism and Sensations* (New Haven: Yale University Press, 1971).

Dahlbom, B., ed., *Dennett and His Critics* (Oxford: Blackwell, 1995).

Damasio, A., *Descartes' Error* (New York: Grossett/Putnam, 1994).

Dennett, D., *Content and Consciousness* (New York: Humanities, 1969).

Dennett, D., *The Intentional Stance* (Cambridge: MIT Press, 1987).

Dennett, D. C., *Consciousness Explained* (Boston: Little Brown, 1991).

Dennett, D. C., *Kinds of Minds: Towards an Understanding of Consciousness* (New York: Basic Books, 1996).

De Waal, F., *Good Natured* (Cambridge: Harvard University Press, 1996).

Dretske, F., *Explaining Behavior* (Cambridge: MIT Press, 1991).

Feigl, H., *The "Mental" and the "Physical"* (Minneapolis: University of Minnesota Press, 1967).

Flanagan, O., *The Science of Mind* (Cambridge: MIT Press, 1984).

Flanagan, O., *Self-Expressions: Mind, Morals, and the Meaning of Life* (New York: Oxford University Press, 1996).

Flew, A., ed., *Body, Mind, and Death* (New York: Macmillan, 1964).

Fodor, J., *Representations* (Cambridge: MIT Press, 1981).

Fodor, J. A., *The Mind Doesn't Work That Way: The Scope and Limits of Computational Psychology* (Cambridge: MIT Press, 2000).

Gregory, R., ed., *The Oxford Companion to the Mind* (Oxford: Oxford University Press, 1987).

Hartman, E., *Substance, Body, and Soul* (Princeton: Princeton University Press, 1977).

Haugeland, J., ed., *Mind Design* (Montgomery, Vt.: Bradford, 1981).

Haugeland, J., *Artificial Intelligence: The Very Idea* (Cambridge: MIT Press, 1985).

Haugeland, J., *Having Thought* (Cambridge: Harvard University Press, 1998).

Hobson, J. A., *Consciousness* (New York: Scientific American Library, 1999).

Hofstadter, D., *Gödel, Escher, Bach* (New York: Basic Books, 1979).

Hofstadter, D. and Dennett, D., eds., *The Mind's I* (New York: Basic Books, 1981).

Lakoff, G. and Johnson, M., *Philosophy in the Flesh* (New York: Basic Books, 1999).

Lovejoy, A., *The Revolt against Dualism* (La Salle: Open Court, 1960).

Lycan, W., *Consciousness* (Cambridge: MIT Press, 1987).

Matson, W., *Sentience* (Berkeley: University of California Press, 1976).

McCauley, R., ed., *The Churchlands and Their Critics* (Oxford: Blackwell, 1996).

McGinn, C., *The Subjective View* (Oxford: Oxford University Press, 1983).

Millikan, R. G., *Language, Thought and Other Biological Categories* (Cambridge: MIT Press, 1983).

Nagel, T., *The View from Nowhere* (Oxford: Oxford University Press, 1986).

Nelson, R., *The Logic of Mind* (Dordrecht: Reidel, 1982).

O'Connor, J., ed., *Modern Materialism: Readings on Mind-Body Identity* (New York: Harcourt, Brace & World, 1969).

Perry, J., *Knowledge, Possibility, and Consciousness* (Cambridge: MIT Press, 2001).

Pinker, S., *How the Mind Works* (New York: Norton, 1997).

Popper, K. and Eccles, J., *The Self and Its Brain* (New York: Springer, 1977).

Port, R. and van Gelder, T., *Mind as Motion: Explorations in the Dynamics of Cognition* (Cambridge: MIT Press, 1995).

Ryle, G., *The Concept of Mind* (New York: Barnes & Noble, 1949).

Searle, J., *The Rediscovery of Mind* (Cambridge: MIT Press, 1992).

Searle, J., *Intentionality* (Cambridge: Cambridge University Press, 1983).

Smith, D. and McIntyre, R., eds., *Husserl and Intentionality* (Dordrecht: Reidel, 1982).

Strawson, P., *Individuals* (Garden City, N.Y.: Doubleday, 1963).

Woodfield, A., ed., *Thought and Object* (Oxford: Oxford University Press, 1982).

Part IV

Freedom

At this moment, you are reading this book; yet you could have been doing something else. You could have chosen to watch television, go to the movies, play tennis, or do any number of things other than read this book. Your reading this book seems to result from an act of free will, and it seems to be in your power to choose to continue or to refrain from reading it. Although these remarks seem obvious, reflection on certain other commonly accepted beliefs have led some philosophers to deny it is ever within our power to do anything other than what we in fact do. That is, they deny the reality of freedom.

Metaphysically, the attacks on freedom have come from several directions. One argument is based on general reflections about truth and logic. According to the law of excluded middle, every proposition is either true or it is false. Thus, for example, the proposition "You will finish reading this introduction tonight" is either now true or now false. If, however, it is now true that you will finish it tonight, then the fact that you will finish it tonight must already exist. If that fact already exists, then you are powerless to not finish it. If, on the other hand, it is now false that you will finish it tonight, then the belief that you can is illusory. In either case, "nothing is or takes place fortuitously, either in the present or in the future, and there are no real alternatives; everything takes place of necessity and is fixed." Although Aristotle himself is at pains to avoid this conclusion, he sees that the argument suggests the law of excluded middle poses a serious challenge to the view that people have free will. The argument says that no person has it within his or her power to alter the course of history. This view is known as *logical fatalism*. Fatalism in this sense should be distinguished from the popular conception of fatalism according to which everything is *fated* or predetermined (by God?) regardless of human choices.

The problem of reconciling a law of logic with human freedom is closely connected with the theological problem of reconciling divine foreknowledge with human freedom. For if God knew *before* you were born that, say, you would finish reading this introduction tonight, then it must have been true before you were born that you would finish it tonight; and so you cannot bring about any alternative. This problem has been the subject of theological and philosophical reflection for centuries, and the selections by Augustine and Rowe contain discussions of the principal solutions to it.

A third attack on freedom comes, not from logic or religion, but from nature, or more specifically, from the connections most people believe exist among events in nature. Most people believe events have causes, and the causes of events "necessitate" the occurrence of those events. That is, given certain laws and initial conditions, then what happens is determined. Thus, hitting a wine glass causes it to shatter. Now, although science has not discovered all the laws governing human actions, it would appear human behavior, like nonhuman behavior, is causally determined. The most basic laws of modern physics are not all deterministic. It is a feature of quantum mechanics that, in the micro-world, some events are random (or certain initial conditions do not necessitate specific later states). But these quantum indeterminacies do not usually affect the behavior of large collections of particles like human bodies and brains. If, then, human actions are causally

determined, it might seem people, contrary to common beliefs, cannot really do other than what they in fact do. Logic, religion, and science each suggest arguments that deny people are really free.

The topic of freedom is related to several of the metaphysical issues presented in Parts I, II, and III. For example, the connection between time and freedom is so close that many have argued that in order to avoid fatalism and preserve human freedom we must abandon the tenseless theory of time defended by D. H. Mellor and D. C. Williams and adopt a tensed theory of time and truth. Regarding the issue of the nature of persons, Thomas Reid and Roderick Chisholm argue that the only way to preserve belief in human freedom is to suppose the self is a substance whose actions are outside the sphere of determinism. On the other hand, if persons are deterministic physical processes, then philosophers must try to find some other analysis of freedom that does justice to the distinction between free acts and compelled acts.

Metaphysical disputes about freedom have important practical and ethical implications. People often praise or blame and reward or punish people for their actions. Philosophical theories about what makes it right to do this involve the notion of responsibility, and the idea of responsibility is usually tied to a person's being free. For example, punishment in the form of retribution is clearly wrong if one cannot do other than what one does (for example, if one is compelled or forced). Punishment whose rationale is correction or prevention of undesirable behavior, however, may be congenial even to determinism. Which social practices should be adopted may then depend upon what kind of freedom, if any, is real.

The selections in Part IV are concerned with articulating and discussing the challenging claim that freedom is not real. The first selection by Aristotle deals with fatalism and the selection by Oaklander attempts to dispel the notion that the tenseless theory implies fatalism or is in any other way a threat to human freedom. In the selection from the *Nicomachean Ethics,* Aristotle offers an analysis of voluntary acts. For Aristotle, voluntary acts have their origins *in the agent*, and the voluntary is that which allows for the possibility of alternative action.

The readings by St. Augustine and Rowe concern the challenge to freedom represented by divine foreknowledge, whereas the selections by Aquinas, Hume, Reid, Moore, and Chisholm concern the challenge to freedom represented by causal determinism. Aquinas first raises the issue of how actions motivated by causes outside of us can be voluntary. Hume's

classic discussion in "On Liberty and Necessity" offer an analysis of the notions of "cause," "necessity," and "determinism" that attempts to dispel that worry. The essay by Frankfurt purports to undermine the common assumption that freedom and responsibility presuppose that we could have done otherwise. The selections by Kane and Dennett debate the question of whether or not the libertarian conception of freedom, which denies causal determinism, can explain the sense in which an action is ultimately up to us. The final essay in this section by Brandom suggests that freedom is not to be associated with the lack of causality, nor its presence, but with being constrained by the norms and social practices of a community.

35. *Fatalism, Voluntary Action, and Choice*

ARISTOTLE

In the first selection from *On Interpretation*, Aristotle raises a typical meta-physical conundrum, a paradox that results from apparently well-grounded intuitions about the world. On the one hand, people usually believe the future is open, in the sense that there are numerous *alternative* courses of actions still open for them to pursue. On the other hand, given any pair of contradictory propositions, say, *X* will occur and *X* will not occur, one is true and the other is false. But if a prediction about the future (*x will* occur) is already true, then the future seems fixed and unavoidable. Conversely, if there are genuine alternatives open in the future, then are some propositions about the future neither true nor false now? Aristotle's response to the dilemma has implications for issues concerning time and truth.

In the selection from the *Nicomachean Ethics*, Aristotle analyzes the nature of voluntary actions and discusses the nature of choice and the role deliberation plays in making choices. Voluntary actions are those in which *"the moving principle is in the agent himself,"* whereas involuntary acts take place under compulsion, "and that is compulsory of which the moving principle is outside. . . . "

On Interpretation

In the case of that which is or which has taken place, propositions, whether positive or negative, must be true or false. Again, in the case of a pair of contradictories, either when the subject is universal and the propositions are of a universal character, or when it is individual, as has been said, one of the two must be true and the other false; whereas when the subject is universal, but the propositions are not of a universal character, there is no such necessity.

When the subject, however, is individual, and that which is predicated of it relates to the future, the case is altered. For if all propositions whether positive or negative are either true or false, then any given predicate must either belong to the subject or not, so that if one man affirms that an event of a given character will take place and another

denies it, it is plain that the statement of the one will correspond with reality and that of the other will not. For the predicate cannot both belong and not belong to the subject at one and the same time with regard to the future.

Thus, if it is true to say that a thing is white, it must necessarily be white; if the reverse proposition is true, it will of necessity not be white. Again, if it is white, the proposition stating that it is white was true; if it is not white, the proposition to the opposite effect was true. And if it is not white, the man who states that it is is making a false statement; and if the man who states that it is white is making a false statement, it follows that it is not white. It may therefore be argued that it is necessary that affirmations or denials must be either true or false.

Now if this be so, nothing is or takes place fortuitously, either in the present or in the future, and there are no real alternatives; everything takes place of necessity and is fixed. For either he that affirms that it will take place or he that denies this is in correspondence with fact, whereas if things did not take place of necessity, an event might just as easily not happen as happen; for the meaning of the word 'fortuitous' with regard to present or

Reprinted from W. D. Ross, ed., *The Oxford Translation of Aristotle*, by permission of Oxford University Press. The selections from "On Interpretation and the Nicomachean Ethnics" originally appeared in Richard McKeon, ed., *The Basic Works of Aristotle* (New York: Random House, 1941), pp. 45–48 and 364–69.

future events is that reality is so constituted that it may issue in either of two opposite directions.

Again, if a thing is white now, it was true before to say that it would be white, so that of anything that has taken place it was always true to say 'it is' or 'it will be.' But if it was always true to say that a thing is or will be, it is not possible that it should not be or not be about to be, and when a thing cannot not come to be, it is impossible that it should not come to be, and when it is impossible that it should not come to be, it must come to be. All, then, that is about to be must of necessity take place. It results from this that nothing is uncertain or fortuitous, for if it were fortuitous it would not be necessary.

Again, to say that neither the affirmation nor the denial is true, maintaining, let us say, that an event neither will take place nor will not take place, is to take up a position impossible to defend. In the first place, though facts should prove the one proposition false, the opposite would still be untrue. Secondly, if it was true to say that a thing was both white and large, both these qualities must necessarily belong to it; and if they will belong to it the next day, they must necessarily belong to it the next day. But if an event is neither to take place nor not to take place the next day, the element of chance will be eliminated. For example, it would be necessary that a sea-fight should neither take place nor fail to take place on the next day.

These awkward results and others of the same kind follow, if it is an irrefragable law that of every pair of contradictory propositions, whether they have regard to universals and are stated as universally applicable, or whether they have regard to individuals, one must be true and the other false, and that there are no real alternatives, but that all that is or takes place is the outcome of necessity. There would be no need to deliberate or to take trouble, on the supposition that if we should adopt a certain course, a certain result would follow, while, if we did not, the result would not follow. For a man may predict an event ten thousand years beforehand, and another may predict the reverse; that which was truly predicted at the moment in the past will of necessity take place in the fullness of time.

Further, it makes no difference whether people have or have not actually made the contradictory statements. For it is manifest that the circumstances are not influenced by the fact of an affirmation or denial on the part of anyone. For events will not take place or fail to take place because it was stated that they would or would not take place, nor is this any more the case if the prediction dates back ten thousand years or any other space of time. Wherefore, if through all time the nature of things was so constituted that a prediction about an event was true, then through all time it was necessary that that prediction should find fulfilment; and with regard to all events, circumstances have always been such that their occurrence is a matter of necessity. For that of which someone has said truly that it will be, cannot fail to take place; and of that which takes place, it was always true to say that it would be.

Yet this view leads to an impossible conclusion; for we see that both deliberation and action are causative with regard to the future, and that, to speak more generally, in those things which are not continuously actual there is a potentiality in either direction. Such things may either be or not be; events also therefore may either take place or not take place. There are many obvious instances of this. It is possible that this coat may be cut in half, and yet it may not be cut in half, but wear out first. In the same way, it is possible that it should not be cut in half; unless this were so, it would not be possible that it should wear out first. So it is therefore with all other events which possess this kind of potentiality. It is therefore plain that it is not of necessity that everything is or takes place; but in some instances there are real alternatives, in which case the affirmation is no more true and no more false than the denial; while some exhibit a predisposition and general tendency in one direction or the other, and yet can issue in the opposite direction by exception.

Now that which is must needs be when it is, and that which is not must needs not be when it is not. Yet it cannot be said without qualification that all existence and nonexistence is the outcome of necessity. For there is a difference between saying that that which is, when it is, must needs be, and simply saying that all that is must needs be, and similarly in the case of that which is not. In the case, also, of two contradictory propositions this holds good. Everything must either be or not be, whether in the present or in the future, but it is not always possible to distinguish and state determinately which of these alternatives must necessarily come about.

Let me illustrate. A sea-fight must either take place tomorrow or not, but it is not necessary that it should take place tomorrow, neither is it necessary that it should not take place, yet it is necessary that it either should or should not take place tomorrow. Since propositions correspond with facts, it is evident that when in future events there is a real alternative, and a potentiality in contrary directions, the corresponding affirmation and denial have the same character.

This is the case with regard to that which is not always existent or not always nonexistent. One of the two propositions in such instances must be true and the other false, but we cannot say determinately that this or that is false, but must leave the alternative undecided. One may indeed be more likely to be true than the other, but it cannot be either actually true or actually false. It is therefore plain that it is not necessary that of an affirmation and a denial one should be true and the other false. For in the case of that which exists potentially, but not actually, the rule which applies to that which exists actually does not hold good. The case is rather as we have indicated.

Nicomachean Ethics, Book III

Since virtue is concerned with passions and actions, and on voluntary passions and actions praise and blame are bestowed, on those that are involuntary pardon, and sometimes also pity, to distinguish the voluntary and the involuntary is presumably necessary for those who are studying the nature of virtue, and useful also for legislators with a view to the assigning both of honours and of punishments.

Those things, then, are thought involuntary, which take place under compulsion or owing to ignorance; and that is compulsory of which the moving principle is outside, being a principle in which nothing is contributed by the person who is acting or is feeling the passion, e.g., if he were to be carried somewhere by a wind, or by men who had him in their power.

But with regard to the things that are done from fear of greater evils or for some noble object (e.g., if a tyrant were to order one to do something base, having one's parents and children in his power, and if one did the action they were to be saved, but otherwise would be put to death), it may be debated whether such actions are involuntary or voluntary. Something of the sort happens also with regard to the throwing of goods overboard in a storm; for in the abstract no one throws goods away voluntarily, but on condition of its securing the safety of himself and his crew any sensible man does so. Such actions, then, are mixed, but are more like voluntary actions; for they are worthy of choice at the time when they are done, and the end of an action is relative to the occasion. Both the terms, then, 'voluntary' and 'involuntary', must be used with reference to the moment of action. Now the man acts voluntarily; for the principle that moves the instrumental parts of the body in such actions is in him, and the things of which the moving principle is in a man himself are in his power to do or not to do. Such actions, therefore, are voluntary, but in the abstract perhaps involuntary; for no one would choose any such act in itself.

For such actions men are sometimes even praised, when they endure something base or painful in return for great and noble objects gained; in the opposite case they are blamed, since to endure the greatest indignities for no noble end or for a trifling end is the mark of an inferior person. On some actions praise indeed is not bestowed, but pardon is, when one does what he ought not under pressure which overstrains human nature and which no one could withstand. But some acts, perhaps, we cannot be forced to do, but ought rather to face death after the most fearful sufferings; for the things that 'forced' Euripides' Alcmaeon to slay his mother seem absurd. It is difficult sometimes to determine what should be chosen at what cost, and what should be endured in return for what gain, and yet more difficult to abide by our decisions; for as a rule what is expected is painful, and what we are forced to do is base, whence praise and blame are bestowed on those who have been compelled or have not.

What sort of acts, then, should be called compulsory? We answer that without qualification actions are so when the cause is in the external circumstances and the agent contributes nothing. But the things that in themselves are involuntary, but now and in return for these gains are worthy of choice, and whose moving principle is in the agent, are in themselves involuntary, but now and in return for these gains voluntary. They are more like voluntary acts; for actions are in the class of particulars, and the particular acts here are voluntary. What sort of things are to be chosen, and in return for what, it is not easy to state; for there are many differences in the particular cases.

But if some one were to say that pleasant and noble objects have a compelling power, forcing us from without, all acts would be for him compulsory; for it is for these objects that all men do everything they do. And those who act under compulsion and unwillingly act with pain, but those who do acts for their pleasantness and nobility do them with pleasure; it is absurd to make external circumstances responsible, and not oneself, as being easily caught by such attractions, and to make oneself responsible for noble acts but the pleasant objects responsible for base acts. The compulsory, then, seems to be that whose moving principle is outside, the person compelled contributing nothing.

Everything that is done by reason of ignorance is *not* voluntary; it is only what produces pain and repentance that is *in*voluntary. For the man who has done something owing to ignorance, and feels not the least vexation at his action, has not acted voluntarily, since he did not know what he was doing, nor yet involuntarily, since he is not pained. Of people, then, who act by reason of ignorance he who repents is thought an involuntary agent, and the man who does not repent may, since he is different, be called a not voluntary agent; for, since he differs from the other, it is better that he should have a name of his own.

Acting by reason of ignorance seems also to be different from acting *in* ignorance; for the man who is drunk or in a rage is thought to act as a result not of ignorance but of one of the causes mentioned, yet not knowingly but in ignorance.

Now every wicked man is ignorant of what he ought to do and what he ought to abstain from, and it is by reason of error of this kind that men become unjust and in general bad; but the term 'involuntary' tends to be used not if a man is ignorant of what is to his advantage—for it is not mistaken purpose that causes involuntary action (it leads rather to wickedness), nor ignorance of the universal (for *that* men are *blamed*), but ignorance of particulars, i.e., of the circumstances of the

action and the objects with which it is concerned. For it is on these that both pity and pardon depend, since the person who is ignorant of any of these acts involuntarily.

Perhaps it is just as well, therefore, to determine their nature and number. A man may be ignorant, then, of who he is, what he is doing, what or whom he is acting on, and sometimes also what (e.g., what instrument) he is doing it with, and to what end (e.g., he may think his act will conduce to some one's safety), and how he is doing it (e.g., whether gently or violently). Now of all of these no one could be ignorant unless he were mad, and evidently also he could not be ignorant of the agent; for how could he not know himself? But of what he is doing a man might be ignorant, as for instance people say 'it slipped out of their mouths as they were speaking,' or 'they did not know it was a secret,' as Aeschylus said of the mysteries, or a man might say he 'let it go off when he merely wanted to show its working,' as the man did with the catapult. Again, one might think one's son was an enemy, as Merope did, or that a pointed spear had a button on it, or that a stone was pumicestone; or one might give a man a draught to save him, and really kill him; or one might want to touch a man, as people do in sparring, and really wound him. The ignorance may relate, then, to any of these things, i.e., of the circumstances of the action, and the man who was ignorant of any of these is thought to have acted involuntarily, and especially if he was ignorant on the most important points; and these are thought to be the circumstances of the action and its end. Further, the doing of an act that is called involuntary in virtue of ignorance of this sort must be painful and involve repentance.

Since that which is done under compulsion or by reason of ignorance is involuntary, the voluntary would seem to be that of which the moving principle is in the agent himself, he being aware of the particular circumstances of the action. Presumably acts done by reason of anger or appetite are not rightly called involuntary. For in the first place, on that showing none of the other animals will act voluntarily, nor will children; and secondly, is it meant that we do not do voluntarily *any* of the acts that are due to appetite or anger, or that we do the noble acts voluntarily and the base acts involuntarily? Is not this absurd, when one and the same thing is the cause? But it would surely be odd to describe as involuntary the things one ought to desire; and we ought both to be angry at certain things and to have an appetite for certain things, e.g., for health and for learning. Also what is involuntary is thought to be painful, but what is in accordance with appetite is thought to be pleasant. Again, what is the difference in respect of involuntariness between errors committed upon calculation and those committed in anger? Both are to be avoided, but the irrational passions are thought not less human than reason is, and therefore also the actions which proceed from anger or appetite are the man's actions. It would be odd, then, to treat them as involuntary.

Both the voluntary and the involuntary having been delimited, we must next discuss choice; for it is thought to be most closely bound up with virtue and to discriminate characters better than actions do.

Choice, then, seems to be voluntary, but not the same thing as the voluntary; the latter extends more widely. For both children and the lower animals share in voluntary action, but not in choice, and acts done on the spur of the moment we describe as voluntary, but not as chosen.

Those who say it is appetite or anger or wish or a kind of opinion do not seem to be right. For choice is not common to irrational creatures as well, but appetite and anger are. Again, the incontinent man acts with appetite, but not with choice; while the continent man on the contrary acts with choice, but not with appetite. Again, appetite is contrary to choice, but not appetite to appetite. Again, appetite relates to the pleasant and the painful, choice neither to the painful nor to the pleasant.

Still less is it anger; for acts due to anger are thought to be less than any others objects of choice.

But neither is it wish, though it seems near to it; for choice cannot relate to impossibles, and if any one said he chose them he would be thought silly; but there may be a wish even for impossibles, e.g., for immortality. And wish may relate to things that could in no way be brought about by one's own efforts, e.g., that a particular actor or athlete should win in a competition; but no one chooses such things, but only the things that he thinks could be brought about by his own efforts. Again, wish relates rather to the end, choice to the means: for instance, we wish to be healthy, but we choose the acts which will make us healthy, and we wish to be happy and say we do, but we cannot well say we choose to be so; for, in general, choice seems to relate to the things that are in our own power.

For this reason, too, it cannot be opinion; for opinion is thought to relate to all kinds of things, no less to eternal things and impossible things than to things in our own power; and it is distinguished by its falsity or truth, not by its badness or goodness, while choice is distinguished rather by these.

Now with opinion in general perhaps no one even says it is identical. But it is not identical even with any kind of opinion; for by choosing what is good or bad we are men of a certain character, which we are not by holding certain opinions. And we choose to get or avoid something good or bad, but we have opinions about what a thing is or whom it is good for or how it is good for him; we can hardly be said to opine to get or avoid anything. And choice is praised for being related to the right object rather than for being rightly related to it, opinion for being truly related to its object. And we choose what we best know to be good, but we opine what we do not quite know; and it is not the same people that are thought to make the best choices and to have the best opinions, but some are thought to have fairly good opinions, but by reason of vice to choose what they should not. If opinion precedes choice or accompanies it, that makes no difference; for it is not this that we are considering, but whether it is *identical* with some kind of opinion.

What, then, or what kind of thing is it, since it is none of the things we have mentioned? It seems to be voluntary, but not all that is voluntary to be an object of choice. Is it, then, what has been decided on by previous deliberation? At any rate choice involves a rational principle and thought. Even the name seems to suggest that it is what is chosen before other things.

36. *Freedom and the New Theory of Time*

L. NATHAN OAKLANDER

In this selection, Oaklander attempts to respond to the various arguments for
the claim that the tenseless theory of time entails a denial of human freedom.
In addition to the alleged implication that Aristotle's argument for logical
fatalism implies the falsity of the tenseless theory, there are various other arguments, including metaphysical, causal, phenomenological, and scientific ones,
that have led some to maintain that the tenseless view is incompatible with
freedom. It is, perhaps, not difficult to see why. If all events are spread out
along the four-dimensional manifold existing tenselessly at the time they do,
regardless of what time it is, can we still maintain that anything we do is up to
us? Oaklander argues that we can, and that the root of many of the arguments
to the contrary results from the confusion of linguistic tense as a feature in
ordinary language with metaphysical TENSE as a feature of reality.

Although McTaggart's famous article on "The
Unreality of Time" initiated the contemporary
debate between tensed and tenseless theories of
time, it was not until the last two or three decades
that the literature and interest in the issue blos-
somed. Undoubtedly, one of the reasons why the
tenser-detenser debate in the philosophy of time
has recently attracted so much attention is its connection with other important issues in philosophy.
The area I wish to connect with the tenser-
detenser controversy is metaphysics or, more
specifically, the problem of human freedom.
Indeed, the connection between time and freedom
is so close that many have argued that in order to
preserve human freedom we must abandon the
tenseless theory of time and adopt the tensed theory. The arguments for this position are not new.
Perhaps the first argument connecting time and
freedom is implicit in Aristotle's discussion of the
sea battle, and it is still common for defenders of
the tensed theory to argue that the tenseless view
is incompatible with human free will.[1]

The criticism that the tenseless theory leads to
a denial of human freedom has been levied on several different fronts. Some have argued that the
tenseless theory implies a *logical* threat to freedom.[2] Since detensers maintain that all events exist
determinately at the moment they do, regardless
of what moment it is, they are committed to the
determinacy of truth-value, and so to the principle
of bivalence. But then, the logical fatalist argues,
that if, for any statement S and any time *t*, S is
either true at *t* or false at *t*, it follows that every
statement, including statements about the future,
is either *now* true or *now* false and that, therefore,
the future (like the past) is fixed and unalterable.

According to others, the tenseless theory
implies a *metaphysical* threat to freedom. For if all
objects in time have a tenseless existence, then
nothing comes into existence or ceases to exist, and
autonomous control over what does or does not
exist is an illusion.[3] Moreover, if detensers maintain, as arguably they must, that objects persist by
perduring, that is, persisting things are wholes composed of temporal parts, then nothing *really*
changes.[4] Without real change, however, we cannot bring about a change in the properties of an
object, and human creativity and freedom are lost.

Furthermore, some have claimed that the
tenseless theory implies a *causal* threat to our freedom. Since, on the tenseless view, all events exist
at the time and place they do, with the qualities
they have, they are determinate in their existence

From L. Nathan Oaklander, "Freedom and the New
Theory of Time." Originally appeared in *Questions of Time
and Tense*, ed. Robin Le Poidevin (Oxford: Clarendon
Press, 1998), pp. 185–205. Reprinted by permission of
Oxford University Press.

and statements about them are determinate in their truth-value. If, however, all temporal objects, and the statements about them, are *determinate,* then everything that takes place is *determined* to be exactly the way it is. Conversely, a critic of tenseless time may argue that the only reason for thinking of the future as determinate is the belief in determinism. But if all events, including human actions, are determined, then they are unfree.[5]

Tensers also argue that the tenseless theory implies a *phenomenological* threat to freedom since it cannot account for our experience of freedom.[6] We experience the future as being an open realm of possibilities, but for the detenser all events are equally real, there being, as Yourgrau puts it, "a *symmetry of past, present and future* with *respect to facility.*"[7] However, if the future is as real as the present, and so already exists or already is a fact, then how can the detenser account for our experience of the role we play in creating the *(not yet existing)* future?

Finally, there is what I will call the *argument from science.* This argument incorporates virtually all of the objections to tenseless time contained in the preceding arguments.[8] It runs something like this. The mathematical representation of physical objects in contemporary physics entails a tenseless theory of time. On this representation time is a space-like dimension along which physical objects lie. It is then argued, as Lucas once put it, that "an inevitable concomitant of this approach [is] that we take a block view of the universe in which the future course of events is already laid out as a path in Minkowski space-time,"[9] which in turn implies the logical, metaphysical, and phenomenological threats to human freedom previously delineated.

Clearly, any complete defense of the tenseless theory of time must address the various charges that it is incompatible with human freedom. To consider all the issues I raised, with the detail and complexity they deserve, would require much more space than I have for this chapter. For that reason, my aim is more modest and the limitations of this essay should be clear at the outset. I am not attempting to give a complete account of human freedom, but only to show that the nature of tenseless time, when properly understood, does not entail a denial of human freedom and that only a host of misinterpretations could lead one to believe that it does.

1. The New Theory of Time

The theory that I wish to defend has been called the "static," "stasis," and "spacelike" theory of time; or, less pejoratively, the "tenseless" or "B-theory" of time. I prefer to call it the "new theory" of time. The other labels, and especially terms such as "spacelike" and "tenseless," can easily lead to misinterpretations. For example, the notion of time being "tenseless" is problematic because it is ambiguous. Tenselessness is a feature of language, and (for some) it is also a feature of reality. Indeed, the distinctive feature of the new theory of time is that tensed (or tenseless) language and TENSED (or TENSEless) reality must be clearly separated, although proponents and opponents of the tenseless theory have not always kept them separate. Early advocates of the tenseless theory argued that metaphysical TENSE was eliminable from reality because grammatical tense was translatable without loss of meaning from ordinary language. On the new theory, the existence of grammatical tense as represented in ordinary language and thought is not to be confused with ontological TENSE, as represented in a tensed theory of time. Thus, on the new theory, the need for tensed discourse in ordinary language does not imply the existence of tensed properties in reality. And conversely, the rejection of ontological TENSE, that is, the denial of tensed properties and tensed facts, does not imply the translatability of tensed language in ordinary discourse. In other words, given that we are representing reality, a tensed language is eliminable in terms of a tenseless one, even though a tensed language cannot be translated in terms of a tenseless one.[10]

To see why tense and tenselessness as applied to language and time must be kept distinct, consider the following sentence-types:

(A) *Oaklander is (present tense) working on a paper on time and freedom.*

and

(B) *Oaklander is (tenselessly) working on a paper on time and freedom on 13 October 1996.*

According to some tensed theorists, (A) literally changes its truth-value in that it expresses a proposition which has different truth-values at different times. For defenders of the new theory, on the other hand, the difference between (A) and (B) consists in two related facts. First, (B) is time indexed and (A) is not, and because of that fact, different tokens of (A) can have different truth-values, whereas different tokens of (B) each have the same truth-value. More generally, sentences with a tenseless copula have an "unchanging" or "permanent" truth-value; they are "always" true (if they ever are), whereas sentences with a tensed copula can "change" their truth-value (i.e., can have tokens with different truth-values) depending on when they are tokened. But why is that so? How is the tenselessness of the copula to be interpreted?

There are three likely possibilities. On one interpretation the tenseless copula is literally without tense, so that (B) is read as:

> (B′) Oaklander's working on a paper on time and freedom has the property of presentness on October 13, 2003.

Alternatively, we can interpret the tenseless copula as *omnitensed* so that (B) is read as:

> (B″) Oaklander is (was and will be) working on a paper on time and freedom on October 13, 2003.[11]

Or, we can interpret the tenseless copula as *timeless* as in "Red is a color" or "Two plus two is equal to four" so that (B) is read as:

> (B‴) Oaklander is (timelessly) working on a paper on time and freedom on 13 October 2003.

Any of these models provide a basis for the "permanent" or "unchanging" truth-value of (B), and the "fact" that (B) is "always" true, but they can also easily give rise to trouble.

Clearly, (B′) is a tenseless sentence in the sense specified. Different tokens of (B′) always have the same truth-value. But either (B′) means that *E* is simultaneous with October 13, 2003, or it means that *E* occurs on October 13, 2003 and *E* has *presentness*. The former interpretation is innocuous whereas the latter commits one to the reality of TENSE and for that reason is unacceptable to the detenser.

Similarly, if one interprets the tenselessness of the copula in (B) as omnitensed (B″), and if one then confuses omni*tensed* language with temporal reality, a tenseless truth like (B) will imply the existence of tensed properties; a thesis adamantly denied by new theorists. Furthermore, if one confuses the "tenseless" sentence (B″) with its truth-conditions (or the fact in virtue of which it is true), then it is a short step to the conclusion that the basis in reality for the permanent truth of (B″) is a state of affairs that *always exists* or *exists at every moment*. Thus, if (B″) represents the nature of time and not just the language we use to communicate about it, then (B″) implies that I am now (always have been and always will be) working on this paper on October 13, 1996, and that is absurd!

The third interpretation of the tenselessness of the copula is equally troublesome. For if the tenseless copula in (B) is construed as the *timeless* copula of, say, "Two plus two is equal to four," and tenseless language is confused with timeless reality, then the objects in the B-series would be timeless, and time and change would be unreal.

C. D. Broad, who thought often and deeply about the problem of time and change, seems to have misinterpreted tenseless time in the ways I have just explained. In his *Examination of McTaggart's Philosophy* Broad says:

> The [tenseless] theory seems to presuppose that all events, past, present, and future, in some sense "co-exist," and stand to each other *timelessly or semipiternally* in determinate relations of temporal precedence. But how are we to think of this "co-existence" of events? It seems to me that the events and their temporal relations are thought of either by analogy with timeless abstract objects such as the integers in their order of magnitude, or by analogy with *simultaneous persistent particulars,* like points of a line in spatial order from left to right. Neither of these analogies will bear thinking out.[12]

I agree that neither of these analogies will bear thinking out, but I disagree that the new theory of time is committed to either of them. On the new theory, temporal relations between events are in some sense analogous to the relations that obtain between universals, but we need not claim that the terms of temporal relations are to be thought of as universals, that is, as timeless abstract objects. Like relations among universals, temporal relations between and among events, and the facts that they enter into, are not located at any time or in any place. Yet, it does not follow that the *terms* of temporal relations coexist timelessly in the way in which universals do. Nor does the eternal truth of "E_1 is earlier than E_2" require E_1 and E_2 to be located at all times. Why, then, might Broad think that events are persistent particulars or timeless objects?

One possible explanation for Broad's mistake is that he does not clearly separate the language which states the truth-conditions of "E_1 is earlier than E_2" from the reality to which that sentence corresponds. By construing the tenselessness of language as either omnitensed or timeless, and then confusing the language of time with the reality of time, one might easily be led to the conclusion that the terms of temporal relations are simultaneous persistent particulars or timeless abstract objects.[13]

A more recent example of the confusion between tenseless language and temporal reality occurs in the writing of Alan Padgett. Padgett argues that what he calls the "stasis" theory is guilty of committing the fallacy of "confusing the logical with the physical."[14] He claims that detensers confuse the logical with the physical when they argue that since something is a fact at time T_3, and it is thus always a fact and can be expressed by a true statement that is always true, then in some way the fact of "the fact at T_3" must always exist.[15] But what exactly is the difference between logical facts and physical facts, and do new theorists actually confuse these two notions? As we shall see, what Padgett says concerning this distinction reflects the blurring of language and reality to which I have been alluding.

Padgett writes:

> There is a distinction between a 'fact' from a logical point of view and a 'physical' fact. A 'fact' from a logical point of view is the truth expressed by a true statement. Thus it is a 'fact' that *2 + 2 = 4*, or that 'London is south of Cambridge'.[16]

In this passage, Padgett's notion of a logical fact equivocates on the phrase "the truth expressed by

a true statement." On the one hand, the truth expressed is the fact or state of affairs that makes a statement true, for example the fact that 2 + 2 = 4. On the other hand, it means the sentence or statement which is true, for example "London is south of Cambridge."[17]

It seems clear, however, that, for Padgett, a logical fact or "truth" expressed by a true statement is not the fact to which it corresponds since he distinguishes logical from physical facts by maintaining that

> A 'physical' fact . . . is an event or some state of affairs *in the world*. I will call such things 'physical states of affairs'. . . . Examples of a physical state of affairs would then be: my having the thought I am having now, the hotness of the sun, and the liquidity of the water in my cup. Now physical states of affairs can only be real or existing events. Thus the difference between the stasis and the process views of time can be put this way: is it now a physical state of affairs that the sun rises (tenselessly!) on July 4, 1776? The process theorist says 'No', and the stasis theorist says 'Yes'. For the stasis view insists that, in some way or other, the event of the sun's rising exists (tenselessly) on July 4, 1776.[18]

Padgett interprets the new theorist to be claiming that since "the sun's rising (tenselessly) on July 4, 1776" is a tenselessly true statement, it follows there now exists (always did exist and always will exist) the physical fact of *the sun's rising on July 4, 1776*. For that reason, he accuses the new theorist of confusing the logical fact or "truth" which is always true, with the physical fact that exists only on July 4, 1776.

Admittedly, it is indeed a fallacy to argue that simply because "E occurs at t_1" *always* expresses a truth, it follows that it is now (always was and always will be) a physical fact that E occurs at t_1, but the new theorist does not commit it. Padgett could only think that it did follow by first confusing tenseless language with omnitensed language and then confusing omnitensed language with temporal reality. To see what other difficulties the failure to keep language and time separate can give rise to, I shall turn to the logical threat to freedom allegedly posed by the new theory, namely, fatalism.

2. Logical Fatalism

Logical fatalism is based upon the principle of bivalence according to which for any sentence S, including those about the future, and any time t, S is either true at t or false at t.[19] If, however, at time t, a sentence about the future is *now* true, or *already* true, then the future is *fixed* and there is nothing we can do to prevent it. And if, at time t, a sentence about the future is *now* false, or *already* false, then there is nothing we can do to bring it about. In either case, as Aristotle puts it, "nothing is or takes place fortuitously, either in the present or in the future, and there are no real alternatives; everything takes place of necessity and is fixed."[20]

The crucial assumption in this argument for fatalism is that if a sentence is now true at time t, then there now exists (or "already exists") at time t a state of affairs in virtue of which it is true. Fortunately, the new theorist need not accept that assumption. Consider the future-tense sentence "There will be a sea fight." According to the new theory as I understand it, the fact in virtue of which that sentence is true will vary depending on the time at which it is uttered or inscribed. For example, if the sentence in question is asserted today, at t_1, then the state of affairs which exists if the sentence is true is *a sea fight occurs later than t_1*. However, that state of affairs is not located at the time at which the future-tense sentence is uttered, and it is not located at any later (or earlier) time. Of course something is located at t_1, namely, the inscription or utterance "There will be a sea fight," and assuming the utterance is true, something is located at a time later than t_1, namely, the sea fight, but the whole state of affairs that *a sea fight occurs later than t_1* is not located at t_1, is not located at t_2, and is not located at any earlier or later time. Indeed, it is not located in time at all.[21]

States of affairs which contain temporal relations between events are *eternal* in the sense of existing outside the network of temporal relations, but not in the sense of existing (or persisting) throughout all of time. Thus, an "eternal" entity is one that neither occupies moments of time, nor exemplifies temporal relations, nor has monadic temporal properties inhering in it. Rather, an eternal entity is related to time in the following way: it

is a whole which contains successive parts. We could say that although an eternal entity is not contained in time, time is contained in it. Thus, the fact that *World War II is later than World War I* is eternal because, although not itself located in time (or a term of a temporal relation), it contains time (a temporal relation) as a constituent. Consequently, the truth of a future-tense sentence does not imply that the future "pre-exists" in the present, or that the future "already exists."

Of course, if one confuses the tenseless sentence "A sea fight occurs later than t_1," which states the truth-conditions of "There will be a sea fight" (uttered at time t_1) with the (TENSEless temporal relational) fact to which it corresponds, namely, *a sea fight occurs later than t_1*, then fatalistic worries will emerge. For the sentence describing the (TENSEless) truth-conditions of a future-tense sentence is tenselessly true, i.e. true *simpliciter*. However, if one confuses true *simpliciter* with true *at every time*, then one will conclude that the tenseless sentence is *always* true. If one then confuses the tenseless sentence with the state of affairs to which it corresponds, one might conclude that it is *always* existing. If, however, *a sea fight's occurring later than t_1*, or *a sea fight's occurring at t_2*, always exists and thus "already" exists at t_1, that is, at a time before the sea fight occurs, then my choice is an illusion, for I can neither bring about nor prevent at t_2 what already exists at t_1. On the other hand, if one recognizes that a future-tense sentence is true in virtue of an event's occurring *later* than the time of the sentence, and not in virtue of anything that is located at the time of utterance, the difficulty vanishes.

My new-theorist response to logical fatalism rests upon the notion of an "eternal" state of affairs. Alan Padgett has criticized my notion of "eternal" temporal relations for again confusing the logical fact that "S_1 is earlier than S_2" which is always true with the physical fact that S_1 and S_2 always exist. Thus, he says:

> The process theorist can agree, if need be, that 'facts' like S_1-earlier-than-S_2 or Alan-born-before-Carl are 'eternal' in that they are omnitensely true. Tensed sentence tokens affirming their existence all make statements which are true, always, were, and always will be. From this it does not follow, however,

that the episodes referred to by S_1, S_2 and S_3 exist eternally, any more than it follows that Carl and I are 'eternally' born, or exist 'eternally'. Oaklander and others who follow this argument have committed the fallacy of confusing the logical with the physical.[22]

I agree that such an inference would be fallacious but deny that I make it. To say that "S_1-is-before-S_2" is always true does not imply that S_1 and S_2 are either eternal, sempiternal, or timeless objects, and Padgett could only think that the new theory would imply that it did by falling prey to the confusion between temporal language and temporal reality discussed throughout this essay.

Although Padgett's argument does not undermine the existence of "eternal" facts (or timeless temporal relations), one might still object that the existence of events that are TENSElessly located at later moments takes away our freedom. For if there is a fact that, say, *I vote for Howard Dean* (assuming he is nominated) *in 2004* (or that *I vote for Dean later than* t_1) then, arguably, that fact *necessitates* the occurrence of my voting for Dean in the year 2004, or synonymously, that it is not within my power, in 2000, to prevent my voting for Dean in 2004. It is not at all clear, however, that the existence of an eternal fact necessitates anything. The necessity does not follow from the principle of bivalence. The law necessitates that one of a pair of contradictory statements is true, but it does not imply that either "*P*" is necessarily true or "*not-P*" is necessarily true. If I vote for Dean in 2004, then my present statement (in 2003) "I will vote for Dean in 2004" is true, and if I do not vote for him then my present statement "I will not vote for Dean in 2004" is true. Thus, which statement is true depends on whether or not the fact *I vote for Dean (approximately one year) later than November 15, 2003* exists or does not exist, but whether or not that fact exists depends upon what I will choose to do on election day, November 2004. In other words, it is my later decision that determines which of two contradictory statements about the future is true, since it is my later decision that determines what eternal fact exists. Thus, the existence of eternal facts is not incompatible with our having it within our power to bring about or prevent certain events. Indeed, it is because we do have it within our power (because we do choose or

do not choose) to bring about or prevent certain events that certain eternal facts exist.[23]

One might still wonder how the existence of facts that are not located in time can depend on something that is located in time. How can the "eternal" fact that *I vote for Dean later than November 15, 2000* depend for its existence on something that occurs in November 2004? Although eternal facts do not exist in time (i.e., as terms of temporal relations), they do contain temporal relations and their relata as constituents. Thus, the fact that I am going to vote for Dean in four years includes my decision next year to vote for Dean. That decision is an event that exists in time, and if it does not occur on November 5, 2004, then there is no such fact as my voting for Dean in 2004. For that reason, the truth of a future-tense sentence does not entail the existence of a fact which in turn determines my choice. Rather, my choice in November 2004 determines what (TENSEless) fact exists, and hence what future-tense sentence is true.

Interestingly, Storrs McCall, a tenser, who once argued that propositions about the future must have an indeterminate truth-value, has recently changed his mind. And what he says on this topic closely reflects the new theorist's view:

> We shall say that the truth of an empirical proposition supervenes upon events in the sense of being wholly dependent upon them, while at the same time events in no way *supervene upon* truth. Thus the truth of the proposition that X is in Warsaw town square at noon next Friday depends upon what happens next Friday, and in this way the sting of 'logical determinism' is drawn. . . . What is true today depends upon what happens tomorrow, not the other way round. The set of true propositions in no way determines what the future is like. Instead, what the future is like determines the set of true propositions.[24]

3. Metaphysical Fatalism

While the logic of temporal language does not commit the new theorist to denying human freedom, the metaphysical implications of the new theory may. In a recent and provocative paper Niall Shanks claims that there are important connections between the free will/determinist debate and some issues in the metaphysics of time.[25] Specifically, he argues that friends of libertarian incompatibilism can find no support in modern indeterministic physics because (1) modern physics implies the S-theory (presumably for spacelike or static theory) of time and (2) if the S-theory is true, then there is no human autonomy.[26] In this section I will consider Shanks's main arguments in defense of (2)—the thesis that the S-theory implies the denial of human autonomy—and argue that they suffer from a pernicious spatialization of (TENSEless) time, and a confusion of common sense with ontology.

To see what is involved in these claims and to justify them let us turn to Shanks's argument in support of (2). Shanks believes that in order to have genuine human autonomy the universe must be open in three senses of the term: one causal and two ontological. In the causal sense, the universe is open if indeterminism is the case, that is, if the location and configurations of physical objects at some time t are underdetermined by (or not all lawfully connected with) earlier states of the universe. In an ontological sense, the universe is open$_1$ if not only is it indeterministic (open$_1$), but also the locations and configurations of physical objects are *autonomously changeable*. "That is, [location and configuration] must be properties of a physical object which admit of alteration and adjustment as a consequence of intervention by, or interaction with an autonomous being."[27] In other words, in an open$_2$ universe, the actions of a causally efficacious (underdetermined) agent are capable of bringing about a *real change* in a physical object. In a third sense, the universe is open$_3$ if there is *ontological indeterminacy*, meaning that "there are many possible futures compatible with their present circumstances, and it is by no means determined or "fixed" at present which of these will come to pass"[28] and thus that the objects of history *do not* tenselessly exist at their respective moments with their respective properties, i.e., the new theory is false. Autonomous action requires openness in each of these senses. For if the universe is either causally determined (closed$_1$) or ontologically *determinate* (closed$_3$) then it is closed$_2$ since no autonomous being is capable of

"bringing about" or "causing" an existential or qualitative change in a physical object, and genuine human autonomy is impossible.

Shanks claims that even though the S-theory *does* allow for the possibility that the universe is indeterministic (or open$_1$), it renders the future fixed (or closed$_3$), and human autonomy impotent (closed$_2$). For on the S-theory, "time is literally a space-like dimension along which an object is extended,"[29] and since "the distinct spatial parts of an object at some given time t enjoy the same existential status . . . the distinct temporal parts of an object will likewise be on a par, ontologically speaking."[30] However if the four-dimensional shapes of physical objects are nothing more than "coexisting temporal parts,"[31] tenselessly existing in different regions of spacetime, "then the objects of history neither begin to exist nor cease to exist."[32] Unfortunately, if objects of history neither begin nor cease to exist, but exist *simpliciter*, then what the future will be is determined or fixed at present, and the belief in autonomous changeability and human autonomy is an illusion.

Shanks's argument, familiar as it is seemingly persuasive, is nevertheless rooted in a web of confusions. We can begin to see what they are by noting that Shanks believes our commonsense intuitions and ordinary language talk about time have implications for ontology. As he says:

> In order to see that the information expressed by the tenses has ontological consequences, it suffices to consider the following fragments of ordinary language: 'Elizabeth I *existed* four hundred years ago', 'Elizabeth II *exists*', and 'Elizabeth III will (possibly) *exist*'. According to common sense, of the three monarchs, only Elizabeth II actually exists. The tenses thus enable ordinary speakers to express existential differences between the objects of history.[33]

Since, however, the tenseless theory treats all objects as *ontologically on a par, tenselessly existing* at the times they do, Shanks concludes that the S-theory must deny our intuitions that only the present exists and that there are existential differences between the objects of history.

It seems to me, however, that Shanks's line of reasoning confuses grammatical tense as represented in ordinary language and thought, with ontological TENSE as represented in the new theory of time. That is, Shanks assumes that, since we use *grammatical* tenses to indicate existential differences between objects of history, it follows that it must be the tensed properties of *pastness, presentness,* and *futurity,* or the tensed facts, It was the case, It will be the case, or It is the case that X is present, that distinguish objects that exist from those which do not. In other words, on the tensed theory, the commonsense platitude "only the present exists" carries ontological weight. On the new theory, on the other hand, there are no such properties (and no such facts), and *in that respect,* time *is* analogous to space. Just as there is no monadic property of *hereness* that distinguishes this place, or the place where I am located, from any other place, there is no monadic property of *presentness* that distinguishes this time, or the time when I am located, from any other time. Thus, time is TENSEless, and all objects are ontologically on a par in that there are no tensed properties that distinguish those events that exist from those that do not. It does not follow that tensed language and thought is translatable in terms of tenseless language, or that we could communicate without tensed language. Nor does it follow that our intuitions about time are mistaken (although they need to be properly interpreted) or that tensed language is false. Indeed, once our ordinary language of time is distinguished from a metaphysically perspicuous language of time, it can be shown how and why our temporal intuitions are true.

As I now write (at 4.00 P.M., November 15, 2003), only those events which are (roughly) simultaneous with my utterances exist and are located at that date. Events which will occur (or TENSElessly occur) on November 23, 2003, eight days later than my writing, do not yet exist in that they are not located at (and do not TENSElessly exist on) November 15, and events which did occur (or TENSElessly occur) on November 14, 2003, one day earlier than my writing, no longer exist in that they are not located at (and do not TENSElessly exist on) November 15 either. Thus, on the new theory our ordinary beliefs that the future is not yet and the past is no longer and the present is now are true but innocuous. Future events are not yet because they are located at times later than my speaking, past events are no longer because they are located at times ear-

lier than my speaking, and only the present exists in the deflationary sense that only those events which are simultaneous with my speaking are located at 4.00 P.M., November 15, 2003. These are the tenseless truths that underlie the intuitions that there are existential differences between objects of history and that only the present exists; the existence of tensed properties or facts has nothing to do with it.

In addition to "tenselessly existing," two other phrases that give rise to trouble are "equally real" and "coexisting." There is, of course, a phenomenological difference between space and time: although we experience objects at different spatial locations as being "equally real" (i.e., occurring at the same time), we do not experience objects at different temporal locations as being *equally* real or *coexisting.* This phenomenological claim is used by tensers to support, on the side of common sense, the claim that the present has a privileged position in the temporal spectrum (i.e., only the present exists), and on the side of ontology the claim that objects in time exist if and only if they exemplify *presentness.*

The fallacy in this line of reasoning consists in its confusing TENSEless time with space. We do experience objects elsewhere in space as coexisting equally with objects that are here, but we do not experience past (earlier) and future (later) events as coexisting with those events that are present. Thus, if one thinks that time is literally like space, then the claim that four-dimensional objects are composed of "coexisting temporal parts" or that all objects in TENSEless time are "equally real" will be taken to deny this phenomenological fact and reduce temporally separate events to simultaneous parts of a presently existing whole. In that case, however, the universe is ontologically determinate (closed$_3$), since what the future will be, is fixed at present, and human autonomy is lost.

Fortunately, such an illicit spatialization of time, along with its dire consequences for human autonomy, is not a necessary part of the new theory of time. On the tenseless theory as Russell, (the early) C. D. Broad, Clifford Williams, Oaklander, and other detensers have conceived of it, temporal relations are primitive and unanalysable relations, and the difference between spatial and temporal relations is an irreducible qualitative difference.[34] The experience of earlier and later upon which the experience of time and change is built is primitive, and is intrinsically different from our experience of one colored patch being to the left of another differently colored patch. For that reason, objects coexist in time in a fundamentally different sense from the way they coexist in space. Thus, time possesses a quality that space does not possess: spatially separated objects can exist at the same time, but temporally separated events cannot occur at the same time. It is this crucial difference between the terms of spatial and temporal relations that is the phenomenological basis of the sense of privilegedness that the present moment possesses.[35]

Of course, there are crucial similarities between space and time as well. Just as temporally separated objects cannot exist at the same time, spatially separated objects cannot exist at the same place, and just as spatially separated objects can exist at the same time, temporally separated objects can exist at the same place. Nevertheless, neither of these analogies between space and time should lead one to deny that on the new theory there is an intrinsic difference between time and space or assert that the terms of the temporal relations of earlier/later coexist in the way in which the terms of the spatial relations of left/right coexist.

Closely connected with the particular interpretation Shanks gives to the S-theory is the claim that "if the S-theory is true, then the objects of history neither begin to exist, nor cease to exist."[36] Once again, if this is true, then nothing could be brought into existence and autonomous existential control (that is, the ability to bring or not bring something into existence) would be impossible. But it is not true.

Consider, for example, the experience of a headache ceasing to exist. It involves first having a headache and at the same time being conscious that one is having a headache. It involves second the consciousness of no longer having a headache. This involves both the awareness of my having various thoughts and feelings, and not having a headache. It also involves the memory of a headache that is not located now, at this moment, but is located (or exists TENSElessly) at an earlier moment. In other words, if I am aware at time$_1$, that I have a headache, and I am aware at a later time$_2$ that I do not have a headache, and I remem-

ber my headache existing at time$_1$, then I am having an experience of my headache ceasing to exist.

What this account of our experience of time makes clear is that the ceasing to exist of a headache (or any other event, for that matter) is a process that takes place at two moments: the last moment of its existence and the first moment of its non-existence. Thus, on the detenser's reading, a headache's ceasing to exist over the interval t_{n-n+1} is its being located up to t_n and thus making the present-tense belief "My headache exists (now)" true up to t_n, and false at t_{n+1} (and later). Similarly, a headache's beginning to exist at t is nothing more than its being located at t and not earlier, and thus making the present-tense belief "My headache exists (now)" true at t and false earlier.

To this it might be objected that since the knowledge of my headache ceasing to exist requires that the *tensed beliefs* "My headache exists (now)" and "My headache did exist" are both true (at different times), there must be *tensed facts* to account for their truth. The inference, however, is fallacious. For if a belief or judgment is indexical, as it is if it is tensed, then its truth-conditions are token-reflexive. So all it takes to make a token of the tensed belief "My headache exists (now)" true is that the headache occurs simultaneously with the belief. And all it takes to make a token of the tensed belief "My headache did exist" true is that the headache ended before I had the belief (or that the belief is held after the end of the headache). If, however, we can make sense of objects coming into existence and ceasing to exist on the new theory, existential control (as reflected, for example, in determining "whether or not to make an apple pie for supper")[37] is still within the grasp of the new theorist.

Human autonomy also requires qualitative control and Shanks attempts to show that to be impossible on the four-dimensionalist account of change, since the four-dimensionalist must reject the commonsense intuition that objects persist with a numerical identity through time. For if the S-theory is true, then Elizabeth II, for example, will be said to have temporal parts in Paris *and distinct temporal parts* in London, it no longer makes sense to say that the object in Paris at t_1 is one and the same object that is now in London at t_2—instead there are distinct temporal parts of a four-dimensional whole at these spacetime locations.[38]

To uncover the confusions that permeate this argument, note that his statement "it no longer makes sense to say that the object in Paris at t_1 is one and the same object that is now in London at t_2" is ambiguous. For the phrase "the object in Paris (P) at t_1" may mean "the temporal part P-at-t_1" (or, more simply, "p_1"). Or, it may also mean "the entity P, of which P-at-t_1 (p_1) is a part." Clearly, if we mean the former, then it is misleading, indeed false, to assert that P-at-t_1 (p_1) is the same person as P-at-t_2 (p_2), but this does not imply that the person of which these two different stages are temporal parts is not the same person at these different times. For on the second interpretation we can say that the person P which at one stage in her life (p_1) is in Paris is the very same person P that at a later stage (p_2) is in London. Thus, the existence of four-dimensional objects, with temporal parts is compatible with thinking of these objects as being the subjects of qualitative change, and with our being able to bring about some of those changes.[39]

It seems, therefore, that some of the crucial intuitions that are employed in the argument for the incompatibility of the new theory of TENSEless time and human freedom, for example that only the present exists, that there are existential differences between the objects of history, that objects can begin to be and cease to be, and that things change, *can* be explained on the new theory. What, then, of Shanks's claim that

> the modality which some people believe the future to have—in the sense that they believe there are many possible futures compatible with their present circumstances, and it is by no means determined or 'fixed' at present which of these will come to pass—must, when analyzed in S-theoretic terms, arise instead merely from ignorance.[40]

If by "determined" *at present* Shanks means that, on the S-theory, the locations and configurations of physical objects at some future time t are causally determined (closed$_1$) by (or lawfully connected with) present states of the universe, then he is falling prey to the confusion between "determined" and "determinate" he sought to avoid. And if by "fixed" *at present* Shanks means that, on the tenseless theory, there *now* exist facts that ground the truth of future contingents, then he is wrong.

For, on the new theory, the truth of "A will do X" when uttered at time t corresponds (in part) to the fact that X *exists (TENSElessly) later than t* (and not to any fact that is located *at t*). On the other hand, if he means that the future is fixed like the past in that we cannot change it, then I would agree. But to say that we cannot change the future is not to say that we do not have a hand in making it, or that our choices do not bring it about.

4. The Phenomenology of Freedom

Nevertheless, there is an intuition that we all share according to which the past is unalterable, fixed, and already settled and thus no longer within our power to control, whereas we are free to make choices that will determine how the future will be. What account of the phenomenological asymmetry of openness with respect to the past and future can the new theorist give? In this concluding section I will mention three possibilities congenial to the new theory that are worthy of further exploration.

The asymmetry of openness is analyzed by David Lewis as an asymmetry of counterfactual dependence. The future depends counterfactually on the present in a way in which the past does not so depend. As Lewis puts it:

> What we can do by way of 'changing the future' . . . is to bring it about that the future is the way it actually will be, rather than any of the other ways it would have been if we acted differently in the present. . . . Likewise, something we ordinarily *cannot* do by way of 'changing the past' is to bring it about that the past is the way it actually was, rather than some other way it would have been if we acted differently in the present.[41]

This suggestion by Lewis is quite plausible and it is compatible with both the new theory and with determinism. My major hesitation concerns Lewis's analysis of counterfactual dependence and the subsequent commitment to possible worlds that it entails. Thus, in order to avoid the thorny problem of giving an adequate account of the truth-conditions of counterfactuals, I therefore prefer, although I will not here explore in any detail, two suggestions put forth by Broad during his (early) detenser stage.

Broad says that there are two senses in which the past is fixed and unalterable, while the future depends, in part, on our volitions. He says:

> (i.) However much I may know about the laws of nature, I cannot make probable inferences from the future to the past, because I am not directly acquainted with the future, but I can make probable inferences from the past to the future; i.e., although every possible proposition about the future is even now determinately true or false, I may be able to judge now, from my knowledge of the past and present and of the laws of nature, that some propositions about future events are much more likely to be true than others. . . .
> (ii.) I know with regard to certain classes of events that such events never occur unless preceded by a desire for their occurrence, and that such desires are generally followed by the occurrence of the corresponding events. But the existence of a desire for x does not increase the probability that x *has* happened. If it did we might be said to affect the past in exactly the same sense in which we can affect the future. Thus the assertion that we can affect the future but not the past seems to come down to this; (a) that propositions about the future can be inferred to be highly probable from a knowledge of the past and present, but not conversely, because of our lack of direct acquaintance with the future; and (b) that the general laws connecting a desire for x with the occurrence of x always contain x as a consequent and never as an antecedent.[42]

According to Broad's first point, the asymmetry of openness is epistemological. The second point seems to me to be more convincing. Our experience of the openness of the future is based upon the awareness that the desire for the occurrence of a certain event is something that is causally efficacious or lawfully connected with the desired event only when the event is *later* than the desire. And our experience of fixity stems from our knowledge that a desire or wish that something *had* happened is not lawfully connected with that event's having happened. For these reasons, we do not experience

the past as something we have any control over, whereas we do experience the future as something over which we do have some control.

I think the new theorist's account of coming into existence and ceasing to exist is relevant here. For the openness of the future is, in part, based on our experience of an event that does not yet exist (i.e., is not located at the time of my decision to bring it about) coming into existence (or being located at a time) after I decide to bring it about. As I argued earlier, the experience of coming to be and ceasing to be is one that the new theorist can accommodate. On the other hand, the experience of the closed past or the fixity of the past stems from the experience or realization that my desire (at t_2) for a certain event to have happened in the past (at t_1) does not bring that event into existence. Similarly, my decision (at t_2) to end an unpleasant event (at t_2) may be lawfully connected with that event ceasing to exist (or not being located at t_3) but my wish (at t_3) for an unpleasant past event (at t_2) not to have happened (or not to be located at t_2) does not make a difference. These experiences, which form the basis of the asymmetry of openness between the future and the past, can be explained on the new theory.

Although much more could and should be said concerning the phenomenology of freedom, these brief remarks suggest the direction a new theorist of time could consistently take. In conclusion, I hope to have developed the new theory sufficiently to convince you that it is not the threat to human freedom that its detractors have claimed it to be.[43]

Endnotes

[1]For recent examples see John R. Lucas, *The Future: An Essay on God, Temporality and Truth* (New York: Blackwell, 1989); Neil Shanks, "Time, Physics, and Freedom," *Metaphilosophy* I (1994): 45–59; and Pallé Yourgrau, *The Disappearance of Time* (New York: Cambridge University Press, 1992).

[2]See, for example, Stephen Cahn, *Fate, Logic and Time* (New Haven: Yale University Press, 1967; repr. Atascadero, Calif.: Ridgeway Publishing Company, 1982). For a good discussion of the connection between time, truth, and fatalism see M. H. Bernstein, *Fatalism* (Lincoln: University of Nebraska Press, 1992).

[3]Cf. Shanks, "Time, Physics, and Freedom," pp. 45–59.

[4]William Carter and H. Scott Hestevold, "Temporal Passage and Temporal Persistence," *American*

Philosophical Quarterly 3112 (1994): 269–83 argue that the tenseless theory implies the doctrine of temporal parts. For arguments that purport to show that nothing really changes on a temporal parts ontology see Lawrence Lombard, *Events: A Metaphysical Study* (New York: Routledge & Kegan Paul, 1986); Lawrence Lombard, "The Doctrine of Temporal Parts and the No Change Objection," *Philosophy and Phenomenological Research* 54, no. 2 (1994): 365–72; and Peter T. Geach, "Some Problems about Time," *Studies in the Philosophy of Thought and Action*, ed. P. F. Strawson (Oxford: Oxford University Press, 1968), pp. 175–91. For a reply to Lombard, see Mark Heller, "Things Change," *Philosophy and Phenomenological Research* (1992): 695–704. For a reply to Geach see L. Nathan Oaklander, *Temporal Relations and Temporal Becoming* (Lanham, Md.: University Press of America, 1984). For a fully developed causal account of tenseless change within a temporal parts ontology see Robin Le Poidevin, *Change, Cause and Contradiction: A Defense of the Tenseless Theory of Time* (London: Macmillan; New York: St Martin's Press, 1991).

[5]Jan Lukasiewicz, "On Determinism," in *Polish Logic*, ed. Storrs McCall (Oxford: Oxford University Press, 1967), pp. 19–39 seems to argue in this fashion. For critiques of the inference from determinate to determined see Adolph Grünbaum, "The Exclusion of Becoming from the Physical World," in *The Concepts of Space and Time*, ed. Milic Capek (Boston: D. Reidel Publishing Co, 1976), pp. 471–500; Oaklander, *Temporal Relations and Temporal Becoming*; Quentin Smith and L. Nathan Oaklander, *Time, Change, and Freedom* (New York: Routledge, 1995); and Donald C. Williams, "The Sea-Fight Tomorrow," in *Structure, Meaning and Method: Essays in Honor of Henry M. Sheffer*, eds. Paul Henle, H. M. Kallen, and S. K. Langer (New York: The Liberal Arts Press, 1951), pp. 282–306.

[6]See Lucas, *The Future: An Essay on God, Temporality and Truth.*

[7]Yourgrau, *The Disappearance of Time*, p. 46.

[8]*Cf. Ibid.*

[9]John R. Lucas, "The Open Future," in *The Nature of Time*, eds. Raymond Rood and Michael Lockwood (Oxford: Basil Blackwell, 1986), pp. 125–34. The quoted passage occurs on p. 130. Lucas himself does not accept this implication of modern physics and adopts a version of the open future theory of time which he argues is compatible with physics. For a recent discussion of the open future theory see Ned Markosian, "The Open Past," *Philosophical Studies* 79 (1995): 95–105.

[10]For recent articles on the new theory and criticism, see the essays by Mellor, MacBeath, Oaklander, Williams, and Smith in part I of *The New Theory of Time*, eds. L. Nathan Oaklander and Quentin Smith (New Haven: Yale University Press, 1994).

[11]Alan Padgett, *God, Eternity and the Nature of Time* (New York: St Martin's Press, 1992) interprets the tenseless copula as omnitensed, and Quentin Smith, *Language and Time* (New York: Oxford University Press, 1993), interprets it as conjunctively (present and future) tensed.

According to the new theory, however, a tenseless copula lacks any tense.

[12]C. D. Broad, *Examination of McTaggart's Philosophy Vol. II, Part I* (Cambridge: Cambridge University Press, 1938). The quoted passage occurs in II, p. 307; emphasis added.

[13]Admittedly, in order to represent reality we must use language, and for that reason temporal language and temporal reality are not entirely distinct. Nevertheless, the new theorist maintains that the language used to represent the metaphysical nature of temporal reality must be without tense since the reality of TENSE (as either properties or facts) entails unacceptable dialectical difficulties (i.e., McTaggart's paradox). For a discussion of McTaggart's paradox and criticisms of recent attempts to avoid it, see Oaklander and Smith, *The New Theory of Time*, Part II and Essays 5–8, 13, and 14.

[14]Padgett, *God, Eternity and Time*, p. 118.

[15]Ibid., p. 119.

[16]Ibid., p. 118.

[17]In correspondence Padgett has replied that "the fact that 'London is south of Cambridge' is a *physical fact;* on p. 118 I am NOT talking about the sentence, 'London is south of Cambridge' but rather the *physical facticity* that this sentence denotes" (e-mail message, 5 June 1996; emphasis added). However, if that is Padgett's view then he is confusing logical and physical facts, since in the passage quoted in the text, Padgett uses "London is south of Cambridge" as an example of a *logical fact.*

[18]Padgett, *God, Eternity and Time*, p. 118; emphasis added.

[19]An anonymous reader correctly noted that the principle of bivalence concerns truth *simpliciter* and *not* truth at a time. Nevertheless, one might confuse the two concepts of truth: because all tokens of a tenseless sentence are true (or false) whenever they are uttered or written, one might mistakenly infer that a tenseless sentence is *always true*, i.e., true at every time, and thus fallaciously conflate the principle of bivalence (for truth *simpliciter*) with the corresponding principle of bivalence (for truth at a time). We shall see that those who attribute logical fatalism to the new theory of time are guilty of that mistaken inference and subsequent confusion. Alternatively, if one holds a tensed view of time one might reject the concept of truth *simpliciter* in favor of the concept of truth at a time. Since, however, according to the detenser, all truth is truth *simpliciter*, any argument against the new theory which is based on the concept of truth at a time (as logical fatalism is) is question-begging and unsound. Recently, Michael Tooley, *Time, Tense and Causation* (Oxford: Oxford University Press, 1997), has argued that an adequate conception of temporal reality requires both conceptions of truth *simpliciter* and truth at a time.

[20]Aristotle, *De Interpretatione: The Basic Works of Aristotle*, ed. Richard McKeon (New York: Random House, 1941), p. 46.

[21]Similarly, the fact that *Socrates is taller than Phaedo* exists outside time, but depends for its existence on Socrates and

Phaedo, who exist in time. Robin Le Poidevin has suggested to me another argument for the claim that facts do not exist in time. Suppose that the fact (call it "F") that *e occurs at t* exists at *t*. Then there is another fact, namely the fact that *F exists at t,* and so on *ad infinitum.* On the other hand, D. H. Mellor has objected to my saying of some facts that they exist outside time. He would say of some facts, not that they do not exist in time, but that they have no limited location in time, and likewise, for space. Thus, the fact, call it *P,* that Mitterrand dies, is located in space and time: Mitterrand dies in Paris in January 1996. On the other hand, the fact, call it *Q,* that Mitterrand dies in Paris in January 1996 is not located in any region *R* of spacetime such that "*Q* in *R*" is true and "*Q* outside *R*" false. For Mellor, this is just a consequence of the fact that all of *P*'s temporal and spatial aspects are already stated in *Q.* As far as responding to the fatalist's argument against the new theory, Mellor's point may be well taken. My preference for treating temporal relational facts as outside time stems from the belief that temporal relations are simple, existents, and atemporal universals. A defense of these views is outside the scope of this essay.

22Padgett, *God, Eternity and Time,* p. 120.

23Perhaps one will ask how, say, Jones is *able* to not eat dinner at t_1, if it is true (or a fact) that Jones does eat dinner at t_1. Very briefly, I would say, that the notion of "ability" or what we "can" do is ambiguous. Relative to one set of facts someone may be able to do something which relative to another set of facts one is unable to do. Thus, given the fact *Jones eats dinner at t_1* there cannot also be the fact *Jones does not eat dinner at t_1,* but given certain other facts which we ordinarily take to be relevant to what we can or cannot do, it can be the case that Jones does not eat dinner at time$_1$. Given facts about Jones's physical capacity to drive a car and to stop by the local pub, his propensity to have a drink, and the typical rush-hour traffic around dinner time, and so on, he can avoid eating dinner at time$_1$ but he will not. See David Lewis, "The Paradoxes of Time Travel," *The Philosophy of Time,* eds. Robin Le Poidevin and Murray MacBeath (Oxford: Oxford University Press, 1993), pp. 135–46.

24Storrs McCall, *A Model of the Universe: Space-Time, Probability, and Decision* (Oxford: Clarendon Press, 1994), p. 14.

25Shanks, "Time, Physics, and Freedom."

26That modern physics implies the tenseless theory is a highly contentious point that Shanks assumes without argument. Recent discussions of the issue occur in Smith, *Language and Time;* Howard Stein, "On Relativity Theory and the Openness of the Future," *Philosophy of Science* 58 (1991): 147–67; and Tooley, *Time, Tense and Causation.*

27Shanks, "Time, Physics, and Freedom," pp. 48–49.

28Ibid., p. 55.

29Ibid., p. 58.

30Ibid., p. 52.

31Ibid., p. 56.

32Ibid., p. 55.

33Ibid., p. 51.

34See Bertrand Russell, "On the Experience of Time," *Monist* 25 (1915): 212–33; C. D. Broad, "Time," *Encyclopedia of Religion and Ethics,* ed. J. Hastings (New York: Scribner Sons, 1921); Clifford Williams, "The Phenomenology of B-Time," *The New Theory of Time,* eds. Oaklander and Smith, pp. 360–72; Oaklander, *Temporal Relations and Temporal Becoming;* Smith and Oaklander, *Time, Change and Freedom.*

35Cf. Williams, "The Phenomenology of B-Time," pp. 360–72. The quoted passage occurs on pp. 365–66. For a causal analysis of tenseless temporal relations see Le Poidevin, *Change, Cause and Contradiction;* and D. H. Mellor, *Real Time* (New York: Cambridge University Press, 1981).

36Shanks, "Time, Physics, and Freedom," p. 55.

37Ibid., p. 57.

38Ibid., p. 52.

39Heller has argued that "once we accept that there really is such a thing as the extended four dimensional whole, there is no good reason to deny that it, and not just its temporal parts, does have properties at various times." (Heller, "Things Change," p. 700. Cf. Essay 29.

40Shanks, "Time, Physics, and Freedom," pp. 54–55.

41David Lewis, "Counterfactual Dependence and Time's Arrow," *Conditionals,* ed. Frank Jackson (New York: Oxford University Press, 1991), pp. 76–101. The quoted passage occurs on p. 53.

42C. D. Broad, "Time," p. 335.

43I wish to thank Ron Hoy, Ned Markosian, Robin Le Poidevin, Hugh Mellor, and Alan White for their very helpful comments on earlier versions of this chapter. I have also benefited from discussions of this chapter at the Mike Morden Memorial Colloquium at Oakland University (in Michigan) and at West Virginia University.

The research for this chapter was supported (in part) by a fellowship from the faculty development fund of the University of Michigan-Flint.

37. Whether There Is Anything Voluntary in Human Acts?

THOMAS AQUINAS

St. Thomas Aquinas (1225–1274) was born in the Castle of Roccasecca, near Aquino, Italy. In addition to his theological writings, of which *The Summa Theologica* is his most famous, he wrote commentaries on Boethius and almost the whole Aristotelian corpus. The brief selection included here considers three objections to Aristotle's definition of "voluntary." These objections set the stage for causal and theological problems of freedom.

We proceed thus to the First Article:

Objection 1. It would seem that there is nothing voluntary in human acts. For that is voluntary *which has its principle within itself,* as Gregory of Nyssa,[1] Damascene[2] and Aristotle[3] declare. But the principle of human acts is not in man himself, but outside him, since man's appetite is moved to act by the appetible object which is outside him, and which is as a *mover unmoved.*[4] Therefore there is nothing voluntary in human acts.

Obj. 2. Further, the Philosopher proves that in animals no new movement arises that is not preceded by another and exterior motion.[5] But all human acts are new, since none is eternal. Consequently, the principle of all human acts is from outside man, and therefore there is nothing voluntary in them.

Obj. 3. Further, he that acts voluntarily can act of himself. But this is not true of man, for it is written (*John* xv. 5): *Without Me you can do nothing.* Therefore there is nothing voluntary in human acts.

On the contrary, Damascene says that *the voluntary is an act consisting in a rational operation.*[6] Now such are human acts. Therefore there is something voluntary in human acts.

I answer that, There must needs be something voluntary in human acts. In order to make this clear, we must take note that the principle of some acts is within the agent, or in that which is moved; whereas the principle of some movements or acts is outside. For when a stone is moved upwards, the principle of this movement is outside the stone; whereas, when it is moved downwards, the principle of this movement is in the stone. Now of those things that are moved by an intrinsic principle, some move themselves, some not. For since every agent or thing moved acts or is moved for an end, as was stated above,[7] those are perfectly moved by an intrinsic principle whose intrinsic principle is one not only of movement but of movement for an end. Now in order that a thing be done for an end, some knowledge of the end is necessary. Therefore, whatever so acts or is so moved by an intrinsic principle that it has some knowledge of the end, has within itself the principle of its act, so that it not only acts, but acts for an end. On the other hand, if a thing has no knowledge of the end, even though it have an intrinsic principle of action or movement, nevertheless, the principle of acting or being moved for an end is not in that thing, but in something else, by which the principle of its action towards an end is imprinted on it. Therefore such things are not said to move themselves, but to be moved by others. But those things which have a knowledge of the end are said to move themselves because there is in them a principle by which they not only act but also act for an end. And, consequently, since both are from an intrinsic principle, *i.e.,* that they act and that they act for an end, the movements and acts of such things are said to be voluntary; for the term *voluntary* signifies that their movements and acts are from their own inclination. Hence it is that, according to the definitions of Aristotle,[8] Gregory of Nyssa[9] and Damascene,[10] the voluntary is

From *Introduction to St. Thomas Aquinas,* ed. with an introduction by Anton C. Pegis (Random House, Inc., 1948). Reprinted by permission of the estate of Anton C. Pegis.

defined not only as having *a principle within* the agent, but also as implying *knowledge*. Therefore, since man especially knows the end of his work, and moves himself, in his acts especially is the voluntary to be found.

Reply Obj. 1. Not every principle is a first principle. Therefore, although it is of the nature of the voluntary act that its principle be within the agent, nevertheless, it is not contrary to the nature of the voluntary act that this intrinsic principle be caused or moved by an extrinsic principle; for it is not of the nature of the voluntary act that its intrinsic principle be a first principle.—Nevertheless, it must be observed that a principle of movement may happen to be first in a genus, but not first absolutely. Thus, in the genus of things subject to alteration, the first principle of alteration is the body of the heavens, which nevertheless is not the first mover absolutely, but is moved locally by a higher mover. And so the intrinsic principle of the voluntary act, *i.e.,* the cognitive and appetitive power, is the first principle in the genus of appetitive movement, although it is moved by an extrinsic principle according to other species of movement.

Reply Obj. 2. New movements in animals are indeed preceded by a motion from without; and this in two respects. First, in so far as by means of an extrinsic motion an animal's senses are confronted with something sensible, which, on being apprehended, moves the appetite. Thus a lion, on seeing the approach of the stag through its movement, begins to be moved towards the stag.—Secondly, in so far as some extrinsic motion produces a physical change in an animal's body, for example, through cold or heat; and when the body is thus affected by the motion of an exterior body, the sensitive appetite likewise, which is the power of a bodily organ, is moved accidentally. Thus, it happens that through some alteration in the body the appetite is roused to the desire of something. But this is not contrary to the nature of voluntariness, as was stated above, for such movements caused by an extrinsic principle are of another genus of movement.

Reply Obj. 3. God moves man to act, not only by proposing the appetible to the senses, or by effecting a change in his body, but also by moving the will itself; for every movement both of the will and of nature proceeds from God as the First Mover. And just as it is not incompatible with nature that the movement of nature be from God as the First Mover, inasmuch as nature is an instrument of God moving it, so it is not contrary to the character of a voluntary act that it proceed from God, inasmuch as the will is moved by God. Nevertheless, both natural and voluntary movements have this in common, that it belongs to the nature of both that they should proceed from a principle within the agent.

Endnotes

[1] Cf. Nemesius, *De Nat. Hom.,* XXXII (PG 40, 728).

[2] *De Fide Orth.,* II, 24 (PG 94, 953).

[3] *Eth.,* III, 1 (1111a 23).

[4] Aristotle, *De An.,* III, 10 (433b 11).

[5] *Phys.,* VIII, 2 (253a 11).

[6] *De Fide Orth.,* II, 24 (PG 94, 953).

[7] Q. 1, a. 2.

[8] *Eth.,* III, 1 (1111a 23).

[9] Cf. Nemesius, *De Nat. Hom.,* XXXII (PG 40, 728).

[10] *De Fide Orth.,* II, 24 (PG 94, 953).

38. *God's Foreknowledge and Human Freedom*

ST. AUGUSTINE

Augustine considers the question Does God's knowledge of what people will do make their choices illusory? Many theists want to answer no since the existence of free will is required by some religious tenets (for example, Why would God punish Adam and Eve if they were not free?). Accordingly, Augustine argues that foreknowledge and human freedom are compatible. He does so by claiming that if God knows one freely chooses to perform a certain action, then one must indeed choose freely. Thus, what one does is the basis for God's knowledge rather than the other way around.

God's Foreknowledge Does Not Exclude Man's Freedom in Sinning

AUGUSTINE:

Surely this is the question that troubles and perplexes you: how can the following two propositions, that [1] God has foreknowledge of all future events, and that [2] we do not sin by necessity but by free will, be made consistent with each other? "If God foreknows that man will sin," you say, "it is necessary that man sin." If man must sin, his sin is not a result of the will's choice, but is instead a fixed and inevitable necessity. You fear now that this reasoning results either in the blasphemous denial of God's foreknowledge or, if we deny this, the admission that we sin by necessity, not by will. Or does some other point bother you?

ERODINS:

No, nothing else right now.

A:

You think that all things of which God has foreknowledge come about by necessity, and not by will?

E:

Absolutely.

A:

Now pay careful attention. Look at yourself a little and tell me this, if you can: how are you going to will tomorrow, to sin or to act rightly?

E:

I do not know.

A:

Do you think that God does not know either?

E:

Of course I do not.

A:

If God knows what you are going to will tomorrow and foresees how all men who exist now or will exist are going to will in the future, He foresees much more what He will do about just men and about wicked ones.

E:

Yes. If God foreknows my deeds, I would say much more confidently that He foreknows His own deeds and foresees most certainly what He will do.

A:

If everything of which God has foreknowledge happens, not by will, but by necessity, shouldn't you be careful lest you say that God does what He is going to do by necessity too, and not by will?

E:

When I said that everything that God foreknows happens by necessity, I meant only those things which occur in His creation, not what occurs in Himself, since these latter are eternal.

A:

By this reasoning, God is not involved in His own creation.

E:

He has decided once and for all how the order of the universe He created is to be carried out, and does not arrange anything by a new act of will.

A:

Does He not make anyone happy?

E:

Yes, He does.

A:

Then He is responsible when someone becomes happy.

E:

Yes.

A:

If, then, for example, you are to be happy a year from now, He will make you happy a year from now.

E:

Yes.

A:

Therefore, God foreknows today what He will do in a year.

E:

He has always foreknown this. I also agree that He also foreknows it now if it is going to be so.

A:

Please tell me: it is not the case, is it, that you are not His creature? Won't your happiness occur in you?

E:

Of course! I am His creature and my happiness will occur in me.

A:

Therefore, your happiness will come about in you, not by will, but by the necessity of God's action.

E:

God's will is my necessity.

A:

So you will be happy against your will!

E:

Had I the power to be happy, I would surely be happy now. I wish to be happy now, and am not, because it is God, not I, who makes me happy.

A:

How clearly truth cries out from you! For you could not maintain that anything is in our power except actions that are subject to our own will. Therefore, nothing is so completely in our power as the will itself, for it is ready at hand to act immediately, as soon as we will. Thus we are right in saying that we grow old by necessity, not by will; or that we die by necessity, not by will, and so on. Who but a madman would say that we do not will with the will?

Therefore, though God foreknows what we shall will in the future, this does not prove that we do not will anything voluntarily. In regard to happiness, you said (as if I would deny it) that you do not make yourself happy. I say, however, that when you are to be happy, you shall not be happy against your will, but because you will to be happy. When, therefore, God foreknows that you will be happy, it cannot be otherwise, or else there would be no such thing as foreknowledge. Nevertheless, we are not forced to believe, as a consequence of this, that you are going to be happy when you do not want to be. This is absurd and far from the truth. Moreover, just as God's foreknowledge, which today is certain of tomorrow's happiness, does not take from you the will to be happy when you begin to be happy; in the same way, a will which deserves blame, if it is going to be blameworthy, will nonetheless remain a will, since God foreknew that it would be so.

See, please, how blindly a man says, "If God has foreknown my will, it is necessary that I will what God foreknows, since nothing can occur except as he has foreknown it. If, moreover, my act of will is subject to necessity, we must admit that I willed it not by will, but by necessity." Strange foolishness! How could it be that nothing happens otherwise than as God foreknew, if He foreknows that something is going to be willed when nothing is going to be willed? I pass over the equally astounding assertion that I just said this man makes: "It is necessary that I will in this way." By assuming necessity, he tries to exclude will. If it is necessary that he will, how can he will, if there is no will?

If he says, in another way, that since it is necessary that he will, this very will is not in his power, he is to be answered with what I just said when I asked whether you would be happy without willing it. You answered that you would be happy if it were in your power to be happy, and that you wanted to, but were not yet able. Then I interposed that the truth had cried out from you because we cannot deny that we have the power, unless we cannot obtain what we will through an act of will or unless the will is absent. When we will, if the will itself is lacking in us, we surely do not will. If it cannot happen that when we will we do not will, then the will is present in the one who wills. And nothing else is in our power except what is present to us when we will. Our will, therefore, is not a will unless it is in our power. And since it is indeed in our power, it is free in us. What we do not, or cannot, have in our power is not free for us. So it follows that we do not deny that God has foreknowledge of all things to be, and yet that we will what we will. For when He has foreknowledge of our will, it is going to be the will that He has foreknown. Therefore, the will is going to be a will because God has foreknowledge of it. Nor can it be a will if it is not in our power. Therefore, God also has knowledge of our power over it. So the power is not taken from me by His foreknowledge; but because of His foreknowledge, the power to will will more certainly be present in me, since God, whose foreknowledge does not err, has foreknown that I shall have the power.

E:
I no longer deny that whatever God foreknows must come to be, and that he foreknows our sins in such a way that our will still remains free in us and lies in our power.

God's Knowledge That Man Will Sin Is Not the Cause of Sin. Hence Punishment for Sin Is Just

A:
What is it, then, that bothers you? Have you perhaps forgotten what our first argument accomplished? Will you deny that we sin by will and not under compulsion from anyone, either higher, lower, or equal?

E:
Of course I do not dare deny any of these points. Yet I still cannot see how God's foreknowledge of our sins can be reconciled with our free choice in sinning. God must, we admit, be just and have foreknowledge. But I would like to know by what justice God punishes sins which must be; or how it is that they do not have to be, when He foreknows that they will be; or why anything which is necessarily done in His creation is not to be attributed to the Creator.

A:
Why do you think that our free choice is opposed to God's foreknowledge? Is it simply because it is foreknowledge or, rather, because it is God's foreknowledge?

E:
Because it is God's.

A:
If you foreknew that someone was going to sin, would it not be necessary for him to sin?

E:
Yes, he would have to sin, for my foreknowledge would not be genuine unless I foreknew what was certain.

A:
Then it is not because it is God's foreknowledge that what He foreknew had to happen, but only because it is foreknowledge. It is not foreknowledge if it does not foreknow what is certain.

E:
I agree. But why are you making these points?

A:
Because unless I am mistaken, your foreknowledge that a man will sin does not of itself necessitate the sin. Your foreknowledge did not force him to sin even though he was, without doubt, going to sin; otherwise you would not foreknow that which was to be. Thus, these two things are not contradictories. As you, by your foreknowledge, know what someone else is going to do of his own will, so God forces no one to sin; yet He foreknows those who will sin by their own will.

Why cannot He justly punish what He does not force to be done, even though He foreknows it? Your recollection of events in the past does not compel them to occur. In the same way God's foreknowledge of future events does not compel them to take place. As you remember certain things that you have done and yet have not done all the things that you remember, so God foreknows all the things of which He Himself is the Cause, and yet He is not the Cause of all that He foreknows. He is not the evil cause of these acts, though He justly avenges them. You may understand from this, therefore, how justly God punishes sins; for He does not do the things which He knows will happen. Besides, if He ought not to exact punishment from sinners because He foresees that they will sin, He ought not to reward those who act rightly, since in the same way He foresees that they will act rightly. On the contrary, let us acknowledge both that it is proper to His foreknowledge that nothing should escape His notice and that it is proper to His justice that a sin, since it is committed voluntarily, should not go unpunished by His judgment, just as it was not forced to be committed by His foreknowledge.

---

39. *Predestination, Divine Foreknowledge, and Human Freedom*

WILLIAM L. ROWE

There are two problems William Rowe, professor of philosophy at Purdue University, addresses in his essay. The first concerns understanding how God could have *ordained* for all eternity what comes to pass, including one's choices; and, at the same time, believing choices are freely chosen. The second problem concerns the conflict between freedom and God's *knowing* from eternity what one will do. Rowe considers various classical solutions to these problems and shows how each of them hinges on definite conceptions of freedom and eternity.

Human Freedom and Divine Predestination

As a seventeen-year-old convert to a quite orthodox branch of Protestantism, the first theological problem to concern me was the question of Divine Predestination and Human Freedom. Somewhere I read the following line from the Westminster Confession: "God from all eternity did . . . freely and unchangeably ordain whatsoever comes to pass." In many ways I was attracted to this idea. It seemed to express the majesty and power of God over all that he had created. It also led me to take an optimistic view of events in my own life and the lives of others, events which struck me as bad or unfortunate. For I now viewed them as planned by God before the creation of the world—thus they must serve some good purpose unknown to me. My own conversion, I reasoned, must also have been ordained to happen, just as the failure of others to be converted must have been similarly ordained. But at this point in my reflections, I hit upon a difficulty, a difficulty that made me think harder than I ever had before in my life. For I also believed that I had chosen God out of my own free will, that each of us is responsible for choosing or rejecting God's way. But how could I be responsible for a choice which, from eternity, God had ordained I would make at that particular moment in my life? How can it be that those who reject God's way do so of their own free will, if God, from eternity, destined them to reject his way? The Westminster Confession itself seemed to

From William L. Rowe, *Philosophy of Religion: An Introduction*, pp. 154–69. Copyright © 1978 by Dickenson Publishing Company, Inc. Reprinted by permission of Wadsworth, Inc.

recognize the difficulty. For its next line read: "Yet . . . thereby is no violence offered to the will of the creatures."

For a time I accepted both Divine Predestination and human freedom and responsibility. I felt that although I could not see how both could be true, they, nevertheless, might both be true, so I accepted them both on faith. But the longer I thought about it the more it seemed to me that they couldn't both be true. That is, I came to the view, rightly or wrongly, that I not only could not see how both could be true, I *could see* that they could not both be true. Slowly I abandoned the belief that before eternity God ordained whatever comes to pass. I took the view, instead, that before eternity God knew whatever comes to pass, including our free choices and acts, but that those choices and acts were not determined in advance.

What I did not know in those early years was that the topics of Predestination, Divine Foreknowledge and Human Freedom had been the focus of philosophical and theological reflection for centuries. In this chapter we shall acquaint ourselves with the various views that have emerged from those centuries of intellectual endeavor, thus enlarging our understanding of the theistic concept of God and one of the problems that has emerged in connection with it.

Freedom of Will or Choice

Perhaps it's best to begin with the idea of human freedom. For, as we shall see, there are two quite different ways in which this idea has been understood, and which way we follow makes a great deal of difference to the topic under consideration. According to the first idea, *acting freely consists in doing what you want or choose to do*. If you want to leave the room but are forcibly restrained from doing so, we certainly would agree that *staying in the room* is not something you do freely. You do not freely stay in the room because it is not what you choose or want to do, it happens against your will.

Suppose we accept this first idea of human freedom, whereby acting freely consists in doing what you want or choose to do. The problem of divine predestination and human freedom will then turn out to be not much of a problem at all. Why so? Well, to take the example of my youthful

conversion, my conversion was free if it was something I wanted to do, chose to do, did not do against my will. Let's suppose, as I believe is true, that my conversion was something I chose to do, wanted to do. Is there any difficulty in believing also that before eternity God ordained that at that particular moment in my life I would be converted? It doesn't seem that there is. For God could simply have ordained also that at that particular moment in my life I would *want* to choose Christ, to follow God's way. If so, then, on our first idea of human freedom, my act of conversion was both a free act on my part and ordained by God from eternity. On our first idea of human freedom, then, there does not seem to be any real conflict between the doctrine of divine predestination and human freedom. Is our first idea of human freedom correct? One reason for thinking that it is not was provided by the English philosopher John Locke (1632–1704). Locke asks us to suppose that a man is brought into a room while asleep. The door, which is the only way out of the room, is then securely bolted from the outside. The man does not know that the door is bolted, does not know, therefore, that he *cannot* leave the room. He awakens, finds himself in the room, looks about and notices that there are friendly people in the room with whom he would like to converse. Accordingly, he decides to stay in the room rather than leave.[1]

What are we to say of this man? Is his act *staying in the room* something he does *freely*? Well, according to our first idea of human freedom, it would seem that it is. For staying in the room is what he wants to do. He considers leaving, not knowing that he cannot leave, but rejects it because he prefers to stay in the room and engage in friendly conversation. But can we really believe that staying in the room is something he does *freely*? After all, it is the only thing that can be done. He stays in the room of *necessity*, for leaving the room is something that is not in his power to do. What is the difference between him and a second man, similarly placed, who wants to leave, but being unable to leave, also stays in the room of necessity? Is the difference that the first man does something freely, whereas, the second man does not? Or is it, rather, that the first man is just more *fortunate* than the second? Each does what he does (stay in the room) of necessity, not freely, but the first man is more fortunate in that what he *must do* turns out to be the very thing that he wants to do. Locke concludes that the first man is not more free than the second, only more fortunate. For freedom, Locke contends, consists in more than simply doing what one wants or chooses, it also must be that *it was in one's power to do otherwise*. And the reason why the first man, no less than the second, did not stay in the room freely is because it was not in his power to do otherwise, to leave the room.

The Power to Do Otherwise

The second idea of human freedom is that we do something freely only if, at the time just before we do it, it is in our power to do otherwise. And I think that on reflection we can see that the second idea is more adequate than the first. Consider, for example, growing old. This is something we do of necessity, not freely. The mere fact that someone prefers to grow old, wants to grow old, is not sufficient for it being true that he or she grows old *freely*—at best we might say that he or she grows old gracefully. Suppose, however, a process is discovered and made available whereby each of us has the power not to grow old in the sense of physical aging. Although time continues to pass, the aging process in our bodies can now be slowed enormously. Under these conditions it could be true that someone grows old freely, for one would not then grow old of necessity, it being in a person's power to do otherwise. The first idea of freedom must be abandoned in favor of the second, more adequate idea.

It is the second idea of freedom that appears to be in conflict with the idea of divine predestination. For if God has determined, from eternity, that I will be converted at a certain moment on a particular day, how can it be in my power just prior to that moment to refrain from being converted? To ascribe such a power to me is to ascribe to me the power to prevent from taking place something that God from eternity has ordained to take place. Surely if from eternity God has determined that something will happen it cannot be in some creature's power to prevent that thing from taking place. Therefore, if from eternity God did ordain whatever comes to pass then there is noth-

ing that happens which we could have prevented from happening. So, since whatever I do has been ordained by God to take place, it is never in my power to do otherwise. And if it is never in my power to do otherwise, then nothing I do is done freely. Human freedom, it seems, is inconsistent with divine predestination.

If the above argument is correct, as I'm inclined to believe it is, the theist must either abandon the belief in human freedom or the doctrine of divine predestination. And it seems reasonable that between the two, the doctrine of divine predestination should be given its walking papers. That God has *ultimate control* over the destiny of his creation and that he *knows* in advance of its happening everything that will happen are ideas that preserve the majesty of God and provide for some degree of human optimism, without requiring that God has *decreed* to happen whatever does happen. And on the surface at least, it does not appear that the doctrine of divine foreknowledge conflicts with human freedom. So perhaps the reasonable thing to do is to reject the doctrine of divine predestination, while preserving the belief in human freedom and the doctrine of divine foreknowledge.

The Conflict between Human Freedom and Divine Foreknowledge

But if God has not ordained from eternity everything that will happen, how is it possible for him to have known from eternity everything that happens? Doesn't the doctrine of divine foreknowledge presuppose the doctrine of divine predestination? Having decreed that something will happen at a certain time would be a way in which God could know in advance that it will happen. But it is not the only way in which God might have possessed such knowledge. We possess telescopes, for example, that enable us to know what is happening at places some distance away, because by means of the telescope we can see them happening. Imagine that God has something like a *time* telescope, a telescope that enables one to see what is happening at times some distance away. By turning the lens one focuses on a certain time, say a thousand years from now, and sees the events that are occurring at that time. With some such image as this we might account for God's foreknowledge without supposing that his knowledge is derived from his prior decree that the events in question will occur. He knows in advance the events that will take place by *foreseeing* them, not by *foreordaining* them. The doctrine of divine foreknowledge, then, does not presuppose the doctrine of divine predestination. And, as we noted earlier, there does not appear to be any conflict between divine foreknowledge and human freedom. For although God's *foreordaining* something makes that something happen, his *foreknowing* does not make it happen. Things occur not because God foreknows them; rather, he foreknows them because they occur.

Unfortunately, things are not so simple as that. There is a serious problem about divine foreknowledge and human freedom. And although we may not be able to solve this problem, it will be instructive to try to understand the problem and see what the various "solutions" are that have been advanced by important philosophers and theologians. Perhaps the best way to start is by stating the problem in the form of an argument, an argument that begins with the doctrine of divine foreknowledge and ends with the denial of human freedom. Once we understand the major premises of the argument, as well as the reasons given in support of them, we will have come to an understanding of one of the major problems theologians have wrestled with for almost two thousand years: the problem of reconciling the doctrine of divine foreknowledge with the belief in human freedom.

1. God knows before we are born everything we will do.

2. If God knows before we are born everything we will do, then it is never in our power to do otherwise.

3. If it is never in our power to do otherwise, then there is no human freedom.

Therefore,

4. There is no human freedom.

The first premise of the argument expresses an apparent implication of the doctrine of divine foreknowledge. The third premise simply states an implication of the second idea of freedom we considered earlier. According to that idea, we do something freely only if, at the time just before we do it, it is in our power to do otherwise. Thus, we concluded that the act of staying in the room was freely done only if, at the time of the decision to stay in the room, it was in the person's power to do otherwise, that is, to leave the room. Since the door was securely bolted from the outside, we concluded that he did not *freely* stay in the room. Now premise (3) merely draws the logical conclusion from this second idea of freedom: if it is *never* in our (any human being's) power to do otherwise, then there is no human freedom. Since the argument is clearly valid, the remaining question concerns premise (2): if God knows before we are born everything we will do then it is never in our power to do otherwise. Why should we accept this premise? Clearly if we replaced the word "knows" with the word "ordains" the statement would be true. But the whole point of abandoning divine predestination in favor of divine foreknowledge was that although (a) if God *ordains* before we are born everything we will do, then it is never in our power to do otherwise, seems surely true, it does not seem to be true that (b) if God *knows* before we are born everything we will do then it is never in our power to do otherwise. Since premise 2 is the same as b why should we now accept it as true? What is the reasoning by which the proponent of this argument hopes to convince us that 2 is true?

The reasoning in support of 2 is complex, so it will be best to develop it by means of an example. Let's suppose it is 2:00 p.m. on a particular Tuesday and that you have a class in philosophy of religion that meets at 2:30. Your friends ask you to go with them to an afternoon movie, but, after considering the proposal, you somehow manage to resist temptation, and elect to attend class instead. It is now 2:45 and your instructor is carrying on about foreknowledge and free will. Somewhat bored, you now wish that you had gone to the movie instead of coming to class. You realize, however, that although you now regret your decision there is nothing that you can do about it. Of course, you could get up from your seat and rush off to see what is left of the movie. But you cannot now, at 2:45, bring it about that you did not go to class at 2:30, you cannot *now* bring it about that you actually went to the movie instead. You can regret what you did, and resolve never to make that mistake again, but, like it or not, you are stuck with the fact that instead of going to the movie you went to class at 2:30. You are stuck with it because it is a *fact about the past* and you cannot *alter the past*. Our inability to alter the past is enshrined in the colloquialism, "There's no use crying over spilt milk." Within limits, however, the future seems open, pliable; we can make it to be one way or another. You believe, for example, that on Thursday, when the class meets again, it will be in your power to go to class and it will be in your power to go to a movie instead. But the past is not open, it is closed, solid like granite, and in no way within your power to alter. As Aristotle observed:

> No one deliberates about the past but only about what is future and capable of being otherwise, while what is past is not capable of not having taken place; hence Agathon is right in saying: "For this alone is lacking, even in God, to make undone things that have once been done."[2]

There are, of course, a large number of facts about the past relative to 2:45 on Tuesday. In addition to the fact that at 2:30 you came to class, there is the fact of your birth, the fact that you became a college student, the fact that Nixon resigned from the Presidency, indeed, all the facts of past history. And what you now know is that at 2:45 it is not in your power to alter *any* of them. There is nothing that is now in your power to do such that were you to do it any of these facts about the past would not have been facts about the past. Pondering your powerlessness over the past, you notice that your instructor has written on the board another fact about the past:

> F. Before you were born God knew that you would come to class at 2:30 this Tuesday.

If God exists and the doctrine of divine foreknowledge is true, F is certainly a fact about the past, and it has been a fact about the past at every moment of your life. It is a fact about the past *now*—at 2:45 on Tuesday—it was a fact about the past *yesterday*, and it will be a fact about the past *tomorrow*. At this point your instructor turns and asks: "Was it in your power at 2:00 to have refrained from coming to class today?" You cer-

tainly think that it was—indeed, you now regret that you did not exercise that power—so the instructor writes on the board:

> A. It was in your power at 2:00 to do something other than come to class at 2:30 this Tuesday.

But now let's think for a bit about F and A. At 2:00, F was a fact about the past. But according to A, it was in your power at 2:00 to do something (go to a movie, say) such that had you done it, what is a fact about the past (F) would not have been a fact about the past. For, clearly, if you had *exercised* your power to refrain from coming to class at 2:30 what God would have known before you were born is not what he in fact knew, that you would come to class this Tuesday, but something quite different, that you would do something else. And this in turn means that if F is a fact about the past—as it surely is if the doctrine of divine foreknowledge is true—and if A is true, then it was in your power at 2:00 this Tuesday to *alter the past*; it was in your power to do something (go to a movie) such that had you done it, what *is* a fact about the past (F) would not have been a fact about the past. If then, *it is never in our power to alter a fact about the past*, it cannot be both that F was a fact about the past and also that it was in your power at 2:00 to refrain from coming to class at 2:30 this Tuesday.

What we have just seen is that given the doctrine of divine foreknowledge and the claim that it is in our power to have done something we did not do, it follows that it was in our power to have altered the past. For given the doctrine of divine foreknowledge it follows that *before you were born* God knew that you would come to class at 2:30 this Tuesday. And if we now claim that *at 2:00* it was in your power to have done otherwise, we imply that at 2:00 it was in your power to alter a fact about the past, the fact that before you were born God knew that you would come to class at 2:30. But we earlier concluded that we are powerless over the past, that facts about the past are not within our power to alter. If we keep to this conviction—as it seems we must—then we must conclude that if God did know before you were born that you would be in class at 2:30 (this Tuesday) then it was *not* in your power at 2:00 to do otherwise. And generalizing from this particular example, we can conclude that if it is never in our power to alter the past, then if God knows before we are born everything we will do then it is never in our power to do otherwise.

We have worked our way through the rather complex reasoning that can be used to support premise 2 of the argument designed to show a conflict between divine foreknowledge and human freedom. That premise, as you recall, says that if God knows before we are born everything we will do then it is never in our power to do otherwise. Reduced to its simplest terms, the reasoning given in support of 2 consists in arguing that if 2 is not true then it is in our power to alter the past. But it is never in our power to alter the past, so 2 must be true. From (i) God knows before we are born everything we will do, and (ii) it is sometimes in our power to do otherwise it follows, so the reasoning goes, that it is sometimes in our power to alter the past. Since it is never in our power to alter the past, premises i and ii can't both be true. Hence, if i is true then ii is false. But to say that it is false is just to say that it is *never* in our power to do otherwise. So if i is true then it is *never* in our power to do otherwise—and this is exactly what premise 2 says.

Some Solutions to the Conflict

We've had a look at perhaps the strongest argument for the view that the doctrine of divine foreknowledge, no less than the doctrine of divine predestination, is in fundamental conflict with the belief in human freedom, an argument that has troubled philosophers and theologians for centuries. It is now time to consider the various "solutions" that have been offered and to assess their strengths and weaknesses.

The argument itself limits the number of possible solutions that can be advanced to the following four:

I. *Rejection of premise 3:* denies that we do something freely only if it is in our power to do otherwise.

II. *Rejection of premise 2:* denies that divine foreknowledge implies that it is never in our power to do otherwise.

III. *Rejection of premise 1:* denies that God has foreknowledge of future events.

IV. *Acceptance of the conclusion 4:* denies that we have human freedom.

Solutions III and IV are "radical" solutions since they amount to a denial either of the doctrine of divine foreknowledge or of human freedom. No theist seriously proposes IV, so we may safely dismiss it. III, however, as we shall see, is the solution preferred by a number of important theologians, including Boethius and Aquinas. Let's consider, then, the first three solutions to this perplexing problem.

The Definition of Freedom

The first solution rejects premise 3 of the argument, charging that 3 expresses a mistaken idea of human freedom. As we saw earlier, there are two different ideas of freedom. According to the first idea, acting freely consists in no more than doing what you want or choose to do; freedom does not require the power to do otherwise. Those who accept this idea of human freedom rightly see no conflict between it and divine foreknowledge. Indeed, as we noted earlier, there is no conflict between this idea of human freedom and the doctrine of divine predestination. A solution along these lines was developed most fully by the American theologian, Jonathan Edwards (1703–58). The adequacy of this solution depends entirely on whether its idea of what human freedom consists in can be defended against the criticisms philosophers have advanced against it.[3] However, having rejected this idea of freedom in favor of the second idea—the idea that we do something freely only if it is in our power to do otherwise—we shall not pursue further this first solution to the problem of divine foreknowledge and human freedom. For given the second idea of human freedom, premise 3 must be accepted as true.

Power to Alter the Past

The second major solution rejects premise 2, thereby denying that divine foreknowledge implies that it is never in our power to do otherwise. Actually, what this solution shows, if successful, is not that 2 is false, but that the reasoning given in support of it is mistaken. What is that reasoning? Well, reduced to its briefest terms, the reasoning is that if 2 is not true then it is in our power to alter facts about the past—facts about what God knew before we were even born. But, so the reasoning goes, it is never in anyone's power to alter the past, therefore 2 must be true. The second solution challenges the claim that it is never in our power to alter the past, arguing that we do have the power to alter certain facts about the past, including certain facts about what God knew before we were even born. This solution was suggested by the most influential philosopher of the fourteenth century, William of Ockham (1285–1349).

The basic point on which the second solution rests involves a distinction between two types of facts about the past: facts which are *simply* about the past, and facts which are *not simply* about the past. To illustrate this distinction, let's consider two facts about the past, facts about the year 1941.

f_1: In 1941 Japan attacks Pearl Harbor.
f_2: In 1941 a war begins between Japan and the United States that lasts five years.

Relative of 1976, f_1 and f_2 are both *simply* about the past. But suppose we consider the year 1943. Relative to 1943, f_1 is a fact that is simply about the past, but f_2 is not simply about the past; f_2 is a fact about the past relative to 1943, for f_2 is, in part, a fact about 1941, and 1941 lies in 1943's past. But f_2, unlike f_1, implies a certain fact about 1944; namely.

f_3: In 1944 Japan and the United States are at war.

Since f_2 implies f_3, a fact about the future relative to 1943, we can say that relative to 1943 f_2 is a fact about the past, but not simply a fact about the past. We have then three facts, f_1, f_2, and f_3, about which we can say that relative to the twenty-first century each is a fact simply about the past. Relative to 1943, however, only f_1 is simply about the past, f_2 is about the past but not simply about the past, and f_3 is not about the past at all.

Having illustrated the distinction between a fact which, relative to a certain time t, is simply about the past and a fact which, relative to t, is not simply about the past, we are now in a position to appreciate its importance. Think of 1943 and the

groups of persons then in power in both Japan and the United States. Neither group had it in its power to do anything about f_1. Both groups may have regretted the actions which brought it about that f_1 is a fact about the past. But it is abundantly clear that among all the things which, in 1943, it was in their power to do, none is such that had they done it, f_1 would not have been a fact about the past. It makes no sense to look back upon *1943* and say that if only one of these groups had then done such-and-such, f_1 would never have been a fact about the past. It makes no sense precisely because, relative to 1943, f_1 is a fact *simply* about the past. Nothing that could have been done by anyone in 1943 would have in any way altered the fact that in 1941 Japan attacked Pearl Harbor.

But what about f_2, the fact that in 1941 a war begins between Japan and the United States that lasts five years. We know that in 1943 neither group did anything that altered this fact about 1941. The question, however, is whether there were things that were not done in 1943, things which, nevertheless, were in the power of one or both of the groups to do, and which, had they been done, a certain fact about 1941, f_2, would not have been a fact at all. Perhaps there were not. Perhaps the momentum of the war was such that neither group had the power to bring it to an end in 1943. Most of us, I suppose, think otherwise. We think that there probably were certain actions that were not, but could have been, taken by one or both of the groups in 1943, actions which had they been taken would have brought the war to an end in 1943. If what we think to be so is so, then it was in the power of one or both of the groups in 1943 to alter a fact about the past; it was in their power in 1943 to do something such that had they done it a certain fact about 1941, f_2, would not have been a fact about 1941. The basic reason why in 1943 f_2 may have been in their power to alter, whereas f_1 certainly was not, is that, unlike f_1, f_2 is not simply about the past relative to 1943, for f_2 implies a certain fact about 1944, that in 1944, Japan and the United States are at war (f_3).

What the above reasoning suggests is that our conviction that the past is beyond our power to affect is certainly true, so far as facts which are simply about the past are concerned. Facts which are about the past, but *not simply* about the past, may not, however, be beyond our power to affect. And what Ockham saw is that the facts about divine foreknowledge which are used as the basis for denying human freedom are facts about the past, but *not simply* about the past. Consider again the fact that before you were born, God knew that you would be in class at 2:30 this Tuesday. We want to believe that at 2:00 it was in your power to do otherwise, to refrain from coming to class at 2:30. To ascribe this power to you implies that it was in your power at 2:00 to alter a fact about the past, the fact that before you were born God knew that you would be in class at 2:30. This fact about the past, however, is not, relative to 2:00, a fact simply about the past. For it implies a fact about the future relative to 2:00, namely, that at 2:30 you are in class. And the solution we are exploring holds that such a fact about the past was in your power to alter if it was in your power at 2:00, as we believe it was, to have gone to a movie instead of coming to class. For it was then in your power to have done something such that had you done it what *is* a fact about a time before you were born *would not have been* a fact at all—instead it would have been a fact that before you were born God knew that you would not be in class at 2:30. Of course, there will still be many facts about God's foreknowledge that are not in your power to alter: all those facts, for example, that relative to the time you are at, are facts simply about the past. The very fact which may have been in your power to alter at 2:00—the fact that before you were born God knew you would be in class at 2:30—is, at 2:45 when you are sitting in class regretting that you did not go to a movie, a fact that cannot *then* (at 2:45) be altered, because at 2:45 it is a fact simply about the past. And there are many facts involving divine foreknowledge that are not simply about the past, which, nevertheless, are not in your power to alter, for the facts that they imply about the future do not fall within the scope of your power. For example, God knew before you were born that the sun would rise tomorrow. This fact about the past is not simply about the past because it implies a fact about tomorrow, that the sun will rise. It is nevertheless, a fact which is not in your power to alter.

We have been considering the second solution to the problem of divine foreknowledge and human freedom. As we saw, this solution consists in denying the reasoning supporting the second premise of the argument by means of which the problem was developed, the premise stating that if God knows before we are born everything we will do it is never in our power to do otherwise. According to the reasoning in support of this premise, given divine foreknowledge, it is in our power to do otherwise only if it is in our power to alter some fact about the past, a fact about what God knew before we were born. The solution we have been considering accepts this point in the reasoning given in support of premise 2, but denies the next point: that it is never in our power to alter the past. The solution argues that some facts about the past are not simply about the past, that some such facts may be within our power to alter, and that the facts about divine foreknowledge used in the reasoning for premise 2 are examples of such facts. So according to the second major solution, we have no good reasons for accepting the second premise of the argument leading from divine foreknowledge to the denial of human freedom. And without such reasons, it has yet to be shown that there is any real difficulty in holding both that God knows before we are born everything we will do and that we sometimes have the power to do otherwise. . . .

The Denial of Foreknowledge

The third and final solution we shall consider rejects premise 1 of the argument, thereby denying that God has foreknowledge of the future events. Earlier I called this a "radical" solution since, unlike the first two solutions, instead of trying to reconcile divine foreknowledge with human freedom, it appears to deny that there is any foreknowledge at all. But, as we shall see, this was the solution preferred by a number of important theologians within the western religious tradition.

There are two different forms of the third solution. According to the first form, statements about certain events in the future, events which might or might not happen, are neither true nor false; they become true (false) when the events they are about actually occur (don't occur). For example, the statement, "You will attend class at a certain hour on a certain day next week" is, on the view we are considering not now true, nor is it false. When next week comes and the hour of that particular day occurs, then the statement will become true if you attend class, and false if you do not. This view concerning statements about the future, a view often ascribed to Aristotle, has the consequence that God does not *now* know whether or not you will attend class at that hour next week, that God does not have foreknowledge of such future events. For knowledge is of what is *true,* and if statements about the future are neither true nor false, they cannot then be known.

The more widely accepted form of the third solution rests upon the idea that God is "eternal" in the second of the two senses introduced in chapter one. There we noted that to be eternal in the first sense is to have infinite duration in both temporal directions. To be eternal in the second sense, however, is to exist outside of time and, therefore, independent of the fundamental law of time according to which every being in time, even an everlasting being, has its life divided into temporal parts. As Boethius wrote:

> For whatever lives in time lives in the present, proceeding from past to future, and nothing is so constituted in time that it can embrace the whole span of its life at once. It has not yet arrived at tomorrow, and it has already lost yesterday; even the life of this day is lived only in each moving, passing moment.[4]

In contrast to things in time, God is viewed as having his infinite, endless life wholly present to himself, all at once. As such, God must be outside of time altogether. For, as we've just seen, whatever is in time has its life divided into temporal parts, only one of which can be present to it at any one time.

The idea that God is eternal in the sense of being outside of time has a direct bearing on the doctrine of divine foreknowledge. For the notion of *fore*knowledge naturally suggests that a being *located* at one point in time knows something that is to take place at some later point in time. Thus we speak of God knowing *at a time before you were born* what you would do at 2:30 this Tuesday. But if God is outside of time then we cannot say that he has a *fore*knowledge of future events, if to do so implies he is located at some point in time and at that point knows what will take place at some *later*

point in time. According to Boethius, Aquinas, and a number of other theologians who hold that God is eternal in the second sense, there is nothing that happens in time that is unknown to God. Every moment in time is ever *present* to God in just the way that what is happening at this particular moment within the field of our vision is present to us. God's knowledge of what to us is past and future is just like the knowledge that we may have of something that is happening in the present. Being above time, God takes in *all* time with one glance just as we who are in time may with a glance take in something that is happening in the present. Speaking of God's knowledge of what takes place in time, Boethius tells us:

> It encompasses the infinite sweep of past and future, and regards all things in its simple comprehension as if they were now taking place. Thus, if you will think about the foreknowledge by which God distinguishes all things, you will rightly consider it to be not a foreknowledge of future events, but knowledge of a never changing present. For this reason, divine foreknowledge is called providence, rather than prevision, because it resides above all inferior things and looks out on all things from their summit.[5]

According to Boethius, God does not, strictly speaking, have *fore*knowledge, for he is not in the position of knowing that something will occur *in advance* of its occurring. And yet God knows everything that has occurred, is occurring, and will occur. But he knows them in the way in which we know what occurs in the present. Perhaps we can clarify his position if we distinguish two senses of "foreknowledge," foreknowledge$_1$ and foreknowledge$_2$. A being foreknows$_1$ some event x, we shall say, provided that the being exists at a certain time *earlier* than when x occurs and knows at that time that x will occur at some later time. This is the sort of foreknowledge which God cannot have if he is eternal in the second sense, for he will not then exist at a certain moment of time, but will be completely outside of time. A being foreknows$_2$ some event x, we shall say, provided that the occurrence of x is *present* to that being but is such that its occurrence is at a moment later than the moment at which we (who are in time) *now* exist. Given that God is eternal in the second sense he cannot have foreknowledge$_1$ of any event, but this does not preclude his having a complete foreknowledge$_2$ of all those events which, from the position of those who exist in time, are yet to come.

We can now see how Boethius and Aquinas solve the problem of divine foreknowledge and human freedom. As we saw, the problem is that to assert both implies that it is sometimes in our power to alter a fact about the past, a fact about what God knew at a time before we were born. If we hold that it is never in our power to alter any fact about the past, it seems we must deny either divine foreknowledge or human freedom. What Boethius and Aquinas point out is that this is a genuine problem only if it is foreknowledge$_1$ that is being ascribed to God. For if God has foreknowledge$_1$, there will be facts about some past time which, if we have human freedom, would have to be within our power to alter. But according to them, we cannot ascribe foreknowledge$_1$ to God, for such ascription implies that God exists in time. God has foreknowledge$_2$ of everything that is yet to come to pass. But foreknowledge$_2$ does not imply that there is some fact about some past time. For God does not exist in time at all. His foreknowledge$_2$ of some event in time is really no different from the knowledge that your instructor had at 2:30 on Tuesday when she saw you entering the classroom. No one thinks that the knowledge obtained by seeing you come into the classroom takes away the power you had earlier to have done something else. Similarly God's foreknowledge$_2$, since it looks down from above time and sees what is future *in time,* but *present* from God's vantage point, imposes no necessity on what it sees. For there is no *past fact* involving God's knowledge which you would have had to alter if you had exercised your power to do otherwise.

In this chapter we have studied one of the ageless problems for theism, the problem of divine foreknowledge and human freedom, and considered in detail the principal solutions which have emerged in the centuries of reflection on the problem. Of the three solutions we've considered only the last two are tenable if, as I've suggested, the

first rests on an inadequate idea of human freedom. The last solution, based as it is on the idea that God exists outside of time, will suffer from any defects associated with that idea. Some philosophers have thought that the idea itself is incoherent, and others have argued that while the idea may be coherent, any being that is eternal in the sense of existing outside of time could never *act within time,* and, therefore, could not create a world or bring about a miracle—activities generally ascribed to the theistic God. We cannot, however, pursue these matters here.[6]

The second solution fits well with the idea that God is eternal in the first sense introduced in chapter one, eternal in the sense of being everlasting, having infinite duration in both temporal directions. On this view, foreknowledge is ascribed to God, but it is argued that insofar as we act freely we do have the power to alter some facts about the past. If both the second and third solutions are successful, then, whether God is held to be eternal in the first or second sense, the problem of divine foreknowledge and human freedom is not an insoluble problem for theism.

Endnotes

[1]John Locke, *An Essay Concerning Human Understanding,* Book II, Chapter XXI, paragraph 10, ed. Peter H. Nidditch (London: Oxford University Press, 1975), p. 238.

[2]Aristotle, *Nicomachean Ethics* VII, 2. 1139^b in *The Basic Works of Aristotle,* ed. Richard McKeon (New York: Random House, 1941).

[3]For a brilliant defense of the first idea of freedom, as well as a response to the objections raised against it, see Jonathan Edwards, *Freedom of the Will,* eds. A. S. Kaufman and W. K. Frankena (Indianapolis: The Bobbs-Merrill Co., 1969).

[4]Boethius, *The Consolation of Philosophy,* Prose VI, tr. Richard Green (New York: The Bobbs-Merrill Company, Inc., 1962).

[5]Boethius, *The Consolation of Philosophy,* Prose VI.

[6]For an excellent study of these problems see Nelson Pike, *God and Timelessness* (New York: Schocken Books Inc., 1970).

40. On Liberty and Necessity

DAVID HUME

In this classic discussion, Hume argues that the truth of causal determinism (what he calls "necessity") does not pose any threat to human freedom (what he calls "liberty"). Hume's position is called "soft determinism" or "compatibilism." According to Hume, all actions are caused, the difference between free and unfree action concerns simply whether or not one can act in accordance with one's will. In his discussion, Hume offers arguments for determinism and for the incompatibility of indeterminism and responsibility.

Part I

It might reasonably be expected, in questions which have been canvassed and disputed with great eagerness since the first origin of science and philosophy, that the meaning of all the terms, at least, should have been agreed upon among the disputants, and our inquiries, in the course of two thousand years, been able to pass from words to the true and real subject of the controversy. For how easy may it seem to give exact definitions of the terms employed in reasoning, and make these definitions, not the mere sound of words, the object of future scrutiny and examination? But if we consider the matter more narrowly, we shall be apt to draw a quite opposite conclusion. From this circumstance alone, that a controversy has been long kept on foot and remains still undecided, we may presume that there is some ambiguity in the expression, and that the disputants affix different ideas to the terms employed in the controversy. For as the faculties of the mind are supposed to be naturally alike in every individual—otherwise nothing could be more fruitless than to reason or dispute together—it were impossible, if men affix the same ideas to their terms, that they could so long form different opinions of the same subject, especially when they communicate their views and each party turn themselves on all sides in search of arguments which may give them the victory over

their antagonists. It is true, if men attempt the discussion of questions which lie entirely beyond the reach of human capacity, such as those concerning the origin of worlds or the economy of the intellectual system or region of spirits, they may long beat the air in their fruitless contests and never arrive at any determinate conclusion. But if the question regard any subject of common life and experience, nothing, one would think, could preserve the dispute so long undecided, but some ambiguous expressions which keep the antagonists still at a distance and hinder them from grappling with each other.

This has been the case in the long-disputed question concerning liberty and necessity, and to so remarkable a degree that, if I be not much mistaken, we shall find that all mankind, both learned and ignorant, have always been of the same opinion with regard to this subject, and that a few intelligible definitions would immediately have put an end to the whole controversy. I own that this dispute has been so much canvassed on all hands, and has led philosophers into such a labyrinth of obscure sophistry, that it is no wonder if a sensible reader indulge his ease so far as to turn a deaf ear to the proposal of such a question from which he can expect neither instruction nor entertainment. But the state of the argument here proposed may, perhaps, serve to renew his attention, as it has more novelty, promises at least some decision of the controversy, and will not much disturb his ease by any intricate or obscure reasoning.

I hope, therefore, to make it appear that all men have ever agreed in the doctrine both of

From David Hume, *An Inquiry Concerning Human Understanding*, Sec. 8. First published in 1748.

necessity and of liberty, according to any reasonable sense which can be put on these terms, and that the whole controversy has hitherto turned merely upon words. We shall begin with examining the doctrine of necessity.

It is universally allowed that matter, in all its operations, is actuated by a necessary force, and that every natural effect is so precisely determined by the energy of its cause that no other effect, in such particular circumstances, could possibly have resulted from it. The degree and direction of every motion is, by the laws of nature, prescribed with such exactness that a living creature may as soon arise from the shock of two bodies, as motion, in any other degree or direction than what is actually produced by it. Would we, therefore, form a just and precise idea of *necessity,* we must consider whence that idea arises when we apply it to the operation of bodies.

It seems evident that, if all the scenes of nature were continually shifted in such a manner that no two events bore any resemblance to each other, but every object was entirely new, without any similitude to whatever had been seen before, we should never, in that case, have attained the least idea of necessity or of a connection among these objects. We might say, upon such a supposition, that one object or event has followed another, not that one was produced by the other. The relation of cause and effect must be utterly unknown to mankind. Inference and reasoning concerning the operations of nature would, from that moment, be at an end; and the memory and senses remain the only canals by which the knowledge of any real existence could possibly have access to the mind. Our idea, therefore, of necessity and causation arises entirely from the uniformity observable in the operations of nature, where similar objects are constantly conjoined together, and the mind is determined by custom to infer the one from the appearance of the other. These two circumstances form the whole of that necessity which we ascribe to matter. Beyond the constant *conjunction* of similar objects and the consequent *inference* from one to the other, we have no notion of any necessity of connection.

If it appear, therefore, that all mankind have ever allowed, without any doubt or hesitation, that these two circumstances take place in the voluntary actions of men and in the operations of mind,

it must follow that all mankind have ever agreed in the doctrine of necessity, and that they have hitherto disputed merely for not understanding each other.

As to the first circumstance, the constant and regular conjunction of similar events, we may possibly satisfy ourselves by the following considerations. It is universally acknowledged that there is a great uniformity among the actions of men, in all nations and ages, and that human nature remains still the same in its principles and operations. The same motives always produce the same actions; the same events follow from the same causes. Ambition, avarice, self-love, vanity, friendship, generosity, public spirit—these passions, mixed in various degrees and distributed through society, have been, from the beginning of the world, and still are, the source of all the actions and enterprises which have ever been observed among mankind. Would you know the sentiments, inclinations, and course of life of the Greeks and Romans? Study well the temper and actions of the French and English: you cannot be much mistaken in transferring to the former *most* of the observations which you have made with regard to the latter. Mankind are so much the same, in all times and places, that history informs us of nothing new or strange in this particular. Its chief use is only to discover the constant and universal principles of human nature by showing men in all varieties of circumstances and situations, and furnishing us with materials from which we may form our observations and become acquainted with the regular springs of human action and behavior. These records of wars, intrigues, factions, and revolutions are so many collections of experiments by which the politician or moral philosopher fixes the principles of his science, in the same manner as the physician or natural philosopher becomes acquainted with the nature of plants, minerals, and other external objects, by the experiments which he forms concerning them. Nor are the earth, water, and other elements examined by Aristotle and Hippocrates more like to those which at present lie under our observation than the men described by Polybius and Tacitus are to those who now govern the world.

Should a traveler, returning from a far country, bring us an account of men wholly different from any with whom we were ever acquainted, men who were entirely divested of avarice, ambition, or revenge, who knew no pleasure but friendship, generosity, and public spirit, we should immediately, from these circumstances, detect the falsehood and prove him a liar with the same certainty as if he had stuffed his narration with stories of centaurs and dragons, miracles and prodigies. And if we would explode any forgery in history, we cannot make use of a more convincing argument than to prove that the actions ascribed to any person are directly contrary to the course of nature, and that no human motives, in such circumstances, could ever induce him to such a conduct. The veracity of Quintus Curtius is as much to be suspected when he describes the supernatural courage of Alexander by which he was hurried on singly to attack multitudes, as when he describes his supernatural force and activity by which he was able to resist them. So readily and universally do we acknowledge a uniformity in human motives and actions as well as in the operations of body.

Hence, likewise, the benefit of that experience acquired by long life and a variety of business and company, in order to instruct us in the principles of human nature and regulate our future conduct as well as speculation. By means of this guide we mount up to the knowledge of men's inclinations and motives from their actions, expressions, and even gestures, and again descend to the interpretation of their actions from our knowledge of their motives and inclinations. The general observations, treasured up by a course of experience, give us the clue of human nature and teach us to unravel all its intricacies. Pretexts and appearances no longer deceive us. Public declarations pass for the specious coloring of a cause. And though virtue and honor be allowed their proper weight and authority, that perfect disinterestedness, so often pretended to, is never expected in multitudes and parties, seldom in their leaders, and scarcely even in individuals of any rank or station. But were there no uniformity in human actions, and were every experiment which we could form of this kind irregular and anomalous, it were impossible to collect any general observations concerning mankind, and no experience, however accurately digested by reflection, would ever serve to any purpose. Why is the aged husbandman more skillful in his calling than the young beginner, but because there is a certain uniformity in the operation of the sun, rain, and earth toward the production of vegetables, and experience teaches the old practitioner the rules by which this operation is governed and directed?

We must not, however, expect that this uniformity of human actions should be carried to such a length as that all men, in the same circumstances, will always act precisely in the same manner, without making any allowance for the diversity of characters, prejudices, and opinions. Such a uniformity, in every particular, is found in no part of nature. On the contrary, from observing the variety of conduct in different men we are enabled to form a greater variety of maxims which still suppose a degree of uniformity and regularity.

Are the manners of men different in different ages and countries? We learn thence the great force of custom and education, which mold the human mind from its infancy and form it into a fixed and established character. Is the behavior and conduct of the one sex very unlike that of the other? It is thence we become acquainted with the different characters which nature has impressed upon the sexes, and which she preserves with constancy and regularity. Are the actions of the same person much diversified in the different periods of his life from infancy to old age? This affords room for many general observations concerning the gradual change of our sentiments and inclinations, and the different maxims which prevail in the different ages of human creatures. Even the characters which are peculiar to each individual have a uniformity in their influence, otherwise our acquaintance with the persons, and our observations of their conduct, could never teach us their dispositions or serve to direct our behavior with regard to them.

I grant it possible to find actions which seem to have no regular connection with any known motives and are exceptions to all the measures of conduct which have ever been established for the government of men. But if we could willingly know what judgment should be formed of such irregular and extraordinary actions, we may consider the sentiments commonly entertained with regard to those irregular events which appear in the course of nature and the operations of eternal objects. All causes are not conjoined to their usual effects with like uniformity. An artificer who handles only dead matter may be disappointed of his aim, as well as the politician who directs the conduct of sensible and intelligent agents.

The vulgar, who take things according to their first appearance, attribute the uncertainty of events to such an uncertainty in the causes as makes the latter often fail of their usual influence, though they meet with no impediment in their operation. But philosophers, observing that almost in every part of nature there is contained a vast variety of springs and principles which are hid by reason of their minuteness or remoteness, find that it is at least possible the contrariety of events may not proceed from any contingency in the cause but from the secret operation of contrary causes. This possibility is converted into certainty by further observation, when they remark that, upon an exact scrutiny, a contrariety of effects always betrays a contrariety of causes and proceeds from their mutual opposition. A peasant can give no better reason for the stopping of any clock or watch than to say that it does not commonly go right. But an artist easily perceives that the same force in the spring or pendulum has always the same influence on the wheels, but fails of its usual effect perhaps by reason of a grain of dust which puts a stop to the whole movement. From the observation of several parallel instances philosophers form a maxim that the connection between all causes and effects is equally necessary, and that its seeming uncertainty in some instances proceeds from the secret opposition of contrary causes.

Thus, for instance, in the human body, when the usual symptoms of health or sickness disappoint our expectation, when medicines operate not with their wonted powers, when irregular events follow from any particular cause, the philosopher and physician are not surprised at the matter, nor are ever tempted to deny, in general, the necessity and uniformity of those principles by which the animal economy is conducted. They know that a human body is a mighty complicated machine, that many secret powers lurk in it which are altogether beyond our comprehension, that to us it must often appear very uncertain in its operations, and that, therefore, the irregular events which outwardly discover themselves can be no proof that the laws of nature are not observed with the greatest regularity in its internal operations and government.

The philosopher, if he be consistent, must apply the same reasonings to the actions and volitions of intelligent agents. The most irregular and unexpected resolutions of men may frequently be accounted for by those who know every particular circumstance of their character and situation. A person of an obliging disposition gives a peevish answer; but he has the toothache, or has not dined. A stupid fellow discovers an uncommon alacrity in his carriage; but he has met with a sudden piece of good fortune. Or even when an action, as sometimes happens, cannot be particularly accounted for, either by the person himself or by others, we know, in general that the characters of men are to a certain degree inconstant and irregular. This is, in a manner, the constant character of human nature, though it be applicable, in a more particular manner, to some persons who have no fixed rule for their conduct, but proceed in a continual course of caprice and inconstancy. The internal principles and motives may operate in a uniform manner, notwithstanding these seeming irregularities—in the same manner as the winds, rains, clouds, and other variations of the weather are supposed to be governed by steady principles, though not easily discoverable by human sagacity and inquiry.

Thus it appears not only that the conjunction between motives and voluntary actions is as regular and uniform as that between the cause and effect in any part of nature, but also that this regular conjunction has been universally acknowledged among mankind and has never been the subject of dispute either in philosophy or common life. Now, as it is from past experience that we draw all inferences concerning the future, and as we conclude that objects will always be conjoined together which we find to have always been conjoined, it may seem superfluous to prove that this experienced uniformity in human actions is a source whence we draw *inferences* concerning them. But in order to throw the argument into a greater variety of lights, we shall also insist, though briefly, on this latter topic.

The mutual dependence of men is so great in all societies that scarce any human action is entirely complete in itself or is performed without some reference to the actions of others, which are requisite to make it answer fully the intention of the agent. The poorest artificer who labors alone expects at least the protection of the magistrate to insure him the enjoyment of the fruits of his labor. He also expects that when he carries his goods to market and offers them at a reasonable price, he shall find purchasers and shall be able, by the money he acquires, to engage others to supply him with those commodities which are requisite for his subsistence. In proportion as men extend their dealings and render their intercourse with others more complicated, they always comprehend in their schemes of life a greater variety of voluntary actions which they expect, from the proper motives, to co-operate with their own. In all these conclusions they take their measures from past experience, in the same manner as in their reasonings concerning external objects, and firmly believe that men, as well as all the elements, are to continue in their operations the same that they have ever found them. A manufacturer reckons upon the labor of his servants for the execution of any work as much as upon the tools which he employs, and would be equally surprised were his expectations disappointed. In short, this experimental inference and reasoning concerning the actions of others enters so much into human life that no man, while awake, is ever a moment without employing it. Have we not reason, therefore, to affirm that all mankind have always agreed in the doctrine of necessity, according to the foregoing definition and explication of it?

Nor have philosophers ever entertained a different opinion from the people in this particular. For, not to mention that almost every action of their life supposes that opinion, there are even few of the speculative parts of learning to which it is not essential. What would become of *history* had we not a dependence on the veracity of the historian according to the experience which we have had of mankind? How could *politics* be a science if laws and forms of government had not a uniform influence upon society? Where would be the foundation of *morals* if particular characters had no certain or determinate power to produce particular sentiments, and if these sentiments had no constant operation on actions? And with what pretense could we employ our *criticism* upon any poet or polite author if we could not pronounce the conduct and sentiments of his actors either natural or unnatural to such characters and in such circumstances? It seems almost impossible, there-

fore, to engage either in science or action of any kind without acknowledging the doctrine of necessity, and this *inference* from motives to voluntary action, from characters to conduct.

And, indeed, when we consider how aptly *natural* and *moral* evidence link together and form only one chain of argument, we shall make no scruple to allow that they are of the same nature and derived from the same principles. A prisoner who has neither money nor interest discovers the impossibility of his escape as well when he considers the obstinacy of the jailer as the walls and bars with which he is surrounded, and in all attempts for his freedom chooses rather to work upon the stone and iron of the one than upon the inflexible nature of the other. The same prisoner, when conducted to the scaffold, foresees his death as certainly from the constancy and fidelity of his guards as from the operation of the ax or wheel. His mind runs along a certain train of ideas: the refusal of the soldiers to consent to his escape; the action of the executioner; the separation of the head and body; bleeding, convulsive motions, and death. Here is a connected chain of natural causes and voluntary actions, but the mind feels no difference between them in passing from one link to another, nor is less certain of the future event than if it were connected with the objects present to the memory or senses by a train of causes cemented together by what we are pleased to call a "physical" necessity. The same experienced union has the same effect on the mind, whether the united objects be motives, volition, and actions, or figure and motion. We may change the names of things, but their nature and their operation on the understanding never change.

Were a man whom I know to be honest and opulent, and with whom I lived in intimate friendship, to come into my house, where I am surrounded with my servants, I rest assured that he is not to stab me before he leaves it in order to rob me of my silver standish; and I no more suspect this event than the falling of the house itself, which is new and solidly built and founded.—*But he may have been seized with a sudden and unknown frenzy.*—So may a sudden earthquake arise, and shake and tumble my house about my ears. I shall, therefore, change the suppositions. I shall say that I know with certainty that he is not to put his hand into the fire and hold it there till it be consumed.

And this event I think I can foretell with the same assurance as that, if he throw himself out of the window and meet with no obstruction, he will not remain a moment suspended in the air. No suspicion of an unknown frenzy can give the least possibility to the former event which is so contrary to all the known principles of human nature. A man who at noon leaves his purse full of gold on the pavement at Charing Cross may as well expect that it will fly away like a feather as that he will find it untouched an hour after. Above one-half of human reasonings contain inferences of a similar nature, attended with more or less degrees of certainty, proportioned to our experience of the usual conduct of mankind in such particular situations.

I have frequently considered what could possibly be the reason why all mankind, though they have ever, without hesitation, acknowledged the doctrine of necessity in their whole practice and reasoning, have yet discovered such a reluctance to acknowledge it in words, and have rather shown a propensity, in all ages, to profess the contrary opinion. The matter, I think, may be accounted for after the following manner. If we examine the operations of body and the production of effects from their causes, we shall find that all our faculties can never carry us further in our knowledge of this relation than barely to observe that particular objects are *constantly conjoined* together, and that the mind is carried, by a *customary transition,* from the appearance of the one to the belief of the other. But though this conclusion concerning human ignorance be the result of the strictest scrutiny of this subject, men still entertain a strong propensity to believe that they penetrate further into the powers of nature and perceive something like a necessary connection between the cause and the effect. When, again, they turn their reflections toward the operations of their own minds and *feel* no such connection of the motive and the action, they are thence apt to suppose that there is a difference between the effects which result from material force and those which arise from thought and intelligence. But being once convinced that we know nothing further of causation of any kind than merely the *constant conjunction* of objects and the consequent *inference* of the mind from one to another, and finding that these two circumstances are universally allowed to have place in voluntary actions, we may be more easily led to

own the same necessity common to all causes. And though this reasoning may contradict the systems of many philosophers in ascribing necessity to the determinations of the will, we shall find, upon reflection, that they dissent from it in words only, not in their real sentiments. Necessity, according to the sense in which it is here taken, has never yet been rejected, nor can ever, I think, be rejected by any philosopher. It may only, perhaps, be pretended that the mind can perceive in the operations of matter some further connection between the cause and effect, and a connection that has not place in the voluntary actions of intelligent beings. Now, whether it be so or not can only appear upon examination, and it is incumbent on these philosophers to make good their assertion by defining or describing that necessity and pointing it out to us in the operations of material causes.

It would seem, indeed, that men begin at the wrong end of this question concerning liberty and necessity when they enter upon it by examining the faculties of the soul, the influence of the understanding, and the operations of the will. Let them first discuss a more simple question, namely, the question of body and brute unintelligent matter, and try whether they can there form any idea of causation and necessity, except that of a constant conjunction of objects and subsequent inference of the mind from one to another. If these circumstances form, in reality, the whole of that necessity which we conceive in matter, and if these circumstances be also universally acknowledged to take place in the operations of the mind, the dispute is at an end; at least, must be owned to be thenceforth merely verbal. But as long as we will rashly suppose that we have some further idea of necessity and causation in the operations of external objects, at the same time that we can find nothing further in the voluntary actions of the mind, there is no possibility of bringing the question to any determinate issue while we proceed upon so erroneous a supposition. The only method of undeceiving us is to mount up higher, to examine the narrow extent of science when applied to material causes, and to convince ourselves that all we know of them is the constant conjunction and inference above mentioned. We may, perhaps, find that it is with difficulty we are induced to fix such narrow limits to human understanding, but we can afterwards find no difficulty when we come to apply this doctrine to the actions of the will. For as it is evident that these have a regular conjunction with motives and circumstances and character, and as we always draw inferences from one to the other, we must be obliged to acknowledge in words that necessity which we have already avowed in every deliberation of our lives and in every step of our conduct and behavior.[1]

But to proceed in this reconciling project with regard to the question of liberty and necessity—the most contentious question of metaphysics, the most contentious science—it will not require many words to prove that all mankind have ever agreed in the doctrine of liberty as well as in that of necessity, and that the whole dispute, in this respect also, has been hitherto merely verbal. For what is meant by liberty when applied to voluntary actions? We cannot surely mean that actions have so little connection with motives, inclinations, and circumstances that one does not follow with a certain degree of uniformity from the other, and that one affords no inference by which we can conclude the existence of the other. For these are plain and acknowledged matters of fact. By liberty, then, we can only mean *a power of acting or not acting according to the determinations of the will;* that is, if we choose to remain at rest, we may; if we choose to move, we also may. Now this hypothetical liberty is universally allowed to belong to everyone who is not a prisoner and in chains. Here then is no subject of dispute.

Whatever definition we may give of liberty, we should be careful to observe two requisite circumstances: *first,* that it be consistent with plain matter of fact; *secondly,* that it be consistent with itself. If we observe these circumstances and render our definition intelligible, I am persuaded that all mankind will be found of one opinion with regard to it.

It is universally allowed that nothing exists without a cause of its existence, and that chance, when strictly examined, is a mere negative word and means not any real power which has anywhere a being in nature. But it is pretended that some causes are necessary, some not necessary. Here then is the advantage of definitions. Let anyone *define* a cause without comprehending, as a part of the definition, a *necessary connection* with its effect, and let him show distinctly the origin of the idea expressed by the definition, and I shall readily give up the whole controversy. But if the foregoing explication of the matter be received,

this must be absolutely impracticable. Had not objects a regular conjunction with each other, we should never have entertained any notion of cause and effect; and this regular conjunction produces that inference of the understanding which is the only connection that we can have any comprehension of. Whoever attempts a definition of cause exclusive of these circumstances will be obliged either to employ unintelligible terms or such as are synonymous to the term which he endeavors to define.[2] And if the definition above mentioned be admitted, liberty, when opposed to necessity, not to constraint, is the same thing with chance, which is universally allowed to have no existence.

Part II

There is no method of reasoning more common, and yet none more blamable, than in philosophical disputes to endeavor the refutation of any hypothesis by a pretense of its dangerous consequences to religion and morality. When any opinion leads to absurdity, it is certainly false; but it is not certain that an opinion is false because it is of dangerous consequence. Such topics, therefore, ought entirely to be forborne as serving nothing to the discovery of truth, but only to make the person of an antagonist odious. This I observe in general, without pretending to draw any advantage from it. I frankly submit to an examination of this kind, and shall venture to affirm that the doctrines both of necessity and liberty, as above explained, are not only consistent with morality, but are absolutely essential to its support.

Necessity may be defined two ways, conformably to the two definitions of *cause* of which it makes an essential part. It consists either in the constant conjunction of like objects or in the inference of the understanding from one object to another. Now necessity, in both these senses (which, indeed, are at bottom the same), has universally, though tacitly, in the schools, in the pulpit, and in common life been allowed to belong to the will of man, and no one has ever pretended to deny that we can draw inferences concerning human actions, and that those inferences are founded on the experienced union of like actions, with like motives, inclinations, and circumstances.

The only particular in which anyone can differ is that either perhaps he will refuse to give the name of necessity to this property of human actions—but as long as the meaning is understood I hope the word can do no harm—or that he will maintain it possible to discover something further in the operations of matter. But this, it must be acknowledged, can be of no consequence to morality or religion, whatever it may be to natural philosophy or metaphysics. We may here be mistaken in asserting that there is no idea of any other necessity or connection in the actions of the body, but surely we ascribe nothing to the actions of the mind but what everyone does and must readily allow of. We change no circumstance in the received orthodox system with regard to the will, but only in that with regard to material objects and causes. Nothing, therefore, can be more innocent at least than this doctrine.

All laws being founded on rewards and punishments, it is supposed, as a fundamental principle, that these motives have a regular and uniform influence on the mind and both produce the good and prevent the evil actions. We may give to this influence what name we please; but as it is usually conjoined with the action, it must be esteemed a *cause* and be looked upon as an instance of that necessity which we would here establish.

The only proper object of hatred or vengeance is a person or creature endowed with thought and consciousness; and when any criminal or injurious actions excite that passion, it is only by their relation to the person, or connection with him. Actions are, by their very nature, temporary and perishing; and where they proceed not from some *cause* in the character and disposition of the person who performed them, they can neither redound to his honor if good, nor infamy if evil. The actions themselves may be blamable; they may be contrary to all the rules of morality and religion; but the person is not answerable for them and, as they proceeded from nothing in him that is durable and constant and leave nothing of that nature behind them, it is impossible he can, upon their account, become the object of punishment or vengeance. According to the principle, therefore, which denies necessity and, consequently, causes, a man is as pure and untainted, after having committed the most horrid crime, as at the first moment of his birth, nor is his character any-

wise concerned in his actions, since they are not derived from it; and the wickedness of the one can never be used as a proof of the depravity of the other.

Men are not blamed for such actions as they perform ignorantly and casually, whatever may be the consequences. Why? But because the principles of these actions are only momentary and terminate in them alone. Men are less blamed for such actions as they perform hastily and unpremeditatedly than for such as proceed from deliberation. For what reason? But because a hasty temper, though a constant cause or principle in the mind, operates only by intervals and infects not the whole character. Again, repentance wipes off every crime if attended with a reformation of life and manners. How is this to be accounted for? But by asserting that actions render a person criminal merely as they are proofs of criminal principles in the mind; and when, by an alteration of these principles, they cease to be just proofs, they likewise cease to be criminal. But, except upon the doctrine of necessity, they never were just proofs, and consequently never were criminal.

It will be equally easy to prove, and from the same arguments, that *liberty*, according to that definition above mentioned, in which all men agree, is also essential to morality, and that no human actions, where it is wanting, are susceptible of any moral qualities or can be the objects of approbation or dislike. For as actions are objects of our moral sentiment so far only as they are indications of the internal character, passions, and affections, it is impossible that they can give rise either to praise or blame where they proceed not from these principles, but are derived altogether from external violence.

I pretend not to have obtained or removed all objections to this theory with regard to necessity and liberty. I can foresee other objections derived from topics which have not here been treated of. It may be said, for instance, that if voluntary actions be subjected to the same laws of necessity with the operations of matter, there is a continued chain of necessary causes, preordained and predetermined, reaching from the Original Cause of all to every single volition of every human creature. No contingency anywhere in the universe, no indifference, no liberty. While we act, we are at the same time acted upon. The ultimate Author of all our volitions is the Creator of the world, who first bestowed motion on this immense machine and placed all beings in that particular position whence every subsequent event, by an inevitable necessity, must result. Human actions, therefore, either can have no moral turpitude at all, as proceeding from so good a cause, or if they have any turpitude, they must involve our Creator in the same guilt, while he is acknowledged to be their ultimate cause and Author. For as a man who fired a mine is answerable for all the consequences, whether the train he employed be long or short, so, wherever a continued chain of necessary causes is fixed, that Being, either finite or infinite, who produces the first is likewise the author of all the rest and must both bear the blame and acquire the praise which belong to them. Our clear and unalterable ideas of morality establish this rule upon unquestionable reasons when we examine the consequences of any human action; and these reasons must still have greater force when applied to the volitions and intentions of a Being infinitely wise and powerful. Ignorance or impotence may be pleaded for so limited a creature as man, but those imperfections have no place in our Creator. He foresaw, he ordained, he intended all those actions of men which we so rashly pronounce criminal. And we must, therefore, conclude either that they are not criminal or that the Deity, not man, is accountable for them. But as either of these positions is absurd and impious, it follows that the doctrine from which they are deduced cannot possibly be true, as being liable to all the same objections. An absurd consequence, if necessary, proves the original doctrine to be absurd in the same manner as criminal actions render criminal the original cause if the connection between them be necessary and inevitable.

This objection consists of two parts, which we shall examine separately:

First, that if human actions can be traced up, by a necessary chain, to the Deity, they can never be criminal, on account of the infinite perfection of that Being from whom they are derived, and who can intend nothing but what is altogether good and laudable. Or, *secondly,* if they be criminal, we must retract the attribute of perfection which we ascribe to the Deity and must acknowledge him to be the ultimate author of guilt and moral turpitude in all his creatures.

The answer to the first objection seems obvious and convincing. There are many philosophers who, after an exact scrutiny of the phenomena of nature, conclude that the WHOLE, considered as one system, is, in every period of its existence, ordered with perfect benevolence; and that the utmost possible happiness will, in the end, result to all created beings without any mixture of positive or absolute ill and misery. Every physical ill, say they, makes an essential part of this benevolent system, and could not possibly be removed, by even the Deity himself, considered as a wise agent, without giving entrance to greater ill or excluding greater good which will result from it. From this theory some philosophers, and the ancient Stoics among the rest, derived topic of consolation under all afflictions, while they taught their pupils that those ills under which they labored were in reality goods to the universe, and that to an enlarged view which could comprehend the whole system of nature every event became an object of joy and exultation. But though this topic be specious and sublime, it was soon found in practice weak and ineffectual. You would surely more irritate than appease a man lying under the racking pains of the gout by preaching up to him the rectitude of those general laws which produced the malignant humors in his body and led them through the proper canals to the sinews and nerves, where they now excite such acute torments. These enlarged views may, for a moment, please the imagination of a speculative man who is placed in ease and security, but neither can they dwell with constancy on his mind, even though undisturbed by the emotions of pain or passion, much less can they maintain their ground when attacked by such powerful antagonists. The affections take a narrower and more natural survey of their object and, by an economy more suitable to the infirmity of human minds, regard alone the beings around us, and are actuated by such events as appear good or ill to the private system.

The case is the same with *moral* as with *physical* ill. It cannot reasonably be supposed that those remote considerations which are found of so little efficacy with regard to the one will have a more powerful influence with regard to the other. The mind of man is so formed by nature that, upon the appearance of certain characters, dispositions, and actions, it immediately feels the sentiment of approbation or blame; nor are there any emotions more essential to its frame and constitution. The characters which engage our approbation are chiefly such as contribute to the peace and security of human society, as the characters which excite blame are chiefly such as tend to public detriment and disturbance; whence it may reasonably be presumed that the moral sentiments arise, either mediately or immediately, from a reflection on these opposite interests. What though philosophical meditations establish a different opinion or conjecture that everything is right with regard to the whole, and that the qualities which disturb society are, in the main, as beneficial, and are as suitable to the primary intention of nature, as those which more directly promote its happiness and welfare? Are such remote and uncertain speculations able to counterbalance the sentiments which arise from the natural and immediate view of the objects? A man who is robbed of a considerable sum, does he find his vexation for the loss anywise diminished by these sublime reflections? Why, then, should his moral resentment against the crime be supposed incompatible with them? Or why should not the acknowledgement of a real distinction between vice and virtue be reconcilable to all speculative systems of philosophy, as well as that of a real distinction between personal beauty and deformity? Both these distinctions are founded in the natural sentiments of the human mind; and these sentiments are not to be controlled or altered by any philosophical theory or speculation whatsoever.

The *second* objection admits not of so easy and satisfactory an answer, nor is it possible to explain distinctly how the Deity can be the immediate cause of all the actions of men without being the author of sin and moral turpitude. These are mysteries which mere natural and unassisted reason is very unfit to handle; and whatever system she embraces, she must find herself involved in inextricable difficulties, and even contradictions, at every step which she takes with regard to such subjects. To reconcile the indifference and contingency of human actions with prescience or to defend absolute decrees, and yet free the Deity from being the author of sin, has been found hitherto to exceed all the power of philosophy. Happy, if she be thence sensible of her temerity, when she pries into these sublime mysteries, and, leaving a scene so full of obscurities and perplexities, return with suitable modesty to her true and proper province, the examination of common life, where she will find difficulties enough to employ her inquiries without launching into so boundless an ocean of doubt, uncertainty, and contradiction.

Endnotes

[1]The prevalence of the doctrine of liberty may be accounted for from another cause, viz., a false sensation, or seeming experience, which we have, or may have, of liberty or indifference in many of our actions. The necessity of any action, whether of matter or of mind, is not, properly speaking, a quality in the agent but in any thinking or intelligent being who may consider the action; and it consists chiefly in the determination of his thoughts to infer the existence of that action from some preceding objects; as liberty, when opposed to necessity, is nothing but the want of that determination, and a certain looseness or indifference which we feel in passing, or not passing, from the idea of one object to that of any succeeding one. Now we may observe that though, in *reflecting* on human actions, we seldom feel such a looseness or indifference, but are commonly able to infer them with considerable certainty from their motives, and from the disposition of the agent; yet it frequently happens that, in *performing* the actions themselves, we are sensible of something like it; and as all resembling objects are readily taken for each other, this has been employed as a demonstrative and even intuitive proof of human liberty. We feel that our actions are subject to our will on most occasions, and imagine we feel that the will itself is subject to nothing, because, when by a denial of it we are provoked to try, we feel that it moves easily every way, and produces an image of itself (or a "velleity," as it is called in the schools), even on that side on which it did not settle. This image, or faint motion, we persuade ourselves, could at that time have been completed into the thing itself, because, should that be denied, we find upon a second trial that at present it can. We consider not that the fantastical desire of showing liberty is here the motive of our actions. And it seems certain that however we may imagine we feel a liberty within ourselves, a spectator can commonly infer our actions from our motives and character; and even where he cannot, he concludes in general that he might, were he perfectly acquainted with every circumstance of our situation and temper, and the most secret springs of our complexion and disposition. Now this is the very essence of necessity, according to the foregoing doctrine.

[2]Thus, if a cause be defined, *that which produces anything,* it is easy to observe *that producing* is synonymous to *causing.* In like manner, if a cause be defined, *that by which anything exists,* this is liable to the same objection. For what is meant by these words, *"by which"?* Had it been said that a cause is *that* after which *anything constantly exists,* we should have understood the terms. For this is, indeed, all we know of the matter. And this constancy forms the very essence of necessity, nor have we any other idea of it.

41. *Of the Liberty of Moral Agents*

THOMAS REID

In contrast to Hume, Reid maintains that some actions are not caused or determined by a person's character, motives, heredity, or background. Reid reasons that if an action is caused by anything other than the agent—Reid's "substantial self"—then it is not one's own will that determines choices; in such cases one's actions are not really free. In Part II, Reid argues for a substantialist conception of the self and its identity through time. Here, Reid connects that notion of the self with a denial that a free self can be caused and a rejection of Hume's views on causation. (See also the Hume selection in Part V.)

The Notions of Moral Liberty and Necessity Stated

By the *liberty* of a moral agent, I understand, a power over the determinations of his own will.

If, in any action, he had power to will what he did, or not to will it, in that action he is free. But if, in every voluntary action, the determination of his will be the necessary consequence of something involuntary in the state of his mind, or of something in his external circumstances, he is not free; he has not what I call the liberty of a moral agent, but is subject to necessity.

This liberty supposes the agent to have understanding and will; for the determinations of the will are the sole object about which this power is employed; and there can be no will, without, at least, such a degree of understanding as gives the conception of that which we will.

The liberty of a moral agent implies, not only a conception of what he wills, but some degree of practical judgment or reason.

For, if he has not the judgment to discern one determination to be preferable to another, either in itself, or for some purpose which he intends, what can be the use of a power to determine? his

From Reid's *Essays on the Active Powers of the Human Mind*, Essay IV, Chapters 1 and 9. First published in 1815.

determinations must be made perfectly in the dark, without reason, motive, or end. They can neither be right nor wrong, wise nor foolish. Whatever the consequences may be, they cannot be imputed to the agent, who had not the capacity of foreseeing them, or of perceiving any reason for acting otherwise than he did.

We may perhaps be able to conceive a being endowed with power over the determinations of his will, without any light in his mind to direct that power to some end. But such power would be given in vain. No exercise of it could be either blamed or approved. As nature gives no power in vain, I see no ground to ascribe a power over the determinations of the will to any being who has no judgment to apply it to the direction of his conduct, no discernment of what he ought or ought not to do.

For that reason, in this Essay, I speak only of the liberty of moral agents, who are capable of acting well or ill, wisely or foolishly, and this, for distinction's sake, I shall call *moral liberty*.

What kind, or what degree of liberty belongs to brute animals, or to our own species, before any use of reason, I do not know. We acknowledge that they have not the power of self-government. Such of their actions as may be called *voluntary*, seem to be invariably determined by the passion or appetite, or affection or habit, which is strongest at the time.

This seems to be the law of their constitution, to which they yield, as the inanimate creation does, without any conception of the law, or any intention of obedience.

But of civil or moral government, which are addressed to the rational powers, and require a conception of the law and an intentional obedience, they are, in the judgment of all mankind, incapable. Nor do I see what end could be served by giving them a power over the determinations of their own will, unless to make them intractable by discipline, which we see they are not.

The effect of moral liberty is, that it is in the power of the agent to do well or ill. This power, like every other gift of God, may be abused. The right use of this gift of God is to do well and wisely, as far as his best judgment can direct him, and thereby merit esteem and approbation. The abuse of it is to act contrary to what he knows, or suspects to be his duty and his wisdom, and thereby justly merit disapprobation and blame.

By *necessity*, I understand the want of that moral liberty which I have above defined.

If there can be a better and a worse in actions on the system of necessity, let us suppose a man necessarily determined in all cases to will and to do what is best to be done, he would surely be innocent and inculpable. But, as far as I am able to judge, he would not be entitled to the esteem and moral approbation of those who knew and believed this necessity. What was, by an ancient author, said of Cato, might indeed be said of him. *He was good because he could not be otherwise.* But this saying, if understood literally and strictly, is not the praise of Cato, but of his constitution, which was no more the work of Cato, than his existence.

On the other hand, if a man be necessarily determined to do ill, this case seems to me to move pity, but not disapprobation. He was ill, because he could not be otherwise. Who can blame him? Necessity has no law.

If he knows that he acted under this necessity, has he not just ground to exculpate himself? The blame, if there be any, is not in him, but in his constitution. If he be charged by his Maker with doing wrong, may he not expostulate with him, and say, why hast thou made me thus? I may be sacrificed at thy pleasure, for the common good, like a man that has the plague, but not for ill desert; for thou knowest that what I am charged with is thy work, and not mine.

Such are my notions of moral liberty and necessity, and of the consequences inseparably connected with both the one and the other.

This moral liberty a man may have, though it do not extend to all his actions, or even to all his voluntary actions. He does many things by instinct, many things by the force of habit without any thought at all, and consequently without will. In the first part of life, he has not the power of self-government any more than the brutes. That power over the determinations of his own will, which belongs to him in ripe years, is limited, as all his powers are; and it is perhaps beyond the reach of his understanding to define its limits with precision. We can only say, in general, that it extends to every action for which he is accountable.

This power is given by his Maker, and at his pleasure whose gift it is, it may be enlarged or diminished, continued or withdrawn. No power in the creature can be independent of the Creator. His hook is in its nose; he can give it line as far as he sees fit, and, when he pleases, can restrain it, or turn it withersoever he will. Let this be always understood, when we ascribe liberty to man, or to any created being.

Supposing it therefore to be true, that man is a free agent, it may be true, at the same time, that his liberty may be impaired or lost, by disorder of body or mind, as in melancholy, or in madness; it may be impaired or lost by vicious habits; it may, in particular cases, be restrained by divine interposition.

We call man a free agent in the same way as we call him a reasonable agent. In many things he is not guided by reason, but by principles similar to those of the brutes. His reason is weak at best. It is liable to be impaired or lost, by his own fault, or by other means. In like manner, he may be a free agent, though his freedom of action may have many similar limitations.

The liberty I have described has been represented by some philosophers as inconceivable, and as involving an absurdity.

"Liberty," they say, "consists only in a power to act as we will; and it is impossible to conceive in any being a greater liberty than this. Hence it follows, that liberty does not extend to the determinations of the will, but only to the actions consequent to its determination, and depending upon the will. To say that we have power to will such an action, is to say, that we may will it, if we will. This supposes the will to be determined by a prior will; and, for the same reason, that will must be determined by a will prior to it, and so on in an infinite series of wills, which is absurd. To act freely, therefore, can mean nothing more than to act voluntarily; and this is all the liberty that can be conceived in man, or in any being."

This reasoning, first, I think, advanced by Hobbes, has been very generally adopted by the defenders of necessity. It is grounded upon a definition of liberty totally different from that which I have given, and therefore does not apply to moral liberty, as above defined.

But it is said that this is the only liberty that is possible, that is conceivable, that does not involve an absurdity.

It is strange indeed! if the word *liberty* has no meaning but this one. I shall mention three, all very common. The objection applies to one of them, but to neither of the other two.

Liberty is sometimes opposed to external force or confinement of the body. Sometimes it is opposed to obligation by law, or by lawful authority. Sometimes it is opposed to necessity.

First, it is opposed to confinement of the body by superior force. So we say a prisoner is set at liberty when his fetters are knocked off, and he is discharged from confinement. This is the liberty defined in the objection; and I grant that this liberty extends not to the will, neither does the confinement, because the will cannot be confined by external force.

Secondly, liberty is opposed to obligation, by law, or lawful authority. This liberty is a right to act one way or another, in things which the law has neither commanded nor forbidden; and this liberty is meant when we speak of a man's natural liberty, his civil liberty, his christian liberty. It is evident that this liberty, as well as the obligation opposed to it, extends to the will: for it is the will to obey that makes obedience: the will to transgress that makes a transgression of the law. Without will there can be neither obedience nor transgression. Law supposes a power to obey or to transgress; it does not take away this power, but proposes the motives of duty and of interest, leaving the power to yield to them, or to take the consequence of transgression.

Thirdly, liberty is opposed to necessity, and in this sense it extends to the determinations of the will only, and not to what is consequent to the will.

In every voluntary action, the determination of the will is the first part of the action, upon which alone the moral estimation of it depends. It has been made a question among philosophers, whether, in every instance, this determination be the necessary consequence of the constitution of the person, and the circumstances in which he is placed? or whether he had not power, in many cases, to determine this way or that?

This has, by some, been called the *philosophical* notion of liberty and necessity; but it is by no means peculiar to philosophers. The lowest of the vulgar have, in all ages, been prone to have recourse to this necessity, to exculpate themselves or their friends in what they do wrong, though, in the general tenor of their conduct, they act upon the contrary principle.

Whether this notion of moral liberty be conceivable or not, every man must judge for himself. To me there appears no difficulty in conceiving it. I consider the determination of the will as an effect. This effect must have a cause which had power to produce it; and the cause must be either the person himself, whose will it is, or some other being. The first is as easily conceived as the last. If the person was the cause of that determination of his own will, he was free in that action, and it is justly imputed to him, whether it be good or bad. But, if another being was the cause of this determination, either by producing it immediately, or by means and instruments under his direction, then the determination is the act and deed of that being, and is solely imputable to him.

But it is said, "That nothing is in our power but what depends upon the will, and therefore the will itself cannot be in our power."

I answer, that this is a fallacy arising from taking a common saying in a sense which it never was intended to convey, and in a sense contrary to what it necessarily implies.

In common life, when men speak of what is, or is not, in a man's power, they attend only to the external and visible effects, which only can be perceived, and which only can affect them. Of these, it is true, that nothing is in a man's power, but what depends upon his will, and this is all that is meant by this common saying.

But this is so far from excluding his will from being in his power, that it necessarily implies it. For to say that what depends upon the will is in a man's power, but the will is not in his power, is to say that the end is in his power, but the means necessary to that end are not in his power, which is a contradiction.

In many propositions which we express universally, there is an exception necessarily implied, and therefore always understood. Thus when we say that all things depend upon God, God himself is necessarily excepted. In like manner, when we say, that all that is in our power depends upon the will, the will itself is necessarily excepted; for if the will be not, nothing else can be in our power. Every effect must be in the power of its cause. The determination of the will is an effect, and therefore must be in the power of its cause, whether that cause be the agent himself, or some other being.

From what has been said in this chapter, I hope the notion of moral liberty will be distinctly understood, and that it appears that this notion is neither inconceivable, nor involves any absurdity or contradiction.

Arguments for Necessity

Another argument that has been used to prove liberty of action to be impossible is, that it implies "an effect without a cause."

To this it may be briefly answered, that a free action is an effect produced by a being who had power and will to produce it; therefore it is not an effect without a cause.

To suppose any other cause necessary to the production of an effect, than a being who had the power and the will to produce it, is a contradiction; for it is to suppose that being to have power to produce the effect, and not to have power to produce it.

But as great stress is laid upon this argument by a late zealous advocate for necessity, we shall consider the light in which he puts it.

He introduces this argument with an observation to which I entirely agree: it is, that to establish this doctrine of necessity, nothing is necessary but that, throughout all nature, the same consequences should invariably result from the same circumstances.

I know nothing more that can be desired to establish universal fatality throughout the universe. When it is proved that, through all nature,

the same consequences invariably result from the same circumstances, the doctrine of liberty must be given up.

To prevent all ambiguity, I grant, that, in reasoning, the same consequences, throughout all nature, will invariably follow from the same premises: because good reasoning must be good reasoning in all times and places. But this has nothing to do with the doctrine of necessity. The thing to be proved, therefore, in order to establish that doctrine, is, that, through all nature, the same events invariably result from the same circumstances.

Of this capital point, the proof offered by that author, is that an event not preceded by any circumstances that determined it to be what it was, would be *an effect without a cause*. Why so? "For," says he, "a *cause* cannot be defined to be any thing but *such previous circumstances as are constantly followed by a certain effect;* the constancy of the result making us conclude, that there must be a *sufficient reason,* in the nature of things, why it should be produced in those circumstances."

I acknowledge that, if this be the only definition that can be given of a cause, it will follow, that an event not preceded by circumstances that determined it to be what it was, would be, not an *effect* without a cause, which is a contradiction in terms, but an *event* without a cause, which I hold to be impossible. The matter therefore is brought to this issue, whether this be the only definition that can be given of a cause?

With regard to this point, we may observe, *first,* that this definition of a cause, bating the phraseology of putting a *cause* under the category of *circumstances,* which I take to be new, is the same, in other words, with that which Mr. Hume gave, of which he ought to be acknowledged the inventor. For I know of no author before Mr. Hume, who maintained, that we have no other notion of a cause, but that it is something prior to the effect, which has been found by experience to be constantly followed by the effect. This is a main pillar of his system; and he has drawn very important consequences from this definition, which I am far from thinking this author will adopt.

Without repeating what I have before said of causes in the first of these Essays, and in the second and third chapters of this, I shall here mention some of the consequences that may be justly deduced from this definition of a cause, that we may judge of it by its fruits.

First, it follows from this definition of a cause, that night is the cause of day, and day the cause of night. For no two things have more constantly followed each other since the beginning of the world.

Secondly, it follows from this definition of a cause, that, for what we know, any thing may be the cause of any thing, since nothing is essential to a cause but its being constantly followed by the effect. If this be so, what is unintelligent may be the cause of what is intelligent; folly may be the cause of wisdom, and evil of good; all reasoning from the nature of the effect to the nature of the cause, and all reasoning from final causes, must be given up as fallacious.

Thirdly, from this definition of a cause, it follows, that we have no reason to conclude, that every event must have a cause: for innumerable events happen, when it cannot be shown that there were certain previous circumstances that have constantly been followed by such an event. And though it were certain, that every event we have had access to observe had a cause, it would not follow, that every event must have a cause: for it is contrary to the rules of logic to conclude, that, because a thing has always been, therefore it must be; to reason from what is contingent, to what is necessary.

Fourthly, from this definition of a cause, it would follow, that we have no reason to conclude that there was any cause of the creation of this world: for there were no previous circumstances that had been constantly followed by such an effect. And, for the same reason, it would follow from the definition, that whatever was singular in its nature, or the first thing of its kind, could have no cause.

Several of these consequences were fondly embraced by Mr. Hume, as necessarily following from his definition of a cause, and as favourable to his system of absolute skepticism. Those who adopt the definition of a cause, from which they follow, may choose whether they will adopt its consequences, or show that they do not follow from the definition.

A *second* observation with regard to this argument is, that a definition of a cause may be given, which is not burdened with such untoward consequences.

Why may not an efficient cause be defined to be a being that had power and will to produce the effect? The production of an effect requires active power, and active power, being a quality, must be in a being endowed with that power. Power without will produces no effect; but, where these are conjoined, the effect must be produced.

This, I think, is the proper meaning of the word *cause*, when it is used in metaphysics; and particularly when we affirm, that every thing that begins to exist must have a cause; and when, by reasoning, we prove, that there must be an eternal First Cause of all things.

Was the world produced by previous circumstances which are constantly followed by such an effect? or, was it produced by a Being that had power to produce it, and willed its production?

In natural philosophy, the word *cause* is often used in a very different sense. When an event is produced according to a known law of nature, the law of nature is called the cause of that event. But a law of nature is not the efficient cause of any event. It is only the rule, according to which the efficient cause acts. A law is a thing conceived in the mind of a rational being, not a thing that has a real existence; and, therefore, like a motive, it can neither act nor be acted upon, and consequently cannot be an efficient cause. If there be no being that acts according to the law, it produces no effect.

This author takes it for granted, that every voluntary action of man was determined to be what it was by the laws of nature, in the same sense as mechanical motions are determined by the laws of motion; and that every choice, not thus determined, "is just as impossible, as that a mechanical motion should depend upon no certain law or rule, or that any other effect should exist without a cause."

It ought here to be observed, that there are two kinds of laws, both very properly called *laws of nature*, which ought not to be confounded. There are moral laws of nature, and physical laws of nature. The first are the rules which God has prescribed to his rational creatures for their conduct. They respect voluntary and free actions only; for no other actions can be subject to moral rules. These laws of nature ought to be always obeyed, but they are often transgressed by men. There is therefore no impossibility in the violation of the moral laws of nature, nor is such a violation an effect without a cause. The transgressor is the cause, and is justly accountable for it.

The physical laws of nature are the rules according to which the Deity commonly acts in his natural government of the world; and, whatever is done according to them, is not done by man, but by God, either immediately, or by instruments under his direction. These laws of nature neither restrain the power of the Author of nature, nor bring him under any obligation to do nothing beyond their sphere. He has sometimes acted contrary to them, in the case of miracles, and, perhaps, often acts without regard to them, in the ordinary course of his providence. Neither miraculous events, which are contrary to the physical laws of nature, nor such ordinary acts of the Divine administration as are without their sphere, are impossible, nor are they *effects without a cause.* God is the cause of them, and to him only they are to be imputed.

That the moral laws of nature are often transgressed by man, is undeniable. If the physical laws of nature make his obedience to the moral laws to be impossible, then he is, in the literal sense, *born under one law, bound unto anther,* which contradicts every notion of a righteous government of the world.

But though this supposition were attended with no such shocking consequence, it is merely a supposition; and until it be proved that every choice, or voluntary action of man, is determined by the physical laws of nature, this argument for necessity is only the taking for granted the point to be proved.

Of the same kind is the argument for the impossibility of liberty, taken from a balance, which cannot move but as it is moved by the weights put into it. This argument, though urged by almost every writer in defence of necessity, is so pitiful, and has been so often answered, that it scarce deserves to be mentioned.

Every argument in a dispute, which is not grounded on principles granted by both parties, is that kind of sophism which logicians call *petitio principii;* and such, in my apprehension, are all the arguments offered to prove that liberty of action is impossible.

It may further be observed, that every argument of this class, if it were really conclusive, must extend to the Deity, as well as to all created beings; and necessary existence, which has always been considered as the prerogative of the Supreme Being, must belong equally to every creature and to every event, even the most trifling.

This I take to be the system of Spinoza, and of those among the ancients, who carried fatality to the highest pitch.

---

42. Free Will

GEORGE E. MOORE

George Edward Moore (1873–1958) taught philosophy at Cambridge University. Early in his career, he and Bertrand Russell led an attack on the metaphysical idealism of Bradley and McTaggart. Moore went on to develop a style of analytical philosophy that gives prominence to commonsense beliefs. In this selection, Moore presents such an analysis of "could have done otherwise." Freedom and responsibility seem to require that it be true that one could, in some sense, do otherwise than what one does. Is determinism compatible with this ability? Moore claims that the important sense of "Could have done otherwise" is simply that "one *would* have done otherwise if one had chosen to do otherwise." Moore argues that people have this ability and that it is compatible with determinism.

Let us begin with the question: Is it ever true that a man *could* have done anything else, except what he actually did do? And, first of all, I think I had better explain exactly how this question seems to me to be related to the question of Free Will. For it is a fact that, in many discussions about Free Will, this precise question is never mentioned at all; so that it might be thought that the two have really nothing whatever to do with one another. And indeed some philosophers do, I think, definitely imply that they *have* nothing to do with one another: they seem to hold that our wills can properly be said to be free even if we *never* can, in any sense at all, do anything else except what, in the end, we actually do do. But this view, if it is held, seems to me to be plainly a mere abuse of language. The statement that we have Free Will is certainly ordinarily understood to imply that we really sometimes have the power of acting differently from the way in which we actually do act; and hence, if anybody tells us that we have Free Will, while at the same time he means to deny that we ever have such a power, he is simply misleading us. We certainly have *not* got Free Will, in the ordinary sense of the word, if we never really *could,* in any sense at all, have done anything else than what we did do; so that, in this respect, the two questions certainly are connected. But, on the other hand, the mere fact (if it is a fact) that we sometimes *can,* in *some* sense, do what we don't do, does not necessarily entitle us to say that we *have* Free Will. We certainly *haven't* got it, *unless* we can; but it doesn't follow that we *have* got it, even if we *can.* Whether we have or not will depend upon the precise sense in which it is true that we can. So that even if we do decide that we really *can* often, in *some* sense, do what we don't do, this decision by itself does not entitle us to say that we have Free Will.

And the first point about which we can and should be quite clear is, I think, this: namely, that we certainly often *can,* in *some* sense, do what we don't do. It is, I think, quite clear that this is so; and also very important that we should realize that it is so. For many people are inclined to assert, quite without qualification: No man ever *could,* on any occasion, have done anything else than what he actually did do on that occasion. By asserting this quite simply, without qualification, they imply, of course (even if they do not mean to imply), that there is *no* proper sense of the word 'could', in which it is true that a man *could* have acted differently. And it is this implication which is, I think, quite certainly absolutely false. For this reason, anybody who asserts, without qualification, 'Nothing ever *could* have happened, except what actually did happen', is making an assertion which is quite unjustifiable, and which he himself cannot help constantly contradicting. And it is important to insist on this, because many people do make this unqualified assertion, without seeing how violently it contradicts what they themselves, and all of us, believe, and rightly believe, at other times. If, indeed, they insert a qualification—if they merely say 'In *one* sense of the word *"could"* nothing ever *could* have happened, except what did happen', then, they may perhaps be perfectly right: we are not disputing that they may. All that we are maintaining is that, in *one* perfectly proper and legitimate sense of the word 'could', and that one of the very commonest senses in which it is used, it is quite certain that some things which didn't happen *could* have happened. And the proof that this is so, is simply as follows.

It is impossible to exaggerate the frequency of the occasions on which we *all* of us make a distinction between two things, neither of which *did* happen—a distinction which we express by saying, that whereas the one *could* have happened, and other could *not.* No distinction is commoner than this. And no one, I think, who fairly examines the instances in which we make it, can doubt about three things: namely (1) that very often there really is *some* distinction between the two things, corresponding to the language which we use; (2) that this distinction, which really *does* subsist between the things, is *the* one which we mean to express by saying that the one was possible and the other impossible; and (3) that this way of expressing it is a perfectly proper and legitimate way. But if so, it absolutely follows that one of the commonest and most legitimate usages of the phrases 'could' and 'could not' is to express a difference, which often really does hold between two things *neither* of which did actually happen. Only a few instances need be given. I *could* have walked a mile in 20 minutes this morning, but I certainly could *not* have run two miles in five minutes. I did not, *in fact,* do either of these two things; but it is pure nonsense to say that the mere fact that I *did* not, does away with the distinction between them, which I express by saying that the one was within my powers, whereas the other was *not. Although* I did neither, yet the one was certainly *possible* to me in a sense in which the other was totally *im*possible. Or, to take another instance: It is true, as a rule, that cats *can* climb trees, whereas dogs *can't.* Suppose that on a particular afternoon neither A's cat nor B's dog *do* climb a tree. It is quite absurd to say that this mere fact proves that we must be wrong if we say (as we certainly often should say) that the cat *could* have climbed a tree, though she didn't, whereas the dog *couldn't.* Or, to take an instance which concerns an inanimate object. Some ships *can* steam 20 knots, whereas others *can't* steam more than 15. And the mere fact that, on a particular occasion, a 20-knot steamer *did* not *actually* run at this speed certainly does not entitle us to say that she *could* not have done so, in the sense in which a 15-knot one *could* not. On the contrary, we all can and should distinguish between cases in which (as, for instance, owing to an accident to her propeller) she did not, *because* she could not, and cases in which she did not, *although* she *could.* Instances of this sort might be multiplied quite indefinitely; and it is surely quite plain that we all of us do *continually* use such language: we continually, when considering two events, neither of which *did* happen, distinguish between them by saying that whereas the one *was* possible, though it didn't happen, the other was *im*possible. And it is surely quite plain that what we mean by this (whatever it may be) is something which is often perfectly true. But, if so, then anybody who

asserts, without qualification, 'Nothing ever *could* have happened, except what did happen', is simply asserting what is false.

It is, therefore, quite certain that we often *could* (in *some* sense) have done what we did not do. And now let us see how this fact is related to the argument by which people try to persuade us that it is *not* a fact.

The argument is well known: it is simply this. It is assumed (for reasons which I need not discuss) that absolutely everything that happens has a *cause* in what precedes it. But to say this is to say that it follows *necessarily* from something that preceded it; or, in other words, that, once the preceding events which are its cause had happened, it was absolutely *bound* to happen. But to say that it was *bound* to happen, is to say that nothing else *could* have happened instead; so that, if *everything* has a cause, *nothing* ever could have happened except what did happen.

And now let us assume that the premise of this argument is correct: that everything really *has* a cause. What really follows from it? Obviously all that follows is that, in *one* sense of the word 'could', nothing ever *could* have happened, except what did happen. This really *does* follow. But, *if* the word 'could' is ambiguous—if, that is to say, it is used in different senses on different occasions—it is obviously quite possible that though, in *one* sense, nothing ever could have happened except what did happen, yet in *another* sense, it may at the same time be perfectly true that some things which did not happen *could* have happened. And can anybody undertake to assert with certainty that the word 'could' is *not* ambiguous? that it may not have more than one legitimate sense? *Possibly* it is not ambiguous; and, *if* it is not, then the fact that some things, which did not happen, *could* have happened, really would contradict the principle that everything has a cause; and, in that case, we should, I think, have to give up this principle, because the fact that we often *could* have done what we did not do, is so certain. But the assumption that the word 'could' is *not* ambiguous is an assumption which certainly should not be made without the clearest proof. And yet I think it often is made, without any proof at all; simply because it does not occur to people that words often are ambiguous. It is, for instance, often assumed, in the Free Will controversy, that the question at issue is solely as to whether everything is caused, or whether acts of will are sometimes uncaused. Those who hold that we *have* Free Will, think themselves bound to maintain that acts of will sometimes have *no* cause; and those who hold that everything is caused think that this proves completely that we have not Free Will. But, in fact, it is extremely doubtful whether Free Will is at all inconsistent with the principle that everything is caused. Whether it is or not, all depends on a very difficult question as to the meaning of the word 'could'. All that is certain about the matter is (1) that, if we have Free Will, it must be true, in *some* sense, that we sometimes *could* have done, what we did not do; and (2) that, if everything is caused, it must be true, in *some* sense, that we *never could* have done, what we did not do. What is very uncertain, and what certainly needs to be investigated, is whether these two meanings of the word 'could' are the same.

Let us begin by asking: What is the sense of the word 'could', in which it is so certain that we often *could* have done, what we did not do? What, for instance, is the sense in which I *could* have walked a mile in 20 minutes this morning, though I did not? There is one suggestion, which is very obvious: namely, that what I mean is simply after all that I could, *if* I had chosen; or (to avoid a possible complication) perhaps we had better say 'that I *should, if* I had chosen'. In other words, the suggestion is that we often use the phrase '*I could*' simply and solely as a short way of saying 'I *should*, if I had chosen.' And in all cases, where it is certainly true that we *could* have done, what we did not do, it is, I think, very difficult to be quite sure that this (or something similar) is *not* what we mean by the word 'could'. The case of the ship may seem to be an exception, because it is certainly not true that she would have steamed 20 knots if *she* had chosen; but even here it seems possible that what we mean is simply that she *would, if the men on board of her* had chosen. There are certainly good reasons for thinking that we *very often* mean by 'could' merely 'would, *if* so and so had chosen.' And if so, then we have a sense of the word 'could' in which the fact that we often *could* have done what we did not do, is perfectly compatible with the principle that everything has a cause: for to say that, *if* I had performed a certain act of will, I should have done something which I did not do, in no way contradicts this principle.

And an additional reason for supposing that this *is* what we often mean by 'could', and one which is also a reason why it is important to insist on the obvious fact that we very often really *should* have acted differently, *if* we had willed differently, is that those who deny that we ever *could* have done anything, which we did not do, often speak and think as if this really did involve the conclusion that we never should have acted differently, even *if* we had willed differently. This occurs, I think, in two chief instances—one in reference to the future, the other in reference to the past. The first occurs when, because they hold that nothing *can* happen, except what *will* happen, people are led to adopt the view called Fatalism—the view that *whatever we will*, the result will always be the same; that it is, therefore, *never* any use to make one choice rather than another. And this conclusion will really follow if by 'can' we mean '*would* happen, even *if* we were to will it'. But it is certainly untrue, and it certainly does not follow from the principle of causality. On the contrary, reasons of exactly the same sort and exactly as strong as those which lead us to suppose that everything has a cause, lead to the conclusion that if we choose one course, the result will *always* be different in *some* respect from what it would have been, if we had chosen another; and we know also that the difference would *sometimes* consist in the fact that *what* we chose would come to pass. It is certainly often true of the future, therefore, that whichever of two actions we *were* to choose, *would* actually be done, although it is quite certain that only one of the two *will* be done.

And the second instance, in which people are apt to speak and think, as if, *because* no man ever *could* have done anything but what he did do, it follows that he would not, even *if* he had chosen, is as follows. Many people seem, in fact, to conclude directly from the first of these two propositions, that we can never be justified in praising or blaming a man for anything that he does, or indeed for making any distinction between what is right or wrong, on the one hand, and what is lucky or unfortunate on the other. They conclude, for instance, that there is never any reason to treat or to regard the voluntary commission of a crime in any different way from that in which we treat or regard the involuntary catching of a disease. The man who committed the crime *could* not, they say, have helped committing it any more than the other man could have helped catching the disease; both events were equally inevitable; and though both may of course be great *misfortunes,* though both may have very bad consequences and equally bad ones—there is no justification whatever, they say, for the distinction we make between them when we say that the commission of the crime was *wrong,* or that the man was morally to blame for it, whereas the catching of the disease was *not* wrong and the man was not to blame for it. And this conclusion, again, will really follow if by 'could not' we mean '*would* not, even if he had willed to avoid it.' But the point I want to make is, that it follows *only* if we make this assumption. That is to say, the mere fact that the man *would* have succeeded in avoiding the crime, *if* he had chosen (which is certainly often true), whereas the other man would *not* have succeeded in avoiding the disease, *even* if he had chosen (which is certainly also often true) gives an ample justification for regarding and treating the two cases differently. It gives such a justification, because, where the occurrence of an event *did* depend upon the will, there, by acting on the will (as we may do by blame or punishment) we have often a reasonable chance of preventing similar events from recurring in the future; whereas, where it did *not* depend upon the will, we have no such chance. We may, therefore, fairly say that those who speak and think, as if a man who brings about a misfortune *voluntarily* ought to be treated and regarded in exactly the same way as one who brings about an equally great misfortune *involuntarily,* are speaking and thinking *as if* it were not true that we ever should have acted differently, even *if* we had willed to do so. And that is why it is extremely important to insist on the absolute certainty of the fact that we often really *should* have acted differently, *if* we had willed differently.

There is, therefore, much reason to think that when we say that we *could* have done a thing which we did not do, we *often* mean merely that we *should* have done it, *if* we had chosen. And if so, then it is quite certain that, in *this* sense, we often really *could* have done what we did not do, and that this fact is in no way inconsistent with the principle that everything has a cause. And for my part I must confess that I cannot feel certain that this may not be *all* that we usually mean and understand by the assertion that we have Free Will; so that those who deny that we have it are really denying (though, no doubt, often unconsciously) that we ever *should* have acted differently, even if we had willed differently. It has been sometimes held that this *is* what we mean; and I cannot find any conclusive argument to the contrary. And if it is *what* we mean, then it absolutely follows that we really *have* Free Will, and also that this fact is quite consistent with the principle that everything has a cause; and it follows also that our theory will be perfectly right, when it makes right and wrong depend on what we *could* have done, *if* we had chosen.

But, no doubt, there are many people who will say that this is *not* sufficient to entitle us to say that we have Free Will; and they will say this for a reason, which certainly has some plausibility, though I cannot satisfy myself that it is conclusive. They will say, namely: Granted that we often *should* have acted differently, *if* we had chosen differently, yet it is not true that we have Free Will, unless it is *also* often true in such cases that we *could* have *chosen* differently. The question of Free Will has been thus represented as being merely the question whether we ever *could* have chosen, what we did not choose, or ever *can* choose, what, in fact, we shall not choose. And since there is some plausibility in this contention, it is, I think, worth while to point out that here again it is absolutely certain that, in two different senses, at least, we often *could* have chosen, what, in fact, we did not choose; and that in neither sense does this fact contradict the principle of causality.

The first is simply the old sense over again. If by saying that we *could* have done, what we did not do, we often mean merely that we *should* have done it, *if* we had chosen to do it, then obviously, by saying that we *could* have chosen to do it, we may mean merely that we *should* have so chosen, *if* we had chosen to *make the choice.* And I think there is no doubt it is often true that we should have chosen to do particular thing *if* we had chosen to make the choice; and that this is a very important sense in which it is often in our power to make a choice. There certainly is such a thing as making an effort to induce ourselves to *choose* a particular course; and I think there is no doubt that often if we *had* made such an effort, we *should* have made a choice, which we did not in fact make.

And besides this, there is another sense in which, whenever we have several different courses of action in view, it is *possible* for us to choose any one of them; and a sense which is certainly of some practical importance, even if it goes no way to justify us in saying that we have Free Will. This sense arises from the fact that in such cases we can hardly ever *know for certain* beforehand, *which* choice we actually *shall* make; and one of the commonest senses of the word 'possible' is that in which we call an event 'possible' when no man can *know for certain* that it will *not* happen. It follows that almost, if not quite always, when we make a choice, after considering alternatives, it *was* possible that we should have chosen one of these alternatives, which we did not actually choose; and often, of course, it was not only possible, but highly probable, that we should have done so. And this fact is certainly of practical importance, because many people are apt much too easily to assume that it is quite certain that they *will not* make a given choice, which they know they ought to make, if it were possible; and their belief that they *will* not make it tends, of course, to prevent them from making it. For this reason it is important to insist that they can hardly ever know for certain with regard to any given choice that they will *not* make it.

It is, therefore, quite certain (1) that we often *should* have *acted* differently, if we had chosen to; (2) that similarly we often should have *chosen* differently, *if* we had chosen so to choose; and (3) that it was almost always *possible* that we should have chosen differently, in the sense that no man could know for certain that we should *not* so choose. All these three things are facts, and all of them are quite consistent with the principle of causality. Can anybody undertake to say for certain that none of these three facts and *no* combination of them will justify us in saying that we have Free Will? Or, suppose it granted that we have not Free Will, unless it is often true that we *could* have chosen, what we did not choose:—Can any defender of Free Will, or any opponent of it, show conclusively that what he means by '*could* have chosen' in this proposition, is anything different from the two certain facts, which I have numbered (2) and (3), or some combination of the two? Many people, no doubt, will still insist that these two facts alone are by no means sufficient to entitle us to say that we have Free Will: that it must be true that we were *able* to choose, in some quite other sense. But nobody, so far as I know, has ever been able to tell us exactly what that sense is. For my part, I can find no conclusive argument to show either that some such other sense of 'can' is necessary, or that it is not.

---

43. *Human Freedom and the Self*

RODERICK M. CHISHOLM

Chisholm argues that to be justified in holding persons responsible for their acts, it must be true that the self is an agent that is not always caused to act by prior events (or by prior desires or motives). He reasons that, if human actions are caused by something prior, then no one could do other than what he or she does. On the other hand, if some actions are uncaused, they are capricious. In either case, it seems wrong to hold people responsible for what they do. Chisholm introduces a special causality—agent (or "immanent") causality—and a special entity—the substantial self—to explain human freedom. In his discussion, Chisholm offers a critique of Moore's compatibilist analysis of "could have done otherwise."

A staff moves a stone, and is moved by a hand, which is moved by a man (Aristotle, *Physics*, 256a).

The metaphysical problem of human freedom might be summarized in the following way: Human beings are responsible agents; but this fact appears to conflict with a deterministic view of human action (the view that every event that is involved in an act is caused by some other event); and it *also* appears to conflict with an indeterministic view of human action (the view that the act, or some event that is essential to the act, is not caused at all.) To solve the problem, I believe, we must make somewhat far-reaching assumptions about the self or the agent—about the man who performs the act.

Perhaps it is needless to remark that, in all likelihood, it is impossible to say anything significant about this ancient problem that has not been said before.[1]

Let us consider some deed, or misdeed, that may be attributed to a responsible agent: one man, say, shot another. If the man *was* responsible for what he did, then, I would urge, what was to happen at the time of the shooting was something that was entirely up to the man himself. There was a moment at which it was true, both that he could have fired the shot and also that he could have refrained from firing it. And if this is so, then, even though he did fire it, he could have done something else instead. (He didn't find himself firing the shot 'against his will', as we say.) I think we can say, more generally, then, that if a man is responsible for a certain event or a certain state of affairs (in our example, the shooting of another man), then that event or state of affairs was brought about by some act of his, and the act was something that was in his power either to perform or not to perform.

But now if the act which he *did* perform was an act that was also in his power *not* to perform, then it could not have been caused or determined by any event that was not itself within his power either to bring about or not to bring about. For example, if what we say he did was really some-

thing that was brought about by a second man, one who forced his hand upon the trigger, say, or who, by means of hypnosis, compelled him to perform the act, then since the act was caused by the *second* man it was nothing that was within the power of the *first* man to prevent. And precisely the same thing is true, I think, if instead of referring to a second man who compelled the first one, we speak instead of the *desires* and *beliefs* which the first man happens to have had. For if what we say he did was really something that was brought about by his own beliefs and desires, if these beliefs and desires in the particular situation in which he happened to have found himself caused him to do just what it was that we say he did do, then, since *they* caused it, *he* was unable to do anything other than just what it was that he did do. It makes no difference whether the cause of the deed was internal or external; if the cause was some state or event for which the man himself was not responsible, then he was not responsible for what we have been mistakenly calling his act. If a flood caused the poorly constructed dam to break, then, given the flood and the constitution of the dam, the break, we may say, *had* to occur and nothing could have happened in its place. And if the flood of desire caused the weak-willed man to give in, then he, too, had to do just what it was that he did do and he was no more responsible than was the dam for the results that followed. (It is true, of course, that if the man is responsible for the beliefs and desires that he happens to have, then he may also be responsible for the things they lead him to do. But the question now becomes: *is* he responsible for the beliefs and desires he happens to have? If he is, then there was a time when they were within his power either to acquire or not to acquire, and we are left, therefore, with our general point.)

One may object: But surely if there were such a thing as a man who is really *good*, then he would be responsible for things that he would do; yet, he would be unable to do anything other than just what it is that he does do, since, being good, he will always choose to do what is best. The answer, I think, is suggested by a comment that Thomas Reid makes upon an ancient author. The author had said of Cato, 'He was good because he could not be otherwise', and Reid observes: 'This saying, if understood literally and strictly, is not the praise of Cato, but of his constitution, which was no

From the Lindley Lecture, 1964, pp. 3–15. Copyright © 1964 by the Department of Philosophy, University of Kansas. Reprinted by permission of the Department of Philosophy, University of Kansas, Lawrence, Kansas.

more the work of Cato than his existence'.[2] If Cato was himself responsible for the good things that he did, then Cato, as Reid suggests, was such that, although he had the power to do what was not good, he exercised his power only for that which was good.

All of this, if it is true, may give a certain amount of comfort to those who are tender-minded. But we should remind them that it also conflicts with a familiar view about the nature of God—with the view that St. Thomas Aquinas expresses by saying that 'every movement both of the will and of nature proceeds from God as the Prime Mover'.[3] If the act of the sinner *did* proceed from God as the Prime Mover, then God was in the position of the second agent we just discussed—the man who forced the trigger finger, or the hypnotist—and the sinner, so-called, was *not* responsible for what he did. (This may be a bold assertion, in view of the history of western theology, but I must say that I have never encountered a single good reason for denying it.)

There is one standard objection to all of this and we should consider it briefly.

The objection takes the form of a stratagem—one designed to show that determinism (and divine providence) is consistent with human responsibility. The stratagem is one that was used by Jonathan Edwards and by many philosophers in the present century, most notably, G. E. Moore.[4]

One proceeds as follows: The expression

1. He could have done otherwise,

it is argued, means no more nor less than

2. If he had chosen to do otherwise, then he would have done otherwise.

(In place of 'chosen,' one might say 'tried', 'set out', 'decided', 'undertaken', or 'willed'.) The truth of statement (2), it is then pointed out, is consistent with determinism (and with divine providence); for even if all of the man's actions were causally determined, the man could still be such that, *if* he had chosen otherwise, then he would have done otherwise. What the murderer saw, let us suppose, along with his beliefs and desires, *caused* him to fire the shot; yet he was such that *if,* just then, he had chosen or decided *not* to fire the shot, then he would not have fired it. All of this is certainly possible. Similarly, we could say,

of the dam, that the flood caused it to break and also that the dam was such that, *if* there had been no flood or any similar pressure, then the dam would have remained intact. And therefore, the argument proceeds, if (2) is consistent with determinism, and if (1) and (2) say the same thing, then (1) is also consistent with determinism; hence we can say that the agent *could* have done otherwise even though he was caused to do what he did do; and therefore determinism and moral responsibility are compatible.

Is the argument sound? The conclusion follows from the premises, but the catch, I think, lies in the first premise—the one saying that statement (1) tells us no more nor less than what statement (2) tells us. For (2), it would seem, could be true while (1) is false. That is to say, our man might be such that, if he had chosen to do otherwise, then he would have done otherwise, and yet *also* such that he could not have done otherwise. Suppose, after all, that our murderer could not have *chosen,* or could not have *decided,* to do otherwise. Then the fact that he happens also to be a man such that, if he had chosen not to shoot he would not have shot, would make no difference. For if he could *not* have chosen *not* to shoot, then he could not have done anything other than just what it was that he did do. In a word: from our statement (2) above ('If he had chosen to do otherwise, then he would have done otherwise'), we cannot make an inference to (1) above ('He could have done otherwise') unless we can *also* assert:

3. He could have chosen to do otherwise.

And therefore, if we must reject this third statement (3), then, even though we may be justified in asserting (2), we are not justified in asserting (1). If the man could not have chosen to do otherwise, then he would not have done otherwise—even if he was such that, if he *had* chosen to do otherwise, then he would have done otherwise.

The stratagem in question, then, seems to me not to work, and I would say, therefore, that the ascription of responsibility conflicts with a deterministic view of action.

Perhaps there is less need to argue that the ascription of responsibility also conflicts with an indeterministic view of action—with the view that the act, or some event that is essential to the act, is not caused at all. If the act—the firing of the shot—was not caused at all, if it was fortuitous or capricious, happening so to speak out of the blue, then, presumably, no one—and nothing—was responsible for the act. Our conception of action, therefore, should be neither deterministic nor indeterministic. Is there any other possibility?

We must not say that every event involved in the act is caused by some other event; and we must not say that the act is something that is not caused at all. The possibility that remains, therefore, is this: We should say that at least one of the events that are involved in the act is caused, not by any other events, but by something else instead. And this something else can only be the agent—the man. If there is an event that is caused, not by other events, but by the man, then there are some events involved in the act that are not caused by other events. But if the event in question is caused by the man then it *is* caused and we are not committed to saying that there is something involved in the act that is not caused at all.

But this, of course, is a large consequence, implying something of considerable importance about the nature of the agent or the man.

If we consider only inanimate natural objects, we may say that causation, if it occurs, is a relation between *events* or *states of affairs.* The dam's breaking was an event that was caused by a set of other events—the dam being weak, the flood being strong, and so on. But if a man is responsible for a particular deed, then, if what I have said is true, there is some event, or set of events, that is caused, *not* by other events or states of affairs, but by the agent, whatever he may be.

I shall borrow a pair of medieval terms, using them, perhaps, in a way that is slightly different from that for which they were originally intended. I shall say that when one event or state of affairs (or set of events or states of affairs) causes some other event or state of affairs, then we have an instance of *transeunt* causation. And I shall say that when an *agent,* as distinguished from an event, causes an event or state of affairs, then we have an instance of *immanent* causation.

The nature of what is intended by the expression 'immanent causation' may be illustrated by this sentence from Aristotle's *Physics:* 'Thus, a staff moves a stone, and is moved by a hand, which is moved by a man' (VII, 5, 256a, 6–8). If the man was responsible, then we have in this illustration a

number of instances of causation—most of them transeunt but at least one of them immanent. What the staff did to the stone was an instance of transeunt causation, and thus we may describe it as a relation between events: 'The motion of the staff caused the motion of the stone.' And similarly for what the hand did to the staff: 'The motion of the hand caused the motion of the staff'. And, as we know from physiology, there are still other events which caused the motion of the hand. Hence we need not introduce the agent at this particular point, as Aristotle does—we *need* not, though we *may.* We *may* say that the hand was moved by the man, but we may *also* say that the motion of the hand was caused by the motion of certain muscles; and we may say that the motion of the muscles was caused by certain events that took place within the brain. But some event, and presumably one of those that took place within the brain, was caused by the agent and not by any other events.

There are, of course, objections to is way of putting the matter; I shall consider the two that seem to me to be most important.

One may object, firstly: 'If the *man* does anything, then, as Aristotle's remark suggests, what he does is to move the *hand.* But he certainly does not *do* anything to his brain—he may not even know that he *has* a brain. And if he doesn't do anything to the brain, and if the motion of the hand was caused by something that happened within the brain, then there is no point in appealing to "immanent causation" as being something incompatible with "transeunt causation"—for the whole thing, after all, is a matter of causal relations among events or states of affairs.'

The answer to this objection, I think, is this: It is true that the agent does not *do* anything with his brain, or to his brain, in the sense in which he *does* something with his hand and does something to the staff. But from this it does not follow that the agent was not the immanent cause of something that happened within his brain.

We should note a useful distinction that has been proposed by Professor A. I. Melden—namely, the distinction between 'making something A happen' and 'doing A'.[5] If I reach for the staff and pick it up, then one of the things that I *do* is just that—reach for the staff and pick it up. And if it is something that I do, then there is a very clear sense in which it may be said to be something that I know that I do. If you ask me, 'Are you doing something, or trying to do something, with the staff?' I will have no difficulty in finding an answer. But in doing something with the staff, I also make various things happen which are not in this same sense things that I do: I will make various air-particles move; I will free a number of blades of grass from the pressure that had been upon them; and I may cause a shadow to move from one place to another. If these are merely things that I make happen, as distinguished from things that I do, then I may know nothing whatever about them: I may not have the slightest idea that, in moving the staff, I am bringing about any such thing as the motion of air-particles, shadows, and blades of grass.

We may say, in answer to the first objection, therefore, that it is true that our agent does nothing to his brain or with his brain; but from this it does not follow that the agent is not the immanent cause of some event within his brain; for the brain event may be something which, like the motion of the air-particles, he made happen in picking up the staff. The only difference between the two cases is this: in each case, he made something happen when he picked up the staff; but in the one case—the motion of the air-particles or of the shadows—it was the motion of the staff that caused the event to happen; and in the other case—the event that took place in the brain—it was this event that caused the motion of the staff.

The point is, in a word, that whenever a man does something A, then (by 'immanent causation') he makes a certain cerebral event happen, and this cerebral event (by 'transeunt causation') makes A happen.

The second objection is more difficult and concerns the very concept of 'immanent causation', or causation by an agent, as this concept is to be interpreted here. The concept is subject to a difficulty which has long been associated with that of the prime mover unmoved. We have said that there must be some event A, presumably some cerebral event, which is caused not by any other event, but by the agent. Since A was not caused by any other event, then the agent himself cannot be said to have undergone any change or produced any other event (such as 'an act of will' or the like) which brought A about. But if, when the agent made A happen, there was no event involved other

than A itself, no event which could be described as *making* A happen, what did the agent's causation consist of? What, for example, is the difference between A's just happening, and the agent's *causing* A to happen? We cannot attribute the difference to any event that took place within the agent. And so far as the event A itself is concerned, there would seem to be no discernible difference. Thus Aristotle said that the activity of the prime mover is nothing in addition to the motion that it produces, and Suarez said that 'the action is in reality nothing but the effect as it flows from the agent'.[6] Must we conclude, then, that there is no more to the man's action in causing event A than there is to the event A's happening by itself? Here we would seem to have a distinction without a difference—in which case we have failed to find a *via media* between a deterministic and an indeterministic view of action.

The only answer, I think, can be this: That the difference between the man's causing A, on the one hand, and the event A just happening, on the other, lies in the fact that, in the first case but not the second, the event A *was* caused and was caused by the man. There was a brain event A; the agent did, in fact, cause the brain event; but there was nothing that he did to cause it.

This answer may not entirely satisfy and it will be likely to provoke the following question: 'But what are you really *adding* to the assertion that A happened when you utter the words "the agent *caused* A to happen"?' As soon as we have put the question this way, we see, I think, that whatever difficulty we may have encountered is one that may be traced to the concept of causation generally—whether 'immanent' or 'transeunt'. The problem, in other words, is not a problem that is peculiar to our conception of human action. It is a problem that must be faced by anyone who makes use of the concept of causation at all; and therefore, I would say, it is a problem for everyone but the complete indeterminist.

For the problem, as we put it, referring just to 'immanent causation,' or causation by an agent, was this: 'What is the difference between saying, of an event A, that A just happened and saying that someone caused A to happen?' The analogous problem, which holds for 'transeunt causation,' or causation by an event, is this: 'What is the difference between saying, of two events A and B, that B happened and then A happened, and saying that B's happening was the *cause* of A's happening?' And the only answer that one can give is this—that in the one case the agent was the cause of A's happening and in the other case event B was the cause of A's happening. The nature of transeunt causation is no more clear than is that of immanent causation.

But we may plausibly say—and there is a respectable philosophical tradition to which we may appeal—that the notion of immanent causation, or causation by an agent, is in fact more clear than that of transeunt causation, or causation by an event, and that it is only by understanding our own causal efficacy, as agents, that we can grasp the concept of *cause* at all. Hume may be said to have shown that we do not derive the concept of *cause* from what we perceive of external things. How, then, do we derive it? The most plausible suggestion, it seems to me, is that of Reid, once again: namely that 'the conception of an efficient cause may very probably be derived from the experience we have had . . . of our own power to produce certain effects.'[7] If we did not understand the concept of immanent causation, we would not understand that of transeunt causation.

It may have been noted that I have avoided the term 'free will' in all of this. For even if there is such a faculty as 'the will', which somehow sets our acts agoing, the question of freedom, as John Locke said, is not the question *'whether the will be free'*; it is the question *'whether a man be free'*.[8] For if there is a 'will', as a moving faculty, the question is whether the man is free to will to do these things that he does will to do—and also whether he is free *not* to will any of those things that he does will to do, and, again, whether he is free to will any of those things that he does not will to do. Jonathan Edwards tried to restrict himself to the question—'Is the man free to do what it is that he wills?'—but the answer to this question will not tell us whether the man is responsible for what it is that he *does* will to do. Using still another pair of medieval terms, we may say that the metaphysical problem of freedom does not concern the *actus imperatus;* it does not concern the question whether we are free to accomplish whatever it is that we will or set out to do; it concerns the *actus elicitus,* the question whether we are free to will or to set out to do those things that we do will or set out to do.

If we are responsible, and if what I have been trying to say is true, then we have a prerogative which some would attribute only to God: each of us, when we act, is a prime mover unmoved. In doing what we do, we cause certain events to happen, and nothing—or no one—causes us to cause those events to happen.

If we are thus prime movers unmoved and if our actions, or those for which we are responsible, are not causally determined, then they are not causally determined by our *desires*. And this means that the relation between what we want or what we desire, on the one hand, and what it is that we do, on the other, is not as simple as most philosophers would have it.

We may distinguish between what we might call the 'Hobbist approach' and what we might call the 'Kantian approach' to this question. The Hobbist approach is the one that is generally accepted at the present time, but the Kantian approach, I believe, is the one that is true. According to Hobbism, if we *know*, of some man, what his beliefs and desires happen to be and how strong they are, if we know what he feels certain of, what he desires more than anything else, and if we know the state of his body and what stimuli he is being subjected to, then we may *deduce*, logically, just what it is that he will do—or, more accurately, just what it is that he will try, set out, or undertake to do. Thus Professor Melden has said that 'the connection between wanting and doing is logical'.[9] But according to the Kantian approach to our problem, and this is the one that I would take, there is no such logical connection between wanting and doing, nor need there even be a causal connection. No set of statements about a man's desires, beliefs, and stimulus situation at any time implies any statement telling us what the man will try, set out, or undertake to do at that time. As Reid put it, though we may 'reason from men's motives to their actions and, in many cases, with great probability', we can never do so 'with absolute certainty'.[10]

This means that, in one very strict sense of the terms, there can be no science of man. If we think of science as a matter of finding out what laws happen to hold, and if the statement of a law tells us what kinds of events are caused by what other kinds of events, then there will be human actions which we cannot explain by subsuming them under any laws. We cannot say, 'It is causally necessary that, given such and such desires and beliefs, and being subject to such and such stimuli, the agent will do so and so'. For at times the agent, if he chooses, may rise above his desires and do something else instead.

But all of this is consistent with saying that, perhaps more often than not, our desires do exist under conditions such that those conditions necessitate us to act. And we may also say, with Leibniz, that at other times our desires may 'incline without necessitating'.

Leibniz's phrase presents us with our final philosophical problem. What does it mean to say that a desire, or a motive, might 'incline without necessitating'? There is a temptation, certainly, to say that 'to incline' means to cause and that 'not to necessitate' means not to cause, but obviously we cannot have it both ways.

Nor will Leibniz's own solution do. In his letter to Coste, he puts the problem as follows: 'When a choice is proposed, for example to go out or not to go out, it is a question whether, with all the circumstances, internal and external, motives, perceptions, dispositions, impressions, passions, inclinations taken together, I am still in a contingent state, or whether I am necessitated to make the choice, for example, to go out; that is to say, whether this proposition true and determined in fact, *In all these circumstances taken together I shall choose to go out,* is contingent or necessary'.[11] Leibniz's answer might be put as follows: In one sense of the terms 'necessary' and 'contingent', the proposition 'In all these circumstances taken together I shall choose to go out', may be said to be contingent and not necessary, and in another sense of these terms, it may be said to be necessary and not contingent. But the sense in which the proposition may be said to be contingent, according to Leibniz, is only this: There is no logical contradiction involved in denying the proposition. And the sense in which it may be said to be necessary is this: Since 'nothing ever occurs without cause or determining reason', the proposition is causally necessary. 'Whenever all the circumstances taken together are such that the balance of deliberation is heavier on one side than on the other, it is certain and infallible that that is the side that is going to win out'. But if what we have been saying is true, the proposition 'In all these circum-

stances taken together I shall choose to go out', may be causally as well as logically contingent. Hence we must find another interpretation for Leibniz's statement that our motives and desires may incline us, or influence us, to choose without thereby necessitating us to choose.

Let us consider a public official who has some moral scruples but who also, as one says, could be had. Because of the scruples that he does have, he would never take any positive steps to receive a bribe—he would not actively solicit one. But his morality has its limits and he is also such that, if we were to confront him with a *fait accompli* or to let him see what is about to happen ($10,000 in cash is being deposited behind the garage), then he would succumb and be unable to resist. The general situation is a familiar one and this is one reason that people pray to be delivered from temptation. (It also justifies Kant's remark: 'And how many there are who may have led a long blameless life, who are only *fortunate* in having escaped so many temptations'.)[12] Our relation to the misdeed that we contemplate may not be a matter simply of being able to bring it about or not to bring it about. As St. Anselm noted, there are at least four possibilities. We may illustrate them by reference to our public official and the event which is his receiving the bribe, in the following way: (i) he may be able to bring the event about himself (*facere esse*), in which case he would actively cause himself to receive the bribe; (ii) he may be able to refrain from bringing it about himself (*non facere esse*), in which case he would not himself do anything to insure that he receive the bribe; (iii) he may be able to do something to prevent the event from occurring (*facere non esse*), in which case he would make sure that the $10,000 was *not* left behind the garage; or (iv) he may be unable to do anything to prevent the event from occurring (*non facere non esse*), in which case, though he may not solicit the bribe, he would allow himself to keep it.[13] We have envisaged our official as a man who can resist the temptation to (i) but cannot resist the temptation to (iv): he can refrain from bringing the event about himself, but he cannot bring himself to do anything to prevent it.

Let us think of 'inclination without necessitation', then, in such terms as these. First we may contrast the two propositions:

1. He can resist the temptation to do something in order to make A happen;

2. He can resist the temptation to allow A to happen (i.e., to do nothing to prevent A from happening).

We may suppose that the man has some desire to have A happen and thus has a motive for making A happen. His motive for making A happen, I suggest, is one that *necessitates* provided that, because of the motive, (1) is false; he cannot resist the temptation to do something in order to make A happen. His motive for making A happen is one that *inclines* provided that, because of the motive, (2) is false; like our public official, he cannot bring himself to do anything to prevent A from happening. And therefore we can say that this motive for making A happen is one that *inclines but does not necessitate* provided that, because of the motive, (1) is true and (2) is false; he can resist the temptation to make it happen but he cannot resist the temptation to allow it to happen.

Endnotes

[1] The general position to be presented here is suggested in the following writings, among others: Aristotle, *Eudemian Ethics*, bk. ii ch. 6; *Nicomachean Ethics*, bk. iii, ch. 1–5; Thomas Reid, *Essays on the Active Powers of Man*; C. A. Campbell, "Is 'Free Will' a Pseudo-Problem?" *Mind*, 1951, 441–65; Roderick M. Chisholm, "Responsibility and Avoidability," and Richard Taylor, "Determination and the Theory of Agency," in *Determinism and Freedom in the Age of Modern Science*, ed. Sidney Hook (New York, 1958).

[2] Thomas Reid, *Essays on the Active Powers of Man*, essay iv, ch. 4 (*Works*, 600).

[3] *Summa Theologica*, First Part of the Second Part, qu. vi ('On the Voluntary and Involuntary').

[4] Jonathan Edwards, *Freedom of the Will* (New Haven, 1957); G. E. Moore, *Ethics* (Home University Library, 1912), ch. 6.

[5] A. I. Melden, *Free Action* (London, 1961), especially ch. 3. Mr. Melden's own views, however, are quite the contrary of those that are proposed here.

[6] Aristotle, *Physics*, bk. iii, ch. 3; Suarez, *Disputations Metaphysicae*, Disputation 18, s. 10.

[7] Reid, *Works*, 524.

[8] *Essay Concerning Human Understanding*, bk. ii, ch. 21.

[9] Melden, 166.

[10] Reid, *Works*, 608, 612.

[11] 'Lettre à Mr. Coste de la Nécessité et de la Contingence' (1707) in *Opera Philosophica*, ed. Erdmann, 447–9.

[12] In the Preface to the *Metaphysical Elements of Ethics*, in *Kant's Critique of Practical Reason and Other Works on the Theory of Ethics*, ed. T. K. Abbott (London, 1959), 303.

[13] Cf. D. P. Henry, 'Saint Anselm's De "Grammatico,"' *Philosophical Quarterly*, x (1960), 115–26. St. Anselm noted that (i) and (iii), respectively, may be thought of as forming the upper left and the upper right corners of a square of opposition, and (ii) and (iv) the lower left and the lower right.

---

44. *Alternate Possibilities and Moral Responsibility*

HARRY FRANKFURT

In the following selection Harry Frankfurt, professor of philosophy at Princeton University, argues that "the principle of alternate possibilities" is mistaken. According to this principle, a person is morally responsible for an action only if he or she could have done otherwise. By means of well-constructed counterexamples, Frankfurt attempts to demonstrate if a person does something that he or she really wanted to do, and not because he or she could not have done otherwise, then even if in fact he or she could not have done otherwise, the person may still be morally responsible for what he or she has done. His thesis, if true, would tend to undercut much of the worry about determinism and criticism of compatibilism.

A dominant role in nearly all recent inquiries into the free-will problem has been played by a principle which I shall call "the principle of alternate possibilities." This principle states that a person is morally responsible for what he has done only if he could have done otherwise. Its exact meaning is a subject of controversy, particularly concerning whether someone who accepts it is thereby committed to believing that moral responsibility and determinism are incompatible. Practically no one, however, seems inclined to deny or even to question that the principle of alternate possibilities (construed in some way or other) is true. It has generally seemed so overwhelmingly plausible that some philosophers have even characterized it as an *a priori* truth. People whose accounts of free will or of moral responsibility are radically at odds evidently find in it a firm and convenient common ground upon which they can profitably take their opposing stands.

But the principle of alternate possibilities is false. A person may well be morally responsible for what he has done even though he could not have done otherwise. The principle's plausibility is an illusion, which can be made to vanish by bringing the relevant moral phenomena into sharper focus.

I.

In seeking illustrations of the principle of alternate possibilities, it is most natural to think of situations in which the same circumstances both bring it about that a person does something and make it impossible for him to avoid doing it. These include, for example, situations in which a person is coerced into doing something, or in which he is impelled to act by a hypnotic suggestion, or in which some inner compulsion drives him to do what he does. In situations of these kinds there are circumstances that make it impossible for the person to do otherwise, and these very circumstances also serve to bring it about that he does whatever it is that he does.

From Harry Frankfurt, "Alternate Possibilities and Moral Responsibility," *The Journal of Philosophy*, 66, No. 23 (December 4, 1969): 829–839. Reprinted by permission of *The Journal of Philosophy* and the author.

However, there may be circumstances that constitute sufficient conditions for a certain action to be performed by someone and that therefore make it impossible for the person to do otherwise, but that do not actually impel the person to act or in any way produce his action. A person may do something in circumstances that leave him no alternative to doing it, without these circumstances actually moving him or leading him to do it—without them playing any role, indeed, in bringing it about that he does what he does.

An examination of situations characterized by circumstances of this sort casts doubt, I believe, on the relevance to questions of moral responsibility of the fact that a person who has done something could not have done otherwise. I propose to develop some examples of this kind in the context of a discussion of coercion and to suggest that our moral intuitions concerning these examples tend to disconfirm the principle of alternate possibilities. Then I will discuss the principle in more general terms, explain what I think is wrong with it, and describe briefly and without argument how it might appropriately be revised.

II.

It is generally agreed that a person who has been coerced to do something did not do it freely and is not morally responsible for having done it. Now the doctrine that coercion and moral responsibility are mutually exclusive may appear to be no more than a somewhat particularized version of the principle of alternate possibilities. It is natural enough to say of a person who has been coerced to do something that he could not have done otherwise. And it may easily seem that being coerced deprives a person of freedom and of moral responsibility simply because it is a special case of being unable to do otherwise. The principle of alternate possibilities may in this way derive some credibility from its association with the very plausible proposition that moral responsibility is excluded by coercion.

It is not right, however, that it should do so. The fact that a person was coerced to act as he did may entail both that he could not have done otherwise and that he bears no moral responsibility for his action. But his lack of moral responsibility is not entailed by his having been unable to do otherwise. The doctrine that coercion excludes moral responsibility is not correctly understood, in other words, as a particularized version of the principle of alternate possibilities.

Let us suppose that someone is threatened convincingly with a penalty he finds unacceptable and that he then does what is required of him by the issuer of the threat. We can imagine details that would make it reasonable for us to think that the person was coerced to perform the action in question, that he could not have done otherwise, and that he bears no moral responsibility for having done what he did. But just what is it about situations of this kind that warrants the judgment that the threatened person is not morally responsible for his act?

This question may be approached by considering situations of the following kind. Jones decides for reasons of his own to do something, then someone threatens him with a very harsh penalty (so harsh that any reasonable person would submit to the threat) unless he does precisely that, and Jones does it. Will we hold Jones morally responsible for what he has done? I think this will depend on the roles we think were played, in leading him to act, by his original decision and by the threat.

One possibility is that Jones$_1$ is not a reasonable man: he is, rather, a man who does what he has once decided to do no matter what happens next and no matter what the cost. In that case, the threat actually exerted no effective force upon him. He acted without any regard to it, very much as if he were not aware that it had been made. If this is indeed the way it was, the situation did not involve coercion at all. The threat did not lead Jones$_1$ to do what he did. Nor was it in fact sufficient to have prevented him from doing otherwise: if his earlier decision had been to do something else, the threat would not have deterred him in the slightest. It seems evident that in these circumstances the fact that Jones$_1$ was threatened in no way reduces the moral responsibility he would otherwise bear for his act. This example, however, is not a counterexample either to the doctrine that coercion excuses or to the principle of alternate possibilities. For we have supposed that Jones$_1$ is a man upon whom the threat had no coercive effect and, hence, that it did not actually deprive him of alternatives to doing what he did.

Another possibility is that Jones$_2$ was stampeded by the threat. Given that threat, he would have performed that action regardless of what decision he had already made. The threat upset him so profoundly, moreover, that he completely forgot his own earlier decision and did what was demanded of him entirely because he was terrified of the penalty with which he was threatened. In this case, it is not relevant to his having performed the action that he had already decided on his own to perform it. When the chips were down he thought of nothing but the threat, and fear alone led him to act. The fact that at an earlier time Jones$_2$ had decided for his own reasons to act in just that way may be relevant to an evaluation of his character; he may bear full moral responsibility for having made *that* decision. But he can hardly be said to be morally responsible for his action. For he performed the action simply as a result of the coercion to which he was subjected. His earlier decision played no role in bringing it about that he did what he did, and it would therefore be gratuitous to assign it a role in the moral evaluation of his action.

Now consider a third possibility. Jones$_3$ was neither stampeded by the threat nor indifferent to it. The threat impressed him, as it would impress any reasonable man, and he would have submitted to it wholeheartedly if he had not already made a decision that coincided with the one demanded of him. In fact, however, he performed the action in question on the basis of the decision he had made before the threat was issued. When he acted, he was not actually motivated by the threat but solely by the considerations that had originally commended the action to him. It was not the threat that led him to act, though it would have done so if he had not already provided himself with a sufficient motive for performing the action in question.

No doubt it will be very difficult for anyone to know, in a case like this one, exactly what happened. Did Jones$_3$ perform the action because of the threat, or were his reasons for acting simply those which had already persuaded him to do so? Or did he act on the basis of two motives, each of which was sufficient for his action? It is not impossible, however, that the situation should be clearer than situations of this kind usually are. And suppose it is apparent to us that Jones$_3$ acted on the basis of his own decision and not because of the threat. Then I think we would be justified in regarding his moral responsibility for what he did as unaffected by the threat even though, since he would in any case have submitted to the threat, he could not have avoided doing what he did. It would be entirely reasonable for us to make the same judgment concerning his moral responsibility that we would have made if we had not known of the threat. For the threat did not in fact influence his performance of the action. He did what he did just as if the threat had not been made at all.

III.

The case of Jones₃ may appear at first glance to combine coercion and moral responsibility, and thus to provide a counterexample to the doctrine that coercion excuses. It is not really so certain that it does so, however, because it is unclear whether the example constitutes a genuine instance of coercion. Can we say of Jones₃ that he was coerced to do something, when he had already decided on his own to do it and when he did it entirely on the basis of that decision? Or would it be more correct to say that Jones₃ was not coerced to do what he did, even though he himself recognized that there was an irresistible force at work in virtue of which he had to do it? My own linguistic intuitions lead me toward the second alternative, but they are somewhat equivocal. Perhaps we can say either of these things, or perhaps we must add a qualifying explanation to whichever of them we say.

This murkiness, however, does not interfere with our drawing an important moral from an examination of the example. Suppose we decide to say that Jones₃ was *not* coerced. Our basis for saying this will clearly be that it is incorrect to regard a man as being coerced to do something unless he does it *because* of the coercive force exerted against him. The fact that an irresistible threat is made will not, then, entail that the person who receives it is coerced to do what he does. It will also be necessary that the threat is what actually accounts for his doing it. On the other hand, suppose we decide to say that Jones₃ *was* coerced. Then we will be bound to admit that

being coerced does not exclude being morally responsible. And we will also surely be led to the view that coercion affects the judgment of a person's moral responsibility only when the person acts as he does because he is coerced to do so— i.e., when the fact that he is coerced is what accounts for his action.

Whichever we decide to say, then, we will recognize that the doctrine that coercion excludes moral responsibility is not a particularized version of the principle of alternate possibilities. Situations in which a person who does something cannot do otherwise because he is subject to coercive power are either not instances of coercion at all, or they are situations in which the person may still be morally responsible for what he does if it is not because of the coercion that he does it. When we excuse a person who has been coerced, we do not excuse him because he was unable to do otherwise. Even though a person is subject to a coercive force that precludes his performing any action but one, he may nonetheless bear full moral responsibility for performing that action.

IV.

To the extent that the principle of alternate possibilities derives its plausibility from association with the doctrine that coercion excludes moral responsibility, a clear understanding of the latter diminishes the appeal of the former. Indeed the case of Jones₃ may appear to do more than illuminate the relationship between the two doctrines. It may well seem to provide a decisive counterexample to the principle of alternate possibilities and thus to show that this principle is false. For the irresistibility of the threat to which Jones₃ is subjected might well be taken to mean that he cannot but perform the action he performs. And yet the threat, since Jones₃ performs the action without regard to it, does not reduce his moral responsibility for what he does.

The following objection will doubtless be raised against the suggestion that the case of Jones₃ is a counterexample to the principle of alternate possibilities. There is perhaps a sense in which Jones₃ cannot do otherwise than perform the action he performs, since he is a reasonable

412 Part IV Freedom

man and the threat he encounters is sufficient to move any reasonable man. But it is not this sense that is germane to the principle of alternate possibilities. His knowledge that he stands to suffer an intolerably harsh penalty does not mean that $Jones_3$, strictly speaking, *cannot* perform any action but the one he does perform. After all it is still open to him, and this is crucial, to defy the threat if he wishes to do so and so accept the penalty his action would bring down upon him. In the sense in which the principle of alternate possibilities employs the concept of "could have done otherwise," $Jones_3$'s inability so resist the threat does not mean that he cannot do otherwise than perform the action he performs. Hence the case of $Jones_3$ does not constitute an instance contrary to the principle.

I do not propose to consider in what sense the concept of "could have done otherwise" figures in the principle of alternate possibilities, nor will I attempt to measure the force of the objection I have just described.[1] For I believe that whatever force this objection may be thought to have can be deflected by altering the example in the following way.[2] Suppose someone—Black, let us say—wants $Jones_4$ to perform a certain action. Black is prepared to go to considerable lengths to get his way, but he prefers to avoid showing his hand unnecessarily. So he waits until $Jones_4$ is about to make up his mind what to do, and he does nothing unless it is clear to him (Black is an excellent judge of such things) that $Jones_4$ is going to decide to do something *other* than what he wants him to do. If it does become clear that $Jones_4$ is going to decide to do something else, Black takes effective steps to ensure that $Jones_4$ decides to do, and that he does do, what he wants him to do.[3] Whatever $Jones_4$'s initial preferences and inclinations then, Black will have his way.

What steps will Black take, if he believes he must take steps, in order so ensure that $Jones_4$ decides and acts as he wishes? Anyone with a theory concerning what "could have done otherwise" means may answer this question for himself by describing whatever measures he would regard as sufficient to guarantee that, in the relevant sense, $Jones_4$ cannot do otherwise. Let Black pronounce a terrible threat, and in this way both force $Jones_4$ to perform the desired action and prevent him from performing a for-

bidden one. Let Black give $Jones_4$ a potion, or put him under hypnosis, and in some such way as these generate in $Jones_4$ an irresistible inner compulsion to perform the act Black wants performed and to avoid others. Or let Black manipulate the minute processes of $Jones_4$'s brain and nervous system in some more direct way, so that causal forces running in and out of his synapses and along the poor man's nerves determine that he chooses to act and that he does act in the one way and not in any other. Given any conditions under which it will be maintained that $Jones_4$ cannot do otherwise, in other words, let Black bring it about that those conditions prevail. The structure of the example is flexible enough, I think, to find a way around any charge of irrelevance by accommodating the doctrine on which the charge is based.[4]

Now suppose that Black never has to show his hand because $Jones_4$, for reasons of his own, decides to perform and does perform the very action Black wants him to perform. In that case, it seems clear, $Jones_4$ will bear precisely the same moral responsibility for what he does as he would have borne if Black had not been ready to take steps to ensure that he do it. It would be quite unreasonable to excuse $Jones_4$ for his action, or to withhold the praise to which it would normally entitle him, on the basis of the fact that he could not have done otherwise. This fact played no role at all in leading him to act as he did. He would have acted the same even if it had not been a fact. Indeed, everything happened just as it would have happened without Black's presence in the situation and without his readiness to intrude into it.

In this example there are sufficient conditions for $Jones_4$'s performing the action in question. What action he performs is not up to him. Of course it is in a way up to him whether he acts on his own or as a result of Black's intervention. That depends upon what action he himself is inclined to perform. But whether he finally acts on his own or as a result of Black's intervention, he performs the same action. He has no alternative but to do what Black wants him to do. If he does it on his own, however, his moral responsibility for doing it is not affected by the fact that Black was lurking in the background with sinister intent, since this intent never comes into play.

V.

The fact that a person could not have avoided doing something is a sufficient condition of his having done it. But, as some of my examples show, this fact may play no role whatever in the explanation of why he did it. It may not figure at all among the circumstances that actually brought it about that he did what he did, so that his action is to be accounted for on another basis entirely. Even though the person was unable to do otherwise, that is to say, it may not be the case that he acted as he did *because* he could not have done otherwise. Now if someone had no alternative to performing a certain action but did not perform it because he was unable to do otherwise, then he would have performed exactly the same action even if he *could* have done otherwise. The circumstances that made it impossible for him to do otherwise could have been subtracted from the situation without affecting what happened or why it happened in any way. Whatever it was that actually led the person to do what he did, or that made him do it, would have led him to do it or made him do it even if it had been possible for him to do something else instead.

Thus it would have made no difference, so far as concerns his action or how he came to perform it, if the circumstances that made it impossible for him to avoid performing it had not prevailed. The fact that he could not have done otherwise clearly provides no basis for supposing that he *might* have done otherwise if he had been able to do so. When a fact is in this way irrelevant to the problem of accounting for a person's action it seems quite gratuitous to assign it any weight in the assessment of his moral responsibility. Why should the fact be considered in reaching a moral judgment concerning the person when it does not help in any way to understand either what made him act as he did or what, in other circumstances, he might have done?

This, then, is why the principle of alternate possibilities is mistaken. It asserts that a person bears no moral responsibility—that is, he is to be excused—for having performed an action if there were circumstances that made it impossible for him to avoid performing it. But there may be circumstances that make it impossible for a person to avoid performing some action without those circumstances in any way bringing it about that he performs that action. It would surely be no good for the person to refer to circumstances of this sort in an effort to absolve himself of moral responsibility for performing the action in question. For those circumstances, by hypothesis, actually had nothing to do with his having done what he did. He would have done precisely the same thing, and he would have been led or made precisely the same way to do it, even if they had not prevailed.

We often do, to be sure, excuse people for what they have done when they tell us (and we believe them) that they could not have done otherwise. But this is because we assume that what they tell us serves to explain why they did what they did. We take it for granted that they are not being disingenuous, as a person would be who cited as an excuse the fact that he could not have avoided doing what he did but who knew full well that it was not at all because of this that he did it.

What I have said may suggest that the principle of alternate possibilities should be revised so as to assert that a person is not morally responsible for what he has done if he did it because he could not have done otherwise. It may be noted that this revision of the principle does not seriously affect the arguments of those who have relied on the original principle in their efforts to maintain that moral responsibility and determinism are incompatible. For if it was causally determined that a person perform a certain action, then it will be true that the person performed it because of those causal determinants. And if the fact that it was causally determined that a person perform a certain action means that the person could not have done otherwise, as philosophers who argue for the incompatibility thesis characteristically suppose, then the fact that it was causally determined that a person perform a certain action will mean that the person performed it because he could not have done otherwise. The revised principle of alternate possibilities will entail, on this assumption concerning the meaning of 'could have done otherwise', that a person is not morally responsible for what he has done if it was causally determined that he do it. I do not believe, however, that this revision of the principle is acceptable.

Suppose a person tells us that he did what he did because he was unable to do otherwise; or suppose he makes the similar statement that he did what he did because he had to do it. We do often accept statements like these (if we believe them) as valid excuses, and such statements may well seem at first glance to invoke the revised principle of alternate possibilities. But I think that when we accept such statements as valid excuses it is because we assume that we are being told more than the statements strictly and literally convey. We understand the person who offers the excuse to mean that he did what he did *only because* he was unable to do otherwise, or *only because* he had to do it. And we understand him to mean, more particularly that when he did what he did it was not because that was what he really wanted to do. The principle: of alternate possibilities should thus be replaced, in my opinion, by the following principle: a person is not morally responsible for what he has done if he did it only because he could not have done otherwise. This principle does not appear to conflict with the view that moral responsibility is compatible with determinism.

The following may all be true: there were circumstances that made it impossible for a person to avoid doing something; these circumstances actually played a role in bringing it about that he did it, so that it is correct to say that he did it because he could not have done otherwise; the person really wanted to do what he did; he did it because it was what he really wanted to do, so that it is not correct to say that he did what he did only because he could not have done otherwise. Under these conditions, the person may well be morally responsible for what he has done. On the other hand, he will not be morally responsible for what he has done if he did it only because he could not have done otherwise, even if what he did was something he really wanted to do.

Endnotes

[1]The two main concepts employed in the principle of alternate possibilities are "morally responsible" and "could have done otherwise." To discuss the principle without analyzing either of these concepts may well seem like an attempt at piracy. The reader should take notice that my Jolly Roger is now unfurled.

[2]After thinking up the example that I am about to develop I learned that Robert Nozick, in lectures given several years ago, had formulated an example of the same general type and had proposed it as a counterexample to the principle of alternate possibilities.

[3]The assumption that Black can predict what $Jones_4$ will decide to do does not beg the question of determinism. We can imagine that $Jones_4$, has often confronted the alternatives—*A* and *B*—that he now confronts and that his face has invariably twitched when he was about to decide to do *A* and never when he was about to decide to do *B*. Knowing this, and observing the twitch, Black would have a basis for prediction. This does, to be sure, suppose that there is some sort of causal relation between $Jones_4$'s, state at the time of the twitch and his subsequent states. But any plausible view of decision or of action will allow that reaching a decision and performing an action both involve earlier and later phases, with causal relations between them, and such that the earlier phases are not themselves part of the decision or of the action. The example does not require that these earlier phases be deterministically related to still earlier events.

[4]The example is also flexible enough so allow for the elimination of Black altogether. Anyone who thinks that the effectiveness of the example is undermined by its reliance on a human manipulator, who imposes his will on $Jones_4$ can substitute for Black a machine programmed to do what Black does. If this is still not good enough, forget both Black and the machine and suppose that their role is played by natural forces involving no will or design at all.

45. *Responsibility, Luck, and Chance: Reflections on Free Will and Indeterminism* *

ROBERT KANE

The apparent problem with indeterminism, at least from the determinist and compatibilist points of view, is that it either undermines freedom and moral responsibility entirely or it requires a mysterious form of causation, labeled "agent causation." If an action is undetermined, then, so the argument goes, it is an arbitrary, capricious, or chance event that is not up to the person who performed it, and so is not freely chosen or one for which we can be held responsible. On the other hand, if the choice of one course of action over another is caused by the agent or self that is not itself caused by anything else, then a special non-scientific type of causation needs to be hypothesized. Robert Kane sets about to defend indeterminism by first arguing that what he calls the *luck principle* (LP):

> (LP)   If an action is *undetermined* at time *t*, then its happening rather than not happening at *t* would be a matter of *chance* or *luck*, and so it could not be a *free* and *responsible* action

is false. He then deals with the second horn of the dilemma by maintaining that in moments of genuine conflict between two courses of action there is a corresponding indeterminacy in the neural processes in our brains, and that when the will chooses one course of action rather than another that corresponds to one of the neural pathways reaching an activation threshold and the action takes place. In this way, Kane believes that indeterminism can avoid both the luck principle and a commitment to agent causality. Robert Kane is a professor of philosophy at the University of Texas at Austin.

Ludwig Wittgenstein[1] once said that to solve the problems of philosophers, you have to think even more crazily than they do" (*ibid.*, p. 75). This task (which became even more difficult after Wittgenstein than it was before him) is certainly required for the venerable problem of free will and determinism.

From Robert Kane, "Responsibility, Luck and Chance: Reflections on Free Will and Indeterminism,: *The Journal of Philosophy*, Vol. 96, No. 5 (May 1999): 217–240. Reprinted by permission of *The Journal of Philosophy* and the author.

I. *The Luck Principle*

Consider the following principle:

> (LP)   If an action is *undetermined* at a time *t*, then its happening rather than not happening at *t* would be a matter of *chance* or *luck,* and so it could not be a *free* and *responsible* action.

This principle (which we may call the *luck principle*, or simply LP) is false, as I shall explain shortly. Yet it seems true. LP and a related principle to be considered later in this paper are fueled by many of those "intuition pumps," in Daniel Dennett's[2] apt expression, which support common intuitions about freedom and responsibility. LP and related principles lie behind the widespread belief that indeterminism, so far from being required for free will and responsibility, would actually undermine free will and responsibility. Dennett does not dwell on the intuition pumps of this sort, as I shall do in this paper. As a compatibilist, he is more interested in criticizing intuition pumps that lead people to think (mistakenly, on his view) that freedom and responsibility are not compatible with determinism, whereas intuition pumps that support LP lead people to think freedom and responsibility are not compatible with *indeterminism*. Yet intuition pumps of the latter kind are every bit as pervasive and influential in free-will debates as those Dennett dwells upon; and they are as much in need of deconstruction, since they play a significant role in leading people to believe that freedom and responsibility must be compatible with determinism.

I think the modern route to compatibilism—which is the reigning view among contemporary philosophers—usually goes through principles like LP at some point or other. In my experience, most ordinary persons start out as natural incompatibilists. They believe there is some kind of conflict between freedom and determinism; and the idea that freedom and responsibility might be compatible with determinism looks to them at first like a "quagmire of evasion" (William James) or "a wretched subterfuge" (Immanuel Kant). Ordinary persons have to be talked out of this natural incompatibilism by the clever arguments of philosophers—who, in the manner of their mentor, Socrates, are only too happy to oblige. To weaken natural incompatibilist instincts, philosophers first argue that what we mean by freedom in everyday life is the power or ability to do whatever we choose or desire to do—in short, an absence of coercion, compulsion, oppression, and other impediments or constraints upon our behavior. They then point out that we can be free in these everyday senses to do what we choose or desire, even if our choices and desires are determined by causes that lie in our past.

But this line of argument does not usually dispose of incompatibilist intuitions by itself. Ordinary persons might grant that many everyday

freedoms are compatible with determinism and still wonder if there is not also some deeper freedom—the freedom to have an *ultimate* say in what we choose or desire to do in the first place—that is incompatible with determinism. (I have argued elsewhere[3] that this deeper freedom is what was traditionally meant by "free *will*.") So the philosophers must add a second step to their case—an argument to the effect that any allegedly deeper freedom (of the will) that is not compatible with determinism is no intelligible freedom at all. And with this step, principles like LP come into the picture. For any freedom not compatible with determinism would require indeterminism; and what is undetermined, it seems, would happen by chance or luck and could not be a free and responsible action. This kind of argument is the one that usually puts the final nail in the coffin of incompatibilist instincts.

When philosophy professors go through this two-stage argument in the modern classroom, they are replicating the standard case against traditional (incompatibilist or libertarian) free will which is one of the defining characteristics of modernity. The goal is to consign incompatibilist freedom to the dustbin of history with other beliefs that a modern scientific age is encouraged to outgrow. Students and ordinary persons subjected to this argument may have an uneasy feeling they are being had by the clever arguments of philosophers. But, also seeing no obvious response, except an appeal to mystery, many of them become compatibilists.

II. *Indeterminism, The Bogeyman*

The second stage of this two-stage argument in support of compatibilism will concern me here, the one that goes through LP and related principles in the attempt to show that indeterminism would not enhance, but in fact would undermine, freedom and responsibility. What is at stake here is not merely the clever arguments of philosophers; for it happens that the case for principles like LP is a powerful one. It *is* difficult to see how indeterminism and chance can be reconciled with freedom and responsibility. Philosophers have tried to bring this out in a number of ways which will be addressed here. We may think of these as the varied intuition pumps that support LP and principles like it.

(1) We are often asked to consider, for example, that whatever is undetermined or happens by chance is not under the *control* of anything, and so is not under the control of the agent. But an action that is not under the control of the agent could not be a free and responsible action. (Here it is evident that the notion of control is involved in the case for LP: indeterminism and chance imply lack of control to a degree that implies lack of freedom and responsibility.)

(2) Another line of argument often heard is this: suppose a choice occurred as the result of an undetermined event (say, a quantum jump) in one's brain. Would that be a free choice? Being undetermined, it would appear to be more of a fluke or accident than a free and responsible action. Some twentieth-century scientists and philosophers have suggested that free will might be rescued by supposing that undetermined quantum events in the brain could be amplified to have large-scale effects on choice or action.[4] Unfortunately, this modern version of the ancient Epicurean "swerve" of the atoms seems to be subject to the same criticisms as its ancient counterpart. It seems that undetermined events in the brain or body, whether amplified or not, would occur spontaneously and would be more of a nuisance—or perhaps a curse, like epilepsy—than an enhancement of freedom and responsibility.

(3) Nor would it help to suppose that the indeterminism or chance came *between* our choices (or intentions) and our actions. Imagine that you are intending to make a delicate cut in a fine piece of cloth, but because of an undetermined twitching in your arm, you make the wrong cut. Here, indeterminism is no enhancement of your freedom, but a *hindrance* or *obstacle* to your carrying out your purposes as intended. Critics of libertarian freedom[5] have often contended that this is what indeterminism would always be—a hindrance or impediment to one's freedom. It would get in the way, *diminishing* control, and hence responsibility, instead of enhancing them.

(4) Even more absurd consequences follow if we suppose that indeterminism or chance is involved in the initiation of overt actions. Arthur Schopenhauer[6] imagined the case of a man who suddenly found his legs start to move *by chance*, carrying him across the room against his wishes. Such caricatures are popular among critics of indeterminist freedom for obvious reasons: undetermined or chance-initiated overt actions would represent the opposite of controlled and responsible actions.

(5) Going a little deeper, one may also note that, if a choice or action is undetermined, it might occur otherwise *given exactly the same past and laws of nature* up to the moment when it does occur. This means that, if Jane is deliberating about whether to vacation in Hawaii or Colorado, and gradually comes to favor and choose Hawaii, she might have chosen otherwise (chosen Colorado), given *exactly the same deliberation* up to the moment of choice that in fact led her to favor and choose Hawaii (exactly the same thoughts, reasonings, beliefs, desires, dispositions, and other characteristics—not a sliver of difference). It is difficult to make sense of this. The choice of Colorado in such circumstances would seem irrational and inexplicable, capricious and arbitrary.[7] If it came about by virtue of undetermined events in Jane's brain, this would not be an occasion for rejoicing in her freedom, but for consulting a neurologist about the waywardness of her neural processes.

(6) At this point, some defenders of incompatibilist freedom appeal to Gottfried Leibniz's[8] celebrated dictum that prior reasons or motives need not determine choice or action, they may merely "incline without necessitating"—that is, they may incline the agent toward one option without determining the choice of that option. This may indeed happen. But it will not solve the present problem; for it is precisely *because* Jane's prior reasons and motives (beliefs, desires, and the like) incline her toward the choice of Hawaii that choosing Colorado by chance at the end of exactly the same deliberation would be irrational and inexplicable. Similarly, if her reasons had inclined her toward Colorado, then choosing Hawaii by chance at the end of the same deliberation would have been irrational and inexplicable. And if prior reasons or motives had not inclined her either way (the celebrated medieval "liberty of indifference") and the choice was a matter of chance, then the choosing of one rather than the other would have been all the more a matter of luck and out of her control. (One

can see why libertarian freedom has often been ridiculed as a mere "liberty of indifference.")

(7) Indeed, critics of indeterminist freedom have often argued that indeterminist free choices must always amount to *random* choices of this sort and hence the outcomes would be matters of mere luck or chance—like spinning a wheel to select among a set of alternatives. Perhaps there is a role for such random choices in our lives when we are genuinely indifferent to outcomes.[9] But to suppose that *all* of our free and responsible choices—including momentous ones, like whether to act heroically or treacherously—had to be by random selection in this way has been regarded by many philosophers as a *reductio ad absurdum* of the view that free will and responsibility require indeterminism.

(8) Consider one final argument which cuts more deeply than the others and to which I shall devote considerable attention. This paper was in fact prompted by new versions of this argument advanced in recent years against my incompatibilist account of free will by Galen Strawson, Alfred Mele, Bernard Berofsky, Bruce Waller, Richard Double, Mark Bernstein, and Ishtiyaque Haji[10]—though the argument is meant to apply generally to any view requiring that free actions be undetermined up to the moment when they occur.

Suppose two agents had exactly the same pasts (as indeterminism requires) up to the point where they were faced with a choice between distorting the truth for selfish gain or telling the truth at great personal cost. One agent lies and the other tells the truth. As Waller puts it, if the pasts of these two agents "are really identical" in every way up to the moment of choice, "and the difference in their acts results from chance," would there "be any grounds for distinguishing between [them], for saying that one deserves censure for a selfish decision and the other deserves praise" (*op. cit.,* p. 151)? Mele poses the problem in terms of a single agent in different possible worlds. Suppose in the actual world, John fails to resist the temptation to do what he thinks he ought to do, arrive at a meeting on time. If he could have done otherwise given the same past, then his counterpart, John* in a nearby possible world, which is the same as the actual world up to the moment of choice, resists the temptation and arrives on time. Mele then argues that, "if there is nothing about the agents'

powers, capacities, states of mind, moral character and the like that explains this difference in outcome, . . . the difference is just a matter of luck" (*op. cit.,* pp. 582–83). It would seem that John* got lucky in his attempt to overcome temptation, whereas John did not. Would it be just to reward the one and punish the other for what appears to be ultimately the luck of the draw?

Considerations such as (1)–(8) lie behind familiar and varied charges that undetermined choices or actions would be "arbitrary," "capricious," "random," "uncontrolled," "irrational," "inexplicable," or "matters of luck or chance," and hence not free and responsible actions. These are the charges which principles like LP are meant to express. Responses to them in the history of philosophy have been many; but none to my mind has been entirely convincing. The charges have often led libertarians—those who believe in an incompatibilist free will—to posit "extra factors" in the form of unusual species of agency or causation (such as noumenal selves, immaterial egos, or nonoccurrent agent causes) to account for what would otherwise be arbitrary, uncontrolled, inexplicable, or mere luck or chance. I do not propose to appeal to any such extra factors in defense of libertarian freedom. Such appeals introduce additional problems of their own without, in my view, directly confronting the deep problems about indeterminism, chance, and luck to which considerations (1)–(8) are pointing. To confront these deep problems directly, I believe one has to rethink issues about indeterminism and responsibility from the ground up, without relying on appeals to extracausal factors—a task to which I now turn.

III. *Indeterminism and Responsibility*

First, one must question the intuitive connection in people's minds between "indeterminism's being involved in something's happening" and "its happening merely as a matter of chance or luck." "Chance" and "luck" are terms of ordinary language which carry the connotation of "its being out of my control" (as in (1) and (4) and above). So using them already begs certain questions, whereas "indeterminism" is a technical term that merely precludes *deterministic* causation (though not causation altogether). Second, one must emphasize that indeterminism does not have to be involved in all free and responsible acts, even for incompatibilists or libertarians.[11] Frequently, we act from a will already formed; and it may well be that our actions are determined in such cases by our then existing characters and motives. On such occasions, to do otherwise by chance *would* be a fluke or accident, irrational and inexplicable, as critics of indeterminist freedom contend (in (3) and (4) above).

Incompatibilists about free will should not deny this. What they should rather say is that when we act from a will already formed (as we frequently do), it is "our own free will" by virtue of the fact that we formed it (at least in part) by earlier choices or actions which were not determined and for which we could have done otherwise voluntarily, not merely as a fluke or accident. I call these earlier undetermined actions *self-forming actions* or SFAs.[12] Undetermined SFAs are a subset of all of the actions done of our own free wills (many of which may be determined by our earlier formed character and motives). But if there were no such undetermined SFAs in our lifetimes, there would have been nothing we could have ever voluntarily done to make ourselves different than we are—a condition that I think is inconsistent with our having the kind of responsibility for being what we are which genuine free will requires.

Now, let us look more closely at these undetermined SFAs. As I see it, they occur at times in life when we are torn between competing visions of what we should do or become. Perhaps we are torn between doing the moral thing or acting from self-interest, or between present desires and long-term goals, or we are faced with difficult tasks for which we have aversions. In all such cases, we are faced with competing motivations and have to make an effort to overcome temptation to do something else we also strongly want. In the light of this picture, I suggest the following incompatibilist account of SFAs.[13] There is a tension and uncertainty in our minds at such times of inner conflict which are reflected in appropriate regions of our brains by movement away from thermodynamic equilibrium—in short, a kind of stirring up of chaos in the brain that makes it sensitive to micro-indeterminacies at the neuronal level. As a result, the uncertainty and inner tension we feel at such soul-searching moments of self-formation is reflected in the indeterminacy of our neural processes themselves. What is experienced phenomenologically as uncertainty corresponds physically to the opening of a window of opportunity that temporarily screens off complete determination by the past. (By contrast, when we act from predominant motives or settled dispositions, the uncertainty or indeterminism is muted. If it were involved then, it *would* be a mere nuisance or fluke, capricious or arbitrary, as critics contend (in (2), (5) and (6) above).)

When we do decide under such conditions of uncertainty, the outcome is not determined because of the preceding indeterminacy—and yet it can be willed (and hence rational and voluntary) either way owing to the fact that in such self-formation, the agents' prior wills are divided by conflicting motives. If we overcome temptation, it will be the result of our effort; and if we fail, it will be because we did not *allow* our effort to succeed. And this is owing to the fact that, while we wanted to overcome temptation, we also wanted to fail, for quite different and incommensurable reasons. When we decide in such circumstances, and the indeterminate efforts we are making become determinate choices, we *make* one set of competing reasons or motives prevail over the others then and there by *deciding*.

Return now to concerns about indeterminism and responsibility in the light of this picture. Consider a businesswoman who faces a conflict in her will of the kind typically involved in such SFAs. She is on the way to a meeting important to her career when she observes an assault in an alley. An inner struggle ensues between her moral conscience, to stop and call for help, and her career ambitions, which tell her she cannot miss this meeting—a struggle she eventually resolves by turning back to help the victim. Now suppose this woman visits some future neuroscientists the next day and they tell her a story about what was going on in her brain at the time she chose, not unlike the story just told. Prior to choice, there was some indeterminacy in her neural processes stirred up by the conflict in her will. The indeterminism made it uncertain (and undetermined) whether she would go back to help or press onward.

Suppose further that two recurrent and connected neural networks are involved in the neuroscientists' story. Such networks circulate impulses and information in feedback loops and generally play a role in complex cognitive processing in the brain of the kind that one would expect to be involved in human deliberation. Moreover, recurrent networks are nonlinear, thus allowing (as some recent research suggests) for the possibility of chaotic activity, which would contribute to the plasticity and flexibility human brains display in creative problem solving (of which practical deliberation is an example).[14] The input of one of these recurrent networks consists of the woman's moral motives, and its output the choice to go back; the input of the other, her career ambitions, and its output, the choice to go on to her meeting. The two networks are connected, so that the indeterminism that made it uncertain that she would do the moral thing was coming from her desire to do the opposite, and vice versa—the indeterminism thus arising, as we said, from a conflict in the will. When her effort to overcome self-interested desires succeeded, this corresponded to one of the neural pathways reaching an activation threshold, overcoming the indeterminism generated by the other.

To this picture, one might now pose the following objection: if it really was undetermined which choice the woman would make (in neural terms, which network would activate) right up to the moment when she chose, it seems that it would be a matter of luck or chance that one choice was made rather than the other, and so she could not be held responsible for the outcome. (Note that this is an expression of LP.) The first step in response is to recall a point made earlier: we must be wary of moving too hastily from "indeterminism is involved in something's happening" to "its happening merely as a matter of chance or luck". "Luck" and "chance" have meanings in ordinary language that mere indeterminism may not have. The second step is to note that indeterminism of itself does not necessarily undermine control and responsibility.[15] Suppose you are trying to think through a difficult problem (say, a mathematical problem) and there is some indeterminacy in your neural processes complicating the task—a kind of chaotic background. It would be like trying to concentrate and solve a problem with

background noise or distraction. Whether you are going to succeed in solving the mathematical problem is uncertain and undetermined because of the distracting neural noise. Yet if you concentrate and solve the problem nonetheless, I think we can say that you did it and are responsible for doing it even though it was undetermined whether you would succeed. The indeterministic noise would have been an obstacle to your solving the problem which you nevertheless overcame by your effort.

There are numerous other examples in the philosophical literature of this kind, where indeterminism functions as an obstacle to success without precluding responsibility. Consider an assassin who is trying to kill the prime minister, but might miss because of some undetermined events in his nervous system which might lead to a jerking or wavering of this arm. If he does hit his target, can he be held responsible? The answer (as J. L. Austin and Philippa Foot[16] successfully argued decades ago) is "yes," because he intentionally and voluntarily succeeded in doing what he was *trying* to do—kill the prime minister. Yet his killing the prime minister was undetermined. We might even say in a sense that he got lucky in killing the prime minister, when he could have failed. But it does not follow, if he succeeds, that killing the prime minister was not his action, not something he did; nor does it follow, as LP would require, that he was not responsible for killing the prime minister. Indeed, if anything is clear, it is that he both killed the prime minister and was responsible for doing so.

Or consider a husband who, while arguing with his wife, swings his arm down in anger on her favorite glass table top, intending to break it. Again we suppose that some indeterminism in the husband's efferent neural pathways makes the momentum of his arm indeterminate, so it is undetermined if the table will break right up to the moment when it is struck. Whether the husband breaks the table or not is undetermined. Yet it does not follow, if he succeeds, that breaking the table was not something he did; nor again does it follow, as LP would require, that he was not responsible for breaking it.[17] The inference sanctioned by LP from "it was undetermined" to "he was not responsible", is not valid. The above cases are counterexamples to it; and there are many more.

IV. *Possible Worlds and* LP*

But one may grant this and still object that counterexamples to LP of these kinds do not amount to genuine exercises of free will involving SFAs, such as the businesswoman's, where there is conflict in the wills of the agents and they are supposed to choose freely and responsibly *whichever* way they choose. If the assassin and husband succeed in doing what they are trying to do (kill the prime minister, break the table) they will do it *voluntarily* (in accordance with their wills) and *intentionally* (knowingly and purposely). But if they *fail* because of the indeterminism, they will not fail voluntarily and intentionally, but "by mistake" or "accident," or merely "by chance." Thus, their "power" to do *otherwise* (if we should even call it a power) is not the usual power we associate with freedom of choice or action in self-formation, where the agents should be able to choose or act either way voluntarily or intentionally. The power to do otherwise of the assassin and the husband is more like Jane's "power" in (5) and (6) of section II, to choose to vacation in Colorado by a fluke or accident, after a long deliberation in which she had come to favor Hawaii.

As a consequence, while LP may fail for cases like those of the assassin, husband, and mathematical problem solver, another luck principle similar to LP might still be applicable to genuine exercises of free will involving SFAs, like the businesswoman's: if it is undetermined at *t* whether an agent *voluntarily* and *intentionally* does A at *t* or *voluntarily* and *intentionally* does otherwise, then the agent's doing one of these rather than the other at *t* would be a matter of *luck* or *chance*, and so could not be a free and responsible action. This principle—let us call it LP*—is fueled by the same intuitions that fuel LP. Indeed, it is a special case of LP, but one that is more difficult to deal with because it is not subject to counterexamples like those of the husband and the assassin; and it seems to be applicable to SFAs, like the businesswoman's, where failure is not merely a matter of mistake or accident.

To explore further the difficulties posed by LP*, let us look at the final and, I think, most powerful of the intuition pumps in support of LP-type principles mentioned in section II, namely, consideration (8). This was the argument of Strawson, Mele, Berofsky, Waller, Double, Bernstein, and Haji about two agents, or one agent in different possible worlds, with the same pasts.

Consider the version of this argument by Mele, which appeared in this JOURNAL and is a particularly revealing and challenging version of it. In the actual world, an agent John succumbs to the temptation to arrive late to a meeting, whereas his counterpart, John*, in a nearby possible world, whose physical and psychological history is the same as John's up to the moment of choice (as indeterminism requires), resists this temptation. Similarly, we can imagine a counterpart to the businesswoman, businesswoman*, in a nearby possible world who goes to her meeting instead of stopping to aid the assault victim, given the same past. But then, Mele argues, "if there is nothing about [these] agents' powers, capacities, states of mind, moral character and the like that explains this difference in outcome," since they are the same up to the moment of choice in the two possible worlds, "then the difference is just a matter of luck" (*op. cit.*, p. 583).[18] It would seem that John* got lucky in his attempt to overcome temptation, whereas John did not; and similarly, the businesswoman got lucky in her attempt to overcome temptations while businesswoman* did not.

Let us first consider a general form of this argument that would support LP.

(a) In the actual world, person *P* (for example, John, the businesswoman) does A at *t*.

On the assumption that the act is undetermined at *t*, we may imagine that:

(b) In a nearby-possible world which is the same as the actual world up to *t*, *P** (*P*'s counterpart with the same past) does otherwise (does *B*) at *t*.

(c) But then (since their pasts are the same), there is nothing about the agents' powers, capacities, states of mind, characters, dispositions. motives, and so on prior to *t* which explains the difference in choices in the two possible worlds.

(d) It is therefore a matter of luck or chance that *P* does A and *P** does *B* at *t*.

(e) P is therefore not responsible (praiseworthy or blameworthy, as the case may be) for A at t (and presumably P^* is also not responsible for B).

Call this the *luck argument*. The key assumption is the assumption of indeterminism, which leads to step (b). The remaining steps are meant to follow from (b), given (a).

Despite the fact that this argument looks like Mele's and has an initial plausibility, it is not his argument—and it is a good thing it is not. For the argument from (a)–(e) is invalid as it stands—for the same reasons that LP was invalid. Consider the husband and husband* (his counterpart in a nearby world who fails to break the wife's table). If the outcome is undetermined, husband and husband* also have "the same powers, capacities, states of mind, characters, dispositions, motives, and so on" up to the moment of breaking or not breaking the table, as the argument requires; and it is a matter of luck or chance that the table breaks in one world and not the other. But for all that, it does not follow, as (e) requires, that the husband is not responsible for breaking the table. The husband would have quite a task persuading his wife that he was not responsible for breaking the table on the grounds that it was a matter of luck or chance that it broke. ("Luck or chance did it, not me" is an implausible excuse.)

But, of course, as we noted, husband* is not also responsible for *failing* to break the table, since he does not fail to break it voluntarily or intentionally. He is responsible only for the attempt, when he fails. Similarly, assassin* would be responsible for the attempted murder of the prime minister, when he missed. What has to be explicitly added to the argument (a)–(e) to avoid counterexamples like these is the LP* requirement that *both P and P* voluntarily* and *intentionally* do A and B respectively in their respective worlds. Specifically, we must add to premise (a) that P voluntarily and intentionally does A at t and to (b), that P^* voluntarily and intentionally does B at t, and then make the corresponding additions to (d) and (e). This will yield what we might call the LP* version of the luck argument rather than the LP version. And the stronger LP* version is clearly the one Mele intends, since John's choice in his example is supposed to be an SFA, like the businesswoman's choice in my example, where the agents

can go either way voluntarily and intentionally. Moreover, this version of the argument—like LP* itself—is immune to counterexamples like those of the husband and the assassin.

V. *Parallel Processing*

Nonetheless, despite immunity from these counterexamples, I think the LP* version of the luck argument, and LP* itself, also fail. But it is far less easy to show why. To do so, we have to take a closer look at SFAs and push the argument beyond where it has come thus far. Let it be granted that the businesswoman's case and other SFAs like John's are not like the examples of the husband and the assassin. The wills of the husband and assassin are already "set" on doing what they intend, whereas the wills of agents in SFAs, like the businesswoman and John, are not already settled or "formed" until they choose (hence the designation "self-forming actions").[19]

Thus, to get from examples like those of the husband and assassin to genuine SFAs, I think we must do two things. First, we must put the indeterminacy involved in the efferent neural pathways of the husband and assassin into the central neural processes of the businesswoman and other agents, like John, who are making efforts of will to overcome moral, prudential, and other temptations. This move has already been made in earlier sections. But to respond to LP* versions of the luck argument, like Mele's, I believe this move must also be combined with another—a kind of "doubling" of the example given earlier of solving the mathematical problem in the presence of background indeterministic noise.[20]

Imagine that the businesswoman is *trying* or making an effort to solve *two* cognitive problems at once, or to complete two competing (deliberative) tasks at once—to make a moral choice and to make a choice for her ambitions (corresponding to the two competing neural networks involved in the earlier description). With respect to each task, as with the mathematical problem, she is being thwarted in her attempt to do what she is trying to do by indeterminism. But in her case, the indeterminism does not have a mere external source; it is coming from her own will, from her desire to do the opposite. Recall that the two crossing neural networks involved are connected, so that the indeterminism which is making it uncertain that she will do the moral thing is coming from her desire to do the opposite, and vice versa. She may therefore fail to do what she is trying to do, just like the assassin, the husband, and the person trying to solve the mathematical problem. But I argue that, if she nevertheless *succeeds,* then she can be held responsible because, like them, she will have succeeded in doing *what she was trying to do.* And the interesting thing is that this will be true of her, *whichever choice is made,* because she was trying to make both choices and one is going to succeed.

Does it make sense to talk about agents trying to do two competing things at once in this way? Well, we know the brain is a parallel processor and that capacity, I believe, is essential for the exercise of free will. In cases of self-formation, agents are simultaneously trying to resolve plural and competing cognitive tasks. They are, as we say, of two minds. But they are not therefore two separate persons. They are not disassociated from either task.[21] The businesswoman who wants to go back and help the assault victim is the same ambitious woman who wants to go on to her meeting and close the sale. She is a complex creature, like most of us who are often torn inside: but hers is the kind of complexity needed for free will. And when she succeeds in doing one of the things she is trying to do, she will endorse that as her resolution of the conflict in her will, voluntarily and intentionally, as LP* requires. She will not disassociate from either outcome, as did Jane (in (5) of section II), who wondered what "happened to" her when she chose Colorado, or like the husband and assassin who did not also want to fail.[22]

But one may still object that the businesswoman makes one choice rather than the other *by chance,* since it was undetermined right up to the last moment which choice she would make. If this is so, we may have the picture of her first making an effort to overcome temptation (to go on to her meeting) and do the moral thing, and then at the last minute "chance takes over" and decides the issue for her. But this is the wrong picture. On the view just described, you cannot separate the indeterminism from the effort to overcome temptation in such a way that *first* the effort occurs *followed by* chance or luck (or vice

versa). One must think of the effort and the indeterminism as fused; the effort *is* indeterminate and the indeterminism is a property of the effort, not something separate that occurs after or before the effort. The fact that the woman's effort of will has this property of being indeterminate does not make it any less her *effort.* The complex recurrent neural network that realizes the effort in the brain is circulating impulses in feedback loops and there is some indeterminacy in these circulating impulses. But the whole process is her effort of will and it persists right up to the moment when the choice is made. There is no point at which the effort stops and chance "takes over." She chooses *as a result of* the effort, even though she might have failed because of the indeterminism.

And just as expressions like "She chose *by* chance" can mislead us in these contexts, so can expressions like "She got lucky". Ask yourself this question: Why does the inference "He got lucky, *so he was not responsible" fail* when it does fail, as in the cases of the husband and the assassin? The first part of an answer goes back to the claim that "luck", like "chance", has question-begging implications in ordinary language which are not necessarily implications of "indeterminism" (which implies only the absence of deterministic causation). The core meaning of "He got lucky", which is implied by indeterminism, I suggest, is that "He succeeded *despite the probability or chance of failure*"; and this core meaning does not imply lack of responsibility, if he succeeds.

If "He got lucky" had further meanings in these contexts often associated with "luck" and "chance" in ordinary usage (for example, the outcome was not his doing, or occurred by *mere* chance, or he was not responsible for it), the inference would not fail for the husband and assassin, as it clearly does. But the point is that these further meanings of "luck" and "chance" do not follow *from the mere presence of indeterminism.* Second, the inference "He got lucky, so he was not responsible" fails because *what* the assassin and husband succeeded in doing was what they were trying and wanting to do all along. Third, *when* they succeeded, their reaction was not "Oh dear, that was a mistake, an accident—something that *happened* to me, not something I *did*." Rather, they *endorsed* the outcomes as something they were trying and wanting to do all along, that is to say, knowingly and purposefully, not by mistake or accident.

But these conditions are satisfied in the businesswoman's case as well, *either way* she chooses. If she succeeds in choosing to return to help the victim (or in choosing to go on to her meeting) (i) she will have "succeeded despite the probability or chance of failure"; (ii) she will have succeeded in doing what she was trying and wanting to do all along (she wanted both outcomes very much, but for different reasons, and was trying to make those reasons prevail in both cases); and (iii) when she succeeded (in choosing to return to help) her reaction was not "Oh dear, that was a mistake, an accident—something that happened to me, not something I did." Rather, she endorsed the outcome as something she was trying and wanting to do all along; she recognized it as her resolution of the conflict in her will. And if she had chosen to go on to her meeting she would have endorsed that outcome, recognizing it as her resolution of the conflict in her will.

VI. *The Luck Argument Revisited*

With this in mind, let us return to the LP* version of the argument from (a)–(e). I said that Mele clearly intends this stronger LP* version of the argument, since the force of his argument depends on the fact that John's choice in his example is an SFA, like the businesswoman's, instead of being like the actions of the husband and assassin. But if this is so, then John's situation will also be like the businesswoman's on the account just given of SFAs. Since both of them are simultaneously trying to do *both* of the things they may do (choose to help or go on, overcome the temptation to arrive late or not), they will do either with intent or on purpose, as a result of wanting and trying to do it—that is, intentionally and voluntarily. Thus, their "failing" to do one of the options will not be a mistake or accident, but a voluntary and intentional doing *of the other*.

Likewise, businesswoman* and John* are simultaneously trying to do both things in their respective worlds; and they will not "fail" to act on moral or weak-willed motives by mistake or accident, as the case may be, but by voluntarily and

intentionally choosing to act on the opposing motives. The point is that in self-formation of these kinds (SFAs), failing is never *just* failing; it is always also a *succeeding* in doing something else we wanted and were trying to do. And we found that one can be responsible for succeeding in doing what one was trying to do, even in the presence of indeterminism. So even if we add the LP* requirement of more-than-one-way voluntariness and intentionality to the argument of (a)–(e), the argument remains invalid for cases like the businesswoman's and other SFAs, like John's.

But one might argue further, as Mele does, that John and John* (and businesswoman and businesswoman*) not only had the same capacities, motives, characters, and the like prior to choice, but they made exactly the same *efforts* as well. And this does seem to suggest that the success of one and failure of the other was a matter of mere luck or chance, so that John and the businesswoman were not responsible. But again the inference is too hasty. Note, first, that husband and husband* also made the same efforts (as well as having the same capacities, motives, and characters) up to the very moment of breaking of the table. Yet it does not follow that the husband is not responsible when he succeeds. And *both* the businesswoman and businesswoman*, and John and John*, are in the position of the husband in their respective worlds, since both will have succeeded in doing what they were trying to do.

But one may still want to object: if the businesswoman and businesswoman*, and John and John*, make exactly the same efforts, how can it *not* be a matter of chance that one succeeds and the other does not, in a way that makes them not responsible? To which I reply: But if they both succeeded in doing what they were trying to do (because they were simultaneously trying to do both things), and then having succeeded, they both *endorsed* the outcomes of their respective efforts (that is, their choices) as what they were trying to do, instead of disowning or disassociating from those choices, how then can we *not* hold them responsible? It just does not follow that, because they made exactly the same efforts, they chose *by* chance.

To say something was done "by chance" usually means (as in the assassin and husband cases when they fail), it was done "by mistake" or "accidentally," "inadvertently," "involuntarily," or "as an unintended fluke." But none of these things holds of the businesswoman and John either way they choose. Unlike husband*, businesswoman* and John do not fail to overcome temptation by mistake or accident, inadvertently or involuntarily. They consciously and willingly fail to overcome temptation *by* consciously and willingly choosing to act in selfish or weak-willed ways. So, just as it would have been a poor excuse for the husband to say to his wife when the table broke that "Luck or chance did it, not me," it would be a poor excuse for businesswoman* and John to say "Luck or chance did it, not me" when they failed to help the assault victim or failed to arrive on time.

Worth highlighting in this argument is the point that we cannot simply say the business-woman and businesswoman* (or John and John*) made exactly the same *effort* (in the singular) in their respective possible worlds and one succeeded while the other failed. We must say they made exactly the same *efforts* (plural) in their respective worlds. Mentioning only one effort prejudices the case, for it suggests that the failure of that effort in one of the worlds was a *mere* mistake or accident, when the fact is that both of the agents (P and P*) made *both* efforts in *both* worlds. In one world, one of the efforts issued in a choice and in the other world, a different effort issued in a different choice; but neither was merely accidental or inad-vertent in either world. I would go even further and say that we may also doubt that the efforts they were both making really were exactly the same. Where events are indeterminate, as are the efforts they were making, there is no such thing as exact sameness or difference of events in different possible worlds. Their efforts were not exactly the same, nor were they exactly different, because they were not exact. They were simply unique.[23]

One might try another line: perhaps we are begging the question in assuming that the out-comes of the efforts of the businesswoman and her counterpart were *choices* at all. If they were not choices to begin with, they could not have been voluntary choices. One might argue this on the grounds that (A) "If an event is undeter-mined, it must be something that merely happens and cannot be somebody's choice"; and (B) "If an event is undetermined, it must be something that merely happens, it cannot be something an agent does (it cannot be an action)." But to see how question-begging these assumptions are, one has only to note that (A) and (B) imply respec-tively (A′) "If an event is a choice, it must be determined" ("All choices are determined") and (B′) "If an event is an action, it must be deter-mined" ("All actions are determined"). Are these supposed to be a priori or analytic truths? If so, then long-standing issues about freedom and determinism would be settled by fiat. If an event were not determined, it could not be a choice or action necessarily or by definition.[24]

This explains the businesswoman's suspicions when she exited the neuroscientists' offices. They told her that when she "chose" to go back to help the assault victim the day before, there was some indeterminism in her neural processes prior to choice. She accepted this as a correct empirical finding. But she was suspicious when the neuro-scientists tried to get her to make the further infer-ence from those findings which she did not really *choose* to help the assault victim yesterday. She refused to accept that conclusion, and rightly so. For in drawing it, they were going beyond their empirical findings and trying to foist on her the a priori assumption that if an event was undeter-mined, it could not have been her choice or could not have been something she did. She rightly saw that there was nothing in the empirical evidence that required her to say that. To choose is con-sciously and deliberately to form an intention to do something; and she did that, despite the inde-terminism in her neural processes (as did business-woman* when she chose to go on to her meeting).

VI. *Final Considerations: Control and Explanation*

But it is one thing to say that she chose and another to say she chose *freely* and *responsibly*. This would require that she not only chose, but had voluntary *control* over her choice either way. We have not talked at length to this point about the matter of control (considerations (1) and (3) of section II) and must now do so. For this may be the reason why we may think the choices made by the businesswoman and businesswoman* (or John and John*) could not be responsible, if they were undetermined. We might deny that they had voluntary control over what they chose, where voluntary control means being able to bring about something in accordance with one's will or purposes (or, as we often say, the ability to bring something about "at will").

One thing does seem to be true about control which critics of indeterminist freedom have always maintained: indeterminism, wherever it appears, does seem to *diminish* rather than enhance agents' voluntary control (consideration (3) of section II). The assassin's voluntary control over whether or not the prime minister is killed (his ability to realize his purpose or what he is trying to do) is diminished by the undetermined impulses in his arm—and so also for the husband and his breaking the table. Moreover, this limitation is connected to another, which I think we must also grant—that indeterminism, wherever it occurs, functions as a *hindrance* or *obstacle* to our purposes that must be overcome by effort (consideration (3)).

But recall that in the businesswoman's case (and for SFAs generally, like John's), the indeterminism that is admittedly diminishing her ability to overcome selfish temptation, and *is* indeed a hindrance to her doing so, is coming from her own will—from her desire and effort to do the opposite—since she is simultaneously trying to realize two conflicting purposes at once. Similarly, her ability to overcome moral qualms is diminished by the fact that she also simultaneously wants and is trying to act on moral reasons. If we could look at each of the two competing neural networks involved separately, abstracting from the other, the situation would look analogous to the situations of the husband and the assassin. The agent would be trying to do something while being hindered by indeterminism coming from an external source. But, in fact, we cannot look at the two networks separately in this way because, in reality, they are connected and interacting. The indeterminism that is a hindrance to her fulfilling one is coming from its interactions with the other. The indeterminism, therefore, does not have an external source. It is internal to her will, and hence to her self, since she identifies with both networks and will identify with the choice reached by either of them as her choice.

The upshot is that, despite the businesswoman's diminished control over *each* option considered separately, due to a conflict in her will, she nonetheless has what I call *plural voluntary control* over the two options considered *as a set* (*ibid.*, pp. 134–43). Having plural voluntary control over a set of options means being able to bring about *whichever* of the options you will or most want, *when* you will to do so, for the reasons you will to do so, without being coerced or compelled in doing so. And the businesswoman (or John) has this power, because whichever of the options she chooses (to help the victim or go on to her meeting) will be *endorsed* by her as what she wills or most wants to do at the moment when she chooses it (though not necessarily beforehand); she will choose it for the reasons she most wants to act on then and there (moral or selfish reasons, as the case may be); she need not have been coerced by anyone else into choosing one rather than the other; and she will not be choosing either compulsively, since neither choice is such that she could not have chosen it then and there, even if she most wanted to.[25]

One must add, of course, that such plural voluntary control is not the same as what may be called *antecedent determining control*—the ability to determine or guarantee which of a set of options will occur *before* it occurs (*ibid.*, p. 144). With respect to undetermined self-forming choices (SFAs), agents cannot determine or guarantee which choice outcome will occur *beforehand;* for that could only be done by predetermining the outcome. But it does not follow that, because one cannot determine which of a set of outcomes will occur before it occurs, one does not determine which of them occurs *when* it occurs. When the conditions of plural voluntary control are satisfied, agents exercise control over their present and future lives then and there by deciding.

But can we not at least say that, if indeterminism is involved, then *which* option is chosen is "arbitrary"? I grant that there is a sense in which this is true. An ultimate arbitrariness remains in all undetermined SFAs because there cannot, in principle, be sufficient or overriding *prior* reasons for making one set of competing reasons prevail over the other. But I argue that such arbitrariness relative to prior reasons tells us something important about free will. It tells us, as I have elsewhere expressed it, that every undetermined self-forming choice (SFA) "is the initiation of a 'value experiment' whose justification lies in the *future* and is not fully explained by the *past*. [Making such a choice], we say in effect, 'Let's try this. It is not required by my past, but is consistent with my past and is one branching pathway my life could now meaningfully take. I am willing to take responsibility for it one way or the other'" (*ibid.*, pp. 145–46). To initiate and take responsibility for such value experiments whose justification lies in the future, is to "take chances" without prior guarantees of success. Genuine self-formation requires this sort of risk-taking and indeterminism is a part of it. If there are persons who need to be certain in advance just exactly what is the best or right thing to do in every circumstance (perhaps to be told so by some human or divine authority), then free will is not for them.

This point also throws light on why the luck argument fails, even in the stronger LP* version, despite its initial plausibility. Consider the move from step (c)—the agents P and P* have the same powers, characters, motives, and the like, prior to t in the two possible worlds—to step (d), which says it was a matter of luck or chance that P did A and P* did B at t. An important reason given for this move was that, if both agents have all the same prior powers, characters, motives, and the like, there can be no "explanation of the difference in choice" between the two agents in terms of their prior reasons or motives; and this is taken to imply that the difference in choices in the two worlds is a matter of luck or chance *in a way* that precludes responsibility.

But this move, like others discussed earlier, is too hasty. The absence of an explanation of the difference in choice in terms of prior reasons does not have the tight connection to issues of responsibility one might initially credit it with. For one thing, the absence of such an explanation does not imply (as I have been arguing throughout this paper) that businesswoman and businesswoman* (John and John*) (1) did not *choose* at all, nor does it imply that they did not both choose (2) *as a result of their efforts*, nor that they did not choose (3) *for reasons* (different reasons, of course) that (4) they most wanted to choose for *when* they chose, nor that they did not choose for those reasons (5) *knowingly* and (6) *on purpose* when they

chose, and hence (7) *rationally*, (8) *voluntarily*, and (9) *intentionally*. None of these conditions is precluded by the absence of an explanation of the difference of choice in terms of prior reasons. Yet these are precisely the kinds of conditions we look for when deciding whether or not persons are responsible.

I suggest that the reason why these conditions are not excluded is that the explanation of the difference of choice in the two possible worlds which is missing is an explanation in terms of *sufficient* or *conclusive* reasons—one that would render an alternative choice, given the same prior reasons, irrational or inexplicable. And, of course, *that* sort of explanation is not possible for undetermined SFAs, when there is conflict in the will and the agent has good (but not decisive or conclusive) prior reasons for going either way. But neither is that sort of explanation required to say that an agent acts as the result of her effort for reasons she most wants to act on then and there. In sum, *you can choose responsibly for prior reasons that were not conclusive or decisive prior to your choosing for them.*

I said a moment ago that such arbitrariness relative to prior reasons tells us something important about free will—that every self-forming choice is the initiation of a value experiment whose justification lies in the future and cannot be fully explained by the past. It is worth adding in this regard that the term "arbitrary" comes from the Latin *arbitrium*, which means "judgment"—as in *liberum arbitrium voluntatis* ("free judgment of the will")—the medieval designation for free will. Imagine a writer in the middle of a novel. The novel's heroine faces a crisis and the writer has not yet developed her character in sufficient detail to say exactly how she will react. The author must make a "judgment" *(arbitrium)* about how she will react that is not determined by the heroine's already formed past, which does not give unique direction. In this sense, the author's judgment of how she will act is "arbitrary," but not entirely so. It has input from the heroine's fictional past and, in turn, gives input to her projected future.

In a similar manner, agents who exercise free will are both authors of, and characters in, their own stories at once. By virtue of "self-forming" judgments of the will *(arbitria voluntatis)*, they are "arbiters" of their own lives, taking responsibility for "making themselves" out of past that, if they are truly free, does not limit their future pathways to one. If someone should charge them with not having a sufficient or conclusive prior reason for choosing as they did, they may reply as follows: "Perhaps so. But that does not mean I did not *choose*, and it does not mean I did not choose for *good* reasons, which I stand by and for which I take responsibility. If I lacked sufficient or conclusive prior reasons, that is because, like the heroine of the novel, I was not a fully formed person before I chose—and still am not, for that matter.[26] Like the author of the novel, I am in the process of writing a story and forming a person (who, in my case, is myself). It is a heavy burden, but an eminently human one."

Endnotes

*This paper was prompted by a recent objection made in various forms against my view and other incompatibilist views of freedom and responsibility by Galen Strawson, Alfred Mele, Bernard Berofsky, Bruce Waller, Richard Double, Mark Bernstein, and Ishtiyaque Haji. (See footnote 10 for references.) The paper has benefitted from interchanges with the above persons and with participants at a conference on my work on free will at the University of Arkansas in September, 1997: Gary Watson, Barry Loewer, Timothy O'Connor, Randolph Clarke, Christopher Hill, and Thomas Senor. It has also benefitted from interchanges in conferences or in correspondence with John Martin Fischer, William Rowe, Nicholas Nathan, David Hodgson, Saul Smilansky, Kevin Magill, Peter van Inwagen, Derk Pereboom, Laura Ekstrom, Hugh McCann, and Ilya Prigogine. I am especially grateful to Mele and Strawson for pursuing me assiduously on these issues since the publication of my latest work, and for perceptive comments on the penultimate draft by Mele, Berofsky, and George Graham.

[1] *Culture and Value* (New York: Blackwell, 1980).

[2] *Elbow Room* (Cambridge: MIT, 1984), chapter 1 and pp. 32–34, 64–65, 119–20, 169–70.

[3] *The Significance of Free Will* (New York: Oxford, 1996), pp. 10–14, 33–37.

[4] For example, physicist A. H. Compton, *The Freedom of Man* (New Haven: Yale, 1935) and neurophysiologist John Eccles, *Facing Reality* (New York: Springer, 1970).

[5] See, for example, Galen Strawson, who argues that, even if free will should be incompatible with determinism, indeterminism would be no help in enhancing either freedom or responsibility—"The Unhelpfulness of Indeterminism," *Philosophy and Phenomenological Research* (forthcoming).

[6] *Essay on the Freedom of the Will* (Indianapolis: Bobbs-Merrill, 1960), p. 47.

[7] This dilemma for incompatibilist accounts of freedom is nicely described by Thomas Nagel, *The View from Nowhere* (New York: Oxford, 1986), chapter 7.

[8] *Selections* (New York: Scribner's, 1951), p. 435.

[9] Stephen M. Cahn makes a persuasive case for there being such a role—"Random Choices," *Philosophy and Phenomenological Research*, XXXVII (1977): 549–51.

[10] Strawson, "The Impossibility of Moral Responsibility," *Philosophical Studies*, LXXV (1994): 5–24. and "The Unhelpfulness of Indeterminism," *op. cit.;* Mele, Review of my *The Significance of Free Will*, this JOURNAL, XCV, 11 (November 1998): 581–84, and "Luck and the Significance of Free Will," *Philosophical Explanations* (forthcoming); Berofsky, "Ultimate Responsibility in a Deterministic World," *Philosophy and Phenomenological Research* (forthcoming); Waller, "Free Will Gone Out of Control," *Behaviorism*, XVI (1988): 149–67; Double, *The Non-reality of Free Will* (New York: Oxford, 1991), p. 140; Bernstein, "Kanean Libertarianism," *Southwest Philosophy Review,* XI (1995): 151–57; Haji, "Indeterminism and Frankfurt-type Examples," *Philosophical Explanations* (forthcoming). Different, but related, concerns about indeterminism and agency are aired by Timothy O'Connor, "Indeterminism and Free Agency: Three Recent Views," *Philosophy and Phenomenological Research*, LIII (1993): 499–526; and Randolph Clarke, "Free Choice, Effort and Wanting More," *Philosophical Explanations* (forthcoming).

[11] I defend this point at length in *Free Will and Values* (Albany: SUNY, 1985), chapters 4 and 5. It is also defended by Peter van Inwagen, "When Is the Will Free" in J. Tomberlin, ed., *Philosophical Perspectives*, Volume 3 (Atascadero, CA: Ridgeview, 1989), pp. 399–422. John Martin Fischer has described the view that van Inwagen and I defend as "restricted libertarianism," and has criticized it in "When the Will Is Free," in Tomberlin, ed., *Philosophical Perspectives*, Volume 6 (Atascadero: Ridgeview, 1992), pp. 423–51. Another critic is Hugh McCann, "On When the Will Is Free," in G. Holmstrom-Hintikka and R. Tuomela, eds., *Contemporary Action Theory*, Volume I (Dordrecht: Kluwer, 1997), pp. 219–32. van Inwagen responds to Fischer in "When Is the Will Not Free?" *Philosophical Studies*, LXXV (1994): 95–114; and I respond in *The Significance of Free Will*, pp. 32–43.

[12] See *The Significance of Free Will*, pp. 74–78. SFAs are also sometimes called "self-forming willings" or SFWs in that work (pp. 125ff.).

[13] This, in broad outline, is the account developed in my *The Significance of Free Will*, chapters 8–10. In later sections below, I make important additions to it in response to criticisms.

[14] See P. Huberman and G. Hogg, "Phase Transitions in Artificial Intelligence Systems," *Artificial Intelligence*, XXXIII (1987): 155–72; C. Skarda and W. Freeman, "How Brains Make Chaos in Order to Make Sense of the World," *Behavior and Brain Sciences*, X (1987): 161–95; A. Babloyantz and A. Destexhe, "Strange Attractors in the Human Cortex," in L. Rensing, ed., *Temporal Disorder in Human Oscillatory Systems* (New York: Springer, 1985), pp. 132–43.

[15] Important recent defenses of the claim that indeterminism does not necessarily undermine control and responsibility include Clarke, "Indeterminism and Control," *American Philosophical Quarterly*, XXXII (1995): 125–58; Carl Ginet, *On Action* (New York: Cambridge, 1990),

chapter 6; O'Connor; and Laura Ekstrom, *Free Will* (Boulder: Westview, forthcoming).

[16]Austin, "Ifs and Cans," in his *Philosophical Papers* (New York: Oxford, 1961), pp. 153–80; Foot, "Free Will as Involving Determinism," in Berofsky, ed., *Free Will and Determinism* (New York: Harper and Row, 1966), pp. 95–108.

[17]We must, of course, assume in both these examples that other (compatibilist) conditions for responsibility are in place—for example, that, despite his anger, the husband was not acting compulsively and would have controlled himself, if he had wished; that he knew what he was doing and was doing it intentionally to anger his wife, and so on (and similarly for the assassin). But the point is that nothing in the facts of either case preclude these assumptions from also being satisfied.

[18]I have elsewhere denied that the pasts of the agents can be exactly the same, since, with indeterminist efforts, there is no exact sameness or difference (*The Significance of Free Will*, pp. 171–74). Mele's argument is designed to work, however, whether this denial of exact sameness is assumed or not. So I do not make an issue of at here.

[19]See *The Significance of Free Will*, pp. 112–14.

[20]This further "doubling" move is consistent with the theory put forward in *The Significance of Free Will*, and presupposes much of that theory, but is not made in that work. It is a further development especially provoked by Mele's argument discussed here as well as by criticisms of other persons since the book's publication, such as Strawson, Berofsky, Nicholas Nathan, Gary Watson, Clarke, O'Connor, Double, and Haji.

[21]I account for this elsewhere in terms of the notion of a "self-network" (*The Significance of Free Will*, pp. 137–42),

a more comprehensive network of neural connections representing the general motivational system in terms of which agents define themselves as agents and practical reasoners. For further discussion of such a notion, see Owen Flanagan, *Consciousness Reconsidered* (Cambridge: MIT, 1992), pp. 207ff.

[22]In response to my claim (*The Significance of Free Will*, p. 215) that "free willers [who engage in SFAs] are always trying to be better than they are by their own lights," by trying to overcome temptations of various sorts, Strawson asks: but can't they also try to be worse than they are?"—"The Unhelpfulness of Indeterminism." He is right, of course; they can. I should have added what I am saying here, that free willers can and do *also* try so be as bad or worse than they are by resisting efforts to be better. Strange creatures indeed.

[23]See *The Significance of Free Will*, pp. 171–74.

[24]*Ibid.*, pp. 133–86, for a fuller account of why indeterminism does not rule out action or choice.

[25]*Ibid.*, pp. 153–38, where a more detailed case is made for each of these claims.

[26]Jan Branson (in "Alternatives of Oneself," *Philosophy and Phenomenological Research* (forthcoming)) has made an important distinction that is relevant here—between choosing "alternatives *for* oneself" and choosing "alternatives *of* oneself." Branson notes that some choices in life are for different courses of action that will make a difference in what sort of person the chooser will become in future. In such cases, agents are not merely choosing alternatives for themselves but are choosing alternatives of themselves. Many SFAs, as I understand them, would be of this kind.

---

46. A Hearing for Libertarianism

DANIEL C. DENNETT

According to libertarianism, to be morally responsible, I have to be the ultimate source of my decision. That can be true only if no earlier influences were sufficient to secure the outcome, that is, only if determinism is not the case. But how can we be the ultimate creator and sustainer of one's ends and purposes without postulating supernatural entities or mysterious forms of causality? In the following selection Dennett asserts that the best libertarian answer to these questions is found in Kane's book *The Significance of Free Will*, and in the previous article. Nevertheless, Dennett argues that Kane cannot find a defensible location for indeterminism within the decision-making process of responsible agents and that Kane's "naturalistic libertarianism" should be rejected. Daniel C. Dennett is University Professor at Tufts University.

The traditional problem of free will is introduced by the proposition that *if determinism is true, then we don't have free will.* This proposition expresses *incompatibilism,* and it certainly seems plausible at the outset. Many who have thought long and hard about it still think it's true, so before returning to my project, which denies it outright, let's take it for a test drive to see what its appeal is, and what its strengths are, as well as its weaknesses.

The Appeal of Libertarianism

If we accept the proposition as it stands, two paths open up, depending on which half of the proposition we cling to:

Hard determinism: Determinism is true, so we don't have free will. Hard-headed scientific types sometimes proclaim their acceptance of this position, even declaring it a no-brainer. Many of them would add: And if determinism is false, we *still* don't have free will—we don't have free will in any case; it's an incoherent concept. But they typically excuse themselves from exploring the question of how they then justify the often strongly held moral convictions that continue to guide their lives. Where does this leave us? What sense are we to make of human striving, praising, blaming? [Earlier], we encountered the spiral into the abyss that beckons at this juncture. Are there any stable alternatives to this threatened moral nihilism? (The hard determinists among you may find in subsequent chapters that your *considered* view is that whereas free will—as you understand the term—truly doesn't exist, something *rather like* free will does exist, and it's just what the doctor ordered for shoring up your moral convictions, permitting you to make the distinctions you need to make. Such a soft landing for a hard determinist is perhaps only terminologically different from *compatibilism,* the view that free will and

From "A Hearing for Libertarianism," from *Freedom Evolves,* by Daniel C. Dennett. Copyright © 2003 by Daniel C. Dennett. Used by permission of Viking Penguin, a division of Penguin Group (USA) Inc.

determinism are compatible after all, the view that I am defending in this book.)

Libertarianism: We do have free will, so determinism must be false; *in*determinism is true. Since, thanks to quantum physicists, the received view among scientists today is that indeterminism *is* true (at the subatomic level and, by implication, at higher levels under various specifiable conditions), this can look like a happy resolution of the problem, but there is a snag: How can the indeterminism of quantum physics be harnessed to give us a clear, coherent picture of a human agent exercising this wonderful free will?

This meaning of *libertarianism,* by the way, has nothing to do with the political sense of the term. There are probably more left-leaning than right-leaning philosophers who defend this kind of libertarianism, but only because there are probably more left-leaning philosophers in general. It might be true that political right-wingers who have thought about it tend to favor free will libertarianism, and religious conservatives are drawn to it, if only by being repelled by all the alternatives, but free will libertarians are not committed to any particular view about the powers of the state vis-à-vis the citizens. They agree that free will depends on indeterminism but they divide rather sharply on the snag just mentioned: How, exactly, could subatomic indeterminism yield free will? One group simply declares that this is somebody else's problem, a job for neuroscientists, perhaps, or physicists. All they are concerned with are what we might call the top-down constraints of moral responsibility: For a human agent to be properly held responsible for something done, it must be the case one way or another that the agent's choice of this action was not determined by the total set of physical conditions that obtained prior to the choice. "We philosophers are in charge of setting the *specs* for a free agent; we leave the problem of *implementation* of those specs to the neuro-engineers." Another smaller group has appreciated that this division of labor is not always a good idea; the very coherence of the libertarian specs is called into question by the difficulties one encounters in trying to implement them. Moreover, it turns out that the attempt to devise a positive account of indeterministic human choice pays dividends that are independent of the assumption of indeterminism.

The best attempt so far is by Robert Kane, in his 1996 book, *The Significance of Free Will.*[1] Only a libertarian account, Kane claims, can provide the feature we—some of us, at least—yearn for, which he calls Ultimate Responsibility. Libertarianism begins with a familiar claim: If determinism is true, then every decision I make, like every breath I take, is an effect, ultimately, of chains of causes leading back into times before I was born. In the previous chapter I argued that determination is not the same as causation, that knowing that a system is deterministic tells you nothing about the interesting causation—or *lack* of causation—among the events that transpire within it; but that's a controversial conclusion, flying in the face of a long tradition. Some may view it as, at best, an eccentric recommendation about how to use the word "cause," so let's set it aside temporarily and see what happens if instead we stick with tradition and treat determinism as the thesis that each state of affairs *causes* the succeeding state. As many have claimed, then, if my decisions are caused by chains of events leading back before my birth, I can be *causally* responsible for the results of my deeds in the same way a tree limb falling in a windstorm can be causally responsible for the death of the person it falls on, but it is not the limb's *fault* that it was only as strong as it was, or that the wind blew so fiercely, or that the tree grew so close to the footpath. To be morally responsible, I have to be the ultimate source of my decision, and that can be true only if no earlier influences were *sufficient* to secure the outcome, which was "truly up to me." Harry Truman had a famous sign on his desk in the Oval Office of the White House: "The Buck Stops Here." A human mind has to be a place where the buck stops, Kane says, and only libertarianism can provide this kind of free will, the kind that can give us Ultimate Responsibility. A mind is an arena of "willings (choices, decisions, or efforts)" and:

> If these willings were in turn caused by something else, so that the explanatory chains could be traced back further to heredity or environment, to God, or fate, then the ultimacy would not lie with the agents but with something else. (Kane 1996, p. 4)

Libertarians have to find a way of breaking these ominous causal chains in the agent at the time of decision, and as Kane acknowledges, the inventory of libertarian models so far devised is a zoo of hopeless monsters. "Libertarians have invoked transempirical power centers, non-material egos, noumenal selves, non-occurrent causes, and a litany of other special agencies whose operations were not clearly explained" (p. 11). He sets out to correct that deficiency.

Before turning to his attempt, however, we should note that some libertarians don't see this as a deficiency. Unrepentant dualists and others actually embrace the idea that it would take a miracle of sorts for there to be free will. They are sure in their bones that free will, real free will, is strictly impossible in a materialist, mechanist, "reductionist" world—and so much the worse for that materialist vision! Consider, for instance, the doctrine known as "agent causation." Roderick Chisholm, the chief architect of the contemporary version of this ancient idea, defines it thus:

> If we are responsible . . . then we have a prerogative which some would attribute only to God: each of us, when we act, is a prime mover unmoved. In doing what we do, we cause certain events to happen, and nothing—or no one—causes us to cause those events to happen. (Chisholm 1964, p. 32)

How do "we" cause these events to happen? How does an *agent* cause an effect without there being an event (in the agent, presumably) that is the cause of that effect (and is itself the effect of an earlier cause, and so forth)? Agent causation is a frankly mysterious doctrine, positing something unparalleled by anything we discover in the causal processes of chemical reactions, nuclear fission and fusion, magnetic attraction, hurricanes, volcanos, or such biological processes as metabolism, growth, immune reactions, and photosynthesis. Is there such a thing? When libertarians insist that there must be, they play into the hands of those at the other pole, the hard determinists, who are content to let the libertarians' uncompromising definition of free will set the terms of the debate, so that they can declare, with science as their ally, so much the worse for free will. I find that those who take it as just obvious that free will is an illusion tend to take their definition of free will from radical agent-causation types.

This polarization is probably inevitable. When the stakes are high, one should be cautious, but excess caution leads to hardened positions and paranoia about "erosion:" If you're not part of the solution, you're part of the problem, as they say. Beware the thin edge of the wedge, the slippery slope. If you give them an inch, they'll take a mile. Caution can also lead to a sort of unwitting self-caricature, however. In their zeal to protect something precious, people sometimes decide to dig the moat too far out, thinking that it is safer to defend too much than risk defending too little. The result is that they end up trying to defend the indefensible, clinging to an extreme position that is actually vulnerable only because of its exaggeration. Absolutism is an occupational hazard in philosophy in any case, since radical, hard-edged positions are easier to define clearly, are more memorable, and tend to attract more attention. Nobody ever became a famous philosopher by being a champion of ecumenical hybridism. On the topic of free will this tendency is amplified and sustained by tradition itself: As philosophers for two millennia have said, either we have free will or we don't; it's all, or nothing at all. And so the various compromise proposals, the suggestions that determinism is compatible with at least *some* kinds of free will, are resisted as bad bargains, dangerous subversions of our moral foundations.

Libertarians have long insisted that the *compatibilist* sorts of free will I am describing and defending are not the real thing at all, and not even an acceptable substitute for the real thing, but rather a "wretched subterfuge," in the oft-quoted phrase of Immanuel Kant. Two can play this disparagement game. Watch. According to us compatibilists, *libertarians* seem to think that you can have free will only if you can engage in what we might call *moral levitation*. Wouldn't it be wonderful to be able to levitate—and then to dash off in any direction with the merest flick of a whim? I'd love to be able to do that, but I can't. It's impossible. There are no such miraculous things as levitators, but there are some pretty good near-levitators: Hummingbirds, helicopters, blimps, and hang gliders come to mind. Near-levitation isn't good enough, though, for libertarians, who say, in effect:

If your feet are on the ground, the decision isn't really yours—it's really planet Earth's decision. The decision isn't *made by you* but is rather a mere summation of causal trains intersecting in your body, a mobile bump on the surface of the planet, buffeted by influences, answerable to gravity. Real autonomy, real freedom, requires that the chooser be somehow suspended, isolated from the push and pull of all those causes, so that when decisions are made nothing causes them except *you!*

Those are the caricatures. They have their uses, but now let's get serious and consider Kane's intrepid attempt to fill in the gaps and provide a libertarian model of responsible decision-making. Acknowledging that "*freedom* is a term with many meanings," Kane grants that "*even if we lived in a determined world,* we could meaningfully distinguish persons who are free from such things as physical restraint, addiction or neurosis, coercion or political oppression, from persons not free from these things, and we could allow that these freedoms would be worth preferring to their opposites even in a determined world" (Kane 1996, p. 15). So some freedoms worth wanting are compatible with determinism, but "human longings transcend" those freedoms; "there is *at least one* kind of freedom that is incompatible with determinism, and it is a *significant kind of freedom worth wanting.*" It is "the power to be the ultimate creator and sustainer of one's own ends or purposes" (p. 15).

It is commonly supposed that in a deterministic world, there are no *real* options, only apparent options. In the previous two chapters, I have shown that this is an illusion, but if it is, it is also remarkably resilient and tempting. If determinism is true, then there is at any instant exactly one physically possible future, so since every choice has already been determined, all of life is just the playing out of a script that was fixed at the dawn of time. With no real options, no branch points in one's trajectory through history, it seems you can hardly be the *author* of your acts; you are more like an actor in a play, speaking your lines with apparent conviction, committing your "crimes" with grace or clumsiness, whichever has been fixed in the stage directions. Compelling, isn't it? But false. Probably the best way to drive home the surprising conclusion that this is just wrong—a panic reaction that is simply not justified by the premise of determinism—is to give the other side their best shot at saying what *would* give us real options The challenge Kane faces is to describe a way our *apparent* decision-making could be *real* decision-making, and he wants to do this without postulating any supernatural entities or mysterious forms of agency. He is, like me, a naturalist, who assumes that we are creatures of the natural order whose mental activity is dependent on the operations of our brains. This requirement of naturalism sets some questions well worth asking. (In later chapters, we'll look more closely at what contemporary cognitive neuroscience and psychology have to say about decision-making, to see what interesting things happen when we get more ambitious and try to put in more of the details.)

Where Should We Put the Much-Needed Gap?

A legendary book review begins, "This book fills a much-needed gap," and whether or not the author of that review meant what he said, Kane definitely needs a gap, a hiatus in determinism, and he wants to install it in what he calls the *faculty of practical reason* in the brain. He describes this faculty in terms of its input, its output, and what sometimes happens during the process that takes it from input to output (see Figure 1). These three phenomena are distinguished by Kane in terms of three senses of *will:*

(i) *desiderative* or *appetitive will:* what I *want, desire,* or *prefer* to do

(ii) *rational will:* what I *choose, decide,* or *intend* to do

(iii) *striving will:* what I *try, endeavor,* or make an *effort* to do. (Kane 1996, p. 26)

Roughly, will of type (i) provides the input to the faculty of practical reason, which yields type (ii) will as output when all goes well. When there is a strain on the machinery we get (iii), which always implies a resistance, generating striving or heightened effort. This all sounds quite familiar and

Figure 1 Faculty of Practical Reasoning

right. When we are undecided, we stoke up our minds with whatever relevant preferences or desires occur to us (i), remind ourselves of relevant facts or beliefs, and then mull. Our mullings, easy or effortful (iii), eventually terminate in decisions (ii). "If there is indeterminacy in free will, on my view, it must come somewhere between the input and the output" (Kane 1996, p. 27).

Kane sets up an example so we can see such a system in action: Consider the case of a businesswoman "who is on the way to a meeting important to her career when she observes an assault in an alley. An inner struggle ensues between her moral conscience, to stop and call for help, and her career ambitions, which tell her she cannot miss this meeting" (Kane 1996, p. 126). He ventures the idea that this struggle might set up two "recurrent and connected neural networks"—one for each side of the issue. These two interconnected networks feed back on each other, interacting in multifarious ways, interfering with each other, and generally churning along until one of them wins the tug-of-war, at which time the system settles, outputting a decision.

> Such networks circulate impulses and information in feedback loops and generally play a role in complex cognitive processing in the brain of the kind that one would expect to be involved in human deliberation. Moreover, recurrent networks are nonlinear, thus allowing (as some recent research suggests) for the possibility of *chaotic activity* [my italics—DCD], which would contribute to the plasticity and flexibility human brains display in creative problem solving (of which practical deliberation is an example). The input of one of these recurrent networks consists of the woman's moral motives, and its output the choice to go back; the input of the other, her career ambitions, and its output, the choice to go on to her meeting. The two networks are connected, so that the *indeterminism that made it uncertain* [my italics—DCD] that she would do the moral thing was coming from her desire to do the opposite, and vice versa—the indeterminism thus arising, as we said, from a conflict in the will. (Kane 1999, pp. 225–26)

Before we go any further, we need to separate two issues that are run together in this passage. The "chaotic activity" Kane mentions here is *deterministic* chaos, the *practical* unpredictability of certain sorts of phenomena that are describable in plain old Newtonian physics. As Kane recognizes, two networks interacting chaotically would not in themselves create any indeterminism, so if there is any "indeterminism that made it uncertain," it has to come from elsewhere. This is a key point. Kane is not alone in seeing the importance of chaos in decision-making, but it is his idea to *supplement* chaos with a smidgen of quantum randomness, following, with many others, in the wake of Roger Penrose (1989, 1994). The question we need to consider is whether any important work is being done by Kane's extra ingredient, and for this we need to get clearer about what a chaotic phenomenon is.

Consider the Hyatt New Departure Ball Bearing exhibit. For many years, the Museum of Science and Technology in Chicago displayed a glass case in which an astonishing phenomenon unfolded, hour after hour. This exhibit, donated by a branch of General Motors, showed an endless parade of little steel balls rolling out of a little hole in the back of the exhibit, falling several feet onto the highly polished top of a beautifully machined cylindrical steel "anvil," bouncing high in the air through a ring that rotated like a coin spun on a tabletop (so that timing the leaps through the rotating ring had to be exquisitely precise), and then bouncing off a second anvil up to a small hole in the back of the case, through which they all made their precise exits: Bounce, bounce, swish, bounce, bounce, swish, hundreds of times an hour. The sign on it said: "This machine demonstrates the accuracy of manufacture and uniformity of physical properties of the balls used in ball bearings." Once the two anvils were properly adjusted, it would run for days on end, with each ball following exactly the trajectory of its predecessor, a perfectly predictable, reliable, deterministic unfolding, a powerful demonstration that physical properties can fix one's destiny—at least if one is a little steel ball. Its predictability could have been shattered, however, by simply doubling the number of anvils (so that each ball had to take four bounces before exiting) and turning the anvils on their sides, so that the balls had to bounce off the rounded walls of the cylinders instead of their ultra-flat tops. The margins of error for machining the balls and adjusting the anvils would shrink vanishingly close to zero.[2] The mere presence of onlookers on the other side of the glass would create enough variable gravitational interference to upset the most exacting of calculations and cause many of the balls to miss their final destinations!

This kind of chaos is deterministic, but not for that reason uninteresting; it could indeed, as Kane says, "contribute to the plasticity and flexibility human brains display." In recent years the powers of such chaos, and "non-linearity" more generally, have been explored and amply demonstrated in many models alluded to by Kane. Some of this research has been heralded by critics as the death knell of Artificial Intelligence or, more specifically, the symbol-crunching variety known as GOFAI— Good Old Fashioned Artificial Intelligence (Haugeland 1985), and the impression has been created in many quarters that non-linear neural networks have wondrous powers altogether off-limits to mere computers, with their clunky, brittle algorithmic programs. But what many fans of neural networks have overlooked is the fact that the very models they advertise to prove their point are *computer* models, not just strictly deterministic but even, down in the engine room, algorithmic. They are non-algorithmic only *at the highest level.* (Can a whole be "freer" than its parts? Here is one way it can.) Even such an astute commentator as Paul Churchland can fall into this tempting trap. Correctly disparaging Roger Penrose's attempt to enlist quantum physics against the dread algorithms of AI, Churchland writes:

> *One need not look so far afield as the quantum realm to find a rich domain of nonalgorithmic processes.* The processes taking place within a *hardware* [my italics—DCD] neural network are typically nonalgorithmic, and they constitute the bulk of the computational activity going on inside our heads. They are nonalgorithmic in the blunt sense that they do not consist in a series of discrete physical states serially traversed under the instructions of a stored set of symbol-manipulating rules. (Paul Churchland 1995, pp. 247–48)

Notice the insertion of the word "hardware" here. Without it, what Churchland says would be false. In fact, all the results he discusses (NETTalk, Elman's grammar-learning networks, Cottrell and Metcalfe's EMPATH, and others) were produced not by "hardware neural networks" but by virtual neural networks simulated on standard computers. And so, at a low level, every one of these demonstrations *did* "consist in a series of discrete physical states serially traversed under the instructions of a stored set of symbol-manipulating rules." This is not the level at which to explain their power, of course, but it is an algorithmic level. Nothing these programs do transcends the limits of Turing computability. Just as we had to go to the chess-playing level to explain the difference in powers between programs A and B . . . we have to go to the neural-network-modeling level to explain the remarkable powers of these simulated networks, but in both cases what is going on at the micro-level is a deterministic, digital, algorithmic process. The very models Churchland discusses so favorably are implemented as computer programs—

algorithms, from the point of view of the limits of computability. So, unless he wants to disavow his own favorite examples, he must grant, after all, that algorithmic processes can exhibit the powers he thinks are crucial to the explanation of mentality. But then his claim that *hardware* neural networks are nonalgorithmic, even if true, would not play any role in explaining the powers they exhibit—since algorithmic approximations thereof have all the necessary powers.[3]

The simple Life world agents . . . and the computer chess programs . . . were both digital and deterministic, and so, for all their extra powers, are computer simulations of non-linear neural networks. Churchland's extra ingredient—hardware in place of virtual machine software—adds nothing to the powers of neural networks. Or if it does, nobody has given us any reason to think so.[4] Does Kane's extra ingredient—quantum level indeterminism—do any more work? To answer this question, we need to consider the details. Where and how should Kane insert the indeterminism he wants?

Kane's Model of Indeterministic Decision-Making

What should the faculty of practical reasoning do, and how should it do it? What are the specs, as an engineer would say, of this deciding-device? Kane tells us that it should somehow discern the weight of the various reasons and preferences fed to it, and tip the scales in favor of the reason the agent "wants to act on more than he or she wants to act on any other reasons (for doing otherwise)." He adds the further proviso that felicitous or successful cases of the faculty in action should not be the result of coercion or compulsion (Kane 1996, p. 30). Kane deliberately leaves open at the outset the question of whether the faculty operates deterministically, since he wants to argue that, for libertarian free will to emerge from the faculty, this extra feature of indeterminism must be installed. In considering the specs for a faculty of practical reason, it helps to go beyond Kane's minimal conditions and consider some of the sorts of *incompetence* you wouldn't want your faculty to exhibit.

(1) It gives no output at all—it's just broken. You are unable to think about what to do next.

(2) It has too narrow a bandwidth (it can't handle simultaneously all your wants or desires or preferences, and thrashes away, unable to digest its huge input).

(3) It gives output too slowly for the world you live in.

(4) It has Hamlet's problem (infinite loop) and delays its output indefinitely.

(5) It fails for particular *sorts* of input (advice from Mom, considerations of patriotism, sex, or tenure . . .).

(6) It gives the *wrong* output for the input (e.g., you definitely *prefer* human rights to having an ice cream at time *t*, but your faculty has you *decide* to buy an ice cream instead of putting the money in the Amnesty International box).

This last suggestion raises an interesting question about weakness of will, and the striving will—Kane's type (iii)—that arises when there is resistance and something has to give. Where is the *clutch* on this mechanism? Is it outside the faculty or inside?

The example given in (6) puts the clutch inside the faculty, allowing unwanted slippage *between* the input and the output: You arrive at an unwanted decision. But apparently there's another sort of case: Your practical reasoning works just fine so that you do *decide* to spend the money on human rights, but (darn it) the clutch slips *after* you make the decision and you end up buying the ice cream instead of doing *what you decided to do*. (See Figure 2.) Are these really two different cases? If so, what is the difference, and why is it important? When is a decision really a decision? This is

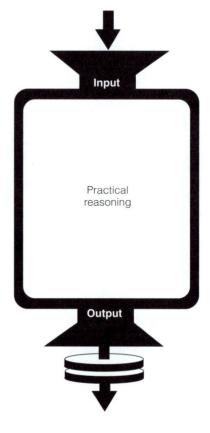

Figure 2 Clutch Positions, Inside and Out

not the only problem about the boundaries that we will encounter.

What if your faculty of practical reasoning were to give different outputs for the very same inputs? Would this be a flaw? Usually we want systems to be reliable, and by this we mean that we count on them always to give the same output—the *best* output, whatever it is—for each possible input. Consider your hand calculator as an example. Sometimes, however, when the best output is not definable or we specifically want the system to introduce "random" variation into the surrounding supersystem, we are content to have it give different outputs for the very same input. The standard way to achieve this is to incorporate a pseudo-random number generator in the system, serving the function of a coin flip (by generating either a 0 or a 1 every time it is asked) or the throw of an ordinary six-sided die (by generating a number between 1 and 6 every time it is asked) or the spin of a wheel of fortune (by generating a number between 1 and *n* every time it is asked). Kane wants something better than pseudo-randomness. He wants genuine randomness, and he proposes to get it by supposing there is some kind of quantum-fluctuation amplifier in the neurons. As we saw in the previous chapter, this wouldn't make his model any more flexible or open-ended, more capable of improving itself or learning. It wouldn't give his system any opportunities it wouldn't get by having a pseudo-random number generator do the work, but that is not its point. Its point is metaphysical, not practical.

In any case, *should* you want your faculty of practical reasoning to give different outputs for the very same inputs? Here we face another boundary problem. What do we count as an input? Does the faculty contain the history of its previous activities, or is it just the content-free mill, the processor, which has to get (parts of) the history fed into it from external memory? (See Figure 3.)

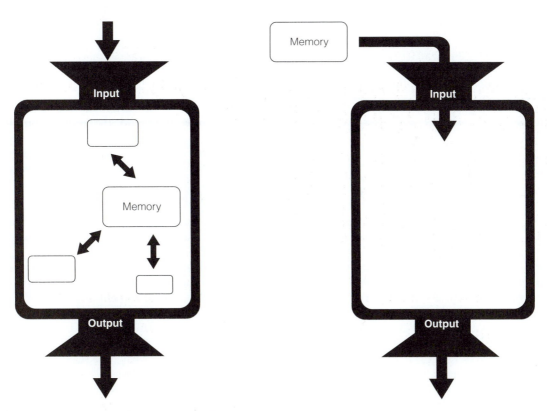

Figure 3 Memory Positions, Inside and Out

You wouldn't want your practical reasoning to be so rigid that it made the same decision every day—for instance, always deciding on a ham sandwich for lunch. But if we include in the input available facts from memory, so that one of the inputs *today* is the fact that you've had a ham sandwich two days running, this makes today's case a different case from yesterday's case, however it is decided. Since people have capacious memories and perceptual sensitivity, they are never in exactly the same state twice, so they can get plenty of variability in the output of their faculties of practical reason by simply feeding in more varied input about their current state and circumstances. Your system of practical reasoning could be as reliable as a hand calculator, *determined* always to give output$_i$ in response to input$_i$ for every value of *i*, and yet still never make the same decision twice—simply because time marches on and the system never faces exactly the same input on two occasions. "That was then, this is now" as the saying goes. [T]he computer chess programs playing against each other might never play the same game twice without ever adjusting *their* faculties of practical reason, all the variations being the result of changes in their inputs over time. You can be perfectly consistent and yet all over the map, if you let the features of the map influence your decision-making.

Now we are ready for Kane's central claim. Suppose your faculty of practical reasoning, unlike the deterministic arrangement just described, was equipped with indeterminism "somewhere between the input and the output." Is this a bug or a feature? How should we imagine this? Should we conceive of the faculty as containing one or more deterministic reasoning modules as subsystems, while also having some indeterministic innards? If we put a random number generator outside the faculty (Figure 4), then the random numbers it generates must be considered to be inputs to the faculty, and the faculty ought to treat them like any other inputs; if it is reliable, it should yield an output *determined* by that input. If, alternatively, we put a random number generator inside the faculty, to let it free up the way the faculty handles its inputs, then the faculty's outputs will *not* be determined by its inputs—but all we've done is drawn the boundary line in a different functional place.

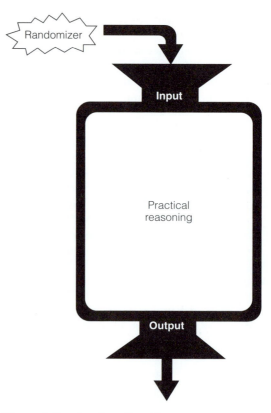

Figure 4 Randomizer Outside

Kane says that the indeterminacy should be "between" the input and the output, but we might well wonder why the indeterminacy couldn't come in *as part of* the input. What difference could it make? I put this question to Kane (in discussing an earlier draft of this chapter), and he had an interesting response:

> There is a reason why it is between input and output and does not come in merely as part of the input. The reason is that what is assumed to go on between input and output is the agent's doing or action (in the form of practical reasoning and efforts issuing in choice). The input (in the form of dispositions, beliefs, desires and the like) is not something the agent here and now controls, though some of it may have been the product of reasoning, efforts or choices made at earlier times. . . . Indeterminism merely at the input stage does not give us robust responsibility. The indeterminism must be an

ingredient not only of what "comes to mind" but of what the agent is actually doing (reasoning, making efforts, making choices) to fully capture libertarian responsibility. If inputs are the result of our doings, OK, but if they just happen to us or occur, that's not good enough even if it's by chance. (Kane, personal correspondence)

Kane wants the indeterminism to be "the result of our doings" rather than randomness that "just happens" in the input. This is easily provided: Have the faculty of practical reasoning *send out for* some randomness whenever, in the midst of its labors, it encounters something it interprets as a blockade of one sort or another—an imponderable choice or meta-choice about which way to turn or what to think about next (Figure 5).

That way, since the randomness will have been "called for" as a result of the specific activities of the faculty, it won't just arrive unbidden from out of the blue. Moreover, the use to which the requested randomness gets put will be deter-

mined by constructive activities of the faculty itself. (If I decide to flip a coin to settle where to dine tonight, it is still my choice; I *made* it settle my choice.) But here again, we are just redrawing the boundary line; anything an *onboard* source of randomness can provide can also be provided in the *input* by an *external* source of randomness that is consulted when needed. As we are beginning to see, the metaphor of the container has to do a lot of work for Kane.

But, for the sake of argument, let's assume that Kane can come up with a good reason to distinguish internal from external sources of randomness. We install the indeterminacy inside the faculty, in between input and output, per his specifications, and then we install the faculty inside the agent. How does it operate in daily life? Kane notes that

> choices or decisions normally terminate processes of deliberation or practical reasoning, but they need not always do so. We need not rule out the possibility of impulsive, spur-of-the-moment, or snap, decisions, which also settle conditions of indecision but arise with minimal or no prior reasoning. Yet, while impulsive or snap decisions can occur, they are less important for free will than decisions that terminate processes of deliberation in which alternatives are reflectively considered. For, in the latter cases, we are more likely to feel we have control over the outcome and "could have done otherwise." (Kane 1996, p. 23)

So we get a picture of *occasional* acts of deliberate choice being the morally significant turning points—"they play a pivotal role" (p. 24)—laying down habits and intentions that are later acted on quite thoughtlessly but still with responsibility. Consider an example of a snap decision. My wife asks me if I can stop by the post office on my way to work and mail a package for her, and I reply almost instantaneously that I can't, because then I'd be late for an appointment with a student. Did I deliberate? Did I engage in a process of practical reasoning? This is not heavy-duty moral decision-making, but this is the stuff from which moral (and immoral) lives are largely composed: hundreds and thousands of minor choice points decided with a moment's consideration, usually

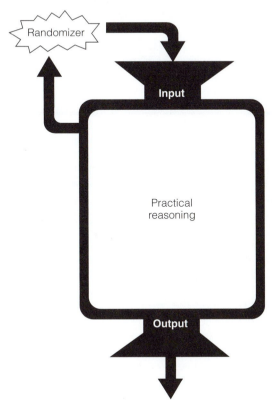

Figure 5 Sending Out for Randomness

with the background of justification kept tacit and unarticulated. How weird it would be if I had responded along these lines: "Well, since you are my wife and we have solemnly promised to help each other, and since I can think of no defect or problem in your request—you haven't asked me to do something physically impossible, or illegal, or self-destructive, for instance—there is undeniably a strong case for my answering, 'Yes, dear.' On the other hand, I have told a student that I would meet with him at nine-thirty, and given the traffic, honoring your request would entail standing him up for at least half an hour. I could try to call him and ask his permission to reschedule, but I might not reach him, and besides, the harder question is whether my mailing the package in so timely a manner is a sufficiently important errand to warrant inconveniencing him. My making the appointment amounted to a promise to him, though not one that couldn't be forgivably broken for cause. . . ." It is perhaps surprising to note that all these considerations (and many more!) really did contribute *somehow* to my snap answer. How so? Well, would I have given an unconsidered snap judgment, positive or negative, if my wife had asked me please to strangle the dentist on my way to work, or drive my car over a cliff? If I had earlier told my student merely that I intended to be in my office at 9:30 for coffee (no promise made or implied), or left the time of the appointment more flexible, or had been talking to him on the phone at the very moment my wife asked, this would have made a difference, surely, in my snap judgment. Even a snap judgment can be remarkably sensitive to myriad features of my world that have conspired over time to create my current dispositional state.

Kane is willing to allow that such a complex dispositional state, which has been building more or less continuously in me since I was a child, may *determine* how I will respond in such a case and in other cases when I do not deliberate. But once again, boundary questions loom. Should we view a snap judgment as *issuing from* the faculty of deliberation (but just so swiftly and effortlessly that the details stay tacit) or should we view the snap decision as issuing more directly from some "lower" faculty or subsystem, the faculty of deliberation being kept in reserve for occasional heavy lifting? It is best, I think, to draw the lines (which

are, after all, just philosophers' lines of analysis, not anatomical boundaries to be discovered) so that even snap judgments get executed, effortlessly, in and by the faculty of practical reasoning. For, as we shall see, Kane holds that whereas the gap of indeterminism is to be located within that faculty (between input and output), the faculty does not always have to avail itself of indeterminism. It can operate deterministically on occasion, even when dealing with high-stakes moral decisions. (Shall I strangle the dentist? Naw.)

Kane is comfortable with this occasional role for determinism in the life of a moral agent, for several reasons. First, it permits him to handle these snap judgment cases realistically. It is just not plausible to maintain that the habits of a lifetime, yielding decisions so predictable you can trust your life to them, are nevertheless indeterministic (except in the limiting sense that there might be one chance in a bazillion that they would be disrupted). Think of your willingness to drive on the highway, facing oncoming cars in the opposite lane with an approach velocity well over 100 miles per hour. Your life depends on the drivers of those cars *not* deciding, as they are free to decide, to swerve suddenly into your lane, just to see what happens. Your equanimity on the highway shows how predictable you assume these total strangers to be. They *could* kill you in a senseless, suicidal *acte gratuit*, but you wouldn't pay a dollar or even a dime for the opportunity to clear the road of all oncoming cars before you ventured out. Second, Kane needs a helping of determinism in order to handle a more serious objection to libertarianism raised by me in *Elbow Room*: the case of Martin Luther.

> "Here I stand," Luther said. "I can do no other." Luther claimed that he could do no other, that his conscience made it *impossible* for him to recant. He might, of course, have been wrong, or have been deliberately overstating the truth. But even if he was— perhaps especially if he was—his declaration is testimony to the fact that we simply do not exempt someone from blame or praise for an act because we think he could do no other. Whatever Luther was doing, he was not trying to duck responsibility. (Dennett 1984, p. 133)

Kane accepts that Luther's decision was the furthest thing from a snap judgment, that it was definitely a morally responsible decision, and that what Luther said about it may well have been true: He could not have done otherwise; he truly was *determined by his faculty of practical reasoning at the time* to stand firm. The case of Luther is not a rare or unimportant sort of case. As we shall see in later chapters, the policy of preparing oneself for tough choices by arranging to be determined to do the right thing when the time comes is one of the hallmarks of mature responsibility, and Kane accepts this. In fact, he builds his account of free will around the idea that for each of us morally responsible agents, there must have been some relatively infrequent occasions in our lives when we have encountered conflicting desires—generating his type (iii) striving will. On some of these occasions we have decided to perform "self-forming actions" (SFAs), which may have a deterministic effect on our subsequent behavior, and only these SFAs need be the result of processes in the faculty of practical reason that are genuinely indeterministic:

> An act like Luther's can be ultimately responsible . . . though determined by his will, *because* the will from which it issued was a will *of his own making,* and in that sense it was his "own" free will. . . . Ultimately responsible acts, or acts done of one's own free will, make up a wider class of actions than those self-forming actions (SFAs) which must be undetermined and such that the agent could have done otherwise. But if no actions were "self-forming" in this way, we would not be *ultimately* responsible for anything we did. (Kane 1996, p. 78)

When I launch a boulder from a catapult toward my enemy, once the boulder is in flight, its trajectory is out of my hands, no longer subject to my will, but its effects on landing are my responsibility, no matter how long the delay. When I launch myself into a trajectory of one sort or another, having taken care to arrange that I will be unable to alter various aspects of that trajectory hereafter, the same conclusion manifestly holds. Reflections like this lead some libertarians to accept that the freedom they seek to install may have to be concentrated in a few windows of opportunity with special properties. (Peter van

Inwagen, for instance, joins Kane on this point, but, unlike Kane, supposes such windows may be quite rare.) But now just what special properties will these be? Kane says that an SFA must meet condition AP:

> (AP) The agent has *alternative possibilities* (or can do otherwise) with respect to A at *t* in the sense that, at *t*, the agent *can* (has the *power* or *ability* to) do A and *can* (has the *power* or *ability* to) *do otherwise.* (Kane 1996, p. 33)

Notice the role of "at *t*" in this formula. Some philosophers can't bear to say simple things, like "Suppose a dog bites a man." They feel obliged instead to say, "Suppose a dog *d* bites a man *m* at time *t*," thereby demonstrating their unshakable commitment to logical rigor, even though they don't go on to manipulate any formulae involving *d, m,* and *t*. Talk about time *t* is ubiquitous in philosophical definitions but seldom given any serious work to do. Here, however, it plays a serious role. This definition speaks about what is the case at each moment in time; it *requires* us to think about *possibilities-at-an-instant.* Kane (p. 87) quotes a rhapsodic passage from William James:

> The great point . . . is that the possibilities are really *here.* . . . At those soul-trying moments when fate's scales seem to quiver, . . . [we acknowledge] that the issue is decided nowhere else than *here* and *now. That* is what gives the palpitating reality to our moral life and makes it tingle . . . with so strange and elaborate an excitement. (James 1897, p. 183)

Let's look more closely at those quivering scales. Imagine that your faculty of practical reason is equipped with a dial, with a needle showing which way the scales are currently tipping as the mulling goes on, hovering between Go and Stay (supposing those are the options you're currently considering) and wandering back and forth, perhaps even quivering, oscillating swiftly between the two values (Figure 6). And suppose that at any moment you can terminate the process of deliberation by pressing the *Now!* button, sealing your choice with whatever side, Go or Stay, happens at that instant to be favored by the deliberation up to then. Suppose, for the moment, that all the

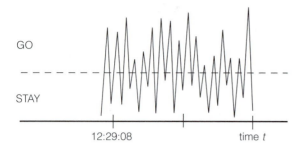

Figure 6 Quivering Needle between Go and Stay

Figure 7 Enlargement of Figure 6, Showing 10-millisecond Period

processing by your faculty of practical reasoning is deterministic; it "sums the weights" by some deterministic function of all the input it has so far considered, and yields a moment-by-moment value that swings this way and that, between Go and Stay, depending on the order in which considerations are processed and reprocessed in the light of further deliberation.

Would condition AP be met in such a case? What would we look for to answer this question? Suppose we looked at the last *minute* of deliberation, and noticed that during that time, the needle oscillated back and forth a dozen times or more, and roughly half the time the needle pointed to Go and half the time the needle pointed to Stay. On that timescale it would certainly look as if both alternatives were *open* (compared, for instance, to a minute during which the needle rested firmly on Stay the entire time). But for Kane (and for James) this is not good enough. For there to be genuine free will, both possibilities have to open *at time t,* the very instant the *Now!* button was pressed. If we then zoomed in on that moment, and noticed that for the last 10 milliseconds before time *t,* the needle was steady on Stay, which was also the decision registered by the pressing of the *Now!* button, it would seem that we had good evidence that the Go option was *not* available at time *t* (see Figure 7).

Ah, but there is a loophole. I imagined that *you* got to press the *Now!* button. Could we introduce indeterminacy by letting the exact timing of the button pressing be "up to you"? Let's suppose, then, that while the mulling process itself is all determined, what is indeterminate is the exact timing of the *Now!* button-press. Sometime in the next 20 milliseconds the button will be pressed, but exactly *when* is strictly (quantum) indeterminate. Then if the quivering between Go and Stay

takes place at a high enough frequency to put both Go and Stay periods into that 20-millisecond window, the actual decision made by the activation of the *Now!* button will be undetermined, utterly and officially unpredictable from a complete description of the universe at the beginning of the window of opportunity (Figure 8).

Unfortunately, it will still not be the case that condition AP is met, due to a flaw in the definition of AP: that pesky "at *t*" clause. It will still be completely predictable that if the decision occurs at millisecond 5, say, it will be a decision to Go, and if it occurs at millisecond 17 it will be a decision to Stay. In fact, for any time *t* in the window of opportunity, it is determined what decision would be made at that instant; what isn't determined is when exactly the decision will be made. The agent is not free *at t* to Go or Stay for *any* value of *t*. But isn't this good enough, so long as the instant of choosing is undetermined? It is tempting to propose a mild revision of condition AP that would then accept our simple model: Let time *t* be smeared over the whole 20-millisecond time window instead of instantaneous, and we're home free, since both Go and Stay coexist at time *t* thus stretched out—and 20 milliseconds is hardly a long period of time.

The needle on the dial, and the button, make this model look awfully "mechanistic," to be sure, but Kane demands this himself. He's crying to be a *naturalist* libertarian, so he wants his model to be scientifically respectable, something the brain could implement, and the dial and the button are just vivid devices for helping us visualize the underlying state of the relevant neural complexity. *Some* sort of physically realizable neural state must implement the current weighting, and *some*

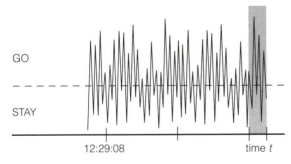

GO

STAY

12:29:08   time *t*

Figure 8 Window of Opportunity

state-transition must implement a decision (yield an output); we can just pretend that the dial transduces the former and the button triggers the latter. So the model illustrates one way—one family of ways—in which subatomic quantum indeterminacy could be amplified into playing a crucial role in decision-making. Moreover, the model seems to satisfy Kane's Ultimacy requirement for SFAs:

> (U) for every X and Y (where X and Y represent occurrences of events and/or states) if the agent is personally responsible for X, and if Y is an *arche*[5] (or sufficient ground or cause or explanation) for X, then the agent must also be personally responsible for Y (Kane 1996, p. 35)

Translation: You can only be personally responsible for one thing if you are personally responsible for everything that is a sufficient condition for it. According to Kane,

> SFAs are the undetermined, regress-stopping voluntary actions (or refrainings) in the life histories of agents chat are required if U is to be satisfied. (Kane 1996, p. 75)

Indeterministic timing of the *Now!* button could make the decision itself indeterministic in cases where both options quiver in a slightly elongated window of opportunity; there wouldn't *be* any sufficient condition for either the Go or Stay decision at any earlier moment, so you could be personally responsible for Go (or Stay) without having to worry about being responsible for any earlier sufficient condition for Go (or Stay). Of course, we still have to find some way of making sense of an indeterministic button pressing being "up to *you*" and not itself just an *external*, random input.

"If You Make Yourself Really Small, You Can Externalize Virtually Everything"[6]

Once again we have a boundary problem, and this time it is major: How can Kane get a quantum indeterminacy to be *inside* the relevant system? To see the difficulty, suppose a bystander yells just as you're about to push the *Now!* button, startling you and thereby hastening your press by five milliseconds, *causing* your press. Is the decision now no longer yours at all? After all, the crucial part of the cause, the part that determined whether to Go or Stay, was itself caused by the bystander's yell (which was caused by the seagull flying by so close, which was caused by the early return of the fishing fleet, which was caused by the resumption of El Niño, which . . . was caused by a butterfly flapping its wings back in 1926). Even if that butterfly wing flap was truly undetermined, the magnified effect of a quantum leap in its tiny brain, this moment of indeterminism is *in the wrong time and place.* The butterfly's moment of freedom back in 1926 isn't what gives you free will today, is it? Kane's libertarianism requires him to break the chain of causation somewhere *in* the agent and *at* the time of decision, the "here and now" requirement spoken of so eloquently by William James. If it really matters, as libertarians think, then we'd better shield your processes of deliberation from all such *external* interference. We'd better insulate the wall that surrounds . . . *you* so that external forces don't interfere with the decision you're cooking up in your internal kitchen, using only the ingredients that *you* have allowed through the door.

This retreat of the Self into a walled enclave within which all the serious work of authorship has to be done parallels another retreat into the center of the brain, the various misbegotten lines of argument and reflection that lead to what I call the Cartesian Theater, the imaginary place in the center of the brain "where it all comes together" for consciousness. *There is no such place,* and any theory that tacitly presupposes that there is should be set aside at once as on the wrong track. All the work done by the imaginary homunculus in the Cartesian Theater must be distributed *in time and space* in the brain. The problem is compounded for Kane, since he has to figure out some way to get the undetermined quantum event to be not just *in you* but *yours*. He wants above all for the decision to be "up to you," but if the decision is undetermined—the defining requirement of libertarianism—it isn't determined by you, whatever you are, because it isn't determined by anything. Whatever you are, you can't *influence* the undetermined event—the whole point of quantum indeterminacy is that such quantum events are not influenced by anything—so you will somehow have to *co-opt* it or *join forces* with it, putting it to use in some intimate way, an *objet trouvé* that you meaningfully incorporate into *your* decision-making in some fashion. But in order to do this, there has to be more to you than just some mathematical point; you have to *be someone;* you have to have parts—memories, plans, beliefs, and desires—that you've acquired along the way. And then all those causal influences from the past, from outside, come crowding back in, contaminating the workshop, preempting your creativity, usurping control of your decision-making. A serious quandary.

The problem, you will recall, was already clearly recognized by William James which he asked, "If a 'free' act be a sheer novelty, that comes not *from* me, the previous me, but *ex nihilo,* and simply tacks itself on to me, how can I, the previous I, be responsible?" Kane makes some useful headway on an answer to this rhetorical question with his idea of "plural rationality" (Kane 1996, Chapter 7). We don't want our free acts to be unmotivated, inexplicable, random lightning bolts without rhyme or reason. We want there to be reasons for them, we want these to be *our* reasons, *and* (if we're libertarians) we want them to meet the AP condition, to be free in the sense that "at time *t*" we "could have done otherwise." One way this could be the case is if you yourself have taken the time and effort to develop two (or more) sets of *competing* reasons. Then both sets of reasons are composed, devised, revised, sanded, and polished *locally,* by yourself. Though you may have borrowed some pieces and ideas from outside, you've made them your own, so these are indeed *do-it-yourself* reasons. Moreover, each set of reasons is at least tentatively endorsed by you. (If one of them wasn't,

there wouldn't have been any fuss, would there? You'd have made a quick—perhaps even snap—decision in favor of the other.) So when deliberation finally terminates, whichever side you come down on is a side you have taken very seriously yourself, right up to the verge of endorsement. Your act amounts to a final verdict, a declaration that makes you the kind of person you are (a Stayer or a Goer)—and *right then* you could have done otherwise.

The point of plural rationality—or "parallel processing," as he more recently calls it (Kane 1999)—is that it builds on an intuition we've always had: You can be rightly held responsible for the outcome of a deed that includes a chance or undetermined element, *if that is what you were trying to accomplish.* The would-be assassin whose lucky long shot hits the prime minister is not absolved on the grounds that it was mere chance—even genuinely indeterministic chance—that he hit his target. By setting up an opponent process pitting two different attempts against each other (e.g., the businesswoman's quandary about whether to do the right thing or advance her career), Kane guarantees that when one of the attempts fails, the other succeeds, and she is rightly held responsible in either case because *that is one of the things she was trying to accomplish.* The fact that she was trying to accomplish two incompatible things at the same time doesn't show that when she manages to accomplish one of them, she *wasn't* trying to accomplish it!

So Kane claims that this embedding of indeterminism in the maelstrom of conflicting reasons, where the agent is actually *trying*—type (iii), the striving will—to get it right, saves the outcome, whichever it is, from being a fluke, a mere accident. Every adult agent will have faced such dilemmas, moral or prudential, and been shaped by them.

> By choosing one way or another in such cases, the agents would be strengthening their moral or prudential characters or reinforcing selfish or imprudent instincts, as the case may be. They would be "making" themselves or "forming" their wills one way or another in a manner that was not determined by past character, motives, and circum-

stances. . . . It is because their efforts are thus a response to inner conflicts embedded in the agents' prior character and motives that their character and motives can explain the conflicts and why the efforts are being made, without also explaining the outcomes of conflicts and the efforts. Prior motives and character provide reasons for going either way, but not decisive reasons explaining which way the agent will inevitably go. (Kane 1996, p. 127)

The idea that someone who has been tested by serious dilemmas of practical reasoning, who has wrestled with temptations and quandaries, is more likely to be "his own man" or "her own woman," a more responsible moral agent than someone who has just floated happily along down life's river taking things as they come, is an attractive and familiar point, but one that has largely eluded philosophers' attention. In most accounts of free will, the occurrence of tough choices in an agent's history plays no marked role and, in fact, is largely ignored, probably because it draws attention to the embarrassing limiting case: Buridan's Ass, who purportedly starves to death because he is equidistant from two piles of food and can't think of a reason for going left rather than right (or vice versa). This "liberty of indifference" has been noted since medieval times, and tie-breaking by flipping a coin has always been a recognized solution to such impasses, a useful prosthesis of the will, one might say, but it doesn't look like a good model for free will. If we theorists find ourselves approaching a view in which our only free choices will be those where we might as well flip a coin, then we must have blundered down the wrong path. Turn back quickly. And so the topic gets ignored. But Kane shows quite convincingly that the incremental character-building that *may* (but also may not) grow out of a lifetime of hard choices taken seriously really does add a "variety of free will worth wanting." There's one big problem with it, however: It doesn't need the indeterminism that inspired its creation. Moreover, it can't harness indeterminism in any way that distinguishes it from determinism, because the "here and now" requirement is not only not well motivated; it is also probably incoherent, as we shall see.

Beware of Prime Mammals

The basic idea is that the *ultimate responsibility* lies where the *ultimate* cause is.

—Robert Kane, *The Significance of Free Will*

You may think you're a mammal, and that dogs and cows and whales are mammals, but really there aren't any mammals at all—there couldn't be! Here's a philosophical argument to prove it (drawn, with alterations, from Sanford 1975).

1. Every mammal has a mammal for a mother.

2. If there have been any mammals at all, there have been only a finite number of mammals.

3. But if there has been even one mammal, then by (1), there have been an infinity of mammals, which contradicts (2), so there can't have been any mammals. It's a contradiction in terms.

Since we know perfectly well that there are mammals, we take this argument seriously only as a challenge to discover what fallacy is lurking within it. Something has to give. And we know in a general way. what has to give: If you go back far enough in the family tree of any mammal, you will eventually get to the therapsids, those strange, extinct bridge species between the reptiles and the mammals. A gradual transition occurred from clear reptiles to clear mammals, with a lot of hard-to-classify intermediaries filling in the gaps. What should we do about drawing the lines across this spectrum of gradual change? Can we identify a mammal, the Prime Mammal, that didn't have a natural for a mother, thus negating premise (1)? On what grounds? Whatever the grounds are, they will be indistinguishable from the grounds we could also use to support the verdict that that animal was *not* a mammal—after all, its mother was a therapsid. What should we do? We should quell our desire to draw lines. We don't need to draw lines. We can live with the quite unshocking and unmysterious fact that, you see, there were all these gradual changes that accumulated over many millions of years and eventually produced undeniable mammals.

Philosophers tend to like the idea of stopping a threatened infinite regress by identifying something that is—must be—the regress-stopper: the Prime Mammal, in this case. It often lands them in doctrines that wallow in mystery, or at least puzzlement, and, of course, it commits them to essentialism in most instances. (The Prime Mammal must be whichever mammal in the set of mammals first had all the *essential* mammalian features. If there is no definable essence of *mammal*, we're in trouble. And evolutionary biology shows us that there are no such essences.)

Kane's theory of free will specifically calls for "regress-stopping" special cases, the self-forming acts, or SFAs.

> If an infinite regress is to be avoided, there must be actions somewhere in the agent's life history for which the agent's predominant motives and the will on which the agent acts were *not already set one way*. (Kane 1996, p. 114)

One might pause to ask how often these important moments tend to occur. Once a day on average, or once a year or once a decade? Do they tend to start at birth, at age five, at puberty? These SFAs look suspiciously like Prime Mammals. It is worrying that while they are key events in the life of any moral agent—the natural rites of passage, one might say, into responsible adulthood—they are practically impossible to discover. There is no way to tell a genuine SFA from a pseudo-SFA, an impostor bout of reasoning that never *actually* availed itself of quantum indeterminism but just cranked out a pseudo-random and hence deterministic result. They would feel the same from the inside and look the same from the outside, no matter how sophisticated our observational apparatus. As Paul Oppenheim has suggested to me, Kane's SFAs can be usefully compared with *speciation events* in evolution, which can only be retrospectively identified. Every birth in every lineage is a potential speciation event, since offspring all have at least minute differences that make them unique, and any difference could be the beginning of something that eventually blooms into speciation. Time will tell. There is nothing *special* at the time about a birth that will turn out to have been a speciation event.[7] Similarly, one should be suspicious of the demand that there be an event—an

SFA—that has some special, intrinsic, local feature that sets it apart from its nearest kin and explains its capacity to found something important. Is it plausible that an agent who hadn't yet experienced one or more of these very special events (but only near misses, pseudo-SFAs) would simply not be responsible for any acts performed? "Yes, these furry warm-blooded things *look* a lot like mammals, and smell and sound like mammals, and are cross-fertile with mammals, but they lack the secret essence; they aren't mammals at all, not really."

Consider Luther in this regard. Kane says: "If he is ultimately accountable for his present act, then at least some of these earlier choices or actions must have been such that he could have done otherwise with respect to them. If this were not the case, nothing he could have ever done would have made any difference to what he was" (Kane 1996, p. 40). And so it makes sense—one might think—to take a good hard look at Luther's biography, to see what kind of upbringing he had, what powerful influences held him in thrall, what catastrophes he endured, and the like. But, in fact, nothing we could discover about such macroscopic details would shed *any light at all* on the question of whether or not Luther had had any genuine SFAs during this period. We could certainly discover that episodes of conflict and soul-searching occurred on various occasions, and we might even confirm that these occasions set up "chaotic" opponent processes in the neural networks from which his decisions eventually emerged. What we could not discover, however, was whether these tugs-of-war had the benefit of genuinely random, as opposed to mere pseudo-random, sources of variability. The price libertarians must pay for sequestering their pivotal moments in subatomic transactions in some privileged place in the brain (at time t) is that they render these all-important pivots undetectable by both the everyday biographer and the fully equipped cognitive neuroscientist. One might think that the difference between Luther$_1$, who was held in a cell during his adolescence for five years and subjected to brainwashing, and Luther$_2$, who had a roughly normal adolescence of triumphs and trials in the knockabout world, would have a bearing on whether there were SFAs in the ancestry of the decision made by Luther$_{today}$. But these salient environmental differences, which intuitively *do* have a bearing on our assessment of Luther's capacity for moral choice, are in no way symptoms of the presence or absence of SFAs. (They are just as irrelevant to the question of whether or not an SFA occurred in Luther as Austin's ten demonstration putts would be to the question of whether or not he was determined to miss the putt at time *t*.) And when we get out our supermicroscopes and look at subatomic activity in the neurons, whatever we see will be equally uninformative about SFAs.

But isn't this inscrutability of ultimate responsibility a problem for every theory? As Kane has said,

> If a young murderer is on trial and we look into his past life of child abuse and peer pressure, we have to make some judgment about how much of his present vicious character from which this act flowed is his own doing and how much is due to outside influences over which he lacked control. Such questions are relevant to determining guilt or innocence and how much punishment should be mitigated on any theory. They are formidably difficult questions to answer no matter what view you take about free will. (Kane, personal correspondence)

This is right, so far as it goes. Variations in life history are indeed relevant to variations in current degree of responsibility, as Kane says, and they are also difficult to investigate, on any theory. But Kane's libertarian view requires an additional investigation that is hard to motivate—impossible, in my opinion. Consider the situation statistically: We sort a hundred murderers by background, from most deprived to most fortunate, to see which should have mitigation, or total exculpation (we'll address those policy issues later). Suppose we find the following: 60 percent show *clear* evidence of major deprivation of the relevant sorts and are hence unproblematic candidates for substantial mitigation; 10 percent are "borderline"—they show quite a lot of deprivation, but how much is too much?—and the remaining 30 percent show normal-to-exemplary upbringings, no signs at all of brain damage, etc. (See Figure 9.) These fortunate individuals emerge, by a process of elimination, as practically indistinguishable

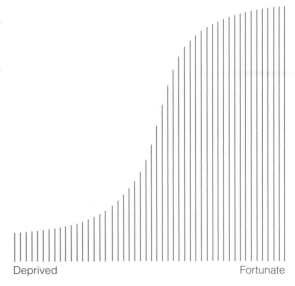

Deprived   Fortunate

Figure 9 The Distribution of Murderers

from each other in all the macroscopic characters that we take to be the necessary conditions for responsibility—the features the 60 percent lack. They are all *apparently* responsible adults. They are all among society's apparent success stories—we raised them right, filled in their gaps, gave them an equal opportunity, and so forth.

Nature doesn't insist on sharp boundaries, but sometimes *we* must draw a line of political policy, simply because we have to have some practical and ostensibly fair way of dealing with specific cases: You can't drive until you are sixteen in most states, and you can't drink until you are twenty-one, no matter how mature you are for your age. Faced with the array of cases illustrated in Figure 9, we would have to find some partly arbitrary way of drawing a line across the penumbral 10 percent, and opinions would no doubt differ on which factors to weight heavily and which to ignore. (If the curve were much steeper, we'd be grateful to discern an apparent joint at which to carve nature; if it were more gradual, our political task would be all the harder.) But Kane's view requires us to reserve judgment about not just the 10 with marginal claims to mitigation but the 30 exemplary candidates as well. Some unknown number—it could be all 30—could turn out to be *entirely* nonresponsible, because all the apparent SFAs in their life histories were pseudo-SFAs. After all, Kane holds that no robot with only a pseudo-random number generator in its system could be responsible *at all,* and yet such a robot might pass all macroscopic tests for humanity perfectly. (Such a robot, unlike a Stepford Wife,[8] would not betray its robotitude by a slavish obsession with some one policy, thanks to the pseudo-random jigglers in its faculty of practical reason that would keep it eternally open-minded.) Indeed, according to Kane's view it is entirely possible that some in the marginal group of 10 are rightly held responsible since they have had some modest number of genuine SFAs in their pasts, in spite of their deprivations, while some of the privileged group of 30 are not fit candidates for moral responsibility at all.

Try to imagine the first defendant (the son of a billionaire, since he'll need an expensive team of lawyers and scientists!) who tries to introduce evidence in court before sentencing, "demonstrating" that his brain lacked the quantum indeterminacies required for responsibility, even though he'd had an exemplary upbringing, was of above average intelligence, etc. It's a tough sell. Why should the *metaphysical* feature of Ultimate Responsibility (supposing Kane has defined a coherent possibility) count more than the macroscopic features that can be defined independently of the issue of quantum indeterminism, and that are well motivated in terms of the decision-making competences that agents have or lack? Indeed, why should metaphysical Ultimate Responsibility count for anything at all? If it can't be motivated as a grounds for treating people differently, why should anyone think it is a variety of free will worth wanting? As Kane himself puts it, "In short, when described from a physical perspective alone, *free will looks like chance*" (Kane 1996, p. 147). And chance looks exactly the same, whether it is genuinely indeterministic or merely pseudo-random or chaotic.

The libertarian, like the essentialist in biology, is captivated with boundaries, in particular the boundaries that delimit the "here" and the "now." But these boundaries, being partly interdefinable, are porous in any case. Suppose the indeterministic neurons in your faculty of practical reasoning died, leaving you disabled for any future SFAs. But suppose, fortunately for you, that the damaged part of your brain could be replaced by an indeter-

ministic prosthetic device implanted in just the right milieu in the healthy part of your brain. A good way to get genuine quantum indeterminism into a physical device is to use a little bit of decaying radium and a Geiger counter, but it might not be healthy to have such a radium randomizer implanted in your brain, so it could be left in the lab, surrounded by a lead shield, and its results could be fed into your brain on demand, by radio link (as in my "Where am I?" story in *Brainstorms,* 1978). The location of the randomizer in the lab obviously shouldn't make a difference, since it is *functionally* inside the system; it would play exactly the same role as the damaged neurons used to play, no matter where it was geographically. But there might be a cheaper, safer way of getting exactly the same effect: We could use genuinely random fluctuations in the light coming from deep space as our trigger, beaming it directly to the transceiver implanted in your brain. Since this signal arrives at the speed of light, there is no way for us to predict what the next fluctuations will be, even though their random source is a star light-years away. But if there is no problem getting your indeterminacy from a distant star, why insist on making it *now* in the first place? *Record* a series of random fluctuations by a radium randomizer over a century, and install that recording from the past as your pseudo-random number generator somewhere in your brain, to be consulted when appropriate.

In *Elbow Room,* I noted the unimportance of the difference between a lottery in which the winning ticket is chosen (randomly) *after* all the tickets are sold, and a lottery in which the winning ticket stub is chosen *before* the tickets are sold. Both are fair lotteries; both give all the purchasers a fair chance of winning.

> If our world is determined, then we have pseudo-random number generators in us, not Geiger counter randomizers. That is to say, if our world is determined, all our lottery tickets were drawn at once, eons ago, put in an envelope for us, and doled out as we needed them through life. (Dennett 1984, p. 121)

Kane has suggested to me (personal correspondence) that "[t]he indeterminacy-producing mechanism must be responsive to the dynamics within the agent's own will and not override them or it would be making the decisions and not the agent." His concern is that a remote source of randomness would threaten your autonomy, and be likely to take control of your thinking processes. Wouldn't it be much safer—and hence more responsible—to keep the randomizer inside you, under your watchful eye in sonic sense? No. Randomness is just randomness; it isn't *creeping* randomness. Programmers routinely insert calls to the random number generator in their programs, not worrying about it somehow getting out of hand and providing chaos where it isn't wanted. Suppose we visualize the brain's dynamics in our Go/Stay example as creating a saddle in a decision landscape, a place where the decision-explorer will eventually slide off the hill into either the Go valley to the north or the Stay valley to the south. (See Figure 10.)

The landscape is generously sprinkled with banana peels—calls to the random number generator that are activated any time the decision-explorer passes over them. This keeps the explorer moving, randomly if necessary, preventing Buridan's Ass from occurring, so the explorer never gets stuck on the flattish ridge of the saddle and dies decisionless. These slippery banana peels are harmless, though, because once a decision starts heading down into one valley or the other, encountering an unnecessary peel can only briefly bump the decision back uphill a bit, delaying for a micro-moment the plunge that has already been settled on, or else hasten its downward slide, without being able to overrule it. Or to use another vivid image popular among modelers, the random number generator simply "shakes" or "jiggles" the landscape ever so incessantly, so that nothing can just stop on the saddle forever—but the shape of the landscape isn't altered at all, so nothing ominous "takes over."

How Can It Be "Up to Me"?

A popular argument with many variations claims to demonstrate the incompatibility of determinism and (morally important) free will as follows:

1. If determinism is true, whether I Go or Stay is completely fixed by the laws of nature and events in the distant past.

2. It is not up to me what the laws of nature are, or what happened in the distant past.

3. Therefore, whether I Go or Stay is completely fixed by circumstances that are not up to me.

4. If an action of mine is not up to me, it is not free (in the morally important sense).

5. Therefore, my action of Going or Staying is not free.

Kane's libertarian response to this compelling argument is to attempt to isolate the indeterminism of libertarian free will in a few crucial episodes of possibility "at time t" and he hopes to locate those episodes inside the agent, both spatially and temporally so the agent's choices can be "up to" the agent. But once he has allowed that the morally relevant effects of these episodes can be widely distributed in time (as in the case of Luther), what work is there left for the boundary of the container to do? If some event in Luther's boyhood can play a crucial role in Luther's responsibility in adulthood for his momentous decision not to recant, why not an event in Luther's mother's life while Martin was but an embryo? Because, presumably, those events occurred not in Luther but outside Luther, in the external environment, however strongly they imposed themselves on him, and hence they were not "up to Luther." Yes, but if "the child is father to the man," isn't young Luther just as

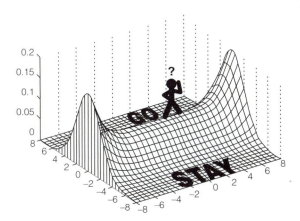

Figure 10 Saddle in a Decision Landscape

external to adult Luther? Why aren't Luther's youthful dispositions, and even his later conscious episodic memories of his youth, themselves rather remote influences "from the outside"? This is a stretched version of the problem we encountered [earlier] . . . when we wondered whether to put the memory inside the faculty of practical reasoning or leave it outside and have portions of it "inputted" when the occasion demanded it. The lines we draw don't do any discernible work for us. And as we will see later, our own moral agency often depends crucially on a little help from our friends without in any way being thereby diminished. The ideal of "do-it-yourself," carried to absolutistic extremes, is superstition. It is true that if you make yourself as small as possible, you can externalize virtually everything. So much the worse for models that push all that matters into a single moment, somewhere in the heart of an atom. If there is a case to be made for libertarianism, it will have to come from some still unexplored quarter, since the best attempt to date, Kane's, ends up in a cul-de-sac. His Ultimate Responsibility requirement turns out, on further examination, to burden the *specs* of a free agent with conditions that are both unmotivated and undetectable. You can demand a car with two steering wheels and a compass in the gas tank, but that doesn't make it worth wanting.

How then should we respond to the incompatibilist argument? Where is the misstep that excuses us from accepting the conclusion? We can now recognize that it commits the same error as the fallacious argument about the impossibility of mammals. Events in the *distant* past were indeed not "up to me," but my choice now to Go or Stay is up to me because its "parents"—some events in the *recent* past, such as the choices I have recently made—were up to me (because *their* "parents" were up to me), and so on, not to infinity, but far enough back to give my *self* enough spread in space and time so that there is a *me* for my decisions to be up to! The reality of a moral me is no more put in doubt by the incompatibilist argument than is the reality of mammals.

Before leaving the topic of libertarianism, we should ask, once more, what the point of it might be. An indeterministic spark occurring at the moment we make our most important decisions couldn't make us more flexible, give us more

opportunities, make us more self-made or autonomous in any way that could be discerned from inside or outside, so why should it matter to us? How could it be a difference that makes a difference? Well, it could be, could it not, that belief in such a spark, like belief in God, changes the whole way you think about the world and your life in it, even if you'll never know (in this lifetime) whether it is true. Yes, the case for belief in indeterminism in action must come down to something like that. But there is an important difference. Even if you can never know, never prove scientifically, that there is a God, it is not hard to explain why a belief in a supreme and merciful Being watching over you might comfort you, give you moral strength and hope, and so forth. The belief in God is not like, say, the belief in Gog (a large sphere of copper that orbits a star outside our light-cone and has the letters GOG stamped prominently on its surface). Anybody is welcome to believe in Gog if it makes them feel good, but why would it? My charge is that libertarians have inflated perfectly reasonable desires for varieties of free will worth wanting into a craving for a variety of free will that would be no more worth wanting than communion with Gog. But it is also true that however misguided such a craving is, it might be unwise to tamper with it. It might be that until or unless a suitable substitute is found, we should tiptoe away from further criticism of this irrational and unmotivated yearning. (*Stop that crow!*) But if that is so, it's too late to put the cat back in the bag. We'd better see what can be done to help people get over their delusion.

Notes on Sources and Further Reading

I drew the importance of chaos to philosophers' attention in *Elbow Room* (Dennett 1984). A more recent compatibilist appreciation of the role of chaos is Matt Ridley 1999, pp. 311–13. On where the buck stops, see *Elbow Room* (p. 76), which also includes discussions of Newtonian chaos (pp. 151–52) and the movable clutch that marks the difference between weakness of will and self-deception.

The discussion of snap judgments in the faculty of practical reason is a descendant of the discussion of *getting a joke* that I offered in *Brainchildren* (Dennett 1998A, p. 86): The complex dispositional state of belief that determines whether or not one will laugh at a joke depends on one's filling in many details left unsaid in the telling. It would be odd to call the unconscious process that triggers an involuntary chuckle *deliberation*, but it is a sophisticated information-transforming process in any case.

See David Velleman's "What Happens When Someone Acts?" (1992) on Chisholm's agent causation, and a possible reduction of it to something more acceptable to a naturalist. . . .

Theorists seldom explicitly endorse the Cartesian Theater, but closet Cartesians can sometimes be teased into the open. For a collection of examples on display, with commentary, see my recent books and articles on consciousness. A similar image of isolation for the sake of authorship inspires, and distorts, some philosophers' thinking about *understanding*. See my "Do-it-yourself Understanding," in *Brainchildren* (Dennett 1998A), on Fred Dretske's attempt to save genuine home-made understanding from pre-fab simulacra that can be bought and installed on the cheap. (According to this vision, robots may seem to understand, but it isn't their understanding, since they didn't make it themselves.)

On Kane's idea of parallel processing: In a piece entitled "On Giving Libertarians What They Say They Want" (in Dennett 1978) I made much the same suggestion, using the example (pp. 294–95) of a woman who had to choose between taking a job at the University of Chicago, and taking a job at Swarthmore; either decision is rational, and even if the choice is undetermined, when she makes whichever choice she makes, there is a good reason for it, and it is *her* reason. But I didn't take the idea very seriously, except as a crumb to throw to libertarians. Kane shows that I underestimated it.

On mammals: There is quite a literature that has grown up in recent years on vagueness and how to deal with it. I recommend in particular Diana Raffman (1996); she has convinced me, but if her discussion doesn't convince you, you can follow her bibliographical references to the rest.

Robert French's (1995) Tabletalk model is a deeply satisfying architecture for the sort of stochastic decision-making process sketched here—a toy world without moral significance, but full of insight. See my Foreword to his book, reprinted in *Brainchildren* (Dennett 1998A).

Kane proposes a distinction between what he calls "Epicurean" and "non-Epicurean" versions of indeterminism (Kane 1996, pp. 172–74). A world of Epicurean indeterminism consists of "forks in history" (modeled on the Epicureans' random swerves) interspersed among things and events with "determinate" properties. In a non-Epicurean world, there is "both indeterminateness of physical properties and the possibility of forks in history." What difference does this make? "An Epicurean world in which undetermined events occurred given an entirely determinate past—a world of chance without indeterminacy—would be a world of mere chance, not free will. There would be no indeterminate 'gestation period' for free acts, so to speak; they would just pop out of a determinate past one way or the other without any preparation in the form of indeterminacy-producing tension, struggle, and conflict" (p. 173). But what about the computer models of non-linear, chaotic, recurrent feedback tugs-of-war? They have *apparent* "gestation periods" as pregnant with (digital approximations of) indeterminacy as you like, but they get their (pseudo-)indeterminism the Epicurean way—with pseudo-random number generators interspersing their outputs among the deterministic subroutines. You can't have it both ways: If, following Paul Churchland, you want to applaud the discovery of the power of non-linear, recurrent networks, in all their non-symbolic, non-rigid, free-wheeling holistic openness, you have to concede that Epicurean algorithmicity suffices to provide it, since that is what the working models are made of.

Endnotes

[1] Followed up with a response to his critics in "Responsibility, Luck, and Chance: Reflections on Free Will and Indeterminism" (1999).

[2] The physicist Michael Berry (1978) has done the calculations for predicting the trajectory of steel balls off the round posts in pinball machines. Three rebounds takes us beyond the limits of feasible calculation.

³This paragraph is drawn, with revisions, from Densmore and Dennett 1999.

⁴There *might* be a reason. . . . It might be that no feasible computer simulation, no virtual world small enough to simulate, can have the mixture of noisiness and quietness required for open-ended creative power. That would not be germane to Churchland's claim about neural networks, but it might be true. The work of Adrian Thompson (e.g., Thompson et al. 1999) on evolutionary electronics suggests from a different quarter that software cannot always substitute for hardware in the exploration of design space. Thompson has created hardware chips with abilities that do not depend on their software-handling capabilities but rely instead on undersigned interactions at the microphysical level that can be selected for by artificial evolution.

⁵*Arche* is Aristotle's term for *origin*.

⁶This was probably the most important sentence in *Elbow Room* (Dennett 1984, p. 143), and I made the stupid mistake of putting it in parentheses. I've been correcting that mistake in my work ever since, drawing out the many implications of abandoning the idea of a punctate self. Of course, what I meant to stress with my ironic formulation

was the converse: You'd be surprised how much you can internalize, if you make yourself large.

⁷Some contemporary creationists have conceded that all living things are related by descent in a tree of life that is billions of years old, and also grant that all the transformations of successive generations within species are accomplished by mindless Darwinian natural selection, but hold out hope that the branching events themselves, the speciations, are, if not miraculous, in need of special help from some intelligent designer (or Intelligent Designer—they claim to be neutral about the identity of the i.d.). This condensation of all the specialness into a magic moment—or a place where it all comes together—is an irresistible motif to some thinkers. The clearest example is Michael Behe (1996); for a discussion of the fallacies involved, see Dennett (1997C).

⁸The 1975 science fiction movie *The Stepford Wives*, by Bryan Forbes (based on Ira Levin's novel), portrayed a town in which the real wives were gradually replaced by mindless robot duplicates who devoted all their energy to housecleaning and taking care of their men.

47. *Freedom and Constraint by Norms*

ROBERT BRANDOM

In the preceding selections, the threats to freedom have come from logic, religion, and nature or causality. They have debated whether, for example, causal determinism is compatible with human freedom, and whether the ability to do otherwise is a necessary condition of human freedom. In the following article, Robert Brandom, a professor of philosophy at the University of Pittsburgh, offers a quite different version of human freedom. Taking his cue from Kant's suggestion that one is free just insofar as he acts according to the dictates of norms or principles, he develops a view of freedom that depends upon being taken to be a member of a community engaging in social practices. To specify a social practice is to specify what counts as the community responding to some candidate act or utterance as a correct performance of that practice. The social practices of the community to which one belongs allow for creative or expressive freedom—the generation of new possibilities—which do not and could not exist outside the framework of norms in the social practices which make up the language of the community.

The issue of human freedom classically arises in the context of appraisal of action according to norms, when we seek an account of praise and blame, approval and disapproval. The issue of

From Robert Brandom, "Freedom and Constraint by Norms," *American Philosophical Quarterly*, Vol. 16, No. 3, 1979, pp. 187–196. Reprinted by permission of the *American Philosophical Quarterly* and the author.

freedom arises again in the political context of an account of the ways in which an individual is and ought to be constrained by norms imposed by his community. One of the most suggestive responses to the first set of concerns has been developed by the Kantian tradition: the doctrine that freedom consists precisely in being constrained by norms rather than merely by causes, answering to what ought to be as well as to what is. Hegel and his admirers, in their turn, have responded to the second sort of concern with an influential doctrine of freedom as consisting of the self-expression made possible by acquiescence in the norms generated by an evolving community (the social synthesis of objective spirit). The central feature determining the character of any vision of human freedom is the account offered of *positive* freedom (freedom to)—those respects in which our activity should be distinguished from the mere lack of external causal constraint (freedom from) exhibited by such processes as the radioactive decay of an atomic nucleus. In this paper I will examine one way of developing Kant's suggestion that one is free just insofar as he acts according to the dictates of norms or principles,[1] and of his distinction between the Realm of Nature, governed by causes, and the Realm of Freedom, governed by norms and principles. Kant's transcendental machinery—the distinction between Understanding and Reason, the free noumenal self expressed somehow as a causally constrained phenomenal self, and so on—can no longer secure this distinction for us. It is just too mysterious to serve as an *explanation* of freedom. Yet some distinction between the realm of facts and the realm of norms must be established if the notion of freedom as normative rather than causal constraint is to be redeemed. In this paper I will present a version of this distinction which was not envisioned by Kant, and show how a novel response to the dispute between naturalists and non-naturalists concerning the relation of fact to norm can be developed out of that rendering. I will then argue that the account of human freedom which results from this story needs to be supplemented in just the ways in which Hegel claimed Kant's account needed to be supplemented, and will recommend an Hegelian self-expressive successor.

I.

In order to clarify the difficult issues associated with accounts of human freedom which center on constraint by norms, we will focus our attention on the special case of norm-governed *linguistic* activity. I am not claiming that there are no significant differences between the way judgments of correctness and incorrectness function for linguistic performances and for actions in general, but I do not think we yet know which differences these are. There are certain respects in which we are surer of what we want to say about the norms that govern language-use than we are about other kinds of norms, so it is reasonable to exploit views about linguistic activity to illuminate the broader issues.

What makes a linguistic performance correct or incorrect, an utterance appropriate or inappropriate? Clearly in some sense the practice of the community which uses utterances of that type generates the standards of correctness by which individual tokenings are to be evaluated. The objective truth or falsehood of claim-making utterances need not concern us here, since appropriate utterances may not be true, and true ones may not be appropriate. I have argued elsewhere[2] that the notions of truth and meaning should be understood as theoretical auxiliaries introduced as part of a certain kind of theory of the practices of using a language which generate norms of appropriateness. For our present purposes we need not invoke these notions, since we need not delve below the level of the practices which constitute the shared use of a language. That it is actual human social practices which determine the correctness as a linguistic performance of an utterance on some particular occasion is clear from the fact that the community whose language is in question could just as well use some other noise on the relevant occasions.

We can express this point in terms of the *conventionality* of the association of particular vocables with standards of usage, so long as we are not seduced by this form of words into thinking of conventions or rules of usage for linguistic expressions as formulated in some ur-language (even mentalese) by the users of the language, an ur-language which they must understand in order to conform to the regularities of usage which constitute the use of the language by that population. We should rather think of those regularities as codified only in the *practices* of competent language-users, including of course the practices of criticizing the utterances of others for perceived failures to conform to the practices governing their linguistic performances and the practices available for adjudicating such disputes as may arise about the appropriateness of some utterance. So long as we think in this way of the norms governing communal usage of linguistic expressions as implicit in the practice of the community, we avoid the pointlessly puzzling regress generated by any rendering of those norms in terms of linguistically expressed) rules or conventions which must themselves be applied correctly.[3] We can still give whatever causal account we like of the objective capacities in virtue of which individuals are able to engage in the complicated practices we attribute to them, for no regress is generated unless we seek to explain the ability to engage in those linguistic practices in some fashion which appeals to prior linguistic abilities, e.g., the following of a rule.[4]

What sort of a thing is the social practice which embodies a standard of correct and incorrect linguistic usage? Differently put, what makes a given act or utterance an instance of, or performance in accord with, some social practice? Consider a community whose members have a practice of greeting each other with gestures. In virtue of what is some particular arm-motion produced on an occasion an appropriate greeting-gesture according to the practice of the community? Clearly, just in case the community takes it to be one, that is, treats it like one. The respect of similarity shared by correct gestures and distinguishing them from incorrect ones is just a *response* which the community whose practice the gesture is does or would make. To specify a social practice is just to specify what counts as the community responding to some candidate act or utterance as a correct performance of that practice. The criteria of identity for social practices appeal to the judgment of the community (where "judgement" here is not to be taken as entailing that the response is an explicit verbal evaluation). What the community says or does, goes, as far as the correctness of performances of their own practices are concerned. Classifying the behavior of a commu-

nity in this way into social practices according to complexly criterioned responses is something that *we* do from the outside, as part of an attempt to understand them. The members of the community need not explicitly split up their activities in the ways we do, though they must do so implicitly, in the sense of responding as we have postulated.

Social practices thus constitute a thing-kind, individuated by communal responses, whose instances are whatever some community takes them to be. *Objective* kinds are those whose instances are what they are regardless of what any particular community takes them to be. *Galaxies more than a hundred light-years from the Earth* is such an objective thing-kind. Linguistic practices determining the appropriateness of utterances on various occasions are social practices rather than objective things according to this classification. It may be that for many of these linguistic practices we cannot specify anthropologically just what it is for the community to treat such an utterance as an appropriate performance (we will have more to say about this issue later, under the heading of translation). But whatever epistemic difficulties of *identification* we may have do not alter the criteria of *identity* of such practices, which consist solely of communal responses to utterances. The language-using community has the last word about the linguistic correctness of the performances of its members. As pointed out before, to say this is not to deny that in addition to appraisals of correctness according to the linguistic social practices one must conform to in order to be speaking the language of the community at all there can be appraisals (for instance of the truth or loudness of an utterance) which concern entirely *objective* features of that utterance—which are what they are independent of the responses of the community to those utterances. Our concern, however, is with those norms conformity to which is a criterion of membership in the linguistic community. The truth of utterances is obviously not one such, else languages would be unlearnable since they would presuppose infallibility. It is, on the other hand, probably a condition of having learned a language containing certain minimal formal devices (the conditional, a truth predicate, etc.) that the majority of one's utterances be *deemed* true by the community. *Taking* something as true is a social practice, not a matter of objective fact, however.

One consequence of the criterial dominion communities enjoy over the social practices they engage in is particularly important for our argument in the next section. Consider what one would have to be able to do in order to characterize a social practice objectively. The practice could be expressed by an objective description of past performances which had been accepted as in accord with the practice (were responded to appropriately), together with an account of the dispositions of the community to respond in the specified manner to future activities. These dispositions would be complex along a number of different dimensions. First, notice that it may well matter in what order different candidate performances come up for consideration. Social practices evolve the way case law does—an issue may be resolved very differently depending upon where in a chain of precedents it comes up for adjudication. Thus the community may accept an act as in accord with a particular practice, and later refuse to accepts acts objectively as similar as you like. In addition to the position of a performance in the tradition of precedent performances which comprise the social practice viewed temporally, we would in general have to take into account the location in the structure of the community at which a performance is initially considered. For the community need not be democratically organized with respect to its social practices. There may be experts with various kinds of special authority with respect to judgments of the appropriateness of a performance, as is the case in English with the correct use of words like "molybdenum," or as could well be the case with the determination of the appropriateness of a bride-price in some tribe.[5] The point is that the past decisions of a community as to what accords with a practice of theirs admits of codification in objective rules only with large areas of indetermination as to future possible performances. And even complete knowledge of the complex dispositions of the community will enable the filling-in of these indeterminate areas only insofar as we can also predict exactly when and where in the social structure each possible case will actually arise. This is a formidable undertaking. The trouble is that the community has total authority over their own practices, so that even if in the past they have exhibited a strong objective regularity in their responses, they may depart from that regularity with impunity at any time and for any or no reason.

There is another source of difficulty in capturing social practices in objective terms, namely the possibility of *nested* social practices. We have been talking so far as if the response which a community must make or be disposed to make to a putative performance in order for it to be in accord with a social practice were always some objectively characterizable response. The objective expression of a social practice is then a matter simply of being able to predict when that response will be elicited from the community, a difficult but not mysterious enterprise. But what if the response which for us identifies some social practice is not an objective response, but rather some performance which must be in accord with *another* social practice? There is clearly no problem envisaging such a situation as long as the second, criterial, social practice is itself definitionally generated by some objective response. This being granted, there is no obstacle to even longer chains, just so they terminate eventually in a practice generated by an objectively characterizable response. The objective description of a social practice of a community for which such chains of social responses were the rule rather than the exception (e.g., linguistic practices) might thus require the prediction of everything anyone in the community would ever do. Although it is not obvious at this point, it will be shown in the next section that we can envisage a situation in which *every* social practice of the community has as is generating response a performance which must be in accord with another social practice. This possibility has profound consequences for our account of the relation of the realm of objective things to the realm of social things.[6]

II.

Simple as this social practice idiom is, it allows us to describe the relation between norm and fact in a new way. To see this, consider the naturalism/non-naturalism dispute about what sort of distinction we are to envision between norms and facts. According to the naturalist, norms are facts, as objective as any other facts (although, of course, naturalists have various views about what sort of facts are important). Accounts of what ought to be may legitimately be inferred from accounts of what is. According to the non-naturalist, on the other hand, norms and facts are different kinds of things, and this ontological difference reflects or is reflected by the impermissibility of inferences of whatever complexity from "is" to "ought." It is clear that social practices, paradigmatically, *linguistic* ones, generate or express norms insofar as those practices are constituted by traditions of judgments of correctness and incorrectness. At least for the case of these norms which are inherent in social practices,[7] the distinction between norm and fact coincides with the distinction between social practices and any matter of objective fact. The naturalist/non-naturalist dispute here translates into a disagreement about the relation of social practices (with their inherent norms) to objective fact. The naturalist sees no distinction of kind operating, and is committed to viewing social practices as complex objective facts concerning the functioning of various communities. The non-naturalist sees a new category of norm or value emerging in these situations.

When the issue is put in these terms, a *via media* accommodating the motivating insights of both view becomes possible. For we need not choose between the claim that there is an objective difference between the social and the objectively factual and the claim that there is no difference at all between them. We may think instead of the difference as genuine, but *social* rather than objective, according to our criterial classification. On this view, whether a certain body of behavior constitutes a set of social practices (and hence expresses a normative constraint on performance) or merely exhibits complex but objective regularities is not a matter of objective fact. It is not, in other words, independent of how any community treats or responds to that body of behavior. The criterial classification of things into objective and social is itself a social, rather than objective or ontological, categorization of things according to whether we treat them as subject to the authority of a community or not. What, then, is the difference between treating some system as a set of social practices and treating it as consisting of objective processes?

For the possibly special case of *linguistic* practices, a straightforward answer is available. We treat some bit of behavior as the expression of a linguistic social practice rather than an objective process when we *translate* it, rather than offering a causal explanation of it. Let us agree to extend the application of the term "translation" to include any transformation of the capacity to engage in one set of social practices into the capacity to engage in some other set of social practices. Transformation of the ability to engage in those practices which constitute the use of German into those which constitute the use of English will then be a special case of general translation. We are considering two ways of coping with some complex behavior. Objectively, any spatio-temporally locatable performance can be described objectively and explained as part of a causal web consisting of other similarly described events. In practice, this sort of explanation of, say, the reliability of some signal as an indicator of red objects, may involve the causal understanding of quite complex facts about the physiology and training of the signal-producer. Instead of attempting such an objective account, we may instead use our own set of social practices as an unexplained explainer, and be responsible for an account of how the system in question *differs* from what we would do in that situation. Insofar as we adopt this second strategy, we expect the system in question to conform to the same sorts of norms of appropriateness and justification of its performances as govern ours. Translating, rather than causally explaining a performance, consists in assimilating it to our own practices, treating it as a dialect of our own practical idiom.[8]

There are two consequences of this distinction which we should notice. First, causal explanations can proceed atomistically, building up the behavior of a complex system out of independently describable behavioral elements. Translations, however, even in our extended sense, must proceed holistically. One assimilates a complex of behavior to a whole set of our own social practices, providing a commentary to control disanalogies and specify the variety and goodness of fit intended. For our own social practices cannot in general be specified in isolation from one another. A performance is in accord with a particular practice of ours just in case it is or would be responded to in a particular way by our community. But that response typically is itself a performance which must be in accord with a social practice, i.e., one which does or would elicit another response in accord with another practice, and so on. From the point of view of an external objective account of our practices, the invocation of a chain of critical-constitutive practices of this sort which didn't end in an objective criterion of correctness would involve us in a vicious explanatory regress or circle. But for us to engage in a web of social practices no such requirement applies. All that is required is sufficient agreement within the community about what counts as an appropriate performance of each of the practices comprising the web; then holistic objective regularities of performance can take the place of appeal to objective criteria of correctness in any particular case. I am not claiming that this situation always arises—we can specify a social practice generated by an objectively characterized response. The point is that it is not a necessary condition of the possibility of our community engaging in a set of social practices that we or anyone else be able to dissect that set into inferential or critical chains of practices, each ultimately governed by some objective response.

Next, notice that on this account, the measure of social practice is *our* social practice. When we treat a performance in this way we treat the performer as a member of *our* community, subject to *our* norms of appropriateness and justification. By translating, rather than causally explaining some performance, we extend our community (the one which engages in the social practices into which we translate the stranger's behavior) so as to include the stranger, and treat his performances as variants of our own. What we should remark about this is that who is or isn't a member of a particular community is a paradigm case of a matter which is social rather than objective according to our criterial classification. The community has final say over who its own members are. That is just the sort of issue that the community could not coherently be claimed to be wrong about. It might be inconvenient, or arbitrary for them to draw the boundaries around "us" in a certain way, but it is clearly not the sort of issue there is an objective fact to be right or wrong about, independent of what the community takes its own membership to be (of course they can *say* false things about who

is in their community—what is decisive according to our criteria is how they behave or respond to the various candidates). So insofar as the distinction between the social and the objective is to be drawn as we have suggested, depending upon whether one copes with the behavior in question by causal explanation and manipulation or by translation, that distinction, while genuine, is social rather than objective, a matter of how the behavior is treated by some community rather than how it is in itself.[9] We will have some more to say about the crucial distinction between translation and explanation in the next section. For now, let us notice the consequences which this way of approaching things has for the larger issues we are concerned with.

If we can make the distinction between translation and causal explanation stick as two distinguishable ways of responding to the same behavior, then we can bypass the naturalism/non-naturalism dispute about the relation of norm to fact. For both parties to that dispute assumed that if there were any distinction between norms and facts it was an *objective* (factual, descriptive) difference. On our account, however, the difference between the normative order expressed in social practices and the factual order expressed in objective events and processes is a social difference in two ways of treating something. The social/objective distinction is social rather than objective.[10] If we now transfer this account of the distinction between the Realm of Nature (fact, description, cause) and the Realm of Freedom (norm, evaluation, practice) back to Kant's original suggestion that freedom consists in constraint by norms rather than simply by causes, the difference between being free and not being free becomes a social rather than an objective difference. The difference between these two "realms" is not an ontological one. The real distinction in the vicinity is between two ways of treating someone's behavior. According to this line of thought, we treat someone as free insofar as we consider him subject to the norms inherent in the social practices conformity to which is the criterion of membership in our community. He is free insofar as he is one of us. Insofar as we cope with him in terms of the causes which objectively constrain him, rather than the norms which constrain him via our practices, we treat him as an object, and unfree. There is no objective fact of the matter concerning his freedom to which we can appeal beyond the judgment of our own community. Of course the community can appeal to what it takes to be objective facts about a candidate for the extended membership granted by translation, but it is how they finally behave toward the candidate that matters. On this view, then, man is not objectively free.[11] Our talk about human freedom is rather a misleading way of talking about the difference between the way in which we treat members of our own community, those who engage in social practices with us, and the attitude we adopt toward those things we manipulate causally. Being constrained by or subject to norms is a matter of belonging to a community, and that is a matter of being *taken* to be a member by the rest of the community.

III.

Reason for doubting that this notion of freedom is a finally satisfactory account emerges when we remember that anything at all can be treated as objective, and can also be treated as social. The two stances do not exclude each other. That any set of spatio-temporally locatable events is in principle capable of an objective causal explanation needs little arguing. It is a regulative ideal of natural science. When we translate another's utterance we need not presume that that utterance cannot also be explained as a part of the objective causal order, that it was not predictable (at least statistically) given sufficient information about the physiology, training, and recent environment of the speaker. Of course in situations where we are not now actually capable of such an explanation in terms of causes, there will be a certain amount of strain involved in treating an utterance as merely caused. But there is no difficulty of principle. Less obviously, anything can be treated as subject to the norms inherent in social practices, with a greater or lesser degree of strain. Thus a tree or a rock can become subject to norms insofar as we consider it as engaging in social practices. We can do this either by giving it a social role, for instance that of an oracle, or simply by translating its performances as utterances. Thus we can take the

groaning of a branch to be the expression of exhaustion, or take the record-changer to be telling us that the record is over. Of course in such cases we must allow that the item in question is only a member of our community in a derivative and second-class fashion, for it is not capable of engaging in very many of our practices, or even of engaging in those very well. This is the strain involved in translating ordinary occurrences rather than simply explaining them, and no doubt this strain is the reason we usually don't do this. But there are border line cases, as with infants, cats, and temperamental automobiles. The force of the claim that the difference between the social and the objective is a difference in how they are treated by some community (by *us*) rather than an objective matter about which we could be right or wrong is that differences in convenience of one kind or another are the only differences to be accommodated here. If we want to treat the tree like one of us, the wind in its branches translated as utterances suggesting various courses of action, debating and justifying these, then the difficulty of finding a scheme which will make the tree sound sensible is the only obstacle.

It does not seem implausible to treat the difference between the social and the objective, and therefore the difference between the normative and the factual, as itself a social difference in this way. There are clear differences between translation and causal explanation of environing occurrences, and it is equally clear how those differences can generate criterial differences in objects treated one way or the other, once we have seen that such criterial classifications are not objective, ontological ones. But the account of freedom which results from conjoining this explanation of the norm/fact distinction to Kant's doctrine that freedom is constraint by norms is unattractive. Hegel objected to Kant's restriction of Reason and the norms and principles involved in it to the purely *formal* features of conduct. He regarded any account of freedom in terms of constraint by norms to be doomed to empty abstractness insofar as it ignores the *content* of the norms involved, linking freedom to the purely formal fact of constraint by some norm or other. The sort of cultural-historical particularity of the content of norms which Hegel sought in vain in Kant is secured by the token-reflexive reference in the formula—to be a Kantian rational-moral agent is to be one of *us*. This establishes only one side of the dialectic of social and individual development which Hegel urges, however. Communal autonomy is a necessary presupposition of the development of individual freedom. This latter, the freedom of the artist and the genius, is not to be identified with the former, the freedom of the peasant and the worthy Pietist. Hegel envisaged a higher form of positive freedom as self-expression and Bildung, enabled by but not reducible to constraint by communal norms. In the rest of this paper we consider such a notion, elaborated from Hegel's hints, but not intended as an exposition of the account presented by Hegel in his own original and ferocious idiom.

As above, we will take our lead from the consideration of the norms which govern linguistic activity. Our concern before was with the social dimension of these norms, with what constitutes membership in the community which has those norms, and consequently with what it is to be constrained by them. Our present concern is not with the nature of such social constraint, but with its issue. In particular, we want to examine the possibility that for some sets of norms, at any rate, constraint can be balanced by the creation of a new sort of "expressive freedom" of the individual. It is a striking fact that learning to engage in the social practices which are the use of a shared language does not simply enable us to use stock expressions ("Pass the salt," "Good morning," and so on) so as to navigate the common social situations which elicit them (communal feeding, working, and so on). In fact most of the sentences that make up our ordinary conversation are sentences that have never been uttered before in the history of the language, as Noam Chomsky has forcefully pointed out.[12] To acknowledge this fact is not to retreat from the characterization of language as a set of social practices in our sense, since it is still the linguistic community which decides whether some novel sentence is appropriately used or not. But we must not think of the social practices governing such communal judgments of appropriateness for novel utterances the way we think of those governing common sentences like "This is red", as the product of selective reinforcement of many different utterances of that very expression on various occasions.[13] Learning the language is not just learning to use a set of stock sentences which everybody else uses too. One has not learned the language, has not acquired the capacity to engage in the social practices which are the use of the language, until one can produce *novel* sentences which the community will deem appropriate, and understand the appropriate novel utterances of other members of the community (where the criterion for this capacity is the ability to make inferences deemed appropriate by the community). This emergent expressive capacity is the essence of natural languages.

We ought to understand this creative aspect of language use as the paradigm of a new kind of freedom, *expressive* freedom. When one has mastered the social practices comprising the use of a language sufficiently, one becomes able to do something one could not do before, to produce and comprehend novel utterances. One becomes capable not only of framing new descriptions of situations and making an indefinite number of novel claims about the world, but also becomes capable of forming new intentions, and hence of performing an indefinite number of novel *actions,* directed at ends one could not have without the expressive capacity of the language. This is a kind of positive freedom, freedom *to* do something rather than freedom *from* some constraint. For it is not as if the beliefs, desires, and intentions one comes to be able to express when one acquires a suitable language have been there all the time, hidden somehow "inside" the individual and kept from overt expression by some sort of constraint. Without a suitable language there are some beliefs, desires, and intentions that one simply cannot have. Thus we cannot attribute to a dog or a prelinguistic child the desire to prove a certain conjectured theorem, the belief that our international monetary system needs reform, or the intention to surpass Blake as a poet of the imagination. One comes to be able to do such things only by becoming able to engage in a wide variety of social practices, making discriminations and inferences and offering justifications concerning the subject matter in question to the satisfaction of the relevant community. And this is to say that it is only by virtue of being constrained by the norms inherent in social practices that one can acquire the freedom of expression which the capacity to produce and understand novel utterances exhibits.

As a form of positive freedom, this expressive capacity does not consist simply in a looseness of fit in the constraining norms. One is able to express novel contents not simply because an utterance can be linguistically appropriate on many different occasions, nor again because the boundaries between appropriate and inappropriate utterances are vague (as is always the case with social practices, whose "boundaries"—the division between what is and what is not in accord with them—are not objective but social, a matter of how the community does or would respond). No novelty is generated by the fact that the constraint constitutive of social practice has such an open texture that lots of antecedently possible performances are acceptable. Expressive freedom consists in the generation of new possibilities of performance which did not and could not exist outside the framework of norms inherent in the social practices which make up the language. One acquires the freedom to believe, desire, and intend the existence of novel states of affairs only insofar as one speaks some language or other, is constrained by some complex of social norms. Expressive freedom is made possible only by constraint by norms, and is not some way of evading or minimizing constraint.

It is clear that not all sets of social practices, in the sense we have given to that term, will generate the sort of expressive freedom which we can discern as enabled by natural languages. So an account of positive freedom modelled on the creative use of language—the possibility of novel performances—will not take that freedom to be constituted by the abstract and purely formal fact that one is constrained by norms (that one engages in the social practices of some community, i.e. is accepted as doing so by some community). Not just constraint by norms but constraint by a particular kind of norms makes possible individual expressive freedom, as Hegel envisaged. Nor should we think of that freedom merely as a fact or a state to be achieved and enjoyed. Expressive freedom, as the capacity to produce an indefinite number of novel appropriate performances in accord with a set of social practices one has mastered, is an ability which must be exercised to be maintained. Following Hegel's hint a little further, we can see the exercise of positive, expres-sive freedom as part of a process of cultivation [Bildung] of the self and of the community. For the capacity of individuals to produce novel performances in accord with a set of social practices makes possible novel social practices as well. For as the community becomes capable of novel responses (themselves subject to judgments of appropriateness), new social practices are generated. A social practice is defined as a respect of similarity evinced by performances which do or would (under circumstances which must be specified whenever we specify a particular practice) elicit some response from the community. Some sets of social practices, paradigmatically natural languages, make possible novel performances on the part of those who participate in them, and these in turn make possible further social practices. Particular novel performances and the social practices which make them possible and are made possible by them, on the one hand, and individuals and the community they comprise on the other, thus develop together in a fashion Hegel marked with the term "dialectical." Thus a child's relative mastery of a natural language first makes possible the production and comprehension of appropriate novel utterances. This capacity in turn enables the child to submit to stricter social linguistic disciplines, such as govern the criticism or production of literary works or legal briefs. At the level of the community, new disciplines are founded by the novel productions of individuals—the social practices which comprise a scientific or academic discipline are produced in this way, and make possible further novel performances and their appreciation. The self-cultivation of an individual consists in the exercise and expansion of expressive freedom by subjecting oneself to the novel discipline of a set of social practices one could not previously engage in, in order to acquire the capacity to perform in novel ways, express beliefs, desires, and intentions one could not previously even have, whether in arts or sports. The cultivation of the community consists in the development of new sets of social practices, at once the result of individual self-cultivation (producing novel performances which, institutionalized as responses to other performances make possible new social practices) and the condition of it. It is in this sense that we speak of the "culture" of a group as the set of social practices they engage in.[14]

It is clearly not possible to specify in advance the expressive capacities of different sets of social practices, for instance in an attempt to compare two languages along this dimension. For the peculiar dialectical pattern of development of expressive capacities itself continually creates novel expressive dimensions by making possible desires and intentions which could not operate at earlier stages in the cultivation of a particular community or individual. Self-cultivating individuals and communities, developing their expressive capacities according to this dialectic of shared practice and novel performance will accordingly be a great deal more difficult to account for in terms of objective causal processes than will social practices which don't make possible indefinite numbers of novel performance-types. Here the quantitative difference in convenience between coping with behavior by treating it as objective and seeking a causal explanation and treating it as social and seeking a translation of it into our own practices assumes such proportions that it is plausible to treat it as a qualitative difference[15] (this does not, of course, entail that we take it as an objective difference rather than as a social difference of how things are treated which is based on the objective difficulty of discovering adequate causal accounts. We are, after all, familiar with objective processes which generate new types of behavior.) Expressive freedom is thus a species of the Kantian genus of freedom as constraint by norms, a specification and supplementation of that general notion.

The final suggestion I want to make by way of recommending this way of talking about human freedom, both individual and social, is to note the sort of legitimation of political and social constraint which it makes possible. Hegel and some of his admirers (notably Marx and T. H. Green) rejected the liberal enlightenment account of justification of constraint of the individual by social and political institutions which had found that justification in the extent to which social organization made possible the greater satisfaction of individual wants, considered as fixed and specifiable in abstraction from the sort of community the individual participates in. The Hegelian tradition was

acutely aware of the debt which an individual's desires owe to his community, but did not wish to succumb entirely to the antidemocratic and antiindividualist implications of an account which made the community paramount. The general form of their resolution of this dilemma, which can be reproduced in less metaphysical terms in the idiom of social practices, is this. Constraint of the individual by the social and political norms inherent in communal practices may be legitimate insofar as that constraint makes possible for the individual an expressive freedom which is otherwise impossible for him. Creative self-cultivation is possible only by means of the discipline of the social practices which constrain one, just as the production of a poem requires not only submission to the exigencies of a shared language, but the stricter discipline of the poetic tradition as well. One must speak some language to say anything at all, and the production and comprehension of novel performances requires a background of shared constraint. Political constraint is illegitimate insofar as it is not in the service of the cultivation of the expressive freedom of those who are constrained by it.

To say this is not so much to present a theory as to present the form of a theory, a way of talking about political legitimation and human freedom, an idiom. It does not, for instance, even begin to settle questions about trade-offs between different varieties of negative and positive freedom. For one cannot project a Utopia from these considerations, nor can one abstractly evaluate political institutions according to the kinds and quality of expressive freedom and self-cultivation they enable and encourage. For it is precisely the production of *novel* expressive possibilities which is admired in this account, and that novelty in principle escapes classification and prediction by a priori theorizing. The idiom of expressive freedom is useful, insofar as it is useful, for those caught up in the dialectic of individual and communal cultivation, of shared practice and novel performance, to reflectively control possible changes in practice within a concrete situation. The value of this idiom, as of any other, consists in the possibilities for novel expression which it engenders, by way of comprehending and directing this dialectical process.[16]

Endnotes

[1] I am not concerned to *expound* Kant (or, later, Hegel), but to develop various consequences of quite general features of his views which can be discussed in abstraction from detailed consideration of particular texts.

[2] "Truth and Assertibility," *The Journal of Philosophy*, vol. 73 (1976), pp. 137–189.

[3] See Ludwig Wittgenstein's, *Investigations* I, Section 198 ff.

[4] The distinction between these two sorts of explanation will be our topic in the next section.

[5] On such linguistic division of labor, and in particular the importance of the possibility of adjudication of some disputes by expert elites to be socially constituted only in the *future*, see Putnam's "Meaning of Meaning" in pp. 215–272 of his *Mind, Language and Reality, Philosophical Papers*, vol. II (Cambridge, 1976).

[6] Among contemporary philosophers, Wilfrid Sellars has made the most of this basic sort of distinction between the objective and the social. He has argued throughout his works for the importance of such a distinction between a causal or descriptive order and a normative order of justification and reason giving (a dualism indebted to Kant, Schopenhauer, and the early Wittgenstein, rather than Descartes). This point is one of the keys to the classic "Empiricism and the Philosophy of Mind" in Sellars' *Science, Perception, and Reality* (London, 1963). See also chapter 7 of *Science and Metaphysics* (London, 1968). Richard Rorty elaborates this perspective in his forthcoming *Philosophy and the Mirror of Nature*, to which I am indebted.

[7] Although I cannot argue the matter here, I believe that the social practice idiom offers a quite general account of the nature of normative constraint. To show this, however, would entail discussing such issues as the relation of moral norms to other sorts of social norms, a project I don't want to enter here.

[8] Jurgen Habermas, in *Knowledge and Human Interests* (Boston, 1971) distinguished the sort of explanation one gives of causal phenomena "logically"—claiming that causal explanation employs a "monologic" of impersonal inference, while interpretation is always "dialogic" in character. While I am not sure what this logical rendering comes to, the account developed here of the difference between the social and objective coincides in many particulars with Habermas' story about the differences between control and conversation.

[9] The point here is reminiscent of D. C. Dennett's views about the justification of the adoption of the "intentional stance" (in "Intentional Systems," *The Journal of Philosophy*, vol. 68 [1971], pp. 87–106). A difference is that social practices need not exhibit any "intentional" character. I have discussed elsewhere (see note 2) some of what is required of a social practice in order for it appropriately to be taken as making a claim that something is the case. I would thus seek to account for intentionality in terms of social practices. J. F. Rosenberg has argued forcefully against the cogency of the reverse order of explana-

tion in the opening chapters of his *Linguistic Representation* (Dordrecht, 1975).

[10] It is a measure of the superiority of this idiom over more traditional ones that the possibility of this sort of view would not come readily to mind so long as the issue is formulated as a norm/fact, or evaluation/description distinction. For what does it mean to say that these distinctions are not factual or descriptive, but normative and evaluative? And yet this is what we are claiming, in the specific sense captured by the social/objective rendering.

[11] Though of course on this account that freedom is not merely subjective and imaginary either. It is rather a social matter, and the criterial classification distinguishes the social from both the subjective (which is whatever some individual takes it to be) and the objective (which is what it is regardless of how anyone takes it to be). I have argued that this criterial classification is itself social rather than objective.

[12] *Aspects of the Theory of Syntax* (Cambridge, Mass., 1965), Chapter One.

[13] W. V. Quine's elephant topiary example in the first chapter of *Word and Object* (Cambridge, 1960), suggests that he has in mind the latter type of sentences exclusively, for it is difficult to see how his story is appropriate to the former.

[14] Defining culture in this way, we may distinguish three sorts of substructure: individual repertorys, traditions, and institutions. Each individual member of the community has a repertory of social practices comprising all those he is capable of engaging in (producing performances appropriate according to) at a particular time. Such a repertory has a history, insofar as it is different at one time than at another. Those practices have in common a particular human being who engages in them. The practices which make up a *tradition* share a common ancestry. A tradition is a tree structure whose nodes are sets of social practices engaged in by individuals (one individual per node, perhaps not his entire repertory) and whose branches are the transmission or training to engage in the social practices are transformed. A social institution is then composed at any time of individuals and sub-sets of their current repertorys which are their *institutional* roles. The development of the institution is the evolution of those roles in their mutual relation.

[15] Although we cannot pursue the matter here, it is plausible to identify the difference between objective causal explanation and translation of social practices (where the criterion for adopting one or the other stance is the appearance of dialectical development by the cultivation of expressive freedom as described above) with the difference which neo-Kantians of the last century perceived between the methods of *Erklärung* and *Verstehen*, which were the distinguishing features of the natural and cultural sciences respectively (and which we might think of as codifying the difference between things which have *natures* and things which have *histories*).

[16] I would like to acknowledge the many helpful comments Richard Rorty and Annette Baier kindly provided on an earlier version.

Further Reading

Ayer, A. J., *Philosophical Essays* (London: Macmillan, 1954, Chapter 12).

Ayers, M. R., *The Refutation of Determinism* (London: Methuen, 1968).

Bernstein, M., *Fatalism* (Lincoln: University of Nebraska, 1992).

Berofsky, B., *Freedom from Necessity: The Metaphysical Basis of Responsibility* (Boston: Routledge & Kegan Paul, 1989).

Berofsky, B., ed., *Free Will and Determinism*. (Princeton, N.J.: Princeton University Press, 1972).

Craig, W. L., *The Only Wise God: The Compatibility of Divine Foreknowledge and Human Freedom* (Grand Rapids, Mich.: Baker Book House, 1987).

Dennett, D., *Elbow Room* (Cambridge, Mass.: MIT Press, 1984).

Double, R., *The Non-Reality of Free Will* (New York: Oxford University Press, 1991).

Dworkin, G., ed., *Determinism, Free Will, and Moral Responsibility* (Englewood Cliffs, N.J.: Prentice-Hall, 1970).

Ekstrum, L. W., *Free Will: A Philosophical Study* (Boulder, Colo.: Westview Press, 2000).

Fischer, J. M., ed., *Moral Responsibility* (Ithaca, N.Y.: Cornell University Press, 1986).

Fischer, J. M., *God, Freedom and Foreknowledge* (Stanford: Stanford University Press, 1989).

Fischer, J. M., *The Metaphysics of Free Will* (Cambridge: Blackwell, 1994).

Fischer, J. M. and Ravizza, M., *Responsibility and Control: A Theory of Moral Responsibility* (New York: Cambridge University Press, 1998).

Forman, F., *The Metaphysics of Liberty* (Dordrecht: Klewer Academic Publishers, 1989).

Frankfurt, H. G., *The Importance of What We Care About: Philosophical Essays* (New York: Cambridge University Press, 1988).

Hampshire, S., *Freedom of the Individual* (New York: Harper & Row, 1965).

Helm, P., ed., *God and Time: Essays on the Divine Nature* (New York: Oxford University Press, 2002).

Honderich, R., *How Free Are You? The Determinism Problem* (New York: Oxford University Press, 2003).

Honderich, T., *A Theory of Determinism* (Oxford: Clarendon Press, 1988).

Honderich, T., ed., *Essay on Freedom of Action* (London: Routledge & Kegan Paul, 1973).

Kane, R., *Free Will and Values* (New York: State University of New York Press, 1985).

Kane, R., *The Significance of Free Will* (New York: Oxford University Press, 1996).

Kane, R., *The Oxford Handbook of Free Will* (New York: Oxford University Press, 2001).

Kane, R., ed., *Free Will* (Malden, Mass.: Blackwell, 2002).

Kenny, A., *Free Will and Responsibility* (Boston: Routledge & Kegan Paul, 1988).

Leftow, B., *Time and Eternity* (Ithaca, N.Y.: Cornell University Press, 1991).

Lehrer, K., ed., *Freedom and Determinism* (New York: Random House, 1966).

Morgenbesser, S. and Walsh, J. J., eds., *Free Will* (Englewood Cliffs, N.J.: Prentice-Hall, 1962).

Padgett, A., *God, Eternity and the Nature of Time* (New York: St. Martin's Press, 1992).

Pereboom, D. *Living without Free Will* (Cambridge: Cambridge University Press, 2001).

Pike, N., *God and Timelessness* (New York: Schocken Books, 1970).

Rowe, W., *Thomas Reid on Freedom and Morality* (Ithaca, N.Y.: Cornell University Press, 1991).

Salmon, W., *Scientific Explanation and the Causal Structure of the World* (Princeton, N.J.: Princeton University Press, 1984).

Taylor, R., *Action and Purpose* (Englewood Cliffs, N.J.: Prentice-Hall, 1960).

Thorton, M., *Do We Have Free Will?* (New York: St. Martin's Press, 1989).

van Inwagen, P., *An Essay on Free Will* (Oxford: Oxford University Press, 1983).

Watson, G., ed., *Free Will* (Oxford: Oxford University Press, 1982).

Widerker, D. and McKenna, M., eds., *Moral Responsibility and Alternative Possibilities* (Aldershot, U.K.: Ashgate, 2003).

Williams, B., *How Free Does the Will Need to Be?* (Lawrence: University of Kansas Philosophy Department, 1986).

Williams, C., *Free Will and Determinism: A Dialogue* (Indianapolis: Hackett, 1980).

Zagzebski, L., *The Dilemma of Freedom and Foreknowledge* (New York: Oxford University Press, 1991).

Zimmerman, M., *An Essay on Human Action* (New York: Peter Lang Publishing, 1984).

Part V

God

Why is God a metaphysical problem? For the ancients the existence of gods was not a metaphysical problem. It was obvious to them that gods existed since it seemed obvious that behavior of nature was benign or malevolent and for some purpose. The ancients had no other paradigm than that of personal agency to describe and to try to explain what was happening. God became a metaphysical problem when religions increasingly conceived of their deity as transcendent, as a different kind of entity somehow prior to or beyond the natural world. Not only did this lead to speculation about the properties of such an entity, but it also lead to skepticism about the transcendent when other modes of explanation claimed to be sufficient for dealing with the natural world. This crisis in theology came to a head with the rise of the new science in the Sixteenth and Seventeenth centuries, and is still with us today. Is there a need for an all-powerful creator and sustainer (on the theistic hypothesis) of the universe, if the behavior of bodies can be predicted without one? And if there is, then how can the existence of such a being be reconciled with moral and natural evils in the world as we find it? With those questions in the background there are at least two kinds of metaphysical issues that arise: What are the properties of God? Can the existence of God be proven?

In this book we are focusing on the question whether the existence of God can be proven. And of the many attempts in history we are focusing on arguments that are in a broad sense cosmological. Is the existence of God required to adequately explain the existence of the natural world? How is the existence of the world, being the way it is, compatible with theories about the properties of God (e.g., perfection)? In the last two decades these questions have been much discussed anew in part because of dramatic advances in scientific cosmology. In recent cosmology several theories (or models) of the early universe (especially those that lend themselves to geometrical or tenseless interpretations) do not posit an "origin" or "creation." For example, different "early" states of the universe might be viewed simply as different locations (parts) of a larger whole. Or, there is an attempt to relate the current "universe" to other or earlier states.* Without mysterious origin events in cosmology, there may be no explanatory need for a creator. And if principles like the conservation of mass-energy are true, then the idea that God must exist to sustain each and every thing might be undermined. We preface recent discussion of some of these issues with classic statements of cosmological arguments by Aquinas and Descartes. If the principle of the conservation of matter-energy is true, then why suppose that God sustains each and every being at every moment of its existence? We begin a discussion of these issues with Aquinas's Five Ways.

Aquinas's second way of proving the existence of God is based on causation. He argues that there cannot be an infinite series of causes in the material world, for then there would be no first cause. However, without a first cause there wouldn't be a first effect, and without a first effect there wouldn't be a second cause or a second effect, and so on. Indeed, without a first cause nothing would exist, but obviously

the world of material causes does exist. Hence, there cannot be an infinite series of causes, but must be a first cause and that first cause is God. Even those sympathetic with Aquinas's conclusion have balked at his premises. For example, while the existence of a first cause is impossible if the series is infinite, to assert that no member of the infinite series is the first cause, that is, an uncaused cause, does not imply that there are no causes and that therefore, nothing exists.

Descartes also argues that there cannot be an infinite series of causes, but that there must be an ultimate cause, which will be God. He bases his reasoning on the principle that "the conservation of a substance, in each moment of its duration, requires the same power and act that would be necessary to create it, supposing it were not yet in existence; so that it is manifestly a dictate of the natural light that conservation and creation differ merely in respect of our mode of thinking [and not in reality]." Given this principle, together with the fact that he exists as a substance that thinks, he argues that whatever the cause that produced him, God must exist as the being that sustains or conserves him in existence at the present moment. In connection with the Cartesian principle regarding creation and conservation, the selections by Quinn and Grünbaum debate whether the energy conservation law is consistent with the divine conservation of the sum total of matter-energy.

Quinn also discusses another version of the cosmological argument, known as the argument from contingency. In its simplest form the argument states that if there are contingent things or facts then there is a necessary being. There are contingent things, so there must be a necessary being, a being upon which dependent or contingent beings depend. A contingent being or fact is a being whose existence or explanation lies outside of itself. Quinn argues that since the conservation law for matter-

---

*As this edition was going to press, a useful article appeared in the May 2004 issue of *Scientific American*, indicative of the current flux of cosmology: Gabriele Veneziano's "The Myth of the Beginning of Time" (pp. 54–65).

energy is contingent there must be an explanation for its existence. The ultimate answer must be accepted as a brute fact or there could be an infinite regress of explanations, but then we can ask: why this hierarchy of explanations rather than some other? Thus, to give a sufficient explanation of the conservation law for matter-energy, indeed, to give a sufficient reason for the existence of the world at all, we need to suppose the existence of a necessary being who exists and cannot not exist; a being that is a sufficient reason for its own existence and for the existence of every other thing and fact that exists. For Grünbaum, on the other hand, the demand for a sufficient reason for the physical existence can be gotten from physics itself, or it is a meaningless quest based on the meaningless idea, that without a supernatural cause existence must arise spontaneously out of nothingness. Rowe points out that the fundamental principle upon which the cosmological argument rests, in the forms we have so far considered it, is the principle of sufficient reason. But what reason do we have to believe that every being and every positive fact must have an explanation?

The cosmological argument highlights God as the all-powerful creator of the universe, but God is alleged to have an infinite number of other perfections, including goodness and existence. In *Meditation V,* Descartes gives a version of the ontological argument, an *a priori* argument for the existence of God based solely on the idea of God. He argues that since the idea of God is the idea of an all-perfect being, and since existence is perfection, we cannot conceive of God except as existing. Since what is inconceivable in thought is inseparable in reality, he concludes that God exists. However, if God exists as an all-good creator and conservator of the universe, as the ontological and cosmological arguments imply, then where do the imperfections we find in the universe come from, and why do they exist? Why do we err and sin, if all our faculties are created by God, why are there terrible natural disasters that seem to result in unwarranted suffering? If we err and sin because our God-given perfect and unlimited free will extends beyond our perfect but limited understanding, then why didn't God in some way limit, without destroying, our freedom to perform egregious actions? And if the evil that exists in this world is rectified by the good that comes out of it, as theists maintain, then why does our experience seldom bear that out? In *Meditation IV,* Descartes attempt to answer some of these questions, and the dialogue by Bruce Russell and Stephen Wykstra attempts to answer others.

48. *The Five Ways*

THOMAS AQUINAS

In the following selection, Thomas Aquinas (1224/5–1274) offers five ways of proving divine existence. Each of these arguments are versions of the cosmological argument in that they start from the fact that there is a world, a world that contains certain general features—e.g., motion, causation, and contingent (dependent) beings—and argues that there must be, e.g., a prime mover, first cause, and necessary being, outside the world. The two most influential of Aquinas' proofs are the second and third ways. The second way is from the idea of causation and argues that there must be a first cause, God, for if the series of causes were infinite, then nothing would exist, but something does exist. The third way is from the idea of contingency. Simply put, the argument asserts that since there are contingent, dependent, beings e.g., human beings, there must be a necessary (independent, self-existent) being outside the realm of contingent beings upon which contingent beings depend. These arguments are refined and criticized in the selections to follow by Descartes, Rowe, Quinn, and Grünbaum.

The First Way: The Argument from Change

The existence of God can be shown in five ways. The first and clearest is taken from the idea of motion. (1) Now it is certain, and our senses corroborate it, that some things in this world are in motion. (2) But everything which is in motion is moved by something else. (3) For nothing is in motion except in so far as it is in potentiality in relation to that towards which it is in motion. (4) Now a thing causes movement in so far as it is in actuality. For to cause movement is nothing else than to bring something from potentiality to actuality; but a thing cannot be brought from potentiality to actuality except by something which exists in actuality, as, for example, that which is hot in actuality, like fire, makes wood, which is only hot in potentiality, to be hot in actuality, and thereby causes movement in it and alters it. (5) But it is not possible that the same thing should be at the same time in actuality and in potentiality in relation to the same thing, but only in relation to different things; for what is hot in actuality cannot at the same time

From *Summa Theologica* by St. Thomas Aquinas, trans. Laurence Shapcote (London: O. P. Benziger Brothers, 1911).

be hot in potentiality, though it is at the same time cold in potentiality. (6) It is impossible, therefore, that in relation to the same thing and in the same way anything should both cause movement and be caused, or that it should cause itself to move. (7) Everything therefore that is in motion must be moved by something else. If therefore the thing which causes it to move be in motion, this too must be moved by something else, and so on. (8) But we cannot proceed to infinity in this way, because in that case there would be no first mover, and in consequence, neither would there by any other mover; for secondary movers do not cause movement except they be moved by a first mover, as, for example, a stick cannot cause movement unless it is moved by the hand. Therefore it is necessary to stop at some first mover which is moved by nothing else. And this is what we all understand God to be.

The Second Way: The Argument from Causation

The Second Way is taken from the idea of the Efficient Cause. (1) For we find that there is among material things a regular order of efficient causes. (2) But we do not find, nor indeed is it possible, that anything is the efficient cause of itself, for in that case it would be prior to itself, which is impossible. (3) Now it is not possible to proceed to infinity in efficient causes. (4) For if we arrange in order all efficient causes, the first is the cause of the intermediate, and the intermediate the cause of the last, whether the intermediate be many or only one. (5) But if we remove a cause the effect is removed; therefore, if there is no *first* among efficient causes, neither will there be a last or an intermediate. (6) But if we proceed to infinity in efficient causes there will be no first efficient cause, and thus there will be no ultimate effect, nor any intermediate efficient causes, which is clearly false. Therefore it is necessary to suppose the existence of some first efficient cause, and this men call God.

The Third Way: The Argument from Contingency

The Third Way rests on the idea of the "contingent" and the "necessary" and is as follows: (1) Now we find that there are certain things in the Universe which are capable of existing and of not existing, for we find that some things are brought into existence and then destroyed, and consequently are capable of being or not being. (2) But it is impossible for all things which exist to be of this kind, because anything which is capable of not existing, at some time or other does not exist. (3) If therefore *all* things are capable of not existing, there was a time when nothing existed in the Universe. (4) But if this is true there would also be nothing in existence now; because anything that does not exist cannot begin to exist except by the agency of something which has existence. If therefore there was once nothing which existed, it would have been impossible for anything to begin to exist, and so nothing would exist now. (5) This is clearly false. Therefore all things are not contingent, and there must be something which is necessary in the Universe. (6) But everything which is necessary either has or has not the cause of its necessity from an outside source. Now it is not possible to proceed to infinity in necessary things which have a cause of their necessity, as has been proved in the case of efficient causes. Therefore it

is necessary to suppose the existence of something which is necessary in itself, not having the cause of its necessity from any outside source, but which is the cause of necessity in others. And this "something" we call God.

The Fourth Way: The Argument from Degrees of Excellence

The Fourth Way is taken from the degrees which are found in things. (1) For among different things we find that one is more or less good or true or noble; and likewise in the case of other things of this kind. (2) But the words "more" or "less" are used of different things in proportion as they approximate in their different ways to something which has the particular quality in the highest degree—e.g., we call a thing hotter when it approximates more nearly to that which is hot in the highest degree. There is therefore something which is true in the highest degree, good in the highest degree and noble in the highest degree; (3) and consequently there must be also something which has being in the highest degree. For things which are true in the highest degree also have being in the highest degree (see Aristotle, *Metaphysics,* 2). (4) But anything which has a certain quality of any kind in the highest degree is also the cause of all the things of that kind, as, for example, fire which is hot in the highest degree is the cause of all hot things (as is said in the same book). (5) Therefore there exists something which is the cause of being, and goodness, and of every perfection in all existing things; and this we call God.

The Fifth Way: The Argument from Harmony

The Fifth Way is taken from the way in which nature is governed. (1) For we observe that certain things which lack knowledge, such as natural bodies, work for an End. This is obvious, because they always, or at any rate very frequently, operate in the same way so as to attain the best possible result. (2) Hence it is clear that they do not arrive at their goal by chance, but by purpose. (3) But those things which have no knowledge do not move towards a goal unless they are guided by someone or something which does possess knowledge and intelligence—e.g., an arrow by an archer. Therefore, there does exist something which possesses intelligence by which all natural things are directed to their goal; and this we call God.

49. *Meditations on First Philosophy*

RENÉ DESCARTES

One of the primary aims of Descartes' *Meditations* is to overcome skepticism by coming up with a criterion of knowledge. He believed that the only way he could definitively establish such a criterion was by proving the existence of God. For only if God existed could he be certain that what he clearly and distinctly conceived to be true was in fact true. Thus, after casting doubt on all his former beliefs, and arriving at his first two truths, namely, I exist, so long as I think, and that I am a thinking thing, Descartes sets his sights on breaking out of the circle of his thoughts by proving the existence of God. His Third Meditation argument for the existence of God is a form of the cosmological argument, since it is based on the fact that there is a world; although in this case the world is quite impoverished containing only himself as a thing or substance that thinks, and his ideas, and he argues that something outside the world is required to explain its existence. Crucial to his argument is the claim that the same power that is needed to create him is needed to sustain him in existence. That is, Descartes asserts the principle that the difference between creation and conservation is a distinction of reason and not of fact. This principle is central in the debate between Quinn and Grünbaum.

In the Fifth Meditation Descartes gives a version of the ontological argument. This is an *a priori* argument in that he reasons solely from the idea of God to the existence of God. The argument is deceptively simply and may be stated as follows: The idea of God is the idea of an infinitely perfect being. Since existence is perfection, it follows that we cannot separate the idea of God from the idea of existence and hence God must necessarily exist. In between these two arguments for the existence of God, Descartes addresses and attempts to solve the problem of error and evil. If, as Descartes believes, God is the all-perfect creator of Descartes, then how come Descartes commits errors of judgment and sins? The problem is to understand how the perfect artisan in the sky can produce a being that is imperfect in that it makes mistakes? Descartes offers several solutions or responses to this problem some of which are explored in more detail in the dialogue by Russell and Wysktra (selection 51). The most developed response that Descartes gives is the free-will solution. According to it, what God gave us when he created us—an unlimited free-will and a finite understanding—are perfect in themselves, but errors arises when the unlimited free will passes judgment on ideas that go beyond the limited understanding. Thus, error and sin do not come from God, which would make God imperfect, but from humans who misuse the perfect faculties that God gave us. In *Meditation IV*, Descartes explains and then attempts to defend the "free-will defense" against several objections.

Meditation III.
Of God: That He Exists.

I will now close my eyes, I will stop my ears, I will turn away my senses from their objects, I will even efface from my consciousness all the images of corporeal things; or at least, because this can hardly be accomplished, I will consider them as empty and false; and thus, holding converse only with myself, and closely examining my nature, I will endeavor to obtain by degrees a more intimate and familiar knowledge of myself. I am a thinking (conscious) thing, that is, a being who doubts, affirms, denies, knows a few objects, and is ignorant of many,—[who loves, hates], wills, refuses, who imagines likewise, and perceives; for, as I before remarked, although the things which I perceive or imagine are perhaps nothing at all apart from me [and in themselves], I am nevertheless assured that those modes of consciousness which I call perceptions and imaginations, in as far only as they are modes of consciousness, exist in me. And in the little I have said I think I have summed up all that I really know, or at least all that up to this time I was aware I knew. Now, as I am endeavoring to extend my knowledge more widely, I will use circumspection, and consider with care whether I can still discover in myself anything further which I have not yet hitherto observed. I am certain that I am a thinking thing; but do I not therefore likewise know what is required to render me certain of a truth? In this first knowledge, doubtless, there is nothing that gives me assurance of its truth except the clear and distinct perception of what I affirm, which would not indeed be sufficient to give me the assurance that what I say is true, if it could ever happen that anything I thus clearly and distinctly perceived should prove false; and accordingly it seems to me that I may now take as a general rule, that all that is very clearly and distinctly apprehended (conceived) is true.

From René Descartes, *Meditations on First Philosophy*. Translated by John Veitch, 1901. First published in 1641.

Nevertheless I before received and admitted many things as wholly certain and manifest, which yet I afterward found to be doubtful. What, then, were those? They were the earth, the sky, the stars, and all the other objects which I was in the habit of perceiving by the senses. But what was it that I clearly [and distinctly] perceived in them? Nothing more than that the ideas and the thoughts of those objects were presented to my mind. And even now I do not deny that these ideas are found in my mind. But there was yet another thing which I affirmed, and which, from having been accustomed to believe it, I thought I clearly perceived, although, in truth, I did not perceive it at all; I mean the existence of objects external to me, from which those ideas proceeded, and to which they had a perfect resemblance; and it was here I was mistaken, or if I judged correctly, this assuredly was not to be traced to any knowledge I possessed (the force of my perception, Lat.).

But when I considered any matter in arithmetic and geometry, that was very simple and easy, as, for example, that two and three added together make five, and things of this sort, did I not view them with at least sufficient clearness to warrant me in affirming their truth? Indeed, if I afterward judged that we ought to doubt of these things, it was for no other reason than because it occurred to me that a God might perhaps have given me such a nature as that I should be deceived, even respecting the matters that appeared to me the most evidently true. But as often as this preconceived opinion of the sovereign power of a God presents itself to my mind, I am constrained to admit that it is easy for him, if he wishes it, to cause me to err, even in matters where I think I possess the highest evidence; and, on the other hand, as often as I direct my attention to things which I think I apprehend with great clearness, I am so persuaded of their truth that I naturally break out into expressions such as these: Deceive me who may, no one will yet ever be able to bring it about that I am not, so long as I shall be conscious that I am, or at any future time cause it to be true that I have never been, it being now true that I am, or make two and three more or less than five, in supposing which, and other like absurdities, I discover a manifest contradiction. And in truth, as I have no ground for believing that Deity is deceitful, and as, indeed, I have not even considered the reasons by which the existence of a Deity of any kind is established, the ground of doubt that rests only on this supposition is very slight, and, so to speak, metaphysical. But, that I may be able wholly to remove it, I must inquire whether there is a God, as soon as an opportunity of doing so shall present itself; and if I find that there is a God, I must examine likewise whether he can be a deceiver; for, without the knowledge of these two truths, I do not see that I can ever be certain of anything. And that I may be enabled to examine this without interrupting the order of meditation I have proposed to myself [which is, to pass by degrees from the notions that I shall find first in my mind to those I shall afterward discover in it], it is necessary at this stage to divide all my thoughts into certain classes, and to consider in which of these classes truth and error are, strictly speaking, to be found.

Of my thoughts some are, as it were, images of things, and to these alone properly belongs the name IDEA; as when I think [represent to my mind] a man, a chimera, the sky, an angel or God. Others, again, have certain other forms; as when I will, fear, affirm, or deny, I always, indeed, apprehend something as the object of my thought, but I also embrace in thought something more than the representation of the object; and of this class of thoughts some are called volitions or affections, and others judgments.

Now, with respect to ideas, if these are considered only in themselves, and are not referred to any object beyond them, they cannot, properly speaking, be false; for, whether I imagine a goat or chimera, it is not less true that I imagine the one than the other. Nor need we fear that falsity may exist in the will or affections; for, although I may desire objects that are wrong, and even that never existed, it is still true that I desire them. There thus only remain our judgments, in which we must take diligent heed that we be not deceived. But the chief and most ordinary error that arises in them consists in judging that the ideas which are in us are like or conformed to the things that are external to us; for assuredly, if we but considered the ideas themselves as certain modes of our thought (consciousness), without referring them to anything beyond, they would hardly afford any occasion of error.

But among these ideas, some appear to me to be innate, others adventitious, and others to be made by myself (factitious); for, as I have the power of conceiving what is called a thing, or a truth, or a thought, it seems to me that I hold this power from no other source than my own nature; but if I now hear a noise, if I see the sun, or if I feel heat, I have all along judged that these sensations proceeded from certain objects existing out of myself; and, in fine, it appears to me that sirens, hippogryphs, and the like, are inventions of my own mind. But I may even perhaps come to be of opinion that all my ideas are of the class which I call adventitious, or that they are all innate, or that they are all factitious; for I have not yet clearly discovered their true origin; and what I have here principally to do is to consider, with reference to those that appear to come from certain objects without me, what grounds there are for thinking them like these objects.

The first of these grounds is that it seems to me I am so taught by nature; and the second that I am conscious that those ideas are not dependent on my will, and therefore not on myself, for they are frequently presented to me against my will, as at present, whether I will or not, I feel heat; and I am thus persuaded that this sensation or idea (*sensum vel ideam*) of heat is produced in me by something different from myself, viz., by the heat of the fire by which I sit. And it is very reasonable to suppose that this object impresses me with its own likeness rather than any other thing.

But I must consider whether these reasons are sufficiently strong and convincing. When I speak of being taught by nature in this matter, I understand by the word nature only a certain spontaneous impetus that impels me to believe in a resemblance between ideas and their objects, and not a natural light that affords a knowledge of its truth. But these two things are widely different; for what the natural light shows to be true can be in no degree doubtful, as, for example, that I am because I doubt, and other truths of the like kind; inasmuch as I possess no other faculty whereby to distinguish truth from error, which can teach me the falsity of what the natural light declares to be true, and which is equally trustworthy; but with respect to [seemingly] natural impulses, I have observed, when the question related to the choice of right or wrong in action, that they frequently led me to take the worse part; nor do I see that I have any better ground for following them in what relates to truth and error. Then, with respect to the other reason, which is that because these ideas do not depend on my will, they must arise from objects existing without me, I do not find it more convincing than the former; for just as those natural impulses, of which I have lately spoken, are found in me, notwithstanding that they are not always in harmony with my will, so likewise it may be that I possess some power not sufficiently known to myself capable of producing ideas without the aid of external objects, and, indeed, it has always hitherto appeared to me that they are formed during sleep, by some power of this nature, without the aid of aught external. And, in fine, although I should grant that they proceeded from those objects, it is not a necessary consequence that they must be like them. On the contrary, I have observed, in a number of instances, that there was a great difference between the object and its idea. Thus, for example, I find in my mind two wholly diverse ideas of the sun; the one, by which it appears to me extremely small draws its origin from the senses, and should be placed in the class of adventitious ideas; the other, by which it seems to be many times larger than the whole earth, is taken up on astronomical grounds, that is, elicited from certain notions born with me, or is framed by myself in some other manner. These two ideas cannot certainly both resemble the same sun; and reason teaches me that the one which seems to have immediately emanated from it is the most unlike. And these things sufficiently prove that hitherto it has not been from a certain and deliberate judgment, but only from a sort of blind impulse, that I believed in the existence of certain things different from myself, which, by the organs of sense, or by whatever other means it might be, conveyed their ideas or images into my mind [and impressed it with their likenesses].

But there is still another way of inquiring whether, of the objects whose ideas are in my mind, there are any that exist out of me. If ideas are taken in so far only as they are certain modes of consciousness, I do not remark any difference or inequality among them, and all seem, in the same manner, to proceed from myself; but, considering them as images, of which one represents one thing and another a different, it is evident that a great diversity obtains among them. For, without doubt, those that represent substances are something more, and contain in themselves, so to speak, more objective reality [that is, participate by representation in higher degrees of being or perfection], than those that represent only modes or accidents; and again, the idea by which I conceive a God [sovereign], eternal, infinite, [immutable], all-knowing, all-powerful, and the creator of all things that are out of himself, this, I say, has certainly in it more objective reality than those ideas by which finite substances are represented.

Now, it is manifest by the natural light that there must at least be as much reality in the efficient and total cause as in its effect; for whence can the effect draw its reality if not from its cause? And how could the cause communicate to it this reality unless it possessed it in itself? And hence it follows, not only that what is cannot be produced by what is not, but likewise that the more perfect, in other words, that which contains in itself more reality, cannot be the effect of the less perfect; and this is not only evidently true of those effects, whose reality is actual or formal, but likewise of ideas, whose reality is only considered as objective. Thus, for example, the stone that is not yet in existence, not only cannot now commence to be, unless it be produced by that which possesses in itself, formally or eminently, all that enters into its composition, [in other words, by that which contains in itself the same properties that are in the stone, or others superior to them]; and heat can only be produced in a subject that was before devoid of it, by a cause that is of an order, [degree or kind], at least as perfect as heat; and so of the others. But further, even the idea of the heat, or of the stone, cannot exist in me unless it be put there by a cause that contains, at least, as much reality as I conceive existent in the heat or in the stone: for although that cause may not transmit into my idea anything of its actual or formal reality, we ought not on this account to imagine that it is less real; but we ought to consider that, [as every idea is a work of the mind], its nature is such as of itself to demand no other formal reality than that which it borrows from our consciousness, of which it is but a mode [that is, a manner or way of thinking]. But in order that an idea may contain this objective reality rather than that, it must doubtless derive it from some cause in which is found at least as much formal reality as the idea contains of objective; for, if we suppose that there is found in an idea anything which was not in its cause, it must of course derive this from nothing. But, however imperfect may be the mode of existence by which a thing is objectively [or by representation] in the understanding by its idea, we certainly cannot, for all that, allege that this mode of existence is nothing, nor, consequently, that the idea owes its origin to nothing. Nor must it be imagined that, since the reality which is considered in these ideas is only objective, the same reality need not be formally (actually) in the causes of these ideas, but only objectively: for, just as the mode of existing objectively belongs to ideas by their peculiar nature, so likewise the mode of existing formally appertains to the causes of these ideas (at least to the first and principal), by their peculiar nature. And although an idea may give rise to another idea, this regress cannot, nevertheless, be infinite; we must in the end reach a first idea, the cause of which is, as it were, the archetype in which all the reality [or perfection] that is found objectively [or by representation] in these ideas is contained formally [and in act]. I am thus clearly taught by the natural light that ideas exist in me as pictures or images, which may, in truth, readily fall short of the perfection of the objects from which they are taken, but can never contain anything greater or more perfect.

And in proportion to the time and care with which I examine all those matters, the conviction of their truth brightens and becomes distinct. But, to sum up, what conclusion shall I draw from it all? It is this: if the objective reality [or perfection] of any one of my ideas be such as clearly to convince me, that this same reality exists in me neither formally nor eminently, and if, as follows from this, I myself cannot be the cause of it, it is a necessary consequence that I am not alone in the world, but that there is besides myself some other being who exists as the cause of that idea; while, on the contrary, if no such idea be found in my mind, I shall have no sufficient ground of assurance of the existence of any other being besides myself; for, after a most careful search, I have, up to this moment, been unable to discover any other ground.

But, among these my ideas, besides that which represents myself, respecting which there can be here no difficulty, there is one that represents a God; others that represent corporeal and inanimate things; others angels; others animals; and, finally, there are some that represent men like myself. But with respect to the ideas that represent other men, or animals, or angels, I can easily suppose that they were formed by the mingling and composition of the other ideas which I have of myself, of corporeal things, and of God, although they were, apart from myself, neither men, animals, nor angels. And with regard to the ideas of corporeal objects, I never discovered in them anything so great or excellent which I myself did not appear capable of originating; for, by considering these ideas closely and scrutinizing them individually, in the same way that I yesterday examined the idea of wax, I find that there is but little in them that is clearly and distinctly perceived. As belonging to the class of things that are clearly apprehended, I recognize the following, viz, magnitude or extension in length, breadth, and depth; figure, which results from the termination of extension; situation, which bodies of diverse figures preserve with reference to each other; and motion or the change of situation; to which may be added substance, duration, and number. But with regard to light, colors, sounds, odors, tastes, heat, cold, and the other tactile qualities, they are thought with so much obscurity and confusion, that I cannot determine even whether they are true or false; in other words, whether or not the ideas I have of these qualities are in truth the ideas of real objects. For although I before remarked that it is only in judgments that formal falsity, or falsity properly so called, can be met with, there may nevertheless be found in ideas a certain material falsity, which arises when they represent what is nothing as if it were something. Thus, for example, the ideas I have of cold and heat are so far from being clear and distinct, that I am unable from them to discover whether cold is only the privation of heat, or heat the privation of cold; or whether they are or are not real qualities: and since, ideas being as it were images there can be none that does not seem to us to represent some object, the idea which represents cold as something real and positive will not improperly be called false, if it be correct to say that cold is nothing but a privation of heat; and so in other cases. To ideas of this kind, indeed, it is not necessary that I should assign any author besides myself: for if they are false, that is, represent objects that are unreal, the natural light teaches me that they proceed from nothing: in other words, that they are in me only because something is wanting to the perfection of my nature; but if these ideas are true, yet because they exhibit to me so little reality that I cannot even distinguish the object represented from non-being, I do not see why I should not be the author of them.

With reference to those ideas of corporeal things that are clear and distinct, there are some which, as appears to me, might have been taken from the idea I have of myself, as those of substance, duration, number, and the like. For when I think that a stone is a substance, or a thing capable of existing of itself, and that I am likewise a substance, although I conceive that I am a thinking and non-extended thing, and that the stone, on the contrary, is extended and unconscious, there being thus the greatest diversity between the two concepts, yet these two ideas seem to have this in common that they both represent substances. In the same way, when I think of myself as now existing, and recollect besides that I existed some time ago, and when I am conscious of various thoughts whose number I know, I then acquire the ideas of duration and number, which I can afterward transfer to as many objects as I please. With respect to the other qualities that go to make up the ideas of corporeal objects, viz, extension, figure, situation, and motion, it is true that they are not formally in me, since I am merely a thinking being; but because they are only certain modes of substance, and because I myself am a substance, it seems possible that they may be contained in me eminently.

There only remains, therefore, the idea of God, in which I must consider whether there is anything that cannot be supposed to originate with myself. By the name God, I understand a substance infinite, [eternal, immutable], independent, all-knowing, all-powerful, and by which I myself, and every other thing that exists, if any such there be, were created. But these properties are so great and excellent, that the more attentively I consider them the less I feel persuaded that the idea I have of them owes its origin to myself alone. And thus it is absolutely necessary to conclude, from all that I have before said, that God exists: for though the idea of substance be in my mind owing to this, that I myself am a substance, I should not, however, have the idea of an infinite substance, seeing I am a finite being, unless it were given me by some substance in reality infinite.

And I must not imagine that I do not apprehend the infinite by a true idea, but only by the negation of the finite, in the same way that I comprehend repose and darkness by the negation of motion and light: since, on the contrary, I clearly perceive that there is more reality in the infinite substance than in the finite, and therefore that in some way I possess the perception (notion) of the infinite before that of the finite, that is, the perception of God before that of myself, for how could I know that I doubt, desire, or that something is wanting to me, and that I am not wholly perfect, if I possessed no idea of a being more perfect than myself, by comparison of which I knew the deficiencies of my nature?

And it cannot be said that this idea of God is perhaps materially false, and consequently that it may have arisen from nothing [in other words, that it may exist in me from my imperfection], as I before said of the ideas of heat and cold, and the like: for, on the contrary, as this idea is very clear and distinct, and contains in itself more objective reality than any other, there can be no one of itself more true, or less open to the suspicion of falsity.

The idea, I say, of a being supremely perfect, and infinite, is in the highest degree true; for although, perhaps, we may imagine that such a being does not exist, we cannot, nevertheless, suppose that his idea represents nothing real, as I have already said of the idea of cold. It is likewise clear and distinct in the highest degree, since whatever the mind clearly and distinctly conceives as real or true, and as implying any perfection, is contained entire in this idea. And this is true, nevertheless, although I do not comprehend the infinite, and although there may be in God an infinity of things that I cannot comprehend, nor perhaps even compass by thought in any way; for it is of the nature of the infinite that it should not be comprehended by the finite; and it is enough that I rightly understand this, and judge that all which I clearly perceive, and in which I know there is some perfection, and perhaps also an infinity of properties of which I am ignorant, are formally or eminently in God, in order that the idea I have of him may become the most true, clear, and distinct of all the ideas in my mind.

But perhaps I am something more than I suppose myself to be, and it may be that all those perfections which I attribute to God, in some way exist potentially in me, although they do not yet show themselves, and are not reduced to act. Indeed, I am already conscious that my knowledge is being increased [and perfected] by degrees; and I see nothing to prevent it from thus gradually increasing to infinity, nor any reason why, after such increase and perfection, I should not be able thereby to acquire all the other perfections of the Divine nature; nor, in fine, why the power I possess of acquiring those perfections, if it really now exist in me, should not be sufficient to produce the ideas of them. Yet, on looking more closely into the matter, I discover that this cannot be; for, in the first place, although it were true that my knowledge daily acquired new degrees of perfection, and although there were potentially in my nature much that was not as yet actually in it, still all these excellences make not the slightest approach to the idea I have of the Deity, in whom there is no perfection merely potentially [but all actually] existent; for it is even an unmistakable token of imperfection in my knowledge, that it is augmented by degrees. Further, although my knowledge increase more and more, nevertheless I am not, therefore, induced to think that it will ever be actually infinite, since it can never reach that point beyond which it shall be incapable of further increase. But I conceive God as actually infinite, so that nothing can be added to his perfection. And, in fine, I readily perceive that the objective being of an idea cannot be produced by a being that is merely potentially existent, which, properly speaking, is nothing, but only by a being existing formally or actually.

And, truly, I see nothing in all that I have now said which it is not easy for any one, who shall carefully consider it, to discern by the natural light; but when I allow my attention in some degree to relax, the vision of my mind being obscured, and, as it were, blinded by the images of sensible objects, I do not readily remember the reason why the idea of a being more perfect than myself, must of necessity have proceeded from a being in reality more perfect. On this account I am here desirous to inquire further, whether I, who possess this idea of God, could exist supposing there were no God. And I ask, from whom could I, in that case, derive my existence? Perhaps from myself, or from my parents, or from some other causes less perfect than God; for anything more perfect, or even equal to God, cannot be thought or imagined. But if I [were independent of every other existence, and] were myself the author of my being, I should doubt of nothing, I should desire nothing, and, in fine, no perfection would be awanting to me; for I should have bestowed upon myself every perfection of which I possess the idea, and I should thus be God. And it must not be imagined that what is now wanting to me is perhaps of more difficult acquisition than that of which I am already possessed; for, on the contrary, it is quite manifest that it was a matter of much higher difficulty that I, a thinking being, should arise from nothing, than it would be for me to acquire the knowledge of many things of which I am ignorant, and which are merely the accidents of a thinking substance; and certainly, if I possessed of myself the greater perfection of which I have now spoken [in other words, if I were the author of my own existence], I would not at least have denied to myself things that may be more easily obtained [as that infinite variety of knowledge of which I am at present destitute]. I could not, indeed, have denied to myself any property which I perceive is contained in the idea of God, because there is none of these that seems to me to be more difficult to make or acquire; and if there were any that should happen to be more difficult to acquire, they would certainly appear so to me (supposing that I myself were the source of the other things I possess), because I should discover in them a limit to my power. And though I were to suppose that I always was as I now am, I should not, on this ground, escape the force of these reasonings, since it would not follow, even on this supposition, that no author of my existence needed to be sought after. For the whole time of my life may be divided into an infinity of parts, each of which is in no way dependent on any other; and, accordingly, because I was in existence a short time ago, it does not follow that I must now exist, unless in this moment some cause create me anew as it were, that is, conserve me. In truth, it is perfectly clear and evident to all who will attentively consider the nature of duration, that the conservation of a substance, in each moment of its duration, requires the same power and act that would be necessary to create it, supposing it were not yet in existence; so that it is manifestly a dictate of the natural light that conservation and creation differ merely in respect of our mode of thinking [and not in reality]. All that is here required, therefore, is that I interrogate myself to discover whether I possess any power by means of which I can bring it about that I, who now am, shall exist a moment afterward: for, since I am merely a thinking thing (or since, at least, the precise question, in the meantime, is only of that part of myself), if such a power resided in me, I should, without doubt, be conscious of it; but I am conscious of no such power, and thereby I manifestly know that I am dependent upon some being different from myself.

But perhaps the being upon whom I am dependent is not God, and I have been produced either by my parents, or by some causes less perfect than Deity. This cannot be: for, as I before said, it is perfectly evident that there must at least be as much reality in the cause as in its effect; and accordingly, since I am a thinking thing and possess in myself an idea of God, whatever in the end be the cause of my existence, it must of necessity be admitted that it is likewise a thinking being, and that it possesses in itself the idea and all the perfections I attribute to Deity. Then it may again be inquired whether this cause owes its origin and existence to itself, or to some other cause. For if it be self-existent, it follows, from what I have before laid down, that this cause is God; for, since it possesses the perfection of self-existence, it must likewise, without doubt, have the power of actually possessing every perfection of which it has the idea—in other words, all the perfections I conceive to belong to God. But if it owe its existence to another cause than itself, we demand again, for a similar reason, whether this second cause exists of itself or through some other, until, from stage to stage we at length arrive at an ultimate cause, which will be God. And it is quite manifest that in

this matter there can be no infinite regress of causes, seeing that the question raised respects not so much the cause which once produced me, as that by which I am at this present moment conserved.

Nor can it be supposed that several causes concurred in my production, and that from one I received the idea of one of the perfections I attribute to Deity, and from another the idea of some other, and thus that all those perfections are indeed found somewhere in the universe, but do not all exist together in a single being who is God; for, on the contrary, the unity, the simplicity, or inseparability of all the properties of Deity, is one of the chief perfections I conceive him to possess; and the idea of this unity of all the perfections of Deity could certainly not be put into my mind by any cause from which I did not likewise receive the ideas of all the other perfections; for no power could enable me to embrace them in an inseparable unity, without at the same time giving me the knowledge of what they were [and of their existence in a particular mode].

Finally, with regard to my parents [from whom it appears I sprung], although all that I believed respecting them be true, it does not, nevertheless, follow that I am conserved by them, or even that I was produced by them, in so far as I am a thinking being. All that, at the most, they contributed to my origin was the giving of certain dispositions (modifications) to the matter in which I have hitherto judged that I or my mind, which is what alone I now consider to be myself, is inclosed; and thus there can here be no difficulty with respect to them, and it is absolutely necessary to conclude from this alone that I am, and possess the idea of a being absolutely perfect, that is, of God, that his existence is most clearly demonstrated.

There remains only the inquiry as to the way in which I received this idea from God; for I have not drawn it from the senses, nor is it even presented to me unexpectedly, as is usual with the ideas of sensible objects, when these are presented or appear to be presented to the external organs of the senses; it is not even a pure production or fiction of my mind, for it is not in my power to take from or add to it; and consequently there but remains the alternative that it is innate, in the same way as is the idea of myself. And, in truth, it is not to be wondered at that God, at my creation, implanted this idea in me, that it might serve, as it were, for the mark of the workman impressed on his work; and it is not also necessary that the mark should be something different from the work itself; but considering only that God is my creator, it is highly probable that he in some way fashioned me after his own image and likeness, and that I perceive this likeness, in which is contained the idea of God, by the same faculty by which I apprehend myself, in other words, when I make myself the object of reflection, I not only find that I am an incomplete, [imperfect] and dependent being, and one who unceasingly aspires after something better and greater than he is; but, at the same time, I am assured likewise that he upon whom I am dependent possesses in himself all the goods after which I aspire [and the ideas of which I find in my mind], and that not merely indefinitely and potentially, but infinitely and actually, and that he is thus God. And the whole force of the argument of which I have here availed myself to establish the existence of God, consists in this, that I perceive I could not possibly be of such a nature as I am, and yet have in my mind the idea of a God, if God did not in reality exist—this same God. I say, whose idea is in my mind—that is, a being who possesses all those lofty perfections, of which the mind may have some slight conception, without, however, being able fully to comprehend them, and who is wholly superior to all defect [and has nothing that marks imperfection]: whence it is sufficiently manifest that he cannot be a deceiver, since it is a dictate of the natural light that all fraud and deception spring from some defect.

But before I examine this with more attention, and pass on to the consideration of other truths that may be evolved out of it, I think it proper to remain here for some time in the contemplation of God himself—that I may ponder at leisure his marvelous attributes—and behold, admire, and adore the beauty of this light so unspeakably great, as far, at least, as the strength of my mind, which is to some degree dazzled by the sight, will permit. For just as we learn by faith that the supreme felicity of another life consists in the contemplation of the Divine majesty alone, so even now we learn from experience that a like meditation, though incomparably less perfect, is the source of the highest satisfaction of which we are susceptible in this life.

Meditation IV.
Of Truth and Error.

I have been habituated these bygone days to detach my mind from the senses, and I have accurately observed that there is exceedingly little which is known with certainty respecting corporeal objects, that we know much more of the human mind, and still more of God himself. I am thus able now without difficulty to abstract my mind from the contemplation of [sensible or] imaginable objects, and apply it to those which, as disengaged from all matter, are purely intelligible. And certainly the idea I have of the human mind in so far as it is a thinking thing, and not extended in length, breadth, and depth, and participating in none of the properties of body, is incomparably more distinct than the idea of any corporeal object; and when I consider that I doubt, in other words, that I am an incomplete and dependent being, the idea of a complete and independent being, that is to say of God, occurs to my mind with so much clearness and distinctness, and from the fact alone that this idea is found in me, or that I who possess it exist, the conclusions that God exists, and that my own existence, each moment of its continuance, is absolutely dependent upon him, are so manifest, as to lead me to believe it impossible that the human mind can know anything with more clearness and certitude. And now I seem to discover a path that will conduct us from the contemplation of the true God, in whom are contained all the treasures of science and wisdom, to the knowledge of the other things in the universe.

For, in the first place, I discover that it is impossible for him ever to deceive me, for in all fraud and deceit there is a certain imperfection: and although it may seem that the ability to deceive is a mark of subtlety or power, yet the will testifies without doubt of malice and weakness; and such, accordingly, cannot be found in God. In the next place, I am conscious that I possess a certain faculty of judging [or discerning truth from error], which I doubtless received from God, along with whatever else is mine; and since it is impossible that he should will to deceive me, it is likewise certain that he has not given me a faculty that will ever lead me into error, provided I use it aright.

And there would remain no doubt on this head, did it not seem to follow from this, that I can never therefore be deceived; for if all I possess be from God, and if he planted in me no faculty that is deceitful, it seems to follow that I can never fall into error. Accordingly, it is true that when I think only of God (when I look upon myself as coming from God, Fr.), and turn wholly to him, I discover [in myself] no cause of error or falsity: but immediately thereafter, recurring to myself, experience assures me that I am nevertheless subject to innumerable errors. When I come to inquire into the cause of these, I observe that there is not only present to my consciousness a real and positive idea of God, or of a being supremely perfect, but also, so to speak, a certain negative idea of nothing, in other words, of that which is at an infinite distance from every sort of perfection, and that I am, as it were, a mean between God and nothing, or placed in such a way between absolute existence and non-existence, that there is in truth nothing in me to lead me into error, in so far as an absolute being is my creator; but that, on the other hand, as I thus likewise participate in some degree of nothing or of nonbeing, in other words, as I am not myself the supreme Being, and as I am wanting in many perfections, it is not surprising I should fall into error. And I hence discern that error, so far as error is not something real, which depends for its existence on God, but is simply defect; and therefore that, in order to fall into it, it is not necessary God should have given me a faculty expressly for this end, but that my being deceived arises from the circumstance that the power which God has given me of discerning truth from error is not infinite.

Nevertheless this is not yet quite satisfactory; for error is not a pure negation, [in other words, it is not the simple deficiency or want of some knowledge which is not due], but the privation or want of some knowledge which it would seem I ought to possess. But, on considering the nature of God, it seems impossible that he should have planted in his creature any faculty not perfect in its kind, that is, wanting in some perfection due to it: for if it be true, that in proportion to the skill of the maker the perfection of his work is greater, what thing can have been produced by the supreme Creator of the universe that is not absolutely perfect in all its parts? And assuredly there is no doubt that God could have created me such as that I should never be deceived; it is certain, likewise, that he always wills what is best: is it better, then, that I should be capable of being deceived than that I should not?

Considering this more attentively, the first thing that occurs to me is the reflection that I must not be surprised if I am not always capable of comprehending the reasons why God acts as he does; nor must I doubt of his existence because I find, perhaps, that there are several other things besides the present respecting which I understand neither why nor how they were created by him; for, knowing already that my nature is extremely weak and limited, and that the nature of God, on the other hand, is immense, incomprehensible, and infinite, I have no longer any difficulty in discerning that there is an infinity of things in his power whose causes transcend the grasp of my mind: and this consideration alone is sufficient to convince me, that the whole class of final causes is of no avail in physical [or natural] things; for it appears to me that I cannot, without exposing myself to the charge of temerity, seek to discover the [impenetrable] ends of Deity.

It further occurs to me that we must not consider only one creature apart from the others, if we wish to determine the perfection of the works of Deity, but generally all his creatures together; for the same object that might perhaps, with some show of reason, be deemed highly imperfect if it were alone in the world, may for all that be the most perfect possible, considered as forming part of the whole universe: and although, as it was my purpose to doubt of everything, I only as yet know with certainty my own existence and that of God, nevertheless, after having remarked the infinite power of Deity, I cannot deny that we may have produced many other objects, or at least that he is able to produce them, so that I may occupy a place in the relation of a part to the great whole of his creatures.

Whereupon, regarding myself more closely, and considering what my errors are (which alone testify to the existence of imperfection in me), I observe that these depend on the concurrence of two causes, viz, the faculty of cognition, which I possess, and that of election or the power of free choice,—in other words, the understanding and the will. For by the understanding alone, I [neither affirm nor deny anything but] merely apprehend (*percipio*) the ideas regarding which I may form a judgment; nor is any error, properly so called, found in it thus accurately taken. And although there are perhaps innumerable objects in the world of which I have no idea in my understanding, it cannot, on that account be said that I am deprived of those ideas [as of something that is due to my nature], but simply that I do not possess them, because, in truth, there is no ground to prove that Deity ought to have endowed me with a larger faculty of cognition than he has actually bestowed upon me; and however skillful a workman I suppose him to be, I have no reason, on that account, to think that it was obligatory on him to give to each of his works all the perfections he is able to bestow upon some. Nor, moreover, can I complain that God has not given me freedom of choice, or a will sufficiently ample and perfect, since, in truth, I am conscious of will so ample and extended as to be superior to all limits. And what appears to me here to be highly remarkable is that, of all the other properties I possess, there is none so great and perfect as that I do not clearly discern it could be still greater and more perfect.

For, to take an example, if I consider the faculty of understanding which I possess, I find that it is of very small extent, and greatly limited, and at the same time I form the idea of another faculty of the same nature, much more ample and even infinite, and seeing that I can frame the idea of it, I discover, from this circumstance alone, that it pertains to the nature of God. In the same way, if I examine the faculty of memory or imagination, or any other faculty I possess, I find none that is not small and circumscribed, and in God immense [and infinite]. It is the faculty of will only, or freedom of choice, which I experience to be so great that I am unable to conceive the idea of another that shall be more ample and extended; so that it is chiefly my will which leads me to discern that I bear a certain image and similitude of Deity. For although the faculty of will is incomparably greater in God than in myself, as well in respect of the knowledge and power that are conjoined with it, and that render it stronger and more efficacious, as in respect of the object, since in him it extends to a greater number of things, it does not, nevertheless, appear to me greater, considered in itself formally and precisely: for the power of will consists only in this, that we are able to do or not to do the same thing (that is, to affirm or deny, to pursue or shun it), or rather in this alone, that in affirming or denying, pursuing or shunning, what is proposed to us by the understanding, we so act that we are not conscious of being determined to a particular action by any external force. For, to the possession of freedom, it is not necessary that I be alike indifferent toward each of two contraries; but, on the contrary, the more I am inclined toward the one, whether because I clearly know that in it there is the reason of truth and goodness, or because God thus internally disposes my thought, the more freely do I choose and embrace it; and assuredly divine grace and natural knowledge, very far from diminishing liberty, rather augment and fortify it. But the indifference of which I am conscious when I am not impelled to one side rather than to another for want of a reason, is the lowest grade of liberty, and manifests defect or negation of knowledge rather than perfection of will; for if I always clearly knew what was true and good, I should never have any difficulty in determining what judgment I ought to come to, and what choice I ought to make, and I should thus be entirely free without ever being indifferent.

From all this I discover, however, that neither the power of willing, which I have received from God, is of itself the source of my errors, for it is exceedingly ample and perfect in its kind; nor even the power of understanding, for as I conceive no object unless by means of the faculty that God bestowed upon me, all that I conceive is doubtless rightly conceived by me, and it is impossible for me to be deceived in it.

Whence, then, spring my errors? They arise from this cause alone, that I do not restrain the will, which is of much wider range than the understanding, within the same limits, but extend it even to things I do not understand, and as the will is of itself indifferent to such, it readily falls into error and sin by choosing the false in room of the true, and evil instead of good.

For example, when I lately considered whether aught really existed in the world, and found that because I considered this question, it very manifestly followed that I myself existed, I could not but judge that what I so clearly conceived was true, not that I was forced to this judgment by any external cause, but simply because great clearness of the understanding was succeeded by strong inclination in the will; and I believed this the more freely and spontaneously in proportion as I was less indifferent with respect to it. But now I not only know that I exist, in so far as I am a thinking being, but there is likewise presented to my mind a certain idea of corporeal nature; hence I am in doubt as to whether the thinking nature which is in me, or rather which I myself am, is different from that corporeal nature, or whether both are merely one and the same thing, and I here suppose that I am as yet ignorant of any reason that would determine me to adopt the one belief in preference to the other; whence it happens that it is a matter of perfect indifference to me which of the two suppositions I affirm or deny, or whether I form any judgment at all in the matter.

This indifference, moreover, extends not only to things of which the understanding has no knowledge at all, but in general also to all those which it does not discover with perfect clearness at the moment the will is deliberating upon them; for, however probable the conjectures may be that dispose me to form a judgment in a particular matter, the simple knowledge that these are merely conjectures, and not certain and indubitable reasons, is sufficient to lead me to form one that is directly the opposite. Of this I lately had abundant experience, when I laid aside as false all that I had before held for true, on the single ground that I could in some degree doubt of it. But if I abstain from judging of a thing when I do not conceive it with sufficient clearness and distinctness, it is plain that I act rightly, and am not deceived; but if I resolve to deny or affirm, I then do not make a right use of my free will; and if I affirm what is false, it is evident that I am deceived; moreover, even although I judge according to truth, I stumble upon it by chance, and do not therefore escape the imputation of a wrong use of my freedom; for it is a dictate of the natural light, that the knowledge of the understanding ought always to precede the determination of the will.

And it is this wrong use of the freedom of the will in which is found the privation that constitutes the form of error. Privation, I say, is found in the act, in so far as it proceeds from myself, but it does not exist in the faculty which I received from God, nor even in the act, in so far as it depends on him; for I have assuredly no reason to complain that God has not given me a greater power of intelligence or more perfect natural light than he has actually bestowed, since it is of the nature of a finite understanding not to comprehend many things, and of the nature of a created understanding to be finite; on the contrary, I have every reason to render thanks to God, who owed me nothing, for having given me all the perfections I possess, and I should be far from thinking that he has unjustly deprived me of, or kept back, the other perfections which he has not bestowed upon me.

I have no reason, moreover, to complain because he has given me a will more ample than my understanding, since, as the will consists only of a single element, and that indivisible, it would appear that this faculty is of such a nature that nothing could be taken from it [without destroying it]; and certainly, the more extensive it is, the more cause I have to thank the goodness of him who bestowed it upon me.

And, finally, I ought not also to complain that God concurs with me in forming the acts of this will, or the judgments in which I am deceived, because those acts are wholly true and good, in so far as they depend on God; and the ability to form them is a higher degree of perfection in my nature than the want of it would be. With regard to privation, in which alone consists the formal reason of error and sin, this does not require the concurrence of Deity, because it is not a thing [or existence], and if it be referred to God as to its cause, it ought not to be called privation, but negation [according to the signification of these words in the schools]. For in truth it is no imperfection in Deity that he has accorded to me the power of giving or withholding my assent from certain things of which he has not put a clear and distinct knowledge in my understanding; but it is doubtless an imperfection in me that I do not use my freedom aright, and readily give my judgment on matters which I only obscurely and confusedly conceive.

I perceive, nevertheless, that it was easy for Deity so to have constituted me as that I should never be deceived, although I still remained free and possessed of a limited knowledge, viz., by implanting in my understanding a clear and distinct knowledge of all the objects respecting which I should ever have to deliberate; or simply by so deeply engraving on my memory the resolution to judge of nothing without previously possessing a clear and distinct conception of it, that I should never forget it. And I easily understand that, in so far as I consider myself as a single whole, without reference to any other being in the universe, I should have been much more perfect than I now am, had Deity created me superior to error; but I cannot therefore deny that it is not somehow a greater perfection in the universe, that certain of its parts are not exempt from defect, as others are, than if they were all perfectly alike.

And I have no right to complain because God, who placed me in the world, was not willing that I should sustain that character which of all others is the chief and most perfect; I have even good reason to remain satisfied on the ground that, if he has not given me the perfection of being superior to error by the first means I have pointed out above, which depends on a clear and evident knowledge of all the matters regarding which I can deliberate, he has at least left in my power the other means, which is, firmly to retain the resolution never to judge where the truth is not clearly known to me: for, although I am conscious of the weakness of not being able to keep my mind continually fixed on the same thought, I can nevertheless by attentive and oft-repeated meditation, impress it so strongly on my memory that I shall never fail to recollect it as often as I require it, and I can acquire in this way the habitude of not erring; and since it is in being superior to error that the highest and chief perfection of man consists, I deem that I have not gained little by this day's meditation, in having discovered the source of error and falsity.

And certainly this can be no other than what I have now explained: for as often as I so restrain my will within the limits of my knowledge, that it forms no judgment except regarding objects which are clearly and distinctly represented to it by the understanding, I can never be deceived; because every clear and distinct conception is doubtless something, and as such cannot owe its origin to nothing, but must of necessity have God for its author—God, I say, who, as supremely perfect, cannot, without a contradiction, be the cause of any error; and consequently it is necessary to conclude that every such conception [or judgment] is true. Nor have I merely learned to-day what I must avoid to escape error, but also what I must do to arrive at the knowledge of truth; for I

will assuredly reach truth if I only fix my attention sufficiently on all the things I conceive perfectly, and separate these from others which I conceive more confusedly and obscurely; to which for the future I shall give diligent heed.

Meditation V.
Of the Essence of Material Things; and, Again, of God; That He Exists.

Several other questions remain for consideration respecting the attributes of God and my own nature or mind. I will, however, on some other occasion perhaps resume the investigation of these. Meanwhile, as I have discovered what must be done and what avoided to arrive at the knowledge of truth, what I have chiefly to do is to essay to emerge from the state of doubt in which I have for some time been, and to discover whether anything can be known with certainty regarding material objects. But before considering whether such objects as I conceive exist without me, I must examine their ideas in so far as these are to be found in my consciousness, and discover which of them are distinct and which confused.

In the first place, I distinctly imagine that quantity which the philosophers commonly call continuous, or the extension in length, breadth, and depth that is in this quantity, or rather in the object to which it is attributed. Further, I can enumerate in it many diverse parts, and attribute to each of these all sorts of sizes, figures, situations, and local motions; and, in fine, I can assign to each of these motions all degrees of duration. And I not only distinctly know these things when I thus consider them in general; but besides, by a little attention, I discover innumerable particulars respecting figures, numbers, motion, and the like, which are so evidently true, and so accordant with my nature, that when I now discover them I do not so much appear to learn anything new, as to call to remembrance what I before knew, or for the first time to remark what was before in my mind, but to which I had not hitherto directed my attention. And what I here find of most importance is, that I discover in my mind innumerable ideas of certain objects, which cannot be esteemed pure negations, although perhaps they possess no reality beyond my thought, and which are not framed by me though it may be in my power to think, or not to think them, but possess true and immutable natures of their own. As, for example, when I imagine a triangle, although there is not perhaps and never was in any place in the universe apart from my thought one such figure, it remains true nevertheless that this figure possesses a certain determinate nature, form, or essence, which is immutable and eternal, and not framed by me, nor in any degree dependent on my thought; as appears from the circumstance, that diverse properties of the triangle may be demonstrated, viz., that its three angles are equal to two right, that its greatest side is subtended by its greatest angle, and the like, which, whether I will or not, I now clearly discern to belong to it, although before I did not at all think of them, when, for the first time, I imagined a triangle, and which accordingly cannot be said to have been invented by me. Nor is it a valid objection to allege, that perhaps this idea of a triangle came into my mind by the medium of the senses, through my having seen bodies of a triangular figure; for I am able to form in thought an innumerable variety of figures with regard to which it cannot be supposed that they were objects of sense, and I can nevertheless demonstrate diverse properties of their nature no less than of the triangle, all of which are assuredly true since I clearly conceive them: and they are therefore something, and not mere negations; for it is highly evident that all that is true is something, [truth being identical with existence]; and I have already fully shown the truth of the principle, that whatever is clearly and distinctly known is true. And although this had not been demonstrated, yet the nature of my mind is such as to compel me to assert to what I clearly conceive while I so conceive it; and I recollect that even when I still strongly adhered to the objects of sense, I reckoned among the number of the most certain truths those I clearly conceived relating to figures, numbers, and other matters that pertain to arithmetic and geometry, and in general to the pure mathematics.

But now if because I can draw from my thought the idea of an object, it follows that all I clearly and distinctly apprehend to pertain to this object, does in truth belong to it, may I not from this derive an argument for the existence of God?

It is certain that I no less find the idea of a God in my consciousness, that is the idea of a being supremely perfect, than that of any figure or number whatever: and I know with not less clearness and distinctness that an [actual and] eternal existence pertains to his nature than that all which is demonstrable of any figure or number really belongs to the nature of that figure or number; and, therefore, although all the conclusions of the preceding Meditations were false, the existence of God would pass with me for a truth at least as certain as I ever judged any truth of mathematics to be, although indeed such a doctrine may at first sight appear to contain more sophistry than truth. For, as I have been accustomed in every other matter to distinguish between existence and essence, I easily believe that the existence can be separated from the essence of God, and that thus God may be conceived as not actually existing. But, nevertheless, when I think of it more attentively, it appears that the existence can no more be separated from the essence of God, than the idea of a mountain from that of a valley, or the equality of its three angles to two right angles, from the essence of a [rectilineal] triangle; so that it is not less impossible to conceive a God, that is, a being supremely perfect, to whom existence is awanting, or who is devoid of a certain perfection, than to conceive a mountain without a valley.

But though, in truth, I cannot conceive a God unless as existing, any more than I can a mountain without a valley, yet, just as it does not follow that there is any mountain in the world merely because I conceive a mountain with a valley, so likewise, though I conceive God as existing, it does not seem to follow on that account that God exists; for my thought imposes no necessity on things; and as I may imagine a winged horse, though there be none such, so I could perhaps attribute existence to God, though no God existed. But the cases are not analogous, and a fallacy lurks under the semblance of this objection: for because I cannot conceive a mountain without a valley, it does not follow that there is any mountain or valley in existence, but simply that the mountain or valley, whether they do or do not exist, are inseparable from each other; whereas, on the other hand, because I cannot conceive God unless as existing, it follows that existence is inseparable from him, and therefore that he really exists: not that this is brought about by my thought, or that it imposes any necessity on things, but, on the contrary, the necessity which lies in the thing itself, that is, the necessity of the existence of God, determines me to think in this way: for it is not in my power to conceive a God without existence, that is, a being supremely perfect, and yet devoid of an absolute perfection, as I am free to imagine a horse with or without wings.

Nor must it be alleged here as an objection, that it is in truth necessary to admit that God exists, after having supposed him to possess all perfections, since existence is one of them, but that my original supposition was not necessary; just as it is not necessary to think that all quadrilateral figures can be inscribed in the circle, since, if I supposed this, I should be constrained to admit that the rhombus, being a figure of four sides, can be therein inscribed, which, however, is manifestly false. This objection is, I say, incompetent; for although it may not be necessary that I shall at any time entertain the notion of Deity, yet each time I happen to think of a first and sovereign being, and to draw, so to speak, the idea of him from the storehouse of the mind, I am necessitated to attribute to him all kinds of perfections, though I may not then enumerate them all, nor think of each of them in particular. And this necessity is sufficient, as soon as I discover that existence is a perfection, to cause me to infer the existence of this first and sovereign being; just as it is not necessary that I should ever imagine any triangle, but whenever I am desirous of considering a rectilineal figure composed of only three angles, it is absolutely necessary to attribute those properties to it from which it is correctly inferred that its three angles are not greater than two right angles, although perhaps I may not then advert to this relation in particular. But when I consider what figures are capable of being inscribed in the circle, it is by no means necessary to hold that all quadrilateral figures are of this number; on the contrary, I cannot even imagine such to be the case, so long as I shall be unwilling to accept in thought aught that I do not clearly and distinctly conceive; and consequently there is a vast difference between false suppositions, as is the one in question, and the true ideas that were born with me, the first and chief of which is the idea of God. For indeed I discern on many grounds that this idea is not facti-

tious depending simply on my thought, but that it is the representation of a true and immutable nature: in the first place because I can conceive no other being, except God, to whose essence existence [necessarily] pertains; in the second, because it is impossible to conceive two or more gods of this kind; and it being supposed that one such God exists, I clearly see that he must have existed from all eternity, and will exist to all eternity; and finally, because I apprehend many other properties in God, none of which I can either diminish or change.

But, indeed, whatever mode of probation I in the end adopt, it always returns to this, that it is only the things I clearly and distinctly conceive which have the power of completely persuading me. And although, of the objects I conceive in this manner, some, indeed, are obvious to every one, while others are only discovered after close and careful investigation; nevertheless after they are once discovered, the latter are not esteemed less certain than the former. Thus, for example, to take the case of a right-angled triangle, although it is not so manifest at first that the square of the base is equal to the squares of the other two sides, as that the base is opposite to the greatest angle; nevertheless, after it is once apprehended, we are as firmly persuaded of the truth of the former as of the latter. And, with respect to God if I were not preoccupied by prejudices, and my thought beset on all sides by the continual presence of the images of sensible objects, I should know nothing sooner or more easily than the fact of his being. For is there any truth more clear than the existence of a Supreme Being, or of God, seeing it is to his essence alone that [necessary and eternal] existence pertains. And although the right conception of this truth has cost me much close thinking, nevertheless at present I feel not only as assured of it as of what I deem most certain, but I remark further that the certitude of all other truths is so absolutely dependent on it that without this knowledge it is impossible ever to know anything perfectly.

For although I am of such a nature as to be unable, while I possess a very clear and distinct apprehension of a matter, to resist the conviction of its truth, yet because my constitution is also such as to incapacitate me from keeping my mind continually fixed on the same object, and as I frequently recollect a past judgment without at the same time being able to recall the grounds of it, it may happen meanwhile that other reasons are presented to me which would readily cause me to change my opinion, if I did not know that God existed; and thus I should possess no true and certain knowledge, but merely vague and vacillating opinions. Thus, for example, when I consider the nature of the [rectilineal] triangle, it most clearly appears to me, who have been instructed in the principles of geometry, that its three angles are equal to two right angles, and I find it impossible to believe otherwise, while I apply my mind to the demonstration; but as soon as I cease from attending to the process of proof, although I still remember that I had a clear comprehension of it, yet I may readily come to doubt of the truth demonstrated, if I do not know that there is a God: for I may persuade myself that I have been so constituted by nature as to be sometimes deceived, even in matters which I think I apprehend with the greatest evidence and certitude, especially when I recollect that I frequently considered many things to be true and certain which other reasons afterward constrained me to reckon as wholly false.

But after I have discovered that God exists, seeing I also at the same time observed that all things depend on him, and that he is no deceiver, and thence inferred that all which I clearly and distinctly perceive is of necessity true: although I no longer attend to the grounds of a judgment, no opposite reason can be alleged sufficient to lead me to doubt of its truth, provided only I remember that I once possessed a clear and distinct comprehension of it. My knowledge of it thus becomes true and certain. And this same knowledge extends likewise to whatever I remember to have formerly demonstrated, as the truths of geometry and the like: for what can be alleged against them to lead me to doubt of them? Will it be that my nature is such that I may be frequently deceived? But I already know that I cannot be deceived in judgments of the grounds of which I possess a clear knowledge. Will it be that I formerly deemed things to be true and certain which I afterward discovered to be false? But I had no clear and distinct knowledge of any of those things, and, being as yet ignorant of the rule by which I am assured of the truth of a judgment, I was led to give my assent to them on grounds which I afterward discovered were less strong than at the time I imagined them to be. What further objection, then, is there? Will it be said that perhaps I am dreaming (an objection I lately myself raised), or that all the thoughts of which I am now conscious have no more truth than the reveries of my dreams? But although, in truth, I should be dreaming, the rule still holds that all which is clearly presented to my intellect is indisputably true.

And thus I very clearly see that the certitude and truth of all science depends on the knowledge alone of the true God, insomuch that, before I knew him, I could have no perfect knowledge of any other thing. And now that I know him, I possess the means of acquiring a perfect knowledge respecting innumerable matters, as well relative to God himself and other intellectual objects as to corporeal nature, in so far as it is the object of pure mathematics [which do not consider whether it exists or not].

50. *The Cosmological Argument*

WILLIAM ROWE

William Rowe is a professor of philosophy at Purdue University. In the following selection Rowe discusses the version of the cosmological argument known as the argument from contingency. One assumption of this argument is the principle of sufficient reason ("PSR" for short). According to PSR, for every thing or fact that exists, there is a sufficient reason or explanation for why it exists. Given this principle, and the fact of the existence of contingent things, it follows that there must be some explanation for the existence of contingent things. If we appeal to a contingent being to explain a contingent being, then the question remains: What is the sufficient reason for that contingent being, and so on? But the argument from contingency is not an argument against an infinite series of contingent beings, since even if the series were infinite we would be lacking an explanation, that is, a sufficient reason, for why there is an infinite series of contingent beings. Indeed, why is there contingent being at all, rather than nothing? The only sufficient reason, so the argument goes, is that there exists a necessary being, a being that is the basis of its own existence and of the existence of everything else that exists. This necessary being is God, and hence God exists. Rowe carefully examines objections to this argument and responses to those objections. He questions whether the PSR deserves our allegiance and concludes that unless we believe that PSR is a fundamental truth of reason, the cosmological argument does not allow us to conclude that God, as a necessary being (a being whose existence is accounted for by its own nature), exists.

Since ancient times thoughtful people have sought to justify their religious beliefs. Perhaps the most basic belief for which justification has been sought is the belief that there is a God. The effort to justify belief in the existence of God has generally started either from facts available to believers and nonbelievers alike or from facts, such as the experience of God, normally available only to believers. In this and the next two chapters, we shall consider some major attempts to justify belief in God by appealing to facts supposedly available to any rational person, whether religious or not. By starting from such facts, theologians and philosophers have developed arguments for the existence of God, arguments which, they have claimed, prove beyond reasonable doubt that there is a God.

From William Rowe, *The Philosophy of Religion: An Introduction*, 3rd ed. (Belmont, CA: Wadsworth, 2001). Reprinted by permission of Wadsworth, a division of Thomson Learning, Inc.

Stating the Argument

Arguments for the existence of God are commonly divided into *a posteriori* arguments and *a priori* arguments. An *a posteriori* argument depends on a principle or premise that can be known only by means of our experience of the world. An *a priori* argument, on the other hand, purports to rest on principles all of which can be known independently of our experience of the world, by just reflecting on and understanding them. Of the three major arguments for the existence of God—the Cosmological, the Design, and the Ontological—only the last of these is entirely *a priori*. In the Cosmological Argument one starts from some simple fact about the world, such as that it contains things which are caused to exist by other things. In the Design Argument a somewhat more complicated fact about the world serves as a starting point, the fact that the world exhibits order and design. In the Ontological Argument, however, one begins simply with a concept of God. In this chapter we shall consider the Cosmological Argument; in the next two chapters we shall examine the Ontological Argument and the Design Argument.

Before we state the Cosmological Argument itself, we shall consider some rather general points about the argument. Historically, it can be traced to the writings of the Greek philosophers, Plato and Aristotle, but the major developments in the argument took place in the thirteenth and in the eighteenth centuries. In the thirteenth century St. Thomas Aquinas put forth five distinct arguments for the existence of God, and of these, the first three are versions of the Cosmological Argument.[1] In the first of these he started from the fact that there are things in the world undergoing change and reasoned to the conclusion that there must be some ultimate cause of change that is itself unchanging. In the second he started from the fact that there are things in the world that clearly are caused to exist by other things and reasoned to the conclusion that there must be some ultimate cause of existence whose own existence is itself uncaused. And in the third argument he started from the fact that there are things in the world which need not have existed at all, things which do exist but which we can easily imagine might not, and reasoned to the conclusion that there must be some being that had to be, that exists and could not have failed to exist. Now it might be objected that even if Aquinas' arguments do prove beyond doubt the existence of an unchanging changer, an uncaused cause, and a being that could not have failed to exist, the arguments fail to prove the existence of the theistic God. For the theistic God, as we saw, is supremely good, omnipotent, omniscient, and creator of but separate from and independent of the world. How do we know, for example, that the unchanging changer isn't evil or slightly ignorant? The answer to this objection is that the Cosmological Argument has two parts. In the first part the effort is to prove the existence of a special sort of being, for example, a being that could not have failed to exist, or a being that causes change in other things but is itself unchanging. In the second part of the argument the effort is to prove that the special sort of being whose

existence has been established in the first part has, and must have, the features—perfect goodness, omnipotence, omniscience, and so on—which go together to make up the theistic idea of God. What this means, then, is that Aquinas' three arguments are different versions of only the first part of the Cosmological Argument. Indeed, in later sections of his *Summa Theologica* Aquinas undertakes to show that the unchanging changer, the uncaused cause of existence, and the being which had to exist are one and the same being and that this single being has all of the attributes of the theistic God.

We noted above that a second major development in the Cosmological Argument took place in the eighteenth century, a development reflected in the writings of the German philosopher, Gottfried Leibniz (1646–1716), and especially in the writings of the English theologian and philosopher, Samuel Clarke (1675–1729). In 1704 Clarke gave a series of lectures, later published under the title *A Demonstration of the Being and Attributes of God.* These lectures constitute, perhaps, the most complete, forceful, and cogent presentation of the Cosmological Argument we possess. The lectures were read by the major skeptical philosopher of the century, David Hume (1711–1776), and in his brilliant attack on the attempt to justify religion in the court of reason, his *Dialogues Concerning Natural Religion,* Hume advanced several penetrating criticisms of Clarke's arguments, criticisms which have persuaded many philosophers in the modern period to reject the Cosmological Argument. In our study of the argument we shall concentrate our attention largely on its eighteenth century form and try to assess its strengths and weaknesses in the light of the criticisms which Hume and others have advanced against it.

The first part of the eighteenth-century form of the Cosmological Argument seeks to establish the existence of a self-existent being. The second part of the argument attempts to prove that the self-existent being is the theistic God, that is, has the features which we have noted to be basic elements in the theistic idea of God. We shall consider mainly the first part of the argument, for it is against the first part that philosophers from Hume to Bertrand Russell have advanced very important objections.

In stating the first part of the Cosmological Argument we shall make use of two important concepts, the concept of a *dependent being* and the concept of a *self-existent being*. By a *dependent being* we mean *a being whose existence is accounted for by the causal activity of other things*. Recalling Anseln's division into the three cases: "explained by another," "explained by nothing," and "explained by itself," it's clear that a dependent being is a being whose existence is explained by another. By *a self-existent being* we mean *a being whose existence is accounted for by its own nature*. This idea, as we saw in the preceding chapter, is an essential element in the theistic concept of God. Again, in terms of Anselm's three cases, a self-existent being is a being whose existence is explained by itself. Armed with these two concepts, the concept of a dependent being and the concept of a self-existent being, we can now state the first part of the Cosmological Argument.

1. Every being (that exists or ever did exist) is either a dependent being or a self-existent being.
2. Not every being can be a dependent being.

Therefore,

3. There exists a self-existent being.

Deductive Validity

Before we look critically at each of the premises of this argument, we should note that this argument is, to use an expression from the logician's vocabulary, *deductively valid*. To find out whether an argument is deductively valid, we need only ask the question: If its premises were true, would its conclusion have to be true? If the answer is yes, the argument is deductively valid. If the answer is no, the argument is deductively invalid. Notice that the question of the validity of an argument is entirely different from the question of whether its premises are in fact true. The following argument is made up entirely of false statements, but it is deductively valid.

1. Babe Ruth is the president of the United States.

2. The president of the United States is from Indiana.

Therefore,

3. Babe Ruth is from Indiana.

The argument is deductively valid because even though its premises are false, if they were true its conclusion would have to be true. Even God, Aquinas would say, cannot bring it about that the premises of this argument are true and yet its conclusion is false, for God's power extends only to what is possible, and it is an absolute impossibility that Babe Ruth be the president, the president be from Indiana, and yet Babe Ruth not be from Indiana.

The Cosmological Argument (that is, its first part) is a deductively valid argument. If its premises are or were true, its conclusion would have to be true. It's clear from our example about Babe Ruth, however, that the fact that an argument is deductively valid is insufficient to establish the truth of its conclusion. What else is required? Clearly that we know or have rational grounds for believing that the premises are true. If we know that the Cosmological Argument is deductively valid, and can establish that its premises are true, we shall thereby have proved that its conclusion is true. Are, then, the premises of the Cosmological Argument true? To this more difficult question we must now turn.

PSR and the First Premise

At first glance the first premise might appear to be an obvious or even trivial truth. But it is neither obvious nor trivial. And if it appears to be obvious or trivial, we must be confusing the idea of a self-existent being with the idea of a being that is not a dependent being. Clearly, it is true that any being is either a dependent being (explained by other things) or it is not a dependent being (not explained by other things). But what our premise says is that any being is either a dependent being (explained by other things) or it is a self-existent being (explained by itself). Consider again Anselm's three cases.

a. explained by another
b. explained by nothing
c. explained by itself

What our first premise asserts is that each being that exists (or ever did exist) is either of sort *a* or of sort *c*. It denies that any being is of sort *b*. And it is this denial that makes the first premise both significant and controversial. The obvious truth we must not confuse it with is the truth that any being is either of sort *a* or not of sort *a*. While this is true it is neither very significant nor controversial.

Earlier we saw that Anselm accepted as a basic principle that whatever exists has an explanation of its existence. Since this basic principle denies that any thing of sort *b* exists or ever did exist, it's clear that Anselm would believe the first premise of our Cosmological Argument. The eighteenth-century proponents of the argument also were convinced of the truth of the basic principle we attributed to Anselm. And because they were convinced of its truth, they readily accepted the first premise of the Cosmological Argument. But by the eighteenth century, Anselm's basic principle had been more fully elaborated and had received a name, the *Principle of Sufficient Reason*. Since this principle (PSR, as we shall call it) plays such an important role in justifying the premises of the Cosmological Argument, it will help us to consider it for a moment before we continue our enquiry into the truth or falsity of the premises of the Cosmological Argument.

PSR, as it was expressed by both Leibniz and Clarke, is a very general principle and is best understood as having two parts. In its first part it is simply a restatement of Anselm's principle that there must be an explanation of the *existence* of any being whatever. Thus if we come upon a man in a room, PSR implies that there must be an explanation of the fact that that particular man exists. A moment's reflection, however, reveals that there are many facts about the man other than the mere fact that he exists. There is the fact that the man in question is in the room he's in, rather than somewhere else, the fact that he is in good health, and the fact that he is at the moment thinking of Paris, rather than, say, London. Now, the purpose of the second part of PSR is to require an explanation of these facts, as well. We may state PSR, therefore, as the principle that *there must be an explanation (a) of the existence of any being, and (b) of any positive fact whatever*. We are now in a position to study the role this very important principle plays in the Cosmological Argument.

Since the proponent of the Cosmological Argument accepts PSR in both its parts, it is clear that he will appeal to its first part, PSRa, as justification for the first premise of the Cosmological Argument. Of course, we can and should enquire into the deeper question of whether the proponent of the argument is rationally justified in accepting PSR itself. But we shall put this question aside for the moment. What we need to see first is whether he is correct in thinking that *if* PSR is true then both of the premises of the Cosmological Argument are true. And what we have just seen is that if only the first part of PSR, that is, PSRa, is true, the first premise of the Cosmological Argument will be true. But what of the second premise of the argument? For what reasons does the proponent think that it must be true?

The Second Premise

According to the second premise, not every being that exists can be a dependent being, that is, can have the explanation of its existence in some other being or beings. Presumably, the proponent of the argument thinks there is something fundamentally wrong with the idea that every being that exists is dependent, that each existing being was caused by some other being which in turn was caused by some other being, and so on. But just what does he think is wrong with it? To help us in understanding his thinking, let's simplify things by supposing that there exists only one thing now, A_1, a living thing perhaps, that was brought into existence by something else, A_2, which perished shortly after it brought A_1, into existence. Suppose further that A_2, was brought into existence in similar fashion some time ago by A_3, and A_3 by A_4, and so forth back into the past. Each of these beings is *a dependent* being, it owes its existence to the preceding thing in the series. Now if nothing else ever existed but these beings, then what the second premise says would not be true. For if every being that exists or ever did exist is an *A* and was produced by a preceding *A*, then every being that exists or ever did exist would be dependent and, accordingly, premise two of the Cosmological Argument would be false. If the proponent of the Cosmological Argument is correct, there must, then, be something wrong with the idea that every being that exists or did exist is an *A* and that they form a causal series. A_1 caused by A_2, A_2 caused by A_3, A_3 caused by A_4, . . . A_n caused by A_{n+1}. How does the proponent of the Cosmological Argument propose to show us that there is something wrong with this view?

A popular but mistaken idea of how the proponent tries to show that something is wrong with the view, that every being might be dependent, is that he uses the following argument to reject it.

1. There must be a *first* being to start any causal series.
2. If every being were dependent there would be no *first* being to start the causal series.

Therefore,

3. Not every being can be a dependent being.

Although this argument is deductively valid, and its second premise is true, its first premise overlooks the distinct possibility that a causal series might be *infinite,* with no first member at all. Thus if we go back to our series of *A* beings, where each *A* is dependent, having been produced by the preceding *A* in the causal series, it's clear that if the series existed it would have no first member, for every *A* in the series there would be a preceding *A* which produced it, *ad infinitum.* The first premise of the argument just given assumes that a causal series must stop with a first member somewhere in the distant past. But there seems to be no good reason for making that assumption.

The eighteenth-century proponents of the Cosmological Argument recognized that the causal series of dependent beings could be infinite, without a first member to start the series. They rejected the idea that every being that is or ever was is dependent not because there would then be no first member to the series of dependent beings, but because there would then be no explanation for the fact that there are and have always been dependent beings. To see their reasoning let's return to our simplification of the supposition that the only things that exist or ever did exist are dependent beings. In our simplification of that supposition only one of the dependent beings exists at a time, each one perishing as it produces the next in the series. Perhaps the first thing to note about this supposition is that there is no individual *A* in the causal series of dependent beings whose existence is unexplained—A_1 is explained by A_2, A_2 by A_3, and A_n by A_{n+1}. So the first part of PSR, PSRa, appears to be satisfied. There is no particular being whose existence lacks an explanation. What, then, is it that lacks an explanation, if every particular *A* in the causal series of dependent beings has an explanation? It is the *series itself* that lacks an explanation. Or, as I've chosen to express it, *the fact that there are and have always been dependent beings.* For suppose we ask why it is that there are and have always been *A*s in existence. It won't do to say that *A*s have always been producing other *A*s—we can't explain why there have always been *A*s by saying there always have been *A*s. Nor, on the supposition that only *A*s have ever existed, can we explain the fact that there have always been *A*s by appealing to something other than an *A*—for no such thing would have existed. Thus the supposition that the only things that exist or ever existed are dependent things leaves us with a fact for which there can be no explanation; namely, the fact that there are dependent beings rather than not.

Questioning the Justification of the Second Premise

Critics of the Cosmological Argument have raised several important objections against the claim that if every being is dependent the series or collection of those beings would have no explanation. Our understanding of the Cosmological Argument, as well as of its strengths and weaknesses, will be deepened by a careful consideration of these criticisms.

The first criticism is that the proponent of the Cosmological Argument makes the mistake of treating the collection or series of dependent beings as though it were itself a dependent being, and, therefore, requires an explanation of its existence. But, so the objection goes, the collection of dependent beings is not itself a dependent being any more than a collection of stamps is itself a stamp.

A second criticism is that the proponent makes the mistake of inferring that because each member of the collection of dependent beings has a cause, the collection itself must have a cause.

But, as Russell noted, such reasoning is as fallacious as to infer that the human race (that is, the collection of human beings) must have a mother because each member of the collection (each human being) has a mother.

A third criticism is that the proponent of the argument fails to realize that for there to be an explanation of a collection of things is nothing more than for there to be an explanation of each of the things making up the collection. Since in the infinite collection (or series) of dependent beings, each being in the collection does have an explanation—by virtue of having been caused by some preceding member of the collection—the explanation of the collection, so the criticism goes, has already been given. As Hume remarked, "Did I show you the particular causes of each individual in a collection of twenty particles of matter, I should think it very unreasonable, should you afterwards ask me, what was the cause of the whole twenty. This is sufficiently explained in explaining the cause of the parts."[2]

Finally, even if the proponent of the Cosmological Argument can satisfactorily answer these objections, he must face one last objection to his ingenious attempt to justify premise two of the Cosmological Argument. For someone may agree that if nothing exists but an infinite collection of dependent beings, the infinite collection will have no explanation of its existence, and still refuse to conclude from this that there is something wrong with the idea that every being is a dependent being. Why, the proponent of the Cosmological Argument might ask, should we think that everything has to have an explanation? What's wrong with admitting that the fact that there are and have always been dependent beings is a *brute fact*, a fact having no explanation whatever? Why does everything have to have an explanation anyway? We must now see what can be said in response to these several objections.

Responses to Criticism

It is certainly a mistake to think that a collection of stamps is itself a stamp, and very likely a mistake to think that the collection of dependent beings is itself a dependent being. But the mere fact that the proponent of the argument thinks that there must be an explanation not only for each member of the

collection of dependent beings but for the collection itself is not sufficient grounds for concluding that he must view the collection as itself a dependent being. The collection of human beings, for example, is certainly not itself a human being. Admitting this, however, we might still seek an explanation of why there is a collection of human beings, of why there are such things as human beings at all. So the mere fact that an explanation is demanded for the collection of dependent beings is no proof that the person who demands the explanation must be supposing that the collection itself is just another dependent being.

The second criticism attributes to the proponent of the Cosmological Argument the following bit of reasoning.

1. Every member of the collection of dependent beings has a cause or explanation.

Therefore,

2. The collection of dependent beings has a cause or explanation.

As we noted in setting forth this criticism, arguments of this sort are often unreliable. It would be a mistake to conclude that a collection of objects is light in weight simply because each object in the collection is light in weight, for if there were many objects in the collection it might be quite heavy. On the other hand, if we know that each marble weighs more than one ounce, we could infer validly that the collection of marbles weighs more than an ounce. Fortunately, however, we don't need to decide whether the inference from 1 to 2 is valid or invalid. We need not decide this question because the proponent of the Cosmological Argument need not use this inference to establish that there must be an explanation of the collection of dependent beings. He need not use this inference because he has in PSR a principle from which it follows immediately that the collection of dependent beings has a cause or explanation. For according to PSR, every positive fact must have an explanation. If it is a fact that there exists a collection of dependent beings then, according to PSR, that fact too must have an explanation. So it is PSR that the proponent of the Cosmological Argument appeals to in concluding that there must be an explanation of the collection of dependent beings, and not some dubious inference from the premise that each member of the collection has an explanation. It seems, then, that neither of the first two criticisms is strong enough to do any serious damage to the reasoning used to support the second premise of the Cosmological Argument.

The third objection contends that to explain the existence of a collection of things is the same thing as to explain the existence of each of its members. If we consider a collection of dependent beings in which each being in the collection is explained by the preceding member that caused it, it's clear that no member of the collection will lack an explanation of its existence. But, so the criticism goes, if we've explained the existence of every member of a collection, we've explained the existence of the collection—there's nothing left over to be explained. This forceful criticism, originally advanced by Hume, has gained considerable support in the modern period. But the criticism rests on an assumption that the proponent of the Cosmological Argument would not accept. The assumption is that to explain the existence of a collection of things it is *sufficient* to explain the existence of every member in the collection. To see what is wrong with this assumption is to understand the basic issue in the reasoning by which the proponent of the Cosmological Argument seeks to establish that not every being can be a dependent being.

In order for there to be an explanation of the existence of the collection of dependent beings, it's clear that the eighteenth-century proponents would require that the following two conditions be satisfied:

C1. There is an explanation of the existence of each of the members of the collection of dependent beings.

C2. There is an explanation of why there are *any* dependent beings.

According to the proponents of the Cosmological Argument, if every being that exists or ever did exist is a dependent being—that is, if the whole of reality consists of nothing more than a collection of dependent beings—C1 will be satisfied, but C2 will not be satisfied. And since C2 won't be satisfied, there will be no explanation of the collection of dependent beings. The third criticism, therefore, says in effect that if C1 is satisfied, C2 will be satisfied, and, since in a collection of dependent

beings each member will have an explanation in whatever it was that produced it, C1 will be satisfied. So, therefore, C2 will be satisfied and the collection of dependent beings will have an explanation.

Although the issue is a complicated one, I think it is possible to see that the third criticism rests on a mistake: the mistake of thinking that if C1 is satisfied C2 must also be satisfied. The mistake is a natural one to make for it is easy to imagine circumstances in which if C1 is satisfied C2 also will be satisfied. Suppose, for example, that the whole of reality includes not just a collection of dependent beings but also a self-existent being. Suppose further that instead of each dependent being having been produced by some other dependent being, every dependent being was produced by the self-existent being. Finally, let us consider both the possibility that the collection of dependent beings is finite in time and has a first member, and the possibility that the collection of dependent beings is infinite in past time, having no first member. Using G for the self-existent being, the first possibility may be diagramed as follows:

G, we shall say, has always existed and always will. We can think of d_1 as some presently existing dependent being, d_2, d_3, and so forth as dependent beings that existed at some time in the past, and d_n as the first dependent being to exist. The second possibility may be portrayed as follows:

On this diagram there is no first member of the collection of dependent beings. Each member of the infinite collection, however, is explained by reference to the self-existent being G which produced it. Now the interesting point about both these cases is that the explanation that has been provided for the members of the collection of dependent beings carries with it, at least in part, an answer to the question of why there are any dependent beings at all. In both cases we may explain why there are dependent

beings by pointing out that there exists a self-existent being that has been engaged in producing
them. So once we have learned that the existence of
each member of the collection of dependent beings
has its existence explained by the fact that G produced it, we have already learned why there are
dependent beings.

Someone might object that we haven't really
learned why there are dependent beings until we
also learn *why* G has been producing them. But, of
course, we could also say that we haven't really
explained the existence of a particular dependent
being, say d_3, until we also learn not just that G
produced it but *why* G produced it. The point we
need to grasp, however, is that once we admit that
every dependent being's existence is explained by
G, we must admit that the fact that there are
dependent beings has also been explained. So it is
not unnatural that someone should think that to
explain the existence of the collection of dependent beings is nothing more than to explain the
existence of its members. For, as we've seen, to
explain the collection's existence is to explain each
member's existence and to explain why there are
any dependent beings at all. And in the examples
we've considered, in doing the one (explaining
why each dependent being exists) we've already
done the other (explained why there are any
dependent beings at all). We must now see, however, that on the supposition that the whole of
reality consists *only* of a collection of dependent
beings, to give an explanation of each member's
existence is not to provide an explanation of why
there are dependent beings.

In the examples we've considered, we have
gone *outside* of the collection of dependent beings
in order to explain the members' existence. But if
the only beings that exist or ever existed are
dependent beings then each dependent being will
be explained by some other dependent being, ad
infinitum. This does not mean that there will be
some particular dependent being whose existence
is unaccounted for. Each dependent being has an
explanation of its existence; namely, in the dependent being which preceded it and produced it. So
C1 is satisfied: there is an explanation of the existence of each member of the collection of dependent beings. Turning to C2, however, we can see
that it will not be satisfied. We cannot explain why
there are (or have ever been) dependent beings by

appealing to all the members of the infinite collection of dependent beings. For if the question to be
answered is why there are (or have ever been) any
dependent beings at all, we cannot answer that
question by noting that there always have been
dependent beings, each one accounting for the
existence of some other dependent being. Thus on
the supposition that every being is dependent, it
seems there will be no explanation of why there
are dependent beings. C2 will not be satisfied.
Therefore, on the supposition that every being is
dependent there will be no explanation of the existence of the collection of dependent beings.

The Truth of PSR

We come now to the final criticism of the reasoning
supporting the second premise of the Cosmological
Argument. According to this criticism, it is admitted that the supposition that every being is dependent implies that there will be a *brute fact* in the
universe, a fact, that is, for which there can be no
explanation whatever. For there will be no explanation of the fact that dependent beings exist and
have always been in existence. It is this brute fact
that the proponents of the argument were describing when they pointed out that if every being is
dependent, the series or collection of dependent
beings would lack an explanation of *its* existence.
The final criticism asks what is wrong with admitting that the universe contains such a brute, unintelligible fact. In asking this question the critic
challenges the fundamental principle, PSR, on
which the Cosmological Argument rests. For, as
we've seen, the first premise of the argument denies
that there exits a being whose existence has no
explanation. In support of this premise the proponent appeals to the first part of PSR. The second
premise of the argument claims that not every
being can be dependent. In support of this premise
the proponent appeals to the second part of PSR,
the part which states that there must be an explanation of any positive fact whatever.

The proponent reasons that if every being
were a dependent being, then although the first
part of PSR would be satisfied—every being would
have an explanation—the second part would be
violated; there would be no explanation for the
positive fact that there are and have always been

dependent beings. For first, since every being is supposed to be dependent, there would be nothing outside of the collection of dependent beings to explain the collection's existence. Second, the fact that each member of the collection has an explanation in some other dependent being is insufficient to explain why there are and have always been dependent beings. And, finally, there is nothing about the collection of dependent beings that would suggest that it is a self-existent collection. Consequently, if every being were dependent, the fact that there are and have always been dependent beings would have no explanation. But this violates the second part of PSR. So the second premise of the Cosmological Argument must be true: Not every being can be a dependent being. This conclusion, however, is no better than the principle, PSR, on which it rests. And it is the point of the final criticism to question the truth of PSR. Why, after all, should we accept the idea that every being and every positive fact must have an explanation? Why, in short, should we believe PSR? These are important questions, and any final judgment of the Cosmological Argument depends on how they are answered.

Most of the theologians and philosophers who accept PSR have tried to defend it in either of two ways. Some have held that PSR is (or can be) known *intuitively* to be true. By this they mean that if we fully understand and reflect on what is said by PSR we can see that it must be true. Now, undoubtedly, there are statements which are known intuitively to be true. "Every triangle has exactly three angles" or "No physical object can be in two different places in space at one and the same time" are examples of statements whose truth we can apprehend just by understanding and reflecting on them. The difficulty with the claim that PSR is known intuitively to be true, however, is that a number of very able philosophers fail on careful reflection to apprehend its truth, and some have developed serious arguments for the conclusion that the principle is in fact false.[3] It is clear, therefore, that not everyone who has reflected on PSR has been persuaded that it is true, and some are persuaded that there are good reasons to think it is false. But while the fact that some able thinkers fail to apprehend the truth of PSR, and may even argue that it is false, is a decisive reason to believe that PSR is not so obvious a truth as say,

"No physical object can be in two different places in space at one and the same time," it falls short of establishing that PSR is not a truth of reason. Here, perhaps, all that one can do is carefully reflect on what PSR says and form one's own judgment on whether it is a fundamental truth about the way reality must be. And if after carefully reflecting on PSR it does strike one in that way, that person may well be rationally justified in taking it to be true and, having seen how it supports the premises of the Cosmological Argument, accepting the conclusion of that argument as true.

The second way philosophers and theologians who accept PSR have sought to defend it is by claiming that although it may not be known to be true, it is, nevertheless, a presupposition of reason, a basic assumption that rational people make, whether or not they reflect sufficiently to become aware of the assumption. It's probably true that there are some assumptions we all make about our world, assumptions which are so basic that most of us are unaware of them. And, I suppose, it might be true that PSR is such an assumption. What bearing would this view of PSR have on the Cosmological Argument? Perhaps the main point to note is that even if PSR is a presupposition we all share, the premises of the Cosmological Argument could still be false. For PSR itself could still be false. The fact, if it is a fact, that all of us *presuppose* that every existing being and every positive fact has an explanation does not imply that no being exists, and no positive fact obtains, without an explanation. Nature is not bound to satisfy our presuppositions. As the American philosopher William James once remarked in another connection, "In the great boarding house of nature, the cakes and the butter and the syrup seldom come out so even and leave the plates so clean."

Our study of the first part of the Cosmological Argument has led us to the fundamental principle on which its premises rest, the Principle of Sufficient Reason. We've seen that unless, on thoughtful reflection, PSR strikes us as something we see with certainty to be true, we cannot reasonably claim to know that the premises of the Cosmological Argument are true. Of course, they might be true. But unless we do know them to be true they cannot *establish* for us the conclusion that there exists a being that has the explanation of its existence within its own nature.

If it were shown, however, that even though we do not *know* that PSR is true we all, nevertheless, *presuppose* PSR to be true, then, whether PSR is true or not, to be consistent we should accept the Cosmological Argument. For, as we've seen, its premises imply its conclusion and its premises do seem to follow from PSR. But no one has succeeded in *showing* that PSR is an assumption that most or all of us share. So our final conclusion must be that, with the exception of those who, on thoughtful reflection, reasonably conclude that PSR is a fundamental truth of reason, the Cosmological Argument does not provide us with good rational grounds for believing that among those beings that exist, there is one whose existence is accounted for by its own nature. And since the classical conception of God is of a being whose existence is accounted for by its own nature, apart from the exception noted, the Cosmological Argument fails to provide us with good rational grounds for believing that God exists.

Endnotes

[1]St. Thomas Aquinas, *Summa Theologica*, 1a. 2, 3, in *The Basic Writings of Saint Thomas Aquinas,* ed. Anton C. Pegis (New York Random House, 1945).

[2]David Hume, *Dialogues Concerning Natural Religion*, pt. IX, ed. H. D. Aiken (New York Hafner Publishing Company, 1948), pp. 59–60.

[3]For a brief account of two of these arguments see the preface to my *The Cosmological Argument* (New York Fordham University Press, 1998).

51. *The "Inductive" Argument from Evil: A Dialogue*

BRUCE RUSSELL AND STEPHEN WYKSTRA

In *Meditation IV* (see Chapter 49), Descartes discusses what is called the logical or "deductive" problem of evil. The logical problem of evil attempts to prove that the existence of God and the existence of evil or error are incompatible and that since there certainly is evil in the world it follows that God does not exist. In the following selection the authors debate the so-called evidential or "inductive" argument from evil. According to this argument, it is not the mere existence that casts doubt on the existence of God, but rather that the existence of what *appears* to be pointless and gratuitous evil. If God exists, He would have prevented such evils from happening, but since He didn't, the inference is that God does not exist. But are some horrendous moral and natural evils *really* pointless? Perhaps if we looked carefully enough we would be able to find the "sufficient good" that is served by allowing this bad thing to occur. Furthermore, is *seeing* no good really evidence that there *is* no such good? The moral depth of the universe might render our knowledge of God's purposes inscrutable. Finally, even if the evidence suggests that there is no good that outweighs the evil; perhaps there is evidence for the existence of God sufficient to balance the negative evidence. These questions are explored in the dialogue by Russell and Wykstra. Bruce Russell is a professor of philosophy at Wayne State University and Stephen Wykstra is a professor of philosophy at Calvin College.

    The following is a conversation between Beatrice Leaver, Athea Ist, and Agnes Tic. Bea and Athea teach philosophy—Bea at a Christian college, and Athea, at a large midwestern university. Agnes is an attorney. Now in their thirties, the women were suitemates in college, together with Iris.

Iris has just lost her six-year old daughter. Bea and Athea have flown to Flint to be with her. They stay with Agnes, who has remained closest to Iris. It is early evening, the day after the burial. Iris, severely depressed, has been hospitalized under medication. Bea and Athea are talking with Agnes in her house.

1. *Evening*
1.1 In Agnes's living room.

ATHEA: I still don't understand how it happened, Agnes. Could you go over it again?

AGNES: Well, here are the essentials. Iris divorced Bo eight months ago, and after Iris met Jim, Bo went over the edge. New Year's Eve, Iris was at the local pub with Jim. Bo came in, and got so abusive he was thrown out. When Jim dropped Iris off, Bo was waiting inside. He threatened her, but Iris took a swing at him and somehow knocked him out. She left him on the floor and went to bed. At 3:45 the brother came in and found Carrie's body. She'd been beaten over most of her body and strangled to death. Bo was arrested, and Iris thinks he did it. She thinks he tried angel dust again that night.

ATHEA: It's all so hard to believe. How is Iris taking it?

AGNES: I'm afraid for her, Athea. She blames herself for not calling the police while Bo was unconscious. She kept saying she couldn't go on living if she didn't believe in a loving God—that "all things work together for good to those who love God." This, for good? To me it is blackness. I keep thinking of Carrie's innocent eyes . . . and I don't know whether Iris can recover again. You know how Carrie's been the center of her life ever since her first husband died.

   And I can't get rid of the thought that this just shouldn't happen. Remember how, when we were seniors, I stopped believing in God? Well, now and then I've wondered if maybe the folks at home weren't right after all; last fall I even tried going to church again. But this thing—I can't see

From Bruce Russell and Stephen Wykstra, "The 'Inductive' Argument from Evil: A Dialogue," *Philosophical Topics*, 16, No. 2 (Fall 1988): 133–60. Reprinted by permission.

how a God could allow it. Of course, I wouldn't say that to Iris. But I've wanted to talk about it with someone. I even dug out my old philosophy book and read an article by an Oxford philosopher named Mackie. Now it hits home.

BEA AND ATHEA *(simultaneously)*: What do you mean?

AGNES *(with a wry smile)*: I'd almost forgotten both of you teach philosophy. Remember our ethics prof? "What exactly do you mean?", he'd ask. Carrie's death makes me think maybe he was right; he claimed that evils like this conclusively prove that there's no God—none like the Baptists believe in, anyhow.

[Athea and Bea are silent.]

AGNES: I know it seems weird, but last night I actually worked out an argument, hoping we could talk like we used to in college. Maybe it's because, not knowing what I believe, I had no words to offer Iris; I could only sit and cry with her. Or maybe I'm using intellectual analysis as a sedative, to escape the pain of these past days.

BEA: Agnes, I don't think there *are* words for a time like this. Saint Paul says "Weep with those who weep"; perhaps your tears were far better than any words could be. But if you think some intellectual analysis will be a respite—well, there are much worse ways of escaping.

ATHEA *(staring into her glass of wine)*: That's for sure. Maybe talking will keep us from drowning in this stuff. Let's hear your proof, Agnes.

AGNES: Okay. I started with two simple ideas. The first is that if God is all-good, as Christians say, he has to be *against* intense suffering, just as a good mother is against her child's suffering. I mean, a good mother does sometimes *allow* her child to suffer greatly—say, by having a tonsilectomy. But she doesn't *like* this suffering, and she's not indifferent about it, either; she's *against* it, in itself. So she would allow it only if this served some purpose—only if she thought this served some sufficient good. And isn't that also true for a good God? To allow such suffering for no purpose would mean God is either indifferent to it, or actually likes it for its own sake. And that would mean he's not wholly good.

Then I tried to clarify what it is to "serve some sufficient good." I saw that it's not enough for allowing the suffering to produce the good. Some painful surgery might produce some good result—but suppose there were some way to get this good equally well, but without the suffering. Some "Plan B," I'll call it. Wouldn't a morally good person have to use the Plan B? And isn't the same true of God, if he is good? I think so. So I wrote:

> If God exists, then (being all-good) he would not allow any instance of intense suffering unless doing so served some sufficient good, and there were no "Plan B"—no equally good way to get this good without such suffering.

From there it was simple logic. God is supposed to be omnipotent, so he can do anything. But then he would always have a "Plan B." It follows, doesn't it, that if God exists, he would not allow any instance of suffering, so no suffering would occur. But it does occur. So it follows that God doesn't exist. It looks like I should give up my indecisive agnosticism and embrace atheism.

ATHEA: You've certainly remembered your logic lessons well, Agnes. But there is a problem with one of your premises. Theism does hold that God is omnipotent, but as some theists explain it, this means that he can do anything power can do. And as Aquinas said, power cannot do self-contradictory things, like make square circles. So even though the theistic God is omnipotent, he might, to obtain certain goods, *have to* allow certain evils. That's the idea behind the "Free Will Defense"—to have creatures with real moral freedom, God has to allow the possibility of the creature choosing evil.

AGNES: I see what you mean. But Athea, you believe that there is no God. Do you have some better argument against theism?

ATHEA: I think so. But it's nearly seven; let's continue over dinner. Shall we go to the Indian restaurant again?

1.2 At the House of India

AGNES: So what is *your* reasoning, Athea?

ATHEA: Like you, Agnes, I believe that a good God would not allow evils like Carrie's death unless doing so served some "sufficient good," as you called it. And I, too, tried to prove there *couldn't* be any such good. But now I think that's the wrong approach. The important thing is the obvious thing: no matter how hard we look, we don't *see* any sufficient good. This itself gives us good reason to believe there is no such good—and hence, no God.

AGNES: But isn't that the "fallacy" of arguing from ignorance? Isn't it like concluding that there is no life on other planets, since we don't know of any?

ATHEA: No, I'm not arguing from our ignorance but from our knowledge. We know of particular evils like Carrie's murder. We also know of many good things, and when we reflect on them, we see that none of them is "God-justifying" with respect to this particular evil. This knowledge that all the goods we *know* of are "non-God-justifying" gives us good reason to think that *all* goods are non-God-justifying. This is an inductive inference of the sort we rely on all the time. For example, that we know of no copper that is insulative gives us good reason to believe that no copper is insulative. That we see no elephant in this room gives us good reason to think there *is* no elephant in the room. These aren't arguments from ignorance; neither is mine.

AGNES: So your argument isn't meant as proof giving 100% certainty, but as inductive evidence justifying a high degree of confidence. Is that what you mean by "good reason"?

ATHEA: Exactly. And because my evidence doesn't give 100% certainty, it could be outweighed if there were enough evidence that God does exist. But I don't think there is. So on the basis of my inductive evidence, I think reason requires us to believe that there is no God-justifying purpose for certain evils, and hence, that God does not exist.

AGNES: That sounds plausible to me. But our philosophy prof always said we should test arguments by seeing if they can survive serious objections. So let's do that with yours. It would be nice if we could write it out premise by premise. Unfortunately we don't have any paper . . .

ATHEA: No problem—philosophers write on whatever is at hand, so I'll just use this napkin. My central argument is this:

(P1) Carrie's murder was, in itself, a very bad thing.
(P2) If there was no sufficiently good point served by allowing this very bad thing to happen, then God, if he exists, would have prevented it.
(P3) There was no sufficiently good point served by allowing this very bad thing.
(C1) Therefore, if God exists, he would have prevented this thing from happening.
(P4) God did not prevent this thing from happening (since it did happen).
(C2) Therefore, God does not exist.

Now premises 1 and 4 seem beyond dispute. And we've already agreed on premise 2 in discussing your argument, Agnes. So the only premise to worry about is P3. And the heart of my case is that we can defend P3 *inductively.* Since this will be a subargument for P3, I'll write it using lower case indices. Bea, could you pass that napkin?

(p1) After careful reflection, we see no good point served by allowing this bad thing to occur.
(p2) If, after careful reflection, we see no sufficiently good point served by allowing some bad thing to occur, then we have some reason to believe there is no sufficiently good point served by allowing it to occur.
(c1) Therefore, we have some reason to believe there is no sufficiently good point served by allowing it to occur.
(p3) We have no outweighing reason to believe the contrary (that there is a sufficiently good point served by allowing this evil).
(p4) If we have some reason to. believe some proposition, and no decent reasons to believe the contrary, then on

balance, reason requires us to believe that proposition.
(c2) Therefore, reason requires us to believe that there is no sufficiently good point served by allowing this bad thing to occur.

(Athea slides the napkin to Bea and Agnes]: Voila!
AGNES: I see what you're doing. You first conclude, at c1, that your inductive evidence gives *some* reason to believe P3 of your main argument. You then infer, at c2, that since there is no evidence to outweigh this reason, we are rationally required to believe P3. Bea, what do you think about this?

BEA: Interesting—by stating her inductive principles as premises p2 and p4, the subargument for P3 has become a deductively valid argument. As you know, I believe in God. Since I reject the conclusion, I've got to look for some false premise, and I think the problem must lie in this subargument from our *not seeing* any God-justifying good. It reminds of those bugs we have here: though you feel their bite, they are so small you can't see 'em, so they're called "*noseeums.*" I'd like to baptize Athea's subargument the "noseeum argument." And I see three things to scrutinize in it.

First, we might scrutinize p1. Don't we see *any* good that might justify God in allowing this evil? What about free will? But suppose that doesn't work, and we see no other sufficient good. We must then look carefully at p2. Is *seeing* no good really evidence that there *is* no such good? Perhaps this "inductive" inference is fallacious in some way. If neither of these work, we might challenge p3. Even if Athea has given us some evidence there is no such good, can't we find positive evidence outweighing this? Evidence that God exists would be evidence that there is some such good even though we don't see it. Are we so sure there isn't evidence for God sufficient to balance Athea's negative evidence?

AGNES: Well, I want to discuss each of them, even if it takes all night. When else will I be able to talk with two philosophers like you? But why don't we pay the tab and go down the street—there's a place called "Mother's" that has absolutely sinful desserts.

1.3 At Mother's

AGNES: Let's begin with p1, then. Bea, what good might justify God's allowing a thing like Carrie's murder? As a Christian, surely you think you see something explaining it.

BEA: Be careful with the "surely" there, Agnes. Christians don't claim *they* are omniscient. But some theists do propose some possible goods that might do the job. In the case of a *moral* evil, like this brutal murder, human choice is clearly involved. On one view, God sets before us options for good and evil, and, to some extent, leaves it *up to us* which we choose. He has placed us in a world in which our choices make real differences, not just to ourselves but to others: whether others flourish or perish is, in many ways, up to us. Isn't it a good thing that we have this kind of significant freedom, and a world in which it can be meaningfully exercised?

AGNES: I suppose it is a good thing. And it does seem that this freedom would be compromised if God always stopped moral evils from occurring. Suppose he made bullets vaporize before they struck humans—or made everyone like superwoman, with no kryptonite around. Then our world would be one in which we could not choose to hurt another. Perhaps we could form intentions to hurt others, but we'd soon learn we couldn't ever carry them out. But then we'd lack freedom. So if God wants a world with this good of freedom in it, doesn't he clearly *have* to allow evils resulting from free choices, including the evil of Carrie's being murdered? What do you say to that, Athea?

ATHEA: Even if I grant that moral freedom is a good thing, there are problems. Couldn't an omnipotent God make us so we are free, but always freely choose to do right? This doesn't seem a contradiction—some Christians even believe that angels like Gabriel are like this. Couldn't Omnipotence make us all like Gabriel? If not, is freedom to *hurt* others really worth the price tag? Like Dostoevsky's "Grand Inquisitor," I'm not sure such freedom is worth the torment of one little child like Carrie.

If these problems are solved, the biggest problem remains. For it would just mean that God, to have such freedom in his universe, must *sometimes* allow moral evils. Not that he'd *always* have to allow them. A mother, to teach her daughter responsibility, must *sometimes* allow what results from her wrong choices. But she needn't *always* do this: she could still intervene *sometimes* to prevent dreadful catastrophes. Similarly, obtaining moral freedom doesn't require God *always* to allow moral evils. So this good doesn't clearly explain, or justify, his allowing the moral evil of Carrie's being murdered.

BEA: I tend to agree. Theists, unlike eighteenth-century deists, believe God is active in his creation. He's not a clockmaker who made the world and left it to run on its own. As a theist, I think that God does *sometimes* intervene to prevent moral evils. It is only his doing this *always* that would destroy freedom.

AGNES: So Athea, how does this help you? We've agreed that if God exists, he will sometimes intervene to reduce evil. So what? In concluding that God doesn't exist, are you supposing that such interventions never occur? What evidence is there for that? Maybe Bo was first going to kill the whole family, and God intervened by helping Iris to knock him out. Bo is no midget, you know.

BEA: No, Agnes; remember how this issue arose. The question was whether we see any good that would justify God's allowing this evil. *You* suggested that to have the good of freedom, God *clearly had to* allow Carrie's murder. This, Athea is saying, falsely assumes that our having freedom requires *no* interventions from God. For we've agreed that God can *sometimes* intervene without destroying this good of freedom.

ATHEA: Thanks, Bea. I see why your students are never sure whose side you are on. But you're exactly right. To see moral freedom as a good justifying God's allowing Carrie's murder, we would have to see that his intervention on *that* occasion would have compromised this good. My argument is that we don't see that at all. In fact, I think (though my argument doesn't demand this) that we see the contrary. If Iris's knocking Bo out the first time (with or without Divine assistance) didn't compromise his freedom, it sure seems that stopping him one more time wouldn't either.

AGNES: Wait a minute. I just remembered a principle from my ethics class. It was that similar cases must be judged similarly. If, under certain circumstances, I should keep a promise, then under similar circumstances, you should too. If one sees no relevant differences in the circumstances, fairness requires there be no difference in one's judgment about what should be done. So if we accept your claim that God should intervene to prevent Bo from carrying out his murderous intention on *this* occasion, won't you have to say that about the *next* occasion too? And so also for the *next* occasion. But that would mean he should *always* so intervene, which you granted is false, for that *would* destroy freedom. Doesn't this refute your claim? Or do you reject the principle about judging similar cases similarly?

ATHEA: No, I don't reject the principle: if the circumstances aren't different, the judgment shouldn't be either. But we need a broad enough notion of "circumstances." If drunk drivers are killing people, it might be right for the police to test randomly selected motorists at checkpoints, but not right to test everyone. One might think that this violates your principle: isn't stopping one like stopping another? Not really. There might be a certain threshold number of people stopped, such that as you pass that threshold you start getting bad effects—say, causing long delays, so that drivers get hostile and cause more accidents than drunkards. The number of drivers you've already checked can be *part* of the circumstances in deciding whether to check one more driver. So you might rightly *not* stop one more driver, because as you reach that threshold, the circumstances *are* different.

So also with divine interventions. It might be right for God (if he existed) sometimes to prevent a person's evil actions, but after a certain number of interventions, a threshold may be reached where further interventions would have very bad effects—say, the person feeling that he lacks real freedom of action. As that "freedom threshold" is reached, it might not be right for God to intervene once more.

BEA: That seems sensible to me, Athea. I would also apply it to God's intervening to prevent "natural evils," due to accidents and the like. The real problem now seems to be this. You allow that to have the good of moral freedom, there are "free-

dom thresholds" which, once reached, would justify God's *allowing* moral evils of murder and the like. But you don't think this good justifies God's allowing this evil of Carrie's death. So you must be supposing the "freedom threshold" has not been reached in this case. What reason is there to suppose that?

AGNES: Can I suggest one? Suppose you were a cop and you saw the little girl being brutalized by someone. Would you have thought: "Well, I've got to be careful; maybe one more intervention will cross some threshold, making the person feel he lacks choice, so he doesn't try to be good any more than I try to fly?" Of course not. If anyone proposed this as an excuse for *your* not intervening, you'd dismiss it as ludicrous. Why should we take it more seriously as an excuse for *God's* not intervening?

BEA: I once heard a similar argument from a philosopher named David Conway. At first it seemed quite compelling. But then I read *The Existence of God* by Richard Swinburne. Swinburne criticizes the assumption that since we'd have a duty to stop something, so would God. There is, he says, no reason to think God is in the same position as we are. For one thing, if God exists he knows much more than we do; and differences in knowledge can make differences in duties. If someone is choking, it might be right for a doctor to cut open his throat, but wrong for me (lacking his medical knowledge or skill) to do so.

ATHEA: I agree, Bea, that one can't simply argue "from us to God." But there's a better way to interpret Conway's argument. What is important is why we think the cop should intervene: we judge that his intervening would not cross any "freedom threshold," that is, would not begin to compromise freedom in a way that produced threshold effects worse than the evil at issue. There may be some such freedom threshold, but we are confident it is not here, or we would not intervene so confidently ourselves.

Here's another idea. *Why* do we think that one more human intervention would not cross any "freedom threshold?" I think it's because we don't *see* how it would. So we are relying on a "noseeum" inference. Well, we also don't see how a further *divine* intervention would cross a "freedom threshold." So isn't a noseeum inference justified here too? Especially since God could intervene covertly, say, by waking Iris with the thought of checking the children. If the freedom threshold wouldn't have been violated by Iris's waking naturally and stopping Bo, why would it by *God's* waking her?

BEA: I don't know, Athea. I think you've put your finger on an important problem, and I don't know how to answer it. It strikes me that the problem also arises for "natural evils," and that even believers can be gripped by it.

Let me explain. We've seen that if God *always* intervened to prevent evils, certain goods might be lost. But theists believe God does *often* guide and protect us. Perhaps we've had loved ones escape tragedy by some fortunate coincidence: believers (if they are not deists) will see this as God's providential care. But what, then, if my child drowns, and wouldn't have, if the lifeguard had only turned his eyes to the corner of the pool? God averted one close call last month; couldn't he avert one more now? It seems so implausible, especially when tragedy strikes close to home. You've helped me see an important problem, and I want to think about it more.

AGNES: It makes me wonder if deism isn't the best theism after all. Your God intervenes to protect little children sometimes, but other times he must regretfully let nature take its toll on them. How does he decide? "Shall I protect this child? Careful now—I've already had to protect X children already this month." I can imagine God thinking: "The heck with this; it's too much fiddling around. I'll just make a universe and let it roll."

BEA: I can feel the pressure toward that way of thinking, though I think it's to be resisted. But for now, I will concede Athea's first premise. We do not see a good justifying God's allowing Carrie's being murdered. Maybe free will is a good justifying God's allowing this; but given Athea's threshold arguments, I don't see *how* it does so. So why don't we turn to p2 in her sub-argument? Suppose we don't see any God-justifying good for this. Is this evidence there *is* no such good?

AGNES: Why don't we continue over a brandy? There's a quiet place, the Barrister, just around the corner.

2. Night
2.1 At the Barrister: Round One.

AGNES: Now that we've got our brandies, let's turn to Athea's p2: "If, after careful reflection, we see no sufficiently good point served by allowing some bad thing to occur, then we have some reason to believe there is no sufficiently good point served by allowing it to occur." Bea, what do you have against this?

BEA: My objection has two points. First, suppose we took p2 as a general rule: our not seeing something after careful looking gives us reason to believe it's not there. Let's call this a "noseeum rule." It seems clear that as a general rule it is false: it works for some cases, but not for others. Seeing no elephant in a normal room, after looking hard, gives us good reason to believe no elephant is in the room. But suppose we wonder if a sandflea is in the room. Looking hard, we see none. Is this good reason to think none is in the room? Clearly, far less so than in the elephant case. How about a strep virus? Does seeing no strep virus give us a reason to think none is in the room? Not any reason worth mentioning, surely. So clearly, the acceptability of a noseeum rule depends on the kind of *critter* at issue. Let's call the following my "expectability principle." If the critter has low "seeability"—if it is the kind of critter that, under the circumstances, you wouldn't expect to see even if it is there—then the noseeum rule is false: not seeing it is *not* evidence it's not there.

My second point is this. We want to know if Athea's noseeum data is evidence that God doesn't exist. At issue is whether there is some good purposed by God, justifying his allowing this murder—some "God-purposed good," let's call it. Does our seeing no such critter give us reason to think none is there? If my first point is correct, this depends upon the "seeability" of such a critter: if there is a God-purposed good for this, would it likely fall within our ken? I think we have good reason to answer "No." A God-purposed good would be more like a strep virus than an elephant. Given my first point, then, the noseeum rule is false for such goods.

AGNES: You say we have good reasons to think that if there is a God-purposed good for this, it would likely be beyond our ken. What are these good reasons?

BEA: Well, I just read one reason in the 1984 issue of the *International Journal for Philosophy of Religion,* which I happen to have with me. Here it is, on page 88, by a Stephen Wykstra:

> We must note, first, that the outweighing good at issue is of a special sort: one purposed by the Creator of all that is, whose vision and wisdom are somewhat greater than ours. How much greater? A modest proposal might be that his wisdom is to ours, roughly as an adult human being's is to a one-month old infant's. (You may adjust the ages and species to to fit your own estimate of how close our knowledge is to omniscience.) If such goods as this do exist, it might not be unlikely that we should discern some of them: even a one-month old infant can perhaps discern, in its inarticulate way, some of the purposes of his mother in her dealings with him. But if the outweighing goods of the sort at issue exist in connection with instances of suffering, that we should discern most of them seems about as likely as that a one-month old infant should discern most of his parents' purposes for those pains which they allow him to suffer. Which is to say, it is not likely at all. So for any selected instance of intense suffering, there is good reason to think that if there is an outweighing good of the sort at issue, we would not have epistemic access to this . . .

ATHEA: Pass that here, Bea. I know this article: Wykstra is criticizing a noseeum argument by William Rowe. But as I recall, it is followed by a reply from Rowe that demolishes Wykstra's argument. Here it is on page 97:

> It's true, as Wykstra observes, that God's mind can grasp goods that are beyond our ken. The idea, then, is that since God grasps goods beyond our ken, we've reason to think it likely that the goods in relation to which God permits many sufferings that occur would be unknown to us. Let's look at Wykstra's reasoning here. He starts with:
>
> 1. God's mind grasps goods beyond our ken.

moves to:

> 2. It is likely that the goods in relation to which God permits sufferings are beyond our ken.

and concludes with:

> 3. It is likely that many of the sufferings in our world do not appear to have a point—we can't see what goods justify God in permitting then.

The difficulty is that the move from (1) to (2) presupposes that the goods in question *have not occurred,* or, at the very least, that if they have occurred they, nevertheless, remain quite unknown to us (in themselves or in their connections with the suffering in our world). And, so far as I can see, the mere assumption that God exists gives us no reason to think that either of these is true. If God exists it is indeed likely, if not certain, that God's mind grasps many good states of affairs which do not obtain and which, *prior to their obtaining,* are such that we are simply unable to think of or imagine them. That much is reasonably clear. But the mere assumption that God exists gives us no reason whatever to suppose *either* that the greater goods in virtue of which he permits most sufferings are goods that come into existence far in the future of the sufferings we are aware of, *or* that once they do obtain we continue to be ignorant of them and their relation to the sufferings.

So Rowe concludes that Wykstra has not justified the claim that if God were to exist, the sufferings in our world would appear to us as they do—that is, that we would see no point to them. Wykstra's argument thus fails.

BEA: But has Rowe correctly represented Wykstra's argument? It seems to me Rowe has missed something—though perhaps Wykstra didn't spell it out sufficiently. Rowe takes Wykstra to *start* from the true claim that God, if he exists, sees goods we don't see; Rowe then objects that this fails to show that God allows present sufferings for the sake of goods we don't see. But I don't think Wykstra means to appeal just to God's superior knowledge. Look again at how he opens:

the good at issue would be "of a special sort," he says, being one *"purposed by the Creator of all that is."* This, ignored by Rowe, makes a big difference.

AGNES: How does it make a difference?

BEA: We can see it this way. First imagine a being who is good, omniscient, and has great powers of intervention, but who is *not* a Creator. He just "came upon" our universe as a brute fact, the way we did, and is hanging around being good. The mere fact that this being sees many goods we don't see—goods thousands of years in the future, for instance—may have little bearing on whether, in allowing some current suffering, this being has in mind one of these goods that are distant or otherwise unknown to us. On this Rowe seems to me to be right. But *now* add the fact that Rowe ignores: that God is *Creator* of all that is. If he exists, then as Job is reminded, he laid the very foundations of our universe: it *proceeded* from his goodness and wisdom. Adding this makes a big difference, because it raises a whole new question: if *our* universe is the *creation* of such a Being, whose wisdom is to ours as an adult's is to a one-month infant's, what should we expect on the present issue?

AGNES: I see that it makes a difference. But how big is it?

BEA: Let me get at that indirectly. We today know something about physical explanations—explanations in terms of electrons, protons, and the like. For most of history, humans didn't even have the concept of such explanation. Around 1600, Francis Bacon had *some* concept of it, but he thought that if men would only apply his experimental method, physics could, in about twenty years, get to the bottom of what causes what. He saw our universe as being, we might put it, "physically shallow"—as having bottom-line physical causes that are, relative to our cognitive abilities, quite near the observable surface. Newton, comparing his greatest discoveries to picking up shells on the ocean's shore, had a contrary view. Four hundred years of science have vindicated Newton. Having descended into a swarm of quarks, leptons, and other denizens of the microtheoretic deep, we are more astonished than ever. The "bottom-line" micro-causes of the observable world lie very deep indeed. We realize our world has extraordinary "physical depth."

Now I want to introduce a similar concept—that of "moral depth." If God exists, then as Athea says, he would allow an evil only if doing so served some outweighing good. Such a good would be the "moral (or axiological) cause" for his allowing the evil. If God exists, there is some such cause for each of his allowings of evil. But here there are two options. We might think that if our universe is the creation of God, these moral causes would likely be "near the observable surface" of their effects. This would be a "Baconian" view of the universe as morally shallow. In contrast, we might judge that if our universe is the creation of God, it would likely have great "moral depth." By this I mean that many of the goods below its puzzling observable surface, many of the moral causes of God's current allowings and intervenings, would be "deep" moral goods. The question is this: if our universe is the creation of God, is it more likely to be morally shallow or morally deep? What Wykstra means to say, I think, is that if our universe is the creation of God, a God with the sort of wisdom and vision entailed by theism, then it is eminently likely that it is morally deep rather than morally shallow. He is not, as Rowe supposes, appealing merely to the fact that God *knows* more than us. He is appealing to the fact that if this sort of God does exist, the axiological foundations of our world were laid by His wisdom and vision.

AGNES: Unless you can read Wykstra's mind, that's a lot to get out of Wykstra's opening words. But I see what you mean, and it does seem to pose a new challenge for Rowe. Athea, I'd like to hear what you think? How about another round of brandy?

2.2 At the Barrister: Round Two

ATHEA: I have a few worries about the claim that if God exists, our universe would likely have moral depth. I take it, Bea, that you mean to define a "morally deep" good so that it would likely be inscrutable to us. But if God is good, and cares about us, wouldn't he want us to be apprised of his game plan? Wouldn't he want the universe to be morally transparent (I prefer this term to "morally shallow") to sensitive creatures like ourselves?

But my main objections to Bea's moral depth line are different than Rowe's. I'm willing to grant, at least for now, that *if* God exists, it may be quite likely that our universe would be morally deep (or, as I'd call it, "morally obscure"). But even granting this, I think your case fails for very different reasons. Here I should acknowledge that I owe these objections to Bruce Russell, a close friend of mine. I think they are on target, and in letters, even Rowe seems to like them.

The first objection is this. To make your case using your expectability principle, you need to show that it is reasonable to believe that if this tragedy has a point (or serves some outweighing good giving it a point), then we would likely not see this point. But you have not shown this. All you have argued is that *if God exists,* then if (though) the suffering has a point, we likely would not see it anyway. But to show what, according to your principle, you need to show, you must now establish the antecedent—that God does exist. Otherwise you beg the question, by assuming that God does exist. Of course, I know that in this context, you don't want to have to show that God exists. In that case, what you really need to show is that it is reasonable to believe that whether God exists or not, if this tragedy serves some outweighing good, we likely would not see it. You haven't done this; that's my first objection.

BEA: There is something that confuses me here, Athea. What you grant I've shown is, it seems to me, all I need to show. But suppose we hear your second objection before examining this.

ATHEA: My second objection is that your expectability principle is false. I shall give what I think is a decisive counterexample to it. To begin, I should introduce a principle that my counterexample rests on. It is this: if, given some evidence e, I am justified in believing some proposition p, and I know that p entails q, then given e, I am also justified in believing q. Call this my "transmission principle."

AGNES: That seems right. Let's hear your counterexample.

ATHEA: Well, consider the fact that I now have the visual sensation of there being a table in front of me. Call this my "visual data." Unless we are skeptics, I take it that we agree that given this visual data, I am justified in believing that I see (really *see*) a (real) table in front of me.

AGNES: Didn't Descartes have some nasty arguments about that—didn't he propose that there might be an "evil demon" who is bent on deceiving me, causing me to have sensations of physical objects that aren't there?

ATHEA: Exactly—that's the next element in my counterexample. Consider the hypothesis that there is an evil demon causing me to have sensations of a non-existent table. Call this the "demon table" hypothesis. Now there are two things we must note about this hypothesis. First, we know that my belief that I see a table in front of me entails that this hypothesis is false. If I see a table in front of me, then there is no evil demon causing me to have sensations of a non-existent table. By my transmission principle, we must then say that I am justified, on my visual data, in believing that the demon table hypothesis is false. And this fact is really just common sense.

But if we accept Bea's expectability principle, we must deny this common sense fact. The demon table hypothesis makes entirely likely (it entails) that I would have just the visual table-data I have; so by her rule, this data cannot be evidence justifying my belief that the demon table hypothesis is false.

AGNES: So you are giving a "Reductio ad Absurdum" of Bea's principle. From her principle, it follows that on my visual data, I am not justified in believing the demon table hypothesis is false. But I *am* justified in believing the demon table hypothesis is false (this is the "common sense" point you support by your principle). So her principle must be mistaken.

But surely there is *something* right in her expectability rule. In the examples she gave—the strep virus and sandflea cases—her rule was very plausible. Can you account for this?

ATHEA: I think there is a correct principle in the neighborhood of Bea's, but it does not give the results she wants. The correct principle is rather complicated. Let's consider an example. Normally our not smelling any sourness in a glass of milk is evidence that it's not sour. But, of course, if you knew you had a cold, your not smelling any sourness wouldn't be evidence that it's not sour. The correct principle explaining this is the following:

If (1) the milk has no sourness that I can discern, *and* (2) I have reason to believe if I have a cold, the milk would have no sourness I could discern even if the milk were sour, *and* (3) I have reason to believe I have a cold, then my not discerning any sourness gives me no reason to think the milk is not sour.

More generally, let X and P be the object and property at issue, and C a condition under which P will be "unseeable." Then:

If (1) X has no P that I can discern, *and* (2) I have reason to believe if C obtains, X would have no P I could discern even if X were P, *and* (3) I have reason to believe C obtains, then my not discerning X as having P gives me no reason to think X is not P.

If we apply *this* principle to a case (X) of tragic suffering which serves no point (P) we can discern, we get:

If (1) the tragedy has no point that I can discern, *and* (2) I have reason to believe if God exists, we likely would not see the point of the tragedy even though it has a point, *and* (3) I have reason to believe God exists, then my discerning no point to the tragedy isn't reason to think it has no point.

AGNES: So you think Bea needs *each* of the three things in the antecedent, but establishes only the first two. This connects back to your first objection then, doesn't it?

ATHEA: Yup.

AGNES: Well, this place is closing. I propose we go down the street to Denny's, and hear Bea's response there.

3. *Toward Morning*
3.1 At Denny's: Coffee Pot #1

AGNES: What about Athea's first objection, Bea? She says you show only that *if* God exists, then if the tragedy has a point, we likely wouldn't see it. You *need* to show that if the tragedy has a point, we likely wouldn't see it. Don't you slide from one to the other, begging the question by supposing that God exists?

BEA: Whether I've begged the question depends on exactly what the question is. Athea adduces her noseeum data as significant evidence that God doesn't exist. Why? Because if God did exist, he would allow a tragedy like Carrie's death only if doing so served some purpose, some sufficient good. So I take the real question to be whether Athea's noseeum data is evidence that there is no such *God-purposed* good. To establish a "No" answer to this question, all I *need* to show is that if there were a *God-purposed* good—one actually purposed by God—which justifies his allowing the tragedy, we likely wouldn't see it. All I *need* to show, in, other words, is that *if* God exists, then if the tragedy serves some good, we likely would not see it. And *that*, Athea allows *I have* shown.

AGNES: What about Athea's cold analogy? There, the question is whether smelling no sourness in the milk is evidence that the milk is not sour. Suppose you wanted to argue it isn't. Surely, as Athea says, you couldn't merely argue that *if* I have a cold, then if the milk is sour, I'd likely smell no sourness anyway. To defeat the nosmellum data, you'd have to go on to establish that I do have a cold. Similarly, to defeat Athea's noseeum data, don't you have to go on to show that God does exist?

BEA: There is a disanalogy between the two cases. Consider the two properties at issue. In the cold case, the issue is whether the milk has the property of being sour. Now there is nothing about this property *itself* that makes the nosmellum data expectable. For precisely this reason, defeating the data requires establishing that some *further* condition obtains (like having a cold), under which, even if the milk has the property, the nosmellum data would be expectable.

In the God case, the issue is whether some suffering has the property of serving some God-purposed good. Here there is something about this putative property *itself*—serving a *God*-purposed good—that leads us to expect that if the tragedy has this property, we'd get our noseeum data anyway. For precisely this reason, we don't need to establish some further condition under which, if the suffering has this property, we'd nevertheless expect the noseeum data.

AGNES: I think I see what you are saying, but Athea's analogy still bothers me.

BEA: Let's loosen the grip of her analogy by considering a different one, which doesn't have the dissimilarity I'm pointing out. Suppose you, an intelligent philosophy undergraduate, find a philosophy manuscript in a dorm room. It has many sentences for which you cannot see any meaning. You are about to dismiss it as nonsense, when it occurs to you that a visiting philosopher might have stayed in the room. And some philosophers, as you know, write papers which are so brilliant and deep that they are intelligible only to a handful of fellow specialists. Perhaps, you conjecture, this manuscript was written by such a philosopher—a Dr. Genius, as you call her.

AGNES: I take it a Dr. Genius does not write gibberish, so if it *was* written by a Dr. Genius, then these sentences would all have meanings, but these would often be beyond my ken—being "Genius-meanings," so to speak.

BEA: Exactly. Of course, you don't *know* whether it was written by a Dr. Genius; this is just one possible hypothesis. Now your noseeum data is that you see no meaning for many sentences in this manuscript. The question is whether this noseeum data is significant evidence against the hypothesis the manuscript is by a Dr. Genius.

AGNES: I don't see that it could be. We've agreed that if it was by Dr. Genius, then one would expect many sentences to have no meanings I could see. Since the noseeum data is just what we'd expect if the hypothesis were true, how can it be evidence *against* the hypothesis?

BEA: But suppose someone objected that all you've shown is that *if* the manuscript is the product of a Dr. Genius, then if some sentence has a meaning, we'd expect not to see its meaning? To avoid begging the question, don't you now have to show it is the product of a Dr. Genius?

AGNES: Of course not. The question is whether the noseeum data is evidence against the claim that some sentence has a meaning-intended-by-Dr.-Genius. To show it isn't, all I'd have to show is

that if it had *that* sort of meaning, we'd expect not to see it anyway. And that's the same as showing that *if* the manuscript was written by Dr. Genius, then if some sentence has a defensible meaning, we'd likely not see it anyway.

BEA: The same for Athea's argument. To defeat her data, I need only show that if some tragedy has a purpose intended by God, we'd likely not be able to discern it. That's the same as showing that if God exists, then if the suffering serves some justifying purpose, we'd likely not see it anyway.

AGNES: Now I see why you think her sour milk analogy is irrelevant. There's nothing about sourness *itself* that makes you expect the nosmellum data; so to defeat such data, you've got to show there is some further condition, like having a cold, which makes this data expectable. But in the God case, your claim is that the very nature of the property at issue—serving a good *intended by God*—leads one to expect the noseeum data. But I'm just repeating what you said, aren't I?

BEA: Yes, but I don't mind. It doesn't happen very often.

AGNES: What about Athea's demon table argument, Bea?

BEA: To begin, we must follow Carnap's distinction between two senses of "confirms." Evidence E confirms hypothesis H in a *static* sense when, *given* E, H is more likely to be true than false. E confirms H in a *dynamic* sense when it *raises* the probability of H higher than it was prior to E. A parallel distinction obviously holds for two senses of "disconfirms."

AGNES: So let H be Iris's hypothesis that Bo is the murderer, and suppose we have evidence showing that the murderer is one of Iris's past boyfriends. Since she's had a number of boyfriends, this evidence might not confirm H in the static sense. But it might well *dynamically* confirm the hypothesis, raising its likelihood from what it was before we had this evidence.

BEA: Exactly. Now I've put this in terms of probabilities. But a similar distinction holds for justification, I think. E justifies H in a static sense when, on E, one is justified in believing H. E justifies H is a dynamic sense when it *increases* the justification of holding the belief, or *contributes* to the beliefs being justified. The key issue is whether Athea's noseeum evidence *dynamically* confirms atheism, increasing its likelihood, or contributing to its justification. That's equivalent to whether it dynamically disconfirms theism, decreasing its likelihood or justification. I argued it doesn't, relying on the "expectability rule" that insofar as E is "expectable" on some hypothesis, it can't dynamically disconfirm the hypothesis.

AGNES: Now let me restate Athea's counterexample. Her visual data justifies her belief that she sees a real table; and this, she knows, entails that it's not a demon table. So by her "transmission principle," her visual data also justifies her belief that its not a demon table. But this means your expectability rule is wrong. For if there were a demon table, we would expect just this visual data; so your principle entails, absurdly, that her visual data *cannot* justify her no-demon-table belief.

BEA: Good job. Now I think this argument equivocates on the term "justifies." Since her visual data justifies her belief that she sees a table, she concludes, by her transmission principle, that it also justifies her no-demon-table belief, and this, she charges, is absurdly denied by my expectability rule. But I think her transmission principle is true *only if* we take "justifies" in its *static* sense; so it only allows her to conclude that her no-demon-table belief is *statically* justified on her data. And my principle does not rule that out. My expectability rule only claims that her visual data cannot *dynamically* justify her no-demon-table belief; it cannot increase its likelihood, or contribute to its justification. Athea's transmission principle—and hence her argument—gives no reason to reject that claim.

AGNES: Maybe not; but is the claim plausible?

BEA: I think so. Suppose Athea wakes up one morning next to her precious antique table. With eyes still closed (perhaps she's been studying too much Descartes), she considers the proposition that an Evil Demon is ready to produce a "demon table" when she wills to open her (demon) eyelids. She believes this hypothesis is false; she rates it as ludicrously improbable; and we, being non-skeptics, deem her justified in this. Now she opens her eyes and has visual table-sensations. We will grant, of course, that on her new visual data, she is still

justified in disbelieving the demon-table hypothesis. But why should we see her visual data as *increasing* this justification, or making less justifiable the demon-table hypothesis?

AGNES: Just one more question. Why do you think her transmission principle is true only in the static sense of "justifies"? If some evidence E increases the likelihood (or justification) of my belief that p, and I know that p entails q, doesn't B increase the likelihood (or justification) of belief q, too?

BEA: Nope. Take the proposition that Athea is a woman philosophy professor. This is a conjunction of three conjuncts: Athea is a woman AND Athea is a prof AND Athea is a philosopher. Now suppose E is that Athea has published in the *American Philosophical Quarterly*. E might greatly raise the likelihood of the third conjunct, and hence, might greatly jack up the likelihood of the whole conjunction. But it needn't raise at all the likelihood of the first conjunct—that Athea is a woman—even though this is entailed by the conjunction. So the transmission principle clearly isn't true if "justifies" is used in the dynamic sense.

AGNES: Is it true even in the static sense? Couldn't the conjunction be more likely true than false *on* some body of evidence, even though one conjunct has a likelihood less than .5 on that evidence? Maybe this conjunct has a likelihood of only .3, but the other two conjuncts have a likelihood of .9; when you average them, the conjunction would have a likelihood of .7, which is more likely true than false.

BEA: No, Agnes, it would be .243. The probability of a conjunction is not the *average* of the probabilities of its conjuncts, but (assuming they are independent) the product of them. So, like the proverbial chain, a conjunction will never be more likely than its least likely conjunct.

AGNES: Oh.

3.2 Coffee Pot #2

ATHEA: Well, we'd better have another pot of coffee. Let's make it decaf, so we can get *some* sleep tonight.

Bea, you said that the real question was whether this evil serves any "God-purposed" good—meaning a good which is both purposed by God in allowing the evil, and sufficient to justify his allowing it. But I don't see that as the original question at all. Let's look at our napkins from House of India. (She shuffles through them until she finds the right one.) Here, look. P3 in the main argument, which my subargument supports, really says that there is no good thing that would *suffice* to justify God, if he exists, in allowing Carrie's murder to happen. Such a good—a God-sufficing good, I shall call it—*could* exist even if it is not purposed by God, and even if God doesn't exist. My argument is that our noseeum data is reason to think there is no such God-sufficing good. And you have given no reason to deny that, for you haven't shown that if there is a God-sufficing good, then we likely wouldn't see it anyway.

So it seems to me you are criticizing a different argument than the one I gave. First you foist on me this argument: if God exists, he would purpose some good in allowing Carrie's death; there is no such God-purposed good; so God doesn't exist. Then you pretend the question is whether my evidence gives reason to believe there is no *God-purposed good*. Well, I agree that our seeing no God-purposed good gives us no reason to believe there is none. But this is a red-herring, diverting us from the argument I actually gave. It's a good thing Agnes had us write it down.

AGNES: So you think Bea's criticism is beside the point because it's not directed at the argument you gave. I guess you'd say the same thing about her Dr. Genius analogy. Suppose that if a sentence was written by Dr. Genius, then we likely wouldn't see the meaning of it. Then Bea is right: our not seeing the meaning of a sentence is no reason to think it wasn't written by Her Brilliancy. But you'd say that, nevertheless, we can be justified in believing that there is no Dr. Genius whose meaning lies behind a sentence that seems gibberish; so also, we can be justified in believing there is no God whose good lies behind suffering that seems pointless.

ATHEA: Exactly. Consider the Cartesian demon again. Surely . . .

BEA: Um, could I interrupt? Athea, you called my moral depth line a red herring. I don't agree, but I see that I didn't make its relevance clear. You're quite right that your original argument was not in terms of God-purposed goods. But I didn't mean to "foist" that on you. I meant that *logically*, the *real* issue is whether your evidence makes it less likely that there is a God-purposed good.

AGNES: But why is this the "real" issue? Athea agrees that her noseeum evidence doesn't make it less likely that there is a God-purposed good. But in her argument, she intended her evidence to justify the claim there is no God-*sufficing* good for E. Since we are evaluating *her* argument, why isn't the "real" issue whether her evidence justifies *that* claim?

BEA: Well, that *too* is the real issue. Here we must be careful: we need to see how the *two* issues are logically related.

Maybe the Dr. Genius case can clarify this. Let's say that a sentence has a "defensible meaning" when it has a meaning on which the sentence is not patently false; and suppose that genius doctors don't write patently false sentences. So if a sentence is by Dr. Genius, it will have a defensible meaning (though one, being genius-intended, that is likely beyond our ken).

Now imagine someone, Rene I'll call him, trying to give evidence against the Dr. Genius hypothesis. Rene concedes that our seeing no meaning for a sentence isn't reason to believe it has no *Genius-intended* meaning, since if it had such a meaning, we likely wouldn't see it anyway. So he argues as follows: "If the sentence is by a Dr. Genius, then it has a *defensible* meaning. But our seeing no meaning to the sentence surely gives us darn good reason to suppose it has no defensible meaning. So it, too, gives us good reason to think it is not by Dr. Genius."

AGNES: This seems like modus tollens. Yet something smells fishy with it, doesn't it?

BEA: And not fresh fish either, I'd say. Notice that "This sentence has a defensible meaning" is less specific than "This sentence has a genius-intended meaning." The former is really a big *disjunctive* claim comprising various possibilities, *one* of which is the latter. To say "the sentence has a defensible meaning" is to say "it has defensible meaning written by a high school student OR it has a defensible meaning intended by an average undergraduate, OR by a bright philosophy major, OR an average graduate student," and so on, til we get to what I'll call "the last little disjunct," namely: . . .

"OR it has a defensible meaning intended by a Dr. Genius."

AGNES: That seems right. But how does it help?

BEA: Well, think of there being some threshold, such that if the evidence reduces the likelihood or credence-worthiness of a statement below that threshold, the statement is unreasonable to believe. Now Rene, while conceding that his evidence does not reduce the likelihood or credence-worthiness of that "last little disjunct," wants to bring the evidence to bear against the big disjunction. But the likelihood of the big disjunction is just the *sum* of the likelihoods of each disjunct (assuming they are, as here, exclusive). Hence, his evidence can't make the disjunction unreasonable to believe unless, prior to the evidence, that last little disjunct was *already* unreasonable to believe. If that last little disjunct was worthy of belief before his noseeum evidence, then the big disjunction will be worthy of belief after the evidence, no matter how successful that evidence is in knocking out the *other* disjuncts.

AGNES: Would this be a similar example? Suppose I am trying to argue against Iris's hypothesis that Bo killed her daughter. Lacking any direct evidence against this, I first point out that her hypothesis entails that one of her ex-boyfriends did it. I then amass evidence disconfirming this big disjunctive claim—evidence, that is, that Jack didn't do it, that Tom didn't do it, and so on for all her former boyfriends except Bo. This approach would be really fishy, wouldn't it? For though my "evidence" might well reduce the likelihood of the big disjunctive claim, it couldn't reduce it below the initial likelihood of Iris's claim that Bo did it. So such evidence couldn't provide reason to reject Iris's claim. Is this similar?

BEA: Exactly. Athea's argument tries to use her noseeum evidence as reason to reject the claim that the tragedy serves a God-sufficing good. But this too is just a big disjunction, one of whose little disjuncts is that the evil serves some God-intended good. I argued that her evidence doesn't *reduce* the likelihood of this crucial little disjunct. Athea *conceded* it doesn't, but charged that this was a red herring. But it's not, because what she concedes is intimately related to the issue of whether her evidence gives reason to reject the

great big disjunctive claim that the evil serves a God-sufficing good. As in your analogy, Agnes, her evidence can't make the big disjunction unworthy of belief unless, prior to her evidence, it was already unreasonable to believe the little disjunct. That's why it was relevant to press the issue about God-intended purposes, although she didn't couch her argument in terms of them. Shall we have some more decaf?

3.3 Coffee Pot #3

AGNES: Athea, you were about to say something about the Cartesian demon. Can we go to that now?

ATHEA: Okay. Bea's analysis seems very insightful, though I want to think about it more. Perhaps I can adapt my demon point to it. Surely, taking everything into account, we are justified in believing there's a table here. It's not that our visual data makes it more likely that there is a real table than a demon table. But it does eliminate, or disconfirm, a lot of *other* possibilities—that there is a Sherman tank here, that there is nothing here, and so on. Now I think that when we get to the question of whether it is a real table or a demon table, the real table hypothesis wins out because it better explains why we have the visual, tactual, and other sensations that we do have.

AGNES: I think I understand, but I don't trust arguments from evil demons. Could you give a more down-to-earth case?

ATHEA: Well, suppose we are at the zoo with a child, looking at what seems just like a zebra. The child imaginatively points out that donkeys might be cleverly painted to look just like zebras; she then wonders if some merry pranksters have done just that in the present case. Now *if* we had some good reason to think there were such donkey-painting pranksters, it might be hard to know what to believe about what we now see. But suppose we don't have good reason to think this. In that case, given our visual data, reason requires us to believe there is a zebra before us. Our visual data does this, in effect, by making it far more likely that there is a zebra before us than that there is some osterich, hippopotamus, or other critter before us—it eliminates a lot of these possibilities, much as in Bea's discussion of possible defensible meanings. To be sure, our data does not disconfirm the painted donkey possibility. But lacking reason to believe there are merry donkey-painting pranksters, this possibility doesn't even get off the ground.

Now return to the God issue. Like our visual striped-critter data, our knowledge of suffering serving no discernible point rules out, or disconfirms, a number of possibilities: that this is a world without evil, for instance, or that it is one all of whose evil serves a point near the surface," or within our intellectual grasp. I guess Bea is right that it does not much disconfirm the claim that each of these evils serves a God-purposed point. But without any reason for thinking that God exists, that hypothesis is like the merry prankster possibility: it doesn't get off the ground.

So I want to say that it really doesn't matter whether evil dynamically or statically justifies us in believing that God doesn't exist, any more than it matters whether our striped-critter data dynamically or statically justifies us in believing the animal in the zoo is not a cleverly painted donkey. Perhaps, as we converse with our imaginative child at the zoo, we are as justified in believing the no-painted-donkey hypothesis *before* having the striped visual data as we were *after* having it. Nevertheless, the data of seeing those black and white stripes serves an important evidential function in the conversation: it *reminds* us that we aren't justified in believing that there are merry donkey-painting pranksters at work here. So also, in conversation with Descartes, our visual table data reminds us that we aren't justified in believing the evil genius hypothesis. In reminding, it forces explicitness. Maybe the data of inscrutable suffering, I now want to say, serves a similar evidential function. Maybe all it does is force explicitness, reminding us that even before the data of inscrutable suffering, we are not justified in believing there is a God. But that is an important function.

[The women are quiet, reflecting on Athea's words.]

AGNES: Why then, Athea, do you think that even before this data, we are justified in believing there is no God?

ATHEA: I still have doubts about whether a loving God would create so morally obscure a world as ours. But I think Bea is right about this: our seeing no sufficient good served by Carrie's death does not count against the claim that there is a God who has made a universe with moral depth. But it now seems to me there is an analogue with creationism. Some creationists argue that the world was made five thousand years ago with signs of apparent great age—fossils and the like—already built into it. I guess the fossil record doesn't count against this version of creationism—it doesn't "dynamically disconfirm" it. But we rightly reject this sort of creationism. So also, barring evidence for the view that God created a morally deep world, I think we must reject this view too. In general, shouldn't we reject views that posit the existence of certain entities—leprechauns, Loch Ness monsters, and the like—unless there is positive reason for their existence?

There are deep issues here. To be justified, must all of our beliefs be supported by evidence, or only some of them? If only some, which ones, and why? There are also questions about what makes one hypothesis a good explanation of certain phenomena—and about whether theism, to avoid irrationality, must provide a good explanation of certain phenomena.

BEA: If you are saying that belief in God requires adequate positive justification if it is to be justified, well, then I agree with you. Of course, I think it *has* the positive justification it requires—though I'm not, as a philosopher, as clear as I would like to be about what it is. There are, as you say, Athea, deep issues here.

But the issue *we* have been discussing is whether the inscrutability of evil counts *against* theism—whether, that is, it puts theistic belief in need of *more* positive justification than it would otherwise require. And I think the comparison with "old-earth creationism" points us back to the right issue here. The problem with old-earth creationism is that to protect itself from the fossil-data, a new addition has been tacked onto the basic creationist claim. To be sure, the fossil data doesn't lower the probability of this *expanded* version of creationism, but the expanded version has, *by* its expanded content, made itself less probable than it was. It has become that much more "top-heavy" relative to the evidence. And I take it that hypotheses are here like tables (real ones, not demon tables): the more top-heavy they are, the more support they require to stand.

But this really points us back to the issue Rowe had raised. Rowe, you remember, challenged Wykstra's claim that theism itself makes it "entirely expectable" that our universe would have "moral depth." The "moral depth" line, Rowe countered, is a significant *"expansion"* of theism, a kind of *ad hoc* addition. I think we are seeing that the issue concerning us tonight depends upon this. If Rowe is right in seeing the moral depth line as a significantly *expanded* version of theism, its immunity against noseeum disconfirmation is purchased at the price of making itself more improbable through added "top-heaviness." I don't think Rowe *is* right; but that does seem to be the real issue.

So we haven't solved the problem; but I think we have narrowed it. For a while it seemed that even if theism *entails* (without "expansion") that our universe would have moral depth, this wouldn't help the theist, because of monstrous problems of circularity, demon tables, and the like. *Those* problems, though interesting, now look more like shadow monsters.

ATHEA: Perhaps so. I too think we've made progress. But it's way past midnight, dear friends, and I'm too tired to say anything with confidence just now. It's time to go back to my place and turn in. We need sleep before we visit Iris in the hospital this afternoon.

AGNES: I just want to thank you both; I haven't had a night like this since our college days. Remember how Iris loved our all-nighters? If only philosophy could help her through her pain now—instead of just giving me a break from it. And I still don't know what I believe.

[Agnes looks out upon the street.]

But it seems a little less dark out there, doesn't it? Do you know, I've never seen the sun come up. I've heard about "false dawn," when sunrise seems near but is really still hours away. But I've never seen that either. Which is this, I wonder?

For the most part, Bea Leaver's arguments come from S. Wykstra, while Athea Ist's arguments come from B. Russell. Russell thanks Wykstra for laboring to improve the dialogical style. Wykstra thanks Russell for initiating and managing the project.

52. *Creation, Conservation and the Big Bang*

PHILIP L. QUINN

Do recent developments in physical cosmology undermine the theological doctrine of divine creation and conservation? The following articles by Philip Quinn and Adolf Grünbaum discuss that question. In the next selection, Quinn attempts to defend the view, found in Descartes (see *Meditation III*), Berkeley, Leibniz, Swinburne, and others, that the same divine power or agency necessary to create a thing from nothing is necessary to conserve it (or keep it) in existence at every moment at which it exists. But is this view consistent with the big bang model(s) of creation, and the conservation law, according to which the sum total of matter-energy in a closed system remains constant throughout a certain interval of time? Quinn argues that his account of divine creation and conservation is consistent with the assumptions of the two big bang models he discusses. Furthermore, he argues that there is a positive case for the theistic hypothesis, namely, that the conservation principle of matter-energy of big bang theories has no explanation if only scientific explanation is allowed. Why is there just that principle of conservation and not some other; why is there a certain amount of matter-energy and not some other amount or none at all? According to Quinn, these are legitimate questions to which science does not have an answer, but the theist does. According to Quinn, if a certain amount of matter-energy exists and it is conserved, then it is because God so wills it. Philip Quinn is a professor of philosophy at the University of Notre Dame.

In a recent paper Adolf Grünbaum has argued that those who think recent physical cosmology poses a problem of matter-energy creation to which there is a theological solution are mistaken (see Grünbaum 1989). In physical cosmology, creation is, he claims, a pseudoproblem. My aim in this essay is to refute that claim.

The essay is divided into five sections. First, I provide some background information about the theological doctrine of divine creation and conservation. By citing both historical and contemporary philosophers, I try to make it clear that there is widespread and continuing agreement among philosophers committed to traditional theism that all contingent things depend for their existence on God whenever they exist and not just when they begin to exist if they do have beginnings. I explicate the particular doctrine of creation ex nihilo set forth by Thomas Aquinas to account for the existence of contingent things that do begin to exist. Second, I propose a fairly precise formulation of the doctrine of divine creation and conservation. My way of stating it is meant to be faithful to the leading ideas in the historical and contemporary sources I have cited, and it has the Thomistic doctrine of creation ex nihilo as a special case. Third, I discuss two classical big bang models of cosmogony, one including an initial singularity and the other not. I argue that only the latter model is inconsistent with the Thomistic doctrine of creation ex nihilo. I go on to contend, however, that neither model is inconsistent with the general account of creation and conservation I have formulated. Fourth, I criticize the view that neither big bang model leaves anything that could be explained unex-

plained and that therefore there is no explanatory work that the doctrine of creation and conservation could do. I argue that in each of these cosmogonic models there is something that either has no explanation at all—if only scientific explanation is allowed—or is explained in terms of causes external to the physical cosmos—if the appeal to theological explanation succeeds. Fifth, and finally, I sketch an extension of the discussion from big bang cosmogonies to steady state and quantum cosmologies. I suggest that they too leave open the question of whether the existence and persistence of matter-energy are inexplicable or are explained by something like the traditional doctrine of divine creation and conservation.

Historical Background

How are we to conceive the manner in which contingent things are supposed to depend for their existence on God? A minimalist account of this dependence is deistic in nature. On this view, God brings all contingent things into existence by creating them. Once having been created, such things continue to exist and operate on their own, without further support or assistance from God. In other words, God is like a watchmaker: Once the watch has been made and wound up, it persists and goes on ticking without further interventions by its maker. Grünbaum assumes this view will shape a creationist reading of big bang theories. It is presupposed in his remark that "God has been thus unemployed, as it were, for about 12 billion years, because the big bang model of the general theory of relativity features the conservation law for matter-energy, which obviously precludes any nonconservative formation of physical entities" (1989, 376).

"Creation, Conservation and the Big Bang" is from *Philosophical Problems of the Internal and External Worlds*, J. Earman, A. I. Janis, G. J. Massey, and N. Rescher, eds. ©1993 by University of Pittsburgh Press. Reprinted by permission of the University of Pittsburgh Press.

It is not now and has not in the past been the view typical of philosophically reflective theists. Going well beyond deistic minimalism, they hold that all contingent things are continuously dependent upon God for their existence. On this view, God not only creates the cosmos of contingent things but also conserves it in existence at every instant when it exists. And divine creation and divine conservation both involve the same power and activity on the part of God. In a famous passage from the *Meditations,* which Grünbaum quotes, Descartes says, "It is as a matter of fact perfectly clear and evident to all those who consider with attention the nature of time, that, in order to be conserved in each moment in which it endures, a substance has need of the same power and action as would be necessary to produce and create it anew, supposing it did not yet exist, so that the light of nature shows us clearly that the distinction between creation and conservation is solely a distinction of the reason" (Descartes 1955, 168). Bishop Berkeley writes to Samuel Johnson, "Those who have all along contended for a material world have yet acknowledged that *natura naturans* (to use the language of the Schoolmen) is God; and that the divine conservation of things is equipollent to, and in fact the same thing with, a continued repeated creation: in a word, that conservation and creation differ only in the *terminus a quo*" (1950, 280).

Leibniz repeatedly endorses this idea. In the *Theodicy* he says, "[W]e must bear in mind that conservation by God consists in the perpetual immediate influence which the dependence of creatures demands. This dependence attaches not only to the substance but also to the action, and one can perhaps not explain it better than by saying, with theologians and philosophers in general, that it is a continued creation" (1952, 139). In the *New Essays Concerning Human Understanding* he remarks, "Thus it is true in a certain sense, as I have explained, that not only our ideas, but also our sensations, spring from within our own soul, and that the soul is more independent than is thought, although it is always true that nothing takes place in it which is not determined, and nothing is found in creatures that God does not continuously create" (1949, 15–16). In the correspondence with Clarke he claims, "The soul knows

things, because God has put into it a principle representative of things without. But God knows things, because he produces them continually" (1956, 41).

Joining the chorus, Jonathan Edwards insists, "God's upholding created substance, or causing its existence in each successive moment, is altogether equivalent to an *immediate production out of nothing,* at each moment, because its existence at this moment is not merely in part from God, but wholly from him; and not in any part, or degree, from its antecedent existence" (1970, 402). So there was striking agreement among the major theistic philosophers of the seventeenth and eighteenth centuries that God not only creates all contingent things but also conserves them in existence, moment by moment, in a way that is tantamount to continuously creating or recreating them.

Nor is this view of divine creation and conservation of merely historical or antiquarian interest. It also commands the loyalty of leading contemporary theistic philosophers. After asking his reader to consider as an example a physical object, a part of the natural world such as a tree, George Mavrodes observes, "If Christian theology is correct, one of the characteristics which this tree has is that it is an entity whose existence is continuously dependent on the activity of God. The existence of something with this characteristic is a perfectly reliable sign of the existence of God" (1970, 70). David Braine makes the point vivid by comparing God to a painter:

It is a corollary of the reality of time that the past and present can have no causal role in that continuance of the substance of things—the continuance of the stuff of the world and the regularities or "nature" on which its continuity depends—which is involved in the future's becoming present. It follows from this that the same power is involved in the causing of this continuance of things (if any cause is needed) as would be involved in the causing of the coming to be of things from nothing. As it were, if the continuance of the world is the result of the continuance of a divine brush stroke, then the same power is exercised at each stage in the continuance of the brush stroke as would have been exercised in the beginning of the brush stroke—if the brush stroke had a beginning. (1988, 180)

As one would expect, Braine then proceeds to offer an argument which, he claims, "compels acceptance that continuance into the future must be caused" (ibid., 198), and from this he concludes that "so-called secondary or natural causation has its reality grounded in the primary causality exercised immediately to every time and place by the First Cause" (ibid.). Richard Swinburne considers the doctrine of creation and conservation to be constitutive of the theistic conception of God. The first volume of his impressive philosophy of religion trilogy begins, "By a theist I understand a man who believes that there is a God. By a 'God' he understand [*sic*] something like a 'person without a body (i.e., a spirit) who is eternal, free, able to do anything, knows everything, is perfectly good, is the proper object of human worship and obedience, the creator and sustainer of the universe'" (1977, 1).

Because he thinks God would hardly be less worthy of worship if he on occasion permitted some other being to create matter, Swanburne attributes to the theist the belief that "God's action (or permission) is needed not merely for things to begin to exist but also for them to continue in existence" (ibid., 128–29). He acknowledges that theists like Aquinas have held that revelation teaches us that the universe is not eternal but had a beginning of existence, but he supposes that this doctrine is not as important in their thought as the doctrine that God is responsible for the existence of the universe whenever it exists. So he attributes to theists the view that "God keeps the universe in being, whether he has been doing so for ever or only for a finite time" (ibid., 129).

The views of Aquinas about creation and conservation are worth examining in more detail. He holds that all contingent things are preserved in being by divine action and not merely by divine permission. All creatures stand in need of such divine preservation, he thinks, because "the being of every creature depends on God, so that not for a moment could it subsist, but would fall into nothingness were it not kept in being by the operation of Divine power" (Aquinas 1981, 511). An interesting objection to this view can be based on the fact that even finite agents can produce effects that persist after they have ceased to act. Thus, to use the examples Aquinas gives, houses continue to stand after their builders have ceased building them, and water remains hot for some time after fire has ceased to heat it. Since God is more powerful than any finite agent, it would seem to be within his power to make something that continues to exist on its own after his activity has ceased. In reply to this objection, Aquinas denies the legitimacy of the comparison of finite agents, which merely cause changes in things that already exist and so are causes of becoming rather than of being, and God, who is the cause of the being of all contingent things. He insists that "God cannot grant to a creature to be preserved in being after the cessation of the Divine influence: as neither can He make it not to have received its being from Himself" (1981, 512). However, just as God acted freely and not from natural necessity in creating contingent things in the first place, so also his conserving activity is free, and any contingent thing would forthwith cease to exist if he were to stop conserving it. This leads Aquinas to return a positive answer to the question of whether God can annihilate anything, "Therefore, just as before things existed, God was free not to give them existence, and not to make them; so after they have been made, He is free not to continue their existence; and thus they would cease to exist; and this would be to annihilate them" (ibid., 514). Annihilation would, of course, not involve a positive destructive act on God's part; it would consist in the mere cessation or withdrawal of his positive conserving activity.

Since Aquinas believes that contingent things have existed for only a finite amount of past time, it might be thought that his view is that the contingent cosmos was created after a prior period of time in which it did not exist. Some of the things he says about creation ex nihilo suggest this doctrine. In an article devoted to the question of whether angels were produced by God from eternity, he maintains that "God so produced creatures that He made them *from nothing;* that is, after they had not been" (ibid., 302). An objection to the view that it is an article of faith that the world began consists of a purported demonstration that the world had a beginning which concludes, "Therefore it must be said that the world was made from nothing; and thus it has being after not being. Therefore it must have begun" (ibid., 242). And, in replying to this objection, Aquinas remarks, "Those who would say that the world was eternal, would say that the world was made by God from nothing, not that it was made after nothing, according to what we understand by the word creation, but that it was not made from anything" (ibid., 243). Again, an objection to the thesis that creation is not a change goes as follows, "Change denotes the succession of one being after another, as stated in *Phys.* v, 1: and this is true of creation, which is the production of being after non-being. Therefore creation is a change" (ibid., 1952, 88). Such passages as these give the impression that, for Aquinas, being created ex nihilo entails existing after a time at which one did not exist. If this impression were accurate, Aquinas would be committed to the view that there was a time when nothing contingent existed before the first contingent things existed.

But Aquinas says things flatly inconsistent with the view that such an entailment exists. Commenting on the first verse of Genesis, according to which in the beginning God created heaven and earth, he contends that time itself was one of the contingent things God created in the beginning. As he interprets scripture, "[F]our things are stated to be created together—viz., the empyrean heaven, corporeal matter, by which is meant the earth, time, and the angelic nature (ibid., 1981, 244). To the objection that time cannot be created in the beginning of time because time is divisible and the beginning of time is indivisible, Aquinas replies, "Nothing is made except as it exists. But nothing exists of time except *now*. Hence time cannot be made except according to some *now*; not because in the first *now* is time, but because from it time begins" (ibid., 245). This reply commits Aquinas to the view that one of the things God made in the beginning was a unique first *now*, from which time began. If this is right, there were no times prior to that time. And since that *now* was made by God together with the empyrean heaven, earth and angels, those contingent things existed at that time. Hence the four first contingent things are, according to Aquinas, such that God made them, and yet there was no time prior to their being made and so no such prior time at which they did not exist.

It is therefore easy to see why Aquinas holds that the creation of the four first things is not a change. In the course of setting forth his views on this topic, he distinguishes three kinds of change. The first involves a single subject being changed from one contrary to another and covers the cases of alteration, increase and decrease, and local motion. The second involves a subject which is actual at one end of the change but only potential at the other and covers the cases of ordinary generation and corruption. The third involves no common subject, actual or potential, but merely continuous time, in the first part of which there is one of two contraries, and in the second part of which there is the other. This last kind is not change properly speaking because it involves imagining time itself as the subject of things that take place in time; it is the sort of thing we are referring to when we say that afternoon changes into evening. According to Aquinas, the creation of the four first things belongs to none of these kinds. His reason for excluding it from the last of them is that "there is no continuous time, if we refer to the creation of the universe, since there was no time when there was no world" (ibid., 1952, 90). But we can conceive of or imagine possible times before the first actual *now*. Thus Aquinas makes this concession:

> And yet we may find a common but purely imaginary subject, in so far as we imagine one common time when there was no world and afterwards when the world had been brought into being. For even as outside the universe there is no real [spatial] magnitude, we can nevertheless picture one to ourselves: so before the beginning of the world there was no time and yet we can imagine one. Accordingly creation is not in truth a change, but only in imagination, and not properly speaking but metaphorically. (Ibid.)

The creation of the four first things is thus not literally but only metaphorically to be counted as a case of change.

Davidsonian charity dictates that we attribute a consistent view to Aquinas if we can find one. I suggest that the way to accomplish this is to take the slogan that creation ex nihilo involves being after not being figuratively in its application to the four first things. What is literally true of them is that they are such that they have existed for only a finite amount of past time and began to exist at the first time. It is therefore literally false that there were times before they existed and, a fortiori, that their creation ex nihilo involves existence temporally after nonexistence. But because we can in imagination extend time back beyond the first real time, we may speak metaphorically of the creation ex nihilo of even the four first things as involving being after not being if we keep in mind that we really have in view something like being (imagined to be) after (imaginary) nonbeing. On this reading of Aquinas, his view of time is the same in some respects as the one embodied in the big bang model that includes the initial singularity. In both cases, time is metrically finite in the past and is also topologically closed because there is a unique first time.

An Account of Divine Creation and Conservation

In order to lend some precision to the subsequent discussion, I draw on an account of divine creation and conservation I have worked out in Quinn (1983, 1988). I begin by stating my ontological assumptions and notational conventions. I assume time is a linear continuum composed of point instants, with t, t', and t'' as variables of quantification ranging over point instants of time. I also assume that there are concrete individuals, with x as a variable of quantification ranging over them. I leave open the question of which things are genuine individuals. Perhaps items of middle-sized dry goods such as tables and chairs are individuals, but maybe they are mere aggregates composed of genuine individuals. For the sake of convenience, I suppose that in discussions of cosmological models in which matter-energy is conserved it is permissible to speak of the sum total of matter-energy as if it were an individual. Finally, I assume that there are states of affairs. Some states of affairs obtain, and others do not.

My account of creation and conservation rests on the further assumption that there is a special two-place relation of divine bringing about defined on ordered pairs of states of affairs. The primitive schematic locution of the account, which

expresses that relation, is this: God willing that x exists at t brings about x existing at t. I leave open the question of whether God and his volitions are timelessly eternal by not building into this locution a variable ranging over times of occurrence of diving willings. Since it is a primitive locution, I have no definition of it to offer, but I can provide a partial informal characterization of it. Obviously it must express a relation of metaphysical dependence or causation. Beyond that, I think this relation must have the following marks in order to serve its theological purposes: totality, exclusivity, activity, immediacy, and necessity. By totality, I mean that what does the bringing about is the total cause of what is brought about; nothing else is required by way of causal contribution in order for the effect to obtain. In particular, divine volitions do not work on independently existing matter, and so no Aristotelian material cause is required for them to produce existence. By exclusivity, I mean that what does the bringing about is the sole cause of what is brought about; causal overdetermination is ruled out. By activity, I mean that the state of affairs that does the bringing about does so in virtue of the exercise of some active power on the part of the individual involved in it. By immediacy, I mean that what does the bringing about causes what is brought about immediately rather than remotely through some extended causal chain or by means of instruments. By necessity, I mean that what does the bringing about in some sense necessitates what is brought about.

Using the primitive locution I have adopted, my account of divine creation and conservation is easy to state. It consists of a single, simple postulate:

POSTULATE 23.I. (P) *For all x and t, if x is contingent and x exists at t, then God willing that x exists at t brings about x existing at t.*

According to this account, then, divine volition brings about the existence of every contingent individual at every instant at which it exists and so brings about the existence of every persisting contingent individual at every instant of, and thus throughout, every interval during which it exists. Since this postulate is consistent with there having been contingent individuals for either an infinite past time or only a finite past time, it nicely captures Swinburne's claim that what is important for theists to hold is that God keeps the universe in being, whether he has been doing so forever or only for a finite time.

How are we to distinguish creation from conservation? According to Scotus, "Properly speaking, then, it is only true to say that a creature is created at the first moment (of its existence) and only after that moment is it conserved, for only then does its being have this order to itself as something that was, as it were, there before. Because of these different conceptual relationships implied by 'create' and 'conserve,' it follows that one does not apply to a thing when the other does" (1975, 276). These remarks motivate the following definitions:

DEFINITION 23.1. (D1) *God creates x at t = def. God willing that x exists at t brings about x existing at t, and there is no t' prior to t such that x exists at t';*

and

DEFINITION 23.2. (D2) *God conserves x at t = def. God willing that x exists at t brings about x existing at t, and there is some t' prior to t such that x exists at t'.*

Notice that the first conjunct in the definiens is exactly the same in both definitions. This feature captures the Cartesian claim that creation and conservation require the same power and action on the part of God as well as Berkeley's claim that conservation is in fact the same thing as continued repeated creation. It also captures Braine's claim that, if the continuance of the world is the result of a conserving divine brush stroke, as it were, then the same power is exercised at each stage as would have been exercised at the beginning of the brush stroke if it had a beginning.

Taken together, (P), (D1) and (D2) have these consequences. God creates every contingent individual at the first instant of its existence, if there is one, and only then; God conserves each contingent individual at every other instant at which it exists. So if there are any contingent individuals whose existence lacks a first instant, either because they have existed for infinite past time or because the finite interval throughout which they have existed is topologically open in the past, God

never creates those individuals, but he nevertheless conserves them whenever they exist. Thus even such individuals would depend on the divine will for their existence at every instant at which they existed.

It is worth noting that an individual whose existence was brought about by God at the first instant of time, supposing there to be one, would satisfy (D1). Hence being created by God does not entail first existing after a temporally prior period of nonexistence. A definition that does yield such a consequence is this:

DEFINITION 23.3. (D3) *God brings x into existence at t after a prior period of its nonexistence = def. God willing that x exists at t brings about x existing at t, there is no t' prior to t such that x exists at t', and there is some t'' prior to t such that x does not exist at t''.*

Being brought by God into existence at a certain time after a prior period of one's nonexistence entails being created by God at that time, but not vice versa. If Aquinas is right that God made the empyrean heaven, the earth and the angels at the first actual *now*, then he created all three of them then but did not then bring any of them into existence after a prior period of its nonexistence, there having been no earlier times to compose such prior periods.

Armed with this account of divine creation and conservation, I next attack the problem of applying it to classical big bang cosmogonic models. Enough has been said by now to make those applications straightforward.

Two Big Bang Models

I follow Grünbaum's presentation in dividing the material to be discussed into two cases. The second but not the first of them is a genuine case of general relativity. In both, matter-energy obeys a conservation law.

As Grünbaum describes it, "*case (i)* features a cosmic time interval that is closed at the big bang instant $t = 0$, and furthermore, *this instant had no temporal predecessor*" (1989, 389). I agree with Grünbaum that in this case it is not legitimate to ask such questions as these: What happened before $t = 0$? What prior events caused matter to come into existence at $t = 0$? Such questions contradict the assumptions of the case by presupposing that there were times before $t = 0$. I also agree that the claim that a sudden violation of matter-energy conservation occurred at $t = 0$ presupposes that there were times before $t = 0$ at which there was either no matter-energy at all or, at least, some amount of it different from that which, according to the assumptions of the case, exists at $t = 0$ and thereafter.

Clearly, however, the application of my account of divine creation and conservation to this case need involve no such presuppositions. Treating the constant sum total of matter-energy as a large contingent individual for purposes of discussion, we can deduce from (P) the claim that, for $t = 0$ and every time thereafter, God willing that this matter-energy exists at that time brings about it existing then. On the basis of (D1), we may claim that God creates this matter-energy at $t = 0$ and only then, and, on the basis of (D2), we may also claim that he conserves it at all times thereafter. All these claims seem to be consistent with the assumptions of the case. We would deny an assumption of the case if we claimed that God brings this matter-energy into existence at $t = 0$ after a prior period of its nonexistence, for those assumptions rule out the existence of any such prior period. But we need not make this claim, and, indeed, had better not do so. Theists should not find this constraint disconcerting. Because the past time of this case is isomorphic to the past time of Thomistic cosmology, the example of Aquinas shows us that theists can and sometimes do claim that God creates things ex nihilo at $t = 0$ without then bringing them into existence after a prior period of their nonexistence. So it appears that the Thomistic cosmology, at least to the extent that it applies to physical things such as matter-energy, is wholly consistent with the assumptions of this case.

This is not so in the other case, which Grünbaum describes as follows:

> *Case (ii)*. This subclass of big bang models differs from those in Case (i) by excluding the mathematical singularity at $t = 0$ as not being an actual moment of time. Thus, their cosmic time interval is *open* in the past by lacking the instant $t = 0$, although the duration of that past interval in years is finite, say 12 billion years or so. But just as in Case (i), no instants of time exist *before $t = 0$* in Case (ii). And despite the equality of finite duration of the time intervals in the two models, the crucial difference between Case (ii) and Case (i) is the following: In Case (ii), *there is no first instant of time at all,* just as there is no left-most point on an infinite Euclidean line that extends in both directions. (1989, 391)

The assumption that there is no first instant of time is, of course, inconsistent with the Thomistic claim that there is a first *now*. However, this inconsistency does not preclude the application of my account of divine creation and conservation to the case. Once again taking the constant sum total of matter-energy to be a large contingent individual, we can deduce from (P) the claim that, for every time after the mathematical singularity at $t = 0$, God willing that this matter-energy exists at that time brings about it existing then. On the basis of (D2), we may go on to claim that God conserves this matter-energy at each of those times. However, because in this case the mathematical singularity is not a time, we must not claim that God creates it at $t = 0$, and a fortiori we must also deny that he brings it into existence at $t = 0$ after a prior period of its nonexistence. So the upshot in this case is that, according to my account, God conserves the sum total of matter-energy whenever it exists, but there is no time at which he creates it or brings it into existence after a prior period of its nonexistence. This claim too seems to be consistent with the assumptions of the case under consideration. In a way, it should not even sound surprising. As Grünbaum has noted elsewhere, Lévy-Leblond has introduced an alternative time-metrization of the case that "confers an infinite duration on the ordinally unbounded past of the Big Bang universe" (Grünbaum 1990, 821). It would, after all, be natural for theists to describe a situation in which the sum total of matter-energy remains constant throughout infinite past time as one in which God always conserves it but never creates it or brings it into existence after a prior period of its nonexistence.

So far I have spoken in a guarded fashion and said only that the claims which result from applying my account of creation and conservation to the two cases being discussed *seem* consistent with their assumptions. But Grünbaum offers an argument which purports to show that this is not so. If it succeeds, the appearances are deceiving. So I must next rebut that argument.

In order to motivate the argument, we may appeal to an historical contrast, which is also cited by Grünbaum, that illustrates the point that physical theories may differ over what they take the unperturbed state or behavior of a system to be. According to Aristotle, Grünbaum tells us:

> When a sublunar body is not acted on by an external force, its *natural,* spontaneous unperturbed behavior is to be at rest at its "proper place", or—if it is not already there—to move vertically toward it. Yet, as we know, Galileo's analysis of the motions of spheres on inclined planes led him to conclude that the empirical evidence speaks against just this Aristotelian assumption. As Newton's First Law of Motion tells us, uniform motion never requires any external force as its cause; only accelerated motion does. (1989, 386)

Grünbaum invokes this notion of freedom from perturbing influences in the following passage, which refers to the remark by Descartes I quoted earlier:

> Similarly, if—as we first learned from the chemist Lavoisier—there is indeed matter-conservation (or matter-energy conservation) in a closed finite system on a macroscopic scale *qua spontaneous, natural, unperturbed behavior of the system,* then Descartes was *empirically* wrong to have assumed that such conservation requires the intervention of an *external cause.* And, if he is thus wrong, then his claim that external divine intervention in particular is needed to keep the table from disappearing into nothingness is based on a false presupposition. (Ibid., 378)

So Grünbaum holds that the presence of a conservation law for matter-energy in our two cases rules out divine conservation of the sum total of matter-energy. If this were so, the claim that God conserves the sum total of matter-energy at all times after $t = 0$ in both cases, which results from applying my account of creation and conservation to them, would be inconsistent with their assumptions.

However, in my opinion, it is not so. We can see why if we reflect a bit on the limits of what we might have learned from Lavoisier. Suppose the empirical evidence supports the hypothesis that the sum total of matter-energy in a closed system remains constant throughout a certain interval of time. The assumption that the system is closed implies that no external physical causes act on it during that interval. But does it also imply that God does not act on the system then? As theists conceive of God, there is no such implication. Divine causality is, as Braine puts it, exercised immediately to every time and place on that conception, and Leibniz too insists that divine causation, when it operates to conserve, is a perpetual immediate influence. That is why, in characterizing the causal relation in my account of creation and conservation, I specified that what does the bringing about causes what is brought about immediately rather than remotely by means of instruments such as secondary physical causes. On this view, it is absurd to suppose that any physical system or region of space-time is closed in the sense of being isolated from divine influence. Hence what we first learned from Lavoisier does not count as an empirical refutation of Descartes. On the contrary, the view that the sum total of matter-energy in a system remains constant, in the absence of external physical influences on the system, only when God conserves it, and would not continue to do so if he did not, is perfectly consistent.

Of course, one might stipulate that a closed system is one unperturbed and uninfluenced by any external cause, natural or supernatural. But then no empirical evidence can suffice to prove that there are in nature any closed systems in this sense, and so theists can consistently maintain that there are none.

In correspondence, Grünbaum has argued that what I have said so far does not get to the heart of the matter. His key thesis, he says, is that the mere physical closure of a system is causally sufficient for the conservation of its matter-energy because the conservation of matter-energy is a matter of natural law. However, this thesis rests on an understanding of the conservation law that theists of the sort I have have been discussing would reject. They would insist that the sum total of matter-energy in a physically closed system remains constant from moment to moment only if God acts to conserve it from moment to moment. Because they hold that divine conserving activity is causally necessary for the conservation of matter-energy even in physically closed systems, such theists would deny that the mere physical closure of a system is causally sufficient for the conservation of its matter-energy. So they would take the true conservation law to contain an implicit ceteris paribus clause about God's will. When spelled out in full detail, the law is to be understood as implying that if a system is physically closed, then the sum total of matter-energy in it remains constant if and only if God wills to conserve that sum total of matter-energy.

It is important to realize that it does not lie within the competence of empirical science to determine whether Grünbaum's understanding of the conservation law is rationally preferable to the theistic understanding I have sketched. The empirical methods of science could not succeed in showing that divine activity does not conserve the matter-energy in physically closed systems. Of course metaphysical naturalism entails that there is no such divine activity, but metaphysical naturalism is not itself entailed by any of the empirically established results of science. All those results are consistent with both theistic and naturalistic metaphysical worldviews. Hence, since the claims about divine conservation made by Descartes are part of a theistic metaphysics, they have not been shown to be empirically wrong by Lavoisier or by any other scientist.

Thus Grünbaum's argument fails. Knowing of no better argument to the same effect, I believe I am entitled to conclude that my claim that God conserves the sum total of matter-energy at all times after $t = 0$ in both big bang cases not only seems to be, but actually is, consistent with the assumptions of those cases. I further conclude that the application of my account of divine creation and conservation to the two big bang cases yields no results that are inconsistent with their assumptions.

Theism and Explanation

Vindicating the consistency of applications of my account of divine creation and conservation to big bang cosmogonic models with the assumptions of those models will contribute to a positive case for theistic belief only if theism, if true, could explain something that has no scientific explanation. Hence the next question I need to address is whether divine creation and conservation are bound to be explanatorily idle or superfluous in physical cosmology. Is there something about the matter-energy of big bang models that has no explanation internal to them? I think there is.

For the sake of simplicity. I assume that scientific explanation in these classical cosmological models is ideally deductive-nomological in form (see Hempel 1965). Roughly put, the idea is that particular facts are explained scientifically by being deduced from laws together with initial or boundary conditions and laws by being deduced from more general laws. Thus, for example, one might explain why there is a certain total amount of matter-energy at a certain time by deducing a statement of that fact from the conservation law for matter-energy and the statement that the same amount existed at a certain earlier time. Of course, one cannot appeal to the amount of matter-energy that existed at an earlier time in order to explain why there is a certain amount of it at $t = 0$ in Grünbaum's Case (i), there being no times earlier than $t = 0$ in that case. But, for two reasons, I do not think that this is a decisive objection to the claim that science leaves nothing which could be explained unexplained. In the first place, because deductive-nomological explanation can proceed either predictively in terms of conditions that obtain before the explanandum or retrodictively in terms of conditions that obtain after the explanandum, the existence of a certain amount of matter-energy at $t = 0$ in Case (i) can be explained retrodictively in terms of the conservation law and the existence of the same amount at a later time. And, in the second place, the existence of a certain amount of matter-energy at any particular past time can be explained predictively in Grünbaum's Case (ii), which is the interesting case from the point of view of general relativity, in terms of the conservation law and the existence of the same amount at an earlier time, because in this case, for every time, there is an earlier.

So the crucial question is whether there would be anything science could not explain even if, because time is unbounded in the past, it is the case that, for every time, the existence of a certain amount of matter-energy at that time can be deduced from the conservation law and the existence of the same amount at an earlier time. Of course, the question will arise both for the unbounded but metrically finite past time of Grünbaum's Case (ii) and for the case in which matter-energy obeys a conservation law throughout metrically infinite, unbounded past time. In my view, there would be in both these cases something that cannot be explained in deductive-nomological terms. Leibniz (1969) gives a striking example that clarifies this:

> For a sufficient reason for existence cannot be found merely in any one individual thing or even in the whole aggregate and series of things. Let us imagine the book on the *Elements of Geometry* to have been eternal, one copy always being made from another; then it is clear that though we can give a reason for the present book based on the preceding book from which it was copied, we can never arrive at a complete reason, no matter how many books we may assume in the past, for one can always wonder why such books should have existed at all times; why there should be books at all, and why they should be written in this way. What is true of books is true also of the different states of the world; every subsequent state is somehow copied from the preceding one (although according to certain laws of change). No matter how far we may have gone back to earlier states, therefore, we will never discover in them a full reason why there should be a world at all, and why it should be such as it is. Even if we should imagine the world to be eternal, therefore, the reason for it would clearly have to be sought elsewhere, since we would still be assuming nothing but a succession of states, in any one of which we can find no sufficient reason, nor can we advance the slightest toward establishing a reason, no matter how many of these states we assume. (P. 486)

Just before he cites this passage, though in a different translation, Swinburne puts the point in terms of explanation and with greater precision in a discussion of the case in which time is metrically infinite in the past. Letting L symbolize the laws of nature, he writes:

> Further, the universe will have during its infinite history, certain constant features, F_1 which are such that given that the universe has these features at a certain time and given L, the universe will always have them. But they are such that the universe could have had a different set of features F_2 equally compatible with L. What kind of features these are will depend on the character of L. But suppose for example that L includes a law of the conservation of matter, then given that there is a quantity M_1 of matter at some time, there will be M_1 at all times—and not merely that quantity of matter, but those particular bits of matter. Yet compatible with L will be the supposition that there was a different quantity M_2 made up of different bits. Then it will be totally inexplicable why the quantity of matter was M_1 rather than M_2. If L does not include laws of the conservation of matter, it is hard to see how it could fail to include laws formulable as conservation laws of some kind (e.g., of energy, or momentum, or spin, or even the density of matter). And so a similar point would arise. Why does the world contain just that amount of energy, no more, no less? L would explain why whatever energy there is remains the same; but what L does not explain is why there is just this amount of energy. (1979, 124–25)

Thus, to return to the Leibnizian example, if there is a law of the conservation of kinds of books, then, given that there are copies of Euclid's *Elements* at some time, there will be copies at all times. But it is compatible with this conservation law to suppose that there were different books than there are. Hence it will be inexplicable by appeal to this law why what is conserved includes Euclid's *Elements* and not Pierre Menard's *Don Quixote* or includes any books at all rather than being a state of booklessness in which no books exist. Similarly, in the big bang cases I have been discussing, given that there is a certain quantity of matter-energy at some time, there will be that quantity at all times. But it is compatible with the conservation law for matter-energy to suppose that there was a different quantity of matter-energy than there actually is. Thus it will be inexplicable by appeal to that law why what is conserved is this particular quantity of matter-energy rather than some other or, for that matter, a state in which there is no matter-energy.

The correct conclusion to draw from these considerations is Swinburne's. Applied to the unbounded but finite past time of Grünbaum's Case (ii), it is that there is no scientific explanation of why there is a certain amount of matter-energy rather than some other amount or none at all, even if, for every time, a statement that this amount exists at that time can be deduced from the conservation law for matter-energy plus a statement that the same amount existed at an earlier time. This is an inexplicable brute fact if only scientific explanation of a deductive-nomological sort is allowed.

There is more. The conservation law for matter-energy is logically contingent. So if it is true, the question of why it holds rather than not doing so arises. If it is a fundamental law and only scientific explanation is allowed, the fact that matter-energy is conserved is an inexplicable brute fact. For all we know, the conservation law for matter-energy may turn out to be a derived law and so deducible from some deeper principle of symmetry or invariance. But if this is the case, the same question can be asked about this deeper principle because it too will be logically contingent. If it is fundamental and only scientific explanation is allowed, then the fact that it holds is scientifically inexplicable. Either the regress of explanation terminates in a most fundamental law or it does not. If there is a deepest law, it will be logically contingent, and so the fact that it holds rather than not doing so will be a brute fact. If the regress does not terminate, then for every law in the infinite hierarchy there is a deeper law from which it can be deduced. hi this case, however, the whole hierarchy will be logically contingent, and so the question of why it holds rather than some other hierarchy will arise. So if only scientific explanation is allowed, the fact that this particular infinite hierarchy of contingent laws holds will be a brute inexplicable fact. Therefore, on the assumption that scientific laws are logically contingent and are explained by being deduced from other laws, there are bound to be inexplicable brute facts if only scientific explanation is allowed.

There are, then, genuine explanatory problems too big, so to speak, for science to solve. If the theistic doctrine of creation and conservation is true, these problems have solutions in terms of agent-causation. The reason why there is a certain amount of matter-energy and not some other amount or none at all is that God so wills it, and the explanation of why matter-energy is conserved is that God conserves it. Obviously nothing I have said proves that the theistic solutions to these problems are correct. I have not shown that it is not an inexplicable brute fact that a certain amount of matter-energy exists and is conserved. For all I have said, the explanatory problems I have been discussing are insoluble. But an insoluble problem is not a pseudoproblem; it is a genuine problem that has no solution. So Grünbaum's claim that creation is a pseudoproblem for big bang cosmogonic models misses the mark.

Steady State and Quantum Cosmologies

Grünbaum's treatment of physical cosmology also contains discussions of the steady state theory of Bondi and Gold and of an account of quantum cosmology by Weisskopf. I conclude with brief remarks on these two cases.

The steady state theory on which Grünbaum focuses his attention postulates conservation of matter-density in an expanding universe and so requires a nonconservative accretion of matter over time. According to Grünbaum, the natural, spontaneous and unperturbed behavior of the physical universe presented by this theory conserves matter-density rather than the total quantity of matter and so requires matter-accretion because the universe is expanding. The key point he makes is this, *"Just as a theory postulating matter-conservation does not require God to prevent the conserved matter from being annihilated, so also the steady-state theory has no need at all for a divine agency to cause its new hydrogen to come into being!"* (1989, 388).

But neither does the steady state theory rule out a divine cause for the coming to be of its new hydrogen. Empirical evidence would warrant the claim that new hydrogen comes into being spontaneously only if spontaneity precluded no more than external physical causes for the postulated matter-accretion. Applied to the new hydrogen of the steady state theory, my account of divine creation and conservation tells us that each new hydrogen atom is either both created and brought into existence after a prior period of its nonexistence by God at the first instant of its existence, if there is one, and thereafter conserved by God, or, if there is a last instant of its nonexistence but no first instant of its existence, conserved by God at all times after the last instant of its nonexistence at which it exists, though neither created nor brought into existence after a prior period of its nonexistence by God. This claim is consistent with the assumptions of the theory. Moreover, the steady state theory, too, poses explanatory problems that science cannot solve. If only scientific explanation is allowed, it will be a brute inexplicable fact that the matter-density has the particular value it does rather than some other value, and the same goes for the fact that a conservation law for matter-density holds or the fact that the deeper laws from which it can be deduced rather than alternatives hold if the conservation principle is a derived law. And, again, if the theistic doctrine of creation and conservation is true, such facts as these have explanations in the divine will. So if the steady state theory were true and such things were facts, theism would not be explanatorily superfluous or idle.

The same is true in the case of quantum cosmology. Following Weisskopf, Grünbaum lays out a cosmogonic scenario. The initial state of the physical cosmos is the true vacuum, which is subject to energy fluctuations but devoid of matter and energy proper. When such fluctuations take place, there is a transition to the false vacuum, which contains energy but not matter. The false vacuum undergoes a rapid inflationary expansion until it reaches a certain size. When it does, the inflationary expansion stops and a true vacuum emerges, but within a microsecond the energy contained in the false vacuum shows up as light and in the form of various particles and antiparticles. Thereafter the universe expands relatively slowly in ways previously familiar, forming in due course atoms, stars, galaxies and so forth. Speaking of the transition from true to false vacuum, Grünbaum says, "Thus, according to quantum theory, this sort of emergence of energy, which is

ex nihilo only in a rather Pickwickian senses proceeds in accord with pertinent physical principles, rather than as a matter of inscrutable external divine causation" (1989, 392).

However, from the fact that, according to quantum cosmology, the emergence of energy proceeds in accord with physical principles it does not follow that there is nothing in this scenario for theism to explain. The litany should by now be familiar. What, if anything, explains the fact that the universe is initially a true vacuum rather than being in some other state? And what, if anything, explains the fact that the particular physical principles in accord with which its evolution from this initial state proceeds rather than others hold? Perhaps these things, if they are facts at all, are inexplicable brute facts. They are if only scientific explanation is allowed. But, then again, perhaps not. If theism is true, they are not.

I confess to a bit of uncertainty about how to apply my account of divine creation and conservation to this scenario, but I will venture a guess. Because the initial true vacuum seems not to be a genuine state of nonbeing, I think it should be described as created by God at the first instant of its existence, if there is one, and conserved by God thereafter for as long as it exists, or, if there is no such first instant, conserved by God as long as it exists. As new individuals come into being later in the scenario, those that have a first instant of existence are then both created by God and brought into existence by God after a prior period of their nonexistence and subsequently conserved by God, and any that have a last instant of nonexistence but no first instant of existence are conserved by God after the last instant of their nonexistence for as long as they exist. And, of course, physical principles describe any empirical regularities there are in the effects of all this divine activity.

I submit that two conclusions are warranted on the basis of the foregoing examination of cosmological theories. First, all the theories surveyed are consistent with my account of divine creation and conservation, and, what is more, none of them gives us any reason for thinking that the theistic doctrine of creation and conservation is false. Second, each of the theories considered gives rise to genuine explanatory problems that science alone cannot solve but that theism, if true, does solve.

In this essay I have not discussed the question of whether physical cosmology provides positive evidential support for the theistic doctrine of creation and conservation. To raise the question is to ask whether there is a successful cosmological argument for the existence of God, and I must reserve for another occasion an exposition of my views on that difficult topic. In closing I will make four brief remarks on the prospects for a successful cosmological argument. First, the version of the argument Grünbaum (1989) criticizes is a particularly simple one, and he makes no effort to show that it was endorsed by any of the historical figures who have made important contributions to philosophical theology. After explicitly noting that there are other versions of the argument, he says "I do *not* claim that my charge of pseudo-problem applies necessarily to all of the questions addressed by these other versions" (ibid., 378). Second, some of these other versions do not suffer from the flaws Grünbaum detects in the version he attacks and are very much worthy of consideration on their own merits. One, to which Grünbaum does refer, is a deductive argument formulated by William Rowe, who finds some of its ideas in an earlier argument constructed by Samuel Clarke. Though he concludes that this argument does not prove the existence of God, Rowe leaves open the possibility that it renders theistic belief reasonable, "I am proposing to the theist that in seeking rational justification for his belief in the conclusion of the Cosmological Argument he would do well to abandon the view that the Cosmological Argument is a proof of theism, and, in its place, pursue the possibility that the Cosmological Argument shows the reasonableness of theistic belief, even though it perhaps fails to show that theism is true" (1975, 269). Another version, to which Grünbaum does not refer, is a Bayesian argument constructed by Swinburne. He argues that the hypothesis of theism is more probable given the existence over time of a complex physical universe than it is on tautological evidence alone, and he further contends that this argument is part of a cumulative case for theism whose ultimate conclusion is that "on our total evidence theism is more probable than not" (1979, 291). Third, because such versions of the argument

appeal only to very general features of the cosmos of contingent things, for example, the fact that it consists at least in part of a complex and enduring physical universe, the details of scientific cosmological theories are apt to have little if any bearing on whether such arguments lend theistic belief evidential support, render it reasonable, or even demonstrate its truth. This is, of course, not to say that such arguments are immunized against philosophical criticism or capable of surviving it in the long run. But, fourth, it does suggest that those who are concerned with the fate of cosmological arguments would do better to study philosophical theology and its history than to immerse themselves in contemporary physics.

At the very end of his paper, Grünbaum says that the traditional cosmological argument for divine creation "dies hard" (1989, 393). My reply is that the tradition contains many such arguments and that it is premature to predict the death of them all.

I am grateful to Alfred J. Freddoso, Adolf Grünbaum, and Ernan McMullin for helpful suggestions. Grünbaum (1991), which appeared in print after this essay had been completed, contains further discussion of the topic of creation as does Grünbaum (1993); I hope to respond to these articles on another occasion.

References

Aquinas, T. 1952. *De Potentia*. Translated by English Dominican Fathers. Westminster, Md.: Newman Press.

———. 1981. *Summa Theologiae*. Translated by English Dominican Fathers. Westminster, Md.: Christian Classics.

Berkeley, G. 1950. *Works*. Vol.2. Edited by A. A. Luce and T. E. Jessop. London: Nelson.

Braine, D. 1988. *The Reality of Time and the Existence of God*. Oxford: Clarendon Press.

Descartes, R. 1955. *Philosophical Works*. Vol. 1. Edited by E. S. Haldane and G. T. R. Ross. New York: Dover.

Edwards, J. 1970. *Works*. Vol. 3. Edited by C. A. Holbrook. New Haven: Yale University Press.

Grünbaum, A. 1989. "The Pseudo-problem of Creation in Physical Cosmology." *Philosophy of Science 56:* 373–94.

———. "Pseudo-creation of the Big Bang." *Nature 344:* 821–22.

———. "Creation as a Pseudo-explanation in Current Physical Cosmology." *Erkenntnis 35:* 233–54.

———. 1993. "Theological Misinterpretations of Current Cosmology." Preprint.

Hempel, C. G. 1965. *Aspects of Scientific Explanation.* New York: Free Press.

Leibniz, G. W. 1949. *New Essays Concerning Human Understanding.* Translated by A. G. Langley. La Salle, Ill.: Open Court.

———. 1952. *Theodicy.* Translated by E. M. Huggard. New Haven: Yale University Press.

———. 1956. *The Leibniz-Clarke Correspondence,* Edited by H. G. Alexander. Manchesrer: Manchester University Press.

———. 1969. *Philosophical Papers and Letters.* Edited by L. E. Loemker. Dordrecht: Reidel.

Mavrodes, G. 1970. *Belief in God.* New York: Random House.

Quinn, P. L. 1983. "Divine Conservation, Continuous Creation, and Human Action." In A. J. Freddoso, ed., *The Existence and Nature of God.* Notre Dame: University of Notre Dame Press.

———. 1988. "Divine Conservation, Secondary Causes, and Occasionalism." In T. V. Morris, ed., *Divine and Human Action.* Ithaca: Cornell University Press.

Rowe, W. 1975. The Cosmological Argument. Princeton: Princeton University Press.

Scotus, J. D. 1975. *God and Creatures: The Quodlibetal Questions.* Translated by F. Alluntis and A. B. Wolter. Princeton: Princeton University Press.

Swinburne, R. 1977. *The Coherence of Theism.* Oxford: Clarendon Press.

———. 1979. *The Existence of God.* Oxford: Clarendon Press.

53. *Theological Misinterpretations of Current Physical Cosmology*

ADOLF GRÜNBAUM

In this selection, Adolf Grünbaum challenges Quinn's cosmological defense of divine creation and conservation in the preceding article. Grünbaum challenges virtually every major point in Quinn's paper. He objects to the idea that divine volitional creations offer an explanation of why there is a world at all. For Grünbaum, "the notion of *timelessly eternal acts of willing* is obscure and elusive to the point of making such divine willings altogether nonexplanatory as causes of the existence of our world" (p. 70). The very question that motivates Quinn's positive reason for God, namely, "Why is something rather than nothing?" is, according to Grünbaum, doubly illegitimate. First, because the sufficient reason for physical existence is found within physics itself (as the reason for energy conservation), and second because it assumes that if there is a physical world at all then it must have arisen spontaneously from utter nothingness. Grünbaum argues that both of these claims are either false or unintelligible. He goes on to argue that contrary to Quinn's claims, the doctrine of physical energy conservation in the big bang cosmology, as well as the physics of the steady-state theories, are logically incompatible with the doctrine of divine conservation. In a sequel to this piece titled, "The Poverty of Theistic Cosmology," forthcoming in *The British Journal for the Philosophy of Science* (2004), Grünbaum continues his attack on versions of the cosmological argument, especially Leibniz's argument from contingency. Adolf Grünbaum is the Mellon Professor of Philosophy of Science, Research Professor of Psychiatry, and Chair of the Center for Philosophy of Science, all at the University of Pittsburgh.

Abstract: In earlier writings, I argued that *neither* of the two major physical cosmologies of the twentieth century *support* divine creation, so that atheism has nothing to fear from the explanations required by these cosmologies. Yet theists ranging from Augustine, Aquinas, Descartes, and Leibniz to Richard Swinburne and Philip Quinn have maintained that, at *every* instant anew, the existence of the world *requires* divine creation *ex nihilo* as its cause. Indeed, according to some such theists, for any given moment *t*, God's volition that the-world-should-exist-at-*t* supposedly *brings about* its actual existence at *t*.

In an effort to establish the current viability of this doctrine of perpetual divine conservation. Philip Quinn[1] argued that it is entirely compatible with *physical* energy conservation in the Big Bang cosmology, as well as with the physics of the steady-state theories.

But I now contend that instead, there is a logical *incompatibility* on both counts. Besides, the stated tenet of divine conservation has an additional defect. It speciously purchases plausibility by trading on the multiply disanalogous volitional explanations of human actions.

---

1. *Introduction*

It has been claimed that the Big Bang Cosmogony—and also the now largely unpopular steady-state cosmology—pose a *scientifically insoluble* problem of matter-energy creation and fail to explain why the world does not lapse into nonbeing at any given moment. We are told that this alleged conundrum is solved by postulating divine intervention as an external cause. If there is a first moment at which the universe begins to exist, we learn, then this creative supernatural intervention occurs at that moment and ever after. In any case,

divine creative intervention is allegedly required *throughout all existing time*, no matter whether the universe has a temporal beginning or not.

In the case of the Big Bang theory, the champions of this thesis have ranged from Pope Pius XII in 1951, as he told the Pontifical Academy of Sciences, to the British astronomer Bernard Lovell, the American astronomer Robert Jastrow, and to the theistic philosophers Richard Swinburne at Oxford and Philip Quinn at Notre Dame University in the United States. Lovell had made the same claim à propos of the steady-state cosmology.

In my earlier papers of 1989 through 1991,[2,3,4,5] I disputed this theological twist. And I maintained more generally that *atheism has nothing to fear at all* from these two major twentieth-century physical cosmologies, because neither of them support the idea of God-the-creator.[6] But, I shall now argue further that, conversely, perpetual divine creationism actually has a great deal to fear from both of these cosmologies.

The familiar meaning of the word "creation" lends itself to the insinuation of a creative role of a supernatural agency *without argument*. As Webster's Dictionary tells us, in its primary use, the term "creation" means: Act of causing to exist, or fact of being brought into existence by divine power or its equivalent; especially the act of bringing the universe or this world into existence out of nothing." Evidently, the transitive verb "to create" calls for a *subject* as well as an object. And in a *cosmological* context, the verb is laden with the notion of a divine *agency* or cause *external* to the entire world.

In a 1989 paper, which was reprinted in John Leslie's 1990 volume *Physical Cosmology and Philosophy,*[7,8] I argued that the question of whether the universe had a temporal origin had been *fallaciously transmuted* into the *pseudo-problem* of the creation of the world with its matter-energy by a cause *external* to the universe.

In a 1991 paper in *Erkenntnis,*[9] I extended my arguments so as to include a critique of the thesis of the English physicist C. J. Isham. According to Isham, the Hartle and Hawking version of quantum cosmology lends itself to supporting Augustinian creation *ex nihilo*. Writing in a 1988 Vatican Observatory volume, Isham[10] extolled as "profound" Augustine's doctrine that

From Adolf Grünbaum, "Theological Misinterpretations of Current Physical Cosmology," *Philo* 1, No. 1 (1998): 15–34. Reprinted by permission of the author and *Philo*.

*This paper is a substantially revised version of an invited article by the same title that appeared in *Foundations of Physics* 26, no. 4 (April 1996): 523–43. A major sequel to it entitled "A New Critique of Theological Interpretations of Physical Cosmology" is now under preparation for later publication.

God created *both* time itself *and* matter. Yet, as I shall explain at the end of Section 5, I contend that Augustine's view is fundamentally unsound.

My 1989 paper[11] provoked three responses, only one of which will concern me here, because it pertains to the most influential of the creationist scenarios: *Perpetual* divine creation.

The theist Philip L. Quinn of Notre Dame University has recently offered a cosmological defense of divine creation and conservation[12] which I shall challenge here.

In the 1989 paper,[13] I had not confined myself to the minimalist doctrine that God created the world all at once. Instead, I had also taken explicit issue with Descartes's thesis of *perpetual divine conservation* of matter vis-à-vis Lavoisier's hypothesis of *natural* spontaneous matter-conservation through time. The Cartesian doctrine asserts that the preservation of matter in existence requires divine *repetition* of an act of creation at every moment. That thesis of *creatio continuans* was espoused by a historically long succession of theists.[14,15] I shall argue, however, that it fails altogether for an array of reasons.

The upshot of this article will strengthen considerably, I trust, my earlier objections to theological creationism. As already noted, previously I had argued mainly that atheism has nothing to fear from the physical cosmologies of the past half century, because they provide no evidential support for divine creation. Philip Quinn's challenge, among others, now prompts me to offer the following *stronger* indictment of creationist natural theology: The Big Bang model of general relativity theory as well as the steady-state theory are *each logically incompatible* with the theological doctrine that divine *creatio continuans* is *required* in both of their worlds. Moreover, that doctrine is vitiated by major epistemological and conceptual difficulties, as I shall try to show.

The well-known American Roman Catholic Jesuit theologian Michael Buckley at Notre Dame University,[16] in a critique of Paul Davies's "wishy-washy" theology, comes fairly close to conceding unintentionally my impending thesis that divine volitional creation offers a *pseudo*explanation, when Buckley makes a major concession concerning the hypothesized process of divine creation. As he admits: "We really do not know how God 'pulls it off.' Catholicism has found no great scandal in this admitted ignorance." But if theology is thus admittedly ignorant, then the theological hypothesis of creation *ex nihilo* adds no articulated *causal* understanding of the existence of matter-energy to *any* physical model of cosmogony! We have no evidence at all for effective volitional actions that are *causally unmediated* by a nervous system and yet conform to the practical syllogism. As we know, in that syllogism an action is explained by a desire-cum-belief set. And it would, of course, be entirely illicit for the theist to trade tacitly on the picture of *transformative* causation to defend creation *ex nihilo*. Yet Pope Pius XII[17] and many, many others have told us that science is explanatorily defective in a basic way without the hypothesis of divine creation *ex nihilo*.

In rejecting creationist theological appropriations of the steady-state and Big Bang cosmologies alike, I need not make any claims concerning their respective technical scientific merits, which are currently oscillating somewhat in the case of the Big Bang model, although the major features of the model continue to command much loyalty from cosmologists. For example, until 1990, when NASA's satellite COBE found wrinkles in the previously uniform density of the cosmic microwave radiation, the Big Bang model conspicuously lacked an explanation of the genesis of the galaxies! But when the Berkeley physicist George Smoot announced the detection of the density fluctuations in April 1991 to the American Physical Society, he electrified the newspapers and some of the faithful by declaring: "If you are religious, this is like looking at God."

Though probably unintended, the journalistic moral seems to be that you have a better chance to behold the Almighty with a differential microwave radiometer than by praying! Yet the evidential fortunes of the *Big Bang theory* are not entirely secure, although it has been almost universally victorious among cosmologists so far over the rival steady-state theories. Now it confronts the embarrassing discrepancy between the age of the oldest stars and the newly calculated lesser age of the universe since the Big Bang. Yet it would seem most recently that the cosmic expansion will continue forever instead of being followed by a cosmic collapse and annihilating crunch. Thus, our own galaxy will be ever more "alone" in the cosmos, a prospect that some people may find depressing but which I myself view with complete equanimity.

The steady-state cosmology now has few adherents among physical scientists, with such notable exceptions as Hoyle and Narlikar and perhaps others. Previously, I criticized the specific theistic reading that the English radio astronomer Sir Bernard Lovell gave of the steady-state world. It is philosophically instructive, however, I believe, that, despite the serious empirical difficulties of the steady-state theory, I examine further critically its theological creationist interpretation, as articulated in 1993 by Quinn. And it will be expeditious to discuss it before I deal with the Big Bang theory.

2. The Steady-State Cosmology

The steady-state theories were pioneered in the late 1940s by Fred Hoyle and by Hermann Bondi and Thomas Gold. Very recently, Hoyle[18] published a modification of his 1948 theory in the journal *Astrophysics and Space Science*. But for my philosophical purposes here, which pertain to attempted *theological appropriations* of physical cosmology, I need to focus on the simplest of the 1948 versions. That original form of the theory features a *violation* of matter-energy conservation by the formation of new matter without any transformative causation, i.e., "out of nothing," whereas the modification of the theory in the 1980s and since no longer features such a violation. At the hands of such astronomers as Lovell,[19,20] divine intervention was claimed to be required by the *non*conservative formation of the new matter that had been deduced in the original 1948 theory. (But in the modified recent version, the positive energy of the new matter is balanced by the negative energy of the so-called C-field.)

The steady-state theory postulated originally *as a matter of natural law* that while the galaxies are receding from each other everywhere in the universe, the matter-*density* nonetheless ubiquitously *remains constant* through time. This constancy is enunciated by the so-called Perfect Cosmological Principle. Hence the name "steady-state" for this cosmic scenario of eternal constancy of density. But, if there is such constancy of density alongside the galactic recession, then com-

pletely *new* matter must pop into existence out of nowhere in violation of matter-conservation, such that it fills, at the requisite rate, the spaces vacated by the galactic recession. Yet the ensuing rate at which the presumed new matter would make its cosmic debut is so small as to presumably elude detection in the laboratory, at least foreseeably.

Lovell[21] asked, in effect: What is the *external cause* of the coming into existence of the new hydrogen atoms in the Bondi and Gold universe, which come into being in violation of matter-energy conservation? Thereupon he complains that the "steady-state theory has no solution to the problem of creation of [new] matter." Note that Lovell uses the theologically tinged causal term "creation," instead of the neutral descriptive term "accretion."

Now observe that Lovell's demand for an *external cause* of the new matter is unfortunately loaded with tacitly taking the law of energy-conservation for granted, as is clear from his complaint[22] that the steady-state theory makes no provision for "the *energy input* which gave rise to the created [hydrogen] atom" (my italics). But the steady-state theory explicitly *denies* that energy-conservation law. Thus, Lovell's conservationist assumption of the need for other energy as the source of the matter "input" *contradicts* the steady-state theory! After all, the steady-state theory had deduced an *altogether natural* violation of energy-conservation from its postulate of density-constancy in an expanding universe. Hence Lovell simply begged the question when he asked for the energy-source or transformative cause of the new hydrogen.

It is granted, of course, that the postulate of density-constancy may be questioned as long as there is insufficient evidence for it. Thus, Lovell and everyone else is entitled to ask for the *observational credentials* of the steady-state theory. But, as we saw, *that* was *not* his question, since he did not challenge that theory epistemologically but only ontologically. I am happy to report that at a 1986 meeting in Locarno, Lovell conceded my point, and he said so in the published proceedings.[23]

In my 1989 article,[24] I had drawn the following conclusion: " . . . in the steady-state theory, . . . *non*-conservative matter-accretion [or popping into existence *ex nihilo*] is claimed to transpire *without any kind of external [or super-*

natural] cause, because it is held to be cosmically the spontaneous, natural, unperturbed behavior of the physical world!"[25, 26] Quinn objects[27]: "But neither does the steady-state theory *rule out* a [required] divine cause for the [eternal] coming to be of its new hydrogen" (my italics). Yet, I shall now argue here against Quinn that his claim of such a required divine creative role is indeed *ruled out* as definitely *inconsistent* with the steady-state cosmology.

As Quinn emphasizes, several contemporary theists besides himself echo the doctrine of *creatio continuans* championed by Aquinas, Descartes, Berkeley, Leibniz, Locke, Jonathan Edwards et al. Thus, Quinn maintains explicitly that perpetual divine creative activity is crucial for such mere physical energy or matter-conservation as holds in a Big Bang universe, no less than for the hypothesized coming into existence of new matter in the steady-state world. And, as Quinn tells us, Richard Swinburne attributes to theists the view that "God keeps the universe in being, whether he has been doing so for ever or only for a finite time."[28] Indeed, the British physicist-theologian John Polkinghorne sees just the doctrine of *perpetual* rather than initial creation as the essence of the Christian scenario, although his views should not be equated with Quinn's in other respects. In short, as Descartes claimed in the Third Meditation, creation and conservation require the same divine power and action. And, as Berkeley explained, divine conservation is simply continued and repeated creation.

Thus, in the traditional theistic account, it is held[29] that "all contingent things are continuously dependent upon God for their existence." I shall challenge that claim as *ill-conceived* from the outset. On Quinn's view,[30] "God not only creates all contingent things but also conserves them in existence, moment by moment, in a way that is tantamount to continuously creating or recreating them" (my italics).

According to Quinn,[31] the relevant "relation of metaphysical dependence or causation" is a primitive relation rendered by the following locution: "God willing that *x*-exists-at-*t* brings about *x*-existing-at-*t*." I disregard here my multiple malaise with this sort of notion of divine *volitional* causation, but just recall my brief objections to it à propos of the Jesuit Buckley's agnostic disclaimer

as to the mediating causal process. Yet, as every paralytic and paraplegic knows all too well, a mediating causal process involving the adequate functioning of the nervous system needs to be specified when we explain *in the context of existing evidence,* say, a particular outcome as the product of human volitional action. If, for example, Jones wants an electric light bulb to be turned on, it won't do to explain the lit state of the bulb by *merely* saying in the manner of the Book of Genesis: "Jones willed: Let there be light"! We have no evidence at all for this kind of unmediated causation, which is reminiscent of *word magic.*

Quinn emphasizes that his relation of divine bringing about volitionally "must have the following marks in order to serve its theological purposes"[32]: (a) " . . . what does the bringing about [i.e., divine volition] is the *total* cause of what is brought about; nothing else is required by way of causal contribution in order for the effect to obtain," because the divine will is causally *sufficient* and (b) " . . . the bringing about is the *sole* cause of what is brought about; causal *overdetermination* is ruled out"[33] (my italics), since it allows more than one sufficient cause.

Quinn is concerned to rule out sufficient causes other than divine volition in order to claim that God's creative and conservative actions are *necessary* for the existence of the physical entities. In short, as Quinn has it, God is the *total* and *only* cause of the existence of things. And the crucial underlying assumption is that this very existence *must have a cause at all,* a posit that I shall discredit in Section 4 below.

Now note that the cardinal postulate of the theories of Hoyle and of Bondi and Gold is the so-called Perfect Cosmological Principle. Rightly or wrongly, it asserts, as a matter of natural law, that there is conservation of matter-*density.* But it is of *decisive* importance that, in conjunction with that law of density-conservation, the so-called expansion of the universe or mutual galactic recession is *causally sufficient* for the *completely natural* coming into existence *ex nihilo* (out of nowhere) of new matter! Equally crucial is the fact that, *without* this cosmic expansion, density-conservation *alone* would *not* issue in matter-accretion.

Thus, Leibniz could get his coveted *sufficient* reason for the existence of the new matter *from the physics itself without God,* if he could have known the content of the 1948 steady-state theory of Bondi and Gold. Indeed, this natural *physical* causal sufficiency is decisive, because it obviously rules out the theistic claim, made by Quinn and Lovell, that external creative divine intervention in the universe is *required* for such formation of new matter.

It has been wrongly claimed that the Bondi and Gold explanation of the rate of the formation of new matter is suspect as being *teleological,* since it is *seemingly* dictated by the *outcome*-state of *density*-conservation during the expansion. But this objection is without merit. Density-conservation is no more teleological than energy-conservation or charge-conservation. The outcome states result from the prior state in accord with the pertinent laws. One might object equally fallaciously, that neutrino-production during radioactive decay, as postulated by Pauli and Fermi, is teleological, because it is governed by the outcome-state of *energy*-conservation, given that the fragments of the radioactive decay have a smaller total mass-energy than their undecayed ancestor. Relatedly, the claim that teleology dictates the formation of new matter in the steady-state world cannot sustain the theistic creationist interpretation of the nonconservative formation of new matter in the steady-state theory.

Thus, contrary to Quinn, the steady-state cosmology is indeed *logically incompatible* with his and Lovell's claim that divine creative intervention is causally necessary for the nonconservative popping into existence of new matter in the steady-state universe.

But that is not all. In Quinn's theistic scenario, we recall, the divine creative will is both the *total* and the *sole* cause of the matter-accretion. This alleged totality and exclusivity of *God's* causal role in the existence of the new matter entails the *bizarre conclusion* that the physics of the steady-state universe makes no causal contribution at all to the popping into existence of the new matter.

Let me emphatically reject as completely futile and evasive the reply that, at any moment in the steady-state world, it is within God's power to *suspend* its density-conservation principle, much as a government can revoke the normativity of its statutory laws. Note at once the dubious analogy between revoking a statutory, *normative* law, which does not describe actual behavior, and "suspending" a *descriptive* law. But suppose that someone would try to disarm the physical causal sufficiency for the genesis of new matter which I have demonstrated, declaring: God does his creative job *indirectly* by keeping the law of density-conservation in place during the cosmic expansion. In this way, it might be thought, the doctrine of required indirect divine creation might be made compatible with the physics after all. But such an attempt to neutralize my critique simply fails.

In the first place, Quinn asserted the logical compatibility of the required theistic creationist scenario with the *assumed truth* of the steady-state cosmology. But that cosmology categorically features *as given* the eternal temporal invariance of density-conservation in an expanding universe. Secondly, but no less importantly, Quinn, citing Leibniz and a 1988 work by David Braine,[34] told us explicitly that divine creative causation is direct in the form of *unmediated* bringing about the existence of matter, rather than only indirect, such as via the density-conservation law. As Quinn explained[35]: In characterizing the causal relation in his account of creation and conservation, he had "specified that what does the bringing about causes what is brought about *immediately* rather than remotely by means of instruments such as secondary physical causes."

Thus it would completely beg the question in this context to seek refuge in the *deus ex machina* of the alleged divine ability to suspend the density-conservation law, as it were, or to stop the expansion of the universe. Theists are free to take that supposed divine ability on faith, if they can clarify just what it means. But that freedom is unavailing, because the context of the entire cosmological debate on divine creation is one of *argument* in natural rather than fideist theology. Thus it would clearly be question-begging, if not simply frivolous, to claim, in effect, that, within the steady-state cosmology, the Perfect Cosmological Principle is tacitly predicated on the proviso that God *refrain* from *suspending* density-conservation and/or from arresting the cosmic expansion. Neither Bondi, nor Gold, nor Hoyle—all reputedly atheists—would dream of such a proviso. And it is not they who are begging the question. *Besides,* the proposed *deus ex machina* of indirect divine creation is plainly *ad hoc,* since no evidence is offered for it at all.

As is now very clear, I trust, the steady-state theory radically belies the inveterate thesis that, *no matter what the physics of our world,* any matter-energy coming into being *ex nihilo* requires an external divine creative cause. And that alone, I claim, clearly discredits the received theistic view as articulated by Quinn. Indeed, it is, I claim, one of the gravest and *most insidious* of errors in the *entire history* of philosophy to legislate the need for external causes independently of what the actual physics of our world may be. I shall now articulate this major moral historically before turning to the Big Bang cosmology. In order to do so, let me now first refine my earlier published statement of the generalized fundamental lesson I draw from the history of science for the issues before us.

3. The *Import of the History of Science for the Postulation of* External *Causes*

Important episodes in the history of science have shown that new evidence or new theoretical insights have warranted fundamental changes in dealing with the following major question: Is it justified, in a given context, to postulate causes *external* to physical or biological systems as *intervening* in them, in order to explain some observed behavior of these systems? The historical evolution of the answers to this question bears directly on the legitimacy of inferring an *external* cause to account for the behavior of the universe as a whole, *or even for its very existence.* Let us see just how.

According to Aristotle. a force is needed as the external cause of a sublunar body's nonvertical motion, even if it moves horizontally with constant velocity. In his physics, the demand for such a disturbing external dynamical cause to explain any such motion arises from the following assump-

tion: When a sublunar body is not acted on by an external force, its *natural,* spontaneous, dynamically unperturbed behavior is to be at rest at its "proper place," or—if it is not already there—to move vertically toward it.

Yet, as we know, Galileo's analysis of the motions of spheres on inclined planes, among other things, led him to conclude that the empirical evidence speaks against just this Aristotelian assumption. As Newton's First Law of Motion tells us, uniform motion *never* requires any external force as its cause; only accelerated motion does. Thus, Galileo and Newton *eliminated* a *supposed external* dynamical cause on *empirical* grounds, explaining that uniform motion can occur spontaneously without such a cause.

But, if so, then the Aristotelian demand for a causal explanation of *any* motion whatever by reference to an external perturbing force is predicated on a *false underlying assumption.*

Clearly, the Aristotelians begged the question by tenaciously continuing to ask: "What net external force, pray tell, keeps a uniformly moving body going?" Thus, scientific and philosophical questions can be anything but innocent by loading the dice with a *petitio principii!*

A brief example from the history of biology, starting with Louis Pasteur but including Oparin and Urey, likewise illustrates a change as to the hypothesized need for external causes in the debate on the feasibility of the spontaneous generation of life from nonliving substances.[36]

I have adduced these examples in addition to the steady-state world to show that a scientific or philosophical theory may be fundamentally mistaken in calling for some sort of external cause to explain certain states of affairs. No physicist or philosopher can be justly criticized for failing to answer a causal question inspired by that mistaken demand for an external cause.[37] Incidentally, I do not deny that in *other* cases, physical evidence may show the need for an external cause where none was theretofore suspected, as noted by the historian Lorraine Darden.

Now let me argue that the stated moral from the particular examples I adduced from the history of science spells a salutary caveat for the purported problem of creation.

4. The Question of the Ratio Essendi as a Pseudoproblem

I claim that the question "Why is there anything at all rather than just nothing?" is a misguided query, at least to the extent that it calls for a cause external to the universe. Thus, it is wrong-headed, I shall now contend, to ask for the external cause or reason of the bare existence and persistence of the world, its so-called *ratio essendi*. But it is vital to distinguish such a supposed *creative* cause or reason, as Aquinas did, from a merely *transformative* cause, which just produces *changes* in things that *already exist* in *some* form, or generates new entities from previously existing objects.

There is a crucial underlying assumption that animates the theological creationist and conservationist *ratio essendi* given by an array of famous theists.

They take it to be axiomatic that *if* there is a physical world *at all,* then its spontaneous, undisturbed or natural state is one of *utter nothingness,* whatever that is. Those many theists who make this dubious assumption have thereby generated grounds for claiming that the very existence of matter, energy, or whatever constitutes a *deviation* from the alleged spontaneity of nothingness. And that supposed deviation must then have a suitably potent *external* cause.

Just this assumption of spontaneous nothingness is at least insinuated by the biblical story of Genesis. But Aquinas and Leibniz, among others, make it explicit. Aquinas used the loaded, question-begging word "creature" to refer to any contingent entity and declared: "the being of *every* creature depends on God, so that not for a moment could it subsist, *but would fall into nothingness* were it not kept in being by the operation of Divine power" (my italics).[38] Thus, here we have the fateful crucial presupposition: There would be no world at all or just nothingness, whatever that is, were it not for divine creative and conservative *intervention.*

But what, I must ask, is the evidence for this philosophically fateful assumption of the spontaneity of nothingness? Why, in the absence of an external supernatural (creative) cause, *should* there be just nothing, even if we are clear what that would mean? Leibniz and Richard Swinburne have offered a defense of the spontaneity of nothing by

arguing from *simplicity* that the nonexistence of the world ("nothingness") is *its [sic]* most probable state. But I argue in my forthcoming "A New Critique of Theological Interpretations of Physical Cosmology" that this defense is completely unavailing.

The baseless tacit presupposition of spontaneous nothingness also contributed to Leibniz's demand for a necessary being to provide a *sufficient reason* for the existence and persistence of contingent things. Yet, *I deny that the mere logical or empirical contingency of the existence of any given particulars can support the spontaneity of utter nothingness* and the need for a logically necessary being as the creator. It will emerge that the theological presupposition of the spontaneity of nothingness lacks even the most rudimentary plausibility. Moreover, some philosophers, such as Henri Bergson, have asserted the unintelligibility of the notion of absolute Nothingness.

As I have just argued, the seminal question as to the *ratio essendi* of the world of contingent beings, far from being innocent and imperative, has forfeited the rationale that animated it at the hands of such major figures as Aquinas and Descartes. Their problem turns out to have been a *pseudo*problem. And their proposed theological resolution of it is a pseudo-*explanation.* One cannot overestimate, I believe, the extent to which the dubious rationale for a *ratio essendi* unconsciously insinuates itself to confer spurious plausibility on that pseudo-explanation. This point must be borne in mind as *prophylaxis* against the insidious temptation to ask for a *creative cause* of the very existence of the *entire world.*

Now let me turn to:

5. The Big Bang Universe of the General Theory of Relativity

Two subtopics will concern us:

A. What is the Big Bang in the Event-Ontology of the General Theory of Relativity? For brevity, I shall hereafter speak of the general theory of relativity as the "GTR."

B. I shall contend that *physical* energy conservation *rules out* divine *creatio continuans.*

A. What Is the Big Bang in the Event-Ontology of the General Theory of Relativity?

In my earlier writings,[39,40,41] I had discussed two Big Bang models, which I called Case (i) and Case (ii) respectively and which I am about to characterize. Yet, as I noted then and will see shortly, Case (i) is *not a bona fide* model of the GTR for reasons given in the *event ontology* of that theory. In the putative Case (i) model, the Big Bang is *supposedly* the temporally first physical event of the space-time, and is said to occur at the instant t = 0. But the Big Bang does not meet the requirements for being a *bona fide* physical event in the GTR. Instead, there is a hole in the space-time manifold at the putative t = 0, such that *at unboundedly ever earlier moments* of time before, say, 14 billion years ago, the space-time metric of the GTR becomes degenerate, and the so-called scalar curvature as well as the density approach infinity.[42] The locution "Big Bang" is a shorthand *façon de parler* for this mathematical behavior of the 4-metric and scalar curvature at *regressively* earlier times.

The physicist John Stachel[43] has justified the view that this singular status robs the Big Bang of its *event-status* in the GTR. As he showed, points of the *theoretical* manifold first *acquire* the physical significance of being *events*, when they stand in the chrono-geometric relations specified by the space-time metric, which familiarly does double duty as the gravitational field in the GTR.

Thus, in the GTR, it turns out that "the notion of an event makes physical sense only when [both] manifold and metric structure are [well] defined around it."[44,45] And in that theory, space-time is taken to be "the collection of all [physical] events." But the Big Bang does *not* qualify as a physical point-event of the space-time to which one could assign three spatial coordinates, and one time coordinate. Therefore, contrary to the Case (i) model, which features a *first* physical event, the past cosmic time-interval is *open* or unbounded, rather than closed or bounded by a first moment, although its metrical duration in years is only *finite*.

Despite the ontological illegitimacy of the Case (i) model, I have discussed it, because Pope Pius XII, Sir Bernard Lovell, and William Craig[46] each claimed support from it for divine creation *ex*

nihilo. Besides, the Case (i) model had figured in the astrophysicist Narlikar's *secular* creationism with which I took issue elsewhere.[47]

But, as we just saw, the Big Bang is actually excluded as not being a physical event occurring at an actual moment of time. Thus understood the relativistically *bona fide* Big Bang models *differ* from those in Case (i) by being temporally *unbounded* (open) in the past. And hence the past physical career of the Big Bang universe *did not include a first physical event or state at which it could be said to have begun*. I designated the *bona fide* temporally unbounded models as *Case (ii) models*.

However, in either Case (i) or Case (ii), the current *age* of the Big Bang universe is *metrically of finite* duration, whose numerical value is under dispute, depending numerically on the time-rate of its expansion.[48] Moreover, there are good reasons in the GTR for claiming that *no instants of physical time whatever* existed *before* that finite time-interval in either Case (i) or Case (ii).[49] Thus, even if the singular Big Bang *were* included as an event having occurred at a *bona fide* moment of time t = 0, this hypothetical instant *had no temporal predecessor*. *A fortiori*, it could *not* have been *preceded* by a state of nothingness, even if the notion of such a state were well-defined.

As we now see, physical processes of some sort *already* existed at every *actual* instant of past time. After all, despite the finite duration of the past, *there was no time* at all at which the physical world did not exist *yet*. Thus, we can say that the Big Bang universe *always* existed, although its age is only, say, somewhere between 8 or 15 times 10^9 years. Here, the word "always" means "for all actual times," but it does not guarantee that time, past or future, is of infinite duration in years.

As we saw, in the Case (i) world, there did not exist any instants of cosmic time before t = 0. Therefore, no supposed earlier cause, either creative or transformative, could possibly have been operative before t = 0. For that reason alone, the Big Bang could not have had any temporally prior creative or transformative cause. Nor could "it" have had a simultaneous cause, creative or otherwise, because there simply was no "it" or instantaneous event that could have been the momentary effect of such a cause. And in the face of the groundlessness of the spontaneity of nothingness, there is no basis for a creative cause of the Big Bang as construed in the Pickwickian sense of a *façon de parler* I mentioned above.

Let me take for granted the altogether reasonable view that only *events* can qualify as the momentary *effects* of other events, or of the action of an agency. As I just argued, the Big Bang is a nonevent, and t = 0 is not at all a *bona fide* time of "its" occurrence. Thus the "Big Bang" *cannot be the effect of any cause in the case of either event-causation or agent-causation alike.* By the same token, a nonexistent event at the putative t = 0 cannot have a cause, *either earlier or simultaneous!* Besides, it cannot have an *earlier* cause, either creative or transformative, if only because there was no earlier time at all. And recall (from Section 4) that I have already undercut the entire rationale for any creative *ratio essendi* anyway by discrediting its assumed spontaneity of nothingness.

B. Physical Energy Conservation versus *Divine* Creatio Continuans

We are ready now to examine Quinn's contention that purportedly *required* divine creation and conservation are entirely consistent with the Big Bang models in both Case (i) and Case (ii). Indeed, Quinn asserts such consistency in all those cases in which *the GTR or any other physical theory* features a *physical* energy-conservation law.

It is very important to bear in mind that the theistic tradition which Quinn tries to defend has insisted aprioristically on the necessity of divine preservation of matter or energy against annihilation, regardless of the particular forms of matter or energy that populate the physical ontologies of successive scientific theories. Thus he is concerned to argue strenuously that the necessity of perpetual divine conservation is logically *compatible* with the old matter-conservation law dating from Lavoisier, and also with such energy-conservation as is valid in GTR universes. Indeed, Quinn and his fellow theists insist quite generally on the logical compatibility of the necessity of divine conservation with whatever *physical* matter-energy conservation law is presumed to be true at any given stage of science. Each such stage features a specific technical physical ontology of matter or energy. But I shall argue

that, instead, there is *incompatibility* between the physical and divine conservation scenarios.

Quinn[50] offers the following definitions of divine creation and conservation, which I find very obscure: (i) God *creates* x at t = $_{def.}$ God willing that x-exists-at-t brings about x-existing-at-t, and there is no t′ prior to t such that x exists at t′, and (ii) God *conserves* x at t = $_{def}$ God willing that x-exists-at-t brings about x-existing-at-t, and there is some t′ prior to t such that x exists at t′.

Quinn[51] points out that his formulations deliberately leave open whether God's volitions or willings "are timelessly eternal by not building into this locution (of divine volitions] a variable ranging over times of occurrence of divine willings." But I submit that the notion of *timelessly eternal acts of willing* is obscure and elusive to the point of making such divine willings altogether nonexplanatory as causes of the existence of our world. Quinn's use of the concept of "willing" clearly draws on the acts of volition familiar from the conative life of humans. But such volitional states are *inherently temporal* rather than "timelessly eternal." Thus, Quinn's divine volitional creation scenario is conceptually elusive. Furthermore, insofar as it is analogous at all to human volitions, there is no evidence whatsoever for the occurrence of such Pickwickian volitions.

Nor do I understand what we are to make of the posited scenario that the instantaneously "ensuing" temporal *bringing about* of the existence-of-x-at-time-t is the *effect* of such an *atemporal* volition. Besides, all of the cases of instantaneous action-at-a-distance familiar from pre-relativistic physics (e.g., gravitational attraction in Newton's law of universal gravitation) feature *causally symmetric laws* of coexistence (*inter*actions), whereas Quinn's instantaneous divine creative causation is claimed to be *causally asymmetric.* Furthermore, let me just recall anew the Jesuit Buckley's agnostic disclaimer that Catholic theology does *not* know *how* God brings about the existence of the world.

It must be borne in mind that the theists whom Quinn claims to vindicate assert the necessity of divine *creatio continuans* unqualifiedly for the lifetime of a tree, for the conservation of the energy in an isolated finite subsystem of the universe, and—when such conservation is defined for the universe as a whole—for the entire cosmos.

We can now turn to Quinn's treatment of the *bona fide* relativistic Big Bang models of Case (ii), featuring a temporally *unbounded* past. He describes his theological scenario for all authentic moments of time as follows[52].

> . . . God *conserves* the sum total of matter-energy whenever it exists, but there is no time at which he creates it or brings it into existence after a prior period of its nonexistence. (my italics)

But, now, my thesis will be the following: Insofar as the GTR does license a matter-energy conservation law for a specified subclass of the Case (ii) Big Bang models or for isolated subsystems of the universe, the physics itself *rules out* Quinn's theological doctrine that physical energy-conservation is only an *epiphenomenon* in the sense of Malebranche's occasionalism, *requiring* repeated divine creation *ex nihilo* at every instant. One form of the energy-conservation law tells us that the total energy-content of an isolated or closed system remains constant naturally and spontaneously. Another form, which is even taught in freshman physics or chemistry, asserts *tout court* that *energy can neither be created nor destroyed.*

To be more specific concerning both cosmological and subcosmological energy-conservation that is licensed by the GTR, consider the spatially closed (or "3-sphere") "Friedmann" Big Bang universe, which exists altogether for only a finite span of time. It is clearly a physically closed system since there is nothing else. When the matter of that universe takes the form of "dust" (i.e., when the pressure in it vanishes), the *total rest-mass of that universe is conserved for the entire time-period of its existence.*[53]

Apart from the stated cosmological rest-mass-conservation law, Wald[54] points out that "in general relativity . . . a conserved total energy of an isolated system [i.e., subsystem of the universe such as a condensed star, immersed in an asymptotically flat spacetime[55]] can be defined." (That total energy is the so-called ADM-energy.[56]) Note that for any particular physical theory *T* such as the GTR, a physical system passes muster as "closed" in the absence of any outflow or influx of the kinds of physical entities that qualify as mass or energy in the ontology of *T*.

In the present Big Bang context, my argument from *physical* energy-conservation against the necessity of divine *creatio continuans* is as follows: *Given the pertinent mass- or energy-conservation law of the Friedmann Big Bang dust world, it follows decisively that the physical closure of this universe is causally sufficient for the conservation of its particular mass-energy-content.* But just that *physical causal sufficiency for energy conservation*, in turn, *rules out* the major claim of theistic creationism that such physical conservation *requires* perpetual divine creative intervention *ab extra as a necessary condition!*

Here, as in the steady-state world, Leibniz can get his sufficient reason for physical existence from the physics itself and would not need God. And, as I have already emphasized twice, Leibniz's *quest* for an External Sufficient Reason was ill-grounded on the alleged spontaneity of nothingness.

It is of cardinal importance to note vis-à-vis Quinn that the causal sufficiency of the physics for energy-conservation which I have claimed is licensed by the *conjunction* of the physical energy-conservation law with the physical closure of the universe, *not* by the physical closure alone. *Mutatis mutandis* for the stated *sub*cosmological systems for which the GTR licenses a conservation law. In short, my thesis of causal sufficiency relies on a solution to the initial value problem.

But Quinn's view of divine conservation as the *total* and *sole* cause of energy-conservation turns this paramount physical process into a mere *epiphenomenon* in the spirit of Malebranche's *occasionalism*. Thereby, Quinn robs the physics of any causal role in energy-conservation, just as he had made the physics causally irrelevant to the genesis of new matter in the steady-state cosmology. Yet, as I have just argued, the *physics* is, in fact, *causally sufficient* in each of the major rival physical cosmologies. And since Quinn claims to accept the physics, his demotion of it to causally ineffectual, and hence also to causally *non*explanatory factors is untenable. Moreover, if he is to be believed, a philosophically enlightened physics teacher ought to explain energy-conservation to students by attributing it *solely* to divine intervention, since the physics does no causally explanatory work in Quinn's scenario.

The bizarre character of that scenario is thrown into still bolder relief, when we consider an *alternative* formulation of the energy-conservation law that is found in standard reference works, such as the *International Encyclopedia of Science,*[57] which *articulates* the statement *"The mass-energy content of an isolated system remains constant."* The articulation follows immediately upon it and reads: *"The energy can be converted from one form to another, but can neither be created nor destroyed."* Hence, even if the system is open, a change in its energy content can occur only by the exportation or importation of energy *not* by its creation *ex nihilo* or *annihilation.*

Thus, the *alternative* formulation of the energy-conservation law *applies alike* to physically open and closed systems. And, importantly, this formulation does not restrict at all the kinds of agencies or devices that are declared *unable* to create or destroy energy. Instead, it asserts the impossibility of its creation or annihilation *tout court* as a law of nature. Therefore, *if* the law is true *and* there is also a God, he is *not almighty.*

Furthermore, since the law declares the impossibility of the annihilation of the energy *tout court* the energy *could* not *lapse into nothingness* in the absence of God. Therefore, contrary to the long theistic tradition of perpetual creation espoused by Quinn, God is clearly *not* needed to *prevent* such supposed spontaneous annihilation by creative intervention. *This is a conclusion of cardinal importance.*

Lastly, let me object to Augustine's version of creation *ex nihilo*. In Book XI of his *Confessions,* he considers a challenger's question "What did God do before He made Heaven and Earth?" But Augustine *rejects* the answer of someone who replied that God was busy preparing hell for those who would ask this question! Instead, he tells us that there simply was no time before creation, because God first had to create *both* time *and* matter. As I remarked at the start, the British physicist C.J. Isham[58] regards Augustine's reply that "time itself was made by God" as "profound."

Yet I consider it very unsatisfactory. What are we to understand by Augustine's assertion that God "brings about" the existence of time itself or creates it? I submit that his claim is either unintelligible or, at best, uselessly circular and unilluminating. In any case, if Augustine means only that time and matter are *existentially coextensive* in the sense of a "relationalist" ontology of time, then, as I have

been at pains to argue, they do not need any *external cause* or creator as the *ratio essendi* of their very existence, let alone a divine one. Furthermore, the locution *"was made,"* as used in regard to the creation of *time itself* must not be allowed to suggest that, like stars or atoms, time itself came into existence *in the course of time.* Such a notion would make *illicit* appeal to some fictitious *supertime.* Therefore, *pace* Isham, the locution *"time itself was made"* by God is senseless here.

Similar objections apply, in my view, to Aquinas's doctrine, reported by Quinn,[59] "that one of two things God made in the beginning was a unique first *now* from which time began."

6. *Quantum Cosmologies*

The so-called quantum cosmologies are quite speculative. And, no self-consistent theory of quantum gravity—uniting quantum theory and general relativity—is currently available.[60] Thus, it may be premature to entrust one's philosophic fortunes to the extant versions of quantum cosmology, let alone to invoke them as support for divine creationism.

Although it is probably the better part of wisdom to wait philosophically until the dust settles in physics, let me just suggest here why, in my view, the creationist cannot get support from quantum cosmology that was *unavailable,* as I have argued, from the pre-quantum Big Bang and steady-state theories. It will turn out that some of the arguments I gave against theistic creationist interpretations of the classical Case (i) and Case (ii) models carry over to the three quantum cosmologies. And, just like the Case (ii) models, the third quantum version does not even provide a point of application for an attempt to argue for *initial* divine creation. Nor does it lend itself to divine *creatio continuans* any more than the other two.

The relevant highlights of the three quantum cosmologies can be briefly described as follows:

1. The semiclassical *inflationary* Big Bang models pioneered by Alan Guth and subsequently modified by Linde, Albrecht, and Steinhardt. In Guth's version, the model is a *modification of the Case (ii) Big Bang world of the GTR* such that (a), between 10^{-35} and 10^{-33} seconds, the expansion

rate was inflationary or enormously higher than thereafter, (b) the Big Bang universe itself originated in quantum fluctuations in *non*gravitational fields. There is a so-called true vacuum featuring quantum energy fluctuations during the first 10^{-35} seconds, which is succeeded by the so-called false vacuum of the inflationary period. In these models, Einstein's GTR field equations are used to derive the false vacuum.

During the inflationary period, *energy-density* is conserved, which means that in analogy to the popping into existence of new *matter* in the old steady-state theory, additional energy pops into existence *during that period*. But it turns out that after this inflationary period, the energy-value returns permanently to the status quo ante. Thus, except for the tiny inflationary period, the model exhibits such physical energy-conservation as is present in the classical Case (ii) model.

Clearly, I can carry over to this semiclassical quantum model my objections to the *theological* interpretations of the Case (ii) models and of the steady-state theory.

2. A second version of quantum cosmology is furnished by the so-called wave-function models.[61,62,63,64] Whereas the semiclassical inflationary models quantize only *non*gravitational fields, the wave-function models quantize all fields. But, like the former, they also feature an inflationary episode. The *temporal* structure of the wave-function models is that of the Case (i) Big Bang model, but with the important difference that there is *no singularity* at the initial state t = 0. Thus, here there is a *bona fide* first state of the universe. But it cannot have an earlier cause, since there is no prior time. Nor is there any basis for thinking that its initial state has a *simultaneous* asymmetric cause supplied by divine volition. We have no empirical evidence at all for the existence of creative causes *ex nihilo*. The demand for such a cause of the very existence of the entire universe is inspired—as I showed in Section 4—by the *groundless* assumption of the spontaneity of nothingness. Moreover, there is no extant viable account of a criterion of asymmetric *instantaneous* causation such that divine volition would qualify under it as the creative cause of the universe. In any case, attributions of volitions to God are completely *ex post facto* and can be invoked unwarrantedly no matter what the facts of the world. Yet the physics of the

wave-function model yields a *probability* for the existence of our world as one member of a set of alternative worlds.

Overall, my objections to a theological reading of the wave-function model can be stated by carrying over those I offered à propos of the classical Case (i) model and against divine conservation à propos of the Case (ii) Big Bang model.

3. The third set of quantum cosmologies, the *vacuum fluctuation* models, are quite distinct from the first two, although there are quantum fluctuations in the course of the careers of the other models as well. Quentin Smith[65] has lucidly outlined a series of these models, beginning with Tryon's in 1973, and including those of Brout, Englert, Gott, and others.

Their cardinal feature is that there is a preexisting background space in which our universe is embedded, and that our world is a quantum fluctuation of the vacuum of this larger space. Yet our world is only one of many vacuum fluctuation worlds that emerge randomly from the embedding vacuum space. As Quentin Smith explains,[66] these models lend themselves to incorporation in Brandon Carter's theory of a World Ensemble explanation of our world, and especially of its "anthropic coincidences."

These models are of interest for various philosophic purposes. But the prior existence of their background space provides no point of application for an attempt to argue for initial divine creation. Nor do they lend themselves to divine *creatio continuans*, any more than any of the others we have considered.

7. Conclusion

I conclude that, in the major cosmologies of the twentieth century, there is no scope at all for a creative role of the deity qua *ratio essendi*.

Endnotes

[1]P. Quinn, "Creation, Conservation and the Big Bang," in *Philosophical Problems of the Internal and External Worlds: Essays on the Philosophy of Adolf Grünbaum*, ed. J. Earman et al. (Pittsburgh: University of Pittsburgh Press, 1993), pp. 589–612.

[2]A. Grünbaum, "The Pseudo-Problem of Creation in Physical Cosmology," *Philosophy of Science* 56 (1989): 373–94.

[3]A. Grünbaum, "The Pseudo-Problem of Creation in Physical Cosmology," in *Physical Cosmology & Philosophy*, ed. J. Leslie (New York: Macmillan, 1990). This is a reprint of Grünbaum, "The Pseudo-Problem of Creation in Physical Cosmology." The paper was also reprinted in *Epistemologia* 12 (1989): 3–32, and in *Free Inquiry* 9 (1990): 48–57.

A German translation, "Die Schöpfung als Scheinproblem der physikalischen Kosmologie," appeared in *Wege der Vernunft, Festschrift*, ed. H. Albert, A. Bohnen, and A. Musgrave (Tübingen: J. C. B. Mohr. 1991), pp. 164–91.

[4]A. Grünbaum, "Pseudo-Creation of the Big Bang," *Nature* 344 (1990): 821–22.

[5]A. Grünbaum, Creation as a Pseudo-Explanation in Current Physical Cosmology," *Erkenntnis* 35 (1991): 233–54.

[6]I have also argued for "The Poverty of Theistic Morality" in my contribution to *Science, Mind and Art*, ed. K. Gavroglu et al. (Boston: Kluwer, 1995), pp. 203–42.

[7]Grünbaum, "The Pseudo-Problem of Creation."

[8]Grünbaum, 'The Pseudo-Problem of Creation," in *Physical Cosmology & Philosophy*.

[9]Grünbaum, "Creation as a Pseudo-Explanation."

[10]C. Isham, "Creation of the Universe as a Quantum Process," in *Physics, Philosophy and Theology: A Common Quest for Understanding*, ed. R. J. Russell et al. (Rome: Vatican Observatory, 1988), p.387.

[11]Grünbaum, "The Pseudo-Problem of Creation."

[12]Quinn. "Creation, Conservation and the Big Bang."

[13]Grünbaum, "The Pseudo-Problem of Creation."

[14]Ibid., p. 378.

[15]Grünbaum. "The Pseudo-Problem of Creation," in *Physical Cosmology & Philosophy*, pp. 96–97.

[16]M. Buckley, "Religion & Science: Paul Davies and John Paul II," *Theological Studies* 51 (1990): 310–24.

[17]Pius XII, "Modern Science and the Existence of God," *The Catholic Mind* 49 (1952): 188, 190.

[18]F. Hoyle, "Light Element Synthesis in Planck Fireballs," *Astrophysics and Spare Science* 198 (1992): 177–93.

[19]A. Lovell, *The Individual and the Universe* (New York: New American Library, 1961).

[20]A. Lovell, "Reason and Faith in Cosmology" (Ragione e Fede in Cosmologia), *Nuovo Civilta Delle Macchine* 4, nos. 3/4 and 15/16 (1986): 101–108.

[21]Lovell, *The Individual and the Universe*, p. 117.

[22]Ibid., p. 124.

[23]Lovell, "Reason and Faith in Cosmology."

[24]Grünbaum, "The Pseudo-Problem of Creation."

[25]Ibid., p. 375.

[26]Grünbaum, "The Pseudo-Problem of Creation," in *Physical Cosmology & Philosophy*, p. 94.

[27]Quinn, "Creation, Conservation and the Big Bang," p. 608.

[28]Ibid., p. 593.

[29]Ibid., p. 590.

[30]Ibid., pp. 591–92.

[31]Ibid., p. 597.

[32]Ibid.

[33]Ibid., pp. 239–41. For an array of difficulties besetting the notion of divine volitional bringing about, see A. Grünbaum, "Origin versus Creation in Physical Cosmology," in *Physik, Philosophie und die Einheit der Wissenschaften*, ed. L Krüger and B. Falkenburg (Heidelberg, Germany: Spektrum Akademischer Verlag, 1995), pp. 221–54.

[34]Quinn, "Creation, Conservation and the Big Bang," p. 602.

[35]Ibid.

[36]A. Grünbaum, *Philosophical Problems of Space and Time*, 2d ed. (Boston: Reidel, 1973), pp. 571–74.

[37]Ibid., pp. 406–407.

[38]Quinn, "Creation, Conservation and the Bag Bang," p. 593, cited from Aquinas's *Summa Theologiae*, p. 511; trans. the English Dominican Fathers, 1981.

[39]Grünbaum, "The Pseudo-Problem of Creation."

[40]Grünbaum, "The Pseudo-Problem of Creation in Physical Cosmology," in *Physical Cosmology & Philosophy*.

[41]Grünbaum, "Pseudo-Creation of the Big Bang."

[42]R. Wald, *General Relativity* (Chicago: University of Chicago Press, 1984), pp. 99–100.

[43]J. Stachel, "The Meaning of General Covariance," in *Philosophical Problems of the Internal and External Worlds: Essays on the Philosophy of Adolf Grünbaum*, ed. J. Earman et al. (Pittsburgh: University of Pittsburgh Press, 1993), pp. 138–44.

[44]Wald, *General Retativity*, p. 213.

[45]S. Hawking and G. Ellis, *The Large-Scale Structure of Space-Time* (New York: Cambridge University Press, 1973), p. 56.

[46]W Craig, "Creation and Big Bang Cosmology," in *Philosophia Naturalis 32*, no. 2 (1994): 217–24. But see my critical reply in the same issue of *Philosophia Naturalis*, pp. 225–36, and Craig's rejoinder there, pp. 237–49.

[47]A. Grünbaum, "Narlikar's 'Creation' of the Big Bang Universe Was a Mere Origination." *Philosophy of Science* 60, no.4 (December 1993): 638–46.

[48]Wald, *General Relativity*, p. 99.

[49]Ibid.

[50]Quinn, "Creation, Conservation and the Big Bang," p. 598.

[51]Ibid., p. 597.

[52]Ibid., pp. 18–19.

[53]Wald, *General Relativity*, p. 100, equation [5.2.19].

[54]Ibid., p. 70 n. 6.

[55] Ibid., p. 269.

[56] Ibid., p. 293.

[57] "Conservation of Mass Energy," *International Encyclopedia of Science*, vol. 1, ed. J. R. Newman (Edinburgh: Thomas Nelson, 1965), p. 276.

[58] Isham, "Creation of the Universe as a Quantum Process," p. 387.

[59] Quinn, "Creation, Conservation and the Big Bang," p. 595.

[60] P. Renteln, "Quantum Gravity," *American Scientist* 79 (1991): 508–27.

[61] J. B. Hartle and S. W Hawking, "Wave Function of the Universe," *Physical Review* D 28 (1983): 2960–75.

[62] S. W. Hawking. "Quantum Cosmology" in *Three Hundred Years of Gravitation*, ed. S. W. Hawking and W. Israel (Cambridge: Cambridge University Press, 1987), pp. 631–51.

[63] A. Vilenkin, "Creation of Universes from Nothing," *Physical Review* 117B (1982): 25–28.

[64] A. Vilenkin, "Birth of Inflationary Universes," *Physical Review* D27 (1983): 2848–55.

[65] Q. Smith, "World Ensemble Explanations," *Pacific Philosophical Quarterly* 67, no. 1 (January 1986): 81–84.

[66] Ibid., pp. 75–86.

Further Reading

Adams, M. M., *Horrendous Evils and the Goodness of God* (Ithaca, N.Y.: Cornell University Press, 1999).

Burrill, D. R., *The Cosmological Argument* (Garden City, N.Y.: Anchor Books, 1967).

Craig, W. L., ed., *The Cosmological Argument from Plato to Leibniz* (Library of Philosophy and Religion), (London: Macmillan, 1980).

Craig, W. L., ed., *Philosophy of Religion: A Reader's Guide* (New Brunswick, N. J.: Rutgers University Press, 2002).

Craig, W. L., and Smith, Q., *Theism, Atheism and Big Bang Cosmology* (Oxford: Clarendon Press, 1993).

Gale, R. M., *On the Nature and Existence of God* (Cambridge: Cambridge University Press, 1991).

Gale, R. M., and Pruss, A. R., eds., *The Existence of God* (Aldershot, U.K.: Ashgate, 2003).

Griffiths, P. J., and Taliaferro, C., eds., *Philosophy of Religion: An Anthology* (Oxford: Blackwell, 2003).

Hick, J., *Evil and the God of Love,* rev. ed. (New York: Harper and Row, 1975).

Hick, J. H., and McGill, A. C., *The Many Faced Argument* (New York: Macmillan, 1967).

Howard-Snyder, D., ed., *The Evidential Argument from Evil* (Bloomington, Ind.: University Press, 1996).

Mackie, J. L., *The Miracle of Theism: Arguments for and against the Existence of God* (Oxford: Clarendon Press; New York: Oxford University Press, 1982).

Martin, M., *Atheism: A Philosophical Justification* (Philadelphia: Temple University Press, 1990).

Oppy, G., *Ontological Arguments and Belief in God* (Cambridge: Cambridge University Press, 1995).

Plantinga, A., *Warranted Christian Belief* (New York: Oxford University Press, 2000).

Swinburne, R., *Providence and the Problem of Evil* (Oxford: Clarendon Press, 1998).

Part VI

Knowing Reality

In the preceding chapters, philosophers have debated the nature or reality of time, identity, mind, and freedom. Along the way, several other topics surfaced; for example, Platonic Forms (or universals), God, and causality. Metaphysics has such an ambitious scope—to provide general understanding of reality—that philosophers are bound to reflect on the enterprise itself. Is metaphysics possible? How should one try to achieve a general account of reality? When these questions are asked, controversies pertaining to the nature of knowledge are bound to arise. In history, one can find many patterns of interaction among theories of knowledge and metaphysics: a philosopher, enthusiastic about some way of knowing, claims his or her method leads to a radically new view

of reality; another is skeptical about this view, and that skepticism may undermine not only the radical view but also the everyday beliefs about reality; a third philosopher argues against skepticism and restores some legitimacy for at least some ordinary view. Though such patterns are oversimplifications, the writings in Part VI reflect some such process at work.

Seventeenth and eighteenth century philosophers were concerned with the challenges new successful theories in physics were posing to traditional beliefs and values. Is the natural world really a material, mechanistic system? Or, more dramatically, are bodies of both the earth and heaven really swarms of material "corpuscles" somehow held together and affecting each other by such invisible forces as

Newton's gravity? Is the human heart a mechanical pump and not the locus of the soul? How are human experiences related to material bodies, and how can the human mind know the true nature of such suddenly foreign things? In Part III, the selection by Descartes represents the struggles of a philosopher (a pre-Newtonian) who helped bring these kinds of questions to general awareness. In Part V, the selection by Descartes shows him attempting to explain how the mind that can know the nature of matter can also prove the existence of God.

Part VI begins with the work of two philosophers who are usually given the epistemological classification of "British empiricists." George Berkeley insists that all knowledge must be based on sense experience. Using this standard, he argues that we have no knowledge of matter apart from experience; or, more strongly, the matter postulated by physicists does not exist! Berkeley views himself as defending the ordinary objects of common experience from the radical metaphysics of materialism. In the end, however, his metaphysics is far from ordinary: reality consists of minds (immaterial spirits) with their perceptions, all perceived by a supreme mind, God.

David Hume is also an empiricist skeptical about what other philosophers claim to know is real. He dismisses *a priori* knowledge as being merely about the relations amongst ideas (e.g., definitions), and he claims all knowledge of what exists depends upon perceptual experience. Against Berkeley, he finds we have no basis in experience for our belief in enduring minds. What, then, is real? For Hume, everything that exists, our selves included, is some pattern of sensations. This metaphysical view is called phenomenalism.

Descartes' dualism, Berkeley's subjective idealism, and Hume's phenomenalism are all linked to two theses made prominent by Descartes. First, knowledge of what is real requires a foundation in the knowing subject.

Second, this foundation is to be found by the examination of mental ideas, where these are assumed to be something like "inner" pictures or representations (where they disagree is about which kinds of ideas should be the foundation). Both theses were challenged by later philosophers, and the challenges had implications for metaphysics. Immanuel Kant (1724–1804) in particular argued that human knowledge does not begin with the inspection of sensations or ideas. Rather, it involves a prior necessary harmony between distinctively human forms of perception and human forms of judgment. However, the function of judgment (propositional beliefs, not just mental pictures) is merely to orient us in the world that we can perceive, and any attempt to extend our beliefs to attain transcendent metaphysical knowledge is doomed to be dysfunctional.

The readings in Part VI leapfrog over Kant and focus on American pragmatism. In the second half of the nineteenth century, Charles Sanders Peirce (1839–1914) is not only suspicious of metaphysicians inspecting their minds but he is also sensitive to new developments in science; for example, the importance of statistics, both in physics and in the study of human behavior, and Darwin's theory of the evolution of biological species. Science is now seen as dynamic and evolving; moreover, science is a community activity. Peirce is happy to shift the character of an individual's belief (and its meaning) from an object of subjective introspection to public action. Pragmatism is often associated with "practical consequences" and with a rejection of metaphysics, and it is easy to find Peirce saying negative things about earlier philosophers. But pragmatism also takes a metaphysical stance, a view about what is real. For Peirce, the real is what the method of science will, in the limit, lead us to accept as true.

Peirce was not only interested in the logic and methods of science; he also developed semiotics, the general theory of signs. He might have thought that everything is a sign of some kind. He wondered about how conventional languages and the symbols of science work. Insofar as he saw such issues as important for philosophy, and insofar as he approached them in a scientific rather than an *a priori* spirit, his work foreshadows later twentieth-century interest in language. The remaining selections in Part VI, though they might seem to be preoccupied with "languages" or "conceptual schemes" can be seen as exploring metaphysical issues implicit in pragmatism.

Wilfrid Sellars takes seriously the thesis that evolving science produces increasingly better pictures of reality. He agrees with Peirce that it will be science that ultimately determines what is real. Sellars's concern is to argue there is no epistemological obstacle to accepting the reality of the theoretical entities of science. He attempts to anticipate how "manifest" (ordinary or obvious) beliefs about persons and their world might be transformed in what he calls the scientific image of reality. Sellars's metaphysics qualifies as optimistic in the sense that he sees science as converging to some definite picture of reality. It also qualifies as revisionary because he claims parts of reality will turn out to be conceived very differently from how we ordinarily conceive them.

In comparison, the selection by Willard Quine might seem skeptical. Though Quine is an advocate of science and approaches language from the perspective of a behaviorist, he maintains what one means—what one is talking or theorizing about—is, in an important way,

indeterminate. Not only is meaning dependent on the language (or theory) one is using, but it is always (even at the limit of ideal science?) vulnerable to reinterpretation in some other equally successful (in the pragmatic sense) language or theory. Such "ontological relativity" suggests one should not attach metaphysical significance to any particular interpretation of one's language or theories.

Some readers may find Sellars's realism too stark; some may find Quine's skepticism about meaning too opaque. Such readers might find comfort in the selection by Richard Rorty. Rorty also claims to be some variety of pragmatist, but he is one who believes that most of our beliefs must be true and no language can be so different that one could not translate into one's own language. Though the title of his article is "The World Well Lost," the world Rorty is willing to lose is the remote one that may or may not correspond to alternative languages or conceptual schemes. Rorty is willing to lose that world so he can hold onto the ordinary world.

Well, we do seem to know what we mean (in spite of Quine's problems), and we do seem to be able to recommend the acceptance of beliefs and theories even if there are equally successful alternatives (think of different interpretations of quantum mechanics) and we are still far from the end of science. So some semantic theories have attempted to avoid quandaries by denying that realism and truth are needed by a semantic theory. In the final essay, William Alston argues we need truth, and so there really is a real world.

54. A Treatise Concerning the Principles of Human Knowledge

GEORGE BERKELEY

George Berkeley (1685–1753) was born and educated in Ireland. He is usually classified as a "British Empiricist" because, like Locke and Hume, he took sensory experience to be the foundation of knowledge. But unlike Locke, he did not embrace the mechanistic and materialistic view of the world that was being impressively pictured in the physics of scientists like Isaac Newton. Locke had tried to show how our knowledge of the material world was based on "ideas" resulting from our causal interaction with material objects, so that there are laws governing the motion (association or combination) of our ideas that are analogous to the laws of mechanics. Berkeley had several worries about Locke's philosophy and about the new physics. The new physics was materialistic and deterministic. And Locke's account of knowledge might lead to skepticism, about both the objects of perception and God. Berkeley's alternative is to be skeptical about the physicist's conception of matter: he denied that we have any knowledge of matter except as perceived. Berkeley's argument for this skepticism becomes a metaphysical theory, often represented by the slogan, "to be is to be perceived." He claims that reality consists of minds (or spirits) and their perceptions. Though often classified as a "subjective idealist," it is important to appreciate that Berkeley did not take himself to be denying the existence of an "external" world of ordinary objects. Rather, he was offering a new metaphysical theory about what those objects really are—collections of ideas. And he was eager to suggest that God perceives objects when individual humans do not. Berkeley was made Bishop of Cloyne in 1734.

Much critical discussion of Berkeley has focused on his account of experience (his account of "ideas") and his theology. His skepticism about the physicist's conception of matter, however, can be seen as foreshadowing some contemporary debates about the metaphysical implications of successful science. Today, some philosophers and some scientists hesitate to affirm the reality of "theoretical" posits like quarks or superstrings. They suggest (in a spirit of "saving the appearances" that goes back to Ptolemy) that such posits are "useful fictions." This is what Berkeley said about the "material corpuscles" of his day (see his 1721 work, *De Motu*).

Introduction

1. Philosophy being nothing else but the study of wisdom and truth, it may with reason be expected that those who have spent most time and pains in it should enjoy a greater calm and serenity of mind, a greater clearness and evidence of knowledge, and be less disturbed with doubts and difficulties than other men. Yet so it is, we see the illiterate bulk of mankind that walk the high-road of plain common sense, and are governed by the dictates of nature, for the most part easy and undisturbed. To them nothing that is familiar appears unaccountable or difficult to comprehend. They complain not of any want of evidence in their senses, and are out of all danger of becoming

A Treatise Concerning the Principles of Human Knowledge was first published in 1710.

Sceptics. But no sooner do we depart from sense and instinct to follow the light of a superior principle, to reason, meditate, and reflect on the nature of things, but a thousand scruples spring up in our minds concerning those things which before we seemed fully to comprehend. Prejudices and errors of sense do from all parts discover themselves to our view; and, endeavouring to correct these by reason, we are insensibly drawn into uncouth paradoxes, difficulties, and inconsistencies, which multiply and grow upon us as we advance in speculation, till at length, having wandered through many intricate mazes, we find ourselves just where we were, or, which is worse, sit down in a forlorn Scepticism.

2. The cause of this is thought to be the obscurity of things, or the natural weakness and imperfection of our understandings. It is said, the faculties we have are few, and those designed by nature for the support and comfort of life, and not to penetrate into the inward essence and constitution of things. Besides, the mind of man being finite, when it treats of things which partake of infinity, it is not to be wondered at if it run into absurdities and contradictions, out of which it is impossible it should ever extricate itself, it being of the nature of infinite not to be comprehended by that which is finite.

3. But, perhaps, we may be too partial to ourselves in placing the fault originally in our faculties, and not rather in the wrong use we make of them. It is a hard thing to suppose that right deductions from true principles should ever end in consequences which cannot be maintained or made consistent. We should believe that God has dealt more bountifully with the sons of men than to give them a strong desire for that knowledge which he had placed quite out of their reach. This were not agreeable to the wonted indulgent methods of Providence, which, whatever appetites it may have implanted in the creatures, doth usually furnish them with such means as, if rightly made use of, will not fail to satisfy them. Upon the whole, I am inclined to think that the far greater part, if not all, of those difficulties which have hitherto amused philosophers, and blocked up the way to knowledge, are entirely owing to ourselves—that we have first raised a dust and then complain we cannot see.

4. My purpose therefore is, to try if I can discover what those Principles are which have introduced all that doubtfulness and uncertainty, those absurdities and contradictions, into the several sects of philosophy; insomuch that the wisest men have thought our ignorance incurable, conceiving it to arise from the natural dulness and limitation of our faculties. And surely it is a work well deserving our pains to make a strict inquiry concerning the First Principles of Human Knowledge, to sift and examine them on all sides, especially since there may be some grounds to suspect that those lets and difficulties, which stay and embarrass the mind in its search after truth, do not spring from any darkness and intricacy in the objects, or natural defect in the understanding, so much as from false Principles which have been insisted on, and might have been avoided.

5. How difficult and discouraging soever this attempt may seem, when I consider how many great and extraordinary men have gone before me in the like designs, yet I am not without some hopes—upon the consideration that the largest views are not always the clearest, and that he who is short-sighted will be obliged to draw the object nearer, and may, perhaps, by a close and narrow survey, discern that which had escaped far better eyes.

6. In order to prepare the mind of the reader for the easier conceiving what follows, it is proper to premise somewhat, by way of Introduction, concerning the nature and abuse of Language. But the unravelling this matter leads me in some measure to anticipate my design, by taking notice of what seems to have had a chief part in rendering speculation intricate and perplexed, and to have occasioned innumerable errors and difficulties in almost all parts of knowledge. And that is the opinion that the mind hath a power of framing abstract ideas or notions of things. He who is not a perfect stranger to the writings and disputes of philosophers must needs acknowledge that no small part of them are spent about abstract ideas. These are in a more especial manner thought to be the object of those sciences which go by the name of Logic and Metaphysics, and of all that which passes under the notion of the most abstracted and sublime learning, in all which one shall scarce find any question handled in such a manner as does not suppose their existence in the mind, and that it is well acquainted with them.

7. It is agreed on all hands that the qualities or modes of things do never really exist each of them apart by itself, and separated from all others, but are mixed, as it were, and blended together, several in the same object. But, we are told, the mind being able to consider each quality singly, or abstracted from those other qualities with which it is united, does by that means frame to itself abstract ideas. For example, there is perceived by sight an object extended, coloured, and moved: this mixed or compound idea the mind resolving into its simple, constituent parts, and viewing each by itself, exclusive of the rest, does frame the abstract ideas of extension, colour, and motion. Not that it is possible for colour or motion to exist without extension; but only that the mind can frame to itself by abstraction the idea of colour exclusive of extension, and of motion exclusive of both colour and extension.

8. Again, the mind having observed that in the particular extensions perceived by sense there is something common and alike in all, and some other things peculiar, as this or that figure or magnitude, which distinguish them one from another; it considers apart or singles out by itself that which is common, making thereof a most abstract idea of extension, which is neither line, surface, nor solid, nor has any figure or magnitude, but is an idea entirely prescinded from all these. So likewise the mind, by leaving out of the particular colours perceived by sense that which distinguishes them one from another, and retaining that only which is common to all, makes an idea of colour in abstract which is neither red, nor blue, nor white, nor any other determinate colour. And, in like manner, by considering motion abstractedly not only from the body moved, but likewise from the figure it describes, and all particular directions and velocities, the abstract idea of motion is framed; which equally corresponds to all particular motions whatsoever that may be perceived by sense.

9. And as the mind frames to itself abstract ideas of qualities or modes, so does it, by the same precision or mental separation, attain abstract ideas of the more compounded beings which include several coexistent qualities. For example, the mind having observed that Peter, James, and John resemble each other in certain common agreements of shape and other qualities, leaves out of the complex or compounded idea it has of Peter, James, and any other particular man, that which is peculiar to each, retaining only what is

common to all, and so makes an abstract idea wherein all the particulars equally partake—abstracting entirely from and cutting off all those circumstances and differences which might determine it to any particular existence. And after this manner it is said we come by the abstract idea of man, or, if you please, humanity, or human nature; wherein it is true there is included colour, because there is no man but has some colour, but then it can be neither white, nor black, nor any particular colour, because there is no one particular colour wherein all men partake. So likewise there is included stature, but then it is neither tall stature, nor low stature, nor yet middle stature, but something abstracted from all these. And so of the rest. Moreover, there being a great variety of other creatures that partake in some parts, but not all, of the complex idea of man, the mind, leaving out those parts which are peculiar to men, and retaining those only which are common to all the living creatures, frames the idea of animal, which abstracts not only from all particular men, but also all birds, beasts, fishes, and insects. The constituent parts of the abstract idea of animal are body, life, sense, and spontaneous motion. By body is meant body without any particular shape or figure, there being no one shape or figure common to all animals, without covering, either of hair, or feathers, or scales, etc., nor yet naked: hair, feathers, scales, and nakedness being the distinguishing properties of particular animals, and for that reason left out of the abstract idea. Upon the same account the spontaneous motion must be neither walking, nor flying, nor creeping; it is nevertheless a motion, but what that motion is it is not easy to conceive.

10. Whether others have this wonderful faculty of abstracting their ideas, they best can tell: for myself, I find indeed I have a faculty of imagining, or representing to myself, the ideas of those particular things I have perceived, and of variously compounding and dividing them. I can imagine a man with two heads, or the upper parts of a man joined to the body of a horse. I can consider the hand, the eye, the nose, each by itself abstracted or separated from the rest of the body. But then whatever hand or eye I imagine, it must have some particular shape and colour. Likewise the idea of man that I frame to myself must be either of a white, or a black, or a tawny, a straight, or a crooked, a tall, or a low, or a middle-sized man. I cannot by any effort of thought conceive the abstract idea above described. And it is equally impossible for me to form the abstract idea of motion distinct from the body moving, and which is neither swift nor slow, curvilinear nor rectilinear; and the like may be said of all other abstract general ideas whatsoever. To be plain, I own myself able to abstract in one sense, as when I consider some particular parts or qualities separated from others, with which, though they are united in some object, yet it is possible they may really exist without them. But I deny that I can abstract from one another, or conceive separately, those qualities which it is impossible should exist so separated; or that I can frame a general notion, by abstracting from particulars in the manner aforesaid—which last are the two proper acceptations of abstraction. And there are grounds to think most men will acknowledge themselves to be in my case. The generality of men which are simple and illiterate never pretend to abstract notions. It is said they are difficult and not to be attained without pains and study; we may therefore reasonably conclude that, if such there be, they are confined only to the learned.

11. I proceed to examine what can be alleged in defence of the doctrine of abstraction, and try if I can discover what it is that inclines the men of speculation to embrace an opinion so remote from common sense as that seems to be. There has been a late deservedly esteemed philosopher who, no doubt, has given it very much countenance, by seeming to think the having abstract general ideas is what puts the widest difference in point of understanding betwixt man and beast. "The having of general ideas," saith he, "is that which puts a perfect distinction betwixt man and brutes, and is an excellency which the faculties of brutes do by no means attain unto. For, it is evident we observe no foot-steps in them of making use of general signs for universal ideas; from which we have reason to imagine that they have not the faculty of abstracting, or making general ideas, since they have no use of words or any other general signs." And a little after: "Therefore, I think, we may suppose that it is in this that the species of brutes are discriminated from men, and it is that proper difference wherein they are wholly separated, and which at last widens to so wide a distance. For, if

they have any ideas at all, and are not bare machines (as some would have them), we cannot deny them to have some reason. It seems as evident to me that they do, some of them, in certain instances reason as that they have sense; but it is only in particular ideas, just as they receive them from their senses. They are the best of them tied up within those narrow bounds, and have not (as I think) the faculty to enlarge them by any kind of abstraction."—*Essay on Human Understanding*, II. xi. 10 and 11. I readily agree with this learned author, that the faculties of brutes can by no means attain to abstraction. But then if this be made the distinguishing property of that sort of animals, I fear a great many of those that pass for men must be reckoned into their number. The reason that is here assigned why we have no grounds to think brutes have abstract general ideas is, that we observe in them no use of words or any other general signs; which is built on this supposition—that the making use of words implies the having general ideas. From which it follows that men who use language are able to abstract or generalize their ideas. That this is the sense and arguing of the author will further appear by his answering the question he in another place puts: "Since all things that exist are only particulars, how come we by general terms?" His answer is: "Words become general by being made the signs of general ideas."—*Essay on Human Understanding*, IV. iii. 6. But it seems that a word becomes general by being made the sign, not of an abstract general idea, but of several particular ideas, any one of which it indifferently suggests to the mind. For example, when it is said "the change of motion is proportional to the impressed force," or that "whatever has extension is divisible," these propositions are to be understood of motion and extension in general; and nevertheless it will not follow that they suggest to my thoughts an idea of motion without a body moved, or any determinate direction and velocity, or that I must conceive an abstract general idea of extension, which is neither line, surface, nor solid, neither great nor small, black, white, nor red, nor of any other determinate colour. It is only implied that whatever particular motion I consider, whether it be swift or slow, perpendicular, horizontal, or oblique, or in whatever object, the axiom concerning it holds equally true. As does the other of every particular extension, it matters not whether line, surface, or solid, whether of this or that magnitude or figure.

12. By observing how ideas become general we may the better judge how words are made so. And here it is to be noted that I do not deny absolutely there are general ideas, but only that there are any abstract general ideas; for, in the passages we have quoted wherein there is mention of general ideas, it is always supposed that they are formed by abstraction, after the manner set forth in sections 8 and 9. Now, if we will annex a meaning to our words, and speak only of what we can conceive, I believe we shall acknowledge that an idea which, considered in itself, is particular, becomes general by being made to represent or stand for all other particular ideas of the same sort. To make this plain by an example, suppose a geometrician is demonstrating the method of cutting a line in two equal parts. He draws, for instance, a black line of an inch in length: this, which in itself is a particular line, is nevertheless with regard to its signification general, since, as it is there used, it represents all particular lines whatsoever; so that what is demonstrated of it is demonstrated of all lines, or, in other words, of a line in general. And, as that particular line becomes general by being made a sign, so the name "line," which taken absolutely is particular, by being a sign is made general. And as the former owes its generality not to its being the sign of an abstract or general line, but of all particular right lines that may possibly exist, so the latter must be thought to derive its generality from the same cause, namely, the various particular lines which it indifferently denotes.

13. To give the reader a yet clearer view of the nature of abstract ideas, and the uses they are thought necessary to, I shall add one more passage out of the *Essay on Human Understanding* (IV. vii. 9) which is as follows: "Abstract ideas are not so obvious or easy to children or the yet unexercised mind as particular ones. If they seem so to grown men it is only because by constant and familiar use they are made so. For, when we nicely reflect upon them, we shall find that general ideas are fictions and contrivances of the mind, that carry difficulty with them, and do not so easily offer themselves as we are apt to imagine. For example, does it not require some pains and skill to form the general idea of a triangle (which is yet none of the most abstract, comprehensive, and dif-

ficult); for it must be neither oblique nor rectangle, neither equilateral, equicrural, nor scalenon, but all and none of these at once? In effect, it is something imperfect that cannot exist, an idea wherein some parts of several different and inconsistent ideas are put together. It is true the mind in this imperfect state has need of such ideas, and makes all the haste to them it can, for the conveniency of communication and enlargement of knowledge, to both which it is naturally very much inclined. But yet one has reason to suspect such ideas are marks of our imperfection. At least this is enough to show that the most abstract and general ideas are not those that the mind is first and most easily acquainted with, nor such as its earliest knowledge is conversant about." If any man has the faculty of framing in his mind such an idea of a triangle as is here described, it is in vain to pretend to dispute him out of it, nor would I go about it. All I desire is that the reader would fully and certainly inform himself whether he has such an idea or no. And this, methinks, can be no hard task for anyone to perform. What is more easy than for anyone to look a little into his own thoughts, and there try whether he has, or can attain to have, an idea that shall correspond with the description that is here given of the general idea of a triangle, which is "neither oblique nor rectangle, neither equilateral, equicrural, nor scalenon, but all and none of these at once?"

14. Much is here said of the difficulty that abstract ideas carry with them, and the pains and skill requisite to the forming them. And it is on all hands agreed that there is need of great toil and labour of the mind, to emancipate our thoughts from particular objects, and raise them to those sublime speculations that are conversant about abstract ideas. From all which the natural consequence should seem to be, that so difficult a thing as the forming abstract ideas was not necessary for communication, which is so easy and familiar to all sorts of men. But, we are told, if they seem obvious and easy to grown men, it is only because by constant and familiar use they are made so. Now, I would fain know at what time it is men are employed in surmounting that difficulty, and furnishing themselves with those necessary helps for discourse. It cannot be when they are grown up, for then it seems they are not conscious of any such painstaking; it remains therefore to be the business of their childhood. And surely the great and multiplied labour of framing abstract notions will be found a hard task for that tender age. Is it not a hard thing to imagine that a couple of children cannot prate together of their sugar-plums and rattles and the rest of their little trinkets, till they have first tacked together numberless inconsistencies, and so framed in their minds abstract general ideas, and annexed them to every common name they make use of?

15. Nor do I think them a whit more needful for the enlargement of knowledge than for communication. It is, I know, a point much insisted on, that all knowledge and demonstration are about universal notions, to which I fully agree: but then it doth not appear to me that those notions are formed by abstraction in the manner premised—universality, so far as I can comprehend, not consisting in the absolute, positive nature or conception of anything, but in the relation it bears to the particulars signified or represented by it; by virtue whereof it is that things, names, or notions, being in their own nature particular, are rendered universal. Thus, when I demonstrate any proposition concerning triangles, it is to be supposed that I have in view the universal idea of a triangle; which ought not to be understood as if I could frame an idea of a triangle which was neither equilateral, nor scalenon, nor equicrural; but only that the particular triangle I consider, whether of this or that sort it matters not, doth equally stand for and represent all rectilinear triangles whatsoever, and is in that sense universal. All which seems very plain and not to include any difficulty in it.

16. But here it will be demanded, how we can know any proposition to be true of all particular triangles, except we have first seen it demonstrated of the abstract idea of a triangle which equally agrees to all? For, because a property may be demonstrated to agree to some one particular triangle, it will not thence follow that it equally belongs to any other triangle, which in all respects is not the same with it. For example, having demonstrated that the three angles of an isosceles rectangular triangle are equal to two right ones, I cannot therefore conclude this affection agrees to all other triangles which have neither a right angle nor two equal sides. It seems therefore that, to be certain this proposition is universally true, we must either make a particular demonstration for every

particular triangle, which is impossible, or once for all demonstrate it of the abstract idea of a triangle, in which all the particulars do indifferently partake and by which they are all equally represented. To which I answer, that, though the idea I have in view whilst I make the demonstration be, for instance, that of an isosceles rectangular triangle whose sides are of a determinate length, I may nevertheless be certain it extends to all other rectilinear triangles, of what sort or bigness soever. And that because neither the right angle, nor the equality, nor determinate length of the sides are at all concerned in the demonstration. It is true the diagram I have in view includes all these particulars, but then there is not the least mention made of them in the proof of the proposition. It is not said the three angles are equal to two right ones, because one of them is a right angle, or because the sides comprehending it are of the same length. Which sufficiently shows that the right angle might have been oblique, and the sides unequal, and for all that the demonstration have held good. And for this reason it is that I conclude that to be true of any obliquangular or scalenon which I had demonstrated of a particular right-angled equicrural triangle, and not because I demonstrated the proposition of the abstract idea of a triangle. And here it must be acknowledged that a man may consider a figure merely as triangular, without attending to the particular qualities of the angles, or relations of the sides. So far he may abstract; but this will never prove that he can frame an abstract, general, inconsistent idea of a triangle. In like manner we may consider Peter so far forth as man, or so far forth as animal without framing the fore-mentioned abstract idea, either of man or of animal, inasmuch as all that is perceived is not considered.

17. It were an endless as well as an useless thing to trace the Schoolmen, those great masters of abstraction, through all the manifold inextricable labyrinths of error and dispute which their doctrine of abstract natures and notions seems to have led them into. What bickerings and controversies, and what a learned dust have been raised about those matters, and what mighty advantage has been from thence derived to mankind, are things at this day too clearly known to need being insisted on. And it had been well if the ill effects of that doctrine were confined to those only who make the most avowed profession of it. When men consider the great pains, industry, and parts that have for so many ages been laid out on the cultivation and advancement of the sciences, and that notwithstanding all this the far greater part of them remains full of darkness and uncertainty, and disputes that are like never to have an end, and even those that are thought to be supported by the most clear and cogent demonstrations contain in them paradoxes which are perfectly irreconcilable to the understandings of men, and that, taking all together, a very small portion of them does supply any real benefit to mankind, otherwise than by being an innocent diversion and amusement—I say the consideration of all this is apt to throw them into a despondency and perfect contempt of all study. But this may perhaps cease upon a view of the false principles that have obtained in the world, amongst all which there is none, methinks, hath a more wide and extended sway over the thoughts of speculative men than this of abstract general ideas.

18. I come now to consider the source of this prevailing notion, and that seems to me to be language. And surely nothing of less extent than reason itself could have been the source of an opinion so universally received. The truth of this appears as from other reasons so also from the plain confession of the ablest patrons of abstract ideas, who acknowledge that they are made in order to naming; from which it is a clear consequence that if there had been no such things as speech or universal signs there never had been any thought of abstraction. See III. vi. 39, and elsewhere of the *Essay on Human Understanding*. Let us examine the manner wherein words have contributed to the origin of that mistake. First then, it is thought that every name has, or ought to have, one only precise and settled signification, which inclines men to think there are certain abstract, determinate ideas that constitute the true and only immediate signification of each general name; and that it is by the mediation of these abstract ideas that a general name comes to signify any particular thing. Whereas, in truth, there is no such thing as one precise and definite signification annexed to any general name, they all signifying indifferently a great number of particular ideas. All which doth evidently follow from what has been already said, and will clearly appear to anyone by a little reflex-

ion. To this it will be objected that every name that has a definition is thereby restrained to one certain signification. For example, a triangle is defined to be "a plain surface comprehended by three right lines," by which that name is limited to denote one certain idea and no other. To which I answer, that in the definition it is not said whether the surface be great or small, black or white, nor whether the sides are long or short, equal or unequal, nor with what angles they are inclined to each other; in all which there may be great variety, and consequently there is no one settled idea which limits the signification of the word triangle. It is one thing for to keep a name constantly to the same definition, and another to make it stand everywhere for the same idea; the one is necessary, the other useless and impracticable.

19. But, to give a farther account how words came to produce the doctrine of abstract ideas, it must be observed that it is a received opinion that language has no other end but the communicating our ideas, and that every significant name stands for an idea. This being so, and it being withal certain that names which yet are not thought altogether insignificant do not always mark out particular conceivable ideas, it is straightway concluded that they stand for abstract notions. That there are many names in use amongst speculative men which do not always suggest to others determinate, particular ideas, or in truth anything at all, is what nobody will deny. And a little attention will discover that it is not necessary (even in the strictest reasonings) significant names which stand for ideas should, every time they are used, excite in the understanding the ideas they are made to stand for—in reading and discoursing, names being for the most part used as letters are in Algebra, in which, though a particular quantity be marked by each letter, yet to proceed right it is not requisite that in every step each letter suggest to your thoughts that particular quantity it was appointed to stand for.

20. Besides, the communicating of ideas marked by words is not the chief and only end of language, as is commonly supposed. There are other ends, as the raising of some passion, the exciting to or deterring from an action, the putting the mind in some particular disposition—to which the former is in many cases barely subservient, and sometimes entirely omitted, when these can be obtained without it, as I think does not unfrequently happen in the familiar use of language. I entreat the reader to reflect with himself, and see if it doth not often happen, either in hearing or reading a discourse, that the passions of fear, love, hatred, admiration, disdain, and the like, arise immediately in his mind upon the perception of certain words, without any ideas coming between. At first, indeed, the words might have occasioned ideas that were fitting to produce those emotions; but, if I mistake not, it will be found that, when language is once grown familiar, the hearing of the sounds or sight of the characters is oft immediately attended with those passions which at first were wont to be produced by the intervention of ideas that are now quite omitted. May we not, for example, be affected with the promise of a good thing, though we have not an idea of what it is? Or is not the being threatened with danger sufficient to excite a dread, though we think not of any particular evil likely to befal us, nor yet frame to ourselves an idea of danger in abstract? If any one shall join ever so little reflexion of his own to what has been said, I believe that it will evidently appear to him that general names are often used in the propriety of language without the speaker's designing them for marks of ideas in his own, which he would have them raise in the mind of the hearer. Even proper names themselves do not seem always spoken with a design to bring into our view the ideas of those individuals that are supposed to be marked by them. For example, when a schoolman tells me "Aristotle hath said it," all I conceive he means by it is to dispose me to embrace his opinion with the deference and submission which custom has annexed to that name. And this effect is often so instantly produced in the minds of those who are accustomed to resign their judgment to authority of that philosopher, as it is impossible any idea either of his person, writings, or reputation should go before. Innumerable examples of this kind may be given, but why should I insist on those things which every one's experience will, I doubt not, plentifully suggest unto him?

21. We have, I think, shewn the impossibility of Abstract Ideas. We have considered what has been said for them by their ablest patrons; and endeavored to show they are of no use for those ends to which they are thought necessary. And

lastly, we have traced them to the source from whence they flow, which appears evidently to be language. It cannot be denied that words are of excellent use, in that by their means all that stock of knowledge which has been purchased by the joint labours of inquisitive men in all ages and nations may be drawn into the view and made the possession of one single person. But at the same time it must be owned that most parts of knowledge have been strangely perplexed and darkened by the abuse of words, and general ways of speech wherein they are delivered. Since therefore words are so apt to impose on the understanding, whatever ideas I consider, I shall endeavour to take them bare and naked into my view, keeping out of my thoughts so far as I am able, those names which long and constant use hath so strictly united with them; from which I may expect to derive the following advantages:

22. First, I shall be sure to get clear of all controversies purely verbal—the springing up of which weeds in almost all the sciences has been a main hindrance to the growth of true and sound knowledge. Secondly, this seems to be a sure way to extricate myself out of that fine and subtle net of abstract ideas which has so miserably perplexed and entangled the minds of men; and that with this peculiar circumstance, that by how much the finer and more curious was the wit of any man, by so much the deeper was he likely to be ensnared and faster held therein. Thirdly, so long as I confine my thoughts to my own ideas divested of words, I do not see how I can easily be mistaken. The objects I consider, I clearly and adequately know. I cannot be deceived in thinking I have an idea which I have not. It is not possible for me to imagine that any of my own ideas are alike or unlike that are not truly so. To discern the agreements or disagreements there are between my ideas, to see what ideas are included in any compound idea and what not, there is nothing more requisite than an attentive perception of what passes in my own understanding.

23. But the attainment of all these advantages doth presuppose an entire deliverance from the deception of words, which I dare hardly promise myself; so difficult a thing it is to dissolve an union so early begun, and confirmed by so long a habit as that betwixt words and ideas. Which difficulty seems to have been very much increased by the doctrine of abstraction. For, so long as men thought abstract ideas were annexed to their words, it doth not seem strange that they should use words for ideas—it being found an impracticable thing to lay aside the word, and retain the abstract idea in the mind, which in itself was perfectly inconceivable. This seems to me the principal cause why those men who have so emphatically recommended to others the laying aside all use of words in their meditations, and contemplating their bare ideas, have yet failed to perform it themselves. Of late many have been very sensible of the absurd opinions and insignificant disputes which grow out of the abuse of words. And, in order to remedy these evils, they advise well, that we attend to the ideas signified, and draw off our attention from the words which signify them. But, how good soever this advice may be they have given others, it is plain they could not have a due regard to it themselves, so long as they thought the only immediate use of words was to signify ideas, and that the immediate signification of every general name was a determinate abstract idea.

24. But, these being known to be mistakes, a man may with greater ease prevent his being imposed on by words. He that knows he has no other than particular ideas, will not puzzle himself in vain to find out and conceive the abstract idea annexed to any name. And he that knows names do not always stand for ideas will spare himself the labour of looking for ideas where there are none to be had. It were, therefore, to be wished that everyone would use his utmost endeavours to obtain a clear view of the ideas he would consider, separating from them all that dress and incumbrance of words which so much contribute to blind the judgment and divide the attention. In vain do we extend our view into the heavens and pry into the entrails of the earth, in vain do we consult the writings of learned men and trace the dark footsteps of antiquity—we need only draw the curtain of words, to hold the fairest tree of knowledge, whose fruit is excellent, and within the reach of our hand.

25. Unless we take care to clear the First Principles of Knowledge from the embarrass and delusion of words, we may make infinite reasonings upon them to no purpose; we may draw consequences from consequences, and be never the wiser. The farther we go, we shall only lose our-

selves the more irrecoverably, and be the deeper entangled in difficulties and mistakes. Whoever therefore designs to read the following sheets, I entreat him to make my words the occasion of his own thinking, and endeavour to attain the same train of thoughts in reading that I had in writing them. By this means it will be easy for him to discover the truth or falsity of what I say. He will be out of all danger of being deceived by my words, and I do not see how he can be led into an error by considering his own naked, undisguised ideas.

A Treatise Concerning the Principles of Human Knowledge

1. It is evident to any one who takes a survey of the objects of human knowledge, that they are either ideas actually imprinted on the senses; or else such as are perceived by attending to the passions and operations of the mind; or lastly, ideas formed by help of memory and imagination—either compounding, dividing, or barely representing those originally perceived in the aforesaid ways. By sight I have the ideas of light and colours, with their several degrees and variations. By touch I perceive hard and soft, heat and cold, motion and resistance, and of all these more and less either as to quantity or degree. Smelling furnishes me with odours; the palate with tastes; and hearing conveys sounds to the mind in all their variety of tone and composition. And as several of these are observed to accompany each other, they come to be marked by one name, and so to be reputed as one thing. Thus, for example a certain colour, taste, smell, figure and consistence having been observed to go together, are accounted one distinct thing, signified by the name apple; other collections of ideas constitute a stone, a tree, a book, and the like sensible things—which as they are pleasing or disagreeable excite the passions of love, hatred, joy, grief, and so forth.

2. But, besides all that endless variety of ideas or objects of knowledge, there is likewise something which knows or perceives them, and exercises divers operations, as willing, imagining, remembering, about them. This perceiving, active being is what I call mind, spirit, soul, or myself. By which words I do not denote any one of my ideas, but a thing entirely distinct from them, wherein, they exist, or, which is the same thing, whereby they are perceived—for the existence of an idea consists in being perceived.

3. That neither our thoughts, nor passions, nor ideas formed by the imagination, exist without the mind, is what everybody will allow. And it seems no less evident that the various sensations or ideas imprinted on the sense, however blended or combined together (that is, whatever objects they compose), cannot exist otherwise than in a mind perceiving them. I think an intuitive knowledge may be obtained of this by any one that shall attend to what is meant by the term exists, when applied to sensible things. The table I write on I say exists, that is, I see and feel it; and if I were out of my study I should say it existed—meaning thereby that if I was in my study I might perceive it, or that some other spirit actually does perceive it. There was an odour, that is, it was smelt; there was a sound, that is, it was heard; a colour or figure, and it was perceived by sight or touch. This is all that I can understand by these and the like expressions. For as to what is said of the absolute existence of unthinking things without any relation to their being perceived, that seems perfectly unintelligible. Their *esse* is *percipi*, nor is it possible they should have any existence out of the minds or thinking things which perceive them.

4. It is indeed an opinion strangely prevailing amongst men, that houses, mountains, rivers, and in a word all sensible objects, have an existence, natural or real, distinct from their being perceived by the understanding. But, with how great an assurance and acquiescence soever this principle may be entertained in the world, yet whoever shall find in his heart to call it in question may, if I mistake not, perceive it to involve a manifest contradiction. For, what are the fore-mentioned objects but the things we perceive by sense? and what do we perceive besides our own ideas or sensations? and is it not plainly repugnant that any one of these, or any combination of them, should exist unperceived?

5. If we thoroughly examine this tenet it will, perhaps, be found at bottom to depend on the doctrine of abstract ideas. For can there be a nicer strain of abstraction than to distinguish the existence of sensible objects from their being perceived, so as to conceive them existing unperceived? Light and colours, heat and cold, extension and figures—in a word the things we see and feel—what are they but so many sensations, notions, ideas, or impressions on the sense? and is it possible to separate, even in thought, any of these from perception? For my part, I might as easily divide a thing from itself. I may, indeed, divide in my thoughts, or conceive apart from each other, those things which, perhaps I never perceived by sense so divided. Thus, I imagine the trunk of a human body without the limbs, or conceive the smell of a rose without thinking on the rose itself. So far, I will not deny, I can abstract—if that may properly be called abstraction which extends only to the conceiving separately such objects as it is possible may really exist or be actually perceived asunder. But my conceiving or imagining power does not extend beyond the possibility of real existence or perception. Hence, as it is impossible for me to see or feel anything without an actual sensation of that thing, so is it impossible for me to conceive in my thoughts any sensible thing or object distinct from the sensation or perception of it.

6. Some truths there are so near and obvious to the mind that a man need only open his eyes to see them. Such I take this important one to be, viz., that all the choir of heaven and furniture of the earth, in a word all those bodies which compose the mighty frame of the world, have not any subsistence without a mind, that their being is to be perceived or known; that consequently so long as they are not actually perceived by me, or do not exist in my mind or that of any other created spirit, they must either have no existence at all, or else subsist in the mind of some Eternal Spirit—it being perfectly unintelligible, and involving all the absurdity of abstraction, to attribute to any single part of them an existence independent of a spirit. To be convinced of which, the reader need only reflect, and try to separate in his own thoughts the being of a sensible thing from its being perceived.

7. From what has been said it follows there is not any other Substance than Spirit, or that which perceives. But, for the fuller proof of this point, let it be considered the sensible qualities are colour, figure, motion, smell, taste, etc., i.e., the ideas perceived by sense. Now, for an idea to exist in an unperceiving thing is a manifest contradiction, for to have an idea is all one as to perceive; that therefore wherein colour, figure, and the like qualities exist must perceive them; hence it is clear there can be no unthinking substance or substratum of those ideas.

8. But, say you, though the ideas themselves do not exist without the mind, yet there may be things like them, whereof they are copies or resemblances, which things exist without the mind in an unthinking substance. I answer, an idea can be like nothing but an idea; a colour or figure can be like nothing but another colour or figure. If we look but never so little into our thoughts, we shall find it impossible for us to conceive a likeness except only between our ideas. Again, I ask whether those supposed originals or external things, of which our ideas are the pictures or representations, be themselves perceivable or no? If they are, then they are ideas and we have gained our point; but if you say they are not, I appeal to any one whether it be sense to assert a colour is like something which is invisible; hard or soft, like something which is intangible; and so of the rest.

9. Some there are who make a distinction betwixt primary and secondary qualities. By the former they mean extension, figure, motion, rest, solidity or impenetrability, and number; by the latter they denote all other sensible qualities, as colours, sounds, tastes, and so forth. The ideas we have of these they acknowledge not to be the resemblances of anything existing without the mind, or unperceived, but they will have our ideas of the primary qualities to be patterns or images of things which exist without the mind, in an unthinking substance which they call Matter. By Matter, therefore, we are to understand an inert, senseless substance, in which extension, figure, and motion do actually subsist. But it is evident from what we have already shown, that extension, figure, and motion are only ideas existing in the mind, and that an idea can be like nothing but another idea, and that consequently neither they nor their archetypes can exist in an unperceiving substance. Hence, it is plain that the very notion of what is called Matter or corporeal substance, involves a contradiction in it.

10. They who assert that figure, motion, and the rest of the primary or original qualities do exist without the mind in unthinking substances, do at the same time acknowledge that colours, sounds, heat, cold, and suchlike secondary qualities, do not—which they tell us are sensations existing in the mind alone, that depend on and are occasioned by the different size, texture, and motion of the minute particles of matter. This they take for an undoubted truth, which they can demonstrate beyond all exception. Now, if it be certain that those original qualities are inseparably united with the other sensible qualities, and not, even in thought, capable of being abstracted from them, it plainly follows that they exist only in the mind. But I desire any one to reflect and try whether he can, by any abstraction of thought, conceive the extension and motion of a body without all other sensible qualities. For my own part, I see evidently that it is not in my power to frame an idea of a body extended and moving, but I must withal give it some colour or other sensible quality which is acknowledged to exist only in the mind. In short, extension, figure, and motion, abstracted from all other qualities, are inconceivable. Where therefore the other sensible qualities are, there must these be also, to wit, in the mind and nowhere else.

11. Again, great and small, swift and slow, are allowed to exist nowhere without the mind, being entirely relative, and changing as the frame or position of the organs of sense varies. The extension therefore which exists without the mind is neither great nor small, the motion neither swift nor slow, that is, they are nothing at all. But, say you, they are extension in general, and motion in general: thus we see how much the tenet of extended movable substances existing without the mind depends on the strange doctrine of abstract ideas. And here I cannot but remark how nearly the vague and indeterminate description of Matter or corporeal substance, which the modern philosophers are run into by their own principles, resembles that antiquated and so much ridiculed notion of *materia prima*, to be met with in Aristotle and his followers. Without extension solidity cannot be conceived; since therefore it has been shewn that extension exists not in an unthinking substance, the same must also be true of solidity.

12. That number is entirely the creature of the mind, even though the other qualities be allowed to exist without, will be evident to whoever considers that the same thing bears a different denomination of number as the mind views it with different respects. Thus, the same extension is one, or three, or thirty-six, according as the mind considers it with reference to a yard, a foot, or an inch. Number is so visibly relative, and dependent on men's understanding, that it is strange to think how any one should give it an absolute existence without the mind. We say one book, one page, one line, etc.; all these are equally units, though some contain several of the others. And in each instance, it is plain, the unit relates to some particular combination of ideas arbitrarily put together by the mind.

13. Unity I know some will have to be a simple or uncompounded idea, accompanying all other ideas into the mind. That I have any such idea answering the word unity I do not find; and if I had, methinks I could not miss finding it: on the contrary, it should be the most familiar to my understanding, since it is said to accompany all other ideas, and to be perceived by all the ways of sensation and reflexion. To say no more, it is an abstract idea.

14. I shall farther add, that, after the same manner as modern philosophers prove certain sensible qualities to have no existence in Matter, or without the mind, the same thing may be likewise proved of all other sensible qualities whatsoever. Thus, for instance, it is said that heat and cold are affections only of the mind, and not at all patterns of real beings, existing in the corporeal substances which excite them, for that the same body which appears cold to one hand seems warm to another. Now, why may we not as well argue that figure and extension are not patterns or resemblances of qualities existing in Matter, because to the same eye at different stations, or eyes of a different texture at the same station, they appear various, and cannot therefore be the images of anything settled and determinate without the mind? Again, it is proved that sweetness is not really in the sapid thing, because the thing remaining unaltered the sweetness is changed into bitter, as in case of a fever or otherwise vitiated palate. Is it not as reasonable to say that motion is not without the mind, since if the succession of ideas in the mind become swifter, the motion, it is acknowledged, shall appear slower without any alteration in any external object?

15. In short, let any one consider those arguments which are thought manifestly to prove that colours and taste exist only in the mind, and he shall find they may with equal force be brought to prove the same thing of extension, figure, and motion. Though it must be confessed this method of arguing does not so much prove that there is no extension or colour in an outward object, as that we do not know by sense which is the true extension or colour of the object. But the arguments foregoing plainly shew it to be impossible that any colour or extension at all, or other sensible quality whatsoever, should exist in an unthinking subject without the mind, or in truth, that there should be any such thing as an outward object.

16. But let us examine a little the received opinion.—It is said extension is a mode or accident of Matter, and that Matter is the substratum that supports it. Now I desire that you would explain to me what is meant by Matter's supporting extension. Say you, I have no idea of Matter and therefore cannot explain it. I answer, though you have no positive, yet, if you have any meaning at all, you must at least have a relative idea of Matter; though you know not what it is, yet you must be supposed to know what relation it bears to accidents, and what is meant by its supporting them. It is evident "support" cannot here be taken in its usual or literal sense—as when we say that pillars support a building; in what sense therefore must it be taken?

17. If we inquire into what the most accurate philosophers declare themselves to mean by material substance, we shall find them acknowledge they have no other meaning annexed to those sounds but the idea of Being in general, together with the relative notion of its supporting accidents. The general idea of Being appeareth to me the most abstract and incomprehensible of all other; and as for its supporting accidents, this, as we have just now observed, cannot be understood in the common sense of those words; it must therefore be taken in some other sense, but what that is they do not explain. So that when I consider the two parts or branches which make the signification of the words material substance, I am convinced there is no distinct meaning annexed to them. But why should we trouble ourselves any farther, in discussing this material substratum or support of figure and motion, and other sensible qualities? Does it not suppose they have an existence without the mind? And is not this a direct repugnancy, and altogether inconceivable?

18. But, though it were possible that solid, figured, movable substances may exist without the mind, corresponding to the ideas we have of bodies, yet how is it possible for us to know this? Either we must know it by sense or by reason. As for our senses, by them we have the knowledge only of our sensations, ideas, or those things that are immediately perceived by sense, call them what you will: but they do not inform us that things exist without the mind, or unperceived, like to those which are perceived. This the materialists themselves acknowledge. It remains therefore that if we have any knowledge at all of external things, it must be by reason, inferring their existence from what is immediately perceived by sense. But what reason can induce us to believe the existence of bodies without the mind, from what we perceive, since the very patrons of Matter themselves do not pretend there is any necessary connexion betwixt them and our ideas? I say it is granted on all hands (and what happens in dreams, phrensies, and the like, puts it beyond dispute) that it is possible we might be affected with all the ideas we have now, though there were no bodies existing without resembling them. Hence, it is evident the supposition of external bodies is not necessary for the producing our ideas; since it is granted they are produced sometimes, and might possibly be produced always in the same order, we see them in at present, without their concurrence.

19. But, though we might possibly have all our sensations without them, yet perhaps it may be thought easier to conceive and explain the manner of their production, by supposing external bodies in their likeness rather than otherwise; and so it might be at least probable there are such things as bodies that excite their ideas in our minds. But neither can this be said; for, though we give the materialists their external bodies, they by their own confession are never the nearer knowing how our ideas are produced; since they own themselves unable to comprehend in what manner body can act upon spirit, or how it is possible it should imprint any idea in the mind. Hence it is evident the production of ideas or sensations in our minds can be no reason why we should suppose Matter or corporeal substances, since that is acknowledged to remain equally inexplicable with or without this supposition. If therefore it were possible for bodies to exist without the mind, yet to hold they do so, must needs be a very precarious opinion; since it is to suppose, without any reason at all, that God has created innumerable beings that are entirely useless, and serve to no manner of purpose.

20. In short, if there were external bodies, it is impossible we should ever come to know it; and if there were not, we might have the very same reasons to think there were that we have now. Suppose—what no one can deny possible—an intelligence without the help of external bodies, to be affected with the same train of sensations or ideas that you are, imprinted in the same order and with like vividness in his mind. I ask whether that intelligence hath not all the reason to believe the existence of corporeal substances, represented by his ideas, and exciting them in his mind, that you can possibly have for believing the same thing? Of this there can be no question—which one consideration were enough to make any reasonable person suspect the strength of whatever arguments he may think himself to have, for the existence of bodies without the mind.

21. Were it necessary to add any farther proof against the existence of Matter after what has been said, I could instance several of those errors and difficulties (not to mention impieties) which have sprung from that tenet. It has occasioned numberless controversies and disputes in philosophy, and not a few of far greater moment in religion. But I shall not enter into the detail of them in this place, as well because I think arguments a posteriori are unnecessary for confirming what has been, if I mistake not, sufficiently demonstrated a priori, as because I shall hereafter find occasion to speak somewhat of them.

22. I am afraid I have given cause to think I am needlessly prolix in handling this subject. For, to what purpose is it to dilate on that which may be demonstrated with the utmost evidence in a line or two, to any one that is capable of the least reflexion? It is but looking into your own thoughts, and so trying whether you can conceive it possible for a sound, or figure, or motion, or colour to exist without the mind or unperceived. This easy trial may perhaps make you see that what you contend for is a downright contradiction. Insomuch that I am content to put the whole upon this issue:—If you can but conceive it possible for one extended movable substance, or, in general, for any one idea, or anything like an idea, to exist otherwise than in a mind perceiving it, I shall readily give up the cause. And, as for all that compages of external bodies you contend for, I shall grant you its existence, though you cannot either give me any reason why you believe it exists, or assign any use to it when it is supposed to exist. I say, the bare possibility of your opinions being true shall pass for an argument that it is so.

23. But, say you, surely there is nothing easier than for me to imagine trees, for instance, in a park, or books existing in a closet, and nobody by to perceive them. I answer, you may so, there is no difficulty in it; but what is all this, I beseech you, more than framing in your mind certain ideas which you call books and trees, and the same time omitting to frame the idea of any one that may perceive them? But do not you yourself perceive or think of them all the while? This therefore is nothing to the purpose; it only shews you have the power of imagining or forming ideas in your mind: but it does not shew that you can conceive it possible the objects of your thought may exist without the mind. To make out this, it is necessary that you conceive them existing unconceived or unthought of, which is a manifest repugnancy. When we do our utmost to conceive the existence of external bodies, we are all the while only contemplating our own ideas. But the mind taking no notice of itself, is deluded to think it can and does conceive bodies existing unthought of or without the mind, though at the same time they are apprehended by or exist in itself. A little attention will discover to any one the truth and evidence of what is here said, and make it unnecessary to insist on any other proofs against the existence of material substance.

24. It is very obvious, upon the least inquiry into our thoughts, to know whether it is possible for us to understand what is meant by the absolute existence of sensible objects in themselves, or without the mind. To me it is evident those words mark out either a direct contradiction, or else nothing at all. And to convince others of this, I know no readier or fairer way than to entreat they would calmly attend to their own thoughts; and if by this attention the emptiness or repugnancy of those expressions does appear, surely nothing more is requisite for the conviction. It is on this therefore that I insist, to wit, that the absolute existence of unthinking things are words without a meaning, or which include a contradiction. This is what I repeat and inculcate, and earnestly recommend to the attentive thoughts of the reader.

25. All our ideas, sensations, notions, or the things which we perceive, by whatsoever names they may be distinguished, are visibly inactive—there is nothing of power or agency included in them. So that one idea or object of thought cannot produce or make any alteration in another. To be satisfied of the truth of this, there is nothing else requisite but a bare observation of our ideas. For, since they and every part of them exist only in the mind, it follows that there is nothing in them but what is perceived: but whoever shall attend to his ideas, whether of sense or reflexion, will not perceive in them any power or activity; there is, therefore, no such thing contained in them. A little attention will discover to us that the very being of an idea implies passiveness and inertness in it, insomuch that it is impossible for an idea to do anything, or, strictly speaking, to be the cause of anything: neither can it be the resemblance or pattern of any active being, as is evident from sect. 8. Whence it plainly follows that extension, figure, and motion cannot be the cause of our sensations. To say, therefore, that these are the effects of powers resulting from the configuration, number, motion, and size of corpuscles, must certainly be false.

26. We perceive a continual succession of ideas, some are anew excited, others are changed or totally disappear. There is therefore some cause of these ideas, whereon they depend, and which produces and changes them. That this cause cannot be any quality or idea or combination of ideas, is clear from the preceding section. I must therefore be a substance; but it has been shewn that there is no corporeal or material substance: it remains therefore that the cause of ideas is an incorporeal active substance or Spirit.

27. A spirit is one simple, undivided, active being—as it perceives ideas it is called the understanding, and as it produces or otherwise operates about them it is called the will. Hence there can be no idea formed of a soul or spirit; for all ideas whatever, being passive and inert (vide sect. 25), they cannot represent unto us, by way of image or likeness, that which acts. A little attention will make it plain to any one, that to have an idea which shall be like that active principle of motion and change of ideas is absolutely impossible. Such is the nature of spirit, or that which acts, that it cannot be of itself perceived, but only by the effects which it produceth. If any man shall doubt of the truth of what is here delivered, let him but reflect and try if he can frame the idea of any power or active being, and whether he has ideas of two principal powers, marked by the names will and understanding, distinct from each other as well as from a third idea of Substance or Being in general, with a relative notion of its supporting or being the subject of the aforesaid powers—which is signified by the name soul or spirit. This is what some hold; but, so far as I can see, the words will, soul, spirit, do not stand for different ideas, or, in truth, for any idea at all, but for something which is very different from ideas, and which, being an agent, cannot be like unto, or represented by, any idea whatsoever. Though it must be owned at the same time that we have some notion of soul, spirit, and the operations of the mind: such as willing, loving, hating—inasmuch as we know or understand the meaning of these words.

28. I find I can excite ideas in my mind at pleasure, and vary and shift the scene as oft as I think fit. It is no more than willing, and straightway this or that idea arises in my fancy; and by the same power it is obliterated and makes way for another. This making and unmaking of ideas doth very properly denominate the mind active. Thus much is certain and grounded on experience; but when we think of unthinking agents or of exciting ideas exclusive of volition, we only amuse ourselves with words.

29. But, whatever power I may have over my own thoughts, I find the ideas actually perceived by Sense have not a like dependence on my will. When in broad daylight I open my eyes, it is not in my power to choose whether I shall see or no, or to determine what particular objects shall present themselves to my view; and so likewise as to the hearing and other senses; the ideas imprinted on them are not creatures of my will. There is therefore some other Will or Spirit that produces them.

30. The ideas of Sense are more strong, lively, and distinct than those of the imagination; they have likewise a steadiness, order, and coherence, and are not excited at random, as those which are the effects of human wills often are, but in a regular train or series, the admirable connexion whereof sufficiently testifies the wisdom and benevolence of its Author. Now the set rules or established methods wherein the Mind we depend on excites in us the ideas of sense, are called the laws of nature; and these we learn by experience, which teaches us that such and such ideas are attended with such and such other ideas, in the ordinary course of things.

31. This gives us a sort of foresight which enables us to regulate our actions for the benefit of life. And without this we should be eternally at a loss; we could not know how to act anything that might procure us the least pleasure, or remove the least pain of sense. That food nourishes, sleep refreshes, and fire warms us; that to sow in the seed-time is the way to reap in the harvest; and in general that to obtain such or such ends, such or such means are conducive—all this we know, not by discovering any necessary connexion between our ideas, but only by the observation of the settled laws of nature, without which we should be all in uncertainty and confusion, and a grown man no more know how to manage himself in the affairs of life than an infant just born.

32. And yet this consistent uniform working, which so evidently displays the goodness and wisdom of that Governing Spirit whose Will constitutes the laws of nature, is so far from leading our thoughts to Him, that it rather sends them wandering after second causes. For, when we perceive certain ideas of Sense constantly followed by other ideas and we know this is not of our own doing, we forthwith attribute power and agency to the ideas themselves, and make one the cause of another, than which nothing can be more absurd and unintelligible. Thus, for example, having observed that when we perceive by sight a certain round luminous figure we at the same time perceive by touch the idea or sensation called heat, we do from thence conclude the sun to be the cause of heat. And in like manner perceiving the motion and collision of bodies to be attended with sound, we are inclined to think the latter the effect of the former.

33. The ideas imprinted on the Senses by the Author of nature are called real things; and those excited in the imagination being less regular, vivid, and constant, are more properly termed ideas, or images of things, which they copy and represent.

But then our sensations, be they never so vivid and distinct, are nevertheless ideas, that is, they exist in the mind, or are perceived by it, as truly as the ideas of its own framing. The ideas of Sense are allowed to have more reality in them, that is, to be more strong, orderly, and coherent than the creatures of the mind; but this is no argument that they exist without the mind. They are also less dependent on the spirit, or thinking substance which perceives them, in that they are excited by the will of another and more powerful spirit; yet still they are ideas, and certainly no idea, whether faint or strong, can exist otherwise than in a mind perceiving it.

34. Before we proceed any farther it is necessary we spend some time in answering objections which may probably be made against the principles we have hitherto laid down. In doing of which, if I seem too prolix to those of quick apprehensions, I hope it may be pardoned, since all men do not equally apprehend things of this nature, and I am willing to be understood by every one.

First, then, it will be objected that by the foregoing principles all that is real and substantial in nature is banished out of the world, and instead thereof a chimerical scheme of ideas takes place. All things that exist, exist only in the mind, that is, they are purely notional. What therefore becomes of the sun, moon and stars? What must we think of houses, rivers, mountains, trees, stones; nay, even of our own bodies? Are all these but so many chimeras and illusions on the fancy? To all which, and whatever else of the same sort may be objected, I answer, that by the principles premised we are not deprived of any one thing in nature. Whatever we see, feel, hear, or anywise conceive or understand remains as secure as ever, and is as real as ever. There is a rerum natura, and the distinction between realities and chimeras retains its full force. This is evident from sect. 29, 30, and 33, where we have shewn what is meant by real things in opposition to chimeras or ideas of our own framing; but then they both equally exist in the mind, and in that sense they are alike ideas.

35. I do not argue against the existence of any one thing that we can apprehend either by sense or reflexion. That the things I see with my eyes and touch with my hands do exist, really exist, I make not the least question. The only thing whose existence we deny is that which philosophers call Matter or corporeal substance. And in doing of this there is no damage done to the rest of mankind, who, I dare say, will never miss it. The Atheist indeed will want the colour of an empty name to support his impiety; and the Philosophers may possibly find they have lost a great handle for trifling and disputation.

36. If any man thinks this detracts from the existence or reality of things, he is very far from understanding what hath been premised in the plainest terms I could think of. Take here an abstract of what has been said:—There are spiritual substances, minds, or human souls, which will or excite ideas in themselves at pleasure; but these are faint, weak, and unsteady in respect of others they perceive by sense—which, being impressed upon them according to certain rules or laws of nature, speak themselves the effects of a mind more powerful and wise than human spirits. These latter are said to have more reality in them than the former:—by which is meant that they are more affecting, orderly, and distinct, and that they are not fictions of the mind perceiving them. And in this sense the sun that I see by day is the real sun, and that which I imagine by night is the idea of the former. In the sense here given of reality it is evident that every vegetable, star, mineral, and in general each part of the mundane system, is as much a real being by our principles as by any other. Whether others mean anything by the term reality different from what I do, I entreat them to look into their own thoughts and see.

37. I will be urged that thus much at least is true, to wit, that we take away all corporeal substances. To this my answer is, that if the word substance be taken in the vulgar sense—for a combination of sensible qualities, such as extension, solidity, weight, and the like—this we cannot be accused of taking away: but if it be taken in a philosophic sense—for the support of accidents or qualities without the mind—then indeed I acknowledge that we take it away, if one may be said to take away that which never had any existence, not even in the imagination.

38. But after all, say you, it sounds very harsh to say we eat and drink ideas, and are clothed with ideas. I acknowledge it does so—the word idea not being used in common discourse to signify the several combinations of sensible qualities which are called things; and it is certain that any expression which varies from the familiar use of language will seem harsh and ridiculous. But this doth not concern the truth of the proposition, which in other words is no more than to say, we are fed and clothed with those things which we perceive immediately by our senses. The hardness or softness, the colour, taste, warmth, figure, or suchlike qualities, which combined together constitute the several sorts of victuals and apparel, have been shewn to exist only in the mind that perceives them; and this is all that is meant by calling them ideas; which word if it was as ordinarily used as thing, would sound no harsher nor more ridiculous than it. I am not for disputing about the propriety, but the truth of the expression. If therefore you agree with me that we eat and drink and are clad with the immediate objects of sense, which cannot exist unperceived or without the mind, I shall readily grant it is more proper or conformable to custom that they should be called things rather than ideas.

39. If it be demanded why I make use of the word idea, and do not rather in compliance with custom call them things; I answer, I do it for two reasons:—first, because the term thing in contradistinction to idea, is generally supposed to denote somewhat existing without the mind; secondly, because thing hath a more comprehensive signification than idea, including spirit or thinking things as well as ideas. Since therefore the objects of sense exist only in the mind, and are withal thoughtless and inactive, I chose to mark them by the word idea, which implies those properties.

40. But, say what we can, some one perhaps may be apt to reply, he will still believe his senses, and never suffer any arguments, how plausible soever, to prevail over the certainty of them. Be it so; assert the evidence of sense as high as you please, we are willing to do the same. That what I see, hear, and feel doth exist, that is to say, is perceived by me, I no more doubt than I do of my own being. But I do not see how the testimony of sense can be alleged as a proof for the existence of anything which is not perceived by sense. We are not for having any man turn sceptic and disbelieve his senses; on the contrary, we give them all the stress and assurance imaginable; nor are there any principles more opposite to Scepticism than those we have laid down, as shall be hereafter clearly shewn.

41. Secondly, it will be objected that there is a great difference betwixt real fire for instance, and the idea of fire, betwixt dreaming or imagining oneself burnt, and actually being so: if you suspect it to be only the idea of fire which you see, do but put your hand into it and you will be convinced with a witness. This and the like may be urged in opposition to our tenets. To all which the answer is evident from what hath been already said; and I shall only add in this place, that if real fire be very different from the idea of fire, so also is the real pain that it occasions very different from the idea of the same pain, and yet nobody will pretend that real pain either is, or can possibly be, in an unperceiving thing, or without the mind, any more than its idea.

42. Thirdly, it will be objected that we see things actually without or at distance from us, and which consequently do not exist in the mind; it being absurd that those things which are seen at the distance of several miles should be as near to us as our own thoughts. In answer to this, I desire it may be considered that in a dream we do oft perceive things as existing at a great distance off, and yet for all that, those things are acknowledged to have their existence only in the mind.

43. But, for the fuller clearing of this point, it may be worth while to consider how it is that we perceive distance and things placed at a distance by sight. For, that we should in truth see external space, and bodies actually existing in it, some nearer, others farther off, seems to carry with it some opposition to what hath been said of their existing nowhere without the mind. The consideration of this difficulty it was that gave birth to my "Essay towards a New Theory of Vision," which was published not long since, wherein it is shewn that distance or outness is neither immediately of itself perceived by sight, nor yet apprehended or judged of by lines and angles, or anything that hath a necessary connexion with it; but that it is only suggested to our thoughts by certain visible ideas and sensations attending vision, which in their own nature have no manner of similitude or relation either with distance or things placed at a distance; but, by a connexion taught us by experience, they come to signify and suggest them to us, after the same manner that words of any language suggest the ideas they are made to stand for; insomuch that a man born blind and afterwards made to see, would not, at first sight, think the things he saw to be without his mind, or at any distance from him. See sect. 41 of the fore-mentioned treatise.

44. The ideas of sight and touch make two species entirely distinct and heterogeneous. The former are marks and prognostics of the latter. That the proper objects of sight neither exist without mind, nor are the images of external things, was shewn even in that treatise. Though throughout the same the contrary be supposed true of tangible objects—not that to suppose that vulgar error was necessary for establishing the notion therein laid down, but because it was beside my purpose to examine and refute it in a discourse concerning Vision. So that in strict truth the ideas of sight, when we apprehend by them distance and things placed at a distance, do not suggest or mark out to us things actually existing at a distance, but only admonish us what ideas of touch will be imprinted in our minds at such and such distances of time, and in consequence of such or such actions. It is, I say, evident from what has been said in the foregoing parts of this Treatise, and in sect. 147 and elsewhere of the Essay concerning Vision, that visible ideas are the Language whereby the Governing Spirit on whom we depend informs us what tangible ideas he is about to imprint upon us, in case we excite this or that motion in our own bodies. But for a fuller information in this point I refer to the Essay itself.

45. Fourthly, it will be objected that from the foregoing principles it follows things are every moment annihilated and created anew. The objects of sense exist only when they are perceived; the trees therefore are in the garden, or the chairs in the parlour, no longer than while there is somebody by to perceive them. Upon shutting my eyes all the furniture in the room is reduced to nothing, and barely upon opening them it is again created. In answer to all which, I refer the reader to what has been said in sect. 3, 4, &c., and desire he will consider whether he means anything by the actual existence of an idea distinct from its being perceived. For my part, after the nicest inquiry I could make, I am not able to discover that anything else is meant by those words; and I once more entreat the reader to sound his own thoughts, and not suffer himself to be imposed on by words. If he can conceive it possible either for his ideas or their archetypes to exist without being perceived, then I give up the cause; but if he cannot, he will acknowledge it is unreasonable for him to stand up in defence of he knows not what, and pretend to charge on me as an absurdity the not assenting to those propositions which at bottom have no meaning in them.

46. It will not be amiss to observe how far the received principles of philosophy are themselves chargeable with those pretended absurdities. It is thought strangely absurd that upon closing my eyelids all the visible objects around me should be reduced to nothing; and yet is not this what philosophers commonly acknowledge, when they agree on all hands that light and colours, which alone are the proper and immediate objects of sight, are mere sensations that exist no longer than they are perceived? Again, it may to some perhaps seem very incredible that things should be every moment creating, yet this very notion is commonly taught in the schools. For the Schoolmen, though they acknowledge the existence of Matter, and that the whole mundane fabric is framed out of it, are nevertheless of opinion that it cannot subsist without the divine conservation, which by them is expounded to be a continual creation.

47. Farther, a little thought will discover to us that though we allow the existence of Matter or corporeal substance, yet it will unavoidably follow, from the principles which are now generally admitted, that the particular bodies, of what kind soever, do none of them exist whilst they are not perceived. For, it is evident from sect. II and the following sections, that the Matter philosophers contend for is an incomprehensible somewhat, which hath none of those particular qualities whereby the bodies falling under our senses are distinguished one from another. But, to make this more plain, it must be remarked that the infinite divisibility of Matter is now universally allowed, at least by the most approved and considerable philosophers, who on the received principles demonstrate it beyond all exception. Hence, it follows there is an infinite number of parts in each particle of Matter which are not perceived by sense. The reason therefore that any particular body seems to be of a finite magnitude, or exhibits only a finite number of parts to sense, is, not because it contains no more, since in itself it contains an infinite number of parts, but because the sense is not acute enough to discern them. In proportion therefore as the sense is rendered more acute, it perceives a greater number of parts in the object, that is, the object appears greater, and its figure varies, those parts in its extremities which were before unperceivable appearing now to bound it in very different lines and angles from those perceived by an obtuser sense. And at length, after various changes of size and shape, when the sense becomes infinitely acute the body shall seem infinite. During all which there is no alteration in the body, but only in the sense. Each body therefore, considered in itself, is infinitely extended, and consequently void of all shape or figure. From which it follows that, though we should grant the existence of Matter to be never so certain, yet it is withal as certain, the materialists themselves are by their own principles forced to acknowledge, that neither the particular bodies perceived by sense, nor anything like them, exists without the mind. Matter, I say, and each particle thereof, is according to them infinite and shapeless, and it is the mind that frames all that variety of bodies which compose the visible world, any one whereof does not exist longer than it is perceived.

48. If we consider it, the objection proposed in sect. 45 will not be found reasonably charged on the principles we have premised, so as in truth to make any objection at all against our notions. For, though we hold indeed the objects of sense to be nothing else but ideas which cannot exist unperceived; yet we may not hence conclude they have no existence except only while they are perceived by us, since there may be some other spirit that perceives them though we do not. Wherever bodies are said to have no existence without the mind, I would not be understood to mean this or that particular mind, but all minds whatsoever. It does not therefore follow from the foregoing principles that bodies are annihilated and created every moment, or exist not at all during the intervals between our perception of them.

49. Fifthly, it may perhaps be objected that if extension and figure exist only in the mind, it follows that the mind is extended and figured; since extension is a mode or attribute which (to speak with the schools) is predicated of the subject in which it exists. I answer, those qualities are in the mind only as they are perceived by it—that is, not by way of mode or attribute, but only by way of idea; and it no more follows the soul or mind is extended, because extension exists in it alone, than it does that it is red or blue, because those colours are on all hands acknowledged to exist in it, and

nowhere else. As to what philosophers say of subject and mode, that seems very groundless and unintelligible. For instance, in this proposition "a die is hard, extended, and square," they will have it that the word die denotes a subject or substance, distinct from the hardness, extension, and figure which are predicated of it, and in which they exist. This I cannot comprehend: to me a die seems to be nothing distinct from those things which are termed its modes or accidents. And, to say a die is hard, extended, and square is not to attribute those qualities to a subject distinct from and supporting them, but only an explication of the meaning of the word die.

50. Sixthly, you will say there have been a great many things explained by matter and motion; take away these and you destroy the whole corpuscular philosophy, and undermine those mechanical principles which have been applied with so much success to account for the phenomena. In short, whatever advances have been made, either by ancient or modern philosophers, in the study of nature do all proceed on the supposition that corporeal substance or Matter doth really exist. To this I answer that there is not any one phenomenon explained on that supposition which may not as well be explained without it, as might easily be made appear by an induction of particulars. To explain the phenomena, is all one as to shew why, upon such and such occasions, we are affected with such and such ideas. But how Matter should operate on a Spirit, or produce any idea in it, is what no philosopher will pretend to explain; it is therefore evident there can be no use of Matter in natural philosophy. Besides, they who attempt to account for things do it not by corporeal substance, but by figure, motion, and other qualities, which are in truth no more than mere ideas, and, therefore, cannot be the cause of anything, as hath been already shewn. See sect. 25.

51. Seventhly, it will upon this be demanded whether it does not seem absurd to take away natural causes, and ascribe everything to the immediate operation of Spirits? We must no longer say upon these principles that fire heats, or water cools, but that a Spirit heats, and so forth. Would not a man be deservedly laughed at, who should talk after this manner? I answer, he would so; in such things we ought to "think with the learned, and speak with the vulgar." They who to demonstration are convinced of the truth of the Copernican system do nevertheless say "the sun rises," "the sun sets," or "comes to the meridian"; and if they affected a contrary style in common talk it would without doubt appear very ridiculous. A little reflexion on what is here said will make it manifest that the common use of language would receive no manner of alteration or disturbance from the admission of our tenets.

52. In the ordinary affairs of life, any phrases may be retained, so long as they excite in us proper sentiments, or dispositions to act in such a manner as is necessary for our well-being, how false soever they may be if taken in a strict and speculative sense. Nay, this is unavoidable, since, propriety being regulated by custom, language is suited to the received opinions, which are not always the truest. Hence it is impossible, even in the most rigid, philosophic reasonings, so far to alter the bent and genius of the tongue we speak, as never to give a handle for cavillers to pretend difficulties and inconsistencies. But, a fair and ingenuous reader will collect the sense from the scope and tenor and connexion of a discourse, making allowances for those inaccurate modes of speech which use has made inevitable.

53. As to the opinion that there are no Corporeal Causes, this has been heretofore maintained by some of the Schoolmen, as it is of late by others among the modern philosophers, who though they allow Matter to exist, yet will have God alone to be the immediate efficient cause of all things. These men saw that amongst all the objects of sense there was none which had any power or activity included in it; and that by consequence this was likewise true of whatever bodies they supposed to exist without the mind, like unto the immediate objects of sense. But then, that they should suppose an innumerable multitude of created beings, which they acknowledge are not capable of producing any one effect in nature, and which therefore are made to no manner of purpose, since God might have done everything as well without them: this I say, though we should allow it possible, must yet be a very unaccountable and extravagant supposition.

54. In the eighth place, the universal concurrent assent of mankind may be thought by some an invincible argument in behalf of Matter, or the existence of external things. Must we suppose the whole world to be mistaken? And if so, what cause can be assigned of so widespread and predominant an error? I answer, first, that, upon a narrow inquiry, it will not perhaps be found so many as is imagined do really believe the existence of Matter or things without the mind. Strictly speaking, to believe that which involves a contradiction, or has no meaning in it, is impossible; and whether the foregoing expressions are not of that sort, I refer it to the impartial examination of the reader. In one sense, indeed, men may be said to believe that Matter exists, that is, they act as if the immediate cause of their sensations, which affects them every moment, and is so nearly present to them, were some senseless unthinking being. But, that they should clearly apprehend any meaning marked by those words, and form thereof a settled speculative opinion, is what I am not able to conceive. This is not the only instance wherein men impose upon themselves, by imagining they believe those propositions which they have often heard, though at bottom they have no meaning in them.

55. But secondly, though we should grant a notion to be never so universally and steadfastly adhered to, yet this is weak argument of its truth to whoever considers what a vast number of prejudices and false opinions are everywhere embraced with the utmost tenaciousness, by the unreflecting (which are the far greater) part of mankind. There was a time when the antipodes and motion of the earth were looked upon as monstrous absurdities even by men of learning: and if it be considered what a small proportion they bear to the rest of mankind, we shall find that at this day those notions have gained but a very inconsiderable footing in the world.

56. But it is demanded that we assign a cause of this prejudice, and account for its obtaining in the world. To this I answer, that men knowing they perceived several ideas, whereof they themselves were not the authors—as not being excited from within nor depending on the operation of their wills—this made them maintain those ideas, or objects of perception had an existence independent of and without the mind, without ever dreaming that a contradiction was involved in those words. But, philosophers having plainly seen that the immediate objects of perception do not exist without the mind, they in some degree corrected the mistake of the vulgar; but at the same time run into another which seems no less absurd, to wit, that there are certain objects really existing without the mind, or having a subsistence distinct from being perceived, of which our ideas are only images or resemblances, imprinted by those objects on the mind. And this notion of the philosophers owes its origin to the same cause with the former, namely, their being conscious that they were not the authors of their own sensations, which they evidently knew were imprinted from without, and which therefore must have some cause distinct from the minds on which they are imprinted.

57. But why they should suppose the ideas of sense to be excited in us by things in their likeness, and not rather have recourse to Spirit which alone can act, may be accounted for, first, because they were not aware of the repugnancy there is, as well in supposing things like unto our ideas existing without, as in attributing to them power or activity. Secondly, because the Supreme Spirit which excites those ideas in our minds, is not marked out and limited to our view by any particular finite collection of sensible ideas, as human agents are by their size, complexion, limbs, and motions. And thirdly, because His operations are regular and uniform. Whenever the course of nature is interrupted by a miracle, men are ready to own the presence of a superior agent. But, when we see things go on in the ordinary course they do not excite in us any reflexion; their order and concatenation, though it be an argument of the greatest wisdom, power, and goodness in their creator, is yet so constant and familiar to us that we do not think them the immediate effects of a Free Spirit; especially since inconsistency and mutability in acting, though it be an imperfection, is looked on as a mark of freedom.

---

55. An *Enquiry Concerning Human Understanding*

DAVID HUME

David Hume (1711–1776) was a Scottish philosopher who was impressed by the success of Newtonian science and who wanted to apply its methods to the study of psychology and the "moral" sciences. As Newton presented his experimental method, he claimed to be against postulating unobservable causes of phenomena; for example, he claimed to discover only the equation for gravity, not its cause. Hume believed all ideas consist of copies of sense impressions, so he analyzed metaphysical ideas (like causality, substance, and God) in terms of sensory experience. Hume also believed the only way to know truths that are not just definitions or truths of logic is by means of perceptual experience. He claimed the analysis of metaphysical ideas and the examination of the adequacy of perceptual support for metaphysical beliefs would lead to skepticism about metaphysics.

. . . [O]bscurity in the profound and abstract philosophy, is objected to, not only as painful and fatiguing, but as the inevitable source of uncertainty and error. Here indeed lies the justest and most plausible objection against a considerable part of metaphysics, that they are not properly a science; but arise either from the fruitless efforts of human vanity, which would penetrate into subjects utterly inaccessible to the understanding, or from the craft of popular superstitions, which, being unable to defend themselves on fair ground,

From Hume's *Enquiry Concerning Human Understanding*, first published in 1748.

raise these entangling brambles to cover and protect their weakness. Chased from the open country, these robbers fly into the forest, and lie in wait to break in upon every unguarded avenue of the mind, and overwhelm it with religious fears and prejudices. The stoutest antagonist, if he remit his watch a moment, is oppressed. And many, through cowardice and folly, open the gates to the enemies, and willingly receive them with reverence and submission, as their legal sovereigns.

But is this a sufficient reason, why philosophers should desist from such researches, and leave superstition still in possession of her retreat? Is it not proper to draw an opposite conclusion, and perceive the necessity of carrying the war into the most secret recesses of the enemy? In vain do we hope, that men, from frequent disappointment, will at last abandon such airy sciences, and discover the proper province of human reason. For, besides, that many persons find too sensible an interest in perpetually recalling such topics; besides this, I say, the motive of blind despair can never reasonably have place in the sciences; since, however unsuccessful former attempts may have proved, there is still room to hope, that the industry, good fortune, or improved sagacity of succeeding generations may reach discoveries unknown to former ages. Each adventurous genius will still leap at the arduous prize, and find himself stimulated, rather than discouraged, by the failures of his predecessors; while he hopes that the glory of achieving so hard an adventure is reserved for him alone. The only method of freeing learning, at once, from these abstruse questions, is to enquire seriously into the nature of human understanding, and show, from an exact analysis of its powers and capacity, that it is by no means fitted for such remote and abstruse subjects. We must submit to this fatigue, in order to live at ease ever after: And must cultivate true metaphysics with some care, in order to destroy the false and adulterate. . . .

Of the Origin of Ideas

Everyone will readily allow that there is a considerable difference between the perceptions of the mind when a man feels the pain of excessive heat or the pleasure of moderate warmth, and when he afterwards recalls to his memory this sensation or anticipates it by his imagination. These faculties may mimic or copy the perceptions of the senses, but they never can entirely reach the force and vivacity of the original sentiment. The utmost we say of them, even when they operate with greatest vigor, is that they represent their object in so lively a manner that we could *almost* say we feel or see it. . . .

Here, therefore, we may divide all the perceptions of the mind into two classes or species, which are distinguished by their different degrees of force and vivacity. The less forcible and lively are commonly denominated "thoughts" or "ideas." The other species want a name in our language, and in most others; I suppose, because it was not requisite for any but philosophical purposes to rank them under a general term or appellation. Let us, therefore, use a little freedom and call them "impressions," employing that word in a sense somewhat different from the usual. By the term "impression," then, I mean all our more lively perceptions, when we hear, or see, or feel, or love, or hate, or desire, or will. And impressions are distinguished from ideas, which are the less lively perceptions of which we are conscious when we reflect on any of those sensations or movements above mentioned.

Nothing, at first view, may seem more unbounded than the thought of man, which not only escapes all human power and authority, but is not even restrained within the limits of nature and reality. To form monsters and join incongruous shapes and appearances costs the imagination no more trouble than to conceive the most natural and familiar objects. And while the body is confined to one planet, along which it creeps with pain and difficulty, the thought can in an instant transport us into the most distant regions of the universe, or even beyond the universe into the unbounded chaos where nature is supposed to lie in total confusion. What never was seen or heard of, may yet be conceived, nor is anything beyond the power of thought except what implies an absolute contradiction.

But though our thought seems to possess this unbounded liberty, we shall find upon a nearer examination that it is really confined within very narrow limits, and that all this creative power of the mind amounts to no more than the faculty of compounding, transposing, augmenting, or diminishing the materials afforded us by the senses and experience. When we think of a golden mountain, we only join two consistent ideas, "gold" and "mountain," with which we were formerly acquainted. A virtuous horse we can conceive, because, from our own feeling, we can conceive virtue; and this we may unite to the figure and shape of a horse, which is an animal familiar to us. In short, all the materials of thinking are derived either from our outward or inward sentiment; the mixture and composition of these belongs alone to the mind and will, or, to express myself in philosophical language, all our ideas or more feeble perceptions are copies of our impressions or more lively ones.

To prove this, the two following arguments will, I hope, be sufficient. *First,* when we analyze our thoughts or ideas, however compounded or sublime, we always find that they resolve themselves into such simple ideas as were copied from a precedent feeling or sentiment. Even those ideas which at first view seem the most wide of this origin are found, upon a nearer scrutiny, to be derived from it. The idea of God, as meaning an infinitely intelligent, wise, and good Being, arises from reflecting on the operations of our own mind and augmenting, without limit, those qualities of goodness and wisdom. We may prosecute this inquiry to what length we please; where we shall always find that every idea which we examine is copied from a similar impression. Those who would assert that this position is not universally true, nor without exception, have only one, and that an easy, method of refuting it by producing that idea which, in their opinion, is not derived from this source. It will then be incumbent on us, if we would maintain our doctrine, to produce the impression or lively perception which corresponds to it.

Secondly, if it happen, from a defect of the organ, that a man is not susceptible of any species of sensation, we always find that he is as little susceptible of the correspondent idea. A blind man can form no notion of colors, a deaf man of sounds. Restore either of them that sense in which he is deficient by opening this new inlet for his sensations, you also open an inlet for the ideas, and he finds no difficulty in conceiving these objects. The case is the same if the object proper for exciting any sensation has never been applied to the organ. A Laplander . . . has no notion of the relish of wine. And though there are few or no instances of a like deficiency in the mind where a person has never felt or is wholly incapable of a sentiment or passion that belongs to his species, yet we find the same observation to take place in a less degree. A man of mild manners can form no idea of inveterate revenge or cruelty, nor can a selfish heart easily conceive the heights of friendship and generosity. It is readily allowed that other beings may possess many senses of which we can have no conception, because the ideas of them have never been introduced to us in the only manner by which an idea can have access to the mind, to wit, by the actual feeling and sensation. . . .

Here, therefore, is a proposition which not only seems in itself simple and intelligible, but, if a proper use were made of it, might render every dispute equally intelligible, and banish all that jargon which has so long taken possession of metaphysical reasonings and drawn disgrace upon them. All ideas, especially abstract ones, are naturally faint and obscure. The mind has but a slender hold of them. They are apt to be confounded with other resembling ideas; and when we have often employed any term, though without a distinct meaning, we are apt to imagine it has a determinate idea annexed to it. On the contrary, all impressions, that is, all sensations either outward or inward, are strong and vivid. The limits between them are more exactly determined, nor is it easy to fall into any error or mistake with regard to them. When we entertain, therefore, any suspicion that a philosophical term is employed without any meaning or idea (as is but too frequent), we need but inquire, *from what impression is that supposed idea derived?* And if it be impossible to assign any, this will serve to confirm our suspicion. By bringing ideas in so clear a light, we may reasonably hope to remove all dispute which may arise concerning their nature and reality.[1]

Skeptical Doubts Concerning the Operations of the Understanding
Part I

All the objects of human reason or inquiry may naturally be divided into two kinds, to wit, "Relations of Ideas," and "Matters of Fact." Of the first kind are the sciences of Geometry, Algebra, and Arithmetic, and, in short, every affirmation which is either intuitively or demonstratively certain. *That the square of the hypotenuse is equal to the square of the two sides* is a proposition which expresses a relation between these figures. *That three times five is equal to the half of thirty* expresses a relation between these numbers. Propositions of this kind are discoverable by the mere operation of thought, without dependence on what is anywhere existent in the universe. Though there never were a circle or triangle in nature, the truths demonstrated by Euclid would forever retain their certainty and evidence.

Matters of fact, which are the second objects of human reason, are not ascertained in the same manner, nor is our evidence of their truth, however great, of a like nature with the foregoing. The contrary of every matter of fact is still possible, because it can never imply a contradiction and is conceived by the mind with the same facility and distinctness as if ever so conformable to reality. *That the sun will not rise tomorrow* is no less intelligible a proposition and implies no more contradiction than the affirmation *that it will rise*. We should in vain, therefore, attempt to demonstrate its falsehood. Were it demonstratively false, it would imply a contradiction and could never be distinctly conceived by the mind.

It may, therefore, be a subject worthy of curiosity to inquire what is the nature of that evidence which assures us of any real existence and matter of fact beyond the present testimony of our senses or the records of our memory. This part of philosophy, it is observable, had been little cultivated either by the ancients or moderns; and, therefore, our doubts and errors in the prosecution of so important an inquiry may be the more excusable while we march through such difficult paths without any guide or direction. They may even prove useful by exciting curiosity and destroying that implicit faith and security which is the bane of all reasoning and free inquiry. The discovery of defects in the common philosophy, if any such there be, will not, I presume, be a discouragement, but rather an incitement, as is usual, to attempt something more full and satisfactory than has yet been proposed to the public.

All reasonings concerning matter of fact seem to be founded on the relation of *cause* and *effect*. By means of that relation alone we can go beyond the evidence of our memory and senses. If you were to ask a man why he believes any matter of fact which is absent, for instance, that his friend is in the country or in France, he would give you a reason, and this reason would be some other fact: as a letter received from him or the knowledge of his former resolutions and promises. A man finding a watch or any other machine in a desert island would conclude that there had once been men in that island. All our reasonings concerning fact are of the same nature. And here it is constantly supposed that there is a connection between the present fact and that which is inferred from it. Were there nothing to bind them together, the inference would be entirely precarious. The hearing of an articulate voice and rational discourse in the dark assures us of the presence of some person. Why? Because these are the effects of the human make and fabric, and closely connected with it. If we anatomize all the other reasonings of this nature, we shall find that they are founded on the relation of cause and effect, and that this relation is either near or remote, direct or collateral. Heat and light are collateral effects of fire, and the one effect may justly be inferred from the other.

If we would satisfy ourselves, therefore, concerning the nature of that evidence which assures us of matters of fact, we must inquire how we arrive at the knowledge of cause and effect.

I shall venture to affirm, as a general proposition which admits of no exception, that the knowledge of this relation is not, in any instance, attained by reasonings *a priori*, but arises entirely from experience, when we find that any particular objects are constantly conjoined with each other. Let an object be presented to a man of ever so strong natural reason and abilities—if that object be entirely new to him, he will not be able, by the most accurate examination of its sensible qualities, to discover any of its causes or effects. Adam, though his rational faculties be supposed, at the very first, entirely perfect, could not have inferred from the fluidity and transparency of water that it would suffocate him, or from the light and warmth of fire that it would consume him. No object ever discovers, by the qualities which appear to the senses, either the causes which produced it or the effects which will arise from it; nor can our reason, unassisted by experience, ever draw any inference concerning real existence and matter of fact.

This proposition, *that causes and effects are discoverable, not by reason, but by experience,* will readily be admitted with regard to such objects as we remember to have once been altogether unknown to us, since we must be conscious of the utter inability which we then lay under of foretelling what would arise from them. Present two smooth pieces of marble to a man who has no tincture of natural philosophy; he will never discover that they will adhere together in such a manner as to require great force to separate them in a direct line, while they make so small a resistance to a lateral pressure. Such events as bear little analogy to the common course of nature are also readily confessed to be known only by experience, nor does any man imagine that the explosion of gunpowder or the attraction of a loadstone could ever be discovered by arguments *a priori.* In like manner, when an effect is supposed to depend upon an intricate machinery or secret structure of parts, we make no difficulty in attributing all our knowledge of it to experience. Who will assert that he can give the ultimate reason why milk or bread is proper nourishment for a man, not for a lion or tiger?

But the same truth may not appear at first sight to have the same evidence with regard to events which have become familiar to us from our first appearance in the world, which bear a close analogy to the whole course of nature, and which are supposed to depend on the simple qualities of objects without any secret structure of parts. We are apt to imagine that we could discover these effects by the mere operation of our reason without experience. We fancy that, were we brought on a sudden into this world, we could at first have inferred that one billiard ball would communicate motion to another upon impulse, and that we needed not to have waited for the event in order to pronounce with certainty concerning it. Such is the influence of custom that where it is strongest it not only covers our natural ignorance but even conceals itself, and seems not to take place, merely because it is found in the highest degree.

But to convince us that all the laws of nature and all the operations of bodies without exception are known only by experience, the following reflections may perhaps suffice. Were any object presented to us, and were we required to pronounce concerning the effect which will result from it without consulting past observation, after what manner, I beseech you, must the mind proceed in this operation? It must invent or imagine some event which it ascribes to the object as its effect; and it is plain that this invention must be entirely arbitrary. The mind can never possibly find the effect in the supposed cause by the most accurate scrutiny and examination. For the effect is totally different from the cause, and consequently can never be discovered in it. Motion in the second billiard ball is a distinct event from motion in the first, nor is there anything in the one to suggest the smallest hint of the other. A stone or piece of metal raised into the air and left without any support immediately falls. But to consider the matter *a priori,* is there anything we discover in this situation which can beget the idea of a downward rather than an upward or any other motion in the stone or metal?

And as the first imagination or invention of a particular effect in all natural operations is arbitrary where we consult not experience, so must we also esteem the supposed tie or connection between the cause and effect which binds them together and renders it impossible that any other effect could result from the operation of that cause. When I see, for instance, a billiard ball moving in a straight line toward another, even suppose motion in the second ball should by accident be suggested to me as the result of their contact or impulse, may I not conceive that a hundred different events might as well follow from that cause? May not both these balls remain at absolute rest? May not the first ball return in a straight line or leap off the second in any line or direction? All these suppositions are consistent and conceivable. Why, then, should we give the preference to one which is no more consistent or conceivable than the rest? All our reasonings *a priori* will never be able to show us any foundation for this preference.

In a word, then, every effect is a distinct event from its cause. It could not, therefore, be discovered in the cause, and the first invention or conception of it *a priori,* must be entirely arbitrary. And even after it is suggested, the conjunction of it with the cause must appear equally arbitrary, since there are always many other effects which, to reason, must seem fully as consistent and natural. In vain, therefore, should we pretend to determine any single event or infer any cause or effect without the assistance of observation and experience.

Hence we may discover the reason why no philosopher who is rational and modest has ever pretended to assign the ultimate cause of any natural operation, or to show distinctly the action of that power which produces any single effect in the universe. It is confessed that the utmost effort of human reason is to reduce the principles productive of natural phenomena to a greater simplicity, and to resolve the many particular effects into a few general causes, by means of reasonings from analogy, experience, and observation. But as to the causes of these general causes, we should in vain attempt their discovery, nor shall we ever be able to satisfy ourselves by any particular explication of them. These ultimate springs and principles are totally shut up from human curiosity and inquiry. Elasticity, gravity, cohesion of parts, communication of motion by impulse—these are probably the ultimate causes and principles which we shall ever discover in nature; and we may esteem ourselves sufficiently happy if, by accurate inquiry and reasoning, we can trace up the particular phenomena to, or near to, these general principles. The most perfect philosophy of the natural kind only staves off our ignorance a little longer, as perhaps the most perfect philosophy of the moral or metaphysical kind serves only to discover larger portions of it. Thus the observation of human blindness and weakness is the result of all philosophy, and meets us, at every turn, in spite of our endeavors to elude or avoid it.

Nor is geometry, when taken into the assistance of natural philosophy, ever able to remedy this defect or lead us into the knowledge of ultimate causes by all that accuracy of reasoning for which it is so justly celebrated. Every part of mixed mathematics proceeds upon the supposition that certain laws are established by nature in her operations, and abstract reasonings are employed either to assist experience in the discovery of these laws or to determine their influence in particular instances where it depends upon any precise degree of distance and quantity. Thus it is a law of motion, discovered by experience, that the moment or force of any body in motion is in the compound ratio or proportion of its solid contents and its velocity, and, consequently, that a small force may remove the greatest obstacle or raise the greatest weight if by any contrivance or machinery we can increase the velocity of that force so as to make it an overmatch for its antagonist. Geometry assists us in the application of this law by giving us the just dimensions of all the parts and figures which can enter into any species of machine, but still the discovery of the law itself is owing merely to experience; and all the abstract reasonings in the world could never lead us one step toward the knowledge of it. When we reason *a priori* and consider merely any object or cause as it appears to the mind, independent of all observation, it never could suggest to us the notion of any distinct object, such as its effect, much less show us the inseparable and inviolable connection between them. A man must be very sagacious who could discover by reasoning that crystal is the effect of heat, and ice of cold, without being previously acquainted with the operation of these qualities.

Part II

But we have not yet attained any tolerable satisfaction with regard to the question first proposed. Each solution still gives rise to a new question as difficult as the foregoing and leads us on to further inquiries. When it is asked, *What is the nature of all our reasonings concerning matter of fact?* the proper answer seems to be, That they are founded on the relation of cause and effect. When again it is asked, *What is the foundation of all our reasonings and conclusions concerning that relation?* it may be replied in one word, *experience*. But if we still carry on our sifting humor and ask, *What is the foundation of all conclusions from experience?* this implies a new question which may be of more difficult solution and explication. Philosophers that give themselves airs of superior wisdom and sufficiency have a hard task when they encounter persons of inquisitive dispositions, who push them from every corner to which they retreat, and who are sure at last to bring them to some dangerous dilemma. The best expedient to prevent this confusion is to be modest in our pretensions and even to discover the difficulty ourselves before it is objected to us. By this means we may make a kind of merit of our very ignorance.

I shall content myself in this section with an easy task and shall pretend only to give a negative answer to the question here proposed. I say, then, that even after we have experience of the operations of cause and effect, our conclusions from that experience are *not* founded on reasoning or any process of understanding. This answer we must endeavor both to explain and to defend.

It must certainly be allowed that nature has kept us at a great distance from all her secrets and has afforded us only the knowledge of a few superficial qualities of objects, while she conceals from us those powers and principles on which the influence of these objects entirely depends. Our senses inform us of the color, weight, and consistency of bread, but neither sense nor reason can ever inform us of those qualities which fit it for the nourishment and support of the human body. Sight or feeling conveys an idea of the actual motion of bodies, but as to what wonderful force or power which would carry on a moving body forever in a continued change of place, and which bodies never lose but by communicating it to others, of this we cannot form the most distant conception. But notwithstanding this ignorance of natural powers[2] and principles, we always presume when we see like sensible qualities that they have like secret powers, and expect that effects similar to those which we have experienced will follow from them. If a body of like color and consistency with that bread which we have formerly eaten be presented to us, we make no scruple of repeating the experiment and foresee with certainty like nourishment and support. Now this is a process of the mind or thought of which I would willingly know the foundation. It is allowed on hands that there is no known connection between the sensible qualities and the secret powers, and, consequently, that the mind is not led to form such a conclusion concerning their constant and regular conjunction by anything which it knows of their nature. As to past *experience,* it can be allowed to give *direct* and *certain* information of those precise objects only, and that precise period of time which fell under its cognizance: But why this experience should be extended to future times and to other objects which, for aught we know, may be only in appearance similar, this is the main question on which I would insist. The bread which I formerly ate nourished me; that is, a body of such sensible qualities was, at that time, endued with such secret powers. But does it follow that other bread must also nourish me at another time, and that like sensible qualities must always be attended with like

secret powers? the consequence seems nowise necessary. At least, it must be acknowledged that there is here a consequence drawn by the mind, a certain step taken, a process of thought, and an inference which wants to be explained. These two propositions are far from being the same: *I have found that such an object has always been attended with such an effect,* and *I foresee that other objects which are in appearance similar will be attended with similar effects.* I shall allow, if you please, that the one proposition may justly be inferred from the other: I know, in fact, that it always is inferred. But if you insist that the inference is made by a chain of reasoning, I desire you to produce that reasoning. The connection between these propositions is not intuitive. There is required a medium which may enable the mind to draw such an inference, if indeed it be drawn by reasoning and argument. What that medium is I must confess passes my comprehension; and it is incumbent on those to produce it who assert that it really exists and is the original of all our conclusions concerning matter of fact.

This negative argument must certainly, in process of time, become altogether convincing if many penetrating and able philosophers shall turn their inquiries this way, and no one be ever able to discover any connecting proposition or intermediate step which supports the understanding in this conclusion. But as the question is yet new, every reader may not trust so far to his own penetration as to conclude, because an argument escapes his inquiry, that therefore it does not really exist. For this reason it may be requisite to venture upon a more difficult task, and, enumerating all the branches of human knowledge, endeavor to show that none of them can afford such an argument.

All reasonings may be divided into two kinds, namely, demonstrative reasoning, or that concerning relations of ideas, and moral reasoning, or that concerning matter of fact and existence. That there are no demonstrative arguments in the case seems evident, since it implies no contradiction that the course of nature may change and that an object, seemingly like those which we have experienced, may be attended with different or contrary effects. May I not clearly and distinctly conceive that a body, falling from the clouds and which in all other respects resembles snow, has yet the taste of salt or feeling of fire? Is there any more intelligible proposition than to affirm that all the trees will flourish in December and January, and will decay in May and June? Now, whatever is intelligible and can be distinctly conceived implies no contradiction and can never be proved false by any demonstrative argument or abstract reasoning *a priori*.

If we be, therefore, engaged by arguments to put trust in past experience and make it the standard of our future judgment, these arguments must be probable only, or such as regard matter of fact and real existence, according to the division above mentioned. But that there is no argument of this kind must appear if our explication of that species of reasoning be admitted as solid and satisfactory. We have said that all arguments concerning existence are founded on the relation of cause and effect, that our knowledge of that relation is derived entirely from experience, and that all our experimental conclusions proceed upon the supposition that the future will be conformable to the past. To endeavor, therefore, the proof of this last supposition by probable arguments, or arguments regarding existence, must be evidently going in a circle and taking that for granted which is the very point in question.

In reality, all arguments from experience are founded on the similarity which we discover among natural objects, and by which we are induced to expect effects similar to those which we have found to follow from such objects. And though none but a fool or madman will ever pretend to dispute the authority of experience or to reject that great guide of human life, it may surely be allowed a philosopher to have so much curiosity at least as to examine the principle of human nature which gives this mighty authority to experience and makes us draw advantage from that similarity which nature has placed among different objects. From causes which appear similar, we expect similar effects. This is the sum of our experimental conclusions. Now it seems evident that, if this conclusion were formed by reason, it would be as perfect at first, and upon one instance, as after ever so long a course of experience; but the case is far otherwise. Nothing so like as eggs, yet no one, on account of this appearing similarity, expects the same taste and relish in all of them. It is only after a long course of uniform experiments in any kind that we attain a firm reliance and secu-

rity with regard to a particular event. Now, where is that process of reasoning which, from one instance, draws a conclusion so different from that which it infers from a hundred instances that are nowise different from that single one? This question I propose as much for the sake of information as with an intention of raising difficulties. I cannot find, I cannot imagine any such reasoning. But I keep my mind still open to instruction if anyone will vouchsafe to bestow it on me.

Should it be said that, from a number of uniform experiments, we *infer* a connection between the sensible qualities and the secret powers, this, I must confess, seems the same difficulty, couched in different terms. The question still occurs, On what process of argument is this *inference* founded? Where is the medium, the interposing ideas which join propositions so very wide of each other? It is confessed that the color, consistency, and other sensible qualities of bread appear not of themselves to have any connection with the secret powers of nourishment and support; for otherwise we could infer these secret powers from the first appearance of these sensible qualities without the aid of experience, contrary to the sentiment of all philosophers, and contrary to plain matter of fact. Here, then, is our natural state of ignorance with regard to the powers and influence of all objects. How is this remedied by experience? It only shows us a number of uniform effects resulting from certain objects, and teaches us that those particular objects, at that particular time, were endowed with such powers and forces. When a new object endowed with similar sensible qualities is produced, we expect similar powers and forces, and look for a like effect. From a body of like color and consistency with bread, we expect like nourishment and support. But this surely is a step or progress of the mind which wants to be explained. When a man says, *I have found, in all past instances, such sensible qualities, conjoined with such secret powers,* and when he says, *similar sensible qualities will always be conjoined with similar secret powers,* he is not guilty of a tautology, nor are these propositions in any respect the same. You say that the one proposition is an inference from the other; but you must confess that the inference is not intuitive, neither is it demonstrative. Of what nature is it then? To say it is experimental is begging the question. For all inferences from experience suppose, as their foundation, that the future will resemble the past and that similar powers will be conjoined with similar sensible qualities. If there be any suspicion that the course of nature may change, and that the past may be no rule for the future, all experience becomes useless and can give rise to no inference or conclusion. It is impossible, therefore, that any arguments are founded on the supposition of that resemblance. Let the course of things be allowed hitherto ever so regular, that alone, without some new argument or inference, proves not that for the future it will continue so. In vain do you pretend to have learned the nature of bodies from your past experience. Their secret nature, and consequently all their efforts and influence, may change without any change in their sensible qualities. This happens sometimes, and with regard to some objects. Why may it not happen always, and with regard to all objects? What logic, what process of argument secures you against this supposition? My practice, you say, refutes my doubts. But you mistake the purport of my question. As an agent, I am quite satisfied in the point; but as a philosopher who has some share of curiosity, I will not say skepticism, I want to learn the foundation of this inference. No reading, no inquiry has yet been able to remove my difficulty or give me satisfaction in a matter of such importance. Can I do better than propose the difficulty to the public, even though, perhaps, I have small hopes of obtaining a solution? We shall at least, by this means, be sensible of our ignorance, if we do not augment our knowledge. . . .

Skeptical Solution of These Doubts

The passion for philosophy, like that for religion, seems liable to this inconvenience, that though it aims at the correction of our manners and extirpation of our vices, it may only serve, by imprudent management, to foster a predominant inclination and push the mind with more determined resolution toward that side which already *draws* too much by the bias and propensity of the natural temper. It is certain that, while we aspire to the magnanimous firmness of the philosophic sage and endeavor to confine our plea-

sures altogether within our own minds, we may, at last, render our philosophy, like that of Epictetus and other Stoics, only a more refined system of selfishness, and reason ourselves out of all virtue as well as social enjoyment. While we study with attention the vanity of human life and turn all our thoughts toward the empty and transitory nature of riches and honors, we are, perhaps, all the while flattering our natural indolence which, hating the bustle of the world and drudgery of business, seeks a pretense of reason to give itself a full and uncontrolled indulgence. There is, however, one species of philosophy which seems little liable to this inconvenience, and that because it strikes in with no disorderly passion of the human mind, nor can mingle itself with any natural affection or propensity; and that is the Academic or Skeptical philosophy. The Academics always talk of doubt and suspense of judgment, of danger in hasty determinations, of confining to very narrow bounds the inquiries of the understanding, and of renouncing all speculations which lie not within the limits of common life and practice. Nothing, therefore, can be more contrary than such a philosophy to the supine indolence of the mind, its rash arrogance, its lofty pretensions, and its superstitious credulity. Every passion is mortified by it, except the love of truth; and that passion never is nor can be carried to too high a degree. It is surprising, therefore, that this philosophy, which in almost every instance must be harmless and innocent, should be the subject of so much groundless reproach and obloquy. But, perhaps, the very circumstance which renders it so innocent is what chiefly exposes it to the public hatred and resentment. By flattering no irregular passion, it gains few partisans. By opposing so many vices and follies, it raises to itself abundance of enemies who stigmatize it as libertine, profane, and irreligious.

Nor need we fear that this philosophy, while it endeavors to limit our inquiries to common life, should ever undermine the reasonings of common life and carry its doubts so far as to destroy all action as well as speculation. Nature will always maintain her rights and prevail in the end over any abstract reasoning whatsoever. Though we should conclude, for instance, as in the foregoing section, that in all reasonings from experience there is a step taken by the mind which is not supported by any argument or process of the understanding, there is no danger that these reasonings, on which almost all knowledge depends, will ever be affected by such a discovery. If the mind be not engaged by argument to make this step, it must be induced by some other principle of equal weight and authority; and that principle will preserve its influence as long as human nature remains the same. What that principle is may well be worth the pains of inquiry.

Suppose a person, though endowed with the strongest faculties of reason and reflection, to be brought on a sudden into this world; he would, indeed, immediately observe a continual succession of objects and one event following another, but he would not be able to discover anything further. He would not at first, by any reasoning, be able to reach the idea of cause and effect, since the particular powers by which all natural operations are performed never appear to the senses; nor is it reasonable to conclude, merely because one event in one instance precedes another, that therefore the one is the cause, the other the effect. The conjunction may be arbitrary and casual. There may be no reason to infer the existence of one from the appearance of the other: and, in a word, such a person without more experience could never employ his conjecture or reasoning concerning any matter of fact or be assured of anything beyond what was immediately present to his memory or senses.

Suppose again that he has acquired more experience and has lived so long in the world as to have observed similar objects or events to be constantly conjoined together—what is the consequence of this experience? He immediately infers the existence of one object from the appearance of the other, yet he has not, by all his experience, acquired any idea or knowledge of the secret power by which the one object produces the other, nor is it by any process of reasoning he is engaged to draw this inference; but still he finds himself determined to draw it, and though he should be convinced that his understanding has no part in the operation, he would nevertheless continue in the same course of thinking. There is some other principle which determines him to form such a conclusion.

This principle is *custom* or *habit*. For whatever the repetition of any particular act or operation produces a propensity to renew the same act or operation without being impelled by any reasoning or process of the understanding, we always say that this propensity is the effect of *custom*. By employing that word we pretend not to have given the ultimate reason of such a propensity. We only point out a principle of human nature which is universally acknowledged, and which is well known by its effects. Perhaps we can push our inquiries no further or pretend to give the cause of this cause, but must rest contented with it as the ultimate principle which we can assign of all our conclusions from experience. It is sufficient satisfaction that we can go so far without repining at the narrowness of our faculties, because they will carry us no further. And it is certain we here advance a very intelligible proposition at least, if not a true one, when we assert that after the constant conjunction of two objects, heat and flame, for instance, weight and solidity, we are determined by custom alone to expect the one from the appearance of the other. This hypothesis seems even the only one which explains the difficulty why we draw from a thousand instances an inference which we are not able to draw from one instance that is in no respect different from them. Reason is incapable of any such variation. The conclusions which it draws from considering one circle are the same which it would form upon surveying all the circles in the universe. But no man, having seen only one body move after being impelled by another, could infer that every other body will move after a like impulse. All inferences from experience, therefore, are effects of custom, not of reasoning.[3]

Custom, then, is the great guide of human life. It is that principle alone which renders our experience useful to us and makes us expect, for the future, a similar train of events with those which have appeared in the past. Without the influence of custom we should be entirely ignorant of every matter of fact beyond what is immediately present to the memory and senses. We should never know how to adjust means to ends or to employ our natural powers in the production of any effect. There would be an end at once of all action as well as of the chief part of speculation. . . .

Of the Idea of Necessary Connection

The great advantage of the mathematical sciences above the moral consists in this, that the ideas of the former, being sensible, are always clear and determinate, the smallest distinction between them is immediately perceptible, and the same terms are still expressive of the same ideas without ambiguity or variation. An oval is never mistaken for a circle, nor a hyperbola for an ellipsis. The isosceles and scalenum are distinguished by boundaries more exact than vice and virtue, right and wrong. If any term be defined in geometry, the mind readily, of itself substitutes on all occasions the definition for the term defined, or, even when no definition is employed, the object itself may be presented to the senses and by that means be steadily and clearly apprehended. But the finer sentiments of the mind, the operations of the understanding, the various agitations of the passions, though really in themselves distinct, easily escape us when surveyed by reflection, nor is it in our power to recall the original object as often as we have occasion to contemplate it. Ambiguity, by this means, is gradually introduced into our reasonings: similar objects are readily taken to be the same, and the conclusion becomes at last very wide of the premises.

One may safely, however, affirm that if we consider these sciences in a proper light, their advantages and disadvantages nearly compensate each other and reduce both of them to a state of equality. If the mind, with greater facility, retains the ideas of geometry clear and determinate, it must carry on a much longer and more intricate chain of reasoning and compare ideas much wider of each other in order to reach the abstruser truths of that science. And if moral ideas are apt, without extreme care, to fall into obscurity and confusion, the inferences are always much shorter in these disquisitions, and the intermediate steps which led to the conclusion much fewer than in the sciences which treat of quantity and number. In reality, there is scarcely a proposition in Euclid so simple as not to consist of more parts than are to be found in any moral reasoning which runs not into chimera and conceit. Where we trace the principles of the human mind through a few steps, we may be very well satisfied with our progress, considering how soon nature throws a bar to all our inquiries concerning causes and reduces us to an acknowledgment of our ignorance. The chief obstacle, therefore, to our improvements in the moral or metaphysical sciences is the obscurity of the ideas and ambiguity of the terms. The principal difficulty in the mathematics is the length of inferences and compass of thought requisite to the forming of any conclusion. And, perhaps, our progress in natural philosophy is chiefly retarded by the want of proper experiments and phenomena, which are often discovered by chance and cannot always be found when requisite, even by the most diligent and prudent inquiry. As moral philosophy seems hitherto to have received less improvement than either geometry or physics, we may conclude that if there be any difference in this respect among these sciences, the difficulties which obstruct the progress of the former require superior care and capacity to be surmounted.

There are no ideas which occur in metaphysics more obscure and uncertain than those of "power," "force," "energy," or "necessary connection," of which it is every moment necessary for us to treat in all our disquisitions. We shall, therefore, endeavor in this Section to fix, if possible, the precise meaning of these terms and thereby remove some part of that obscurity which is so much complained of in this species of philosophy.

It seems a proposition which will not admit of much dispute that all our ideas are nothing but copies of our impressions, or, in other words, that it is impossible for us to *think* of anything which we have not antecedently *felt*, either by our external or internal senses. I have endeavored to explain and prove this proposition, and have expressed my hopes that by a proper application of it men may reach a greater clearness and precision in philosophical reasonings than what they have hitherto been able to attain. Complex ideas may, perhaps, be well known by definition, which is nothing but an enumeration of those parts or simple ideas that compose them. But when we have pushed up definitions to the most simple ideas and find still some ambiguity and obscurity, what resources are we then possessed of? By what invention can we throw light upon these ideas and render them altogether precise and determinate to our intellectual view? Produce the impressions or original sentiments from which the ideas are copied. These impressions are all strong and sensible. They admit not of ambiguity. They are not only placed in a full light themselves, but may throw light on their correspondent ideas, which lie in obscurity. And by this means we may perhaps obtain a new microscope or species of optics by which, in the moral sciences, the most minute and most simple ideas may be so enlarged as to fall readily under our apprehension and be equally known with the grossest and most sensible ideas that can be the object of our inquiry.

To be fully acquainted, therefore, with the idea of power or necessary connection, let us examine its impression and, in order to find the impression with greater certainty, let us search for it in all the sources from which it may possibly be derived.

When we look about us toward external objects and consider the operation of causes, we are never able, in a single instance, to discover any power or necessary connection, any quality which binds the effect to the cause and renders the one an infallible consequence of the other. We only find that the one does actually in fact follow the other. The impulse of one billiard ball is attended with motion in the second. This is the whole that appears to the *outward* senses. The mind feels no sentiment or *inward* impression from this succession of objects; consequently, there is not, in any single particular instance of cause and effect, anything which can suggest the idea of power or necessary connection.

From the first appearance of an object we never can conjecture what effect will result from it. But were the power or energy of any cause discoverable by the mind, we could foresee the effect, even without experience, and might, at first, pronounce with certainty concerning it by the mere dint of thought and reasoning.

In reality, there is no part of matter that does ever, by its sensible qualities, discover any power or energy, or give us ground to imagine that it could produce anything, or be followed by any other object, which we could denominate its effect. Solidity, extension, motion—these qualities are all complete in themselves and never point out any other event which may result from them. The scenes of the universe are continually shifting, and one object follows another in an uninterrupted succession; the power or force which actuates the whole machine is entirely concealed from us and never discovers itself in any of the sensible qualities of body. We know that, in fact, heat is a constant attendant of flame; but what is the connection between them we have no room so much as to conjecture or imagine. It is impossible, therefore, that the idea of power can be derived from the contemplation of bodies in single instances of their operation, because no bodies ever discover any power which can be the original of this idea.[4]

Since, therefore, external objects as they appear to the senses give us no idea of power or necessary connection by their operation in particular instances, let us see whether this idea be derived from reflection on the operations of our own minds and be copies from any internal impression. It may be said that we are every moment conscious of internal power while we feel that, by the simple command of our will, we can move the organs of our body or direct the faculties of our mind. An act of volition produces motion in our limbs or raises a new idea in our imagination. This influence of the will we know by consciousness. Hence we acquire the idea of power or energy, and are certain that we ourselves and all other intelligent beings are possessed of power. This idea, then, is an idea of reflection since it arises from reflecting on the operations of our own mind and on the command which is exercised by will both over the organs of the body and faculties of the soul.

We shall proceed to examine this pretension and, first, with regard to the influence of volition over the organs of the body. This influence, we may observe, is a fact which, like all other natural events, can be known only by experience, and can never be foreseen from any apparent energy or power in the cause which connects it with the effect and renders the one an infallible consequence of the other. The motion of our body follows upon the command of our will. Of this we are every moment conscious. But the means by which this is effected, the energy by which the will performs so extraordinary an operation—of this we are so far from being immediately conscious that it must forever escape our most diligent inquiry.

For, *first,* is there any principle in all nature more mysterious than the union of soul with body, by which a supposed spiritual substance acquires such an influence over a material one that the most refined thought is able to actuate the grossest matter? Were we empowered by a secret wish to remove mountains or control the planets in their orbit, this extensive authority would not be more extraordinary, nor more beyond our comprehension. But if, by consciousness, we perceived any power or energy in the will, we must know this power; we must know its connection with the effect; we must know the secret union of soul and body, and the nature of both these substances by which the one is able to operate in so many instances upon the other.

Secondly, we are not able to move all the organs of the body with a like authority, though we cannot assign any reason, besides experience, for so remarkable a difference between one and the other. Why has the will an influence over the tongue and fingers, not over the heart or liver? This question would never embarrass us were we conscious of a power in the former case, not in the latter. We should then perceive, independent of experience, why the authority of the will over the organs of the body is circumscribed within such particular limits. Being in that case fully acquainted with the power or force by which it operates, we should also know why its influence reaches precisely to such boundaries, and no further.

A man suddenly struck with a palsy in the leg or arm, or who had newly lost those members, frequently endeavors, at first, to move them and employ them in their usual offices. Here he is as much conscious of power to command such limbs as a man in perfect health is conscious of power to actuate any member which remains in its natural state and condition. But consciousness never deceives. Consequently, neither in the one case nor in the other are we ever conscious of any power. We learn the influence of our will from experience alone. And experience only teaches us how one event constantly follows another, without instructing us in the secret connection which binds them together and renders them inseparable.

Thirdly, we learn from anatomy that the immediate object of power in voluntary motion is not the member itself which is moved, but certain muscles and nerves and animal spirits, and, perhaps, something still more minute and more unknown, through which the motion is successively propagated ere it reach the member itself whose motion is the immediate object of volition.

Can there be a more certain proof that the power by which this whole operation is performed, so far from being directly and fully known by an inward sentiment or consciousness, is to the last degree mysterious and unintelligible? Here the mind wills a certain event; immediately another event, unknown to ourselves and totally different from the one intended, is produced. This event produces another, equally unknown, till, at last, through a long succession the desired event is produced. But if the original power were felt, it must be known; were it known, its effect must also be known, since all power is relative to its effect. And, *vice versa,* if the effect be not known, the power cannot be known nor felt. How indeed can we be conscious of a power to move our limbs when we have no such power, but only that to move certain animal spirits which, though they produce at last the motion of our limbs, yet operate in such a manner as is wholly beyond our comprehension?

We may therefore conclude from the whole, I hope, without any temerity, though with assurance, that our idea of power is not copied from any sentiment or consciousness of power within ourselves when we give rise to animal motion or apply our limbs to their proper use and office. . . .

But to hasten to a conclusion of this argument, which is already drawn out to too great a length: We have sought in vain for an idea of power or necessary connection in all the sources from which we would suppose it to be derived. It appears that in single instances of the operation of bodies we never can, by our utmost scrutiny, discover anything but one event following another, without being able to comprehend any force or power by which the cause operates or any connection between it and its supposed effect. The same difficulty occurs in contemplating the operations of mind on body, where we observe the motion of the latter to follow upon the volition of the former, but are not able to observe or conceive the tie which binds together the motion and volition, or the energy, by which the mind produces this effect. The authority of the will over its own faculties and ideas is not a whit more comprehensible, so that, upon the whole, there appears not, throughout all nature, any one instance of connection which is conceivable by us. All events seem entirely loose and separate. One event follows another, but we never can observe any tie between them. They seem *conjoined*, but never *connected*. But as we can have no idea of anything which never appeared to our outward sense or inward sentiment, the necessary conclusion *seems* to be that we have no idea of connection or power at all, and that these words are absolutely without any meaning when employed either in philosophical reasonings or common life.

But there still remains one method of avoiding this conclusion, and one source which we have not yet examined. When any natural object or event is presented, it is impossible for us, by any sagacity or penetration, to discover, or even conjecture, without experience, what event will result from it, or to carry our foresight beyond that object which is immediately present to the memory and senses. Even after one instance or experiment where we have observed a particular event to follow upon another, we are not entitled to form a general rule or foretell what will happen in like cases, it being justly esteemed an unpardonable temerity to judge the whole course of nature from one single experiment, however accurate or certain. But when one particular species of events has always, in all instances, been conjoined with another, we make no longer any scruple of foretelling one upon the appearance of the other, and of employing that reasoning which can alone assure us of any matter of fact or existence. We then call the one object "cause," the other "effect." We suppose that there is some connection between them, some power in the one by which it infallibly produces the other and operates with the greatest certainty and strongest necessity.

It appears, then, that this idea of a necessary connection among events arises from a number of similar instances which occur, of the constant conjunction of these events; nor can that idea ever be suggested by any one of these instances surveyed in all possible lights and positions. But there is nothing in a number of instances, different from every single instance, which is supposed to be exactly similar, except only that after a repetition of similar instances the mind is carried by habit, upon the appearance of one event, to expect its usual attendant and to believe that it will exist. This connection, therefore, which we *feel* in the mind, this customary transition of the imagination from one object to its usual attendant, is the sentiment or impression from which we form the idea of power or necessary connection. Nothing further is the case. Contemplate the subject on all sides, you will never find any other origin of that idea. This is the sole difference between one instance, from which we can never receive the idea of connection, and a number of similar instances by which it is suggested. The first time a man saw the communication of motion by impulse, as by the shock of two billiard balls, he could not pronounce that the one event was *connected*, but only that it was *conjoined* with the other. After he has observed several instances of this nature, he then pronounces them to be *connected*. What alteration has happened to give rise to this new idea of *connection*? Nothing but that he now *feels* these events to be *connected* in his imagination, and can readily foretell the existence of one from the appearance of the other. When we say, therefore, that one object is connected with another, we mean only that they have acquired a connection in our thought and gave rise to this inference by which they become proofs of each other's existence—a conclusion which is somewhat extraordinary, but which seems founded on sufficient evidence. Nor will its evidence be weakened by any general diffidence of the understanding or skeptical suspicion concerning every conclusion which is new and extraordinary. No conclusions can be more agreeable to skepticism than such as make discoveries concerning the weakness and narrow limits of human reason and capacity.

And what stronger instance can be produced of the surprising ignorance and weakness of the understanding than the present? For surely, if there be any relation among objects which it imports us to know perfectly, it is that of cause and effect. On this are founded all our reasonings concerning matter of fact or existence. By means of it alone we attain any assurance concerning objects which are removed from the present testimony of our memory and senses. The only immediate utility of all sciences is to teach us how to control and regulate future events by their causes. Our thoughts and inquiries are, therefore, every moment employed about this relation; yet so imperfect are the ideas which we form concerning it that it is impossible to give any just definition of cause, except what is drawn from something extraneous and foreign to it. Similar objects are always conjoined with similar. Of this we have experience. Suitably to this experience, therefore, we may define a cause to be *an object followed by another, and where all the objects, similar to the first, are followed by objects similar to the second.* Or, in other words, *where, if the first object had not been, the second never had existed.* The appearance of a cause always conveys the mind, by a customary transition, to the idea of the effect. Of this also we have experience. We may, therefore, suitably to this experience, form another definition of cause and call it *an object followed by another, and whose appearance always conveys the thought to that other.* But though both these definitions be drawn from circumstances foreign to the cause, we cannot remedy this inconvenience or attain any more perfect definition which may point out that circumstance in the cause which gives it a connection with its effect. We have no idea of this connection, nor even any distinct notion what it is we desire to know when we endeavor at a conception of it. We say, for instance, that the vibration of this string is the cause of this particular sound. But what do we mean by that affirmation? We either mean *that this vibration is followed by this sound, and that all similar vibrations have been followed by similar sounds;* or, *that this vibration is followed by this sound, and that, upon the appearance of one, the mind anticipates the senses and forms immediately an idea of the other.* We may consider the relation of cause and effect in either of these two lights; but beyond these we have no idea of it.[5]

To recapitulate, therefore, the reasonings of this Section: Every idea is copied from some preceding impression or sentiment; and where we cannot find any impression, we may be certain that there is no idea. In all single instances of the operation of bodies or minds there is nothing that produces any impression, nor consequently can suggest any idea, of power or necessary connection. But when many uniform instances appear, and the same object is always followed by the same event, we then begin to entertain the notion of cause and connection. We then *feel* a new sentiment or impression, to wit, a customary connection in the thought or imagination between one object and its usual attendant; and this sentiment is the original of that idea which we seek for. For as this idea arises from a number of similar instances, and not from any single instance, it must arise from that circumstance in which the number of instances differ from every individual instance. But this customary connection or transition of the imagination is the only circumstance in which they differ. In every other particular they are alike. The first instance which we saw of motion, communicated by the shock of two billiard balls (to return to this obvious illustration), is exactly similar to any instance that may at present occur to us, except only that we could not at first *infer* one event from the other, which we are enabled to do at present, after so long a course of uniform experience. I know not whether the reader will readily apprehend this reasoning. I am afraid that, should I multiply words about it or throw it into a greater variety of lights, it would only become more obscure and intricate. In all abstract reasonings there is one point of view which, if we can happily hit, we shall go further toward illustrating the subject than by all the eloquence and copious expression in the world. This point of view we should endeavor to reach, and reserve the flowers of rhetoric for subjects which are more adapted to them. . . .

The chief objection against all *abstract* reasonings is derived from the ideas of space and time; ideas, which, in common life and to a careless view, are very clear and intelligible, but when they pass through the scrutiny of the profound sciences (and they are the chief object of these sciences) afford principles, which seem full of absurdity and contradiction. No priestly *dogmas,* invented on purpose to tame and subdue the rebellious reason of mankind, ever shocked common sense more than the doctrine of the infinite divisibility of extension, with its consequences; as they are pompously displayed by all geometricians and metaphysicians, with a kind of triumph and exultation. A real quantity, infinitely less than any finite quantity, containing quantities infinitely less than itself, and so on *in infinitum;* this is an edifice so bold and prodigious, that it is too weighty for any pretended demonstration to support, because it shocks the clearest and most natural principles of human reason.[6] But what renders the matter more extraordinary, is, that these seemingly absurd opinions are supported by a chain of reasoning, the clearest and most natural; nor is it possible for us to allow the premises without admitting the consequences. . . .

The absurdity of these bold determinations of the abstract sciences seems to become, if possible, still more palpable with regard to time than extension. An infinite number of real parts of time, passing in succession, and exhausted one after another, appears so evident a contradiction, that no man, one should think, whose judgment is not corrupted, instead of being improved, by the sciences, would ever be able to admit of it.

Yet still reason must remain restless, and unquiet, even with regard to that scepticism, to which she is driven by these seeming absurdities and contradictions. How any clear, distinct idea can contain circumstances, contradictory to itself, or to any other clear, distinct idea, is absolutely incomprehensible; and is, perhaps, as absurd as any proposition, which can be formed.

. . . [H]ere is the chief and most confounding objection to *excessive* scepticism, that no durable good can ever result from it; while it remains in its full force and vigour. We need only ask such a sceptic, *What his meaning is? And what he proposes by all these curious researches?* He is immediately at a loss, and knows not what to answer. A Copernican or Ptolemaic, who supports each his different system of astronomy, may hope to produce a conviction, which will remain constant and durable, with his audience. A Stoic or Epicurean displays principles, which may not only be durable, but which have an effect on conduct and behaviour. But a Pyrrhonian cannot expect, that his philosophy will have any constant influence on the mind: Or if it had, that its influence would be beneficial to society. On the contrary, he must acknowledge, if he will acknowledge any thing, that all human life must perish, were his principles universally and steadily to prevail. All discourse, all action would immediately cease; and men remain in a total lethargy, till the necessities of nature, unsatisfied, put an end to their miserable existence. It is true; so fatal an event is very little to be dreaded. Nature is always too strong for principle. And though a Pyrrhonian may throw himself or others into a momentary amazement and confusion by his profound reasonings; the first and most trivial event in life will put to flight all his doubts and scruples, and leave him the same, in every point of action and speculation, with the philosophers of every other sect, or with those who never concerned themselves in any philosophical researches. When he awakes from his dream, he will be the first to join in the laugh against himself, and to confess, that all his objections are mere amusement, and can have no other tendency than to show the whimsical condition of mankind, who must act and reason and believe; though they are not able, by their most diligent enquiry, to satisfy themselves concerning the foundation of these operations, or to remove the objections, which may be raised against them.

There is, indeed, a more *mitigated* scepticism or *academical* philosophy, which may be both durable and useful, and which may, in part, be the result of this Pyrrhonism, or *excessive* scepticism, when its undistinguished doubts are, in some measure, corrected by common sense and reflection. The greater part of mankind are naturally apt to be affirmative and dogmatical in their opinions; and while they see objects only on one side, and have no idea of any counterpoising argument, they throw themselves precipitately into the principles, to which they are inclined; nor have they any indulgence for those who entertain opposite sentiments. To hesitate or balance perplexes their understanding, checks their passion, and suspends their action. They are, therefore, impatient till they escape from a state, which to them is so uneasy; and they think, that they can never remove themselves far enough from it, by the violence of their affirmations and obstinacy of their belief. But could such dogmatical reasoners become sensible of the strange infirmities of human understanding, even in its most perfect state, and when most accurate and cautious in its determinations; such a reflection would naturally inspire them with more modesty and reserve, and diminish their fond opinion of themselves, and their prejudice against antagonists. The illiterate may reflect on the disposition of the learned, who, amidst all the advantages of study and reflection, are commonly still diffident in their determinations: And if any of the learned be inclined, from their natural temper, to haughtiness and obstinacy, a small tincture of Pyrrhonism might abate their pride, by showing them, that the few advantages, which they may have attained over their fellows, are but inconsiderable, if compared with the universal perplexity and confusion, which is inherent in human nature. In general, there is a degree of doubt, and caution, and modesty, which, in all kinds of scrutiny and decision, ought for ever to accompany a just reasoner.

Another species of *mitigated* scepticism, which may be of advantage to mankind, and which may be the natural result of the Pyrrhonian doubts and scruples, is the limitation of our enquiries to such subjects as are best adapted to the narrow capacity of human understanding. The *imagination* of man is naturally sublime, delighted with whatever is remote and extraordinary, and running, without control, into the most distant parts of space and time in order to avoid the objects, which custom has rendered too familiar to it. A correct *Judgment* observes a contrary method, and avoiding all distant and high enquiries, confines itself to common life, and to such subjects as fall under daily practice and experience; leaving the more sublime topics to the embellishment of poets and orators, or to the arts of priests and politicians. To bring us to so salutary a determination, nothing can be more serviceable, than to be once thoroughly convinced of the force of the Pyrrhonian doubt, and of the impossibility, that any thing, but the strong power of natural instinct, could free us from it. Those who have a propensity of philosophy, will still continue their researches; because they reflect, that, besides the immediate pleasure, attending such an occupation, philosophical decisions are nothing but the reflections of common life, methodized and corrected. But they will never be tempted to go beyond common life, so long as they consider the imperfection of those faculties which they employ, their narrow reach, and their inaccurate operations. While we cannot give a satisfactory reason, why we believe, after a thousand experiments, that a stone will fall, or fire bum; can we ever satisfy ourselves concerning any determination, which we may form, with regard to the origin of worlds, and the situation of nature, from, and to eternity?

This narrow limitation, indeed, of our enquiries, is, in every respect, so reasonable, that it suffices to make the slightest examination into the natural powers of the human mind, and to compare them with their objects, in order to recommend it to us. We shall then find what are the proper subjects of science and enquiry.

It seems to me, that the only objects of the abstract sciences or of demonstration are quantity and number, and that all attempts to extend this more perfect species of knowledge beyond these bounds are mere sophistry and illusion. As the component parts of quantity and number are entirely similar, their relations become intricate and involved; and nothing can be more curious, as well as useful, than to trace, by a variety of mediums, their equality or inequality, through their different appearances. But as all other ideas are clearly distinct and different from each other, we can never advance farther, by our utmost scrutiny, than to observe this diversity, and, by an obvious reflection, pronounce one thing not to be another. Or if there be any difficulty in these decisions, it proceeds entirely from the undeterminate meaning of words, which is corrected by juster definitions. That *the square of the hypothenuse is equal to the squares of the other two sides,* cannot be known, let the terms be ever so exactly defined, without a train of reasoning and enquiry. But to convince us of this proposition, *that where there is no property, there can be no injustice,* it is only necessary to define the terms, and explain injustice to be a violation of property. This proposition is, indeed, nothing but a more imperfect definition. It is the same case with all those pretended syllogistical reasonings, which may be found in every other branch of learning, except the sciences of quantity and number; and these may safely, I think, be pronounced the only proper objects of knowledge and demonstration.

All other enquiries of men regard only matter of fact and existence; and these are evidently incapable of demonstration. Whatever *is* may *not be.* No negation of a fact can involve a contradiction. The nonexistence of any being, without exception, is as clear and distinct an idea as its existence. The proposition, which affirms it not to be, however false, is no less conceivable and intelligible, than that which affirms it to be. The case is different with the sciences, properly so called. Every proposition, which is not true, is there confused and unintelligible. That the cube root of 64 is equal to the half of 10, is a false proposition, and can never be distinctly conceived. But that Caesar, or the angel Gabriel, or any being never existed, may be a false proposition, but still is perfectly conceivable, and implies no contradiction.

The existence, therefore, of any being can only be proved by arguments from its cause or its effect; and these arguments are founded entirely on experience. If we reason *a priori,* any thing may appear able to produce any thing. The falling of a pebble may, for aught we know, extinguish the sun; or the wish of a man control the planets in their orbits. It is only experience, which teaches us the nature and bounds of cause and effect, and enables us to infer the existence of one object from that of another.[7] Such is the foundation of moral reasoning, which forms the greater part of human knowledge, and is the source of all human action and behaviour.

Moral reasonings are either concerning particular or general facts. All deliberations in life regard the former; as also all disquisitions in history, chronology, geography, and astronomy.

The sciences, which treat of general facts, are politics, natural philosophy, physics, chemistry, etc., where the qualities, causes and effects of a whole species of objects are enquired into.

Divinity or Theology, as it proves the existence of a Deity, and the immortality of souls, is composed partly of reasonings concerning particular, partly concerning general facts. It has a foundation in *reason,* so far as it is supported by experience. But its best and most solid foundation is *faith* and divine revelation.

Morals and criticism are not so properly objects of the understanding as of taste and sentiment. Beauty, whether moral or natural, is felt, more properly than perceived. Or if we reason concerning it, and endeavour to fix its standard, we regard a new fact, to wit, the general taste of mankind, or some such fact, which may be the object of reasoning and enquiry.

When we run over libraries, persuaded of these principles, what havoc must we make? If we take in our hand any volume; of divinity or school metaphysics, for instance; let us ask, *Does it contain any abstract reasoning concerning quantity or number?* No. *Does it contain any experimental reasoning concerning matter of fact and existence?* No. Commit it then to the flames: For it can contain nothing but sophistry and illusion.

Endnotes

[1] It is probable that no more was meant by those who denied innate ideas than that all ideas were copies of our impressions, though it must be confessed that the terms which they employed were not chosen with such caution, nor so exactly defined, as to prevent all mistakes about their doctrine. For what is meant by "innate"? If "innate" be equivalent to "natural," then all the perceptions and ideas of the mind must be allowed to be innate or natural, in whatever sense we take the latter word, whether in opposition to what is uncommon, artificial, or miraculous. If by innate he meant contemporary to our birth, the dispute seems to be frivolous, nor is it worth while to inquire at what time thinking begins, whether before, at, or after our birth. Again, the word "idea" seems to be commonly taken in a very loose sense by Locke and others, as standing for any of our perceptions, our sensations and passions, as well as thoughts. Now, in this sense, I should desire to know what can be meant by asserting that selflove, or resentment of injuries, or the passion between the sexes is not innate?

But admitting these terms "impressions" and "ideas" in the sense above explained, and understanding by "innate" what is original or copied from no precedent perception, then may we assert that all our impressions are innate, and our ideas not innate.

To be ingenuous, I must own it to be my opinion that Locke was betrayed into this question by the schoolmen, who, making use of undefined terms, draw out their disputes to a tedious length without ever touching the point in question. A like ambiguity and circumlocution seem to run through that philosopher's reasonings, on this as well as most other subjects.

[2] The word "power" is here used in a loose and popular sense. The more accurate explication of it would give additional evidence to this argument.

[3] Nothing is more usual than for writers, even on *moral, political,* or *physical* subjects, to distinguish between *reason* and *experience,* and to suppose that these species of argumentation are entirely different from each other. The former are taken for the mere result of our intellectual faculties, which, by considering *a priori* the nature of things, and examining the effects that must follow from their operation, establish particular principles of science and philosophy. The latter are supposed to be derived entirely from sense and observation, by which we learn what has actually resulted from the operation of particular objects, and are thence able to infer what will for the future result from them. Thus, for instance, the limitations and restraints of civil government and a legal constitution may be defended, either from *reason,* which, reflecting on the great frailty and corruption of human nature, teaches that no man can safely be trusted with unlimited authority; or from *experience* and history, which inform us of the enormous abuses that ambition in every age and country has been found to make of so imprudent a confidence.

The same distinction between reason and experience is maintained in all our deliberations concerning the conduct of life, while the experienced statesman, general physician, or merchant, is trusted and followed, and the unpracticed novice, with whatever natural talents endowed, neglected and despised. Though it be allowed that reason may form very plausible conjectures with regard to the consequences of such a particular conduct in such particular circumstances, it is still supposed imperfect without the assistance of experience, which is alone able to give stability and certainty to the maxim derived from study and reflection.

But notwithstanding that this distinction be thus universally received, both in the active and speculative scenes of life, I shall not scruple to pronounce that it is, at bottom, erroneous, or at least superficial.

If we examine those arguments which, in any of the sciences above mentioned, are supposed to be the mere effects of reasoning and reflection, they will be found to terminate at last in some general principle or conclusion for which we can assign no reason but observation and experience. The only difference between them and those maxims which are vulgarly esteemed the result of pure experience is that the former cannot be established without some process of thought, and some reflection on what we have observed, in order to distinguish its circumstances and trace its consequences—whereas, in the latter, the experienced event is exactly and fully similar to that which we infer as the result of any particular situation. The history of a Tiberius or a Nero makes us dread a like tyranny, were our monarchs freed from the restraints of laws and senates: but the observation of any fraud or cruelty in private life is sufficient, with the aid of a little thought, to give us the same apprehension, while it serves as an instance of the general corruption of human nature, and shows us the danger which we must incur by reposing an entire confidence in mankind. In both cases, it is experience which is ultimately the foundation of our inference and conclusion.

There is no man so young and inexperienced as not to have formed from observation many general and just maxims concerning human affairs and the conduct of life; but it must be confessed that when a man comes to put these in practice he will be extremely liable to error, till time and further experience both enlarge these maxims, and teach him their proper use and application. In every situation or incident there are many particular and seemingly minute circumstances which the man of greatest talents is at first apt to overlook, though on them the justness of his conclusions, and consequently the prudence of his conduct, entirely depend. Not to mention that, to a young beginner, the general observations and maxims occur not always on the proper occasions, nor can be immediately applied with due calmness and distinction. The truth is, an inexperienced reasoner could be no reasoner at all were he absolutely inexperienced; and when we assign that character to anyone, we mean it only in a comparative sense, and suppose him possessed of experience in a smaller and more imperfect degree.

⁴Mr. Locke says that, finding from experience that there are several new productions in matter, and concluding that there must somewhere be a power capable of producing them, we arrive at last by this reasoning at the idea of power. But no reasoning can ever give us a new, original simple idea, as this philosopher himself confesses. This, therefore, can never be the origin of that idea.

⁵According to these explications and definitions, the idea of *power* is relative as much as that of *cause;* and both have a reference to an effect, or some other event constantly conjoined with the former. When we consider the *unknown* circumstance of an object by which the degree or quantity of its effect is fixed and determined, we call that its power. And accordingly, it is allowed by all philosophers that the effect is the measure of the power. But if they had any idea of power as it is in itself, why could they not measure it in itself? The dispute, whether the force of a body in motion be as its velocity, or the square of its velocity; this dispute, I say, needed not be decided by comparing its effects in equal or unequal times, but by direct mensuration and comparison.

As to the frequent use of the words "force," "power," "energy," etc., which everywhere occur in common conversation as well as in philosophy, that is no proof that we are acquainted, in any instance, with the connecting principle between cause and effect, or can account ultimately for the production of one thing by another. These words, as commonly used, have very loose meanings annexed to them, and their ideas are very uncertain and confused. No animal can put external bodies in motion without the sentiment of a *nisus* or endeavor; and every animal has a sentiment or feeling from the stroke or blow of an external object that is in motion. These sensations, which are merely animal, and from which we can *a priori* draw no inference, we are apt to transfer to inanimate objects, and to suppose that they have some such feelings whenever they transfer or receive motion. With regard to energies, which are exerted without our annexing to them any idea of communicated motion, we consider only the constant experienced conjunction of the events; and as we *feel* a customary connection between the ideas, we transfer that feeling to the objects, as nothing is more usual than to apply to external bodies every internal sensation which they occasion.

⁶Whatever disputes there may be about mathematical points, we must allow that there are physical points; that is, parts of extension, which cannot be divided or lessened, either by the eye or imagination. These images, then, which are present to the fancy or senses, are absolutely indivisible, and consequently must be allowed by mathematicians to be infinitely less than any real part of extension; and yet nothing appears more certain to reason, than that an infinite number of them composes an infinite extension. How much more an infinite number of those infinitely small parts of extension, which are still supposed infinitely divisible?

⁷That impious maxim of the ancient philosophy, *Ex nihilo, nihil fit* [From nothing, nothing comes], by which the creation of matter was excluded, ceases to be a maxim, according to this philosophy. Not only the will of the supreme Being may create matter; but, for aught we know *a priori,* the will of any other being might create it, or any other cause, that the most whimsical imagination can assign.

56. *The Fixation of Belief*

CHARLES S. PEIRCE

Charles Sanders Peirce (1839–1914) was an American philosopher who is most famous as a founder of pragmatism. Pragmatism is a movement variously articulated by Peirce, Chauncey Wright, William James, and John Dewey. As a movement, pragmatism is often linked to a rejection of *a priori* metaphysics in favor of beliefs that have practical or useful consequences. In Peirce's work, however, he offers theories of meaning and scientific method that have metaphysical implications. For Peirce meaning is not determined by introspection of ideas or by *a priori* analysis of propositions; rather it is determined by actions and their consequences. And belief is primarily a habit (a way of behaving) rather than just a state of mind. Peirce does not make these claims merely as criticisms of traditional philosophy. He incorporates them in his analysis of science, in his search for the logic of science. Importantly, Peirce does not view science as complete or as needing a metaphysical foundation provided by philosophy. Instead, science is dynamic, evolving, and it promises to be the arbiter of what is real. For Peirce, reality is what a community of investigators (scientists) will come to agree is truly represented at the ideal limit of their inquiries.

Peirce was the son of a prominent American mathematician, and he went on himself to work as a mathematician and scientist. While in Cambridge, Massachusetts, he interacted frequently with other participants in what later would be called the pragmatist movement. For a short time he taught philosophy at Johns Hopkins University, but he was not offered a permanent position. The selections included here were originally published as part of a series of articles in *Popular Science Monthly.*

I.

Few persons care to study logic, because everybody conceives himself to be proficient enough in the art of reasoning already. But I observe that this satisfaction is limited to one's own ratiocination, and does not extend to that of other men.

We come to the full possession of our power of drawing inferences, the last of all our faculties; for it is not so much a natural gift as a long and difficult art. The history of its practice would make a grand subject for a book. The medieval schoolman, following the Romans, made logic the earliest of a boy's studies after grammar, as being very easy. So it was as they understood it. Its fundamental principle, according to them, was, that all knowledge rests either on authority or reason; but that whatever is deduced by reason depends ultimately on a premiss derived from authority. Accordingly, as soon as a boy was perfect in the syllogistic procedure, his intellectual kit of tools was held to be complete.

To Roger Bacon, that remarkable mind who in the middle of the thirteenth century was almost a scientific man, the schoolmen's conception of reasoning appeared only an obstacle to truth. He saw that experience alone teaches anything—a proposition which to us seems easy to understand, because a distinct conception of experience has been handed down to us from former generations; which to him likewise seemed perfectly clear, because its difficulties had not yet unfolded themselves. Of all kinds of experience, the best, he thought, was interior illumination, which teaches many things about Nature which the external senses could never discover, such as the transubstantiation of bread.

Four centuries later, the more celebrated Bacon, in the first book of his *Novum Organum*, gave his clear account of experience as something which must be open to verification and reexamination. But, superior as Lord Bacon's conception is to earlier notions, a modern reader who is not in awe of his grandiloquence is chiefly struck by the inadequacy of his view of scientific procedure. That we have only to make some crude experiments, to draw up briefs of the results in certain blank forms, to go through these by rule, checking off everything disproved and setting down the alternatives, and that thus in a few years physical science would be finished up—what an idea! "He wrote on science like a Lord Chancellor," indeed, as Harvey, a genuine man of science said.

The early scientists, Copernicus, Tycho Brahe, Kepler, Galileo, Harvey, and Gilbert, had methods more like those of their modern brethren. Kepler undertook to draw a curve through the places of Mars;[1] and to state the times occupied by the planet in describing the different parts of that curve; but perhaps his greatest service to science was in impressing on men's minds that this was the thing to be done if they wished to improve astronomy; that they were not to content themselves with inquiring whether one system of epicycles was better than another but that they were to sit down to the figures and find out what the curve, in truth, was. He accomplished this by his incomparable energy and courage, blundering along in the most inconceivable way (to us), from one irrational hypothesis to another, until, after trying twenty-two of these, he fell, by the mere exhaustion of his invention, upon the orbit which a mind well furnished with the weapons of modern logic would have tried almost at the outset.

In the same way, every work of science great enough to be well remembered for a few generations affords some exemplification of the defective state of the art of reasoning of the time when it was written; and each chief step in science has been a lesson in logic. It was so when Lavoisier and his contemporaries took up the study of Chemistry. The old chemist's maxim had been, "*Lege, lege, lege, labora, ora, et relege.*" Lavoisier's method was not to read and pray, but to dream that some long

and complicated chemical process would have a certain effect, to put it into practice with dull patience, after its inevitable failure, to dream that with some modification it would have another result, and to end by publishing the last dream as a fact: his way was to carry his mind into his laboratory, and literally to make of his alembics and cucurbits instruments of thought, giving a new conception of reasoning as something which was to be done with one's eyes open, in manipulating real things instead of words and fancies.

The Darwinian controversy is, in large part, a question of logic. Mr. Darwin proposed to apply the statistical method to biology. The same thing has been done in a widely different branch of science, the theory of gases. Though unable to say what the movements of any particular molecule of gas would be on a certain hypothesis regarding the constitution of this class of bodies, Clausius and Maxwell were yet able, eight years before the publication of Darwin's immortal work, by the application of the doctrine of probabilities, to predict that in the long run such and such a proportion of the molecules would, under given circumstances, acquire such and such velocities; that there would take place, every second, such and such a relative number of collisions, etc.; and from these propositions were able to deduce certain properties of gases, especially in regard to their heat-relations. In like manner, Darwin, while unable to say what the operation of variation and natural selection in any individual case will be, demonstrates that in the long run they will, or would, adapt animals to their circumstances. Whether or not existing animal forms are due to such action, or what position the theory ought to take, forms the subject of a discussion in which questions of fact and questions of logic are curiously interlaced.

II.

The object of reasoning is to find out, from the consideration of what we already know, something else which we do not know. Consequently, reasoning is good if it be such as to give a true conclusion from true premises, and not otherwise. Thus, the question of validity is purely one of fact and not of thinking. A being the facts stated in the premises and B being that con-cluded, the question is, whether these facts are really so related that if A were B would generally be. If so, the inference is valid; if not, not. It is not in the least the question whether, when the premisses are accepted by the mind, we feel an impulse to accept the conclusion also. It is true that we do generally reason correctly by nature. But that is an accident; the true conclusion would remain true if we had no impulse to accept it; and the false one would remain false, though we could not resist the tendency to believe in it.

We are, doubtless, in the main logical animals, but we are not perfectly so. Most of us, for exam-ple, are naturally more sanguine and hopeful than logic would justify. We seem to be so constituted that in the absence of any facts to go upon we are happy and self-satisfied; so that the effect of expe-rience is continually to contract our hopes and aspirations. Yet a lifetime of the application of this corrective does not usually eradicate our sanguine disposition. Where hope is unchecked by any experience, it is likely that our optimism is extrav-agant. Logicality in regard to practical matters (if this be understood, not in the old sense, but as consisting in a wise union of security with fruitful-ness of reasoning) is the most useful quality an ani-mal can possess, and might, therefore, result from the action of natural selection; but outside of these it is probably of more advantage to the animal to have his mind filled with pleasing and encouraging visions, independently of their truth, and thus, upon unpractical subjects, natural selection might occasion a fallacious tendency of thought.

That which determines us, from given pre-misses, to draw one inference rather than another, is some habit of mind, whether it be constitutional or acquired. The habit is good or otherwise, according as it produces true conclusions from true premises or not; and an inference is regarded as valid or not, without reference to the truth or falsity of its conclusion specially, but according as the habit which determines it is such as to produce true conclusions in general or not. The particular habit of mind which governs this or that inference may be formulated in a proposition whose truth depends on the validity of the inferences which the habit determines; and such a formula is called a *guiding principle* of inference. Suppose, for example, that we observe that a rotating disk of copper quickly comes to rest when placed between the poles of a magnet, and we infer that this will happen with every disk of copper. The guiding principle is, that what is true of one piece of copper is true of another. Such a guiding principle with regard to copper would be much safer than with regard to many other substances—brass, for example.

A book might be written to signalize all the most important of these guiding principles of rea-soning. It would probably be, we must confess, of no service to a person whose thought is directed wholly to practical subjects, and whose activity moves along thoroughly-beaten paths. The prob-lems that present themselves to such a mind are matters of routine which he has learned once for all to handle in learning his business. But let a man venture into an unfamiliar field, or where his results are not continually checked by experience, and all history shows that the most masculine intellect will ofttimes lose his orientation and waste his efforts in directions which bring him no nearer to his goal, or even carry him entirely astray. He is like a ship in the open sea, with no one on board who understands the rules of navigation. And in such a case some general study of the guid-ing principles of reasoning would be sure to be found useful.

The subject could hardly be treated, however, without being first limited; since almost any fact may serve as a guiding principle. But it so happens that there exists a division among facts, such that in one class are all those which are absolutely essential as guiding principles, while in the others are all which have any other interest as objects of research. This division is between those which are necessarily taken for granted in asking why a cer-tain conclusion is thought to follow from certain premises, and those which are not implied in such a question. A moment's thought will show that a variety of facts are already assumed when the logi-cal question is first asked. It is implied, for instance, that there are such states of mind as doubt and belief—that a passage from one to the other is possible, the object of thought remaining the same, and that this transition is subject to some rules by which all minds are alike bound. As these are facts which we must already know before we can have any clear conception of reasoning at all, it cannot be supposed to be any longer of much interest to inquire into their truth or falsity.

On the other hand, it is easy to believe that those rules of reasoning which are deduced from the very idea of the process are the ones which are the most essential; and, indeed, that so long as it conforms to these it will, at least, not lead to false conclusions from true premises. In point of fact, the importance of what may be deduced from the assumptions involved in the logical question turns out to be greater than might be supposed, and this for reasons which it is difficult to exhibit at the outset. The only one which I shall here mention is, that conceptions which are really products of logical reflection, without being readily seen to be so, mingle with our ordinary thoughts, and are frequently the causes of great conclusion. This is the case, for example, with the conception of quality. A quality, as such, is never an object of observation. We can see that a thing is blue or green, but the quality of being blue and the quality of being green are not things which we see; they are products of logical reflections. The truth is, that common-sense, or thought as it first emerges above the level of the narrowly practical, is deeply imbued with that bad logical quality to which the epithet *metaphysical* is commonly applied; and nothing can clear it up but a severe course of logic.

III.

We generally know when we wish to ask a question and when we wish to pronounce a judgment, for there is a dissimilarity between the sensation of doubting and that of believing.

But this is not all which distinguishes doubt from belief. There is a practical difference. Our beliefs guide our desires and shape our actions. The Assassins, or followers of the Old Man of the Mountain, used to rush into death at his least command, because they believed that obedience to him would insure everlasting felicity. Had they doubted this, they would not have acted as they did. So it is with every belief, according to its degree. The feeling of believing is a more or less sure indication of there being established in our nature some habit which will determine our actions. Doubt never has such an effect.

Nor must we overlook a third point of difference. Doubt is an uneasy and dissatisfied state from which we struggle to free ourselves and pass into the state of belief; while the latter is a calm and satisfactory state which we do not wish to avoid, or to change to a belief in anything else.[2] On the contrary, we cling tenaciously, not merely to believing, but to believing just what we do believe.

Thus, both doubt and belief have positive effects upon us, though very different ones. Belief does not make us act at once, but puts us into such a condition that we shall behave in some certain way, when the occasion arises. Doubt has not the least such active effect, but stimulates us to inquiry until it is destroyed. This reminds us of the irritation of a nerve and the reflex action produced thereby; while for the analogue of belief, in the nervous system, we must look to what are called nervous associations—for example, to that habit of the nerves in consequence of which the smell of a peach will make the mouth water.

IV.

The irritation of doubt causes a struggle to attain a state of belief. I shall term this struggle *inquiry,* though it must be admitted that this is sometimes not a very apt designation.

The irritation of doubt is the only immediate motive for the struggle to attain belief. It is certainly best for us that our beliefs should be such as may truly guide our actions so as to satisfy our desires; and this reflection will make us reject every belief which does not seem to have been so formed as to insure this result. But it will only do so by creating a doubt in the place of that belief. With the doubt, therefore, the struggle begins, and with the cessation of doubt it ends. Hence, the sole object of inquiry is the settlement of opinion. We may fancy that this is not enough for us, and that we seek, not merely an opinion, but a true opinion. But put this fancy to the test, and it proves groundless; for as soon as a firm belief is reached we are entirely satisfied, whether the belief be true or false. And it is clear that nothing out of the sphere of our knowledge can be our object, for nothing which does not affect the mind can be the motive for mental effort. The most that can be maintained is, that we seek for a belief that we shall *think* to be true. But we think each one of our beliefs to be true, and, indeed, it is mere tautology to say so.

That the settlement of opinion is the sole end of inquiry is a very important proposition. It sweeps away, at once, various vague and erroneous conceptions of proof. A few of these may be noticed here.

1. Some philosophers have imagined that to start an inquiry it was only necessary to utter a question whether orally or by setting it down upon paper, and have even recommended us to begin our studies with questioning everything! But the mere putting of a proposition into the interrogative form does not stimulate the mind to any struggle after belief. There must be a real and living doubt, and without this all discussion is idle.
2. It is a very common idea that a demonstration must rest on some ultimate and absolutely indubitable propositions. These, according to one school, are first principles of a general nature; according to another, are first sensations. But, in point of fact, an inquiry, to have that completely satisfactory result called demonstration, has only to start with propositions perfectly free from all actual doubt. If the premises are not in fact doubted at all, they cannot be more satisfactory than they are.
3. Some people seem to love to argue a point after all the world is fully convinced of it. But no further advance can be made. When doubt ceases, mental action on the subject comes to an end; and, if it did go on, it would be without a purpose.

V.

If the settlement of opinion is the sole object of inquiry, and if belief is of the nature of a habit, why should we not attain the desired end, by taking as answer to a question any we may fancy, and constantly reiterating it to ourselves, dwelling on all which may conduce to that belief, and learning

to turn with contempt and hatred from anything that might disturb it? This simple and direct method is really pursued by many men. I remember once being entreated not to read a certain newspaper lest it might change my opinion upon free-trade. "Lest I might be entrapped by its fallacies and misstatements," was the form of expression. "You are not," my friend said, "a special student of political economy. You might, therefore, easily be deceived by fallacious arguments upon the subject. You might, then, if you read this paper, be led to believe in protection. But you admit that free-trade is the true doctrine; and you do not wish to believe what is not true." I have often known this system to be deliberately adopted. Still oftener, the instinctive dislike of an undecided state of mind, exaggerated into a vague dread of doubt, makes men cling spasmodically to the views they already take. The man feels that, if he only holds to his belief without wavering, it will be entirely satisfactory. Nor can it be denied that a steady and immovable faith yields great peace of mind. It may, indeed, give rise to inconveniences, as if a man should resolutely continue to believe that fire would not burn him, or that he would be eternally damned if he received his *ingesta* otherwise than through a stomach-pump. But then the man who adopts this method will not allow that its inconveniences are greater than its advantages. He will say, "I hold steadfastly to the truth, and the truth is always wholesome." And in many cases it may very well be that the pleasure he derives from his calm faith overbalances any inconveniences resulting from its deceptive character. Thus, if it be true that death is annihilation, then the man who believes that he will certainly go straight to heaven when he dies, provided he have fulfilled certain simple observances in this life, has a cheap pleasure which will not be followed by the least disappointment. A similar consideration seems to have weight with many persons in religious topics, for we frequently hear it said, "Oh, I could not believe so-and-so, because I should be wretched if I did." When an ostrich buries its head in the sand as danger approaches, it very likely takes the happiest course. It hides the danger, and then calmly says there is no danger, and, if it feels perfectly sure there is none, why should it raise its head to see? A man may go through life, systematically keeping out of view all that might cause a change in his opinions, and if he only succeeds—basing his method, as he does, on two fundamental psychological laws—I do not see what can be said against his doing so. It would be an egotistical impertinence to object that his procedure is irrational, for that only amounts to saying that his method of settling belief is not ours. He does not propose to himself to be rational, and, indeed, will often talk with scorn of man's weak and illusive reason. So let him think as he pleases.

But this method of fixing belief, which may be called the method of tenacity, will be unable to hold its ground in practice. The social impulse is against it. The man who adopts it will find that other men think differently from him, and it will be apt to occur to him, in some saner moment, that their opinions are quite as good as his own, and this will shake his confidence in his belief. This conception, that another man's thought or sentiment may be equivalent to one's own, is a distinctly new step, and a highly important one. It arises from an impulse too strong in man to be suppressed, without danger of destroying the human species. Unless we make ourselves hermits, we shall necessarily influence each other's opinions; so that the problem becomes how to fix belief not in the individual merely, but in the community.

Let the will of the state act, then, instead of that of the individual. Let an institution be created which shall have for its object to keep correct doctrines before the attention of the people, to reiterate them perpetually, and to teach them to the young; having at the same time power to prevent contrary doctrines from being taught, advocated, or expressed. Let all possible causes of a change of mind be removed from men's apprehensions. Let them be kept ignorant, lest they should learn of some reason to think otherwise than they do. Let their passions be enlisted, so that they may regard private and unusual opinions with hatred and horror. Then, let all men who reject the established belief be terrified into silence. Let the people turn out and tar-and-feather such men, or let inquisitions be made into the manner of thinking of suspected persons, and when they are found guilty of forbidden beliefs, let them be subjected to some signal punishment. When complete agreement could not otherwise be reached, a general massacre of all who have not thought in a certain way has proved a very effective means of settling opinion in a country. If the power to do this be wanting, let a list of opinions be drawn up, to which no man of the least independence of thought can assent, and let the faithful be required to accept all these propositions, in order to segregate them as radically as possible from the influence of the rest of the world.

This method has, from the earliest times, been one of the chief means of upholding correct theological and political doctrines, and of preserving their universal or catholic character. In Rome, especially, it has been practised from the days of Numa Pompilius to those of Pius Nonus. This is the most perfect example in history; but wherever there is a priesthood—and no religion has been without one—this method has been more or less made use of. Wherever there is an aristocracy, or a guild, or any association of a class of men whose interests depend, or are supposed to depend, on certain propositions, there will be inevitably found some traces of this natural product of social feeling. Cruelties always accompany this system; and when it is consistently carried out, they become atrocities of the most horrible kind in the eyes of any rational man. Nor should this occasion surprise, for the officer of a society does not feel justified in surrendering the interests of that society for the sake of mercy, as he might his own private interests. It is natural, therefore, that sympathy and fellowship should thus produce a most ruthless power.

In judging this method of fixing belief, which may be called the method of authority, we must, in the first place, allow its immeasurable mental and moral superiority to the method of tenacity. Its success is proportionately greater; and, in fact, it has over and over again worked the most majestic results. The mere structures of stone which it has caused to be put together—in Siam, for example, in Egypt, and in Europe—have many of them a sublimity hardly more than rivaled by the greatest works of Nature. And, except the geological epochs, there are no periods of time so vast as those which are measured by some of these organized faiths. if we scrutinize the matter closely, we shall find that there has not been one of their creeds which has remained always the same; yet the change is so slow as to be imperceptible during one person's life, so that individual belief remains sensibly fixed. For the mass of mankind, then, there is perhaps no better method than this. If it is their highest impulse to be intellectual slaves, then slaves they ought to remain.

But no institution can undertake to regulate opinions upon every subject. Only the most important ones can be attended to, and on the rest men's minds must be left to the action of natural causes. This imperfection will be no source of weakness so long as men are in such a state of culture that one opinion does not influence another—that is, so long as they cannot put two and two together. But in the most priest-ridden states some individuals will be found who are raised above that condition. These men possess a wider sort of social feeling; they see that men in other countries and in other ages have held to very different doctrines from those which they themselves have been brought up to believe; and they cannot help seeing that it is the mere accident of their having been taught as they have, and of their having been surrounded with the manners and associations they have, that has caused them to believe as they do and not far differently. Nor can their candour resist the reflection that there is no reason to rate their own views at a higher value than those of other nations and other centuries; thus giving rise to doubts in their minds.

They will further perceive that such doubts as these must exist in their minds with reference to every belief which seems to be determined by the caprice either of themselves or of those who originated the popular opinions. The willful adherence to a belief, and the arbitrary forcing of it upon others, must, therefore, both be given up. A different new method of settling opinions must be adopted, that shall not only produce an impulse to believe, but shall also decide what proposition it is which is to be believed. Let the action of natural preferences be unimpeded, then, and under their influence let men, conversing together and regarding matters in different lights, gradually develop beliefs in harmony with natural causes. This method resembles that by which conceptions of art have been brought to maturity. The most perfect example of it is to be found in the history of metaphysical philosophy. Systems of this sort have not usually rested upon any observed facts, at least not in any great degree. They have been chiefly adopted because their fundamental propositions seemed "agreeable to reason." This is an apt expression; it does not mean that which agrees with experience, but that which we find ourselves inclined to believe. Plato, for example, finds it agreeable to reason that the distances of the celestial spheres from one another should be proportional to the different lengths of strings which produce harmonious chords. Many philosophers have been led to their main conclusions by considerations like this; but this is the lowest and least developed form which the method takes, for it is clear that another man might find Kepler's theory, that the celestial spheres are proportional to the inscribed and circumscribed spheres of the different regular solids, more agreeable to *his* reason. But the shock of opinions will soon lead men to rest on preferences of a far more universal nature. Take, for example, the doctrine that man only acts selfishly—that is, from the consideration that acting in one way will afford him more pleasure than acting in another. This rests on no fact in the world, but it has had a wide acceptance as being the only reasonable theory.

This method is far more intellectual and respectable from the point of view of reason than either of the others which we have noticed. But its failure has been the most manifest. It makes of inquiry something similar to the development of taste; but taste, unfortunately, is always more or less a matter of fashion, and accordingly metaphysicians have never come to any fixed agreement, but the pendulum has swung backward and forward between a more material and a more spiritual philosophy, from the earliest times to the latest. And so from this, which has been called the *a priori* method, we are driven, in Lord Bacon's phrase, to a true induction. We have examined into this *a priori* method as something which promised to deliver our opinions from their accidental and capricious element. But development, while it is a process which eliminates the effect of some casual circumstances, only magnifies that of others. This method, therefore, does not differ in a very essential way from that of authority. The government may not have lifted its finger to influence my convictions; I may have been left outwardly quite free to choose, we will say, between monogamy and polygamy, and, appealing to my conscience only, I may have concluded that the latter practice is in itself licentious. But when I come to see that the chief obstacle to the spread of Christianity among a people of as high culture as the Hindoos has been a conviction of the immorality of our way of treating women, I cannot help seeing that, though governments do not interfere, sentiments in their development will be very greatly determined by accidental causes. Now, there are some people, among whom I must suppose that my reader is to be found, who, when they see that any belief of theirs is determined by any circumstance extraneous to the facts, will from that moment not merely admit in words that that belief is doubtful, but will experience a real doubt of it, so that it ceases to be a belief.

To satisfy our doubts, therefore, it is necessary that a method should be found by which our beliefs may be determined by nothing human, but by some external permanency—by something upon which our thinking has no effect. Some mystics imagine that they have such a method in a private inspiration from on high. But that is only a form of the method of tenacity, in which the conception of truth as something public is not yet developed. Our external permanency would not be external, in our sense, if it was restricted in its influence to one individual. It must be something which affects, or might affect, every man. And, though these affections are necessarily as various as are individual conditions, yet the method must be such that the ultimate conclusion of every man shall be the same. Such is the method of science. Its fundamental hypothesis, restated in more familiar language, is this: There are Real things, whose characters are entirely independent of our opinions about them; those Reals affect our senses according to regular laws, and, though our sensations are as different as are our relations to the objects, yet, by taking advantage of the laws of perception, we can ascertain by reasoning how things really and truly are; and any man, if he have sufficient experience and he reason enough about it, will be led to the one True conclusion. The new conception here involved is that of Reality. It may be asked how I know that there are any Reals. If this hypothesis is the sole support of my method of inquiry, my method of inquiry must not be used to support my hypothesis. The reply is this: 1. If investigation cannot be regarded as proving that there are Real things, it at least does not lead to a contrary

conclusion; but the method and the conception on which it is based remain ever in harmony. No doubts of the method, therefore, necessarily arise from its practice, as is the case with all the others. 2. The feeling which gives rise to any method of fixing belief is a dissatisfaction at two repugnant propositions. But here already is a vague concession that there is some *one* thing which a proposition should represent. Nobody, therefore, can really doubt that there are Reals, for, if he did, doubt would not be a source of dissatisfaction. The hypothesis, therefore, is one which every mind admits. So that the social impulse does not cause men to doubt it. 3. Everybody uses the scientific method about a great many things, and only ceases to use it when he does not know how to apply it. 4. Experience of the method has not led us to doubt it, but, on the contrary, scientific investigation has had the most wonderful triumphs in the way of settling opinion. These afford the explanation of my not doubting the method or the hypothesis which it supposes; and not having any doubt, nor believing that anybody else whom I could influence has, it would be the merest babble for me to say more about it. If there be anybody with a living doubt upon the subject, let him consider it.

To describe the method of scientific investigation is the object of this series of papers. At present I have only room to notice some points of contrast between it and other methods of fixing belief.

This is the only one of the four methods which presents any distinction of a right and a wrong way. If I adopt the method of tenacity, and shut myself out from all influences, whatever I think necessary to doing this, is necessary according to that method. So with the method of authority: the state may try to put down heresy by means which, from a scientific point of view, seem very ill-calculated to accomplish its purposes; but the only test *on that method* is what the state thinks; so that it cannot pursue the method wrongly. So with the *a priori* method. The very essence of it is to think as one is inclined to think. All metaphysicians will be sure to do that, however they may be inclined to judge each other to be perversely wrong. The Hegelian system recognizes every natural tendency of thought as logical, although it be certain to be abolished by countertendencies. Hegel thinks there is a regular system in the succession of these tendencies, in consequence of which, after drifting one way and the other for a long time, opinion will at last go right. And it is true that metaphysicians do get the right ideas at last; Hegel's system of Nature represents tolerably the science of his day; and one may be sure that whatever scientific investigation shall have put out of doubt will presently receive *a priori* demonstration on the part of the metaphysicians. But with the scientific method the case is different. I may start with known and observed facts to proceed to the unknown; and yet the rules which I follow in doing so may not be such as investigation would approve. The test of whether I am truly following the method is not an immediate appeal to my feelings and purposes, but, on the contrary, itself involves the application of the method. Hence it is that bad reasoning as well as good reasoning is possible; and this fact is the foundation of the practical side of logic.

It is not to be supposed that the first three methods of settling opinion present no advantage whatever over the scientific method. On the contrary, each has some peculiar convenience of its own. The *a priori* method is distinguished for its comfortable conclusions. It is the nature of the process to adopt whatever belief we are inclined to, and there are certain flatteries to the vanity of man which we all believe by nature, until we are awakened from our pleasing dream by rough facts. The method of authority will always govern the mass of mankind; and those who wield the various forms of organized force in the state will never be convinced that dangerous reasoning ought not to be suppressed in some way. If liberty of speech is to be untrammeled from the grosser forms of constraint, then uniformity of opinion will be secured by a moral terrorism to which the respectability of society will give its thorough approval. Following the method of authority is the path of peace. Certain non-conformities are permitted; certain others (considered unsafe) are forbidden. These are different in different countries and in different ages; but, wherever you are, let it be known that you seriously hold a tabooed belief, and you may be perfectly sure of being treated with a cruelty less brutal but more refined than hunting you like a wolf. Thus, the greatest intellectual benefactors of mankind have never dared, and dare not now, to utter the whole of their thought; and thus a shade of *prima facie* doubt is cast upon every proposition which is considered essential to the security of society. Singularly enough, the persecution does not all come from without; but a man torments himself and is oftentimes most distressed at finding himself believing propositions which he has been brought up to regard with aversion. The peaceful and sympathetic man will, therefore, find it hard to resist the temptation to submit his opinions to authority. But most of all I admire the method of tenacity for its strength, simplicity, and directness. Men who pursue it are distinguished for their decision of character, which becomes very easy with such a mental rule. They do not waste time in trying to make up their minds what they want, but, fastening like lightning upon whatever alternative comes first, they hold to it to the end, whatever happens, without an instant's irresolution. This is one of the splendid qualities which generally accompany brilliant, unlasting success. It is impossible not to envy the man who can dismiss reason, although we know how it must turn out at last.

Such are the advantages which the other methods of settling opinion have over scientific investigation. A man should consider well of them; and then he should consider that, after all, he wishes his opinions to coincide with the fact, and that there is no reason why the results of those three first methods should do so. To bring about this effect is the prerogative of the method of science. Upon such considerations he has to make his choice—a choice which is far more than the adoption of any intellectual opinion, which is one of the ruling decisions of his life, to which, when once made, he is bound to adhere. The force of habit will sometimes cause a man to hold on to old beliefs, after he is in a condition to see that they have no sound basis. But reflection upon the state of the case will overcome these habits, and he ought to allow reflection its full weight. People sometimes shrink from doing this, having an idea that beliefs are wholesome which they cannot help feeling rest on nothing. But let such persons suppose an analogous though different case from their own. Let them ask themselves what they would say to a reformed Mussulman who should hesitate to give up his old notions in regard to the relations of the sexes; or to a reformed Catholic who should still shrink from reading the Bible. Would they not say that these persons ought to consider the matter fully, and clearly understand the new doctrine, and then ought to embrace it, in its entirety? But, above all, let it be considered that what is more wholesome than any particular belief is integrity of belief, and that to avoid looking into the support of any belief from a fear that it may turn out rotten is quite as immoral as it is disadvantageous. The person who confesses that there is such a thing

as truth, which is distinguished from falsehood simply by this, that if acted on it should, on full consideration, carry us to the point we aim at and not astray, and then, though convinced of this, dares not know the truth and seeks to avoid it, is in a sorry state of mind indeed.

Endnotes

[1]Not quite so, but as nearly so as can be told in a few words.

[2]I am not speaking of secondary effects occasionally produced by the interference of other impulses.

How to Make Our Ideas Clear

CHARLES S. PEIRCE

I.

Whoever has looked into a modern treatise on logic of the common sort, will doubtless remember the two distinctions between *clear* and *obscure* conceptions, and between *distinct* and *confused* conceptions. They have lain in the books now for nigh two centuries, unimproved and unmodified, and are generally reckoned by logicians as among the gems of their doctrine.

A clear idea is defined as one which is so apprehended that it will be recognized wherever it is met with, and so that no other will be mistaken for it. If it fails of this clearness, it is said to be obscure.

This is rather a neat bit of philosophical terminology; yet, since it is clearness that they were defining, I wish the logicians had made their definition a little more plain. Never to fail to recognize an idea, and under no circumstances to mistake another for it, let it come in how recondite a form it may, would indeed imply such prodigious force and clearness of intellect as is seldom met with in

this world. On the other hand, merely to have such an acquaintance with the idea as to have become familiar with it, and to have lost all hesitancy in recognizing it in ordinary cases, hardly seems to deserve the name of clearness of apprehension, since after all it only amounts to a subjective feeling of mastery which may be entirely mistaken. I take it, however, that when the logicians speak of "clearness," they mean nothing more than such a familiarity with an idea, since they regard the quality as but a small merit, which needs to be supplemented by another, which they call *distinctness*.

A distinct idea is defined as one which contains nothing which is not clear. This is technical language; by the *contents* of an idea logicians understand whatever is contained in its definition. So that an idea is *distinctly* apprehended, according to them, when we can give a precise definition of it, in abstract terms. Here the professional logicians leave the subject; and I would not have troubled the reader with what they have to say, if it were not such a striking example of how they have been slumbering through ages of intellectual activity, listlessly disregarding the enginery of modern thought, and never dreaming of applying its

From *Popular Science Monthly* 12 (January 1878), 286–302.

lessons to the improvement of logic. It is easy to show that the doctrine that familiar use and abstract distinctness make the perfection of apprehension has its only true place in philosophies which have long been extinct; and it is now time to formulate the method of attaining to a more perfect clearness of thought, such as we see and admire in the thinkers of our own time.

When Descartes set about the reconstruction of philosophy, his first step was to (theoretically) permit scepticism and to discard the practice of the schoolmen of looking to authority as the ultimate source of truth. That done, he sought a more natural fountain of true principles, and thought he found it in the human mind; thus passing, in the directest way, from the method of authority to that of apriority, as described in my first paper. Self-consciousness was to furnish us with our fundamental truths, and to decide what was agreeable to reason. But since, evidently, not all ideas are true, he was led to note, as the first condition of infallibility, that they must be clear. The distinction between an idea *seeming* clear and really being so, never occurred to him. Trusting to introspection, as he did, even for a knowledge of external things, why should he question its testimony in respect to the contents of our own minds? But then, I suppose, seeing men, who seemed to be quite clear and positive, holding opposite opinions upon fundamental principles, he was further led to say that clearness of ideas is not sufficient, but that they need also to be distinct, i.e., to have nothing unclear about them. What he probably meant by this (for he did not explain himself with precision) was, that they must sustain the test of dialectical examination; that they must not only seem clear at the outset, but that discussion must never be able to bring to light points of obscurity connected with them.

Such was the distinction of Descartes, and one sees that it was precisely on the level of his philosophy. It was somewhat developed by Leibnitz. This great and singular genius was as remarkable for what he failed to see as for what he saw. That a piece of mechanism could not do work perpetually without being fed with power in some form, was a thing perfectly apparent to him; yet he did not understand that the machinery of the mind can only transform knowledge, but never originate it, unless it be fed with facts of observation. He thus missed the most essential point of the Cartesian philosophy, which is, that to accept propositions which seem perfectly evident to us is a thing which, whether it be logical or illogical, we cannot help doing. Instead of regarding the matter in this way, he sought to reduce the first principles of science to two classes, those which cannot be denied without self-contradiction, and those which result from the principle of sufficient reason (of which more anon), and was apparently unaware of the great difference between his position and that of Descartes. So he reverted to the old trivialities of logic; and, above all, abstract definitions played a great part in his philosophy. It was quite natural, therefore, that on observing that the method of Descartes labored under the difficulty that we may seem to ourselves to have clear apprehensions of ideas which in truth are very hazy, no better remedy occurred to him than to require an abstract definition of every important term. Accordingly, in adopting the distinction of *clear* and *distinct* notions, he described the latter quality as the clear apprehension of everything contained in the definition; and the books have ever since copied his words. There is no danger that his chimerical scheme will ever again be overvalued. Nothing new can ever be learned by analyzing definitions. Nevertheless, our existing beliefs can be set in order by this process, and order is an essential element of intellectual economy, as of every other. It may be acknowledged, therefore, that the books are right in making familiarity with a notion the first step toward clearness of apprehension, and the defining of it the second. But in omitting all mention of any higher perspicuity of thought, they simply mirror a philosophy which was exploded a hundred years ago. That much-admired "ornament of logic"—the doctrine of clearness and distinctness—may be pretty enough, but it is high time to relegate to our cabinet of curiosities the antique *bijou*, and to wear about us something better adapted to modern uses.

The very first lesson that we have a right to demand that logic shall teach us is, how to make our ideas clear; and a most important one it is, depreciated only by minds who stand in need of it. To know what we think, to be masters of our own meaning, will make a solid foundation for great and weighty thought. It is most easily learned by those whose ideas are meagre and restricted; and far happier they than such as wallow helplessly in a rich mud of conceptions. A nation, it is true, may, in the course of generations, overcome the disadvantage of an excessive wealth of language and its natural concomitant, a vast, unfathomable deep of ideas. We may see it in history, slowly perfecting its literary forms, sloughing at length its metaphysics, and, by virtue of the untirable patience which is often a compensation, attaining great excellence in every branch of mental acquirement. The page of history is not yet unrolled that is to tell us whether such a people will or will not in the long run prevail over one whose ideas (like the words of their language) are few, but which possesses a wonderful mastery over those which it has. For an individual, however, there can be no question that a few clear ideas are worth more than many confused ones. A young man would hardly be persuaded to sacrifice the greater part of his thoughts to save the rest; and the muddled head is the least apt to see the necessity of such a sacrifice. Him we can usually only commiserate, as a person with a congenital defect. Time will help him, but intellectual maturity with regard to clearness is apt to come rather late. This seems an unfortunate arrangement of Nature, inasmuch as clearness is of less use to a man settled in life, whose errors have in great measure had their effect, than it would be to one whose path lay before him. It is terrible to see how a single unclear idea, a single formula without meaning, lurking in a young man's head, will sometimes act like an obstruction of inert matter in an artery, hindering the nutrition of the brain, and condemning its victim to pine away in the fullness of his intellectual vigor and in the midst of intellectual plenty. Many a man has cherished for years as his hobby some vague shadow of an idea, too meaningless to be positively false; he has, nevertheless, passionately loved it, has made it his companion by day and by night, and has given to it his strength and his life, leaving all other occupations for its sake, and in short has lived with it and for it, until it has become, as it were, flesh of his flesh and bone of his bone; and then he has waked up some bright morning to find it gone, clean vanished away like the beautiful Melusina of the fable, and the essence of his life gone with it. I have myself known such a man; and who can tell how many histories of circle-squarers, metaphysi-

cians, astrologers, and what not, may not be told in the old German story?

═══

II.

The principles set forth in the first part of this essay lead, at once, to a method of reaching a clearness of thought of higher grade than the "distinctness" of the logicians. It was there noticed that the action of thought is excited by the irritation of doubt, and ceases when belief is attained; so that the production of belief is the sole function of thought. All these words, however, are too strong for my purpose. It is as if I had described the phenomena as they appear under a mental microscope. Doubt and Belief, as the words are commonly employed, relate to religious or other grave discussions. But here I use them to designate the starting of any question, no matter how small or how great, and the resolution of it. If, for instance, in a horse-car, I pull out my purse and find a five-cent nickel and five coppers, I decide, while my hand is going to the purse, in which way I will pay my fare. To call such a question Doubt, and my decision Belief is certainly to use words very disproportionate to the occasion. To speak of such a doubt as causing an irritation which needs to be appeased, suggests a temper which is uncomfortable to the verge of insanity. Yet, looking at the matter minutely, it must be admitted that, if there is the least hesitation as to whether I shall pay the five coppers or the nickel (as there will be sure to be, unless I act from some previously contracted habit in the matter), though irritation is too strong a word, yet I am excited to such small mental activity as may be necessary to deciding how I shall act. Most frequently doubts arise from some indecision, however momentary, in our action. Sometimes it is not so. I have, for example, to wait in a railway-station, and to pass the time I read the advertisements on the walls. I compare the advantages of different trains and different routes which I never expect to take, merely fancying myself to be in a state of hesitancy, because I am bored with having nothing to trouble me. Feigned hesitancy, whether feigned for mere amusement or with a lofty purpose, plays a great part in the production of scientific inquiry.

However the doubt may originate, it stimulates the mind to an activity which may be slight or energetic, calm or turbulent. Images pass rapidly through consciousness, one incessantly melting into another, until at last, when all is over—it may be in a fraction of a second, in an hour, or after long years—we find ourselves decided as to how we should act under such circumstances as those which occasioned our hesitation. In other words, we have attained belief.

In this process we observe two sorts of elements of consciousness, the distinction between which may best be made clear by means of an illustration. In a piece of music there are the separate notes, and there is the air. A single tone may be prolonged for an hour or a day, and it exists as perfectly in each second of that time as in the whole taken together; so that, as long as it is sounding, it might be present to a sense from which everything in the past was as completely absent as the future itself. But it is different with the air, the performance of which occupies a certain time, during the portions of which only portions of it are played. It consists in an orderliness in the succession of sounds which strike the ear at different times; and to perceive it there must be some continuity of consciousness which makes the events of a lapse of time present to us. We certainly only perceive the air by hearing the separate notes; yet we cannot be said to directly hear it, for we hear only what is present at the instant, and an orderliness of succession cannot exist in an instant. These two sorts of objects, what we are *immediately* conscious of and what we are *mediately* conscious of, are found in all consciousness. Some elements (the sensations) are completely present at every instant so long as they last, while others (like thought) are actions having beginning, middle, and end, and consist in a congruence in the succession of sensations which flow through the mind. They cannot be immediately present to us, but must cover some portion of the past or future. Thought is a thread of melody running through the succession of our sensations.

We may add that just as a piece of music may be written in parts, each part having its own air, so various systems of relationship of succession subsist together between the same sensations. These different systems are distinguished by having different motives, ideas, or functions. Thought is only one such system, for its sole motive, idea, and function is to produce belief, and whatever does not concern that purpose belongs to some other system of relations. The action of thinking may incidentally have other results; it may serve to amuse us, for example, and among *dilettanti* it is not rare to find those who have so perverted thought to the purposes of pleasure that it seems to vex them to think that the questions upon which they delight to exercise it may ever get finally settled; and a positive discovery which takes a favorite subject out of the arena of literary debate is met with ill-concealed dislike. This disposition is the very debauchery of thought. But the soul and meaning of thought, abstracted from the other elements which accompany it, though it may be voluntarily thwarted, can never be made to direct itself toward anything but the production of belief Thought in action has for its only possible motive the attainment of thought at rest; and whatever does not refer to belief is no part of the thought itself.

And what, then, is belief? It is the demi-cadence which closes a musical phrase in the symphony of our intellectual life. We have seen that it has just three properties: First, it is something that we are aware of; second, it appeases the irritation of doubt; and, third, it involves the establishment in our nature of a rule of action, or, say for short, a *habit*. As it appeases the irritation of doubt, which is the motive for thinking, thought relaxes, and comes to rest for a moment when belief is reached. But, since belief is a rule for action, the application of which involves further doubt and further thought, at the same time that it is a stopping-place, it is also a new starting-place for thought. That is why I have permitted myself to call it thought at rest, although thought is essentially an action. The *final* upshot of thinking is the exercise of volition, and of this thought no longer forms a part; but belief is only a stadium of mental action, an effect upon our nature due to thought, which will influence future thinking.

The essence of belief is the establishment of a habit; and different beliefs are distinguished by the different modes of action to which they give rise. If beliefs do not differ in this respect, if they appease the same doubt by producing the same rule of action, then no mere differences in the manner of consciousness of them can make them different beliefs, any more than playing a tune in different keys is playing different tunes. Imaginary distinctions are often drawn between beliefs which differ only in their mode of expression;—the wrangling which ensues is real enough, however. To believe that any objects are arranged among themselves as in Fig. 1, and to believe that they are arranged in Fig. 2, are one and the same belief, yet it is conceivable that a man should assert one proposition and deny the other. Such false distinctions do as much harm as the confusion of beliefs really different, and are among the pitfalls of which we ought constantly to beware, especially when we are upon metaphysical ground. One singular deception of this sort, which often occurs, is to mistake the sensation produced by our own unclearness of thought for a character of the object we are thinking. Instead of perceiving that the obscurity is purely subjective, we fancy that we contemplate a quality of the object which is essentially mysterious; and if our conception be afterward presented to us in a clear form we do not recognize it as the same, owing to the absence of the feeling of unintelligibility. So long as this deception lasts, it obviously puts an impassable barrier in the way of perspicuous thinking; so that it equally interests the opponents of rational thought to perpetuate it, and its adherents to guard against it.

Another such deception is to mistake a mere difference in the grammatical construction of two words for a distinction between the ideas they express. In this pedantic age, when the general mob of writers attend so much more to words than to things, this error is common enough. When I just said that thought is an *action*, and that it consists in a *relation*, although a person performs an action but not a relation, which can only be the result of an action, yet there was no inconsistency in what I said, but only a grammatical vagueness.

From all these sophisms we shall be perfectly safe so long as we reflect that the whole function of thought is to produce habits of action; and that whatever there is connected with a thought, but irrelevant to its purpose, is an accretion to it, but no part of it. If there be a unity among our sensations which has no reference to how we shall act on a given occasion, as when we listen to a piece of music, why we do not call that thinking. To develop its meaning, we have, therefore, simply to determine what habits it produces, for what a thing means is simply what habits it involves. Now, the identity of a habit depends on how it might lead us to act, not merely under such circumstances as are likely to arise, but under such as might possibly occur, no matter how improbable they may be. What the habit is depends on *when* and *how* it causes us to act. As for the *when*, every stimulus to action is derived from perception as for the *how*, every purpose of action is to produce some sensible result. Thus, we come down to what is tangible and conceivably practical, as the root of every real distinction of thought, no matter how subtle it may be; and there is no distinction of meaning so fine as to consist in anything but a possible difference of practice.

To see what this principle leads to, consider in the light of it such a doctrine as that of transub-

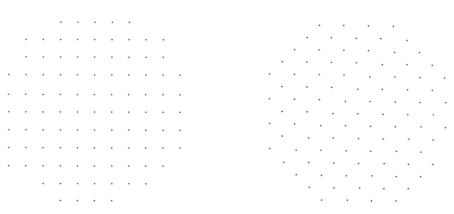

Figure 1   *Figure 2*

stantiation. The Protestant churches generally hold that the elements of the sacrament are flesh and blood only in a tropical sense; they nourish our souls as meat and the juice of it would our bodies. But the Catholics maintain that they are literally just meat and blood; although they possess all the sensible qualities of wafercakes and diluted wine. But we can have no conception of wine except what may enter into a belief, either—

1. That this, that, or the other, is wine; or,
2. That wine possesses certain properties.

Such beliefs are nothing but self-notifications that we should, upon occasion, act in regard to such things as we believe to be wine according to the qualities which we believe wine to possess. The occasion of such action would be some sensible perception, the motive of it to produce some sensible result. Thus our action has exclusive reference to what affects the senses, our habit has the same bearing as our action, our belief the same as our habit, our conception the same as our belief, and we can consequently mean nothing by wine but what has certain effects, direct or indirect, upon our senses; and to talk of something as having all the sensible characters of wine, yet being in reality blood, is senseless jargon. Now, it is not my object to pursue the theological question; and having used it as a logical example I drop it, without caring to anticipate the theologian's reply. I only desire to point out how impossible it is that we should have an idea in our minds which relates to anything but conceived sensible effects of things. Our idea of anything *is* our idea of its sensible effects; and if we fancy that we have any other we deceive ourselves, and mistake a mere sensation accompanying the thought for a part of the thought itself. It is absurd to say that thought has any meaning unrelated to its only function. It is foolish for Catholics and Protestants to fancy themselves in disagreement about the elements of the sacrament, if they agree in regard to all their sensible effects, here and hereafter.

It appears, then, that the rule for attaining the third grade of clearness of apprehension is as follows: Consider what effects, that might conceivably have practical bearings, we conceive the object of our conception to have. Then, our conception of these effects is the whole of our conception of the object.

III.

Let us illustrate this rule by some examples; and, to begin with the simplest one possible, let us ask what we mean by calling a thing *hard*. Evidently that it will not be scratched by many other substances. The whole conception of this quality, as of every other, lies in its conceived effects. There is absolutely no difference between a hard thing and a soft thing so long as they are not brought to the test. Suppose, then, that a diamond could be crystallized in the midst of a cushion of soft cotton, and should remain there until it was finally burned up. Would it be false to say that that diamond was soft? This seems a foolish question, and would be so, in fact, except in the realm of logic. There such questions are often of the greatest utility as serving to bring logical principles into sharper relief than real discussions ever could. In studying logic we must not put them aside with hasty answers, but must consider them with attentive care, in order to make out the principles involved. We may, in the present case, modify our question, and ask what prevents us from saying that all hard bodies remain perfectly soft until they are touched, when their hardness increases with the pressure until they are scratched. Reflection will show that the reply is this: there would be no *falsity* in such modes of speech. They would involve a modification of our present usage of speech with regard to the words hard and soft, but not of their meanings. For they represent no fact to be different from what it is; only they involve arrangements of facts which would be exceedingly maladroit. This leads us to remark that the question of what would occur under circumstances which do not actually arise is not a question of fact, but only of the most perspicuous arrangement of them. For example, the question of free-will and fate in its simplest form, stripped of verbiage, is something like this: I have done something of which I am ashamed; could I, by an effort of the will, have resisted the temptation, and done otherwise? The philosophical reply is, that this is not a question of fact, but only of the arrangement of facts. Arranging them so as to exhibit what is particularly pertinent to my question—namely, that I ought to blame myself for having done wrong—it is perfectly true to say that, if I had willed to do otherwise than I did, I should have done otherwise. On the other hand, arranging the facts so as to exhibit another important consideration, it is equally true that, when a temptation has once been allowed to work, it will, if it has a certain force, produce its effect, let me struggle how I may. There is no objection to a contradiction in what would result from a false supposition. The *reductio ad absurdum* consists in showing that contradictory results would follow from a hypothesis which is consequently judged to be false. Many questions are involved in the free-will discussion, and I am far from desiring to say that both sides are equally right. On the contrary, I am of opinion that one side denies important facts, and that the other does not. But what I do say is, that the above single question was the origin of the whole doubt; that, had it not been for this question, the controversy would never have arisen; and that this question is perfectly solved in the manner which I have indicated.

Let us next seek a clear idea of Weight. This is another very easy case. To say that a body is heavy means simply that, in the absence of opposing force, it will fall. This (neglecting certain specifications of how it will fall, etc., which exist in the mind of the physicist who uses the word) is evidently the whole conception of weight. It is a fair question whether some particular facts may not *account* for gravity; but what we mean by the force itself is completely involved in its effects.

This leads us to undertake an account of the idea of Force in general. This is the great conception which, developed in the early part of the seventeenth century from the rude idea of a cause, and constantly improved upon since, has shown us how to explain all the changes of motion which bodies experience, and how to think about all physical phenomena; which has given birth to modem science, and changed the face of the globe; and which, aside from its more special uses, has played a principal part in directing the course of modem thought, and in furthering modem social development. It is, therefore, worth some pains to comprehend it. According to our rule, we must begin by asking what is the immediate use of thinking about force; and the answer is, that we thus account for changes of motion. If bodies were left to themselves, without the intervention of forces, every motion would continue unchanged both in velocity and in direction. Furthermore, change of motion never takes place abruptly; if its direction is changed, it is always through a curve without angles; if its velocity alters, it is by degrees. The gradual changes which are constantly taking place are conceived by geometers to be compounded together according to the rules of the parallelogram of forces. If the reader does not already know what this is, he will find it, I hope, to his advantage to endeavor to follow the following explanation; but if mathematics are insupportable to him, pray let him skip three paragraphs rather than that we should part company here.

A *path* is a line whose beginning and end are distinguished. Two paths are considered to be equivalent, which, beginning at the same point, lead to the same point. Thus *the two paths, A B C D E* and *A F G H E,* are equivalent. Paths which do not begin at the same point are considered to be equivalent, provided that, on moving either of them without turning it, but keeping it always parallel to its original position, when its beginning coincides with that of the other path, the ends also coincide. Paths are considered as geometrically added together, when one begins where the other ends; thus the path *A E* is conceived to be a sum of *A B, B C, C D,* and *D E.* In the parallelogram of Fig. 4 the diagonal *A C* is the sum of *A B* and *B C,* or, since *A D* is geometrically equivalent to *B C, A C* is the geometrical sum of *A B* and *A D.*

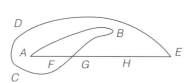

Figure 3

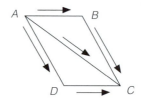

Figure 4

All this is purely conventional. It simply amounts to this: that we choose to call paths having the relations I have described equal or added. But, though it is a convention, it is a convention with a good reason. The rule for geometrical addition may be applied not only to paths, but to any other things which can be represented by paths. Now, as a path is determined by the varying direction and distance of the point which moves over it from the starting-point, it follows that anything which from its beginning to its end is determined by a varying direction and a varying magnitude is capable of being represented by a line. Accordingly, *velocities* may be represented by lines, for they have only directions and rates. The same thing is true of *accelerations,* or changes of velocities. This is evident enough in the case of velocities; and it becomes evident for accelerations if we consider that precisely what velocities are to positions—namely, states of change of them—that accelerations are to velocities.

The so-called "parallelogram of forces" is simply a rule for compounding accelerations. The rule is, to represent the accelerations by paths, and then to geometrically add the paths. The geometers, however, not only use the "parallelogram of forces" to compound different accelerations, but also to resolve one acceleration into a sum of several. Let *A B* (Fig. 5) be the path which represents a certain acceleration—say, such a change in the motion of a body that at the end of one second the body will, under the influence of that change, be in a position different from what it would have had if its motion had continued unchanged such that a path equivalent to *A B* would lead from the latter position to the former. This acceleration may be considered as the sum of the accelerations represented by *A C* and *C B*. It may also be considered as the sum of the

very different accelerations represented by *A D* and *D B*, where *A D* is almost the opposite of *A C*. And it is clear that there is an immense variety of ways in which *A B* might be resolved into the sum of two accelerations.

After this tedious explanation, which I hope, in view of the extraordinary interest of the conception of force, may not have exhausted the reader's patience, we are prepared at last to state the grand fact which this conception embodies. This fact is that if the actual changes of motion which the different particles of bodies experience are each resolved in its appropriate way, each component acceleration is precisely such as is prescribed by a certain law of Nature, according to which bodies, *in the relative positions which the bodies in question actually have at the moment*[1], always receive certain accelerations, which, being compounded by geometrical addition, give the acceleration which the body actually experiences.

This is the only fact which the idea of force represents, and whoever will take the trouble clearly to apprehend what this fact is, perfectly comprehends what force is. Whether we ought to say that a force *is* an acceleration, or that it *causes* an acceleration, is a mere question of propriety of language, which has no more to do with our real meaning than the difference between the French idiom *"Il fait froid"* and its English equivalent *"It is cold."* Yet it is surprising to see how this simple affair has muddled men's minds. In how many profound treatises is not force spoken of as a "mysterious entity," which seems to be only a way of confessing that the author despairs of ever getting a clear notion of what the word means! In a recent admired work on Analytic Mechanics it is stated that we understand precisely the effect of force, but what force itself is we do not understand! This is simply a self-contradiction. The idea which the word force excites in our minds has no other function than to affect our actions, and these actions can have no reference to force otherwise than through its effects. Consequently, if we know what the effects of force are, we are acquainted with every fact which is implied in saying that a force exists, and there is nothing more to know. The truth is, there is some vague notion afloat that a question may mean something which the mind cannot conceive; and when some hair-splitting philosophers have been confronted with the

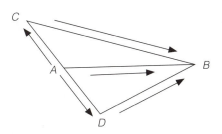

Figure 5

absurdity of such a view, they have invented an empty distinction between positive and negative conceptions, in the attempt to give their non-idea a form not obviously nonsensical. The nullity of it is sufficiently plain from the considerations given . . . and, apart from those considerations, the quibbling character of the distinction must have struck every mind accustomed to real thinking.

IV.

Let us now approach the subject of logic, and consider a conception which particularly concerns it, that of *reality*. Taking clearness in the sense of familiarity, no idea could be clearer than this. Every child uses it with perfect confidence, never dreaming that he does not understand it. As for clearness in its second grade, however, it would probably puzzle most men, even among those of a reflective turn of mind, to give an abstract definition of the real. Yet such a definition may perhaps be reached by considering the points of difference between reality and its opposite, fiction. A figment is a product of somebody's imagination; it has such characters as his thought impresses upon it. That those characters are independent of how you or I think is an external reality. There are, however, phenomena within our own minds, dependent upon our thought, which are at the same time real in the sense that we really think them. But though their characters depend on how we think, they do not depend on what we think those characters to be. Thus, a dream has a real existence as a mental phenomenon, if somebody has really dreamt it; that he dreamt so and so, does not depend on what anybody thinks was dreamt, but is completely independent of all opinion on the subject. On the other hand, considering, not the fact of dreaming, but the thing dreamt, it retains its peculiarities by virtue of no other fact than that it was dreamt to possess them. Thus we may define the real as that whose characters are independent of what anybody may think them to be.

But, however satisfactory such a definition may be found, it would be a great mistake to suppose that it makes the idea of reality perfectly clear. Here, then, let us apply our rules.

According to them, reality, like every other quality, consists in the peculiar sensible effects which things partaking of it produce. The only effect which real things have is to cause belief, for all the sensations which they excite emerge into consciousness in the form of beliefs. The question therefore is, how is true belief (or belief in the real) distinguished from false belief (or belief in fiction). Now, as we have seen in the former paper, the ideas of truth and falsehood, in their full development, appertain exclusively to the experiential method of settling opinion. A person who arbitrarily chooses the propositions which he will adopt can use the word truth only to emphasize the expression of his determination to hold on to his choice. Of course, the method of tenacity never prevailed exclusively; reason is too natural to men for that. But in the literature of the dark ages we find some fine examples of it. When Scotus Erigena is commenting upon a poetical passage in which hellebore is spoken of as having caused the death of Socrates, he does not hesitate to inform the inquiring reader that Helleborus and Socrates were two eminent Greek philosophers, and that the latter, having been overcome in argument by the former, took the matter to heart and died of it! What sort of an idea of truth could a man have who could adopt and teach, without the qualification of a perhaps, an opinion taken so entirely at random? The real spirit of Socrates, who I hope would have been delighted to have been "overcome in argument," because he would have learned something by it, is in curious contrast with the naive idea of the glossist, for whom (as for "the born missionary" of today) discussion would seem to have been simply a struggle. When philosophy began to awake from its long slumber, and before theology completely dominated it, the practice seems to have been for each professor to seize upon any philosophical position he found unoccupied and which seemed a strong one, to intrench himself in it, and to sally forth from time to time to give battle to the others. Thus, even the scanty records we possess of those disputes enable us to make out a dozen or more opinions held by different teachers at one time concerning the question of nominalism and realism. Read the opening part of the *Historia Calamitatum* of Abelard, who was certainly as philosophical as any of his contemporaries, and see the spirit of combat which it breathes. For him, the truth is simply his particular stronghold. When the method of authority prevailed, the truth meant little more than the Catholic faith. All the efforts of the scholastic doctors are directed toward harmonizing their faith in Aristotle and their faith in the Church, and one may search their ponderous folios through without finding an argument which goes any further. It is noticeable that where different faiths flourish side by side, renegades are looked upon with contempt even by the party whose belief they adopt; so completely has the idea of loyalty replaced that of truth-seeking. Since the time of Descartes, the defect in the conception of truth has been less apparent. Still, it will sometimes strike a scientific man that the philosophers have been less intent on finding out what the facts are, than on inquiring what belief is most in harmony with their system. It is hard to convince a follower of the *a priori* method by adducing facts; but show him that an opinion he is defending is inconsistent with what he has laid down elsewhere, and he will be very apt to retract it. These minds do not seem to believe that disputation is ever to cease; they seem to think that the opinion which is natural for one man is not so for another, and that belief will, consequently, never be settled. In contenting themselves with fixing their own opinions by a method which would lead another man to a different result, they betray their feeble hold of the conception of what truth is.

On the other hand, all the followers of science are animated by a cheerful hope that the processes of investigation, if only pushed far enough, will give one certain solution to each question to which they apply it. One man may investigate the velocity of light by studying the transits of Venus and the aberation of the stars; another by the oppositions of Mars and the eclipses of Jupiter's satellites; a third by the method of Fizeau; a fourth by that of Foucault; a fifth by the motions of the curves of Lissajoux; a sixth, a seventh, an eighth, and a ninth, may follow the different methods of comparing the measures of statical and dynamical electricity. They may at first obtain different results, but, as each perfects his method and his processes, the results are found to move steadily together toward a destined centre. So with all scientific research. Different minds may set out with the most antagonistic views, but the progress of investigation carries them by a force outside of themselves to one and the same conclusion. This activity of thought by which we are carried, not where we wish, but to a fore-ordained goal, is like the operation of destiny. No modification of the point of view taken, no selection of other facts for study, no natural bent of mind even, can enable a man to escape the predestinate opinion. This great hope is embodied in the conception of truth and reality. The opinion which is fated[2] to be ultimately agreed to by all who investigate, is what we mean by the truth, and the object represented in this opinion is the real. That is the way I would explain reality.

But it may be said that this view is directly opposed to the abstract definition which we have given of reality, inasmuch as it makes the characters of the real depend on what is ultimately thought about them. But the answer to this is that, on the one hand, reality is independent, not necessarily of thought in general, but only of what you or I or any finite number of men may think about it; and that, on the other hand, though the object of the final opinion depends on what that opinion is, yet what that opinion is does not depend on what you or I or any man thinks. Our perversity and that of others may indefinitely postpone the settlement of opinion; it might even conceivably cause an arbitrary proposition to be universally accepted as long as the human race should last. Yet even that would not change the nature of the belief, which alone could be the result of investigation carried sufficiently far; and if, after the extinction of our race, another should arise with faculties and disposition for investigation, that true opinion must be the one which they would ultimately come to. "Truth crushed to earth shall rise again," and the opinion which would finally result from investigation does not depend on how anybody may actually think. But the reality of that which is real does depend on the real fact that investigation is destined to lead, at last, if continued long enough, to a belief in it.

But I may be asked what I have to say to all the minute facts of history, forgotten never to be recovered, to the lost books of the ancients, to the buried secrets.

> "Full many a gem of purest ray serene
>   The dark, unfathomed caves of ocean
>   bear;
> Full many a flower is born to blush unseen,
>   And waste its sweetness on the desert air."

Do these things not really exist because they are hopelessly beyond the reach of our knowledge? And then, after the universe is dead (according to the prediction of some scientists), and all life has ceased forever, will not the shock of atoms continue though there will be no mind to know it? To this I reply that, though in no possible state of knowledge can any number be great enough to express the relation between the amount of what rests unknown to the amount of the known, yet it is unphilosophical to suppose that, with regard to any given question (which has any clear meaning), investigation would not bring forth a solution of it, if it were carried far enough. Who would have said, a few years ago, that we could ever know of what substances stars are made whose light may have been longer in reaching us than the human race has existed? Who can be sure of what we shall not know in a few hundred years? Who can guess what would be the result of continuing the pursuit of science for ten thousand years, with the activity of the last hundred? And if it were to go on for a million, or a billion, or any number of years you please, how is it possible to say that there is any question which might not ultimately be solved?

But it may be objected, "Why make so much of these remote considerations, especially when it is your principle that only practical distinctions have a meaning?" Well, I must confess that it makes very little difference whether we say that a stone on the bottom of the ocean, in complete darkness, is brilliant or not—that is to say, that it *probably* makes no difference, remembering always that that stone *may* be fished up tomorrow. But that there are gems at the bottom of the sea, flowers in the untraveled desert, etc., are propositions which, like that about a diamond being hard when it is not pressed, concern much more the arrangement of our language than they do the meaning of our ideas.

It seems to me, however, that we have, by the application of our rule, reached so clear an apprehension of what we mean by reality, and of the fact which the idea rests on, that we should not, perhaps, be making a pretension so presumptuous as it would be singular, if we were to offer a metaphysical theory of existence for universal acceptance among those who employ the scientific method of fixing belief. However, as metaphysics is a subject much more curious than useful, the knowledge of which, like that of a sunken reef, serves chiefly to enable us to keep clear of it, I will not trouble the reader with any more ontology at this moment. I have already been led much further into that path than I should have desired; and I have given the reader such a dose of mathematics, psychology, and all that is most abstruse, that I fear he may already have left me, and that what I am now writing is for the compositor and proof-reader exclusively. I trusted to the importance of the subject. There is no royal road to logic, and really valuable ideas can only be had at the price of close attention. But I know that in the matter of ideas the public prefer the cheap and nasty; and in my next paper I am going to return to the easily intelligible, and not wander from it again. The reader who has been at the pains of wading through this paper, shall be rewarded in the next one by seeing how beautifully what has been developed in this tedious way can be applied to the ascertainment of the rules of scientific reasoning.

We have, hitherto, not crossed the threshold of scientific logic. It is certainly important to know how to make our ideas clear, but they may be ever so clear without being true. How to make them so, we have next to study. How to give birth to those vital and procreative ideas which multiply into a thousand forms and diffuse themselves everywhere, advancing civilization and making the dignity of man, is an art not yet reduced to rules, but of the secret of which the history of science affords some hints.

Endnotes

[1]Possibly the velocities also have to be taken into account.

[2]Fate means merely that which is sure to come true, and can nohow be avoided. It is a superstition to suppose that a certain sort of events are ever fated, and it is another to suppose that the word fate can never be freed from its superstitious taint. We are all fated to die.

57. *Philosophy and the Scientific Image of Man*

WILFRID SELLARS

Modern science has stimulated contemporary philosophy in many ways. Are scientific theories successful because they truly describe reality (scientific realism) or are they just useful tools for predicting observable phenomena (instrumentalism)? If scientific theories purport to describe reality, then what should one conclude when they seem to conflict with traditional beliefs that have become deeply embedded in our ordinary view of reality? This problem has been a recurrent theme in Parts I–IV. In "Philosophy and the Scientific Image of Man," Wilfrid Sellars diagnoses the general problem. He claims ordinary views of reality have their roots in what he calls the "manifest image"—a network of beliefs that originally centered on the concept of a person. The "scientific image," in contrast, consists of a description of reality "derived from the fruits of postulational theory construction." Sellars interprets a variety of historically important philosophical positions in terms of different ways the scientific image might be thought to be related to the manifest image.

Providing an account of persons becomes the chief obstacle to the completeness and superiority of the scientific image. Regarding persons, Sellars offers a functionalist account of thinking, and he suggests that science will evolve to accommodate sensory qualities. He denies that normative descriptions of persons can be reduced to scientific descriptions, but claims it will be possible to enrich the scientific image with normative language without jeopardizing the scientific image's claim to be a complete description of reality. Sellars (1912–1989) taught philosophy at the University of Pittsburgh.

The Philosophical Quest

The aim of philosophy, abstractly formulated, is to understand how things in the broadest possible sense of the term hang together in the broadest possible sense of the term. Under 'things in the broadest possible sense' I include such radically different items as not only 'cabbages and kings', but numbers and duties, possibilities and finger snaps, aesthetic experience and death. To achieve success in philosophy would be, to use a contemporary turn of phrase, to 'know one's way around' with respect to all these things, not in that unreflective way in which the centipede of the story knew its way around before it faced the question, 'how do I walk?' but in that reflective way which means that no intellectual holds are barred.

Knowing one's way around is, to use a current distinction, a form of 'knowing *how*' as contrasted with 'knowing *that*'. There is all the difference in the world between knowing *how* to ride a bicycle and knowing *that* a steady pressure by the legs of a balanced person on the pedals would result in forward motion. Again, to use an example somewhat closer to our subject, there is all the difference in the world between knowing *that* each step of a given proof in mathematics follows from the preceding steps, and knowing *how* to find a proof. Sometimes being able to find a proof is a matter of being able to follow a set procedure; more often it

"Philosophy and the Scientific Image of Man" by Wilfrid Sellars is from *Frontiers of Science and Philosophy*, Robert G. Colodny, editor. © 1962 by the University of Pittsburgh Press. Reprinted by permission of the University of Pittsburgh Press.

is not. It can be argued that anything which can be properly called 'knowing how to do something' presupposes a body of knowledge *that;* or, to put it differently, knowledge of truth or facts. If this were so, then the statement that 'ducks know *how* to swim' would be as metaphorical as the statement that they know *that* water supports them. However this may be, knowing how to do something at the level of characteristically human activity presupposes a great deal of knowledge *that,* and it is obvious that the reflective knowing one's way around in the scheme of things, which is the aim of philosophy, presupposes a great deal of reflective knowledge of truths.

Now the subject-matter of this knowledge of truths which is presupposed by philosophical 'know-how', falls, in a sense, completely within the scope of the special disciplines. Philosophy in an important sense has no special subject-matter which stands to it as other subject-matters stand to other special disciplines. If philosophers did have such a special subject-matter, they could turn it over to a new group of specialists as they have turned other special subject-matters to non-philosophers over the past 2500 years, first with mathematics, more recently psychology and sociology, and, currently, certain aspects of theoretical linguistics. What is characteristic of philosophy is not a special subject-matter, but the aim of knowing one's way around with respect to the subject-matters of all the special disciplines.

Now the special disciplines know their way around in their subject-matters, and each learns to do so in the process of discovering truths about its own subject-matter. But each special discipline must also have a sense of how its bailiwick fits into the countryside as a whole. This sense in many cases amounts to a little more than the unreflective 'knowing one's way around' which is a common possession of us all. Again, the specialist must have a sense of how not only his subject-matter, but also the methods and principles of his thinking about it fit into the intellectual landscape. Thus, the historian reflects not only on historical events themselves, but on what it is to think historically. It is part of his business to reflect on his own thinking—its aim, its criteria, its pitfalls. In dealing with historical questions, he must face and answer questions which are not, themselves, in a primary sense historical questions. But he deals with these questions as they arise in the attempt to answer specifically historical questions.

Reflection on any special discipline can soon lead one to the conclusion that the *ideal* practitioner of that discipline would see his special subject-matter and his thinking about it in the light of a reflective insight into the intellectual landscape as a whole. There is much truth in the Platonic conception that the special disciplines are perfected by philosophy, but the companion conception that the philosopher must know his way around in each discipline as does the specialist, has been an ever more elusive ideal since the scientific revolution began. Yet if the philosopher cannot hope to know his way around in each discipline as does the specialist, there is a sense in which he can know his way around with respect to the subject-matter of that discipline, and must do so if he is to approximate to the philosophic aim.

The multiplication of sciences and disciplines is a familiar feature of the intellectual scene. Scarcely less familiar is the unification of this manifold which is taking place by the building of scientific bridges between them. I shall have something to say about this unification later in this chapter. What is not so obvious to the layman is that the task of 'seeing all things together' has itself been (paradoxically) broken down into specialities. And there *is* a place for specialization in philosophy. For just as one cannot come to know one's way around in the highway system as a whole without knowing one's way around in the parts, so one can't hope to know one's way around in 'things in general,' without knowing one's way around in the major groupings of things.

It is therefore, the 'eye on the whole' which distinguishes the philosophical enterprise. Otherwise, there is little to distinguish the philosopher from the persistently reflective specialist; the philosopher of history from the persistently reflective historian. To the extent that a specialist is more concerned to reflect on how his work as a specialist joins up with other intellectual pursuits, than in asking and answering questions within his speciality, he is said, properly, to be philosophically minded. And, indeed, one can 'have one's eye on the whole' without staring at it all the time. The latter would be a fruitless enterprise. Furthermore, like other specialists, the philosopher who specializes may derive much of his sense of the whole from the pre-reflective orientation which is our common heritage. On the other hand, a philosopher could scarcely be said to have his eye on the whole in the relevant sense, unless he has reflected on the nature of philosophical thinking. It is this reflection on the place of philosophy itself, in the scheme of things which is the distinctive trait of the philosopher as contrasted with the reflective specialist; and in the absence of this critical reflection on the philosophical enterprise, one is at best but a potential philosopher.

It has often been said in recent years that the aim of the philosopher is not to discover new truths, but to 'analyse' what we already know. But while the term 'analysis' was helpful in its implication that philosophy as such makes no *substantive* contribution to what we know, and is concerned in some way to improve the *manner* in which we know it, it is most misleading by its contrast to 'synthesis'. For by virtue of this contrast these statements suggest that philosophy is ever more myopic, tracing parts within parts, losing each in turn from sight as new parts come into view. One is tempted, therefore, to contrast the analytic conception of philosophy as myopia with the synoptic vision of true philosophy. And it must be admitted that if the contrast between 'analysis' and 'synthesis' were the operative connotation in the metaphor, then a purely analytic philosophy would be a contradiction in terms. Even if we construe 'analysis' on the analogy of making ever smaller scale maps of the same overall terrain, which does more justice to the synoptic element, the analogy disturbs because we would have to compare philosophy to the making of small-scale maps from an original large-scale map; and a smaller scale map in this sense is a triviality.

Even if the analogy is changed to that of bringing a picture into focus, which preserves the synoptic element and the theme of working within the framework of what is already known while adding a dimension of gain, the analogy is disturbing in two respects. (*a*) It suggests that the special disciplines are confused; as though the scientist had to wait for the philosopher to clarify his subject-matter, bring it into focus. To account for the creative role of philosophy, it is not necessary

to say that the scientist doesn't know his way around in his own area. What we must rather say is that the specialist knows his way around in his own neighbourhood, as his neighbourhood, but doesn't know his way around in it in the same way *as a part of the landscape as a whole.*

(*b*) It implies that the essential change brought about by philosophy is the standing out of detail within a picture which is grasped as a whole from the start. But, of course, to the extent that there is *one* picture to be grasped reflectively as a whole, the unity of the reflective vision is a task rather than an initial datum. The search for this unity at the reflective level is therefore more appropriately compared to the contemplation of a large and complex painting which is not seen as a unity without a prior exploration of its parts. The analogy, however, is not complete until we take into account a *second* way in which unity is lacking in the original datum of the contemporary philosopher. For he is confronted not by one picture, but, *in principle,* by *two* and, in fact, by *many.* The plurality I have in mind is not that which concerns the distinction between the fact finding, the ethical, the aesthetic, the logical, the religious, and other aspects of experience, for these are but aspects of one complex picture which is to be grasped reflectively as a whole. As such, it constitutes one term of a crucial duality which confronts the contemporary philosopher at the very beginning of his enterprise. Here the most appropriate analogy is stereoscopic vision, where two differing perspectives on a landscape are fused into one coherent experience.

For the philosopher is confronted not by one complex many-dimensional picture, the unity of which, such as it is, he must come to appreciate; but by *two* pictures of essentially the same order of complexity, each of which purports to be a complete picture of man-in-the-world, and which, after separate scrutiny, he must fuse into one vision. Let me refer to these two perspectives, respectively, as the *manifest* and the *scientific* images of man-in-the-world. And let me explain my terms. First, by calling them images I do not mean to deny to either or both of them the status of 'reality.' I am, to use Husserl's term, 'bracketing' them, transforming them from ways of experiencing the world into objects of philosophical reflection and evaluation. The term 'image' is usefully ambiguous. On the one hand it suggests the contrast between an object, e.g., a tree, and a projection of the object on a plane, or its shadow on a wall. In this sense, an image is as much an existent as the object imaged, though, of course, it has a dependent status.

In the other sense, an 'image' is something imagined, and that which is imagined may well not exist, although the imagining of it does—in which case we can speak of the image as *merely* imaginary or unreal. But the imagined *can* exist; as when one imagines that someone is dancing in the next room, and someone is. This ambiguity enables me to imply that the philosopher is confronted by two projections of man-in-the-world on the human understanding. One of these projections I will call the manifest image, the other the scientific image. These images exist and are as much a part and parcel of the world as this platform or the Constitution of the United States. But in addition to being confronted by these images as existents, he is confronted by them as images in the sense of 'things imagined'—or, as I had better say at once, *conceived;* for I am using 'image' in this sense as a metaphor for conception, and it is a familiar fact that not everything that can be conceived can, in the ordinary sense, be imagined. The philosopher, then, is confronted by two conceptions, equally public, equally non-arbitrary, of man-in-the-world and he cannot shirk the attempt to see how they fall together in one stereoscopic view.

Before I begin to explain the contrast between 'manifest' and 'scientific' as I shall use these terms, let me make it clear that they are both 'idealizations' in something like the sense in which a frictionless body or an ideal gas is an idealization. They are designed to illuminate the inner dynamics of the development of philosophical ideas, as scientific idealizations illuminate the development of physical systems. From a somewhat different point of view they can be compared to the 'ideal types' of Max Weber's sociology. The story is complicated by the fact that each image has a history, and while the main outlines of what I shall call the manifest image took shape in the mists of pre-history, the scientific image, promissory notes apart, has taken shape before our very eyes.

The Manifest Image

The 'manifest' image of man-in-the-world can be characterized in two ways, which are supplementary rather than alternative. It is, first, the framework in terms of which man came to be aware of himself as man-in-the-world. It is the framework in terms of which, to use an existentialist turn of phrase, man first encountered himself—which is, of course, when he came to be man. For it is no merely incidental feature of man that he has a conception of himself as man-in-the-world, just as it is obvious, on reflection, that 'if man had a radically different conception of himself he would be a radically different kind of man'.

I have given this quasi-historical dimension of our construct pride of place, because I want to highlight from the very beginning what might be called the paradox of man's encounter with himself, the paradox consisting of the fact that man couldn't be man until he encountered himself. It is this paradox which supports the last stand of Special Creation. Its central theme is the idea that anything which can properly be called conceptual thinking can occur only within a framework of conceptual thinking in terms of which it can be criticized, supported, refuted, in short, evaluated. To be able to think is to be able to measure one's thoughts by standards of correctness, of relevance, of evidence. In this sense a diversified conceptual framework is a whole which, however sketchy, is prior to its parts, and cannot be construed as a coming together of parts which are already conceptual in character. The conclusion is difficult to avoid that the transition from pre-conceptual patterns of behaviour to conceptual thinking was a holistic one, a jump to a level of awareness which is irreducibly new, a jump which was the coming into being of man.

There is a profound truth in this conception of a radical difference in level between man and his precursors. The attempt to understand this difference turns out to be part and parcel of the attempt to encompass in one view the two images of man-in-the-world which I have set out to describe. For, as we shall see, this difference in level appears as an irreducible discontinuity in the *manifest* image, but as, in a sense requiring careful analysis, a reducible difference in the *scientific* image.

I have characterized the manifest image of man-in-the-world as the framework in terms of which man encountered himself. And this, I believe, is a useful way of characterizing it. But it is also misleading, for it suggests that the contrast I am drawing between the manifest and the scientific images, is that between a pre-scientific, uncritical, naïve conception of man-in-the-world, and a reflected, disciplined, critical—in short a scientific—conception. This is not at all what I have in mind. For what I mean by the manifest image is a refinement or sophistication of what might be called the 'original' image; a refinement to a degree which makes it relevant to the contemporary intellectual scene. This refinement or sophistication can be construed under two headings; *(a)* empirical; *(b)* categorial.

By empirical refinement, I mean the sort of refinement which operates within the broad framework of the image and which, by approaching the world in terms of something like the canons of inductive inference defined by John Stuart Mill, supplemented by canons of statistical inference, adds to and subtracts from the contents of the world as experienced in terms of this framework and from the correlations which are believed to obtain between them. Thus, the conceptual framework which I am calling the manifest image is, in an appropriate sense, itself a scientific image. It is not only disciplined and critical; it also makes use of those aspects of scientific method which might be lumped together under the heading 'correlational induction'. There is, however, one type of scientific reasoning which it, by stipulation, does *not* include, namely that which involves the postulation of imperceptible entities, and principles pertaining to them, to explain the behaviour of perceptible things.

This makes it clear that the concept of the manifest image of man-in-the-world is not that of an historical and bygone stage in the development of man's conception of the world and his place in it. For it is a familiar fact that correlational and postulational methods have gone hand in hand in the evolution of science, and, indeed, have been dialectically related; postulational hypotheses presupposing correlations to be explained, and suggesting possible correlations to be investigated. The notion of a purely correlational scientific view of things is both an historical and a methodological fiction. It involves abstracting correlational fruits from the conditions of their discovery, and the theories in terms of which they are explained. Yet it is a useful fiction (and hence no *mere* fiction), for it will enable us to define a way of looking at the world which, though disciplined and, in a limited sense, scientific, contrasts sharply with an image of man-in-the-world which is implicit in and can be constructed from the postulational aspects of contemporary scientific theory. And, indeed, what I have referred to as the 'scientific' image of man-in-the-world and contrasted with the 'manifest' image, might better be called the 'postulational' or 'theoretical' image. But, I believe, it will not be too misleading if I continue, for the most part, to use the former term.

Now the manifest image is important for our purpose, because it defines one of the poles to which philosophical reflection has been drawn. It is not only the great speculative systems of ancient and medieval philosophy which are built around the manifest image, but also many systems and quasi-systems in recent and contemporary thought, some of which seem at first sight to have little if anything in common with the great classical systems. That I include the major schools of contemporary Continental thought might be expected. That I lump in with these the trends of contemporary British and American philosophy which emphasize the analysis of 'common sense' and 'ordinary usage', may be somewhat more surprising. Yet this kinship is becoming increasingly apparent in recent years and I believe that the distinctions that I am drawing in this chapter will make possible an understanding and interpretation of this kinship. For all these philosophies can, I believe, be fruitfully construed as more or less adequate accounts of the manifest image of man-in-the-world, which accounts are then taken to be an adequate and full description in general terms of what man and the world really are.

Let me elaborate on this theme by introducing another construct which I shall call—borrowing a term with a not unrelated meaning—the perennial philosophy of man-in-the-world. This construct, which is the 'ideal type' around which philosophies in what might be called, in a suitably broad sense, the Platonic tradition cluster, is simply the manifest image endorsed as real, and its outline taken to be the large-scale map of reality to which science brings a needle-point of detail and an elaborate technique of map-reading.

It will probably have occurred to you by now that there are negative over-tones to both constructs: the 'manifest image' and the 'perennial philosophy'. And, in a certain sense, this is indeed the case. I *am* implying that the perennial philosophy is analogous to what one gets when one looks through a stereoscope with one eye dominating. The manifest image dominates and mislocates the scientific image. But if the perennial philosophy of man-in-the-world is in this sense distorted, an important consequence lurks in the offing. For I have also implied that man is *essentially* that being which conceives of itself *in terms of the image which the perennial philosophy refines and endorses.* I seem, therefore, to be saying that man's conception of himself in the world does not easily accommodate the scientific image; that there is a genuine tension between them; that man is not the sort of thing he conceives himself to be; that his existence is in some measure built around error. If this were what I wished to say, I would be in distinguished company. One thinks, for example, of Spinoza, who contrasted man as he falsely conceives himself to be with man as he discovers himself to be in the scientific enterprise. It might well be said that Spinoza drew a distinction between a 'manifest' and a 'scientific' image of man, rejecting the former as false and accepting the latter as true.

But if in Spinoza's account, the scientific image, as he interprets it, dominates the stereoscopic view (the manifest image appearing as a tracery of explainable error), the very fact that I use the analogy of stereoscopic vision implies that as I see it the manifest image is not overwhelmed in the synthesis.

But before there can be any point to these comparisons, I must characterize these images in more detail, adding flesh and blood to the bare bones I have laid before you. I shall devote the remainder of this section and the following section to developing the manifest image. In the concluding sections I shall characterize the scientific image, and attempt to describe certain key features of how the two images blend together in a true stereoscopic view.

I distinguished above between two dimensions of the refinement which turned the 'original' image into the 'manifest' image: the empirical and

the categorial. Nothing has been said so far about the latter. Yet it is here that the most important things are to be said. It is in this connection that I will be able to describe the general structure of the manifest image.

A fundamental question with respect to any conceptual framework is 'of what sort are the basic objects of the framework?' This question involves, on the one hand, the contrast between an object and what can be true of it in the way of properties, relations, and activities; and, on the other, a contrast between the basic objects of the framework and the various kinds of groups they can compose. The basic objects of a framework need not be things in the restricted sense of perceptible physical objects. Thus, the basic objects of current theoretical physics are notoriously imperceptible and unimaginable. Their basic-ness consists in the fact that they are not properties or groupings of anything more basic (at least until further notice). The questions, 'are the basic objects of the framework of physical theory *thing-like*? and if so, to what extent?' are meaningful ones.

Now to ask, 'what are the basic objects of a (given) framework?' is to ask not for a *list*, but a *classification*. And the classification will be more or less 'abstract' depending on what the purpose of the inquiry is. The philosopher is interested in a classification which is abstract enough to provide a synoptic view of the contents of the framework but which falls short of simply referring to them as objects or entities. Thus we are approaching an answer to the question, 'what are the basic objects of the manifest image?' when we say that it includes persons, animals, lower forms of life and 'merely material' things, like rivers and stones. The list is not intended to be complete, although it is intended to echo the lower stages of the 'great chain of being' of the Platonic tradition.

The first point I wish to make is that there is an important sense in which the primary objects of the manifest image are *persons*. And to understand how this is so, is to understand central and, indeed, crucial themes in the history of philosophy. Perhaps the best way to make the point is to refer back to the construct which we called the 'original' image of man-in-the-world, and characterize it as a framework in which *all* the 'objects' are persons. From this point of view, the refinement of the 'original' image into the manifest image, is the gradual 'depersonalization' of objects other than persons. That something like this has occurred with the advance of civilization is a familiar fact. Even persons, it is said (mistakenly, I believe), are being 'depersonalized' by the advance of the scientific point of view.

The point I now wish to make is that although this gradual depersonalization of the original image is a familiar idea, it is radically misunderstood, if it is assimilated to the gradual abandonment of a superstitious belief. A primitive man did not *believe* that the tree in front of him was a person, in the sense that he thought of it both as a tree *and* as a person, as I might think that this brick in front of me is a doorstop. If this were so, then when he abandoned the idea that trees were persons, his concept of a tree could remain unchanged, although his beliefs about trees would be changed. The truth is, rather, that *originally* to be a tree was *a way of being a person*, as, to use a close analogy, to be a woman is a way of being a person, or to be a triangle is a way of being a plane figure. That a woman is a person is not something that one can be said to *believe;* though there's enough historical bounce to this example to make it worth-while to use the different example that one cannot be said to believe that a triangle is a plane figure. When primitive man ceased to think of what we called trees as persons, the change was more radical than a change in belief; it was a change in category.

Now, the human mind is not limited in its categories to what it has been able to refine out of the world view of primitive man, any more than the limits of what we can conceive are set by what we can imagine. The categories of theoretical physics are not essences distilled from the framework of perceptual experience, yet, if the human mind can conceive of *new* categories, it can also refine the old; and it is just as important not to over-estimate the role of creativity in the development of the framework in terms of which you and I experience the world, as it is not to under-estimate its role in the scientific enterprise.

I indicated above that in the construct which I have called the 'original' image of man-in-the-world, all 'objects' are persons, and all kinds of objects ways of being persons. This means that the sort of things that are said of objects in this framework are the sort of things that are said of persons. And let me make it clear that by 'persons', I do not

mean 'spirit' or 'mind'. The idea that a man is a team of two things, a mind *and* a body, is one for which many reasons of different kinds and weights have been given in the course of human intellectual development. But it is obvious, on reflection, that whatever philosophers have made of the idea of a *mind,* the pre-philosophical conception of a 'spirit', where it is found, is that of a ghostly *person,* something analogous to flesh and blood persons which 'inhabits' them, or is otherwise intimately connected with them. It is, therefore, a development *within the framework of persons,* and it would be incorrect to construe the manifest image in such a way that persons are composite objects. On the other hand, if it is to do its work, the manifest framework must be such as to make meaningful the assertion that what we ordinarily call persons are composites of a person proper and a body—and, by doing so, make meaningful the contrary view that although men have many different types of ability, ranging from those he has in common with the lowest of things, to his ability to engage in scientific and philosophical reflection, he nevertheless is one object and not a team. For we shall see that the essential dualism in the manifest image is not that between mind and body as substances, but between two radically different ways in which the human individual is related to the world. Yet it must be admitted that most of the philosophical theories which are dominated by the manifest image are dualist in the substantive sense. There are many factors which account for this, most of which fall outside the scope of this essay. Of the factors which concern us, one is a matter of the influence of the developing scientific image of man, and will be discussed in the following section. The other arises in the attempt to make sense of the manifest image in its own terms.

Now to understand the manifest image as a refinement or depersonalization of the 'original' image, we must remind ourselves of the range of activities which are characteristic of persons. For when I say that the objects of the manifest image are primarily persons, I am implying that what the objects of this framework primarily *are* and *do,* is what persons are and do. Thus persons are 'impetuous' or 'set in their ways'. They apply old policies or adopt new ones. They do things from habit or ponder alternatives. They are immature or have an established character. For my present purposes, the most important contrasts are those between actions which are expressions of character and actions which are *not* expressions of character, on the one hand, and between habitual actions and deliberate actions, on the other. The first point that I want to make is that only a being capable of deliberation can properly be said to act, either impulsively or from habit. For in the full and non-metaphorical sense an action is the sort of thing that can be done deliberately. We speak of actions as *becoming* habitual, and this is no accident. It is important to realize that the use of the term 'habit' in speaking of an earthworm as acquiring the habit of turning to the right in a T-maze, is a metaphorical extension of the term. There is nothing dangerous in the metaphor until the mistake is made of assuming that the habits of persons are the same sort of thing as the (metaphorical) 'habits' of earthworms and white rats.

Again, when we say that something a person did was an expression of his character, we mean that it is 'in character'—that it was to be expected. We do not mean that it was a matter of *habit*. To be *habitual* is to be 'in character', but the converse is not true. To say of an action that it is 'in character', that it was to be expected, is to say that it was predictable—not, however, predictable 'no holds barred,' but predictable with respect to evidence pertaining to what the person in question has done in the past, and the circumstances as he saw them in which he did it. Thus, a person cannot, *logically* cannot, *begin* by acting 'in character', any more than he can *begin* by acting from habit.

It is particularly important to see that while to be 'in character' is to be predictable, the converse is not true. It does not follow from the fact that a piece of human behaviour is predictable, that it is an expression of character. Thus the behaviour of a burnt child with respect to the fire is predictable, but not an expression of character. If we use the phrase, 'the nature of a person', to sum up the predictabilities *no holds barred* pertaining to that person, then we must be careful not to equate the *nature* of a person with his *character,* although his character will be a 'part' of his nature in the broad sense. Thus, if everything a person did were predictable (in principle), given sufficient knowledge about the person and the circumstances in which he was placed, and was, therefore, an 'expression of his nature,' it would not follow that everything the per-

son did was an expression of his *character*. Obviously, to say of a person that everything that he does is an expression of his character is to say that his life is simply a carrying out of formed habits and policies. Such a person is a type only approximated to in real life. Not even a mature person always acts in character. And as we have seen, it cannot possibly be true that he has always acted in character. Yet, if determinism is true, everything he has done has been an expression of his 'nature'.

I am now in a position to explain what I mean when I say that the primary objects of the manifest image are persons. I mean that it is the modification of an image in which *all* the objects are capable of *the full range* of personal activity, the modification consisting of a gradual pruning of the implications of saying with respect to what *we* would call an inanimate object, that it *did* something. Thus, in the original image to say of the wind that it blew down one's house would imply that the wind *either* decided to do so with an end in view, and might, perhaps, have been persuaded not to do it, *or* that it acted thoughtlessly (either from habit or impulse), or, perhaps, inadvertently, in which case other appropriate action on one's part might have awakened it to the enormity of what it was about to do.

In the early stages of the development of the manifest image, the wind was no longer conceived as acting deliberately, with an end in view; but rather from habit or impulse. Nature became the locus of 'truncated persons'; that which things could be expected to do, its habits; that which exhibits no order, its impulses. Inanimate things no longer 'did' things in the sense in which persons do them—not, however, because a *new* category of impersonal things and impersonal processes has been achieved, but because the category of *person* is now applied to these things in a pruned or truncated form. It is a striking exaggeration to say of a person, that he is a 'mere creature of habit and impulse', but in the early stages of the development of manifest image, the world includes truncated persons which *are* mere creatures of habit, acting out routines, broken by impulses, in a life which never rises above what ours is like in our most unreflective moments. Finally, the sense in which the wind 'did' things was pruned, save for poetic and expressive purposes—and, one is tempted to add, for philosophical purposes—of implications pertaining to 'knowing what one is doing' and 'knowing what the circumstances are'.

Just as it is important not to confuse between the 'character' and the 'nature' of a person, that is to say, between an action's being predictable with respect to evidence pertaining to prior action, and its being predictable no holds barred, so it is important not to confuse between an action's being *predictable* and its being *caused*. These terms are often treated as synonyms, but only confusion can arise from doing so. Thus, in the 'original' image, one person causes another person to do something he otherwise would not have done. But most of the things people do are not things they are *caused* to do, even if what they do is highly predictable. For example: when a person has well-established habits, what he does in certain circumstances is highly predictable, but it is not for that reason *caused*. Thus the category of causation (as contrasted with the more inclusive category of predictability) betrays its origin in the 'original' image. When all things were persons it was certainly not a framework conception that everything a person did was caused; nor, of course, was it a framework principle that everything a person did was predictable. To the extent that relationships between the truncated 'persons' of the manifest framework were analogous to the causal relationships between persons, the category itself continued to be used, although pruned of its implications with respect to plans, purposes, and policies. The most obvious analogue at the inanimate level of causation in the original sense is one billiard ball causing another to change its course, but it is important to note that no one who distinguishes between causation and predictability would ask, 'what *caused* the billiard ball on a smooth table to continue in a straight line?' The distinctive trait of the scientific revolution was the conviction that all events are predictable from relevant information about the context in which they occur, not that they are all, in any ordinary sense, caused.

Classical Philosophy and the Manifest Image

I have characterized the concept of the manifest image as one of the poles towards which philosophical thinking is drawn. This commits me, of course, to the idea that the manifest image is not a mere external standard, by relation to which one interested in the development of philosophy classifies philosophical positions, but has in its own way an objective existence in philosophical thinking itself, and, indeed, in human thought generally. And it can influence philosophical thinking only by having an existence which transcends in some way the individual thought of individual thinkers. I shall be picking up this theme shortly, and shall ask how an image of the world, which, after all, is a way of thinking, *can* transcend the individual thinker which it influences. (The general lines of the answer must be obvious, but it has implications which have not always been drawn.) The point I wish to make now is that since this image has a being which transcends the individual thinker, *there is truth and error with respect to it, even though the image itself might have to be rejected, in the last analysis, as false.*

Thus, whether or not the world as we encounter it in perception and self-awareness is ultimately real, it is surely incorrect, for example, to say as some philosophers have said that the physical objects of the encountered world are 'complexes of sensations' or, equally, to say that apples are not *really* coloured, or that mental states are 'behavioural dispositions', or that one cannot intend to do something without knowing that one intends to do it, or that to say that something is good is to say that one likes it, etc. For there is a correct and an incorrect way to describe this objective image which we have of the world in which we live, and it is possible to evaluate the correctness or incorrectness of such a description. I have already claimed that much of academic philosophy can be interpreted as an attempt by individual thinkers to delineate the manifest image (not recognized, needless to say, as such) an image which is both immanent in and transcendent of their thinking. In this respect, a philosophy can be evaluated as perceptive or imperceptive, mistaken or correct, even though one is prepared to say that the image they delineate is but one way in which reality appears to the human mind. And it is, indeed, a task of the first importance to delineate this image, particularly in so far as it concerns man himself, for, as was pointed out before, man is what he is because he thinks of himself in terms of this image, and the latter must be understood before it is proper to ask, 'to what extent does manifest man survive in the synoptic view which does equal justice to the scientific image which now confronts us?'

I think it correct to say that the so-called 'analytic' tradition in recent British and American philosophy, particularly under the influence of the later Wittgenstein, has done increasing justice to the manifest image, and has increasingly succeeded in isolating it in something like its pure form, and has made clear the folly of attempting to replace it *piecemeal* by fragments of the scientific image. By doing so, it is made apparent, and has come to realize, its continuity with the perennial tradition.

Now one of the most interesting features of the perennial philosophy is its attempt to understand the status in the individual thinker of the framework of ideas in terms of which he grasps himself as a person in the world. How do individuals come to be able to think in terms of this complex conceptual framework? How do they come to have this image? Two things are to be noticed here: (1) The manifest image does not present conceptual thinking as a complex of items which, considered in themselves and apart from these relations, are not conceptual in character. (The most plausible candidates are images, but all attempts to construe thoughts as complex patterns of images have failed, and, as we know, were bound to fail.) (2) Whatever the ultimate constituents of conceptual thinking, the process itself as it occurs in the individual mind must echo, more or less adequately, the intelligible structure of the world.

There was, of course, a strong temptation not only to think of the constituents of thinking as qualitatively similar to the constituents of the world, but also to think of the world as causing constituents to occur in patterns which echo the patterns of events. The attempt, by precursors of scientific psychology, to understand the genesis of conceptual thinking in the individual in terms of an 'association' of elemental processes which were not themselves conceptual, by a direct action of the physical environment on the individual— the paradigm case being the burnt child fearing the fire—was a premature attempt to construct a scientific image of man.

The perennial tradition had no sympathy with such attempts. It recognized *(a)* that association of *thoughts* is not association of images, and, as presupposing a framework of conceptual thinking, cannot account for it; *(b)* that the direct action of perceptible nature, *as perceptible,* on the *individual* can account for associative connection, *but not the rational connections of conceptual thinking.*

Yet somehow the world *is* the cause of the individual's image of the world, and, as is well-known, for centuries the dominant conception of the perennial tradition was that of a direct causal influence of the world as intelligible on the individual mind. This theme, initiated by Plato, can be traced through Western thought to the present day. In the Platonic tradition this mode of causation is attributed to a being which is analogous, to a greater or lesser degree, to a person. Even the Aristotelian distinguishes between the way in which sensations make available the intelligible structure of things to man, and the way in which contingencies of perceptual experience establish expectations and permit a non-rational accommodation of animals to their environment. And there is, as we know today, a sound core to the idea that while reality is the 'cause' of the human conceptual thinking which represents it, this causal role cannot be equated with a conditioning of the individual by his environment in a way which could in principle occur without the mediation of the family and the community. The Robinson Crusoe conception of the world as generating conceptual thinking directly in the individual is too simple a model. The perennial tradition long limited itself to accounting for the presence in the individual of the framework of conceptual thinking in terms of a unique kind of action of reality as intelligible on the individual mind. The accounts differed in interesting respects, but the main burden remained the same. It was not until the time of Hegel that the essential role of the group as a mediating factor in this causation was recognized, and while it is easy for us to see that the immanence and transcendence of conceptual frameworks with respect to the individual thinker is a social phenomenon, and to find a recognition of this fact implicit in the very form of our image of man in the world, it was not until the nineteenth century that this feature of the manifest image was, however inadequately, taken into account.

The Platonic theory of conceptual abilities as the result of the 'illumination' of the mind by intelligible essences limited the role of the group and, in particular, the family to that of calling these abilities into play—a role which could, in principle, be performed by perceptual experience—and to that of teaching the means of giving verbal expression to these abilities. Yet the essentially social character of conceptual thinking comes clearly to mind when we recognize that there is no thinking apart from common standards of correctness and relevance, which relate what *I do* think to what *anyone ought to* think. The contrast between 'I' and 'anyone' is essential to rational thought.

It is current practice to compare the inter-subjective standards without which there would be no thinking, to the inter-subjective standards without which there would be no such a thing as a game; and the acquisition of a conceptual framework to learning to play a game. It is worth noting, however, that conceptual thinking is a unique game in two respects: *(a)* one cannot learn to play it by being told the rules; *(b)* whatever else conceptual thinking makes possible—and without it there is nothing characteristically human—it does so by virtue of containing a way of representing the world.

When I said that the individual as a conceptual thinker is essentially a member of a group, this does not mean of course, that the individual cannot exist apart from the group, for example as sole survivor of an atomic catastrophe, any more than the fact that chess is a game played by two people means that one can't play chess with oneself. A group isn't a group in the relevant sense unless it consists of a number of individuals each of which thinks of himself as 'I' in contrast to 'others'. Thus a group exists in the way in which members of the group represent themselves. Conceptual thinking is not by accident that which is *communicated* to others, any more than the decision to move a chess piece is by accident that which finds an expression in a move on a board between two people.

The manifest image must, therefore, be construed as containing a conception of itself as a group phenomenon, the group mediating between the individual and the intelligible order. But any attempt to *explain* this mediation within the framework of the manifest image was bound to fail, for the manifest image contains the resources for such an attempt only in the sense that it provides the foundation on which scientific theory can build an explanatory framework; and while conceptual structures of this framework are *built on*

the manifest image, they are not definable within it. Thus, the Hegelian, like the Platonist of whom he is the heir, was limited to the attempt to understand the relation between intelligible order and individual minds in analogical terms.

It is in the *scientific* image of man in the world that we begin to see the main outlines of the way in which man came to have an image of himself-in-the-world. For we begin to see this as a matter of evolutionary development, as a group phenomenon, a process which is illustrated at a simpler level by the evolutionary development which explains the correspondence between the dancing of a worker bee and the location, relative to the sun, of the flower from which he comes. This correspondence, like the relation between man's 'original' image and the world, is incapable of explanation in terms of a direct conditioning impact of the environment on the individual as such.

I have called attention to the fact that the manifest image involves two types of causal impact of the world on the individual. It is, I have pointed out, this duality of causation and the related irreducibility, within the manifest image of conceptual thinking in all its forms to more elementary processes, which is the primary and essential dualism of the perennial philosophy. The dualistic conception of mind and body characteristic of, but by no means an invariable feature of, *philosophia perennis,* is in part an inference from this dualism of causation and of process. In part, however, as we shall see, it is a result of the impact of certain themes present in even the smallest stages of the developing scientific image.

My primary concern in this essay is with the question, in what sense, and to what extent, does the manifest image of man-in-the-world survive the attempt to unite this image in one field of intellectual vision with man as conceived in terms of the postulated objects of scientific theory? The bite to this question lies, we have seen, in the fact that man is that being which conceives of itself in terms of the manifest image. To the extent that the manifest does not survive in the synoptic view, to that extent man himself would not survive. Whether the adoption of the synoptic view would transform man in bondage into man free, as Spinoza believed, or man free into man in bondage, as many fear, is a question that does not properly arise until the claims of the scientific image have been examined.

The Scientific Image

I devoted my attention in the previous sections to defining what I called the 'manifest' image of man-in-the-world. I argued that this image is to be construed as a sophistication and refinement of the image in terms of which man first came to be aware of himself as man-in-the-world; in short, came to be man. I pointed out that in any sense in which this image, in so far as it pertains to man, is a 'false' image, this falsity threatens man himself, inasmuch as he is, in an important sense, the being which has this image of himself. I argued that what has been called the perennial tradition in philosophy—*philosophia perennis*—can be construed as the attempt to understand the structure of this image, to know one's way around in it reflectively with no intellectual holds barred. I analysed some of the main features of the image and showed how the categories in terms of which it approaches the world can be construed as progressive prunings of categories pertaining to the person and his relation to other persons and the group. I argued that the perennial tradition must be construed to include not only the Platonic tradition in its broadest sense, but philosophies of 'common sense' and 'ordinary usage'. I argued what is common to all these philosophies is an acceptance of the manifest image as the *real*. They attempt to understand the achievements of theoretical science in terms of this framework, subordinating the categories of theoretical science to its categories. I suggested that the most fruitful way of approaching the problem of integrating theoretical science with the framework of sophisticated common sense into one comprehensive synoptic vision is to view it not as a piecemeal task—e.g., first a fitting together of the common sense conception of physical objects with that of theoretical physics, and then, as a separate venture, a fitting together of the common sense conception of man with that of theoretical psychology—but rather as a matter of articulating two whole ways of seeing the sum of things, two images of man-in-the-world and attempting to bring them together in a 'stereoscopic' view.

My present purpose is to add to the account I have given of the manifest image, a comparable sketch of what I have called the scientific image, and to conclude this essay with some comments on the respective contributions of these two to the unified vision of man-in-the-world which is the aim of philosophy.

The scientific image of man-in-the-world is, of course, as much an idealization as the manifest image—even more so, as it is still in the process of coming to be. It will be remembered that the contrast I have in mind is not that between an *unscientific* conception of man-in-the-world and a *scientific* one, but between that conception which limits itself to what correlational techniques can tell us about perceptible and introspectible events and that which postulates imperceptible objects and events for the purpose of explaining correlations among perceptibles. It was granted, of course, that in point of historical fact many of the latter correlations were suggested by theories introduced to explain previously established correlations, so that there has been a dialectical interplay between correlational and postulational procedures. (Thus we might not have noticed that litmus paper turns red in acid, until this hypothesis had been suggested by a complex theory relating the absorption and emission of electromagnetic radiation by objects to their chemical composition; yet in principle this familiar correlation could have been, and, indeed, was, discovered before any such theory was developed.) Our contrast then, is between two ideal constructs: *(a)* the correlational and categorial refinement of the 'original image', which refinement I am calling the manifest image; *(b)* the image derived from the fruits of postulational theory construction which I am calling the scientific image.

It may be objected at this point that there is no such thing as *the* image of man built from postulated entities and processes, but rather as many images as there are sciences which touch on aspects of human behaviour. And, of course, in a sense this is true. There *are* as many scientific images of man as there are sciences which have something to say about man. Thus, there is man as he appears to the theoretical physicist—a swirl of physical particles, forces, and fields. There is man as he appears to the biochemist, to the physiologist, to the behaviourist, to the social scientist; and all of these images are to be contrasted with man as he appears to himself in sophisticated common sense, the manifest image which even today contains most of what he knows about himself at the properly human level. Thus the conception of *the* scientific or postulational image is an idealization in the sense that it is a conception of an integration of a manifold of images, each of which is the application to man of a framework of concepts which have a certain autonomy. For each scientific theory is, from the standpoint of methodology, a structure which is built at a different 'place' and by different procedures within the intersubjectively accessible world of perceptible things. Thus 'the' scientific image is a construct from a number of images, each of which is *supported* by the manifest world.

The fact that each theoretical image is a construction on a foundation provided by the manifest image, and *in this methodological sense* presupposes the manifest image, makes it tempting to suppose that the manifest image is prior in a *substantive* sense; that the categories of a theoretical science are logically dependent on categories pertaining to its methodological foundation in the manifest world of sophisticated common sense in such a way that there would be an absurdity in the notion of a world which illustrated its theoretical principles *without also illustrating the categories and principles of the manifest world*. Yet, when we turn our attention to 'the' scientific image which emerges from the several images proper to the several sciences, we note that although the image is *methodologically* dependent on the world of sophisticated common sense, and in this sense does not stand on its own feet, yet it purports to be a *complete* image, i.e., to define a framework which could be the *whole truth* about that which belongs to the image. Thus although methodologically a development *within* the manifest image, the scientific image presents itself as a *rival* image. From its point of view the manifest image on which it rests is an 'inadequate' but pragmatically useful likeness of a reality which at first finds its adequate (in principle) likeness in the scientific image. I say, 'in principle', because the scientific image is still in the process of coming into being— a point to which I shall return at the conclusion of this chapter.

To all of which, of course, the manifest image or, more accurately, the perennial philosophy which endorses its claims, replies that the scientific image cannot replace the manifest without rejecting its own foundation.

But before attempting to throw some light on the conflicting claims of these two world perspec-

tives, more must be said about the constitution of *the* scientific image from the several scientific images of which it is the supposed integration. There is relatively little difficulty about telescoping *some* of the 'partial' images into one image. Thus, with due precaution, we can unify the biochemical and the physical images; for to do this requires only an appreciation of the sense in which the objects of biochemical discourse can be equated with complex patterns of the objects of theoretical physics. To make this equation, of course, is not to equate the sciences, for as sciences they have different procedures and connect their theoretical entities via different instruments to intersubjectively accessible features of the manifest world. But diversity of this kind is compatible with intrinsic 'identity' of the theoretical entities themselves, that is, with saying that biochemical compounds are 'identical' with patterns of sub-atomic particles. For to make this 'identification' is simply to say that the *two* theoretical structures, each with its own connection to the perceptible world, could be replaced by *one* theoretical framework connected *at two levels of complexity* via different instruments and procedures to the world as perceived.

I distinguished above between the unification of the postulated *entities* of two sciences and the unification of the *sciences*. It is also necessary to distinguish between the unification of the theoretical *entities* of two sciences and the unification of the theoretical *principles* of the two sciences. For while to say that biochemical substances are complexes of physical particles is in an important sense to imply that the laws obeyed by biochemical substances are 'special cases' of the laws obeyed by physical particles, there is a real danger that the sense in which this is so may be misunderstood. Obviously a specific pattern of physical particles cannot obey different laws in biochemistry than it does in physics. It may, however, be the case that the behaviour of very complex patterns of physical particles is related in no simple way to the behaviour of less complex patterns. Thus it may well be the case that the only way in which the laws pertaining to those complex systems of particles which are biochemical compounds could be *discovered* might be through the techniques and procedures of biochemistry, i.e., techniques and procedures appropriate to dealing with biochemical substances.

There is, consequently, an ambiguity in the statement: The laws of biochemistry are 'special cases' of the laws of physics. It may mean: *(a)* biochemistry needs no variables which cannot be defined in terms of the variables of atomic physics; *(b)* the laws relating to certain complex patterns of sub-atomic particles, the counterparts of biochemical compounds, are related in a simple way to laws pertaining to less complex patterns. The former, of course, is the only proposition to which one is committed by the identification of the theoretical objects of the two sciences in the sense described above.

Similar considerations apply, *mutatis mutandis,* to the physiological and biochemical images of man. To weld them into one image would be to show that physiological (particularly neurophysiological) entities can be equated with complex biochemical systems, and, therefore, that in the weaker sense, at least, the theoretical principles which pertain to the former can be interpreted as 'special cases' of principles pertaining to the latter.

More interesting problems arise when we consider the putative place of man as conceived in behaviouristics in 'the' scientific image. In the first place, the term 'behaviouristic psychology' has more than one meaning, and it is important for our purpose to see that in at least one sense of the term, its place is not in the scientific image (in the sense in which I am using the term) but rather in the continuing correlational sophistication of the manifest image. A psychology is behaviouristic in the broad sense, if, although it permits itself the use of the full range of psychological concepts belonging to the manifest framework, it always confirms hypotheses about psychological events in terms of behavioural criteria. It has no anxieties about the concepts of sensation, image, feeling, conscious or unconscious thought, all of which belong to the manifest framework; but requires that the occurrence of a feeling of pain, for example, be asserted only on behavioural grounds. Behaviourism, thus construed, is simply good sense. It is not necessary to redefine the language of mental events in terms of behavioural criteria in order for it to be true that observable behaviour provides evidence for mental events. And, of course, even in the common sense world, even in the manifest image, perceptible behaviour is the only *intersubjective* evidence for mental events.

Clearly 'behaviourism' in this sense does not preclude us from paying attention to what people say about themselves. For *using autobiographical statements as evidence for* what a person is thinking and feeling is different from simply *agreeing with* these statements. It is part of the force of autobiographical statements in ordinary discourse—not unrelated to the way in which children learn to make them—that, other things being equal, if a person says, 'I am in state φ', it is reasonable to believe that he is in state φ; the probability ranging from almost certainty in the case of, 'I have a toothache', to considerably less than certainty in the case of, 'I don't hate my brother'. The discounting of verbal and non-verbal behaviour as evidence is not limited to professional psychologists.

Thus, behaviourism in the first sense is simply a sophistication within the manifest framework which relies on pre-existent evidential connections between publicly observable verbal and non-verbal behaviour on the one hand and mental states and processes on the other, and should, therefore, be considered as belonging to the manifest rather than the scientific image as I have defined in these terms. Behaviourism in a second sense not only restricts its evidential base to publicly observable behaviour, but conceives of its task as that of finding correlations between constructs which it introduces and defines in terms of publicly accessible features of the organism and its environment. The interesting question in this connection is: 'Is there reason to think that a framework of correlation between constructs of this type could constitute a scientific understanding of human behaviour?' The answer to this question depends in part on how it is interpreted, and it is important to see why this is so.

Consider first the case of animal behaviour. Obviously, we know that animals are complex physiological systems and, from the standpoint of a finer-grained approach, biochemical systems. Does this mean that a science of animal behaviour has to be formulated in neurophysiological or biochemical terms? In one sense the answer is 'obviously not'. We bring to our study of animal behaviour a background knowledge of some of the relevant large-scale variables for describing and predicting the behaviour of animals in relation to their environments. The fact that these large-scale variables (the sort of thing that are grouped under such headings as 'stimulus', 'response', 'goal behaviour', 'deprivation', etc.) are such that we can understand the behaviour of the animal in terms of them is something which is not only suggested by our background knowledge, but is, indeed, *explained* by evolutionary theory. But the correlations themselves can be discovered by statistical procedures; and, of course, it is important to establish these correlations. Their discovery and confirmation by the procedures of behaviouristics must, of course, be distinguished from their *explanation* in terms of the postulated entities and processes of neurophysiology. And, indeed, while physiological considerations may *suggest* correlations be tested, the correlations themselves must be establishable independently of physiological consideration, if, and this is a 'definitional' point, they are to belong to a distinguishable science of behaviour.

Thus if we mean by 'earthworm behaviouristics' the establishing of correlations in large-scale terms pertaining to the earthworm and its environment, there may not be much to it, for a correlation does not belong to 'earthworm behaviouristics' unless it is a correlation in these large-scale terms. On the other hand, it is obvious that not every scientific truth about earthworms is a part of earthworm behaviouristics, unless the latter term is so stretched as to be deprived of its distinctive sense. It follows that one cannot explain everything an earthworm does in terms of earthworm behaviouristics *thus defined*. Earthworm behaviouristics works within a background knowledge of 'standard conditions'—conditions in which correlations in terms of earthworm behaviour categories *are* sufficient to explain and predict what earthworms do in so far as it can be described in these categories. This background knowledge is obviously an essential part of the scientific understanding of what earthworms do, though not a part of earthworm behaviouristics, for it is simply the application to earthworms of physics, chemistry, parasitology, medicine, and neurophysiology.

We must also take into consideration the fact that most of the interesting constructs of correlational behaviouristics will be 'iffy' properties of organisms, properties to the effect that *if* at that time a certain stimulus *were* to occur, a certain response *would be* made. Thus, to use an example from an-other field, we are able to correlate the

fact that a current has been run through a helix in which a piece of iron has been placed, with the 'iffy' property of being such that if an iron filing *were* placed near it, the latter *would be* attracted.

Now it may or may not be helpful at a given stage of scientific development, to suppose that 'iffy' properties of organisms are connected with states of a postulated system of entities operating according to certain postulated principles. It is helpful, if the postulated entities are sufficiently specific and can be connected to a sufficient diversity of large-scale behavioural variables to enable the prediction of new correlations. The methodological utility of postulational procedures for the behaviouristics of lower organisms has, perhaps, been exaggerated, primarily because until recently little was known in neurophysiology which was suited to throw much light on correlations at the large-scale level of behaviouristics. In human behaviouristics, however, the situation has been somewhat different from the start, for an important feature of characteristically human behaviour is that any two successive pieces of observable behaviour *essentially* involve complex, very complex, 'iffy' facts about what the person *would have said or done* at each intervening moment *if he had been asked certain questions;* and it happens that our background knowledge makes reasonable the supposition that these 'iffy' facts obtain *because an inner process is going on which is, in important respects, analogous to overt verbal behaviour, and each stage of which would find a natural expression in overt speech.*

Thus it *does* prove helpful in human behaviouristics to postulate an inner sequence of events in order to interpret what could *in principle* be austerely formulated as correlations between behavioural states and properties, including the *very* important and, indeed, *essential* 'iffy' ones. But, and this is an important point, the postulated episodes are not postulated on neurophysiological grounds—at least this was not true until very recently, but because of our background knowledge that something analogous to speech goes on while people are sitting 'like bumps on a log'.

For our present purposes it does not make too much difference whether we say that human behaviouristics *as such* postulates inner speechlike processes, or that whatever their contribution to explanation or discovery, these processes fall by definition outside behaviouristics proper. Whether or not human behaviouristics, as a distinctive science, includes any statements about postulated entities, the correlations it establishes must find their counterparts in the postulational image, as was seen to be true in the case of the correlations established by earthworm behaviouristics. Thus, the scientific explanation of human behaviour must take account of those cases where the correlations characteristic of the organism in 'normal' circumstances break down. And, indeed, no behaviourist would deny that the correlations he seeks and establishes are in some sense the counterparts of neurophysiological and, consequently, biochemical connections, nor that the latter are special cases within a spectrum of *biochemical* connections (pertaining to human organisms), many of which are reflected in observable phenomenon which, *from the standpoint of behaviouristics*, represent breakdowns in explanation. I shall, therefore, provisionally assume that although behaviouristics and neurophysiology remain distinctive sciences, the correlational content of behaviouristics points to a structure of postulated processes and principles which telescope together with those of neurophysiological theory, with all the consequences which this entails. On this assumption, if we trace out these consequences, the scientific image of man turns out to be that of a complex physical system.

The Clash of the Images

How, then, are we to evaluate the conflicting claims of the manifest image and the scientific image thus provisionally interpreted to constitute *the* true and, in principle, *complete* account of man-in-the-world?

What are the alternatives? It will be helpful to examine the impact of the earlier stages of postulational science on philosophy. Some reflections on the Cartesian attempt at a synthesis are in order, for they bring out the major stresses and strains involved in any attempt at a synoptic view. Obviously, at the time of Descartes theoretical science had not yet reached the neurophysiological level, save in the fashion of a clumsy promissory note. The initial challenge of the scientific image was directed at the manifest image of inanimate

nature. It proposed to construe physical things, in a manner already adumbrated by Greek atomism, as systems of imperceptible particles, lacking the perceptible qualities of manifest nature. Three lines of thought seemed to be open: (1) Manifest objects are identical with systems of imperceptible particles in that simple sense in which a forest is identical with a number of trees. (2) Manifest objects are what really exist; systems of imperceptible particles being 'abstract' or 'symbolic' ways of representing them. (3) Manifest objects are 'appearances' to human minds of a reality which is constituted by systems of imperceptible particles. Although (2) merits serious consideration, and has been defended by able philosophers, it is (1) and (3), particularly the latter, which I shall be primarily concerned to explore.

First, some brief remarks about (1). There is nothing immediately paradoxical about the view that an object can be both a perceptible object with perceptible qualities *and* a system of imperceptible objects, none of which has perceptible qualities. Cannot systems have properties which their parts do not have? Now the answer to this question is 'yes', if it is taken in a sense of which a paradigm example would be the fact that a system of pieces of wood can be a ladder, although none of its parts is a ladder. Here one might say that for the system as a whole to be a ladder is for its parts to be of such and such shapes and sizes and to be related to one another in certain ways. Thus there is no trouble about systems having properties which its parts do not have *if these properties are a matter of the parts having such and such qualities and being related in such and such ways.* But the case of a pink ice cube, it would seem clear, cannot be treated in this way. It does not seem plausible to say that for a system of particles to be a pink ice cube is for them to have such and such imperceptible qualities, and to be so related to one another as to make up an approximate cube. *Pink* does not seem to be made up of imperceptible qualities in the way in which being a ladder is made up of being cylindrical (the rungs), rectangular (the frame), wooden, etc. The manifest ice cube presents itself to us as something which is pink through and through, as a pink continuum, all the regions of which, however small, are pink. It presents itself to us as *ultimately homogeneous;* and an ice cube variegated in colour is, though not homogeneous in its specific colour, 'ultimately homoge-neous', in the sense to which I am calling atten-tion, with respect to the generic trait of being coloured.

Now reflection on this example suggests a principle which can be formulated approximately as follows:

> If an object is *in a strict sense* a system of objects, then every property of the object must consist in the fact that its constituents have such and such qualities and stand in such and such relations or, roughly, every property of a system of objects consists of properties of, and relations between, its constituents.

With something like this principle in mind, it was argued that if a physical object is *in a strict sense* a system of imperceptible particles, then it cannot as a whole have the perceptible qualities characteristic of physical objects in the manifest image. It was concluded that manifest physical objects are 'appearances' *to human perceivers* of systems of imperceptible particles which is alter-native (3) above.

This alternative, (3), however, is open to an objection which is ordinarily directed not against the alternative itself, but against an imperceptive formulation of it as the thesis that the perceptible things around us 'really have no colour'. Against *this* formulation the objection has the merit of call-ing attention to the fact that in the manifest frame-work it is as absurd to say that a visible object has no colour, as it is to say of a triangle that it has no shape. However, against the above formulation of alternative (3), namely, that *the very objects them-selves* are appearances to perceivers of systems of imperceptible particles, the objection turns out on examination to have no weight. The objection for which the British 'common sense' philosopher G. E. Moore is directly or indirectly responsible, runs:

> Chairs, tables, etc., as we ordinarily think them to be, can't be 'appearances' of sys-tems of particles lacking perceptible quali-ties, because we *know* that there are chairs, tables, etc., and it is a framework feature of chairs, tables, etc., that they have percepti-ble qualities.

It simply *disappears* once it is recognized that, properly understood, the claim that physical objects do not really have perceptible qualities is not analogous to the claim that something gener-ally believed to be true about a certain kind of thing is actually false. It is not the denial of a belief *within a framework*, but a challenge to the frame-work. It is the claim that although the framework of perceptible objects, the manifest framework of everyday life, is adequate for the everyday purposes of life, it is ultimately inadequate and should not be accepted as an account of what there is *all things considered*. Once we see this, we see that the argument from 'knowledge' cuts no ice, for the reasoning:

> We know that there are chairs, pink ice cubes, etc. (physical objects). Chairs, pink ice cubes are coloured, are perceptible objects with perceptible qualities. Therefore, percep-tible physical objects with perceptible quali-ties exist

operates *within* the framework of the manifest image and cannot *support* it. It fails to provide a point of view outside the manifest image from which the latter can be evaluated.

A more sophisticated argument would be to the effect that we successfully find our way around in life by using the conceptual framework of coloured physical objects in space and time, there-fore, this framework represents things as they re-ally are. This argument has force, but is vulnerable to the reply that the success of living, thinking, and acting in terms of the manifest framework can be accounted for by the framework which pro-poses to replace it, by showing that there are suffi-cient structural similarities between manifest objects and their scientific counterparts to account for this success.[1]

One is reminded of a standard move designed to defend the reality of the manifest image against *logically* rather than *scientifically* motivated con-siderations. Thus it has been objected that the framework of physical objects in space and time is incoherent, involving antinomies or contradic-tions, and that therefore this framework is unreal. The counter to this objection has often been, not a painstaking refutation of the arguments claiming to show that the framework is incoherent, but rather something along the following lines:

> *We know* that this collision occurred at a dif-ferent place and time than that collision.

Therefore, the statement that the first collision occurred at a different place and time from the other collision *is true*.

Therefore, the statement that the two collisions occurred at different times and places *is consistent*.

Therefore, statements about events happening at various times and places are, as such, consistent.

This argument, like the one we have already considered, does not prove what it sets out to prove, because it operates within the framework to be evaluated, and does not provide an external point of view from which to defend it. It makes the tacit assumption that if a framework is inconsistent, its incoherence must be such as to lead to retail and immediate inconsistencies, as though it would force people using it to contradict themselves on every occasion. This is surely false. The framework of space and time could be internally inconsistent, and yet be a successful conceptual tool at the retail level. We have examples of this in mathematical theory, where inconsistencies can be present which do not reveal themselves in routine usage.

I am not, however, concerned to argue that the manifest image is unreal because ultimately incoherent in a narrowly conceived logical sense. Philosophers who have taken this line have either *(a)* left it at that (Hume; scepticism), or *(b)* attempted to locate the source of the inconsistency in features of the framework, and interpreted reality as an inadequately known structure *analogous* to the manifest image, but lacking just those features which are responsible for the inconsistency. In contrast to this, the critique of the manifest image in which we are engaged is based on logical considerations in a broader and more constructive sense, one which compares this image unfavourably with a *more* intelligible account of what there is.

It is familiar fact that those features of the manifest world which play no role in mechanical explanation were relegated by Descartes and other interpreters of the new physics to the minds of the perceiver. Colour, for example, was said to exist only in sensation; its *esse* to be *percipi*. It was argued, in effect, that what scientifically motivated reflection recognizes to be states of the perceiver are conceptualized in ordinary experience as traits of independent physical things, indeed that these supposed independent coloured things are actually conceptual constructions which ape the mechanical systems of the real world.

The same considerations which led philosophers to deny the reality of perceptible things led them to a dualistic theory of man. For if the human body is a system of particles, the body cannot be the subject of thinking and feeling, *unless thinking and feeling are capable of interpretation as complex interactions of physical particles;* unless, that is to say, the manifest framework of man as *one* being, a *person* capable of doing radically different kinds of things can be replaced without loss of descriptive and explanatory power by a postulational image in which he is a complex of physical particles, and all his activities a matter of the particles changing in state and relationship.

Dualism, of course, denied that either sensation or feeling or conceptual thinking could in this sense be construed as complex interactions of physical particles, or man as a complex physical system. They were prepared to say that a *chair* is really a system of imperceptible particles which 'appears' in the manifest framework as a 'coloured solid' (cf., our example of the ice cube), but they were not prepared to say that man himself was a complex physical system which 'appears' to itself to be the sort of thing man is in the manifest image.

Let us consider in more detail the Cartesian attempt to integrate the manifest and the scientific images. Here the interesting thing to note is that Descartes took for granted (in a promissory-noteish kind of way) that the scientific image would include items which would be the counterparts of the sensations, images, and feelings of the manifest framework. These counterparts would be complex states of the brain which, obeying purely physical laws, would resemble and differ from one another in a way which corresponded to the resemblances and differences between the conscious states with which they were correlated. Yet, as is well-known, he denied that there were brain states which were, in the same sense, the cerebral counterparts of conceptual thinking.

Now, if we were to ask Descartes, 'Why can't we say that sensations "really are" complex cerebral processes as, according to you, we *can* say that physical objects "really are" complex systems of imperceptible particles?' he would have a number of things to reply, some of which were a consequence of his conviction that sensation, images, and feelings belong to the same family as believing, choosing, wondering, in short are low-grade examples of conceptual thinking and share its supposed irreducibility to cerebral states. But when the chips are down there would remain the following argument:

> We have pulled perceptible qualities out of the physical environment and put them into sensations. If we now say that all there really is to sensation is a complex interaction of cerebral particles, then we have taken them out of our world picture altogether. We will have made it unintelligible how things could even *appear* to be coloured.

As for conceptual thinking, Descartes not only refused to identify it with neurophysiological process, he did not see this as a live option, because it seemed obvious to him that no complex neurophysiological process could be sufficiently analogous to conceptual thinking to be a serious candidate for being what conceptual thinking 'really is'. It is not as though Descartes granted that there might well be neurophysiological processes which are strikingly analogous to conceptual thinking, but which it would be philosophically incorrect to *identify* with conceptual thinking (as he had identified physical objects of the manifest world with systems of imperceptible particles). He did not take seriously the idea that there *are* such neurophysiological processes.

Even if he had, however, it is clear that he would have rejected this identification on the ground that we had a 'clear and distinct', well-defined idea of what conceptual thinking is before we even suspected that the brain had anything to do with thinking. Roughly: we know what thinking is without conceiving of it as a complex neurophysiological process, therefore, it cannot *be* a complex physiological process.

Now, of course, the same is true of physical objects. We knew what a physical object was long before we knew that there were imperceptible physical particles. By parity of reasoning we should conclude that a physical object cannot *be* a complex of imperceptible particles. Thus, if Descartes had had reason to think that neurophysiological processes strikingly analogous to conceptual think-

ing exist, it would seem that he should *either* have changed his tune with respect to physical objects *or* said that conceptual thinking *really is* a neurophysiological process.

Now in the light of recent developments in neurophysiology, philosophers have come to see that there is no reason to suppose there can't be neurophysiological processes which stand to conceptual thinking as sensory states of the brain stand to conscious sensations. And, indeed, there have not been wanting philosophers (of whom Hobbes was, perhaps, the first) who have argued that the analogy should be viewed philosophically as an *identity*, i.e., that a world picture which includes *both* thoughts *and* the neurophysiological counterparts of thoughts would contain a redundancy; just as a world picture which included *both* the physical objects of the manifest image *and* complex patterns of physical particles would contain a redundancy. But to this proposal the obvious objection occurs, that just as the claim that 'physical objects are complexes of imperceptible particles' left us with the problem of accounting for the status of the perceptible qualities of manifest objects, so the claim that 'thoughts, etc., are complex neuro-physiological processes' leaves us with the problems of accounting for the status of the *introspectable qualities* of thoughts. And it would seem obvious that there is a vicious regress in the claim that these qualities exist in introspective awareness of the thoughts which seem to have them, but not in the thoughts themselves. For, the argument would run, surely introspection is itself a form of thinking. Thus one thought (Peter) would be robbed of its quality only to pay it to another (Paul).

We can, therefore, understand the temptation to say that even if there are cerebral processes which are strikingly analogous to conceptual thinking, they are processes which *run parallel* to conceptual thinking (and cannot be identified with it) as the sensory states of the brain *run parallel* to conscious sensation. And we can, therefore, understand the temptation to say that all these puzzles arise from taking seriously the claim of *any* part of the scientific image to be *what really is,* and to retreat into the position that reality is the world of the manifest image, and that all the postulated entities of the scientific image are 'symbolic tools' which function (something like the distance-measuring devices which are rolled around on maps) to help us find our way around in the world, but do not themselves describe actual objects and processes. On this view, the theoretical counterparts of *all* features of the manifest image would be *equally* unreal, and that philosophical conception of man-of-the-world would be correct which endorsed the manifest image and located the scientific image within it as a conceptual tool used by manifest man in his capacity as scientist.

The Primacy of the Scientific Image: A Prolegomenon

Is this the truth of the matter? Is the manifest image, subject, of course, to continual empirical and categorial refinements, the measure of what there really is? I do not think so. I have already indicated that of the three alternatives we are considering with respect to the comparative claims of the manifest and scientific images, the first, which, like a child, says 'both', is ruled out by a principle which I am not defending in this chapter, although it does stand in need of defence. The second alternative is the one I have just reformulated and rejected. I propose, therefore, to re-examine the case against the third alternative, the primacy of the scientific image. My strategy will be to argue that the difficulty, raised above, which seems to stand in the way of the identification of thought with cerebral processes, arises from the mistake of supposing that in self-awareness conceptual thinking presents itself to us in a qualitative guise. Sensations and images *do,* we shall see, present themselves to us in a qualitative character, a fact which accounts for the fact that they are stumbling blocks in the attempt to accept the scientific image as real. *But* one scarcely needs to point out these days that however intimately conceptual thinking is related to sensations and images, it cannot be equated with them, nor with complexes consisting of them.

It is no accident that when a novelist wishes to represent what is going on in the mind of a person, he does so by 'quoting' the person's thoughts as he might quote what a person says. For thoughts not only are the sort of things that find overt expression in language, we conceive of them as analogous to overt discourse. Thus, *thoughts* in the manifest image are conceived not in terms of their 'quality', but rather as inner 'goings-on' which are analogous to speech, and find their overt expression in speech—though they can go on, of course, in the absence of this overt expression. It is no accident that one learns to think in the very process of learning to speak.

From this point of view one can appreciate the danger of misunderstanding which is contained in the term 'introspection'. For while there is, indeed, an analogy between the direct knowledge we have of our own thoughts and the perceptual knowledge we have of what is going on in the world around us, the analogy holds only in as much as both self-awareness and perceptual observation are basic forms of non-inferential knowledge. They differ, however, in that whereas in perceptual observation we know objects as being of a certain quality, in the direct knowledge we have of what we are thinking (e.g., I am thinking that it is cold outside) what we know non-inferentially is that *something analogous to and properly expressed by the sentence, 'It is cold outside', is going on in me.*

The point is an important one, for if the concept of a thought is the concept of an inner state analogous to speech, this leaves open the possibility that the inner state conceived in terms of this analogy is *in its qualitative character* a neurophysiological process. To draw a parallel: if I begin by thinking of the cause of a disease as a substance (to be called 'germs') which is analogous to a colony of rabbits, in that it is able to reproduce itself in geometrical proportion, but, unlike rabbits, imperceptible and, when present in sufficient number in the human body, able to cause the symptoms of disease, and to cause epidemics by spreading from person to person, there is no logical barrier to a subsequent identification of 'germs' thus conceived with the *bacilli* which microscopic investigation subsequently discovers.

But to point to the analogy between conceptual thinking and overt speech is only part of the story, for of equally decisive importance is the analogy between speech and what sophisticated computers can do, and finally, between computer circuits and conceivable patterns of neurophysiological organization. All of this is more or less speculative, less so now than even a few years ago. What interests the philosopher is the matter of principle; and here the first stage is decisive—the recognition that the concept of a thought is a concept by analogy. Over and above this all we need is to recognize the force of Spinoza's statement: 'No one has thus far determined what the body can do nor no one has yet been taught by experience what the body can do merely by the laws of nature insofar as nature is considered merely as corporeal and extended' (*Ethics,* Part Three, Prop. II [note]).

Another analogy which may be even more helpful is the following: suppose we are watching the telegraphic report of a chess game in a foreign country.

White	*Black*
P—K3	P—QB3

And suppose that we are sophisticated enough to know that chess pieces can be made of all shapes and sizes, that chess boards can be horizontal or vertical, indeed, distorted in all kinds of ways provided that they preserve certain topological features of the familiar board. Then it is clear that while we will think of the players in the foreign country as moving kings, pawns, etc., castling and check-mating, our concepts of the pieces they are moving and the moving of them will be simply the concept of items and changes which play a role analogous to the pieces and moves which take place when *we* play chess. We know that the items must have some intrinsic quality (shape, size, etc.), but we think of these qualities as 'those which make possible a sequence of changes which are structurally similar to the changes which take place on our own chess boards'.

Thus our concept of 'what thoughts are' might, like our concept of what a castling is in chess, be abstract in the sense that it does not concern itself with the *intrinsic* character of thoughts, *save as items which can occur in patterns of relationships which are analogous to the way in which sentences are related to one another and* to the contexts in which they are used.

Now if thoughts are items which are conceived in terms of the roles they play, then there is no barrier *in principle* to the identification of conceptual thinking with neurophysiological process. There would be no 'qualitative' remainder to be accounted for. The identification, curiously enough, would be even more straightforward than the identification of the physical things in the manifest image with complex systems of physical particles. And in this key, if not decisive, respect, the respect in which both images are concerned with conceptual thinking (which is the distinctive trait of man), *the manifest and scientific images could merge without clash in the synoptic view.*

How does the situation stand in respect to sensation and feeling? Any attempt at identification of these items with neurophysiological process runs into a difficulty to which reference has already been made, and which we are now in a position to make more precise. This difficulty accounts for the fact that, with few exceptions, philosophers who have been prepared to identify conceptual thinking with neurophysiological process have *not* been prepared to make a similar identification in the case of sensation.

Before restating the problem let us note that curiously enough, there is more similarity between the two cases than is commonly recognized. For it turns out on reflection that just as conceptual thinking is construed in the manifest image by analogy with overt speech, so sensation is construed by analogy with its external cause, sensations being the states of persons which correspond, in their similarities and differences to the similarities and differences of the objects which, in standard conditions, bring them about. Let us assume that this is so. But if it is so, why not suppose that the inner-states which *as sensations* are conceived by analogy with their standard causes, are *in propria persona* complex neurophysiological episodes in the cerebral cortex? To do so would parallel the conclusion we were prepared to draw in the case of conceptual thinking.

Why do we feel that there would be something extremely odd, even absurd, about such a supposition? The key to the answer lies in noticing an important difference between identifying thoughts with neurophysiological states and identifying sensations with neurophysiological states. Whereas both thoughts and sensations are conceived by analogy with publicly observable items, in the former case the analogy concerns the *role* and hence leaves open the possibility that thoughts are radically different *in their intrinsic character* from the verbal behaviour by analogy with which they are conceived. But in the case of sensations, the analogy concerns the quality itself. Thus a 'blue and triangular sensation' is conceived by analogy with the blue and triangular (facing) surface of a physical object which, when looked at in daylight, is its cause. The crucial issue then is this: can we define, in the framework of neurophysiology, states which are sufficiently analogous in their *intrinsic* character to sensations to make identification plausible?

The answer seems clearly to be 'no'. This is not to say that neurophysiological states cannot be defined (in principle) which have a high degree of analogy to the sensations of the manifest image. That this can be done is an elementary fact in psycho-physics. The trouble is, rather, that the feature which we referred to as 'ultimate homogeneity', and which characterizes the perceptible qualities of things, e.g., their colour, seems to be essentially lacking in the domain of the definable states of nerves and their interactions. Putting it crudely, colour expanses in the manifest world consist of regions which are themselves colour expanses, and these consist in their turn of regions which are colour expanses, and so on; whereas the state of a group of neurons, though it has regions which are also states of groups of neurons, has ultimate regions which are *not* states of groups of neurons but rather states of single neurons. And the same is true if we move to the finer grained level of biochemical process.

Nor do we wish to say that the ultimate homogeneity of the sensation of a red rectangle is a matter of each physical particle in the appropriate region of the cortex *having* a colour; for whatever other difficulties such a view would involve, it doesn't make sense to say of the particles of physical theory that they are coloured. And the principle of reducibility, which we have accepted without argument, makes impossible the view that groups of particles can have properties which are not 'reducible to' the properties and relations of the members of the group.

It is worth noting that we have here a recurrence of the essential features of Eddington's 'two tables' problem—the two tables being, in our terminology, the table of the manifest image and the table of the scientific image. There the problem was to 'fit together' the manifest table with the scientific table. Here the problem is to fit together the manifest sensation with its neurophysiological

counterpart. And, interestingly enough, the problem in both cases is essentially the same: *how to reconcile the ultimate homogeneity of the manifest image with the ultimate non-homogeneity of the system of scientific objects.*

Now we are rejecting the view that the scientific image is a mere 'symbolic tool' for finding our way around in the manifest image; and we are accepting the view that the scientific account of the world is (in principle) the adequate image. Having, therefore, given the perceptible qualities of manifest objects their real locus in sensation, we were confronted with the problem of choosing between dualism or identity with respect to the relation of conscious sensations to their analogues in the visual cortex, and the above argument seems to point clearly in the dualistic direction. The 'ultimate homogeneity' of perceptible qualities, which, among other things, prevented *identifying* the perceptible qualities of physical objects with complex properties of systems of physical particles, stands equally in the way of *identifying*, rather than *correlating*, conscious sensations with the complex neural processes with which they are obviously connected.

But such dualism is an unsatisfactory solution, because *ex hypothesi* sensations are essential to the explanation of how we come to construct the 'appearance' which is the manifest world. They are essential to the explanation of how there even *seem* to be coloured objects. But the scientific image presents itself as a closed system of explanation, and *if the scientific image is interpreted as we have interpreted it up to this point* the explanation will be in terms of the constructs of neurophysiology, which, according to the argument, *do not involve the ultimate homogeneity, the appearance of which in the manifest image is to be explained.*

We are confronted, therefore, by an antinomy, *either, (a)* the neurophysiological image is *incomplete,* and must be supplemented by new objects ('sense fields') which do have ultimate homogeneity, and which somehow make their presence felt in the activity of the visual cortex as a system of physical particles; or, *(b)* the neurophysiological image is complete and the ultimate homogeneity of the sense qualities (and, hence, the sense qualities, themselves) is *mere appearance* in the very radical sense of not existing in the spatiotemporal world at all.

Is the situation irremediable? Does the assumption of the reality of the scientific image lead us to a dualism of particles and sense fields? of matter and 'consciousness'? If so, then, in view of the obviously intimate relation between sensation and conceptual thinking (for example, in perception), we must surely regress and take back the identification or conceptual thinking with neurophysiological process which seemed so plausible a moment ago. We could then argue that although in the absence of other considerations it would be plausible to equate conceptual thinking with neurophysiological process, when the chips are *all* down, we must rather say that although conceptual thinking and neurophysiological process are each analogous to verbal behaviour as a public social phenomenon (the one by virtue of the very way in which the very notion of 'thinking' is formed; the other as a scientifically ascertained matter of fact), they are also *merely* analogous to one another and cannot be identified. If so, the manifest and the scientific conception of *both* sensations *and* conceptual thinking would fit into the synoptic view as parallel processes, a dualism which could only be avoided by interpreting the scientific image *as a whole* as a 'symbolic device' for coping with the world as it presents itself to us in the manifest image.

Is there any alternative? As long as the ultimate constituents of the scientific image are particles forming ever more complex systems of particles, we are inevitably confronted by the above choice. But the scientific image is not yet complete; we have not yet penetrated all the secrets of nature. And if it should turn out that particles instead of being the primitive entities of the scientific image could be treated as singularities in a space-time continuum which could be conceptually 'cut up' without significant loss—*in inorganic contexts, at least*—into interacting particles, then we would not be confronted at the level of neurophysiology with the problem of understanding the relation of *sensory consciousness* (with its ultimate homogeneity) to *systems of particles*. Rather, we would have the alternative of saying that although for many purposes the central nervous system can be construed without loss as a complex system of physical particles, *when it comes to an adequate understanding of the relation of sensory consciousness to* neurophysiological process, we must penetrate to the non-particulate foundation of the particulate image, and recognize that in this non-particulate image the qualities of sense are a dimension of natural process which occurs only in connection with those complex physical processes which, when 'cut up' into particles in terms of those features which are the least common denominators of physical process—present in inorganic as well as organic processes alike—become the complex system of particles which, in the current scientific image, is the central nervous system.

Putting Man into the Scientific Image

Even if the constructive suggestion of the preceding section were capable of being elaborated into an adequate account of the way in which the scientific image could recreate in its own terms the sensations, images, and feelings of the manifest image, the thesis of the primacy of the scientific image would scarcely be off the ground. There would remain the task of showing that categories pertaining to man as a *person* who finds himself confronted by standards (ethical, logical, etc.) which often conflict with his desires and impulses, and to which he may or may not conform, can be reconciled with the idea that man is what science says he is.

At first sight there would seem to be only one way of recapturing the specifically human within the framework of the scientific image. The categories of the person might be reconstructed without loss in terms of the fundamental concepts of the scientific image in a way analogous to that in which the concepts of biochemistry are (in principle) reconstructed in terms of subatomic physics. To this suggestion there is, in the first place, the familiar objection that persons as responsible agents who make genuine choices between genuine alternatives, and who could on many occasions have done what in point of fact they did not do, simply *can't* be construed as physical systems (even broadly interpreted to include sensations and feelings) which evolve in accordance with laws of nature (statistical or non-statistical). Those who make the above move can be expected to reply (drawing on distinctions developed in the first section) that the concepts in terms of which we think of a person's 'character', or the fact that 'he could have done otherwise,' or that 'his actions are predictable' would appear in the reconstruction as extraordinarily complex defined concepts not to be confused with the concepts in terms of which we think of the 'nature' of NaCl, or the fact that 'system X would have failed to be in state S given the same initial conditions' or that 'it is predictable that system X will assume state S given these initial conditions.' And I think that a reply along these lines could be elaborated which would answer *this* objection to the proposed reconstruction of categories pertaining to persons.

But even if the proposed reconstruction could meet what might be called the 'free will' objection, it fails decisively on another count. For it can, I believe, be conclusively shown that such a reconstruction is *in principle* impossible, the impossibility in question being a strictly logical one. (I shall not argue the point explicitly, but the following remarks contain the essential clues.) If so, that would seem to be the end of the matter. Must we not return to a choice between *(a)* a dualism in which men as scientific objects are contrasted with the 'minds' which are the source and principle of their existence as persons; *(b)* abandoning the reality of persons as well as manifest physical objects in favour of the exclusive reality of scientific objects; *(c)* returning once and for all to the thesis of the merely 'calculational' or 'auxiliary' status of theoretical frameworks and to the affirmation of the primacy of the manifest image?

Assuming, in accordance with the drift of the argument of this chapter, that none of these alternatives is satisfactory, is there a way out? I believe there is, and that while a proper exposition and defence would require at least the space of this whole volume, the gist can be stated in short compass. To say that a certain person desired to do A, thought it his duty to do B but was forced to do C, is not to *describe* him as one might describe a scientific specimen. One does, indeed, describe him, but one does something more. And it is this something more which is the irreducible core of the framework of persons.

In what does this something more consist? First, a relatively superficial point which will guide the way. To think of a featherless biped as a person is to think of it as a being with which one is bound up in a network of rights and duties. From this point of view, the irreducibility of the personal is the irreducibility of the 'ought' to the 'is.' But even more basic than this (though ultimately, as we shall see, the two points coincide), is the fact that to think of a featherless biped as a person is to construe its behaviour in terms of actual or potential membership in an embracing group each member of which thinks of itself as a member of the group. Let us call such a group a 'community'. Once the primitive tribe, it is currently (almost) the 'brotherhood' of man, and is potentially the 'republic' of rational beings (cf., Kant's 'Kingdom of Ends'). An individual may belong to many communities, some of which overlap, some of which are arranged like Chinese boxes. The most embracing community to which he belongs consists of those with whom he can enter into meaningful discourse. The scope of the embracing community is the scope of 'we' in its most embracing non-metaphorical use. 'We', in this fundamental sense (in which it is equivalent to the French *'on'* or English *'one'*), is no less basic than the other 'persons' in which verbs are conjugated. Thus, to recognize a featherless biped or dolphin or Martian as a person is to think of oneself and it as belonging to a community.

Now, the fundamental principles of a community, which define what is 'correct' or 'incorrect', 'right' or 'wrong', 'done' or 'not done', are the most general common *intentions* of that community with respect to the behaviour of members of the group. It follows that to recognize a featherless biped or dolphin or Martian as a person requires that one think thoughts of the form, 'We (one) shall do (or abstain from doing) actions of kind A in circumstances of kind C.' To think thoughts of this kind is not to *classify* or *explain,* but to *rehearse an intention.*[2]

Thus the conceptual framework of persons is the framework in which we think of one another as sharing the community intentions which provide the ambience of principles and standards (above all, those which make meaningful discourse and rationality itself possible) within which we live our own individual lives. A person can almost be defined as a being that has intentions. Thus the conceptual framework of persons is not something that needs to be *reconciled with* the scientific image, but rather something to be *joined* to it. Thus, to complete the scientific image we need to enrich it *not* with more ways of saying what is the case, but with the language of community and individual intentions, so that by construing the actions we intend to do and the circumstances in which we intend to do them in scientific terms, we *directly* relate the world as conceived by scientific theory to our purposes, and make it *our* world and no longer an alien appendage to the world in which we do our living. We can, of course, as matters now stand, realize this direct incorporation of the scientific image into our way of life only in imagination. But to do so is, if only in imagination, to transcend the dualism of the manifest and scientific images of man-in-the-world.

Endnotes

[1] It might seem that the manifest framework accounts for the success of the scientific framework, so that the situation is symmetrical. But I believe that a more penetrating account of theoretical explanation than I have been able to sketch in this chapter would show that this claim is illusory.

[2] Community intentions ('One shall . . .') are not just private intentions (I shall . . .') which everybody has. (This is another way of putting the above mentioned irreducibility of 'we.') There is, however, a logical connection between community and private intentions. For one does not really share a community intention unless, however often one may rehearse it, it is reflected, where relevant, in the corresponding private intention.

58. *Ontological Relativity*

WILLARD V. O. QUINE

Rationalists were confident reason could grasp the meaning of ideas and show that some beliefs correspond to reality. Empiricists like Hume doubted one could know anything about the causes of ideas beyond their relations to other components of experience, like sensations; but they too were confident that an analysis of ideas would result in definite knowledge of their meaning and that some knowledge of the relations among them could be a priori. Much twentieth-century philosophy shared this optimism about meaning, though the focus shifted from meaning as a psychological phenomenon to meaning as it is expressed in languages. Philosophers hoped the analysis of language (whether "ordinary language," scientific languages, or ideal languages constructed with the aid of formal logic) would help settle metaphysical disputes. Frequently, however, these analyses embodied controversial metaphysical assumptions, as has been made clear by the work of Willard Van Orman Quine (1908–2000), who was professor of philosophy at Harvard University.

Quine is a logician who approached language from a naturalistic point of view—skeptical about both abstract Platonic entities and private mental entities. In 1951, he published "Two Dogmas of Empiricism," an influential paper that denied there are any analytic truths (beliefs that might be known a priori to be true just by virtue of meaning); and he has continued to argue that there is no a priori knowledge of meaning that solves metaphysical problems. Quine insists theories of meaning should be based on data consisting of overt behavior, but then theories of meaning encounter many of the philosophical problems that other scientific theories face—for example, theories are "underdetermined by data" in the sense that several different theories could be compatible with (or explain) the data. In "Ontological Relativity," Quine shows how his important theses about meaning (indeterminancy of translation and inscrutibility of reference) lead to the conclusion that there is no absolute way to say what a language (or a scientific or formal theory) is about. Thus, ontological claims are always *relative:* "It makes no sense to say what the objects of a theory are, beyond saying how to interpret or reinterpret the theory in another." And there are numerous alternative theories, which, Quine hopes, evolve in accordance with scientific principles.

I.

I listened to Dewey on Art as Experience when I was a graduate student in the spring of 1931. Dewey was then at Harvard as the first William James Lecturer. I am proud now to be at Columbia as the first John Dewey Lecturer.

Philosophically I am bound to Dewey by the naturalism that dominated his last three decades. With Dewey I hold that knowledge, mind, and meaning are part of the same world that they have to do with, and that they are to be studied in the same empirical spirit that animates natural science. There is no place for a prior philosophy.

When a naturalistic philosopher addresses himself to the philosophy of mind, he is apt to talk of language. Meanings are, first and foremost, meanings of language. Language is a social art which we all acquire on the evidence solely of other people's overt behavior under publicly recognizable circumstances. Meanings, therefore, those very models of mental entities, end up as grist for the behaviorist's mill. Dewey was explicit on the point: "Meaning . . . is not a psychic existence; it is primarily a property of behavior."[1]

Once we appreciate the institution of language in these terms, we see that there cannot be, in any useful sense, a private language. This point was stressed by Dewey in the twenties. "Soliloquy," he wrote, "is the product and reflex of converse with others." Further along he expanded the point thus: "Language is specifically a mode of interaction of at least two beings, a speaker and a hearer; it presupposes an organized group to which these creatures belong, and from

whom they have acquired their habits of speech. It is therefore a relationship." Years later, Wittgenstein likewise rejected private language. When Dewey was writing in this naturalistic vein, Wittgenstein still held his copy theory of language.

The copy theory in its various forms stands closer to the main philosophical tradition, and to the attitude of common sense today. Uncritical semantics is the myth of a museum in which the exhibits are meanings and the words are labels. To switch languages is to change the labels. Now the naturalist's primary objection to this view is not an objection to meanings on account of their being mental entities, though that could be objection enough. The primary objection persists even if we take the labeled exhibits not as mental ideas but as Platonic ideas or even as the denoted concrete objects. Semantics is vitiated by a pernicious mental-ism as long as we regard a man's semantics as somehow determinate in his mind beyond what might be implicit in his dispositions to overt behavior. It is the very facts about meaning, not the entities meant, that must be construed in terms of behavior.

There are two parts to knowing a word. One part is being familiar with the sound of it and being able to reproduce it. This part, the phonetic part, is achieved by observing and imitating other people's behavior, and there are no important illusions about the process. The other part, the semantic part, is knowing how to use the word. This part, even in the paradigm case, is more complex than the phonetic part. The word refers, in the paradigm case, to some visible object. The learner has now not only to learn the word phonetically, by hearing it from another speaker; he also has to see the object; and in addition to this, in order to capture the relevance of the object to the word, he has to see that the speaker also sees the object. Dewey summed up the point thus: "The characteristic theory about *B*'s understanding of *A*'s sounds is that he responds to the thing from the standpoint of *A*." Each of us, as he learns his language, is a student of his neighbor's behavior; and conversely, insofar as his tries are approved or corrected, he is a subject of his neighbor's behavioral study.

The semantic part of learning a word is more complex than the phonetic part, therefore, even in simple cases: we have to see what is stimulating the other speaker. In the case of words not directly ascribing observable traits to things, the learning process is increasingly complex and obscure; and obscurity is the breeding place of mentalistic semantics. What the naturalist insists on is that, even in the complex and obscure parts of language learning, the learner has no data to work with but the overt behavior of other speakers.

When with Dewey we turn thus toward a naturalistic view of language and a behavioral view of meaning, what we give up is not just the museum figure of speech. We give up an assurance of determinacy. Seen according to the museum myth, the words and sentences of a language have their determinate meanings. To discover the meanings of the native's words we may have to observe his behavior, but still the meanings of the words are supposed to be determinate in the native's *mind,* his mental museum, even in cases where behavioral criteria are powerless to discover them for us. When on the other hand we recognize with Dewey that "meaning . . . is primarily a property of behavior," we recognize that there are no meanings, nor likenesses nor distinctions of meaning, beyond what are implicit in people's dispositions to overt behavior. For naturalism the question whether two expressions are alike or unlike in meaning has no determinate answer, known or unknown, except insofar as the answer is settled in principle by people's speech dispositions, known or unknown. If by these standards there are indeterminate cases, so much the worse for the terminology of meaning and likeness of meaning.

To see what such indeterminacy would be like, suppose there were an expression in a remote language that could be translated into English equally defensibly in either of two ways, unlike in meaning in English. I am not speaking of ambiguity within the native language. I am supposing that one and the same native use of the expression can

be given either of the English translations, each being accommodated by compensating adjustments in the translation of other words. Suppose both translations, along with these accommodations in each case, accord equally well with all observable behavior on the part of speakers of the remote language and speakers of English. Suppose they accord perfectly not only with behavior actually observed, but with all dispositions to behavior on the part of all the speakers concerned. On these assumptions it would be forever impossible to know of one of these translations that it was the right one, and the other wrong. Still, if the museum myth were true, there would be a right and wrong of the matter; it is just that we would never know, not having access to the museum. See language naturalistically, on the other hand, and you have to see the notion of likeness of meaning in such a case simply as nonsense.

I have been keeping to the hypothetical. Turning now to examples, let me begin with a disappointing one and work up. In the French construction "ne . . . rien" you can translate "rien" into English as "anything" or as "nothing" at will, and then accommodate your choice by translating "ne" as "not" or by construing it as pleonastic. This example is disappointing because you can object that I have merely cut the French units too small. You can believe the mentalistic myth of the meaning museum and still grant that "rien" of itself has no meaning, being no whole label; it is part of "ne . . . rien," which has its meaning as a whole.

I began with this disappointing example because I think its conspicuous trait—its dependence on cutting language into segments too short to carry meanings—is the secret of the more serious cases as well. What makes other cases more serious is that the segments they involve are seriously long: long enough to be predicates and to be true of things and hence, you would think, to carry meanings.

An artificial example which I have used elsewhere[2] depends on the fact that a whole rabbit is present when and only when an undetached part of a rabbit is present; also when and only when a temporal stage of a rabbit is present. If we are wondering whether to translate a native expression "gavagai" as "rabbit" or as "undetached rabbit part" or as "rabbit stage," we can never settle the matter simply by ostension—that is, simply by repeatedly querying the expression "gavagai" for the native's assent or dissent in the presence of assorted stimulations.

Before going on to urge that we cannot settle the matter by non-ostensive means either, let me belabor this ostensive predicament a bit. I am not worrying, as Wittgenstein did, about simple cases of ostension. The color word "sepia," to take one of his examples,[3] can certainly be learned by an ordinary process of conditioning, or induction. One need not even be told that sepia is a color and not a shape or a material or an article. True, barring such hints, many lessons may be needed, so as to eliminate wrong generalizations based on shape, material, etc., rather than color, and so as to eliminate wrong notions as to the intended boundary of an indicated example, and so as to delimit the admissible variations of color itself. Like all conditioning, or induction, the process will depend ultimately also on one's own inborn propensity to find one stimulation qualitatively more akin to a second stimulation than to a third; otherwise there can never be any selective reinforcement and extinction of responses.[4] Still, in principle nothing more is needed in learning "sepia" than in any conditioning or induction.

But the big difference between "rabbit" and "sepia" is that whereas "sepia" is a mass term like "water," "rabbit" is a term of divided reference. As such it cannot be mastered without mastering its principle of individuation: where one rabbit leaves off and another begins. And this cannot be mastered by pure ostension, however persistent.

Such is the quandary over "gavagai": where one gavagai leaves off and another begins. The only difference between rabbits, undetached rabbit parts, and rabbit stages is in their individuation. If you take the total scattered portion of the spatiotemporal world that is made up of rabbits, and that which is made up of undetached rabbit parts, and that which is made up of rabbit stages, you come out with the same scattered portion of the world each of the three times. The only difference is in how you slice it. And how to slice it is what ostension or simple conditioning, however persistently repeated, cannot teach.

Thus consider specifically the problem of deciding between "rabbit" and "undetached rabbit part" as translation of "gavagai." No word of the native language is known, except that we have

settled on some working hypothesis as to what native words or gestures to construe as assent and dissent in response to our pointings and queryings. Now the trouble is that whenever we point to different parts of the rabbit, even sometimes screening the rest of the rabbit, we are pointing also each time to the rabbit. When, conversely, we indicate the whole rabbit with a sweeping gesture, we are still pointing to a multitude of rabbit parts. And note that we do not have even a native analogue of our plural ending to exploit, in asking "gavagai"? It seems clear that no even tentative decision between "rabbit" and "undetached rabbit part" is to be sought at this level.

How would we finally decide? My passing mention of plural endings is part of the answer. Our individuating of terms of divided reference, in English, is bound up with a cluster of interrelated grammatical particles and constructions: plural endings, pronouns, numerals, the "is" of identity, and its adaptations "same" and "other." It is the cluster of interrelated devices in which quantification becomes central when the regimentation of symbolic logic is imposed. If in his language we could ask the native, "Is this *gavagai* the same as that one?" while making appropriate multiple ostensions, then indeed we would be well on our way to deciding between "rabbit," "undetached rabbit part," and "rabbit stage." And of course the linguist does at length reach the point where he can ask what purports to be that question. He develops a system for translating our pluralizations, pronouns, numerals, identity, and related devices contextually into the native idiom. He develops such a system by abstraction and hypothesis. He abstracts native particles and constructions from observed native sentences and tries associating these variously with English particles and constructions. Insofar as the native sentences and the thus associated English ones seem to match up in respect of appropriate occasions of use, the linguist feels confirmed in these hypotheses of translation—what I call *analytical hypotheses*.[5]

But it seems that this method, though laudable in practice and the best we can hope for, does not in principle settle the indeterminacy between "rabbit," "undetached rabbit part," and "rabbit stage." For if one workable overall system of analytical hypotheses provides for translating a given native expression into "is the same as," perhaps another equally workable but systematically different system would translate that native expression rather into something like "belongs with." Then when in the native language we try to ask "Is this *gavagai* the same as that?" we could as well be asking "Does this *gavagai* belong with that?" Insofar, the native's assent is no objective evidence for translating "gavagai" as "rabbit" rather than "undetached rabbit part" or "rabbit stage."

This artificial example shares the structure of the trivial earlier example "ne . . . rien." We were able to translate "rien" as "anything" or as "nothing," thanks to a compensatory adjustment in the handling of "ne." And I suggest that we can translate "gavagai" as "rabbit" or "undetached rabbit part" or "rabbit stage," thanks to compensatory adjustments in the translation of accompanying native locutions. Other adjustments still might accommodate translation of "gavagai" as "rabbithood," or in further ways. I find this plausible because of the broadly structural and contextual character of any considerations that could guide us to native translations of the English cluster of inter-related devices of individuation. There seem bound to be systematically very different choices, all of which do justice to all dispositions to verbal behavior on the part of all concerned.

An actual field linguist would of course be sensible enough to equate "gavagai" with "rabbit," dismissing such perverse alternatives as "undetached rabbit part" and "rabbit stage" out of hand. This sensible choice and others like it would help in turn to determine his subsequent hypotheses as to what native locutions should answer to the English apparatus of individuation, and thus everything would come out all right. The implicit maxim guiding his choice of "rabbit," and similar choices for other native words, is that an enduring and relatively homogeneous object, moving as a whole against a contrasting background, is a likely reference for a short expression. If he were to become conscious of this maxim, he might celebrate it as one of the linguistic universals, or traits of all languages, and he would have no trouble pointing out its psychological plausibility. But he would be wrong; the maxim is his own imposition, toward settling what is objectively indeterminate. It is a very sensible imposition, and I would recommend no other. But I am making a philosophical point.

It is philosophically interesting, moreover, that what is indeterminate in this artificial example is not just meaning, but extension; reference. My remarks on indeterminacy began as a challenge to likeness of meaning. I had us imagining "an expression that could be translated into English equally defensibly in either of two ways, unlike in meaning in English." Certainly likeness of meaning is a dim notion, repeatedly challenged. Of two predicates which are alike in extension, it has never been clear when to say that they are alike in meaning and when not; it is the old matter of featherless bipeds and rational animals, or of equiangular and equilateral triangles. Reference, extension, has been the firm thing; meaning, intension, the infirm. The indeterminacy of translation now confronting us, however, cuts across extension and intension alike. The terms "rabbit," "undetached rabbit part," and "rabbit stage" differ not only in meaning; they are true of different things. Reference itself proves behaviorally inscrutable.

Within the parochial limits of our own language, we can continue as always to find extensional talk clearer than intensional. For the indeterminacy between "rabbit," "rabbit stage," and the rest depended only on a correlative indeterminacy of translation of the English apparatus of individuation—the apparatus of pronouns, pluralization, identity, numerals, and so on. No such indeterminacy obtrudes so long as we think of this apparatus as given and fixed. Given this apparatus, there is no mystery about extension; terms have the same extension when true of the same things. At the level of radical translation, on the other hand, extension itself goes inscrutable.

My example of rabbits and their parts and stages is a contrived example and a perverse one, with which, as I said, the practicing linguist would have no patience. But there are also cases, less bizarre ones, that obtrude in practice. In Japanese there are certain particles, called "classifiers," which may be explained in either of two ways. Commonly they are explained as attaching to numerals, to form compound numerals of distinctive styles. Thus take the numeral for 5. If you attach one classifier to it you get a style of "5" suitable for counting animals; if you attach a different classifier, you get a style of "5" suitable for counting slim things like pencils and chopsticks; and so on. But another way of viewing classifiers is to view them not as constituting part of the numeral, but as constituting part of the term—the term for "chopsticks" or "oxen" or whatever. On this view the classifier does the individuative job that is done in English by "sticks of" as applied to the mass term "wood," or "head of" as applied to the mass term "cattle."

What we have on either view is a Japanese phrase tantamount say to "five oxen," but consisting of three words;[6] the first is in effect the neutral numeral "5," the second is a classifier of the animal kind, and the last corresponds in some fashion to "ox." On one view the neutral numeral and the classifier go together to constitute a declined numeral in the "animal gender," which then modifies "ox" to give, in effect, "five oxen." On the other view the third Japanese word answers not to the individuative term "ox" but to the mass term "cattle"; the classifier applies to this mass term to produce a composite individuative term, in effect "head of cattle"; and the neutral numeral applies directly to all this without benefit of gender, giving "five head of cattle," hence again in effect "five oxen."

If so simple an example is to serve its expository purpose, it needs your connivance. You have to understand "cattle" as a mass term covering only bovines, and "ox" as applying to all bovines. That these usages are not the invariable usages is beside the point. The point is that the Japanese phrase comes out as "five bovines," as desired, when parsed in either of two ways. The one way treats the third Japanese word as an individuative term true of each bovine, and the other way treats that word rather as a mass term covering the unindividuated totality of beef on the hoof. These are two very different ways of treating the third Japanese word; and the three-word phrase as a whole turns out all right in both cases only because of compensatory differences in our account of the second word, the classifier.

This example is reminiscent in a way of our trivial initial example, "ne . . . rien." We were able to represent "lien" as "anything" or as "nothing," by compensatorily taking "ne" as negative or as vacuous. We are able now to represent a Japanese word either as an individuative term for bovines or as a mass term for live beef, by compensatorily taking the classifier as declining the numeral or as individuating the mass term. However, the triviality of the one example does not quite carry over to the other. The early example was dismissed on the ground that we had cut too small; "lien" was too short for significant translation on its own, and "ne . . . rien" was the significant unit. But you cannot dismiss the Japanese example by saying that the third word was too short for significant translation on its own and that only the whole three-word phrase, tantamount to "five oxen," was the significant unit. You cannot take this line unless you are prepared to call a word too short for significant translation even when it is long enough to be a term and carry denotation. For the third Japanese word is, on either approach, a term: on one approach a term of divided reference, and on the other a mass term. If you are indeed prepared thus to call a word too short for significant translation even when it is a denoting term, then in a back-handed way you are granting what I wanted to prove: the inscrutability of reference.

Between the two accounts of Japanese classifiers there is no question of right and wrong. The one account makes for more efficient translation into idiomatic English; the other makes for more of a feeling for the Japanese idiom. Both fit all verbal behavior equally well. All whole sentences, and even component phrases like "five oxen," admit of the same net overall English translations on either account. This much is invariant. But what is philosophically interesting is that the reference or extension of shorter terms can fail to be invariant. Whether that third Japanese word is itself true of each ox, or whether on the other hand it is a mass term which needs to be adjoined to the classifier to make a term which is true of each ox—here is a question that remains undecided by the totality of human dispositions to verbal behavior. It is indeterminate in principle; there is no fact of the matter. Either answer can be accommodated by an account of the classifier. Here again, then, is the inscrutability of reference—illustrated this time by a humdrum point of practical translation.

The inscrutability of reference can be brought closer to home by considering the word "alpha," or again the word "green." In our use of these words and others like them there is a systematic ambiguity. Sometimes we use such words as concrete general terms, as when we say the grass is green, or that some inscription begins with an alpha. Sometimes on the other hand we use them as abstract singular terms, as when we say that green is a color and alpha is a letter. Such ambiguity is encouraged by the fact that there is nothing in ostension to distinguish the two uses. The pointing that would be done in teaching the concrete general term "green," or "alpha," differs none from the pointing that would be done in teaching the abstract singular term "green" or "alpha." Yet the objects referred to by the word are very different under the two uses; under the one use the word is true of many concrete objects, and under the other use it names a single abstract object.

We can of course tell the two uses apart by seeing how the word turns up in sentences: whether it takes an indefinite article, whether it takes a plural ending, whether it stands as singular subject, whether it stands as modifier, as predicate complement, and so on. But these criteria appeal to our special English grammatical constructions and particles, our special English apparatus of individuation, which, I already urged, is itself subject to indeterminacy of translation. So, from the point of view of translation into a remote language, the distinction between a concrete general and an abstract singular term is in the same predicament as the distinction between "rabbit," "rabbit part," and "rabbit stage." Here then is another example of the inscrutability of reference, since the difference between the concrete general and the abstract singular is a difference in the objects referred to.

Incidentally we can concede this much indeterminacy also to the "sepia" example, after all. But this move is not evidently what was worrying Wittgenstein.

The ostensive indistinguishability of the abstract singular from the concrete general turns upon what may be called "deferred ostension," as opposed to direct ostension. First let me define direct ostension. The *ostended point,* as I shall call it, is the point where the line of the pointing finger first meets an opaque surface. What characterizes *direct ostension,* then, is that the term which is being ostensively explained is true of something that contains the ostended point. Even such direct ostension has its uncertainties, of course, and these are familiar. There is the question how wide an environment of the ostended point is meant to be covered by the term that is being ostensively

explained. There is the question how considerably an absent thing or substance might be allowed to differ from what is now ostended, and still be covered by the term that is now being ostensively explained. Both of these questions can in principle be settled as well as need be by induction from multiple ostensions. Also, if the term is a term of divided reference like "apple," there is the question of individuation: the question where one of its objects leaves off and another begins. This can be settled by induction from multiple ostensions of a more elaborate kind, accompanied by expressions like "same apple" and "another," if an equivalent of this English apparatus of individuation has been settled on; otherwise the indeterminacy persists that was illustrated by "rabbit," "undetached rabbit part," and "rabbit stage."

Such, then, is the way of direct ostension. Other ostension I call *deferred.* It occurs when we point at the gauge, and not the gasoline, to show that there is gasoline. Also it occurs when we explain the abstract singular term "green" or "alpha" by pointing at grass or a Greek inscription. Such pointing is direct ostension when used to explain the concrete general term "green" or "alpha," but it is deferred ostension when used to explain the abstract singular terms; for the abstract object which is the color green or the letter alpha does not contain the ostended point, nor any point.

Deferred ostension occurs very naturally when, as in the case of the gasoline gauge, we have a correspondence in mind. Another such example is afforded by the Gödel numbering of expressions.[7] Thus if 7 has been assigned as Gödel number of the letter alpha, a man conscious of the Gödel numbering would not hesitate to say "Seven" on pointing to an inscription of the Greek letter in question. This is, on the face of it, a doubly deferred ostension: one step of deferment carries us from the inscription to the letter as abstract object, and a second step carries us thence to the number.

By appeal to our apparatus of individuation, if it is available, we can distinguish between the concrete general and the abstract singular use of the word "alpha"; this we saw. By appeal again to that apparatus, and in particular to identity, we can evidently settle also whether the word "alpha" in its abstract singular use is being used really to name the letter or whether, perversely, it is being used to name the Gödel number of the letter. At any rate we can distinguish these alternatives if also we have located the speaker's equivalent of the numeral "7" to our satisfaction; for we can ask him whether alpha *is 7*.

These considerations suggest that deferred ostension adds no essential problem to those presented by direct ostension. Once we have settled upon analytical hypotheses of translation covering identity and the other English particles relating to individuation, we can resolve not only the indecision between "rabbit" and "rabbit stage" and the rest, which came of direct ostension, but also any indecision between concrete general and abstract singular, and any indecision between expression and Gödel number, which come of deferred ostension. However, this conclusion is too sanguine. The inscrutability of reference runs deep, and it persists in a subtle form even if we accept identity and the rest of the apparatus of individuation as fixed and settled; even, indeed, if we forsake radical translation and think only of English.

Consider the case of a thoughtful protosyntactician. He has a formalized system of first-order proof theory, or protosyntax, whose universe comprises just expressions, that is, strings of signs of a specified alphabet. Now just what sorts of things, more specifically, are these expressions? They are types, not tokens. So, one might suppose, each of them is the set of all its tokens. That is, each expression is a set of inscriptions which are variously situated in space-time but are classed together by virtue of a certain similarity in shape. The concatenate $x ⌢ y$ of two expressions x and y, in a given order, will be the set of all inscriptions each of which has two parts which are tokens respectively of x and y and follow one upon the other in that order. But $x ⌢ y$ may then be the null set, though x and y are not null; for it may be that inscriptions belonging to x and y happen to turn up head to tail nowhere, in the past, present, or future. This danger increases with the lengths of x and y. But it is easily seen to violate a law of protosyntax which says that $x = z$ whenever $x ⌢ y = z ⌢ y$.

Thus it is that our thoughtful protosyntactician will not construe the things in his universe as sets of inscriptions. He can still take his atoms, the single signs, as sets of inscriptions, for there is no risk of nullity in these cases. And then, instead of taking his strings of signs as sets of inscriptions, he can invoke the mathematical notion of sequence and take them as sequences of signs. A familiar way of taking sequences, in turn, is as a mapping of things on numbers. On this approach an expression or string of signs becomes a finite set of pairs each of which is the pair of a sign and a number.

This account of expressions is more artificial and more complex than one is apt to expect who simply says he is letting his variables range over the strings of such and such signs. Moreover, it is not the inevitable choice; the considerations that motivated it can be met also by alternative constructions. One of these constructions is Gödel numbering itself, and it is temptingly simple. It uses just natural numbers, whereas the foregoing construction used sets of one-letter inscriptions and also natural numbers and sets of pairs of these. How clear is it that at just *this* point we have dropped expressions in favor of numbers? What is clearer is merely that in both constructions we were artificially devising models to satisfy laws that expressions in an unexplicated sense had been meant to satisfy.

So much for expressions. Consider now the arithmetician himself, with his elementary number theory. His universe comprises the natural numbers outright. Is it clearer than the protosyntactician's? What, after all, is a natural number? There are Frege's version, Zermelo's, and von Neumann's, and countless further alternatives, all mutually incompatible and equally correct. What we are doing in any one of these explications of natural number is to devise set-theoretic models to satisfy laws which the natural numbers in an unexplicated sense had been meant to satisfy. The case is quite like that of protosyntax.

It will perhaps be felt that any set-theoretic explication of natural number is at best a case of *obscurum per obscurius;* that all explications must assume something, and the natural numbers themselves are an admirable assumption to start with. I must agree that a construction of sets and set theory from natural numbers and arithmetic would be far more desirable than the familiar opposite. On the other hand our impression of the clarity even of the notion of natural number itself has suffered somewhat from Gödel's proof of the impossibility of a complete proof procedure for elementary number theory, or, for that matter, from Skolem's and Henkin's observations that all laws of natural numbers admit nonstandard models.[8]

We are finding no clear difference between *specifying* a universe of discourse—the range of the variables of quantification—and *reducing* that universe to some other. We saw no significant difference between clarifying the notion of expression and supplanting it by that of number. And now to say more particularly what numbers themselves are is in no evident way different from just dropping numbers and assigning to arithmetic one or another new model, say in set theory.

Expressions are known only by their laws, the laws of concatenation theory, so that any constructs obeying those laws—Gödel numbers, for instance—are *ipso facto* eligible as explications of expression. Numbers in turn are known only by their laws, the laws of arithmetic, so that any constructs obeying those laws—certain sets, for instance—are eligible in turn as explications of number. Sets in turn are known only by their laws, the laws of set theory.

[Bertrand] Russell pressed a contrary thesis, long ago. Writing of numbers, he argued that for an understanding of number the laws of arithmetic are not enough; we must know the applications, we must understand numerical discourse embedded in discourse of other matters. In applying number, the key notion, he urged, is *Anzahl:* there are *n* so-and-sos. However, Russell can be answered. First take, specifically, *Anzahl*. We can define "there are *n* so-and-sos" without ever deciding what numbers are, apart from their fulfillment of arithmetic. That there are *n* so-and-sos can be explained simply as meaning that the so-and-sos are in one-to-one correspondence with the numbers up to *n*.[9]

Russell's more general point about application can be answered too. Always, if the structure is there, the applications will fall into place. As paradigm it is perhaps sufficient to recall again this reflection on expressions and Gödel numbers: that even the pointing out of an inscription is no final evidence that our talk is of expressions and not of Gödel numbers. We can always plead deferred ostension.

It is in this sense true to say, as mathematicians often do, that arithmetic is all there is to number. But it would be a confusion to express this point by saying, as is sometimes said, that numbers are any things fulfilling arithmetic. This formulation is wrong because distinct domains of objects yield distinct models of arithmetic. Any progression can be made to serve; and to identify all progressions with one another, e.g., to identify the progression of odd numbers with the progression of evens, would contradict arithmetic after all.

So, though Russell was wrong in suggesting that numbers need more than their arithmetical properties, he was right in objecting to the definition of numbers as any things fulfilling arithmetic. The subtle point is that any progression will serve as a version of number so long and only so long as we stick to one and the same progression. Arithmetic is, in this sense, all there is to number: there is no saying absolutely what the numbers are; there is only arithmetic.[10]

II.

I first urged the inscrutability of reference with the help of examples like the one about rabbits and rabbit parts. These used direct ostension, and the inscrutability of reference hinged on the indeterminacy of translation of identity and other individuative apparatus. The setting of these examples, accordingly, was radical translation: translation from a remote language on behavioral evidence, unaided by prior dictionaries. Moving then to deferred ostension and abstract objects, we found a certain dimness of reference pervading the home language itself.

Now it should be noted that even for the earlier examples the resort to a remote language was not really essential. On deeper reflection, radical translation begins at home. Must we equate our neighbor's English words with the same strings of phonemes in our own mouths? Certainly not; for sometimes we do not thus equate them. Sometimes we find it to be in the interests of communication to recognize that our neighbor's use of some word, such as "cool" or "square" or "hopefully," differs from ours, and so we translate that word of his into a different string of phonemes in our idiolect. Our usual domestic rule of translation is indeed the homophonic one, which simply carries each string of phonemes into itself; but still we are always prepared to temper homophony with what Neil Wilson has called the "principle of charity." We will construe a neighbor's word heterophonically now and again if thereby we see our way to making his message less absurd.

The homophonic rule is a handy one on the whole. That it works so well is no accident, since imitation and feedback are what propagate a language. We acquired a great fund of basic words and phrases in this way, imitating our elders and encouraged by our elders amid external circumstances to which the phrases suitably apply. Homophonic translation is implicit in this social method of learning. Departure from homophonic translation in this quarter would only hinder communication. Then there are the relatively rare instances of opposite kind, due to divergence in dialect or confusion in an individual, where homophonic translation incurs negative feedback. But what tends to escape notice is that there is also a vast mid-region where the homophonic method is indifferent. Here, gratuitously, we can systematically reconstrue our neighbor's apparent references to rabbits as really references to rabbit stages, and his apparent references to formulas as really references to Gödel numbers and vice versa. We can reconcile all this with our neighbor's verbal behavior, by cunningly readjusting our translations of his various connecting predicates so as to compensate for the switch of ontology. In short, we can reproduce the inscrutability of reference at home. It is of no avail to check on this fanciful version of our neighbor's meanings by asking him, say, whether he really means at a certain point to refer to formulas or to their Gödel numbers; for our question and his answer—"By all means, the numbers"—have lost their title to homophonic translation. The problem at home differs none from radical translation ordinarily so called except in the willfulness of this suspension of homophonic translation.

I have urged in defense of the behavioral philosophy of language, Dewey's, that the inscrutability of reference is not the inscrutability of a fact; there is no fact of the matter. But if there is really no fact of the matter, then the inscrutability of reference can be brought even closer to home than the neighbor's case; we can apply it to ourselves. If it is to make sense to say even of oneself that one is referring to rabbits and formulas and not to rabbit stages and Gödel numbers, then it should make sense equally to say it of someone else. After all, as Dewey stressed, there is no private language.

We seem to be maneuvering ourselves into the absurd position that there is no difference on any terms, interlinguistic or intralinguistic, objective or subjective, between referring to rabbits and referring to rabbit parts or stages; or between referring to formulas and referring to their Gödel numbers. Surely this is absurd, for it would imply that there is no difference between the rabbit and each of its parts or stages, and no difference between a formula and its Gödel number. Reference would seem now to become nonsense not just in radical translation but at home.

Toward resolving this quandary, begin by picturing us at home in our language, with all its predicates and auxiliary devices. This vocabulary includes "rabbit," "rabbit part," "rabbit stage," "formula," "number," "ox," "cattle"; also the two-place predicates of identity and difference, and other logical particles. In these terms we can say in so many words that this is a formula and that a number, this a rabbit and that a rabbit part, this and that the same rabbit, and this and that different parts, *in just those words*. This network of terms and predicates and auxiliary devices is, in relativity jargon, our frame of reference, or coordinate system. Relative to *it* we can and do talk meaningfully and distinctively of rabbits and parts, numbers and formulas. Next, as in recent paragraphs, we contemplate alternative denotations for our familiar terms. We begin to appreciate that a grand and ingenious permutation of these denotations, along with compensatory adjustments in the interpretations of the auxiliary particles, might still accommodate all existing speech dispositions. This was the inscrutability of reference, applied to ourselves; and it made nonsense of reference. Fair enough; reference *is* nonsense except relative to a coordinate system. In this principle of relativity lies the resolution of our quandary.

It is meaningless to ask whether, in general, our terms "rabbit," "rabbit part," "number," etc., really refer respectively to rabbits, rabbit parts, numbers, etc., rather than to some ingeniously permuted denotations. It is meaningless to ask this absolutely; we can meaningfully ask it only relative to some background language. When we ask, "Does 'rabbit' really refer to rabbits?" someone can counter with the question: "Refer to rabbits in what sense of 'rabbits'?" thus launching a regress; and we need the background language to regress into. The background language gives the query sense, if only relative sense; sense relative in turn to it, this background language. Querying reference in any more absolute way would be like asking for absolute position, or absolute velocity, rather than position or velocity relative to a given frame of reference. Also it is very much like asking whether our neighbor may not systematically see everything upside down, or in complementary color, forever undetectably.

We need a background language, I said, to regress into. Are we involved now in an infinite regress? If questions of reference of the sort we are considering make sense only relative to a background language, then evidently questions of reference for the background language make sense in turn only relative to a further background language. In these terms the situation sounds desperate, but in fact it is little different from questions of position and velocity. When we are given position and velocity relative to a given coordinate system, we can always ask in turn about the placing of origin and orientation of axes of that system of coordinates; and there is no end to the succession of further coordinate systems that could be adduced in answering the successive questions thus generated.

In practice of course we end the regress of coordinate systems by something like pointing. And in practice we end the regress of background languages, in discussions of reference, by acquiescing in our mother tongue and taking its words at face value.

Very well; in the case of position and velocity, in practice, pointing breaks the regress. But what of position and velocity apart from practice? what of the regress then? The answer, of course, is the relational doctrine of space; there is no absolute position or velocity; there are just the relations of coordinate systems to one another, and ultimately of things to one another. And I think that the parallel question regarding denotation calls for a parallel answer, a relational theory of what the objects of theories are. What makes sense is to say not what the objects of a theory are, absolutely speaking, but how one theory of objects is interpretable or reinterpretable in another.

The point is not that bare matter is inscrutable: that things are indistinguishable except by their properties. That point does not

need making. The present point is reflected better in the riddle about seeing things upside down, or in complementary colors; for it is that things can be inscrutably switched even while carrying their properties with them. Rabbits differ from rabbit parts and rabbit stages not just as bare matter, after all, but in respect of properties; and formulas differ from numbers in respect of properties. What our present reflections are leading us to appreciate is that the riddle about seeing things upside down, or in complementary colors, should be taken seriously and its moral applied widely. The relativistic thesis to which we have come is this, to repeat: it makes no sense to say what the objects of a theory are, beyond saying how to interpret or reinterpret that theory in another. Suppose we are working within a theory and thus treating of its objects. We do so by using the variables of the theory, whose values those objects are, though there be no ultimate sense in which that universe can have been specified. In the language of the theory there are predicates by which to distinguish portions of this universe from other portions, and these predicates differ from one another purely in the roles they play in the laws of the theory. Within this background theory we can show how some subordinate theory, whose universe is some portion of the background universe, can by a reinterpretation be reduced to another subordinate theory whose universe is some lesser portion. Such talk of subordinate theories and their ontologies *is* meaningful, but only relative to the background theory with its own primitively adopted and ultimately inscrutable ontology.

To talk thus of theories raises a problem of formulation. A theory, it will be said, is a set of fully interpreted sentences. (More particularly, it is a deductively closed set: it includes all its own logical consequences, insofar as they are couched in the same notation.) But if the sentences of a theory are fully interpreted, then in particular the range of values of their variables is settled. How then can there be no sense in saying what the objects of a theory are?

My answer is simply that we cannot require theories to be fully interpreted, except in a relative sense, if anything is to count as a theory. In specifying a theory we must indeed fully specify, in our own words, what sentences are to comprise the theory, and what things are to be taken as values of the variables, and what things are to be taken as satisfying the predicate letters; insofar we do fully interpret the theory, *relative* to our own words and relative to our overall home theory which lies behind them. But this fixes the objects of the described theory only relative to those of the home theory; and these can, at will, be questioned in turn.

One is tempted to conclude simply that meaninglessness sets in when we try to pronounce on everything in our universe; that universal predication takes on sense only when furnished with the background of a wider universe, where the predication is no longer universal. And this is even a familiar doctrine, the doctrine that no proper predicate is true of everything. We have all heard it claimed that a predicate is meaningful only by contrast with what it excludes, and hence that being true of everything would make a predicate meaningless. But surely this doctrine is wrong. Surely self-identity, for instance, is not to be rejected as meaningless. For that matter, any statement of fact at all, however brutally meaningful, can be put artificially into a form in which it pronounces on everything. To say merely of Jones that he sings, for instance, is to say of everything that it is other than Jones or sings. We had better beware of repudiating universal predication, lest we be tricked into repudiating everything there is to say.

Carnap took an intermediate line in his doctrine of universal words, or *Allwörter*, in *The Logical Syntax of Language*. He did treat the predicating of universal words as "quasi-syntactical"—as a predication only by courtesy, and without empirical content. But universal words were for him not just any universally true predicates, like "is other than Jones or sings." They were a special breed of universally true predicates, ones that are universally true by the sheer meanings of their words and no thanks to nature. In his later writing this doctrine of universal words takes the form of a distinction between "internal" questions, in which a theory comes to grips with facts about the world, and "external" questions, in which people come to grips with the relative merits of theories.

Should we look to these distinctions of Carnap's for light on ontological relativity? When we found there was no absolute sense in saying what a theory is about, were we sensing the infactuality of what Carnap calls "external questions"? When

we found that saying what a theory is about did make sense against a background theory, were we sensing the factuality of internal questions of the background theory? I see no hope of illumination in this quarter. Carnap's universal words were not just any universally true predicates, but, as I said, a special breed; and what distinguishes this breed is not clear. What I said distinguished them was that they were universally true by sheer meanings and not by nature; but this is a very questionable distinction. Talking of "internal" and "external" is no better.

Ontological relativity is not to be clarified by any distinction between kinds of universal predication—unfactual and factual, external and internal. It is not a question of universal predication. When questions regarding the ontology of a theory are meaningless absolutely, and become meaningful relative to a background theory, this is not in general because the background theory has a wider universe. One is tempted, as I said a little while back, to suppose that it is; but one is then wrong.

What makes ontological questions meaningless when taken absolutely is not universality but circularity. A question of the form "What is an *F*?" can be answered only by recourse to a further term: "An *F* is a *G*." The answer makes only relative sense: sense relative to the uncritical acceptance of "*G*."

We may picture the vocabulary of a theory as comprising logical signs such as quantifiers and the signs for the truth functions and identity, and in addition descriptive or nonlogical signs, which, typically, are singular terms, or names, and general terms, or predicates. Suppose next that in the statements which comprise the theory, that is, are true according to the theory, we abstract from the meanings of the nonlogical vocabulary and from the range of the variables. We are left with the logical form of the theory, or, as I shall say, the *theory form*. Now we may interpret this theory form anew by picking a new universe for its variables of quantification to range over, and assigning objects from this universe to the names, and choosing sub-sets of this universe as extensions of the one-place predicates, and so on. Each such interpretation of the theory form is called a model of it, if it makes it come out true. Which of these models is meant in a given actual theory cannot, of course, be guessed from the theory form. The intended references of the names and predicates have to be learned rather by ostension, or else by paraphrase in some antecedently familiar vocabulary. But the first of these two ways has proved inconclusive, since, even apart from indeterminacies of translation affecting identity and other logical vocabulary, there is the problem of deferred ostension. Paraphrase in some antecedently familiar vocabulary, then, is our only recourse; and such is ontological relativity. To question the reference of all the terms of our all-inclusive theory becomes meaningless, simply for want of further terms relative to which to ask or answer the question.

It is thus meaningless within the theory to say which of the various possible models of our theory form is our real or intended model. Yet even here we can make sense still of there being many models. For we might be able to show that for each of the models, however unspecifiable, there is bound to be another which is a permutation or perhaps a diminution of the first.

Suppose for example that our theory is purely numerical. Its objects are just the natural numbers. There is no sense in saying, from within that theory, just which of the various models of number theory is in force. But we can observe even from within the theory that, whatever 0, 1, 2, 3, etc. may be, the theory would still hold true if the 17 of this series were moved into the role of 0, and the 18 moved into the role of 1, and so on.

Ontology is indeed doubly relative. Specifying the universe of a theory makes sense only relative to some background theory, and only relative to some choice of a manual of translation of the one theory into the other. Commonly of course the background theory will simply be a containing theory, and in this case no question of a manual of translation arises. But this is after all just a degenerate case of translation still—the case where the rule of translation is the homophonic one.

We cannot know what something is without knowing how it is marked off from other things. Identity is thus of a piece with ontology. Accordingly it is involved in the same relativity, as may be readily illustrated. Imagine a fragment of economic theory. Suppose its universe comprises persons, but its predicates are incapable of distinguishing between persons whose incomes are equal. The interpersonal relation of equality of income enjoys, within the theory, the substitutiv-

ity property of the identity relation itself; the two relations are indistinguishable. It is only relative to a background theory, in which more can be said of personal identity than equality of income, that we are able even to appreciate the above account of the fragment of economic theory, hinging as the account does on a contrast between persons and incomes.

A usual occasion for ontological talk is reduction, where it is shown how the universe of some theory can by a reinterpretation be dispensed with in favor of some other universe, perhaps a proper part of the first. I have treated elsewhere[12] of the reduction of one ontology to another with help of a *proxy function:* a function mapping the one universe into part or all of the other. For instance, the function "Gödel number of" is a proxy function. The universe of elementary proof theory or protosyntax, which consists of expressions or strings of signs, is mapped by this function into the universe of elementary number theory, which consists of numbers.

The proxy function used in reducing one ontology to another need not, like Gödel numbering, be one-to-one. We might, for instance, be confronted with a theory treating of both expressions and ratios. We would cheerfully reduce all this to the universe of natural numbers, by invoking a proxy function which enumerates the expressions in the Gödel way, and enumerates the ratios by the classical method of short diagonals. This proxy function is not one-to-one, since it assigns the same natural number both to an expression and to a ratio. We would tolerate the resulting artificial convergence between expressions and ratios, simply because the original theory made no capital of the distinction between them; they were so invariably and extravagantly unlike that the identity question did not arise. Formally speaking, the original theory used a two-sorted logic.

For another kind of case where we would not require the proxy function to be one-to-one, consider again the fragment of economic theory lately noted. We would happily reduce its ontology of persons to a less numerous one of incomes. The proxy function would assign to each person his income. It is not one-to-one; distinct persons give way to identical incomes. The reason such a reduction is acceptable is that it merges the images of only such individuals as never had been distinguishable by the predicates of the original theory. Nothing in the old theory is contravened by the new identities.

If on the other hand the theory that we are concerned to reduce or reinterpret is straight protosyntax, or a straight arithmetic of ratios or of real numbers, then a one-to-one proxy function is mandatory. This is because any two elements of such a theory are distinguishable in terms of the theory. This is true even for the real numbers, even though not every real number is uniquely specifiable; any two real numbers x and y are still distinguishable, in that $x < y$ or $y < x$ and never $x < x$. A proxy function that did not preserve the distinctness of the elements of such a theory would fail of its purpose of reinterpretation.

One ontology is always reducible to another when we are given a proxy function f that is one-to-one. The essential reasoning is as follows. Where P is any predicate of the old system, its work can be done in the new system by a new predicate which we interpret as true of just the correlates fx of the old objects x that P was true of. Thus suppose we take fx as the Gödel number of x, and as our old system we take a syntactical system in which one of the predicates is "is a segment of." The corresponding predicate of the new or numerical system, then, would be one which amounts, so far as its extension is concerned, to the words "is the Gödel number of a segment of that whose Gödel number is." The numerical predicate would not be given this devious form, of course, but would be rendered as an appropriate purely arithmetical condition.

Our dependence upon a background theory becomes especially evident when we reduce our universe U to another V by appeal to a proxy function. For it is only in a theory with an inclusive universe, embracing U and V, that we can make sense of the proxy function. The function maps U into V and hence needs all the old objects of U as well as their new proxies in V.

The proxy function need not exist as an object in the universe even of the background theory. It may do its work merely as what I have called a "virtual class,"[13] and Gödel has called a "notion."[14] That is to say, all that is required toward a function is an open sentence with two free variables, provided that it is fulfilled by exactly one value of the first variable for each object of the

old universe as value of the second variable. But the point is that it is only in the background theory, with its inclusive universe, that we can hope to write such a sentence and have the right values at our disposal for its variables.

If the new objects happen to be among the old, so that V is a subclass of U, then the old theory with universe U can itself sometimes qualify as the background theory in which to describe its own ontological reduction. But we cannot do better than that; we cannot declare our new ontological economies without having recourse to the uneconomical old ontology.

This sounds, perhaps, like a predicament: as if no ontological economy is justifiable unless it is a false economy and the repudiated objects really exist after all. But actually this is wrong; there is no more cause for worry here than there is in *reductio ad absurdum*, where we assume a falsehood that we are out to disprove. If what we want to show is that the universe U is excessive and that only a part exists, or need exist, then we are quite within our rights to assume all of U for the space of the argument. We show thereby that if all of U were needed then not all of U would be needed; and so our ontological reduction is sealed by *reductio ad absurdum*.

Toward further appreciating the bearing of ontological relativity on programs of ontological reduction, it is worth while to reexamine the philosophical bearing of the Löwenheim-Skolem theorem. I shall use the strong early form of the theorem,[15] which depends on the axiom of choice. It says that if a theory is true and has an indenumerable universe, then all but a denumerable part of that universe is dead wood, in the sense that it can be dropped from the range of the variables without falsifying any sentences.

On the face of it, this theorem declares a reduction of all acceptable theories to denumerable ontologies. Moreover, a denumerable ontology is reducible in turn to an ontology specifically of natural numbers, simply by taking the enumeration as the proxy function, if the enumeration is explicitly at hand. And even if it is not at hand, it exists; thus we can still think of all our objects as natural numbers, and merely reconcile ourselves to not always knowing, numerically, which number an otherwise given object is. May we not thus settle for an all-purpose Pythagorean ontology out-right?

Suppose, afterward, someone were to offer us what would formerly have qualified as an ontological reduction—a way of dispensing in future theory with all things of a certain sort *S*, but still leaving an infinite universe. Now in the new Pythagorean setting his discovery would still retain its essential content, though relinquishing the form of an ontological reduction; it would take the form merely of a move whereby some numerically unspecified numbers were divested of some property of numbers that corresponded to *S*.

Blanket Pythagoreanism on these terms is unattractive, for it merely offers new and obscurer accounts of old moves and old problems. On this score again, then, the relativistic proposition seems reasonable: that there is no absolute sense in speaking of the ontology of a theory. It very creditably brands this Pythagoreanism itself as meaningless. For there is no absolute sense in saying that all the objects of a theory are numbers, or that they are sets, or bodies, or something else; this makes no sense unless relative to some background theory. The relevant predicates—"number," "set," "body," or whatever—would be distinguished from *one another* in the background theory by the roles they play in the laws of that theory.

Elsewhere [*The Way of Paradox*] I urged in answer to such Pythagoreanism that we have no ontological reduction in an interesting sense unless we can specify a proxy function. Now where does the strong Löwenheim-Skolem theorem leave us in this regard? If the background theory assumes the axiom of choice and even provides a notation for a general selector operator, can we in these terms perhaps specify an actual proxy function embodying the Löwenheim-Skolem argument?

The theorem is that all but a denumerable part of an ontology can be dropped and not be missed. One could imagine that the proof proceeds by partitioning the universe into denumerably many equivalence classes of indiscriminable objects, such that all but one member of each equivalence class can be dropped as superfluous; and one would then guess that where the axiom of choice enters the proof is in picking a survivor from each equivalence class. If this were so, then with help of Hilbert's selector notation we could indeed express a proxy function. But in fact the

Löwenheim-Skolem proof has another structure. I see in the proof even of the strong Löwenheim-Skolem theorem no reason to suppose that a proxy function can be formulated anywhere that will map an indenumerable ontology, say the real numbers, into a denumerable one.

On the face of it, of course, such a proxy function is out of the question. It would have to be one-to-one, as we saw, to provide distinct images of distinct real numbers; and a one-to-one mapping of an indenumerable domain into a denumerable one is a contradiction. In particular it is easy to show in the Zermelo-Fraenkel system of set theory that such a function would neither exist nor admit even of formulation as a virtual class in the notation of the system.

The discussion of the ontology of a theory can make variously stringent demands upon the background theory in which the discussion is couched. The stringency of these demands varies with what is being said about the ontology of the object theory. We are now in a position to distinguish three such grades of stringency.

The least stringent demand is made when, with no view to reduction, we merely explain what things a theory is about, or what things its terms denote. This amounts to showing how to translate part or all of the object theory into the background theory. It is a matter really of showing how we *propose*, with some arbitrariness, to relate terms of the object theory to terms of the background theory; for we have the inscrutability of reference to allow for. But there is here no requirement that the background theory have a wider universe or a stronger vocabulary than the object theory. The theories could even be identical; this is the case when some terms are clarified by definition on the basis of other terms of the same language.

A more stringent demand was observed in the case where a proxy function is used to reduce an ontology. In this case the background theory needed the unreduced universe. But we saw, by considerations akin to *reductio ad absurdum*, that there was little here to regret.

The third grade of stringency has emerged now in the kind of ontological reduction hinted at by the Löwenheim-Skolem theorem. If a theory has by its own account an indenumerable universe, then even by taking that whole unreduced theory as background theory we cannot hope to produce a proxy function that would be adequate to reducing the ontology to a denumerable one. To find such a proxy function, even just a virtual one, we would need a background theory essentially stronger than the theory we were trying to reduce. This demand cannot, like the second grade of stringency above, be accepted in the spirit of *reductio ad absurdum*. It is a demand that simply discourages any general argument for Pythagoreanism from the Löwenheim-Skolem theorem.

A place where we see a more trivial side of ontological relativity is in the case of a finite universe of named objects. Here there is no occasion for quantification, except as an inessential abbreviation; for we can expand quantifications into finite conjunctions and alternations. Variables thus disappear, and with them the question of a universe of values of variables. And the very distinction between names and other signs lapses in turn, since the mark of a name is its admissibility in positions of variables. Ontology thus is emphatically meaningless for a finite theory of named objects, considered in and of itself. Yet we are now talking meaningfully of such finite ontologies. We are able to do so precisely because we are talking, however vaguely and implicitly, within a broader containing theory. What the objects of the finite theory are, makes sense only as a statement of the background theory in its own referential idiom. The answer to the question depends on the background theory, the finite foreground theory, and, of course, the particular manner in which we choose to translate or embed the one in the other.

Ontology is internally indifferent also, I think, to any theory that is complete and decidable. Where we can always settle truth values mechanically, there is no evident internal reason for interest in the theory of quantifiers nor, therefore, in values of variables. These matters take on significance only as we think of the decidable theory as embedded in a richer background theory in which the variables and their values are serious business.

Ontology may also be said to be internally indifferent even to a theory that is not decidable and does not have a finite universe, if it happens still that each of the infinitely numerous objects of the theory has a name. We can no longer expand quantifications into conjunctions and alternations, barring infinitely long expressions. We can, how-

ever, revise our semantical account of the truth conditions of quantification, in such a way as to turn our backs on questions of reference. We can explain universal quantifications as true when true under all substitutions; and correspondingly for existential. Such is the course that has been favored by Leśniewski and by Ruth Marcus.[16] Its nonreferential orientation is seen in the fact that it makes no essential use of namehood. That is, additional quantifications could be explained whose variables are placeholders for words of any syntactical category. *Substitutional* quantification, as I call it, thus brings no way of distinguishing names from other vocabulary, nor any way of distinguishing between genuinely referential or value-taking variables and other place-holders. Ontology is thus meaningless for a theory whose only quantification is substitutionally construed; meaningless, that is, insofar as the theory is considered in and of itself. The question of its ontology makes sense only relative to some translation of the theory into a background theory in which we use referential quantification. The answer depends on both theories and, again, on the chosen way of translating the one into the other.

A final touch of relativity can in some cases cap this, when we try to distinguish between substitutional and referential quantification. Suppose again a theory with an infinite lot of names, and suppose that, by Gödel numbering or otherwise, we are treating of the theory's notations and proofs within the terms of the theory. If we succeed in showing that every result of substituting a name for the variable in a certain open sentence is true in the theory, but at the same time we disprove the universal quantification of the sentence,[17] then certainly we have shown that the universe of the theory contained some nameless objects. This is a case where an absolute decision can be reached in favor of referential quantification and against substitutional quantification, without ever retreating to a background theory.

But consider now the opposite situation, where there is no such open sentence. Imagine on the contrary that, whenever an open sentence is such that each result of substituting a name in it can be proved, its universal quantification can be proved in the theory too. Under these circumstances we can construe the universe as devoid of nameless objects and hence reconstrue the quantifications as substitutional, but we need not. We could still construe the universe as containing nameless objects. It could just happen that the nameless ones are *inseparable* from the named ones, in this sense: it could happen that all properties of nameless objects that we can express in the notation of the theory are shared by named objects.

We could construe the universe of the theory as containing, e.g., all real numbers. Some of them are nameless, since the real numbers are indenumerable while the names are denumerable. But it could still happen that the nameless reals are inseparable from the named reals. This would leave us unable within the theory to prove a distinction. between referential and substitutional quantification.[18] Every expressible quantification that is true when referentially construed remains true when substitutionally construed, and vice versa.

We might still make the distinction from the vantage point of a background theory. In it we might specify some real number that was nameless in the object theory; for there are always ways of strengthening a theory so as to name more real numbers, though never all. Further, in the background theory, we might construe the universe of the object theory as exhausting the real numbers. In the background theory we could, in this way, clinch the quantifications in the object theory as referential. But this clinching is doubly relative: it is relative to the background theory and to the interpretation or translation imposed on the object theory from within the background theory.

One might hope that this recourse to a background theory could often be avoided, even when the nameless reals are inseparable from the named reals in the object theory. One might hope by indirect means to show within the object theory that there are nameless reals. For we might prove within the object theory that the reals are indenumerable and that the names are denumerable and hence that there is no function whose arguments are names and whose values exhaust the real numbers. Since the relation of real numbers to their names would be such a function if each real number had a name, we would seem to have proved within the object theory itself that there are nameless reals and hence that quantification must be taken referentially.

However, this is wrong; there is a loophole. This reasoning would prove only that a relation of all real numbers to their names cannot exist as an entity in the universe of the theory. This reasoning denies no number a name in the notation of the theory, as long as the name relation does not belong to the universe of the theory. And anyway we should know better than to expect such a relation, for it is what causes Berry's and Richard's and related paradoxes.

Some theories can attest to their own nameless objects and so claim referential quantification on their own; other theories have to look to background theories for this service. We saw how a theory might attest to its own nameless objects, namely, by showing that some open sentence became true under all constant substitutions but false under universal quantification. Perhaps this is the only way a theory can claim referential import for its own quantifications. Perhaps, when the nameless objects happen to be inseparable from the named, the quantification used in a theory cannot meaningfully be declared referential except through the medium of a background theory. Yet referential quantification is the key idiom of ontology. Thus ontology can be multiply relative, multiply meaningless apart from a background theory. Besides being unable to say in absolute terms just what the objects are, we are sometimes unable even to distinguish objectively between referential quantification and a substitutional counterfeit. When we do relativize these matters to a background theory, moreover, the relativization itself has two components: relativity to the choice of background theory and relativity to the choice of how to translate the object theory into the background theory. As for the ontology in turn of the background theory, and even the referentiality of its quantification—these matters can call for a background theory in turn.

There is not always a genuine regress. We saw that, if we are merely clarifying the range of the variables of a theory or the denotations of its terms, and are taking the referentiality of quantification itself for granted, we can commonly use the object theory itself as background theory. We found that when we undertake an ontological reduction, we must accept at least the unreduced theory in order to cite the proxy function; but this we were able cheerfully to accept in the spirit of *reductio ad absurdum* arguments. And now in the end we have found further that if we care to question quantification itself, and settle whether it imports a universe of discourse or turns merely on substitution at the linguistic level, we in some cases have genuinely to regress to a background language endowed with additional resources. We seem to have to do this unless the nameless objects are separable from the named in the object theory.

Regress in ontology is reminiscent of the now familiar regress in the semantics of truth and kindred notions—satisfaction, naming. We know from Tarski's work how the semantics, in this sense, of a theory regularly demands an in some way more inclusive theory. This similarity should perhaps not surprise us, since both ontology and satisfaction are matters of reference. In their elusiveness, at any rate—in their emptiness now and again except relative to a broader background—both truth and ontology may in a suddenly rather clear and even tolerant sense be said to belong to transcendental metaphysics.[19],[20]

Endnotes

[1]J. Dewey, *Experience and Nature* (La Salle, Ill.: Open Court, 1925, 1958), pp. 170–185.

[2]Quine, *Word and Object* (Cambridge, Mass.: MIT Press, 1960), §12.

[3]L. Wittgenstein, *Philosophical Investigations* (New York: Macmillan, 1953), p. 14.

[4]Cf. *Word and Object*, §17.

[5]*Word and Object*, §15.

[6]To keep my account graphic I am counting a certain postpositive particle as a suffix rather than a word.

[7] [Gödel numbering is a way of using numbers as a code for symbols.—Ed.]

[8]See Leon Henkin, "Completeness in the theory of types," *Journal of Symbolic Logic* 15 (1950), 81–91, and references therein.

[9]For more on this theme see my *Set Theory and Its Logic* (Cambridge, Mass.: Harvard, 1963, 1969), §11.

[10]Paul Benacerraf, "What numbers cannot be," *Philosophical Review* 74 (1965), 47–73, develops this point. His conclusions differ in some ways from those I shall come to.

[11]N. L. Wilson, "Substances without substrata," *Review of Metaphysics* 12 (1959), 521–539, p. 532.

[12]Quine, *The Ways of Paradox* (New York: Random House, 1966), pp. 204 ff.; or see *Journal of Philosophy*, 1964, pp. 214 ff.

[13]Quine, *Set Theory and Its Logic*, §2 ff.

[14]Kurt Gödel, *The Consistency of the Continuum Hypothesis* (Princeton, N.J.: The University Press, 1940), p. 11.

[15]Thoralf Skolem, "Logisch-kombinatorische Untersuchungen über die Erfüllbarkeit oder Beweisbarkeit mathematischer Sätze nebst einem Theorem über dichte Mengen," *Skrifter utgit av Videnskapsselskapet i Kristiania*, 1919, 37 pp. Translation in Jean van Heijenoort, ed., *From Frege to Gödel: Source Book in the History of Mathematical Logic* (Cambridge, Mass.: Harvard, 1967), pp. 252–263.

[16]Ruth B. Marcus, "Modalities and intensional languages," *Syntheses* 13 (1961), 303–322. I cannot locate an adequate statement of Stanisław Leśniewski's philosophy of quantification in his writings; I have it from his conversations. E. C. Luschei, in *The Logical Systems of Leśniewski* (Amsterdam: North-Holland, 1962), pp. 108 ff. confirms my attribution but still cites no passage.

[17]Such is the typical way of a numerically insegregative system, misleadingly called "ω-inconsistent." See my *Selected Logic Papers* (New York: Random House, 1966), pp. 118 ff., or *Journal of Symbolic Logic*, 1953, pp. 122 ff.

[18]This possibility was suggested by Saul Kripke.

[19]In developing these thoughts I have been helped by discussions with Saul Kripke, Thomas Nagel, and especially Burton Dreben.

[20] [Note added later.] Besides such ontological reduction as is provided by proxy functions (cf. pp. 526–528), there is that which consists simply in dropping objects whose absence will not falsify any truths expressible in the notation. Commonly this sort of deflation can be managed by proxy functions, but R. E. Grandy has shown me that sometimes it cannot. Let us by all means recognize it then as a further kind of reduction. In the background language we must, of course, be able to say what class of objects is dropped, just as in other cases we had to be able to specify the proxy function. This requirement seems sufficient still to stem any resurgence of Pythagoreanism on the strength of the Löwenheim-Skolem theorem.

59. *The World Well Lost*

RICHARD RORTY

Scientific realists like Sellars suggest reality may be quite different from how we ordinarily perceive and think it to be. But "ontological relativists" like Quine point out that there may be deep reasons why any theory or language can be reinterpreted in terms of other theories or languages, and this may give the impression that any claim to say what is real is just one of many equally cogent rival interpretations. Should one, then, be skeptical of claims about what the world really is? How should one choose which interpretation or which theory to believe among all the rivals that are equally compatible with the data?

In "The World Well Lost," Richard Rorty, professor of comparative literature and philosophy at Stanford University, argues that the skepticism generated by the idea of radically different conceptual frameworks (or languages) is mistaken. Rorty thinks most beliefs must be true and will survive conceptual change. If so, the challenge of radically different conceptual frameworks is overrated. He diagnoses the skeptical threat as stemming, in part, from the idea of the world as a remote Kantian thing-in-itself, which makes different frameworks true or false, and recommends abandoning this notion of the world. As a pragmatist, he is content to continue working with the world as conceived in the bulk of our beliefs.

The notion of alternative conceptual frameworks has been a commonplace of our culture since Hegel. Hegel's historicism gave us a sense of how there might be genuine novelty in the development of thought and of society. Such a historicist conception of thought and morals was, we may see by hindsight, rendered possible by Kant, himself the least historicist of philosophers. For Kant perfected and codified the two distinctions that are necessary to develop the notion of an "alternative conceptual framework"—the distinction between spontaneity and receptivity and the distinction between necessary and contingent truth. Since Kant, we find it almost impossible not to think of the mind as divided into active and passive faculties, the former using concepts to "interpret" what "the world" imposes on the latter. We also find it difficult not to distinguish between those concepts which the mind could hardly get along without and those which it can take or leave alone—and we think of truths about the former concepts as "necessary" in the most proper and paradigmatic sense of the term. But as soon as we have this picture of the mind in focus, it occurs to us, as it did to Hegel, that those all-important a priori concepts, those which determine what our experience or our morals will be, might have been different. We cannot, of course, imagine what an experience or a practice *that* different would be like, but we can abstractly suggest that the men of the Golden Age, or the inhabitants of the Fortunate Isles, or the mad, might shape the intuitions that are our common property in different molds, and might thus be conscious of a different "world."

Various attacks on the contrast between the observed and the theoretical (in, e.g., Kuhn, Feyerabend, and Sellars) have led recently to a new appreciation of Kant's point that to change one's concepts would be to change what one experiences, to change one's "phenomenal world." But

From Richard Rorty, "The World Well Lost," *Consequences of Pragmatism* (University of Minnesota Press, 1982), pp. 3–18. Copyright © 1982 by the University of Minnesota Press. Reprinted by permission of the University of Minnesota Press. Originally published in the *Journal of Philosophy*, vol. lxix (1972), pp. 649-665.

Part VI Knowing Reality

this appreciation leads us to question the familiar distinction between spontaneity and receptivity. The possibility of different conceptual schemes highlights the fact that a Kantian unsynthesized intuition can exert no influence on how it is to be synthesized—or, at best, can exert only an influence we shall have to describe in a way as relative to a chosen conceptual scheme as our description of everything else. Insofar as a Kantian intuition is effable, it is just a perceptual judgment, and thus not *merely* "intuitive." Insofar as it is ineffable, it is incapable of having an explanatory function. This dilemma—a parallel to that which Hegelians raised concerning the thing-in-itself—casts doubt on the notion of a faculty of "receptivity." There seems no need to postulate an intermediary between the physical thrust of the stimulus upon the organ and the full-fledged conscious judgment that the properly programmed organism forms in consequence. Thus there is no need to split the organism up into a receptive wax tablet on the one hand and an "active" interpreter of what nature has there imprinted on the other. So the Kantian point that different a priori concepts would, if there could be such things, give a different phenomenal world gives place either to the straightforward but paradoxical claim that different concepts give us different worlds, or to dropping the notion of "conceptual framework" altogether. "Phenomenal" can no longer be given a sense, once Kantian "intuitions" drop out. For the suggestion that our concepts shape neutral material no longer makes sense once there is nothing to serve as this material. The physical stimuli themselves are not a useful substitute, for the contrast between the "posits" which the inventive mind constructs to predict and control stimuli, and the stimuli themselves, can be no more than a contrast between the effable world and its ineffable cause.[1]

The notion of *alternative* conceptual frameworks thus contains the seeds of doubt about the root notion of "conceptual framework," and so of its own destruction. For once the faculty of receptivity and, more generally, the notion of neutral material becomes dubious, doubt spreads easily to the notion of conceptual thought as "shaping" and thus to the notion of the World-Spirit moving from one set of a priori concepts to the next.

But the doubts about the Hegelian picture produced by an attack on the given/interpretation distinction are vague and diffuse by comparison with those which result from attacking the necessary/contingent distinction. Quine's suggestion that the difference between a priori and empirical truth is merely that between the relatively difficult to give up and the relatively easy brings in its train the notion that there is no clear distinction to be drawn between questions of meaning and questions of fact. This, in turn, leaves us (as Quine has pointed out in criticizing Carnap) with no distinction between questions about alternative "theories" and questions about alternative "frameworks."[2] The philosophical notion of "meaning," against which Quine is protesting is, as he says, the latest version of the "idea idea"—a philosophical tradition one of whose incarnations was the Kantian notion of "concept." The notion of a choice among "meaning postulates" is the latest version of the notion of a choice among alternative conceptual schemes. Once the necessary is identified with the analytic and the analytic is explicated in terms of meaning, an attack on the notion of what Harman has called the "philosophical" sense of 'meaning' becomes an attack on the notion of "conceptual framework" in any sense that assumes a distinction of kind between this notion and that of "empirical theory."[3]

So far we have seen how criticisms of givenness and of analyticity both serve to dismantle the Kantian notion of "conceptual framework"—the notion of "concepts necessary for the constitution of experience, as opposed to concepts whose application is necessary to control or predict experience." I have been arguing that without the notions of "the given" and of "the a priori" there can be no notion of "the constitution of experience." Thus there can be no notion of alternative experiences, or alternative worlds, to be constituted by the adoption of new a priori concepts. But there is a simpler and more direct objection to the notion of "alternative conceptual framework," to which I now wish to turn. This objection has recently been put forward, in connection with Quine's thesis of indeterminacy, by Davidson and Stroud.[4] The argument is verificationist, and turns on the unrecognizability of persons using a conceptual framework different from our own (or, to put it another way, the unrecognizability as a *language* of anything that is not translatable into English). The connection between Quine's attack on "conventionalist" notions of meaning and this verification-ist argument is supposed to be as follows: if one thinks of "meaning" in terms of the discovery of the speech dispositions of foreigners rather than in terms of mental essences (ideas, concepts, chunks of the crystalline structure of thought), then one will not be able to draw a clear distinction between the foreigner's using words different in meaning from any words in our language and the foreigner's having many false beliefs. We can and must play off awkward translations against ascriptions of quaint beliefs, and vice versa, but we will never reach the limiting case of a foreigner all or most of whose beliefs must be viewed as false according to a trans-lating scheme that pairs off all or most of his terms as identical in meaning with some terms of English. We will not reach this case (so the Davidsonian argument goes) because any such translation scheme would merely show that we had not suc-ceeded in finding a translation at all.

But (to extend Davidson's argument a bit) if we can never find a translation, why should we think that we are faced with language users at all? It is, of course, possible to imagine humanoid organisms making sounds of great variety at one another in very various circumstances with what appear to be various effects upon the interlocutors' behavior. But suppose that repeated attempts sys-tematically to correlate these sounds with the organisms' environment and behavior fail. What should we say? One suggestion might be that the analytic hypotheses we are using in our tentative translation schemes use concepts that we do not share with the natives—because the natives "carve up the world" differently, or have different "qual-ity spaces" or something of the sort. But could there be a way of deciding between this suggestion and the possibility that the organisms' sounds are *just* sounds? Once we imagine different ways of carving up the world, nothing could stop us from attributing "untranslatable languages" to *anything* that emits a variety of signals. But, so this verifica-tionist argument concludes, this degree of open-endedness shows us that the purported notion of an untranslatable language is as fanciful as that of an invisible color.

It is important to note that Quinean argu-ments against analyticity and for the indeterminacy of translation are not necessary for this argument. The argument stands on its own feet—Quine's

only contribution to it being to disparage the pos-sibility that 'meaning' can mean something more than what is contextually defined in the process of predicting the foreigner's behavior. To adopt this view of meaning is all that is required to suggest that the notion of "people who speak our lan-guage but believe nothing that we believe" is inco-herent.[5] To *show* that it is incoherent, however—to complete the argument—one would have to show in detail that no amount of nonlin-guistic behavior by the foreigner could be suffi-cient to underwrite a translation that made all or most of his beliefs false.[6] For it might be the case, for example, that the way in which the foreigner dealt with trees while making certain sounds made it clear that we had to translate some of his utter-ances as "These are not trees," and so on for every-thing else with which he had dealings. Some of his utterances might be translated as: "I am not a per-son," "These are not words," "One should never use *modus ponens* if one wishes valid arguments," "Even if I were thinking, which I am not, that would not show that I exist." We might ratify these translations by showing that his nonlinguis-tic ways of handling himself and others showed that he actually did hold such paradoxical beliefs. The only way to show that this suggestion cannot work, would be actually to tell the whole story about this hypothetical foreigner. It might be that a story could be told to show the coherence of these false beliefs with each other and with his actions, or it might not. To show that Davidson and Stroud were right would be to show that, indeed, no such story was tellable.

There is, I think, no briefer way to decide on the soundness of this a priori argument against the possibility of alternative conceptual frameworks than to run over such possible stories. But this inconclusiveness is a feature this argument has in common with all interesting verificationist anti-skeptical arguments. It conforms to the following pattern: (1) the skeptic suggests that our own beliefs (about, e.g., other minds, tables and chairs, or how to translate French) have viable alternatives which unfortunately can never be known to hold but which justify the suspension of judgment; (2) the anti-skeptic replies that the very meaning of the terms used shows that the alternatives sug-gested are not merely dubious but in principle unverifiable, and thus not reasonable alternatives at all; (3) the skeptic rejoins that verificationism confuses the *ordo essendi* with the *ordo cognoscendi* and that it may well be that some alternative is true even though we shall never know that it is; (4) the anti-skeptic replies that the matter is not worth debating until the skeptic spells out the suggested alternative in full detail, and insinuates that this cannot be done; (5) the controversy degenerates into a dispute about assuming the burden of proof, with the skeptic claiming that it is not up to him to build up a coherent story around his suggested alternative but rather up to the anti-skeptic to show a priori that this cannot be done.

In the case at hand, the skeptic is the fan of "alternative conceptual frameworks," practicing his skepticism on a global scale by insinuating that our entire belief structure might dissolve, leaving not a wrack behind, to be replaced by a complete but utterly dissimilar alternative. The Davidsonian anti-skeptic is in the position of asking how one could come to call any pattern of behavior evidence for such an alternative. The skeptic replies that perhaps we could *never* come to do so, but this merely shows how complete our egocentric predicament is. And so it goes.[7]

In this case, however (unlike the case of limited skepticism about whether, e.g., 'pain' or 'red' means to me what it does to you) the skeptic's global approach gives him a significant dialectical advantage. For he can here sketch what might bring about the actualization of his suggested alternative without being caught up in disagreement about how to interpret concrete experimental results. He can simply refer us to ordinary scientific and cultural progress extrapolated just beyond the range of science fiction. Consider, he will say, the following view of man's history and prospects. Our views about matter and motion, the good life for man, and much else have changed in subtle and complicated ways since the days of the Greeks. Many of the planks in Neurath's boat have been torn up and relaid differently. But since (1) we can describe why it was "rational" for each such change to have occurred, and (2) *many* more of our beliefs are the same as Greek beliefs than are different (e.g., our belief that barley is better than nettles and freedom than slavery, that red is a color, and that lightning often precedes thunder), we should not yet wish to talk about "an alternative conceptual framework." And yet we must

admit that even the relatively slight refurbishings of the boat which have occupied the past two thousand years are enough to give us considerable difficulty in knowing just *how* to translate some Greek sentences, and just *how* to explain the "rationality" of the changes that have intervened. Again, the various shifts that have taken place in our understanding of the subject matter of the beliefs we purportedly "share" with the Greeks (resulting from, e.g., the development of new strains of nettles, new forms of slavery, new ways of producing color perceptions, and new explanations of the sound of the thunder and the look of the lightning) make us a little dubious about the claim to shared belief. They create the feeling that here too we may be imposing on history rather than describing it. Let us now extrapolate from ourselves to the Galactic civilization of the future, which we may assume to have moved and reshaped 10^{50} planks in the boat we are in, whereas since Aristotle we have managed to shift only about 10^{20}. Here the suggestion that we interpret these changes as a sequence of rational changes in views about a common matter seems a bit forced, and the fear that even the most empathic Galactic historians of science "won't really understand us properly" quite appropriate. So, our skeptic concludes, the Davidson-Stroud point that to describe in detail the Galactic civilization's beliefs is automatically to make them merely alternative theories within a common framework is not enough. Granting this point, we can still see that it is rational to expect that the incommunicably and unintelligibly novel will occur, even though, *ex hypothesi,* we can neither write nor read a science-fiction story that describes Galactic civilization. Here, then, we have a case in which there really is a difference between the *ordo cognoscendi* and the *ordo essendi,* and no verificationist argument can apply.

To intensify the antinomy we confront here, let us agree for the sake of argument that it is a necessary condition for an entity to be a person that it have or once have had the potentiality for articulating beliefs and desires comparable in quantity and complexity to our own. The qualifications are required if we are to include infants and the insane while excluding dogs and the simpler sort of robots. But the same qualifications will, of course, give trouble when we come to cases where it is not clear whether we are educating a person by developing his latent potentialities (as by teaching a child a language) or transforming a thing into a person (as by clamping some additional memory units onto the robot). Bating this difficulty for the moment, however, let us simply note that this formulation has the consequence that ascribing personhood, ascribing a language, and ascribing beliefs and desires go hand in hand. So, if Davidson is right, ascribing personhood and ascribing mostly the *right* beliefs and mostly the *appropriate* desires go hand in hand. This means that we shall never be able to have evidence that there exist persons who speak languages in principle untranslatable into English or hold beliefs all or most of which are incompatible with our own.

Despite this, however, we can extrapolate to a story about how just such persons might come into existence. So it seems that the world may come to be full of persons whom we could never conceivably recognize as such. A Galactic time-traveler come among us, we now realize, would eventually be forced to abandon his original presumption that we were persons when he failed to correlate our utterances with our environment in any way that enabled him to construct an English-Galactic lexicon. Our initial assumption that the Galactic emissary was a person would be frustrated by the same sort of discovery. How sad that two cultures who have so much to offer each other should fail to recognize each other's existence! What pathos in the thought that we, time-traveling among our Neanderthal ancestors, might stand to them as the Galactic stands to us! But the situation is even worse than that, for reasons I hinted at earlier. We can now see that, for all we know, our *contemporary* world is filled with unrecognizable persons. Why should we ignore the possibility that the trees and the bats and the butterflies and the stars all have their various untranslatable languages in which they are busily expressing their beliefs and desires to one another? Since their organs suit them to receive such different stimuli and to respond in such different ways, it is hardly surprising that the syntax and the primitive predicates of their languages bear no relation to our own.

The inclusion of this last possibility may suggest that something has gone wrong. Perhaps we should not have been so ready to admit the possi-

bility of extrapolation. Perhaps we were too hasty in thinking that attributions of personhood and of articulate belief went hand in hand—for surely we know in advance that butterflies are not persons and therefore know in advance that they will have no beliefs to express. For myself, however, I see nothing wrong with the proposed extrapolation, and I do not see what 'known in advance not to be a person' could mean when applied to the butterfly save that the butterfly doesn't seem human. But there is no particular reason to think that our remote ancestors or descendants would seem human right off the bat either. Let the notion of a person be as complex and multiply criterioned as you please, still I do not think that it will come unstuck from that of a complex interlocked set of beliefs and desires, nor that the latter notion can be separated from that of the potentiality for translatable speech. So I think that to rule the butterflies out is to rule out the Galactics and the Neanderthals, and that to allow extrapolation to the latter is to allow for the possibility that the very same beliefs and desires which our Galactic descendants will hold are being held even now by the butterflies. We can dig in our heels and say that terms like 'person', 'belief', 'desire', and 'language' are ultimately as token-reflexive as 'here' and 'now' or 'morally right', so that in each case essential reference is made to where *we* are. But that will be the *only* way of ruling out the Galactic, and thus the *only* way of ruling out the butterfly.

If this seems puzzling, I think it will seem less so if we consider some parallels. Suppose we say that there is no poetry among the Patagonians, no astronomy among the aborigines, and no morality among the inhabitants of the planet Mongo. And suppose a native of each locale, protesting against our parochial view, explains that what they have is a *different* sort of poetry, astronomy, or morals, as the case may be. For the Patagonian, neither Homer nor Shelley nor Mallarmé nor Dryden look in the least like poets. He admits, however, that Milton and Swinburne are both faintly reminiscent, in the same only vaguely describable respect, of the paradigms of Patagonian poesy. Those paradigms strike him as clearly fulfilling some of the roles in his culture which our poets fulfill in ours, though not all. The aborigine knows nothing of the equinoxes and the solstices, but he does distinguish planets from stars. However, he uses the same term to refer to planets, meteors, comets, and the sun. The stories he tells about the movements of these latter bodies are bound up with a complicated set of stories about divine providence and cure of diseases, whereas the stories told about the stars have to do exclusively with sex. The inhabitants of the planet Mongo appear shocked when people tell the truth to social equals, and surprised and amused when people refrain from torturing helpless wanderers. They seem to have no taboos at all about sex, but a great many about food. Their social organizations seem held together half by a sort of lottery, and half by brute force. The inhabitants of Mongo, however, profess to be revolted by the Earthlings' failure to grasp the moral point of view, and by our apparent confusion of morality with etiquette and with expedients for ensuring social order.

In the three cases just cited the question, Is it a different *sort* of poetry (or astronomy, or morality), or do they simply have *none?* is obviously not the sort of question it is very important to answer. I suggest that the question, Are the Galactics, or the butterflies, different sorts of persons than ourselves or not persons at all? is also not very important. In the three cases mentioned, one can extend the argument indefinitely by pressing for further details. In the global case, where *ex hypothesi* no translation scheme will work, we cannot. But in the global case (having beliefs *tout court*), as in the particular cases of having beliefs about astronomy or about right and wrong, what is in question is just the best way of predicting, controlling, and generally coping with the entities in question. In the course of figuring this out, we encounter some of the same hard questions I referred to above— the questions that arise when coping with such borderline cases as fetuses, prelinguistic infants, computers, and the insane—Do they have civil rights? Must we try to justify ourselves to them? Are they thinking or acting on instinct? Are they holding beliefs or merely responding to stimuli? Is that a word to which they assign a sense, or are they just sounding off on cue? I doubt that many philosophers believe any longer than procedures for answering such questions are built into "our language" waiting to be discovered by "conceptual analysis." But if we do not believe this, perhaps we can be content to say, in the global case, that the question, Might there be alternative con-

ceptual frameworks to our own, held by persons whom we could never recognize as persons? is the same case. I doubt that we can ever adumbrate general ways of answering questions like, Is it a conceptual framework very different from our own, or is it a mistake to think of it as a language at all? Is it a person with utterly different organs, responses, and beliefs, with whom communication is thus forever impossible, or rather just a complexly behaving thing?

This "don't-care" conclusion is all I have to offer concerning the antinomy created by the Davidson-Stroud argument on the one hand and the skeptic's extrapolation on the other. But this should not be thought of as denigrating the importance of what Davidson and Stroud are saying. On the contrary, I think that, having seen through this antinomy and having noticed the relevance of the original argument to our application of the notion of "person," we are now in a better position to see the importance that it has. This importance can be brought out by (a) looking at the standard objection to the coherence theory of truth ("it cuts truth off from the world") and (b) recurring to our previous discussion of the Kantian roots of the notion of "conceptual framework."

Consider first the traditional objection to coherence theories of truth which says that, although our only *test* of truth must be the coherence of our beliefs with one another, still the *nature* of truth must be "correspondence to reality." It is thought a sufficient argument for this view that Truth is One, whereas alternative equally coherent sets of beliefs are Many.[8] In reply to this argument, defenders of coherence and pragmatic theories of truth have argued that our so-called "intuition" that Truth is One is simply the expectation that, if all perceptual reports were in, there would be one optimal way of selecting among them and all other possible statements so as to have one ideally proportioned system of true beliefs. To this reply, the standard rebuttal is that there would clearly be many such possible systems, among which we could choose only on aesthetic grounds. A further, and more deeply felt, rebuttal is that it is the *world* that determines the truth. The accident of which glimpses of the world our sense organs have vouchsafed us, and the further accidents of the predicates we have entrenched or the theories whose proportions please us, may determine what we have a right to believe. But how could they determine the *truth?*[9]

Now the Davidson-Stroud argument supplies a simple, if temporizing, answer to this standard objection to the coherence theory. Since most of our beliefs (though not any particular one) simply *must* be true—for what could count as evidence that the vast majority of them were not?—the specter of alternative conceptual frameworks shrinks to the possibility that there might be a number of equally good ways to modify slightly our present set of beliefs in the interest of greater predictive power, charm, or what have you. The Davidson-Stroud point makes us remember, among other things, what a very small proportion of our beliefs are changed when our paradigms of physics, or poetry, or morals, change—and makes us realize how few of them *could* change. It makes us realize that the number of beliefs that changed among the educated classes of Europe between the thirteenth and the nineteenth centuries is ridiculously small compared to the number that survived intact. So this argument permits us to say: it is just not the case that there are "alternative" coherent global sets of beliefs. It is perfectly true that there will always be areas of inquiry in which alternative incompatible sets of beliefs are "tied." But the fact that we shall *always* be holding mostly true beliefs and, thus, presumably be "in touch with the world" the vast majority of the time makes this point seem philosophically innocuous. In particular, the claim that, since Truth is One and, therefore, is "correspondence," we must resurrect a foundationalist epistemology to explain "how knowledge is possible" becomes otiose.[10] We shall automatically be "in touch with the world" (most of the time) whether or not we have any incorrigible, or basic, or otherwise privileged or foundational statements to make.

But this way of dealing with the claim that "it is the *world* that determines what is true" may easily seem a fraud. For, as I have been using it, the Davidson-Stroud view seems to perform the conjuring trick of substituting the notion of "the unquestioned vast majority of our beliefs" for the notion of "the world." It reminds us of such coherence theorists as Royce, who claim that our notion of "the world" is just the notion of the ideally coherent contents of an ideally large mind, or of the pragmatists' notion of "funded experi-

ence"—those beliefs which are not at the moment being challenged, because they present no problems and no one has bothered to think of alternatives to them. In all these cases—Davidson and Stroud, Royce, Dewey—it may well seem that the issue about truth is just being ducked. For our notion of the world—it will be said—is not a notion of unquestioned beliefs, or unquestionable beliefs, or ideally coherent beliefs, but rather of a hard, unyielding, rigid *être-en-soi* which stands aloof, sublimely indifferent to the attentions we lavish upon it. The true realistic believer will view idealisms and pragmatisms with the same suspicion with which the true believer in the God of our Fathers will view, for example, Tillich's talk of an "object of ultimate concern."[11]

Now, to put my cards on the table, I think that the realistic true believer's notion of the world is an obsession rather than an intuition. I also think that Dewey was right in thinking that the only intuition we have of the world as determining truth is just the intuition that we must make our new beliefs conform to a vast body of platitudes, unquestioned perceptual reports, and the like. So I am happy to interpret the upshot of the Davidson-Stroud argument in a Deweyan way.

But I have no arguments against the true believer's description of our so-called "intuitions." All that can be done with the claim that "only the *world* determines truth" is to point out the equivocation in the realists' own use of 'world'. In the sense in which "the world" is just whatever that vast majority of our beliefs not currently in question are currently thought to be about, there is of course no argument.[12] If one accepts the Davidson-Stroud position, then "the world" will just be the stars, the people, the tables, and the grass—all those things which nobody except the occasional "scientific realist" philosopher thinks might not exist. The fact that the vast majority of our beliefs must be true will, on this view, guarantee the existence of the vast majority of the things we now think we are talking about. So in one sense of 'world'—the sense in which (except for a few fringe cases like gods, neutrinos, and natural rights) we now know perfectly well what the world is like and could not possibly be wrong about it—there is no argument about the point that it is the world that determines truth. All that "determination" comes to is that our belief that snow is white is true because snow is white, that our beliefs about the stars are true because of the way the stars are laid out, and so on.

But this trivial sense in which "truth" is "correspondence to reality" and "depends upon a reality independent of our knowledge" is, of course, not enough for the realist.[13] What he wants is precisely what the Davidson-Stroud argument prevents him from having—the notion of a world *so* "independent of our knowledge" that it might, for all we know, prove to contain none of the things we have always thought we were talking about. He wants to go from, say, "we might be wrong about what the stars are" to "none of the things we talk about might be anything like what we think they are." Given this projection from, as Kant would say, the "conditioned" to the "unconditioned," it is no wonder that antinomies are easily generated.

The notion of "the world" as used in a phrase like 'different conceptual schemes carve up the world differently' must be the notion of something *completely* unspecified and unspecifiable—the thing-in-itself, in fact. As soon as we start thinking of "the world" as atoms and the void, or sense data and awareness of them, or "stimuli" of a certain sort brought to bear upon organs of a certain sort, we have changed the name of the game. For we are now well within some particular theory about how the world is. But for purposes of developing a controversial and nontrivial doctrine of truth as correspondence, only an utterly vague characterization in some such terms as 'cause of the impacts upon our receptivity and goal of our faculty of spontaneity' will do. "Truth" in the sense of "truth taken apart from any theory" and "world" taken as "what determines such truth" are notions that were (like the terms "subject" and "object", "given" and "consciousness") made for each other. Neither can survive apart from the other.

To sum up this point, I want to claim that "the world" is either the purely vacuous notion of the ineffable cause of sense and goal of intellect, or else a name for the objects that inquiry at the moment is leaving alone: those planks in the boat which are at the moment not being moved about. It seems to me that epistemology since Kant has shuttled back and forth between these two meanings of the term "world", just as moral philosophy since Plato has shuttled back and forth between 'the Good' as a name for an ineffable touchstone

of inquiry which might lead to the rejection of *all* our present moral views, and as a name for the ideally coherent synthesis of as many of those views as possible. This equivocation seems to me essential to the position of those philosophers who see "realism" or "the correspondence theory of truth" as controversial or exciting theses.

To remove altogether the "realistic" temptation to use the word 'world' in the former vacuous sense, we should need to eschew once and for all a whole galaxy of philosophical notions that have encouraged this use—in particular, the Kantian distinctions I discussed at the outset. For suppose we have a simple theory of the eye of the mind either getting, or failing to get, a clear view of the natures of kinds of things—the sort of theory we get, say, in parts of Aristotle's *Posterior Analytics.* Then the notion of alternative sets of concepts will make no clear sense. *Noûs* cannot err. It is only when we have some form of the notion that the mind is split between "simple ideas" or "passively received intuitions" on the one hand and a range of complex ideas (some signifying real, and some only nominal, essences) on the other, that *either* the coherence theory of truth *or* the standard objections to it can begin to look plausible. Only then is the notion plausible that inquiry consists in getting our "representations" into shape, rather than simply describing the world. If we no longer have a view about knowledge as the result of manipulating *Vorstellungen,* then I think we can return to the simple Aristotelian notion of truth as correspondence with reality with a clear conscience—for it will now appear as the uncontroversial triviality that it is.

To develop this claim about the way in which Kantian epistemology is linked with the notion of a nontrivial correspondence theory of truth and thus with the "realist's" notion of "the world" would require another paper, and I shall not try to press it further. Instead I should like to conclude by recalling some of the historical allusions I have made along the way, in order (as Sellars says) to place my conclusions in philosophical space. I said at the outset that the notion of "conceptual framework" and, thus, that of "alternative conceptual framework" depend upon presupposing some standard Kantian distinctions. These distinctions have been the common target of Wittgenstein, Quine, Dewey, and Sellars. I can now express the same point by saying that the notion of "the world" that is correlative with the notion of "conceptual framework" is simply the Kantian notion of a thing-in-itself, and that Dewey's dissolution of the Kantian distinctions between receptivity and spontaneity and between necessity and contingency thus leads naturally to the dissolution of the true realistic believer's notion of "the world." If you start out with Kant's epistemology, in short, you will wind up with Kant's transcendental metaphysics. Hegel, as I suggested earlier, kept the epistemology, but tried to drop the thing-in-itself, thus making himself, and idealism generally, a patsy for realistic reaction. But Hegel's historical sense—the sense that nothing, including an a priori concept, is immune from cultural development—provided the key to Dewey's attack on the epistemology that Hegel shared with Kant. This attack was blunted by Dewey's use of the term "experience" as an incantatory device for blurring every possible distinction, and so it was not until more sharply focused criticisms were formulated by Wittgenstein, Quine, and Sellars that the force of Dewey's point about "funded experience" as the "cash-value" of the notion of "the world" could be seen. But now that these criticisms have taken hold, the time may have come to try to recapture Dewey's "naturalized" version of Hegelian historicism. In this historicist vision, the arts, the sciences, the sense of right and wrong, and the institutions of society are not attempts to embody or formulate truth or goodness or beauty. They are attempts to solve problems—to modify our beliefs and desires and activities in ways that will bring us greater happiness than we have now. I want to suggest that this shift in perspective is the natural consequence of dropping the receptivity/spontaneity and intuition/concept distinctions, and more generally of dropping the notion of "representation" and the view of man that Dewey has called "the spectator theory" and Heidegger, the "identification of *physis* and *idea*." Because the idealists kept this general picture and occupied themselves with redefining the "object of knowledge," they gave idealism and the "coherence theory" a bad name—and realism and the "correspondence theory" a good one. But if we can come to see both the coherence and correspondence theories as noncompeting trivialities, then we may finally move beyond realism and ide-

alism. We may reach a point at which, in Wittgenstein's words, we are capable of stopping doing philosophy when we want to.

Endnotes

[1]T. S. Kuhn, "Reflections on My Critics," in I. Lakatos and A. Musgrave, eds., *Criticism and the Growth of Knowledge* (New York: Cambridge, 1970), p. 276, says that "the stimuli to which the participants in a communication breakdown respond are, under pain of solipsism, the same" and then continues by saying that their "programming" must be so also, since men "share a history . . . a language, an everyday world, and most of a scientific one." On the view I should like to support, the *whole* anti-solipsist burden is borne by the "programming," and the "stimuli" (like the noumenal unsynthesized intuitions) drop out. If a stimulus is thought of as somehow "neutral" in respect to different conceptual schemes, it can be so only, I would argue, by becoming "a wheel that can be turned though nothing else moves with it." (Cf. Ludwig Wittgenstein, *Philosophical Investigations* [New York: Macmillan, 1958], I, 271.)

[2]See W. V. Quine, "On Carnap's View on Ontology," in *The Ways of Paradox* (New York: Random House, 1966), pp. 126–134.

[3]See Gilbert Harman, "Quine on Meaning and Existence, I," *Review of Metaphysics,* XXI, 1 (September 1967): 124–151, p. 142.

[4]I first became aware of this argument, and of the importance of the issues I am here discussing, on reading the sixth of the Locke Lectures which Davidson gave at Oxford in 1970. These lectures are at present still unpublished, and I am most grateful to Davidson for permission to see the manuscript, and also the manuscript of his 1971 University of London Lectures on "Conceptual Relativism"—the more especially as I want to turn Davidson's argument to purposes for which he would have slim sympathy. After reading Davidson's unpublished material, I read Barry Stroud's presentation of a partially similar argument in "Conventionalism and the Indeterminacy of Translation," in *Words and Objections: Essays on the Work of W. V. Quine,* ed. Davidson and J. Hintikka (Doredrecht: Reidel, 1969), esp. pp. 89–96. Stroud and Davidson concur in rejecting the notion of "alternative conceptual frameworks," but Davidson goes on to draw explicitly the radical conclusion that "most of our beliefs must be true." It is this latter conclusion on which I shall be focusing in this paper. (Addendum, 1981: Although Davidson has not yet published his Locke Lectures in full, the material most relevant to this paper has appeared in his "On the Very Idea of a Conceptual Scheme," *Proceedings of the American Philocophical Association,* 17 (1973–74), pp. 5–20.)

[5]I have argued elsewhere ("Indeterminacy of Translation and of Truth," *Synthese,* 23 [1972]: 443–462) that Quine's doctrine that there is no "matter of fact" for translations to be right or wrong about, is philosophical overkill, and that the "idea idea" is adequately discredited by attacks on the Kantian distinctions discussed above.

[6]The importance of this point was shown me by Michael Friedman. I am grateful also to Michael Williams for criticisms of my general line of argument.

[7]I have tried to develop this view of the course of the argument between verificationists and skeptics in "Verificationism and Transcendental Argument, *Noûs,* V, 1 (February 1971); 3–14; and in "Criteria and Necessity," *Noûs,* VIII, 4 (November 1973): 313–329.

[8]For a formulation of this objection, see John L. Pollock, "Perceptual Knowledge," *Philosophical Review,* LXXX, 3 (July 1971): 290–292.

[9]This sort of question is at the root of the attempt to distinguish between a "theory of truth" and a "theory of evidence" in reply to such truth-as-assertibility theorists as Sellars—see Harman's criticism of Sellars on this point in "Sellars' Semantics," *Philosophical Review,* LXXIX, 3 (July 1970): 404–419, pp. 409ff., 417ff.

[10]See Pollock, op. cit., for a defense of the claim that, once we reject a coherence theory of justification, such an explanation in foundationalist terms becomes necessary.

[11]For examples of the programmatic passion that realism can inspire, see the "Platform of the Association for Realistic Philosophy" in *The Return to Reason,* ed. John Wild (Chicago: Henry Regnery, 1953); and the "Program and First Platform of Six Realists," in Edwin B. Holt et al., *The New Realism* (New York: Macmillan, 1912), pp. 471ff.

[12]I say "are currently thought to be about" rather than "are about" in order to skirt an issue that might be raised by proponents of a "causal theory of reference." Such a theory might suggest that we are in fact now talking about (referring to) what the Galactics will be referring to, but that the Galactics might know what this was and we might not. (The relevance of such theories of reference was pointed out to me by Michael Friedman and by Fred Dretske.) My own view, which I cannot develop here, is that an attempt to clarify epistemological questions by reference to "reference" will always be explaining the obscure by the more obscure—explicating notions ("knowledge," "truth") which have some basis in common speech in terms of a contrived and perpetually controversial philosophical notion.

[13]I do not wish to be taken as suggesting the triviality of Tarski's semantic theory, which seems to me not a theory relevant to epistemology (except perhaps, as Davidson has suggested, to the epistemology of language learning). I should regard Tarski as founding a new subject, not as solving an old problem. I think that Davidson is right in saying that, in the sense in which Tarski's theory is a correspondence theory, "it may be the case that no battle is won, or even joined between correspondence theories and others" ("True to the Facts," *Journal of Philosophy,* LXVI, 21 [Nov. 6, 1969]: 748–764, p. 761). The philosophically controversial "correspondence theory of truth" to which coherence and pragmatic theories were supposed alternatives is not the theory Strawson (quoted by Davidson, op. cit., p. 763) identifies as "to say that a statement is true is to say that a certain speech-episode is related in a certain conventional way to something in the world exclusive of itself." For this latter view would, as far as it goes, be perfectly acceptable to, e.g., Blanshard or Dewey.

60. *Yes, Virginia, There Is a Real World*

WILLIAM P. ALSTON

Quine hoped that theories and languages (especially scientific ones) would evolve in accordance with scientific principles, and so, in spite of his thesis of ontological relativity presented in selection 58, he tended to view himself as part of the pragmatist tradition. But how can we know what we mean if there is ontological relativity, and how can we reason about and assess theories that are still far from the ideal truth of final science? Some philosophers of language attempted to sidestep these problems by offering semantic theories that are non-realist—that is, they attempt to account for meaning while avoiding realist assumptions about reference or truth. If we cannot tie semantic theories to independent reality, should we concede that meaning and something like warranted assertibility is relative to evidence or coherence or . . . ? Should we concede that there is no "real world" corresponding to the correct use of our languages, theories, and concepts? In this selection, William P. Alston attempts to defend realism against some of these "anti-realist" arguments. William Alston is Emeritus Professor of Philosophy at Syracuse University.

My topic this evening is realism, which I come not to bury but to praise. More specifically, I shall be casting a critical eye on some recent divagations from the straight and narrow path of realism, and I shall be considering whether these tempting byways do really exist. My contention shall be that there is, in truth, but the one path through the forest, and that what have been taken as alternative routes, are but insubstantial phantoms.

I.

But first I must explain what view this is that will be so earnestly commended. Many a position wears the name of "realism," and with most of them I shall not be concerned.

As a first shot, let's say that Realism is here being understood as the view that whatever there is, is what it is regardless of how we think of it. Even if there were no human thought, even if there were no human beings, whatever there is other than human thought (and what depends on that, causally or logically) would still be just what it actually is.

As just stated, the position is quite compatible with there being nothing except human thought and what depends on that. So watery a potion is unsuitable for this high occasion. Let's turn it into wine by a codicil to the effect that there is something independent of human thought.

Realism, so stated, is a bit hard to get hold of. It will prove useful to concentrate instead on a certain consequence around which many of the historic battles have raged. If there is a reality independent of our thought, it obviously behooves us to find out as much about it as possible. This means that our thought and discourse will be (largely) directed to thinking (saying) it like it is. Believing (saying) what is true rather than what is false will be the primary goal of cognition; *where we have said what is true iff what we were talking about is as we have said it to be.*[1] I shall call this the realistic conception of truth, and where 'true' and its cognates are used in the sequel with-

out further qualification, this is the intended meaning. So the consequence in question is: *The primary goal of human thought and discourse is to believe (say) what is true in the realistic sense.* Although this is the full statement of the consequence, I shall be working with a somewhat less inflated form:

> Our statements are issued with a (realistic) truth claim (a claim to truth in the realist sense).

I agree with Hilary Putnam[2] that a distinguishing feature of the realistic sense of 'true' is that it is logically possible for even the best attested statement to be false, where the attestation is in terms of "internal" criteria like coherence with the total system of beliefs, being self-evident, being a report of current experience, or being the best explanation of something or other. That is what is "realistic" about this concept of truth. In the final analysis what makes our statement true or false is the way things are (the things the statement is about); not the reasons, evidence, or justification we have for it.

Our thesis is marked by exemplary modesty. It only requires that we hold our statements subject to assessment in terms of truth and falsity. A bolder thesis would be that we sometimes succeed in making statements that are true rather than false. I shall not be so rash this evening; it will not be necessary, since the issues I will be considering concern the viability of the realistic *concept* of truth and its attempted substitutes. Therefore it will be sufficient to consider whether we can, and whether we must, make statements with that kind of claim.

But even within this ambit we can distinguish more and less modest claims. Let me illustrate this point with respect to singular subject–predicate statements. Suppose I assert that this cup is empty. According to the above formulation of the realist thesis, that statement is true or false, depending on whether what the statement is about is as it is said to be. That formulation *pre-supposes* that I have succeeded at least to the extent of picking out a particular referent about which to make a statement. But even if I had failed in that referential task (there is nothing that I would be prepared to recognize as what I was saying to be empty), I would still be saying something intelligible that could be assessed for its success in "saying it like it is." There is, notori-

Originally published in *Proceedings and Addresses of the American Philosophical Association* vol. 52, No. 6 (1979): 779–808. Reprinted by permission of the American Philosophical Association and the author.

ously, controversy over whether, in that case, I said anything that could be evaluated as true or false. Be that as it may, a realistic thesis more modest than ours could be formulated as follows: a statement is put forward with the claim that what it is about, if there is anything it is about, is as it is said to be. I shall not carry modesty to those lengths in this paper; I shall be rash enough to assume that we often do succeed in making a statement about something. If anyone feels that this unfairly begs an important question against the anti-realist, he may substitute the more guarded formulation without disrupting the ensuing discussion.

Here are a few additional exegetical notes:

(1) I have presented the thesis in terms both of thought and discourse (beliefs and statements). To sharpen the focus, I shall henceforward restrict the discussion to statements. I do this not because I consider statement more fundamental than belief, my bent is the opposite one. It is rather that statements are more "out in the open" and, hence, the structure is more readily identified and denominated.

(2) My formulation is limited to statements that can be said to be about something(s). This will take in a wider territory than is sometimes supposed, e.g., not only singular statements but also universal and existential generalizations if we can think of the latter as being "about" all the values of the variables. Other kinds of statements, e.g., subjunctive conditionals, will be harder to fit into this model. But enough statements clearly do fit to give our discussion a point.

(3) Whether my version of realism boils down to a "correspondence" theory of truth depends on how that term is construed. If correspondence theory of truth merely holds that the truth-value of a statement depends on how it is with what the statement is about, rather than on, e.g., its relations to other statements, then of course this is a (the) correspondence theory. But that term is often reserved for theories that take truth to consist in some structural isomorphism, or mirroring or picturing relation between statements (propositions) and facts. Nothing of that sort is implied by my thesis.

(4) In espousing realism in this fundamental sense I am not committed to acknowledging the independent reality of any particular kinds of entities—material substances, numbers, classes, properties, facts, propositions, quanta, angels, or whatever. The thesis is quite neutral as to what is real; it merely holds that our attempts at knowledge are to be evaluated in terms of whether we succeed in picking out something(s) real and saying them to be as they are. Thus it is not tied to most of the views called "realism"—"Platonic" realism about abstract objects, perceptual realism about commonsense physical objects, "scientific" realism about theoretical entities, and so on. These are all much more specific doctrines than the one being defended here.

Because of this my thesis is not necessarily opposed to many of the positions with which realism is commonly contrasted—idealism (in most uses of that term), phenomenalism, verificationism, even conventionalism as applied to some restricted domain, such as scientific theories. If idealism is the view that reality is basically mental or spiritual in character, whether this be a Berkeleyan, Leibnizian, or Hegelian[3] version of that thesis, then idealism allows particular statements (about spirits, monads, the Absolute, or whatever) to be true or false in a realistic sense. If you're attributing to the Absolute characteristics it really has, you are speaking truly; if not, not.

I note in this connection that in the March 1979 issue of the *Journal of Philosophy* an excellent article by Coln McGinn, entitled "An a priori argument for realism" begins with the sentence:

> Except in the vulgar sense, one is not a realist *tout court;* one is a realist with respect to some or other type of subject matter—or better, with respect to particular classes of statements.

As Thomas Reid said, in connection with Hume's contract between the vulgar and the philosophical opinions concerning the immediate objects of perception, "In this division, to my great humiliation, I find myself classed with the vulgar."

Realism, as I have defined it, may seem to the uninitiated to be so minimal as to be trivially true. But notoriously, even so minimal a doctrine as this has been repeatedly denied; and the denials supported by elaborate and ingenious argumentation. Nineteenth-century idealism and pragmatism were in good part devoted to attacking realism and searching for an alternative. Thus F. H. Bradley tells us that truth is "that which satisfies the intellect,"[4] "an ideal expression of the Universe, at once coherent and comprehensive,"[5] and Brand Blanshard that a proposition is true if it coheres with an all comprehensive and fully articulated whole.[6] From the pragmatist side, C. S. Peirce's well-known view is that "the opinion which is fated to be ultimately agreed to by all who investigate, is what we mean by the truth,"[7] while William James writes that "true ideas are those that we can assimilate, validate, corroborate, and verify."[8] John Dewey holds true ideas to be those that are instrumental to "an active reorganization of the given environment, a removal of some specific trouble and perplexity."[9] These philosophers would make the truth of the statement that snow is white to consist in something other than snow's *being* white. More recently, Hilary Putnam, who for years had been presenting a highly visible target to the anti-realist, has now been kind enough to turn the other cheek and present an equally prominent target to the realist. In his recent Presidential Address to the Eastern Division,[10] he argues that it is incoherent to suppose that a theory that satisfies all epistemic criteria might be false.

After having dominated the field for some time, the idealist and pragmatist movements provoked a vigorous realist reaction in the late nineteenth and early twentieth century in the redoubtable persons of Frege, Husserl, Moore, and Russell. It is not my intention this evening to do an instant replay of these epic battles, even though it might result in changing some earlier calls by the arbiters of philosophic fashion. Rather, I shall look at some recent anti-realist tendencies. Though these are by no means unconnected with their distinguished precedents, they also present some apparently new features.

My procedure will be as follows. First, I shall look at some anti-realist arguments, or trends of thought, and find them lacking in merit. Second, I shall consider some attempts to work out a non-realist position, and conclude that no coherent alternative has been provided. At that point the defense will rest.

II.
A.

Under the first rubric I will begin by taking a very brief look at the Quinean theses of indeterminacy of translation and inscrutability of reference. I have no time to enter the formidable thickets of Quinean exegesis, and so I refrain from asking whether Quine is a realist, or whether Quine himself takes these theses to have an anti-realist thrust. But they have frequently been so taken, a tendency encouraged by Quine's use of the label "ontological relativism." Just what bearing do these celebrated doctrines have on the matter? It seems to me somewhat less direct than ordinarily supposed. They don't exactly contradict realism; rather, they strike at a presupposition of the question for which realism is one possible answer. They make, or seem to make, it impossible to raise the question. What indeterminacy of translation and inscrutability of reference most directly imply is that our thought and discourse is irremediably indeterminate in a throughgoing and shocking fashion. To wit, there is no particular determinate content to any assertion. Because of the indeterminacy of translation, there are indefinitely many versions of what it is I am saying about an object in any assertion I make. And because of inscrutability of reference, there are indefinitely many versions of what I would be saying it about if there were any particular thing I were saying. Viewed in a larger context, this is simply an extreme version of forms of indeterminacy that have long been recognized as affecting much of our speech. It is uncontroversial that people frequently use words in an ambiguous or confused manner, so that there is no precise answer to the question: "What is he saying?" And again it is uncontroversial that there are breakdowns in reference in which it is in principle indeterminate to what the speaker meant to be referring. Quine is simply holding, with what justice I shall not inquire, that such indeterminacies ineluctably affect all speech. Now it has long been recognized by realists that a statement will have a definite truth-value only to the extent that it has a definite content. If I am not saying anything definite, it will be correspondingly indefinite whether what I say is true or false. If, e.g., the meaning of 'religion' does nor involve precise necessary and sufficient conditions for something's being a religion, then there is no definite answer to the question whether the Ethical Culture movement is a religion. Since the Quinean doctrines under consideration imply that all our utterances are in this condition, they imply that the issue of realism cannot arise anywhere in human discourse. Anti-realism goes down the drain along with realism. For the remainder of this section I shall concentrate on arguments that have been thought to support an anti-realist answer to the question to which realism is another answer.

B.

Next let's take a brief look at some echoes of nineteenth-century idealism—the attack on the "Given." This familiar theme of Hegelianism and pragmatism has reappeared in partially novel garb in the work of Quine, Sellars, and others. As in the previous century, it is denied that there are any fixed immutable certainties, any statements totally immune to revision or rejection, any points at which an objective fact itself is directly given to us, so that all we need to do is to note it. Since it is assumed, wrongly in my opinion, that unless a statement satisfies these descriptions it cannot be justified save by its support from other statements, these denials issue in some form of a coherence or contextualist epistemology. Insofar as there is novelty in the recent attack on fixed, isolated, intuitive certainties, it comes from the "linguistic turn," e.g., the resting of epistemic status on conditions of assertability in a language community.

So far this is epistemology. What does it have to do with truth and reality? Not all the recent opponents of the given have followed their idealist and pragmatist forebears in rejecting a realist conception of truth. The story of where Sellars, e.g., stands on this matter is too complex to be gone into here. But at least one contemporary thinker has drawn anti-realist morals from this epistemology. In his book, *Philosophy and the Mirror of Nature*, Richard Rorty writes:

> Shall we take . . . "S knows non-inferentially that P" . . . as a remark about the status of S's reports among his peers, or shall we take it as a remark about the relation between nature and its mirror?[11] The first alternative leads to

a pragmatic view of truth . . . (on) the second alternative . . . truth is something more than what Dewey called "warranted assertability": more than what our peers will, *ceteris paribus*, let us get away with saying . . . To choose between these approaches is to choose between truth as "what it is good for us to believe" and truth as "contact with reality."[12]

Why should we suppose realism to depend on the existence of fixed intuitive certainties? Perhaps the argument goes like this. If we are to have any reason for supposing that any of our statements are realistically true, there must be some points at which we have direct access to the way things are in themselves. If some objective states of affairs are directly presented to consciousness, so that here we have the fact itself and not just our own "interpretation," then at those points at least, we can tell whether a statement is telling it like it is. But if we never enjoy any such intuitive apprehensions of objective reality, how could we ever tell whether any statement is or is not in accord with the facts. And if it is in principle impossible to determine this, it is idle, meaningless, or empty, to claim such an accord or to wonder whether it obtains.

This argument is in two stages. (1) Without fixed intuitive certainties we have no way of telling whether any statement is realistically true. (2) Hence it is unintelligible, or otherwise out of order, to employ this dimension of evaluation. Both steps seem to me unwarranted.

The first stage is, at best, question begging. The basic issue here is the status and evaluation of epistemic principles. The argument obviously assumes that a valid (reasonable, justified) set of epistemic principles might be such that a statement could satisfy sufficient conditions for acceptability without our having any reason to think it realistically true. But that is just what a realist would deny. From a realist point of view, epistemic justification is intimately connected with truth; not necessarily so closely connected that justification entails truth, but at least so closely connected that justification entails a considerable probability of truth. An epistemic principle that laid down sufficient principles of justification such that we could know that a statement satisfied them while having no reason to think it true, would *ipso facto* be unacceptable.

Another way of putting this last point: this first stage of the argument is one form of the old contention that "we can't get outside our thought and experience to compare it with reality." Therefore we had better renounce any ambition to make our thought conform to "reality" and concentrate instead on tidying up its internal structure. But from a realist point of view this picture of being trapped inside our own thought, unable to get a glimpse of what it is like outside, is radically misleading—even if we do lack fixed intuitive certainties. For whenever we have knowledge, that is *ipso facto* a case of getting a glimpse of the reality "outside." However we get this knowledge, it wouldn't be knowledge unless the belief in question were conformed to its referent(s).[13] It is unfortunate picture-thinking to suppose that only some specially direct or intuitive knowledge constitutes finding out what something is really like.

The second stage of the argument is plain unvarnished verificationism. If there is no way of telling whether a given statement is realistically true, then we can attach no sense (or, if you prefer, no cognitive or factual meaning) to the supposition that it is true. It would be pleasant to suppose that verificationism is now in such ill repute that to tar the argument with this brush would be condemnation enow. But, alas, such is not the case. The verificationist criterion has conclusively and repeatedly been found wanting; but perhaps excessive attention to technical details has obscured the basic point of these criticisms. If the underlying causes of the disease are not clearly identified, relapses are to be expected. The basic point is simply this. Except for such statements as are directly testable, no statement can be empirically tested in isolation. We must conjoin it with other statements if we are to derive any directly testable consequences. And for any sentence, no matter how meaningless, we can find some set of sentences that together with the former will yield observation sentences not derivable from that set alone. Thus the capacity of a sentence to contribute to the generation of directly testable consequences completely fails to discriminate between the meaningful and the meaningless. We do, of course, make distinctions between those sentences that do, and those that do not, enter *fruitfully* into empirically testable systems, though it is either very difficult or impossible to formulate precise

criteria for this. But this distinction also fails to coincide with the distinction between meaningful and meaningless, as is shown by the fact that one and the same statement, e.g., "Matter is composed of tiny indivisible particles," will enter into such combinations fruitfully at one period but not at another.[14]

C.

Rorty's argument can be generally characterized as moving from epistemology to ontology, from considerations concerning the epistemic status of statements to conclusions concerning their capacity to "reveal" reality. I now want to consider some further arguments of this general sort, which differ from the argument just discussed in being of a relativistic character. Although Rorty's argument depends on rejecting classical foundationalism, it does not question (1) the existence of a single set of epistemological principles that (2) yield a unique result in each individual instance. The two lines of thought I shall now consider each deny one of these assumptions.

The first assumption is rejected by, e.g., the language-game approach that stems from the later work of Wittgenstein and is found full-blown in Peter Winch and D. Z. Phillips. Here the idea is that there are radically different criteria of justification and rationality for different spheres of discourse—commonsense talk about the physical environment, talk about personal agents, moral discourse, religious discourse, scientific theorizing, reports of dreams, experiential reports, etc. Observation is crucial for physical-object talk, the authority of sacred books and holy persons for religious discourse, and the sincere asseveration of the subject for reports of experience. It is a piece of outrageous imperialism to suppose that any single requirement for justification applies across the board.

What bearing is this supposed to have on realism? Well, first there is a straight verificationist argument from the fact that different language-games have different criteria of truth to the conclusion that they employ different concepts of truth. This argument presupposes a stronger form of verificationism. Rorty's argument only required us to suppose that being empirically testable is a necessary condition of meaningfulness for sentences. But here we need the additional assumption that the mode of verification constitutes the meaning. We need this stronger thesis if we are to infer a difference in the meaning of 'true' in different language-games from differences in the *way* of verifying truth-ascriptions in different language-games. This stronger verificationist thesis can hardly be in a more favorable position than the weaker one, since it entails the latter.

The language-game approach also generates arguments of a more distinctive sort, though I cannot see that they fare any better.

(1) The irreducible plurality of language-games militates against the realist position in another way. The ontologies of different language-games do not all fit into any single scheme. There is no place in physical space for minds, sense-data, or God. Agency cannot be located in the interstices of the physiological causal network. Nor is there any overarching neutral position from which particular language-games can be criticized and their subject matters integrated into a single framework. Therefore it seems quite unjustified to suppose that the success of a statement in some particular language-game depends on whether it conforms to the constitution of something called "reality."

This argument also depends on verificationism. It argues from our inability to see whether, or how, different sorts of entities fit into one scheme, to the unintelligibility of supposing that they do. But, more basically, the argument suffers from a naïvely simplistic conception of reality. Why suppose that reality, if there be such, must fall into some single pattern? Why shouldn't reality be as many-mansioned as you like? Why should there not be even more kinds of entities in heaven and earth than are dreamt of in our language-games? And if there is some significant degree of unity to it all, why should we expect to be able to discern it? Even if we can't integrate agency and physical causation in a single "space," they may, for all that, be what they are apart from our attempts to conceptualize them. The argument suffers from a grievous lack of ontological imagination.

(2) We find in the writings of Sprachspielists, as well as in their historical relativist forebears, the insistence that *our* concepts of truth and reality are rooted in *our* forms of life, *our* practices—linguistic and non-linguistic. From this the inference is drawn that truth cannot consist in conformity to

the way things are "outside" our thought and practice. But this is just the old question-begging argument that we "can't get outside our own thought and experience to compare it with reality." Of course, when we use the term 'true' or any other term, we are using *our* language, if we know what we are talking about. Who else's language might we be using? (I could have been speaking French or Bantu instead, but that is presumably not to the point.) But this has absolutely no implications for the *content* of what I am saying, or for the ways in which it is properly evaluated. The fact that when I say anything I am using the language I am using, which is rooted in the social practices it is rooted in, is a miserable truism that has no bearing on our problem. It leaves completely open the question of whether, in saying what I say, I am claiming to refer to something that exists independent of our discourse, and whether this is an intelligible or reasonable claim to make.[15]

D.

Although Sprachspielism is relativistic in the sense that it takes any particular cognitive success to be relative to some particular language-game, it is not so relativistic as to suppose that different language-games yield mutually incompatible results. On the contrary, it considers different language-games to be too different to be in competition for the same prize. We now turn to a more extreme relativism, which denies the second of the assumptions listed earlier—that our epistemological principles yield a unique result in each application.

This line of thought has taken many forms from the ancient Greek sophists to the present. Its most prominent recent incarnation is in the work of Feyerabend and Kuhn. Here is a highly oversimplified version. In the development of a science we have a succession of "theoretical (or conceptual) frameworks" or "paradigms." Each of these paradigms is self-enclosed in something like the way Winch and Phillips think of a language-game as being self-enclosed. The constituent terms get their meanings by their place in the framework; observations are conceptualized and reported in these terms; and hypotheses are evaluated in terms of how well they explain data so construed, and in terms of how well they solve the problems generated by that paradigm. Hence we are unable to choose between rival theoretical frameworks in terms of one or another contestant.

The position is usually not held in so extreme a form, but I wanted to present it as such so as to see what bearing it would have on realism. The obvious argument is this. All our conclusions are relative to the assumptions and conceptual framework of a given paradigm, which has indefinitely many alternatives. Therefore we can never have reason to think that any of our conclusions are in conformity with reality itself. Hence the realist notion of truth is inapplicable to our discourse. Clearly this is but another rerun of the same old verificationist argument. And again the same comments are applicable.

These, I take it, are the epistemological arguments against realism that are most prominent on the current scene. I have not contested their epistemological premises, though I do not accept them in every case, but instead have concentrated on showing that even with these premises the arguments are far from cogent.

E.

Finally, there is the direct application of verificationism to the crucial implication of realism mentioned above, viz., that however well confirmed, justified, or rationally acceptable a statement may be, it is logically possible that it be false. The argument is very simple. We have, *ex hypothesi,* ruled out any possible reason for supposing the statement false. Therefore we cannot attach any meaning to the denial that it is true. This is clearly nor just an argument against realism, but also an argument for the equation of 'true' and 'justified' (or 'could be justified'), or at least for the substitution of the latter for the former. In only slightly different garb it is the main argument of Peirce, James, and Dewey for their several pragmatic conceptions of truth. It is given a fancy logical dress in Hilary Putnam's recent Presidential Address to the Eastern Division, but the verificationist underpinning is the same in all its versions. And about this enough has been said.

I conclude from this discussion that the recent opponents of realism have failed to shake our commonsense confidence in that doctrine. They have not done significantly better than Hegel, Bradley, James, and Dewey; in fact, their arguments turn out to be warmed-over scraps from the idealist, pragmatist and positivist traditions, masked by a few ingenious sauces from La Nouvelle Cuisine.

III.

However, on this solemn occasion I am not content with simply shooting down the arguments of opponents. A more fitting aspiration would be to show that there is no coherent alternative to realism. Unfortunately, I can see no way to do this other than by examining all sufficiently promising alternatives. This is, of course, a very large task, and I shall only be able to make a start.

The most obvious move for the anti-realist is to *define* truth in terms of whatever he takes to be the appropriate standards for accepting a statement. A common thread in the arguments we have been considering is the verificationist objection to the idea that there is something involved in a statement's *being* true over and above the grounds we can have for regarding it as true. Such arguments naturally lead to an identification of a statement's being true with there being adequate grounds for taking it to be true (not, of course, with anyone's seeing that there are adequate grounds). Thus the truth of a statement, S, will be identified with S's cohering with the rest of one's beliefs, with S's leading, or having the capacity to lead, to fruitful consequences, with S's satisfying the standards of the particular language-game in which it is a move, with S's being one of the survivors at the ideal limit of scientific inquiry, or whatever.[16]

Instead of proposing a non-realist analysis of 'true', the anti-realist may instead (more candidly, in my view) propose that we abandon the concept of truth and talk instead of justification, confirmation, or verification. Thus Dewey once advocated dropping 'true' in favor of 'warrantedly assertable'. It will be easier to focus the discussion if I stick with the version in which some non-realist analysis of 'true' is given.

As is implicit in the list just given, these non-realist theories differ along various dimensions. They may be atomistic or holistic; i.e., they may attach justification conditions to individual statements or only to larger systems; in the latter case what it is for a particular statement to be true is to belong to a system that, as a whole, satisfies certain constraints. Again, they may seek to give a single account of justification for *all* statements, like the traditional coherence theories, or they may hold, like Sprachspielism, that different accounts are to be given for different realms of discourse. The question I want to explore is whether *any* verificationist account of truth can be intelligibly and coherently spelled out (while not completely losing touch with its subject matter), without involving or presupposing the realist concept of truth.

A.

The first place a realist will look for a chink in the armor is the status of the higher-level epistemic judgments like S_1—'S would be included in the ultimate scientific theory'.[17] Isn't Peirce implicitly thinking of this as true in the realist sense? In asserting S, isn't he thinking that it is really the case that if scientific inquiry were pushed to the limit, S would still be there? If so, we have extruded (real) truth from first-level statements, only to have it reappear on a second level.[18] But suppose that Peirce retorts that he is prepared to treat these second-level statements in the same way, i.e., hold their truth to consist in their membership in the ultimate scientific theory. In that case he will be faced with an infinite regress. For this will set up a still higher-level statement S^2—'S_1 would be included in the ultimate scientific theory'. And if that in turn is treated in the same way. . . .

I am uncertain as to the force of this realist criticism. It is unclear to me whether this regress as any more vicious than a variety of other infinite regresses with which we are saddled anyway, e.g., the regress of truth levels, or the regress of levels of justification. Hence I will pass on to difficulties that seem to me to be clearly fatal.

B.

The real crusher for the anti-realist is the question "How are we to interpret the statements to which you apply your concept of truth?" What is crushing about this question? Well, the point is that on a natural, intuitive way of understanding statement content (of specifying what is being asserted in a given statement), that content carries with it the applicability of the realist concept of truth. Let's continue to restrict the discussion to those statements that can plausibly be thought of as being "about something(s)." For such a statement, the natural way of specifying content, of making explicit what statement it is, is to specify the referent(s), and to make explicit what is being asserted of that referent(s). But if that is what makes the statement the statement it is, then there is no alternative to supposing that the statement is true *iff* the referent(s) is as it is being said to be. If what I did in a certain utterance was to refer to snow and say of it that it is white, what alternative is there to holding that my statement is true *iff* snow is white?[19] You can't in one and the same breath construe the statement as a commitment to X's being Φ, and also deny that the statement is true *iff* X is Φ. To understand statement content in this familiar way is to subject it to realistic truth-conditions. It is incoherent to say "What I asserted was that snow is white (or what I did in my assertion was to refer to snow and say of it that it is white), but the truth of my assertion does not ride on whether snow *is* white." This is to take away with one hand what was offered with the other. The realistic concept of truth is indissolubly bound up with this familiar way of specifying statement content.[20] If I am correct in this, the anti-realist will have to provide some other way of specifying *what* is being asserted—other than "The speaker referred so snow and said of it that it is white."

If we ask whether anti-realists have recognized the necessity for an alternative reading, the picture appears so be a mixed one. I believe that idealists in the Hegelian tradition have generally been alive to the issue. Consider Bradley's view of the nature of judgment, as involving a separation of the 'that' and the 'what', and a vain attempt to reunite them in the forms of predication, together with the view that the essential aim of thought is to produce a comprehensive, coherent totality that would be identical with reality. This is an attempt to give an account of what we are up to in statement making that is fundamentally different from the familiar account and that is in harmony with a coherence account of the nature of truth. Again, we can see Dewey's emphasis on the "instrumental" function of ideas and judgments as the germ of a different kind of alternative account. If what we are up to in statement making is not attempting to tell is like it is with particular referents or classes thereof, but rather providing effective guidance to our active commerce with the environment (allowing, as I would not, that the latter can be separated from the former), then it might be not incoherent to hold that the fundamental dimension of evaluation for statements is their effectiveness in this role. In many cases, however, one is left with the impression that the anti-realist takes individual statements in the same old way, but simply proposes to change the account of what it is for them to be *true*. If the above argument is correct, this is just what she cannot do.

A thoroughgoing anti-anti-realist argument would involve a careful scrutiny of all the noteworthy attempts, actual and possible, to devise a mode of statement-interpretation suitable for their purposes. However, I fear that an examination of such darkly labyrinthine authors as Bradley and Dewey would be beyond the bounds of this lecture even if we were at the beginning rather than, as I hasten to assure you, in the latter half. Instead, I shall consider some moves that are more in accord with the dominant temper of Anglo-American philosophy of the last half-century, moves that might well tempt anti-realists, and in some cases actually have.

(1) The anti-realist may try to turn the above argument back on her opponent in the following manner. "The argument depends on the claim that statemental content is tied to truth-conditions. Well and good; two can play as this game. If a realist construal of statements yields realist truth-conditions, then non-realist truth-conditions can be associated with a corresponding mode of assigning statement-content. If what is takes for a statement, S, so be true is that it belong to the ultimate scientific theory (call that 'T') then we will simply assign to S the content— *S belongs to T*."

However tempting this may sound in the abstract, as soon as it is stated explicitly, is clearly displays its absurdity. How could is be that asserting that *S* is asserting that *S* has some property or other? How could S *be* some higher-level statement about S, i.e., be a higher-level statement than itself? How can a statement be a statement about itself, rasher than itself?

A contemporary anti-realist like Dummett, or (the most recent) Putnam, would not be

moved by this. They would just take it as illustrating the futility of working with *statements* or *propositions* as our basic units, instead of sentences in a language. Of course, we can't regard a statement as being a statement about itself, instead of being itself. But we do not find the same absurdity in the suggestion that each of our statements makes a claim about a certain sentence, even the very sentence used so make that statement. Let's follow recent fashion and take a theory so consist of a set of sentences. Then we may formulate the following Peircean view of statement interpretation. When I assertorically utter "Lead melts as 327 degrees F," what I am claiming is: "The sentence 'Lead melts at 327 degrees F' will (would) be included in the final scientific theory, T."[21]

But though this escapes the absurdity of denying that a statement is identical with itself, it suffers the same unhappy fate that befalls other attempts to substitute sentences for beliefs, propositions, or statements. Here, as elsewhere, it turns out that even the closest possible statement about language will fail to have the same force as the original. In this case (passing over the *parochiality* involved in supposing that the *ultimate* scientific theory will consist of English sentences) the difficulty is that whether the sentence in question figures in T depends, *inter alia,* on what that sentence will mean by the time the final consummation is achieved. If the sentence means something different from what it means now, it may not be included, even if T does include a statement to the effect that lead melts at 327 degrees F. Thus, on this interpretation, when we assert "Lead melts as 327 degrees F," we are, in part, making a claim about the future history of the English language. This radically distorts our intent. Sometimes we are talking about language, but most of the time we are not.

Of course, this view may be so construed that our statement has to do not with a mere phonological string (which might receive various semantic interpretations) but with the semantically interpreted sentence "Lead melts as 327 degrees F." But that is to throw us back on the absurdities of treating a statement as being about itself. For a semantic interpretation of an assertoric sentence is precisely designed to determine a statement-content; is specifies *what* is asserted when the sentence is used assertorically. Therefore this latest proposal amounts to assigning two different contents to the statement: the one determined by the presupposed semantic interpretation, and the one built on that—to the effect that the sentence used to express the first content will be in T. Again we lapse into incoherence.

(2) The moral of this story is that we can't identify a statement with a statement about *itself*, whether about its epistemic status or about the sentence used to make is. But the diagnosis suggests a simple remedy. Why not take S to be, not the statement that S satisfies certain epistemic conditions, but rather the statement of those conditions themselves? For each statement, S, we will choose conditions the satisfaction of which will guarantee that the statement has the desired epistemic status, but we will construe S not as the statement that S has that status, but rather as the affirmation of those conditions.

It would seem that this kind of first-level interpretation is not available for holistic theories that identify the truth of S with the way it fits into some system—the final scientific theory, the most coherent and comprehensive theory of truth, or the ongoing enterprise of coping with the environment. Here a blanket statement that makes reference to S (to the way S fits into some system) is all we have to work with. But an empirical verifiability theory of truth looks more promising. If we can specify conditions under which S would be verified, why not identify what is stated by S with the satisfaction of those conditions?

Interpretations like this were prominent in twentieth-century phenomenalism and in early logical positivism. ("The meaning of a statement is its method of verification.")[22] And recently Michael Dummett has suggested the possibility of replacing (realist) truth-conditions with "verification-conditions" in giving a semantic description of a language. Let's use as our example an oversimplified statement of C. I. Lewis's version of phenomenalism.[23] A singular attribution of a property to a physical object, like 'This container is made of glass', is to be construed as the assertion of an indefinitely large conjunction of subjunctive conditionals like the following:

1. If I were to seem to dash this container to the floor, I would seem to see the container shattering.

2. If I were to seem to thump this container with my finger, I would hear a certain kind of ringing sound.

Each of these "terminating judgments" is supposed to have the virtue of being decisively verified or falsified by "sensory presentations." And the verification of the whole set would *be* the verification of the original statement, since they are one and the same.[24]

It has been frequently argued and, I think, to good effect, that projects like Lewis's cannot be carried out, that no purely phenomenalistic statement is equivalent to any physical-object statement. I don't want to get into all of that. I merely want to ask whether, assuming that some such project can be carried through, it enables us to avoid the realistic concept of truth. And here I am not asking whether the concept of verification can be cut loose from dependence on the concept of truth, as it would have to be if it is to be used in an analysis of truth. Clearly the ordinary meaning of 'verify' is simply *show (ascertain) to be true*. But this is not to the present point, since the second-level concept of verification does not enter into the proposed interpretation of first-level statements like 'This container is made of paper'.

The crucial point, rather, is this. Let's say that S is taken to be the assertion that p. q, . . . , where these are verifying conditions, whether stated in Lewis's way or in some other. We have given a propositional content to S that differs from the familiar one. But in giving it this new content, are we not thereby committed to realistic truth-conditions for *that* content as firmly as we were with the earlier one? Instead of simply attributing a property to the object referred to by 'this container', we are asserting a number of contingencies in sense experience. But with respect to each of those contingencies are we not asserting that it in fact obtains—that if I were to seem to dash this container to the floor, it would seem to break? But if so, then again I am saying something that is true *iff* that consequence would result from that activity.[25] Once more, I cannot both be making that claim and denying that whether the claim is true rides on whether things would come out that way under those conditions. In fact, this is the way in which the matter has been viewed by most phenomenalists and other verificationists. They were far from wanting to jettison the realistic concept of truth. They simply wanted to put restrictions on what sorts of statements are susceptible of (realistic) truth and falsity.

One might think that the failure to slough off realistic truth-conditions comes from making the verificationist interpretation match the original too closely. By insisting on conditions of conclusive verification, we have guaranteed that the translation says just the same as the original, and that is why we wind up with realistic truth claims after all. This suggests that we should follow the pilgrimage of logical positivism from conclusive verification to "confirmation." Perhaps we should interpret our statements in terms of what would provide (more or less strong) confirmation, rather than in terms of what would conclusively verify. But this suggestion is even more incoherent than its predecessor. We cannot judge a certain condition to be merely providing some evidence for S, rather than conclusively verifying it, except against the background of a conception of what would render S *true* or, if you like, of what would conclusively verify S. Why do we suppose that determining that X's malleable is only some evidence for X's being gold, but does not conclusively establish that it is gold? Because we have enough of an idea of what it is for X to *be* gold to see that it is possible for something to be malleable and yet not be gold.

Contrariwise, if we simply take some "confirmation condition" as giving the content of a statement, then it follows that we can't be taking it to be merely non-conclusively confirming. If what I am asserting when I utter 'X is gold' is that X is malleable, then is cannot be denied that the malleability of X makes my assertion true. A set of conditions cannot be merely confirming evidence, and also constitute the content of what was said.

Nor will it be more efficacious to construe our interpretation as made up of conditions of "acceptance." Again, if we mean to contrast conditions of acceptance with conditions of truth or verification, we still have the latter in the background; we have neither eliminated them, nor dissolved their tie with statement content. If, on the other hand, we are serious in taking our to-called conditions of acceptance to specify statement-consent, we are thereby precluded from regarding them as conditions of acceptance rather than of truth.

Thus these verificationist moves are to no avail. When we identify statement-consent in terms of test, verification, or confirmation conditions, we do not evade realistic truth-conditions; rather, we introduce certain restrictions on what can be asserted, thereby generating parallel restrictions on what it takes to make statements true. When all the smoke has cleared, it is still a matter of what is talked about being as it is said to be.

The language-game, and other relativistic approaches such as Quine's "ontological relativism," may *seem* to provide a different way out. Instead of trying to get away from interpreting statements in terms of the familiar machinery of reference, predication, and truth, we simply hang onto all that, but regard it, in each instance, as relative to a certain language-game (paradigm, scheme of translation). In a normal utterance of 'Snow is white', we are, indeed, referring to snow and predicating whiteness of it; and so what we say is true *iff* snow is white. But this is all relative to the "commonsense physical world language-game." We can only pick out a referent, identify a property predicated, and adjudge truth by the standards internal to that language-game. There is no way in which we can raise the question, absolutely, as to what is referred to in that statement, or as to the conditions under which it is true. All such semantic notions exist only in relativized forms. When we try to drop the qualification, the concept dissolves.

But what does it mean to say that 'Snow is white' is true *in the commonsense physical world language-game*, rather than just true *tout court*?

(1) There is an innocuous interpretation according to which it is in L that S is true, because L is where S is. That is, S is constructed from the conceptual resources of L; that statement-content emerges from that conceptual practice. Clearly on this interpretation 'S is true in L' will be true for some L, for any true statement, S, assuming that every statement can be assigned to as least one language-game. But this is innocuous because the relativity does not affect the notion of truth. On this reading 'S is true in L' is just a conjunction of 'S is in L' and 'S is true *(tout court)*'.

(2) It could mean—we're just pretending, rather than claiming that S is *really* true, as in "It is true that Bunter is Lord Peter's butler in Dorothy Sayer's mysteries." But presumably this is not what

is intended, for this reading depends on a contrast with "really true" (absolutely)—not to mention the fact that a Sprachspielist would not be prepared to assimilate all language-games to fiction.

(3) What is left to us? Only the obvious, straightforward suggestion that 'S is true in L' means—'S passes the tests of L for being true'. But the second occurrence of 'true' has to be taken as employing the *verboten* absolute concept. For if we try to make that occurrence express a relativistic concept of truth in some L, that will require a similar explanation, and an infinite regress looms.

These all too brief considerations indicate that notions like 'true' and 'refers' stubbornly resist relativization. Once admitted, they point inevitably to what there is, whatever webs of thought we weave.

(3) The non-realist interpretations that emerge from currently fashionable modes of thought have all backfired. The moral I draw from this cautionary tale is that most non-realists have seriously underestimated the magnitude of their task. They have failed to appreciate how violent a break is required with our customary ways of viewing thought and discourse. They have failed to grasp the central point that if they are to abandon the realistic concept of truth, they must give up thinking of our thought and discourse in terms of reference, and the other semantic notions based on that—saying this or that *of* what is referred to, quantification over what is (or could be) referred to, and so on. They have supposed that they can continue to construe discourse in these terms, while attaching a relativistic rider to these semantic notions, or by substituting some specially tailored propositional content for the more familiar ones. But it just doesn't work. To repeat the main point once more, so long as we think of our utterances as being about something(s), there is no escape from the realistic truth formula. So long as it is correct to say that you are talking about this container, or dogs, or the quality of mercy, then there is no escape from the recognition that what you say is true *iff* what you are talking about is as you say it to be. If, on the other hand, it could be made out that it is a mistake to think of statemental utterances as

being *about* anything, then clearly the realistic truth concept does not apply. If there is nothing I am talking about, my utterance can hardly be evaluated in terms of whether what it is about is as I say is to be. If the non-realist is to make her position stick, she will have to find some adequate non-referential account of statemental discourse.

How might this be done? Well, there is the Bradleian idea that the aim of thought is to develop a comprehensive, coherent system of concepts, where this aim is so conceived that if it were fully realized, the system would *be* Reality as a whole. Here the relation with reality is not secured by way of reference to particular objects in each judgment (belief, statement), but rather by way of the fact that Reality is what would constitute the complete fulfillment of the aim of thought. Whether this is a radically non-referential conception depends on whether we can understand the incomplete stages of this quest without thinking of ourselves as referring either to the concepts themselves, or to their extensions or instances. A still more radical alternative would be an explicitly non-intentionalistic account of speech as complexly conditioned behavior, as in B. F. Skinner's book *Verbal Behavior*. Whether *this* is really a radically non-referential account will depend, *inter alia*, on whether the account itself can be an account of speech without itself being about something, viz., speech.

Obviously I can't discuss these putatively non-referential accounts at the tag-end of this paper. I shall have to confine myself to the following remark. Even if doubts of the sort just expressed could be stilled, and one or more such accounts could be formulated without embodying or presupposing references at some point, the question would still remain whether reference is being sold at too dear a price. We would have to give up such cherished ideas to that we can pick out objects of various sorts and characterize them, correctly and incorrectly, and that in the course of this enterprise we sometimes communicate information about the world that guides our behavior as well as satisfies our intellectual curiosity. Unless the arguments against realism are considerably stronger than I found them to be earlier in this essay, the game, clearly, is not worth the candle.

IV.

Yes, Virginia, there is a real world. Not, or not only, in the hearts and minds of men. Not, or not only, in the language-games we play, in the schemes of translation we devise, or in the epistemic standards we acknowledge. But in that ineluctable, circumambient web of fact to the texture of which we must needs do homage, lest, though we speak with the tongues of men and of angels, and have not truth, our logos is become as sounding symbols or as tinkling paradigms.

Endnotes

Presidential Address delivered before the Seventy-Seventh Annual Western Division Meeting of the American Philosophical Association in Denver, Colorado, 20 May, 1979.

[1] I take this to be simply a slightly more explicit formulation of the view classically expressed by Aristotle in *Metaphysics* (101 lb, 27) as " . . . to say of what is that it is, and of what is not that it is not, is true."

[2] See Hilary Putnam, "Realism and reason," *Proceedings and Addresses of the American Philosophical Association* 50 (1977), p. 4–5.

[3] To be sure, Hegel's philosophy as a whole contains elements that are incompatible with realism in my sense. Here I am only concerned with the Hegelian or "absolute" version of the particular thesis that reality is basically spiritual in character.

[4] F. H. Bradley, *Essays on Truth and Reality* (Oxford: Clarendon Press, 1914), p. 1.

[5] F. H. Bradley, *Essays on Truth and Reality* (Oxford: Clarendon Press, 1914) p. 223.

[6] Brand Blanshard, *The Nature of Thought* (London: George Allen & Unwin Ltd., 1939), vol. 2, p. 264.

[7] C. S. Peirce, "How to make our ideas clear," in C. Hartshorne and P. Weiss (eds), *Collected Papers* (Cambridge, Mass.: Harvard University Press, 1934), p. 268.

[8] William James, *Pragmatism* (Cambridge, Mass.: Harvard University Press, 1975), p. 97.

[9] John Dewey, *Reconstruction in Philosophy* (New York: Henry Holt & Co., 1920), p. 156.

[10] Putnam, "Realism and reason."

[11] This last is Rorty's picturesque way of saying, "taking it as involving an immediate awareness that *p*, or as involving the fact that *p*'s being directly presented to consciousness."

[12] Richard Rorty, *Philosophy and the Mirror of Nature* (Princeton: Princeton University Press, 1979), pp. 175–6.

[13] Hence the well-advised tendency of some anti-realists to renounce the concept of knowledge for justified belief, or warranted assertability.

[14] In this connection we may note that the verifiability criterion forces us into a caricature of the process of scientific inquiry. Often this involves generating some hypothesis ('Electric current is a flow of tiny particles') and then looking around for some way to test it. Free of verificationist blinders, it seems obvious that this process is guided throughout by our understanding of the hypothesis we do not yet see how to test. (We haven't yet found a promising way of embedding it in a larger system that will generate directly testable consequences.) But verificationism would have it that what we were doing was looking for a meaning to bestow on a certain sentence! And if that were what we were doing, why should it matter which of indefinitely many empirically respectable meanings we chose?

[15] We might also note that though this argument is found principally in the writings of Sprachspielists, it does not in any way depend on the multiplicity of language-games. These truisms would be equally true if our discourse were restricted to a single language-game.

[16] It may be suggested that I should have taken "redundancy" or "disappearance" theories as equally obvious alternatives for the anti-realist. These theories deny that the statement 'It is true that S' has any more "cognitive" or "assertoric" content (makes any further truth claim!) than S. The function of 'It's true' is simply to endorse someone else's statement that S, or to assert that S in a specially emphatic way, or the like. But the relation of the redundancy theory to realism is unclear. It does *look* anti-realist, if we aren't asserting anything (over and above S) in saying 'It's true that S', then we aren't asserting, among other things, that what S is about as it is said to be in asserting S. Nevertheless, the opposition might be only skin deep. If the redundancy theory is merely a view as to how the *word* 'true' or phrases like 'It's true' are used, then it is quite compatible with the view that realism is right about the primary aim of thought, and about the most fundamental dimension of evaluation of statements; the disagreement would only be over whether the word 'true' is properly used to express this.

[17] We might also raise questions about the status of epistemic principles like "The ultimate scientific theory must satisfy the following constraints . . ."

[18] This realist rejoinder is reminiscent of a variety of *tu quoque's* in which one who denies that there are X's is charged with assuming X's himself. Thus the skeptic who denies that anyone knows anything is charged wish himself claiming to know something—viz., that no one knows anything. Again, the mechanist or behaviorist who writes books to prove that men are not actuated by purposes, is charged with displaying an example of what he is claiming not to exist. It is generally true in these cases that the denial of X's on a first level is held to involve the admission of X's on a higher level.

[19] The use of the Tarskian paradigm is not inadvertent. Unlike those who see the whole Tarskian treatment of truth as a series of technical gimmicks, I feel that Tarski's criterion of adequacy embodies a fundamental feature of our concept of truth. But I read it somewhat differently from many other admirers. The fact that 'S is true *iff* S' is a conceptual truth is often taken to show that the former doesn't say anything more than the latter, and that truth-

talk is eliminable. But in opposition to this reductive reading, I prefer to concentrate on the other direction of equivalence and give it an inflationary reading. That is, the notion of what is takes for the statement to be true is already embodied, implicitly, in the statement-content; in explicitly saying that S is true, we are just bringing to light what is already embedded in the first-level statement.

[20]This contention can be rerun for the question "What is it to *understand* a given statement or to know what statement is being made on a given occasion?" For what one has to know to know that is precisely what we have been calling statement-content. So again we cannot say: "In order to know what statement P asserted at *t*, what we have to know is that P referred to snow and said of is that is was white; and yes the truth of what P said does not ride on whether snow is white."

[21]Hilary Putnam considers an interpretation like this in the second of his John Locke lectures, *Meaning and the Moral Sciences* (London: Routledge and Kegan Paul, 1978).

[22]To be sure, the mid-twentieth-century advocates of this mode of interpretation were not concerned to reject a realist theory of truth, and rightly so, as we shall see. Nevertheless, their verificationist brand of statement-interpretation might well appear attractive to an anti-realist who is grappling with the problem currently under consideration.

[23]See C. I. Lewis, *Analysis of Knowledge and Valuation* (La Salle, Ill.: Open Court, 1946), ch. 8.

[24]Of course, there are many alternative ways of stating verification-conditions for statements. They may be stated in terms of what would have to be experienced in order to verify it, or, as with Lewis, in terms of the experiencing of it. On the former alternative the conditions may be phenomenalistic or physicalistic. They may or may not be such as to provide a practicable possibility of complete verification of falsification. And so on.

[25]It must be admitted that conditionals, especially subjunctive conditions, pose special difficulties for the determination of realistic truth-conditions. But these are problems that arise for any view that allows conditionals (and how can they be avoided?) It is just that subjunctive conditionals loom much larger on the view under discussion.

Further Reading

Alston, W., *A Realist Conception of Truth* (Ithaca, N.Y.: Cornell University Press, 1996).

Aune, B., *Metaphysics: The Elements* (Minneapolis: University of Minnesota Press, 1985).

Ayer, A. J., *Philosophy in the Twentieth Century* (New York: Vintage, 1984).

Benardete, José, *Metaphysics: The Logical Approach* (New York: Oxford University Press, 1989).

Bergmann, G., *Logic and Reality* (Madison: University of Wisconsin Press, 1964).

Brent, J., *Charles Sanders Peirce, A Life* (Bloomington: Indiana University Press, 1993).

Campbell, L., *Metaphysics: An Introduction* (Belmont, Calif.: Dickenson, 1976).

Carr, B., *Metaphysics: An Introduction* (Atlantic Highlands, N. J.: Humanities Press, 1988).

Churchland, P., and Hooker, C., eds., *Images of Science* (Chicago: University of Chicago Press, 1985).

Coburn, R., *The Strangeness of the Ordinary: Problems and Issues in Contemporary Metaphysics* (Savage, Maryland: Barnes and Noble Imports, 1990).

Cornman, J., *Metaphysics, Reference, and Language* (New Haven, Conn.: Yale University Press, 1966).

Davidson, D. and Hintikka, J., eds., *Words and Objections: Essays on the Work of W. V. Quine* (Dordrecht: Reidel, 1969).

Delaney, C., Loux, M., Gutting, G., and Solomon, W., *The Synoptic Vision: Essays in the Philosophy of Wilfrid Sellars* (Notre Dame, Ind.: University of Notre Dame Press, 1977).

Dummett, M., *The Logical Basis of Metaphysics* (Cambridge: Harvard University Press, 1991).

Evans, G., and McDowell, J., eds., *Truth and Meaning: Essays in Semantics* (Oxford: Oxford University Press, 1976).

Feigl, H., Sellars, W., and Lehrer, K., eds., *New Readings in Philosophical Analysis* (New York: Appleton-Century-Crofts, 1972).

Feyerabend, P., *Realism, Rationalism, and Scientific Method, Philosophical Papers,* Vol. I (Cambridge: Cambridge University Press, 1986).

Goodman, N., *Languages of Art* (New York: Bobbs-Merrill, 1968).

Goodman, N., *Ways of Wordmaking* (Indianapolis: Hackett, 1978).

Hacking, I., *Why Does Language Matter to Philosophy?* (Cambridge: Cambridge University Press, 1975).

Hahn L. and Schilpp, P., eds., *The Philosophy of W. V. Quine,* Vol. XVIII, The Library of Living Philosophers (La Salle, Ill.: Open Court, 1986).

Hamlyn, D., *Metaphysics* (Cambridge: Cambridge University Press, 1984).

Heidegger, M., *Introduction to Metaphysics* (Garden City, N.Y.: Doubleday & Co., 1961).

Heidegger, M., *Being and Time.* (J. Macquarrie and E. Robinson, trans.) (New York: Harper and Row, 1962).

Houser, N., and Kloesel, C., eds., *The Essential Peirce, Selected Philosophical Writings,* Vols. I and II (Bloomington: Indiana University Press, 1992).

Korner, S., *Metaphysics: Its Structure and Function* (New York: Cambridge University Press, 1984).

Leplin, J., ed., *Scientific Realism* (Berkeley: University of California Press, 1984).

Lewis, D., *Philosophical Papers,* Vol. I & II (New York: Oxford University Press, 1983).

McDowell, J., *Mind and World* (Cambridge: Harvard University Press, 1994).

Menand, L., *The Metaphysical Club* (New York: Farrar, Straus and Giroux, 2001).

Passmore, J., *A Hundred Years of Philosophy* (New York: Basic Books, 1966).

Passmore, J., *Recent Philosophers* (La Salle, Ill.: Open Court, 1985).

Peacocke, C., *Being Known* (Oxford: Oxford University Press, 1999).

Putnam, H., *Realism and Reason, Philosophical Papers,* Vol. 3 (New York: Cambridge University Press, 1983).

Putnam, H., *The Many Faces of Realism* (La Salle, Ill.: Open Court, 1987).

Quine, W., *From a Logical Point of View* (Cambridge, Mass.: Harvard University Press, 1953).

Quine, W., *Word and Object* (Cambridge: Massachusetts Institute of Technology Press, 1960).

Quine, W., *Ontological Relativity and Other Essays* (New York: Columbia University Press, 1969).

Quine, W., *Roots of Reference* (La Salle, Ill.: Open Court, 1973).

Romanos, G., *Quine and Analaytic Philosophy* (Cambridge: Massachusetts Institute of Technology Press, 1983).

Rorty, R., ed., *The Linguistic Turn* (Chicago: University of Chicago Press, 1967).

Rorty, R., *Philosophy and the Mirror of Nature* (Princeton: Princeton University Press, 1979).

Rorty, R., *Consequences of Pragmatism* (Minneapolis: University of Minnesota Press, 1982).

Rorty, R., *Contingency, Irony, and Solidarity* (New York: Cambridge University Press, 1989).

Rosenberg, J., *Linguistic Representation* (Dordrecht: Reidel, 1974)

Russell, B., *Problems of Philosophy* (New York: Oxford University Press, 1959).

Schilpp, P. A., ed., *The Philosophy of Rudolf Carnap,* Vol. XI, The Library of Living Philosophers, (La Salle, Ill.: Open Court, 1963).

Sellars, W., *Science, Perception, and Reality* (New York: Routledge & Kegan Paul, 1963).

Sellars, W., *Science and Metaphysics* (London: Routledge & Kegan Paul, 1968).

Solomon, R. C., *From Rationalism to Existentialism* (New York: Harper & Row, 1972).

Solomon, R. C., *Continental Philosophy Since 1750* (Oxford: Oxford University Press, 1988).

Strawson, P., *Individuals: An Essay in Descriptive Metaphysics* (London: Methuen, 1959).

van Fraassen, B., *The Scientific Image* (New York: Oxford University Press, 1980).

van Fraassen, B., *The Empirical Stance* (New Haven: Yale University Press, 2002).

Van Inwagen, P., *Metaphysics* (Oxford: Oxford University Press, 1990).